D1134647

1 2 APR 2024

WITHDRAWN

College of Ripon & York St. John

3 8025 00299518 4

121012 .

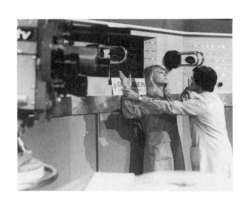

A for Andromeda to *Zoo Time*

A for Andromeda

A·to·Z

Zoo Time

The TV holdings of
the National Film and
Television Archive
1936·1979

Edited by Simon Baker
and Olwen Terris

University College of
Ripon & York St. John
YORK CAMPUS
REFERENCE ONLY
NOT TO BE TAKEN OUT
OF THE LIBRARY

BRITISH FILM INSTITUTE

bfi

BFI PUBLISHING

First published in 1994 by the
British Film Institute
21 Stephen Street
London W1P 1PL

The British Film Institute exists to encourage the
development of film, television and video in the
United Kingdom, and to promote knowledge,
understanding and enjoyment of the culture of the
moving image. Its activities include the National
Film and Television Archive; the National Film
Theatre; the Museum of the Moving Image; the
London Film Festival; the production and
distribution of film and video; funding and support
for regional activities; Library and Information
Services; Stills, Posters and Designs; Research;
Publishing and Education; and the monthly *Sight
and Sound* magazine.

Copyright © British Film Institute 1994

This book has been published as a contribution to
the celebrations of the centenary of the cinema in
the United Kingdom, which are being organised
by Cinema 100 on behalf of all sectors of the
industry.

Cinema 100 aims to ensure that everyone is aware
of the Centenary; that filmgoing audiences
increase; that knowledge of the cinema industry's
history and culture is enhanced; and that the
cinema's second century is heralded.

British Library Cataloguing-in-Publication Data.
A catalogue record for this book is available from
the British Library.

ISBN: 0–85170–420–4

Cover design by John Gibbs

Typesetting by
Fakenham Photosetting Limited, Fakenham,
Norfolk
Printed in Great Britain by
Page Bros Limited, Norwich

Small photos on cover and half-title:
Julie Christie in *A for Andromeda* (BBC)
Desmond Morris in *Zoo Time* (Granada)

Contents

Foreword

THE LAST introduction to a catalogue we were asked to contribute was for the Ann Summers 1985 winter collection of see-through overcoats and transparent gumboots. We weren't paid for that either but we eagerly accepted the commission in the vain hope that the same conditions would apply as to this one. Namely free access to any of the contents that took our fancy.

This is by any standards a truly remarkable collection of archive material which can be viewed by anybody with a few years to spare. We can personally vouchsafe that all the items are available as we sat through the entire collection one week last year at the National Film Theatre armed only with a thermos flask and a fast forward button which we applied liberally during the Potter's Wheel on the principle that if you have seen one potter's wheel you've seen them all. We applied the same criteria to the Windmill, the Sea Coming In, the Tankfull of Tropical Fish and other such Top Ten programmes of the 1950s. This most enjoyable task was interrupted on the fourth day by a BBC detector van demanding to see a current television licence – which of course they didn't have. A quick 'phone call to J. Paul Getty Junior quickly rectified this embarrassing oversight.

We must congratulate Steve Bryant and his colleagues in assembling this collection, which in this modern era of the moving image compares in importance with the library at Alexandria. We ourselves have special reason to be grateful to them for their expertise in restoring to viewability some antiquated tapes of *Steptoe and Son* which we had recorded on an equally antiquated machine to ensure against the unlikely event of the BBC losing them – which of course they did. The salvaging of this early material ranks in complexity with the job done on the Dead Sea Scrolls.

Anybody faintly connected with the industry or interested in the preservation and documentation of how we lived in the Twentieth Century owes a great debt to the foresight and dedication of the National Film and Television Archive. And now we are going to enjoy our fee. A free look at something. Oh God, there's so much to choose from. Shall it be Mrs Bradshaw's Lodger, the 'Esso Sign Means Happy Motoring', or Brideshead Revisited? Decisions, decisions, all the time decisions!

RAY GALTON and ALAN SIMPSON

Introduction

THE IMPORTANCE of the National Film Archive's espousal of British television in the late 50s (and even then it was dangerously close to being too little, too late) cannot be overstressed. Since then, our commitment to this, the 20th century's most dynamic medium of art, entertainment, information and communication, has grown to the point where we are possibly the world's largest independent archive dedicated to the preservation of national television output, and in January 1993 the scale of this commitment was recognised by the words '. . . and Television' being added to our title.

As the Archive's Keeper of Television, Steve Bryant, describes in his introduction to this catalogue, it was during the 80s that the Archive achieved the funding and capacity to systematise its acquisition of television programmes, and what was a small but steady flow became a river – too large now for the entire collection to be contained in one volume.

What this catalogue does, therefore, is round up everything that has survived and been preserved in the NFTVA since the beginnings of television transmission in this country up until the end of the 70s, when the wholesale use of videotape had made acquisition a matter of relative ease. There are tragic gaps and losses, some inevitable, some through thoughtlessness or wanton neglect – but even so, there are 10,000 entries in this book, reflecting the entire gamut of drama, light entertainment, sport and current affairs from the first forty years of British television for which there is now such a nostalgic appetite.

The British Film Institute, no less than the NFTVA, has fully embraced television in its cultural remit, and with the BFI currently celebrating its 60th birthday, the Archive about to do the same, and the centenary of moving pictures knocking on our door, this seems a timely moment to reveal the richness of our historic television collection and invite its perusal by researchers and browsers alike. We do so with pleasure and a certain amount of satisfaction at what has been achieved, against the odds, in this area of our conservation work.

CLYDE JEAVONS
Curator, National Film and Television Archive

Acknowledgments

The National Film and Television Archive is grateful to the many people and organisations who assisted in the preparation of this catalogue. Thanks must be extended to Wilf Stevenson, Director of the British Film Institute, for his support of the project and for the provision of financial resources which made publication possible.

The considerable task of researching the information for *A for Andromeda to Zoo Time* within the tight schedule would have been impossible without the considerable assistance and expert knowledge of Tise Vahimagi. He willingly and efficiently worked on all aspects of text preparation, in particular with research on individual programmes and series, the preparation of the genre index, proof-reading and the selection of stills. We are most grateful to him.

The efficient downloading of data from the BFI's database to machine-readable files for typesetting was the work of the Computer Unit, in particular Frank Carberry and Mark Richardson to whose enthusiasm and expertise we are indebted. For expert advice on typesetting and design layout we thank Ed Buscombe, Roma Gibson and John Smoker (BFI Publishing) and John Gibbs; thanks also to the Stills, Posters & Designs collection of the NFTVA and the BFI's Library and Information Service.

Sincere thanks for sharing their knowledge on the content of individual programmes and the history of the collection as a whole are extended to colleagues in TV Acquisitions. Thanks too go to the staff, both past and present, in the Cataloguing Section who have given help and support throughout the project and made the experience of producing this publication a pleasant and happy one.

For assistance in finding transmission dates, confirming titles and in clarifying ambiguous information, we acknowledge the help of the film libraries and press departments of the various ITV companies.

Individuals who have given freely of their time to advise and comment in numerous ways include Markku Salmi, Aileen Cook, Tony Mechele, Elaine Burrows, Julie Rigg, Bryony Dixon, Sandie Brown, Charles Hicks and Gordon Terris.

Finally the editors would like to thank Clyde Jeavons and Anne Fleming, Curator and Deputy Curator of the NFTVA for their unwavering commitment to and support for this catalogue.

SIMON BAKER
OLWEN TERRIS
National Film and Television Archive, Cataloguing Section
June 1993

The Television Collection at the National Film and Television Archive

THIS CATALOGUE contains details of all the television programmes and programme items dating from before 1980, held in the National Film and Television Archive (formerly the National Film Archive), which is a division of the British Film Institute. The only exceptions are news items and commercials, which have been excluded for reasons of space. As such, the catalogue obviously includes many of the most significant and successful broadcasts in British television history, but the methods by which the material has been acquired have been various and opportunistic, resulting in a collection which, though impressive, is uneven and requires some explanation if it is to be fully understood.

The National Film Archive was founded in 1935, the year before the world's first regular high-definition television service was established by the BBC. The Archive's aim subsequently has been to acquire, preserve and make permanently available a national collection of moving images which have lasting value as examples of the art and history of cinema and television, or as a documentary record of the twentieth century. However, unlike some other countries, Britain has never had a law of statutory deposit for moving images, such as exists for printed matter, so that the acquisition of that national collection has depended upon grants, donations and the expenditure of very limited acquisition budgets from the public purse. Consequently, the Archive has not always contained everything its keepers would have liked to include; while, on the other hand, it has taken in substantial and often comprehensive collections of material which have, for whatever reason, been made available to it.

Television was initially a minor part of the Archive's operations and it was not until 1959 that the first Television Officer was appointed. The following year the Archive signed a deposit agreement with the BBC, the first of its kind, which laid down the conditions under which programmes deposited by the Corporation or purchased by the Archive were to be held, thus satisfying the demands of copyright law. This was followed by similar agreements with the various ITV companies. In 1961 the British Film Institute formally acknowledged a television commitment and in 1962 a Television Selection Committee, made up of critics, programme makers and archivists, was set up to choose which programmes should be acquired by the Archive. Even so, the emphasis was on 'films for television' and much material on videotape was unfortunately rejected in the sixties at the same time as the television companies themselves were unsure of the viability of preserving programmes on tape.

Throughout the sixties the rate of acquisition of television material was very low and restricted by lack of funds. Nevertheless, copies of many important programmes from that era and from the comparatively small number of items which had survived from the previous decade, were purchased and preserved. These tended to be those programmes which the Selection Committee considered of particular importance, such as *The Wednesday Play: Cathy Come Home* (BBC), *Lord Reith Looks Back* (BBC), *The Lover* (Rediffusion) or *A Wedding on Saturday* (Granada). In addition, the Archive's other acquisition areas, concerned with cinema and documentary material, selected considerable amounts of television material from series such as *Cinema* and *World in Action* (Granada), both of which are reflected in this catalogue.

Some special collections of television material from the early decades, such as all the nitrate film material from the BBC's *Television Newsreel* (not listed in this catalogue) also came the Archive's way, both at the time and in more recent years. For instance, when Rediffusion, the ITV contractor for the London area, went out of existence in 1968, the Archive picked up most of what was left of its programme archive, with the exception of the extremely important collection of film material associated with the current affairs series *This Week* from 1956 to 1968. However, the *This Week* material was eventually acquired by the Archive in the mid 1970s and takes up a large section of these pages. Also acquired in recent years was what remained of the large number of light entertainment programmes produced for Rediffusion in the late fifties by Jack Hylton Television Productions, featuring such performers as Tony Hancock, Arthur Askey and the Crazy Gang. These programmes appear throughout the catalogue, as indeed do all the Rediffusion programmes preserved by the Archive.

The fragile nature of archival provision in an ITV system in which companies had no guaranteed long-term survival was recognised in 1969, when the Independent Television Companies Association (now the Independent Television Association) provided the National Film Archive with the first of a series of annual grants to be used for the purchase of copies of extra ITV programmes for preservation. In 1969 the grant was ten thousand pounds, enough to buy 75 programmes, and it was gradually increased in later years, so that many more ITV than BBC programmes were acquired by purchase in the seventies.

In 1982 Channel 4 opted, from its very beginning, to provide similar grant monies and in 1985 the Archive changed its main method of acquisition from purchase to direct recording off-air, to broadcast standard, using the grant monies for this purpose, a much more cost-effective method. Today, the National Film and Television Archive records, for preservation and access, about 25% of the output of ITV and Channel 4, over 5,000 programmes per annum, plus a limited but not insubstantial number of BBC and satellite items. As this material falls outside the scope of this catalogue it will need to be itemised in forthcoming volumes. However, material from before 1980 which has been repeated on-air in recent years and recorded by the Archive has been included.

Since August 1990 the Archive has also provided an access service to current BBC programmes by recording viewing cassette copies only of the complete output of both BBC TV channels, which means that some material from before 1980, which has been recently repeated, will be available for viewing. This recording operation is too extensive to allow for the cataloguing of individual programmes, so that these pre-1980 items are not included here, although dial-in access to the BBC's own database means that Archive staff can identify what is held on request.

Also included in this catalogue is the pre-1980 material which has recently been donated by the companies and which has shown as dramatic an increase as that acquired through the use of grant monies. The reason for this is that there are large collections of programmes on the obsolete 2″ videotape format which the companies must transfer to a modern format if they are to be used. This does not always happen, but, whether the transfers are made or not, many tapes are tending to end up with the Archive, which has the facilities to provide the companies with copies on request. Companies which have recently been transferring their 2″ collections and depositing the masters with the Archive include Granada, LWT and Yorkshire, while Tyne Tees simply deposited its entire 2″ collection as it stood, which explains why this catalogue contains a large amount of material from that company from the seventies.

The catalogue contains all the programmes in the Archive's possession at the end of July 1992, which means that, in terms of much of the 2″ videotape material continuously coming in, parts of it will already be out-of-date. For instance, Granada is constantly transferring episodes of *Coronation Street*, of which it holds every one made, and depositing the masters with the Archive, so it has been necessary to indicate this in the catalogue rather than attempt to list the individual episodes held at the cut-off point. However, the database is constantly being updated so that Archive staff can answer enquiries as to the contents of the collection, and updated catalogues can be published in future. Indeed, this will prove very necessary if all the material which it is anticipated may come the Archive's way in future does in fact arrive. This includes the BBC's collection of over 50,000 2″ videotapes, yet to be transferred, and almost the entire contents of the Thames archive.

Because the Archive is constantly making new copies of its holdings in the interests of both preservation and access, the catalogue does not indicate on which format the programmes listed are held. These range from 16 mm and 35 mm film to the whole variety of videotape formats, past and present. The Archive always endeavours to hold both preservation master material and viewing copies, but this is not always possible and, where only single copies exist, preservation takes priority over access, although there are some items, particularly those acquired after screenings on the BFI's South Bank complex, which are held only on U-matic cassette but are available for viewing.

Under the terms of the Archive's agreement with donating organisations, and because of contractual and copyright considerations, viewing of the programmes held in the collection is limited to *bona fide* students and researchers engaged in serious research, and is confined to British Film Institute premises. This usually means the Institute's Central London offices, where the Archive's public access sections are located, although the collection itself is actually kept in optimum preservation conditions at the purpose-built J. Paul Getty Jnr. Conservation Centre, Berkhamsted. Viewings are arranged by appointment through the Archive's Viewing Service and are charged at specially subsidised rates, far below the commercial viewing rates charged by the companies themselves. As indicated above, only when viewing material exists can viewing take place, although the Archive is constantly seeking to enlarge its viewing collection and video technology can make this relatively cheap and easy.

One particular collection is worthy of note in this context. Over the past few years the Archive has been acquiring classic ballet and contemporary dance performances from the BBC under the terms of an agreement with the Society for Dance Research which pays for the copying of the material in return for free viewing access to its members. A similar scheme for drama productions is being developed and it is hoped that other specialist areas of study may consider the merits of ensuring that important television recordings can be made available to those who would most benefit from their accessibility.

There are other outlets for public access to the Archive's television collection. Programmes are frequently supplied for screening in the regular Television on BFI South Bank evenings and at regional film theatres throughout the country. The permanent exhibits at the Museum of the Moving Image on the South Bank also contain much Archive material, and the BFI is currently exploring ways of making a collection of classic programmes available through a videotheque facility and by cooperation with the *TV Heaven* project at the National Museum of Photography, Film and Television in Bradford.

In addition to these uses, the collection is also available for use by the television companies themselves. Donor companies are automatically entitled to copies of their own productions while the Archive's Production Library supplies copies of extracts for use in new productions, provided that copyright clearance has been made and that it is not more appropriate for the material to be supplied by the original broadcaster. One recent production for which the Archive supplied a large amount of material, both in terms of extracts and complete programmes, was Channel 4's *TV Heaven* series.

One other form of acquisition is worth mentioning in conclusion. They are not indicated as such, but several of the items in this catalogue were thought to have been lost, having been discarded by their originating company at a time when archival concerns were not so well established as they are today. However, such lost treasures do occasionally come to light from sources such as overseas television companies, the original production personnel or even private

xiv

collectors. Probably the most spectacular recovery of recent years at the National Film and Television Archive was the difficult restoration, from antique half-inch open reel tapes, of eight missing episodes of *Steptoe and Son* (BBC), which had been kept by the writers, Ray Galton and Alan Simpson. These have since been screened at the South Bank, repeated on BBC Television and released on BBC Home Video, proving beyond a doubt the value of maintaining television archives and keeping our television heritage alive.

STEVE BRYANT
Keeper of Television
National Film and Television Archive

Arrangement of the Catalogue

THE CATALOGUE is arranged alphabetically by series title and main titles which do not form part of a series. Within a series, episode titles are filed in transmission date order, from earliest to the latest.

The episode title index (for anthology drama and some documentary series where individual episodes have become well known in their own right) directs users from the episode title to the series. For example, the user looking in the index under the play title LET'S MURDER VIVALDI will be directed to The **WEDNESDAY PLAY** series where the full entry will be found.

Production Countries
The vast majority of programmes in the catalogue were produced in Great Britain. Where a programme was produced in another country this is indicated in brackets after the programme or series title. A list of the country codes is given on page xvii.

Production Companies
The production company is given in brackets after the programme or series title. A co-production is indicated by the use of a hyphen, e.g. Film Partnership-BBC. A list of abbreviations is given on page xvii.

Transmission Dates
Every effort has been made to give a transmission date for each programme listed and for the transmission date span of a series. Where this information is missing, and only a year is given, the details were not available from the production companies. This is a problem made more difficult by the fact that many companies in this period have since lost their franchise and records of transmission dates have not always been logged with the new company. The television journals (*Radio Times* and *TV Times*) often cite only the series title in their listings rather than the episode title, making the identification of an exact transmission date more problematical. It should be noted that transmission dates in this catalogue are taken from the London-based editions of the *Radio Times* and *TV Times*.

Production and Cast Credits
Directors, producers, scriptwriters, cast and leading players (for serials and drama series) are listed for each programme. Other credits such as choreographer, narrator, reporter, etc. are given as appropriate. Where this information is missing the credit details were not available from the *Radio Times* or *TV Times*. The abbreviations used are listed on page xvii.

Indexes
Episode and Alternative Title Index
The alternative title index directs the user from the name of the episode title to the series of which it forms part. The transmission date follows the title to facilitate the finding of the main entry chronologically within the series.

Users are reminded that the episode title index applies to episodes within anthology drama series and for episodes of documentary series where individual episodes have become well-known in their own right.

Following international cataloguing standards titles have been given in the language of the country of production. References from the English language title are given in the index.

Genre Index
The list of genre headings groups together programmes and series within a common theme. It brings together, for example, the quiz shows, medical dramas and sitcoms.

Where a heading generates a large number of titles, for example, arts and social documentaries, the user is directed to other headings which may also be of interest. Some of these may be broad subject headings; for example, the researcher looking under 'Social Documentaries' will be prompted to look

Abbreviations

at related headings such as 'Housing' or 'Trade Unionism'. Other subject headings have been introduced for ease of use to highlight topics such as 'Royalty' and 'Health and Medicine'.

Episode titles within the same series are filed in transmission date order; titles which are the same are distinguished by the year of transmission; series with the same title but made by different companies are distinguished.

TV companies

ABC (for GB; US and Australian – country code will appear before company e.g. (AU ABC 12/9/1978))
AU ABC (Australian Broadcasting Corporation)
US ABC (American Broadcasting Company)
ATV (Associated Television)
BBC (British Broadcasting Corporation)
CBC (Canadian Broadcasting Corporation)
CBS (Columbia Broadcasting System)
HTV (Harlech Television)
ITC (Incorporated Television Company)
LWT (London Weekend Television)
NBC (National Broadcasting Company)
NOS (Nederlandse Omroep Stichting/ Netherlands Broadcasting Corporation)
RTVE
TVS (Television South)
TWW (Television West and Wales)

Co-productions entered as follows: –
BBC-WGBH
Piccolo Films-ITC

Country codes

AU	Australia
CA	Canada
CN	People's Republic of China
DD	German Democratic Republic (East Germany)
DE	German Federal Republic (West Germany)
ES	Spain
FR	France
GB	Great Britain
IE	Ireland
IT	Italy
JP	Japan
NL	The Netherlands
SE	Sweden
SU	Soviet Union
US	United States of America

Credits

adapt	adapter
assoc.p	associate producer
auth	author (of the original work/ play/story)
chor	choreographer
comm	commentator
creator	creator
d	director
exec.p	executive producer
intro	introduction
lp	leading players
m	music
nar	narrator
ntx	not transmitted
p	producer
ph	photography
pres	presenter
reader	reader
regular(s)	regular cast
rep	reporter
sc	scriptwriter
trans	translation
tx	transmitted
voice	voice(s)
with	with

British Television Companies

For fuller information on the holdings of these companies and access to them the *Researcher's Guide to British Film & Television Collections* 4th rev ed., edited by James Ballantyne, published 1993 by the British Universities Film & Video Council, is recommended.

ABC Television
Began transmission 24/9/1955; ended 28/7/1968. Became **Associated Television** (ATV) 30/7/1968–31/12/1981. Combined with Rediffusion to form **Thames Television** 30/7/1968.

Anglia Television Ltd
Began transmission 27/10/1959

Anglia Television Ltd
Programme Library
Anglia House
NORWICH NR21 3JG
0603 615151 fax 0603 631032

Associated Television (ATV)
Began transmission with London (Weekend) franchise 24/9/1955; ended 28/7/1968, then **London Weekend Television** 2/8/1968. Held Midlands (Weekday) franchise 17/2/1956–31/12/81, became **Central Independent Television** 1/1/1982. See also **ITC**.

BBC
Access to all libraries is through BBC Enterprises.

Requests for footage to:
Sales Manager Library Sales
BBC Enterprises Ltd
Woodlands
LONDON W12 0TT
081–758 8444/5 fax 081–847 4267

Complete programmes handled by:
BBC Enterprises Ltd
Woodlands
80 Wood Lane
LONDON W12 0TT
081–576 0202 or 081–743 5588
fax 081–749 0538

Border Television
Began transmission 1/9/1961

Border Television Film & VTR Library
Border Television plc
CARLISLE
Cumbria CA1 3NT
0228 25101 fax 0228 41384

Central Independent Television
Began transmission 1/1/1982 following restructuring of ATV. There are separate news libraries in Nottingham (0602 863322 ext. 5204) and Abingdon (0235 554123 ext. 141).

Central Independent Television
Film and Tape Libraries
Central House
Broad Street
BIRMINGHAM B1 2JP
021–643 9898 fax 021–616 1088

Channel Television
Began transmission 1/9/1962

The Television Centre
La Pouquelaye
St HELIER
Jersey JE2 3ZD
0534 68999 fax 0534 59446

Grampian Television
Began transmission 30/9/1961

Grampian Television
Queen's Cross
ABERDEEN AB9 2XJ
0224 646464 fax 0224 635127

Granada Television
Began transmission 3/5/1956

Granada Television Ltd
MANCHESTER M60 9EA
061–832 7211 fax 061–839 6558

Associated Television (ATV) and Granada Television became seven-day contractors in 1968.

HTV
Began transmission 4/3/1968

Television Centre
HTV
Culverhouse Cross
CARDIFF CF5 6XJ
0222 590590 fax 0222 598544

ITN

ITN Library Sales
200 Gray's Inn Road
LONDON WC1X 8XZ
071–430 4453 fax 071–430 4453

Library covers news bulletins and
coverage from 1955 to date.

ITC

ITC Library Sales
No. 1 Wadsworth Business Centre
21 Wadsworth Road
PERIVALE
Middx UB6 7JD
081–998 0066 fax 081–998 5905

The library deals with material from
Associated Television from 1955–1981/2.

London Weekend Television (LWT)
Began transmission 2/8/1968

London Television Centre
Upper Ground
LONDON SE1 9LT
071–261 3690/3771 fax 071–261 3456

Rediffusion
Began transmission 22/9/1955; ended
29/7/1968. Name changed from
Associated-Rediffusion in July 1964.
Combined with ABC to form **Thames
Television**
30/7/1968–31/12/92, then Carlton
Television.

Scottish Television
Began transmission 31/8/1957

Scottish Television plc
Cowcaddens
GLASGOW G2 3PR
041–332 9999 fax 041–332 6982

Southern Television
Began transmission 30/7/1958; ended
31/12/1981. Became **TVS** (Television
South) 1/1/1982–31/12/1992, then
Meridian.

TVS
Began transmission 1/1/1982; ended
31/12/1992; then Meridian.

The Television Centre
SOUTHAMPTON SO9 5HZ
0703 634211 fax 0703 639057

Thames Television
Began transmission 30/7/1968; ended
31/12/92. Then Carlton Television.

Thames Television plc
306–316 Euston Road
LONDON NW1 3BB
071–387 9494 fax 071–383 2015

TWW
Began transmission 14/1/1958; ended
3/3/1968. Then **HTV**.

Tyne Tees Television
Began transmission 15/1/1959

Tyne Tees Television
Television Centre
City Road
NEWCASTLE UPON TYNE NE1 2AL
091–261 0181 fax 091–261 2302

Ulster Television
Began transmission 31/10/1959

Ulster Television Ltd
Havelock
Ormeau Road
BELFAST BT7 1EB
0232 328122 fax 0232 246695

Westward Television
Began transmission 29/4/61; ended
11/8/1981. Became TSW (Television
South West) 12/8/1981–31/12/1992, then
Westcountry Television.

TSW Broadcasting Ltd
Derry's Cross
PLYMOUTH
Devon P11 2SP
0752 663322 fax 0752 671970

Yorkshire Television
Began transmission 29/7/1968

Yorkshire Television Programme
Library
Television Centre
LEEDS
West Yorkshire LS3 1JS
0532 438283 fax 0532 445107

The Catalogue

A

A FOR ANDROMEDA
(BBC 3/10–14/11/1961)
Seven-part science-fiction series.
The LAST MYSTERY 14/11/1961
Incomplete last episode.
p Michael Hayes, Norman Jones;
sc Fred Hoyle, John Elliot
lp Peter Halliday; Esmond Knight;
Patricia Kneale; Julie Christie; Noel Johnson;
Jack May

A.V. LAIDER (BBC 3/12/1955)
Adaptation of the story by Sir Max Beerbohm
set in a seaside hotel in 1908.
d Victor Menzies; *adapt* George F. Kerr
lp Richard Hurndall; Keith Pyott;
Norman Claridge; Pauline Loring;
Maureen O'Reilly; Richard Bebb

ABC OF ABC: A SOUVENIR WITH MUSIC
(ABC 30/4/1966)
A celebration and look back at ten years of ABC
Television.
p Reginald Collin; *sc* Ray Bottomley;
with Eamonn Andrews, Barry Westwood,
Billie Whitelaw, Cliff Richard, Alun Owen

ABOUT ANGLIA (Anglia 1959–90)
Local news magazine programme.
ABOUT ANGLIA 24/6/1970

ABOUT BRITAIN (ITV various 1972–84)
Daytime half-hour slot on the ITV network used
by regional companies with programmes filmed
in their own areas.
The DANCING WATERS (Tyne Tees 5/6/1973)
Two different communities who live on the
banks of the River Coquet in Northumberland.
d Tony Kysh
ONE MAN AND HIS CITY (Tyne Tees 2/4/1974)
Dr Henry Miller gives a tour of Newcastle.
d Andrea Wonfor
SELKIRK COMMON RIDING (Border 24/10/1974)
The annual march at Selkirk.
d John Pattison Tomkins
EVERYONE'S A WINNER IN GATESHEAD
(Tyne Tees 20/8/1975)
The achievements of Brendan Foster as manager
of Gateshead's sports and recreation
department, and the impact on the town of the
new sports stadium.
d Jeremy Lack
FISHERMAN OF CLOVELLY (HTV 9/10/1975)
Life in Clovelly and a profile of the village's last
remaining fisherman, John Heddon, in his 70s.
d Sebastian Robinson; *p* Ron Evans;
comm Tony Holme
BUCCLEUCHS OF THE BORDER
(Border 7/1/1976)
An interview with the ninth Duke of Buccleuch;
and the agriculture in the Border region of
England and Scotland.
d Norman Fraser
LAND OF THE GIANT LEEKS
(Tyne Tees 4/7/1976)
Competition among villagers for first prize at the
Monkton Village Leek Show, Jarrow.
d Jeremy Lack; *exec.p* Leslie Barrett
JOSS (Border 13/10/1976)
Portrait of Joss Naylor, champion fell runner.
d William Cartner; *p* Ken De Vonald
An ENGLISHMAN'S CASTLE
(Tyne Tees 28/1/1977)
How George Howard runs his stately home –
Castle Howard – which is open to the public.
d Tony Kysh; *exec.p* Leslie Barrett
PITMAN PAINTER (Tyne Tees 4/2/1977)
Artist Norman Cornish, a former miner, who
lives and works in his home town of
Spennymoor, Co. Durham.
d Andrea Wonfor
TELL THEM YOU COME FROM GOSFORTH
(Tyne Tees 7/2/1977)
A celebration of one hundred years of Gosforth
Rugby Union Club.
d Jeremy Lack; *p* Alan Powell
WALKING WESTWARD (Westward 1/4/1977)
Clive Gunnell visits the Nimrod squadron at
RAF St. Mawgan in Cornwall.
d Clive Gunnell

WOR BOBBY (Tyne Tees 15/7/1977)
Profile of stand-up comic Bobby Thompson, an
entertainer in the north-east of England.
d Roger Cheveley; *p/sc* Michael McHugh
Y GWR O GWR YR ARAN (HTV 5/10/1978)
The life of handicapped schoolteacher Frank
Letch of Llanuwchllyn, Gwynnedd.
d Gareth Wynn Jones; *p* Gwyn Erfyl
An HONEST DAY'S TOIL (Tyne Tees 12/2/1979)
A farm where shire horses still do most of the
work on the land.
p David Thomasson
IS EVERYBODY HAPPY (Tyne Tees 9/4/1979)
St. Stephen's community and church centre in
South Shields.
d Bernard Preston; *p* John Fleight
SHETLAND AND THE GIFT HORSE
(Scottish TV 27/6/1979)
A visit to Shetland to discover what effect the oil
bonanza has had on the islands and their
inhabitants.
d Don Cumming; *exec.p* Ken Blackie;
rep Paul Murricane
HALLELUJAH HOLIDAY (Tyne Tees 4/7/1979)
Members of The Movement for World
Evangelisation at a Christian Crusade week at
Butlins, Filey Bay.
d Mike Ruggins; *p* Maxwell Deas

ABOUT RELIGION (ATV 1956–65)
Series on religious issues.
CHRIST IN JEANS 23/3/1958
A discussion on religion and everyday life.
p Michael Regington
EPILEPSY 11/8/1963
The problems faced by epileptics and the current
methods of treatment available.
d Shaun O'Riordan; *sc* Monica Furlong;
intro Peter Barkworth

ABOUT TURN (Grampian)
Regional interview series.
ODETTE 2/8/1979
d Tom Fawcett

ABROAD WITH BEHAN (Tyne Tees 1968)
A series of six regional programmes in which
Irish poet Brendan Behan interviews various
people.
DAME IRENE WARD 19/9/1968
EMANUEL SHINWELL 26/9/1968

ACCESS (Tyne Tees 1973)
Open access programme featuring causes from
local groups.
DISABLEMENT INCOMES GROUP 16/7/1973
Sir Keith Joseph answers questions raised by
disabled people who are not receiving maximum
state benefits.

ACCOLADE (Rediffusion 11/1/1967)
Extract from the London Evening Standard's
Drama Awards for 1966.
d Jim Pople, Peter Moffatt; *p* Elkan Allan

ACROSS THE HEART (AU ABC 11/4/1963)
A review of Queen Elizabeth II's tour of
Australia.

ACT OF FAITH (BBC 22/5/1962)
The story of the building and adornment of the
new Coventry Cathedral. With Basil Spence,
Jacob Epstein, John Piper, Graham Sutherland,
and John Campbell Hutton.
d John Read; *p/sc* Robin Whitworth;
comm Leo Genn

ADAM ADAMANT LIVES! (BBC 1966–67)
Fantasy-drama series about an Edwardian
adventurer resurrected from suspended
animation to fight modern-day crime.
The TERRIBLY HAPPY EMBALMERS
4/8/1966
d Paul Ciappessoni; *p* Verity Lambert;
sc Brian Clemens
lp Gerald Harper; Juliet Harmer; Jack May;
John Scott; John Le Mesurier; Deryck Guyler

ADAM SMITH (Granada 1972–73)
Drama series about the life of a church minister.
EPISODE 12 9/4/1972
d Richard Martin; *p* June Howson; *sc* Ben Rae
lp Andrew Keir; Robert James; Brown Derby;
Helen Norman; Brigit Forsyth

The ADDAMS FAMILY
(US Filmways TV Productions 1964–66)
Comedy series based on the cartoon characters
created by Charles Addams for 'The New
Yorker' magazine.
The ADDAMS FAMILY GOES TO SCHOOL
18/9/1964
d Arthur Hiller; *p* Nat Perrin;
sc Ed James, Seaman Jacobs
lp John Astin; Carolyn Jones; Jackie Coogan;
Ted Cassidy; Blossom Rock; Ken Weatherwax;
Lisa Loring; Allyn Joslyn; Madge Blake;
Rolfe Sedan

ADVENTURE (BBC 1961–65)
Series of films taken by travellers and explorers
on their expeditions throughout the world. Series
edited by David Attenborough.
SCOTT'S LAST JOURNEY 3/4/1962
A commemoration of the 50th anniversary of the
death of Captain Robert Scott.
p John Read; *sc* Martin Chisholm;
nar Richard Dimbleby
DALAI LAMA 29/6/1962
The Dalai Lama, his tour of Tibet and his
inauguration.
pres Brian Branston; *nar* David Attenborough
BALLOON FROM ZANZIBAR 23/8/1962
Anthony Smith and cameraman Douglas Botting
fly by balloon from Zanzibar to the mainland of
Africa.
ph Douglas Botting, Alan Root;
pres Brian Branston; *nar* Anthony Smith
QUEST UNDER CAPRICORN
26/4–31/5/1963
A limited series of programmes on the people
and animals living in the deserts and tropical
swamps of the Northern Territory of Australia.
p/nar David Attenborough; *ph* Eugene Carr
QUEST UNDER CAPRICORN: THE DESERT
GODS 26/4/1963
QUEST UNDER CAPRICORN: THE HERMITS OF
BORROLOOLA 3/5/1963
QUEST UNDER CAPRICORN: BUFFALO, GEESE
AND MEN 10/5/1963
QUEST UNDER CAPRICORN: THE ARTISTS OF
ARNHEM LAND 17/5/1963
QUEST UNDER CAPRICORN: BUSH
WALKABOUT 24/5/1963
QUEST UNDER CAPRICORN: THE FIRST
AUSTRALIANS 31/5/1963

ADVENTURE PLAYGROUND
(BBC 19/4/1963)
The conversion of waste ground in Grimsby into
a playground for children.
d Stephen Peet, Tom Foley,
Maddalena Fagandini; *pres* Patrick Dowling

ADVENTURE WEEKLY (BBC 1968–70)
Series for children featuring five youngsters who
start their own newspaper.
d Barry Letts; *p* John McRae
regulars Brent Oldfield; Len Jones;
Bartlett Mullins; Frank Barry; Elizabeth Dear
UNITED EFFORT 6/1/1969
sc Shaun Sutton
lp Morris Perry; Ian Ellis; Barry Lowe;
John Woodnutt
The SIEGE 17/3/1969
sc Victor Pemberton
lp Barbara Leake; David Graham;
Michael Wisher

The ADVENTURER (ITC 1972–74)
Spy series featuring an undercover agent posing
as an international film star. *p* Monty Berman
regulars Gene Barry; Barry Morse;
Catherine Schell; Stuart Damon
POOR LITTLE RICH GIRL 7/10/1972
d Cyril Frankel; *sc* Paul Clay
lp Judy Geeson; John Savident;
Maurice Browning

The ADVENTURER cont.

HAS ANYONE HERE SEEN KELLY? 1973
d Val Guest; *sc* Tony Williamson
lp Anouska Hempel; Rio Fanning; Sandor Eles
The BRADLEY WAY 15/9/1973
d Val Guest; *sc* Gerald Kelsey
lp Richard Marner; Janet Key;
Joanna Dunham
SKELETON IN THE CUPBOARD 22/9/1973
d Cyril Frankel; *sc* Donald James
lp Roy Kinnear; Sylvia Syms;
Richard Vernon; Basil Dignam
COUNTERSTRIKE 7/12/1973
d Paul Dickson; *sc* Tony Williamson
lp Stephan Kulik; Kara Wilson;
George Mikel
LOVE ALWAYS, MAGDA 14/12/1973
d Cyril Frankel; *sc* Philip Broadley
lp Kieron Moore; Cyd Hayman; Paul Maxwell
DEADLOCK 28/12/1973
d Val Guest; *sc* Donald James
lp Mervyn Johns; Jennie Linden;
Wolfe Morris
I'LL GET THERE SOMETIME 11/1/1974
d Val Guest; *sc* Tony Williamson
lp Patrick Jordan; Pippa Steel;
Frank Barrie
TO THE LOWEST BIDDER 18/1/1974
d Val Guest; *sc* Donald James
lp Anthony Nicholls; Jane Asher; Sheila Gish
GOING, GOING... 25/1/1974
d Val Guest; *sc* Gerald Kelsey
lp Arnold Diamond; Burt Kwouk; Norman Bird
The SOLID GOLD HEARSE 1/3/1974
d Val Guest; *sc* Tony Williamson
lp Sydney Tafler; Kevin Stoney; Janos Kurucz
MAKE IT A MILLION 8/3/1974
d Barry Morse; *sc* Tony Williamson
lp Paul Eddington; Ronald Radd;
Joanna Jones
ICONS ARE FOREVER 15/3/1974
d Cyril Frankel; *sc* Tony Williamson
lp Stephanie Beacham; Noel Willman;
Alfred Marks

The ADVENTURES OF AGGIE
(ME Films 1956–57)
Thriller series featuring a globe-trotting fashion
expert.
CUT GLASS 27/4/1957
d John Guillermin; *p* Michael Sadler;
sc Ernest Borneman, Martin Stern
lp Joan Shawlee; Christopher Lee;
Ernst Ulman; Peter Bull; John Miller

The ADVENTURES OF ROBIN HOOD
(Sapphire Films 1955–60)
Adventure series based on the Robin Hood
legend.
The MONEYLENDER 2/10/1955
d Ralph Smart; *p* Hannah Weinstein;
sc Eric Heath
lp Richard Greene; Alan Wheatley; Alfie Bass;
Leo McKern; Bruce Seton

The ADVENTURES OF SHERLOCK
HOLMES (US Sheldon Reynolds, 1954–55)
Syndicated American series, filmed in Europe,
featuring Ronald Howard as Sherlock Holmes
and Howard Marion-Crawford as Dr Watson.
The CASE OF A PERFECT HUSBAND 1955
The CASE OF HARRY CROCKER 1955
The CASE OF THE BAKER STREET
BACHELORS 1955
The CASE OF THE BAKER STREET
NURSEMAID 1955
The CASE OF THE CHRISTMAS PUDDING 1955
The CASE OF THE DIAMOND TOOTH 1955
The CASE OF THE EXHUMED CLIENT 1955
The CASE OF THE FRENCH INTERPRETER 1955
The CASE OF THE GREYSTONE
INSCRIPTION 1955
The CASE OF THE IMPOSTER MYSTERY 1955
The CASE OF THE IMPROMPTU
PERFORMANCE 1955
The CASE OF THE NEUROTIC DETECTIVE 1955
The CASE OF THE PENNSYLVANIA GUN 1955
The CASE OF THE REDHEADED LEAGUE 1955
The CASE OF THE RELUCTANT
CARPENTER 1955
The CASE OF THE ROYAL MURDER 1955
The CASE OF THE SHOELESS 1955
The CASE OF THE SHY BALLERINA 1955

The CASE OF THE SINGING VIOLIN 1955
The CASE OF THE SPLIT TICKET 1955
The CASE OF THE TEXAS COWGIRL 1955
The CASE OF THE THISTLE KILLER 1955
The CASE OF THE TYRANT'S DAUGHTER 1955
The CASE OF THE UNLUCKY GAMBLER 1955
The CASE OF THE VANISHED DETECTIVE 1955
The CASE OF THE VIOLENT SUITOR 1955
The CASE OF THE WINTHROP LEGEND 1955
The MOTHER HUBBARD CASE 1955

The ADVENTURES OF THE SCARLET
PIMPERNEL (Towers of London 1955–56)
Adventure series based on Baroness Orczy's
stories about the Scarlet Pimpernel during the
period of the French Revolution.
The WINGED MADONNA 7/2/1956
d Wolf Rilla;
p Marius Goring, Dennis Vance;
sc Joel Murcott, Ralph Bettinson
lp Marius Goring; Anthony Newlands;
Renee Goddard; Nicholas Bruce;
Stanley Van Beers

The ADVENTURES OF TWIZZLE
(Rediffusion 1959–62)
Puppet series for children.
The ADVENTURES OF TWIZZLE 1959
d Gerry Anderson; *p/sc* Roberta Leigh

AFRICAN REVOLUTIONARY – JULIUS
NYERERE (BBC 20/1/1966)
A portrait of the Tanzanian President, Julius
Nyerere.
d/p Michael Gill; *nar* Erskine Childers

AFTER A LIFETIME
(Kestrel Films-LWT 18/7/1971)
The family of a militant trade unionist gather in
Liverpool for his funeral and wake.
d Ken Loach; *p* Tony Garnett;
sc Neville Smith
lp Bill Dean; Neville Smith; Edie Brooks;
Jimmy Coleman; Peter Kerrigan;
Johnny Gee

AFTER JULIUS (Yorkshire TV 1979)
Trilogy by Elizabeth Jane Howard, adapted from
her novel of the same name. Describes the
events of a weekend in 1959; a reunion between
the widow and daughters of a man who
disappeared at Dunkirk in 1940.
d John Glenister; *exec.p* David Cunliffe;
sc Elizabeth Jane Howard
lp Faith Brook; Petra Markham;
Paul Copley; John Carson; Cyd Hayman;
Freda Bamford; Alison Key; Trevor Bowen
EPISODE 1: FRIDAY 20/4/1979
EPISODE 2: SATURDAY 21/4/1979
EPISODE 3: SUNDAY 22/4/1979

AFTER MIDNIGHT (Rediffusion 21/9/1959)
Michael Ingrams looks at London between
midnight and dawn.
d/sc Michael Ingrams

AFTERNOON (Thames 1977–79)
Daytime magazine programme. Previously called
GOOD AFTERNOON (1974–77).
BERYL BAINBRIDGE 8/12/1977
Mavis Nicholson interviews the novelist Beryl
Bainbridge.

An AFTERNOON AT THE FESTIVAL
(Yorkshire TV 6/5/1973)
Film director Leo is trying to sell his latest epic
at a film festival when he meets music student,
Anita.
d Donald McWhinnie; *exec.p* Peter Willes;
sc David Mercer
lp Leo McKern; Adrienne Corri; Jeremy Kemp;
Rosalind Ayres; Donald Pickering

AGAINST THE CROWD
(ATV 13/7–17/8/1975)
A series of seven plays concerned with
individuals who find themselves opposed to the
views of the majority.
p Nicholas Palmer

POOR BABY 20/7/1975
d Paul Annett; *sc* Fay Weldon
lp Amanda Murray; Edward Hardwicke;
Patricia Garwood; William Hoyland;
Carole Hayman
CARBON COPY 3/8/1975
d Piers Haggard; *sc* Howard Schumann
lp Don Warrington; Judy Campbell;
Simon Lack; Kate Nicholls; Brian Stirner
WE ARE ALL GUILTY 17/8/1975
d Don Leaver; *sc* Kingsley Amis
lp Peter Vaughan; Terence Budd;
Marjie Lawrence; Don Henderson;
Linda Robson

The AGE OF UNCERTAINTY (BBC 1977)
Thirteen-part series charting the rise and crisis of
modern industrial society, presented by
Professor John Kenneth Galbraith.
The PROPHETS AND PROMISE OF CLASSICAL
CAPITALISM 10/1/1977
The men who laid the foundations of economics,
Adam Smith, David Ricardo and Thomas
Malthus.
p Dick Gilling
The MANNERS AND MORALS OF HIGH
CAPITALISM 17/1/1977
The effects today of attitudes of the rich in the
last century.
p Mick Jackson
KARL MARX – THE MASSIVE DISSENT 24/1/1977
The life and work of Karl Marx.
p Dick Gilling
The COLONIAL IDEA 31/1/1977
Colonialism from the Crusades to the present.
p Mick Jackson
LENIN AND THE GREAT UNGLUING 7/2/1977
Lenin and the coming of the Russian
Revolution.
p Dick Gilling
The RISE AND FALL OF MONEY 14/2/1977
The history of money.
p David Kennard
MANDARIN REVOLUTION 21/2/1977
The Depression and John Maynard Keynes'
policies.
p Dick Gilling
The FATAL COMPETITION 28/2/1977
The origins of the Cold War.
p David Kennard
The BIG CORPORATION 7/3/1977
The rise of corporate industry.
p David Kennard
LAND AND THE PEOPLE 14/3/1977
A solution to end poverty in the world.
p David Kennard
The METROPOLIS 21/3/1977
The city as the focus of the problems of modern
society.
p Mick Jackson
DEMOCRACY, LEADERSHIP AND COMMITMENT
28/3/1977
Professor Galbraith's views on democracy.
p Adrian Malone
WEEKEND IN VERMONT 2/4/1977
Views expressed on the themes outlined in the
series, with various contributors, including
Edward Heath, Henry Kissinger, Gyorgy
Arbatov and Shirley Williams.
p Mick Jackson, David Kennard

AGONY (LWT 1979–81)
Sitcom about a magazine 'agony aunt' and the
troubles she has solving the problems of her
family and friends, as well as her readers.
HELP 11/3/1979
d/p John Reardon;
sc Len Richmond, Anna Raeburn
lp Maureen Lipman; Simon Williams;
Diana Weston; Maria Charles; Jan Holden;
Peter Blake

AIN'T MISBEHAVIN' (ATV 25/7/1979)
Adaptation of the stage musical based on the
works of Fats Waller.
p Colin Clews
lp Evan Bell; Andre De Shields;
Annie Joe Edwards; Jozella Reed;
Charlaine Woodard

AIRPORT (Rediffusion 23/9/1964)
A day in the life of Heathrow Airport, London.
d Charles Squires

ALCHERINGA (AU ABC 1963)
Twelve-part series about the Australian
Aborigines.
HUNTING AN EMU 11/10/1963
The daily life of the Aborigines before
Europeans arrived in Australia.
d/sc Frank Few

The ALCOHOLIC (Rediffusion 18/5/1960)
The study of alcoholism as a disease.
d Peter Morley; *sc* Cyril Bennett

ALFRED HITCHCOCK PRESENTS
(US Shamley Productions 1955–62)
Drama anthology hosted by Alfred Hitchcock.
MR. BLANCHARD'S SECRET 23/12/1956
d/p Alfred Hitchcock; *sc* Sarett Rudley;
auth Emily Neff
lp Robert Horton; Meg Mundy;
Mary Scott; Dayton Lummis; Eloise Hardt
The PERFECT CRIME 20/10/1957
d Alfred Hitchcock;
p Joan Harrison, Alfred Hitchcock;
sc Stirling Silliphant; *auth* Ben Ray Redman
lp Vincent Price; James Gregory; Mark Dana;
Marianne Stewart; Gavin Gordon
MISS PAISLEY'S CAT 22/12/1957
d Jus Addiss; *p* Joan Harrison;
sc Marian Cockrell; *auth* Roy Vickers
lp Dorothy Stickney; Raymond Bailey;
Harry Tyler
LAMB TO THE SLAUGHTER 13/4/1958
d Alfred Hitchcock; *p* Joan Harrison;
sc/auth Roald Dahl
lp Barbara Bel Geddes; Allan Lane;
Harold J. Stone; Ken Clark; Robert C. Ross
A DIP IN THE POOL 1/6/1958
d Alfred Hitchcock;
p Joan Harrison, Alfred Hitchcock;
sc Robert Dennis; *auth* Roald Dahl
lp Keenan Wynn; Louise Platt; Fay Wray;
Philip Bourneuf; Doreen Lang
The CRYSTAL TRENCH 1/1/1959
d Alfred Hitchcock; *p* Joan Harrison;
sc Stirling Silliphant; *auth* A.E.W. Mason
lp James Donald; Patricia Owens;
Harold Dyrenforth; Ben Astar; Oscar Beregi
SIX PEOPLE, NO MUSIC 4/1/1959
d Norman Lloyd; *p* Joan Harrison;
sc Richard Berg; *auth* Garson Kanin
lp John McGiver; Peggy Cass; Howard Smith;
Joby Baker; Wilton Graff; Joe Hamilton
BANQUO'S CHAIR 3/5/1959
d Alfred Hitchcock;
p Joan Harrison, Alfred Hitchcock;
sc Francis Cockrell; *auth* Rupert Croft-Cooke
lp Reginald Gardiner; John Williams;
Kenneth Haigh; Max Adrian
ARTHUR 27/9/1959
d Alfred Hitchcock;
p Joan Harrison, Alfred Hitchcock
sc James P. Cavanagh; *auth* Arthur Williams
lp Laurence Harvey; Hazel Court;
Robert Douglas; Barry Harvey; Patrick Macnee
MRS. BIXBY AND THE COLONEL'S COAT
27/9/1960
d Alfred Hitchcock;
p Joan Harrison, Alfred Hitchcock;
sc Halsted Welles; *auth* Roald Dahl
lp Audrey Meadows; Les Tremayne;
Stephen Chase; Sally Hughes; Howard Caine;
Maidie Norman

ALFRED MARKS TIME
(Jack Hylton TV Productions 1956–61)
Comedy-music series.
d Douglas Hurn; *m* Steve Race and his
Orchestra;
with Alfred Marks, Paddie O'Neil,
Ray Ellington and his Quartet
ALFRED MARKS TIME 2/2/1959
with Leslie Mitchell, Jimmy Hanley,
Glen Mason, John Abineri, Anita West
ALFRED MARKS TIME 2/3/1959
with Leslie Mitchell

ALFRED MARKS TIME 16/3/1959
with Robert Rietty, John Abineri,
R.S.M. Brittain, William Sylvester,
Miriam Karlin, Anita West, Leslie Mitchell
ALFRED MARKS TIME 30/3/1959
with Spike Milligan, Sydney Tafler,
Michael Balfour, Robert Rietty, Sandra Dorne,
Amy Dalby, John Abineri, R.S.M. Brittain,
Dick Vosburgh
ALFRED MARKS TIME 13/4/1959
sc Dick Vosburgh, Eric Merriman, Barry Took;
with R.S.M. Brittain, Leslie Mitchell,
Dulcie Gray, Irene Handl, Libby Morris,
Murray Kash, Freddie Earle

ALGERIA (ATV 4/4/1962)
Henry Fairlie relates the story of the war in
Algeria, illustrating its progress with newsreel
material.
p Michael Redington;
sc Henry Fairlie, Sydney Elliott, Tony Firth;
nar Henry Fairlie

ALGERIA – TEN YEARS AFTER
(ATV 9/5/1972)
James Cameron reports on Algeria ten years
after independence.
p Richard Marquand

ALICE IN WONDERLAND (BBC 28/12/1966)
Adaptation of Lewis Carroll's fantasy.
d/p/adapt Jonathan Miller
lp Ann-Marie Mallik; Freda Dowie;
Jo Maxwell-Muller; Alan Bennett;
Finlay Currie; Leo McKern; Peter Sellers;
Michael Redgrave; John Gielgud;
Malcolm Muggeridge; Michael Gough;
Wilfrid Brambell; John Bird; Wilfrid Lawson;
Avril Elgar; Peter Cook

The ALIEN SKY (BBC 26/1/1956)
Drama set in India at the time of Independence.
d John Jacobs; *sc/auth* Paul Scott
lp Stephen Murray; Helen Haye;
Roger Delgado; Sheila Burrell; Zia Mohyeddin;
Hugh McDermott

The ALISTAIR MACLEAN STORY
(Westward 20/4/1973)
Barry Norman interviews the novelist Alistair
MacLean.
d/p Peter Yolland

**ALIVE AND KICKING – BRITISH
POETS** (LWT 1971)
Series featuring British poets.
BRIAN PATTEN 6/6/1971
Adrian Mitchell introduces a reading by Brian
Patten.
d David J. Chapman

ALL ABOUT ANIMALS (BBC 31/10/1955)
Programme for children. George Cansdale
presents a film about animal life.

ALL CREATURES GREAT AND SMALL
(BBC 1978–90)
Series based on the popular books of 'James
Herriot', the pseudonym of a Yorkshire
veterinary surgeon.
regulars Christopher Timothy; Robert Hardy
HORSE SENSE 8/1/1978
d Terence Dudley; *p* Bill Sellars;
sc Brian Clark
lp Carol Drinkwater; Mary Hignett; Paul Luty
DOG DAYS 15/1/1978
d Peter Moffatt; *p* Bill Sellars;
sc Brian Finch
lp Peter Davison; Margaretta Scott;
Mary Hignett; George Malpas; George Selway

ALL GOOD THINGS (TWW 3/3/1968)
The last programme transmitted by Television
Wales and West. Those appearing include
Bernard Braden, Morecambe and Wise, Ivor
Emmanuel, Clifford Evans, Anita Harris,
Manfred Mann and Stan Stennett.
d John Scriminger

ALL IN A DAY (BBC 1971–74)
A series of films concentrating on a few hours of
intense activity in the lives of individuals.
p Michael Wooller
The LAUNCH 25/8/1971
The building of the 'Texaco Great Britain'
supertanker.
d Rex Bloomstein
The NEWS 1/9/1971
Seven film cameras show how reporters gather
news, how the editor handles the news, and how
all combine to make up 20 minutes of a
television news broadcast.
d Tim King
The SIEGE 8/9/1971
Six hundred members of the Sealed Knot Society
re-enact the siege of Warwick Castle in 1642.
d Anna Benson-Gyles
The AUCTION 15/9/1971
The sale of a Stradivarius violin at Sotheby's
auction house.
d Rex Bloomstein

ALL OUR YESTERDAYS (Granada 1960–73)
Documentary series using newsreels to cover the
events of 25 years ago.
pres Brian Inglis
ALL OUR YESTERDAYS 11/12/1961
King Edward VIII and the Abdication crisis.
d Peter Plummer; *p* Jeremy Isaacs
ALL OUR YESTERDAYS 21/6/1965
The German occupation of France, the fall of
France and the evacuation of Dunkirk.
d Cormac Newell; *p* Bill Grundy
ALL OUR YESTERDAYS 2/8/1965
The civilian soldiers of the Local Defence
Volunteers during World War II.
d Cormac Newell; *p* Bill Grundy
ALL OUR YESTERDAYS 9/8/1965
Britain under the threat of a German invasion
during World War II.
d Cormac Newell; *p* Bill Grundy
The BATTLE OF ARNHEM: PART 1 13/9/1969
The position of the opposing Allied and German
forces before Arnhem, with comments from Sir
Brian Horrocks.
d Richard Guinea; *exec.p* James Butler
The BATTLE OF ARNHEM: PART 2 20/9/1969
Sir Brian Horrocks discusses the outcome of the
Arnhem operation.
d Richard Guinea; *exec.p* James Butler
CONCENTRATION CAMP PRISONERS
19/4/1970
Interviews with ex-prisoners who talk about
conditions in the concentration camps of Nazi
Germany.
d Richard Guinea; *p* Michael Murphy
LAURENS VAN DER POST AS A JAPANESE
PRISONER-OF-WAR 25/8/1970
Laurens Van Der Post discusses his time as a
prisoner-of-war.
d Richard Guinea; *p* Michael Murphy
BOTTOMLEY ON INDIA 27/9/1970
Arthur Bottomley MP discusses his experiences
in India in 1945 when a member of the
Parliamentary Mission.
d Richard Guinea; *p* Michael Murphy
LAURENS VAN DER POST ON THE FAR EAST
15/11/1970
Interview with Laurens Van Der Post, who
discusses Indonesian nationalism and the
destruction of the Dutch Empire.
d Richard Guinea; *p* Michael Murphy
ROBERTSON HARE 1971 *ntx*
Interview with actor Robertson Hare.
SIR MILES THOMAS 31/1/1971
Sir Miles Thomas discusses the problems of the
aircraft industry, the flying boat and the motor
car immediately after World War II.
d Richard Guinea; *p* Michael Murphy
TOM DRIBERG 14/3/1971
Tom Driberg discusses his experiences as a war
correspondent in South East Asia at the end of
World War II.
d Richard Guinea; *p* Michael Murphy
SIR ROBERT BIRLEY 16/5/1971
Birley describes his work as Educational Adviser
to the Military Governor of Germany after
World War II.
d Richard Guinea; *p* Michael Murphy

ALL OUR YESTERDAYS *cont.*

INTERVIEW WITH NORMAN RICHARD
COLLINS 13/6/1971
Norman Richard Collins and the early days of
television when he was Controller of BBC
Television, 1947–50.
d Richard Guinea; *p* Michael Murphy
PALESTINE: SIR JOHN GLUBB 18/7/1971
Interview with Sir John Glubb, writer and Chief
of General Staff of the Arab Legion in Amman,
Jordan, 1939–56.
d Richard Guinea; *p* Michael Murphy
SIR ANTHONY MILWARD 1/8/1971
Sir Anthony Milward and the formation of
British European Airways in 1946.
d Richard Guinea; *p* Michael Murphy
CYRIL CONNOLLY 29/8/1971
Cyril Connolly discusses the theatre and film
industry in 1946.
d Richard Guinea; *p* Michael Murphy
SIR ELWYN JONES INTERVIEW
9/10/1971
Sir Elwyn Jones talks about the Nuremberg
Trials where he was a member of the British War
Crimes Executive.
d Richard Guinea; *p* Michael Murphy
LAURENS VAN DER POST ON JAPANESE
SURRENDER 13/11/1971
Laurens Van Der Post talks about the Japanese
surrender and the setting up of the Indonesian
Republic in 1946.
d Richard Guinea; *p* Michael Murphy
BRITISH OCCUPATION OF PALESTINE:
INTERVIEW WITH ILLEGAL IMMIGRANT
20/11/1971
Interview with Herman Haas, an illegal
immigrant to Palestine in 1946.
d Richard Guinea; *p* Michael Murphy
LORD LONGFORD 11/12/1971
Lord Longford talks about post-war Germany
when he was Minister responsible for Germany
in the Attlee Government.
d Michael Becker; *p* Michael Murphy
J.L. MANNING 15/1/1972
Sports writer J.L. Manning discusses the state of
British sport in 1947.
d Michael Becker; *p* Douglas Terry
JAMES CAMERON ON INDIA 19/2/1972
James Cameron discusses the events leading to
Indian Independence.
d Michael Becker; *p* Douglas Terry
LORD HINTON 26/2/1972
Lord Hinton discusses the restoration of power
after the great fuel crisis in 1947.
d Michael Becker; *p* Douglas Terry
DILYS POWELL 11/3/1972
Dilys Powell discusses the films of 1947.
d Michael Becker; *p* Douglas Terry
TOWN PLANNING IN POST-WAR
BRITAIN 18/3/1972
Lord Llewelyn-Davies and Lord Silkin discuss
post-war town planning.
d Michael Becker; *p* Douglas Terry
MICHAEL POWELL INTERVIEW 23/4/1972
Brian Inglis looks back at the state of the British
film industry in 1947, with Michael Powell and
Dilys Powell.
d Michael Becker; *p* Douglas Terry
LAURENS VAN DER POST ON
INDONESIA 23/7/1972
Laurens Van Der Post discusses the hostility in
Indonesia in 1947 between the Nationalists and
the Dutch.
d Michael Becker; *p* Douglas Terry

ALL THE QUEEN'S MEN (ATV 23/11/1966)
The public, military and private lives of men in
the Household Brigade of Guards.
d/p Kevin Billington

ALPHA BETA
(Memorial Enterprises 1/1/1974)
Drama which studies stages in the disintegration
of a marriage.
d Anthony Page; *p* Timothy Burrill;
sc E.A. Whitehead
lp Albert Finney; Rachel Roberts

ALRIGHT NOW (Tyne Tees 1979)
Regional rock music magazine programme.
p Malcolm Gerrie
BOB GELDOF 1979
SUZI QUATRO 1979
SHOWBIZ KIDS/PENETRATION 6/4/1979
DIRE STRAITS/POLICE 13/4/1979
ALRIGHT NOW 26/4/1979
CHRIS REA/YOUNG BUCKS/ROD STEWART
27/4/1979
PUNILUX/GOLDIE 4/5/1979
THIN LIZZIE/JUNCO PATNERS/ERIC BURDON
11/5/1979
STEVE GIBBONS/GUITAR SPECIAL 18/5/1979
LINDISFARNE 25/5/1979
The CLASH/TOM ROBINSON BAND 19/6/1979

ALTERNATIVE 3 (Anglia 20/6/1977)
A spoof programme about the supposed
disappearance of scientists.
d Christopher Miles; *sc* David Ambrose;
pres Tim Brinton

ALWAYS ON WEDNESDAY (BBC 16/9/1967)
Nadia Boulanger instructing young French
violinist Patrice Fontanarosa.
d/p Anthony Wilkinson; *comm* Kenneth van
Barthold

AMADEUS (BBC 6/5/1973)
A tribute to celebrate the 25th anniversary of the
musical partnership of Norbert Brainin,
Seigmund Nissel, Peter Schidlof and Martin
Lovett – The Amadeus String Quartet.
d Roy Tipping; *intro* John Amis

AMAHL AND THE NIGHT VISITORS
(BBC 24/12/1959)
A Christmas story with music.
d Christian Simpson; *m* Gian-Carlo Menotti
lp Christopher Nicholls; Forbes Robinson;
Elsie Morrison; John Kentish; Hervey Alan;
Thomas Baptiste; Molly Kenny

AMERICA ABROAD (Rediffusion 30/5/1962)
The work of the American Peace Corps in
Cambodia, South Vietnam, Pakistan and Ghana.
d Michael Ingrams; *p* Peter Hunt

AMERICA NOW (Rediffusion 27/8/1957)
Michael Ingrams visits American families in
Georgia, Los Angeles, the Midwest and New
York.
d/sc Michael Ingrams; *p* Caryl Doncaster

AMERICA – ON THE EDGE OF
ABUNDANCE (Rediffusion 27/1/1965)
An examination of the growth of the affluent
society in America.
d Bill Morton; *nar* James Cameron

AMERICA – THE DOLLAR POOR
(Rediffusion 3/2/1965)
The poor in America.
d Randal Beattie

The ANATOMY OF FIRST AID
(ABC 17/4–10/7/1966)
Thirteen-part instructional series.
The BASIC PRINCIPLES 17/4/1966
d Marjory Ruse; *sc/pres* Michael Winstanley

ANCESTRAL VOICES (BBC 17/5–14/6/1976)
Series of programmes about early musical
instruments.
MUSIC OF EARLY INSTRUMENTS
17/5/1976
David Munrow recreates the music of the flute.
d Paul Kriwaczek; *p* Victor Poole;
sc David Munrow

ANCIENT MONUMENTS OF EGYPT
(BBC 8/3/1960)
The monuments and villages to be submerged by
the Aswan Dam.
comm Robin Scott

...AND MOTHER MAKES THREE
(Thames 1971–73)
Sitcom featuring a struggling mother and her two
sons.
THANK HEAVEN FOR LITTLE GIRLS? 5/10/1972
d/p Peter Frazer-Jones; *sc* Richard Waring
lp Wendy Craig; Richard Coleman;
Valerie Lush; Robin Davies; David Parfitt;
Miriam Mann; Charles Hill

The ANDERSON PLATOON
(FR Radiodiffusion Télévision Française;
BBC *tx* 18/5/1967)
Six weeks in the life of an American platoon in
Vietnam, commanded by 24–year-old
Lieutenant Joseph Anderson.
d Pierre Schoendoerffer

The ANDERSONVILLE TRIAL
(US KCET Los Angeles 17/5/1970)
Made-for-TV film, originally shown as the
premiere edition of 'Hollywood Television
Theatre' (1970–73). A military trial set during
the American Civil War and based on real events
in Andersonville, Georgia. Based on Saul
Levitt's 1959 play.
d George C. Scott; *p* Lewis Freedman;
sc Saul Levitt
lp Cameron Mitchell; William Shatner;
Jack Cassidy; Martin Sheen; Richard Basehart;
Whit Bissell; Harry Townes; Buddy Ebsen;
John Anderson; Lou Frizzell; Michael Burns;
Albert Salmi

ANDRES SEGOVIA: THE SONG OF THE
GUITAR (Allegro Films 27/4/1977)
Documentary on the Spanish guitarist.
d/comm Christopher Nupen;
sc/nar Andrés Segovia

ANDY (Scottish TV 12/5/1972)
Variety show hosted by Andy Stewart.
d/p Clarke Tait

ANGELS (BBC 1975–83)
Drama series set in a nurses' training hospital;
from 1979 adopted a soap opera format.
INITIATION 8/9/1975
d Ken Hannam; *p* Ron Craddock;
sc Adele Rose
lp Clare Clifford; Julie Dawn Cole;
Lesley Dunlop; Karan David; Erin Geraghty;
Christine Akehurst; Faith Brook; June Watson;
Esmond Webb
MY PATIENT 20/9/1976
d Tristan De Vere Cole; *p* Ron Craddock;
sc Susan Pleat
lp Julie Dawn Cole; Daphne Heard;
Jessie Matthews; Clare Clifford; Mai Bacon;
Linda Polan; Rosamund Greenwood;
Johnny Wade

ANGLIA TELEVISION OPENING NIGHT
TRANSMISSION (Anglia 27/10/1959)
Programmes from the opening night of Anglia
TV, includes 'Introducing Anglia', 'The Birth of
a Regiment', news items on a visit to Cambridge
by Winston Churchill and an interview with the
new Bishop of Norwich.

ANGOLA – SPRING 1976 (ATV 9/6/1976)
A report on developments in Angola after the
victory of the Popular Movement for the
Liberation of Angola (MPLA).
d John Sheppard

ANIMAL STORY (Granada 1959–62)
Series on aspects of animal behaviour.
FAMILY PORTRAIT 10/4/1961
Studies the chimpanzee, orang-utang and the
gorilla.
p Milton Shulman; *sc* Philip Oakes;
comm Desmond Morris

ANNA KARENINA (BBC 3/11/1961)
Adaptation of the Leo Tolstoy novel.
p Rudolph Cartier; *sc* Marcelle-Maurette;
trans E.J. King Bull; *adapt* Donald Bull
lp Claire Bloom; Sean Connery;
Jack Watling; Valerie Taylor;
Daphne Anderson; June Thorburn

The ANNE SHELTON SHOW
(Jack Hylton TV Productions 1958–59)
Variety show, with Anne Shelton, Billy Ternent
and his Orchestra, and The Beryl Stott Singers.
The ANNE SHELTON SHOW 5/1/1959
d Bill Hitchcock;
with Joe Lynch, Bill Maynard, Thora Hird
The ANNE SHELTON SHOW 12/1/1959
d Bill Hitchcock; *with* Joe Lynch,
Alfred Marks, Paddie O'Neil
The ANNE SHELTON SHOW 19/1/1959
d Bill Hitchcock;
sc Dick Vosburgh, Brad Ashton;
with Joe Lynch, Danny Ross, Kenneth Connor
The ANNE SHELTON SHOW 26/1/1959
d Bill Hitchcock;
sc Dick Vosburgh, Brad Ashton;
with Joe Lynch, Terry Scott, Deryck Guyler,
Dickie Valentine, Libby Morris
The ANNE SHELTON SHOW 9/2/1959
d Bill Hitchcock;
sc Dick Vosburgh, Brad Ashton;
with David Tomlinson, Kenneth Connor,
Harry Fowler, Warren Mitchell
The ANNE SHELTON SHOW 23/2/1959
d Bill Hitchcock;
sc Dick Vosburgh, Brad Ashton;
with Bud Flanagan, Dick Bentley, Dick Emery
The ANNE SHELTON SHOW 9/3/1959
d Michael Westmore;
sc Dick Vosburgh, Brad Ashton;
with Edmund Purdom, Irene Handl,
Kenneth Connor, Libby Morris
The ANNE SHELTON SHOW 6/4/1959
d Michael Westmore;
sc Dick Vosburgh, Brad Ashton;
with Terry Scott, Peter Butterworth,
Harry Fowler

ANNO DOMINI (BBC 1974–76)
Religious, moral and ethics series. See also The
ANNO DOMINI INTERVIEW series (1977).
SOUTH KOREA 25/5/1975
Made with the help of Amnesty International.
The political situation in South Korea after the
repressive regime of President Pak during 1975.
p Vanya Kewley, Peter Armstrong;
pres Colin Morris
PARADISE LOST 7/11/1976
The widespread abuse of human rights in
Paraguay.
p/rep Vanya Kewley

The ANNO DOMINI INTERVIEW
(BBC 1977)
Series of interviews with personalities who
discuss their beliefs. See also ANNO DOMINI
series (1974–76).
ENOCH POWELL 6/2/1977
Colin Morris talks to Enoch Powell MP.
p Dennis Sullivan
DENNIS POTTER 13/2/1977
Colin Morris talks to television playwright and
critic Dennis Potter.
p Dennis Sullivan

ANOTHER BOUQUET (LWT 7/1–18/2/1977)
Sequel to Andrea Newman's BOUQUET OF
BARBED WIRE (1976) which continues the
domestic trials of a middle-class family.
EPISODE 6: EMERGENCIES 11/2/1977
d/p John Frankau; *sc* Andrea Newman
lp Frank Finlay; Deborah Grant; James Aubrey;
Sheila Allen; Elizabeth Romilly; Fred Bryant;
Philip Madoc

ANOTHER SUNDAY AND SWEET F.A.
(Granada 9/1/1972)
A dedicated local soccer referee is brought to the
depths of disillusionment with the game when he
officiates at an encounter between two local
sides.
d Michael Apted; *p* Peter Eckersley;
sc Jack Rosenthal
lp David Swift; Freddie Fletcher;
Gordon McGrase; Fred Feast; Joe Gladwin;
Duggie Brown

ANOTHER WORLD (Granada 1961–65)
Wildlife/nature programme.
FEATHERED HORDES 12/8/1963
The habits of the starling.
p Douglas Fisher
The THREE THAT GOT AWAY 14/4/1964
The coypu in Britain.
p Douglas Fisher; *nar* Michael Smee
The FEATHERS OF DEATH 28/4/1964
Hawks and the tradition of falconry.
p Douglas Fisher; *nar* Michael Smee

ANTONY AND CLEOPATRA
(ATV 28/7/1974)
The Royal Shakespeare Company's 1972
production, re-staged for television.
d Trevor Nunn, Jon Scoffield
lp Janet Suzman; Richard Johnson;
Patrick Stewart; Corin Redgrave;
Tim Pigott-Smith

ANTHONY QUINN (BBC 30/8/1960)
Anthony Quinn, John Paddy Carstairs, Peter
Coe, Robert MacDermott and Anthony Quinton
in an informal discussion on acting and the
actor's responsibilities towards the author and
society.
p John Warrington

The APHRODITE INHERITANCE
(BBC 1979)
Eight-part serial thriller set in Cyprus.
p Andrew Osborn; *sc* Michael J. Bird
lp Peter McEnery; Godfrey James;
Alexandra Bastedo; Stefan Gryff; Brian Blessed;
Paul Maxwell; Tony Doyle; William Wilde
EPISODE 1: A DEATH IN THE FAMILY 3/1/1979
EPISODE 2: A LAMB TO THE SLAUGHTER
10/1/1979
d Terence Williams
EPISODE 3: HERE WE COME GATHERING
17/1/1979
d Terence Williams
EPISODE 4: A FRIEND IN NEED 24/1/1979
d Terence Williams
EPISODE 5: COME INTO MY PARLOUR 31/1/1979
d Terence Williams
EPISODE 6: SAID THE SPIDER TO THE FLY
7/2/1979
d Terence Williams
EPISODE 7: THE EYES OF LOVE 14/2/1979
d Viktors Ritelis
EPISODE 8: TO TOUCH A RAINBOW 21/2/1979
d Viktors Ritelis

APPLAUSE! APPLAUSE!
(Thames 23/7–26/8/1969)
Six-part series on music hall entertainers.
d/sc Margery Baker; *nar* John Stone
GEORGE FORMBY 23/7/1969
The story of George Formby and his singing
career.
LUCAN AND MCSHANE 26/8/1969
Arthur Lucan and Kitty McShane.

APPOINTMENT WITH (Granada 1960–63)
Interview series.
APPOINTMENT WITH ARTHUR MILLER 1/7/1960
Arthur Miller talks to Malcolm Muggeridge.
d Douglas Hurn; *p* Patricia Lagone
APPOINTMENT WITH SIR ROY WELENSKY
KCMG 1961
Sir Roy Welensky discusses racial policy, the
Commonwealth, South Africa, imperial rule and
mixed marriages.
d Pauline Shaw; *p* Patricia Lagone
APPOINTMENT WITH VICKY 23/2/1962
Malcolm Muggeridge talks to political cartoonist
Vicky about humour, the effects of satire on
politics and his personal philosophy.
d Wilfred Fielding; *p* Patricia Lagone
APPOINTMENT WITH AUDEN, ISHERWOOD,
SPENDER AND CONNOLLY 23/3/1962
A discussion chaired by Malcolm Muggeridge.
The writers (W.H.Auden, Christopher
Isherwood, Stephen Spender and Cyril
Connolly) discuss their political attitudes, their
work in the 1930s and present writings.
d Michael Scott; *p* Patricia Lagone

APPOINTMENT WITH DRAMA (BBC 1955)
Anthology drama series.
The APOLLO OF BELLAC 12/8/1955
p Tony Richardson; *sc* Henry Mara;
auth Jean Giraudoux
lp Natasha Parry; Denholm Elliott;
Gerald Lawson; Mark Dignam; Violet Gould;
Jane Henderson

AQUARIUS (LWT 1970–77)
Arts series. Developed into The SOUTH BANK
SHOW (1978–).
A PINTER PREMIERE 3/10/1970
Donald Pleasence gives a solo rendition of an
extract from Harold Pinter's 'Tea Party'.
d Derek Bailey; *assoc.p* Russell Harty;
ed Humphrey Burton
DENIS MITCHELL: TELEVISION'S
MASTER FILM MAKER 17/10/1970
A profile of television documentary film-maker
Denis Mitchell.
d Derek Bailey, Michael Darlow;
assoc.p Russell Harty; *ed* Humphrey Burton
ELTON JOHN – MR. SUPERFUNK
3/4/1971
Elton John talks about the pop world and his
place in it. He is seen rehearsing recent
compositions, and performing at a concert.
d Derek Bailey; *assoc.p* Russell Harty;
ed Humphrey Burton
PRESSURE COOKIE 26/6/1971
A behind-the-scenes look at the recording of an
episode of the television series BUDGIE (1971–
72), with Adam Faith, director Mike Newell and
producer Verity Lambert.
d Derek Bailey; *assoc.p* Russell Harty;
ed Humphrey Burton
COOKHAM TO CALVARY 18/3/1972
A study of the life and work of artist Stanley
Spencer.
p Russell Harty; *ed* Humphrey Burton
The BEST TELEVISION IN THE WORLD? 1/4/1972
A report on the Monte Carlo Television Festival,
introduced by Humphrey Burton. What other
countries think of British television.
d Derek Bailey; *p* Michael Peacock;
ed Humphrey Burton
ALFRED THE GREAT 5/8/1972
Alfred Hitchcock is interviewed by Humphrey
Burton about his work in the cinema and his
latest film 'Frenzy'. Hitchcock at work on
location for 'Frenzy'.
d Derek Bailey; *p* Humphrey Burton
The UNKNOWN WARRIOR 19/11/1972
A profile of English composer Havergal Brian.
d Barrie Gavin; *ed* Humphrey Burton
HELLO DALI! 11/11/1973
Russell Harty visits Salvador Dali on his
Mediterranean estate in Spain, talks to the artist
about his life, wealth and art and is shown
around his private museum.
d Bruce Gowers; *p* Russell Harty
AQUARIUS INTERNATIONAL MUSIC FESTIVAL
22/9/1974
A concert at the Royal Festival Hall, with
Mstislav Rostropovich, Galina Vishnevskaya,
and The New Philharmonia Orchestra. The
music includes Haydn's Cello Concerto in C
major, the Letter Song from 'Eugene Onegin'
and Tchaikovsky's Symphony No. 6.
d David Heather; *p* Humphrey Burton
The GREAT GONDOLA RACE: PART 1
2/3/1975
Preparations for the annual historical regatta in
Venice. The decay of the city's architecture
through age and industrial pollution.
d/p Humphrey Burton; *assoc.p* Tanya Bruce-
Lockhart
The GREAT GONDOLA RACE: PART 2
9/3/1975
The annual gondola race along the Grand Canal
in Venice. A profile of former champion Albino
dei Rossi.
d/p Humphrey Burton
A-RONNE 13/11/1976
Television version of Luciano Berio's
composition 'A-Ronne', performed by Swingle
II, with inventive use of electronics.
d/p Bryan Izzard; *ed* Derek Bailey

AQUARIUS cont.

HE IS A CAMERA 27/11/1976
Film-makers Joris Ivens and partner Marceline Loridan talk about their work.
d Bryan Izzard; *p* Derek Bailey;
assoc.p Tanya Bruce-Lockhart; *intro* Peter Hall
The FOUR SEASONS 1/1/1977
Flautist James Galway, accompanied by The Zagreb Soloists, plays Vivaldi's 'The Four Seasons'.
d/p Bryan Izzard; *ed* Derek Bailey

The ARAB EXPERIENCE
(Yorkshire TV 2/4–8/7/1975)
Three-part examination of Arab society and Islamic faith.
d/p/nar Antony Thomas
The LEGACY OF FAISAL 2/4/1975
Saudi Arabian society under King Faisal.
LEBANON 8/7/1975
A report on Islam in the Arab world and on the situation in Lebanon and Syria, which includes actuality film of a pilgrimage to Mecca and an interview with Kamal Jumblatt.

ARAB FERMENT
(Television Reporters International 1963)
Three films looking at Saudi Arabia, Egypt and the Arab-Israeli conflict.
A LAND AWAKE 10/3/1963A report on Nasser's Egypt. President Nasser discusses the extension of the Egyptian revolution to other Arab countries.
rep/comm Robert Kee

The ARCATA PROMISE
(Yorkshire TV 22/9/1974)
Drama.
d David Cunliffe; *exec.p* Peter Willes;
sc David Mercer
lp Anthony Hopkins; Kate Nelligan; John Fraser

ARE YOU BEING SERVED? (BBC 1973–85)
Sitcom set in the department store of Grace Brothers.
regulars Trevor Bannister; Mollie Sugden; Frank Thornton; John Inman; Wendy Richard; Arthur Brough; Nicolas Smith; Harold Bennett
'DEAR SEXY KNICKERS...' 21/3/1973
p David Croft; *sc* Jeremy Lloyd, David Croft
lp Robert Raglan; Derek Smith
OUR FIGURES ARE SLIPPING 28/3/1973
d Bernard Thompson; *p* David Croft;
sc Jeremy Lloyd, David Croft
lp Stephanie Gathercole; Peter Needham
CAMPING IN 4/4/1973
p David Croft; *sc* Jeremy Lloyd, David Croft
lp Larry Martyn; James Copeland;
Anita Richardson; Pamela Manson;
Stephanie Gathercole
HIS AND HERS 11/4/1973
p David Croft; *sc* Jeremy Lloyd, David Croft
lp Joanna Lumley; Larry Martyn;
Margaret Flint; Evan Ross
COLD COMFORT 21/3/1974
p Harold Snoad;
sc Jeremy Lloyd, David Croft,
Michael Knowles
lp Larry Martyn; Hilda Fenemore;
Helen Lambert; Robert Mill; Carolyn Hudson
BIG BROTHER 4/4/1974
p Harold Snoad; *sc* Jeremy Lloyd,
David Croft, Michael Knowles
lp Larry Martyn; Donald Morley;
Robert Raglan; Stephanie Reeve;
Joyce Cummings
OH! WHAT A TANGLED WEB 13/5/1976
d Ray Butt; *p* David Croft;
sc Jeremy Lloyd, David Croft
lp Arthur English; Diana King; Melita Manger;
Penny Irving; Michael Stainton

ARENA (BBC 1975–)
Arts and entertainment series.
MY WAY 12/3/1979
The song 'My Way' interpreted by Frank Sinatra, Sid Vicious, Elvis Presley and others.
d Nigel Finch; *p* Alan Yentob

ARLECCHINO (IT Polytel International;
BBC tx 27/8/1977)
Italian television production of the play by Carlo Goldoni.
d Giorgio Strehler
lp Gianrico Tedeschi; Ginella Bertacchi;
Enzo Tarascio; Giancarlo Dettori

ARMCHAIR MYSTERY THEATRE
(ABC 1960–65)
Anthology drama series.
EYE WITNESS 5/6/1960
d Charles Jarrott;
p Leonard White, Sydney Newman;
sc Leslie Sands; *intro* Donald Pleasence
lp Diana Wynyard; Paul Daneman;
Margaret Griffin; Margaret Stallard; John Morris
FLIGHT FROM TREASON 10/7/1960
d Dennis Vance; *p* Leonard White;
sc James Mitchell; *pres* Donald Pleasence
lp John Gregson; Robert Brown; Ian Hendry;
Roger Delgado; Avril Elgar; Donald Churchill
TIME OUT OF MIND 19/7/1964
d Guy Verney; *p* Leonard White;
sc John Hopkins
lp Ian Hendry; John Bentley;
Miranda Connell; Maurice Good;
Elizabeth Shepherd; Billy Cornelius

ARMCHAIR THEATRE (ABC 1956–68;
Thames 1969–74)
Anthology drama series.
p Sydney Newman (1958–62),
Leonard White (1963–69)
NOW LET HIM GO 15/9/1957
d/p Dennis Vance; *sc* J.B. Priestley
lp Hugh Griffith; June Thorburn;
Peter Halliday; John Schlesinger;
Beatrice Varley; Philip Ray; Redmond Phillips;
Gerald Lawson
The LADY OF THE CAMELIAS 16/2/1958
d George More O'Ferrall;
p George More O'Ferrall, Dennis Vance;
sc Norman Ginsbury, Jacques Sarch;
auth Alexandre Dumas
lp Ann Todd; David Knight; Pamela Buck;
Patience Collier; Barbara Everest; Violetta
The EMPEROR JONES 30/3/1958
p Ted Kotcheff; *sc* Terry Southern;
auth Eugene O'Neill
lp Kenneth Spencer; Harry H. Corbett;
Connie Smith; Uriel Porter; Van Boolen
WOLF PACK 13/4/1958
d Wilfrid Eades; *sc* Jon Manchip White
lp David Davies; Maurice Colbourne;
Geoffrey Chater; Ian Bannen; Richard Gale;
Denys Graham
BREACH OF MARRIAGE 4/5/1958
d John Nelson Burton; *sc* Dan Sutherland
lp Roddy McMillan; Freda Bamford;
Shay Gorman; Basil Dignam; Nan Munro;
Sarah Lawson; Neil McCallum
The TERRORIST 26/10/1958
d George More O'Ferrall; *sc* John Kruse
lp Sebastian Shaw; Ann Beach;
Margaretta Scott; Yolanda; Joseph Attard;
Paul Stassino
The GREATEST MAN IN THE WORLD 9/11/1958
d Ted Kotcheff; *sc* Reuben Ship;
auth James Thurber
lp Ludovic Kennedy; Gerry Wilmot;
Macdonald Parke; Donald Pleasence;
Wensley Pithey; Michael Balfour;
Patrick McGoohan
HOT SUMMER NIGHT 1/2/1959
d Ted Kotcheff; *sc* Ted Willis
lp John Slater; Ruth Dunning; Andree Melly;
Harold Scott; Lloyd Reckord; Joyce Howard
The SCENT OF FEAR 13/9/1959
d John Llewellyn Moxey; *sc* Ted Willis
lp Dorothy Tutin; Anthony Quayle;
Neil McCallum; Frederick Schiller;
Alexis Chesnakov; David Ritch; Wolfe Morris;
Walter Gotell; John Carson
AFTER THE SHOW 20/9/1959
d Ted Kotcheff; *sc* Angus Wilson
lp Hermione Baddeley; Jeremy Spenser;
Carmel McSharry; Ann Lynn; Hilda Barry;
Paul Whitsun-Jones
SMALL FISH ARE SWEET 8/11/1959
d Alan Cooke; *sc* Peter Luke
lp Donald Pleasence; Katharine Blake;
Harold Scott; Felicity Ross; Murray Melvin

The LAST OF THE BRAVE 15/11/1959
d Philip Saville; *sc* Stanley Mann
lp Donald Wolfit; Paul Massie; Keith Smith;
Rosemary Scott; Ivor Dean; Sheila Allen
LORD ARTHUR SAVILE'S CRIME
3/1/1960
d Alan Cooke;
sc Constance Cox, Gerald Savory;
auth Oscar Wilde
lp Robert Coote; Terry-Thomas;
Eric Pohlmann; Ernest Thesiger;
June Thorburn; Ambrosine Phillpotts;
Arthur Lowe
WHERE I LIVE 10/1/1960
d Ted Kotcheff; *sc* Clive Exton
lp Ruth Dunning; Robert Brown; Lloyd Lamble;
Madge Ryan; Paul Curran
AFTER THE FUNERAL 3/4/1960
d Ted Kotcheff; *sc* Alun Owen
lp William Lucas; Hugh David; Charles Carson;
Rachel Thomas; Dorothea Phillips; Sylvia Kay
A NIGHT OUT 24/4/1960
d Philip Saville; *sc* Harold Pinter
lp Tom Bell; Madge Ryan; David Baron;
Philip Locke; Edmond Bennett;
Vivien Merchant; Arthur Lowe
LENA, O MY LENA 25/9/1960
d Ted Kotcheff; *sc* Alun Owen
lp Billie Whitelaw; Peter McEnery;
Colin Blakely; Patrick O'Connell; Keith Smith;
Scott Forbes
I'LL HAVE YOU TO REMEMBER
23/10/1960
d Ted Kotcheff; *sc* Clive Exton
lp Stephen Murray; Ruth Dunning
HONEYMOON POSTPONED 29/1/1961
d John Knight; *sc* Bill Naughton
lp Paul Rogers; Patience Collier; Alison Bayley;
Lois Daine; Harry Hutchinson; Derren Nesbitt
The WAYS OF LOVE 9/4/1961
d Ted Kotcheff; *sc* Alun Owen
lp Kenneth Haig; Donald Houston;
Elwyn Brook-Jones; Peter Halliday; Elvi Hale;
Zena Walker
The ROSE AFFAIR 8/10/1961
d Charles Jarrott; *sc* Alun Owen
lp Anthony Quayle; Naunton Wayne;
Natasha Parry; Dudley Foster; Joseph O'Conor
The TROUBLE WITH OUR IVY 19/11/1961
d Charles Jarrott; *sc* David Perry
lp John Barrie; Laurence Hardy;
Gretchen Franklin; Dandy Nichols;
Roddy McMillan
NIGHT CONSPIRATORS 6/5/1962
d Philip Saville; *sc* Robert Muller
lp Peter Wyngarde; John Robinson;
John Arnatt; Cyril Luckham; Ronald Radd;
Peter Arne
The HARD KNOCK 8/7/1962
d Ted Kotcheff; *sc* Alun Owen
lp Colin Blakely; J.G. Devlin; Frank Finlay;
Sylvia Kay; Ronald Lacey; Lynne Furlong
AFTERNOON OF A NYMPH 30/9/1962
d Philip Saville; *sc* Robert Muller
lp Janet Munro; Ian Hendry; Betty Bascomb;
Jeremy Lloyd; Jackie Lane; Patrick Holt;
Aubrey Morris
ALWAYS SOMETHING HOT 28/10/1962
d Philip Saville; *sc* Donald Churchill
lp Ronald Lacey; Frank Finlay; Patrick Duggan;
Will Stampe; Jay Huguely; Michael Lehrer;
Philip Locke
HEAR THE TIGER SEE THE BAY
23/12/1962
d Charles Jarrott; *sc* Alun Richards
lp Ethel Gabriel; Dandy Nichols;
Norman Wynne; Fredrick Steger;
Terence Knapp; Clifford Evans
INTO THE DARK 3/2/1963
d Ted Kotcheff; *sc* Ken Taylor
lp Peter Sallis; Norman Rossington;
Wendy Craig
The PARADISE SUITE 17/2/1963
d Philip Saville; *sc* Robert Muller
lp Carroll Baker; Sam Wanamaker; Ian Holm;
Derek Smith; Jess Conrad
LITTLE DORIS 13/10/1963
d Charles Jarrott; *sc* David Perry
lp Vivienne Martin; Gladys Henson;
Bryan Mosley; Royston Tickner; Ian Wilson

A WAY OF LIVING 22/12/1963
d Alan Cooke; sc David Mercer
lp David Buck; David Davies; Bert Palmer;
Ruth Kettlewell; Rosemary Nicols
SHARP AT FOUR 12/1/1964
d Guy Verney; sc Donald Churchill
lp Derek Godfrey; Rosemary Leach;
Percy Steven; Marcus Hammond; Mona Bruce;
John Standing
PRISONER AND ESCORT 5/4/1964
d Philip Saville; sc Charles Wood
lp Alfred Lynch; Norman Rossington;
June Barry; Tim Preece
PLEASURE WHERE SHE FINDS IT 3/5/1964
d Charles Jarrott; sc Robert Muller
lp Nigel Stock; Rosemary Leach; Richard Pasco;
Anthony Bate
THAT'S WHERE THE TOWN'S GOING 7/6/1964
d Charles Jarrott; sc Tad Mosel
lp Margaret Johnson; Patricia Marmont;
David Bauer; Larry Cross; Monica Merlin
The TRIAL OF DR. FANCY
13/9/1964
d Ted Kotcheff; sc Clive Exton
lp Kynaston Reeves; Barry Jones; Nigel Stock;
Ronald Hines; Walter Hudd; Dandy Nichols
The CHERRY ON TOP 27/9/1964
d Guy Verney; sc Donald Churchill
lp Robert Lang; Pauline Yates;
Peggy Sinclair; Anthony Dawes; Vivien Lloyd;
Kay Gallie
The IMPORTANCE OF BEING EARNEST
15/11/1964
d Bill Bain; auth Oscar Wilde
lp Ian Carmichael; Susannah York;
Patrick Macnee; Fenella Fielding; Pamela Brown
I TOOK MY LITTLE WORLD AWAY 14/3/1965
d Peter Hammond; sc John Hopkins
lp Susannah York; John Robinson;
John Ronane; Neil Robertson; Janet Rowsell
The PARAFFIN SEASON 4/12/1965
d Guy Verney; sc Donald Churchill
lp Norman Rossington; Pauline Yates;
Joss Ackland; Mona Bruce; George Baker;
Tessa Wyatt
A COLD PEACE 18/12/1965
d Don Leaver; sc Robert Muller
lp Ian Hendry; Britt Ekland; Roy Dotrice;
Isabel Dean; David Phethean; Kathleen Breck
The PITY OF IT ALL 22/1/1966
d Patrick Dromgoole; sc Stan Barstow
lp Billie Whitelaw; Nigel Stock; Maureen Pryor;
John McKelvey; Ann Firbank; Jack Watson
MAN WITHOUT A MORTGAGE 19/3/1966
d Guy Verney; sc Donald Churchill
lp Donald Churchill; Terence Alexander;
Fabia Drake; Anne Godfrey;
Margaret Anderson
The NIGHT BEFORE THE MORNING AFTER
2/4/1966
d Kim Mills; sc Jack Rosenthal
lp Bernard Lee; Julia Foster;
Betty Marsden; Rodney Bewes;
Trevor Bannister; Coral Atkins
PRETTY POLLY 23/7/1966
d Bill Bain; sc/pres William Marchant;
auth Noël Coward
lp Lynn Redgrave; Donald Houston;
Dandy Nichols; Zia Mohyeddin; Gwenda Wilson
The ONE EYED MONSTER 6/8/1966
d Robert Tronson; sc Allan Prior
lp Rupert Davies; Rex Garner;
Pauline Williams; Ronald Bridges;
Edward Caddick
The FLOATING POPULATION 28/1/1967
d Jonathan Alwyn; sc Donald Churchill
lp Ian Bannen; Wendy Craig; George Day;
Anthony Collin; Sheridan Grant; Leslie Dwyer
A MAGNUM FOR SCHNEIDER 4/2/1967
This original play was the inspiration for the
later CALLAN series (ABC 1967; Thames
1969–72).
d Bill Bain; sc James Mitchell
lp Edward Woodward; Joseph Furst;
Peter Bowles; Ronald Radd; Russell Hunter;
Ivor Dean; Martin Wyldeck
WHAT'S WRONG WITH HUMPTY DUMPTY?
11/2/1967
d Charles Jarrott; sc Hugh Whitemore
lp Donald Houston; Katharine Blake;
Lynn Redgrave; John Clark

EASIER IN THE DARK 25/2/1967
d Don Leaver; sc Robert Muller
lp Shelley Winters; Michael Bryant;
John Garrie; Neville Becker; Mollie Peters
CALL ME DADDY 8/1/1967
d Alvin Rakoff; sc Ernest Gebler
lp Donald Pleasence; Judy Cornwell;
Derek Carpenter
I AM OSANGO 15/4/1967
d Bill Bain; sc Giles Cooper
lp Roy Dotrice; Lynn Redgrave;
Kathleen Michael; Ken Jones; Leon Sinden;
Mollie Sugden
LOVE LIFE 29/7/1967
d Guy Verney; sc Hugh Leonard
lp George Baker; Diana Coupland;
Carmen Munroe; Martin Dempsey;
Bill Golding; Pauline Collins
The EDUCATION OF CORPORAL HALLIDAY
5/8/1967
d Bill Bain; sc Robert Holles
lp George Sewell; Gary Bond; Bernard Archard;
John Keightley; Peter Williams; John Nettleton
POOR CHERRY 9/9/1967
d Piers Haggard; sc Fay Weldon
lp Dilys Laye; Peter Arne; Judy Cornwell;
Gwen Nelson; Jane Birkin; John Wood
The BLOOD KNOT 1968 ntx
d Charles Jarrott; sc Athol Fugard
lp Ian Bannen
The WIND IN A TALL PAPER CHIMNEY 7/2/1968
d Peter Sasdy; sc Robert Holles
lp Donald Sinden; Bernard Cribbins;
David Stoll; John Steiner; Judy Cornwell
SAY GOODNIGHT TO YOUR GRANDMA
27/10/1970
d Jim Goddard; p John Kershaw;
sc Colin Welland
lp Madge Ryan; Colin Welland;
Susan Jameson; Mona Bruce; Ralph Watson;
Jack Smethurst
The LOVING LESSON 31/8/1971
d Mike Vardy; sc Donald Churchill
lp Colette O'Neil; Donald Churchill;
Diane Grayson; Nicholas Clay; Michael Standing
A BIT OF A LIFT 25/9/1973
d Dennis Vance; p Joan Kemp-Welch;
sc Donald Churchill
lp Ann Beach; Ronald Fraser;
Donald Churchill; Bill Horsley; Stafford Gordon
VERITE 23/10/1973
d Piers Haggard; p Joan Kemp-Welch;
sc Howard Schuman
lp Annabel Leventon; Richard Morant;
Tim Curry; Matthew Scurfield; Nadim Sawalha;
Beth Porter
The VIRGINS 25/6/1974
d Graham Evans; p Kim Mills;
sc Hugh Leonard
lp Godfrey Quigley; David Kelly;
Moira Redmond; William Bond;
Brenda Fricker; Brian Phelan

ARMCHAIR 30 (Thames 1973)
Anthology drama series.
CAPTAIN VIDEO'S STORY 27/11/1973
d Anthea Browne-Wilkinson;
p Joan Kemp-Welch; sc Howard Schuman
lp Barbara Ewing; Derek Fowlds;
Barrie Cookson; Alison Coleridge

ARMCHAIR THRILLER (ABC 1967)
Anthology drama series.
ENGLAND MY ENGLAND 29/4/1967
d Don Leaver; p Richard Bates;
sc Julian Bond
lp Paul Eddington; Rachel Gurney;
Hugh Burden; Robert Crewdson;
Kenneth Watson; Malcolm Terris

ARNHEM: THE STORY OF AN ESCAPE
(BBC 17/11/1976)
Dramatisation of the book 'Travel by Dark'. The
story of Colonel Warrack who was captured at
Arnhem and escaped from a prisoner-of-war
camp in Germany.
d Clive Rees;
p Innes Lloyd, Stephan Felsenthal;
auth Graeme Warrack
lp John Hallam; Marie-Louise Stheins;
Mark Russel; Paul Copley; Wolf Kahler;
Gavin Campbell; John Nettles

AROUND THE BEATLES
(Rediffusion 6/5/1964)
Pop music show featuring The Beatles, with Cilla
Black, Sounds Incorporated, Long John Baldry,
P.J. Proby and Millie.
p Jack Gold, Rita Gillespie

ARTHUR C. CLARKE: 2001 IDEAS
OF THE PROPHET OF THE SPACE AGE
(Yorkshire TV 11/4/1972)
The work of science-fiction writer Arthur C.
Clarke and his life in Ceylon.
d Ian McFarlane; p/sc Michael Deakin;
intro Simon Welfare

The ARTHUR HAYNES SHOW (ATV 1963)
Comedy and variety series featuring Arthur
Haynes.
The ARTHUR HAYNES SHOW 19/1/1963
p Colin Clews; sc Johnny Speight
with Nicholas Parsons, Joe Henderson,
Susan Maughan, Jack Parnell and his Orchestra

ARTHUR'S ANNIVERSARY
(Rediffusion 15/3/1957)
Arthur Askey celebrates thirty years in show
business.
d Eric Fawcett; sc Sid Colin

ARTICLE 237–A REPORT ON THE
NEW EUROPE (Rediffusion 31/10/1962)
The EEC, how it works, and what would happen
to the Community if the United Kingdom
joined. Includes an interview with Jean Monnet,
'Father' of the Common Market.
d Rollo Gamble; p Peter Hunt;
sc Peter Hunt, Rollo Gamble

The ARTIST SPEAKS (BBC 1958–60)
Series in which various artists discuss their work.
Earlier series billed as BRITISH ART AND
ARTISTS (1957–58).
MICHAEL AYRTON 11/7/1960
The work of artist and sculptor Michael Ayrton.
p/sc John Read

ARTISTS AT WORK (LWT 18/11–23/12/1973)
Six-part series on artists.
STANLEY BOARDMAN 18/11/1973
Jeff Nuttall talks to the artist about his first
exhibition of work held at the Cliffe Castle
Museum, Keighley.
d David Coulter; p Ann Wolff;
pres Jeff Nuttall

ARTISTS MUST LIVE (BBC 30/6/1953)
The relationship between artist and patron
discussed by an art critic and a number of
painters and sculptors, including John Piper,
Keith Vaughan, Patrick Heron, Rodrigo
Moynihan, Ivon Hitchens, Reg Butler and
Clifford Ellis.
d John Read; p John Elliot;
nar Basil Taylor

ARTISTS' NOTEBOOKS (BBC 1964)
Educational series for sixth formers.
LEONARDO DA VINCI (1452–1519) 2/11/1964
The life and work of Leonardo da Vinci.
d/p Michael Gill;
sc John Broadbent, Michael Gill;
nar Tony Church; voice Cyril Shaps
WILLIAM HOGARTH (1697–1764) 16/11/1964
Notebooks, diaries, letters and other sources
illustrating the life, work and aspirations of the
painter.
d/p Barbara Parker; nar Tony Church;
voice Patrick Troughton
EUGENE DELACROIX (1798–1863) 23/11/1964
The life and work of Delacroix based upon the
journals he kept between 1822–24 and from 1847
to his death in 1863.
p/sc Michael Gill; nar Tony Church;
voice William Squire
VINCENT VAN GOGH (1853–1890) 30/11/1964
The life and work of Van Gogh.
p/sc Michael Gill; nar Tony Church;
voice Alan Dobie

ARTUR RUBINSTEIN PLAYS BEETHOVEN (BBC 7/1/1968)
Artur Rubenstein talks to Richard Baker about his attitude to life and music and is seen playing Beethoven's Piano Concerto no.4 in G Major at the Royal Festival Hall with the London Philharmonic Orchestra.
d Antony Craxton

AS I WAS SAYING (BBC 10/9–15/10/1955)
Six original portraits in crime by Berkely Mather.
p Andrew Osborn
An EYE FOR DETAIL 10/9/1955
lp Ronald Simpson; James Fox; Ballard Berkeley; Sam Kydd; Henry Oscar; Victor Rietti; Tom Clegg
A DEAL IN DIVING 1/10/1955
lp Beatrice Varley; Laidman Browne; Ronald Simpson; James Fox; Carl Bernard; Willoughby Goddard; Robert Raikes; John Schlesinger

The ASCENT OF MAN (BBC 1973)
Series in thirteen parts on the scientific evolution of mankind.
d Mick Jackson, David Kennard (part 5 only); *p* Dick Gilling; *pres* Dr Jacob Bronowski
LOWER THAN THE ANGELS 5/5/1973
The changes, both anatomical and intellectual, which brought about man's superiority.
The HARVEST OF THE SEASONS 12/5/1973
The discovery of agriculture and the domestication of plants and animals.
The GRAIN IN THE STONE 19/5/1973
The origin of science in the action of the hand.
The HIDDEN STRUCTURE 26/5/1973
The beginnings of chemistry, in the ancient metallurgy of China and Japan, and in alchemy.
The MUSIC OF THE SPHERES 2/6/1973
The evolution of mathematics, following the spread of Greek ideas through Islam to Moorish Spain and Renaissance Europe.
The STARRY MESSENGER 9/6/1973
The origin of the Scientific Revolution in the battle between progress and dogma, symbolised by the trial of Galileo.
The MAJESTIC CLOCKWORK 16/6/1973
The revolution that took place in the Newtonian universe of mass, space and time when Einstein introduced his Theory of Relativity.
The DRIVE FOR POWER 23/6/1973
How the American, French and the Industrial Revolutions revised the concepts of power.
The LADDER OF CREATION 30/6/1973
Charles Darwin and Alfred Russell Wallace had the same idea simultaneously. An account of the way their theories helped scientists like Louis Pasteur to ascribe to life a biochemical nature.
WORLD WITHIN WORLD 7/7/1973
The world inside the atom.
KNOWLEDGE OF CERTAINTY 14/7/1973
Dr Bronowski lectures about information and responsibility and the moral dilemma of the scientist.
GENERATION UPON GENERATION 21/7/1973
The revolution mathematics and physics brought to biology.
The LONG CHILDHOOD 28/7/1973
The way each age and culture has limited the opportunities of children, turning them at a too early age into carbon copies of their parents.

The ASH TREE (BBC 23/12/1975)
A nephew is haunted because of the testimony of his great uncle.
d Lawrence Gordon Clark; *p* Rosemary Hill; *adapt* David Rudkin; *auth* M.R. James
lp Edward Petherbridge; Lucy Griffiths; Lalla Ward; David Pugh; Preston Lockwood; Barbara Ewing

ASIAN HIGHWAY
(AU ABC 10/3/1965)
Part two of a documentary on the Asian Highway – a United Nations sponsored project to build a road from Turkey to South Vietnam.

ASK THE FAMILY (BBC 1971–82)
Family quiz show; presented by Robert Robinson.
ASK THE FAMILY 20/3/1978
d Rosalind Gold; *p* Robert Toner
ASK THE FAMILY 6/8/1979
d Rosalind Gold; *p* Robert Toner

ASSIGNMENT FOREIGN LEGION
(Intelfilms 1956–58)
Adventure series featuring the exploits of the French Foreign Legion.
Host/nar Merle Oberon
The STRIPES OF SERGEANT SCHWEIGER 15/9/1956
d Lance Comfort; *p* E.M. Smedley Aston; *sc* Paul Monash
lp Anton Diffring; Geoffrey Keen; Karel Stepanek; Alex Gallier
The MAN WHO FOUND FREEDOM 22/9/1956
d Lance Comfort; *p* E.M. Smedley Aston
lp Lee Patterson; Leonard Sachs; Norah Gorsen; Jacques Gey
The BARONESS 29/9/1956
d Michael McCarthy; *p* E.M. Smedley Aston; *sc* Max Ehrlich
lp Merle Oberon; Tom Conway; Betty McDowall; Laurence Payne; Arthur Gomez
The THIN LINE 10/11/1956
d Don Chaffey; *p* E.M. Smedley Aston; *sc* W. Stanley Moss, Reed de Rouen
lp Patrick Barr; John Loder; Denis Shaw; Felix Felton
DOLLAR A YEAR MAN 24/11/1956
d Lance Comfort; *p* E.M. Smedley Aston; *sc* A.R. Rawlinson
lp Anton Diffring; Bill Fraser; Lesley Nunnerley; Gaylord Cavallaro
FINGER YOUR NECK 1/12/1956
d Don Chaffey; *p* E.M. Smedley Aston; *sc* James Carhart, Nicholas Winter
lp Merle Oberon; William Sylvester; Norman Rossington; Conrad Phillips
A PONY FOR JOE CRAZY HORSE 29/12/1956
d David MacDonald; *p* E.M. Smedley Aston; *sc* Carey Wilber
lp Martin Benson; Lionel Jeffries; Norman Rossington; John Schlesinger

AT A TIME LIKE THIS: PAY SCHOOLS
(BBC 1968)
Four-part documentary series about private education; part of the 'At a Time Like This' series (1967–75).
ed Desmond Wilcox, Bill Morton; *rep* Trevor Philpott.
The OFFICERS MUST BE TOUGHER THAN THE TROOPS 1/3/1968
Education at a modern public school, Milton Abbey.
MANNERS, MODESTY AND THE PRESERVATION OF INNOCENCE 8/3/1968
A study of Lawnside, Malvern, an old established boarding school for girls.
BOSS DELIVERS THE GOODS 15/3/1968
Public school attitudes and methods of education, as seen at Millfield School.
FIVE HOURS OF LESSONS? – IT'S A CRIME 22/3/1968
The methods of teaching at a progressive public school, Kilquhanity House, Galloway.

AT HOME WITH DR. EVADNE HINGE AND DAME HILDA BRACKET (Scottish TV 23/9/1977)
Female impersonators Hinge and Bracket.
p David Bell
lp George Logan; Patrick Fyffe

AT LAST THE 1948 SHOW (Rediffusion 1967)
Comedy series featuring gags and sketches.
exec.p David Frost
AT LAST THE 1948 SHOW 22/3/1967
d Ian Fordyce; *sc/with* Tim Brooke-Taylor, Graham Chapman, John Cleese, Marty Feldman
note: five compilations of the series also held.

AT NO. 10 DOWNING STREET
(BBC 31/8/1959)
President Dwight Eisenhower's arrival, with Prime Minister Harold Macmillan, at Downing Street.

ATOM SPIES (Anglia 9/6/1979)
Dramatisation of the events behind post-war spies Klaus Fuchs, Bruno Pontecorvo and Alan Nunn May.
d Alan Gibson; *p* John Rosenberg; *sc* Ian Curteis
lp Andrew Ray; Michael Craig; Ray Smith; Peter Jeffrey; John Franklyn-Robbins; Edward Wilson

ATROCITY 1914 (US CBS 13/10/1964)
Germany's war on Belgium in which troops brutalised the Belgian people and ransacked the countryside, destroying many ancient and historic places, among them the renowned library at Louvain.
p Isaac Kleinerman, John Sharnik; *sc* Irve Tunick; *nar* Robert Ryan

Der ATTENTÄTER
(DE Bavaria Atelier Gesellschaft 9/11/1969; BBC *tx* 8/2/1972)
Drama-documentary on the assassination attempt on Hitler on 8th November 1939. BBC English language transmission as 'The Assassin'.
d Rainer Erler; *sc* Hans Gottschalk
lp Fritz Hollenbeck; Ulrich Matschoss; Ingeborg Lapsien; Lothar Grützner

An AUDIENCE WITH JASPER CARROTT
(LWT 6/1–3/3/78))
Comedy series featuring Birmingham comedian Jasper Carrott.
An AUDIENCE WITH JASPER CARROTT 6/1/1978
d/p Paul Smith

The AUTHOR OF BELTRAFFIO
(LWT 13/11/1976)
The British contribution to a five-part series of Henry James stories made for French television in 1974.
d Tony Scott; *p* Stephen Bayly; *sc* Robin Chapman; *auth* Henry James
lp Tom Baker; Georgina Hale; Michael J. Shannon; Catherine Willmer; Stefan Gates; Preston Lockwood

The AVENGERS (ABC 1961–69)
Adventure-fantasy series featuring a pair of Government agents. See also The NEW AVENGERS (1976–77).
regulars Patrick Macnee (1961–69); Honor Blackman (1961–64); Diana Rigg (1965–67); Linda Thorson (1968–69)
DEATH OF A GREAT DANE 17/11/1962
d Peter Hammond; *p* Leonard White; *sc* Roger Marshall, Jeremy Scott
lp Billy Milton; Herbert Nelson; Leslie French; Clare Kelly
MAN IN THE MIRROR 24/2/1963
d Kim Mills; *p* John Bryce; *sc* Geoffrey Orme, Anthony Terpiloff
lp Julie Stevens; Daphne Anderson; Ray Barrett; Julian Somers
The GILDED CAGE 9/11/1963
d Bill Bain; *p* John Bryce; *sc* Roger Marshall
lp Neil Wilson; Norman Chappell; Frederick Abbott; Alan Haywood
The LITTLE WONDERS 11/1/1964
d Laurence Bourne; *p* John Bryce; *sc* Eric Paice
lp Tony Steedman; Lois Maxwell; David Bauer; Rosemarie Dunham; John Cowley; Frank Maher
MANDRAKE 25/1/1964
d Bill Bain; *p* John Bryce; *sc* Roger Marshall
lp George Benson; Philip Locke; John Le Mesurier; Madge Ryan; Annette Andre
The SECRETS BROKER 1/2/1964
d Jonathan Alwyn; *p* John Bryce; *sc* Ludovic Peters
lp Avice Landon; Valentino Musetti; John Stone; Ronald Allen; Jennifer Wood

A SURFEIT OF H$_2$O 19/11/1965
d Sidney Hayers; p Julian Wintle;
sc Colin Finbow
lp Noel Purcell; Albert Lieven; Sue Lloyd;
Talfryn Thomas; John Kidd; Geoffrey Palmer
The HOUR THAT NEVER WAS 26/11/1965
d Gerry O'Hara; p Julian Wintle;
sc Roger Marshall
lp Gerald Harper; Dudley Foster;
Roy Kinnear; Roger Booth; Daniel Moynihan
DIAL A DEADLY NUMBER 3/12/1965
d Don Leaver; p Julian Wintle;
sc Roger Marshall
lp Clifford Evans; Jan Holden;
Anthony Newlands; John Carson; Peter Bowles
The MAN-EATER OF SURREY GREEN 10/12/1965
d Sidney Hayers; p Julian Wintle;
sc Philip Levene
lp Derek Farr; Athene Seyler; Gillian Lewis;
Alan Carter; Edwin Finn
TWO'S A CROWD 17/12/1965
d Roy Ward Baker; p Julian Wintle;
sc Philip Levene
lp Warren Mitchell; Maria Machado;
Alec Mango; Wolfe Morris; Julian Glover
TOO MANY CHRISTMAS TREES 23/12/1965
d Roy Ward Baker; p Julian Wintle;
sc Tony Williamson
lp Mervyn Johns; Edwin Richfield;
Jeannette Sterke; Alex Scott
SILENT DUST 31/12/1965
d Roy Ward Baker; p Julian Wintle;
sc Roger Marshall
lp William Franklyn; Jack Watson;
Conrad Phillips; Norman Bird; Joanna Wake
ROOM WITHOUT A VIEW 7/1/1966
d Roy Ward Baker; p Julian Wintle;
sc Roger Marshall
lp Paul Whitsun-Jones; Peter Jeffrey;
Richard Bebb; Philip Latham; Peter Arne
SMALL GAME FOR BIG HUNTERS
14/1/1966
d Gerry O'Hara; p Julian Wintle;
sc Philip Levene
lp Bill Fraser; James Villiers;
Liam Redmond; A.J. Brown; Tom Gill
The GIRL FROM AUNTIE 21/1/1966
d Roy Ward Baker; p Julian Wintle;
sc Roger Marshall
lp Liz Fraser; Alfred Burke;
Bernard Cribbins; David Bauer; Mary Merrall
The 13th HOLE 28/1/1966
d Roy Ward Baker; p Julian Wintle;
sc Tony Williamson
lp Patrick Allen; Hugh Manning; Peter Jones;
Victor Maddern; Francis Matthews
A TOUCH OF BRIMSTONE 18/2/1966
d James Hill; p Julian Wintle;
sc Brian Clemens
lp Peter Wyngarde; Colin Jeavons;
Carol Cleveland; Robert Cawdron;
Jeremy Young
FROM VENUS WITH LOVE 13/1/1967
d Robert Day;
p Albert Fennell, Brian Clemens;
sc Philip Levene
lp Barbara Shelley; Philip Locke;
Jon Pertwee; Derek Newark; Jeremy Lloyd
The GAME 2/10/1968
d Robert Fuest;
p Albert Fennell, Brian Clemens;
sc Richard Harris
lp Peter Jeffrey; Garfield Morgan;
Anthony Newlands
LOOK (STOP ME IF YOU'VE HEARD
THIS ONE) BUT THERE WERE THESE
TWO FELLERS 4/12/1968
d James Hill;
p Albert Fennell, Brian Clemens;
sc Dennis Spooner
lp Jimmy Jewel, Julian Chagrin; John Cleese
The INTERROGATORS 1/1/1969
d Charles Crichton;
p Albert Fennell, Brian Clemens;
sc Richard Harris, Brian Clemens
lp Christopher Lee; David Sumner; Philip Bond;
Patrick Newell; Neil McCarthy; Neil Stacy

The ROTTERS 8/1/1969
d Robert Fuest;
p Albert Fennell, Brian Clemens;
sc David Freeman
lp Gerald Sim; Jerome Willis;
Eric Barker; Patrick Newell; John Nettleton;
Rhonda Parker
The MORNING AFTER 29/1/1969
d John Hough;
p Albert Fennell, Brian Clemens;
sc Brian Clemens
lp Peter Barkworth; Joss Ackland;
Brian Blessed
The CURIOUS CASE OF THE COUNTLESS
CLUES 5/2/1969
d Don Sharp;
p Albert Fennell, Brian Clemens;
sc Philip Levine
lp Kenneth Cope; Tony Selby; Peter Jones
LOVE ALL 19/2/1969
d Peter Sykes;
p Albert Fennell, Brian Clemens;
sc Tony Williamson
lp Liam Redmond; Robert Urquhart;
Brook Williams; Dudley Foster; Patrick Newell
WHO WAS THAT MAN I SAW YOU WITH?
19/3/1969
d Don Chaffey;
p Albert Fennell, Brian Clemens;
sc Jeremy Burnham
lp Alan Wheatley; Alan Browning;
William Marlowe; Bryan Marshall
HOMICIDE AND OLD LACE 26/3/1969
d John Hough; p Albert Fennell, Brian Clemens;
sc Malcolm Hulke, Terrance Dicks
lp Patrick Newell; Joyce Carey;
Mary Merrall; Gerald Harper; Rhonda Parker;
Keith Baxter
THINGUMAJIG 2/4/1969
d Leslie Norman;
p Albert Fennell, Brian Clemens;
sc Terry Nation
lp Dora Reisser; Jeremy Lloyd;
Iain Cuthbertson; Willoughby Goddard
MY WILDEST DREAM 7/4/1969
d Robert Fuest;
p Albert Fennell, Brian Clemens;
sc Philip Levene
lp Edward Fox; Peter Vaughan;
Derek Godfrey; Susan Travers; Philip Madoc
REQUIEM 16/4/1969
d Don Chaffey;
p Albert Fennell, Brian Clemens;
sc Brian Clemens
lp Angela Douglas; John Cairney; John Paul;
Patrick Newell; Denis Shaw
TAKE OVER 23/4/1969
d Robert Fuest;
p Albert Fennell, Brian Clemens;
sc Terry Nation
lp Tom Adams; Elizabeth Sellars;
Michael Gwynn; Hilary Pritchard
PANDORA 30/4/1969
d Robert Fuest;
p Albert Fennell, Brian Clemens;
sc Brian Clemens
lp Patrick Newell; Julian Glover;
James Cossins; Peter Madden
GET-A-WAY 14/5/1969
d Don Sharp;
p Albert Fennell, Brian Clemens;
sc Philip Levene
lp Peter Bowles; Barry Lineman; Andrew Keir
BIZARRE 21/5/1969
d Leslie Norman;
p Albert Fennell, Brian Clemens;
sc Brian Clemens
lp Fulton Mackay; Roy Kinnear; John Sharp

The AWEFUL MR. GOODALL
(LWT 5/4–10/5/1974)
Robert Urquhart stars as a retired MI5 agent
whose past keeps intruding into his present.
INDISCRETION 12/4/1974
d Jim Goddard; p Richard Bates;
sc Trevor Preston
lp Robert Urquhart; Donald Burton;
Peter Jeffrey; Geraldine Newman; Stephen Greif

B

B-P SERVICE IN WESTMINSTER ABBEY
(BBC 1965)
Guides and scouts arriving in Westminster
Abbey, the wreath laying ceremony in honour of
Lord Baden-Powell.

BABYLON (LWT 25/11–30/12/1979)
Current affairs series for the black community.
d Howard Ross; p Michael Attwell;
pres Lincoln Browne
YOUNG BLACKS AND BRITISH EDUCATION
25/11/1979
Young black people talk about the problems
they face at school.
BLACKS AND TRADITIONAL WHITE POLITICS
30/12/1979
The rejection of traditional British politics by
young West Indians.

BACKS TO THE LAND (Anglia 1977)
Comedy series about members of the Women's
Land Army during the early 1940s.
d David Askey; assoc.p Robert Bell;
sc David Climie
A MISS IS AS GOOD AS A MALE 15/4/1977
lp Marilyn Galsworthy; Teresa Stevens;
Philippa Howell; David Troughton;
Michael Troughton; John Stratton
The MAGNETIC POLE 30/12/1977
lp Teresa Stevens; Pippa Page;
Philippa Howell; Charles Lamb;
Stephanie Fayerman; John Stratton;
Geraldine Newman

BALLET SHOES (BBC 5/10–9/11/1975)
Six-part serial based on the novel by Noel
Streatfield which tells the story of Pauline,
Petrova and Posy, the three adopted daughters
of an eccentric professor.
EPISODE 1 5/10/1975
d Timothy Combe; p John McRae;
sc John Wiles
lp Jane Slaughter; Sarah Prince;
Elizabeth Morgan; Barbara Lott; Angela Thorne

BARBARA HEPWORTH (BBC 17/9/1961)
Barbara Hepworth and her sculptures at St. Ives.
d/sc John Read; nar Bernard Miles

BARBARA HEPWORTH (Westward 1/4/1968)
The evolution of the work of sculptor Barbara
Hepworth.

The BARDNEY POP FESTIVAL
(Anglia 1972)
A compilation of four local news reports
covering the events surrounding the Festival held
during May 1972.

BARLOW AT LARGE (BBC 1971–73)
Police series featuring characters from Z CARS
(1962–78) and SOFTLY, SOFTLY (1966–70).
STRAYS 7/2/1973
d Gilchrist Calder; p Keith Williams;
sc Elwyn Jones
lp Stratford Johns; Neil Stacy; Norman Comer;
Victor Beaumont; Donald Sumpter

The BARNSTORMERS (BBC 10/9/1969)
Stanley Holloway reminisces about the early
days of his career and the early days of variety.
d G.B. Lupino; sc Austin Steele

The BARON (ITC 1966–67)
Adventures of an international antique dealer
and occasional undercover operative of British
Intelligence.
p Monty Berman
regulars Steve Forrest; Sue Lloyd;
Colin Gordon; Paul Ferris
DIPLOMATIC IMMUNITY 17/4/1966
d Leslie Norman; sc Dennis Spooner
lp Dora Reisser; Frank Gatliff;
Robert Crewdson; Michael Wolf
RED HORSE, RED RIDER 24/4/1966
d John Llewellyn Moxey; sc Terry Nation
lp Jane Merrow; Frank Wolff; John Bennett;
Edward Brayshaw; Harold Goldblatt

The BARON cont.

SOMETHING FOR A RAINY DAY
15/5/1966
d Cyril Frankel; *sc* Terry Nation
lp Patrick Allen; Michael Gwynn; Ann Lynn;
Lois Maxwell; Derek Newark
ENEMY OF THE STATE 22/5/1966
d Jeremy Summers; *sc* Dennis Spooner
lp Anton Diffring; Joseph Furst;
John Abineri; Michael Wolf; Brian Phelan;
Richard Carpenter
AND SUDDENLY YOU'RE DEAD
29/5/1966
d Cyril Frankel;
sc Terry Nation, Dennis Spooner
lp Kay Walsh; Alan MacNaughton;
Vladek Sheybal; Bernard Kay
YOU CAN'T WIN THEM ALL 8/10/1966
d Don Chaffey; *sc* Dennis Spooner
lp Sam Wanamaker; Reginald Marsh;
David Burke; John Bown; Peter Bowles
MASQUERADE 15/10/1966
Part one of a two-part story.
d Cyril Frankel; *sc* Terry Nation
lp Bernard Lee; Yvonne Furneaux;
John Carson
A MEMORY OF EVIL 12/11/1966
d Don Chaffey; *sc* Terry Nation
lp Robert Hardy; Ann Bell;
Edwin Richfield; Frederick Bartman;
John Rollason
LONG AGO AND FAR AWAY 19/11/1966
d Robert Asher; *sc* Dennis Spooner
lp Barrie Ingham; Douglas Wilmer;
Alex Scott; Eric Pohlmann; Paul Stassino
The MAZE 26/11/1966
d Jeremy Summers; *sc* Tony O'Grady
lp Alan MacNaughton; Don Borisenko;
Glynn Edwards; David Morrell
STORM WARNING: PART 1 31/12/1966
d Gordon Flemyng; *sc* Terry Nation
lp Dudley Sutton; Reginald Marsh;
John Woodvine; Derek Newark
STORM WARNING: PART 2: THE ISLAND
7/1/1967
d Gordon Flemyng; *sc* Terry Nation
lp Dudley Sutton; Reginald Marsh;
Derek Newark; David Healy
TIME TO KILL 14/1/1967
d Jeremy Summers; *sc* Dennis Spooner
lp David Garth; Peter Bowles;
George Murcell; Hamilton Dyce;
Geraldine Moffatt
NIGHT OF THE HUNTER 21/1/1967
d Roy Ward Baker; *sc* Terry Nation
lp Derek Godfrey; Katharine Blake;
Zeph Gladstone; Walter Gotell
ROUNDABOUT 11/2/1967
d Robert Tronson; *sc* Terry Nation
lp June Ritchie; Edwin Richfield;
Annette Andre; Lisa Daniely; Norman Bird
The HIGH TERRACE 18/2/1967
d Robert Asher; *sc* Dennis Spooner
lp Max Adrian; Jan Holden;
John Collin; Veronica Hurst
COUNTDOWN 4/3/1967
d Robert Asher; *sc* Terry Nation
lp Edward Woodward; Philip Locke;
Harold Lang; Michael Wynne

BARRIE WITH LOVE
(Yorkshire TV 27/6–11/7/1973)
Series of three plays by J.M. Barrie.
The TWELVE POUND LOOK 27/6/1973
d Mike Newell; *exec.p* Peter Willes
lp Michael Denison; Judy Cornwell;
Gwen Watford; Jeffrey Segal

BARRY SHEENE – DAYTONA 1975
(Thames 25/6/1975)
The crash suffered by motor cyclist Barry Sheene
while practising for the Daytona 200 race in
Florida, and his subsequent struggle to recover
from injury.
d/p Frank Cvitanovich

The BASIL BRUSH SHOW (BBC 1968–80)
Entertainment series for children, hosted by a
puppet fox.
The BASIL BRUSH SHOW 19/2/1970
p Johnny Downes; *sc* George Martin;
pres Derek Fowlds; *with* Gil Dova

The BASIL BRUSH SHOW 30/1/1972
p Johnny Downes; *sc* George Martin;
pres Derek Fowlds

BAT MASTERSON
(US Ziv Television Programs 1959–61)
Western series.
PIGEON AND HAWK 21/1/1960
d Alan Crosland Jr;
p Frank Pittman, Andy White;
sc John Tucker Battle; *auth* Richard O'Connor
lp Gene Barry; Lisa Montell;
Howard Petrie; Hugh Sanders; Rand Brooks;
Mickey Simpson

The BATTLE OF ARNHEM (Anglia 16/9/1969)
A study of the Battle of Arnhem in September
1944. Those taking part are General Sir John
Hackett, Major Generals R. R. Urquhart, John
Frost, Sir Alan Adair, Panzer General Willi
Bittrich, Brigadier Charles MacKenzie, Flight
Lt. Jimmy Edwards, and Jeanne Christine
Lamberts.
d Harry Aldous; *p/sc/nar* Michael Robson

BATTLEGROUND (Tyne Tees 1978)
Regional documentary series looking at famous
battles.
d Gavin Taylor; *p* Alex Murchie
EDGEHILL 23/2/1978
The NILE 23/3/1978
FRANCE 20/4/1978
GETTYSBURG 27/4/1978

BBC-3 (BBC 1965–66)
Satirical review of current events, combining
music, comedy and discussion.
BBC-3 16/10/1965
d/p Ned Sherrin;
with John Bird, Robert Robinson, Lynda Baron,
David Battley, Bill Oddie, Leonard Rossiter,
Alan Bennett
BBC-3 30/10/1965
d Darrol Blake; *p* Ned Sherrin;
with John Bird, Robert Robinson, Lynda Baron,
David Battley, Bill Oddie, Leonard Rossiter,
Alan Bennett

BBC TELEVISION SHAKESPEARE
(BBC 1978–85)
Adaptations of the plays by William
Shakespeare.
p Cedric Messina
ROMEO AND JULIET 3/12/1978
d Alvin Rakoff
lp Patrick Ryecart; Rebecca Saire;
Celia Johnson; Michael Hordern;
John Gielgud; David Sibley; Jack Carr;
Bunny Reed; Christopher Strauli; Alan Rickman
RICHARD II 10/12/1978
d David Giles
lp Derek Jacobi; Jon Finch;
John Gielgud; Wendy Hiller; Richard Owens;
Mary Morris; Jeffrey Holland; Charles Gray
AS YOU LIKE IT 17/12/1978
d Basil Coleman
lp Helen Mirren; Brian Stirner; Angharad Rees;
Richard Pasco; James Bolam
MEASURE FOR MEASURE 18/2/1979
d Desmond Davis
lp Kate Nelligan; Tim Pigott-Smith;
Kenneth Colley; Christopher Strauli;
John McEnery; Jacqueline Pearce;
Frank Middlemass; Alun Armstrong;
Adrienne Corri
HENRY IV: PART TWO 16/12/1979
d David Giles
lp David Gwillim; Jon Finch;
Anthony Quayle; Robert Eddison;
Brenda Bruce; Michele Dotrice; Frances Cuka;
Rob Edwards; Martin Neil
HENRY V 23/12/1979
d David Giles
lp David Gwillim; Alec McCowen;
Jocelyne Boisseau; Martin Smith; Rob Edwards;
Roger Davenport; Clifford Parrish;
Derek Hollis; Robert Ashby

BEARCATS
(US Filmways TV Productions 1971)
Adventure series set in the American Southwest
of 1914.
The BIG GUNS 1971
d Alf Kjellin;
p Morton Fine, David Friedkin;
sc Sam Roeca, James L. Henderson
lp Rod Taylor; Dennis Cole;
Leslie Nielsen; George Murdock; Stacy Harris;
Arthur Batanides
The RETURN OF ESTABAN 1971
d Herb Wallerstein;
p Morton Fine, David Friedkin;
sc Edward J. Lakso
lp Rod Taylor; Dennis Cole; Henry Darrow;
Kathryn Hays; Brioni Farrell; William Smith

BEASTLY TIME: ROYAL WELSH 1904–
1979 (HTV 22/7/1977)
A history of the Royal Welsh Agricultural Show.

BEASTS (ATV 16/10–20/11/1976)
Anthology of macabre dramas written by Nigel
Kneale.
DURING BARTY'S PARTY 23/10/1976
d Don Taylor; *p* Nicholas Palmer
lp Elizabeth Sellars; Anthony Bate; Colin Bell;
Norman Mitchell; John Rhys-Davies

BEAT CITY (Rediffusion 24/12/1963)
Daniel Farson visits Liverpool to discover its pop
music heritage; with Gerry and The Pacemakers,
Rory Storm and The Hurricanes, Faron's
Flamingoes, Earl Preston and The T.T.'s, The
Chants, Chick Graham and The Coasters, The
Spinners, Jacqueline McDonald, Birdie
O'Donnell, Billy Kietly and Paul Cunningham.
d Charles Squires; *sc* Daniel Farson

The BEATLES AT SHEA STADIUM
(NEMS Enterprises 1/3/1966)
The Beatles' first concert (15/8/1965) at the Shea
Stadium, near New York, during their tour of
the United States. Other performers include
Sounds Incorporated, Brenda Holloway, King
Curtis, and The Discotheque Dancers.
p Bob Precht

BEATRIX POTTER – THE PRIVATE
WORLD (Yorkshire TV 16/5/1972)
The life of Beatrix Potter drawn from her diaries
and from reminiscences of those who knew her.
d Duncan Dallas; *exec.p* Tony Essex

BEAUTY AND THE BEAST (BBC 27/1/1965)
Ballet based on the fairy tale, with music by
Maurice Ravel and choreography by John Cranko.
with Doreen Wells, Richard Farley

BEAUTY, BONNY, DAISY, VIOLET, GRACE
AND GEOFFREY MORTON
(Thames 1/10/1974)
The farm of Geoffrey Morton in Yorkshire on
which he uses shire horses instead of tractors.
d Frank Cvitanovich

BEFORE THE MONSOON (ATV 1979)
Three-part documentary on India.
d/p Michael Grigsby
PART 1: ROOTS OF VIOLENCE 27/11/1979
Conditions in India which led to the State of
Emergency in 1975.
PART 2: STATE OF EMERGENCY 4/12/1979
Indian people tell of their own experiences
during the nineteen-month state of emergency.
PART 3: SEEDS OF DEMOCRACY 11/12/1979
Indian villagers and workers talk of the changes
they would like to see take place in India.

BEFORE YOUR VERY EYES (ATV 1956–57)
Comedy series with Arthur Askey. Originally
shown under 'Jack Hylton Presents' billing.
d/p Kenneth Carter
BEFORE YOUR VERY EYES 24/2/1956
BEFORE YOUR VERY EYES 9/3/1956
BEFORE YOUR VERY EYES 23/3/1956
BEFORE YOUR VERY EYES 6/4/1956
BEFORE YOUR VERY EYES 20/4/1956

Studio of ATV.

Above: *Take Your Pick* (Rediffusion).
Michael Miles.

Right: *What's My Line?* (BBC). The panel,
left to right, David Nixon, Lady Barnett,
Barbara Kelly, Maurice Edelman MP.
Host is Eamonn Andrews.

Above: *Pinky and Perky* (BBC). Jan and
Vlasta Dalibor with Pinky and Perky.

Left: *Enid Blyton's Famous Five* (Southern
TV). Marcus Harris, Gary Russell,
Michele Gallagher; seated Jennifer
Thanisch.

The Evacuees (BBC). Steven Serember and Gary Carp.

Alice in Wonderland (BBC). Left to right, Peter Cook, Wilfrid Lawson, Michael Gough, Anne Marie Mallick.

BEFORE YOUR VERY EYES 2/12/1957
BEFORE YOUR VERY EYES 16/12/1957

BEHIND THE LINES: ERITREA
(ATV 24/4/1979)
The attempt by the Eritrean People's Liberation
Front to mobilise village society in Eritrea.
d Roger James

**BEHIND THE MIRROR: A PROFILE OF
DOUGLAS SIRK** (BBC 30/4/1979)
Interview with film-maker Douglas Sirk.
d Sue Mallinson; *p* Mark Shivas

La BELLE VIE (FR Antenne 2 1979)
Comedy set in Munich in 1918.
d Lazare Iglesis; *sc* Jean Anouilh
lp Jacques François; Jean Le Poulain;
Hélène Perdrière; Mala Simon;
Alain Mottet; Madeleine Barbulée;
Jean-Pierre Bouvier

The BENEDICT PLAN (BBC 6/12/1955)
A play for children.
p Pamela Brown; *sc* Sheilah Ward
lp Ralph Tovey; Evelyn Lund; Michael Caridia;
Fraser White; Anthony Selby; Anthony Verner

BENJAMIN BRITTEN AND HIS FESTIVAL
(BBC 22/11/1967)
The organisation of the Aldeburgh Festival by
Benjamin Britten. Includes Julian Bream, The
Vienna Boys Choir, Sviatoslav Richter, Henry
Moore, Sir William Walton, Peter Pears, Joyce
Grenfell and The King's College Choir.
d Tony Palmer;
p Nathan Kroll, Humphrey Burton;
nar Patrick Allen

The BENNY HILL SHOW (Thames 1969–89)
Comedy show featuring Benny Hill.
The BENNY HILL SHOW 24/3/1971
d John Robins; *p* John Robins;
with Andree Melly, Bob Todd, Nicholas Parsons

BENTINE (Thames 22/9/1975)
Comedy programme.
d Leon Thau; *p* David Clark;
sc Michael Bentine; *with* Michael Bentine,
Geoffrey Bayldon, James Berwick, Jack Haig,
Nat Jackley, Jan Hunt, Barrie Manning,
Kevin Moran

The BERLIN STORY (Rediffusion 21/9/1960)
Henry Fairlie tells the story of Berlin from 1945
to 1960 and suggests why it is the flash-point in
East-West relations.
d Graham Watts; *p* Caryl Doncaster

BERNADETTE DEVLIN (ATV 21/4/1970)
A profile of Bernadette Devlin, MP for Mid-
Ulster.
d/p John Goldschmidt

BERT D'ANGELO/SUPERSTAR
(US QM Productions 1976)
San Francisco-based police detective series.
exec.p Quinn Martin
regular Paul Sorvino
MURDER IN VELVET 21/2/1976
d David Friedkin; *sc* Larry Alexander
lp Dennis Patrick, Robert Pine,
Shelly Novack, George Dzundza, Wynn Irwin,
Leigh McCloskey, Lisa Lyon, Anne Helm
REQUIEM FOR A RIP OFF 29/5/1976
d William Hale; *sc* Martin Roth
lp David Huffman; Scott Colomby;
Devon Ericson; Corinne Michaels
SERPENT'S TOOTH 10/7/1976
d Walter Grauman; *sc* Marion Hargrove
lp Reni Santoni; Trish Stewart

BERTRAM MILLS CIRCUS (BBC 17/12/1959)
A Royal Performance of Bertram Mills Circus at
Olympia, London, in the presence of Princess
Margaret, in aid of the Olympic Games and
International Equestrian Fund.
p Derek Burrell-Davis

BERTRAND RUSSELL REFLECTS
(Rediffusion 24/3/1958)

BERYL'S LOT (Yorkshire TV 1973–77)
Domestic drama series.
SAFETY FIRST 5/12/1975
d David Reynolds; *p* Jacky Stoller;
sc Kevin Laffan
lp Carmel McSharry; Mark Kingston;
Clare Kelly; Jeffery Kissoon; Robert Keegan;
Jill Gascoine

The BEST OF YARWOOD (BBC 23/4/1976)
Features impersonator Mike Yarwood.
d Alan Boyd; *p* John Ammonds;
sc Eric Davidson

BEST SELLERS
(Rediffusion 3/1–1/3/1967)
Documentary series on popular novelists.
THOMAS HARDY 1/3/1967
The novels of Thomas Hardy with Lord David
Cecil.
d John Rhodes; *p* Peter Hunt;
reader Ralph Wightman

BETJEMAN AT RANDOM
(Rediffusion 1/8–22/8/1966)
Four-part series in which John Betjeman talks
about and reads poetry; with studio guests.
SIR CHARLES TENNYSON 1/8/1966
p Geoffrey Hughes
WILLIAM BEALBY-WRIGHT 8/8/1966
p Geoffrey Hughes

BETJEMAN'S LONDON
(Rediffusion 14/8–18/9/1967)
Six-part series in which John Betjeman visits
various London landmarks.
The ROYAL MINT 28/8/1967
d Graham Watts; *p* Geoffrey Hughes

**BETTE DAVIS: AMERICAN FILM
INSTITUTE SALUTE** (US Filmways
TV Productions 21/3/1977)
A tribute to actress Bette Davis.
d/p Robert Scheerer; *sc* Rod Warren;
pres Jane Fonda

BETWEEN THE WARS (LWT 11/5–15/6/1973)
Six plays specially adapted from English short
stories written in the 1920s and '30s.
The SILVER MASK 15/6/1973
d Alastair Reid; *p* Verity Lambert;
auth Hugh Walpole; *adapt* Trevor Griffiths
lp Joyce Redman; Scott Antony; Joan Peart;
Anthony Roye; Tara Soppet; Zoë Wanamaker

BETWEEN TWO RIVERS (BBC 3/6/1960)
After three years at Oxford, Dennis Potter
returns to his village between the Severn and the
Wye and describes the changes in the life of the
village and in the relations between himself and
family and friends.
p Anthony De Lotbinière; *sc* Dennis Potter

The BEVERLY HILLBILLIES
(US Filmways TV Productions 1962–71)
Sitcom about a family of hillbillies who become
rich and move to Beverly Hills.
regulars Buddy Ebsen; Irene Ryan; Nancy Kulp;
Raymond Bailey; Max Baer Jr; Donna Douglas
GREAT FEUD 12/12/1962
p Paul Henning
lp Ken Drake; Lyle Talbot;
Sirry Steffen; Arthur Gould-Porter
NO PLACE LIKE HOME 26/12/1962
p Paul Henning
lp Bea Benaderet; Paul Winchell;
Frank Wilcox

BEYOND BELIEF (ATV 1970)
Light-hearted revue series.
BEYOND BELIEF 18/10/1970
d/p John Scholz-Conway;
sc Les Lilley, Chic Jacob,
Chris Allen, Brian Freeman, Alec Myles,
Nicolette McKenzie, Philip Parsons,
Melvyn Hayes; *with* Carmel Cryan, Mark Eden,
Melvyn Hayes, Anthony Jackson,
Nicolette McKenzie, The Settlers

**The BIG BANDS FROM THE
DORCHESTER**
(BBC 14/4–26/5/1974)
Seven-part music series.
p Stanley Dorfman
COUNT BASIE AND HIS ORCHESTRA 14/4/1974
STAN KENTON AND HIS ORCHESTRA 21/4/1974
BUDDY RICH AND HIS BAND 5/5/1974
WOODY HERMAN AND HIS BAND 12/5/1974
DUKE ELLINGTON AND HIS ORCHESTRA
19/5/1974

**BIG BOB JOHNSON AND HIS FANTASTIC
SPEED CIRCUS** (US Playboy Productions
16/4/1979)
Big Bob Johnson and his two assistants are stunt
drivers who don't have a lot of success. They
believe they may have hit the big time when
someone offers a large sum to race a Rolls-
Royce, to satisfy the conditions of a will.
d Jack Starrett; *p* Joseph Cantman;
sc Bob Comfort, Rick Kellard
lp Maud Adams; Constance Forslund;
Robert Stoneman; Charles Napier;
William Daniels

BIG BREADWINNER HOG
(Granada 11/4–30/5/1969)
Crime thriller series featuring a young and
ruthless gangster.
EPISODE 1: A PROMISING, IF IMPULSIVE
PUPIL... 11/4/1969
d Mike Newell; *p/sc* Robin Chapman
lp Peter Egan; Rosemary McHale;
Donald Burton; Timothy West; Tony Steedman;
Eileen Huxtable

BIG BROTHER
(LWT 30/8–4/10/1970)
Series of six plays created by William Greatorex
and based on the Orwellian concept of 'Big
Brother', operating under many guises in 1970s
Britain.
A TOUCH OF THE JUMBOS 4/10/1970
d Cyril Coke; *exec.p* Peter Wildeblood;
sc Peter Draper
lp Robert Hardy; David Bauer; Hilary Tindall;
Graham James; Janet Key; Tom Chatto;
Alex Davion

BIG DEAL AT GOTHENBURG
(Tyne Tees 7/9/1966)
Brian Widlake reports on shipbuilding in
Sweden, and provides an assessment of British
competition.
d/p Robert Tyrrell

BIG JACK'S OTHER WORLD
(Tyne Tees 2/11/1971)
Footballer Jack Charlton visits his home town of
Ashington, Northumberland.
d Jeremy Lack

The BIG SHOW (Tyne Tees 15/1/1959)
Variety show featuring Dickie Henderson, Jill
Day, Bill Maynard, Jack Payne, Bill Travers and
Linden Travers.
p Bill Lyon-Shaw

BIG TIME (BBC 20/4/1961)
An unconventional approach to the theme of
juvenile delinquency featuring three would-be
'underworld' characters.
p Don Taylor; *sc* Jimmy MacReady
lp Tony Garnett; Robert Scroggins;
Stratford Johns; Edward Evans

The BIG VALLEY (US Four Star-Margate
1965–69)
Western drama series featuring a ranching family
and set in California of the 1870s.
PALMS OF GLORY 15/9/1965
d William A. Graham;
p Jules Levy, Arthur Gardner, Arnold Laven;
sc Christopher Knopf
lp Richard Long; Peter Breck; Lee Majors;
Linda Evans; Barbara Stanwyck

The BIG VALLEY *cont.*

The RIVER MONARCH 6/4/1966
d Sutton Roley;
p Jules Levy, Arthur Gardner, Arnold Laven;
sc Joseph Mazzuca, Carey Wilber,
Mel Goldberg; *auth* Carey Wilber
lp Richard Long; Peter Breck; Lee Majors;
Linda Evans; Barbara Stanwyck; Chips Rafferty;
Katherine Justice; Curt Conway

BILL BRAND (Thames 7/6–16/8/1976)
Eleven-part political drama based around the
exploits of a Socialist candidate in a north of
England constituency.
p Stuart Burge; *sc* Trevor Griffiths
regular Jack Shepherd
NOW AND IN ENGLAND 28/6/1976
d Michael Lindsay-Hogg
lp Lynn Farleigh; Alan Badel; Cherie Lunghi;
Robert Hardy; Peter Copley
RESOLUTION 12/7/1976
d Stuart Burge
lp Arthur Lowe; Alan Badel; Robert East;
Rosemary Martin; Gary Roberts
TRANQUILITY OF THE REALM 19/7/1976
d Roland Joffé
lp Karen Silver; Lynn Farleigh; Cherie Lunghi;
Philip Cox; Ann Pennington
RABBLES 26/7/1976
d Stuart Burge
lp Alan Badel; Cherie Lunghi; Allan Surtees;
James Garbutt; John Barrett
ANYBODY'S 2/8/1976
d Roland Joffé
lp Alan Badel; Geoffrey Palmer;
Stephanie Cole; Peter Copley; Rosemary Martin
REVISIONS 9/8/1976
d Stuart Burge
lp Alan Badel; Rosemary Martin;
Douglas Campbell; Lynn Farleigh;
Peter Davison
IT IS THE PEOPLE WHO CREATE 16/8/1976
d Roland Joffé
lp Karen Silver; Jonathan Pryce;
Rosemary Martin; Colin Douglas; Peter Copley

The BILLION DOLLAR SHOW
(Scottish TV 1/1/1967)
The extensive organisation and preparatory work
behind Expo 67 at Montreal.
d Don Cumming

The BILLY COTTON BAND SHOW
(BBC 1956–65)
Variety series featuring Billy Cotton, Alan
Breeze, and Kathie Kay. See also The WAKEY
WAKEY TAVERN (1959).
The BILLY COTTON BAND SHOW 24/12/1961
p Bill Cotton; *sc* Jimmy Grafton
with Eric Sykes, Hattie Jacques, Jeremy Lloyd,
The High-Lights, The Leslie Roberts
Silhouettes, John Williams, Mrs Mills

BILLY LIAR (LWT 1973–74)
Comedy series based on the play by Keith
Waterhouse and Willis Hall
BILLY'S NIGHT IN 7/12/1973
d/p Stuart Allen;
sc Keith Waterhouse, Willis Hall
lp Jeff Rawle; Colin Jeavons;
George A. Cooper; Pamela Vezey; Sally Watts;
May Warden

BILLY – VIOLENCE IN A FAMILY
(Thames 15/11/1977)
A study of a seventeen-year-old from Glasgow
with a history of aggression.
d/p Michael Whyte

BIOSCOPE BYGONES
(Anglia 10/5–14/6/1971)
Documentary series looking at early cinema.
Part of the long-running BYGONES series
(1968–81).
NATURE IN REVOLT 6/5/1971
Dick Joice and John Huntley introduce extracts
from early newsreels on natural disasters,
including the 1906 San Francisco earthquake,
hurricanes in Miami and the eruption of Mount
Etna.
d Les Caynes

BIOSCOPE DAYS (BBC 1978)
Five-part documentary series on early British
films.
BIOSCOPE DAYS 10/5/1978
The surviving films of early Brighton-based film-
maker George Albert Smith.
p Patrick Taggart; *pres* John Huntley

BIRD'S EYE VIEW (BBC 1969–71)
Series on the British countryside.
A GREEN AND PLEASANT LAND 22/6/1969
Aerial views of Britain.
p David Gerrard; *nar* Alan Dobie
JOHN BULL'S WORKSHOP 30/11/1969
The rise of industry in Britain.
p John Bird; *nar* Alan Dobie
A LAND FOR ALL SEASONS 18/4/1971
British countryside throughout one year in
poetry, music and aerial pictures.
p John Bird

BIRDS ON THE WING (BBC 1971)
Sitcom.
BIRDS ON THE WING 16/7/1971
p Graeme Muir; *sc* Peter Yeldham
lp Richard Briers; Julia Lockwood;
Anne Rogers; Robert Lee

The BIRTH OF ITV (Thames 16/9/1976)
The events and personalities behind the birth of
commercial television in Great Britain. With
Norman Collins, Christopher Mayhew, Sir John
Rodgers, Lord Selwyn-Lloyd, Lord Gordon
Walker, Grace Wyndham Goldie, Harman
Grisewood, Mark Chapman-Walker and
Malcolm Muggeridge.
d Peter Tiffin; *p* David Elstein

A BIT OF VISION (Yorkshire TV 6/8/1972)
The meeting of the families of a successful writer
and a resentful director form a picture of marital
chaos and professional instability.
d Marc Miller; *p* Peter Willes;
sc Charles Wood
lp Roy Dotrice; Clive Revill; Adrienne Corri;
Annette Crosbie; John Carson; John White

BITTER HARVEST (ATV 23/10/1973)
The struggle of the United Farm Workers, led by
Caesar Chavez, to gain recognition in the USA
as the union representing agricultural labour.
d Maurice Hatton;
p Charles Stewart, Maurice Hatton

BLACK AND BLUE
(BBC 14/8–18/9/1973)
Series of six black comedy plays.
SECRETS 14/8/1973
d James Cellan Jones; *p* Mark Shivas;
sc Michael Palin, Terry Jones;
lp Warren Mitchell; Julian Holloway;
David Collings; Clifford Rose; George Innes

**The BLACK AND WHITE MINSTREL
SHOW** (BBC 1958–78)
Song and dance variety show with The George
Mitchell Minstrels.
The BLACK AND WHITE MINSTREL SHOW
13/1/1962
d George Inns
with Leslie Crowther, Margo Henderson,
Semprini, George Chisholm and his Jazzers
The BLACK AND WHITE MINSTREL SHOW
3/7/1971
p Ernest Maxin
with The Monarchs, Jimmy Marshall
The BLACK AND WHITE MINSTREL SHOW
20/2/1972
p Ernest Maxin
The BLACK AND WHITE MINSTREL SHOW
27/2/1972
p Ernest Maxin
The BLACK AND WHITE MINSTREL SHOW
19/3/1972
p Ernest Maxin

BLACK MAN'S BURDEN (Thames 14/9/1971)
Excerpt from the programme containing an
interview with Julius Nyerere of Tanzania about
the problems facing the Third World.
d/sc Richard Broad; *p* Ian Martin

**BLACK MARRIES WHITE – THE LAST
BARRIER** (Rediffusion 29/4/1964)
Partners of mixed marriages talk about the
problems they face.
d Peter Morley

BLACK NATIVITY (Rediffusion 25/12/1964)
Black American presentation of the nativity
story from the New York stage production by
Langston Hughes.
d Ronald Marriott

BLACK ON WHITE (BBC 28/11/1954)
Historical events during the last 200 years as
seen by British cartoonists and caricaturists from
Hogarth to David Low.
d John Read; *sc* Reg Groves;
comm Alistair Cooke

BLACKMAIL (Rediffusion 1965–66)
Drama series centered around the theme of
blackmail.
p Stella Richman
KILL ME 17/9/1965
d Marc Miller; *sc* Alexander Baron
lp Joss Ackland; Eric Pohlmann;
Lennard Pearce; John Quayle; Gillian Webb;
Jean Marlow
CUT YOURSELF A SLICE OF THROAT 15/10/1965
d Stuart Burge; *sc* Peter Draper
lp Diane Cilento; Gwendolyn Watts;
Derrick Sherwin; Aubrey Richards;
Gary Raymond
SNAKES AND LADDERS 5/11/1965
d Peter Moffatt; *sc* Douglas Livingstone
lp Anthony Sagar; Diana King; Doreen Andrew;
Francis Attard; Gerald Rowland
The TAMING OF TROOPER TANNER 25/11/1965
d Marc Miller; *sc* Robert Holles
lp John Carson; John Quentin; George Innes;
Colin Spaull; Mopileola Daramola
The HUNTING OF AUBREY HOPKISS 7/11/1966
d Marc Miller; *sc* Robert Holles
lp Roy Dotrice; Gwen Cherrell; Derek Newark;
Arthur Brough; Mary Kenton; Melissa Stribling

BLACKPOOL NIGHT OUT (ABC 12/9/1965)
Variety show from the ABC Theatre, Blackpool.
d Pat Johns; *sc* John Morley, Brad Ashton;
with Mike and Bernie Winters, Cilla Black,
Ray Alan, The New Faces, Lionel Blair,
Bob Sharples

The BLACKPOOL SHOW (ABC 31/7/1966)
Variety show from Blackpool.
p Mark Stuart; *sc* John Muir, Eric Green;
pres Tony Hancock; *with* Jeannie Carson,
Bob Monkhouse, Freddy Davies,
The Rockin' Berries, John Junkin,
The Peter Gordeno Dancers,
The ABC Television Showband, Bob Sharples

BLAKE'S 7 (BBC 1978–81)
Science-fiction series.
regulars Gareth Thomas; Paul Darrow;
Michael Keating; Jan Chappell; Sally Knyvette;
David Jackson; Peter Tuddenham
The WAY BACK 2/1/1978
d Michael E. Briant; *p* David Maloney;
sc Terry Nation
lp Robert Beatty; Robert James; Jeremy Wilkin;
Michael Halsey; Pippa Steel
SPACE FALL 9/1/1978
d Pennant Roberts; *p* David Maloney;
sc Terry Nation
lp Glyn Owen; Leslie Schofield; Norman Tipton;
David Hayward; Brett Forrest; Tom Kelly
PROJECT AVALON 27/2/1978
d Michael E. Briant; *p* David Maloney;
sc Terry Nation
lp Stephen Greif; Jacqueline Pearce;
Julia Vidler; David Bailie; Glynis Barber;
John Baker; John Rolfe
BREAKDOWN 6/3/1978
d Vere Lorrimer; *p* David Maloney;
sc Terry Nation
lp Julian Glover; Ian Thompson;
Christian Roberts

BOUNTY 13/3/1978
d Pennant Roberts; p David Maloney;
sc Terry Nation
lp T.P. McKenna; Carinthia West; Mark York;
Marc Zuber
DELIVERANCE 20/3/1978
d Michael E. Briant; p David Maloney;
sc Terry Nation
lp Tony Caunter; Suzan Farmer; James Lister

BLESS 'EM ALL! (BBC 9/5/1955)
A television variety show on the tenth
anniversary of VE-Day. With Vera Lynn, Jack
Warner, Bobby Alderson, Robert Easton,
Richard Murdoch, Kenneth Horne, Sam Costa,
Eric Barker, Pearl Hackney, Charlie Chester,
Teddy Haskell, Renee Baxter, The Windmill
Girls, Doris Hare, and Bob Harvey. Introduced
by John Snagge, Richard Dimbleby, Ralph
Reader, and Jean Metcalfe.
p Derek Burrell-Davis

BLESS ME, FATHER (LWT 1978–81)
Sitcom set in 1950, about an eccentric parish
priest and his young curate.
BAPTISM OF FIRE 24/9/1978
d/p David Askey; sc Peter de Rosa
lp Arthur Lowe; Daniel Abineri;
Gabrielle Daye; Susan Sheridan

BLESS THIS HOUSE (Thames 1971–76)
Sitcom.
d/p William G. Stewart
regulars Sid James; Diana Coupland;
Robin Stewart; Sally Geeson
The DAY OF REST 23/3/1971
sc Dave Freeman
lp James Cossins; Juliet Harmer
MAKE LOVE...NOT WAR 30/3/1971
sc Carla Lane, Myra Taylor
lp Anthony Jackson; Patsy Rowlands
The BIGGEST WOODWORM IN THE WORLD
28/10/1974

BLOW-OUT AT BRAVO (Grampian 1/5/1977)
Day by day account of the blow-out on the
North Sea oil rig 'Bravo' and its subsequent
capping by Red Adair's team.

BLUE PETER (BBC 1958–)
Series for children.
BLUE PETER ROYAL SAFARI 11/4/1971
Princess Anne with presenter Valerie Singleton
on safari in Kenya.
p Biddy Baxter, Edward Barnes

The BLUES AND GOSPEL TRAIN
(Granada 19/8/1964)
Blues and gospel music performed on a suburban
station in Manchester. With Sister Rosetta
Tharpe, Muddy Waters, Cousin Joe Pleasants,
Sonny Terry and Brownie McGhee, Otis Spann,
Willie Smith and Ransome Knowling.
d Philip Casson; p John Hamp

The BOB HOPE SHOW (Granada 1956)
Variety show.
The BOB HOPE SHOW 9/5/1956
d Bill Ward; p Jack Hope;
with Yana, Richard Wattis; The Bernard
Brothers, Zena Marshall
The BOB HOPE SHOW 23/5/1956
with Fernandel, Diana Dors, Yana,
Richard Wattis, Zena Marshall,
Ted Heath and his Band

The BOB MONKHOUSE COMEDY HOUR
(Thames 1972–73)
Comedy series.
The BOB MONKHOUSE DISTURBANCE
22/11/1972
Comedy show hosted by Bob Monkhouse and
featuring William Franklyn, Barbara Mitchell,
Clement Freud, Bob Todd, Joe Baker, Melvyn
Hayes, Katie Boyle, Stanley Unwin and Diana
Dors.
d/p Terry Henebery;
sc Bob Monkhouse, Tony Hawes, Wally Malston

The BOB MONKHOUSE SHOW
(Thames 1973)
Comedy series.
The BOB MONKHOUSE OFFENSIVE 18/4/1973
Comedy show hosted by Bob Monkhouse
satirising the 'permissive society' and its critics.
Also featuring Alfred Marks, Barbara Windsor,
Jack Douglas and Bernard Hepton.
d/p Terry Henebery;
sc Bob Monkhouse, Tony Hawes

The BODKIN CLUB (BBC 1963)
Puppet series.
BEAUTY AND THE BEAST 23/7/1963
d/p Gordon Murray

BOD YN GENEDI (HTV 12/1/1979)
A Welsh view of Scotland as it nears the
referendum for devolution.
d Owen Griffith; pres Gerallt Jones

The BODY IN QUESTION
(BBC 6/11/1978–12/2/1979)
A series of thirteen programmes in which Dr
Jonathan Miller examines various aspects of the
human body.
NAMING OF PARTS 6/11/1978
d Jonathan Crane, Fisher Dilke;
p Patrick Uden; sc Jonathan Miller
HOW DO YOU FEEL? 20/11/1978
d Jonathan Crane, Fisher Dilke;
p Patrick Uden; sc Jonathan Miller

BOLD VENTURE (US Ziv Television Programs
1959–61)
Syndicated action series set in the Caribbean.
BOLD VENTURE 1959
d William Conrad;
p/sc David Friedkin, Morton Fine
lp Dane Clark; Joan Marshall; Bernie Gozier;
Phillip Pine; Ted De Corsia; Helen Kleeb

**BOLTON WANDERERS v MANCHESTER
CITY** (Granada 17/11/1979)
Coverage of the football match.

BONANZA (US NBC 1959–73)
Western series.
SAN FRANCISCO HOLIDAY 2/4/1960
d Arthur Lubin; p David Dortort;
sc Thomas Thompson
lp Michael Landon; Lorne Greene;
Robert Nichols; Dan Blocker; Pernell Roberts;
O.Z. Whitehead

BONNY! (BBC 1974)
Series for children.
BLACKBEARD'S GOLD 18/3/1974
p Paul Ciani; sc John Morley
lp Una Mclean; Walter Carr; Alex McAvoy;
Ian Collier; John Yule; Gordon Belbin;
Alastair McDonald

The BOOK PROGRAMME (BBC 1973–)
Documentary series covering literature and
publishing.
V.S. NAIPAUL 24/3/1979
d Sandra Gregory; p Peter Foges;
pres Robert Robinson; reader Ronald Pickup

A BOOK WITH CHAPTERS IN IT
(BBC 8/12/1961)
Drama about the complications of adult life as
seen through the eyes of a lonely young boy.
p Eric Tayler; sc Jack Pulman
lp Ruth Dunning; Bruce Prochnik;
Maureen Pryor; Peter Vaughan; Beckett Bould

BOOTSIE AND SNUDGE (Granada 1960–63)
Sitcom featuring the two characters from 'The
Army Game'; following their misadventures in
Civvy-street.
BEING NICE TO BOOTSIE 7/3/1963
d Eric Fawcett; p Milo Lewis;
sc Jack Rosenthal, Harry Driver
lp Alfie Bass; Bill Fraser; Robert Dorning;
Clive Dunn; William Sherwood

The BORDERERS (BBC 1968–70)
Adventure series set in the seventeenth-century
Scottish Borders.
regulars Iain Cuthbertson; Michael Gambon;
Joseph Brady; Edith MacArthur
WITCH HUNT 14/1/1969
d Moira Armstrong; p Anthony Coburn;
sc Vincent Tilsley
lp Roy Sampson; Elaine Boyle
BLOODFEUD 18/2/1969
d Eric Price; p Peter Graham Scott;
sc George F. Kerr
lp Ross Campbell; Nell Brennan;
Margaret Greig; Ian Gardiner; Stuart Mungall;
Jane Walker
OUTLAW 11/3/1969
d Moira Armstrong; p Peter Graham Scott;
sc Bruce Stewart
lp Ian McCulloch; Leonard Maguire;
Heather Bell; Michael McKevitt
DISPOSSESSED 25/3/1969
d James Gatward; p Peter Graham Scott;
sc Bill Craig, Julian Nees
lp John Thaw; Vivien Heilbron

BORN AND BRED (Thames 1978–80)
Comedy series about the various branches of a
big south London family.
HOW DO YOU FEEL WHEN YOU MARRY YOUR
IDEAL? 4/10/1978
d/p Peter Duguid; sc Douglas Livingstone
lp Max Wall; Constance Chapman; Susan Tracy;
Gorden Kaye; Kate Williams; Joan Sims

BORN CHINESE (BBC 4/5/1965)
The way of life for a Chinese family in Hong
Kong.
d/p Richard Cawston; comm Anthony Lawrence

BORN TO BE SMALL (ATV 6/12/1971)
Documentary asking the question of how does
the world seem to the many men and women
who are often, and hurtfully, described as dwarfs
and midgets.
d Tony Snowdon; p Derek Hart

BOUQUET OF BARBED WIRE
(LWT 9/1–20/2/1976)
Seven-part drama series about a middle-class
family breaking apart. Followed by ANOTHER
BOUQUET (1977).
d/p Tony Wharmby; sc Andrea Newman;
regulars Frank Finlay; Susan Penhaligon;
Sheila Allen; James Aubrey
EPISODE 1: HOME-COMING 9/1/1976
lp Ann Beach; Roland Curram
EPISODE 2: INTRODUCTIONS 16/1/1976
lp Deborah Grant; Marilyn Finlay; Wendy Wax;
Roland Curram; Ann Beach
EPISODE 3: DIVERSIONS 23/1/1976
lp Paul Stacey; Jeremy Stacey; Deborah Grant;
Roland Curram
EPISODE 4: FESTIVITIES 30/1/1976
lp Roland Curram; Deborah Grant; Eric Carte;
Marilyn Finlay; Carol Drinkwater
EPISODE 5: REPERCUSSIONS 6/2/1976
lp David Horovitch; Deborah Grant;
Zuleika Robson
EPISODE 7: LEAVE-TAKING 20/2/1976
lp Deborah Grant; Eric Carte; Roland Curram

BOURBON STREET BEAT
(US Warner Bros 1959–60)
Detective series.
The TASTE OF ASHES 5/10/1959
d Leslie H. Martinson; p Harry Tatelman;
sc Charles Hoffman, Al C. Ward;
auth Howard Browne
lp Richard Long; Andrew Duggan;
Arlene Howell; Van Williams; Joanna Moore;
Fredd Wayne

BOY DOMINIC (Yorkshire TV 1974)
Adventure series for children set in 1820.
Followed by the sequel DOMINIC (1976).
p Terence Williams
regulars Richard Todd; Hildegard Neil;
Murray Dale; Brian Blessed
LOST AT SEA 24/3/1974
d Gareth Davies; sc Keith Dewhurst
lp Mary Morris; Ivor Dean

BOY DOMINIC cont.

LODGINGS TO LET 31/3/1974
d John Davies; *sc* Nick McCarty
lp Dinah Glaskin; Ruth Kettlewell
The MAN WHO LOVED CHILDREN 7/4/1974
d John Davies; *sc* John Brason
lp Reginald Marsh; Nancie Jackson
CAPTAIN DARKNESS 14/4/1974
d Gareth Davies; *sc* Keith Dewhurst
lp Leslie Schofield; Jonathan Arundel
FAIR GAME 21/4/1974
d Gareth Davies; *sc* Penelope Lively
lp Peter Cellier; Jonathan Arundel
MEDICINE MAN 28/4/1974
d John Davies; *sc* Nick McCarty
lp Ruth Kettlewell; Basil Henson
The MAN WITH THE PAINTED FACE 5/5/1974
d John Davies; *sc* John Brason
lp Ruth Kettlewell; Gary Raymond
A FROG HE WOULD A WOOING GO 12/5/1974
d Jeremy Summers; *sc* Nick McCarty
lp Ruth Kettlewell; Ivor Dean; David Knight
SERMONS AND SNUFF 19/5/1974
d Jeremy Summers; *sc* Penelope Lively
lp Ruth Kettlewell; Brian Wilde
FRIENDS OF THE FAMILY 26/5/1974
d Terence Williams; *sc* Penelope Lively
lp Ruth Kettlewell; Maxine Audley;
Julian Glover
GHOST IN GREENWICH 2/6/1974
d Terence Williams; *sc* Nick McCarty
lp Ruth Kettlewell; Ivor Dean
LADY BULMAN REGRETS 9/6/1974
d John Davies; *sc* Denis Constanduros
lp Ruth Kettlewell; Mary Morris;
Julian Glover
CHARLES AND EMMA 16/6/1974
d John Davies; *sc* Denis Constanduros
lp Honora Burke; Gillian Bailey

The BOY FROM NAZARETH
(Tyne Tees 1976–77)
Six-part regional series for children in which
stories from The Bible are related by means of
drawings, magic and songs.
d James Goldby; *pres* Roy North
The SOWER 10/10/1976
lp Cindy Kent
The BOY FROM NAZARETH 28/11/1976
lp Cindy Kent
The GOOD SAMARITAN 16/1/1977
lp Cindy Kent; Richard Kayes

The BRADFORD GODFATHER
(Yorkshire TV 10/3/1976)
Documentary portrait of the head of the
Pakistani community in Bradford and his visit to
Pakistan.
d/p John Willis, Paul Dunstan;
sc Paul Dunstan

BRAIN AND BEHAVIOUR
(BBC 11/8–29/9/1964)
Series of eight programmes which examines the
link between the mind and the body.
p John Drummond
US AND THEM 11/8/1964
The difference between humans and animals
with regard to basic impulses.
The PHYSICAL FRAMEWORK 18/8/1964
The human brain as compared to an animal's.
INSTINCT AND REACTION 25/8/1964
The child in its earliest years and the part
heredity plays.
REASON OVER REFLEX 1/9/1964
Normality and abnormality in childhood.

BREAKING POINT (ATV 19/12/1978)
Police racism in Great Britain and the growing
militancy of all sections of the black community
in the face of police harassment.
d Menelik Shabazz; *p* Malcolm Feuerstein

The BRIAN CONNELL INTERVIEW
(Anglia 1971–80)
Interview series
LORD BLACKETT 4/10/1971
d Peter Joy
BERNARD LEVIN 1/8/1976
FIELD MARSHALL LORD CARVER 27/7/1977

BRIMSTONE AND TREACLE
(BBC 1976 *ntx*)
The devil, in the guise of a young man called
Martin, involves himself with the family of a girl
who is physically and mentally disabled after a
road accident. Martin rapes the girl which
miraculously restores her health. *tx* 25/8/1987.
d Barry Davis; *p* Kenith Trodd;
sc Dennis Potter
lp Denholm Elliott; Michael Kitchen;
Patricia Lawrence; Michelle Newell;
Paul Williamson

BRITISH ART AND ARTISTS (BBC 1957–58)
Documentary series. Followed by The ARTIST
SPEAKS (1958–60).
HENRY MOORE – A SCULPTOR'S LANDSCAPE
29/6/1958
An interpretation of the work of Henry Moore.
d/p/sc John Read; *nar* Ralph Richardson

BRITISH EMPIRE: ECHOES OF
BRITANNIA'S RULE
(BBC-Time Life 11/1–4/4/1972)
Thirteen-part documentary series on the British
Empire.
OH! THE JUBILEE! 11/1/1972
Queen Victoria's Diamond Jubilee of 1897 as a
celebration of the British Empire.
p Tom Haydon
REMEMBER CAWNPORE! 25/1/1972
The East India Company's control of India and
the Indian Mutiny of 1857.
p Michael Weigall
ALL FRONTIER AND NOTHING ELSE 1/2/1972
The colonisation of Canada by the British and its
defence against the expansionism of the USA.
p Dominic Flessati
IN DARKEST AFRICA 8/2/1972
The attitudes of Victorian Britain towards
Africa, the colonisation of Southern Africa, and
the war with the Zulus.
p Anthony Isaacs
SCRAMBLE FOR AFRICA 22/2/1972
Cecil Rhodes' plans for a Cape-to-Cairo railway,
and the conflict with the Boers leading to the
Boer War.
p Anthony Isaacs
NEW GODS FOR OLD 14/3/1972
The conflict in Africa between traditional values
and those of the British colonisers.
p Anthony Isaacs
The GIFT OF ENDLESS DREAMS 21/3/1972
The story of the British Empire in the Far East,
centred on Singapore, the significance of the fall
and surrender of Singapore to the Japanese.
p Tom Haydon
The SETTING OF THE SUN 4/4/1972
The post-war independence movements in
Britain's former African colonies and the
creation of The Commonwealth.
p Anthony Isaacs

The BRITISH ROCK AND POP AWARDS
1976 (ATV 27/1/1977)
Highlights from the award ceremony in
celebration of the 'Daily Mirror' Readers' 1976
pop awards. Includes: David Essex, The Bay
City Rollers, Paul McCartney, Wings, Eric
Faulkner, Real Thing, Status Quo, Noel
Edmonds, Kiki Dee, Elton John and John Miles.
p Hector Stewart; *pres* Maurice Kinn

The BRITISH SITUATION (Thames 1978 *ntx*)
Comedy written for the 1978 Edinburgh
Television Festival, in response to the Festival's
request for a paper on stereotyping on television.
d Marilyn Gaunt; *p* Andrew Brown;
sc Howard Schuman
lp Denis Lawson; Ian McDiarmid;
Eleanor Bron; Richard Beckinsale

BRITISH SOCIAL HISTORY (BBC 1969)
History series for schools.
The BIG CITIES 26/11/1969
p John Radcliffe; *pres* Robin Ray

BROAD ACRES (BBC 2/2/1965)
The pattern of life and work on the estate of
Castle Howard, Yorkshire, under its owner
George Howard.
p Don Haworth; *nar* David Mahlowe

BROKEN HILL – WALLED CITY
(Yorkshire TV 25/8/1970)
Alan Whicker visits the Australian mining town
of Broken Hill, and interviews Joe Keenan,
president of The Barrier Industrial Council.
d/p Michael Blakstad; *pres* Alan Whicker

BRONCO (US Warner Bros 1958–62)
Western series.
The INVADERS 23/1/1961
lp Ty Hardin; Gerald Mohr; Walter Sande;
Shirley Knight

The BRONTËS OF HAWORTH
(Yorkshire TV 30/9–21/10/1973)
Four-part drama series about the Brontë family.
REWARDING DESTINY 21/10/1973
d/p Marc Miller; *sc* Christopher Fry
lp Alfred Burke; Michael Kitchen;
Vickery Turner; Rosemary McHale;
Ann Penfold; Barbara Leigh-Hunt

The BROTHERS (BBC 1972–76)
Drama series about a family involved in the road
haulage industry and their firm Hammond
Transport.
CONFRONTATION 24/3/1972
d Philip Dudley; *p* Gerard Glaister;
sc N.J. Crisp
lp Jean Anderson; Glyn Owen; Jennifer Wilson;
Richard Easton; Robin Chadwick;
Hilary Tindall; Julia Goodman
MANOEUVRES 3/10/1976
d Timothy Combe; *p* Bill Sellars;
sc Brian Finch
lp Jean Anderson; Patrick O'Connell;
Kate O'Mara; Robin Chadwick; Terence Frisby;
Liza Goddard; Colin Baker

BRUCE FORSYTH AND THE
GENERATION GAME (BBC 1971–77)
Game show; hosted by Bruce Forsyth and
Anthea Redfern.
BRUCE FORSYTH AND THE GENERATION
GAME
30/11/1974
d Alan Boyd; *p* James Moir

The BRUCE FORSYTH SHOW
(ABC 27/8/1967)
Variety show.
p Keith Beckett; *sc* Sid Green, Dick Hills;
with Dudley Moore, Anita Harris

BRUTE FORCE AND FINESSE
(BBC 16/2/1965)
New methods of shaping materials including the
electron beam, the lost wax process and the
plasma torch.
p Max Morgan-Witts

The BUDGET 1956 (19/4/1956)
Budget reply: Shadow Chancellor, Harold
Wilson is interviewed by Robert McKenzie, Mr
Hodson, and Harold Wincott in response to
Macmillan's 1956 budget.

The BUDGET 1957 (10/4/1957)
Harold Wilson, Shadow Chancellor, answers
questions from Robert McKenzie in response to
the budget introduced the day before.

The BUDGET 1958 (16/4/1958)
Robert McKenzie interviews Harold Wilson
about the Conservative budget introduced the
day before.

The BUDGET 1959 (19/4/1959)
Kenneth Harris questions Harold Wilson about
the Conservative budget.

The BUDGET 1960 (8/4/1960)
Kenneth Harris interviews Harold Wilson in
response to the previous day's budget.

The BUDGET 1961 (18/4/1961)
Kenneth Harris interviews Harold Wilson in
response to the previous day's budget.

The BUDGET (ITN-Rediffusion 9/4/1962)
Analysis of the Chancellor's budget speech by
Brian Connell, Ian Trethowan, Andrew
Schonfield and George Ffitch.
d John Phillips; *p* David Hennessy

The BUDGET 1962 (10/4/1962)
Robin Day interviews James Callaghan in
response to Selwyn Lloyd's budget.

**The BUDGET 1963–JAMES CALLAGHAN
M.P. FOR THE OPPOSITION** (4/4/1963)
Callaghan for the opposition Labour Party
responds to the Conservative budget of the
previous day.

**The BUDGET – JAMES CALLAGHAN M.P.
FOR THE OPPOSITION** (15/4/1964)
Robin Day interviews James Callaghan about
the 1964 Conservative budget.

The BUDGET (MR CALLAGHAN 1965)
(6/4/1965)
Kenneth Harris interviews James Callaghan
about the measures in his 1965 budget.

The BUDGET 1967 (11/4/1967)
Robin Day interviews James Callaghan about his
1967 budget.

**The BUDGET: RT. HON. ROY JENKINS
REPLIES FOR THE OPPOSITION**
(22/3/1972)
Shadow Chancellor Roy Jenkins attacks the
measures taken in Mr Barber's 1972 budget.

BUDGET RESPONSE – DENIS HEALEY
(7/3/1973)
Shadow Chancellor Denis Healey responds to
the 1973 Conservative budget.

**The BUDGET: DENIS HEALEY – THREE
DAY WEEK – MINI BUDGET REPLY**
(18/12/1973)
Denis Healey replies to the mini budget
introduced by Anthony Barber.

**The BUDGET – CHANCELLOR OF THE
EXCHEQUER** (26/3/1974)
Denis Healey introduces a budget. He outlines
the economic situation and what needs to be
done.

The BUDGET – DENIS HEALEY
(12/11/1974)
Chancellor Healey makes a broadcast outlining
the measures he has taken in his 1974 budget.

**The BUDGET: THE RT. HON. DENIS
HEALEY, M.P. FROM NO. 11 DOWNING
STREET** (15/4/1975)
Denis Healey broadcasts on the evening of
presenting his 1975 budget.

**The BUDGET – CHANCELLOR OF THE
EXCHEQUER** (6/4/1976)
Denis Healey introduces the measures he has
taken in the 1976 budget.

BUDGIE (LWT 1971–72)
Light-hearted series about a London spiv;
featuring Adam Faith in the title role.
p Verity Lambert;
sc Willis Hall, Keith Waterhouse
A PAIR OF CHARLIES 4/6/1971
d Mike Newell; *auth* Jack Trevor Story
lp Iain Cuthbertson; Lynn Dalby;
George Innes; Reg Lye; Jack Shepherd
DREAMING OF THEE 21/4/1972
d Michael Lindsay-Hogg
lp Iain Cuthbertson; Jimmy Gardner;
James Bolam; Bill Dean; Georgina Hale
LOUIE THE RING IS DEAD AND BURIED
IN KENSAL GREEN CEMETERY 5/5/1972
d Michael Lindsay-Hogg
lp Lynn Dalby; Iain Cuthbertson;
June Lewis; Fraser Kerr; Roger Hume
The JUMP UP BOYS 12/5/1972
d Michael Lindsay-Hogg
lp Iain Cuthbertson; Lynn Dalby;
Derek Newark; Jack Shepherd; Peggy Aitchison

OUR STORY SO FAR 19/5/1972
d Mike Newell
lp Derek Newark; James Warrior; Rio Fanning
DO ME A FAVOUR 26/5/1972
d Moira Armstrong
lp Derek Jacobi; Roy Hanlon; Ken Wynne
GLORY OF FULHAM 2/6/1972
d Michael Lindsay-Hogg
lp Joe Zaranoff; Kevin Moran; Kathleen Heath
TWENTY FOUR THOUSAND BALL POINT PENS
9/6/1972
d Alan Gibson
lp Kenneth Cranham; Alfie Bass;
Christopher Benjamin
KING FOR A DAY 16/6/1972
d Moira Armstrong
lp John Rhys-Davies; David Bauer;
John J. Carney
The OUTSIDE MAN 23/6/1972
d Michael Lindsay-Hogg
lp George A. Cooper; Jack Shepherd;
James Grout
The MAN OUTSIDE 30/6/1972
d Michael Lindsay-Hogg
lp John Rhys-Davies; George A. Cooper
BRIEF ENCOUNTER 7/7/1972
d Michael Lindsay-Hogg
lp Margaret Nolan; George A. Cooper;
Iain Cuthbertson; Eamonn Boyce; Lynn Dalby
RUN RABBIT, RUN RABBIT, RUN, RUN, RUN
14/7/1972
d Mike Newell
lp Iain Cuthbertson; John Rhys-Davies;
Lynn Dalby; Margaret Nolan; Gretchen Franklin

The BUILDING OF THE BOMB
(BBC 2/3/1965)
Scientists involved in the race to produce the
first atomic bomb reflect on their experiences:
with J. Robert Oppenheimer, Werner von
Heisenberg, Otto Frisch, James Tuck and
Edward Teller.
p Robert Reid; *sc* Antony Jay;
interv Stephen Black; *nar* René Cutforth

A BUNCH OF FIVES (ATV 1977–78)
Drama series for children set in 'Oxford Lane
School', a comprehensive school.
The CRITIC 25/5/1977
d John Sichel; *p* Colin Rogers;
sc Paula Milne
lp Lesley Manville; Jamie Foreman;
Andrew Rinous; Richard Willis; Julia Carey

BUNNY (Thames 11/12/1972)
How a five-year old boy suffering from brain
damage has responded to a radical form of
therapy developed in the USA.
d Frank Cvitanovich; *p* Jeremy Isaacs;
nar Midge Mackenzie

BURKE'S LAW
(US Four Star-Barbety 1963–65)
Drama series featuring a millionaire police
captain and the assorted eccentrics he encounters
while solving murders.
WHO KILLED THE STRANGLER? 6/1/1965
d Sam C. Freedle; *p* Aaron Spelling;
sc Larry Gordon
lp Gene Barry; Regis Toomey; Leon Lontoc;
Frankie Avalon; Jeanne Crain;
Annette Funicello; Una Merkel;
Robert Middleton; Gary Conway

The BURNING FIERY FURNACE
(BBC 24/11/1968)
A parable for church performance by William
Plomer set to music by Benjamin Britten and
recorded in Orford Parish Church.
d/p Brian Large

BURNS (Border 24/1/1978)
John Cairney's one-man show telling the story of
Scotland's best-known native son and poet.
d/p Norman Fraser
lp John Cairney

BY ALAN BENNETT – SIX PLAYS
(LWT 2/12/1978–24/2/1979)
Series of six plays written by Alan Bennett.
The OLD CROWD 27/1/1979
d Lindsay Anderson; *p* Stephen Frears
lp Jill Bennett; Isabel Dean; Valentine Dyall;
Frank Grimes
AFTERNOON OFF 3/2/1979
d/p Stephen Frears
lp Peter Butterworth; Thora Hird; Anna Massey;
John Normington; Elizabeth Spriggs

BYGONES (Anglia 1969–81)
Documentary series.
WHERE ARE THE CLOWNS? 22/12/1977
Clowns at Gerry Cottle's circus and the annual
memorial service for Grimaldi.
WAGONS AND CARRIAGES 23/2/1978
Horse-drawn carriages in Bedfordshire and
Cambridgeshire.
IMPERIAL WAR MUSEUM 20/10/1978
TRADITIONAL ROPES AND A VICTORIAN
PHARMACY 2/3/1979

C

CAESAR AND CLEOPATRA
(Southern TV 4/1/1977)
Adaptation of the George Bernard Shaw play.
d James Cellan Jones;
p David Susskind, Duane Bogie;
sc Audrey Maas
lp Alec Guinness; Geneviève Bujold;
Margaret Courtenay; Jolyon Bates;
Noel Willman; David Steuart; Gareth Thomas;
Iain Cuthbertson; Michael Bryant; Clive Francis

The CAESARS (Granada 22/9–27/10/1968)
Series of six plays based on the lives of the
Emperors of Rome.
CLAUDIUS 27/10/1968
d Derek Bennett; *p/sc* Philip Mackie
lp Freddie Jones; Ralph Bates; John Paul;
Barbara Murray; Nicola Pagett;
John Normington; Mark Hawkins;
Roger Hammond; Ian Fleming;
Ronald Mee; Gerald Harper

CALENDAR (Yorkshire TV 1969–)
Local news programme. See also CALENDAR
PEOPLE, CALENDAR SPECIAL and GOOD
MORNING CALENDAR (1977).
The MUSIC MAKERS – LORD HAREWOOD
23/10/1978
First of two programmes about the launch of
English National Opera North.
pres Richard Whiteley
The MUSIC MAKERS – DAVID LLOYD JONES
30/10/1978
Second of two programmes about the launch of
English National Opera North.
pres Richard Whiteley
The GRUMBLEWEEDS – SHURA CHERKASSKY
29/6/1979

CALENDAR PEOPLE (Yorkshire TV)
Local news progamme.
HAROLD WILSON INTERVIEW 12/2/1976

CALENDAR SPECIAL (Yorkshire TV)
Series of one-off specials from the local news
programme, CALENDAR.
The BATTLE FOR HUMBERSIDE 8/5/1977
Council election campaigns in Hull and
Scunthorpe.
d Jim McCan; *pres* Guy Williams;
rep Edwina Taterley

CALL FOR ACTION (BBC 25/8–29/9/1960)
Six-part series on the work of emergency rescue
services.
RESCUE UNDERGROUND 15/9/1960
Dramatises an underground rescue operation in
a coal mine.
p Geoffrey Baines; *sc* Budge Cooper

CALL MY BLUFF (BBC 1965–1988)
Word game show hosted by Robert Robinson.
CALL MY BLUFF 25/11/1974
d Michael Goodwin; *with* Patrick Campbell,
Glenys Roberts, Paul Daneman, Frank Muir,
Hannah Gordon, Barry Norman

CALLAN (ABC/Thames 1967–73)
Drama series about an agent, inspired by the play A MAGNUM FOR SCHNEIDER shown in the ARMCHAIR THEATRE series (4/2/1967).
regular Edward Woodward
The GOOD ONES ARE ALL DEAD 8/7/1967
d Toby Robertson; *exec.p* Lloyd Shirley;
sc James Mitchell
lp Ronald Radd; Anthony Valentine;
Powys Thomas; Linda Marlowe;
Tom Kempinski; David Lander;
Russell Hunter; Lisa Langdon
YOU SHOULD HAVE GOT HERE SOONER 12/8/1967
d Piers Haggard; *exec.p* Lloyd Shirley;
sc James Mitchell
lp Ronald Radd; Derek Newark;
Russell Hunter; Anthony Valentine;
Jon Laurimore; Bernard Stone; Lisa Langdon;
Pinkie Johnstone; Anne Blake; Philip Ryan;
Stanley Stewart
The MOST PROMISING GIRL OF HER YEAR 15/1/1969
d Peter Duguid; *p* Reginald Collin;
sc James Mitchell
lp Michael Goodliffe; Raymond Young;
Anthony Valentine; Clifford Rose;
Russell Hunter; Joan Crane; Peter Blythe;
David Hargreaves

CALLAS SINGS TOSCA (ATV 1964)
Maria Callas singing Act II of Franco Zeffirelli's production of 'Tosca', with Renato Cioni, Tito Gobbi, Dennis Wicks, Robert Bowman and the Orchestra and Chorus of the Royal Opera House, Covent Garden.
p Bill Ward; *pres* David Webster

CAMERA IN ACTION
(Granada 10/8–31/8/1965)
Four-part series about photography as a documentary record.
A PROSPECT OF WHITBY 17/8/1965
Photographic study of Whitby seen through the work of Frank Meadow Sutcliffe.
d Peter Jones; *p* Mike Wooller;
nar Derek Granger

CAMPAIGN REPORT (BBC 1979)
Coverage of the 1979 General Election.
CAMPAIGN REPORT 19/4/1979
Election news programme, includes James Callaghan, David Steel, Michael Heseltine on housing, Sir Robert Mark and Margaret Thatcher.

The CANADIANS (Scottish TV 1/1/1966)
Documentary about life in Canada including footage of Canadian football, ice hockey, icebergs, Winnipeg, Toronto, and Scottish immigrants.
d Don Cummings

The CANAL CHILDREN
(BBC 10/11–15/12/1976)
Drama series for children.
d John Prowse; *exec.p* Anna Home;
sc Brian Wright
regulars Andrew O'Connor; Maxime Gordon;
Gwen Cherrell; Eric Porter; Barbara Hickmott;
William Wilde
A GONGOOZLER 10/11/1976
lp Peter Berry; Don McKillop
BUGGETS AND TONNAGE 17/11/1976
lp Peter Berry; Don McKillop; Brian Wright
POOR MAN'S MORRIS 24/11/1976
GUNPOWDER 1/12/1976
lp Peter Berry
The SECRET AGENT 8/12/1976
lp Peter Berry

CANDIDA (BBC 29/12/1961)
p Naomi Capon; *auth* George Bernard Shaw
lp Wendy Craig; Patrick Allen;
Peter McEnery; Peter Sallis;
Rosamund Greenwood; Michael Brennan

CANNON (US QM Productions 1971–76)
Detective series.
regular William Conrad
ARENA OF FEAR 19/12/1973
lp John Marley; Pat Renella;
Nick Nolte; James McCallion; Jess Walton;
John Ward; Alan Dexter; Reta Shaw
The STALKER 20/3/1974
The ICEMAN 1/10/1975
lp Robert Foxworth; Andrew Parks;
John Milford; Dennis Patrick; Margaret Impert
Paul Lambert
The MAN WHO DIED TWICE 15/10/1975
lp Leslie Nielsen; Leslie Charleson;
James Gregory; Michael Baseleon

CANNONBALL (US Normandie Productions 1958)
Syndicated adventure/drama series concerning two truck drivers.
MARK TIME 1958
p Ruby Abel; *sc* Ed Adamson
lp Paul Birch; William Campbell

CAPTAIN PUGWASH (BBC 1957–65)
Animation. The adventures of the pirate Captain Pugwash and his crew.
anim Oliver Postgate
CAPTAIN PUGWASH 15/4/1959
CAPTAIN PUGWASH 27/5/1959
CAPTAIN PUGWASH 1/7/1959
SURPRISE ATTACK 18/11/1959
The POWDER MAGAZINE 3/1/1960
The CAPTAIN'S DREAM 19/1/1960
ABANDON SHIP 6/4/1960
A NEW SHIP 22/6/1960
ON TRIAL 15/3/1961
The TEST 4/8/1961
CROWN JEWELS 25/10/1961
The DOCTOR 26/11/1961
MAN OVERBOARD 8/3/1962
TUG O'WAR 24/7/1962
PLEASURE CRUISE 26/2/1963
The TWINS 21/6/1963
The WRECKERS 25/7/1963

CAPTAIN R.N. (Yorkshire TV 5/8/1969)
A portrait of a serving officer in the Royal Navy.
d Michael Tuchner; *p* Michael Deakin;
intro Jonathan Aitken

CAR 54, WHERE ARE YOU?
(US NBC 1961–63)
Comedy series set in a police precinct in the Bronx.
SOMETHING NICE FOR SOL 24/9/1961
d/p Nat Hiken
lp Joe E. Ross; Fred Gwynne;
Gerald Hiken

The CARETAKER (Rediffusion 25/10/1966)
Performance of Pinter's play.
d Marc Miller; *exec.p* Peter Willes;
sc Harold Pinter
lp Roy Dotrice; Ian McShane; John Rees

CASABLANCA (US Warner Bros 1955–56)
Series based on the classic 1942 film of the same name. One of several rotating series shown under the title WARNER BROTHERS PRESENTS.
regulars Charles McGraw; Marcel Dalio
HAND OF FATE 29/11/1955
d John Peyser; *p* Jerome Robinson;
sc Nelson Gidding
lp Ludwig Stossel; Dan Seymour;
Kurt Katch
FATEFUL NIGHT 10/1/1956
d John Peyser; *p* Jerome Robinson
sc Nelson Gidding; *auth* Robert Libott
lp Lisa Daniels; Lester Matthews;
Karin Booth; Dan Seymour
SATAN'S VEIL 31/1/1956
d Alvin Ganzer; *p* Jerome Robinson;
sc Norman Lessing, Nelson Gidding
auth Eric Ambler
lp Rossana Rory; Dan Seymour; Clarence Muse
KILLER AT LARGE 28/2/1956
d Don Weis; *p* Jerome Robinson;
sc Seeleg Lester
lp Eduard Franz; Corey Allen;
Fred Villani

DEADLOCK 24/4/1956
d Don Weis; *p* Jerome Robinson;
sc Nelson Gidding
lp Olive Sturgess; Peter Van Eyck;
Clarence Muse

CASANOVA (BBC 1971)
Series based on the life of the eighteenth-century lover.
p Mark Shivas; *sc* Dennis Potter
regulars Frank Finlay; Norman Rossington
STEED IN THE STABLE 16/11/1971
d John Glenister
lp George Benson; Zienia Merton;
Christine Noonan; Victor Baring;
Geoffrey Wincott
ONE AT A TIME 23/11/1971
d John Glenister
lp Patrick Newell; David Swift;
Elaine Donnelly; Julia Cornelius;
Brigid Erin Bates
MAGIC MOMENTS 30/11/1971
d Mark Cullingham
lp Patrick Newell; Frederick Peisley;
Lyn Yeldham; Rowan Wylie; Tim Thomas
WINDOW, WINDOW 7/12/1971
d John Glenister
lp David Swift; Ania Marson;
Jean Holness; Norman Tyrrell; Simon Barclay
FEVERS OF LOVE 14/12/1971
d Mark Cullingham
lp Patrick Newell; Valerie Gearon;
Basil Clarke; Gillian Brown
GOLDEN APPLES 21/12/1971
d Mark Cullingham
lp Graham Crowden; Gillian Hills;
John Ringham; Roger Hammond;
Patrick Newell

A CASE FOR EXPANSION
(BBC 26/3–16/4/1968)
Four-part documentary series on different aspects of town expansion.
GROWTH 2/4/1968
Considers the problems involved in attracting industry to towns.
p Michael Bunce; *intro* Wyndham Thomas

The CASE OF YOLANDE McSHANE
(Yorkshire TV 24/8/1977)
Di Burgess reports on the case of Yolande McShane who was found guilty of attempting to assist the suicide of her mother.
d John Willis;
exec.p Michael Deakin, John Fairley

The CASES OF EDDIE DRAKE
(US I.M.P.R.O. 1949)
Private eye series set in New York. Originally transmitted on CBS, dropped after nine episodes and then syndicated on American television 1951–52.
DROP DEAD! 1951
d Paul Garrison;
p Harlan Thompson, Herbert L. Strock;
sc Jason James
lp Don Haggerty; Lynne Roberts;
Theodore Von Eltz; Lowell Gilmore;
Frank Gerstle; Jean Dean

The CATHODE COLOURS THEM HUMAN
(CA CBC; GB *tx* 27/4/1965)
The influence of television on the public's political views, and the extent to which politicians depend on their television image.
d Cicely Burwash; *p* Patrick Watson;
nar John Drainie

CATHOLICS (HTV 14/4/1974)
Adapted by Brian Moore from his novel, concerning the plight of a divided man, an abbot who finds himself in conflict with both the Vatican and his inner convictions.
d Jack Gold; *p* Barry Levinson;
sc Brian Moore
lp Trevor Howard; Cyril Cusack;
Martin Sheen; Andrew Keir; Michael Gambon;
Raf Vallone

CBI CONFERENCE (BBC 5/11/1979)
Coverage of the 1979 Confederation of British Industry (CBI) Conference.

CBS EVENING NEWS WITH WALTER CRONKITE (US CBS 22/10/1966)
News items include: Viet Cong terrorism – bombing of railway; item on the conspiracy theory in relation to John F. Kennedy's assassination.
d Fred Stollmack;
p Sanford Socolow, Russ Bensley;
pres Walter Cronkite;
rep Dan Rather, Morley Safer

CBS NEWS SPECIAL (US CBS)
Series of documentaries investigating topical issues.
The SUMMIT – A REPORT ON GENEVA 17/7/1955
Roundup of events and opinion relating to the Big Four (France, Great Britain, USA, and USSR) summit in Geneva on 18th July 1955.
d Vern Diamond; *p* Ernest Leiser;
pres Howard K. Smith;
rep Eric Sevareid, Robert Pierpoint, Richard C. Hottelet; *with* Edward Crankshaw
The PENTAGON PAPERS: A CONVERSATION WITH DANIEL ELLSBERG 23/6/1971
Interview with former Pentagon Aide, Daniel Ellsberg, about 'The Pentagon Papers' which discussed American involvement in Vietnam and eventually led to the withdrawal of the USA from the conflict.

CBS REPORTS (US CBS 1959–)
Investigative documentary series, derived from the SEE IT NOW series (1951–58). Transmitted 1959–60 irregularly as series of specials. First transmitted regularly as CBS REPORTS in 1961.
INFLUENTIAL AMERICANS 30/11/1960
Modern teaching methods.
p Fred W. Friendly
The BUSINESS OF HEALTH: MEDICINE, MONEY AND POLITICS 2/2/1961
Existing health insurance plans and controversial proposals to increase coverage through federal legislation and national health and welfare programmes.
d Robert Downey; *p* Stephen Fleischman;
rep Howard K. Smith
CROSSROADS AFRICA: PILOT FOR A PEACE CORPS 16/3/1961
The work of 14 college students in the Republic of Guinea under the auspices of Operation Crossroads Africa Inc., a project similar to John F. Kennedy's Peace Corps programmes. [This report marked Edward R. Murrow's last assignment for CBS News].
p Edward Magruder Jones;
pres Edward R. Murrow;
rep Howard K. Smith
HARVEST OF SHAME 21/3/1961
Migrant farm workers in the United States.
d David Lowe
BRITAIN: BLOOD, SWEAT AND TEARS PLUS 20 30/3/1961
Looks at Britain as an industrial power with a growing middle class, also its role in NATO and as a member of the British Commonwealth. Prime Minister Harold Macmillan, and the Labour Party leader Hugh Gaitskell, explain their positions on nuclear arms. With Alan Sillitoe, Shelagh Delany, Arnold Wesker, Bertrand Russell and Robert Boothby.
p William K. McClure; *pres* Eric Sevareid
The TRIALS OF CHARLES DE GAULLE 30/5/1961
Algeria since 1945.
d George A. Vicas
WHO SPEAKS FOR BIRMINGHAM? 28/6/1961
Race relations in Birmingham, Alabama following the mob violence surrounding the 'freedom riders'.
d Fred W. Friendly
UFO: FRIEND, FOE OR FANTASY 10/5/1966
An investigation into the UFO mystery.
p William K. McClure, Joseph Wershba, Jack Beck; *rep* Walter Cronkite, Bill Stout, Frank Kearns

CBS SPECIAL REPORTS (US CBS 1959–60)
Investigative documentary series. Shown on CBS on an irregular basis.
BRITAIN GOES TO THE POLLS 4/10/1959
Report on British national elections.
pres Robert Trout; *rep* Eric Sevareid, David Schoenbrun, Alexander Kendrick
BIOGRAPHY OF A MISSILE 27/10/1959
Filmed diary of the life story of a Juno II intermediate range ballistic missile. Featured are explanations and interviews with missile scientists, Wernher von Braun, Kurt Debus, Fritz Mueller, Otto Hoberg, James Van Allen, and William Pickering.
p Edward R. Murrow, Fred W. Friendly;
rep Jack Beck
The YEAR OF THE POLARIS 11/10/1960
A special report on the Polaris intermediate range nuclear missile and the Fleet ballistic missile submarine from which the Polaris can be launched.
p Fred W. Friendly, Jack Beck;
rep Edward R. Murrow

The CEDAR TREE (ATV 1976–79)
Drama series/soap opera dealing with the domestic incidents in a large country house during the 1930s.
p Ian Fordyce
regulars Philip Latham; Susan Engel; Jennifer Lonsdale; Sally Osborn; Susan Skipper; Joyce Carey; Cyril Luckham
ANNE: PART 1 27/9/1976
d Dorothy Denham; *sc* Alfred Shaughnessy
lp Jean Taylor Smith; Peter Copley
ANNE: PART 2 28/9/1976
d Dorothy Denham; *sc* Alfred Shaughnessy
lp Jean Taylor Smith; Peter Copley
FETE ACCOMPLI: PART 1 29/11/1976
d John Scholz-Conway; *sc* T.E.B. Clarke
lp Kate Coleridge; Ed Bishop
FETE ACCOMPLI: PART 2 30/11/1976
d John Scholz-Conway; *sc* T.E.B. Clarke
lp Kate Coleridge; Ed Bishop

CELEBRATION (Granada 1979–)
Granada series initially acting as a showcase for local entertainment from the North West, later as a general arts programme.
CELEBRATION 15/11/1979
CELEBRATION 22/11/1979
CELEBRATION 6/12/1979
CELEBRATION 13/12/1979
CELEBRATION 20/12/1979

CELEBRATION OF STEAM (Tyne Tees 1/1/1976)
The celebration that took place to commemorate the 150th anniversary of the Stockton to Darlington railway.

CELEBRITY (Rediffusion 1959)
Interview series.
LORD BRABAZON OF TARA 19/8/1959
Lord Brabazon of Tara, pioneer aviator, motorist and politician, talks to Kenneth Harris about his background, his interest in cars, his political career, and attitude to death.
d Sheila Gregg
CLIFF RICHARD 30/9/1959
Cliff Richard talks to Daniel Farson about his views on the older generation, his fans and how he became a singing star.
d Geoffrey Hughes
HENRY FONDA 7/10/1959
Michael Ingrams interviews Henry Fonda, who talks about his life and career, politics, his daughter Jane, and his future plans.
d Michael Ingrams

CELEBRITY SQUARES (ATV 1975–79)
Quiz series hosted by Bob Monkhouse.
CELEBRITY SQUARES 28/3/1976
d Paul Stewart Laing;
with Arthur Mullard, William Rushton, Charlie Drake, Sara Leighton, Pat Coombs, Diana Dors, Pete Murray, Magnus Pyke, Dickie Davies.

CENSORED SCENES FROM KING KONG (BBC 1974 *ntx*)
d Brian Farnham; *p* Mark Shivas;
sc Howard Schuman

CENTRE PLAY (BBC 1973–77)
Anthology drama series.
ARTICLE 5 1975 *ntx*
d John Bruce; *p* Anne Head; *auth* Brian Phelan

CHALK AND CHEESE (Thames 2/4–14/5/1979)
Sitcom about quarrelling neighbours.
FRIENDS AND NEIGHBOURS 9/4/1979
lp Michael Crawford; Robin Hawdon; Julia Goodman

CHALLENGE OF THE SEXES (Southern TV 26/2–19/3/1976)
Top sportsmen and women challenge each other at various sports.
SNOOKER, ATHLETICS, RODEO, WATER SKIING 19/3/1977
Snooker, Fred Davis v. Vera Selby; athletics, Glen Cohen v. women's relay team; rodeo, Sheila Bussey v. Larry Mahan; and water skiing, John Arthur v. Kathy Hume.
d Anthony Howard; *pres* Brough Scott;
comm Rachel Heyhoe-Flint, David Bobin, Suzy Chaffee, Vin Scully

The CHAMPIONS (ITC 1969–71)
Fantasy-adventure series about three 'superhuman' special agents. [Series was first shown in some ITV regions in 1968.]
p Monty Berman
regulars Stuart Damon; Alexandra Bastedo; William Gaunt; Anthony Nicholls
The BEGINNING 26/11/1969
d Cyril Frankel; *sc* Dennis Spooner
lp Felix Aylmer; Kenneth J. Warren; Joseph Furst; Eric Young; Burt Kwouk
The INVISIBLE MAN 3/12/1969
d Cyril Frankel; *sc* Donald James
lp Peter Wyngarde; James Culliford; Basil Dignam; Aubrey Morris; Steve Plytas
The EXPERIMENT 17/12/1969
d Cyril Frankel; *sc* Tony Williamson
lp David Bauer; Allan Cuthbertson; Caroline Blakiston; Philip Bond; Nicholas Courtney
TO TRAP A RAT 14/1/1970
d Sam Wanamaker; *sc* Ralph Smart
lp Guy Rolfe; Edina Ronay; Michael Standing; Toke Townley; Kate O'Mara; John Lee
The IRON MAN 21/1/1970
d John Llewellyn Moxey; *sc* Philip Broadley
lp George Murcell; Patrick Magee; Robert Crewdson; Michael Mellinger; Steven Berkoff
The GHOST PLANE 28/1/1970
d John Gilling; *sc* Donald James
lp Andrew Keir; Hilary Tindall; Michael Wynne; Dennis Chinnery; Tony Steedman
The SEARCH 25/2/1970
d Leslie Norman; *sc* Dennis Spooner
lp John Woodvine; Reginald Marsh; Joseph Furst; Patricia English; Ernst Walder
The SURVIVORS 18/3/1970
d Cyril Frankel; *sc* Donald James
lp Clifford Evans; Donald Houston; John Tate; Bernard Kay; Frederick Schiller
The FANATICS 16/9/1970
d John Gilling; *sc* Terry Nation
lp Gerald Harper; Donald Pickering; Julian Glover; David Burke; David Morrell
GET ME OUT OF HERE 7/10/1970
d Cyril Frankel; *sc* Ralph Smart
lp Frances Cuka; Ronald Radd; Philip Madoc; Eric Pohlmann
OPERATION DEEP-FREEZE 15/10/1970
d Paul Dickson; *sc* Gerald Kelsey
lp Patrick Wymark; Robert Urquhart; Walter Gotell; Peter Arne; Dallas Cavell
The NIGHT PEOPLE 21/10/1970
d Robert Asher; *sc* Donald James
lp Terence Alexander; Adrienne Corri; David Lodge; Anne Sharp; Michael Bilton

The INTERROGATION 4/11/1970
d Cyril Frankel; *sc* Dennis Spooner
lp Colin Blakely
NUTCRACKER 16/12/1970
d Roy Ward Baker; *sc* Philip Broadley
lp William Squire; David Langton;
Michael Barrington; John Franklyn-Robbins;
John Bown
A CASE OF LEMMINGS 6/1/1971
d Paul Dickson; *sc* Philip Broadley
lp Edward Brayshaw; John Bailey;
Jeanne Roland; Michael Graham;
Olive McFarland
PROJECT ZERO 13/1/1971
d Don Sharp; *sc* Tony Williamson
lp Rupert Davies; Peter Copley;
Geoffrey Chater; Reginald Jessup; Jan Holden
FULL CIRCLE 17/2/1971
d John Gilling; *sc* Donald James
lp Patrick Allen; Martin Benson;
John Nettleton; Gabrielle Drake; Jack Gwillim

A CHANGE IN MIND
(Yorkshire TV 21/2–7/3/1978)
Three-part documentary series on psycho-
medical problems.
WHAT MAKES YOU TIC? 21/2/1978
Record of an American sufferer from the rare
disease Tourette's Syndrome.
d David Green; *exec.p* Duncan Dallas

CHARLES ENDELL ESQUIRE (Scottish TV
1979–80)
Series featuring the underworld character who
first appeared in LWT's BUDGIE series in 1971.
GLASGOW BELONGS TO ME 28/7/1979
d Gerry Mill; *p* Rex Firkin;
sc Robert Banks Stewart
lp Iain Cuthbertson; Annie Ross;
Tony Osoba; Bernard Archard; Rikki Fulton

CHARLEY'S AUNT (Yorkshire TV 29/12/1977)
Eric Sykes' adaptation of the comedy of
Brandon Thomas.
d/p Graeme Muir; *sc* Eric Sykes;
auth Brandon Thomas
lp Eric Sykes; Jimmy Edwards; Barbara Murray;
Gerald Flood; Alun Lewis; Osmund Bullock

CHARLIE MUFFIN (Euston Films 11/12/1979)
Spy thriller featuring a down-at-heel agent who
is odd man out in his department of British
Intelligence.
d Jack Gold;
p Ted Childs, Norton Knatchbull;
sc Keith Waterhouse; *auth* Brian Freemantle
lp David Hemmings; Sam Wanamaker;
Jennie Linden; Pinkas Braun; Ian Richardson;
Ralph Richardson

The CHARLTON BOYS
(Thames 2/11/1968)
A profile of footballers Bobby and Jack
Charlton.
d Frank Cvitanovich

CHARLTON'S CHAMPIONS
(Tyne Tees 24/4–15/5/1974)
Four-part series about Middlesbrough football
club.
MIDDLESBROUGH FC 24/4/1974
d Tony Kysh, Andrea Wonfor, Jeremy Lack;
exec.p Leslie Barrett

The CHEATERS (Danzigers 1962–63)
Drama series featuring the cases of an insurance
company investigator. [Series was first shown in
some ITV regions in 1960.]
p Edward J. Danziger, Harry Lee Danziger
regulars John Ireland; Robert Ayres
FIRE! 14/4/1962
d Frank Marshall
lp Basil Dignam; Peter Elliot;
Carl Duering; Reginald Marsh
KNIGHT OF THE ROAD 2/5/1962
d Max Varnel
lp Richard Vernon; Raymond Rollett;
John McLaren; Robert Webber
A HOOD FROM CANADA 26/5/1962
d Max Varnel
lp Marion Mathie; Glyn Houston;
Rowland Bartrop; Colin Tapley

The HANDS OF ADRIAN 9/6/1962
d Frank Marshall
lp Delphi Lawrence; Robert Rietty;
Ian Fleming; Ann Hanslip; Jack MacNaughton
FOR THE PRICE OF TWO 24/6/1962
d Godfrey Grayson
lp Rosemary Dorken; Reginald Marsh;
Totti Truman Taylor; Bettina Milne
LEGS 50,000 EACH 1/7/1962
d Max Varnel
lp Jackie Lane; Glen Mason;
Robert Dorning; Judy Carne; John Witty
The MAN WHO WOULDN'T BE PAID
8/7/1962
d Godfrey Grayson
lp Ian Fleming; George Merritt;
Wendy Williams; Roy Purcell
CARNIVAL CASE 15/7/1962
d Frank Marshall
lp Paul Eddington; John Gabriel; Ann Lynn;
Michael Peake; Arnold Bell
A TALE OF TWO SHIPS 5/8/1962
d Max Varnel
lp Francis De Wolfe; Sandor Eles;
John Bennett; Sally Smith; Bruce Beeby
The CASE OF GEORGE PETERSON 12/8/1962
lp Kevin Stoney; Robert Dorning;
Ann Hanslip; Anton Rodgers
MIGHTY WARRIOR 19/8/1962
d Godfrey Grayson
lp Ballard Berkeley; Gaylord Cavallaro;
John Scott; Reginald Marsh
The DASHING MAJOR 26/8/1962
d Frank Marshall
lp Ralph Truman; Joan Newell;
Willoughby Goddard; Howard Lang; Brian Peck
FLASH IN THE SKY 2/9/1962
d Frank Marshall
lp William Fox; Hy Hazell;
Humphrey Lestocq; Steve Plytas; Mary Kenton
QUESTION OF MURDER 9/9/1962
d Godfrey Grayson
lp Viola Keats; Richard Vernon; John Carson;
Jennifer Jayne; Patrick Holt
DIAMOND STUDDED MALARIA 6/1/1963
d Max Varnel
lp Bill Nagy; Glyn Houston;
Roddy McMillan; Lionel Ngakane
GREEN FOR DANGER 13/1/1963
d Max Varnel
lp Margaretta Scott; Steve Plytas; Hugh Cross;
Michael Balfour; Colin Tapley
KILLIAN'S CUT 27/1/1963
d Max Varnel
lp Valentine Dyall; Peter Howell; Ann Lynn;
Raymond Young; Larry Noble
The BITE 3/2/1963
d Frank Marshall
lp Jill Ireland; Susan Swinford;
David Courtnay; Gillian Vaughan
A CASE OF LARCENY 10/2/1963
d Max Varnel
lp Sean Kelly; John Bennett;
Sally Bazely; Susan Richards; Colin Tapley
The SAFE WAY 3/3/1963
d Frank Marshall
lp John Carson; Kenneth Edwards;
Robert Cawdron; Dorinda Stevens
TIME TO KILL 24/3/1963
d Frank Marshall
lp Peter Butterworth; Max Butterfield;
John Bennett; Tony Thawnton
SCHEMERS 31/3/1963
d Max Varnel
lp Margot Vanderburgh; Kitty Bluett;
Robert Raglan; Brian Cobby
SLOPE OF DEATH 7/4/1963
d Max Varnel
lp Peter Williams; Maurice Kaufmann;
Naomi Chance; June Cunningham
BACK OF BEYOND 14/4/1963
d Max Varnel
lp Joseph Tomelty; Harriett Johns;
Ballard Berkeley; Barbara Ferris
The ROCKER 21/4/1963
d Max Varnel
lp Oliver Johnson; Victor Platt;
Frederick Piper; Patricia English
The AFFAIRS OF THE HEART 5/5/1963
d Max Varnel
lp Bruce Beeby; Lisa Daniely; Jack May;
Geoffrey Denton

CHECK IT OUT (Tyne Tees 1979)
Regional teenage programme.
CHECK IT OUT 1/7/1979
Sex education for young people. Includes an
interview with singer Kate Bush.
d Gavin Taylor; *p* Andrea Wonfor
CHECK IT OUT 31/7/1979
The problem of teenage drinking.
d Gavin Taylor; *p* Andrea Wonfor

CHECKMATE (US JaMco Productions
1960–62)
Crime drama series revolving around a trio of
criminologists working as Checkmate Inc.
VOYAGE INTO FEAR 6/5/1961
d Jules Bricken; *p* Dick Berg;
sc Edmund Morris, Harold Clements
lp Anthony George; Doug McClure;
Sebastian Cabot; Joan Fontaine; Scott Brady;
Robert Webber

CHEERIO LOU (BBC 13/3/1961)
An East End family receives notice that their
house is to be demolished.
p Don Taylor; *sc* Leonard Webb
lp Margery Withers; Daniel Moynihan;
Brian Wright; Frank Atkinson; Jayne Muir;
Carl Bernard; Rita Webb

CHELSEA FLOWER SHOW
(Rediffusion 28/5/1964)
Celia Irving talks to growers about their
preparations for the Chelsea Flower Show.
d Jim Pople

CHEYENNE (US Warner Bros 1955–63)
Western series.
regular Clint Walker
JULESBURG 20/9/1955
d Richard L. Bare; *p* Harve Foster;
sc Charles Lang
lp L.Q. Jones; Ray Teal; Adelle August;
Edwin Rand; Tom Monroe
BORDER SHOWDOWN 22/11/1955
d Richard L. Bare;
p Harve Foster, Arthur W. Silver;
sc Clark E. Reynolds, Dean Reisner
lp L.Q. Jones; Myron Healey;
Richard Reeves; Adele Mara; Lisa Montell
The OUTLANDER 13/12/1955
d Richard L. Bare; *p* Roy Huggins;
sc R. Wright Campbell; *auth* Douglas Heyes
lp Onslow Stevens; Doris Dowling;
Leo Gordon; Jack Pepper
The TRAVELLERS 3/1/1956
d Richard L. Bare; *p* Roy Huggins;
sc Kenneth Higgins;
auth Walter Doniger, S. Lewis Meltzer
lp James Gleason; Diane Brewster;
Morris Ankrum; Robert Armstrong;
Joseph Breen
RENDEZVOUS AT RED ROCK 21/2/1956
d Richard L. Bare; *p* Roy Huggins;
sc D.D. Beauchamp
lp Gerald Mohr; Douglas Fowley;
Steve Darrell; Joel Ashley; Gregg Barton
ONE WAY TICKET 19/2/1962
d Otto Lang; *p* Burt Dunne;
sc Robert Hamner
lp Phil Carey

CHICAGO: PORTRAIT OF A CITY
(BBC 21/2/1961)
Documentary reflecting an Englishman's first
impression of Chicago and all its moods by day
and by night. [Banned in the USA for 6 years.]
d/p Denis Mitchell; *comm* Studs Terkel

A CHILD OF THE SIXTIES (LWT 27/12/1969)
Gyles Brandreth, president of the Oxford
Union, looks back over the last decade with
Lady Longford, Fred W. Friendly, Iain
MacLeod, and Michael Foot.
d Peter Morley

The CHILD WANTS A HOME
(Anglia 13/4–18/5/1978)
Six-part documentary series on the rewards and
demands of adoption.

DECIDING 13/4/1978
Carole Mowlam and Phillip Whitehead introduce a programme about deciding to adopt; with Mary James, Mike Turner and Bob and Shirley Lines.
d Francis Fuchs; *p* John Lloyd Fraser
FOSTERING 11/5/1978
Views on fostering expressed by parents and children, and a discussion between Christine Reeves, Director of the National Foster Care Association, and Raissa Page of the National Children's Bureau.
d Francis Fuchs

CHILDHOOD (Granada 21/4–26/5/1974)
Series of six plays showing the world as children see it.
THERE IS A HAPPY LAND 5/5/1974
d Barry Davis; *p* James Brabazon;
sc Keith Waterhouse
lp Paul Woodhead; Bryan Pringle;
Susan Braddock; David Stevens; Pat Wallis

CHILDREN AND MATHEMATICS
(BBC 2–23/10/1966)
Four educational programmes aimed at parents and teachers.
WE STILL NEED ARITHMETIC 2/10/1966
p Edward Goldwyn; *pres* Jim Boucher

CHILDREN GROWING UP
(BBC 15/10–12/11/1970)
Documentary series on the development of children. See also CHILDREN GROWING UP – FIVE PLUS (1972).
MAKING SENSE 22/10/1970
How a child sees and makes sense of the world.
p Eurfron Gwynne Jones

CHILDREN GROWING UP – FIVE PLUS
(BBC 10/4–8/5/1972)
Documentary series on the development of children. Continuing from the series CHILDREN GROWING UP (1970).
HOME AND AWAY 10/4/1972
The attitudes of children to starting school.
p Eurfron Gwynne Jones

CHILDREN OF ABERFAN (ATV 17/1/1978)
Documentary observing the effect of the 1966 Aberfan disaster on the families who survived it.
d/p/sc Peter Denton; *nar* Michael Aspel

CHILDREN OF ESKDALE (Yorkshire TV 3/4/1973)
The life of a farmer and his family on a small farm in Eskdale, Yorkshire.
d/p Barry Cockcroft

CHILDREN OF REVOLUTION
(Intertel-Rediffusion 21/7/1965)
The lives of young people in Czechoslovakia.
d Randal Beattie; *exec.p* David Windlesham;
sc/nar Robert Kee

The CHILDREN OF THE NEW FOREST
(BBC 1977)
Five-part serial based on the book by Captain Marryat.
d John Frankau; *p* Barry Letts;
sc William Pointer
regulars John Carson; Donald Sumpter;
Graham Seed; Richard Gibson;
Arthur Campbell; Edwina Ashton;
Timandra Alwyn
PART 1 13/11/1977
lp Philip Bond; Kendrick Owen; Jeremy Clyde;
Andrew Lodge; Guy Slater; Caroline Blakiston
PART 2 20/11/1977
lp Philip Bond; Kendrick Owen;
Robert Keegan; Jack May; Raymond Platt;
Andrew McCulloch
PART 3 27/11/1977
lp Philip Bond; Kendrick Owen;
Robert Keegan; Raymond Platt;
Leonard Gregory; Rebecca Croft
PART 4 4/12/1977
lp Philip Bond; Robert Keegan;
Raymond Platt; Leonard Gregory;
Rebecca Croft; Jack May

PART 5 11/12/1977
lp Robert Keegan; Rebecca Croft; Jack May;
Brigid Erin Bates; Christopher Guinee

A CHILD'S PLACE (BBC 1979)
A series about children's rights, made for the International Year of the Child.
p Suzanne Davies
KIDS AT SCHOOL 4/6/1979
KIDS IN CARE 5/6/1979
KIDS AT HOME 6/6/1979
KIDS AND PLAY SPACE 7/6/1979
KIDS AND THE WELFARE STATE 8/6/1979

CHINA NOW (ITC 1964)
Three-part documentary series looking at China.
p Francis Megahy
The NEW MOOD 17/2/1964
Felix Greene describes his impressions of the new mood in China since his visit three years earlier.
The COMMUNE 24/2/1964
Felix Greene describes the changes in the social and economic lives of peasants in China.
INDUSTRY AND LEADERSHIP 2/3/1964
Felix Greene reports on industry in China, and interviews Chou En-Lai.

The CHRISTIANS (Granada 2/8–25/10/1977)
Thirteen-part documentary history of Christianity.
A PECULIAR PEOPLE 2/8/1977
d Carlos Pasini; *p* Mike Murphy;
nar Bamber Gascoigne

CHRISTIANS AT WAR – TWO FAMILIES IN BELFAST (BBC 12/8/1970)
A comparison between the way of life and outlook of two families, one Protestant, the other Catholic, living in Belfast.
d Ivor Dunkerton, Storry Walton;
rep Jim Douglas Henry, Harold Williamson

CHRONICLE (BBC 1966–)
Series on archaeology and history.
The TREASURE OF PRIAM 3/12/1966
The story of Heinrich Schliemann, the first man to excavate the site of the ancient city of Troy.
d Julia Cave; *p* Paul Johnstone;
nar Magnus Magnusson
ABU SIMBEL (Sveriges Radio 5/8/1967)
The removal to higher ground of the Abu Simbel temples, threatened with inundation after the construction of the Aswan high dam. Shown under the title 'Shall the Waters Prevail?'.
The MAN WHO WAS GIVEN A GASWORKS 20/4/1968
A new museum in County Durham with a collection reflecting life in the North East: an interview with Frank Atkinson, Director of the Bowes Museum, Barnard Castle.
d Ray Sutcliffe; *p* Paul Johnstone
'THERE IS NO CONQUEROR...' THE STORY OF THE MOORS IN SPAIN 11/10/1969
The story of the Muslim civilisation in Andalusia.
p Ken Shepheard; *nar* Michael Adams
The CATACOMBS OF SAKKARA 11/4/1970
The story of the discovery by Professor Walter Emery of the catacombs of Isis in Egypt.
d Paul Jordan; *p* Paul Johnstone
CRACKING THE STONE AGE CODE 31/10/1970
Professor Alexander Thom, whose theories about 'sophisticated mathematicians and astronomers' of the Stone Age revolutionised the archaeological establishment.
d David Collison; *sc/nar* Magnus Magnusson
The LOST WORLD OF THE MAYA 6/10/1972
Dr Eric Thompson explores the Maya civilisation of Central America and examines the damage done by looters who remove relics from the jungle.
p David Collison; *sc/intro* Magnus Magnusson
LONGBOW 12/2/1973
Robert Hardy traces the story of the longbow, from its Stone Age origins to its use at the Battle of Crécy in 1346.
d Roy Davies; *exec.p* Paul Johnstone

SIR MORTIMER: DIGGING UP PEOPLE 26/3/1973
Archaeologist Sir Mortimer Wheeler, in the company of Magnus Magnusson, looks at the landmarks in the earlier part of his career.
p David Collison
SIR MORTIMER: THE VICEROY SENT FOR ME 2/4/1973
Archaeologist Sir Mortimer Wheeler looks at the events of the latter half of his career.
p David Collison; *intro* Magnus Magnusson
The SCROLLS FROM THE SON OF A STAR 12/2/1976
The story of the search and discovery of historical documents dating from AD 70.
d/sc Irene Shubik; *nar* Magnus Magnusson
TOMB OF THE LOST KING 20/4/1979
The story of 40 years of detective work that finally led Professor Manolis Andronicos to the lost city of Aegae.
p/sc Roy Davies
SHIPWRECK 11/5/1979
The recovery of the Spanish Armada ship Trinidad Valencera which was grounded off the Donegal coast in 1588.
p Ray Sutcliffe; *nar* Andrew Faulds

CHURCHILL AND THE GENERALS
(BBC 23/9/1979)
Play which explores Churchill's relationships with his generals in World War II.
d Alan Gibson; *p* Alan Shallcross;
sc Ian Curteis
lp Timothy West; Ian Richardson;
Robert Dysart; Patrick Magee; Eric Porter;
Geoffrey Keen; Joseph Cotten

CHURCHILL FUNERAL
(Rediffusion 30/1/1965)
The state funeral of Sir Winston Churchill.
d Peter Morley

CHURCHILL OBITUARY
(Rediffusion 24/1/1965)
A review of the career of Sir Winston Churchill.

CHURCHILL'S PEOPLE
(BBC 20/12/1974–23/6/1975)
Twenty-six-part series of plays based on Winston Churchill's 'A History of the English Speaking Peoples'.
LIBERTY TREE 26/5/1975
The Boston Tea Party 1773.
d Alvin Rakoff; *sc* Howard Schuman
lp Derek Francis; Elvi Hale;
Geoffrey Palmer; Jeremy Irons;
Thomas Heathcote; Lynne Dearth

Y CHWARELWR (BBC 27/5/1975)
p Gareth Price

CICERO: THE QUEEN'S DRUM HORSE
(BBC 4/6/1977)
The story of a young foal which became the Queen's drum horse.
d Kevin Connor; *p* Terence Dudley;
sc Anthony Read
lp John Hallam; Tod Carty; Bill Gavin;
Leon Sinden

CIDER WITH ROSIE (BBC 25/12/1971)
Laurie Lee's recollection of boyhood in a Cotswold village during the early 1920s, based on his book of the same name.
d Claude Whatham; *p* Ann Kirch;
sc Hugh Whitemore
lp Rosemary Leach; Stephen Grendon;
Philip Hawkes; Peter Chandler;
Andrew Webber; Trevor Bannister

CILLA (BBC 1968–76)
Music/comedy series featuring singer Cilla Black.
CILLA 12/2/1969
d Vernon Lawrence; *p* Michael Hurll;
host Cilla Black; *with* Georgie Fame,
Dusty Springfield, Tom Ward,
The Irving Davies Dancers, Tim Brooke-Taylor,
Graham Chapman, Graeme Garden
CILLA (PRODUCTION MATERIAL) 27/1/1973
p Sydney Lotterby; *p* Michael Hurll;
with Cilla Black, T. Rex, Cliff Richard,
Kenny Lynch, Marc Bolan, Eddie Waring

CILLA AT THE SAVOY
(Rediffusion 6/7/1966)
Cilla Black recorded during her cabaret season at the Savoy Hotel.
d John Robins; *p* Brian Epstein;
with Cilla Black, Peter Gordeno,
The Savoy Dancers, George Martin and his Orchestra

CINDERELLA (BBC 26/12/1958)
Performance of a play based on the classic fairy tale with music specially composed by John Hotchkis.
p Shaun Sutton; *sc* C.E. Webber
lp June Thorburn; John Fabian;
Peter Sallis; Joan Benham; Edna Petrie;
Frazer Hines

CINDERELLA (Granada 13/4/1960)
The Royal Ballet Company perform Sir Frederick Ashton's 'Cinderella'. Dancers include Margot Fonteyn, Michael Somes, Annette Page, Alexander Grant, Gerd Larsen, Rosemary Lindsay, Merle Park and Georgina Parkinson.
d Mark Stuart

CINEMA (Granada 1964–75)
Documentary series looking at various personalities involved with cinema.
p Mike Wooller (1964–65), Derek Granger (1964), Graeme McDonald (1965–66), Brian Armstrong (1/10/65; 1969), Peter Plummer (1966), Peter Wildeblood (1966–67), Michael Ryan (1967–68), Mark Shivas (1968–69), John Hamp (1969; 1970–71), Michael Murphy (1969), Arthur Taylor (1971–73; 1975), Pauline Shaw (1974)
DICK VAN DYKE 1964
Dick Van Dyke is interviewed about his career.
ROSS HUNTER 1964
Ross Hunter talks about his career in the cinema.
HONOR BLACKMAN 30/9/1964
Bamber Gascoigne interviews Honor Blackman and introduces excerpts from her films.
d Peter Jones
DIRK BOGARDE 1965
An interview with Dirk Bogarde.
RAQUEL WELCH 1965
An interview with Raquel Welch.
RICHARD BROOKS 1965
Profile of film director Richard Brooks.
ROGER CORMAN 1965
The film career of Roger Corman.
ANTHONY ASQUITH 22/1/1965
The film career of Anthony Asquith.
OTTO PREMINGER 16/7/1965
Derek Granger interviews Otto Preminger.
PETER O'TOOLE 10/9/1965
Michael Scott introduces a film profile of Peter O'Toole.
d Graeme McDonald
WILLIAM WYLER 19/11/1965
William Wyler talks about his career as a film director.
CLIFF RICHARD 1966
Cliff Richard talks about his career in films.
DAVID NIVEN 1966
Interview with David Niven.
JOSEPH COTTEN 1966
Joseph Cotten talks about his acting career.
RICHARD FLEISCHER 1966
Richard Fleischer talks about his career as a film director.
PETER USTINOV 21/1/1966
Michael Scott interviews Peter Ustinov and introduces extracts from some of his films.
d Philip Casson
BRYAN FORBES 28/1/1966
Michael Scott interviews Bryan Forbes about his career in films.
d Philip Casson
CHARLTON HESTON 4/2/1966
Michael Scott interviews Charlton Heston about his roles in films.
d Philip Casson
CARL FOREMAN 18/3/1966
Michael Scott interviews Carl Foreman about his films.
d Philip Casson

JOAN CRAWFORD 6/5/1966
Michael Scott talks to Joan Crawford about her life and work in Hollywood.
d Philip Casson
ALFRED HITCHCOCK 20/5/1966
Michael Scott interviews Alfred Hitchcock and introduces extracts from some of his films.
d Philip Casson
CARL FOREMAN 1967
Carl Foreman talks about his films to Michael Scott.
CECIL BEATON 1967
Cecil Beaton, photographer and designer, talks about his work for the cinema.
DAVID JANSSEN 1967
Michael Scott interviews David Janssen about his film and television career, especially the part he played in the television series, 'The Fugitive'.
HOWARD HAWKS 1967
Michael Scott interviews film director Howard Hawks.
JAMES COBURN 1967
Michael Scott interviews and looks at the career of James Coburn.
JAMES STEWART 1967
Michael Scott interviews James Stewart about his career.
JERRY LEWIS 1967
Michael Scott looks at the career of Jerry Lewis.
JOAN FONTAINE 1967
Michael Scott interviews Joan Fontaine about her career.
JOSHUA LOGAN 1967
Michael Scott interviews Joshua Logan.
MARK ROBSON 1967
Michael Scott talks to Mark Robson about his films.
d Richard Guinea
MARTIN RITT 1967
Michael Scott interviews Martin Ritt.
MICHAEL CAINE 1967
Michael Scott talks to Michael Caine about his films.
OMAR SHARIF 1967
Omar Sharif is interviewed by Michael Scott.
PETER CUSHING 1967
Michael Scott talks to Peter Cushing about his career.
REX HARRISON 1967
Michael Scott talks to Rex Harrison about his career.
SIDNEY LUMET 1967
Michael Scott interviews Sidney Lumet.
STANLEY KRAMER 1967
Michael Scott talks to Stanley Kramer about his career in the cinema.
VANESSA REDGRAVE 1967
Michael Scott interviews Vanessa Redgrave about some of her cinema roles.
WALTER MATTHAU 1967
Michael Scott talks to Walter Matthau about his career.
WOLF MANKOWITZ 1967
Michael Scott interviews screenwriter Wolf Mankowitz.
OTTO PREMINGER 24/8/1967
Michael Scott talks to Otto Preminger about his career.
TOMMY STEELE 20/12/1967
Michael Scott interviews Tommy Steele about his career, and the new production of 'Half a Sixpence'.
d Eric Prytherch
GEORGE CUKOR 1968
George Cukor is interviewed about his career in films.
BOB HOPE 5/6/1968
Michael Scott interviews Bob Hope and reviews his career with extracts from some of his films.
STAR 15/7/1968
Interviews with director Robert Wise and stars Julie Andrews and Daniel Massey, of the film 'Star'.
BRIAN AHERNE 18/10/1968
Interview with actor Brian Aherne.
JOANNE WOODWARD 14/11/1968
Mark Shivas talks with Joanne Woodward.
d Eric Prytherch
PROFILE OF A STAR 4/12/1968
Vanessa Redgrave discusses with Mark Shivas the making of 'The Seagull'.
d Eric Prytherch

EDWARD DMYTRYK 12/12/1968
Mark Shivas interviews director Edward Dmytryk.
d Eric Prytherch
EDWARD EVERETT HORTON 1969
Edward Everett Horton talks about his career as a film actor.
HAL WALLIS 1969
Michael Parkinson interviews Hal Wallis and discusses his career as a film maker.
d Michael Becker
KEN ANNAKIN 1969
Michael Parkinson interviews Ken Annakin about his work.
d Michael Becker
LIONEL JEFFRIES 1969
Lionel Jeffries talks about his career in films.
RALPH RICHARDSON 1969
Ralph Richardson discusses his career as a film actor.
d Michael Becker
SEAN CONNERY 30/1/1969
Michael Parkinson interviews Sean Connery about his career in the cinema.
d Eric Prytherch
GINA LOLLOBRIGIDA 7/2/1969
Gina Lollobrigida talks about her career as a film actress.
RICHARD ATTENBOROUGH 3/1969
d Eric Prytherch; *interv* Michael Parkinson
JOHN SCHLESINGER 18/9/1969
Michael Parkinson interviews film director John Schlesinger.
d Michael Becker
JOHN BARRY 2/10/1969
Michael Parkinson interviews John Barry about his film music.
d Michael Becker
STANLEY DONEN 23/10/1969
Michael Parkinson interviews film director Stanley Donen.
d Michael Becker
BRYAN FORBES 30/10/1969
Michael Parkinson interviews Bryan Forbes about his work in the cinema.
d Michael Becker
DANNY KAYE 6/11/1969
Michael Parkinson interviews Danny Kaye about his career in the cinema.
d Michael Becker
ELIA KAZAN 18/12/1969
Michael Parkinson interviews Elia Kazan about his career as a film director.
d Michael Becker
JON VOIGHT 1970
Jon Voight talks about his film career.
LEE MARVIN 1970
Michael Parkinson talks to Lee Marvin and reviews his film career.
d Michael Becker
JEAN SIMMONS 21/4/1970
Michael Parkinson talks to Jean Simmons about her film career.
d Michael Becker
MICHAEL CAINE 10/7/1970
Michael Parkinson talks to Michael Caine and reviews his film career.
d Michael Becker
CINEMA CITY 1/10/1970
Michael Parkinson reviews the Cinema City exhibition at the Round House, London.
d John Hamp
OMAR SHARIF 1/10/1970
Michael Parkinson talks to Omar Sharif and reviews his film career.
d Michael Becker
RICHARD FLEISCHER 8/10/1970
Michael Parkinson talks to film director Richard Fleischer.
d Michael Becker
ROD STEIGER 29/10/1970
Michael Parkinson interviews Rod Steiger.
d Michael Becker
GENE KELLY 12/11/1970
Michael Parkinson interviews Gene Kelly.
d Michael Becker
SIR LAURENCE OLIVIER 19/11/1970
Michael Parkinson interviews Sir Laurence Olivier and reviews his film career.
MARGARET LEIGHTON 1971
Margaret Leighton discusses her film career.
d Michael Becker

MICHAEL KLINGER 1971
Michael Klinger is interviewed about his career
as a film producer.
d Michael Becker
RODDY MCDOWELL 1971
Michael Parkinson interviews Roddy McDowell
about his early acting career and his later work
as a film director.
RON MOODY 1971
Ron Moody discusses his film career.
SIDNEY GILLIAT 1971
Sidney Gilliat discusses his film career.
d Michael Becker
SAM PECKINPAH 7/1/1971
Interview with film director Sam Peckinpah.
MICK JAGGER 14/1/1971
Mick Jagger discusses his film career.
d John Downie
LIONEL JEFFRIES 21/1/1971
Lionel Jeffries talks about his film career.
JOHN TREVELYAN 28/1/1971
John Trevelyan is interviewed about his work as
Britain's official film censor.
RICHARD ATTENBOROUGH 4/2/1971
d Roger Tucker
GEORGE MELLY 11/2/1971
Interview with film critic George Melly.
MICHAEL CRAWFORD 18/2/1971
The film career of Michael Crawford.
d Roger Tucker
TREVOR HOWARD 25/2/1971
Michael Parkinson interviews Trevor Howard.
d Roger Tucker
CHRISTOPHER LEE 4/3/1971
Michael Parkinson interviews Christopher Lee
and reviews his career as a film actor.
d Roger Tucker
DIRK BOGARDE 18/3/1971
Michael Parkinson talks to Dirk Bogarde and
reviews his career as a film actor.
d Michael Becker
RAY MILLAND 25/3/1971
Ray Milland talks about his film career.
HOWARD KEEL 8/4/1971
Michael Parkinson interviews Howard Keel and
reviews his film career.
d Michael Becker
DUSTIN HOFFMAN 22/4/1971
Michael Parkinson interviews Dustin Hoffman
and reviews his film career.
d Michael Becker
FRANKIE HOWERD 6/5/1971
Michael Parkinson interviews Frankie Howerd
about his film career.
d Michael Becker
DAVID NIVEN 13/5/1971
David Niven talks about his film career to
Michael Parkinson.
d Michael Becker
ROBERT MORLEY 20/5/1971
Michael Parkinson interviews Robert Morley.
d Michael Becker
JOHN BOULTING 3/6/1971
Michael Parkinson interviews John Boulting and
reviews his film career.
d Michael Becker
JOHN MILLS 10/6/1971
Michael Parkinson interviews John Mills and
reviews his film career.
d Michael Becker
ROBERT WISE 1/7/1971
Michael Parkinson interviews film director
Robert Wise.
d Michael Becker
PETER FINCH 8/7/1971
Peter Finch discusses his film career.
d Michael Becker
PAUL SCOFIELD 21/7/1971
Paul Scofield discusses his film career.
d Michael Becker
SHELLEY WINTERS 29/7/1971
d Michael Becker
JACK NICHOLSON 1/8/1971
Michael Parkinson interviews Jack Nicholson
and reviews his career in films.
d Michael Becker
VANESSA REDGRAVE 5/8/1971
Vanessa Redgrave discusses her film career.
d Michael Becker

ROBERT MULLIGAN 12/8/1971
Robert Mulligan talks about his career as a film
director.
d Michael Becker
TOM COURTENAY 26/8/1971
Tom Courtenay discusses his film career.
JOSEPH LOSEY 2/9/1971
Joseph Losey is interviewed about his career as a
film director.
d Michael Becker
WOODY ALLEN 9/9/1971
Interview with Woody Allen about his film
career.
d Michael Becker
OLIVER REED 30/9/1971
Oliver Reed talks about his film career.
d Michael Becker
RACHEL ROBERTS 14/10/1971
Rachel Roberts discusses her acting career.
DAVID ROSE 21/10/1971
David Rose talks about film music.
d Michael Becker
MICHAEL WINNER 4/11/1971
Michael Winner is interviewed about his career
as a film director.
d Michael Becker
BOB SIMMONS 18/11/1971
Film stuntman Bob Simmons talks about his
work.
d Michael Becker
TELLY SAVALAS 25/11/1971
Telly Savalas discusses his film career.
d Michael Becker
FRANKLIN SCHAFFNER 2/12/1971
Franklin Schaffner talks about the films he has
directed.
d Michael Becker
NORMAN JEWISON 9/12/1971
Norman Jewison discusses his film career.
d Michael Becker
RICHARD HARRIS 30/12/1971
Richard Harris talks about his film career.
d Michael Becker
MIA FARROW 1972
The film career of Mia Farrow.
CARL FOREMAN 6/1/1972
The film career of Carl Foreman.
d Michael Becker
HENRY MANCINI 13/1/1972
The film music of Henry Mancini.
d Michael Becker
GENE HACKMAN 27/1/1972
Gene Hackman talks about his film career.
d Michael Becker
NED SHERRIN 3/2/1972
Ned Sherrin talks about his career as a film
producer.
d Michael Becker
ROMAN POLANSKI 10/2/1972
Roman Polanski talks about his film career.
JAMES STEWART 17/2/1972
James Stewart talks about his career as a film
actor.
d Michael Becker
MICKEY ROONEY 24/2/1972
Mickey Rooney talks about his film career.
CHARLTON HESTON 2/3/1972
Charlton Heston is interviewed about his career
in films.
SUSANNAH YORK 9/3/1972
Susannah York talks about her career in films.
OSWALD MORRIS 23/3/1972
Interview with film cameraman Oswald Morris.
d Richard Guinea
NIGEL DAVENPORT 30/3/1972
Nigel Davenport talks about his film career.
DANA ANDREWS 6/4/1972
Dana Andrews talks about his career in films.
OTTO PREMINGER 13/4/1972
Otto Preminger talks about his film career.
HARRY BELAFONTE 20/4/1972
The film career of Harry Belafonte.
d Michael Becker
GARSON KANIN 27/4/1972
Garson Kanin talks about his film career, and his
work with Spencer Tracy and Katherine
Hepburn.
MEL FERRER 11/5/1972
The film career of Mel Ferrer.
DONALD PLEASENCE 18/5/1972
The film career of Donald Pleasence.

ROBERT WAGNER 25/5/1972
Robert Wagner talks about his film career.
PETER YATES 1/6/1972
Peter Yates talks about his film career.
ALAN BATES 8/6/1972
An interview with Alan Bates about his career in
films.
MELVILLE SHAVELSON 8/6/1972
Melville Shavelson talks about his career as a
screenwriter.
LEE REMICK 15/6/1972
The film career of Lee Remick.
YUL BRYNNER 22/6/1972
Yul Brynner talks about his film career.
SIMON WARD 20/7/1972
Simon Ward talks about his film career.
BURT LANCASTER 10/8/1972
Clive James interviews Burt Lancaster about his
film career.
d Richard Guinea
ROBERT MITCHUM 17/8/1972
Clive James interviews Robert Mitchum.
d Richard Guinea
JOHN HUSTON 14/9/1972
Clive James interviews John Huston.
d Richard Guinea
PETER SELLERS 19/10/1972
Clive James interviews Peter Sellers.
d Richard Guinea
RICHARD BURTON 26/10/1972
Clive James interviews Richard Burton.
d Richard Guinea
STANLEY BAKER 2/11/1972
Clive James talks to Stanley Baker.
d Richard Guinea
PETER USTINOV 16/11/1972
Clive James interviews Peter Ustinov.
d Richard Guinea
SEAN CONNERY 4/1/1973
Clive James looks at Sean Connery's film career.
d Richard Guinea
DON SIEGEL 24/5/1973
Brian Trueman interviews Don Siegel.
d Pauline Shaw
STERLING HAYDEN 31/5/1973
Brian Trueman interviews Sterling Hayden
about his career as a film actor.
d Pauline Shaw
MALCOLM MCDOWELL 7/6/1973
Malcolm McDowell talks to Brian Trueman
about his career as a film actor.
p Pauline Shaw
JOE MANKIEWICZ 12/7/1973
Joseph Mankiewicz talks about his career to
Brian Trueman.
d Pauline Shaw
DONALD SUTHERLAND 4/10/1973
Donald Sutherland talks to Brian Trueman
about his career as a film actor.
d Pauline Shaw
ROBERT ALTMAN 25/10/1973
Brian Trueman interviews film director Robert
Altman.
d Pauline Shaw
JAMES COBURN 22/11/1973
James Coburn talks about his career as a film
actor to Brian Trueman.
d Pauline Shaw
LIV ULLMAN 6/12/1973
Liv Ullman talks to Brian Trueman about her
career as a film actress.
d Pauline Shaw
RAY HARRYHAUSEN 20/12/1973
Ray Harryhausen talks to Brian Trueman about
his career in the cinema.
d Pauline Shaw
FRANK FINLAY 1974
The film acting career of Frank Finlay.
YVONNE BLAKE 1974
The film career of Yvonne Blake.
FRED ZINNEMANN 14/2/1974
Fred Zinnemann and his career as a film
director.
RYAN O'NEAL 21/2/1974
Ryan O'Neal and his career as a film actor.
NATALIE WOOD 4/4/1974
Brian Trueman interviews Natalie Wood about
her career as a film actress.
JACK NICHOLSON 30/5/1974
Brian Trueman interviews Jack Nicholson about
his career in films.

IRVIN KERSHNER 11/7/1974
Brian Trueman interviews Irvin Kershner about his career as a film director.
PETER HUNT 5/9/1974
Brian Trueman interviews film director Peter Hunt.
SHEPPERTON STUDIOS 6/10/1974
Brian Trueman visits Shepperton Studios.
COLIN WELLAND 13/10/1974
Colin Welland takes a personal look at some post-war British films reflecting changing social attitudes. He reviews two new films: 'The Odessa File' and 'Conrack'.
d Pauline Shaw
JACK HALEY JNR 3/11/1974
Benny Green interviews Jack Haley Jnr.
DIRK BOGARDE 10/11/1974
George Melly interviews Dirk Bogarde about his film career.
JAMES CAAN 17/11/1974
Brian Trueman interviews James Caan about his film career.
ANITA LOOS 24/11/1974
Benny Green interviews Anita Loos.
PETER BOGDANOVICH 29/8/1975
David Shipman interviews Peter Bogdanovich.
d Michael Becker

CINEMA TODAY (BBC 1959–62)
Series covering various aspects of the cinema and film industry.
EXPERIMENTAL FILMS 8/12/1959
Karel Reisz introduces extracts from experimental films and interviews Richard Williams and Jack Gold. Films used are 'Generation', 'The Wardrobe', 'Concerto for Sub-Machine Gun', 'Dom', 'L' Opera Mouffe', 'Little Island', 'Neighbours', 'It's a Grand Life', 'The Savage Eye', 'Lourdes et ses Miracles', and 'The Visit'.
p Victor Poole
WEST GERMANY 16/5/1960
Derek Prouse interviews Wolfgang Staudte.
p Victor Poole
SEYMOUR CASSEL 19/7/1960
Derek Prouse interviews Seymour Cassel, who talks about the number of American films being made in New York rather than Hollywood.
d Victor Poole
WAR 11/11/1960
Derek Prouse examines war as it is portrayed on film, with extracts from 'All Quiet on the Western Front', 'La Grande Illusion', 'Paths of Glory', 'The Way Ahead' and 'The Unknown Soldier'.
p Victor Poole

CIRCUIT ELEVEN MIAMI
(BBC 27/8–27/10/1979)
Thirteen-part documentary series on law and order in Florida, including coverage of court-room proceedings.
EXECUTION 27/10/1979
The execution of John Spenkelink, the first in Florida for 15 years.
p Mark Anderson

CITIZEN 63 (BBC 28/8–25/9/1963)
Documentary series which looks at particular individuals and their lives.
BARRY LANGFORD 28/8/1963
The new breed of British businessman in the 1960s looking at the life and work of Barry Langford, antique dealer and pop-music agent.
p John Boorman
MARION KNIGHT 11/9/1963
The story of an attractive and rebellious girl at a secondary modern school.
p John Boorman

CITIZEN SMITH (BBC 1977–80)
Sitcom with Robert Lindsay as Wolfie Smith, the 'Che Guevara of Tooting'.
p Dennis Main Wilson; *sc* John Sullivan
regulars Robert Lindsay; Mike Grady;
Hilda Braid; Cheryl Hall; Peter Vaughan
CROCODILE TEARS 3/11/1977
lp Tony Millan
GUESS WHO'S COMING TO DINNER 10/11/1977
lp Stephen Greif

The HOSTAGE 1/12/1977
lp Stephen Greif; Tony Millan;
Patricia Denys
SPEED'S RETURN 1/12/1978
lp Stephen Greif; Tony Millan;
George Sweeney; Anna Nygh
The PARTY'S OVER 25/10/1979
lp Tony Steedman

CITY (BBC 9/3–13/4/1979)
A series of six films about inner cities.
PARADISE LOST 9/3/1979
A school in the depressed Chapeltown area of Leeds prepares its annual play; this year, based on Milton's 'Paradise Lost'.
p Gerry Troyna

CITY ON THE BORDER (BBC 30/5/1978)
One week spent in the city of Londonderry.
d Colin Thomas, Colin Rose,
Philip Donnellan; *p* Michael Croucher

The CITY ON THE STEPPE
(Granada 17/12/1975)
Surviving traditions in Mongolia.
d/p Brian Moser

CIVILISATION (BBC 1969)
Documentary series in which Sir Kenneth Clark examines the ideas and values which to him give meaning to the term Western Civilisation.
d Michael Gill;
p Peter Montagnon, Michael Gill
The SKIN OF OUR TEETH 23/2/1969
The Dark Ages, the six centuries following the collapse of the Roman Empire.
The GREAT THAW 2/3/1969
The sudden reawakening of European civilisation in the twelfth century.
ROMANCE AND REALITY 9/3/1969
The architectural achievements of the later Middle Ages in France and Italy.
MAN – THE MEASURE OF ALL THINGS 16/3/1969
Florence and other centres of Renaissance civilisation.
The HERO AS ARTIST 23/3/1969
Papal Rome in the early sixteenth century; Michelangelo, Raphael and da Vinci.
PROTEST AND COMMUNICATION 30/3/1969
The Reformation artist in Germany, France and Elizabethan Great Britain.
GRANDEUR AND OBEDIENCE 6/4/1969
Rome of the Counter-Reformation and the glory of St. Peter's.
The LIGHT OF EXPERIENCE 13/4/1969
Realism in Dutch painting and new developments in science.
The PURSUIT OF HAPPINESS 20/4/1969
The nature of eighteenth-century music (with examples from Bach, Handel, Haydn and Mozart).
The SMILE OF REASON 27/4/1969
Revolutionary change in eighteenth-century Paris and its salons.
The WORSHIP OF NATURE 4/5/1969
The sudden decline of Christianity, about the year 1730, as the chief creative force in western civilisation.
The FALLACIES OF HOPE 11/5/1969
The aftermath of the French Revolution.
HEROIC MATERIALISM 18/5/1969
Contrasts the materialistic achievements of the past 100 years (engineering and science) with the equally remarkable influence of such humanitarian reformers as Wilberforce and Shaftesbury.

A CLAN FOR ALL SEASONS
(Scottish TV 1/1/1973)
A visit to Dunvegan Castle on the Isle of Skye to meet the Clan MacLeod, including Dame Flora MacLeod, 28th Chief of the Clan.
d David Dunn; *p* Russell Galbraith

CLASS OF '74 (Yorkshire TV 10/9/1974)
Paul Dunstan reports on the ambitions and prospects of three sixteen-year-old girls at Ryburn School, Sowerby Bridge, Yorkshire: Julie Senior, Kathleen Snell and Jacqueline Ingham.
d Barry Cockcroft; *exec.p* John Fairley

CLAYHANGER (ATV 1/1–24/6/1976)
Twenty-six-part adaptation of Arnold Bennett's trilogy of novels set against the background of the Staffordshire Potteries in the late nineteenth century.
EPISODE 15: THE CHAIN IS BROKEN 8/4/1976
d David Reid;
p David Reid, Douglas Livingstone;
sc Douglas Livingstone
lp Peter McEnery; Harry Andrews;
Thelma Whiteley; Benjamin Whitrow;
Joyce Redman; Anne Carroll; Patricia Garwood;
John Horsley; Clive Swift

The CLIFTON HOUSE MYSTERY
(HTV 8/10–12/11/1978)
Six-part supernatural mystery serial for children.
EPISODE 2 15/10/1978
d Hugh David; *p* Leonard White;
sc Harry Moore, Daniel Farson
lp Robert Morgan; Joshua Le Touzel;
Ingrid Hafner; Amanda Kirby;
Sebastian Breaks; June Barrie; Margery Withers

A CLIMATE OF FEAR (BBC 22/6/1962)
Second of a trilogy of plays; sequel to WHERE THE DIFFERENCE BEGINS (1961); followed by the third play 'The Birth of a Private Man' (1963).
p Don Taylor; *sc* David Mercer
lp Tony Garnett; Arch Taylor;
William Gaunt; John Stratton;
Anthony Higginson; Douglas Wilmer;
Pauline Letts; Geoffrey Bayldon; Sarah Badel

CLOCHEMERLE (BBC-Bavaria Atelier, Munich 1972)
Adaptation, in nine parts, of Gabriel Chevallier's humorous story about the controversy surrounding the construction of a 'public convenience' in the centre of a French village.
p Michael Mills;
sc Ray Galton, Alan Simpson;
nar Peter Ustinov
regulars Cyril Cusack; Roy Dotrice;
Wendy Hiller; Kenneth Griffith; Cyd Hayman;
Micheline Presle; Catherine Rouvel;
Barry Linehan
PART 1: THE MAGNIFICENT IDEA OF BARTHELEMY PIECHUT, THE MAYOR 18/2/1972
lp Mandy Jenner; Ian Gray; Freddie Earlle;
Bernard Bresslaw; Miriam Raymond;
Christian Roberts
PART 2: THE TRIUMPHANT INAUGURATION OF A MUNCIPAL AMENITY 25/2/1972
lp Hugh Griffith; Aubrey Wood;
Meredith Edwards
PART 3: THE SPIRITED PROTEST OF JUSTINE PUTET 3/3/1972
lp Freddie Earlle; Bernard Bresslaw;
Miriam Raymond
PART 4: THE AWFUL AWAKENING OF CLAUDIUS BRODEQUIN 10/3/1972
lp James Wardroper; Georgina Moon;
Richard Shaw
PART 5: THE PAINFUL INFLICTION OF NICHOLAS THE BEADLE 17/3/1972
lp Freddie Earlle; Bernard Bresslaw
PART 6: THE SCANDALOUS OUTCOME OF A NIGHT OF DESTRUCTION 24/3/1972
lp Freddie Earlle; Wolfe Morris
PART 7: THE INEXORABLE POWER OF THE THIRD REPUBLIC 31/3/1972
lp Nigel Green; Dennis Price;
Raymond Gerome
PART 8: THE DREADED ARRIVAL OF CAPTAIN TARDIVAUX 7/4/1972
lp Nigel Green; Freddie Earlle
PART 9: THE GLORIOUS TRIUMPH OF BARTHELMY PIECHUT 14/4/1972
lp Nigel Green; Dennis Price; Freddie Earlle

CLOSE-UP (Rediffusion 1960–63)
Documentary series on the cinema.
LOCATION STORY OF THE GUNS OF NAVARONE 24/11/1960
A behind-the-scenes look at the making of 'The Guns of Navarone'.
d Jonathan Alwyn; *p* Ray Dicks

DOLORES HART 1962
Two interviews with the American actress,
Dolores Hart.
d Harry Sloan; *pres* Nick Barker
JAMES MASON 1962
PETER USTINOV 1962
Nick Barker introduces Peter Ustinov and shows
extracts from his films.
d Adrian Brown

CLOSE-UP (CA CBC)
Documentary series.
SIR ANTHONY EDEN 17/12/1959
An interview with Sir Anthony Eden in Canada.
**DON'T LABEL ME: A REPORT ON BRITISH
GUIANA** 1/10/1961
Politics in British Guiana (the former British
colony now known as Guyana).

CLOTHES THAT COUNT
(BBC 10/10–12/12/1967)
A series of ten programmes for home
dressmakers.
The SHIRTWAISTER 24/10/1967
d Bryn Brooks

CLOUDS OF GLORY (Granada 1978)
Two films about William Wordsworth and
Samuel Taylor Coleridge.
d Ken Russell; *p* Norman Swallow;
sc Ken Russell, Melvyn Bragg
WILLIAM AND DOROTHY 9/7/1978
lp David Warner; Felicity Kendal;
Preston Lockwood; Amanda Murray;
Robin Bevan; Susan Withers; Antony Carrick;
Patricia Quinn
The RIME OF THE ANCIENT MARINER 16/7/1978
lp David Hemmings; Peter Dodd;
Patricia Garwood; Ben Aris; Kika Markham;
Murray Melvin; Diana Mather; David Warner;
Felicity Kendal

COLDITZ (BBC-Universal TV 1972–73;
BBC 1974)
Drama series set in the prisoner-of-war
stronghold of Colditz Castle during World
War II.
GONE AWAY: PART 1 18/1/1973
d William Slater; *p* Gerard Glaister;
sc John Brason
lp Robert Wagner; David McCallum;
Edward Hardwicke; Jack Hedley;
Christopher Neame; Bernard Hepton
SENIOR AMERICAN OFFICER 4/3/1974
d Philip Dudley; *p* Gerard Glaister;
sc Ivan Moffat
lp Robert Wagner; Daniel O'Herlihy;
Al Mancini; Hugh Sullivan; Robert MacLeod;
Anthony Valentine; David McCallum;
Bernard Hepton; Jack Hedley

COLLISION COURSE (Granada 20/2/1979)
Recreates the dramatic moments before and
after the 1976 mid-air collision between a British
Airways Trident and a Yugoslav charter plane.
d Leslie Woodhead; *p* David Boulton;
sc Martin Thompson
lp Antony Sher; David De Keyser;
Nick Brimble; David Beames; Alec Sabin;
Malcolm Reynolds

The COLONY (BBC 16/6/1964)
Documentary impression of some of the people
of the West Indies now living in Birmingham.
d Philip Donnellan

COME BACK MRS NOAH (BBC 13/12/1977)
Pilot episode for a six-part sitcom, transmitted in
1978, set in the near future about a housewife
who accidentally gets launched into orbit as a
member of a space crew.
p David Croft; *sc* David Croft, Jeremy Lloyd
lp Mollie Sugden; Ian Lavender;
Donald Hewlett; Michael Knowles;
Robert Gillespie; Gorden Kaye

COME IN, IF YOU CAN GET IN
(Tyne Tees 1979)
Regional weekly entertainment programme
featuring excerpts from current shows and
appearances from personalities visiting the
region.

COME IN, IF YOU CAN GET IN 23/2/1979
The nature of comedy.
d Graham Bye, Tony Kysh; *p* Heather Ging
COME IN, IF YOU CAN GET IN 16/3/1979
Film production in the north east of England.
d Tony Kysh, Graham Bye; *p* Heather Ging
COME IN, IF YOU CAN GET IN 30/3/1979
Discussion on the theatre and acting.
d Graham Bye, Walter Storey, Tony Kysh;
p Heather Ging

**COME OUT ALAN BROWNING – WE
KNOW YOU'RE IN THERE**
(Tyne Tees 28/12/1979)
Alan Browning, the actor, searches for his roots
in his hometown Sunderland
d Jeremy Lack; *sc* Andrea Masefield

COME OUT FIGHTING (Granada 19/9/1967)
The daily life of boxer Harry Scott.
d Frank Cvitanovich

...COME TO AN END (TWW 3/3/1968)
Sir John Betjeman says farewell on behalf of
Television Wales and West.

COME TO YOUR SENSES
(BBC 7/1–11/2/1979)
A six-part journey through the world of the
senses.
The MIND'S EYE 14/1/1979
How the eye recognises images.
d Chris Serle; *p* Michael Garrod;
pres Clive Holloway

The COMEDIANS (Granada 1971–85)
Fast-paced comedy series in which the acts of
stand-up comedians were split up into separate
jokes and interspliced.
The COMEDIANS 12/6/1971
d Walter Butler; *p* John Hamp;
with Duggie Brown, Frank Carson,
Mike Coyne, Ken Goodwin, Bernard Manning,
Paul Melba, George Roper, Charlie Williams,
Sheps Banjo Band
The COMEDIANS 18/2/1972
d Walter Butler; *p* John Hamp;
with Ken Goodwin, Charlie Williams,
George Roper, Bernard Manning,
Frank Carson, Mike Reid, Sheps Banjo Band
The COMEDIANS 30/11/1979
d David Warwick; *exec.p* John Hamp;
with Hal Nolen, Charlie Daze, Roy Walker,
Lennie Windsor, Brian Carroll, Lee Wilson,
Bob Curtiss, George King, Mick Miller,
Stan Boardman, Mike Kelly, Harry Scott

The COMEDY OF ERRORS (ATV 18/4/1978)
Adaptation, for television, of the Royal
Shakespeare Company's stage production.
d Philip Casson; *p* Peter Roden
lp Brian Coburn; Griffith Jones; Roger Rees;
Mike Gwilym; Michael Williams;
Nickolas Grace; Judi Dench; Francesca Annis;
Paul Brooke

COMEDY PLAYHOUSE (BBC 1961–74)
A series of one-off plays which acted as a
showcase for potential comedy series.
The OFFER 5/1/1962
Became the basis for the series STEPTOE AND
SON (1962–74).
p Duncan Wood;
sc Alan Simpson, Ray Galton
lp Harry H. Corbett; Wilfrid Brambell
The MATE MARKET 3/1/1964
p Dennis Main Wilson; *sc* Gerry Jones
lp Jeremy Young; Lance Percival;
Francesca Annis; Jean Conroy; Dilys Laye;
Richard Caldicot
LAST OF THE SUMMER WINE 4/1/1973
Became the basis for the series LAST OF THE
SUMMER WINE (1973–).
p James Gilbert; *sc* Roy Clarke
lp Michael Bates; Bill Owen; Peter Sallis;
John Comer; Jane Freeman; Kathy Staff

COMMAND IN BATTLE (BBC 1958–59)
Eight-part series with Field Marshal
Montgomery about his strategies during World
War II.
p Michael Bowen

INTRODUCTION 7/12/1958
Field Marshal Montgomery introduces the series
by summarising his handling of the Battles of
Alamein and Mareth, the Normandy campaign,
and the Allied progress along the Rhine.
The BATTLE OF ALAMEIN 12/12/1958
Montgomery takes command of the 8th Army.
The BATTLE OF MARETH 19/12/1958
Using film, a map and a scale model to illustrate
his talk, Field Marshal Montgomery describes
the piercing of the Mareth Line by the 8th Army
and linking up with the 1st Army and American
troops. This victory heralded the defeat of
German forces and the end of the war in North
Africa.
The INVASION OF SICILY AND ITALY 26/12/1958
The part played by the 8th Army in the invasion
of Sicily and Italy up to the Battle of the River
Sangro.
d John Fearon
The NORMANDY CAMPAIGN 2/1/1959
The build-up to and course of the Allies'
invasion of Normandy during World War II.
The WINTER OF 1944 9/1/1959
The course of the Allied campaign during the
winter of 1944.
The SURRENDER ON LÜNEBURG HEATH
16/1/1959
The final months of the Allied advance on the
Western Front, and the German surrender on
Lüneburg Heath.
LOOKING BACK 23/1/1959
Richard Dimbleby and Charles Collingwood
interview Field Marshal Montgomery about his
views on the current international situation, and
about aspects of his personality as revealed in
the COMMAND IN BATTLE series.

The COMMANDERS (BBC 1972–73)
Seven-part documentary series on the the
military leaders of World War II.
p Harry Hastings; Patricia Meehan
**GEORGI ZHUKOV, MARSHAL OF THE SOVIET
UNION** 5/12/1972
The commander who survived Stalin's purges of
the 1930s, who dared to argue with the Russian
dictator and who finally led the Red Army to
victory against the Nazis.
**GENERAL OF THE ARMY, DWIGHT D.
EISENHOWER** 12/12/1972
Eisenhower's decision to invade Europe in the
appalling weather of June 1944.
BILL SLIM, FIELD MARSHALL – BRITISH ARMY
25/9/1973
A survey of the career of Field Marshal Bill
Slim, commander in World War II.

**The COMMON MARKET – THE PRIME
MINISTER THE RT. HON. HAROLD
MACMILLAN** (20/9/1962)
Harold Macmillan reports to the nation on the
Commonwealth Prime Ministers' Conference to
discuss Britain's membership of the EEC.

COMPACT (BBC 1962–65)
Bi-weekly series set in the offices of a women's
magazine.
COMPACT 4/1/1962
d Christopher Barry; *p* Alan Bromly;
sc Hazel Adair, Peter Ling
lp Jean Harvey; Moray Watson;
Marcia Ashton; Justine Lord; Nicholas Selby;
Tamara Fuerst; Betty Cooper; Monica Evans

COMPASS (Ulster TV 1979)
Ulster magazine programme about religious
affairs.
COMPASS 5/2/1979
Frank Hanna interviews Father John Doherty,
Rev. Gerrard Patton, Rev. A.H. Graham and
Edgar Turner.
p Alan Hailes, Robin Roddie,
P.F. Scott, Derek Murray
COMPASS 11/3/1979
Frank Hanna interviews Dr Harry Morton,
Brian McKeown, David Hamilton and Michael
Barry.
p Alan Hailes, Robin Roddie,
P.F. Scott, Derek Murray

The COMPLAISANT LOVER
(BBC 20/10/1961)
Production of the comedy play about a
womaniser.
p Stuart Burge; *sc* Graham Greene
lp Andrew Cruickshank; Alan Badel;
William Mervyn; Tracey Lloyd;
Rosalie Crutchley

**A COMPLETELY DIFFERENT WAY OF
LIFE?** (ATV 11/5/1971)
The activities of the St. Anne's Community Craft
Centre, a commune in Nottingham.
d/p Chris Menges

CONCENTRATION (Granada 1959–60)
Quiz programme hosted by Chris Howland.
CONCENTRATION 12/4/1960
d Peter Mullings

CONFESSION (Granada 3/7–4/9/1970)
Anthology drama series.
ALLERGY 28/8/1970
d Mike Newell; *p* Peter Eckersley;
sc Cecil Taylor
lp Gordon Jackson; Hannah Gordon;
Maurice Roëves

CONFLICT (US Warner Bros 1956–57)
Anthology drama series.
GIRL ON THE SUBWAY 8/1/1957
d John Rich; *p* Roy Huggins;
sc Everett Freeman, Harry Kurnitz
lp Natalie Wood; Charles Ruggles;
James Garner; Murray Hamilton; Nicky Blair;
James Flavin; June Blair
A QUESTION OF LOYALTY 2/4/1957
d Walter Doniger; *p* Roy Huggins;
sc Howard Browne
lp Dennis Hopper; Gerald Mohr; Pat McVey;
Paul Richards; Judi Boutin; Kenneth Alton;
Allison Hayes
NO MAN'S ROAD 30/4/1957
d Leslie H. Martinson; *p* Roy Huggins;
sc Robert Schaefer, Eric Friewald;
auth John Wells
lp Dennis Hopper; Karen Sharpe;
Rafael Campos; Ken Lynch; Ainslie Pryor;
Jody McCrea
PATTERN FOR VIOLENCE 14/5/1957
d Leslie H. Martinson; *p* Roy Huggins;
sc Howard Browne
lp Jack Lord; Karen Steele; Ainslie Pryor;
Meg Randall; Kay Stewart; Charles Evans
EXECUTION NIGHT 28/5/1957
d Douglas Heyes; *p* Roy Huggins;
sc Frederick Brady; *auth* Thomas Walsh
lp Virginia Mayo; Edmund Lowe;
Efrem Zimbalist Jr; Jay Novello; Floyd Simmons

The CONGO I KNEW (BBC 1963)
Two-part compilation film of material filmed on
safari in 1935, from Morocco to the Belgian
Congo.
d/p Armand Denis
PART ONE: THE ELEPHANTS OF GANGALA-NA-
BODIO 13/12/1963
PART TWO: GIANTS AND PYGMIES 20/12/1963

CONJUGAL RIGHTS (Yorkshire TV 1973)
Series of three plays based on the emotional
entanglements of six people.
d Marc Miller; *exec.p* Peter Willes;
sc Philip Mackie
lp Julian Holloway; Ann Bell; Ian Holm;
Julian Glover; Sarah Badel; Barbara Ferris
ALAN AND ROSAMUND 8/1/1973
CHARLES AND PAULA 15/1/1973
MICHAEL AND JENNY 22/1/1973

CONNECTIONS (BBC 17/10–19/12/1978)
Series of ten programmes, presented by James
Burke, which examines various events in history.
p Mick Jackson, David Kennard; *sc* James Burke
The TRIGGER EFFECT 17/10/1978
DEATH IN THE MORNING 24/10/1978

CONNOLLY (Scottish TV 31/12/1976)
Scottish comedian Billy Connolly, with singers
Gallagher and Lyle.
p David Bell

CONQUEST (US CBS 1957–60)
Charles Collingwood examines major technical
and medical advances.
WHAT MAKES US HUMAN? 9/9/1960
Experiments on pigeons carried out at Harvard
University to investigate conditioning processes.
d Michael Sklar
ESCAPE FROM DANGER 23/9/1960
Escape without apparatus from a submerged
submarine; parachuting from a balloon at
80,000 ft.
d Michael Sklar

**The CONSECRATION OF COVENTRY
CATHEDRAL** (BBC 25/5/1962)
The Bishop of Coventry, Dr C.K.N. Bardsley
performs the consecration ceremony in the
presence of Queen Elizabeth II, Princess
Margaret and the Earl of Snowdon; Dr Arthur
Michael Ramsey delivers a sermon.
p Barrie Edgar

**The CONSERVATIVE PARTY
CONFERENCE 1958** (BBC 11/10/1958)
The Conservative Party conference at Blackpool,
October 1958. Debates include housing,
taxation, education, foreign affairs, the
economy. Kenneth Harris interviews Iain
MacLeod, Henry Brooke, Lord Hailsham, John
Tilney, R.A. Butler, Geoffrey Howe, Selwyn
Lloyd, Peter Thorneycroft and Derick
Heathcoat-Amory; Harold Macmillan's closing
speech.
p John Grist; *rep* Robert Kee

CONSETT – THE END OF THE ROAD
(Tyne Tees 12/12/1979)
The demise of the steel-making industry in
Consett, Co. Durham.

CONTACT (BBC 10/10–12/12/1976)
Ten-part series for the physically disabled.
PLUGGING THE GAPS 24/10/1976
The deficiencies in statutory provisions for
disabled people, with Corbet Woodall and Jill
Lumb.
p Charles Pascoe

CONTRACT 736 (Scottish TV 1/10/1967)
The construction of the liner 'Queen Elizabeth
II' on Clydebank and its impact on the life of the
local shipbuilding community.
d Ted Williamson; *p* George Reid

CONTRASTS (BBC 1967–69)
A series of music and arts features.
The BUILDINGS OF ENGLAND 3/12/1968
A study of Nikolaus Pevsner, the author of 'The
Buildings of England'.
p David Cheshire

CONTROVERSY (BBC 1971–75)
Series of discussion programmes.
BRITAIN NEEDS COMMON MARKET NOW
20/5/1975
Debate on Britain and the EEC, with Andrew
Shonfield and Robin Day.
d Michael Lumley; *p* Jack Saltman

CONVERSATIONS AT CRANBORNE
(BBC 15/10/1970)
Patrick Garland interviews Lord David Cecil.
p Tristram Powell

COPPELIA (BBC 27/10/1957)
Ballet performance.
p/adapt Margaret Dale
with Nadia Nerina, Robert Helpmann,
Donald Britton, Alexis Chesnakov

The CORONATION (BBC 2/6/1953)
The Coronation of Queen Elizabeth II.
comm Berkeley Smith, Chester Wilmot,
Max Robertson, Michael Henderson, Mary Hill,
Brian Johnston, Bernard Braden,
Richard Dimbleby

CORONATION STREET (Granada 1960–)
Long-running soap opera revolving around the
characters living in the fictitious northern
England town of Weatherfield. Originally
devised by Tony Warren as a twelve-part serial
and developed into a bi-weekly soap opera.
p Stuart Latham (1960–61; 1964),
Derek Granger (1961–62), Harry V. Kershaw
(1962–67), Margaret Morris (1963–64),
Tim Aspinall (1964), Richard Everitt (1965),
Howard Baker (1965), Peter Eckersley (1966),
Jack Rosenthal (1967), Michael Cox (1967),
Richard Doubleday (1968), John Finch (1968–
69), June Howson (1970), Leslie Duxbury (1971;
1974–75), Brian Armstrong (1971–1972),
Eric Prytherch (1972–74), Susi Hush (1974–75),
Bill Podmore (1976–79)
note: the NFTVA holds a comprehensive
collection of the series transmitted up to and
including 1979.

The COSMOLOGISTS (BBC 12/3/1963)
The views of five leading astronomers, Fred
Hoyle, Bernard Lovell, Herman Bondi, and
Margaret and Geoffrey Burbidge on the creation
of the universe.
p Philip Daly; *interv* Stephen Black

The COST OF LOVING
(Yorkshire TV 1977)
A series of seven plays each set in the imaginary
Northern town of Cressley.
p James Ormerod; *sc* Stan Barstow
EPISODE 1: ALBERT'S PART 25/9/1977
d David Reynolds
lp Colin Welland; Anna Cropper;
Derek Francis; Ray Mort
EPISODE 2: ESTUARY 2/10/1977
d David Reynolds
lp Robert Longden; Ann Lynn
EPISODE 3: MADGE 9/10/1977
d James Ormerod
lp Lynn Farleigh; Robert McDermott;
Robert Brown; Jessica Benton
EPISODE 4: THE YEARS BETWEEN 16/10/1977
d James Ormerod
lp Patricia Routledge; John Ronane;
Philip Stone; James Hazeldine
EPISODE 5: THE ASSAILANTS 23/10/1977
d James Ormerod
lp Tony Beckley; Jo Rowbottom;
Joseph Brady
EPISODE 6: FLESH, PINK AND BLACK 30/10/1977
d James Ormerod
lp Jack Watson; Rosemary Martin;
Diana Rayworth
EPISODE 7: THE HUMAN ELEMENT 6/11/1977
d David Reynolds
lp Paula Wilcox; Tim Woodward;
Teddy Turner; Jeff Rawle; Ken Kitson;
Tony Melody

**COUGH AND YOU'LL DEAFEN
THOUSANDS** (BBC 12/11/1972)
A history of the BBC and the technical
innovations of its engineers.
d Michael Currer-Briggs; *p* Peter Bradford;
comm Dudley Foster, Frank Gillard,
John Snagge

COULD YOUR STREET BE NEXT?
(ATV 20/8/1973)
The effects of a road-widening scheme in
London.
d/p Charles Stewart

The COUNT OF MONTE CRISTO
(US Vision Productions–TPA 1955)
Adventure series loosely based on the Dumas
novel, where Edmond Dantes becomes a fighter
for justice once he assumes the title of the Count
of Monte Cristo.
The SARDINIA AFFAIR 1955
lp George Dolenz; Nick Cravat

COUNTERPOINT (Ulster TV)
Current affairs and local issues programme.
EMMA – A DAY AT A TIME 26/1/1978
A day in the life of Emma, the spastic daughter
of an Ulster Methodist minister, who has had a
small book of prayers published.
d Andrew Crockhart

RAPE OF THE SHANKHILL 1/7/1978
The redevelopment of the housing in Shankhill, with comments from local politicians.
d Alan Hailes, Derek Murray;
p Derek Murray
HEAR TODAY 8/3/1979

COUNTRY FOCUS (Grampian)
Northern Scottish farming magazine programme.
COUNTRY FOCUS 1979
Items on the EEC, the warble fly, Scottish Young Farmers, crofting on the west coast, guinea fowl production in Aberdeen and market gardening.
d Graham McLeish

COUNTRY MATTERS (Granada 1972–73)
Drama series based on stories by H.E. Bates and A.E. Coppard.
p Derek Granger
CRAVEN ARMS 20/8/1972
d David Giles; *sc* James Saunders;
auth A.E. Coppard
lp Ian McKellen; Prunella Ransome; Susan Penhaligon; Marilyn Taylerson; Joe Holmes
The MILL 27/8/1972
d Donald McWhinnie; *sc* James Saunders;
auth H.E. Bates
lp Brenda Bruce; Ray Smith; Rosalind Ayres; Robert Keegan; Maria Charles; Tom Chadbon
The SULLENS SISTERS 3/9/1972
d Barry Davis; *sc* Hugh Leonard;
auth A.E. Coppard
lp Peter Firth; Penelope Wilton; Clare Sutcliffe; Gillian Martell; Queenie Watts; Trevor Bannister
CRIPPLED BLOOM 10/9/1972
d Barry Davis; *sc* Jeremy Paul;
auth A.E. Coppard
lp Joss Ackland; Pauline Collins; Anna Cropper; George Waring; Meg Johnson
The WATERCRESS GIRL 17/9/1972
d Barry Davis; *sc* Hugh Leonard;
auth A.E. Coppard
lp Susan Fleetwood; Gareth Thomas; John Welsh
BREEZE ANSTEY 24/9/1972
d Peter Wood; *sc* Hugh Whitemore;
auth H.E. Bates
lp Morag Hood; Meg Wynn Owen; Joan Newell; Tenniel Evans; Rachel Kempson; Bernard Archard
The LITTLE FARM 28/1/1973
d Silvio Narizzano; *sc* Hugh Leonard;
auth H.E. Bates
lp Bryan Marshall; Barbara Ewing; Michael Elphick
The BLACK DOG 4/2/1973
d John MacKenzie; *adapt* James Saunders;
auth A.E. Coppard
lp Jane Lapotaire; Stephen Chase; Glyn Houston; June Watson; Dorothy Black; Edward Peel; Fred Feast
The HIGGLER 11/2/1973
d Richard Martin; *sc* Hugh Leonard;
auth A.E. Coppard
lp Keith Drinkel; Mary Wimbush; Rosalie Crutchley; Jane Carr; Sheila Ruskin
The SIMPLE LIFE 18/2/1973
d Silvio Narizzano; *sc* Hugh Whitemore;
auth H.E. Bates
lp Maggie Fitzgibbon; Robert Urquhart; Peter Firth
An ASPIDISTRA IN BABYLON 25/2/1973
d Richard Everitt; *sc* Jeremy Paul;
auth H.E. Bates
lp Carolyn Courage; Jeremy Brett; Agnes Laughlan; Renee Asherson; Mary Healey
The RING OF TRUTH 4/3/1973
d Donald McWhinnie; *sc* Julian Mitchell;
auth H.E. Bates
lp Prunella Scales; Nicholas Hoye; Ray Mort
The FOUR BEAUTIES 11/3/1973
d Donald McWhinnie; *sc* Hugh Leonard;
auth H.E. Bates
lp Zena Walker; Michael Kitchen

A COURIS THING (BBC 31/3/1968)
The work being done to preserve English windmills, and a record of a windmill working.
p/sc Malcolm Freegard

CRACKERJACK (BBC 1955–84)
Variety show series for children with resident presenters and special guests, consisting of comic sketches and competitions with prizes.
CRACKERJACK 19/3/1958
p Johnny Downes;
sc David Whittaker, Ronnie Corbett, Michael Darbyshire; *pres* Eamonn Andrews;
with Ronnie Corbett, Winifred Atwell, Michael Darbyshire

CRADLE OF ENGLAND
(BBC 18/7–22/8/1972)
A series of six programmes giving a view of man and his expanding society as seen in the archaeological landscape of the south of England.
p Hugh Pitt; *pres* Barry Cunliffe
ORDER OUT OF CHAOS 18/7/1972
Pre-Roman society and monuments, including Avebury and Stonehenge.
The AGE OF AFFLUENCE 15/8/1972
Roman civilisation and prosperity.

The CRAFTSMEN (Anglia 1969)
Craft series.
The SLATER 4/9/1969
The THATCHER 11/9/1969

CRAFTSMEN (BBC 7/1–4/3/1971)
A series of nine films which demonstrates craftsmanship.
p John Read
DAVID COLEMAN, CABINETMAKER 14/1/1971
Making reproduction antique furniture in a workshop in Stebbing, Essex.
IMAGES IN GLASS 21/1/1971
Making of Caithness glass at a factory in Wick.

CRANE (Rediffusion 1963–65)
Adventure series featuring the activities of a Moroccan-based smuggler.
regulars Patrick Allen; Sam Kydd; Gerald Flood; Laya Raki
The CANNABI SYNDICATE 16/4/1963
d Richard Doubleday; *p* Jordan Lawrence;
sc Ludovic Peters
lp Peter Reynolds; Bruce Montague; Derek Benfield; David Graham
A CARGO OF CORNFLOUR 4/1/1965
d Ian Fordyce; *p* Jordan Lawrence;
sc Denis Butler
lp David Nettheim; Terence Soall; Leonard Trolley; Peter Bowles; Edina Ronay; John Hollis

The CRAZY GANG'S PARTY
(Rediffusion 23/12/1957)
Comedy-variety special, originally billed under 'Jack Hylton presents'.
d Michael Westmore; *with* The Crazy Gang (Bud Flanagan, Jimmy Nervo, Teddy Knox, Charlie Naughton, Jimmy Gold, Eddie Gray), Peter Glaze, Alfred Marks, Chesney Allen, Arthur Askey

CREDO (LWT 1978–84)
Religious series.
TOMAS O'FIAICH, ARCHBISHOP OF ARMAGH AND ROMAN CATHOLIC PRIMATE OF ALL IRELAND 18/3/1979
Report from Armagh on the man expected to be made cardinal.
d Michael Snow; *p* Michael Braham

CRICKET WITH TREVOR BAILEY
(Rediffusion 1956)
LEG BREAKS AND OFF BREAKS 4/6/1956
Trevor Bailey coaches young cricketers.

CRIME (BBC 1960)
Documentary series of six programmes examining the prevalence of crime in Britain.
p Derek Holroyde; *pres* Christopher Mayhew
WHO GETS HURT? 26/7/1960
The reasons that lead men to break the law, and the ways in which they are dealt with under the British penal system.
BAD CHARACTERS 2/8/1960
An enquiry into criminals and what leads them to break the law.

INSIDE 9/8/1960
The life of prisoners inside Dartmoor prison and Armley gaol, Leeds.
STEPS TOWARDS FREEDOM 16/8/1960
The attitude of prison staff and prisoners towards rehabilitation. Filmed at Leyhill Open Prison and the training prison at Wakefield.
CAUGHT YOUNG 23/8/1960
Christopher Mayhew investigates why some juvenile offenders continue with a life of crime despite frequent periods in detention.
OUTSIDE 30/8/1960
The way ex-prisoners are treated, with Barbara Wootton, Dr Terence Morris, Professor W.J.H. Sprott and Merfyn Turner.

CRIME AND PUNISHMENT (BBC 1979)
Three-part adaptation of the novel by Fyodor Dostoyevsky.
d Michael Darlow; *p* Jonathan Powell;
sc Jack Pulman
regulars John Hurt; Siân Phillips; Frank Middlemass; Beatrix Lehmann; Timothy West
PART 1 22/5/1979
lp Simon Rouse; Tom Wilkinson; Olwen Griffiths; Anne Orwin
PART 2 29/5/1979
lp Anthony Bate; David Troughton; Carinthia West
PART 3 5/6/1979
lp Anthony Bate; Colin Higgins; Gordon Gostelow

The CRIME OF THE CENTURY
(BBC 1/12/1956–5/1/1957)
Six-part thriller serial set in London.
EPISODE 1: DEATH OF A CANARY 1/12/1956
p Andrew Osborn; *sc* Michael Gilbert
lp Edward Chapman; William Lucas; Gene Anderson; Brian Peck

CRIME SQUAD (ATV 10/4/1973)
The work of the Birmingham-based No.4 Regional Crime Squad.
p/sc David C. Rea; *nar* Peter Williams

CRISIS AT 'THE OBSERVER'
(BBC 13/10/1975)
A day-by-day account of the crisis facing 'The Observer' newspaper threatened with closure.
p/sc Elwyn Parry-Jones

CRISIS ON WHEELS (ATV 29/6/1966)
Documentary in a blend of styles which puts the case against the motor car and its domination of modern life.
d Kevin Brownlow; *p/sc* Stuart Hood
nar Derek Hart

CRISS CROSS QUIZ (Granada 1957–67)
Quiz game based on noughts-and-crosses.
CRISS CROSS QUIZ 1/10/1960
d Les Chatfield; *pres* Barbara Kelly
CRISS CROSS QUIZ 1967
pres Jeremy Hawk

CROSSROADS (ATV 1964–88)
Soap opera set in a motel in the West Midlands.
CROSSROADS 5/12/1968
d Rollo Gamble; *p* Reg Watson;
sc Mark Haywood
lp Noele Gordon; Ronald Allen
CROSSROADS 10/6/1969
d Rollo Gamble; *p* Reg Watson;
sc Ray Mansell
lp Noele Gordon; Susan Hanson; William Avenell; Jacqueline Holborough
CROSSROADS 3/4/1975
d Sid Kilby; *p* Jack Barton;
sc Peter Ling, Joan Paget, Michala Crees, Malcolm Hulke
lp Noele Gordon; Ronald Allen; John Bentley; Roger Tonge; Edward Clayton; Jane Rossington; Jack Woolgar; Ann George; David Fennell; Susan Hanson

CROWD OF THE DAY (BBC 19/8/1975)
14 June 1975: Australia play the West Indians at cricket. Film of crowd's reactions and preparations for the game, including scenes of a ticketless fan outside the Oval trying various methods to break into the ground.
p Michael Blakey

CROWN COURT (Granada 1972–84)
Daytime courtroom drama series in which the outcome is decided by a jury picked from the public.
The JU-JU LANDLORD: EPISODE 1 3/3/1976
d Steve Butcher; *p* Dennis Woolf;
sc Buchi Emecheta
lp Alan Rowe; Thomas Baptiste;
Suzanne Stone; Louis Mahoney;
Freddie Fletcher
The JU-JU LANDLORD: EPISODE 2 4/3/1976
d Steve Butcher; *p* Dennis Woolf;
sc Buchi Emecheta
lp as above
The JU-JU LANDLORD: EPISODE 3 5/3/1976
d Steve Butcher; *p* Dennis Woolf;
sc Buchi Emecheta
lp as above
LOLA: EPISODE 1 8/12/1976
d Colin Bucksey; *p* Dennis Woolf;
sc David Yallop
lp Judy Parfitt; Ben Kingsley;
Philip Sayer; Nicholas Ball; John Leyton;
Colette O'Neill
LOLA: EPISODE 2 9/12/1976
d Colin Bucksey; *p* Dennis Woolf;
sc David Yallop
lp as above
LOLA: EPISODE 3 10/12/1976
d Colin Bucksey; *p* Dennis Woolf;
sc David Yallop
lp as above

CROWN MATRIMONIAL
(LWT 22/12/1974)
Dramatic presentation of the events surrounding the abdication of King Edward VIII in 1936.
d Alan Bridges;
sc Royce Ryton, Audrey Maas;
auth Royce Ryton
lp Greer Garson; Peter Barkworth;
Maxine Audley; Brian Wilde; Amanda Reiss;
Andrew Ray

The CRUCIFIXION
(Rediffusion 27/3/1959)
Crucifixion and resurrection story as seen in pictures and sculptures on altars in Austrian village churches.
p Cecil Lewis

CUBA...SI! (Granada 29/9–20/10/1961)
Four-part documentary series on Cuba.
d James Hill; *p* Tim Hewat;
nar Bill Grundy
PART 1 29/9/1961
The story of Cuba from Columbus to Castro.
PART 3 13/10/1961
One of Havana's cigar-makers tells the story of his city.
PART 4 20/10/1961
Cuba in 1961 and what impact its revolution will have on the rest of the world.

CUBA – THE MISSILE CRISIS
(US NBC 26/5/1964)
The role of President J.F. Kennedy in the Cuban missile crisis of October 1962 recalled by McGeorge Bundy and Theodore Sorenson, two of his closest advisers.
d Fred Freed

CUIR CAR (Grampian 1977–80)
Gaelic series for children.
CUIR CAR 30/4/1977

CULLODEN (BBC 15/12/1964)
A documentary reconstruction of the Battle of Culloden in 1746, the last battle to be fought on British soil, and its aftermath.
d/p/sc Peter Watkins
lp George McBean; Alan Pope

CURRY AND CHIPS
(LWT 21/11–26/12/1969)
Sitcom with a controversial background, featuring an immigrant Pakistani worker and a liberal-minded factory foreman.
CURRY AND CHIPS 21/11/1969
d/p Keith Beckett; *sc* Johnny Speight
lp Eric Sykes; Spike Milligan;
Norman Rossington; Kenny Lynch;
Geoffrey Hughes

CUT AND THRUST
(BBC 7/1–25/2/1973)
Eight-part series on fencing.
The FIGHT BUSINESS 21/1/1973
d John Rickword; *p* John Dobson;
pres David Vine

CYCLING HOLIDAY (BBC 31/7/1956)
A play for children.
p Joy Harington; *sc* Henry Treece
lp Freda Bamford; Danny Hayes;
Patrick Troughton; Donald Morley;
Joseph Chelton

The CYRIL FLETCHER SHOW
(Jack Hylton TV Productions 9/4–14/5/1959)
Six music-and-comedy shows featuring comedian Cyril Fletcher.
The CYRIL FLETCHER SHOW 9/4/1959
d Milo Lewis; *sc* Johnny Speight
with Cyril Fletcher, Betty Astell,
Pat Coombs, Ian Francis, Ian Wilson

D

DADDY KISS IT BETTER
(Yorkshire TV 29/7/1968)
Drama observing the petty wrangling of domestic life.
d Christopher Hodson; *exec.p* Peter Willes;
sc Peter Nichols
lp Michael Craig; Dilys Laye; Percy Herbert;
Hilda Braid; Jane Bolton; Pauline Challoner

DAD'S ARMY (BBC 1968–77)
Sitcom about the Home Guard in a small seaside town during World War II.
p David Croft
sc Jimmy Perry, David Croft
regulars Arthur Lowe; John Le Mesurier;
Clive Dunn; John Laurie; James Beck;
Arnold Ridley; Ian Lavender; Frank Williams;
Bill Pertwee; Edward Sinclair
SOMETHING NASTY IN THE VAULT 9/10/1969
lp Janet Davies; Robert Dorning;
Norman Mitchell
The DAY THE BALLOON WENT UP 30/10/1969
lp Nan Braunton; Jennifer Browne;
Andrew Carr; Therese McMurray;
Kenneth Watson; Harold Bennett; Jack Haig
NO SPRING FOR FRAZER 4/12/1969
lp Harold Bennett; Joan Cooper;
Ronnie Brandon
PUT THAT LIGHT OUT 6/11/1970
lp Avril Angers; Stuart Sherwin; Gordon Peters
The TWO AND A HALF FEATHERS 13/11/1970
lp John Cater; Queenie Watts; Linda James;
Gilda Perry; John Ash; Parnell McGarry;
Wendy Richard
The TEST 27/11/1970
lp Don Estelle; Harold Bennett;
Freddie Trueman
UNWANTED GUESTS 11/12/1970
lp Rose Hill; Don Estelle
The FALLEN IDOL 18/12/1970
lp Geoffrey Lumsden; Rex Garner;
Michael Knowles; Anthony Sagar;
Tom Mennard; Robert Raglan
BATTLE OF THE GIANTS 27/12/1971
lp Geoffrey Lumsden; Robert Raglan;
Charles Hill; Colin Bean
TIME ON MY HANDS 29/12/1972
lp Harold Bennett; Colin Bean; Joan Cooper;
Eric Longworth; Christopher Sandford
The DEADLY ATTACHMENT 31/10/1973
lp Philip Madoc; Robert Raglan; Colin Bean

DAFT AS A BRUSH (BBC 24/9/1975)
A love story set in Yorkshire.
d Stephen Frears; *p* Graeme McDonald;
sc Adrian Mitchell
lp Lynn Redgrave; Jonathan Pryce;
David Daker; Betsy Blair; Celia Hewitt;
Harry Markham

DAISY, DAISY (Granada 23/1–12/5/1978)
Puppet series for children featuring the characters Wriggle and Splodge.
BRUSHES 23/1/1978
d Pat Baker; *p* Stephen Clarke;
sc Barry Hill, Anne Mountfield;
pres Alan Rothwell, Jan Harvey

The DALE THAT DIED
(Trident Television 21/10/1975)
The story of Joe Gibson, the last remaining farmer living and working in Grisedale, Yorkshire.
d Barry Cockcroft; *exec.p* John Fairley;
rep Paul Dunstan

DAME EDITH SITWELL (BBC 16/9/1959)
A sequence of poems chosen from a recital given by Dame Edith Sitwell at the Edinburgh Festival, 1959.

The DAME OF SARK (Anglia 29/12/1976)
Dramatisation of the fight for survival by the Dame of Sark during the German occupation of the Channel Islands in World War II.
d Alvin Rakoff; *p* John Jacobs;
adapt David Butler; *auth* William Douglas-Home
lp Celia Johnson; Peter Dyneley; Tony Britton;
Natalie Caron; Simon Cadell; John Quentin

The DANCING PRINCESSES
(BBC 17/12/1978)
Musical based on a story by the Brothers Grimm.
d Ben Rea; *p* David Turnbull;
sc John Tully
lp Joseph O'Connor; Angus Lennie;
Christopher Biggins; Bosco Hogan;
Rosalie Crutchley

DANGER MAN (ITC 1960–61; 1964–69)
Secret agent adventure series featuring Patrick McGoohan as NATO troubleshooter John Drake.
p Ralph Smart (1960–61);
Aida Young (1964–65); Sidney Cole (1964–69)
VIEW FROM THE VILLA 11/9/1960
d Terry Bishop;
sc Brian Clemens, Ralph Smart
lp Barbara Shelley; Delphi Lawrence; John Lee;
Colin Douglas; Philip Latham
TIME TO KILL 18/9/1960
d Ralph Smart;
sc Ian Stuart Black, Brian Clemens;
auth Brian Clemens
lp Sarah Lawson; Lionel Murton;
Derren Nesbitt; Carl Jaffe; Louise Collins
JOSETTA 25/9/1960
d Michael Truman; *sc* Ralph Smart
lp Kenneth Haigh; Julia Arnall;
Campbell Singer; Randall Kinkead
The BLUE VEIL 2/10/1960
d Charles Frend;
sc Don Ingalls, Ralph Smart
lp Laurence Naismith; Lisa Gastoni;
Ferdy Mayne; Joseph Cuby; Peter Thornton
The LOVERS 9/10/1960
d Peter Graham Scott;
sc Jo Eisinger, Doreen Montgomery
lp Maxine Audley; Michael Ripper;
Ewen Solon; Carl Bernard; Hermione Gregory
The GIRL IN PINK PYJAMAS 16/10/1960
d Peter Graham Scott;
sc Ian Stuart Black, Ralph Smart;
auth Brian Clemens
lp Angela Browne; John Crawford;
Alan Tilvern; Robert Raglan; Richard Warner
POSITION OF TRUST 23/10/1960
d Ralph Smart; *sc* Jo Eisinger;
auth Ralph Smart
lp Donald Pleasence; Lois Maxwell;
John Phillips; Irene Prador; Martin Benson

The LONELY CHAIR 30/10/1960
d Charles Frend;
sc John Roddick, Ralph Smart
lp Hazel Court; Sam Wanamaker;
Richard Wattis; Patrick Troughton;
Howard Pays
The SANCTUARY 6/11/1960
d Charles Frend;
sc John Roddick, Ralph Smart
lp Kieron Moore; Wendy Williams;
Barry Keegan; Charles Farrell; Shay Gorman
An AFFAIR OF STATE 13/11/1960
d Peter Graham Scott; *sc* Oscar Brodny
lp Patrick Wymark; John Le Mesurier;
Dorothy White; Warren Mitchell;
Fenella Fielding
The KEY 20/11/1960
d Seth Holt; *sc* Jack Whittingham;
auth Ralph Smart
lp Robert Flemyng; Monique Ahrens;
Charles Carson; Charles Gray
The SISTERS 27/11/1960
d Seth Holt; *sc* Jo Eisinger;
auth Brian Clemens
lp Mai Zetterling; Barbara Murray;
Richard Wattis; Sydney Tafler;
Anthony Dawson
The PRISONER 4/12/1960
d Terry Bishop;
sc Ralph Smart, Robert Stewart
lp William Sylvester; June Thorburn;
William Lucas; Michael Peake
COLONEL RODRIGUEZ 18/12/1960
d Julian Amyes; *sc* Ralph Smart
lp Noel Willman; Maxine Audley;
Honor Blackman; Ronald Allen;
Campbell Singer
The NURSE 25/12/1960
d Peter Graham Scott;
sc Ralph Smart, Brian Clemens
lp Ellen Moore; Jack MacGowran;
Eric Pohlmann; Robert Ayres; Heather Chasen
The ISLAND 1/1/1961
d C.M. Pennington-Richards;
sc Brian Clemens, Ralph Smart
lp Allan Cuthbertson; Peter Stephens;
Ann Firbank; Michael Ripper; Ronan O'Casey
FIND AND RETURN 8/1/1961
d Seth Holt; *sc* Jo Eisinger
lp Moira Lister; Donald Pleasence;
Richard Wattis; Paul Stassino; Zena Marshall
The GIRL WHO LIKED GI'S 15/1/1961
d Michael Truman; *sc* Marc Brandel
lp Anna Gaylor; Anthony Bushell; Paul Maxwell
NAME, DATE AND PLACE 22/1/1961
d Charles Frend;
sc Ralph Smart, John Roddick
lp Cyril Raymond; Richard Wattis;
Kathleen Byron; Jean Marsh
VACATION 29/1/1961
d Patrick McGoohan; *sc* Ralph Smart
lp Jacqueline Ellis; Barrie Ingham;
Lawrence Davidson; John Wynyard
The CONSPIRATORS 5/2/1961
d Michael Truman;
sc Ralph Smart, John Roddick
lp Patricia Driscoll; Terence Longdon;
Hugh Moxey; Alfred Burke
The HONEYMOONERS 12/2/1961
d Charles Frend;
sc Ralph Smart, Lewis Davidson
lp Ronald Allen; Sally Bazely;
Michael Peake; Kerrigan Prescott
The GALLOWS TREE 19/2/1961
d Michael Truman;
sc Ralph Smart, Marc Brandel
lp Wendy Craig; Paul Rogers;
Raymond Huntley; Ewan Roberts;
Andrew Crawford
The RELAXED INFORMER 26/2/1961
d Anthony Bushell;
sc Ralph Smart, Robert Stewart
lp Duncan Lamont; Moira Redmond;
Paul Maxwell; Brian Rawlinson;
Stanley Van Beers
The BROTHERS 5/3/1961
d Charles Frend; *sc* Ralph Smart
lp Lisa Gastoni; George Coulouris;
Ronald Fraser; Derren Nesbitt; John Woodvine

The JOURNEY ENDS HALFWAY 12/3/1961
d Clive Donner; *sc* Ian Stuart Black
lp Paul Daneman; Willoughby Goddard;
Anna May Wong; Paul Hardtmuth
BURY THE DEAD 19/3/1961
d Clive Donner; *sc* Ralph Smart;
auth Brian Clemens
lp Beverly Garland; Dermot Walsh;
Paul Stassino; Patrick Troughton; Robert Shaw
SABOTAGE 26/3/1961
d Peter Graham Scott;
sc Michael Pertwee, Ian Stuart Black
lp Maggie Fitzgibbon; Yvonne Romain;
Oliver Burt; Alex Scott
The LEAK 9/4/1961
d Anthony Bushell;
sc Ralph Smart, Brian Clemens
lp Zena Marshall; Bernard Archard;
Marne Maitland; Joseph Cuby; Eric Pohlmann
The TRAP 16/4/1961
d C.M. Pennington-Richards;
sc Ralph Smart, John Roddick
lp Jeanne Moody; Noel Trevarthen;
Maria Burke; Alan Gifford; Louise Collins
The ACTOR 23/4/1961
d Michael Truman; *sc* Marc Brandel
lp Rupert Davies; Gary Cockrell;
Julie Allan; Patsy Rowlands; Burt Kwouk
HIRED ASSASSIN 30/4/1961
d Charles Frend;
sc Ralph Smart, John Roddick
lp Alan Wheatley; Cyril Shaps;
Frank Thornton; Judy Carne
The COYANNIS STORY 7/5/1961
d Peter Graham Scott; *sc* Jo Eisinger
lp John Phillips; Charles Gray;
Heather Chasen; Liam Gaffney; Peter Welch
FIND AND DESTROY 14/5/1961
d Charles Frend;
sc Ralph Smart, John Roddick
lp Peter Arne; Nadja Regin; Peter Sallis;
Helen Horton; Ronald Leigh-Hunt; Alec Mango
UNDER THE LAKE 21/5/1961
d Seth Holt; *sc* Jack Whittingham
lp Christopher Rhodes; Hermione Baddeley;
Moira Redmond; Lionel Murton;
Roger Delgado; Walter Gotell
DEAD MAN WALKS 28/5/1961
d Charles Frend;
sc Ralph Smart, Brian Clemens
lp Richard Wattis; Marla Landi;
Julia Arnall; Richard Pearson; Michael Ripper
DEADLINE 4/6/1961
d Peter Graham Scott; *sc* Jo Eisinger;
auth Ian Stuart Black
lp William Marshall; Edric Connor;
Barbara Chilcott; Christopher Carlos;
Earl Cameron; Lionel Ngakane
YESTERDAY'S ENEMIES 10/10/1964
d Charles Crichton; *sc* Donald Jonson
lp Maureen Connell; Joan Hickson;
Howard Marion-Crawford; Anton Rodgers;
The PROFESSIONALS 17/10/1964
d Michael Truman;
sc Wilfred Greatorex, Louis Marks
lp Helen Cherry; Nadja Regin; Alex Scott;
John Welsh; Noel Johnson; Jerry Stovin
The GALLOPING MAJOR 31/10/1964
d Peter Maxwell; *sc* David Stone
lp William Marshall; Errol John;
Earl Cameron; Edric Connor; Arnold Diamond;
Jill Melford
FAIR EXCHANGE 7/11/1964
d Charles Crichton;
sc Wilfred Greatorex, Marc Brandel
lp Lelia Goldoni; James Maxwell;
Raymond Adamson
FISH ON THE HOOK 14/11/1964
d Robert Day;
sc John Roddick, Michael Pertwee
lp Dawn Addams; Zena Marshall;
Terence Longdon; Martin Miller; Peter Bowles;
Vladek Sheybal
A DATE WITH DORIS 12/12/1964
d Quentin Lawrence; *sc* Philip Broadley
lp James Maxwell; Ronald Radd
DON'T NAIL HIM YET 19/12/1964
d Michael Truman; *sc* Philip Broadley
lp Sheila Allen; John Fraser; Wendy Richard

THAT'S TWO OF US SORRY 16/1/1965
d Quentin Lawrence; *sc* Jan Read
lp Francesca Annis; Finlay Currie;
Nigel Green; Duncan Lamont
SUCH MEN ARE DANGEROUS 23/1/1965
d Don Chaffey; *sc* Ralph Smart
lp Jack MacGowran; Zia Mohyeddin;
Jack Gwillim; John Cairney; Alan Wheatley
WHATEVER HAPPENED TO GEORGE FOSTER?
30/1/1965
d Don Chaffey; *sc* David Stone
lp Jill Melford; Joyce Carey;
Colin Douglas; Adrienne Corri; Bernard Lee;
Patsy Smart
A ROOM IN THE BASEMENT 6/2/1965
d Don Chaffey; *sc* Ralph Smart
lp William Lucas; Michael Gwynn;
Jane Merrow
The AFFAIR AT CASTELVARA 13/2/65
d Quentin Lawrence; *sc* James Foster
lp Sonia Fox; Eric Pohlmann;
Harold Goldblatt; Martin Benson; André Morell
The MIRROR'S NEW 6/3/1965
d Michael Truman; *sc* Philip Broadley
lp Donald Houston; David Hutcheson;
Wanda Ventham; Nicola Pagett
The BLACK BOOK 26/9/1965
d Michael Truman; *sc* Philip Broadley
lp Georgina Ward; Griffith Jones;
Jack Gwillim; Patricia Haines; Mike Pratt
STING IN THE TAIL 10/10/1965
d Peter Yates; *sc* Philip Broadley
lp Ronald Radd; Derren Nesbitt;
John Standing; Jeanne Roland
ENGLISH LADY TAKES LODGERS 17/10/1965
d Michael Truman; *sc* David Stone
lp Gabriella Licudi; Robert Urquhart;
Howard Marion-Crawford; Frederick Bartman
The MERCENARIES 31/10/1965
d Don Chaffey; *sc* Ralph Smart
lp Patricia Donahue; John Slater;
Percy Herbert; Peter Arne; Frederick Peisley;
Jack Gwillim
ARE YOU GOING TO BE MORE PERMANENT?
5/12/1965
d Don Chaffey; *sc* Philip Broadley
lp Susan Hampshire; Maxwell Shaw;
Howard Goorney
MAN ON THE BEACH 19/12/1965
d Peter Yates; *sc* Philip Broadley
lp Barbara Steele; Glyn Houston;
David Hutcheson; Peter Hughes; Clifton Jones
SAY IT WITH FLOWERS 2/1/1966
d Peter Yates;
sc Ralph Smart, Jacques Gillis
lp Ian Hendry; John Phillips; Jemma Hyde;
Gretchen Franklin
The MAN WHO WOULDN'T TALK 9/1/1966
d Michael Truman;
sc Ralph Smart, Donald Jonson
lp Jane Merrow; Norman Rodway;
Ralph Michael; Brian Worth; Mike Pratt;
Roy Marsden
SOMEONE IS LIABLE TO GET HURT 16/1/1966
d Michael Truman;
sc Philip Broadley, Ralph Smart
lp Maurice Denham; Zia Mohyeddin;
Geraldine Moffatt; Earl Cameron
DANGEROUS SECRET 23/1/1966
d Stuart Burge;
sc Ralph Smart, Donald Jonson
lp Derek Francis; John Brooking
I CAN ONLY OFFER YOU SHERRY 30/1/1966
d George Pollock; *sc* Ralph Smart
lp Wendy Craig; Warren Mitchell;
Anthony Newlands; Bernard Archard;
Henry Gilbert
The HUNTING PARTY 6/2/1966
d Pat Jackson; *sc* Philip Broadley
lp Moira Lister; Denholm Elliott;
Edward Underdown; John Welsh; Alan White
TWO BIRDS WITH ONE BULLET 13/2/1966
d Peter Yates; *sc* Pat Silver
lp Geoffrey Keen; Lelia Goldoni;
Paul Curran; Richard O'Sullivan
I AM AFRAID YOU HAVE THE WRONG NUMBER
13/3/1966
d George Pollock; *sc* Ralph Smart
lp Paul Eddington; Jeanne Moody;
Vincent Harding

DANGER MAN *cont.*

The MAN WITH THE FOOT 20/3/1966
d Jeremy Summers; *sc* Raymond Bowers
lp Bernard Lee; Robert Urquhart;
Paul Curran; Isobel Black; Hugh McDermott
PAPER CHASE 27/3/1966
d Patrick McGoohan;
sc Philip Broadley, Ralph Smart
lp Joan Greenwood; Kenneth J. Warren;
Aubrey Morris; Ferdy Mayne; Sandor Eles
NOT SO JOLLY ROGER 3/4/1966
d Don Chaffey; *sc* Tony Williamson
lp Edwin Richfield; Wilfred Lawson;
Lisa Daniely; Patsy Ann Noble
SHINDA SHIMA 26/2/1967
d Peter Yates; *sc* Norman Hudis
lp Yoko Tani; Kenneth Griffith;
George Coulouris; Maxine Audley;
David Toguri

**The DANGEROUS DAYS OF KIOWA
JONES** (US Youngstein and Karr Productions
25/12/1966)
Made-for-TV Western; originally made for
American television as pilot for unsold series.
d Alex March;
p Max E. Youngstein, David Karr;
sc Frank Fenton, Robert E. Thompson;
auth Clifton Adams
lp Robert Horton; Diane Baker; Sal Mineo;
Nehemiah Persoff; Gary Merrill; Zalman King;
Harry Dean Stanton

The DARK LADY OF THE SONNETS
(BBC 2/10/1955)
Adaptation of the play by George Bernard Shaw
set in 1600 in which William Shakespeare meets
Queen Elizabeth I.
p Douglas Allen
lp Alan MacNaughtan; Beatrix Lehmann;
Barbara Murray; George Woodbridge

DATELINE (ITN 1965–66)
News and current affairs series.
RHODESIA – IAN SMITH AND THE PRESS
18/11/1965
At a press conference in Salisbury, Ian Smith
answers questions on Rhodesia's Unilateral
Declaration of Independence.

DATELINE SCOTLAND (Scottish TV)
Local current affairs series.
GLASGOW POLICE 1965

The DAWSON PATROL
(CA CBC 30/12/1978)
Film, based on a true incident. Four Mounties
set out in the winter of 1910 to establish a new
record of 20 days to travel the 500 miles to the
Yukon town of Dawson.
d/exec.p Peter Kelly; *sc* George R. Robertson;
nar Leslie Nielsen
lp Peter Henry; Neil Dianard;
James B. Douglas; George R. Robertson

The DAY BEFORE YESTERDAY
(Thames 1970)
Six-part documentary series examining Britain
during the years 1945–1963.
p Phillip Whitehead; *sc/nar* Robert Kee
WE ARE THE MASTERS 1/9/1970
Britain under the Labour Government of
1945–51.
REALITIES OF POWER 8/9/1970
The problems of the post-war world faced by
Britain's Foreign Secretary Ernest Bevin in 1945.
SET THE PEOPLE FREE 15/9/1970
The events of Winston Churchill's premiership,
1951–55.
A POLITICAL TRAGEDY 22/9/1970
The career of Anthony Eden and his resignation
after the Suez crisis.
FIGHT AND FIGHT AGAIN 29/9/1970
The struggle in the 1950's between the Gaitskell
and Bevanite factions of the Labour Party, and
the emergence of Harold Wilson.
The RISE AND FALL OF SUPERMAC 6/10/1970
The career of Harold Macmillan.

DAY BY DAY (Southern TV 1963–81)
Local magazine programme series.
PREVIEW AND THE OPENING OF BROADLANDS
15/5/1979
21 YEARS 28/12/1979

A DAY OUT (BBC 24/12/1972)
A group of men and youths of a cycling club
leave the soot and smoke of Halifax one summer
Sunday in 1911. Partly set at Fountains Abbey.
d Stephen Frears; *p* Innes Lloyd;
sc Alan Bennett
lp David Waller; James Cossins;
John Normington; Philip Locke; David Hill;
Brian Glover; Paul Shane

The DAY WAR BROKE OUT
(Thames 15/7/1975)
Entertainment during World War II, with
reminiscences from Bing Crosby, George Elrick,
Bill Fraser, Margaret Lockwood, Vera Lynn,
Richard Murdoch, Victor Sylvester, Tommy
Trinder and Jack Warner.
d/p/sc John Robins

DAYS OF HOPE (BBC 1975)
A drama series of four films about life from the
Great War to the General Strike of 1926.
d Ken Loach; *p* Tony Garnett;
sc Jim Allen
1916: JOINING UP 11/9/1975
lp Paul Copley; Pamela Brighton;
Nikolas Simmonds; Helen Beck;
Clifford Kershaw; Peter Russell; Fred Feast
1921 18/9/1975
lp Paul Copley; Gary Roberts;
Jean Spence; Christine Anderson;
Robert Bradley
1924 25/9/1975
lp Paul Copley; Pamela Brighton;
Nikolas Simmonds; Brian Hawksley; Bert King;
Patrick Barr; Peter Kerrigan
1926: GENERAL STRIKE 2/10/1975
lp Paul Copley; Pamela Brighton;
Nikolas Simmonds; Russell Waters; Neil Seiler;
Brian Harrison; Dai C. Davies

DE GAULLE – THE FREE FRENCHMAN
(BBC 10/11/1972)
A portrait of Charles de Gaulle.
d Michel Droit

The DEAD END LADS (ATV 10/8/1972)
Youth unemployment in Britain.
d/p John Goldschmidt; *nar* Ashley Bruce

DEAR OCTOPUS
(Yorkshire TV 26/12/1972)
Dodie Smith's play in which four generations of
a family meet to celebrate a golden wedding.
d Joan Kemp-Welch; *p* Peter Willes
lp Peter Barkworth; Lally Bowers;
Hannah Gordon; Cyril Luckham;
Nora Swinburne; Anna Massey

DEATH BY MISADVENTURE?
(Granada 14–28/11/1967)
Three-part documentary series on disasters.
AIRSHIP R.101 21/11/1967
The circumstances surrounding the R101 airship
disaster on October 4th 1930. Interviews with
eyewitnesses and relatives of the victims.
d Michael Cox; *exec.p* Mike Wooller;
nar Frank Ducan; *reader* Cyril Shaps

The DEATH OF ADOLF HITLER
(LWT 7/1/1973)
Play that records the last ten days of Hitler's life.
d/p Rex Firkin; *sc* Vincent Tilsley;
nar David De Keyser
lp Frank Finlay; Caroline Mortimer;
Michael Sheard; Ed Devereaux; Oscar Quitak;
Robert Cawdron; Tony Steedman

DEATH OR GLORY BOY
(Yorkshire TV 10–24/3/1974)
Trilogy of plays about a grammar school boy
joining the army.

EARLY BREAKFAST 24/3/1974
d Marc Miller; *exec.p* Peter Willes;
sc Charles Wood
lp Robert Coleby; Christopher Blake;
David Dixon; Jon Glover; Graham Seed

DECISION (Rediffusion 1963)
Discussion series.
HAROLD WILSON 16/7/1963
A number of politicians and political
commentators give their views on Harold Wilson
at the time of his election to the leadership of the
Labour Party.
d Michael Westmore; *intro* Quentin Crewe

DECISION (Granada 27/1–10/2/1976)
Three films that show how a nationalised
industry, a local council and a giant oil company
come to their decisions.
STEEL – THE KORF CONTRACT 27/1/1976
A detailed study of how the British Steel
Corporation decided whether to purchase two
German-made plants for the production of iron
in pellet form.
d/p Roger Graef; *pres* Mike Scott

DECISION: BRITISH COMMUNISM
(Granada 1978)
Three-part study of the British Communist Party
and democracy.
d/p Roger Graef
LIBERTY 25/7/1978
The split between the leadership and hard-liners
in the Party who believe the new
Eurocommunist line is a betrayal of Marxist
principles.
EQUALITY 1/8/1978
Back stage meetings and corridor discussions
during the Party's 1977 Congress.
FRATERNITY 8/8/1978
The Party's relations with the Soviet Union.

The DEEP CONCERN (BBC 7/6–12/7/1979)
A six-part thriller.
p David Rose; *sc* Elwyn Jones
regulars Bernard Lloyd; Yolande Bavan;
Ronald Hines; Beth Porter; Tim Preece;
Neil Cunningham; Katharine Schofield;
Hilary Mason; Sebastian Abineri
EPISODE 1: ARRIVALS AND DEPARTURES
7/6/1979
d Richard Callanan
EPISODE 2: RETURN AND DESPATCH 14/6/1979
d Richard Callanan
lp Allan Lander
EPISODE 3: BURIALS AND TRAPPINGS
21/6/1979
d Jonathan Alwyn
lp Allan Lander; Geoff Hannan;
John Crocker
EPISODE 4: EXPOSURE AND EXPLOSION
28/6/1979
d Jonathan Alwyn
lp Allan Lander; John Crocker
EPISODE 5: CANVAS AND CONTAINERS
5/7/1979
d Richard Callanan
lp Michael Troughton; Diana Weston;
Michael Harbour

DEEP SOUTH (Granada 21/1/1969)
An analysis of the problems faced by black
people in the Mississippi delta.
d/p Michael Grigsby

DEFEAT IN THE WEST
(Rediffusion 29/5/1963)
An examination of the reasons for Germany's
defeat in World War II, using German wartime
newsfilm. Taking part in the programme are
Generals Gunther Blumentritt and Walter
Warlimont.
d Peter Morley; *sc/nar* Paul Johnson

The DEFENDERS
(US Plautus Productions 1961–65)
Courtroom drama series created by and based on
an original story by Reginald Rose.

The NAKED HEIRESS 7/4/1962
d Jack Smight; *p* Herbert Brodkin;
sc Alvin Boretz, David Shaw
lp E.G. Marshall; Robert Reed;
Salome Jens; Howard St. John; Glenda Farrell;
Robert Goodier; Conrad Nagel
The VOICES OF DEATH 15/9/1962
d Stuart Rosenberg; *p* Bob Markell;
sc Reginald Rose
lp Ruth Roman; E.G. Marshall;
Robert Reed; J.D. Cannon; Judson Laire;
Doro Merande

The DELIVERERS (ATV 22/1/1964)
The V-bombers and the men who fly them.
p Francis Megahy

DEMOCRACY AT WORK
(BBC 8/1–12/3/1978)
A series of ten programmes for trade unionists.
COMPANY PENSIONS – WHO CARES? 5/2/1978
How unions are bargaining about company
pensions.
d Nick Gosling; *p* John Twitchin;
pres Alan Grant

**DEMONSTRATION FILM: OPENING OF
MIDLAND TELEVISION STUDIOS**
(BBC 29/12/1955)
The opening of the Birmingham Studio with
presenter J.J. Duncan; Controller of BBC
Midlands, H.J. Dunkerley; Lord Mayor of
Birmingham, A.L. Gibson; and Desmond
Morris.

DENNIS THE MENACE
(US Dariell Productions 1959–63)
Comedy series based on the 'Dennis the Menace'
comic strip by Hank Ketcham. Shown in Britain
under the title 'Just Dennis' to avoid confusion
with the 'Beano' character.
DENNIS GOES TO THE MOVIES 4/10/1959
d William D. Russell; *p* James Fonda;
sc William Cowley, Peggy Chantler
lp Herbert Anderson; Jay North;
Gloria Henry; Joseph Kearns; Gilbert Smith;
Madge Blake

DEPARTMENT 'S' (ITC 1969)
Detective drama series featuring an offshoot
branch of Interpol. Series continued with
JASON KING (1971–73).
p Monty Berman
regulars Peter Wyngarde; Joel Fabiani;
Rosemary Nicols; Dennis Alaba Peters
SIX DAYS 10/1/1969
d Cyril Frankel; *sc* Gerald Kelsey
lp Bernard Horsfall; Peter Bromilow;
Tony Steedman; Geraldine Moffatt;
Peter Bowles
The TROJAN TANKER 17/1/1969
d Ray Austin; *sc* Philip Broadley
lp Patricia Haines; Simon Oates; Bill Nagy
PIED PIPER OF HAMBLEDOWN 31/1/1969
d Roy Ward Baker; *sc* Donald James;
auth Dennis Spooner
lp Richard Vernon; Gina Warwick;
Jeremy Young; Stanley Beard; Peter Lawrence
ONE OF OUR AIRCRAFT IS EMPTY 7/2/1969
d Paul Dickson; *sc* Tony Williamson
lp Anton Rodgers; Basil Dignam;
Gillian Lewis; Edina Ronay; John Gabriel;
Angela Lovell
HANDICAP DEAD 21/2/1969
d John Gilling;
sc Philip Broadley, Dennis Spooner
lp Dawn Addams; Neil McCallum;
Dudley Sutton; Jennifer Clulow; John Bailey
BLACKOUT 2/3/1969
d Ray Austin; *sc* Philip Broadley
lp Neil Hallett; Sue Lloyd;
Richard Caldicot; David Sumner;
Caron Gardner
The DOUBLE DEATH OF CHARLIE CRIPPEN
9/3/1969
d John Gilling; *sc* Leslie Darbon
lp Peter Arne; Edward De Souza;
John Savadent; Yolande Turner;
Veronica Carlson

The TREASURE OF THE COSTA DEL SOL
16/3/1969
d John Gilling; *sc* Philip Broadley
lp George Pastell; Isla Blair;
John Louis Mansi; Peter Thomas; David Prowse
WHO PLAYS THE DUMMY? 23/3/1969
d John Gilling; *sc* Tony Williamson
lp Alan MacNaughton; Kate O'Mara;
George Pastell; John Bindon
The MAN WHO GOT A NEW FACE 30/3/1969
d Cyril Frankel; *sc* Philip Broadley
lp Alexandra Bastedo; Adrienne Corri;
Eric Pohlmann; Arnold Diamond
Les FLEURS DU MAL 6/4/1969
d Cyril Frankel; *sc* Philip Broadley
lp Donal Donnelly; Michael Gothard;
Edina Ronay; Alex Scott; John Tate
DEAD MEN DIE TWICE 20/4/1969
d Ray Austin; *sc* Philip Broadley
lp Kieron Moore; Barbara Murray;
Alan Lake; David Bauer
The LAST TRAIN TO REDBRIDGE 4/5/1969
d John Gilling; *sc* Gerald Kelsey
lp Leslie Sands; Patricia English; Derek Newark
The MAN FROM 'X' 18/5/1969
d Gil Taylor; *sc* Tony Williamson
lp John Nettleton; Wanda Ventham;
Duncan Lamont
DEATH, ON REFLECTION 25/5/1969
d Ray Austin; *sc* Dennis Spooner
lp Jennifer Hilary; Guy Rolfe
The PERFECT OPERATION 8/6/1969
d Cyril Frankel; *sc* Leslie Darbon
lp Cyril Luckham; Ronald Radd;
Jean Marsh; Martin Miller; Ronald Leigh-Hunt
The DUPLICATED MAN 15/6/1969
d Paul Dickson; *sc* Harry W. Junkin
lp Robert Urquhart; Ann Bell;
Guy Deghy; Sarah Lawson; Basil Dignam
The MAN IN THE ELEGANT ROOM 3/8/1969
d Cyril Frankel; *sc* Terry Nation
lp Stratford Johns; Toby Robins;
Peter Reynolds; John Hallam
SPENCER BODILY IS SIXTY YEARS OLD
10/8/1969
d Leslie Norman; *sc* Harry W. Junkin
lp Iain Cuthbertson; Patricia Donahue;
Warren Stanhope
A FISH OUT OF WATER 17/8/1969
d Cyril Frankel; *sc* Philip Broadley
lp Maggie Wright; Lee Montague;
Cyril Shaps
SMALL WAR OF NERVES 24/8/1969
d Leslie Norman; *sc* Harry W. Junkin
lp Frederick Jaeger; Anthony Hopkins;
Isobel Black
The BONES OF BYRON BLAIN 31/8/1969
d Paul Dickson; *sc* Dennis Spooner
lp John Carson; John Barron; Patrick Barr;
Gerald Campion
SOUP OF THE DAY 7/9/1969
d Leslie Norman; *sc* Leslie Darbon
lp Patrick Mower; Anthony Valentine;
Michael Coles; Ronald Lacey; Peter Arne;
Isobel Black

The DEPUTY
(US Top Gun Company 1959–61)
Western series featuring a chief marshal and a
young deputy sheriff, set in Arizona in the 1880s.
The TRULY YOURS 9/4/1960
d David Butler; *p* Michael Kraike;
sc Montgomery Pittman, Herb Purdum
lp Henry Fonda; Allen Case; James Coburn;
Anthony Caruso; Miriam Colon

DERBY DAY (LWT 28/5/1971)
Russell Harty reports on the social aspects of
Derby Day at Epsom, 1970.
d Charlie Squires; *rep* Russell Harty

DES O'CONNOR ENTERTAINS
(ATV 1974–76)
Variety show hosted by comedian/singer Des
O'Connor.
DES O'CONNOR ENTERTAINS 4/6/1976
d/p Colin Clews;
sc Mike Craig, Lawrie Kinsley,
Ron McDonnell, Des O'Connor;
with Des O'Connor, Lena Zavaroni,
Joan Sanderson, Martin Dale,
Jennie Lee-Wright, Eli Woods, Johnny Vyvyan,
Felix Bowness, Dash's Chimpanzees,
Jack Parnell and his Orchestra

DESIGN BY FIVE (BBC 2/2–2/3/1979)
Series of five programmes in which various
personalities have rooms designed for them.
A DINING ROOM FOR HENRY COOPER 2/3/1979
A dining room for Mr and Mrs Henry Cooper
designed by Sue Rowlands.
p Paul Kriwaczek

DESTINATION AMERICA
(Thames 25/5–13/7/1976)
Eight-part documentary series looking at
immigration to the USA.
CITY OF THE BIG SHOULDERS 22/6/1976
Polish settlers in Chicago in the late nineteenth
and twentieth centuries.
p David Gill; *nar* Iain Cuthbertson

DESTRUCTION OF THE INDIAN
(BBC 19/7–2/8/1962)
Three programmes about the Indians of Brazil.
CARNIVAL OF VIOLENCE 2/8/1962
The lives of the impoverished Peruvian Indians.
(An ADVENTURE presentation).
d Adrian Cowell; *pres* Harry Hastings

The DETECTIVES
(US Four Star-Hastings 1959–62)
Police detective series.
KIN FOLK 20/1/1961
lp Robert Taylor; Tige Andrews;
Dabbs Greer; Lonny Chapman; L.Q. Jones

The DEVIL'S MUSIC (BBC 9–30/7/1979)
Four-part series re-edited from the original
(five-part) transmission of 14/11–12/12/1976.
CRAZY BLUES 16/7/1979
Blues musicians filmed in the USA in 1976.
Alexis Korner presents Laura Dukes, Sam
Chatman, Big Joe Williams, Little Brother
Montgomery and James Dashay.
p Giles Oakley, Maddalena Fagandini

DIAL 999 (Towers of London 1958–59)
Police detective series featuring Robert Beatty as
a Det-Inspector of the Canadian Mounties who
is attached to the Metropolitan Police.
The KILLING JOB 6/7/1958
p Harry Alan Towers
lp Duncan Lamont; William Hartnell;
Peter Bull; Patricia Laffan; Sydney Tafler;
Vera Day
24 HOURS 7/9/1958
p Harry Alan Towers; *sc* Edward J. Mason
lp Robert Arden; Joy Owen;
Leslie Sarony; George Street; John Witty
77 BUS 25/10/1958
p Harry Alan Towers; *sc* Edward J. Mason
lp John Warwick; John Salew;
June Rodney; Robert Cawdron
DOWN TO THE SEA 24/1/1959
p Harry Alan Towers
lp Jack Melford; John Cazabon;
Gordon Jackson; Edward Judd

DIAMOND SPECTACULAR (BBC 1970)
Coverage of the Diamond Jubilee spectacular
given by Girl Guides at the Empire Pool,
Wembley.
d Joyce Boucher; *d* Frank Whitten;
comm Geoffrey Wheeler

DIAMONDS IN THE SKY
(BBC 1/11–13/12/1979)
Documentary series on air travel.
CONQUERING THE ATLANTIC 22/11/1979
The history of commercial aviation.
p Harry Hastings, John Purdie,
Colin Luke; *intro* Julian Pettifer

DIAMONDS IN THE SKY *cont.*

DEALING DOWN THE LINE 6/12/1979
The need for ground crews throughout the world
to cope with problems which may arise for an
international airway.
p Harry Hastings, John Purdie,
Colin Luke; *intro* Julian Pettifer

DIARY OF A YOUNG MAN
(BBC 8/8–12/9/1964)
Six-part series about two young Northerners in
London.
SURVIVAL 8/8/1964
d Ken Loach; *p* James MacTaggart;
sc Troy Kennedy Martin, John McGrath
lp Victor Henry; Richard Moore; Nerys Hughes;
Sally Mates; Frank Williams

DICK AND THE DUCHESS (Sheldon
Reynolds Production 1958–59)
Comedy adventure series featuring an American
insurance investigator living in London and
married to an English duchess.
BANK ROBBERY 14/11/1958
lp Patrick O'Neal; Hazel Court;
Richard Wattis; Michael Shepley; Sydney Tafler
WILD PARTY 19/2/1959
lp Patrick O'Neal; Hazel Court;
Richard Wattis; Warren Mitchell;
Ronnie Stevens; Roddy Hughes
MAUDE 5/3/1959
lp Patrick O'Neal; Hazel Court;
Richard Wattis; Jean St. Clair;
Richard Goolden; Viola Lyel

The DICK CAVETT SHOW
(US ABC 1969–75)
Chat show.
SIR LAURENCE OLIVIER 17/2/1974
Dick Cavett interviews Laurence Olivier.

DICK POWELL'S ZANE GREY THEATRE
(US Four Star-Zane Grey 1956–61)
Western anthology series based on adaptations
of stories by Western author Zane Grey.
VILLAGE OF FEAR 1/3/1957
d Christian I. Nyby; *p* Hal Hudson;
sc Anthony Ellis
lp David Niven; George Wallace

DICKENS OF LONDON
(Yorkshire TV 28/9–21/12/1976)
Thirteen-part drama series tracing the early life
of novelist Charles Dickens.
p Marc Miller; *sc* Wolf Mankowitz
regulars Roy Dotrice, Diana Coupland
EPISODE 1: MASK 28/9/1976
d Marc Miller
lp Simon Bell; Bill Reimbold; Lynsey Baxter
EPISODE 2: DEED 5/10/1976
d Marc Miller
lp Simon Bell; John F. Landry; Claire McLellan
EPISODE 3: BLACKING 12/10/1976
d Michael Ferguson
lp Simon Bell; John F. Landry; Dudley Jones
EPISODE 4: LOVE 19/10/1976
d Marc Miller
lp Gene Foad; Karen Dotrice; Holly Palance
EPISODE 5: SUCCESS 26/10/1976
d Marc Miller
lp Gene Foad; Karen Dotrice;
Raymond Francis; Graham Faulkner
EPISODE 6: FAME 2/11/1976
d Michael Ferguson
lp Gene Foad; Patsy Kensit; Lois Baxter;
Adrienne Burgess; Graham Faulkner
EPISODE 7: MONEY 9/11/1976
d Michael Ferguson
lp Gene Foad; Adrienne Burgess;
Lois Baxter; Graham Faulkner

DICKIE HENDERSON HALF-HOUR
(Jack Hylton TV Productions 1958–60)
Comedy and variety series.
d Bill Hitchcock
regulars Dickie Henderson; Anthea Askey;
Eve Lister; Bernard Hunter
DICKIE HENDERSON HALF-HOUR 4/7/1958
with Ilene Day, June Cunningham,
Tom Payne, Claire Gordon
DICKIE HENDERSON HALF-HOUR 11/7/1958
sc Jack Greenhalgh; *with* Freddie Mills

DICKIE HENDERSON HALF-HOUR 18/7/1958
sc Jack Greenhalgh; *with* Eric Delaney,
Len Lowe, Diane Todd
DICKIE HENDERSON HALF-HOUR 25/7/1958
sc Jack Greenhalgh; *with* Len Lowe, Jill Day
DICKIE HENDERSON HALF-HOUR 1/8/1958
sc Jack Greenhalgh; *with* Patricia Moore
DICKIE HENDERSON HALF-HOUR 8/8/1958
with William Sylvester, Len Lowe,
Sara Leighton, Marion Keene
DICKIE HENDERSON HALF-HOUR 15/8/1958
with Freddie Mills, Len Lowe, Ilene Day
DICKIE HENDERSON HALF-HOUR 22/8/1958
with Freddie Mills
DICKIE HENDERSON HALF-HOUR 29/8/1958
with Marion Keene
DICKIE HENDERSON HALF-HOUR 5/9/1958
with Marion Keene
DICKIE HENDERSON HALF-HOUR 12/9/1958
with June Cunningham, Diane Todd
DICKIE HENDERSON HALF-HOUR 4/5/1959
sc Jimmy Grafton; *with* Clive Dunn
DICKIE HENDERSON HALF-HOUR 11/5/1959
sc Jimmy Grafton; *with* Clive Dunn
DICKIE HENDERSON HALF-HOUR 18/5/1959
sc Jimmy Grafton
DICKIE HENDERSON HALF-HOUR 25/5/1959
sc Jimmy Grafton; *with* Lionel Murton
DICKIE HENDERSON HALF-HOUR 1/6/1959
sc Jimmy Grafton; *with* Renate Holm
DICKIE HENDERSON HALF-HOUR 8/6/1959
sc Jimmy Grafton; *with* Marion Keene
DICKIE HENDERSON HALF-HOUR 15/6/1959
sc Jimmy Grafton; *with* Marion Keene
DICKIE HENDERSON HALF-HOUR 22/6/1959
sc Jimmy Grafton
with Freddie Mills, Lionel Murton

The DICKIE HENDERSON SHOW
(Rediffusion 1960–68)
Sitcom series.
d Bill Hitchcock
regulars Dickie Henderson; June Laverick;
John Parsons; Lionel Murton
The PSYCHIATRIST 14/11/1960
sc Jimmy Grafton, Jeremy Lloyd
lp Alfred Marks; Pat Coombs;
Judy Cornwell
The ROMANCE 1962
lp Richard Wattis
LEARNER DRIVER 1963
PARKING METER 1963
The STAMP COLLECTOR 16/1/1963
sc Jimmy Grafton
lp Fred Stone; George Benson;
Deryck Guyler
The STATELY HOME 24/4/1963
sc Jimmy Grafton, Stan Mars, Jeremy Lloyd
lp Andrew Bowen; Paul Williamson; Tom Gill

DISAPPEARING WORLD (Granada 1970–)
Documentary series which looks at the customs
and way of life of the tribes of Africa, Asia and
North and South America.
A CLEARING IN THE JUNGLE 19/5/1970
The Panare tribe of the Northern Amazon
region.
d/p Charlie Nairn
LAST OF THE CUIVA 8/6/1971
The Cuiva Indians of Colombia, a group of
nomadic hunters who are under threat from
cattle ranchers and colonists desperate for land.
d/p Brian Moser
EMBERA – THE END OF THE ROAD 15/6/1971
The Embera people of Colombia, under threat
from the construction of the last section of the
Pan-American highway.
d/p Brian Moser
WAR OF THE GODS 22/6/1971
Protestant and Catholic missionaries are
competing to convert the Maku and Barasana
Colombian Indians to Christianity, thereby
endangering their ancient culture.
d/p Brian Moser
The TUAREGS 18/4/1972
The Tuareg, a nomadic tribe of Berbers living in
the Sahara desert, are finding their economy in a
state of collapse due to a combination of climatic
and political conditions.
d/p Charlie Nairn

MEO 4/7/1972
The Meo are hill tribesmen scattered over Laos
and Southern China. They live a peaceful
existence and are primitive agriculturalists but
their way of life is being disrupted by the war in
Laos.
d/p Brian Moser
KATARAGAMA 20/11/1973
Once a year there is a festival at the central
shrine of the Hindu god Kataragama, in the
jungle of South East Ceylon.
d/p Charlie Nairn
The MEHINACU 20/11/1974
Shows some of the more important rituals of the
Mehinacu, a small tribe living in Central Brazil.
d Carlos Pasini; *sc* Mark Ash;
nar Mark Edwards
MASAI WOMEN 27/11/1974
A study of the Masai people of Kenya's Rift
Valley.
d Chris Curling
MASAI MANHOOD 8/4/1975
Anthropologist Melissa Llewelyn-Davies
examines the progress to adulthood of young
Masai men.
d Chris Curling
ESKIMOS OF POND INLET – THE PEOPLE'S
LAND 12/1/1976
The Pond Inlet Eskimos, caught between
encroaching western values and their own
traditional culture.
d Michael Grigsby
SOME WOMEN OF MARRAKESH 26/1/1977
The women of Marrakesh; edition produced by a
female camera team.
d/p Melissa Llewelyn-Davies; *ph* Diane Tammes

DISCO 2 (BBC 1970–71)
Contemporary music series, that later developed
into The OLD GREY WHISTLE TEST
(1971–85).
DISCO 2 17/10/1970
Mike Harding presents the rock musicians LA
(alias Love Affair), Jimmy Campbell, and Rare
Bird, with film of the band UFO.
p Steve Turner; *pres* Mike Harding
DISCO 2 3/6/1971
Includes Muddy Waters, Chuck Berry, Assegai,
Otis Redding, and Mick Jagger.
p Granville Jenkins

DISCOVERING JAPANESE ART
(ATV 2–16/12/1963)
Three talks by Sir Kenneth Clark.
The SHADOW OF CHINA 2/12/1963
Sir Kenneth Clark examines the sculpture of
Japan.
p Michael Redington

DISCOVERY (Granada 1959–64)
Scientific series for schools.
NUCLEIC ACIDS 15/10/1961
Sir Alexander Todd talks about his interest in
inorganic chemistry and research leading to the
discovery of nucleic acids.
The SCIENCE OF LIFE: ACCIDENT OR DESIGN?
12/11/1961
Sir James Gray, the biologist, talks about the
characteristics that distinguish the animate from
the inanimate.

DISCOVERY (Yorkshire TV 1974–76)
Series on ideas and discoveries in science.
AWAKENINGS 24/2/1974
A report on the use, in the USA, of the drug
L-Dopa in the treatment of Parkinson's Disease.
The drug was used on victims of a sleeping
sickness epidemic of 1917. The neurologist
involved, Dr Oliver Sacks, appears in the
programme.
exec.p Duncan Dallas; *rep* Simon Welfare
The BUTTERFLY AND THE BABY 16/3/1975
A method of preventing rhesus disease in babies,
based on the work of Professor Philip Sheppard.
d Barry Cockcroft; *rep* Simon Welfare

DISCOVERY AND DESIGN
(BBC 2–30/1/1967)
Five-part series on the aims and methods of
science and engineering. (Produced as a part of
the 'Outlook' programme.)

WHAT IS ENGINEERING? 30/1/1967
d Harry B. Levinson; *p* James McCloy

DISCOVERY AND EXPERIENCE
(BBC 12/1–23/3/1966)
Series for parents and teachers about primary school children. (Produced as a part of the 'Outlook' programme.)
CITY INFANTS 2/3/1966
Some of the new methods of teaching primary school children and the children's response to them. Illustrates one of the results of educational research into the mental processes of young children.
p Eileen Molony; *comm* Nora Goddard
HOW DO CHILDREN THINK? 16/3/1966
Dr Ruth Beard reconstructs some of the experiments which the Swiss psychologist Piaget designed to investigate children's mental development.
p Eileen Molony
WHAT ABOUT IT? 23/3/1966
Questions about the ten previous programmes are put by parents and teachers to Molly Brearley, Principal of the Froebel Educational Institute; Ronald Wastnedge and Dr Geoffrey Matthews, organisers of The Nuffield Teaching Project; Tom John, Head of Tower Hill Primary School.
p Eileen Molony

DISPUTE (BBC 1967)
A two-part film recording disputes between the personnel director of a Coventry car delivery firm and the representative of the Transport and General Workers' Union.
d Jack Gold, Ken Ashton, Paul Watson
ROUND I 27/4/1967
The sacking of a shop-steward.
ROUND II 4/5/1967
Planned redundancies.

DIVIDED WE STAND (Scottish TV 1973)
A survey of the history and current problems of the Scottish Co-operative movement.
d Ted Williamson

DIXON OF DOCK GREEN (BBC 1955–76)
Drama series based on the adventures of a London policeman. Jack Warner continues his role from Ted Willis' original screenplay and play of the 1950 film, 'The Blue Lamp'.
regulars Jack Warner, (early series);
Peter Byrne; Arthur Rigby; Moira Mannion;
Neil Wilson; Jeannette Hutchinson
The ROTTEN APPLE 11/8/1956
p Douglas Moodie; *sc* Ted Willis
lp Geoffrey Wincott; Paul Eddington;
Geoffrey King; Christopher Hodge;
Robert Cawdron
The ROARING BOY 18/8/1956
p Douglas Moodie; *sc* Ted Willis
lp Kenneth Cope; Phoebe Hodgson;
Jennifer Wilson; Ray Jackson
IN LAW 1/9/1956
p Douglas Moodie; *sc* Ted Willis;
lp Margaret Allworthy; Valerie Gaunt;
Jean Trend; Jefferson Clifford
LOOTERS LTD. 29/3/1975
d Mary Ridge; *sc* Gerald Kelsey
lp Sam Kydd; Robin Ford; Terry Cowling;
Alan Leith; Nicholas Donnelly; Margery Mason

DIZZY GILLESPIE (BBC 17/10/1975)
Dizzy Gillespie in concert at Ronnie Scott's with a British band; playing with his own quartet; and talking to Tony Cash about his career.
p Tony Cash

The DO GOODERS (LWT 2/11–7/12/1979)
Documentary series examining the role of social workers.
CASH OR CARE 23/11/1979
The way in which social workers are increasingly having to cope with clients' financial problems and areas in which they have no professional jurisdiction.
d John Longley; *p/nar* David Tereschchuk

The DO-IT-YOURSELF FILM ANIMATION SHOW (BBC 21/4–19/5/1974)
Series highlighting animation techniques.
SOUND AND FURY 19/5/1974
British animation techniques with animator Bob Godfrey and guest Ron Geesin.
d Anna Jackson; *p* David Hargreaves

DO NOT ADJUST YOUR SET
(Rediffusion 1967–69)
Comedy series for children written by and starring Michael Palin, Terry Jones and Eric Idle.
d Daphne Shadwell; *p* Humphrey Barclay;
with The Bonzo Dog Doo-Dah Band,
Denise Coffey, David Jason
DO NOT ADJUST YOUR SET NO. 1 26/12/1967
DO NOT ADJUST YOUR SET NO. 2 4/1/1968
DO NOT ADJUST YOUR SET NO. 5 25/1/1968
DO NOT ADJUST YOUR SET NO. 6 1/2/1968
DO NOT ADJUST YOUR SET NO. 9 22/2/1968
DO NOT ADJUST YOUR SET NO. 10 29/2/1968
DO NOT ADJUST YOUR SET NO. 11 7/3/1968
DO NOT ADJUST YOUR SET NO. 12 14/3/1968
DO NOT ADJUST YOUR SET NO. 13 21/3/1968
DO NOT ADJUST YOUR STOCKING 25/12/1968
Denise Coffey, Eric Idle, David Jason, Terry Jones, Michael Palin, The Bonzo Dog Doo-Dah Band and Captain Fantastic (David Jason) in a special Christmas Day edition of the comedy series.
d Adrian Cooper;
sc Eric Idle, Terry Jones, Michael Palin

DO YOU REMEMBER?
(Yorkshire TV 14/5–4/6/1978; 2/7/1978)
Series of five plays by leading writers.
NIGHT SCHOOL 14/5/1978
d Marc Miller; *p* John Kaye Cooper;
sc Harold Pinter
lp Ian Holm; Brenda Bruce; Jean Kent;
Mel Martin; Sydney Tafler; Paul Dawkins

DO YOU REMEMBER VIETNAM?
(ATV 3/10/1978)
Life in Vietnam after three years of peace.
d/p David Munro

DOCTOR AT LARGE (LWT 1971)
Follow-up series to DOCTOR IN THE HOUSE (1969–70), originally based on the comic tales of medical life by Richard Gordon, and followed by DOCTOR IN CHARGE (1972–73).
NO ILL FEELING! 30/5/1971
Note: The characters Mr and Mrs Griffith in this episode, played by guests Timothy Bateson and Eunice Black, are the prototypes of Basil and Sybil Fawlty in the FAWLTY TOWERS series (1975).
d Alan Wallis; *exec.p* Humphrey Barclay;
sc John Cleese
lp Barry Evans; George Layton;
Brian Oulton; Timothy Bateson; Eunice Black;
Lucy Griffiths; Roy Kinnear; Geoffrey Davies

DR. FINLAY'S CASEBOOK (BBC 1962–71)
Drama series revolving around a village doctor's practice in Scotland during the 1920s.
regulars Andrew Cruickshank;
Barbara Mullen; Bill Simpson
POLYGRAPH 27/12/1963
d William Slater; *p* Campbell Logan;
sc Jan Read
lp Effie Morrison; Mary Webster;
Michael Graham; David Orr
A TEST OF INTELLIGENCE 12/1/1964
d Julia Smith; *sc* Donald Bull
lp Patrick Troughton; Derek Keith;
Gavin Crombie; Gareth Tandy; Eric Woodburn
SPIRIT OF DR. MCGREGOR 26/4/1964
d Julia Smith; *p* Andrew Osborn;
sc Jan Read
lp Fay Compton; Stephanie Bidmead;
Robert James; Michael Elder
A RIGHT TO LIVE 24/1/1965
d Gerard Glaister; *p* Andrew Osborn;
sc Doreen Montgomery
lp Noel Johnson; Jennie Linden;
Bryan Marshall; Maureen Crombie

The GATE OF THE YEAR 28/2/1965
d John Fabian; *p* Gerard Glaister;
sc John Lucarotti, Donald Bull
lp Eric Woodburn; Elaine Mitchell;
Kay Galli; Elizabeth Wallace
OFF THE HOOK 7/3/1965
d Prudence Fitzgerald; *p* Gerard Glaister;
sc Vincent Tilsley
lp Clement McCallin; Fulton Mackay;
Vivien Heilbron
The PHANTOM PIPER OF TANNOCHBRAE 21/11/1965
d Paul Ciappessoni; *p* Gerard Glaister;
sc Alan Gosling
lp Andrew Keir; Ian Colin; Kevin Stoney;
Douglas Storm
CRUSADE 24/4/1966
d Julia Smith; *p* Gerard Glaister;
sc Elaine Morgan
lp Patrick Troughton; Anne Kristen;
Margaret Greig; Archie Duncan
GIFTS OF THE MAGI 25/12/1966
d Joan Craft; *p* Douglas Allen;
sc Harry Green
lp Helen Christie; Lynette Meredith;
Elizabeth Kentish; Molly Urquhart;
Eric Woodburn
TELL ME TRUE 20/11/1967
d Laurence Bourne; *p* Royston Morley;
sc Harry Green
lp Jack May; Jill Richards; May Warden;
Molly Urquhart
CONSCIENCE CLAUSE 21/1/1968
d Laurence Bourne; *p* Royston Morley;
sc Elaine Morgan
lp Peter Jeffrey; Andrew Crawford;
Declan Mulholland; Amanda Walker
LACK OF COMMUNICATION 13/7/1969
d Tina Wakerell; *p* Royston Morley;
sc Martin Hall, David Hopkins
lp Billy Russell; Effie Morrison;
Martin Boddey; Myra Forsyth
COMING THRU' THE RYE 27/9/1970
d Eric Hills; *p* John Henderson;
sc Anthony Steven
lp James Hayter; Don McKillop;
Honora Burke; Elspeth Charlton

DOCTOR IN CHARGE (LWT 1972–73)
Medical sitcom; continuing from DOCTOR AT LARGE (1971).
The EPIDEMIC 6/10/1973
d Bryan Izzard; *p* Humphrey Barclay;
sc Phil Redmond
lp Robin Nedwell; George Layton;
Geoffrey Davies; Sally Stephens; Ernest Clark;
Tony Robinson

DOCTOR IN THE HOUSE (LWT 1969–70)
Medical sitcom based on Richard Gordon's original novel. Followed by DOCTOR AT LARGE (1971).
IF IN DOUBT, CUT IT OUT 23/8/1969
d David Askey; *p* Humphrey Barclay;
lp Barry Evans; Ernest Clark;

DR. KILDARE
(US Arena Productions-MGM 1961–66)
Medical drama based on the characters created by author Max Brand, and the 1940s films.
WINTER HARVEST 19/10/1961
d Lamont Johnson; *p* Herbert Hirschman;
sc John Furia Jr
lp Richard Chamberlain; Raymond Massey;
Charles Bickford; Hershel Bernardi
HASTINGS FAREWELL 1/11/1962
d Ralph Senensky
lp Richard Chamberlain; Raymond Massey;
Beverly Garland; Harry Guardino

DOCTOR ON THE GO (LWT 1975–77)
Medical sitcom; continuing from 'Doctor at Sea'.
HAPPY EVER AFTER 10/4/1977
d Bryan Izzard; *p* Humphrey Barclay;
sc Bernard McKenna
lp Robin Nedwell; Geoffrey Davies;
Oliver Maguire; Ernest Clark; Andrew Knox;
Jacquie-Ann Carr

DR. PRICE 1800–1893 (HTV 10/10/1972)
Dramatised documentary of the life of Dr
William Price of Llantrisant.
d/p Terry Delacey; *sc* Ewart Alexander
lp William Squire; Meg Wynn Owen

DR. WHO (BBC 1963–)
Science fiction series featuring the intergalactic
exploits of an enigmatic time traveller.
p Verity Lambert (1963–65);
John Wiles (1965–66); Innes Lloyd (1966–68);
Peter Bryant (1967–69); Derrick Sherwin (1970);
Barry Letts (1970–75);
Philip Hinchcliffe (1975–77);
Graham Williams (1977–80)
Title role William Hartnell (1963–66);
Patrick Troughton (1966–69);
Jon Pertwee (1970–74); Tom Baker (1974–81)
An UNEARTHLY CHILD 1963 *ntx*
Original first episode of the series which was
never transmitted and formed the basis for the
episode transmitted on 23/11/1963. This edition
was finally transmitted on 26/8/1991.
d Waris Hussein; *sc* Anthony Coburn
lp Carole Ann Ford; Jacqueline Hill;
William Russell
An UNEARTHLY CHILD 23/11/1963
d Waris Hussein; *sc* Anthony Coburn
lp Carole Ann Ford; Jacqueline Hill;
William Russell
The CAVE OF SKULLS 30/11/1963
d Waris Hussein; *sc* Anthony Coburn
lp William Russell; Jacqueline Hill;
Carole Ann Ford; Derek Newark
The FOREST OF FEAR 7/12/1963
d Waris Hussein; *sc* Anthony Coburn
lp Carole Ann Ford; William Russell;
Jacqueline Hill; Eileen Way
The FIREMAKER 14/12/1963
d Waris Hussein; *sc* Anthony Coburn
lp Carole Ann Ford; William Russell;
Jacqueline Hill; Howard Lang; Jeremy Young
The DALEKS: THE DEAD PLANET 21/12/1963
d Christopher Barry; *sc* Terry Nation
lp William Russell; Jacqueline Hill;
Carole Ann Ford
The DALEKS: THE SURVIVORS 28/12/1963
d Christopher Barry; *sc* Terry Nation
lp William Russell; Jacqueline Hill;
Carole Ann Ford
The DALEKS: THE ESCAPE 4/1/1964
d Richard Martin; *sc* Terry Nation
lp William Russell; Jacqueline Hill;
Carole Ann Ford; John Lee; Philip Bond
The DALEKS: THE AMBUSH 11/1/1964
d Christopher Barry; *sc* Terry Nation
lp William Russell; Jacqueline Hill;
Carole Ann Ford; Alan Wheatley; John Lee
The DALEKS: THE ORDEAL 25/1/1964
d Richard Martin; *sc* Terry Nation
lp William Russell; Jacqueline Hill;
Carole Ann Ford; Philip Bond;
Marcus Hammond
The DALEKS: THE RESCUE 1/2/1964
d Richard Martin; *sc* Terry Nation
lp William Russell; Jacqueline Hill;
Carole Ann Ford; Philip Bond
The EDGE OF DESTRUCTION: THE EDGE OF
DESTRUCTION 8/2/1964
d Richard Martin; *sc* David Whitaker
lp Carole Ann Ford; Jacqueline Hill;
William Russell
The EDGE OF DESTRUCTION: THE BRINK OF
DISASTER 15/2/1964
d Frank Cox; *sc* David Whitaker
lp Carole Ann Ford; Jacqueline Hill;
William Russell
The KEYS OF MARINUS: THE SEA OF DEATH
11/4/1964
d John Gorrie; *sc* Terry Nation
lp Carole Ann Ford; Jacqueline Hill;
William Russell; George Coulouris
The KEYS OF MARINUS: THE VELVET WEB
18/4/1964
d John Gorrie; *sc* Terry Nation
lp Carole Ann Ford; Jacqueline Hill;
William Russell; Robin Phillips;
Katharine Schofield

The KEYS OF MARINUS: THE SCREAMING
JUNGLE 25/4/1964
d John Gorrie; *sc* Terry Nation
lp Carole Ann Ford; Jacqueline Hill;
William Russell; Robin Phillips;
Katharine Schofield
The KEYS OF MARINUS: THE SNOWS OF
TERROR 2/5/1964
d John Gorrie; *sc* Terry Nation
lp Carole Ann Ford; Jacqueline Hill;
William Russell; Robin Phillips;
Katharine Schofield
The KEYS OF MARINUS: SENTENCE OF DEATH
9/5/1964
d John Gorrie; *sc* Terry Nation
lp Carole Ann Ford; Jacqueline Hill;
William Russell; Robin Phillips;
Katharine Schofield
The KEYS OF MARINUS: THE KEYS OF
MARINUS 16/5/1964
d John Gorrie; *sc* Terry Nation
lp William Russell; Jacqueline Hill;
Carole Ann Ford; Donald Pickering;
Henley Thomas
The AZTECS: THE TEMPLE OF EVIL 23/5/1964
d John Crockett; *sc* John Lucarotti
lp Carole Ann Ford; Jacqueline Hill;
William Russell; Robin Phillips;
Katharine Schofield
The AZTECS: THE WARRIORS OF DEATH
30/5/1964
d John Crockett; *sc* John Lucarotti
lp Carole Ann Ford; Jacqueline Hill;
William Russell; Keith Pyott; John Ringham
The AZTECS: THE BRIDE OF SACRIFICE
6/6/1964
d John Crockett; *sc* John Lucarotti
lp Carole Ann Ford; Jacqueline Hill;
William Russell; Keith Pyott; John Ringham
The AZTECS: THE DAY OF DARKNESS 13/6/1964
d John Crockett; *sc* John Lucarotti
lp Carole Ann Ford; Jacqueline Hill;
William Russell; Keith Pyott; John Ringham
The SENSORITES: THE STRANGERS IN SPACE
20/6/1964
d Mervyn Pinfield; *sc* Peter R. Newman
lp Carole Ann Ford; Jacqueline Hill;
William Russell; Stephen Dartnell;
Ilona Rodgers
The SENSORITES: THE UNWILLING WARRIORS
27/6/1964
d Mervyn Pinfield; *sc* Peter R. Newman
lp Carole Ann Ford; Jacqueline Hill;
William Russell; Stephen Dartnell;
Ilona Rodgers
The SENSORITES: HIDDEN DANGER 11/7/1964
d Mervyn Pinfield; *sc* Peter R. Newman
lp Carole Ann Ford; Jacqueline Hill;
William Russell; Stephen Dartnell;
Ilona Rodgers
The SENSORITES: KIDNAP 25/7/1964
d Mervyn Pinfield; *sc* Peter R. Newman
lp Carole Ann Ford; Jacqueline Hill;
William Russell; Stephen Dartnell;
Ilona Rodgers
The SENSORITES: A DESPERATE VENTURE
1/8/1964
d Mervyn Pinfield; *sc* Peter R. Newman
lp Carole Ann Ford; Jacqueline Hill;
William Russell; Stephen Dartnell;
Ilona Rodgers
PLANET OF GIANTS: PLANET OF GIANTS
31/10/1964
d Mervyn Pinfield; *sc* Louis Marks
lp Jacqueline Hill; Carole Ann Ford;
Alan Tilvern; Frank Crawshaw
PLANET OF GIANTS: DANGEROUS JOURNEY
7/11/1964
d Mervyn Pinfield; *sc* Louis Marks
lp Jacqueline Hill; Carole Ann Ford;
Alan Tilvern; Frank Crawshaw;
Reginald Barratt
PLANET OF GIANTS: CRISIS 14/11/1964
d Mervyn Pinfield; *sc* Louis Marks
lp Jacqueline Hill; Carole Ann Ford;
Alan Tilvern; Reginald Barratt; Fred Ferris;
William Russell
The DALEK INVASION OF EARTH: WORLD'S
END 21/11/1964
d Richard Martin; *sc* Terry Nation
lp William Russell; Jacqueline Hill;
Carole Ann Ford; Bernard Kay; Peter Fraser

The DALEK INVASION OF EARTH: THE DALEKS
28/11/1964
d Richard Martin; *sc* Terry Nation
lp William Russell; Jacqueline Hill;
Carole Ann Ford; Alan Judd; Bernard Kay
The DALEK INVASION OF EARTH: DAY OF
RECKONING 5/12/1964
d Richard Martin; *sc* Terry Nation
lp William Russell; Jacqueline Hill;
Carole Ann Ford; Alan Judd; Bernard Kay
The DALEK INVASION OF EARTH: THE END OF
TOMORROW 12/12/1964
d Richard Martin; *sc* Terry Nation
lp William Russell; Jacqueline Hill;
Carole Ann Ford; Alan Judd; Bernard Kay
The DALEK INVASION OF EARTH: THE WAKING
ALLY 19/12/1964
d Richard Martin; *sc* Terry Nation
lp William Russell; Jacqueline Hill;
Carole Ann Ford; Alan Judd; Bernard Kay
The DALEK INVASION OF EARTH: FLASHPOINT
26/12/1964
d Richard Martin; *sc* Terry Nation
lp William Russell; Jacqueline Hill;
Carole Ann Ford; Alan Judd; Bernard Kay
The RESCUE: THE POWERFUL ENEMY 2/1/1965
d Christopher Barry; *sc* David Whitaker
lp William Russell; Jacqueline Hill;
Maureen O'Brien; Ray Barrett; Tom Sheridan
The RESCUE: DESPERATE MEASURES 9/1/1965
d Christopher Barry; *sc* David Whitaker
lp William Russell; Jacqueline Hill;
Maureen O'Brien; Ray Barrett; Tom Sheridan
The ROMANS: THE SLAVE TRADERS 16/1/1965
d Christopher Barry; *sc* Dennis Spooner
lp William Russell; Jacqueline Hill;
Maureen O'Brien; Derek Sydney;
Nicholas Evans
The ROMANS: ALL ROADS LEAD TO ROME
23/1/1965
d Christopher Barry; *sc* Dennis Spooner
lp William Russell; Jacqueline Hill;
Maureen O'Brien; Derek Sydney; Barry Jackson
The ROMANS: CONSPIRACY 30/1/1965 *ntx*
d Christopher Barry; *sc* Dennis Spooner
lp William Russell; Jacqueline Hill;
Maureen O'Brien
The ROMANS: INFERNO 6/2/1965
d Christopher Barry; *sc* Dennis Spooner
lp William Russell; Jacqueline Hill;
Maureen O'Brien; Derek Sydney;
Peter Diamond
The WEB PLANET: THE WEB PLANET 13/2/1965
d Richard Martin; *sc* Bill Strutton
lp William Russell; Jacqueline Hill;
Maureen O'Brien
The WEB PLANET: THE ZARBI 20/2/1965
d Richard Martin; *sc* Bill Strutton
lp William Russell; Jacqueline Hill;
Maureen O'Brien
The WEB PLANET: ESCAPE TO DANGER
27/2/1965
d Richard Martin; *sc* Bill Strutton
lp William Russell; Jacqueline Hill;
Maureen O'Brien
The WEB PLANET: CRATER OF NEEDLES
6/3/1965
d Richard Martin; *sc* Bill Strutton
lp William Russell; Jacqueline Hill;
Maureen O'Brien; Roslyn De Winter;
Arne Gordon
The WEB PLANET: INVASION 13/3/1965
d Richard Martin; *sc* Bill Strutton
lp William Russell; Jacqueline Hill;
Maureen O'Brien; Roslyn De Winter;
Arne Gordon
The WEB PLANET: THE CENTRE 20/3/1965
d Richard Martin; *sc* Bill Strutton
lp William Russell; Jacqueline Hill;
Maureen O'Brien; Roslyn De Winter;
Arne Gordon
The SPACE MUSEUM: THE SPACE MUSEUM
24/4/1965
d Mervyn Pinfield; *sc* Glyn Jones
lp Maureen O'Brien; William Russell;
Jacqueline Hill; Peter Sanders; Peter Craze
The SPACE MUSEUM: THE DIMENSIONS OF
TIME 1/5/1965
d Mervyn Pinfield; *sc* Glyn Jones
lp Maureen O'Brien; William Russell;
Jacqueline Hill; Richard Shaw; Jeremy Bulloch

The SPACE MUSEUM: THE SEARCH 8/5/1965
d Mervyn Pinfield; *sc* Glyn Jones
lp Maureen O'Brien; William Russell;
Jacqueline Hill; Richard Shaw; Jeremy Bulloch
The SPACE MUSEUM: THE FINAL PHASE
15/5/1965
d Mervyn Pinfield; *sc* Glyn Jones
lp Maureen O'Brien; William Russell;
Jacqueline Hill; Richard Shaw; Jeremy Bulloch
The CHASE: THE DEATH OF TIME 29/5/1965
d Richard Martin; *sc* Terry Nation
lp Maureen O'Brien; William Russell;
Jacqueline Hill; Ian Thompson; Hywel Bennett
The CHASE: FLIGHT THROUGH ETERNITY
5/6/1965
d Richard Martin; *sc* Terry Nation
lp Maureen O'Brien; William Russell;
Jacqueline Hill; Arne Gordon; Peter Purves
The CHASE: JOURNEY INTO TERROR 12/6/1965
d Richard Martin; *sc* Terry Nation
lp Maureen O'Brien; William Russell;
Jacqueline Hill; John Maxim; Malcolm Rogers
The CHASE: THE DEATH OF DR. WHO 19/6/1965
d Richard Martin; *sc* Terry Nation
lp Maureen O'Brien; William Russell;
Jacqueline Hill; Edmund Warwick
The CHASE: THE PLANET OF DECISION
26/6/1965
d Richard Martin; *sc* Terry Nation
lp Maureen O'Brien; William Russell;
Jacqueline Hill; Peter Purves; Derek Ware
The TIME MEDDLER: THE MEDDLING MONK
10/7/1965
d Douglas Camfield; *sc* Dennis Spooner
lp Maureen O'Brien; Peter Purves;
Peter Butterworth
The ARK: THE STEEL SKY 5/3/1966
d Michael Imison;
sc Paul Erickson, Lesley Scott
lp Jackie Lane; Peter Purves; Eric Elliott;
Inigo Jackson; Roy Spencer
The ARK: THE PLAGUE 12/3/1966
d Michael Imison;
sc Paul Erickson, Lesley Scott
lp Jackie Lane; Peter Purves; Eric Elliott;
Inigo Jackson; Roy Spencer
The ARK: THE RETURN 19/3/1966
d Michael Imison;
sc Paul Erickson, Lesley Scott
lp Jackie Lane; Peter Purves; Terence Woodfield
The ARK: THE BOMB 26/3/1966
d Michael Imison;
sc Paul Erickson, Lesley Scott
lp Jackie Lane; Peter Purves; Terence Woodfield
The GUNFIGHTERS: A HOLIDAY FOR THE
DOCTOR 30/4/1966
d Rex Tucker; *sc* Donald Cotton
lp Peter Purves; Jackie Lane;
William Hurndell; Maurice Good; David Cole
The MOONBASE: PART 4 4/3/1967
d Morris Barry; *sc* Kit Pedler
lp Patrick Barr; Frazer Hines;
André Maranne; Michael Wolf; Anneke Wills
The EVIL OF THE DALEKS: PART 2 27/5/1967
d Derek Martinus; *sc* David Whitaker
lp Griffith Davies; Robert Jewell;
Frazer Hines; John Bailey; Geoffrey Colville
The WHEEL IN SPACE: PART 6 1/6/1968
d Tristan De Vere Cole; *sc* David Whitaker;
auth Kit Pedler
lp Frazer Hines; Wendy Padbury; Eric Flynn;
Donald Sumpter; Clare Jenkins
DOMINATORS: PART 1 10/8/1968
d Morris Barry; *sc* Norman Ashby
lp Patrick Allen; Ronald Allen;
Kenneth Ives; Frazer Hines; Wendy Padbury;
Arthur Cox
DOMINATORS: PART 2 17/8/1968
d Morris Barry; *sc* Norman Ashby
lp Walter Fitzgerald; Frazer Hines;
Wendy Padbury; Ronald Allen; Kenneth Ives;
Arthur Cox
DOMINATORS: PART 3 24/8/1968
d Morris Barry; *sc* Norman Ashby
lp Walter Fitzgerald; Ronald Allen;
Arthur Cox; Kenneth Ives
DOMINATORS: PART 4 31/8/1968
d Morris Barry; *sc* Norman Ashby
lp Walter Fitzgerald; Ronald Allen;
Arthur Cox; Kenneth Ives

DOMINATORS: PART 5 7/9/1968
d Morris Barry; *sc* Norman Ashby
lp Ronald Allen; Arthur Cox;
Kenneth Ives; Felicity Gibson
The MIND ROBBER: PART 1 14/9/1968
d David Maloney; *sc* Peter Ling
lp Emrys Jones
The MIND ROBBER: PART 2 21/9/1968
d David Maloney; *sc* Peter Ling
lp Emrys Jones; Wendy Padbury;
Frazer Hines; Bernard Horsfall; Philip Ryan
The MIND ROBBER: PART 3 28/9/1968
d David Maloney; *sc* Peter Ling
lp Emrys Jones; Bernard Horsfall;
Frazer Hines; Wendy Padbury; Christine Pirie
The MIND ROBBER: PART 4 5/10/1968
d David Maloney; *sc* Peter Ling
lp Frazer Hines; Emrys Jones;
Bernard Horsfall; Sue Pulford;
Christopher Robbie
The MIND ROBBER: PART 5 12/10/1968
d David Maloney; *sc* Peter Ling
lp Emrys Jones; Bernard Horsfall;
Christopher Robbie; Christine Pirie
The INVASION: EPISODE 8 21/12/1968
d Douglas Camfield; *sc* Derrick Sherwin;
auth Kit Pedler
lp Kevin Stoney; Sally Faulkner;
John Levine; Clifford Earl; Wendy Padbury
The KROTONS: PART 1 28/12/1968
d David Maloney; *sc* Robert Holmes
lp James Copeland; Terence Brown;
Madeleine Mills; Gilbert Wynne; Philip Madoc
The KROTONS: PART 2 4/1/1969
d David Maloney; *sc* Robert Holmes
lp Wendy Padbury; James Copeland;
Gilbert Wynne; Madeleine Mills
The KROTONS: PART 3 11/1/1969
d David Maloney; *sc* Robert Holmes
lp Wendy Padbury; James Cairncross;
James Copeland; Philip Madoc; Gilbert Wynne
The KROTONS: PART 4 18/1/1969
d David Maloney; *sc* Robert Holmes
lp Wendy Padbury; James Cairncross;
James Copeland; Philip Madoc; Gilbert Wynne
The SEEDS OF DEATH: PART 1 25/1/1969
d Michael Ferguson; *sc* Brian Hayles
lp Frazer Hines; Ronald Leigh-Hunt;
Philip Ray; Terry Scully; Harry Towb
The SEEDS OF DEATH: PART 2 1/2/1969
d Michael Ferguson; *sc* Brian Hayles
lp Frazer Hines; Wendy Padbury;
Ronald Leigh-Hunt; Louise Pajo; Philip Ray
The SEEDS OF DEATH: PART 3 8/2/1969
d Michael Ferguson; *sc* Brian Hayles
lp Frazer Hines; Ronald Leigh-Hunt;
Louise Pajo; Philip Ray; Terry Scully
The SEEDS OF DEATH: PART 4 15/2/1969
d Michael Ferguson; *sc* Brian Hayles
lp Frazer Hines; Ronald Leigh-Hunt;
Louise Pajo; Philip Ray; Terry Scully
The SEEDS OF DEATH: PART 5 22/2/1969
d Michael Ferguson; *sc* Brian Hayles
lp Frazer Hines; Ronald Leigh-Hunt;
Louise Pajo; Philip Ray; Terry Scully
The SEEDS OF DEATH: PART 6 1/3/1969
d Michael Ferguson; *sc* Brian Hayles
lp Frazer Hines; Ronald Leigh-Hunt;
Louise Pajo; Philip Ray; Alan Bennion
The WAR GAMES: PART 1 19/4/1969
d David Maloney;
sc Terrance Dicks, Malcolm Hulke
lp Frazer Hines; Jane Sherwin;
David Savile; Terence Bayler; Noel Coleman
The WAR GAMES: PART 2 26/4/1969
d David Maloney;
sc Terrance Dicks, Malcolm Hulke
lp Frazer Hines; Hubert Rees;
Noel Coleman; Richard Steele; Jane Sherwin
The WAR GAMES: PART 3 3/5/1969
d David Maloney;
sc Terrance Dicks, Malcolm Hulke
lp Frazer Hines; David Savile;
Jane Sherwin; Hubert Rees; David Valla
The WAR GAMES: PART 4 10/5/1969
d David Maloney;
sc Terrance Dicks, Malcolm Hulke
lp Frazer Hines; Jane Sherwin;
Bill Hutchinson; Terry Adams; Rudolph Walker

The WAR GAMES: PART 5 17/5/1969
d David Maloney;
sc Terrance Dicks, Malcolm Hulke
lp Frazer Hines; David Savile;
Jane Sherwin; David Garfield; Rudolph Walker
The WAR GAMES: PART 6 24/5/1969
d David Maloney;
sc Terrance Dicks; Malcolm Hulke
lp Frazer Hines; David Savile; James Bree;
Vernon Dobtcheff; Edward Brayshaw
The WAR GAMES: PART 7 31/5/1969
d David Maloney;
sc Terrance Dicks, Malcolm Hulke
lp Frazer Hines; David Savile;
Edward Brayshaw; Philip Madoc; Noel Coleman
The WAR GAMES: PART 8 7/6/1969
d David Maloney;
sc Terrance Dicks, Malcolm Hulke
lp Frazer Hines; David Savile; James Bree;
Philip Madoc; Edward Brayshaw
The WAR GAMES: PART 9 14/6/1969
d David Maloney;
sc Terrance Dicks, Malcolm Hulke
lp Frazer Hines; David Savile;
Edward Brayshaw; James Bree; Philip Madoc
The WAR GAMES: PART 10 21/6/1969
d David Maloney;
sc Terrance Dicks, Malcolm Hulke
lp Frazer Hines; Bernard Horsfall;
Trevor Martin; Clyde Pollitt; Clare Jenkins
SPEARHEAD FROM SPACE: PART 1 3/1/1970
d Derek Martinus; *sc* Robert Holmes
lp Caroline John; John Breslin; Neil Wilson;
Talfryn Thomas; Hugh Burden
SPEARHEAD FROM SPACE: PART 2 10/1/1970
d Derek Martinus; *sc* Robert Holmes
lp Caroline John; John Breslin; Hugh Burden;
John Woodnutt; George Lee
SPEARHEAD FROM SPACE: PART 3 17/1/1970
d Derek Martinus; *sc* Robert Holmes
lp Caroline John; Hugh Burden;
John Woodnutt; John Breslin; Derek Smee
SPEARHEAD FROM SPACE: PART 4 24/1/1970
d Derek Martinus; *sc* Robert Holmes
lp Caroline John; Hamilton Dyce; Hugh Burden;
John Woodnutt; John Breslin
The AMBASSADORS OF DEATH: EPISODE 1
21/3/1970
d Michael Ferguson; *sc* David Whitaker
lp Robert Cawdron; Ronald Allen;
Michael Wisher; John Abineri
The AMBASSADORS OF DEATH: EPISODE 5
18/4/1970
d Michael Ferguson; *sc* David Whitaker
lp Caroline John; Cyril Shaps;
William Dysart; Ronald Allen; John Abineri
The CLAWS OF AXOS: EPISODE 1 13/3/1971
d Michael Ferguson;
sc Bob Baker, Dave Martin
lp Katy Manning; Michael Walker;
David March; Peter Bathurst; Nicholas Courtney
The CLAWS OF AXOS: EPISODE 2 20/3/1971
d Michael Ferguson;
sc Bob Baker, Dave Martin
lp Katy Manning; Nicholas Courtney;
Bernard Holley; Peter Bathurst; Roger Delgado
The CLAWS OF AXOS: EPISODE 3 27/3/1971
d Michael Ferguson;
sc Bob Baker, Dave Martin
lp Katy Manning; Bernard Holley;
Paul Grist; Nicholas Courtney; Roger Delgado
The CLAWS OF AXOS: EPISODE 4 3/4/1971
d Michael Ferguson;
sc Bob Baker, Dave Martin
lp Katy Manning; Donald Hewlett;
Roger Delgado; Nicholas Courtney;
Richard Franklin
The DAEMONS: EPISODE 4 12/6/1971
d Christopher Barry; *sc* Guy Leopold
lp Katy Manning; Roger Delgado;
Damaris Hayman; Richard Franklin;
John Levene
The DAY OF THE DALEKS: EPISODE 1 1/1/1972
d Paul Bernard; *sc* Louis Marks
lp Katy Manning; Jean McFarlane;
Wilfred Carter; Tim Condren; Nicholas
Courtney
The DAY OF THE DALEKS: EPISODE 2 8/1/1972
d Paul Bernard; *sc* Louis Marks
lp Katy Manning; John Scott Martin;
Oliver Gilbert; Peter Messaline; Jimmy Winston

The DAY OF THE DALEKS: EPISODE 3 15/1/1972
d Paul Bernard; *sc* Louis Marks
lp Katy Manning; John Scott Martin;
Oliver Gilbert; Peter Messaline
The DAY OF THE DALEKS: EPISODE 4 22/1/1972
d Paul Bernard; *sc* Louis Marks
lp Katy Manning; John Scott Martin;
Oliver Gilbert; Peter Messaline; Aubrey Woods
The SEA DEVILS: EPISODE 1 26/2/1972
d Michael Briant; *sc* Malcolm Hulke
lp Katy Manning; Roger Delgado;
Edwin Richfield; Clive Morton; Royston Tickner
The SEA DEVILS: EPISODE 2 4/3/1972
d Michael Briant; *sc* Malcolm Hulke
lp Katy Manning; Edwin Richfield;
Roger Delgado; Clive Morton;
Declan Mulholland
The SEA DEVILS: EPISODE 3 11/3/1972
d Michael Briant; *sc* Malcolm Hulke
lp Katy Manning; Roger Delgado;
Clive Morton; Edwin Richfield; Donald Sumpter
The SEA DEVILS: EPISODE 4 18/3/1972
d Michael Briant; *sc* Malcolm Hulke
lp Katy Manning; Roger Delgado;
Clive Morton; Edwin Richfield; June Murphy
The SEA DEVILS: EPISODE 5 25/3/1972
d Michael Briant; *sc* Malcolm Hulke
lp Katy Manning; Edwin Richfield;
June Murphy; Roger Delgado;
Peter Forbes-Robertson
The SEA DEVILS: EPISODE 6 1/4/1972
d Michael Briant; *sc* Malcolm Hulke
lp Katy Manning; Edwin Richfield;
Roger Delgado; Peter Forbes-Robertson;
June Murphy
The MUTANTS: EPISODE 1 8/4/1972
d Christopher Barry;
sc Bob Baker, Dave Martin
lp Katy Manning; Paul Whitsun-Jones;
Christopher Coll; Rick James; James Mellor
The MUTANTS: EPISODE 3 22/4/1972
d Christopher Barry;
sc Bob Baker, Dave Martin
lp Katy Manning; Rick James;
James Mellor; Paul Whitsun-Jones;
George Pravda
The MUTANTS: EPISODE 4 29/4/1972
d Christopher Barry;
sc Bob Baker, Dave Martin
lp Katy Manning; Christopher Coll;
Rick James; Garrick Hagon; John Hollis
The MUTANTS: EPISODE 5 6/5/1972
d Christopher Barry;
sc Bob Baker, Dave Martin
lp Katy Manning; Garrick Hagon;
Rick James; Christopher Coll;
Paul Whitsun-Jones
The MUTANTS: EPISODE 6 13/5/1972
d Christopher Barry;
sc Bob Baker, Dave Martin
lp Katy Manning; George Pravda;
Paul Whitsun-Jones; Rick James; Garrick Hagon
The TIME MONSTER: EPISODE 1 20/5/1972
d Paul Bernard; *sc* Robert Sloman
lp Roger Delgado; Katy Manning;
Nicholas Courtney; John Levene;
Wanda Moore; Ian Collier
The TIME MONSTER: EPISODE 2 27/5/1972
d Paul Bernard; *sc* Robert Sloman
lp Roger Delgado; Katy Manning;
Nicholas Courtney; John Levene;
Wanda Moore; Ian Collier
The TIME MONSTER: EPISODE 3 3/6/1972
d Paul Bernard; *sc* Robert Sloman
lp Roger Delgado; Katy Manning;
Nicholas Courtney; John Levene; Wanda Moore
The TIME MONSTER: EPISODE 4 10/6/1972
d Paul Bernard; *sc* Robert Sloman
lp Roger Delgado; Katy Manning;
Nicholas Courtney; John Levene; Wanda Moore
The TIME MONSTER: EPISODE 5 17/6/1972
d Paul Bernard; *sc* Robert Sloman
lp Roger Delgado; Katy Manning;
Donald Eccles; George Cormack;
Susan Penhaligon
The TIME MONSTER: EPISODE 6 24/6/1972
d Paul Bernard; *sc* Robert Sloman
lp Roger Delgado; Susan Penhaligon;
Ingrid Pitt; George Cormack; Katy Manning

The THREE DOCTORS: EPISODE 1 30/12/1972
d Lennie Mayne;
sc Bob Baker, Dave Martin
lp Jon Pertwee; Patrick Troughton;
William Hartnell; Laurie Webb; Rex Robinson;
Patricia Prior; Nicholas Courtney; Katy Manning
The THREE DOCTORS: EPISODE 2 6/1/1973
d Lennie Mayne;
sc Bob Baker, Dave Martin
lp Jon Pertwee; Patrick Troughton;
William Hartnell; Katy Manning; John Levene;
Nicholas Courtney; Clyde Pollitt;
Graham Leaman
The THREE DOCTORS: EPISODE 3 13/1/1973
d Lennie Mayne;
sc Dave Martin, Bob Baker
lp Jon Pertwee; Patrick Troughton;
William Hartnell; Nicholas Courtney;
John Levene; Katy Manning; Rex Robinson;
Stephen Thorne
The THREE DOCTORS: EPISODE 4 20/1/1973
d Lennie Mayne;
sc Bob Baker, Dave Martin
lp Jon Pertwee; Patrick Troughton;
William Hartnell; Stephen Thorne;
Nicholas Courtney; Katy Manning; John Levene
The CARNIVAL OF MONSTERS: EPISODE 1
27/1/1973
d Barry Letts; *sc* Robert Holmes
lp Katy Manning; Michael Wisher;
Terence Lodge; Cheryl Hall; Leslie Dwyer
The CARNIVAL OF MONSTERS: EPISODE 2
3/2/1973
d Barry Letts; *sc* Robert Holmes
lp Katy Manning; Peter Halliday;
Terence Lodge; Michael Wisher; Cheryl Hall
The CARNIVAL OF MONSTERS: EPISODE 3
10/2/1973
d Barry Letts; *sc* Robert Holmes
lp Katy Manning; Terence Lodge;
Leslie Dwyer; Peter Halliday; Cheryl Hall
The CARNIVAL OF MONSTERS: EPISODE 4
17/2/1973
d Barry Letts; *sc* Robert Holmes
lp Katy Manning; Leslie Dwyer;
Peter Halliday; Cheryl Hall; Michael Wisher
FRONTIER IN SPACE: EPISODE 6 31/3/1973
d Paul Bernard; *sc* Malcolm Hulke
lp Roger Delgado; Vera Fusek;
Peter Birrel; Ramsay Williams
PLANET OF THE DALEKS: EPISODE 1 7/4/1973
d David Maloney; *sc* Terry Nation
lp Katy Manning; Bernard Horsfall;
Prentis Hancock; Tim Preece
PLANET OF THE DALEKS: EPISODE 2 14/4/1973
d David Maloney; *sc* Terry Nation
lp Katy Manning; Bernard Horsfall;
Tim Preece; Prentis Hancock; Roy Skelton
PLANET OF THE DALEKS: EPISODE 4 28/4/1973
d David Maloney; *sc* Terry Nation
lp Katy Manning; Tim Preece; Jane How;
Bernard Horsfall; Prentis Hancock
PLANET OF THE DALEKS: EPISODE 5 5/5/1973
d David Maloney; *sc* Terry Nation
lp Katy Manning; Prentis Hancock;
Bernard Horsfall; Tim Preece; Jane How
PLANET OF THE DALEKS: EPISODE 6 12/5/1973
d David Maloney; *sc* Terry Nation
lp Katy Manning; Bernard Horsfall;
Tim Preece; Jane How; Alan Tucker
The GREEN DEATH: EPISODE 1 19/5/1973
d Michael Briant; *sc* Robert Sloman
lp John Scott Martin; Jerome Willis;
Ben Howard; Tony Adams; Katy Manning;
Nicholas Courtney
The GREEN DEATH: EPISODE 2 26/5/1973
d Michael Briant; *sc* Robert Sloman
lp Jerome Willis; Ben Howard; Tony Adams;
Mostyn Evans; Stewart Bevan; Katy Manning;
Nicholas Courtney
The GREEN DEATH: EPISODE 3 2/6/1973
d Michael Briant; *sc* Robert Sloman
lp Jerome Willis; Ben Howard; Tony Adams;
Stewart Bevan; Katy Manning;
Nicholas Courtney; Talfryn Thomas
The GREEN DEATH: EPISODE 4 9/6/1973
d Michael Briant; *sc* Robert Sloman
lp Jerome Willis; Ben Howard; Tony Adams;
Stewart Bevan; Katy Manning;
Nicholas Courtney; John Dearth;
Mitzi Mckenzie

The GREEN DEATH: EPISODE 5 16/6/1973
d Michael Briant; *sc* Robert Sloman
lp Jerome Willis; Stewart Bevan;
Katy Manning; Nicholas Courtney; John Dearth
The GREEN DEATH: EPISODE 6 23/6/1973
d Michael Briant; *sc* Robert Sloman
lp Jerome Willis; Stewart Bevan;
Katy Manning; Nicholas Courtney; John Dearth
The TIME WARRIOR: PART 1 15/12/1973
d Alan Bromly; *sc* Robert Holmes
lp John J. Carney; Sheila Fay;
Kevin Lindsay; Nicholas Courtney;
Elisabeth Sladen
The TIME WARRIOR: PART 2 22/12/1973
d Alan Bromly; *sc* Robert Holmes
lp John J. Carney; Kevin Lindsay;
Elisabeth Sladen; David Daker; Jeremy Bulloch
The TIME WARRIOR: PART 3 29/12/1973
d Alan Bromly; *sc* Robert Holmes
lp John J. Carney; Kevin Lindsay;
Elisabeth Sladen; David Daker; Jeremy Bulloch
The TIME WARRIOR: PART 4 5/1/1974
d Alan Bromly; *sc* Robert Holmes
lp John J. Carney; Kevin Lindsay;
Elisabeth Sladen; David Daker; Jeremy Bulloch
INVASION OF THE DINOSAURS: EPISODE 6
16/2/1974
d Paddy Russell; *sc* Malcolm Hulke
lp John Bennett; Richard Franklin;
Martin Jarvis; Colin Bell
DEATH TO THE DALEKS: EPISODE 1 23/2/1974
d Michael Briant; *sc* Terry Nation
lp Terry Walsh; Elisabeth Sladen;
Duncan Lamont; John Abineri; Julian Fox
DEATH TO THE DALEKS: EPISODE 2 2/3/1974
d Michael Briant; *sc* Terry Nation
lp Joy Harrison; Michael Wisher;
John Scott Martin; Murphy Grumbar; Cy Town
DEATH TO THE DALEKS: EPISODE 3 9/3/1974
d Michael Briant; *sc* Terry Nation
lp Joy Harrison; Michael Wisher;
John Scott Martin; Murphy Grumbar; Cy Town
DEATH TO THE DALEKS: EPISODE 4 16/3/1974
d Michael Briant; *sc* Terry Nation
lp Joy Harrison; Michael Wisher;
John Scott Martin; Murphy Grumbar; Cy Town
The MONSTER OF PELADON: EPISODE 1
23/3/1974
d Lennie Mayne; *sc* Brian Hayles
lp Ralph Watson; Donald Gee; Gerald Taylor;
Nina Thomas; Frank Gatliff; Elisabeth Sladen
The MONSTER OF PELADON: EPISODE 2
30/3/1974
d Lennie Mayne; *sc* Brian Hayles
lp Ralph Watson; Donald Gee; Nina Thomas;
Frank Gatliff; Stuart Fell; Elisabeth Sladen
The MONSTER OF PELADON: EPISODE 3
6/4/1974
d Lennie Mayne; *sc* Brian Hayles
lp Ralph Watson; Donald Gee; Nina Thomas;
Frank Gatliff; Stuart Fell; Elisabeth Sladen
The MONSTER OF PELADON: EPISODE 4
13/4/1974
d Lennie Mayne; *sc* Brian Hayles
lp Ralph Watson; Donald Gee; Nina Thomas;
Frank Gatliff; Stuart Fell; Elisabeth Sladen
The MONSTER OF PELADON: EPISODE 5
20/4/1974
d Lennie Mayne; *sc* Brian Hayles
lp Donald Gee; Nina Thomas;
Frank Gatliff; Stuart Fell; Elisabeth Sladen
The MONSTER OF PELADON: EPISODE 6
27/4/1974
d Lennie Mayne; *sc* Brian Hayles
lp Donald Gee; Nina Thomas; Stuart Fell;
Ysanne Churchman; Elisabeth Sladen
GENESIS OF THE DALEKS: EPISODE 1 8/3/1975
d David Maloney; *sc* Terry Nation
lp Elisabeth Sladen; Ian Martin;
Michael Wisher; Peter Miles; Dennis Chinnery
GENESIS OF THE DALEKS: EPISODE 2 15/3/1975
d David Maloney; *sc* Terry Nation
lp Elisabeth Sladen; Ian Martin;
Michael Wisher; Peter Miles; Dennis Chinnery
GENESIS OF THE DALEKS: EPISODE 3 22/3/1975
d David Maloney; *sc* Terry Nation
lp Elisabeth Sladen; Ian Martin;
Michael Wisher; Peter Miles; Dennis Chinnery
GENESIS OF THE DALEKS: EPISODE 4 29/3/1975
d David Maloney; *sc* Terry Nation
lp Elisabeth Sladen; Ian Martin;
Michael Wisher; Peter Miles; Dennis Chinnery

The TERROR OF THE ZYGONS: EPISODE 1
30/8/1975
d Douglas Camfield; *sc* Robert Banks Stewart
lp Hugh Martin; Elisabeth Sladen;
Ian Marter; John Woodnutt; John Levene
The TERROR OF THE ZYGONS: EPISODE 2
6/9/1975
d Douglas Camfield; *sc* RobertBanks Stewart
lp Hugh Martin; Elisabeth Sladen;
Ian Marter; John Levene; Nicholas Courtney
The TERROR OF THE ZYGONS: EPISODE 3
13/9/1975
d Douglas Camfield; *sc* Robert Banks Stewart
lp Hugh Martin; Elisabeth Sladen;
Ian Marter; John Woodnutt; Angus Lennie
The BRAIN OF MORBIUS: EPISODE 1 3/1/1976
d Christopher Barry; *sc* Robin Bland
lp Elisabeth Sladen; John Scott Martin;
Colin Fay; Philip Madoc; Cynthia Grenville
The BRAIN OF MORBIUS: EPISODE 2 10/1/1976
d Christopher Barry; *sc* Robin Bland
lp Elisabeth Sladen; Colin Fay;
Philip Madoc; Cynthia Grenville
The BRAIN OF MORBIUS: EPISODE 3 17/1/1976
d Christopher Barry; *sc* Robin Bland
lp Elisabeth Sladen; Colin Fay;
Philip Madoc; Cynthia Grenville
The BRAIN OF MORBIUS: EPISODE 4 24/1/1976
d Christopher Barry; *sc* Robin Bland
lp Elisabeth Sladen; Colin Fay;
Philip Madoc; Cynthia Grenville
The HAND OF FEAR: EPISODE 1 2/10/1976
d Lennie Mayne;
sc Bob Baker, Dave Martin
lp Elisabeth Sladen; Roy Pattison;
David Purcell; Rex Robinson; Renu Setna
The HAND OF FEAR: EPISODE 2 9/10/1976
d Lennie Mayne;
sc Bob Baker, Dave Martin
lp Elisabeth Sladen; Glyn Houston;
Francis Pidgeon; Roy Boyd
The HAND OF FEAR: EPISODE 3 16/10/1976
d Lennie Mayne;
sc Bob Baker, Dave Martin
lp Elisabeth Sladen; Roy Boyd;
Glyn Houston; Judith Paris; Francis Pidgeon
The HAND OF FEAR: EPISODE 4 23/10/1976
d Lennie Mayne;
sc Bob Baker Dave Martin
lp Elisabeth Sladen; Judith Paris;
Roy Skelton; Stephen Thorne
The DEADLY ASSASSIN: EPISODE 3 13/11/1976
d David Maloney; *sc* Robert Holmes
lp George Pravda; Bernard Horsfall;
Erik Chitty
The TALONS OF WENG-CHIANG: EPISODE 3
12/3/1977
d David Maloney; *sc* Robert Holmes
lp Louise Jameson; John Bennett;
Deep Roy; Trevor Baxter; Michael Spice
The SUN MAKERS: EPISODE 3 10/12/1977
d Pennant Roberts; *sc* Robert Holmes
lp Roy Macready; Richard Leech;
Jonina Scott; Michael Keating
The PIRATE PLANET: EPISODE 1 30/9/1978
d Pennant Roberts; *sc* Douglas Adams
lp Mary Tamm; Bruce Purchase;
Andrew Robertson; Bernard Finch; John Leeson
The PIRATE PLANET: EPISODE 2 7/10/1978
d Pennant Roberts; *sc* Douglas Adams
lp Mary Tamm; Bruce Purchase;
Andrew Robertson; Rosalind Lloyd;
David Warwick
The PIRATE PLANET: EPISODE 3 14/10/1978
d Pennant Roberts; *sc* Douglas Adams
lp Mary Tamm; Bruce Purchase;
Andrew Robertson; David Sibley;
Bernard Finch
The PIRATE PLANET: EPISODE 4 21/10/1978
d Pennant Roberts; *sc* Douglas Adams
lp Mary Tamm; Bruce Purchase;
Andrew Robertson; David Sibley;
Rosalind Lloyd

DOLLY (Yorkshire TV 2–16/5/1973)
Series based on 'The Dolly Dialogues' by
Anthony Hope, first published in 1894.
The HOUSE OPPOSITE 2/5/1973
d John Frankau; *exec.p* Peter Willes;
sc Philip Mackie
lp Daniel Massey; Felicity Kendal;
Walter Forsbrugh; Guy Slater; Martin Boddey;
Faith Brook; Petra Davies; Richard Vernon

DOMINIC (Yorkshire TV 1976)
Eight-part adventure series for children; sequel
to BOY DOMINIC (1974).
p Hugh David
regulars Richard Todd; John Hallam;
Murray Dale
HANGMAN'S HOLLOW 15/2/1976
d Hugh David; *sc* Keith Dewhurst
lp Ruth Kettlewell; Jerold Wells; Donald Morley
The HUNTER 22/2/1976
d Hugh David; *sc* Keith Dewhurst
lp Jerold Wells; Trevor Smith;
Ruth Kettlewell; Stacey Tendeter;
Gordon Gostelow
MISS SARAH 29/2/1976
d David Reynolds; *sc* Keith Dewhurst
lp Jerold Wells; Trevor Smith;
Ruth Kettlewell; Gordon Gostelow; Ken Kitson;
Gerry Cowan; Stacey Tendeter
The CRYPT 7/3/1976
d David Reynolds; *sc* Keith Dewhurst
lp Gordon Gostelow; Edwin Richfield;
Stacey Tendeter
The BROTHERHOOD 14/3/1976
d David Reynolds; *sc* Keith Dewhurst
lp Edwin Richfield; Eric Francis;
Stacey Tendeter; Gordon Gostelow;
Gerry Cowan
LUCY AND HARRIET 21/3/1976
d David Reynolds; *sc* Keith Dewhurst
lp Edwin Richfield; Eric Francis;
Stacey Tendeter; Gordon Gostelow;
Gerry Cowan; Louise Jameson
TWENTY YEARS AGO 28/3/1976
d Hugh David; *sc* David Corbey
lp Gordon Gostelow; Edwin Richfield;
Thorley Walters; Louise Jameson
BEYOND GRAVITY 4/4/1976
d Hugh David; *sc* David Corbey
lp Gordon Gostelow; Edwin Richfield;
Stacey Tendeter; Thorley Walters;
Ruth Kettlewell; Louise Jameson

DON'T KNOCK THE ROCK
(Granada 5/12/1977)
Compilation of material from two Granada
music specials from 1964, 'It's Little Richard'
and 'Whole Lotta Shakin' Goin' On' with Jerry
Lee Lewis, Little Richard, Gene Vincent,
Sounds Incorporated, The Shirelles, The
Animals, and The Nashville Teens.
d Philip Casson; *p* John Hamp

The DOOMSDAY FLIGHT
(US Universal TV 13/12/1966)
Thriller concerning a bomb that has been
planted on an airliner, set to detonate when the
plane descends to 4,000 ft. Originally shown on
television in the USA, theatrically released in
Europe.
d William A. Graham; *p* Frank Price;
sc Rod Serling
lp Jack Lord; Edmond O'Brien;
Van Johnson; Katherine Crawford; John Saxon;
Richard Carlson; Michael Sarrazin;
Edward Asner

DOOMWATCH (BBC 1970–72)
Science-fiction drama series featuring a
government department that keeps an eye on all
forms of scientific research in order to prevent
them getting out of hand.
The RED SKY 6/4/1970
d Jonathan Alwyn; *p* Terence Dudley;
sc Kit Pedlar, Gerry Davis
lp John Paul; Simon Oates; Robert Powell;
Joby Blanshard; Wendy Hall; Paul Eddington

The DOUBLE LIFE OF HENRY PHYFE
(US Filmways TV Productions 1966)
Sitcom with Red Buttons as a mild accountant
impersonating his dead double, who was an
intelligence agent.
DOUBLE LIFE OF HENRY PHYFE (PILOT) 1966
d Charles R. Rondeau; *p* Luther Davis;
sc Hannibal Coons, Harry Winkler
lp Red Buttons; Fred Clark; Zeme North;
Tom D'Andrea; Lisa Seagram; Richard Crane
DOUBLE LIFE OF HENRY PHYFE 1966
d Theodore J. Flicker; *p/sc* Luther Davis
lp Red Buttons; Fred Clark; Zeme North;
Rob Kilgallen; Leon Askin; Severn Darden;
Chanin Hale; Lauren Gilbert

DOUBLE SENTENCE (ATV 17/4/1973)
Documentary about the problems faced by
prisoners' wives and families.
p Chris Fox

DOUBLE YOUR MONEY
(Rediffusion 1955–68)
Quiz show hosted by Hughie Green; based on
CBS's 'The $64,000 Question'.
DOUBLE YOUR MONEY 1955
DOUBLE YOUR MONEY 1955
DOUBLE YOUR MONEY 1955
DOUBLE YOUR MONEY 26/9/1955
DOUBLE YOUR YEN 1962
A version of the show from Tokyo.
DOUBLE YOUR MONEY 1966
Hughie Green comperes a special edition of his
quiz show at the Tower of London, with
Yeoman warders (Beefeaters) and visitors.
Prizes are awarded in National Savings and
securities, as part of the 50th anniversary
celebrations of National Savings Certificates.
Interview with Sir Miles Thomas.
d Peter Croft
DOUBLE YOUR MONEY 22/11/1966
d Peter Croft; *with* Monica Rose
DOUBLE YOUR MONEY 11/3/1968
p Don Gale; *with* Monica Rose, Audrey Graham
DOUBLE YOUR MONEY 15/7/1968
p Don Gale; *with* Monica Rose, Audrey Graham
DOUBLE YOUR MONEY 22/7/1968
Special edition of the quiz programme, hosted by
Hughie Green in Adelaide, Australia. Last of
the series.
p Don Gale; *with* Monica Rose, Audrey Graham

DOUBTS AND CERTAINTIES
(BBC 1964–75)
Series of conversations with a religious theme.
ROBERT MCKENZIE TALKS TO MARGARET
MEAD 28/3/1968
A discussion on racial prejudice and man's need
for religion.
p Oliver Hunkin
MARTIN LUTHER KING 4/4/1968
Gerald Priestland interviews Martin Luther
King.
p Oliver Hunkin

DOUGLAS EDWARDS WITH THE NEWS
(US CBS 26/6/1956)
pres Douglas Edwards

DOUGLAS FAIRBANKS JR., PRESENTS
(Douglas Fairbanks Productions 1952–57)
Douglas Fairbanks Jr hosted and sometimes
appeared in this syndicated anthology series of
dramas produced in Britain.
The SILENT MAN 27/1/1954
lp Tilda Thamar; Robert Ayres
LITTLE BIG SHOT 18/5/1955
d/p Lance Comfort;
sc William Wiener, Herbert Abbott Spiro
lp Diana Wynyard; Diana Decker;
Hartley Power; Peter Dyneley
BETTER MOUSETRAPS 6/2/1956
d Harold Huth;
sc Pauline Stone, Michael Cosgrove
lp Ella Raines; Paul Carpenter
The PRESENT 13/2/1956
sc Michael Voysey
lp James Kenney; Carol Marsh;
Anne Blake; Humphrey Morton;
Joby Blanshard; Angela Crow

DOUGLAS FAIRBANKS JR., PRESENTS *cont.*

JASON'S HOUSE 20/2/1956
d Derek Twist; *sc* Jerry McGill
NO SAMPLES 27/2/1956
lp Betty McDowall; Ron Randell; Al Mulock
A WALK IN THE WILDERNESS 5/3/1956
lp Douglas Fairbanks Jr; Roddy McDowall
FIRST DAY 19/3/1956
d Harold Huth; *sc* Paul Dudley;
auth Bernard Glemser
lp Tom McCauley; Frances Latemore;
Mary Steele
The INTRUDER 2/4/1956
BELOVED STRANGER 3/9/1956
lp Douglas Fairbanks Jr; Ella Raines
TIMMY THE SHANKS 17/9/1956
d/p Harold Huth; *sc* Paul Vincent Carroll
lp Richard O'Sullivan; Eddie Byrne;
Bee Duffell; Peggy Marshall; Victor Brooks;
Kevin Kelly
THIS LAST TOUR 15/10/1956
lp Charlotte Thiele
SOMEONE OUTSIDE 22/10/1956
d Lance Comfort; *sc* Martin Worth
lp Lois Maxwell; Maurice Kaufmann;
Anton Diffring; Cyril Shaps; Jean Driant
ONE CAN'T HELP FEELING SORRY 29/10/1956
d/p Harold Smith; *sc* Frank D. Gilroy
lp Douglas Fairbanks Jr; Lois Maxwell;
Rolf Von Nauckhoff
HOMECOMING 12/11/1956
d Joseph Sterling; *sc* Joseph Schull
lp Barry Foster; Barbara Mullen;
Eynon Evans; Anne Paige; Glyn Houston;
Fanny Carby
RENDEZVOUS AT DAWN 19/11/1956
lp Robert Beatty
TO WHAT GREAT HEIGHTS 3/12/1956
lp Robert Beatty; Sean Barrett

DOWAGER IN HOT PANTS
(Thames 17/8/1971)
Accounts of life in Hollywood from Adolph
Zukor, Sharon Farrell, Betty Blythe, Pamela
Kellino; Babe London, Ben Lane and Stanley
Kramer.
d/p Jack Gold

DRAMA '62 (ATV 1962)
Anthology drama series.
LONESOME ROAD 21/1/1962
A London accountant travelling home by train to
Woking reluctantly engages in conversation with
an apparently insensitive and over-talkative
fellow passenger.
p Donald McWhinnie; *sc* Giles Cooper
lp Michael Gough; Ronald Fraser;
Gwen Cherrell; Michael Harding; Bart Allison

DRAMA '64 (ATV 1964)
Anthology drama series.
A FEAR OF STRANGERS 10/5/1964
A Chief Inspector of police, who is awaiting a
board of inquiry into allegations of brutality,
tries to force a confession of murder from a West
Indian musician.
d Herbert Wise; *sc* Leon Griffiths
lp Stanley Baker; Earl Cameron;
Garfield Morgan; Peter Williams; Neil Wilson;
Ray Austin

The DREAM MACHINE (ATV 11/11/1964)
A backstage view of a production of a television
show, 'Six Wonderful Girls'.
d Denis Mitchell; *p* Francis Essex;
sc S.C. Green, R.M. Hills
with Francis Essex, Roy Knight,
Honor Blackman, Cleo Laine, Dora Bryan,
Millicent Martin, Adele Leigh, Nadia Nerina

A DREAM OF TREASON (BBC 7/8/1960)
Play about the predicament of a Deputy Head of
the News Department at the Foreign Office who,
before a conference, betrays the text of a secret
Foreign Office document to a French newspaper.
p John Jacobs; *sc* Anthony Steven;
auth Maurice Edelman
lp Tony Britton; Andrew Cruickshank;
Judith Stott; Ernest Clark; Anthony Sharp

The DUCHESS OF DUKE STREET
(BBC 1976–77)
Drama series based on the life of Louisa Trotter,
proprietor of the Bentinck Hotel, Duke St.,
London.
A PRESENT SOVEREIGN 4/9/1976
d Bill Bain; *p/sc* John Hawkesworth
lp Gemma Jones; Donald Burton;
Christopher Cazenove; George Pravda;
June Brown; Doreen Mantle; Susan Brown

DUCHESS OF KENT OBITUARY
(Rediffusion 27/8/1968)
Review of the life of Princess Marina, Duchess
of Kent.

DUDH KOSI – RELENTLESS RIVER OF
EVEREST (HTV 28/12/1977)
A six-strong British team canoe down the Dudh
Kosi, whose source is 20,000ft up on the slopes
of Everest.
exec.p Aled Vaughan; *nar* Ian McNaught-Davis

DUMMY (ATV 9/11/1977)
Dramatised documentary concerning Sandra X,
a young, deaf girl who became a prostitute.
d/p Franc Roddam; *sc* Hugh Whitemore
lp Geraldine James; Kelvyn Harrison

The DUPONT SHOW OF THE WEEK
(US NBC 1961–64)
A mixture of documentaries, musical shows and
drama presentations.
HURRICANE! 27/5/1962
The progress of hurricane 'Carla', which struck
Texas in September 1961.
p Al Wasserman, Irving Gitlin;
sc Craig Gilbert; *nar* Dane Clarke

DUSTY (BBC 1966–67)
Music and comedy series starring Dusty
Springfield.
DUSTY 1/9/1966
p Stanley Dorfman; *with* Woody Allen
DUSTY 19/9/1967
p Stanley Dorfman; *with* Scott Walker

DUWIAU AC ARWYR (BBC)
Welsh language series about legends.
PERSEUS A'R GORGON 20/11/1978

DYLAN THOMAS'S ME AND MY BIKE
(BBC 3/1/1979)
Emlyn Williams guides the viewer through a
fantasy about a young stable-lad who falls under
the spell of a penny-farthing bicycle in this
operetta performed by puppets.
p Derek Trimby
lp Emlyn Williams; Timothy German

E

The EAMONN ANDREWS SHOW
(ABC 1965–69)
Talk show hosted by Eamonn Andrews.
The EAMONN ANDREWS SHOW 8/5/1966
Eamonn Andrews and guests celebrate the 10th
anniversary of the opening of ITV in the North
of England, from the Hotel Piccadilly,
Manchester,
d Neville Wortman; *p* Malcolm Morris
with Harry H. Corbett, Billie Whitelaw,
Jackie Trent, Bob Sharples, Gerry Marsden
The EAMONN ANDREWS SHOW 7/1/1968
p Gordon Reece
with Muhammad Ali, David Susskind

EARL MOUNTBATTEN OF BURMA
(Rediffusion 23/4/1959)
Lord Mountbatten, interviewed by Ludovic
Kennedy, talks about his naval career and the
current role of the Royal Navy within NATO.
d Rollo Gamble

ED AND ZED! (BBC 24/10–19/12/1970)
Comedy and pop series for children, presented
by Ed Stewart and robot assistant Zed.
ED AND ZED! 21/11/1970
p Paul Ciani; *sc* Paul Ciani, Jack Tinker

EDEN AND AFTER (Scottish TV 1/11/1973)
The impact on the island community of Unst of
the discovery of North Sea oil.
d Geoff Rimmer

The EDGE OF THE SIXTIES
(BBC 27–30/12/59)
Four-part series looking at the first sixty years of
the twentieth century.
V.E. PLUS TEN 30/12/1959
Lord Boothby introduces a review of the major
events in Britain and Europe since V.E. Day.
d Richard Cawston

EDITH EVANS (Yorkshire TV 6/3/1973)
Bryan Forbes talks to Dame Edith Evans about
her life and career.
d Bryan Forbes

The EDITORS (BBC 1973–81)
Documentary series looking at the press and
media.
IMMIGRANT PRESS 13/6/1976
Interview with four editors about the Southall
Protest March.
d Brian James; *p* Elwyn Parry-Jones
The ETHICS OF TV DOCUMENTARIES 28/8/1977
George Scott questions the power and privilege
of modern communicators – the editors of
newspapers, books and periodicals, radio and
television. Includes clips from The CASE OF
YOLANDE McSHANE (1977).
d David Taft; *p* Elwyn Parry-Jones

EDWARD AND MRS SIMPSON
(Thames 1978)
A dramatic reconstruction, in seven parts, of the
romance between Edward VIII and Mrs Wallis
Simpson, which led to the Abdication in 1936.
d Waris Hussein; *p* Andrew Brown;
sc Simon Raven
regulars Edward Fox; Cynthia Harris
EPISODE 1: The LITTLE PRINCE 8/11/1978
lp Marius Goring; Jeremy Child;
Kika Markham; Cherie Lunghi
EPISODE 2: VENUS AT THE PROW 15/11/1978
lp Marius Goring; Andrew Ray;
David Waller; Peggy Ashcroft; Maurice Denham
EPISODE 3: The NEW KING 22/11/1978
lp Andrew Ray; Peggy Ashcroft;
Nigel Hawthorne; John Shrapnel
EPISODE 4: The DIVORCE 29/11/1978
lp David Waller; Maurice Denham;
Nigel Hawthorne; John Shrapnel
EPISODE 5: The DECISION 6/12/1978
lp Andrew Ray; Peggy Ashcroft;
Nigel Hawthorne; Jessie Matthews;
David Waller
EPISODE 6: PROPOSALS 13/12/1978
lp Peggy Ashcroft; Nigel Hawthorne;
David Waller; John Shrapnel
EPISODE 7: ABDICATION 20/12/1978
lp Peggy Ashcroft; Andrew Ray;
Amanda Reiss; John Schrapnel;
Nigel Hawthorne

EH JOE (BBC 4/7/1966)
Written specially for television the play features
only one visible character, Joe, who does not
speak throughout the play, and the voice of an
unseen woman whom Joe once loved.
d Alan Gibson; *p* Michael Bakewell;
sc Samuel Beckett
lp Jack MacGowran; Siân Phillips

EIGHT FACES OF GOD
(Tyne Tees 11/6/1975)
p Maxwell Deas

EIGHTEEN MONTHS TO BALCOMBE
STREET (LWT 19/2/1977)
Dramatised documentary on the IRA bombers
and events leading to the siege of Balcombe
Street, London. [The programme was
unscheduled and transmitted only a week after
the trial of the men involved in the Balcombe
Street siege.]
d Stephen Frears; *p* Barry Cox;
sc John Shirley
lp Niall O'Brien; Daragh O'Malley;
John Murphy; Raymond Campbell;
Andrew Byatt

EIN TAG
(DE Norddeutscher Rundfunk 6/5/1965;
BBC *tx* 10/12/1977)
Egon Monk's dramatic reconstruction of a day in
a German concentration camp, made as a factual
report on the daily routine in a camp in January
1939.
d Egon Monk;
sc Gunther R. Lys, Egon Monk,
Claus Hubalek
lp Hartmut Reck; Heinz Giese;
Ernst Ronnecker; Ernst Jacobi;
Eberhard Fechner

EINSTEIN (BBC 27/4/1965)
A biography of Albert Einstein; those taking
part include Hedwig Born, Thomas Bucky,
Helen Dukas, Patrick Gordon-Walker, Banesh
Hoffmann and J. Robert Oppenheimer.
p/sc Robert Reid; *nar* John Stockbridge

EL GRECO
(US Times Four Productions 22/4/1973)
The artist's paintings compared with film of the
actual locations.
d Robert Delaney

The ELEANOR ROOSEVELT STORY
(BBC 27/12/1966)
A film biography of a President Roosevelt's wife
who became a political figure in her own right.
d Richard Kaplan; *p* Sidney Glazier

ELECTION FORUM (BBC 1966)
Coverage of the 1966 General Election.
JO GRIMOND 8/3/1966
Robin Day, Ian Trethowan and Kenneth Harris
interview Jo Grimond, putting to him questions
set by viewers.
EDWARD HEATH 9/3/1966
Robin Day, Ian Trethowan and Kenneth Harris
interview Edward Heath, putting to him
questions set by viewers.
HAROLD WILSON 10/3/1966
Robin Day, Ian Trethowan and Kenneth Harris
interview Harold Wilson, putting to him
questions set by viewers.

ELECTION 1974 (BBC 28/2/1974)
Coverage of the February l974 General Election.
d Keith Clement

ELECTION RESULTS (ITN 8/10/1959)
Report of the General Election results as they
are declared throughout the country. Reports
from the political parties' headquarters;
Professor M.G. Kendall in Stafford analyses
swings and predicts results using 'Deuce' the
electronic computer of the English Electric
Company.
d John Rhodes, Graham Watts;
p James Bredin;
pres Ian Trethowan, Brian Connell

ELECTION RESULTS 1959
(BBC 9/10/1959)
Richard Dimbleby, David Butler and Robert
McKenzie comment on the results from the 1959
General Election.

ELECTION ROUND-UP (BBC 9/10/1959)
An analysis of the results of the 1959 General
Election, introduced by Richard Dimbleby, with
contributions from David Butler, Cliff
Michelmore, Robert McKenzie and others, plus
comments from Harold Macmillan, Hugh
Gaitskell, Frank Byers, Lord Boothby, and Tom
Driberg.

ELECTION 70 (BBC 1970)
Coverage of the 1970 General Election.
QUESTION TIME 9/6/1970
Journalists who work in the south east of
England question party representatives on
regional election issues.
p John Morrell; *pres* Bob Wellings

ELECTION 74 (BBC 1974)
Coverage of the October 1974 General Election.
HERE IS THE RESULT 10/10/1974
Coverage of the October 1974 General Election
results, with Alastair Burnet, David Butler,
Graham Pyatt, Robert McKenzie, and Robin
Day.
d Keith Clement

ELECTRA (Rediffusion 28/11/1962)
A production of Sophocles' play by the Piraikon
Greek Tragedy Theatre.
d Joan Kemp-Welch; *p* Dimitrios Rondiris
lp Aspassia Papathanassiou; Dimitri Veakis;
Georgia Saris; Dimitris Malavetas;
Anthi Kariofili

ELIZABETH R (BBC 17/2–24/3/1971)
Six-part drama series on the life of Elizabeth I of
England.
p Rod Graham
regular Glenda Jackson
The LION'S CUB 17/2/1971
d Claude Whatham; *sc* John Hale
lp Ronald Hines; Daphne Slater;
Rachel Kempson; Rosalie Crutchley;
Bernard Hepton; Peter Jeffrey
SHADOW IN THE SUN 3/3/1971
d Richard Martin; *sc* Julian Mitchell
lp Ronald Hines; Robert Hardy;
Stephen Murray; Michael Williams;
Margaretta Scott; Angela Thorne
HORRIBLE CONSPIRACIES 10/3/1971
d Rod Graham; *sc* Hugh Whitemore
lp Stephen Murray; Vivian Pickles;
David Collings; Hamilton Dyce; Brian Wilde;
Malcolm Hayes
SWEET ENGLAND'S PRIDE 24/3/1971
d Rod Graham; *sc* Ian Rodger
lp Ronald Hines; Robin Ellis;
John Nettleton; Nicholas Selby;
Patrick O'Connell; Angela Thorne; Peter Egan

ELLA (Granada 22/4/1964)
A concert broadcast from the Free Trade Hall,
Manchester, with Ella Fitzgerald, The Oscar
Peterson Trio, and The Roy Eldridge Quartet.
d Philip Casson; *p* John Hamp

EMERGENCY – WARD 10 (ATV 1957–67)
Hospital drama series set in the fictional hospital
of Oxbridge.
EMERGENCY – WARD 10 19/5/1959
d Christopher Morahan; *p* Antony Kearey;
sc Tessa Diamond
lp Charles Tingwell; Jill Browne;
Frederick Bartman; Barbara Clegg;
Desmond Carrington; Geoffrey Adams;
Jan Holden
EMERGENCY – WARD 10 22/5/1959
d Christopher Morahan; *p* Antony Kearey;
sc Margot Bennett
lp Charles Tingwell; Jill Browne;
Frederick Bartman; Barbara Clegg;
Desmond Carrington; John Carson

EMMERDALE FARM (Yorkshire TV 1972–)
Farming soap opera set in the Yorkshire Dales.
Changed its name to 'Emmerdale' in 1989.
EMMERDALE FARM 9/10/1973
d Michael Snow; *p* Robert D. Cardona;
sc Kevin Laffan
lp Toke Townley; George Little;
Sheila Mercier; Carolyn Moody; Patrick Holt;
Daphne Green; Ronald Magill;
Geoffrey Burridge; Frederick Pyne;
Andrew Burt; Frazer Hines; Arthur Pentelow;
Eric Allan; Diane Grayson
EMMERDALE FARM 15/10/1973
d/p Robert D. Cardona; *sc* Kevin Laffan
lp as above
EMMERDALE FARM 16/10/1973
d/p Robert D. Cardona; *sc* Kevin Laffan
lp as above

EMPIRE ROAD (BBC 1978–79)
Drama series featuring a West Indian community
in Birmingham.
WEDDING 25/10/1979
d Horace Ové; *p* Peter Ansorge;
sc Michael Abbensetts
lp Norman Beaton; Nalini Moonasar;
Wayne Laryea; Corinne Skinner-Carter;
Joe Marcell; Rosa Roberts; Trevor Butler;
Vincent Taylor

The EMPTY QUARTER (BBC 26/8/1967)
Reconstructed record of explorer Thesiger's
desert treks in 1946 contrasting Arab life then
and now.
p Richard Taylor; *nar* Wilfred Thesiger

**EMU'S BROADCASTING COMPANY
(EBC1)** (BBC 1975–80)
Series for children featuring Rod Hull and his
puppet Emu.
EMU'S BROADCASTING COMPANY (EBC1)
12/11/1976
d Hazel Lewthwaite; *p* Peter Ridsdale Scott;
sc Rod Hull; *with* Billy Dainty, Barbara New
EMU'S BROADCASTING COMPANY (EBC1)
14/11/1977
d Hazel Lewthwaite; *p* Peter Ridsdale Scott;
sc Rod Hull; *with* Billy Dainty, Barbara New

END OF PART ONE (LWT 1979–80)
Comedy series.
END OF PART ONE 15/4/1979
p Simon Brett;
sc Andrew Marshall, David Renwick
lp Denise Coffey; Tony Aitken;
Fred Harris; Sue Holderness; Dudley Stevens

ENDURANCE (Ulster TV 17/8/1966)
James Fisher tells the story of Shackleton's
1914–16 Endurance expedition to Antarctica.
p E.V.H. Emmett

The ENEMIES WITHIN
(Television Reporters International
26/4–7/6/1964)
Three reports on recent scientific and medical
advances.
CANCER 26/4/1964
A report by Robert Kee on attitudes to, and
treatment of, cancer. Includes J.B.S. Haldane
reading a poem about his own experience of
cancer.

ENEMY AT THE DOOR (LWT 1978–80)
Drama series about the German occupation of
the Channel Islands during World War II.
p Michael Chapman
regulars Alfred Burke; Emily Richard;
Richard Heffer
BY ORDER OF THE FÜHRER 21/1/1978
d Bill Bain; *sc* Michael Chapman
lp Peter Williams; Martin Fisk;
Bernard Horsfall; Antonia Pemberton;
Richard Hurndall
The LIBRARIAN 28/1/1978
d Tony Wharmby; *sc* N.J. Crisp
lp Peter Williams; Bernard Horsfall;
Antonia Pemberton; Helen Shingler;
John Malcolm
AFTER THE BALL 4/2/1978
d Christopher Hodson; *sc* James Doran
lp Bernard Horsfall; Antonia Pemberton;
John Malcolm; Simon Cadell; Simon Lack
STEEL HAND FROM THE SEA 11/2/1978
d Christopher Hodson; *sc* Kenneth Clark
lp Bernard Horsfall; Antonia Pemberton;
Simon Cadell; Martyn Jacobs; Anthony Read
The LAWS AND USAGES OF WAR 18/2/1978
d Christopher Hodson; *sc* Kenneth Clark
lp Bernard Horsfall; Antonia Pemberton;
John Malcolm; Simon Cadell; Simon Lack
V FOR VICTORY 25/2/1978
d Bill Bain; *sc* Robert Barr
lp Bernard Horsfall; John Malcolm;
Simon Cadell; Simon Gipps-Kent;
Peter Woodward
The POLISH AFFAIRE 4/3/1978
d Christopher Hodson; *sc* Michael Chapman
lp Bernard Horsfall; Antonia Pemberton;
Simon Cadell; Simon Lack; Robert Flemyng

ENEMY AT THE DOOR *cont.*

OFFICERS OF THE LAW 11/3/1978
d Jonathan Alwyn; *sc* James Doran
lp Bernard Horsfall; Antonia Pemberton;
John Malcolm; Simon Lack; John Nettles
The JERRYBAG 18/3/1978
d Bill Bain; *sc* N.J. Crisp
lp Bernard Horsfall; Antonia Pemberton;
Norma Streader; David Beames
TREASON 25/3/1978
d Jonathan Alwyn; *sc* Kenneth Clark
lp Simon Cadell; Simon Lack;
Helen Shingler; James Maxwell; Joss Ackland
PAINS AND PENALTIES 1/4/1978
d Bill Bain; *sc* John Kershaw
lp Bernard Horsfall; Antonia Pemberton;
John Malcolm; Simon Lack; John Normington
The PRUSSIAN OFFICER 8/4/1978
d Jonathan Alwyn; *sc* James Doran
lp Bernard Horsfall; John Malcolm;
Simon Cadell; Simon Lack; Helen Shingler
JUDGEMENT OF SOLOMON 15/4/1978
d Bill Bain; *sc* Michael Chapman
lp Bernard Horsfall; Antonia Pemberton;
Helen Shingler; John Malcolm; Simon Cadell

ENGLAND, THEIR ENGLAND
(ATV 1978–84)
Documentary series produced by ATV, later by
Central TV.
I DON'T THINK TWICE ABOUT MY KINKY MAIL
4/12/1978
A portrait of a woman wrestler which contrasts
her role as mum and housewife with her career.
d David C. Rea; *exec.p* Brian Lewis
MIDLAND YOUTH JAZZ ORCHESTRA 15/3/1979
An ORDER FROM AMERICA 29/3/1979
An American contemplative order of nuns who
live in a closed community.
d Albert Wallace; *p* Brian Lewis
A FORCE OF WOMEN 23/4/1979
The women's police force in Nottinghamshire.
d David Goldsmith; *exec.p* Brian Lewis

ENGLAND v. HUNGARY
(Rediffusion 5/5/1965)
Soccer international at Wembley Stadium.
d Grahame Turner;
comm Gerry Loftus, Johnny Haynes

ENGLAND v. POLAND
(Granada 5/1/1966)
Edited highlights of the soccer international at
Goodison Park.
d Eric Harrison; *comm* Gerry Loftus

ENGLAND v. ROMANIA
(BBC 15/1/1969)
Edited highlights of the match at Wembley.
p Alec Weeks; *comm* Kenneth Wolstenholme

ENGLAND v. SPAIN
(Rediffusion 24/5/1967)
Soccer international at Wembley Stadium.
d Grahame Turner; *comm* Hugh Jones

ENGLAND v. WEST GERMANY
(Rediffusion 23/2/1966)
Soccer international at Wembley Stadium.
d Grahame Turner; *comm* Barry Davies

ENGLAND v. YUGOSLAVIA
(Rediffusion 4/5/1966)
Soccer international at Wembley Stadium.
d Steve Minchin; *comm* Gerry Loftus

The ENGLISH CARDINAL (BBC 21/4/1966)
Malcolm Muggeridge interviews Cardinal
Heenan, Archbishop of Westminster, who
explains what his faith means to him and how he
sees his role in propagating it.
d Kevin Billington

An ENGLISH SUMMER (BBC 18/9/1960)
Battle of Britain drama set during the summer of
1940 on a Fighter Squadron Station in the South
East of England.
p Peter Hammond; *sc* Ronald Adam
lp Joseph O'Conor; Kevin Stoney;
Tim Seely; Richard Carpenter; Donald Churchill

ENID BLYTON'S FAMOUS FIVE
(Southern TV 1978)
Adventure series for children.
FIVE GET INTO TROUBLE: PART 1:
PRISONERS 19/11/1978
d/p Sidney Hayers; *sc* Richard Sparks
lp Michael Hinz; Sue Best; Marcus Harris;
Jennifer Thanisch; Gary Russell;
Michele Gallagher
FIVE GET INTO TROUBLE: PART 2:
CONSPIRACIES 26/11/1978
d/p Sidney Hayers; *sc* Richard Sparks
lp Michael Hinz; Sue Best; Marcus Harris;
Jennifer Thanisch; Gary Russell;
Michele Gallagher

ENOUGH TO EAT (ATV 1965–66)
Educational series for schools showing the
different ways people of the world obtain their
food.
A DUTCH FARM 7/2/1966
Carol Chell introduces a schools programme on
a dairy farm in the Polderland of North Holland.
d Victor Rudolf

ENTERPRISE (Anglia 1977–84)
Documentary series about businesses.
BROOM BOATS; VW – MILTON KEYNES;
CORBY; BABY BUGGIES 19/8/1977
Series of filmed reports about a local boat
builder; the arrival of Volkswagen in Milton
Keynes; a factory in Corby; and baby buggies.
p John Swinfield
The CASE FOR FRUIT AND NUT 26/6/1979
An interview with Sir Adrian Cadbury, chairman
of Cadbury Schweppes, about the confectionery
industry and the British economy.
d Bryan Shiner; *p* John Swinfield

The ENTERTAINERS (Grampian 1977–81)
Popular music series.
SPOOKEY 23/11/1979
The group Spookey filmed in concert.
d Alan Franchi

The ENTERTAINERS (Granada 25/3/1964 *ntx*)
Documentary giving an insight into the daily
lives of various entertainers, including singers,
strippers, wrestlers and others, who share a
rooming house in a northern city. Banned by the
ITA owing to the striptease sequence but
transmitted on 13/1/1965. [First documentary to
be shot entirely on videotape].
d John McGrath; *p* Denis Mitchell

ENTERTAINING MR. SLOANE
(Rediffusion 15/7/1968)
d Peter Moffatt; *auth* Joe Orton
lp Sheila Hancock; Edward Woodward;
Clive Francis; Arthur Lovegrove

**ENTHRONEMENT OF THE ARCHBISHOP
OF CANTERBURY** (BBC 27/6/1961)
An edited recording of the enthronement of
Arthur Michael Ramsey at Canterbury
Cathedral.
d Antony Craxton

The EPIC THAT NEVER WAS
(BBC 24/12/1965)
Dirk Bogarde tells the story of Alexander
Korda's attempt to film 'I Claudius', with
extracts from the material that was shot, and
recollections from Josef Von Sternberg, Robert
Graves, Emlyn Williams, Merle Oberon and
Flora Robson.
p Bill Duncalf

EPIDEMIC (BBC 26/1/1961)
Dramatisation about the disastrous effects of an
unexpected smallpox epidemic in a small town in
the North of England.
d/sc Robert Barr

EPILOGUE (Tyne Tees)
Religious series.
MOHAMMED ALI ON TYNE TEES EPILOGUE
1/10/1977

ERICA ON EMBROIDERY
(US WGBH Boston; BBC *tx* 10/10–19/12/1976)
Eleven-part series on sewing.
SATIN STITCH 10/10/1976
Erica Wilson demonstrates satin stitch.
d James Field; *p* Margaret MacLeod

ESPIONAGE
(Plautus Productions-ITC 1963–64)
Anglo-US drama series on the theme of
espionage, with stories ranging from the
eighteenth century to the modern day.
NEVER TURN YOUR BACK ON A FRIEND
4/1/1964
d Michael Powell; *p* George Justin;
sc Mel Davenport
lp George Voskovec; Donald Madden;
Mark Eden; Julian Glover; Pamela Brown

ETON (BBC 28/9/1965)
A typical schoolday at Eton College.
p Anthony De Lotbinière; *comm* René Cutforth

The EUROPEAN CHAMPIONS' CUP FINAL
(ES RTVE 28/5/1969)
Live coverage from Spain of the European Final
between A.C. Milan and Ajax Amsterdam.
comm Kenneth Wolstenholme

The EUROPEAN CHAMPIONS' CUP FINAL
(IT Radiotelevisione Italiana 25/5/1977)
Liverpool v. Borussia Moenchengladbach match
played at the Olympic Stadium, Rome.
p Alec Weeks, Martin Hopkins;
comm Barry Davies

**EUROPEAN CUP FINAL: BENFICA v.
MANCHESTER UNITED** (BBC 29/5/1968)
Live coverage of the final from Wembley.
intro David Coleman;
comm Kenneth Wolstenholme

**EUROPEAN CUP WINNERS' CUP FINAL:
LIVERPOOL v. BORUSSIA DORTMUND**
(BBC 5/5/1966)
Live coverage of the final from Hampden Park,
Glasgow.
comm Kenneth Wolstenholme

A EUROPEAN JOURNEY (Granada 1972–73)
René Cutforth and Denis Mitchell journey
across Europe.
ITALY INTO FRANCE 31/1/1972
René Cutforth and Denis Mitchell leave Italy for
France, on a journey through less frequented
areas of the Common Market countries.
d Denis Mitchell

The EVACUEES (BBC 5/3/1975)
Drama about two Jewish boys evacuated to
Blackpool from Manchester during World
War II.
d Alan Parker; *p* Mark Shivas;
sc Jack Rosenthal
lp Maureen Lipman; Gary Carp;
Margery Mason; Steven Serember; Ray Mort

EVERYMAN (BBC 1977–)
Documentary series on religious and moral
issues.
RASTAMAN 26/6/1977
The Rastafarians of Jamaica who believe that the
late Haile Selassie of Ethiopia is God.
d/p Vanya Kewley
BLASPHEMY AT THE OLD BAILEY 18/9/1977
Dramatised documentary on the recent trial for
blasphemy at the Old Bailey, which was begun
by Mary Whitehouse against the homosexual
newspaper 'Gay News'.
d Hugh David; *p* Daniel Wolf;
rep Peter France
lp Donald Eccles; Norman Rodway;
Gareth Thomas; Terence Hardiman;
Peter Machin
HOW IS IT IN CRACOW? 22/10/1978
Reactions in Poland to the election of John Paul
II as Pope.

The IMMORTALISTS 11/11/1979
Study of Trans Time Inc., who offer cryonic suspension services to the Californian rich, so that they can be deep frozen on death in order to wait for a cure to the cause of death.
p Chris Fox

EVERYONE MATTERS (BBC 8/6/1965)
Documentary about a north London school for girls and its headmistress, Dame Kitty Anderson.
p Stephen Hearst

EVERYONE'S GONE TO THE MOON
(Rediffusion 9/5/1967)
The life and training of astronauts in the Houston Manned Spacecraft Centre.
d Ian McFarlane; *p* James Butler;
sc/nar Peter Williams

EXPANSIONS: MARKOVA
(Scottish TV 25/5/1972)
Alicia Markova coaches dancers from the Scottish Theatre Ballet for a performance of 'Giselle'.
d Brian Mahoney

The EXPERT (BBC 1968–76)
Crime series revolving around the cases of a forensic pathologist.
IT CAN'T BE DONE 12/7/1968
d Paul Ciappessoni; *p* Gerard Glaister;
sc John Pennington
lp Marius Goring; Ann Morrish;
Victor Winding; Michael Farnsworth;
Sally Nesbitt
The YELLOW TORRISH 25/4/1969
d Prudence Fitzgerald; *p* Gerard Glaister;
sc Mervyn Haisman, Henry Lincoln
lp Marius Goring; Ann Morrish;
Victor Winding; Michael Farnsworth;
Valerie Murray

EXPLORERS (BBC 14/9–16/11/1975)
Ten-part series featuring dramatisations of famous journeys of exploration.
The STORY OF ROALD AMUNDSEN 14/9/1975
Roald Amundsen's journey to the South Pole.
d David Cobham; *p* Michael Latham;
sc Ian Rodger; *intro/nar* David Attenborough
lp Per Theodore Haugen
The STORY OF CAPTAIN JAMES COOK
2/11/1975
Captain James Cook and his voyage of discovery to Australia in 1770.
d John Irvin; *p* Michael Latham;
sc Hammond Innes;
intro/nar David Attenborough

EXTRA ITEM (BBC 19/8/1956)
A play for children.
p Barbara Hammond; *sc* Frederick H. Wiseman
lp Melvyn Hayes; Anthony Green;
Christine Stirling; Michael Corcoran;
Sally Travers; Campbell Gray

EXTRAORDINARY (Yorkshire TV 1977–80)
Series for children investigating unexplained phenomena.
EXTRAORDINARY 14/6/1977
d/p Ian Bolt; *sc/pres* Alan Brien;
with Julian Orchard

EYE ON RESEARCH (BBC 1957–61)
Documentary series on scientific developments.
TEST FLIGHT 12/5/1959
Squadron Leader S.J. Hubbard, flying the supersonic Fairey Delta II, shows how aerodynamic theories and wind tunnel tests are checked in actual flight at speeds of over 1000 mph.
p Philip Daly
ANOTHER CHILD'S POISON 26/5/1959
A report on evidence which claims that some forms of mental deficiency are caused by normal foods which some children find difficult to break down.
p Philip Daly

FULL FATHOM FIVE 30/6/1959
The Scripps Institute of Oceanography of the University of California, one of the world's main centres for research into the ocean's potential as a source of food, medicines and minerals.
d Norman Weisman
The ELECTRON MICROSCOPE 28/3/1960
The uses of electron microscopes, with practical examples explained by David E. Bradley, of AEI, Robert W. Horne of the Cavendish Laboratory, Dr Hugh Huxley of University College, London, Peter Forsyth of the Royal Aircraft Establishment, and James Menter.
p Gerald Leach; *pres* Raymond Baxter
SHAPES OF LIFE 3/5/1960
A discussion with Dr Max Ferdinand Perutz and Dr John Cowdery Kendrew about their research into the structure of proteins. With Professor J.D. Bernal.
p Philip Daly; *p* Gerald Leach
The INDOOR OCEAN 26/4/1961
A visit to the ship-testing tank at Feltham.
d Philip Daly, John Vernon;
sc Gordon Rattray Taylor;
pres Raymond Baxter

EYE TO EYE (BBC 1957–58)
A series of documentary films.
NIGHT IN THE CITY 14/6/1957
Life in a provincial city from evening to dawn. Includes film of a faith healing session at the Sharon Gospel Church in Manchester.
d Denis Mitchell
ONION JOHNNY 20/9/1957
The life of the onion-sellers from Roscoff (Brittany), who spend several months annually in Britain selling onions.
d Stephen Hearst; *p* Richard Cawston;
sc Stephen Hearst, Richard Cawston;
comm Jacques Brunius

EYES OF A CHILD (Film Partnership-BBC 7/8/1961)
Life at a school for the blind at Sevenoaks, Kent.
d/sc Henry Lewes; *p* Robert M. Angell

F

F. SCOTT FITZGERALD AND 'THE LAST OF THE BELLES'
(US Titus Productions 7/1/1974)
A play within a play. A dramatisation of F. Scott and Zelda Fitzgerald's first meeting intertwined with the fictional story he wrote about the love between a young World War I soldier and a Southern belle.
d George Schaefer; *p* Robert Buzz Berger;
sc James Costigan
lp Richard Chamberlain; Blythe Danner;
Leslie Williams; Albert Stratton;
Susan Sarandon

FABIAN OF THE YARD
(Trinity Productions 1954–57)
One of the first crime series to be shown on UK television. Featuring stories from the real-life casebook of Chief Inspector Fabian.
regular Bruce Seton
BOMBS IN PICCADILLY 1955 *ntx*
AGAINST THE EVIDENCE 8/1/1955
p John Larkin;
lp Peter Copley
The COWARD 19/3/1955
COCKTAIL GIRL 24/1/1956
d Charles Saunders; *p* John Larkin
lp Kathleen Byron; Hugh Latimer;
Ewan Roberts; Wensley Pithey; Conrad Phillips

The FABULOUS ELVIS
(US NBC 3/12/1968; BBC *tx* 31/12/1969)
A television spectacular marking Elvis Presley's first appearance before a live audience in seven years.
d/p Steve Binder

The FACE OF THE UNKNOWN
(BBC 16/8/1960)
Donald Holms introduces science fiction films, with extracts from 'Man in Space', 'The War of the Worlds', 'Them', 'Invasion of the Body-snatchers', 'Forbidden Planet', and 'The Time Machine'.
p Richard Evans; *sc* Derek Hill;
pres Donald Holms

FACE THE MUSIC (BBC 1972–76)
Musical game show with celebrity guests.
pres Joseph Cooper
FACE THE MUSIC 16/7/1973
Contestants are Joyce Grenfell, Patrick Moore, and Robin Ray, with a guest appearance by Joan Cross.
d Denis Moriarty; *p* Walter Todds

FACE THE NATION (US CBS 1954–)
Current affairs programme. Series of interviews with political figures.
HUGH GAITSKELL 13/1/1957
Hugh Gaitskell faces questions from John Madigan, Peter Lisagor, and Howard K. Smith. Chaired by Stuart Novins
EDWARD HEATH 1961
The LORD BOOTHBY 1961
MOSHE DAYAN 1961

FACE THE PRESS (Tyne Tees 1968–87)
Journalists question a figure in the news.
HRH THE DUKE OF EDINBURGH 20/3/1968
The Duke of Edinburgh answers questions on contemporary Britain, put to him by Brian Redhead, William Hardcastle and Harold Evans, chaired by Ludovic Kennedy.
d Jim Parker; *p* Frank Entwistle
EMANUEL SHINWELL MP 4/12/1968
VALERY NIKITIN 26/1/1969
The London correspondent of 'Tass' answers questions from a panel of journalists; the topics covered include the situation in Czechoslovakia.
SIR OSWALD MOSLEY 2/2/1969
pres Ludovic Kennedy
ARNOLD TOYNBEE 23/3/1969
pres Ludovic Kennedy
GENERAL SIR WILLIAM WALKER 26/2/1973
MRS ANNE ARMSTRONG 4/7/1976
d Andrea Wonfor; *p* Michael Partington;
interv Katherine Whitehorn, Peter Jenkins, Harold Evans
DAVID STEEL 11/7/1976
d Malcolm Dickinson; *p* Michael Partington
GOUGH WHITLAM 18/7/1976
d Tony Kysh; *p* Michael Partington;
interv Peregrine Worsthorne, Paul Johnson
MICHAEL FOOT 1/8/1976
d Tony Kysh; *p* Michael Partington;
interv Harold Evans
ENOCH POWELL 8/8/1976
d Tony Kysh; *p* Michael Partington;
interv George Ffitch
MRS BROOKES 19/9/1976
MICK MCGAHEY 6/7/1977
LORD ROBENS 13/7/1977
VICTOR MATTHEWS 31/7/1977
PETER PARKER 7/8/1977
d Tony Kysh; *p* Michael Partington;
pres George Ffitch
MARGARET THATCHER 28/8/1977
d Tony Kysh; *p* Michael Partington
SIR MARCUS SIEFF 6/8/1978
d Malcolm Dickinson;
p Michael Partington, Alex Murchie;
pres George Ffitch
LAURIE McMENEMY 13/8/1978
DAVID McNEE 20/8/1978
d Malcolm Dickinson;
p Michael Partington, Alex Murchie
MOSS EVANS 3/9/1978
d Tony Kysh; *p* Michael Partington
JAMES PRIOR 10/9/1978
d Tony Kysh; *p* Michael Partington
JAMES ANDERTON 29/7/1979
ABEL MUZOREWA 5/8/1979
d Lisle Willis; *interv* Anthony Howard
SID WEIGHELL 4/11/1979
d Lisle Willis
WILLIAM WHITELAW 11/11/1979
d Lisle Willis; *p* David Jones;
interv Anthony Howard

FACE TO FACE (BBC 1959–62)
Influential series of in-depth interviews.
p Hugh Burnett; *interv* John Freeman
PROFESSOR JUNG 22/10/1959
HENRY MOORE 21/2/1960
AUGUSTUS JOHN 15/5/1960
SIR ROY WELENSKY 29/5/1960
EVELYN WAUGH 26/6/1960
GILBERT HARDING 18/9/1960
GENERAL VON SENGER UND ETTERLIN
2/10/1960
LORD REITH 30/10/1960
SIMONE SIGNORET 13/11/1960
VICTOR GOLLANCZ 27/11/1960
OTTO KLEMPERER 8/1/1961
MARTIN LUTHER KING 29/10/1961

FACES OF COMMUNISM
(Yorkshire TV 26/4–24/5/1978)
Robert Kee reports on different Marxist
societies.
PEOPLE'S REPUBLIC OF THE CONGO: THE
COMEDY'S GOT TO STOP 3/5/1978
The equation of the teachings of Marx and Lenin
with tribalism and subsistence economy.
p John Fanshawe

The FACTS ARE THESE
(Granada 1969–73)
Programmes on health education for schools and
colleges.
DYING FOR A SMOKE? 1969
The medical effects of smoking are outlined.
Sportsmen, George Best, Geoff Boycott and
Mark Cox warn of the harmful effects of
smoking.
d/p Pauline Shaw
FIXED FOR DEATH 27/4/1969
Registered drug addicts talk about their
addiction.
d/p Pauline Shaw
The OTHER SIDE OF LOVE 15/5/1969
An explanation of how venereal disease is
caught; advice about treatment and contact
tracing is also given.
d Pauline Shaw
UNDERSTANDING CANCER 1970
The nature of cancer as an illness and the need
for early detection if it is to be successfully
cured.
p Pauline Shaw
LOVE NOW PAY LATER 22/2/1973
Sex education for school children.
p Pauline Shaw

The FALKLANDS AFFAIR (Anglia 25/6/1968)
Life in the Falkland Islands and the fears of the
islanders that they might be annexed by
Argentina.
d Peter Robinson; *intro* Brian Connell

**The FALL AND RISE OF REGINALD
PERRIN** (BBC 1976–79)
Comedy series about a middle-aged man's revolt
at his middling successful, middling contented
life.
p Gareth Gwenlan; *sc* David Nobbs
regulars Leonard Rossiter; Pauline Yates;
John Barron
The FALL AND RISE OF REGINALD PERRIN
8/9/1976
lp Sue Nicholls; John Horsley;
Trevor Adams
The FALL AND RISE OF REGINALD PERRIN
15/9/1976
lp Terence Conoley; Sue Nicholls;
Trevor Adams; Bruce Bould; John Horsley;
Geoffrey Palmer
The FALL AND RISE OF REGINALD PERRIN
22/9/1976
lp Sue Nicholls; Tim Preece;
David Warwick; Geoffrey Palmer
The FALL AND RISE OF REGINALD PERRIN
29/9/1976
lp Terence Conoley; Sue Nicholls;
Tim Barrett; Trevor Adams; Bruce Bould
The FALL AND RISE OF REGINALD PERRIN
6/10/1976
lp Sue Nicholls; Terence Conoley;
Bruce Bould; Trevor Adams; John Horsley

The FALL AND RISE OF REGINALD PERRIN
13/10/1976
lp Bruce Bould; Trevor Adams;
Sally-Jane Spencer; Anne Cunningham;
Ken Wynne
The FALL AND RISE OF REGINALD PERRIN
20/10/1976
lp Sue Nicholls; Geoffrey Palmer;
Trevor Adams; Bruce Bould
The FALL AND RISE OF REGINALD PERRIN
21/9/1977
lp Sue Nicholls; Bruce Bould;
Trevor Adams; Sally-Jane Spencer; Tim Preece
The FALL AND RISE OF REGINALD PERRIN
28/9/1977
lp Glynn Edwards; Sue Nicholls; Bruce Bould;
Trevor Adams; Sally-Jane Spencer; Tim Preece
The FALL AND RISE OF REGINALD PERRIN
5/10/1977
lp Glynn Edwards; Geoffrey Palmer;
Sally-Jane Spencer; Tom Preece; Sue Nicholls;
Trevor Adams
The FALL AND RISE OF REGINALD PERRIN
12/10/1977
lp Sally-Jane Spencer; Tim Preece;
Bruce Bould; Trevor Adams; Sue Nicholls
The FALL AND RISE OF REGINALD PERRIN
19/10/1977
lp Sue Nicholls; Trevor Adams; Bruce Bould
The FALL AND RISE OF REGINALD PERRIN
26/10/1977
lp Geoffrey Palmer; John Horsley;
Derry Power; Sue Nicholls; Tim Preece;
Sally-Jane Spencer; Bruce Bould
The FALL AND RISE OF REGINALD PERRIN
2/11/1977
lp Geoffrey Palmer; John Horsley;
Sue Nicholls; Tim Preece; Sally-Jane Spencer;
Trevor Adams; Bruce Bould
The FALL AND RISE OF REGINALD PERRIN
29/11/1978
lp John Horsley; Trevor Adams;
Bruce Bould; Theresa Watson; Leslie Schofield;
Sue Nicholls; Sally-Jane Spencer
The FALL AND RISE OF REGINALD PERRIN
6/12/1978
lp John Horsley; Trevor Adams;
Bruce Bould; Theresa Watson; Leslie Schofield;
Sue Nicholls; Sally-Jane Spencer;
Geoffrey Palmer
The FALL AND RISE OF REGINALD PERRIN
20/12/1978
lp Joseph Brady; Leslie Schofield;
Trevor Adams; Sally-Jane Spencer; Sue Nicholls
The FALL AND RISE OF REGINALD PERRIN
27/12/1978
lp Joseph Brady; John Horsley;
Bruce Bould; Theresa Watson; Trevor Adams
The FALL AND RISE OF REGINALD PERRIN
3/1/1979
lp Geoffrey Palmer; Bruce Bould;
Theresa Watson; Trevor Adams; Sue Nicholls
The FALL AND RISE OF REGINALD PERRIN
10/1/1979
lp Leslie Schofield; Joseph Brady;
Geoffrey Palmer; John Horsley;
Sally-Jane Spencer
The FALL AND RISE OF REGINALD PERRIN
24/1/1979
lp John Horsley; Trevor Adams;
Sue Nicholls; Geoffrey Palmer; Bruce Bould

**The FALL AND RISE OF THE HOUSE OF
KRUPP** (ATV 17/2/1965)
The Krupp family, and the rebuilding of their
armaments industry after the World Wars. Those
taking part include Lord Shawcross, Lord
Robertson, Airey Neave, Goronwy Rees,
Terence Prittie, Professor Francis Carsten and
Gottfried Treviranus.
d Victor Rudolf; *p/sc* Peter Batty;
nar Bernard Archard

FALL OF EAGLES
(BBC 15/3–7/6/1974)
Thirteen-part drama series tracing the history of
the old monarchies of Europe.

EPISODE 6: ABSOLUTE BEGINNERS 19/4/1974
d Gareth Davies; *p* Stuart Burge;
sc Trevor Griffiths
lp Charles Kay; Patrick Stewart;
Lynn Farleigh; Paul Eddington;
Michael Kitchen; Bruce Purchase

FALSTAFF (BBC 15/9/1960)
A performance of Verdi's 'Falstaff' by The
Glyndebourne Festival Chorus and Ballet and
The Royal Philharmonic Orchestra conducted by
Vittorio Gui.
d Peter Ebert
lp Hugues Cuenod; Geraint Evans;
Ilva Ligabue; Anna Maria Rota;
Oralia Dominguez; Sesto Bruscantini

FALSTAFF (Southern TV 29/4/1978)
The Glyndebourne Festival production of
Verdi's 'Falstaff', with the London Philharmonic
Orchestra conducted by John Pritchard.
p David Heather
lp Donald Gramm; Reni Penkova;
Kay Griffel; Nucci Condo; Elizabeth Gale

The FAMILY (BBC 3/4–26/6/1974)
Fly-on-the-wall record of the daily life of the
Wilkins family of Reading.
The FAMILY 10/4/1974
The relationship between the eldest daughter
and her fiancé, who lodges with the Wilkins.
d Franc Roddam; *p* Paul Watson
The FAMILY 12/6/1974
The Wilkins discuss their holiday plans and their
eldest daughter's wedding arrangements.
d Franc Roddam; *p* Paul Watson

A FAMILY AT WAR (Granada 1970–72)
Drama series about a middle-class Liverpool
family during World War II.
p Richard Doubleday
regulars Lesley Nunnerley; Barbara Flynn;
Keith Drinkel; Coral Atkins; Colin Douglas;
Colin Campbell; Shelagh Fraser; Peter Finch;
Janet Tute
The GATE OF THE YEAR 12/5/1970
d Michael Cox; *sc* John Finch
lp Patrick Troughton; Arthur Cox;
Jessica Spencer; Margery Mason; Ian Thompson
The BREACH IN THE DYKE 19/5/1970
d Tim Jones; *sc* Alexander Baron
lp Richard Beckinsale; John McKelvey;
Tony Anholt; Patrick Troughton; Billy Murray
The WAR OFFICE REGRETS 26/5/1970
d Michael Cox; *sc* John Finch
lp James Beck; John McKelvey;
Rosemarie Dunham; Patrick Troughton;
Margery Mason
FOR STRATEGIC REASONS 2/6/1970
d Tim Jones; *sc* Harry V. Kershaw
lp Derek Anders; Jeremy Wilkin;
Richard Vanstone; Michael Williams; Bill Lyons
The NIGHT THEY HIT NUMBER EIGHT 9/6/1970
d June Howson; *sc* John Finch
lp Bryan Mosley; Harry Markham;
Julie Goodyear; David Bradley
ONE OF OURS 14/7/1970
d Tim Jones; *sc* Leslie Sands
lp Michael Harbour; Brett Usher;
Rowena Cooper; Gordon Griffin; Philip Brack
BROTHERS IN WAR 21/7/1970
d Michael Cox; *sc* Alexander Baron
lp David Dixon; Rowena Cooper;
Christopher Renshaw; David Lincoln
YIELDING PLACE TO NEW 16/2/1972
d Richard Doubleday; *sc* John Finch
lp Ian Thompson; John Nettles;
John McKelvey; Trevor Bowen;
Georgine Anderson

FAMILY BY CHOICE (Thames 14/11/1972)
Life in the commune founded in London by
Catherine Ginsberg.
d Udi Eichler; *p* Jolyon Wimhurst;
comm Michael Channon

The FAMILY OF MAN (BBC 18/5–29/6/1970)
A series of seven films comparing family life in
different parts of the world.
p/sc John Percival

MARRIED LIFE 18/5/1970
A comparison of marriage in five different places: India; New Guinea; Botswana; Esher, Surrey and Colne, Lancashire.
CHILDREN 25/5/1970
The raising of children in Colne, Lancashire; Esher, Surrey; India; Botswana; and New Guinea.
TEENAGERS 1/6/1970
A comparison of teenagers in different cultures, including India, Britain and New Guinea.
WEDDINGS 8/6/1970
A comparison of weddings in five different places: Esher, Surrey; Colne, Lancashire; Andheri, India; Khegudi, Botswana; and Buk, New Guinea.
BIRTH 15/6/1970
A comparison of pregnancy and childbirth in five different places: Lancashire; Esher, Surrey; New Guinea, India and Hong Kong.
OLD AGE 22/6/1970
The problems of old age and social attitudes towards old people in Colne, Lancashire; Esher, Surrey; Buk, New Guinea; Heri, India; and Khegudi, Botswana.
DEATH 29/6/1970
Attitudes towards death in Colne, Lancashire; Esher, Surrey; India, New Guinea and Hong Kong.

FAMINE (Rediffusion 13/6/1967)
Report on the famine in Bihar, India.
d/p Jack Gold

FANATICS (Granada 12/12/1962)
Documentary on the Suffragette movement.
d Mike Wooler; *p* Philip Mackie;
sc Pat Williams; *nar* Siân Phillips

The FANTASTIC FOUR
(US Hanna-Barbera Productions 1967–70)
Cartoon series about four trouble-shooters with extraordinary powers; based on the characters appearing in Marvel Comics.
MOLECULE MAN 1970

A FAR BETTER PLACE (Thames 4/4/1972)
The evacuation of St. Kilda in 1930, the island today and interviews with former islanders now living on the mainland of Scotland.
d/sc Tom Steel; *exec.p* Jeremy Isaacs;
nar Ian Gilmour

FAREWELL ARABIA
(Rediffusion 29/8/1967)
How Sheikh Zaid of Abu Dhabi is using his country's new-found wealth from oil. The traditional way of life in Abu Dhabi is contrasted with developments in construction, the army, education and health helped by Western expertise.
d Randal Beattie; *sc/nar* David Holden

FAREWELL TO THE VIC (BBC 15/6/1963)
The closing moments of The Old Vic Company's final production, 'Measure for Measure'. Looking back at the theatre's history are Robert Atkins, Michael Benthall, John Blatchley, Richard Burton, Michael Elliott, Edith Evans, John Gielgud, Alec Guinness, Tyrone Guthrie, John Neville, and Laurence Olivier.
d David Jones, Mary Evans;
p David Jones; *intro* Michael Flanders

FARM AND COUNTRY NEWS (Westward)
Regional news magazine programme.
FARM AND COUNTRY NEWS 1975

FARMING OUTLOOK (Tyne Tees)
Regional documentary and news programme for farmers.
FARMING OUTLOOK 7/7/1974
FARMING OUTLOOK 13/10/1974
FARMING OUTLOOK 1/12/1974
FARMING OUTLOOK 5/3/1978
SMITHFIELD 1978 9/12/1978
HIGHLAND SHOW 24/6/1979
SMITHFIELD SHOW 9/12/1979

FARSON'S GUIDE TO THE BRITISH
(Rediffusion 1959–60)
Documentary series.
CATS 3/12/1959
The British passion for cats.
d Sheila Gregg; *sc* Jacqueline Charrott-Lodwidge; *rep* Daniel Farson

FASCINATING FACTS (BBC 1963)
Series for children which looks at old sayings and beliefs.
FASCINATING FACTS 10/7/1963
d Patrick Dowling; *p* John Irwin;
pres Donal Donnelly

FAT MAN ON A BEACH (HTV 12/11/1974)
An illustration of B.S. Johnson's unconventional approach to his work showing him on a beach in the Lleyn Peninsula, alone and talking to camera.
d Michael Bakewell; *exec.p* Aled Vaughan

FATHER, DEAR FATHER (Thames 1968–73)
Sitcom about a philandering father and his two daughters.
d/p William G. Stewart;
sc Johnnie Mortimer, Brian Cooke
regulars Patrick Cargill; Natasha Pyne;
Ann Holloway; Noel Dyson
The RETURN OF THE MUMMY 19/11/1968
lp Sally Bazely; Ursula Howells;
Patrick Holt; Roy Denton
THIS IS YOUR WIFE 12/5/1970
lp Ursula Howells; Joyce Carey;
Jan Holden; Michael Segal; Paul Whitsun-Jones
ONE DOG AND HIS MAN 19/5/1970
lp Michael Segal; Diane King

The FAVOURITES (BBC 25/3/1966)
The training of racehorses Freddie and Jay Trump by Reg Tweedie in Berwickshire and Fred Winter in Berkshire, respectively, during the three weeks before the 1965 Grand National. Shows preparations before the race and the race itself.
p Anthony De Lotbinière; *sc* John Lawrence;
comm John Lawrence, Derek Hart

FAWLTY TOWERS (BBC 1975; 1979)
Comedy series revolving around a belligerent hotel proprietor and his put-upon staff.
p John Howard Davies (1975),
Douglas Argent (1979);
sc John Cleese, Connie Booth
regulars John Cleese; Prunella Scales;
Andrew Sachs; Connie Booth
A TOUCH OF CLASS 19/9/1975
lp David Simeon; Ballard Berkeley;
Lionel Wheeler; Robin Ellis
GOURMET NIGHT 17/10/1975
lp Steve Plytas; André Maranne;
Ballard Berkeley; Jeffrey Segal;
Allan Cuthbertson
COMMUNICATION PROBLEMS 19/2/1979
d Bob Spiers
lp Mervyn Pascoe; Robert Lankesheer;
Joan Sanderson; Johnny Shannon;
The PSYCHIATRIST 26/2/1979
d Bob Spiers
lp Nicky Henson; Basil Henson;
Elspet Gray; Luan Peters; Brian Hall;
Gilly Flower
WALDORF SALAD 5/3/1979
d Bob Spiers
lp Anthony Dawes; June Ellis;
Terence Conoley; Dorothy Frere; Beatrice Shaw
The KIPPER AND THE CORPSE 12/3/1979
d Bob Spiers
lp Mavis Pugh; Ballard Berkeley;
Geoffrey Palmer; Len Marten; Derek Royle
The ANNIVERSARY 26/3/1979
[Originally billed for tx on 19/3/1979 but actually shown a week later.]
d Bob Spiers
lp Brian Hall; Ken Campbell; Una Stubbs;
Pat Keen; Robert Arnold; Roger Hume

BASIL THE RAT 25/10/1979
[Sixth and final episode of the second series was not transmitted, due to industrial action, until some seven months later; then billed as a 'Special'.]
d Bob Spiers
lp John Quarmby; Brian Hall;
Gilly Flower; Renee Roberts; Stuart Sherwin

The FELONY SQUAD
(US Twentieth Century-Fox TV 1966–69)
Drama series about the on- and off-duty lives of three Los Angeles police detectives.
BETWEEN TWO FIRES 21/11/1966
d Laslo Benedek; *p* Richard Newton;
sc Harold Gast
lp Howard Duff; Ben Alexander;
Dennis Cole; Kevin McCarthy; Richard Evans

FERMTOWN FOLK (Grampian)
Regional series.
The HORSE FAIR 1/6/1979

FESTIVAL 40 (BBC 1976)
Celebration of the 40th anniversary of BBC Television.
WHAT DO YOU THINK OF IT SO FAR? 29/8/1976
Discussion on the impact of television on our lives.
p Peter Foges; *intro* David Frost;
with Huw Wheldon, Asa Briggs,
John Whale, Fred W. Friendly, Barbara Walters

FESTIVAL OF FAMILY CLASSICS
(US 1972–73)
Syndicated animation series for children, shown on local US television stations.
JACK O'LANTERN 1972
CINDERELLA 17/9/1972

FEVER OF THE DEEP
(Southern TV 4/1/1972)
Narcosis, a form of mild hysteria that affects divers who dive beyond the proper limits.
d Mike Connor; *sc* Graham Hurley;
nar Patrick Allen

A FEW CASTLES IN SPAIN
(BBC 6/1/1966)
Alan Whicker talks to the Duke and Duchess of Alba and their family, and visits palaces in Madrid and Seville.
d/p Kevin Billington

A FEW NOTES ON OUR FOOD PROBLEM
(US 1978)
Underlines the threat of starvation as population growth continues to outstrip food production.
d James Blue

FIDEL CASTRO SPEAKS
(SE Sveriges Radio; BBC *tx* 13/6/1977)
Interview with Fidel Castro in which he gives his interpretation of Cuban events of the last twenty years. He explains his country's special affinity with Angola and comments on other aspects of Cuba's foreign relations.
d Gaetano Pagano

5TH ANNIVERSARY (Scottish TV 1962)
The fifth anniversary of Scottish Television.

FIFTY YEARS A WINNER
(BBC 2/12/1965)
A portrait of, and interview with, the scientist Sir Lawrence Bragg.
d/p Philip Daly; *sc* Antony Jay;
interv Barry Westwood

FIFTY YEARS OF THE R.A.F.
(BBC 28/3/1968)
Documentary to mark the half-centenary of the Royal Air Force.
p Harry Hastings; *sc* Douglas Botting;
nar Michael Flanders

The FIGHT FOR YORK MINSTER
(Anglia 1/12/1967)
The work of preserving York Minster.

The FIGHT GAME: IS IT SPORT – OR WAR? (BBC 11/6/1973)
A documentary about boxing based on the radio ballad by Ewan MacColl, Peggy Seeger and Charles Parker.
p/sc Philip Donnellan;
with Bobby Arthur, John Conteh, Pat Dwyer, Bunny Johnson, Mark Rowe, Bunny Sterling

La FILLE MAL GARDEE (BBC 27/12/1962)
Studio production of the ballet, choreographed by Frederick Ashton.
d/p Margaret Dale
with Nadia Nerina; David Blair;
Stanley Holden; Leslie Edwards;
Alexander Grant

FILM NIGHT (BBC 1969–76)
Documentary series on the cinema.
PETER SELLERS AND SPIKE MILLIGAN 8/11/1970
Tony Bilbow talks to Spike Milligan and Peter Sellers before an audience at the Round House during the Cinema City Exhibition.
p Barry Brown
STACY KEACH 15/12/1972
Stacy Keach talks about his film career to Sheridan Morley and Philip Jenkinson.
p Barry Brown

FILM PROFILE (BBC 1955–62)
Special editions of this programme were presented from 1955; then from 1959–62 alternating with The CINEMA TODAY (1959–62) series and continuing after, on an irregular schedule.
J. LEE THOMPSON 19/10/1959
Robert Robinson introduces a profile of film director J. Lee Thompson.
d Richard Evans
WILLIAM WYLER 15/1/1960
Dilys Powell introduces a profile of William Wyler.
p Victor Poole
EDITH EVANS 2/8/1960
Edith Evans discusses her career with Derek Prouse.
d Victor Poole
FRED ZINNEMANN 17/2/1961
Donald Holms interviews Fred Zinnemann.
d Richard Evans
SIR MICHAEL BALCON 12/9/1961
Sir Michael Balcon is interviewed by Robert Robinson.
p Christopher Doll
JEANNE MOREAU 1963
Jeanne Moreau is interviewed by Derek Prouse.
d Victor Poole

FINDING OUT
(Rediffusion 1964–66)
Educational series for schools.
The TAP 15/3/1965
How water taps work.
d Angela Holder; *sc* Peter Pickering;
pres Penny Whittam

FIREBALL XL5
(AP Films Production 1962–63)
Animated science-fiction puppet series set in the twenty-first century.
WINGS OF DANGER 3/2/1963
d David Elliott; *p* Gerry Anderson;
sc Alan Fennell; *voice* Paul Maxwell,
Sylvia Anderson, David Graham, John Bluthal,
Gerry Anderson
CONVICT IN SPACE 10/2/1963
d Bill Harris; *p* Gerry Anderson;
sc Alan Fennell; *voice* Paul Maxwell,
Sylvia Anderson, David Graham, John Bluthal,
Gerry Anderson

The FIRECHASERS (ITC 20/3/1979)
Crime thriller about a female reporter investigating a crime of arson.
d Sidney Hayers; *p* Julian Wintle;
sc Philip Levene
lp Chad Everett; Anjanette Comer;
Keith Barron; Joanne Dainton; Rupert Davies

FIRING LINE
(BBC-SECA 26/8–16/9/1973)
A series of four programmes in which American politician William F. Buckley Jr discusses a series of issues with his guests.
FIRING LINE 16/9/1973
Dee Wells, Louis Heren and Anthony Howard question William F. Buckley Jr on his political beliefs.
d Christopher Hodson;
p Warren Steibel, Peter Chafer

The FIRST CASUALTY
(Thames 16/11/1971)
The use of propaganda during World War I.
d/p Peter Morley; *sc/pres* John Terraine;
nar Alec Mango, Allan Hargreaves

FIRST HAND (BBC 1957)
Documentary series examining historical events and developments.
AIRSHIPS 25/10/1957
Peter West presents a history of the airship, from the hot-air balloon to the Zeppelin.
p Nancy Thomas, Paul Johnstone

FIRST IN – LAST OUT
(Southern TV 25/6/1968)
The role of the Royal Marine Commandos during the evacuation of Aden.
p Terry Johnston; *rep* Christopher Wain

FIRST REPORT (ITN 1973–76)
Lunchtime news programme.
MACMILLAN'S MEMOIRS LAUNCHED 25/9/1973
The reception at the Dorchester to mark the publication of Harold Macmillan's memoirs; includes speeches by Macmillan and Harold Wilson.

FIVE FINGERS
(US Twentieth Century-Fox TV 1959–60)
Secret agent drama based on the film of the same title made in 1952, and in turn derived from the L.C. Moyzisch book 'Operation Cicero'.
DOSSIER 10/10/1959
d Montgomery Pittman; *p* Herbert B. Swope Jr;
sc Robert Dennis
lp David Hedison; Luciana Paluzzi;
Edgar Bergen; John Williams; Paul Burke;
Kurt Kreuger

FIVE REVOLUTIONARY PAINTERS
(ATV 1959)
Five-part study of great artists.
p Michael Redington; *pres* Kenneth Clark
GOYA 19/10/1959
PIETER BRUEGHEL THE ELDER 16/11/1959
CARAVAGGIO 30/11/1959
REMBRANDT 14/12/1959
VAN GOGH 28/12/1959

FLAIR (Rediffusion 1/4/1959)
Fashion programme for Courtaulds and Kaysar stockings.
d Bill Turner; *with* Derek Waring, Nola Rose

FLAMBARDS
(Yorkshire TV 2/2–20/4/1979)
Twelve-part drama serial adapted from Kathleen Peyton's novels and set among the Essex country society prior to World War I.
p Leonard Lewis
regulars Edward Judd; Alan Parnaby;
Steve Grives; Christine McKenna
EPISODE 2: ENTRY TO A NEW WORLD 9/2/1979
d Leonard Lewis; *sc* Alex Glasgow
lp Sebastian Abineri; Rosalie Williams;
Frank Mills; George Mikell; David Huscroft
EPISODE 3: LADY BOUNTIFUL 16/2/1979
d Michael Ferguson; *sc* William Humble
lp Anton Diffring; David Huscroft;
Sebastian Abineri; Sally Sanders; Frank Mills
EPISODE 4: POINT TO POINT 23/2/1979
d Lawrence Gordon Clark; *sc* Alex Glasgow
lp Anton Diffring; Rosalie Williams;
Ted Carroll; Geoffrey Tomlinson;
David Huscroft
EPISODE 5: THE COLD LIGHT OF DAY 2/3/1979
d Michael Ferguson; *sc* William Humble
lp Anton Diffring; Barkley Johnson;
John Ringham; Mike Perry; Carol Leader

EPISODE 6: THE EDGE OF THE CLOUD 9/3/1979
d Leonard Lewis; *sc* Alan Plater
lp John Jardine; David Huscroft;
Peter Settelen; John Ringham; Olive Pendleton
EPISODE 7: FLYING HIGH 16/3/1979
d Michael Ferguson; *sc* Alex Glasgow
lp Peter Settelen; Carol Leader;
David Huscroft; John Ringham; Olive Pendleton
EPISODE 8: SING NO SAD SONGS 23/2/1979
d Leonard Lewis; *sc* Alan Plater
lp Sebastian Abineri; Carol Leader;
David Huscroft; John Ringham;
Aubrey Richards
EPISODE 9: NEW BLOOD 30/3/1979
lp Sebastian Abineri; Alan Downer
EPISODE 10: PRISONERS OF WAR 6/4/1979
lp Sebastian Abineri; Alan Downer;
Frank Mills; Rosalie Williams; Max Smith
EPISODE 11: WHAT ARE SERVANTS FOR? 13/4/1979
lp Sebastian Abineri; Alan Downer;
Carol Leader; Frank Mills; Rosalie Williams
EPISODE 12: INHERITANCE 20/4/1979
lp Sebastian Abineri; Alan Downer;
Carol Leader; Rosalie Williams; Frank Mills

FLAT BUST (Yorkshire TV 10/2/1979)
Play about a young girl who travels to Leeds in search of her future.
d/p Michael Ferguson; *sc* Peter Draper
lp Alyson Spiro; Alan Starkey;
Chris Barrington; Roger Brierley; Joe Gladwin

FLIGHT OF THE HERON
(Scottish TV 28/2–17/4/1968)
An eight-part dramatisation for children of D.K. Broster's novel.
EPISODE 1: CAPTURE 28/2/1968
d/p Brian Mahoney; *sc* Moultrie R. Kelsall
lp Ian McCulloch; Finlay Currie;
Sheila Whittingham; Jon Laurimore
EPISODE 2: REBELLION 6/3/1968
d/p Brian Mahoney; *sc* Moultrie R. Kelsall
lp Finlay Currie; Ian McCulloch;
Sophie Stewart; Jon Laurimore;
Sheila Whittingham

FLYING DOCTOR (ABC 1960–61)
Drama series featuring the hazardous work of The Royal Flying Doctor Service in the Australian Outback.
d/p David MacDonald
regulars Richard Denning; Jill Adams;
Alan White; Peter Madden
The SECRET 18/6/1960
sc Philip Levene
lp Paul Massie; James Copeland;
Ann Sears; Russell Walters;
Giacomo Rossi Stuart
STRANGER IN DISTRESS 16/4/1961
sc Michael Noonan
lp James Copeland; Russell Napier;
Colin Tapley; Patrick Troughton; Ronald Fraser
WOMAN HUNT 25/11/1961
sc Philip Levene
lp Sheila Allen; Madge Ryan;
Martin Wyldeck; Richard Burrell;
Leigh Madison

FOOTBALL LEAGUE CUP FINAL: MANCHESTER CITY v. NEWCASTLE UNITED (ITV Sport 29/2/1976)
Highlights of the final of the Football League Cup played at Wembley on Saturday 28/2/1976.
p Bob Gardam; *comm* Brian Moore

FOR THE LOVE OF ADA (Thames 1970–71)
Comedy series telling the story of a love affair between two sprightly characters enjoying their autumn years of retirement.
The WEDDING 26/10/1970
p Ronnie Baxter;
sc Vince Powell, Harry Driver
lp Irene Handl; Wilfred Pickles;
Barbara Mitchell; Jack Smethurst;
Colin Welland; Anna Turner; Bert Palmer;
Anna Wing; Norman Shelley

Above: *Wednesday Special* 17/1/1975 *The Naked Civil Servant* (Thames). Quentin Crisp and John Hurt.

Left: *No Man's Land* (Granada). John Gielgud and Ralph Richardson.

Below: *Bouquet of Barbed Wire* 9/1/1976 *Homecoming* (LWT). Frank Finlay and Susan Penhaligon.

Left: *Nineteen Eighty Four* (BBC). From left to right, Harry Dane (standing), Wilfrid Brambell (on knees), Peter Cushing (centre), and Campbell Gray.

Below: *The Human Jungle* 18/2/1965 *Struggle for a Mind* (ABC). Herbert Lom and Joan Collins.

Right: *The Power Game* (ATV). Patrick Wymark.

Below: *The Prisoner* 3/12/1967 *Checkmate* (Everyman-ITC). Patrick McGoohan and Ronald Radd.

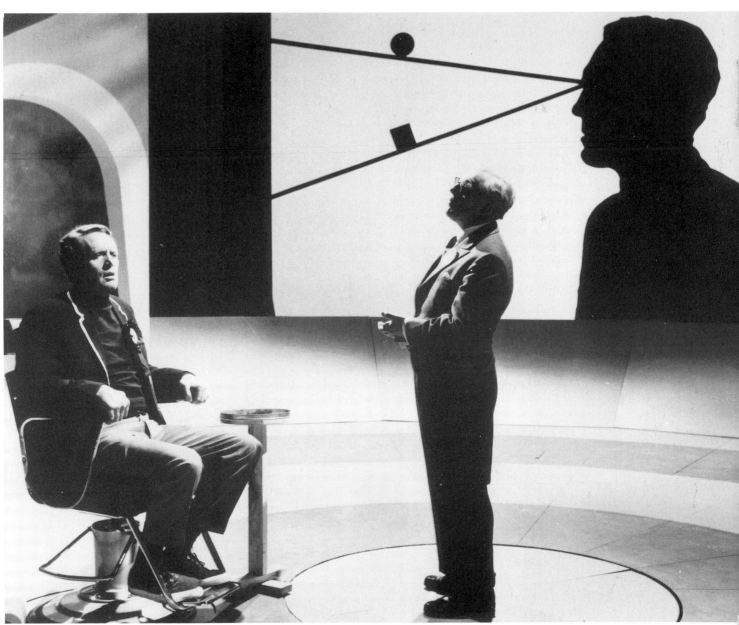

The Avengers (ABC). Patrick Macnee and Diana Rigg.

FOR THE RECORD (LWT 1968–69)
Interview series.
GEORGE BROWN 4/8/1968
George Brown is interviewed by Alan Watson and looks back over his political career and his relationships with prominent members of the Labour movement.
d Tim Slessor; *exec.p* Terry Hughes
BARBARA CASTLE 20/10/1968
Margaret Laing interviews Barbara Castle upon her appointment to the Department of Employment and Productivity.
JACK DASH 24/1/1969
Alan Watson talks to Jack Dash about his attitude to the British Communist Party, the situation in Czechoslovakia, and his relationship with the dockers.
d Tim Slessor; *exec.p* Terry Hughes
GEORGE BEST 31/1/1969
Michael Parkinson interviews footballer George Best.
d Tim Slessor; *exec.p* Terry Hughes

FORMAT V (ATV)
Regional documentary series.
SAVE OUR SPOUSES 2/11/1978
The suffering of second wives to balance the focus placed on first wives.
d John Pullen; *p* Graham Mole;
pres Wendy Jones
The WHOLE WORLD IN HIS HANDS 9/11/1978
Child impressionist Paul Harding performs on the club circuit.
d Michael Connor; *p* Graham Mole

The FORSYTE SAGA (BBC 1967)
Dramatisation of John Galsworthy's novel in twenty-six parts.
p Donald Wilson
regulars Kenneth More; Eric Porter;
Fay Compton; Joseph O'Conor; John Welsh;
George Woodbridge; A.J. Brown;
Nora Nicholson; Nora Swinburne;
Kynaston Reeves; John Baskcomb;
Fanny Rowe; Margaret Tyzack; John Barcroft;
Sarah Harter; Ursula Howells; Lana Morris;
Nyree Dawn Porter; Dallia Penn;
Terence Alexander; June Barry; Michael York;
Suzanne Neve; Jonathan Burn; Anne De Vigier;
Richard Armour; Martin Jarvis;
Susan Hampshire
EPISODE 1: FAMILY FESTIVAL 7/1/1967
d David Giles; *sc* Donald Wilson
lp Susan Pennick; Maggie Jones;
Deddie Davies; Jenny Laird; Campbell Singer;
Anna Korwin
EPISODE 2: FAMILY SCANDAL 14/1/1967
d David Giles; *sc* Donald Wilson
lp Mischa De La Motte; Clifford Parrish;
Deddie Davies; Jenny Laird; Campbell Singer
EPISODE 3: PURSUIT OF HAPPINESS 21/1/1967
d David Giles; *sc* Donald Wilson
lp Garry Marsh; Maggie Jones;
Mischa De La Motte; Michael Mulcaster;
Jenny Laird; Campbell Singer
EPISODE 4: DINNER AT SWITHIN'S 28/1/1967
d David Giles; *sc* Constance Cox
lp Mischa De La Motte; Bart Allison;
Michael Mulcaster; Maggie Jones; John Caesar
EPISODE 5: MAN OF PROPERTY 4/2/1967
d David Giles; *sc* Constance Cox
lp John Bennett; Maggie Jones;
Bart Allison; Gillian Martell; Jackie Smith
EPISODE 6: DECISIONS 11/2/1967
d David Giles; *sc* Donald Wilson
lp John Bennett; Bart Allison;
Clifford Parrish; Olwen Brooks
EPISODE 7: INTO THE DARK 18/2/1967
d David Giles; *sc* Constance Cox
lp Olwen Brooks; Jeanne Le Bars;
John Bennett; Christopher Hodge; Charles West
EPISODE 8: INDIAN SUMMER OF A FORSYTE 25/2/1967
d David Giles; *sc* Donald Wilson
lp Roy Denton; Malya Nappi;
Jackie Smith; Bridget Turner
EPISODE 9: IN CHANCERY 4/3/1967
d David Giles; *sc* Lawrie Craig
lp Bridget Turner; Garry Marsh;
Michael Pemberton; Ellen Pollock; Faith Hines

EPISODE 10: CHALLENGE 11/3/1967
d David Giles; *sc* Lawrie Craig
lp James Wardroper; Mischa De La Motte;
Jeffrey Segal; Alan Judd; Ellen Pollock
EPISODE 11: IN THE WEB 18/3/1967
d David Giles; *sc* Lawrie Craig
lp Mischa De La Motte; Derek Smith;
Maggie Jones; Bridget Turner; Susan Manderson
EPISODE 12: BIRTH OF A FORSYTE 25/3/1967
d David Giles; *sc* Lawrie Craig
lp Bridget Turner; Cameron Miller;
Ellen Pollock; Maggie Jones; Lee Fox
EPISODE 13: ENCOUNTER 1/4/1967
d James Cellan Jones; *sc* Vincent Tilsley
lp Maggie Jones; Christopher Benjamin;
Nicholas Pennell; John Dunn-Hill
EPISODE 14: CONFLICT 8/4/1967
d James Cellan Jones; *sc* Vincent Tilsley
lp Christopher Benjamin; Nicholas Pennell;
Julia Whyte; Patricia Leventon
EPISODE 15: TO LET 15/4/1967
d James Cellan Jones; *sc* Vincent Tilsley
lp Christopher Benjamin; Patricia Leventon;
Maggie Jones; Julia Whyte
EPISODE 16: FAMILY WEDDING 22/4/1967
d James Cellan Jones; *sc* Anthony Steven
lp Nicholas Pennell; Cyril Luckham;
Robin Phillips; Brenda Cowling; Terry Scully
EPISODE 17: WHITE MONKEY 29/4/1967
d James Cellan Jones; *sc* Anthony Steven
lp Nicholas Pennell; Robin Phillips;
Terry Scully; Geraldine Sherman; Ian Fleming
EPISODE 18: AFTERNOON OF A DRYAD 6/5/1967
d James Cellan Jones; *sc* Anthony Steven
lp Nicholas Pennell; Terry Scully;
Geraldine Sherman; Cyril Luckham;
Derek Francis
EPISODE 19: NO RETREAT 13/5/1967
d James Cellan Jones; *sc* Anthony Steven
lp Nicholas Pennell; Brenda Cowling;
Terry Scully; Julia Whyte; Cyril Luckham
EPISODE 20: SILENT WOOING 20/5/1967
d David Giles; *sc* Anthony Steven
lp Karin Fernald; Hal Hamilton;
Cyril Luckham; Nicholas Pennell; Tenniel Evans
EPISODE 21: ACTION FOR LIBEL 27/5/1967
d David Giles; *sc* Anthony Steven
lp Nicholas Pennell; Margaret Tyzack;
Julia Whyte; Caroline Blakiston; Cyril Luckham
EPISODE 22: SILVER SPOON 3/6/1967
d David Giles; *sc* Anthony Steven
lp John Phillips; Cyril Luckham;
George Benson; Julia Whyte; Nicholas Pennell
EPISODE 23: STRIKE 10/6/1967
d David Giles; *sc* Donald Wilson
lp Nicholas Pennell; Caroline Blakiston;
George Benson; Karin Fernald; Ralph Michael
EPISODE 24: AFTERNOON AT ASCOT 17/6/1967
d David Giles; *sc* Donald Wilson
lp Maggie Jones; Nicholas Pennell;
Karin Fernald; Julia Whyte; Peter Copley;
Rose Power
EPISODE 25: PORTRAIT OF FLEUR 24/6/1967
d David Giles; *sc* Donald Wilson
lp George Benson; Karin Fernald;
Bryan Marshall; Clive Morton; Nicholas Pennell
EPISODE 26: SWAN SONG 1/7/1967
d David Giles; *sc* Donald Wilson
lp Nicholas Pennell; Hilda Barry;
Noel Howlett; Tina Matthews; Karin Fernald

The 44TH ANNUAL OSCAR AWARDS (US Academy of Motion Picture Arts and Sciences 12/4/1972)
Item from the programme in which Charles Chaplin receives a special Oscar award.
d Marty Pasetta

FORTY MILLION SHOES
(CA CBC-Intertel; GB *tx* 21/3/1962)
Brazil, as seen through the eyes of five of its citizens.
d/p Douglas Leiterman

FORWARD TO RETIREMENT
(BBC 1966)
Documentary series on how to make the most of retirement.
SHOULD THE FIRM HELP? 30/1/1966
d Michael Blakstad; *p* Beryl Radley;
intro Hugh Barrett; *interv* Joan Bakewell

KEEPING HEALTHY 27/2/1966
d Michael Blakstad; *p* Beryl Radley;
intro Hugh Barrett; *interv* Joan Bakewell
ORGANISING A PRE-RETIREMENT COURSE 20/3/1966
d Michael Blakstad; *p* Beryl Radley;
intro Hugh Barrett

The FOSTERS (LWT 1976–77)
Sitcom about the life of a south London black family.
The WINDFALL 11/6/1976
d/p Stuart Allen; *sc* Alan Mannings;
adapt Jon Watkins
lp Isabelle Lucas; Lenny Henry;
Sharon Rosita; Lawrie Mark; Carmen Munro;
Norman Beaton

The FOUNDATION (ATV 1977–78)
Drama series set in the world of big business.
SEPARATION 2/9/1977
d Robert Tronson; *p* John Cooper;
sc Richard Gregson
lp Lynette Davies; John Barron;
Sandor Eles; William Gaunt;
Geoffrey Whitehead; Ellis Dale

4472 – FLYING SCOTSMAN (BBC 11/8/1968)
The last journey of the Flying Scotsman on 1/5/l968 from King's Cross to Edinburgh.
d Tony Wheeler

The FOUR FREEDOMS
(ATV 11/2–11/3/1962)
A series of five programmes surveying how President Roosevelt's 'Four Freedoms' have been interpreted over the years.
The FREEDOM TO WORSHIP 18/2/1962
Dr Arthur Michael Ramsey, Father Martin D'Arcy and Dr Donald Soper discuss religious freedom.
p James Ferman; *sc/nar* Paul Johnson

FOUR GREAT PAINTERS
(BBC 23/1–13/2/1970)
Profiles of modern artists.
HEAD OVER HEELS – MARC CHAGALL 30/1/1970
Marc Chagall working at his studios near Nice. Review of his life and work.
p John Read; *nar* Robert Cushman

FOUR OF HEARTS
(Rediffusion 27/9–18/10/1965)
A quartet of individual plays designed to showcase the talents of actor Patrick Wymark.
THIS YEAR'S GIRL 11/10/1965
d Cyril Coke; *sc* Allan Prior
lp Patrick Wymark; Carol Mowlam;
Sonia Dresdel; Charles Victor;
Marcus Hammond

FOUR STAR PLAYHOUSE
(US Four Star Productions 1952–56)
Anthology series revolving around the single performances of its four stars: Charles Boyer, Dick Powell, Ida Lupino and David Niven. In some episodes actors other than the 'four' took the lead role.
TUNNEL OF FEAR 19/1/1956
d Roy Kellino; *p* David Niven;
sc Roland Winters, Frederic Brady
lp David Niven; Cedric Hardwicke;
Alex Frazer; Keith McConnell; Leslie Denison
YELLOWBELLY 12/7/1956
d Laslo Benedek; *p* Warren Lewis;
sc Al C. Ward; *auth* Douglas Lansford
lp Frank Lovejoy; Maxine Cooper;
Bart Burns; Harry Lauter; Jeanette Nolan

14TH JULY – PARIS (BBC 14/7/1956)
Bastille day celebrations in Paris.

Les FRANÇAIS CHEZ VOUS
(FR Radiodiffusion-Television Francaise 1960)
A series of French language lessons.
Les CHEVAUX 1960
d Georges Rouquier; *exec.p* Gérard Abensour;
sc Georges Bayard
DANS DEUX HEURES 1960
d Roger Iglesis; *sc* Jean Guenot;
with Jacques Marin, Michel Serrault

Les FRANÇAIS CHEZ VOUS *cont.*

IL N'EN RESTE PLUS 1960
d Roger Iglesis; *sc* Jean Guenot;
with Elina Labourdette
IL Y A BEAUCOUP DE PLACE 1960
d Roger Iglesis; *sc* Jean Guenot
La MEILLEURE OCCASION 1960
d Roger Iglesis; *sc* Jean Guenot

FRANCE (BBC 16/11–14/12/1970)
Five-part documentary series on changing society
in modern France.
THAT'S THE WAY WE ARE 16/11/1970
The craftsmen and shopkeepers of France.
d Peter Jarvis; *p* Howard Smith;
pres John Ardagh

The FRANCE I LOVE (BBC 6/9/1977)
Impressions of the French people at work and at
leisure.
d Erik Durschmied

**FRANCIS BACON: FRAGMENTS OF A
PORTRAIT** (BBC 18/9/1966)
A study of the painter Francis Bacon and an
assessment of his work.
d/p/sc Michael Gill; *interv* David Sylvester;
nar Alan Dobie

FRANCIS DURBRIDGE PRESENTS
(BBC 1961–1980)
Series of thrillers written for television by
Francis Durbridge.
The DESPERATE PEOPLE: EPISODE 1 24/2/1963
p Alan Bromly
lp Denis Quilley; Hugh Cross;
Gerard Heinz; June Ellis; Philip Guard;
Barry Jackson
The DESPERATE PEOPLE: EPISODE 2 3/3/1963
lp Denis Quilley; Hugh Cross;
David William; June Ellis; Shirley Cain;
Renny Lister
The DESPERATE PEOPLE: EPISODE 3 10/3/1963
lp Denis Quilley; Hugh Cross;
Stanley Meadows; Peter Ducrow; Garard Green;
June Ellis
The DESPERATE PEOPLE: EPISODE 4 17/3/1963
lp Denis Quilley; Hugh Cross;
Stanley Meadows; Nigel Hawthorne;
Hilary Crane
The DESPERATE PEOPLE: EPISODE 5 24/3/1963
lp Denis Quilley; Hugh Cross;
Stanley Meadows; Shirley Cain; Clifford Earl
The DESPERATE PEOPLE: EPISODE 6 31/3/1963
lp Denis Quilley; Hugh Cross;
Stanley Meadows; Renny Lister;
Nigel Hawthorne
MELISSA: EPISODE 1 26/4/1964
d/p Alan Bromly
lp Tony Britton; Petra Davies;
Brian Wilde; Kerry Jordan; Helen Christie
MELISSA: EPISODE 2 3/5/1964
lp Tony Britton; Brian Wilde;
Kerry Jordan; Helen Christie; Brian McDermott
MELISSA: EPISODE 3 10/5/1964
lp Tony Britton; Kerry Jordan;
Helen Christie; Brian McDermott;
Martin Norton
MELISSA: EPISODE 4 17/5/1964
lp Tony Britton; Brian Wilde;
Brian McDermott; Anthony Sagar;
Carole Mowlam
MELISSA: EPISODE 5 24/5/1964
lp Tony Britton; Brian Wilde;
Norman Scace; Elizabeth Weaver;
Michael Collins

FRANCO PROFILE (ITN 20/11/1975)
Compilation film of the life of General Franco.

**FRANK SINATRA SPECIAL: OL' BLUE
EYES IS BACK**
(US Bristol Productions 18/11/1973)
Show celebrating Sinatra's return to show-
business in 1973. Musical arrangements by
Don Costa and Gordon Jenkins.
d Marty Pasetta; *p* Howard W. Koch

FRANKIE LAINE (BBC 20/8/1976)
Special solo performance recorded during
Laine's UK tour.
d Tony Harrison; *p* Peter Ridsdale-Scott

FRED HOYLE'S UNIVERSE
(BBC 27/12/1964)
Astronomer Fred Hoyle describes the revolution
in astronomy in his lifetime, and visits the Mount
Palomar optical telescope.
d/p Philip Daly; *sc* Gordon Rattray Taylor;
comm Peter Hawkins

FREDDIE STARR'S VARIETY MADHOUSE
(LWT 1979)
Light entertainment series featuring comedian
Freddie Starr.
FREDDIE STARR'S VARIETY MADHOUSE
10/11/1979
p Ken O'Neill; *with* Russ Abbot,
Mike Newman, Bella Emberg, Norman Collier

FREE SPEECH (ATV 1974–75)
Discussion series.
DISCUSSION ON ENOCH POWELL'S ADOPTION
FOR SOUTH DOWN 8/9/1974
A discussion of the move by Enoch Powell to the
Ulster Unionists. Those taking part are A.J.P.
Taylor, Malcolm Muggeridge, Lord George-
Brown, and Peregrine Worsthorne, with Derek
Hart in the chair.
d Tim Watson; *p* John Irwin

**FREEDOM ROAD: SONGS OF NEGRO
PROTEST** (Rediffusion 5/2/1964)
Programme which relates by means of music,
song and picture, black people's unceasing
struggle for racial equality.
d Robert Fleming; *p/sc* Elkan Allan;
with Cleo Laine, Cy Grant, Madeleine Bell,
Nadia Cattouse, Lucky McKenzie,
Pearl Prescod, George Webb, The Woodpeckers

FRENCH NARROW GAUGE (BBC 1/7/1962)
A record of trains on the P.O. Correze Line of
the SNCF which runs from Tulle to Argentat.
d John Adams, Patrick Whitehouse

FRIDAY LIVE (Tyne Tees 1978)
Regional live discussion programme.
FRIDAY LIVE 23/2/1978

FRIDAY NIGHT WITH THE CRAZY GANG
(Rediffusion 5/10/1956)
d Michael Westmore; *with* Rosalina Neri,
Bud Flanagan, Jimmy Nervo, Teddy Knox,
Charlie Naughton, Jimmy Gold

The FRIGHTENERS (LWT 1972–1973)
Thirteen-part drama series featuring ordinary
people threatened by situations out of their
control.
The MANIPULATORS 28/7/1972
d Mike Hodges; *p* Geoffrey Hughes;
sc Mike Hodges
lp Bryan Marshall; Stanley Lebor;
Brian Grellis; David Sands; David Healey;
Kara Wilson

FROM A BIRD'S EYE VIEW
(Sheldon Leonard Productions 1973–75)
Comedy-drama series following the lives of two
air stewardesses.
regulars Millicent Martin; Patte Finley
The MATCHMAKERS 1973 *ntx*
d Ralph Levy; *p* Jack Greenwood;
sc Pat Dunlop; *auth* Reuben Ship
lp Evelyn Keyes; Noel Hood; Art Gross
The DIFFICULT PASSENGER 16/9/1973
d Ralph Levy; *p* Jack Greenwood;
sc T.E.B. Clarke
lp Peter Jones; Robert Coote;
Jess Conrad; Mavis Villiers
NEVER PUT IT IN WRITING 23/9/1973
d Ralph Levy; *p* Jack Greenwood;
sc John Muir, Eric Green
lp Peter Jones; Noel Hood;
Angus Lennie; Arthur Mullard
WIFE TROUBLE 30/9/1973
d Ralph Levy; *p* Jack Greenwood;
sc T.E.B. Clarke
lp Peter Jones; Dora Reisser; Neil Stacy
HOME IS WHERE THE HEART IS 28/10/1973
d Ralph Levy; *p* Jack Greenwood;
sc Anthony Marriott, Scott Finch
lp Peter Jones; Robert Cawdron;
Frank Thornton

HIGHLAND FLING 18/11/1973
d John Robins; *p* Jack Greenwood;
sc Tom Brennard, Roy Bottomley
lp Peter Jones; Clive Dunn;
John Laurie; Noel Hood
I TOO WAS A NOVICE 25/11/1973
d Peter Duffell; *p* Jack Greenwood;
sc Brad Ashton
lp Peter Jones; George Tovey;
Gay Hamilton
RUSSIAN ROULETTE – MILLIE STYLE 9/12/1973
d Ralph Levy; *p* Jack Greenwood;
sc Lewis Schwarz
lp Yuri Borienko; Peter Jones;
Robert Cawdron
SICILIAN AFFAIR 1/3/1975
d John Robins; *p* Jack Greenwood;
sc John Warren, John Singer
lp Alexandra Bastedo; Franco Derosa;
Aubrey Morris
ALL IN A DAY'S WORK 8/3/1975
d Ralph Levy; *p* Jack Greenwood;
sc Stan Cutler; Martin Donovan
lp Edward Judd; Robert Howay;
Robert Rietty
WITNESS FOR THE PERSECUTION 29/3/1975
d Peter Duffell;
p Jack Greenwood, Pat Dunlop
lp Peter Jones; Reginald Barratt;
Ferdy Mayne

FROM INNER SPACE
(ABC 17/4–15/5/1966)
Five-part religious programme.
GEORGE FOX 1966
The life and vision of George Fox, founder of
the Quakers.
p Mike Vardy
lp Tom Criddle; Julian Glover;
Terry Scully; Leon Sinden; Jerome Willis

FRONT PAGE DETECTIVE
(US Jerry Fairbanks 1951–53)
Early crime drama featuring a crusading
newspaper columnist.
The DEVIL'S BIBLE 1951
d Arnold Webster; *exec.p* Jerry Fairbanks;
sc Irwin Ashkenazy
lp Edmund Lowe; Paula Drew;
John Davidson; Norman Budd;
Virginia Christine
A FRIEND OF THE CORPSE 1951
d Arnold Wester; *exec.p* Jerry Fairbanks
lp Edmund Lowe; Sarah Spencer;
Ben Welden; John Ridgely; Dani Sue Nolan

FRONTIERS OF DISCOVERY
(Anglia 3/8–15/11/1979)
Six-part science series.
SCIENCE AND LIFE 15/11/1979

FRONTIERS OF SCIENCE
(BBC 12/11–10/12/1968)
A series of five programmes on current research
into the brain.
UNITS OF PERCEPTION 19/11/1968
Dr Christopher Evans and E.F. Evans of Keele
University discuss the work being done by
psychologists and physiologists to crack the code
the brain uses to perceive the outside world.
p Eurfron Gwynne Jones

FROST ON FRIDAY (LWT 1968–69)
Interview series hosted by David Frost.
GENERAL DAYAN 23/8/1968
d Ian Fordyce; *p* Geoffrey Hughes
BALDUR VON SCHIRACH 13/9/1968
d Ian Fordyce; *p* Geoffrey Hughes
IAN SMITH 20/9/1968
d Ian Fordyce; *p* Geoffrey Hughes

FROST ON SATURDAY (LWT 1968–69)
Discussion show hosted by David Frost.
MUSIC HALL 28/9/1968
David Frost interviews Randolph Sutton and
Hetty King.
p.assoc Peter Baker, Neil Shand

FROST OVER ENGLAND (BBC 26/3/1967)
Comedy show compered by David Frost which
was the BBC entry and ultimate winner of the
1967 Montreux Festival. Repeated 14/8/76 in
BBC's FESTIVAL 40 series.
p James Gilbert; *with* Ronnie Barker,
John Cleese, Ronnie Corbett, Sheila Steafel,
Julie Felix

The FROST PROGRAMME
(Rediffusion/LWT 1966–73)
Interview series with David Frost
IAN SMITH 9/12/1966
Ian Smith is interviewed by telephone, following
the Rhodesian Government's rejection of
Britain's plans for a new constitution.
d Ian Fordyce; *p* Geoffrey Hughes
The RT. HON. GEORGE BROWN 2/2/1967
d Steve Minchin; *p* Geoffrey Hughes
DR. EMIL SAVUNDRA 3/2/1967
Emil Savundra is interviewed by David Frost
about the collapse of his car insurance company.
Programme gave rise to the term 'trial by
television'.
d Steve Minchin; *p* Geoffrey Hughes
DISCUSSION ON MEDITATION 4/10/1967
David Frost leads a discussion on meditation
with John Lennon, George Harrison, John
Mortimer and John Allison.
d William G. Stewart; *p* Geoffrey Hughes
EDWARD HEATH 13/10/1967
d William G. Stewart; *p* Geoffrey Hughes
FRANK COUSINS 18/10/1967
David Frost talks with Frank Cousins, Sir Max
Aitken, Bob Butlin, Jim Conway, Robert
Maxwell and Joe Hyman.
d William G. Stewart; *p* Geoffrey Hughes
RANDOLPH CHURCHILL 19/10/1967
d William G. Stewart; *p* Geoffrey Hughes
MIKE HOARE 19/10/1967
Mike Hoare, mercenary soldier in the Congo, is
interviewed.
d William G. Stewart
LESLIE THOMAS & VIETNAM WAR
DEMONSTRATORS 3/11/1967
d William G. Stewart; *p* Geoffrey Hughes
OSWALD MOSLEY 15/11/1967
d William G. Stewart; *p* Geoffrey Hughes
KING HUSSEIN 16/11/1967
d William G. Stewart; *p* Geoffrey Hughes
KENNETH KAUNDA 6/12/1967
The first part of the programme includes a
telephone interview with Kenneth Kaunda
followed by a studio discussion between Patrick
Keatley of 'The Guardian' and Julian Amory.
d William G. Stewart; *p* Geoffrey Hughes
JERRY RUBIN AND ROBERT ARDREY 7/11/1970
David Frost talks to Jerry Rubin and Robert
Ardrey. The 'Yippies' take over the show during
the transmission.
d David Coulter; *p* Geoffrey Hughes;
sc Nicolas Barrett
SHEIKH MUJIB 16/1/1972
David Frost interviews the President of
Bangladesh, Sheikh Mujib ur Rahman.
d Bruce Gowers; *p* John Birt
The MINERS' STRIKE 30/1/1972
David Frost discusses the miners' strike with
Welsh miners and their families.
d Bruce Gowers; *p* John Birt
The ULSTER CRISIS: WHEN WILL IT ALL END?
6/2/1972
David Frost discusses the situation in Ulster with
representatives of Catholic and Protestant
opinion.
d Bruce Gowers; *p* John Birt
ULSTER 24/3/1972
David Frost discusses with representatives of
Catholic and Protestant opinion the situation in
Ulster following the introduction of direct rule
from Westminster.
d Bruce Gowers
LIFE BEGINS AT SEVENTY 4/11/1973
David Frost interviews a number of elderly
people.
d Bruce Gowers; *p* Peter Baker

G

GALLERY (BBC 1962–65)
Series dealing with current events in Britain.
LORD HAILSHAM 13/6/1963
Robert McKenzie interviews Lord Hailsham
following the resignation of John Profumo.
p John Grist
PRE-LABOUR CONFERENCE SCARBOROUGH
1963 29/9/1963
Ian Trethowan previews the 1963 Labour Party
Conference. Robin Day interviews Harold
Wilson. Ian Trethowan interviews Lord Attlee.
The PRIME MINISTER AND MR ROBERT
MENZIES 17/6/1965
Presented by Ian Trethowan. At a debate of the
Oxford Union a speaker justifies the American
action in Vietnam. The programme then
announces the news that a 'peace conference'
has been set up, beginning with a fact-finding
mission to Vietnam, led by Harold Wilson;
Robin Day interviews Harold Wilson and Sir
Robert Menzies.
p Anthony Whitby

GALLOWAY CEILIDH (Border 2/3/1979)
Songs and stories from Galloway. With Robin
Hall, Jimmy McGregor, Mona Stewart and
David Hannay.
p Norman Fraser

GALTON AND SIMPSON PLAYHOUSE
(Yorkshire TV 17/2–7/4/1977)
Series of comedies written by Ray Galton and
Alan Simpson.
CAR ALONG THE PASS 17/2/1977
d/p Vernon Lawrence
lp Arthur Lowe; Mona Washbourne;
Anton Diffring; Aubrey Morris; André Maranne

GALTON & SPEIGHT'S TEA LADIES
(BBC 4/1/1979)
Comedy show set in the House of Commons.
p Dennis Main Wilson;
sc Ray Galton, Johnny Speight
lp Mollie Sugden; Dandy Nichols;
Patricia Hayes; John Quayle

The GAMBLERS (Rediffusion 1967–68)
A collection of individual plays with a central
theme.
TYCOON OF THE YEAR 23/11/1967
d Herbert Wise; *p* Tim Aspinall;
sc Roger Marshall
lp Lee Montague; George Selway;
Janet Davies; Godfrey Quigley;
Michael Barrington
The MAN BENEATH 7/12/1967
d Herbert Wise; *p* Tim Aspinall;
sc Jim Allen
lp Bernard Lee; Leslie Sands;
Timothy Bateson; Michael Wynne; Vera Cook
The BRIDGE 21/12/1967
d Gareth Davies; *p/sc* Tim Aspinall
lp Ronald Lacey; Colin Farrell;
Neville Buswell; Godfrey James; Brian Cox
THIRTY STRETCH 28/2/1968
d Alastair Reid; *p* Tim Aspinall;
sc Jimmy O'Connor
lp John Binden; Jerome Willis;
Robert Russell; Liam Redmond; Llewellyn Rees

The GAMBLING CITY (Rediffusion 22/2/1967)
The gambling city of Las Vegas.
d Charlie Squires; *nar* Robert Kee

GANGSTERS (BBC 1976; 1978)
Crime series set in the Birmingham underworld.
Developed from the play GANGSTERS shown
in the PLAY FOR TODAY series *tx* 9/1/1975.
INCIDENT 2 16/9/1976
d Alastair Reid; *p* David Rose;
sc Philip Martin
lp Maurice Colbourne; Ahmed Khalil;
Paul Barber; Oscar James; Oswald Lindsay

GARDENERS' WORLD (BBC 1968–)
Gardening series.
GARDENERS' WORLD 19/10/1979
p John Kenyon; *pres* Peter Seabrook

GARNOCK WAY (Scottish TV)
Soap opera.
GARNOCK WAY 1/4/1976
GARNOCK WAY 14/9/1978
GARNOCK WAY 21/9/1978
GARNOCK WAY 28/9/1978

The GATHERING STORM (BBC 1/12/1974)
A biographical film about Winston Churchill.
d Herbert Wise;
p Jack Le Vien, Andrew Osborn;
sc Colin Morris
lp Richard Burton; Virginia McKenna;
Robert Beatty; Robert Hardy; Ian Bannen;
Angharad Rees; Lesley Dunlop; Clive Francis

GAY OPERETTA
(Jack Hylton TV Productions 1959)
A series of condensed popular operettas.
COUNTESS MARITZA 6/11/1959
d Mark Lawton
lp Victoria Elliott; William McAlpine;
Margaret Nisbett; Eric Shilling
The MERRY WIDOW 13/11/1959
d Mark Lawton
lp Peter Grant; June Bronhill;
Marion Lowe; Howell Glynne; Rowland Jones
The GIPSY BARON 27/11/1959
d Mark Lawton; *intro* Derek Oldham
lp Alexander Young; Joan Stuart;
Nancy Creighton

GAYS: SPEAKING UP (Thames 3/8/1978)
An audience of homosexuals and lesbians
discusses with Llew Gardner what it means to be
gay in Britain.
d Vincent Stafford; *p* James Farrant

GENERAL ELECTION RESULTS 1959
(BBC 8/10/1959)
Richard Dimbleby, David Butler and Robert
McKenzie comment on the incoming results
from the 1959 General Election.
d Grace Wyndham Goldie, Michael Peacock

GENERAL HOSPITAL (ATV 1972–79)
Soap opera set in a busy Midlands hospital.
GENERAL HOSPITAL 19/10/1972
d Shaun O'Riordan; *p* Ian Fordyce;
sc Max Marquis
lp David Garth; Lewis Jones; James Kerry;
Ian White; Ronald Leigh-Hunt; Peggy Sinclair
GENERAL HOSPITAL 20/10/1972
d Shaun O'Riordan; *p* Ian Fordyce;
sc Max Marquis
lp David Garth; Lewis Jones; James Kerry;
Ian White; Ronald Leigh-Hunt;
Lynda Bellingham; Judy Buxton
STITCH IN TIME 10/9/1976
d Keith Farthing; *p* Royston Morley;
sc David Fisher
lp David Garth; Lewis Jones; Tony Adams;
Carl Rigg; Louis Mahoney; Eric Lander

GENERAL STRIKE REPORT
(Yorkshire TV 3/5–12/5/1976)
Ten-part series representing the General Strike
of 1926 as a series of current affairs reports.
MAY 3, 1926 3/5/1976
A survey of the first day of the General Strike.
p James Farrant

GENERATIONS APART
(BBC 17/10–31/10/1970)
Three documentaries charting the differences in
generations and outlook of groups and
individuals.
TWO GIRLS IN HAMPSHIRE 31/10/1970
The opposing views of two girls from the same
school in Aldershot.
d Jenny Barraclough; *rep* John Pitman

GENETTE (Westward 23/11/1979)
An investigative report and reconstruction of the
circumstances surrounding the disappearance of
schoolgirl Genette Tate from the West Devon
village of Aylesbeare.

The GENUINE ARTICLE (BBC 2/5–12/6/1979)
Series on how to recognise fakes and frauds.
PAINTINGS 23/5/1979
p John Mansfield, Robin Bootle;
pres John Fitzmaurice Mills

GEORDIE SCENE (Tyne Tees)
Music series.
GEORGIE FAME 16/1/1975
PROCOL HARUM 21/3/1976

GEORGE AND MILDRED (Thames 1976–78)
Sitcom based on the the landlord characters first
seen in MAN ABOUT THE HOUSE
(1973–76).
BABY TALK 27/9/1976
d/p Peter Frazer-Jones;
sc Johnnie Mortimer, Brian Cooke
lp Brian Murphy; Yootha Joyce;
Norman Eshley; Sheila Fearn;
Nicholas Bond Owen

GEORGIA O'KEEFE
(US WNET/Thirteen; BBC tx 4/7/1979)
Documentary about the artist; interviewed at her
studio home in New Mexico while overseeing the
production of a new book on her work.
Assessments of her work are given by the critics
Barbara Rose and Daniel Catton Rich.
d Perry Miller Adato

**GERALD MOORE INTRODUCES
LEONTYNE PRICE** (BBC 4/6/1959)
Performance by vocalist Leontyne Price.
pres Walter Todds

GERMAINE GREER v. USA (ATV 9/11/1971)
Germaine Greer touring the USA to promote
her book 'The Female Eunuch'.
d Charles Mapleston; *p* Brigid Segrave

GERT AND DAISY
(Jack Hylton TV Productions 1959)
Comedy series set in a theatrical boarding house
featuring Elsie and Doris Waters.
d Milo Lewis;
sc Lewis Schwarz, Malcolm Hulke, Eric Paice;
regulars Hugh Paddick; Patsy Rowlands;
Dudy Nimmo; Jennifer Browne; Julian D'Albie
GERT AND DAISY 10/8/1959
GERT AND DAISY 17/8/1959
GERT AND DAISY 24/8/1959
GERT AND DAISY 31/8/1959
GERT AND DAISY 7/9/1959
GERT AND DAISY 16/9/1959

GET IT TOGETHER (Granada 1977–81)
Series of pop music programmes, featuring
studio performances by groups and singers.
GET IT TOGETHER 10/10/1978
d Nicholas Ferguson; *p* Muriel Young;
pres Linda Fletcher, Roy North;
with Abba, Chris Blake, Honey Brown, Hunter,
Allan David

GET SOME IN! (Thames 1975–78)
Sitcom set in a National Service RAF camp
during 1955.
LILLEY'S BOOTS 13/11/1975
d/p Michael Mills;
sc John Esmonde, Bob Larbey
lp Tony Selby; David Janson;
Robert Lindsay; Gerard Ryder; Brian Pettifer;
David Quilter; Mark Dunn

The GHOST SONATA (BBC 16/3/1962)
d/p Stuart Burge; *auth* August Strindberg
lp Robert Helpmann; Beatrix Lehmann;
John Rae; Jeremy Brett; Linda Gardner;
Yvonne Coulette

GHOST SQUAD (ATV 1961–63)
Detective/undercover drama series.
p Connery Chappell;
regulars Donald Wolfit; Michael Quinn
TICKET FOR BLACKMAIL 9/9/1961
d Norman Harrison; *sc* Lindsay Galloway
lp Petra Davies; Paul Stassino;
Ronald Leigh-Hunt; Alex Scott; Donald Morley

BULLET WITH MY NAME ON IT 16/9/1961
d Don Sharp; *sc* Lindsay Galloway
lp Angela Browne; Catherine Feller;
Alfred Burke; Peter Williams; William Greene
HONG KONG STORY 23/9/1961
d Don Sharp; *sc* Lindsay Galloway
lp Neil Hallett; Anthony Marlowe;
Angela Browne; Julie Allan; Bill Kerr
HIGH WIRE 30/9/1961
d Norman Harrison; *sc* Lewis Davidson
lp Angela Browne; William Hartnell;
Anne Wakefield; Collette Wilde; John Cairney
BROKEN DOLL 7/10/1961
d Don Sharp; *sc* Patrick Campbell
lp Julia Arnall; Simon Lack;
Jean Anderson; Harry Locke; Gabriella Licudi
The EYES OF THE BAT 14/10/1961
d Don Sharp; *sc* Robert Stewart
lp William Lucas; Jean Clarke;
Lionel Murton; Edward Cast; Donald Churchill
STILL WATERS 21/10/1961
d Robert Lynn; *sc* Max Marquis
lp John Carson; Angela Browne;
Stratford Johns; Victor Beaumont;
Patricia Marmont
ASSASSIN 28/10/1961
d Robert Lynn;
sc Dick Sharples, Gerald Kelsey
lp George Coulouris; Angela Browne;
Norman Bird; Jill Ireland; Joseph Furst
DEATH FROM A DISTANCE 4/11/1961
d Robert Lynn; *sc* Lindsay Galloway
lp William Sylvester; Hazel Court;
John Le Mesurier; Anton Diffring;
Angela Browne
CATSPAW 7/10/1962
d Robert Lynn; *sc* Bill Craig
lp Paul Stassino; Michael Goodliffe;
Moira Redmond; Bill Nagy; Angela Browne
PRINCESS 14/10/1962
d Robert Lynn;
sc Dick Sharples, Gerald Kelsey
lp Honor Blackman; Warren Mitchell;
Barbara Evans; Angela Browne; Robert Rietty

GHOSTS (BBC 26/1/1962)
p George R. Foa; *auth* Henrik Ibsen
lp Katina Paxinou; Paul Rogers;
Barry Foster; Prunella Scales; Esmond Knight

GHOSTS (Yorkshire TV 26/7/1977)
d David Cunliffe; *auth* Henrik Ibsen
lp Dorothy Tutin; Richard Pasco;
Ronald Fraser; Brian Deacon; Julia Foster

The GHOSTS OF MOTLEY HALL
(Granada 1976–78)
Fantasy series for children.
The CHRISTMAS SPIRIT 26/12/1976
d/p Quentin Lawrence; *sc* Richard Carpenter
lp Arthur English; Freddie Jones;
Nicholas Le Prevost; Sean Flanagan
PHANTOMIME 26/12/1977
d/p Quentin Lawrence; *sc* Richard Carpenter
lp Arthur English; Freddie Jones;
Nicholas Le Prevost; Sean Flanagan

GIDEON'S WAY (ATV 1964–66)
Detective series following the investigations of
Commander George Gideon of Scotland Yard;
based on the character created by author John
Creasey, writing as J.J. Marric.
p Robert S. Baker, Monty Berman
regulars John Gregson; Alexander Davion;
Daphne Anderson
The V MEN 17/10/1964
d Cyril Frankel; *sc* Alun Falconer
lp Roland Culver; Keith Baxter;
Angela Douglas; Allan Cuthbertson;
Basil Dignam
RHYME AND THE REASON 24/10/1964
d John Gilling; *sc* Jack Whittingham
lp Jo Rowbottom; Alan Rothwell;
Edward Evans; Clare Kelly; Carol White
The TIN GOD 7/11/1964
d John Gilling; *sc* Harry W. Junkin
lp Derren Nesbitt; Jennifer Wilson;
John Hurt; Arthur Lovegrove; Michael Cashman
STATE VISIT 14/11/1964
d John Llewellyn Moxey; *sc* Jim O'Connolly
lp Alfie Bass; Catherine Lacey;
Basil Dignam; Gerald Harper

The LADY-KILLER 5/12/1964
d Leslie Norman; *sc* David Chantler
lp Ray Barrett; Rosemary Leach;
Justine Lord; John Tate; Timothy Bateson
BIG FISH, LITTLE FISH 19/12/1964
d Cyril Frankel; *sc* Alun Falconer
lp Angela Baddeley; Jack MacGowran;
Maxwell Shaw; Sydney Tafler; Avis Bunnage
The HOUSEKEEPER 2/1/1965
d Leslie Norman; *sc* David Chantler
lp Kay Walsh; Harry Fowler;
Oliver Johnson; Marjie Lawrence; John Dearth
The NIGHTLIFERS 9/1/1965
d John Llewellyn Moxey; *sc* Iain MacCormick
lp Anton Rodgers; Derek Fowlds;
Jean Marsh; Annette Andre; Pauline Munro
FALL HIGH, FALL HARD 16/1/1965
d Leslie Norman; *sc* Malcolm Hulke
lp Donald Houston; Sarah Lawson;
Victor Maddern; Glyn Houston;
Gordon Gostelow
SUBWAY TO REVENGE 3/4/1965
d Roy Ward Baker; *sc* Norman Hudis
lp Anne Lawson; Donald Churchill;
Bryan Pringle; Esmond Knight; Noel Dyson
The WALL 10/4/1965
d Leslie Norman; *sc* David Chantler
lp John Barrie; Ann Bell; Megs Jenkins;
Richard Carpenter; Pauline Yates;
Bernard Brown
GANG WAR 17/4/1965
d Quentin Lawrence; *sc* David Chantler
lp Jane Merrow; Ray Brooks; Ronald Lacey;
Frederick Bartman; Donald Morley
The ALIBI MAN 24/4/1965
d Cyril Frankel; *sc* Iain MacCormick
lp Jack Hedley; Sheila Allen;
Jennifer Daniel; James Culliford
The PROWLER 1/5/1965
d Robert Tronson; *sc* Harry W. Junkin
lp David Collings; Fanny Rowe;
Gillian Lewis; Rosemary Dunham;
Thomas Heathcote
BOY WITH GUN 27/2/1966
d Jeremy Summers; *sc* Iain MacCormick
lp Anthony Bate; George Sewell;
Michael Craze; Michael Standing;
Ruth Trouncer
The MILLIONAIRE'S DAUGHTER 20/11/1966
d Cyril Frankel; *sc* Norman Hudis
lp Donald Sutherland; Don Borisenko;
David Bauer; Lois Maxwell; Georgina Ward

The GIFT (Anglia 13/12/1978)
The Sainsbury Centre for Visual Arts designed
by Norman Foster for the University of East
Anglia.
d Ron Downing

The GIFT OF FRIENDSHIP
(Yorkshire TV 24/9/1974)
d Mike Newell; *exec.p* Peter Willes;
sc John Osborne
lp Alec Guinness; Michael Gough;
Sarah Badel; Leueen MacGrath; John Role

**GILBERT AND SULLIVAN – THE
IMMORTAL JESTERS** (BBC 1961)
Three-part drama series on the lives of Gilbert
and Sullivan.
d/p Graeme Muir; *sc* Michael Voysey
regulars Alan Wheatley; Ernest Clark;
Lyndon Brook; Mary McKenzie; Mairhi Russell
PART 1: OVERTURE 10/12/1961
PART 2: THE GOLDEN YEARS 17/12/1961
PART 3: SHADOWS AND SUNSHINE 23/12/1961

GILLIGAN'S ISLAND
(US Gladasya Productions 1964–67)
Comedy series concerning a colourful group of
passengers shipwrecked on a remote Pacific
island.
TWO ON A RAFT 21/9/1964
d John Rich; *p* Sherwood Schwartz;
sc Laurence J. Cohen, Fred Freeman
lp Bob Denver; Alan Hale Jr;
Jim Backus; Natalie Schafer; Tina Louise;
Russell Johnson; Dawn Wells

GISELLE (BBC 23/11/1958)
Ballet performance by the Royal Ballet, choreographed by G. Coralli and G. Perrot. The Royal Opera House Orchestra is conducted by Hugo Rignold.
p Margaret Dale; *with* Nadia Nerina, Nikolai Fadeyechev, Niels Bjørn Larsen, Lydia Sokolova; Margaret Hill; Julia Farron

GIULINI CONDUCTS (BBC 27/7/1965)
Richard Baker introduces the New Philharmonic Orchestra conducted by Carlo Maria Giulini, playing Mozart's Symphony No. 39 and De Falla's suite 'El amor brujo'.
p Antony Craxton

GIVE US A CLUE (Thames 1979–)
Game show based on the parlour game of charades.
GIVE US A CLUE 2/1/1979
d Alan Wallis; *p* Juliet Grimm;
host Michael Aspel; *with* Una Stubbs, Liz Fraser, Judy Geeson, Lionel Blair

The GLITTERING PRIZES (BBC 1976)
Six plays by Frederic Raphael following the lives of a group of Cambridge students.
p Mark Shivas
EPISODE 1: EARLY LIFE 21/1/1976
d Waris Hussein
lp Tom Conti; Barbara Kellermann;
Elizabeth Spriggs; David Robb; Natasha Morgan
EPISODE 2: LOVE LIFE 28/1/1976
d Robert Knights
lp Tom Conti; Angela Down;
Barbara Kellermann; Anna Carteret;
John Gregg
EPISODE 3: PAST LIFE 4/2/1976
d Waris Hussein
lp Tom Conti; Barbara Kellermann;
Eric Porter; Miriam Margolyes; Leonard Sachs
EPISODE 4: COUNTRY LIFE 11/2/1976
d Waris Hussein
lp Angela Down; Malcolm Stoddard;
Anna Carteret; John Gregg; Tim Preece;
Nigel Havers
EPISODE 5: ACADEMIC LIFE 18/2/1976
d Robert Knights
lp Dinsdale Landen; Austin Denny;
Clive Merrison; Suzanne Stone;
Carolle Rousseau
EPISODE 6: DOUBLE LIFE 25/2/1976
d Robert Knights
lp Tom Conti; Barbara Kellermann;
Mark Wing-Davey; Emily Richard; Prunella Gee

GLOBE THEATRE (BBC)
BBC series featuring foreign productions. Transmission dates are for BBC.
SMOG (DE 5/11/1974)
Documentary drama about the dangers of smog.
d Wolfgang Petersen; *auth* Wolfgang Menge
LITTLE MAN LASSE (SE Sveriges Radio 3/12/1974)
d Christer Dahl;
auth Christer Dahl, Lasse Stromstedt, Bodil Martensson
lp Hans Mosesson; Christina Evers
The TIME OF YOUR LIFE (SE Sveriges Radio 26/7/1978)
A play about a woman suffering from a brain tumour.
d Gun Jonsson; *sc* Anna-Maria Hagerfors
lp Gösta Bredefeldt; Mona Malm;
Johan Wahlström; Anna-Lo Sundberg;
Sebastian Hakansson

The GLUMS (LWT 1979)
Comedy series taken from the original radio show 'Take It From Here'.
The GLUMS 2/12/1979
d John Reardon; *p* Simon Brett;
sc Denis Norden, Frank Muir
lp Jimmy Edwards; Ian Lavender;
Patricia Brake; Michael Stainton; John Barron;
Norman Bird

GO GO GO SAID THE BIRD
(Rediffusion 26/10/1966)
Four young people pinpoint the attitudes that have contributed to the phenomenon of swinging London.
d John Irvin; *p* Richard De La Mare;
comm Nik Cohn

GOING TO WORK (BBC 1964–71)
Careers service series for young people.
CATERING 5/10/1964
Visits to a school of catering, a factory canteen, a school kitchen and a hospital.
p Peter Scroggs
PARKS AND GARDENS 17/10/1966
Working in parks and gardens.
p Wynne Lloyd; *intro* Peter West
MOTOR INDUSTRY APPRENTICE 6/3/1967
The apprentice training school and the assembly line of one of Britain's largest car manufacturers.
p Gordon Croton; *intro* Peter West
HORTICULTURE 29/1/1968
The range of jobs available in the horticulture industry.
p Len Brown; *intro* Peter West
WORKING FOR NOTHING 13/5/1968
Report on the social and community work done by pupils at schools in Chesterfield and Shropshire.
p John Parry; *intro* Peter West
WORK FOR THE HANDICAPPED 27/5/1968
p Gordon Croton; *intro* Peter West
WHAT I THINK...24/6/1968
The experiences of two school-leavers and their reactions to their first year at work.
p John Prescott Thomas; *intro* Peter West
WORKING FOR THE COUNCIL 30/9/1968
Chester City and Cheshire County Councils and the career opportunities they offer to school leavers.
p John Prescott Thomas; *intro* Peter West
HAIRDRESSING 3/2/1969
Peter West looks at the career opportunities for young people in hairdressing.
p John Prescott Thomas; *intro* Peter West
The PHOTO BUSINESS 17/11/1969
Opportunities in commercial photography for school leavers.
d Barbara Parker
DAY RELEASE 8/3/1971
p Andrew Neal
JOBS FOR LATER ON 3/5/1971
A Birmingham taxi-driver and a buyer from a London department store, both in their mid-20s, show that some jobs are well worth waiting for.
p Len Brown; *comm* Nigel Anthony
BEING YOUR OWN BOSS 17/5/1971
Self-employment.
p Paul Mitchell
HOTELS AND RESTAURANTS 11/10/1971
p Julian Aston; *nar* Nigel Anthony

The GOLD ROBBERS
(LWT 6/6–29/8/1969)
Crime series.
The GREAT BULLION ROBBERY 6/6/1969
d Don Leaver; *p* John Hawkesworth;
. *sc* John Hawkesworth, Glyn Jones
lp Peter Vaughan; Richard Leech;
Donald Morley; Michael Barrington;
Artro Morris

The GOLD RUN (Yorkshire TV 12/4/1969)
The lives of African workers in the South African gold mines.
d/p Antony R. Thomas

The GOLDEN BOWL
(BBC 4/5–8/6/1972)
A six-part dramatisation of the Henry James novel.
EPISODE 1: PRINCE 4/5/1972
d James Cellan Jones; *p* Martin Lisemore;
sc Jack Pulman
lp Cyril Cusack; Daniel Massey;
Gayle Hunnicutt; Barry Morse; Jill Townsend;
Kathleen Byron

EPISODE 6: END GAME 8/6/1972
d James Cellan Jones; *p* Martin Lisemore;
sc Jack Pulman
lp Cyril Cusack; Daniel Massey;
Gayle Hunnicutt; Jill Townsend; Barry Morse;
Kathleen Byron

GOLDEN DRAMA (ATV 31/1/1965)
An excerpt from a programme about British stage drama; an extract of the National Theatre's production of Farquhar's 'The Recruiting Officer', presented at the Queen's Theatre.
d Bill Ward; *p* Cecil Clarke
lp Laurence Olivier

GOLDEN GALA (ATV 9/7/1978)
A charity show at the London Palladium to celebrate the 50th Anniversary of equal voting rights for women.
d/p Wendy Toye; *sc* Caryl Brahms,
Garry Chambers, Ronald Chesney,
John Dankworth, Benny Green,
Peter Greenwell, Charlotte Mitchell,
Rosemary Ann Sissons, Peter Vincent,
Bronwen Williams, Ronald Wolfe;
with Isobel Barnett, Katie Boyle,
Eleanor Bron, Dulcie Gray, Jean Kent,
Margaret Lockwood, Geraldine McEwan,
Muriel Pavlow, Janet Suzman, Billie Whitelaw
Googie Withers

The GOLDEN SHOT (ATV 1967–75)
Game show based on markmanship using a free-standing crossbow, shooting at moving or stationary targets.
The GOLDEN SHOT 4/2/1968
d Anton Bowler; *p* Colin Clews;
with Bob Monkhouse, Ivor Emmanuel,
Morgan James, Carol Dilworth, Andrea Lloyd

The GOLDEN YEARS OF ALEXANDER KORDA (BBC 27/12/1968)
An account of Korda's career in Britain, with reminiscences from actors and collaborators, and extracts from his films.
d/p/sc Robert Vas; *nar* Kenneth More;
with Elisabeth Bergner, Mary Morris,
John Clements, Ian Dalrymple,
Douglas Fairbanks Jr, John Justin,
Elsa Lanchester, Vivien Leigh, James Mason,
Muir Mathieson, Merle Oberon,
Ralph Richardson, Flora Robson, Miklös Rözsa,
R.C. Sherriff, Ann Todd

GOLDWATER – MAN OUT OF THE WEST
(Rediffusion 28/10/1964)
John Freeman presents a biographical study of senator Barry Goldwater.
d James Butler

GOOD AFTERNOON (Thames 1974–77)
Magazine programme. Later became AFTERNOON (1977–79)
APRIL ASHLEY 17/3/1977
Mavis Nicholson interviews April Ashley who underwent a sex change operation in the 1960s.
d Adrian Brown; *pres* Mavis Nicholson

GOOD GIRL (Yorkshire TV 27/7–31/8/1974)
Comedy series starring Julia Foster as an 'unbridled' do-gooder.
DOES THE ROAD WIND UPHILL 24/8/1974
d David Cunliffe; *exec.p* Peter Willes;
sc Philip Mackie
lp Julia Foster; Peter Barkworth;
Peter Bowles; Brian Deacon; John Shrapnel;
Joan Hickson

GOOD HEALTH (ATV)
Series on health and safety for school children.
WHO NEEDS A CHIMNEY IN THE HEAD?
25/11/1975
Discourages school children from smoking.
d Dilys Howell
lp Victor Woolf; David Biddle
WATCH OUT! 1976
Reminds children to 'play safe' and avoid potential dangers on the road, at home and in play.
d Albert Wallace

The GOOD LIFE (BBC 1975–77)
Sitcom about a couple's attempts to be totally
self-sufficient in affluent Surbiton.
d/p John Howard Davies;
sc John Esmonde, Bob Larbey
regulars Richard Briers; Felicity Kendal;
Paul Eddington; Penelope Keith
PLOUGH YOUR OWN FURROW 4/4/1975
SAY LITTLE HEN...? 11/4/1975
PIGS' LIB 25/4/1975
The THING IN THE CELLAR 2/5/1975
The PAGAN RITE 9/5/1975
The GURU OF SURBITON 12/12/1975
lp Bruce Bould; Irene Richard
MUTINY 9/1/1976
lp Reginald Marsh
GOING TO POT? 23/1/1976
lp Charmian May
EARLY BIRDS 10/9/1976
The HAPPY EVENT 17/9/1976
lp George Innes
A TUG OF THE FORELOCK 24/9/1976
I TALK TO THE TREES 1/10/1976
lp Noel Howlett; Joyce Windsor;
Raymond Mason
AWAY FROM IT ALL 10/4/1977
The GREEN DOOR 17/4/1977
lp Jane Hilary; Toria Fuller

GOOD MORNING CALENDAR
(Yorkshire TV 1977)
Local news magazine programme. See also
CALENDAR (1969–)
GOOD MORNING CALENDAR 25/5/1975
Everton beat Newcastle; Police Federation
Conference; review of morning papers; weather;
birthdays; horoscope.
d David Milland; *p* John Meade

GOOD MORNING DAWN
(Scottish TV 31/8/1977)
Preparations for the annual Bo'ness Industrial
Fair.
p Chris Fox

GOOD MORNING NORTH
(Tyne Tees 13/5/1977)
News magazine programme transmitted as part
of a breakfast-time television experiment.

The GOOD OLD DAYS (BBC 1953–83)
Variety show featuring music hall acts;
introduced by Leonard Sachs from the City
Varieties, Leeds.
The GOOD OLD DAYS 16/4/1960
p Barney Colehan; *with* The Gaunt Brothers,
The Falcons, June Merlin and her doves, Jimmy
Gay, Harry Bailey and Nancy and Molly Munks.
The GOOD OLD DAYS 7/6/1977
p Barney Colehan;
with Max Bygraves; Jessie Matthews;
Millicent Martin; Julia McKenzie; Sheila Steafel

GOOD SAILING (BBC 16/4–18/6/1969)
Ten-part instructional series.
RACING 7/5/1969
p Brenda Horsfield; *intro* Jack Knights
CRUISER HANDLING 4/6/1969
p Brenda Horsfield; *intro* Alec Miller

**The GOOD, THE BAD AND THE
INDIFFERENT** (Yorkshire TV 19/10/1976)
A personal view of the Church of England by
Antony Thomas.
d/sc/nar Antony Thomas; *exec.p* Michael Deakin

GOODBYE LONGFELLOW ROAD
(Yorkshire TV 8/3/1977)
Documentary telling the story of a London
street, showing poor housing conditions and
corruption in local government.
d/p John Willis;
exec.p John Fairley, Michael Deakin

The GOODIES (BBC 1970–77)
Anarchic comedy series written by the three
performers.
sc/with Graeme Garden, Bill Oddie,
Tim Brooke-Taylor

MONTREUX 72 9/4/1972
The BBC entry for the Golden Rose of
Montreux.
d Jim Franklin; *p* John Howard Davies
lp Michael Aspel; Corbet Woodall;
Milton Reid
FRANKENFIDO 10/3/1975
p Jim Franklin
KUNG FU KAPERS 24/3/1975
p Jim Franklin

GOSLING'S TRAVELS (Granada 1974–75)
Reporter Ray Gosling tours Britain.
CARAVAN STRIP 6/8/1974
Ray Gosling visits the caravan sites on the North
Wales coast between Rhyl and Abergele.
d Philip Trevelyan

The GOVERNMENT INSPECTOR
(BBC 9/2/1958)
Adaptation of Gogol's satirical 1836 play set in
provincial Russia about a young man mistaken
for an incognito inspector by the town officials.
p Alan Bromly; *sc* Barry Thomas;
auth Nikolai Gogol
lp Tony Hancock; Reginald Barratt;
Wilfrid Brambell; Roy Dotrice

GOYA: THE WINTER EXHIBITION
(BBC 7/2/1964)
Sir Gerald Kelly at The Royal Academy of Arts
discusses some of the paintings in the current
Goya exhibition.
d Innes Lloyd; *p* Bill Duncalf;
comm Gerald Kelly

GRACELESS GO I (HTV 8/10/1974)
Drama about a psychiatrist.
d Patrick Dromgoole; *p* Peter Miller;
auth/sc Anthony Storey
lp Stanley Baker; Rachel Roberts
Ian McKellen; Peter Sallis

The GRAFTERS (Rediffusion 18/11/1964)
Open-air market traders and the life of Joe
Edwards, a famous grafter from Barnsley
market.
d Charlie Squires

GRAHAM'S GANG
(BBC 21/11–19/12/1977; 14/2–14/3/1979)
Comedy series for children.
d Marilyn Fox; *exec.p* Anna Home;
sc John Challen
regulars Lloyd Mahoney; Tommy Pender;
Neill Lillywhite; Alan Corbett; Mark Francis;
Melanie Gibson
The GREAT OUTDOORS 28/11/1977
lp George A. Cooper; Jesse Birdsall;
James McCormack, David Nunn; Ivor Danvers
WILLIAM'S WEEK 5/12/1977
lp Peter Cellier; Christopher Owen;
Marcia Gresham; Steve Fletcher; Colm Daly
KIDNAP 12/12/1977
lp David Corti; Suzan Cameron;
Michael Troughton; Sheila Ferris
CAMERADERIE 19/12/1977
lp Jesse Birdsall; James McCormack;
Steve Fletcher; Colm Daly; Norman Bird;
Ivor Salter
ACTION! 14/2/1979
lp Katherine Hughes
REMEMBER REMEMBER 21/2/1979
lp George A. Cooper; Paddy Joyce;
Frank Jarvis; Malcolm Rogers; Charles Stewart
MILDRED'S PARTY 28/2/1979
lp Katherine Hughes; Jo Rowbottom;
Ivor Salter; John Blundell; Malcolm McFee
ONLY FOOLING 7/3/1979
lp Keith James; Jean Marlow
CORDIAL INTENT 14/3/1979
lp Katherine Hughes; Elizabeth Rees;
Marion Gay; Brigit Forsyth; Bill McGuirk

GRAMPIAN TODAY (Grampian)
Regional news magazine.
GRAMPIAN TODAY 22/11/1979

GRANDSTAND (BBC 1958–)
Sports programme.
GRANDSTAND 19/8/1971
Includes an Olympic preview, racing from
Haydock, show jumping, and rugby league –
Salford v Leeds.
pres Frank Bough
GRANDSTAND 6/1/1973
Includes racing from Haydock, ski-jumping from
Garmisch and New Zealand v England at
Twickenham.
pres Frank Bough

GRANGE HILL (BBC 1978–)
Drama series about the children and staff of the
fictitious Grange Hill Comprehensive School.
d Colin Cant; *exec.p* Anna Home;
sc Phil Redmond
regulars Robert Morgan; Terry Sue Patt;
George Armstrong; Miriam Mann; Todd Carty;
Gary Fetterplace; Abigail Brown;
Lucinda Duckett; Julia Gale; Michelle Herbert;
Graham Ashley; Roger Sloman;
Michael Percival; Peggy Sinclair
GRANGE HILL 8/2/1978
lp Christopher Hall; James Jebbia;
Stella Haime; Hilary Crane; Dorothea Phillips;
Pamela Vezey
GRANGE HILL 15/2/1978
lp Donald Waugh; Carol Daniels;
Perry Benson; Brenda Cavendish
GRANGE HILL 22/2/1978
lp Kim Neve; Tilly Vosburgh; Karen Snow
GRANGE HILL 1/3/1978
lp Christopher Hall; Donald Waugh;
Paul McCarthy; James Jebbia; Christopher Coll
GRANGE HILL 8/3/1978
lp Kim Neve; Karen Snow; Jill Dixon;
Blake Butler; Pamela Vezey; Jean Boht
GRANGE HILL 15/3/1978
lp Christopher Hall; Donald Waugh;
James Jebbia; Jumoke Debayo; Hilary Crane
GRANGE HILL 22/3/1978
lp Vincent Hall; Donald Waugh;
Kim Benson; Clive Gehle; Simon Henderson
GRANGE HILL 29/3/1978
lp Ann Mannion; Tim Slender;
Vincent Hall; Donald Waugh; Kim Benson
GRANGE HILL 5/4/1978
lp Vincent Hall; Kim Benson;
Robert Collins; Simon Henderson;
Franco Manzi
GRANGE HILL 2/1/1979
lp Kim Benson; Lindy Brill;
Abigail Arundel; Ruth Davies; Alan Gibson

GRASS ROOTS (BBC 4/10/1961)
Denis Mitchell's impression of the small
American town of Princeton, Kentucky.
d Denis Mitchell

GREAT ACTING (BBC 1965–66)
Interview series with actors.
MICHAEL REDGRAVE 19/2/1966
Michael Redgrave talks to Richard Findlater on
the stage of the Yvonne Arnaud Theatre,
Guildford, and in the studio.
p Hal Burton

GREAT BRITONS (BBC 25/7–29/8/1978)
Six-part series on personalities in British history.
DAVID LLOYD GEORGE 22/8/1978
Lloyd George's life from childhood in Wales
through his career as a lawyer, politician,
Chancellor and Prime Minister.
p Malcolm Brown; *sc/intro* John Grigg

GREAT CAPTAINS
(BBC 22/12/1960–18/4/1961)
Four-part series on great military leaders.
p Thérèse Denny; *nar* Brian Horrocks
OLIVER CROMWELL 22/12/1960
DUKE OF MARLBOROUGH 24/1/1961
ADMIRAL LORD NELSON 28/2/1961
DUKE OF WELLINGTON 18/4/1961

**The GREAT DEBATE – ENOCH POWELL
AND TREVOR HUDDLESTON**
(LWT 12/10/1969)
Trevor Huddleston and Enoch Powell debate the
issue of race relations in Britain.

GREAT DIRECTORS (BBC 1974)
Documentary series on film directors.
HARRY WATT 20/9/1974
Harry Watt is interviewed by Gordon Jackson at
Ealing Studios. He looks back at his career as a
film director, with extracts from some of his
films.
d Tony Staveacre

The GREAT LITTLE TRAINS OF WALES
(HTV 1976)
Documentary series.
LLANBERIS LAKE RAILWAY AND THE
SNOWDON MOUNTAIN RAILWAY 19/5/1976
The Llanberis Lake Railway, which was built to
transport slate from the Dinorwic Quarries to
the coast.
d/p John Mead; *comm* Wynford Vaughan-
Thomas

The GREAT NORTH SEA GAMBLE
(Tyne Tees 4/8/1965)
The economic and political significance of the oil
and gas which may be discovered in the North
Sea.
d Peter Dunbar; *p* Robert Tyrrell;
sc Frank Entwisle, Robert Tyrrell;
nar Anthony Brown

GREAT PARKS OF THE WORLD
(BBC 22/6–27/7/1972)
Documentary series on national parks.
BAYERISCHER WALD 22/6/1972
p Peter Bale
NAIROBI 29/6/1972
p Richard Brock
The HIGH TATRAS 6/7/1972
p Peter Crawford
FUJI-HAKONE-IZU 13/7/1972
p Peter Bale

The GREATEST SHOW ON EARTH (US
Desilu Productions-Cody Productions 1963–64)
Inspired by the 1952 film of the same name and
featuring dramatic stories involving the life of
circus folk.
CORSICANS DON'T CRY 14/1/1964
d Vincent McEveety; *p* Bob Rafelson;
sc Paul Mason; *auth* Anthony Spinner
lp Jack Palance; Steven Hill;
Stuart Erwin; Ann Adler; Carl Carlsson;
Pamela Curran

The GREEN TABLE (BBC 13/4/1967)
A performance of the ballet 'The Green Table'
by the Folkwangballet. Choreography by Kurt
Jooss.
d/p Peter Wright; *with* Winifred Krisch,
Michael Diekamp, Pina Bausch

The GROUP (BBC 5/10–16/11/1965)
Documentary series which looks at various
groups brought together by a common interest,
such as work or pleasure.
The EGGHEADS 9/11/1965
The stages in the preparation of an advertising
campaign for the Egg Marketing Board by
Mather & Crowther.
d/p Michael Croucher

The GROWING TOWN (BBC 1961)
Five-part series for sixth formers on the
development on the rise of town and city.
d/p Peter Dunkley; *pres* Michael Calthrop
The MEDIEVAL TOWN 30/10/1961
A study of life in the medieval towns of York,
Edinburgh and Bruges.
The GEORGIAN TOWN 6/11/1961
The growth of the medieval town led to the
Georgian architects' answers to a pressing
problem in the form of new towns, as in
Edinburgh.
The INDUSTRIAL TOWN 13/11/1961
The nineteenth-century town reflects the impact
of the technologies of steam and iron both in its
size and form.
The CONTEMPORARY TOWN 20/11/1961
Some of the contemporary solutions to bring the
amenity of open space into a crowded
environment.

A LOOK AT THE FUTURE 27/11/1961
Looks at Harlow, Sheffield and London. With
Lewis Mumford and Percy Johnson-Marshall.

GUARDIANS (LWT 10/7–2/10/1971)
Thirteen-part drama series set in the totalitarian
state of a future Britain.
HEAD OF STATE 24/7/1971
d Robert Tronson; *p* Andrew Brown;
auth John Bowen;
lp Cyril Luckham; Edward Petherbridge;
Kenneth Gilbert; Michael Smee; Derek Smith

The GUN (BBC 12/7–13/9/1976)
Ten-part documentary on the development and
history of the gun.
ACCURATE AT A MILE 6/9/1976
The Enfield rifle.
p Ray Sutcliffe, Paul Jordan;
intro Christopher Roads; *comm* Duncan Carse

H

**H.R.H. PRINCE PHILIP – INTERVIEW WITH
WALTER CRONKITE** (US 17/11/1971)

H.R.H. PRINCESS ELIZABETH
(BBC 1947)
Compilation film to mark Princess Elizabeth's
21st birthday on April 21st, 1947.

HADLEIGH (Yorkshire TV 1969–76)
Series featuring the owner of a stately home.
p Jacky Stoller
regulars Gerald Harper;
Ambrosine Phillpotts; Jenny Twigge
The STORY OF A PANIC 5/3/1976
d Derek Bennett; *sc* David Ambrose
lp Richard Vernon; Anthony Corlan;
Peter Dennis; Richard Easton
GOD SAVE US FROM MORALISTS 12/3/1976
d Derek Bennett; *sc* David Ambrose
lp Gerald James; Mark Dignam;
Richard Vernon; Anthony Corlan; Peter Dennis
BLOODLINE 19/3/1976
d Derek Bennett; *sc* Peter Whitbread
lp Gary Waldhorn; Eric Pohlmann;
Susanne Roquette
ECHOES 26/3/1976
d Jim Goddard; *sc* Raymond Bowers
lp Gerald James; Anthony Corlan;
Peter Dennis
DIVORCE 2/4/1976
d Christopher Hodson; *sc* Ian Curteis
lp Peter Dennis; Shane Rimmer;
Geoffrey Lumsden; Marc Zuber
The CHARM FACTOR 9/4/1976
d Tony Wharmby; *sc* Raymond Bowers
lp Anthony Corlan; Peter Dennis;
Myra Frances; Colin Farrell; Peter Sallis
FILM STORY 16/4/1976
d Tony Wharmby; *sc* Owen Holder
lp Michael Johnson; Stephanie Beacham
HONG KONG ROCK 23/4/1976
d Jim Goddard; *sc* David Ambrose
lp Nancy Kwan; David Waller;
Joop Doderer
A HOUSEHOLD OF GAMBLERS 30/4/1976
d Derek Bennett; *sc* Patsy Trench
lp Peter Dennis; Noel Johnson;
Lois Baxter
TIME OUT 7/5/1976
d Christopher Hodson; *sc* Ian Curteis
lp Gerald James; Joanna Dunham;
Patricia Haines; Geoffrey Chater;
Joan Haythorne
INCIDENT 14/5/1976
d David Reynolds; *sc* Tim Couper
lp Peter Dennis; Ann Penfold;
Ralph Michael; James Grout
FAVOURS 21/5/1976
d Tony Wharmby; *sc* David Ambrose
lp Peter Dennis; Myra Frances;
Michael Elphick; Gordon Jackson; David Ryall
BROKE 28/5/1976
d Brian Farnham; *sc* Ian Curteis
lp Peter Dennis; Myra Frances;
John Woodvine; Michael Aldridge

HALF HOUR STORY
(Rediffusion 1967–68; Thames 1971)
Anthology drama series. Series was re-presented
in early 1971, containing new material among
repeated episodes.
p Stella Richman
SHELTER 19/5/1967
d Alan Clarke; *sc* Alun Owen
lp Wendy Craig; Colin Blakely
MYSELF, I'VE GOT NOTHING AGAINST
SOUTH KEN 9/6/1967
d Nicholas Ferguson; *sc* Julian Bond
lp George Baker; Gwen Cherrell
HAWKS AND DOVES 19/7/1967
d Nicholas Ferguson; *sc* Philip Purser
lp Robert Flemyng; Petra Davies
The 45TH UNMARRIED MOTHER 9/8/1967
d Adrian Cooper; *sc* Fay Weldon
lp Jennie Linden; Maureen Pryor
FRIENDS 6/9/1967
d Michael Lindsay-Hogg; *sc* Cecil P. Taylor
lp George Cole; Bernard Lee
BUG 13/9/1967
d William G. Stewart; *sc* Peter Draper
lp Bob Monkhouse; Bill Owen
IN LOVING MEMORY OF... 2/1/1968
d Marc Miller; *sc* Ewart Alexander
lp Virginia McKenna; Margaret Rawlings
GOODNIGHT ALBERT 6/2/1968
d Alan Clarke; *sc* Roy Minton
lp Victor Henry; Gwen Nelson
VENUS RISING 13/2/1968
d Nicholas Ferguson; *sc* Fay Weldon
lp Avis Bunnage; Angela Douglas
The PUB FIGHTER 27/2/1968
d Marc Miller; *sc* Jim Allen
lp John Collin; Diana Coupland
NATURAL JUSTICE 13/3/1968
d Marc Miller; *sc* Robert Holler
lp Glynn Edwards; George Benson
STELLA 19/6/1968
d Alan Clarke; *sc* Alun Owen
lp Geraldine Moffat; Ray Smith
The FIFTY-SEVENTH SATURDAY 3/7/1968
d Alan Clarke; *sc* William Trevor
lp Ronald Fraser; Frances White
HAPPY ANNIVERSARY 10/7/1968
d Michael Lindsay-Hogg; *sc* Cecil P. Taylor
lp John Welsh; Sylvia Coleridge
GEORGE'S ROOM 5/2/1971
d Alan Clarke; *sc* Alun Owen
lp John Neville; Geraldine Moffat

HALF-TIME BRITAIN? (BBC 8/12/1964)
Industrial management and production in Britain
compared to the USA and Western European
countries.
p Glyn Jones; *comm* Derek Cooper

HALLMARK HALL OF FAME
(US NBC 1952–)
Drama showcase series.
KING RICHARD II 24/1/1954
d George Schaefer; *p* Albert McCleery;
sc Maurice Evans
lp Maurice Evans; Kent Smith;
Sarah Churchill; Frederic Worlock;
Bruce Gordon
MACBETH 28/11/1954
d/p George Schaefer; *adapt* Maurice Evans
lp Maurice Evans; Judith Anderson;
Staats Cotsworth; Richard Waring;
Peter Fernandez
The TAMING OF THE SHREW 18/3/1956
d George Schaefer; *p* Maurice Evans;
adapt Michael Hogan, William Nichols
lp Maurice Evans; Lilli Palmer;
Diane Cilento; Philip Bourneuf
The CRADLE SONG 6/5/1956
d George Schaefer; *p* Maurice Evans;
adapt James Costigan
lp Judith Anderson; Siobhan Mckenna;
Evelyn Varden; Barry Jones; Deirdre Owen;
Anthony Franciosa
MAN AND SUPERMAN 25/11/1956
d/p George Schaefer; *sc* Joseph Schrank;
auth George Bernard Shaw
lp Maurice Evans; Joan Greenwood;
Walter Greaza

HALLMARK HALL OF FAME cont.

TWELFTH NIGHT 15/12/1957
d David Greene; *p* Robert Hartung;
adapt William Nichols
lp Maurice Evans; Rosemary Harris;
Howard Morris; Max Adrian
HAMLET 17/11/1970
d Peter Wood; *p* George Lemaire;
adapt John Barton
lp Richard Chamberlain; Michael Redgrave;
Ciaran Madden; Margaret Leighton;
Richard Johnson; John Gielgud; Martin Shaw

HAMLET AT ELSINORE
(BBC-Danmarks Radio 19/4/1964)
Extracts from the outside broadcast production
of 'Hamlet', performed at Kronborg Castle,
Elsinore, Denmark.
d Philip Saville; *p* Peter Luke
lp Christopher Plummer; Robert Shaw;
Alec Clunes; June Tobin; Jo Maxwell Muller;
Michael Caine; Roy Kinnear;
Donald Sutherland; Steven Berkoff

HANCOCK (BBC 1961)
Comedy series. A continuation of HANCOCK'S
HALF HOUR (1956–60).
p Duncan Wood; *sc* Alan Simpson, Ray Galton
regular Tony Hancock
The LIFT 16/6/1961
lp Colin Gordon; Jack Watling;
John Le Mesurier; Hugh Lloyd;
Charles Lloyd Pack
The BLOOD DONOR 23/6/1961
lp Patrick Cargill; June Whitfield

HANCOCK'S HALF HOUR
(BBC 1956–60)
Comedy series.
p Duncan Wood; *sc* Alan Simpson, Ray Galton
regular Tony Hancock
The ALPINE HOLIDAY 1/4/1957
lp June Whitfield; Richard Wattis;
Kenneth Williams; John Vere
THERE'S AN AIRFIELD AT THE BOTTOM OF MY
GARDEN 16/12/1957
lp Sid James; Dick Emery; John Vere;
Cameron Hall
ERICKSON THE VIKING 26/12/1958
lp Sid James; Pat Coombs; John Vere;
Laurie Webb
The TRAIN JOURNEY 23/10/1959
lp Sid James; Raymond Huntley
SPANISH INTERLUDE 20/11/1959
lp Sid James; Roger Delgado;
Ronnie Brody; Annabelle Lee; Paddy Edwards;
Lynne Cole
FOOTBALL POOLS 27/11/1959
lp Sid James; Sidney Vivian;
Hugh Lloyd; Robert Dorning; Tom Clegg
The COLD 4/3/1960
lp Sid James; John Le Mesurier
Patricia Hayes
The MISSING PAGE 11/3/1960
lp Sid James; Hugh Lloyd;
George Couloris; Gordon Phillott;
Kenneth Kove; Totti Truman Taylor

HAND IN GLOVE (Rediffusion 26/9/1955)
Adventure story for children.
d Cliff Owen; *auth* Mary Cathcart Borer
lp Janet Harrison; Diana Beavers;
Fella Edmonds; Ross Goodall, Huw Evans;
Sylvia Marriott; Olga Dickie; Lloyd Pearson

HANDEL'S MESSIAH FROM YORK
MINSTER (Yorkshire TV 18/12/1977)
Part 1 of Handel's oratorio plus the Hallelujah
Chorus given in York Minster with the
Huddersfield Choral Society, the choristers of
York Minster and the Northern Sinfonia
Orchestra conducted by Owain Arwel Hughes.
d David Heather; *p* Peter Max-Wilson
with Stuart Burrows, Elizabeth Harwood,
Norma Procter, John Shirley-Quirk

HANDS ACROSS THE SKY
(BBC 7/2/1960)
A comic opera by Antony Hopkins with Eric
Shilling, Julia Shelley, James Maxwell and
Stephen Manton.
p Charles Lefeaux

HANG UP YOUR BRIGHTEST
COLOURS...THE LIFE AND DEATH OF
MICHAEL COLLINS (ATV 1973 *ntx*)
Documentary on the life of Michael Collins,
hero of the Irish struggle for independence
following the Easter Uprising of 1916.
pres Kenneth Griffiths

HAPPY DAYS (BBC 13/10/1979)
Production of Samuel Beckett's play first
performed at the Royal Court Theatre, London
in May 1979. Shown as part of the 'In
Performance' series.
d Samuel Beckett; *p* Tristram Powell
lp Billie Whitelaw; Leonard Fenton

HAPPY SOUNDS (Tyne Tees 27/12/1971)
Pantomime stars Ray Fell and Bryan Burdon
play host to some north east children and
introduce Julie Rogers. Music by The Ken
Maddison Trio.
d Tony Kysh; *p* Christopher Palmer

HARD TIMES (Granada 25/10–15/11/1977)
Four-part adaptation of Charles Dickens' novel
about life in Victorian industrial society.
EPISODE 1 25/10/1977
d John Irvin; *p* Peter Eckersley;
sc Arthur Hopcraft
lp Patrick Allen; Timothy West;
Alan Dobie; Barbara Ewing; Rosalie Crutchley

HARDCASE
(US Hanna-Barbera Productions 1/2/1972)
This Western drama was the first live-action film
from the animated-cartoon producers.
d John Llewellyn Moxey; *p* Matthew Rapf;
sc Harold Jack Bloom, Sam Rolfe
lp Clint Walker; Stefanie Powers;
Pedro Armendariz Jr; Alex Karras;
Luis Mirando

The HARDEST WAY UP
(Thames 16/3/1971)
The British expedition to climb the south face of
Annapurna led by Chris Bonington; expedition
members include Don Whillans, Dougal Haston,
Mick Burke and Ian Clough.
p/sc John Edwards

HAROLD WILSON PRIME MINISTERIAL
BROADCAST (14/10/1974)
A broadcast after Harold Wilson's re-election in
October 1974 in which he stresses the need for
national unity.

HAROLD WILSON – RIGHT OF REPLY –
COAL DISPUTE (28/2/1972)
Harold Wilson gives a ministerial broadcast in
reply to Prime Minister Edward Heath's
broadcast on the 1972 coal dispute.

HAROLD WILSON – RIGHT TO REPLY –
POWER CRISIS (14/12/1973)
Harold Wilson addresses the problem that
Britain faces and outlines some of the solutions
he would propose.

HARRIET (HTV 29/6–3/8/1976)
Regional series.
...AT WAR 3/8/1976
Programme for children in which Harriet
Crawler joins up with the Order of the Sealed
Knot as a cavalier and re-enacts the Royal Battle
for the City of Gloucester.
d Tony Palmer

HARRY BELAFONTE (BBC 17/8/1958)
Belafonte sings before a studio audience.
p Bryan Sears

HARRY'S OUT (Thames 13/6/1972)
Documentary about the way of life and ideas of
a petty criminal in London.
p/sc Ken Ashton

HAUNTED (Granada 1974)
Drama series with supernatural overtones.
The FERRYMAN 23/12/1974
d John Irvin; *p* David Granger;
sc Julian Bond; *auth* Kingsley Amis
lp Jeremy Brett; Natasha Parry;
Geoffrey Chater; Lesley Dunlop;
Andrew Bradford; Ray Mort

HAVE A HARRY BIRTHDAY
(Yorkshire TV 11/10/1978)
Comedy, song and dance on the theme of
birthdays.
d/p Vernon Lawrence;
sc Barry Cryer, Spike Mullins,
Peter Vincent, Peter Robinson
lp Harry Secombe; Pat Coombs;
Lorna Dallas; Robert Dorning; Fred Evans

HAVE GUN – WILL TRAVEL
(US CBS 1957–63)
Western series starring Richard Boone as a
sophisticated gunfighter-for-hire.
THREE BELLS TO PERDIDO 13/9/1957
d Sam Peckinpah; *p* Julian Claman;
sc Herb Meadow, Sam Rolfe
lp Janice Rule
SOMETHING TO LIVE FOR 20/12/1958
d Andrew V. McLaglen;
sc John Tucker Battle, Don Ingalls
lp Rayford Barnes; Nancy Hadley;
Malcolm Atterbury; Tom Brown;
John Anderson

HAZELL (Thames 1978–79)
Investigations of an ex-policeman turned private
eye.
regular Nicholas Ball
HAZELL AND THE WALKING BLUR 30/1/1978
d Brian Farnham; *p* June Roberts;
sc Richard Harris
lp Barbara Young; Bill Henderson;
Diana Rowan; James Faulkner; Fiona Mollison
HAZELL MEETS THE FIRST ELEVEN 13/2/1978
d Moira Armstrong; *p* June Roberts;
sc Tony Hoare, Gordon Williams
lp James Faulkner; Fiona Mollison;
Bryan Coleman; David Robb; Fiesta Mei Ling
HAZELL AND THE BAKER STREET SLEUTH
19/4/1979
d Brian Farnham;
sc Gordon Williams, Terry Venables
HAZELL AND THE GREASY GUNNERS 28/6/1979
d Gerry Mill; *p* Tim Aspinall;
sc Brian Glover
lp Paul Satvender; Alex Scott;
Derek Ware; Cyd Hayman; Riba Akabusi

HEAD ON (Granada 1961)
Series in which celebrities are confronted with
filmed assessments of themselves made by
friends and rivals.
RANDOLPH CHURCHILL 9/8/1961
d Norman Dunkles; *p* Milton Shulman;
intro Henry Fairlie

HEALTHY EATING (Tyne Tees 1977)
Regional series on food.
d/p Lisle Willis;
pres Alec Taylor, Diana MacAdie
HEALTHY EATING 3/7/1977
HEALTHY EATING 17/7/1977
HEALTHY EATING 24/7/1977

HEART OF THE CITY (Tyne Tees 22/4/1979)

HEART TO HEART (Yorkshire TV 1976–79)
Discussion/interview series.
JANE BOARDMAN 26/10/1977
Jane Boardman, a 19-year-old with a history of
aggression, talks to Colin Morris about her
worries.
d Lesley Smith; *exec.p* John Fairley

The HEARTBEAT OF FRANCE
(Rediffusion 14/6/1961)
France and the French people.
d Peter Morley; *sc* Cyril Bennett;
nar Peter Finch

HEARTLAND (ATV 1979–80)
Series of plays on the theme of love.
ALICE TRYING 10/8/1979
d Don Leaver; *p* Nicholas Palmer;
sc Donald Churchill;
lp Judy Parfitt; Donald Churchill;
Edward Judd; Lynda Baron; Richard Hope

The HECKLERS (BBC 30/3/1967)
An American view of a British general election.
d Joseph Strick

HEDDA GABLER
(US Talent Associates 28/12/1962)
d Alex Segal;
p David Susskind, Lars Schmidt,
Norman Rutherford; *sc* Phil Reisman;
auth Henrik Ibsen
lp Ingrid Bergman; Michael Redgrave;
Ralph Richardson; Trevor Howard;
Dilys Hamlett

HEIL CAESAR (BBC 12–26/11/1973)
Adaptation of Shakespeare's 'Julius Caesar'
transposed to a modern day setting. Shown in
three programmes as a part of the day-time
transmission for schools.
p Ronald Smedley; *sc* John Bowen
lp Anthony Bate; John Stride; Peter Howell;
David Allister; Frank Middlemass;
Angela Thorne
PART 2: MURDER OF A PRESIDENT 19/11/1973
PART 3: DEFEAT 26/11/1973

HELEN – A WOMAN OF TODAY
(LWT 21/9–14/12/1973)
Thirteen-part drama series about the breakdown
of a marriage.
FRANK 21/9/1973
d Jim Goddard; *p* Richard Bates;
sc David Butler
lp Alison Fiske; Martin Shaw;
Christopher Ballantyne; Diana Hutchinson
HELEN 14/12/1973
d Tony Wharmby; *p* Richard Bates;
sc David Butler
lp Alison Fiske; Martin Shaw;
Diana Hutchinson; Christopher Ballantyne;
Margery Withers

HELPING HAND (Tyne Tees 1979)
Series which looks at the problems facing
disabled people in Britain, and how their lives
may be made easier.
d Tony Bulley; *p* Audrey Holmes;
intro Joe Hennessy, Pattie Coldwell
FOUR MILLION PEOPLE 25/11/1979
Shows some severely handicapped people who
have succeeded in overcoming their handicaps.
Explains how to guide blind people, and the
teaching of the newly blind on the use of the
long cane.
OUT AND ABOUT 2/12/1979
The difficulties of access to buildings for people
in wheelchairs.
HIDDEN DISABILITIES 23/12/1979
Deals with a number of disabilities, including
epilepsy, angina, and diabetes. Shows the work
of volunteers in speech therapy clubs.
INDEPENDENCE 30/12/1979
Young disabled children in play activities which
force them to exert themselves and which have
the effect of strengthening limbs and increasing
mobility.

HENRY MOORE (BBC 30/4/1951)
A survey of sculptor Henry Moore. Moore is
shown at work on his bronze 'Reclining Figure'
commissioned by the Arts Council of Great
Britain.
p John Read; *comm* Bernard Miles

HERE AND NOW
(Rediffusion 1961–1963)
Topical magazine programme.
BILLY WALKER 23/3/1962
Billy Walker's career prior to his first
professional fight.
d Geoffrey Hughes; *p* Ray Dicks;
intro Huw Thomas

CHILDREN'S ART 18/4/1962
Michael Ingrams introduces children's art.
d Mark Lawton; *p* Michael Ingrams
LONDON UNIVERSITY 20/6/1962
Huw Thomas and Michael Ingrams investigate
life and work at the University of London.
d Don Gale; *p* Michael Ingrams
TEA TASTERS 28/6/1962
Michael Ingrams looks at the work of tea tasters.
d Don Gale; *p* Michael Ingrams;
intro Huw Thomas
LADY MAYORESS 5/7/1962
Michael Ingrams looks at the life of a lady
mayoress.
d Bill Hitchcock; *p* Michael Ingrams;
intro Huw Thomas
SANDHURST 8/8/1962
Life at the Royal Military College, Sandhurst.
d Robert Fleming; *p* Michael Ingrams;
intro Huw Thomas
NATIONAL FILM ARCHIVE 2/1/1963
Huw Thomas interviews Ernest Lindgren,
curator of the National Film Archive.
d Jim Pope; *p* Michael Ingrams;
intro Huw Thomas

Las HERMANAS (BBC 21/2/1965)
Dance film. Five sisters, still subject to their
mother's authority, restlessly await the arrival of
the local gigolo as a suitor for the eldest.
Choreographed by Kenneth MacMillan
p Peter Wright; *auth* Federico Garcia Lorca;
with Marcia Haydee, Ray Barra,
Ruth Papendick, Georgina Parkinson,
Monica Mason, Sheila Humphreys,
Jennifer Layland

The HERO OF MY LIFE
(Thames 9/6/1970)
Film about the life of Charles Dickens, to mark
the centenary of his death.
d Michael Darlow;
p Michael Darlow, Bruce Norman;
sc Bruce Norman; *comm* David March
lp Michael Jayston; Amanda Reiss;
Isla Blair; Jo Rowbottom; Sheila Grant;
Ciaran Madden

A HERO'S RETURN (BBC 7/7/1967)
The knighting of Sir Francis Chichester by
Queen Elizabeth II following his return from a
solo round-the-world yacht voyage.
p Paul Bonner; *comm* Richard Baker

HESS (Scottish TV 30/9/1978)
Reconstruction of the ill-fated flight of Rudolf
Hess to Scotland at the beginning of the war in a
vain attempt to make a peace settlement.
d Tina Wakerell; *p* Rex Firkin;
sc Ian Curteis
lp Wolf Kahler; John Stride; David Robb;
Geoffrey Chater; Mark Dignam;
Shaughan Seymour; Kevin Brennan;
Paul Darrow; Leonard Maguire

HEUTE DIREKT (BBC 1979–81)
German language teaching series.
HEUTE DIREKT 4/6/1979
d Patrick Harpur; *p* Barbara Derkow;
pres Corinna Schnabel

The HILL OF THE RED FOX (BBC 1975)
Adventure serial for children in six parts; based
on the novel by Allan Campbell McLean.
d Bob McIntosh; *p* Pharic MacLaren;
sc Scot Finch
regulars Mark Rogers; Donald Douglas
PART 1 24/9/1975
lp Ellen McIntosh; Iris Russell;
John Shedden
PART 2 1/10/1975
lp Bernard Horsfall; Gillian Barclay;
Marjorie Thomson
PART 3 8/10/1975
lp Bernard Horsfall; Peter Copley;
Gillian Barclay
PART 4 15/10/1975
lp Bernard Horsfall; Gillian Barclay;
Marjorie Thomson
PART 5 22/10/1975
lp Bernard Horsfall; Peter Copley;
Paul Young

PART 6 29/10/1975
lp Ellen McIntosh; Bernard Horsfall;
Peter Copley

HINE (ATV 7/4–30/6/1971)
Thirteen-part drama series about an arms dealer.
SURVIVAL OF THE CREEPS 16/6/1971
d Robert Tronson; *p* Wilfred Greatorex;
sc Arden Winch
lp Barrie Ingham; Paul Eddington;
John Steiner; Sarah Craze; Morris Perry;
Timothy West

**The HIPPODROME CIRCUS – GREAT
YARMOUTH** (BBC 9/8/1968)
Excerpts from the 1968 Chipperfield Circus, with
The Trio Lorch, Mario and Partner, Noe Noe
and Company, Bob Bramson, The Tisza Troupe
and The Digger Pugh Girls.

HITCHCOCK ON GRIERSON
(Scottish TV 1970)

HOLLYWOOD: THE DREAM FACTORY
(US MGM 21/6/1972)
A history of MGM film studios. Shown as an
'ABC Monday Night Special'.
p Nicholas Noxton, Irwin Rosten,
Bud Friedgen; *sc* Irwin Rosten
nar Dick Cavett

HOLLYWOOD – THE FABULOUS ERA
(US David L. Wolper Productions 26/9/1963)
Hollywood from the beginning of sound to the
present day.
d David L. Wolper

HOME AND AWAY (Granada 14/2–27/3/1972)
Seven-part drama series.
The COLD WIND DOTH BLOW 14/2/1972
d Donald McWhinnie; *p* Kenith Trodd;
sc Julia Jones
lp Gillian Raine; Tony Melody;
Rosalind Ayres; Stephen Temperley; Peter Firth

HOME AT THE HIRSEL
(Tyne Tees 22/10/1974)
Robert Kee interviews Sir Alec Douglas-Home.
d Jeremy Lack; *p* Frank Entwisle

HOME COOKING (BBC 25/4–27/6/1965)
Ten-part cookery series.
CASSEROLES AND ROASTS 16/5/1965
d Margaret McCall; *p* Beryl Radley;
pres Fanny Craddock

A HOME FOR THE ORCHESTRA
(Southern TV 5/10/1978)

HOME-MADE FOR THE HOME
(Tyne Tees 1978)
How to make items for the home.
d/p Lisle Willis; *pres* Alison Brierly
HOME-MADE FOR THE HOME 18/7/1978
Patchwork by both hand and machine with
Mary Bromly.
HOME-MADE FOR THE HOME 25/7/1978
Crochet for making cushions and clothes, and
the basic knots of macramé for making things
with string.
HOME-MADE FOR THE HOME 8/8/1978
Nellie Renton demonstrates cane handicrafts.
How to make a handbag from canvas, corduroy
or leather with Malcolm Parsons.
HOME-MADE FOR THE HOME 22/8/1978
Making toys with Barbara Rowe and Colin Sims.
HOME-MADE FOR THE HOME 5/9/1978
Home-made jewellery with Ann E. Gill and
Connie Dodds.
HOME-MADE FOR THE HOME 19/9/1978
Renovating old furniture with Eileen Elliott and
Heulwen Fellows.
HOME-MADE FOR THE HOME 3/10/1978
Spinning, weaving and dyeing.

HOME NURSING (Tyne Tees 1976)
Advice on how to look after a sick, convalescing
or disabled person at home. Based on the British
Red Cross Society's demonstration-cards
'Nursing for the Family'.

HOW'S YOUR FATHER? *cont.*

WEDDING BELLS 3/4/1979
lp Giles Watling; Debby Cumming;
Fanny Carby; Sonia Graham; Keith Jayne

HUGGY BEAR (Yorkshire TV 11/4/1976)
A dentist is torn between the affections of two
women – his fiancée and his nurse.
d David Cunliffe; *exec.p* Peter Willes;
sc David Mercer
lp Bill Wallis; Maurice Denham;
Joyce Heron; Paddy Joyce; Aimée Delamain;
Sharon Mughan; Molly Weir

The HUMAN JUNGLE
(Independent Artists Production-ABC 1963–65)
Drama series featuring the cases of a London
psychiatrist.
p Julian Wintle, Leslie Parkyn
regulars Herbert Lom; Sally Smith;
Mary Yeomans; Michael Johnson; Mary Steele
THIN ICE 20/4/1963
d John Ainsworth; *sc* Robert Stewart
lp Jacqueline Lacey; George A. Cooper;
John McLaren
The LOST HOURS 27/4/1963
d Sidney Hayers; *sc* John Kruse
lp Leonard Sachs; Ursula Howells;
Patrick Whyte; Joyce Heron; Coral Morphew
TIME CHECK 8/6/1963
d Alan Cooke; *sc* Lewis Davidson
lp Melvyn Hayes; Gerald James;
Fabia Drake; Mitzi Rogers; Warren Mitchell
STRUGGLE FOR A MIND 18/2/1965
d Sidney Hayers; *sc/auth* John Kruse
lp Joan Collins; Clifford Evans;
Derek Godfrey; Kay Walsh; Margaret Whiting
The TWENTY-FOUR HOUR MAN 4/3/1965
d Robert Day; *sc* Robert Banks Stewart
lp Johnny Sekka; Dolores Mantez;
Inigo Jackson; Patrick McAlinney;
Donald Morley
SOLO PERFORMANCE 11/3/1965
d Roy Ward Baker; *sc* Bill MacIlwraith
lp Margaret Lockwood; James Villiers;
Rona Anderson; Basil Hoskins; Doreen Dawn
The MAN WHO FELL APART 8/4/1965
d Roy Ward Baker; *sc* Jon Rollason
lp Rita Tushingham; Barbara Shelley;
Alan Dobie; Janet Kelly; Patrick O'Connell;
John Rae
DUAL CONTROL 15/4/1965
d Roy Ward Baker; *sc* Anne Francis
lp Peggy Cummins; Dennis Price;
Lyndon Brook; Annette Andre; Rona Anderson
SKELETON IN THE CUPBOARD 22/4/1965
d Roy Ward Baker; *sc* Bill MacIlwraith
lp Roger Livesey; Sonia Dresdel;
Nora Nicholson; Ann Firbank;
Allan Cuthbertson
ENEMY OUTSIDE 6/5/1965
d Roy Ward Baker; *sc* Bill MacIlwraith
lp Tony Tanner; Lloyd Reckord;
Barbara Ferris; Avis Bunnage; Rona Anderson

HUNT v. LAUDA (LWT 24/10/1976)
The Japanese Grand Prix in which James Hunt
won the World Drivers' Championship.

HUNTER'S WALK (ATV 1973–76)
Police drama series set in Northamptonshire.
REASONABLE SUSPICION 9/7/1973
d Robert Tronson; *p* John Cooper;
sc Richard Harris
lp Ewan Hooper; Davyd Harries;
Brendan Price; Duncan Preston; Charles Rea;
Mary Tamm

The HUNTING OF THE SNARK
(Rediffusion 26/12/1967)
Animated version of the poem by Lewis Carroll.
d Diana Potter; *nar* Michael Hordern

HURRICANE HIGGINS (Thames 4/9/1972)
John Morgan presents a profile of snooker player
Alex Higgins.
d Chris Goddard; *p* Ian Martin

The HURT MIND (BBC 1–29/1/1957)
Five-part documentary series on mental health.
p Andrew Miller-Jones

PUT AWAY 1/1/1957
An account of a brief stay in a mental hospital,
showing facilities available for the treatment of
the mentally ill.
BREAKDOWN 8/1/1957
Some of the causes of mental breakdown and
disturbance.
PSYCHOLOGICAL TREATMENT 15/1/1957
Some of the non-physical methods of treatment
by which people are helped to overcome their
mental disabilites.
PHYSICAL TREATMENT 22/1/1957
Leading psychiatrists and research workers
describe the more recent physical treatments for
mental illness.

A HYMN FOR TODAY
(Southern TV 2/4/1972)
The final of a competition to find new hymns.
The entries are sung by The Nigel Brooke
Singers.
p Bob Leng; *pres* Fred Dineage;
with Berkeley Smith

I

I AM AN ENGINEER
(Yorkshire TV 1968–69)
Series on engineering and its importance in
society.
JOHN BRITTEN – AERONAUTICAL ENGINEER
20/5/1969
An account of John Britten's aircraft company,
now in liquidation. Shows the construction of the
Britten Norman Islander, a highly successful,
unique and inexpensive aeroplane.
d Graham Watts

I BELIEVE... (Granada 12/11–17/12/1962)
Series in which leading exponents of religious
and philosophical beliefs express their views.
A HUMANIST – PROFESSOR A.J. AYER
26/11/1962
Malcolm Muggeridge interviews Professor
Alfred J. Ayer about his beliefs.
d Max Morgan-Witts; *p* Patricia Lagone

I, CLAUDIUS (BBC 1976)
Twelve-part serial adapted from Robert Graves'
Roman history about the family of Emperor
Augustus.
d Herbert Wise; *p* Martin Lisemore;
sc Jack Pulman
regular Derek Jacobi
EPISODE 1: A TOUCH OF MURDER 20/9/1976
lp Siân Phillips; Brian Blessed;
Christopher Guard; John Paul; Frances White;
George Baker; Angela Morant; Sheila Ruskin;
Ian Ogilvy; Margaret Tyzack
EPISODE 2: WAITING IN THE WINGS 27/9/1976
lp George Baker; Kevin Stoney;
Frances White; Margaret Tyzack;
Simon MacCorkindale; Esmond Knight;
Siân Phillips; Brian Blessed
EPISODE 3: WHAT SHALL WE DO ABOUT
CLAUDIUS? 4/10/1976
lp Brian Blessed; Siân Phillips;
George Baker; Fiona Walker; Margaret Tyzack;
Patricia Quinn
EPISODE 4: POISON IS QUEEN 11/10/1976
lp John Evitts; David Robb;
Brian Blessed; George Baker; Siân Phillips;
Patricia Quinn; Patrick Stewart
EPISODE 5: SOME JUSTICE 18/10/1976
lp Siân Phillips; David Robb;
Roy Purcell; Fiona Walker; Robert Morgan;
George Baker; Patrick Stewart; Siân Phillips;
Margaret Tyzack; Stratford Johns
EPISODE 6: QUEEN OF HEAVEN 25/10/1976
lp Fiona Walker; Edward Jewesbury;
Isabel Dean; Peter Williams; Siân Phillips;
George Baker; Patrick Stewart; John Hurt;
Patricia Quinn; James Faulkner;
Margaret Tyzack
EPISODE 7: REIGN OF TERROR 1/11/1976
lp Margaret Tyzack; Kate Lansbury;
Karin Foley; Patricia Quinn; George Baker;
Charles Kay; John Rhys-Davies; John Hurt
EPISODE 8: ZEUS, BY JOVE! 8/11/1976
lp George Baker; John Rhys-Davies;
John Hurt; Lockwood West; James Faulkner;
Margaret Tyzack

EPISODE 9: HAIL WHO? 15/11/1976
lp John Hurt; Jo Rowbottom; Anne Dyson;
Bruce Purchase; Jan Carey; Sally Bazely;
Norman Eshley; Freda Dowie; Sheila White;
Norman Rossington; Bernard Hill
EPISODE 10: FOOL'S LUCK 22/11/1976
lp Neal Arden; Lyndon Brook;
Bernard Hill; Geoffrey Hinsliff; James Faulkner;
Sheila White; Bernard Hepton; Moira Redmond
EPISODE 11: A GOD IN COLCHESTER
29/11/1976
lp Sheila White; Bernard Hepton;
John Cater; Charlotte Howard; George Innes;
Moira Redmond; James Faulkner;
Jo Rowbottom
EPISODE 12: OLD KING LOG 6/12/1976
lp Christopher Biggins; Barbara Young;
Bernard Hepton; John Cater; Roger Bizley;
Peter Bowles; Brian Blessed; Siân Phillips;
Margaret Tyzack; George Baker; John Hurt

I DIDN'T KNOW YOU CARED
(BBC 1975–79)
Comedy series adapted by Peter Tinniswood
from his own novels, 'A Touch of Daniel', 'I
Didn't Know You Cared' and ''Cept You're a
Bird'.
AFTER THE BALL WAS OVER 17/9/1975
p Bernard Thompson; *sc* Peter Tinniswood
lp Robin Bailey; John Comer; Liz Smith;
Stephen Rea; Anita Carey; Gretchen Franklin

IF THERE WEREN'T ANY BLACKS YOU'D
HAVE TO INVENT THEM (LWT 4/8/1968)
Sardonic comedy set in a cemetery where a
young man is accused by a blind man of being
black. [Script originally commissioned by the
BBC but later acquired by ITV.]
d Charles Jarrott; *sc* Johnny Speight
lp Frank Thornton; Ronald Radd;
Moray Watson; Leslie Sands; Jimmy Hanley;
Nerys Hughes

IF THERE WEREN'T ANY BLACKS YOU'D
HAVE TO INVENT THEM (LWT 3/3/1974)
[This version originally scheduled for *tx* 3/2/1974]
d Bill Hays; *p* Rex Firkin;
sc Johnny Speight
lp Leonard Rossiter; Michael Bryant;
Richard Beckinsale; Bob Hoskins; Ken Wynne;
Geoffrey Bayldon; John Nightingale;
Vicki Michelle

I'M GOING TO ASK YOU TO GET UP OUT
OF YOUR SEAT (BBC 24/11/1966)
Evangelist Billy Graham and his Greater
London Crusade, held at Earls Court in June
1966.
d Richard Cawston

I'M JUST A SIMPLE MAN
(BBC 12/6/1977)
John Read re-assesses L.S. Lowry's paintings
and drawings.
p/sc John Read

I'M THE WORLD'S BEST WRITER –
THERE'S NOTHING MORE TO SAY
(Yorkshire TV 13/12/1971)
Alan Whicker interviews Harold Robbins and
looks at his life in New York and the south of
France.
d Peter Robinson; *exec.p* Tony Essex

IMAGES (Thames 3/8/1972)
Examines the stereotypes projected by the
media, with Imogen Hassall and Matthew
Scurfield.
d Francis Fuchs; *p* Ian Martin

IMPACT (Tyne Tees 1979)
Regional current affairs programme.
PUBLIC SPENDING CUTS 20/5/1979
IMPACT 27/5/1979

The IMPORTANT THING IS LOVE
(ATV 9/2/1970)
A documentary about lesbians.
p Brigid Seagrave

IN LOVING MEMORY
(Yorkshire TV 1979–86)
Sitcom about an undertaking business in the
northern town of Oldshaw during the late 1920s.
d/p Ronnie Baxter; *sc* Dick Sharples
regulars Thora Hird; Christopher Beeny
IN LOVING MEMORY 21/5/1979
lp Freddie Jones; Avis Bunnage
GONE DANCING 4/6/1979
lp Colin Farrell; Lori Wells;
Sherrie Hewson
The RIVALS 11/6/1979
lp Avis Bunnage; Sheila Steafel;
Rose Power; Richard Wilson; Paul Luty;
Mary Larkin
PORK 18/6/1979
lp Colin Farrell; Avis Bunnage;
Joan Sims; Rose Power; Paul Luty;
Johnny Allan
COME BACK LITTLE MALCOLM 25/6/1979
lp Avis Bunnage; Peter Hill;
Christine Hargreaves; Christian Rodska
ONIONS 2/7/1979
lp Colin Farrell; Rose Power

IN PRAISE OF LOVE
(Anglia 14/3/1976)
Television production of the play by Terence
Rattigan.
d Alvin Rakoff; *p* John Jacobs
lp Kenneth More; Claire Bloom;
Paul Maxwell; Joseph Blatchley

IN PRISON (BBC 19/4/1957)
The daily lives of the male and female inmates of
Strangeways prison, Manchester. The governor,
Gilbert Hair, talks about the prisoners'
problems.
d Roy Harris

IN THE NAME OF FRANCE
(BBC 19/8/1969)
The story of the German occupation of France
and of the French resistance movement. Includes
interviews with Xavier Vallat and Georges
Bidault.
p Julien Jacottet; *comm* James Cameron

The INCREDIBLE ROBERT BALDICK
(BBC 2/10/1972)
Drama about a Victorian ghost hunter
[Pilot for an unrealised series; postponed from
tx 6/9/1972].
d Cyril Coke; *p* Anthony Coburn;
sc Terry Nation
lp Robert Hardy; Reginald Marsh;
James Cossins; Ron Welling; Julian Holloway;
John Rhys-Davies; David Mobley

The INDOOR LEAGUE
(Yorkshire TV 31/1/1974)
Fred Trueman introduces a number of indoor
games contests including table football, darts and
skittles.
d Peter Jones; *p* Sid Waddell;
comm Dave Lanning, Keith Macklin

INDUSTRIAL GRAND TOUR
(BBC 27/7–28/9/1972; 15/7–19/8/1974)
Series looking at Britain's industrial heritage.
p Ray Sutcliffe; *nar* Kenneth Hudson
DINORWIC SLATE QUARRY 10/8/1972
The slate quarry at Dinorwic in Wales.
HIGHER MILL 17/8/1972
A textile mill in Helmshore, Lancashire,
powered by water.
d/p David Collison; *nar* Neil Cossons
SHEFFIELD 7/9/1972
The industrial history of Sheffield, includes
surviving original forges in operation.
nar Kenneth Hawley
TOLGUS TIN 21/9/1972
Traditional methods of tin production at the
Tolgus Tin Works in Cornwall.
The TOOLMAKER 15/7/1974
The central London forge of Harold Pound, an
edge toolmaker.
The PAPER MAKERS 22/7/1974
Paper making by hand in Somerset.

The CAMERA MAKER 29/7/1974
The London workshop of Arthur and Frederick
Gandolfi, makers of plate cameras.
p Ann Turner; *nar* Kenneth Hudson
The TANNERS 5/8/1974
The tradition of oak-bark leather tanning
maintained by the Croggan brothers in Cornwall.
The IRON MAKERS 12/8/1974
The making of wrought-iron at the Atlas forge,
Bolton.
The BREWERS 19/8/1974
The work of a traditional English brewery at
Hook Norton, Oxfordshire.

The INFORMER
(Rediffusion 1966–67)
Crime series about a debarred barrister who tries
to repair his career and marriage.
GET OFF MY BACK 1/8/1966
d Peter Collinson;
p Stella Richman, Peter Collinson;
sc Geoffrey Bellman, John Whitney
lp Ian Hendry; Jean Marsh; Heather Sears;
Eric Pohlmann; Neil Hallett; John Allison
YOUR MONEY OR YOUR LIFE 13/12/1967
d Christopher Hodson; *p* John Whitney;
sc Jeremy Paul
lp Ian Hendry; Jean Marsh; Neil Hallett;
Tony Selby; Patrick McAlinney; Annette Carell

INSIDE (Granada 5/1–2/2/1965)
Five-part documentary series examining aspects
of the British penal system.
d Michael Grigsby;
p Elaine Grand, Michael Grigsby;
nar Reginald Marsh
YOUNG OFFENDERS 12/1/1965
Detention centres and borstals, and the attitudes
of some of the inmates.
WOMEN IN PRISON 19/1/1965
Present day conditions in women's prisons and
the problems that women prisoners have to cope
with during and after imprisonment.

INSIDE EUROPE (Granada 1978–79)
Current affairs series which considers the major
topics affecting Europe.
BIG DEAL: THE SALE OF THE CENTURY
20/3/1979
The process by which Norway, Belgium, Holland
and Denmark came to choose the F16 as a new
NATO aircraft.
d John Sheppard; *sc* David Boulton;
rep Andrew Cockburn

INSIDE STORY (BBC 1974–80)
Documentary series.
MAREK 14/5/1975
An unsuccessful heart operation.
d Mark Anderson; *p* Roger Mills
LIZ THOMAS 28/5/1975
The work of an English nurse in Saigon.
p Anthony De Lotbinière
MINI 11/6/1975
Methods used by the Social Services in dealing
with problem children and their families.
d Franc Roddam; *p* Roger Mills
The SENTENCE 5/8/1976
Re-enactment of the trial of a man accused of
petty theft; an account of contemporary attitudes
and procedures in the British judicial system.
d Rex Bloomstein; *p* Roger Mills
The APPEAL 19/8/1976
A tribunal hearing in which a Pakistani man's
right to keep his wife and child in Britain is
decided.
d Rex Bloomstein; *p* Roger Mills
BEHIND THE FRONT 15/2/1978
The National Front movement in Britain.
d Mark Anderson; *p* Roger Mills
The END OF THE LINE 19/5/1978
The training given to volunteers who wish to
become Samaritans.
d Richard Benton; *p* Roger Mills

INSIDE THE FOREIGN OFFICE
(Rediffusion 31/10/1967)
An investigation into the workings of the
Foreign Office.
d James Butler; *p/sc* Clive Irving;
nar John Cleese

INTERNATIONAL DETECTIVE
(Delfry Production 1959–61)
Crime drama series following the investigations
of Ken Franklin, a detective working for an
international detective agency.
regular Arthur Fleming
The PRESCOTT CASE 9/4/1960
d Jeremy Summers; *p* Gordon L.T. Scott;
sc Gordon Wellesley
lp Lisa Gastoni; Neil McCallum;
Adam Kean; Tommy Duggan; Louise Collins
The BARNABY CASE 21/5/1960
d A. Edward Sutherland; *p* Gordon L.T. Scott
lp Ronan O'Casey
The SANTENO CASE 31/7/1960
d Jeremy Summers; *p* Gordon L.T. Scott
lp Betta St. John; Francis De Wolff;
Harold Lang; Bernard Cribbins; Derek Sydney
The BISMARK CASE 14/8/1960
d A. Edward Sutherland; *p* Gordon L.T. Scott;
sc A.R. Rawlings
lp William Franklyn; Lisa Daniely;
Edwin Richfield; Willoughby Goddard;
John Abineri
The ROSARIO CASE 23/10/1960
d Jeremy Summers; *p* Gordon L.T. Scott;
sc Lester Fuller
lp Virgilio Texera; Vera Fusek;
Elizabeth Wallace; Hannah Maria Miller
The WASHINGTON CASE 30/10/1960
d A. Edward Sutherland; *p* Gordon L.T. Scott;
sc Guy Morgan
lp William Franklyn; Lisa Gastoni;
Charles Richardson; Jean Serrett; Magda Miller

**INTERNATIONAL FOOTBALL: ENGLAND
v. RUMANIA** (BBC 15/1/1969)
Highlights of the match from Wembley Stadium.
comm Kenneth Wolstenholme

**INTERNATIONAL FOOTBALL: ENGLISH
LEAGUE v. SCOTTISH LEAGUE**
(Tyne Tees 16/3/1966)
Edited recording of the match between the
English and Scottish leagues, at St. James' Park,
Newcastle.
d Christopher Palmer; *comm* John Camkin

**INTERNATIONAL FOOTBALL: HOLLAND
vs. ENGLAND** (BBC 5/11/1969)
Recorded highlights of the match.

The INTERNATIONAL POP PROMS
(Granada 1976–77)
Originally a ten-part series of concerts, with later
'specials'.
p John Hamp; *d* Nicholas Ferguson
The INTERNATIONAL POP PROMS 13/3/1976
The INTERNATIONAL POP PROMS 20/3/1976
The INTERNATIONAL POP PROMS 3/4/1976
The INTERNATIONAL POP PROMS 17/4/1976
The INTERNATIONAL POP PROMS 24/4/1976
The INTERNATIONAL POP PROMS 28/12/1976
The INTERNATIONAL POP PROMS 13/7/1977

INTERPOL CALLING
(Rank-Wrather 1959–60)
Crime detective series featuring the cases of the
Paris-based International Police organisation.
p Anthony Perry, Connery Chapel
regulars Charles Korvin; Edwin Richfield
The THIRTEEN INNOCENTS 13/9/1959
d C.M. Pennington-Richards; *sc* David Chantler
lp Peter Illing; Patrick Troughton;
Guy Deghy; Larry Burns
MONEY GAME 20/9/1959
d C.M. Pennington-Richards; *sc* Lewis Davidson
lp Walter Rilla; Ferdy Mayne;
Delphi Lawrence; Phil Brown; Walter Gotell
The SLEEPING GIANT 27/9/1959
d C.M. Pennington-Richards; *sc* Larry Forrester
lp John Crawford; David Cameron;
Esmond Knight; Oliver Burt; Jack Stewart;
Rufus Cruickshank
The TWO-HEADED MONSTER 4/10/1959
d C.M. Pennington-Richards; *sc* David Chantler
lp Marla Landi; Alan Tilvern;
George Pastell; Robert Cawdron
The LONG WEEKEND 11/10/1959
d Charles Frend; *sc* David Chantler
lp David Kossoff; John Le Mesurier;
Balbina; André Maranne

INTERPOL CALLING cont.

YOU CAN'T DIE TWICE 18/10/1959
d C.M. Pennington-Richards;
sc Barbara Hammer, Leonard Fincham
lp Cec Linder; Gerard Heinz;
Arnold Diamond; Colette Wilde; Leonard Sachs
PRIVATE VIEW 1/11/1959
d C.M. Pennington-Richards; sc Robert Stewart
lp Michael Goodliffe; Moira Redmond;
Ernest Clark; Leslie French
AIR SWITCH 15/11/1959
d C.M. Pennington-Richards;
sc Gilbert Winfield, Leonard Fincham
lp Colin Croft; John Van Eyssen;
Trevor Reid; Lloyd Lamble; Dorinda Stevens
ANGOLA BRIGHTS 22/11/1959
d C.M. Pennington-Richards; sc Larry Forrester
lp Rupert Davies; Alfred Burke;
Philip Ray; Arthur Gomez; Julian Sherrier
CHINESE MASK 29/11/1959
d C.M. Pennington-Richards; sc Lewis Davidson
lp Bill Nagy; Jan Holden;
Howard Marion-Crawford; Brown Derby;
Zed Zakari
SLAVE SHIP 6/12/1959
d C.M. Pennington-Richards;
sc Geoffrey Orme, Edwin Richfield,
Gilbert Winfield
lp David Davies; Meredith Edwards;
Harold Kasket; Cyril Shaps; Oscar Quitak;
Errol John
LAST MAN LUCKY 20/12/1959
d C.M. Pennington-Richards; sc Neville Dasey
lp Annabel Maule; Sandra Dorne;
Michael Brennan; Ewan MacDuff;
Donald Stewart
NO FLOWERS FOR ONO 27/12/1959
d C.M. Pennington-Richards; sc Robert Stewart
lp Victor Beaumont; Kevin Stoney;
Leigh Madison; Bruno Barnabe;
Edward Jewesbury
The THOUSAND MILE ALIBI 10/1/1960
d George Pollock;
sc John Kruse, Leonard Fincham
lp Paul Eddington; George Pastell;
Rowland Bartrop; Margaret Diamond;
Brian Worth
ACT OF PIRACY 17/1/1960
d C.M. Pennington-Richards;
sc Edwin Richfield, John Kruse
lp Richard Gale; Reed De Rouen;
Steve Plytas; Alec Mango
GAME FOR THREE HANDS 24/1/1960
d C.M. Pennington-Richards; sc Robert Stewart
lp Peter Dyneley; Alan Gifford;
Paula Byrne; Russell Waters;
Charles Richardson
The COLLECTOR 31/1/1960
d C.M. Pennington-Richards;
sc Wilton Schiller, David Chantler
lp Leonard Sachs; Paul Stassino;
Christina Gregg; Richard Leech
The HEIRESS 7/2/1960
d C.M. Pennington-Richards;
sc Philip Chambers, Leonard Fincham,
Max Marquis
lp Julia Lockwood; Maurice Kaufmann;
Betty McDowall; Donald Morley
FINGERS OF GUILT 28/2/1960
d Robert Lynn;
sc Robert Stewart, Tom Hutchinson,
Ernie Player
lp Bill Nagy; John Salew; June Merlin
The GIRL WITH GREY HAIR 6/3/1960
d Charles Frend;
sc Leonard Fincham, Robert Stewart,
Michael Hankinson
lp Mary Laura Wood; Elisabeth Wilson;
Ronald Leigh-Hunt; George Pastell
TRIAL AT CRANBY'S CREEK 13/3/1960
d C.M. Pennington-Richards; sc Larry Forrester
lp Tommy Duggan; Rowland Bartrop;
Leslie Watson; Felicity Young; Charles Houston
ASCENT TO MURDER 20/3/1960
d Robert Lynn; sc Larry Forrester
lp Ursula Howells; Anthony Dawson;
Howard Marion-Crawford; Gordon Tanner;
Julian Sherrier
WHITE BLACKMAIL 3/4/1960
d Robert Lynn; sc Robert Stewart
lp Nanette Newman; Douglas Wilmer;
Francis Matthews; Robert Gallico; Mary Morris

EIGHT DAYS INCLUSIVE 1/5/1960
d C.M. Pennington-Richards; sc Robert Stewart
lp Glyn Owen; Rona Anderson; Robert Hunter
DRESSED TO KILL 8/5/1960
d Robert Lynn;
sc David Chantler, Robert Stewart
lp David Knight; Hazel Court;
Frederick Jaeger; Paula Byrne
The ABSENT ASSASSIN 5/6/1960
d Robert Lynn; sc Larry Forrester
lp Donald Pleasence; Frederick Piper;
Russell Waters; John Longden

INTERVIEW WITH PRINCESS ANNE
(BBC 5/9/1971)
An interview with Princess Anne after the
Burghley European Championships three-day
event.

INTIMATE STRANGERS
(LWT 20/9–13/12/1974)
Thirteen-part drama series about a man suffering
a heart attack and the effects it has on his work
and family.
INTIMATE STRANGERS 4/10/1974
d Jim Goddard; p Richard Bates;
sc Julian Bonds
lp Anthony Bate; Patricia Lawrence

The **INVADERS** (US QM Productions 1967–68)
Science-fiction series.
The EXPERIMENT 17/1/1967
d Joseph Sargent; p Alan Armer;
sc Anthony Spinner
lp Roy Thinnes; Roddy McDowall;
Laurence Naismith; Harold Gould; Dabbs Greer
The SAUCER 12/9/1967
d Jesse Hibbs; p Alan Armer;
sc Daniel B. Ullman
lp Roy Thinnes; Anne Francis;
Charles Drake; Dabney Coleman
The WATCHERS 19/9/1967
d Jesse Hibbs; p Alan Armer;
sc Jerry Sohl, Earl Hamner Jr
lp Roy Thinnes; Shirley Knight;
Kevin McCarthy; Leonard Stone; Walter Brooke

INVESTITURE AT CAERNARVON
(HTV 1/7/1969)
The investiture of Prince Charles as Prince of
Wales at Caernarvon Castle.
d Peter Morley

INVISIBLE ARMIES (BBC 9/3–30/3/1958)
Four-part serial for children about how Louis
Pasteur revolutionised medical science.
p Rex Tucker; sc Nesta Pain
regular Hugh David
PART 1 9/3/1958
lp Margaret Barton; Lockwood West;
Gladys Spencer; Norman Shelley; Gerald Cross
PART 2 16/3/1958
d Nesta Pain
lp Margaret Barton; Philip Ray;
Frances Guthrie; Gerald C. Lawson;
Philip Lennard
PART 3 23/3/1958
lp Margaret Barton; Oliver Burt;
Barry MacGregor; Alan Edwards;
George A. Cooper

The INVISIBLE MAN
(Official Films-ITP 1958–59)
The science-fantasy adventures of Dr Peter
Brady, a British scientist who has the power of
invisibility.
p Ralph Smart
regulars Lisa Daniely; Deborah Watling
The LOCKED ROOM 1958
d C.M. Pennington-Richards;
sc Lindsay Galloway; auth Ralph Smart
lp Zena Marshall; Rupert Davies;
Noel Coleman; Lloyd Lamble
PICNIC WITH DEATH 1958
d C.M. Pennington-Richards;
sc Leonard Fincham, Leslie Arliss;
auth Leonard Fincham
lp Derek Bond; Faith Brook;
Michael Ripper

The MINK COAT 9/11/1958
d C.M. Pennington-Richards;
sc Ian Stuart Black; auth Lenore J. Coffee
lp Hazel Court; Derek Godfrey
BLIND JUSTICE 16/11/1958
d C.M. Pennington-Richards; sc Ralph Smart
lp Honor Blackman; Philip Friend;
Robert Raglan; Jack Watling; Leslie Phillips
JAILBREAK 23/11/1958
d C.M. Pennington-Richards; sc Ian Stuart Black
lp Dermot Walsh; Denny Dayvis;
Michael Brennan

IS ART NECESSARY? (ATV 1958)
Arts series.
SHOULD EVERY PICTURE TELL A STORY?
14/4/1958
Three experts in different fields give their
opinion of the importance of the narrative
element in painting.
p Quentin Lawrence; intro Kenneth Clark

ISADORA (BBC 22/9/1966)
Drama based on the life of Isadora Duncan.
d/p Ken Russell;
sc Sewell Stokes, Ken Russell
lp Vivian Pickles; Peter Bowles;
Alexei Jawdokimov; Murray Melvin;
Jeanne Le Bars

ISLAND OF DESTINY (TWW 1960)

ISTANBUL EXPRESS
(US Universal TV 22/10/1968)
International espionage thriller intended as a
series pilot but released theatrically outside
the USA.
d/p Richard Irving;
sc Richard Levinson, William Link
lp Gene Barry; Senta Berger; John Saxon;
Tom Simcox; Mary Ann Mobley; John Marley

IT AIN'T HALF HOT MUM
(BBC 1974–81)
Comedy featuring a British Army entertainment
troupe in India during the 1940s.
QUIT INDIA 3/1/1974
p David Croft;
sc Jimmy Perry, David Croft
lp Michael Bates; George Layton;
Windsor Davies; Melvyn Hayes;
Donald Hewlett; Christopher Mitchell;
Don Estelle

IT HAPPENED TO ME (BBC 1959–61)
Interview series.
MARY LINDELL 26/1/1960
Hywel Davies interviews Mary Lindell about her
work with the French underground during the
war, and her present work with the RAF
Escaping Society.
d/p Alan Rees
ERNIE THOMAS 23/2/1960
Hywel Davies interviews Ernie Thomas, a canal
freight contractor, and some of his colleagues
about their life on the Shropshire Union canal.
d Gordon Mackay; p James Buchan
COCO THE CLOWN 15/12/1960
Hywel Davies interviews Coco the Clown
(Nicolai Poliakoff) about how he became
involved in road safety campaigns for children.
d Gordon Mackay, James Buchan;
p James Buchan

IT NEVER SEEMED TO RAIN
(Yorkshire TV 27/5/1969)
A party of elderly people visit Scarborough after
an absence of fifty years; included is film of
Scarborough in 1913.
exec.p Tony Essex; nar Alec Mango

The ITALIA TRAGEDY (BBC 4/7/1967)
The story of Umberto Nobile and his attempt to
fly over the North Pole in the airship 'Italia', and
his rescue.
p Harry Hastings; sc Douglas Botting;
nar Robert Hardy

ITALIAN WAY (BBC 25/3–6/5/1975)
Seven-part series which highlights Italian life.
SONG OF THE WAVE 25/3/1975
A look at Siena.
The RACE OF SAINTS 15/4/1975
The customs of the inhabitants of Gubbio in
Umbria.
d Michael Croucher

IT'LL BE ALRIGHT ON THE NIGHT
(LWT 18/9/1977)
Compilation of comic outtakes (errors usually
edited out of films and television programmes).
d/p Paul Smith; *pres* Denis Norden

IT'LL BE ALRIGHT ON THE NIGHT 2
(LWT 28/10/1979)
Compilation of comic outtakes.
d/p Paul Smith; *pres* Denis Norden

ITN REPORTS (ITN)
Early evening news programme.
SURVEY OF THE YEAR'S NEWS 29/12/1965
A survey of the news events of 1965: fighting
between India and Pakistan; Vietnam; Greece;
riots in Los Angeles; the South Wales coalfields;
and Rhodesia.
d Robert Verrall

The ITN STORY (ITN 7/7/1977)
The 'official' history of the past twenty-one years
of Independent Television News.
p Michael Weigall; *nar* Reginald Bosanquet;
with Christopher Chataway, Robin Day

IT'S A SQUARE WORLD (BBC 1960–64)
BBC live/tape comedy show written by and
starring Michael Bentine. Includes some
eccentric animation.
IT'S A SQUARE WORLD 19/4/1962
p John Street;
sc Michael Bentine, John Law;
pres Michael Bentine; *with* Dick Emery,
Frank Thornton, Harold Berens, Joe Gibbons,
Leon Thau, Anthea Wyndham
IT'S A SQUARE WORLD (GOLDEN ROSE OF
MONTREUX 1963) 19/4/1963
Compilation of the best of previous programmes
for the BBC entry in the l963 Golden Rose of
Montreux festival.
p James Gilbert;
sc Michael Bentine, John Law;
with Michael Bentine, Ronnie Barker
IT'S A SQUARE WORLD 1964
p John Street; *with* Michael Bentine,
Leon Thau, Deryck Guyler, Clive Dunn,
Joe Gibbons
IT'S A SQUARE WORLD 1964
d Roger Gage; *p* G.B. Lupino;
with Michael Bentine, Joe Gibbons,
Alec Bregonzi, Leon Thau, Dick Emery
IT'S A SQUARE WORLD 1964
p Joe McGrath;
sc Michael Bentine, John Law;
with Michael Bentine, Clive Dunn,
Frank Thornton, Leon Thau, Freddie Earle,
Joe Gibbons

IT'S DARK DOWN THERE
(ATV 20/2/1968)
The closure of the Trimdon Grange pit in
Durham; the feelings of the miners and local
inhabitants; the effect of the closure on their
lives.
d/p Alex Valentine

ITV OPENING NIGHT AT THE GUILDHALL
(Rediffusion 22/9/1955)
Speeches by the Lord Mayor, the Postmaster
General and the Chairman of the ITA, at the
Guildhall banquet to mark the inauguration of
the first independent television service for the
London area.

**ITV OPENING NIGHT – PREVIEW OF
REDIFFUSION AND ABC PROGRAMMES**
(Rediffusion 22/9/1955)
A preview introducing the personalities and
programmes which will be seen on the new
Rediffusion and ABC Television service.

ITV OPENING NIGHT – TRAILER
(Rediffusion 22/9/1955)
Prologue to ITV's opening transmission from
London, outlining the origins of ITV and
Rediffusion's good intentions.

ITV PLAYHOUSE (ITV various 1977–82)
Series of single plays produced by various ITV
companies; previously called PLAYHOUSE
(1964–74).
PHILBY, BURGESS & MACLEAN
(Granada 31/5/1977)
d Gordon Flemyng; *sc* Ian Curteis
lp Anthony Langdon; Richard Hurndall
LAST SUMMER (Thames 21/6/1977)
d Stephen Frears; *p* Barry Hanson;
sc Peter Prince
lp Richard Mottau; Patrick Murray;
Richard Beckinsale; Michael Elphick
COLD HARBOUR (Thames 25/4/1978)
d Stephen Frears; *p* Barry Hanson;
sc Peter Prince
lp Leticia Garrido; Lindsay Ingram;
Antony Sher; Barbara Hicks; Bill Paterson;
Michael Elphick
I'M A DREAMER MONTREAL (Thames 6/3/1979)
d Brian Farnham; *p* Robert Buckler;
sc Stewart Parker
lp Bryan Murray; Vass Anderson;
Jeananne Crowley; James Duggan;
Jeremy Nicholas
NO MAMA NO (Thames 27/3/1979)
d Roland Joffé; *p* Robert Buckler;
sc Verity Bargate
lp Victoria Fairbrother; Tim Pigott-Smith
The BLACKTOFT DIARIES – TRUE OR FALSE?
(Yorkshire TV 10/4/1979)
d Leonard Lewis; *sc* Alan Plater;
intro/nar James Cameron
lp Jo Kendall; Alan Downer;
Roger Milner; Daphne Oxenford;
William Simons

J

JACK HYLTON'S MONDAY SHOW
(Rediffusion-Jack Hylton TV Productions 1958)
Variety show
JACK HYLTON'S MONDAY SHOW 10/2/1958
d Bill Hitchcock;
sc Eric Merriman, Barry Took;
with Rosalina Neri, Dick Bentley,
Leonard Weir, Billy Ternent and his Orchestra
JACK HYLTON'S MONDAY SHOW 17/2/1958
Variety show, from aboard a Britannia flight to
New York.
d Ted Lloyd; *assoc.p* Bambi Harris;
sc Jimmy Coghill; *with* Rosalina Neri,
Hughie Green, Winifred Atwell,
Billy Ternent and his Orchestra
A DAY IN NEW YORK 3/3/1958
d Bambi Harris; *sc* Jimmy Coghill;
with Hughie Green, Peter Ustinov,
Mary Ure
JACK HYLTON'S MONDAY SHOW 7/4/1958
d Bill Hitchcock;
sc Eric Merriman, Barry Took;
with Rosalina Neri, Dick Bentley,
Leonard Weir, Lionel Blair and his Dancers,
Billy Ternent and his Orchestra
JACK HYLTON'S MONDAY SHOW 26/5/1958
d Eric J. Croall;
sc Jimmy Coghill, Bill Smith;
with Hughie Green, Billy Ternent and his
Orchestra

JACK THE RIPPER
(BBC 13/7–17/8/1973)
A six-part series in which Stratford Johns and
Frank Windsor (in their roles as Det. Chief
Supts. Barlow and Watt of Z CARS) investigate
the Whitechapel murders of 1888.
EPISODE 6: HIGHEST IN THE LAND? 17/8/1973
d David Wickes;
p Paul Bonner, Leonard Lewis;
sc Elwyn Jones, John Lloyd

JACKANORY (BBC 1965–)
Story-telling series for children.
ANANSI AND THE TIGER STORIES 1968

JACKIE 'TV' PALLO v. BOBBY GRAHAM
(ATV 14/4/1971)
All-in wrestling bouts, Jackie Pallo v. Bobby
Graham, John Cortez v. Johnnie Williams.
d Tony Parker

JACKS AND KNAVES
(BBC 16/11–7/12/1961)
Four comedy-drama stories focusing on the work
of policemen in Liverpool. Inspired the drama
series Z CARS (1962–78).
The INTERROGATION 23/11/1961
p Gilchrist Calder; *sc* Colin Morris
lp John Barrie

JACK'S HORRIBLE LUCK (BBC 14/8/1961)
Adventures of a happy-go-lucky sailor whose
ship puts into Liverpool.
p Gerard Glaister; *sc* Henry Livings
lp Barry Foster; Wilfrid Brambell;
Stan Simmons; Blake Butler; June Murphy;
Fred Ferris

JACQUELINE DU PRE MASTERCLASS
(BBC 25/9–16/10/1979)
Series of four programmes, recorded at the
Guildhall School of Music and Drama, in which
cellist Jacqueline Du Pré gives a masterclass.
JACQUELINE DU PRE MASTERCLASS 25/9/1979
d Keith Cheetham

JAMIE AND THE MAGIC TORCH
(Thames 1978–1979)
Animation series of the adventures of Jamie and
his dog, Wordsworth, and the magic torch.
d Keith Scroble, Chris Taylor;
p Brian Cosgrove, Mark Hall;
sc/nar Brian Trueman
HIDDEN PERSUASION 3/4/1978
The DIRTY SUBMARINE 10/4/1978
YOO-HOO YETI! 17/4/1978
A NARROW ESCAPE 24/4/1978
A POLICEMAN'S LOT 1/5/1978
The FLOSSED WORLD 8/5/1978
HELP! HELP! 15/5/1978
The DOWNSIDE-UPPER 19/5/1978
ONE CLOUDY DAY 22/5/1978
JEEPERS CREEPERS 5/6/1978
The UNEXPECTED VISITOR 12/6/1978
BIG MAGIC 19/6/1978
JAMIE'S BIRTHDAY PARTY 26/6/1978
The RUNAWAY TROMBONIUM 25/6/1979
The HAIR-STACK 2/7/1979
SYM-PHONEY 9/7/1979
The FLYING RABBIT 16/7/1979
The WICKED WAND 23/7/1979
NATIONAL WELLIBOB DAY 30/7/1979
SPADE-WORK 6/8/1979
UNIDENTIFIED FLYING ELEPHANT 13/8/1979
ARTHUR'S DETOUR 20/8/1979
JAMIE AND THE MAGIC TORCH 27/8/1979
JAMIE AND THE MAGIC TORCH 3/9/1979
JAMIE AND THE MAGIC TORCH 10/9/1979
JAMIE AND THE MAGIC TORCH 17/9/1979

The JAPANESE EXPERIENCE
(Yorkshire TV 1974)
Three-part documentary series on Japan.
d/p/comm Antony Thomas
The ROAD TO KAMAGASAKI 16/4/1974
The influence of the yakuza in Japanese society.
The Zen-ai Kaigl, headed by Keizo Takei.
HOLY GROWTH 23/4/1974
The social effects of Japan's commitment to
industrial growth, which looks at the lives of a
business executive and his family and at
production line workers on an annual outing to
the seaside.
The ABBOT OF HOKE-KYO 30/4/1974
Investigates the mercury pollution at Minamata,
and the opposition to the projected airport at
Narita. Three options for Japanese society are
also examined: the Communist answer, the
political/religious brotherhood of the Sokkagaki,
who believe in a return to the values of
Buddhism, and the solution of the 'Abbot of
Hoke-Kyo' and his ultra-conservative followers.

JASON KING (Scoton-ITC 1971–73)
Continuing the adventures of Jason King,
originally seen as a member of
DEPARTMENT 'S' (1969).
p Monty Berman
regulars Peter Wyngarde; Ann Sharp;
Dennis Price; Ronald Lacey
A DEADLY LINE IN DIGITS 4/12/1971
d Jeremy Summers; *sc* Tony Williamson
lp Donald Houston; Joanna Jones;
Freddie Jones; Jan Waters; Philip Stone;
Barry Lowe
A PAGE BEFORE DYING 18/12/1971
d Jeremy Summers; *sc* Tony Williamson
lp Carl Duering; Harry Landis;
Richard Wyler; Philip Madoc
VARIATIONS ON A THEME 1/1/1972
d Cyril Frankel; *sc* Philip Broadley
lp Julian Glover; Ralph Bates;
Eric Pohlmann; Walter Hertner; Basil Dignam;
Alexandra Bastedo
BURIED IN THE COLD, COLD GROUND 5/3/1972
d Jeremy Summers; *sc* Philip Broadley
lp Michele Dotrice; Frederick Jaeger;
Gary Raymond; Lewis Fiander; Jane Lapotaire
ALL THAT GLISTERS: PART 1 19/3/1972
d Cyril Frankel; *sc* Philip Broadley
lp Lee Patterson; Clinton Greyn;
Anton Rodgers; Joanna Dunham;
Madeleine Smith
UNEASY LIES THE HEAD 9/4/1972
d Cyril Frankel; *sc* Donald James
lp Lance Percival; Juliet Harmer;
Harold Kasket; Sandor Eles
IT'S TOO BAD ABOUT AUNTIE 7/5/1972
d Jeremy Summers; *sc* Harry W. Junkin
lp Sarah Lawson; Jack Watling;
Allen Bickford; Dinsdale Landen; Norman Bird;
Fiona Lewis
STONES OF VENICE 14/5/1972
d Jeremy Summers; *sc* Donald James
lp Roger Delgado; Anna Gael;
William Squire; John Ronane; Irene Prador;
Imogen Hassall
CHAPTER ONE: THE COMPANY I KEEP 4/6/1972
d Cyril Frankel; *sc* Donald James
lp Toby Robbins; Ronald Radd;
Paul Whitsun-Jones; Paul Stassino;
Stephanie Beacham
TOKI 16/7/1972
d Jeremy Summers; *sc* Philip Broadley
lp Kieron Moore; Felicity Kendal;
Tony Beckley; David Buck; Simon Lack
IF IT'S GOT TO GO – IT'S GOT TO GO 5/1/1973
d Cyril Frankel; *sc* Tony Williamson
lp Felix Aylmer; John Le Mesurier;
Jennifer Hilary; Yootha Joyce; Guy Deghy

JAZZ 625 (BBC 1964–66)
Jazz music series.
EARL 'FATHA' HINES 27/7/1966
Humphrey Lyttelton introduces Earl Hines, Ron
Mathewson and Lennie Hastings.
p Terry Henebery

JAZZ AT THE PHILHARMONIC: PART 2
(BBC 26/11/1967)
Norman Gartz introduces a jazz concert
featuring Teddy Wilson, Coleman Hawkins,
Benny Carter, Dizzy Gillespie, Clark Terry,
Zoot Sims, James Moody, T-Bone Walker,
Bob Cranshaw and Louis Belson.
p Terry Henebery

JET PROPELLED (BBC 19/5/1966)
The history and development of jet engines. Sir
Frank Whittle and his colleagues talk about their
achievements.
d/p Ramsay Short; *sc* Gordon Thomas;
comm John Stockbridge

JIM BULLOCK – MINER EXTRAORDINARY
(Yorkshire TV 22/7/1969)
Jim Bullock, founder of the first union for mine
managers, recalls his career in the mining
industry.
d Duncan Dallas; *sc* Michael Deakin

JIM'LL FIX IT (BBC 1975–)
Series in which Jimmy Saville makes people's
dreams come true.
OLAVE, LADY BADEN-POWELL AND JIM'LL FIX
IT INTERVIEW 1977
Lady Baden-Powell 'comes out of seclusion' to
speak to a Brownie who wrote to Jim'll Fix It.
She talks about the history of the guide and
scout movement.

JIMMY CARTER MEETS THE GEORDIES
(Tyne Tees 6/5/1977)
The President of the USA, Jimmy Carter, visits
the north-east of England.
d Lewis Williams

The JO STAFFORD SHOW (ATV 1961–62)
Thirteen-part, fortnightly transmitted, variety
show hosted by American singer Jo Stafford.
The JO STAFFORD SHOW 7/10/1961
d Jo Douglas; *p* Bill Ward;
sc Marilyn Bergman, Alan Bergman,
Eddie Maguire; *with* Ella Fitzgerald,
Kathleen Harrison, Claire Bloom

The JOAN BAKEWELL INTERVIEW
(Scottish TV 12/9–21/11/1977)
Six-part interview series.
JOHN MCGRATH 17/10/1977
R.D. LAING 21/11/1977

JOBY (Yorkshire TV 1975)
Stan Barstow's two-part study of an eleven-year-
old boy discovering life at the outbreak of war in
1939.
d James Ormerod; *exec.p* Peter Willes;
sc/auth Stan Barstow
PART 1 12/1/1975
lp Patrick Stewart; Richard Tolan;
Diana Davies; Geoffrey Tomlinson;
David Clayforth; Jean Lloyd; Lorraine Peters;
Sharon Gower; Joanne Whalley; Frances Cox
PART 2 19/1/1975
lp Richard Tolan; Lorraine Peters;
Sharon Gower; Alick Hayes; Patrick Stewart;
Joanne Whalley

JOE THE CHAINSMITH (BBC 7/11/1958)
Joe Mallen is the foreman of a team which hand-
forges heavy iron chains – the traditional craft of
Cradley Heath, Staffordshire.
sc/p Philip Donnellan

JOHN CRAVEN'S NEWSROUND
(BBC 1972–87)
Series of news bulletins aimed at children,
covering the main news items of the day;
presented by John Craven. Known as
'Newsround' from 1988.
JOHN CRAVEN'S NEWSROUND 10/11/1975
JOHN CRAVEN'S NEWSROUND 11/11/1975

The JOHN CURRY ICE SPECTACULAR
(LWT 25/12/1976)
Ice skating show starring John Curry, making his
first television appearance since turning
professional.
d/p Jon Scoffield; *with* Millicent Martin,
Julia McKenzie, David Kernan, Wayne Sleep,
Peggy Fleming

JOHN HUME'S DERRY
(IE Radio Telefís Éireann 1/10/1969)
Londonderry's history leading up to the
outbreak of violence in 1968–69.
p Noel D. Greene

JOHNNY GO HOME
(Yorkshire TV 22/7/1975)
A two-part investigation (shown on the same
evening) of the dangers facing teenagers who
leave home for the bright lights of London.
d/p John Willis
PART ONE: END OF THE LINE
The true story of Annie who ran away from
home when she was 10; and of Tommy who left
Glasgow, aged 14.
PART TWO: The MURDER OF BILLY TWO-TONE
Investigation uncovering the story of the murder
of homeless youngster Billy 'Two-Tone'
McPhee.

JOHNNY STACCATO
(US Revue Studios 1959–60)
Private detective series set in New York.
COLLECTOR'S ITEM 31/12/1959
d John Cassavetes; *p* Everett Chambers;
sc Stanford Whitmore
lp John Cassavetes; Eduardo Ciannelli;
Rupert Crosse; Juano Hernandez

JOKES A JOKE (LWT 6/9–25/10/1975)
Members of the public tell jokes to camera.
LEEDS 4/10/1975
p David Bell

The JOLLY BEGGARS
(Scottish TV 25/1/1979)
Scottish Opera production of Robert Burns' 'The
Jolly Beggars'.
d Jim McCann;
p Bryan Izzard, Peter Ebert

JONI MITCHELL IN CONCERT
(BBC 17/5/1971)
p Stanley Dorfman

A JOURNEY OF UNDERSTANDING
(ATV 1961)
Tour of the Middle East by Archbishop Fisher,
November-December 1960.
d Michael Redington

JOURNEY TO THE UNKNOWN
(Hammer Film Productions-Twentieth Century-
Fox TV 1968–69)
Fantasy-suspense anthology series.
GIRL OF MY DREAMS 26/9/1968
d Peter Sasdy; *p* Anthony Hinds;
sc Robert Bloch, Michael J. Bird;
auth Richard Matheson
lp Michael Callan; Justine Lord;
Zena Walker; Jan Holden; David Lampton

The JUDGES (Thames 12/10/1971)
Bryan Magee talks to Sir Frederick Sellers, Lord
Devlin and Lord Radcliffe about their work as
judges and their reaction to criticism of the
judiciary.
d Peter Tiffin

JUKE BOX JURY (BBC 1959–67)
Pop music series, in which guests discuss and
judge the latest record releases.
JUKE BOX JURY 29/10/1960
David Jacobs presents; *with* studio guests
Carmen McRae, Nancy Spain and Pete Murray.
p Stewart Morris

The JULIAN BREAM CONSORT
(BBC 31/7/1961)
Julian Bream plays Elizabethan popular music.
p Walter Todds; *intro* Julian Bream

JUMP FOR JOY
(Jack Hylton TV Productions 4/7/1957)
A telerecorded excerpt from the Southsea Pier
Theatre of the summer show.
d Peter Croft;
pres Chesney Allen, Jack Hylton;
with Reg Dixon

The JUMPERS (Westward 4/11/1969)
A behind-the-scenes look at international show-
jumping meetings and local gymkhanas.
p/sc Hugh Pitt; *nar* John Pett;
with David Broome, Anneli Drummond-Hay

JUMPING FOR THE JELLY-BEANS
(BBC 21/5/1973)
Professor Fred Herzberg talks to an audience of
British managers on his thesis that people have
two distinct kinds of needs at work. The first is
how they are treated at work (with regards to
salary, supervision and working conditions,
which he calls 'hygiene' needs). The second is
that people are motivated by what they do at
work. His talk covers the areas of job
enrichment, work expansion and
communication.
p Peter Riding

JUNE EVENING (BBC 10/7/1960)
The life and humour of a street in Bolton,
Lancashire on an evening in June 1921.
p Vivian A. Daniels; *sc/auth* Bill Naughton
lp John Sharp; Leslie Cotton;
Marjorie Rhodes; Nan Marriott-Watson;
Brian Peck; Jennifer Moss; Davy Jones;
Patricia Haines; Violet Carson; Colin Douglas;
Patricia Hayes

JUST GRACIE (BBC 26/12/1960)
Gracie Fields, with Bert Waller at the piano and
The Rita Williams Singers.
p G.B. Lupino

JUST ONE KID (ATV 11/6/1974)
Documentary of life for a Jewish child growing
up in the East End of London between the wars,
recalled by Alfred Maron; with dramatised
sequences featuring actors and children of the
Jewish Free School.
d/p John Goldschmidt

JUST ONE MORE WAR (ATV 26/4/1977)
Documentary about war photographer Don
McCullin.
d Jana Bokova; *p* Brian Lewis

JUST THE JOB (BBC 2/1–17/3/1969)
Ten programmes on career opportunities for
young adults.
WHAT ABOUT INDUSTRY? 3/2/1969
The career prospects for young adults in
industry.
d Tony Roberts; *p* John Dutot

JUST WILLIAM (LWT 1977–78)
Adaptations of the 'Just William' books by
Richmal Crompton.
The SWEET LITTLE GIRL IN WHITE 27/2/1977
d/p John Davies; *sc* Keith Dewhurst
lp Adrian Dannatt; Diana Dors;
Diana Fairfax; Bonnie Langford;
Michael McVey; Tim Rose; Craig McFarlane;
Selina Cadell; John Stratton

JUSTICE (Yorkshire TV 1971–74)
Drama series about a female barrister.
p James Ormerod, Jacky Stoller (3rd series,
1974)
regular Margaret Lockwood
The MOST IMPORTANT THING OF ALL 8/10/1971
d James Ormerod; *sc* James Mitchell
lp William Franklyn; Victor Maddern;
Philip Latham; Carleton Hobbs;
Sebastian Breaks
BY ORDER OF THE MAGISTRATES 15/10/1971
d Tony Wharmby; *sc* Edmund Ward
lp Ronald Leigh-Hunt; John Collin;
Rosemarie Dunham; Eric Woofe
WITNESSES COST EXTRA 22/10/1971
d James Ormerod; *sc* John Malcolm
lp Derek Francis; Philip Stone;
George A. Cooper; Raymond Huntley;
John Harvey
The RAIN IT RAINETH 29/10/1971
d Tony Wharmby; *sc* Ray Jenkins
lp Michael Coles; Hilda Fenemore;
Leon Vitali; Peter Blythe; Derek Lamden;
Ian Sharp; Carleton Hobbs
WITHIN A YEAR AND A DAY 5/11/1971
d Christopher Hodson; *sc* Ray Jenkins
lp Michael Coles; Hilda Fenemore;
Leon Vitali; Peter Blythe; Derek Lamden;
Ian Sharp; Philip Stone
TO HELP AN OLD SCHOOL FRIEND 12/11/1971
d Christopher Hodson; *sc* James Mitchell
lp Roger Livesey; Joan Haythorne;
Geoffrey Whitehead; Amanda Murray;
Brian Wilde
NO FLOWERS – BY REQUEST 19/11/1971
d Christopher Hodson; *sc* David Lees
lp Jack Watson; Robert Keegan;
Richard Beckinsale; Norman Jones;
Bernard Brown; Carl Rigg
WHEN DID YOU FIRST FEEL THE PAIN?
26/11/1971
d Tony Wharmby; *sc* John Malcolm
lp Barry Keegan; John Stone;
Gwendolyn Watts; Peter Sallis; Carleton Hobbs;
Claire Nielson

A NICE STRAIGHTFORWARD TREASON
3/12/1971
d Christopher Hodson; *sc* James Mitchell
lp John Stone; Paul Eddington;
Elizabeth Bell; Colin Rix; Milos Kirek;
James Walsh
PEOPLE HAVE TOO MANY RIGHTS 10/12/1971
d James Ormerod; *sc* John Malcolm
lp John Stone; Philip Stone; Guy Slater;
Hector Ross; Cyril Shaps; Christopher Malcolm
YOU DIDN'T PAY FOR JUSTICE 17/12/1971
d Christopher Hodson; *sc* James Mitchell
lp Anthony Valentine; Frances White;
Amber Kammer; John Graham; James Ottaway
A LICENCE TO BUILD YOUR OWN MONEY
7/1/1972
d Christopher Hodson; *sc* James Mitchell
lp Joss Ackland; Philip Stone;
Michael Gwynn; Maria Aitken; Michael Godfrey
A DUTY TO THE COURT 14/1/1972
d James Ormerod
lp Barbara Jefford; Percy Herbert;
Peter Cellier; John Westbrook; Carleton Hobbs
CONSPIRACY 9/2/1973
d James Ormerod; *sc* John Batt
lp John Stone; T.P. McKenna;
Donald Burton; Raymond Huntley; Lois Baxter;
Philip Stone
MALICIOUS DAMAGE 16/2/1973
d James Ormerod; *sc* Kevin Laffan
lp John Stone; Paul Eddington;
Norman Eshley; Fiona Gaunt; Philip Stone;
Sharon Mughan
A LIBEL AMONG FRIENDS 23/2/1973
d Tony Wharmby; *sc* Bill MacIlwraith
lp John Stone; Philip Stone;
Donald Houston; Barbara Leigh-Hunt;
Ronald Leigh-Hunt
The WHOLE TRUTH 2/3/1973
d Alan Bromly; *sc* Bill MacIlwraith
lp John Stone; Philip Stone;
Brian Blessed; Frederick Jaeger; Sheila Reid;
Michael Gover; John Carlin
ONE FOR THE ROAD 9/3/1973
d Tony Wharmby; *sc* Bill MacIlwraith
lp John Stone; Philip Stone;
Carmel McSharry; Geoffrey Whitehead;
Frank Mills
DIVORCE 16/3/1973
d Tony Wharmby; *sc* Kevin Laffan
lp John Stone; Philip Stone; Sue Lloyd;
Mary Merrall; John Turner; Robin Wentworth
AFTER ALL, WHAT IS A LIE? 23/3/1973
d Alan Bromly; *sc* John Batt
lp John Stone; Philip Stone;
Basil Dignam; Derek Newark; Brian Wilde
HARRIET PETERSON v. DR. MOODY 30/3/1973
d Tony Wharmby; *sc* Henry Cecil
lp John Stone; Philip Stone;
Carolyn Courage; Clifford Evans; Russell Napier
FOR THOSE IN PERIL 6/4/1973
d Alan Bromly; *sc* Bill MacIlwraith
lp John Stone; Philip Stone;
Paul Hardwick; Ray McAnally;
Carolyn Courage
DUMMY SCOULAR AGAINST THE CROWN
13/4/1973
d James Ormerod; *sc* Kevin Laffan
lp Philip Stone; Joseph Brady;
Derek Francis; Tony Steedman; John Stone;
Clifford Rose
NOBODY'S THAT GOOD 20/4/1973
d Alan Bromly; *sc* John Batt
lp John Stone; Philip Stone;
Carolyn Courage; John Bryans; Faith Kent;
John Nettleton; Angela Thorne; Mark Colleano
COVENANT FOR QUIET ENJOYMENT 27/4/1973
d James Ormerod; *sc* John Batt
lp John Stone; Philip Stone;
Carolyn Courage; John Bryans; John Nettleton;
Angela Thorne; Mark Colleano
TRESPASS TO THE PERSON 4/5/1973
d James Ormerod; *sc* John Batt
lp John Stone; Philip Stone;
Glyn Houston; Angela Thorne;
Michael Elphick; Rod Beacham
TRIAL FOR MURDER 17/5/1974
d John Frankau; *sc* David Ambrose
lp Anthony Valentine; John Stone;
Lynn Farleigh; Geoffrey Bayldon;
John Woodnutt

The PRICE OF INNOCENCE 24/5/1974
d Mark Cullingham; *sc* John Batt
lp Anthony Valentine; John Stone;
Robin Bailey; Ralph Michael; John Shrapnel;
Hilary Mason
DUTY OF CARE 31/5/1974
d Mark Cullingham; *sc* John Batt
lp John Stone; Geoffrey Keen;
Philip Bond; Brewster Mason; Jim Norton;
Pat Keen
GROWING UP 7/6/1974
d Tony Wharmby; *sc* Ian Curteis
lp Anthony Valentine; John Stone;
William Lucas; Michael Coles; Gerald Sim;
Jill Gascoine
The FINE LINE OF DUTY 21/6/1974
d John Frankau; *sc* David Ambrose
lp John Stone; Anton Rodgers;
Helen Lindsay; Noel Willman; Ronald Adam
IT'S ALWAYS A GAMBLE 28/6/1974
d Brian Farnham; *sc* David Ambrose
lp Anthony Valentine; Cyril Luckham;
Donald Douglas; Alun Armstrong;
David Horovitch
MATRIMONIAL MALICE 5/7/1974
d Mark Cullingham; *sc* Bill MacIlwraith
lp Carolyn Seymour; John Stone;
Gareth Thomas; James Maxwell; Brian Oulton
PERSONA NON GRATA 12/7/1974
d Tony Wharmby; *sc* Bill MacIlwraith
lp John Stone; Anthony Valentine;
Ed Devereaux; James Cossins; Nancy Waite;
Joe Gladwin; Angus Lennie
TWICE THE LEGAL LIMIT 19/7/1974
d Brian Farnham; *sc* John Batt
lp John Stone; Anthony Valentine;
William Fox; Noel Johnson; Ralph Michael;
Basil Henson
UNDER SUSPICION 26/7/1974
d Brian Farnham; *sc* David Ambrose
lp John Stone; Anthony Valentine;
Tony Melody; Ray Mort; Sarah Douglas;
Jenny Laird
DECISIONS, DECISIONS 2/8/1974
d Brian Farnham; *sc* Eric Wendell
lp John Stone; Anthony Valentine;
Rowena Cooper; Richard Vernon; Jenny Till;
Ed Devereaux; Sarah Douglas
POINT OF DEATH 9/8/1974
d Tony Wharmby; *sc* Bruce Stewart
lp John Stone; William Russell;
Barbara Shelley; James Maxwell; Judy Buxton
COLLISION COURSE 16/8/1974
d Tony Wharmby; *sc* Bill MacIlwraith
lp John Stone; Fulton Mackay;
Alan MacNaughton; Tony Jay; Jennie Stoller

K

K.M. & L.M.: THE CLAIMS OF FRIENDSHIP
(BBC 12/6/1973)
Lesley Moore recalls her friendship with
Katherine Mansfield.
d/sc Tristram Powell; *nar* Bridget Armstrong

KAREN – A TODAY REPORT
(Thames 12/11/1976)
Documentary about a 16 year-old delinquent girl
who has been in borstals and prisons over a
period of four years.

KASKAD (SE Sveriges Radio 8/8/1962)
Variety entertainment featuring Eartha Kitt, Jan
Malmsjo, Lill Lindfors and others.
d Åke Falck

KEEPING IN STEP (Rediffusion 1958)
Documentary series.
d Rollo Gamble; *rep* Daniel Farson
The STOCK EXCHANGE 1958
The PUBLIC SCHOOL 1/1/1958
Winchester College.
sc Daniel Farson, Geoffrey Golden
BOTH ENDS OF THE MUSICAL SCALE 8/1/1958
The British pastime of dancing.
sc Stanley Craig, Daniel Farson
CHILDREN'S PARTIES 15/1/1958
Daniel Farson visits the party of journalist's
daughter Tina Noble and talks to 'Uncle Bertie',
the party's magician.
sc Elkan Allan

KEEPING IN STEP cont.

The WEDDING 22/1/1958
Daniel Farson attends a wedding and interviews
the bride, bridegroom, in-laws, toastmaster, and
a canon of the church.
sc Stanley Craig; Daniel Farson
BRIGADE OF GUARDS 29/1/1958
sc Geoffrey Golden, Stanley Craig,
Daniel Farson
THIS ENGLAND 2/4/1958
Daniel Farson interviews various people,
including Adam Faith, about social change.

KENNETH HARRIS INTERVIEWS
(BBC 1972–73)
Interview series.
p Elwyn Parry-Jones
DR. PIETRO BASSETTI 25/3/1973
Dr Pietro Bassetti of Italy, a millionaire,
industrialist and budding politician.
d Simon Wadleigh
PROFESSOR KURT HANSEN 15/4/1973
Hansen, chairman of Bayer, Germany – the
company which invented Aspirin – views the role
and responsibility of powerful industrialists in
the new Europe.
d Simon Wadleigh

The KENNY EVERETT VIDEO SHOW
(Thames 1978–80)
Comedy series featuring Kenny Everett and the
dance group Hot Gossip.
The KENNY EVERETT VIDEO SHOW 24/7/1978
d/p David Mallett;
sc Barry Cryer, Ray Cameron, Kenny Everett
The KENNY EVERETT VIDEO SHOW 19/2/1979
d/p David Mallett;
sc Barry Cryer, Ray Cameron, Kenny Everett

KHRUSHCHEV AND BERLIN
(US NBC 13/2/1962)
Chet Huntley analyses Krushchev's policies on
Berlin.
p Irving Gitlin

KHYBER (Granada 27/6/1979)
The history of the North West Frontier.
Interviews with Pathans about their relationship
with the British.
d/p Andre Singer; *sc* Charles Allen;
nar Leo McKern

KIDS (LWT 27/4–20/7/1979)
Thirteen-part drama series about children in
care; shot largely on location.
LUCILLE 11/5/1979
d/p John Frankau
lp James Hazeldine; Sarah Neville;
Caroline Mortimer; Neil Nisbet

KILVERT'S DIARY (BBC 1977–78)
Dramatised serialisation of the diaries of the
Rev. Francis Kilvert.
d Peter Hammond; *p* Rosemary Hill;
sc James Andrew Hall
regular Timothy Davies
An ANGEL SATYR WALKS THESE HILLS
21/10/1977
lp Mervyn Johns; Emrys James
VILLAGING 28/10/1977
lp Charles Turner; Raymond Young;
Rita Davies; Denis Carey; Rachel Thomas
The BOIL 4/11/1977
lp Tim Preece; Hugh Latimer;
Rhoda Lewis; Maggie Wilkinson
SCHOOL INSPECTION 11/11/1977
lp Raymond Young; Rita Davies;
John Nicholls; Deborah Cliffe;
Edward Burnham
The MAD WOMAN 18/11/1977
lp Freda Jackson; David Garfield
ST. VALENTINE'S DAY 25/11/1977
lp Tim Preece
A SWEET SUSPICION OF SPRING 2/12/1977
lp Patricia Healey; Richard Goolden
The SOLITARY 9/12/1977
lp John Cording; Sebastian Shaw
TWO SERMONS 16/12/1977
lp Phyllida Law
JUNKETTINGS 23/12/1977
lp Hugh Latimer; Rhoda Lewis;
Clifford Evans

DAISY THOMAS 6/1/1978
lp Victoria Plucknett; Rhoda Lewis;
Clifford Evans
The BLACK MOUNTAIN 13/1/1978
lp Lucy Griffiths
The OLD SOLDIER 20/1/1978
lp Susan Richards; Esmond Knight
TEN MILES FOR A KISS 27/1/1978
lp Chloe Franks
FATHER IGNATIUS 3/2/1978
lp Chrissy Iddon; Sean Mathias;
Michael Aldridge
A BABY AT THE VICARAGE 10/2/1978
lp Maggie Wilkinson; Dudley Owen;
Maureen Pryor
A WET AFTERNOON 17/2/1978
lp Nicholas Jones
BIRTHDAY 24/2/1978
lp Rhoda Lewis; Hugh Latimer

KIND OF EXILE (ATV 13–27/7/1971)
Trilogy of biographical programmes about three
individuals who have all moved from their
birthplace to another land.
SIR OSWALD MOSLEY 27/7/1971
A profile of Sir Oswald Mosley and his views on
the future of Britain.
d/p Robin Brown

KING
(US Abby Mann Productions-Filmways TV
Productions 12–14/2/1978)
Mini-series. A drama about the career of Martin
Luther King Jr from his days as a Baptist
minister in the South of the 1950s until his
assassination in 1968.
d/sc Abby Mann; *p* Paul Maslansky
lp Paul Winfield; Cicely Tyson;
Tony Bennett; Roscoe Lee Browne;
Lonny Chapman; Ossie Davis; Cliff DeYoung;
Al Freeman Jr; Clu Gulager; Steven Hill;
William Jordan; Warren Kemmerling;
Lincoln Kilpatrick

KING OF THE CASTLE
(HTV 8/5–19/6/1977)
Seven-part serial for children.
EPISODE 1 8/5/1977
d Peter Hammond; *p* Leonard White;
sc Bob Barker, Dave Martin
lp Philip Da Costa; Milton Johns;
Fulton Mackay; Talfryn Thomas; Derek Smith;
Jamie Foreman; Kevin Hudson;
Angela Richards; Sean Lynch

KINGDOM IN THE JUNGLE
(ATV 14/12/1971)
The work of the Villas-Boas brothers with the
primitive tribes on the Xingu reserve in Brazil.
See also The TRIBE THAT HIDES FROM
MAN.
d/p Adrian Cowell

KINGDOM IN THE NORTH (BBC 19/5/1953)
Life in Northumberland and Durham.
d Anthony De Lotbinière; *p* John Elliot

A KING'S REVOLUTION
(Rediffusion 1/1/1964)
The Shah of Iran tells of his plan to transform
Iran into a progressive, industrial nation.
d Randal Beattie; *sc* Paul Johnson;
nar Andrew Faulds

KINGS ROW (US Warner Bros. 1955–56)
Drama series which was developed from the
1941 film of the same name. Part of WARNER
BROTHERS PRESENTS series.
LADY IN FEAR 13/9/1955
d Paul Stewart; *p* Roy Huggins;
sc Jameson Brewer; *auth* Henry Bellamann
lp Jack Kelly; Nan Leslie; Robert Horton;
Peggy Webber; Victor Jory

KIRKBY: A SELF PORTRAIT
(Granada 20/1/1975)
Kirkby, Lancashire and its problems as seen by
its residents.
d Steve Morrison

KIRKBY, PORTRAIT OF A TOWN
(Granada 19/2/1973)
Ray Gosling gives a personal impression of
Kirkby, Lancashire.

KITTY CLIVE (BBC 27/3/1956)
A comedy for children about the eighteenth-
century comedienne of Drury Lane.
p Naomi Capon; *sc* Estelle Holt
lp Peter Sallis; Jill Balcon;
Denise Hirst; Pauline Winter; John Van Eyssen;
William Mervyn; Faith Brook; Peter Augustine

KITTY – RETURN TO AUSCHWITZ
(Yorkshire TV 6/11/1979)
Kitty Hart, a radiographer in Birmingham,
returns to Auschwitz with her son, reliving
memories of her internment in the concentration
camp.
p Peter Morley, Kevin Sim

KNITTING FASHION (BBC 11/10–13/12/1976)
A series of ten programmes demonstrating both
the basic and the advanced techniques of knitting
and crochet.
p Jenny Rogers; *intro* Jan Leeming
TAKE A SQUARE 18/10/1976
CRAFT AND ART 13/12/1976

The KNOWLEDGE (Euston Films 27/12/1979)
Comedy about how a group of prospective
London taxi drivers obtain the 'Knowledge' of
the city.
d Bob Brooks; *p* Christopher Neame;
sc Jack Rosenthal
lp Mick Ford; Maureen Lipman;
Nigel Hawthorne; Kim Taylforth;
Jonathan Lynn; David Ryall; Michael Elphick

KOJAK (US Universal TV 1973–78)
Police series featuring a group of Manhattan-
based detectives.
OUT OF THE FRYING PAN... 2/11/1975
d Charles Dubin; *p* James McAdams;
sc Jack Laird
lp Telly Savalas; Kevin Dobson;
George Savalas; Richard Venture;
Eugene Roche; Joseph Stern; Lee Weaver

KOK (SE Sveriges Radio 12/1/1962)
d/p Eric Nilsson

KONTAKION (Thames 20/4/1973)
A performance of 'Kontakion', depicting events
in the life of Christ, danced by William Louther,
Robert North and London Contemporary
Dance; with music conducted and played by
Peter Maxwell-Davies with The Fires of London.
d Anton Bowler; *exec.p* Marjory Ruse

L

L.S. LOWRY (BBC 17/5/1957)
A study of the painter L.S. Lowry and of the
locations from which he works.
d/p/sc John Read; *nar* L. S. Lowry

The LABOUR PARTY CONFERENCE –
BLACKPOOL (BBC 1/10/1956)
Report on the first day of the Labour Party
conference. Edited extracts and a studio
interview with Frank Cousins. Summary from
David Butler.

The LABOUR PARTY CONFERENCE –
BLACKPOOL (BBC 2/10/1956)
Report from the second day of the Labour Party
conference. Extracts from the proceedings,
interview with Aneurin Bevan. Summary from
David Butler.

The LABOUR PARTY CONFERENCE –
BLACKPOOL (BBC 3/10/1956)
Report from the third day of the Labour Party
conference. Extracts from the conference, the
debate on the pamphlet 'Towards Equality';
interview with Marcia Williams. Summary from
David Butler.

**The LABOUR PARTY CONFERENCE –
BLACKPOOL** (BBC 4/10/1956)
Report from the fourth day of the Labour Party
conference. Extracts from the debate on colonial
policy, interview with Hugh Gaitskell. Summary
from David Butler.

**The LABOUR PARTY CONFERENCE –
BRIGHTON** (BBC 30/9/1957)
The Labour Conference debates Conservative
economic policy, nationalised industries, and the
Rent Act. Harold Wilson is interviewed.

**The LABOUR PARTY CONFERENCE –
BRIGHTON** (BBC 1/10/1957)
Extracts from the Labour Conference debate on
pensions; Richard Crossman is interviewed as is
Aneurin Bevan; David Butler comments on the
elections to the National Executive.

**The LABOUR PARTY CONFERENCE –
BRIGHTON** (BBC 2/10/1957)
Extracts from the debate on the document
'Labour's Future Plan'. Robert McKenzie sums
up.

**LABOUR PARTY CONFERENCE
SCARBOROUGH 1958: FIRST DAY**
(ITN 29/9/1958)
Extracts from Hugh Gaitskell on Quemoy and
the education debate. Reginald Bosanquet
interviews Alice Bacon (Sound only). Introduced
by Robin Day.

**LABOUR PARTY CONFERENCE
SCARBOROUGH 1958: SECOND DAY**
(ITN 30/9/1958)
Analysis of elections to NEC and extracts from
the debate on agriculture. Interview with Hugh
Gaitskell (Sound only). Introduced by Robin
Day.

**LABOUR PARTY CONFERENCE
SCARBOROUGH 1958: THIRD DAY**
(ITN 1/10/1958)
Extract from debate on Labour's Economic
Plan. Robin Day interviews Harold Wilson.

**LABOUR PARTY CONFERENCE
SCARBOROUGH 1958: FOURTH DAY**
(ITN 2/10/1958)
Extracts from H-bomb debate and an interview
with Aneurin Bevan. Introduced by Reginald
Bosanquet.

**The LABOUR PARTY CONFERENCE
(SCARBOROUGH 1958: DAY 1)**
(BBC 29/9/1958)
Extracts from the debates on Quemoy and
education, Kenneth Harris interviews Hugh
Gaitskell, Frank Cousins, and Tom Driberg.
Robert Kee speaks to American journalist Don
Cook.

**The LABOUR PARTY CONFERENCE
(SCARBOROUGH 1958: DAY 2)**
(BBC 30/9/1958)
Extracts from the debate on agriculture.
Kenneth Harris interviews Eirene White and
Morgan Phillips. Robert Kee talks to journalists
Sydney Jacobson and W. Margo

**The LABOUR PARTY CONFERENCE
(SCARBOROUGH 1958: DAY 3)**
(BBC 1/10/1958)
Extracts from the debate on the executive policy
document 'Plan for Progress'. Kenneth Harris
interviews Harold Wilson, Alan Birch and
Jennie Lee.

**The LABOUR PARTY CONFERENCE
(SCARBOROUGH 1958: DAY 4)**
(BBC 2/10/1958)
Extracts fom the debates on foreign policy and
nuclear disarmament. Kenneth Harris interviews
Nye Bevan and Hugh Gaitskell. Robert Kee
talks to Harold Clay who first attended the
conference in 1914.

The LABOUR PARTY CONFERENCE 1960
(BBC 3/10/1960)
Robert Kee and Kenneth Harris discuss the
tension over the defence debate. Contributions
from E.J. Hill, and Harris interviews Tom
Driberg.

The LABOUR PARTY CONFERENCE 1960
(BBC 5/10/1960)
Extracts from the defence debate. Kenneth
Harris interviews Hugh Gaitskell, Bill Carron,
Frank Cousins and George Brown. Long extracts
from Gaitskell's 'Fight, fight and fight again'
speech.

The LABOUR PARTY CONFERENCE 1960
(BBC 6/10/1960)
Extracts from a debate on nationalisation.
Kenneth Harris interviews Anthony Crossman
on the difference between Tory and Labour
conferences and Barbara Castle on the nature of
the make-up of the Labour Party's membership.

LABOUR PARTY CONFERENCE 1961
(BBC 2/10/1961)
Extracts from the debate on expulsion of the
E.T.U. (Electrical Trades Union), government's
interference in free wage bargaining and on
'Signposts to the Sixties'. Kenneth Harris
interviews James Callaghan and Frank Cousins.
p John Grist, Jack Ashley

LABOUR PARTY CONFERENCE 1961
(BBC 3/10/1961)
Extracts from Blackpool of debates on education
and equality, and public ownership. Kenneth
Harris interviews Anthony Greenwood and
Hugh Gaitskell.
p John Grist, Jack Ashley

LABOUR PARTY CONFERENCE 1961
(BBC 4/10/1961)
Extracts from the debates on foreign policy and
defence. Kenneth Harris interviews Frank
Cousins and Hugh Gaitskell.
p John Grist, Jack Ashley

LABOUR PARTY CONFERENCE 1961
(BBC 5/10/1961)
Extracts from the Angola debate and the EEC
debate. Kenneth Harris interviews Jennie Lee,
Michael Foot, George Brown and Richard
Crossman.

**LABOUR PARTY CONFERENCE 1962:
FIRST DAY** (BBC 1/10/1962)
Extracts from the Brighton Conference debates
on transport. Kenneth Harris interviews Ray
Gunter on transport, Richard Crossman on
pensions and Jennie Lee on the state of the
Party.

**LABOUR PARTY CONFERENCE 1962:
SECOND DAY** (BBC 2/10/1962)
Extracts from the health service debate. Kenneth
Harris interviews James Callaghan about the loss
of his seat on the NEC. An angry exchange
between Kenneth Harris and George Brown.

**LABOUR PARTY CONFERENCE 1962:
THIRD DAY** (BBC 3/10/1962)
Extracts from the debate on the EEC. Kenneth
Harris talks about Labour as a party particularly
in the light of the coming election and the EEC
with journalists Geoffrey Goodman, John Cole
and Peregrine Worsthorne.

**LABOUR PARTY CONFERENCE 1962:
FOURTH DAY** (BBC 4/10/1962)
Extracts from debates on regional policy and
nationalisation. Kenneth Harris interviews
Harold Wilson and sums up the conference.

**LABOUR PARTY CONFERENCE,
SCARBOROUGH 1963: FIRST DAY**
(BBC 30/9/1963)
Ian Trethowan reports on the first day. Extracts
from the opening address; housing and transport
debates. Trethowan interviews Michael Foot.
Robin Day interviews Patrick Gordon-Walker
and Anthony Greenwood.

**LABOUR PARTY CONFERENCE,
SCARBOROUGH 1963: SECOND DAY**
(BBC 1/10/1963)
Extracts from major speech by Harold Wilson.
Richard Crossman on organising university
research. Ian Trethowan interviews George
Brown; Robin Day sums up the health service
debate.

**LABOUR PARTY CONFERENCE,
SCARBOROUGH 1963: THIRD DAY**
(BBC 2/10/1963)
Extracts from major speech by George Brown.
Incomes policy debate highlights. Robin Day
interviews James Callaghan.

**LABOUR PARTY CONFERENCE,
SCARBOROUGH 1963: FOURTH DAY**
(BBC 3/10/1963)
Robin Day interviews Harold Wilson and Ian
Trethowan reports on the day's proceedings and
sums up the whole conference.

**LABOUR PARTY CONFERENCE 1964 –
DAY 1** (BBC 12/12/1964)
Extracts from speeches by Anthony Greenwood
and Harold Wilson. Robin Day interviews
Greenwood.
d Mary Evans; *p* Anthony Whitby

**LABOUR PARTY CONFERENCE 1964 –
DAY 2** (BBC 13/12/1964)
Robin Day interviews George Brown and
Harold Wilson on the Labour Party's first eight
weeks in office.
d Mary Evans; *p* Anthony Whitby

**LABOUR PARTY CONFERENCE 1979
(MONDAY)** (BBC 1/10/1979)
Live coverage of various important debates.
p Peter Kenyatta; *rep* David Dimbleby,
Robert McKenzie, Robin Day

**LABOUR PARTY CONFERENCE 1979
(TUESDAY)** (BBC 2/10/1979)
Live coverage of various important debates.
p Peter Kenyatta; *rep* David Dimbleby,
Robert McKenzie, Robin Day

**LABOUR PARTY CONFERENCE 1979
(WEDNESDAY)** (BBC 3/10/1979)
Live coverage of various important debates.
p Peter Kenyatta; *rep* David Dimbleby,
Robert McKenzie, Robin Day

**LABOUR PARTY CONFERENCE 1979
(THURSDAY)** (BBC 4/10/1979)
Live coverage of various important debates.
p Peter Kenyatta; *rep* David Dimbleby,
Robert McKenzie, Robin Day

**LABOUR PARTY CONFERENCE 1979
(FRIDAY)** (BBC 5/10/1979)
Live coverage of various important debates.
p Peter Kenyatta; *rep* David Dimbleby,
Robert McKenzie, Robin Day

LACE (BBC 6/10/1951)
Richard Dimbleby visits Nottingham Museum
with Reg Barnes, a past president of the Lace
Federation.

**Der LACHENDE MANN: BEKENNTNISSE
EINES MÖRDERS** (DD DEFA 9/2/1966)
An interview with the mercenary soldier
Siegfried Müller about his beliefs, his career and
his activities in the Congo during the civil war.
The interview is complemented with stills and
with footage of white mercenaries in action
against African rebels in the Congo.
d Gerhard Scheumann, Walter Heynowski

LADIES NIGHT (ATV)
Regional documentary.
HYPNOTISM AND ACUPUNCTURE 18/1/1978
GAY WOMEN 22/2/1978

The LADY AND THE FOOL (BBC 3/5/1959)
A ballet created by John Cranko for the Royal
Ballet first performed in 1954. Charles
Mackerras conducts the Royal Opera House
Orchestra.
p Margaret Dale; *with* Svetlana Beriosova,
Ronald Hynd, Ray Powell

The LADY OF THE CAMELLIAS
(BBC 13/12–20/12/1976)
Two-part dramatisation of the novel by
Alexandre Dumas.
PART 1 13/12/1976
d Robert Knights; *p* Richard Beynon;
adapt Edmond Gosse
lp Kate Nelligan; Peter Firth; Garrick Hagon;
Deborah Fallender; Brian Tully;
James Hazeldine

The LARGEST THEATRE IN THE WORLD
(BBC 1962–71)
A Eurovision venture in which nine countries
broadcast a series of individual plays at the same
time.
The TEA PARTY 25/3/1965
d Charles Jarrott; *p* Sydney Newman;
sc Harold Pinter
lp Leo McKern; Vivien Merchant;
Jennifer Wright; John Le Mesurier;
Charles Gray

**The LAST DICTATOR – STROESSNER'S
PARAGUAY** (Yorkshire TV 7/4/1970)
Alan Whicker reports on the political situation in
Paraguay under its President Don Alfredo
Stroessner.
d/p Michael Blakstad

The LAST GOON SHOW OF ALL
(BBC 26/12/1972)
Comedy programme, with Peter Sellers, Harry
Secombe, Spike Milligan, Max Geldray and the
Ray Ellington Quartet.
p Douglas Hespe; *sc* Spike Milligan

The LAST HUNTERS (Westward 19/7/1977)
The fishermen of Newlyn and how their close-
knit community is affected by international
politics and highly organised commercial
methods.
d/p John Pett

The LAST JOURNEY (Granada 9/4/1972)
The last days in the life of Leo Tolstoy, whose
passionate concern for the people of Russia
began to destroy his relationship with his wife
Sonya.
d/p Peter Potter; *sc* James Forsyth
lp Peggy Ashcroft; Harry Andrews;
Patrick Allen; Ian McKellen; Paul Eddington;
John Stratton

The LAST LIGHTHOUSE (BBC 6/2/1974)
Tony Parker visits Bishop Rock lighthouse off
the Scilly Isles and talks to the men who work
there.
d David Gerrard; *p* Paul Bonner

LAST OF THE BASKETS (Granada 1971–72)
Comedy series featuring Arthur Lowe as a
gentleman's gentleman to a broken-down earl.
The HOUND OF THE BASKETS 31/1/1972
d/p Bill Podmore; *sc* Andy Maher
lp Arthur Lowe; Ken Jones;
Patricia Hayes; Ambrosine Phillpotts

The LAST OF THE MOHICANS
(BBC 17/1–7/3/1971)
Eight-part adaptation of the J. Fenimore Cooper
novel.
EPISODE 1 17/1/1971
d David Maloney; *p* John McRae;
sc Harry Green
lp Andrew Crawford; Tim Goodman;
Kenneth Ives; John Abineri; Richard Warwick;
Philip Madoc

LAST OF THE SUMMER WINE
(BBC 1973–)
Comedy series about three middle-aged,
redundant men who fill their time talking and
walking in and around their small Yorkshire
town; developed from the COMEDY
PLAYHOUSE entry LAST OF THE SUMMER
WINE (4/1/1973).
COMPO'S SUITS 10/12/1973
p James Gilbert; *sc* Roy Clarke
lp Michael Bates; Bill Owen;
Peter Sallis; John Comer; Jane Freeman;
Ronald Lacey; Mollie Maureen
SOME ENCHANTED EVENING 26/3/1975
p Bernard Thompson; *sc* Roy Clarke
lp Michael Bates; Peter Sallis;
Bill Owen; Kathy Staff

The LAST WORD (BBC 1955)
A chess game played in Kiel in 1925 between
Brinkmann (white) and an amateur (black).
d Lester Bookbinder

LATE CALL (BBC 1975)
Four-part adaptation of the Angus Wilson novel
about an elderly couple moving in with their son
and his family in a new town.
d Philip Dudley; *p* Ken Riddington;
sc Dennis Potter
regulars Dandy Nichols; Leslie Dwyer;
Michael Bryant; Daniélle Carson
EPISODE 1 1/3/1975
lp Sarah Sutton; John Dawson;
Patricia Mort; Anne Blake; Rosalyn Elvin;
Timothy Morand; Nigel Crewe
EPISODE 2 8/3/1975
lp Timothy Morand; Nigel Crewe;
Rosalyn Elvin; Sarah Sutton; Mary Chester;
Elizabeth Chambers; Geoffrey Adams;
Fanny Carby
EPISODE 3 15/3/1975
lp Fanny Carby; Timothy Morand;
Nigel Crewe; Rosalyn Elvin; Geoffrey Adams;
Rosemarie Dunham; Nicholas McArdle;
Sarah Sutton
EPISODE 4 22/3/1975
lp Kathryn Leigh-Scott; Alison Dowling;
Philip Bond; Hugh Sullivan; Timothy Morand;
Nigel Crewe; Rosemarie Dunham;
Nicholas McArdle; Rosalyn Elvin; John Cater;
Raymond Mason

LATE NIGHT DRAMA (ITV various 1974)
Anthology drama series.
I KNOW WHAT I MEANT (Granada 10/7/1974)
d Jack Gold; *p* Michael Cox; *sc* the White House
tapes and public statements, edited by David
Edgar
lp Nicol Williamson; Bob Sherman;
James Berwick; John Bay; Shane Rimmer
ITEM (HTV 7/8/1974)
d Patrick Dromgoole; *p* Leonard White;
sc Bob Baker, Dave Martin
lp Freddie Jones; Bernard Hepton;
Alfred Lynch; Alaric Cotter; June Barrie
STARMAKER (Granada 4/9/1974)
d Peter Plummer; *p* Dennis Woolf;
sc Ray Davies
lp Ray Davies; June Ritchie; The Kinks
MS OR JILL AND JACK (Yorkshire TV 11/9/1974)
d Mike Newell; *sc* John Osborne
lp Jill Bennett; John Standing;
Wendy Gifford; Michael Byrne; Denis Lawson

LATE NIGHT LINE-UP (BBC 1964–77)
Review and discussion series.
LATE NIGHT LINE-UP 15/9/1972
Profile of writer Johnny Speight, creator of the
television series TILL DEATH US DO PART
(1965–75), with numerous clips from the series.
ed Rowan Ayers; *with* Johnny Speight
CATCH 44 23/10/1972
An American access programme by prisoners of
the Billerica House of Correction.

LATE SUMMER AFFAIR (BBC 1/6/1962)
With his wife and children away at the seaside, a
man finds himself on the loose for the first time
in eight years and in the mood for romance.
p Eric Tayler; *sc* Leo Lehman
lp Nigel Stock; Wendy Craig;
Jessie Evans; Brian Wilde; Reginald Marsh;
Frazer Hines

LAUDES EVANGELII (Rediffusion 31/3/1961)
A mystery play based on an Umbrian text.
d Joan Kemp-Welch; *exec.p* Norman Marshall;
auth Giorgio Signorini
lp Angelo Pietri; Tatiana Massine;
Gerard Ohn; Tatiana Orlova; Nicola Petrov

LAURENCE OLIVIER PRESENTS
(Granada 1976–78)
Laurence Olivier presents a series of 'best plays'
from a given year.
The COLLECTION 5/12/1976
d Michael Apted;
p Laurence Olivier, Derek Granger;
sc Harold Pinter
lp Alan Bates; Malcolm McDowell;
Laurence Olivier; Helen Mirren
HINDLE WAKES 19/12/1976
d/p June Howson, Laurence Olivier;
auth Stanley Houghton
lp Jack Hedley; Pat Heywood;
Donald Pleasence; Rosemary Leach;
Roy Dotrice; Rosalind Ayres; Marjorie Sudell;
Joe Holmes; Peter Wallis; Pat Wallis;
Trevor Eve; Judi Bowker

LAW AND ORDER (BBC 1978)
Four interlocking plays looking at aspects of
crime and punishment.
d Les Blair; *p* Tony Garnett;
sc G.F. Newman
A DETECTIVE'S TALE 6/4/1978
lp Derek Martin; Ken Campbell; Alan Ford;
Roy Sone
A VILLAIN'S TALE 13/4/1978
lp Peter Dean; Derek Martin;
Deirdre Costello; Alan Ford
A BRIEF'S TALE 20/4/1978
lp Ken Campbell; Peter Dean;
Deirdre Costello; Derek Martin
A PRISONER'S TALE 27/4/1978
lp Peter Dean; Deirdre Costello;
Edward Cast; Roger Booth

The LAW OF THE PLAINSMAN
(US Four Star-Cardiff-NBC 1959–60)
Western series focusing on the partnership
between an educated Indian and a New Mexico
deputy marshal.
FULL CIRCLE 8/10/1959
lp Michael Ansara; Dayton Lummis;
Lyle Bettger; Gail Kobe; Wayne Rogers

The LAWYERS (BBC 24/11/1960)
A behind the scenes look at the legal profession.
p/sc Richard Cawston; *comm* Colin Wills

LEFT, RIGHT AND CENTRE (ATV 1978–81)
Regional political current affairs series.
NATIONAL COAL BOARD 18/9/1978
with Eric Varley
POLITICAL EDUCATION 16/10/1978
with Shirley Williams, Rhodes Boyson
LEFT, RIGHT AND CENTRE 6/11/1978
SPIES 4/12/1978
with Chapman Pincher
SECRET BALLOTS 8/1/1979
with Jim Prior

LENA AND BONNIE (LWT 26/3/1978)
Variety show starring Lena Zavaroni and Bonnie
Langford.
d/p John Kaye Cooper; *sc* Ken Hoare

LET'S MAKE MUSIC (BBC 5/1–5/3/1964)
Series of ten educational programmes on musical
instruments, music and musicians.
The ORCHESTRA 5/3/1964
p Victor Poole; *intro* Antony Hopkins

LET'S PRETEND...THE MAKE BELIEVE WORLD OF DAPHNE DU MAURIER
(Westward 13/12/1977)
An interview with author, Daphne du Maurier.
d Christian Browning; *p* John Pett;
pres Cliff Michelmore

LET'S TWIST IN PARIS (Rediffusion 8/5/1962)
David Frost introduces a dancing contest to find the best performers of the twist in Paris.
d Rollo Gamble; *intro* David Frost

The LEVIN INTERVIEW
(Rediffusion 1966–67)
Bernard Levin interviews various public figures. [Not to be confused with 'Levin Interviews' (BBC 1980)].
BERNARD HOLLOWOOD 31/1/1966
Bernard Hollowood, the editor of 'Punch'.
d Michael Currer-Briggs
WOODROW WYATT M.P. 14/2/1966
d Michael Currer-Briggs
DR. JOOST DE BLANK 21/2/1966
The most reverend Dr Joost de Blank, Archbishop of Capetown 1957–1963.
d Michael Currer-Briggs
DR. LOUIS JACOBS 28/2/1966
Rabbi Louis Jacobs, a critic of the traditional views of Judaism.
d Michael Currer-Briggs
DR. JOHN TREASURE 5/4/1966
Dr John Treasure, a director of one of Britain's largest advertising agencies.
d Michael Currer-Briggs
ANTON WALLICH-CLIFFORD 13/7/1966
Anton Wallich-Clifford, the founder of the Simon Community Trust.
d Michael Currer-Briggs
SHEILA ANDREWS 20/7/1966
Sheila Andrews, broadcaster and writer.
d Michael Currer-Briggs
LORD MONTGOMERY 5/9/1966
d Geoffrey Hughes
DAME REBECCA WEST 12/9/1966
d Steve Minchin
ALEXANDRE KERENSKI 1967
ROBERT KENNEDY 1967
SIR JOHN ROTHENSTEIN 20/2/1967
Sir John Rothenstein, the director of the Tate Gallery.
d John Phillips
ROBERT BOLT 13/3/1967
d John Phillips
ORSON WELLES 3/4/1967
d John Phillips
SIR MICHAEL TIPPETT 17/4/1967
d Sheila Gregg
RANDOLPH CHURCHILL 1/5/1967
d Terry Yarwood
JOHN HUSTON 15/5/1967
d Jim Pople
S.J. PERELMAN 5/6/1967
d John Phillips
OSBERT LANCASTER 19/6/1967
d John Phillips

The LIBERAL PARTY ASSEMBLY 1961
(BBC 1961)
Robert Kee introduces a report on the final day of the Assembly in Edinburgh. Extracts from debates on the UN and education. Speech by Jo Grimond. Kenneth Harris interviews Jo Grimond.

The LIFE AND WORK OF AN M.P.
(BBC 1969)
The daily life of a Member of Parliament, David Steel.

A LIFE APART (Granada 13/2/1973)
The hazards faced by Fleetwood trawlermen during a typical trip to Icelandic fishing grounds, and the problems faced by their families ashore.
d/p Michael Grigsby

A LIFE AT STAKE (BBC 17/2–14/4/1978)
Eight-part series of dramatised re-enactments of stories which made headlines.

HOUSTON...WE'VE GOT A PROBLEM 31/3/1978
The Apollo XIII moon shot.
d Ben Rea;
sc Brian Clark, Jim Hawkins
lp Ed Bishop; Keith Alexander;
Bob Sherman; Jerry Harte

LIFE BEFORE BIRTH (BBC 14/6–12/7/1960)
Five-part scientific documentary series on the beginnings of life from conception to birth.
d Brenda Horsfield; *p* James McCloy;
intro David Lutyens
CONCEPTION 21/6/1960
Professor Peter Leslie Krohn, Doctor Alan Parkes and Lord Rothschild discuss recent scientific research on the first hours of life.
The VITAL LINK 5/7/1960
A review of current research into the functions of the placenta, with Professors J.D. Boyd, F.W. Brambell, A. Jost and Peter Brian Medawar.
The LINK IS BROKEN 12/7/1960
The drastic adaptations made by new born infants in order to survive outside the mother's womb.

LIFE BEGINS AT FORTY
(Yorkshire TV 1978; 1980)
Sitcom about a middle-aged couple coming to terms with parenthood.
d/p Graeme Muir; *sc* Jan Butlin
regulars Derek Nimmo; Rosemary Leach; Rosemary Martin; Michael Graham Cox
AND BABY MAKES THREE 13/6/1978
lp Robert Raglan; Robin Halstead
FIT FOR NOTHING 20/6/1978
lp Fanny Rowe; Sheila Raynor
ANOTHER FINE MESS 27/6/1978
lp Robin Halstead
FOREIGN AFFAIRS 4/7/1978
lp Nikki Kelly; Michael Remick
HAPPY FAMILIES 11/7/1978
lp Geoffrey Sumner; Fanny Rowe; Janina Faye
POT LUCK 18/7/1978
lp Geoffrey Sumner; Marilyn Galsworthy
ALARMS AND EXCURSIONS 25/7/1978
lp Fanny Rowe; Norman Bird

LIFE BY MISADVENTURE
(Southern TV 7/8/1973)
The work of plastic surgeon James Ellsworth Laing in treating severely burned patients at Odstock Hospital, Salisbury.
d Graham Hurley; *comm* James Montgomery

LIFE ON EARTH (BBC 1979)
Natural history series in thirteen parts, presented by David Attenborough.
exec p Christopher Parsons
The INFINITE VARIETY 16/1/1979
The beginnings of life on earth.
BUILDING BODIES 23/1/1979
How various forms evolved from the first primitive animals of the sea.
The FIRST FORESTS 30/1/1979
The emergence of plants and animals on dry land.
The SWARMING HORDES 6/2/1979
The relationship between plants and insects
CONQUEST OF THE WATERS 13/2/1979
A study of fish.
INVASION OF THE LAND 20/2/1979
The development of amphibians.
VICTORS OF THE DRY LAND 27/2/1979
The development of the reptiles.
LORDS OF THE AIR 6/3/1979
The emergence of birds.
The RISE OF THE MAMMALS 13/3/1979
The development of marsupials in Australia.
THEMES AND VARIATIONS 20/3/1979
The wide variety that exists amongst mammals looking at bats, ant-eaters and whales.
The HUNTERS AND HUNTED 27/3/1979
Animals hunting for food and their prey.
LIFE IN THE TREES 3/4/1979
Primates in Madagascar, Japan and Central Africa.
The COMPULSIVE COMMUNICATORS 10/4/1979
The development of the human being.

A LIFE WITH CRIME (BBC 4/3–8/4/1979)
Series looking at crime from various viewpoints.
PUBLIC ENEMY NO. 1 4/3/1979
Ex-convict John McVicar and his life of crime.
d Michael Hogan; *p* Lavinia Warner;
pres Ludovic Kennedy

LIFE WITH THE LYONS
(Rediffusion 1957–60)
Family sitcom featuring real-life family Bebe Daniels, Ben Lyon, Barbara Lyon and Richard Lyon. [BBC had also presented Life With the Lyons during 1955–56]
d John Phillips
GREEN-EYED MONSTER 17/9/1957
sc Bebe Daniels, Bob Ross, Bob Block
lp Jack Buchanan; Molly Weir; Frank Pettitt
GOING, GOING, GONE 12/11/1957
sc Bob Ross, Bebe Daniels, Bob Block
lp Molly Weir; Doris Rogers; Hugh Morton; Rex Rashley; Benn Simons
THIRTEEN SHOP-LIFTING DAYS TO CHRISTMAS 12/12/1958
sc Bob Ross, Bebe Daniels, Bob Black, Ronnie Hanbury
lp Susan Richmond; Wilfred Babbage; Peter Glaze; Michael Partridge; Robin Ford; Wilfrid Brambell; Lilian Grassom
The SHERIFF OF FRACTURED WRIST 26/12/1958
sc Bob Block, Bebe Daniels, Ronnie Hanbury
lp Alfred Marks; Molly Weir; Frank Pemberton; Redvers Kyle; Tony Day
CATTLE AUCTION 1960
d John Phillips
lp Dickie Valentine; Doris Rogers; Molly Weir; Peter Hawkins; Wilfrid Brambell
DANGER – WOMAN AT WORK 1960
d John Phillips
lp Molly Weir; Carl Bernard; Ruth Gower; Douglas Bradley-Smith
LEAVE IT TO THE WOMEN 1960
d John Phillips
lp Hughie Green; Joan Ingram; Rufus Cruickshank; Molly Weir
HOME SWEET HOMICIDE 8/1/1960
sc Bebe Daniels, Bob Block, Ronnie Hanbury
lp Molly Weir; Wilfrid Brambell; Doris Rogers

LIFELINE (BBC 1957–60)
Medical/psychological series.
VENEREAL DISEASE 10/11/1959
The social and medical problems caused by venereal diseases.
p Hugh Burnett
A.I.D. 29/7/1960
A discussion of artificial insemination by donor.
d Hugh Burnett

LIFESTYLE (ITV various)
Regional documentary series.
ONE OF OUR AIRFIELDS (Anglia 4/10/1976)
How a group of enthusiasts are helping to preserve a wartime airfield and establishing a unique collection of historic aircraft.
CATHERINE COOKSON (Tyne Tees 1977)
The world of novelist Catherine Cookson.
WORKING MEN'S CLUB (Tyne Tees 5/1/1978)
Working men's clubs in the north east of England.
d David Goldsmith
IN THE ARMY NOW (Tyne Tees 26/6/1978)
Recruits on a British Army basic training course at Catterick Garrison.
d Francis Fuchs; *p* Leslie Barrett

The LIGHTNING WAR (Rediffusion 1/8/1967)
Charles Douglas-Home introduces a report on how Israel won the Six Day War.
d John Phillips

The LIKELY LADS (BBC 1964–66)
North east-based sitcom featuring the social misadventures of two young characters, played by Rodney Bewes and James Bolam. Their further mishaps were presented in the sequel series WHATEVER HAPPENED TO THE LIKELY LADS? (1973–74).
sc Ian La Frenais, Dick Clement

THE LIKELY LADS *cont.*

ENTENTE CORDIALE 16/12/1964
p Dick Clement
lp Joan Pickering; Don McKillop;
Bartlett Mullins; Sheila Fearn
The OTHER SIDE OF THE FENCE 6/1/1965
p Dick Clement
lp Anneke Wills; Didi Sullivan;
Don McKillop; Bartlett Mullins; Richard Moore
ROCKER 18/6/1966
p Dick Clement
lp Carole Mowlam; Derek Sydney;
Patti Dalton
GOODBYE TO ALL THAT 23/7/1966
p Dick Clement
lp Sheila Fearn; Olive Milbourne;
Alex McDonald; Barry Stanton; Bartlett
Mullins; Don McKillop; Irene Richmond

The LIMITS OF GROWTH (Thames 6/6/1972)
The implications of the Club of Rome M.I.T.
report on the environmental and ecological
problems brought by industrial and economic
development. See also LIMITS OF GROWTH
DISCUSSION shown in the SOMETHING TO
SAY series tx 6/6/1972.
d Richard Broad, Ken Craig

The LINEHAMS OF FOSDYKE
(Yorkshire TV 24/4/1973)
The Lineham family, who gain their living from
The Wash by traditional methods, such as raking
cockles, dredging for mussels, shooting ducks
and skinning seals.
d Barry Cockcroft, John Willis;
p John Willis

The LINEUP (US CBS 1954–60)
San Francisco-based police drama series.
The RADIO CASE 1955
d Hollingsworth Morse; *p* Jaime Del Valle;
sc Fred Eggers
lp Warner Anderson; Tom Tully;
Marshall Reed; Mario Silletti;
Argentina Brunetti; William Newell;
Steve Pendleton

LINK (ATV 1976–1982; Central 1982–)
Current affairs magazine programme for the
disabled.
A TOWN FULL OF WHEELCHAIR USERS 5/9/1976
d Jonathan Wright Miller; *p* Richard Creasey;
pres Rosalie Wilkins, John Sheppard,
Tony Northmore

The LION AND THE EAGLE
(Intertel 7/12/1966)
Alistair Cooke reviews the course of the Anglo-
American alliance from Pearl Harbor to
Vietnam.
d Randal Beattie

LITTLE BLUE (Yorkshire TV 1976–77)
Animation series for children featuring a young
elephant character.
The DANCING DISPLAY 20/1/1977
d Digby Turpin; *p* Joy Whitby;
sc Iris Purcell, Harold Purcell
HAYTHORNE FAIR 24/2/1977
d Digby Turpin; *p* Joy Whitby;
sc Iris Purcell, Harold Purcell

LITTLE LORD FAUNTLEROY
(BBC 21/11–26/12/76)
Six-part serialisation of the novel by Frances
Hodgson Burnett.
d Paul Annett; *p* Barry Letts;
sc Jack Gerson
regular Glenn Anderson
PART 2 28/11/1976
lp Jennie Linden; Betty McDowall;
Preston Lockwood; Paul Rogers;
Ray Armstrong
PART 3 5/12/1976
lp Jennie Linden; Betty McDowall;
Preston Lockwood; Paul Rogers; Ian Thompson
PART 4 12/12/1976
lp Jennie Linden; Preston Lockwood;
Paul Rogers; Ray Armstrong; Ian Thompson;
Mischa De La Motte

PART 5 19/12/1976
lp Jennie Linden; Betty McDowall;
Preston Lockwood; Paul Rogers;
Ray Armstrong
PART 6 26/12/1976
lp Jennie Linden; Preston Lockwood;
Paul Rogers; Ray Armstrong; Valerie Lush;
Tony Beckley

The LIVELY ARTS (BBC 1976–78)
Arts series.
SHADES: THREE PLAYS BY SAMUEL BECKETT
17/4/1977
Documents the early life of Samuel Beckett;
Martin Esslin talks about the playwright.
Includes performances of 'Ghost Trio', '…But
the Clouds…' and 'Not I'.
d Donald McWhinnie, Anthony Page;
p Tristram Powell; *sc* Samuel Beckett;
intro Melvyn Bragg
lp Billie Whitelaw; Ronald Pickup

The LIVER BIRDS (BBC 1969–78)
Comedy series featuring the adventures of two,
young, single women sharing a flat in Liverpool.
The LIVER BIRDS 18/2/1972
p Sydney Lotterby;
sc Jack Seddon, David Pursall
lp Polly James; Nerys Hughes; Ken Jones;
Artro Morris; Mollie Sugden; Ivan Beavis;
Cyril Shaps

The LIVING CAMERA
(US Time-Life Broadcast-Drew Associates
1960–63)
Documentary series.
EDDIE 1960
A record of Eddie Sachs, racing driver.
d Richard Leacock, Robert L. Drew
AGA KHAN 1961
A record of Shah Karim Aga Khan IV.
d Richard Leacock, Robert L. Drew
MOONEY VS. FOWLE 1961
The training of two high school football teams
and the subsequent match.
d Richard Leacock, Robert L. Drew

LIVING FOR KICKS
(Rediffusion 2/3/1960)
Daniel Farson investigates the lives of teenagers.
Includes comments on the investigation by the
Countess of Albemarle.
d Rollo Gamble

LIVING IT UP
(Jack Hylton TV Productions 1957–58)
Comedy series with Arthur Askey.
LIVING IT UP 10/5/1957
d Eric Fawcett
lp Richard Murdoch; Anthea Askey;
Danny Ross
LIVING IT UP 27/10/1958
d Bill Hitchcock;
sc Sid Colin, Talbot Rothwell
lp Richard Murdoch; Danny Ross;
Hugh Morton; Billy Percy

The LIVING WALL (Tyne Tees 10/6/1974)
Follows author and journalist Hunter Davies on
a four week walk along Hadrian's Wall, from
Wallsend to Bowness, and presents his view of
what life was like between 122 and 126 AD when
the wall was built.
d Jeremy Lack; *exec.p* Leslie Barrett;
sc Hunter Davies, Michael McHugh

LIVING WITH A GIANT
(Rediffusion 21/2/1962)
A film about Canada and its relationship with
the United States.
d Rollo Gamble; *sc* Elkan Allan

LIVING WITH DANGER (BBC 1/8–5/9/1958)
Six-part documentary series about people who
risk their lives in their work.
BLUE WATCH 8/8/1958
Work of the Fire Service as demonstrated by
men of Blue Watch Leytonstone Fire Station and
Wickford Fire Station.
p Maurice Harvey; *comm* Frank Johnson

LIVING WITH THE GERMANS
(ATV 20/2/1963)
The life of British soldiers and their families in
Germany.
p James Bredin; *rep* David Holden

LOCAL ISSUE – CHELTENHAM
(BBC 12/2/1960)
A meeting of Cheltenham Council to decide if
the town should retain the word 'Spa' and
encourage industry.
rep Robert Reid

LONDON HEATHROW (BBC 24/5/1977)
Behind the scenes at Heathrow airport.
p Anthony De Lotbinière; *nar* Raymond Baxter

LONDON PLAYHOUSE
(Rediffusion 1955–56)
Anthology drama series.
The HOUSE IN ATHENS 1956
d Alan Bromly; *sc* N. Richard Nash
lp Sylvia Syms; David Peel; Mary Clare;
Alec Mango; Ina De La Haye; John Salew;
John G. Heller; George Roderick
The GUV'NOR 19/1/1956
d Peter Graham Scott;
sc Tudor Gates, Patrick Brawn
lp Michael Hordern; Coral Browne;
Jimmy Hanley; Nigel Davenport;
Edward Mulhare; Sam Kydd; Alan Gifford

The LONDON PROGRAMME (LWT 1975–)
Documentary-current affairs programme looking
at issues involving London.
GAMBLING 29/6/1975
A report on gambling in London.
d John Reardon; *p* Barry Cox;
rep Godfrey Hodgson
The NATIONAL FRONT 15/5/1977
A report on the aims of, and personalities
involved in, the National Front.
d Bob Bee, Michael Snow

The LONDON SYMPHONY ORCHESTRA
(Rediffusion 1964)
The London Symphony Orchestra, led by Erich
Gruenberg, and conducted by Adrian Boult,
play Elgar's Enigma Variations (nos. 8 & 9)
accompanied by countryside scenes; and
Beethoven's Symphony No.3
d Peter Moffat

**LONDON TO BRIGHTON IN FOUR
MINUTES** (BBC 22/4/1953)
An experiment in slow speed camera technique.
The journey of the Brighton Belle train from
London Victoria to Brighton is filmed at 2 fps.

The LONDON WEEKEND SHOW
(LWT 1976–79)
Current affairs programme dealing with aspects
of London.
PUNK ROCK 28/11/1976
Janet Street-Porter reports on punk rock groups.
d Bruce MacDonald; *p* Andy Mayer
The YOUNG NATIONAL FRONT 30/10/1977
Report on the Young National Front and its
activities in schools in and around London.
d Bruce MacDonald; *p* Andy Mayer

LONDONERS (Rediffusion 1968)
Ludovic Kennedy looks at London and its
people.
d Terry Yarwood, John Phillips

**LONDON'S FESTIVAL BALLET IN
GRADUATION BALL** (BBC 27/12/1960)
A ballet by David Lichine. Geoffrey Corbett
conducts the London Philharmonic Orchestra.
p Margaret Dale; *with* Belinda Wright,
Vassilie Trunoff, Janet Kedge

The LONG DAY (TWW 15/7/1963)
A report on Dartmoor prison, including
interviews with prisoners, prison officers and
villagers.
p/sc Mike Towers; *interv* John Mead

LONG DAY'S JOURNEY INTO NIGHT
(ATV 22/4/1973)
d Peter Wood, Michael Blakemore;
auth Eugene O'Neill
lp Constance Cummings; Maureen Lipman;
Laurence Olivier; Ronald Pickup; Denis Quilley

The LONG SEARCH (BBC 19/9–12/12/1977)
Thirteen-part documentary series looking at the
religions of the world.
pres Ronald Eyre
THREE HUNDRED AND THIRTY MILLION GODS
19/9/1977
Hinduism in India.
p Peter Montagnon
THERE IS NO GOD BUT GOD 17/10/1977
Islam in Egypt.
p Peter Montagnon
The WAY OF THE ANCESTORS 7/11/1977
The land of the Torajas in the Celebes.
p Peter Montagnon

**The LONG STRUGGLE: THE RISE OF THE
WELFARE STATE** (BBC 30/10/1962)
The story of Britain from the end of the
nineteenth century to 1960. It examines the rise
of the Welfare State, with rare film from archives
and film collections of important events and the
personalities of 1900–60.
p Thérèse Denny; *nar* Malcolm Muggeridge

The LONG VIEW (BBC 23/9/1958)
Film preservation by the National Film Archive;
the vaults at Aston Clinton; testing nitrate film
for deterioration; repairing and printing fragile
film.
d Richard Evans; *p* Victor Poole

LONGCHAMP RACES (BBC 18/5/1972)
Queen Elizabeth II and the Duke of Edinburgh
attend the 'Coupe de Sa Majesté, La Reine
Elizabeth II', at Longchamp racecourse.

The LONGEST DECADE
(Ulster TV 29/10/1978)
The story of the civil strife in Ulster and how the
population lives with it.
d Andrew Crockart; *p* Rory Fitzpatrick

LOOK (BBC 1955–68)
Natural history series.
pres Peter Scott
WOODPECKERS 15/1/1955
Includes Heinz Sielmann's film from 1954.
The BEST OF WALTER HIGHAM 21/4/1961
A compilation of films about birds made by
Walter Higham.
p Eileen Molony
The GULL WATCHERS 22/6/1964
Observational and experimental work on the
black-headed gull, carried out at the Ravenglass
Nature Reserve by Niko Tinbergen and his
students.
d Hugh Falkus
The SIGN READERS 28/12/1964
Observational work carried out at the
Ravenglass Nature Reserve in Cumberland by
Niko Tinbergen and Monica Impekoven.
d Hugh Falkus
The BEACHCOMBERS 30/11/1965
A record of the observational and experimental
work carried out by Niko Tinbergen at the
Ravenglass Nature Reserve.
d/sc/nar Hugh Falkus

A LOOK AT LIV
(SE Strengholt TV; BBC *tx* 3/10/1979)
Liv Ullman discusses her career and relationship
with Ingmar Bergman.
d Richard Kaplan

LOOK HERE (LWT 1978–81)
Monthly documentary series about television.
See also LOOK HERE SPECIAL.
LIGHT ENTERTAINMENT 27/5/1978
Looks at light entertainment; sex on television;
participation in television documentaries; and
sport on television.
d Clive Halls; *p* Rod Allen

NORTHERN IRELAND/FOOTBALL 8/7/1978
Discussion on television's coverage of Northern
Ireland with Richard Francis, Philip Schlesinger
and Nick Ross; presentation of football with Ed
Buscombe and Sam Leitch.
d Clive Halls; *p* Rod Allen
EDINBURGH TV FESTIVAL 2/9/1978
Andrew Neil reports on the Edinburgh
Television Festival.
d Clive Halls; *p* Rod Allen
The FOURTH CHANNEL DEBATE 25/11/1979
The Fourth Channel debate and Richard Francis'
explanation of the BBC's position on the
controversy regarding PANORAMA footage of
the IRA at Carrickmore.
d David Coulter; *p* Rod Allen

LOOK HERE SPECIAL (LWT 1978–81)
One-off specials from the LOOK HERE series,
a monthly documentary series about television.
The QUESTION OF VIOLENCE ON TELEVISION
5/11/1978
d Bob Bee; *p* Rod Allen

LOOK IN (Rediffusion 1959)
Documentary series.
HYPNOTISM 3/2/1959
A Harley Street doctor explains to Michael
Ingrams the medical uses of hypnotism, and
demonstrates its use on two patients.
d Ian Fordyce
DUSTMEN 10/2/1959
Michael Ingrams follows a dustcart on a refuse
collection round in Westminster, and interviews
the dustmen, inspector, foreman and driver
about the job.
d Ian Fordyce; *p* Michael Ingrams
OLD PEOPLE: PART 1 12/5/1959
Michael Ingrams talks to the residents and
matrons of old people's homes at Eastways Park,
Hackney and Luxborough Lodge, Marylebone,
and to an elderly couple who look after
themselves.
d Cyril Butcher; *p* Michael Ingrams
DOWSING 2/6/1959
Mr Latham, a dowser, demonstrates to Michael
Ingrams the techniques of water-divining, and
successfully locates a stream.
d Bill Morton
ACUPUNCTURE 16/6/1959
Dr Roger de la Fuyé demonstrates the treatment
of illness by acupuncture, first on a woman
patient and then on the commentator, Michael
Ingrams. Small needles are inserted into each of
Ingrams' temples, to cure a headache, and also
in his hands, forearms and calves.
d Bill Morton
MIDWIVES 7/7/1959
Michael Ingrams reports on a typical day's work
for a midwife and interviews Barbara Cartland
about the shortage of trained midwives.
d Michael Ingrams

LOOK IN ON LONDON
(Rediffusion 1956)
Documentary series looking at various aspects of
London life.
d Michael Ingrams
SEWERMEN 1/1/1956
Michael Ingrams goes down a sewer and talks to
sewermen about their work. The pumps in action
at the mains drainage station. The operation of a
sewage works.
STREET CLEANERS 13/6/1956
Michael Ingrams interviews a street cleaner in
Maida Vale and is shown round his slum
dwelling. The conveyance of rubbish by barge
from Westminster depot to Pitsea, from where it
is taken by truck to marshland for use in land
reclamation.
ALMS HOUSES 20/6/1956
Michael Ingrams interviews men at the 'Manor
House' lodging establishment, Camberwell,
where a bed can be had for 2/6 (two shillings and
six old pence). Camberwell Reception Centre,
which caters for the completely penniless. The
Superintendent, Mr J.W. Shorter, is interviewed
on the entrance routine.
W.V.S 11/7/1956
Michael Ingrams looks at the work done by the
Women's Voluntary Service to help old people.
p Caryl Doncaster

BARGEES 30/7/1956
Shots of barges on a canal followed by lock gates
opening and closing whilst the commentary
points out that London is still a centre for canal
traffic.
INCURABLES 6/8/1956
Michael Ingrams talks to staff and patients at the
Royal Hospital and Home for Incurables at
Putney.
HYDE PARK 20/8/1956
Scenes in Hyde Park. Michael Ingrams
interviews people at Speakers' Corner. Groups
represented at the corner include the Coloured
Workers' Welfare Association, the Ireland for
the Irish movement, the London Anarchist
group, and the Socialist Party of Great Britain.

LOOK OF THE WEEK (BBC 1966–67)
Arts programme.
LOOK OF THE WEEK 14/5/1967
Robert Robinson talks to Dame Laura Knight
about her current exhibition; Pink Floyd play
'Games for May' and Hans Keller interviews
Roger Waters and Syd Barrett; Robinson
interviews Christopher Isherwood about his new
novel 'A Meeting by the River'.
d Darrol Blake; *p* Lorna Pegram;
pres Robert Robinson

LOOK OUT (Tyne Tees 1977)
Regional programme for children.
STUFF 27/10/1977
Science and scientific experiments.
d Tony Kysh; *p* Andrea Wonfor

**LOOK OUT OF LONDON – NORTHERN
JOURNEY** (Rediffusion 1956)
Journey along the Grand Union Canal from
London to Birmingham and on to Manchester.
d Michael Ingrams
REGENT DOCKS, STEPNEY 2/10/1956
Dockers queuing for work at Regent Docks in
London; at their club Michael Ingrams talks to
the dockers about the lives they lead and the
state of the docks industry.
BIRMINGHAM YOUTH CLUB 13/11/1956
Interviewer talks to boys belonging to youth
clubs and others who express little or no interest
in such centres.
REPERTORY 4/12/1956
Michael Ingrams talks to the stage director and
to actors of the Windsor Repertory Company at
the Windsor Theatre in Salford as they prepare
for an evening's performance.

LOOK STRANGER (BBC 1970–76)
Documentary series looking at places and people
in Britain.
PINT TO PINT POET 14/9/1976
Documentary on pub comedian Harry Harrison.
p John Kenyon; *with* René Cutforth

LOOKING ABOUT (Rediffusion 1962)
Programme for schools.
RAISING THE VASA 29/10/1962
The engineering techniques involved in raising
the 'Vasa' from Stockholm harbour.
d Richard Doubleday

LOOKING AT TELEVISION
(Yorkshire TV 27/4–29/6/1977)
Series for school children which encourages
discussion of television.
d/p Richard Handford; *pres* Peter Fiddick
OPEN THE BOX! 27/4/1977
The way we use television, how television uses
us, and how we could change it if we wanted to.
BEHIND THE SCREENS 11/5/1977
How Britain's television system works and who
makes the decisions as to what is shown.
MAKE BELIEVE 18/5/1977
The presentation of drama on television.
NARROWCASTING 25/5/1977
A discussion of access programmes such as the
BBC's OPEN DOOR series, and of how
television caters for minority groups.
The SHOW BUSINESS 1/6/1977
Discusses the series ROCK FOLLIES (1976).
NOTHING BUT THE TRUTH 15/6/1977
The presentation of news bulletins and
documentaries on television.

LOOKING AT TELEVISION *cont.*

GIVE US A BREAK 22/6/1977
Advertising and television.
FUTUREVISION 29/6/1977
The future of television in Britain – discussion on the Annan Report and new technological developments such as ORACLE/CEEFAX, new lightweight equipment, cablevision and video recorders.

LOOKING FOR CLANCY
(BBC 24/5–21/6/1975)
Five-part adaptation of the book by Frederic Mullally.
EPISODE 1 24/5/1975
d Bill Hays; *p* Richard Beynon;
sc Jack Pulman
lp Robert Powell; Keith Drinkel

LOOKOUT (BBC 1960–61)
Documentary series.
The PEOPLE WHO CARE 18/1/1961
A London County Council nursery school at Cobham, Surrey.
d J. Glyn Jones; *pres* John Tidmarsh

LORD BEAVERBROOK (BBC 14/5/1952)
Lord Beaverbrook talks about volume 4 of 'The History of The Times' and about Lord Northcliffe.

LORD BEAVERBROOK (BBC 5/11/1959)
Lord Beaverbrook looks round his home town of Newcastle, New Brunswick, and Fredericton, where he has given money to industry and the arts, and talks about his relationship with Winston Churchill, his meeting with Rudolph Hess, and of current East-West relations.
d Anthony De Lotbinière

LORD DERBY (TWW 3/3/1968)
Chairman of Television Wales and West, Lord Derby, introduces the company's final transmission, ALL GOOD THINGS.

LORD EMSWORTH AND THE LITTLE FRIEND (BBC 22/8/1956)
P.G. Wodehouse story made into a play for television; originally shown under the daytime 'Children's Television' banner. [A BBC telerecording of the broadcast on 20/3/56].
p Rex Tucker; *sc* C.E. Webber
lp John Miller; Joan Sanderson;
Brenda Dean; Margaret McCourt; John Hall;
Rufus Cruickshank; Raymond Rollett

LORD REITH LOOKS BACK (BBC 1967)
Three-part film in which Lord Reith, the BBC's first Director-General is interviewed by Malcolm Muggeridge.
d/p Stephen Peet
I WAS MEANT TO DO SOMETHING IN THE WORLD 23/11/1967
Malcolm Muggeridge interviews Lord Reith on his Glasgow upbringing, World War I, and his appointment as General Manager of the BBC.
I FOUND THE BBC OR THE BBC FOUND ME 30/11/1967
Malcolm Muggeridge interviews Lord Reith on events during his time at the BBC, including the General Strike, the Abdication, and the coming of television.
I WAS NOT FULLY STRETCHED 3/12/1967
Malcolm Muggeridge interviews Lord Reith on his career after leaving the BBC.

LOST HEARTS (BBC 25/12/1973)
A ghost story.
d Lawrence Gordon Clark; *p* Rosemary Hill;
sc Robin Chapman; *auth* M.R. James
lp Joseph O'Conor; Susan Richards;
Simon Gipps-Kent; James Mellor

The LOST WORLD OF THE KALAHARI
(BBC 1956)
Laurens van der Post, in a series of six programmes, tells of an expedition into the Kalahari Desert he had recently made with the collaboration of the BBC.
p Andrew Miller Jones
PART 1: VANISHED PEOPLE 15/6/1956
PART 2: FIRST ENCOUNTER 22/6/1956

PART 3: SPIRITS OF THE SLIPPERY HILLS 29/6/1956
PART 4: LIFE IN THE THIRSTLAND 6/7/1956
PART 5: GREAT ELAND 13/7/1956
PART 6: RAIN SONG 20/7/1956

LOVE AND KISSES (BBC 4/11–2/12/1955)
Five-part comedy series.
d Richard Bird;
p Bill Luckwell, Derek Winn;
sc Glenn Melvyn
lp Arthur Askey; Glenn Melvyn;
Lally Bowers; Anthea Askey; Danny Ross;
Ian Gardiner; Barbara Miller; Bernard Graham;
Leonard Williams; Margaret Anderson
LOVE AND KISSES 4/11/1955
LOVE AND KISSES 11/11/1955
BILL'S BRIGHT IDEAS 18/11/1955

LOVE FOR LYDIA (LWT 9/9–2/12/1977)
Adaptation of H.E. Bates' romantic novel.
EPISODE 2: 16/9/1977
d/p Tony Wharmby; *sc* Julian Bond
lp Mel Martin; Christopher Blake;
Beatrix Lehmann; Rachel Kempson;
Michael Aldridge; Charles Lamb; Jeremy Irons

LOVE FROM A-Z
(US David L. Wolper Productions 10/7/1974)
A concert from the Rainbow Theatre, London featuring Charles Aznavour and Liza Minnelli.
d Mel Stuart

LOVE STORY (ATV 1963–74)
Anthology drama series.
MAKE IT A HABIT 8/7/1963
p Hugh Rennie; *sc* Stanley Mann
lp Mark Eden; Susan Maryott;
Jennifer Wilson; Walter Brown; Juno Stevas;
Stephen Follet; Mary Fouracres
La MUSICA 6/12/1965
d John Nelson Burton; *p* Josephine Douglas;
auth Marguerite Duras
lp Vanessa Redgrave; Michael Craig;
Rosalind Atkinson; David March;
Edward Higgins

LOVE THY NEIGHBOUR
(Thames 1972–76)
Sitcom revolving around the misunderstandings of a white family and a black family living next door to each other.
LOVE THY NEIGHBOUR 13/4/1972
d/p Stuart Allen;
sc Vince Powell, Harry Driver
lp Jack Smethurst; Kate Williams;
Rudolph Walker; Nina Baden-Semper;
Harry Littlewood; George Roderick

LOVELY COUPLE (LWT 7/4–30/6/1979)
Sitcom about a couple's plans to wed.
CHANGE PARTNERS 21/4/1979
p/d Derrick Goodwin; *sc* Christopher Wood
lp Elaine Donnelly; Anthony O'Donnell;
Maggie Jones; David Lodge

The LOVER (Rediffusion 28/3/1963)
d Joan Kemp-Welch; *sc* Harold Pinter
lp Alan Badel; Vivien Merchant;
Michael Forrest

The LOVER (Yorkshire TV 9/1/1977)
Pinter's 1963 television play re-staged, with Merchant reviving her original role.
d James Ormerod; *exec.p* Peter Willes;
sc Harold Pinter
lp Patrick Allen; Vivien Merchant;
Robert Swales

The LOVERS (Granada 1970–71)
Comedy series about a young couple's uneven relationship.
EPISODE 1: 27/10/1970
d Michael Apted; *p/sc* Jack Rosenthal
lp Paula Wilcox; Richard Beckinsale; Joan Scott
BRAINWASHED 17/11/1970
d Michael Apted; *p/sc* Jack Rosenthal
lp Richard Beckinsale; Paula Wilcox;
Maureen Lipman; John Flanagan

LSO – THE MUSIC MEN
(Rediffusion 22/9/1965)
The world of orchestral players – their life, music, problems and dedication. Scenes of rehearsals with conductors Colin Davis and Istvan Kertesz.

LUKE'S KINGDOM
(Trident International-TCN9 1976)
Adventures set in the early nineteenth century telling the hardships and heartaches of those British people who helped to found Australia.
p Tony Essex
regulars Oliver Tobias; James Condon;
Elizabeth Crosby; Gerrard Maguire
EPISODE 1: A SORT OF GENTLEMAN 31/3/1976
d Ken Hannam; *sc* Keith Raine
lp Barry Hill; John Clayton; Willie Fennel
EPISODE 2: THE LAND LOVERS 7/4/1976
d Ken Hannam; *sc* John Dorsman
lp Kenneth Laird; Judy Morris; Colin Croft
EPISODE 3: THE BAIT 14/4/1976
d Peter Hammond; *sc* Elizabeth Kata
lp Edmund Pegge; Willie Fennel; Les Foxcroft
EPISODE 4: A MAN WORSE THAN CORMAC 21/4/1976
d Peter Weir; *sc* Brian Wright
lp John Cousins; Shirley Cameron;
Bettina Kenter
EPISODE 5: A WOMAN WAITING 28/4/1976
d Peter Hammond; *sc* Donald Bull
lp David Baxter; Edmund Pegge; Shirley Cameron
EPISODE 6: THE MAN FROM HOME 5/5/1976
d Peter Hammond; *sc* Robert Wales
lp Christopher Haywood; Bettina Kenter;
Shirley Cameron
EPISODE 7: THE SURVEYOR 12/5/1976
d Gareth Davies; *sc* Keith Raine
lp Alfred Bell; Les Foxcroft; Willie Fennel
EPISODE 8: THE KING'S GENTLEMAN 19/5/1976
d Peter Hammond; *sc* John Dorsman
lp Alfred Bell; Joseph Furst; Bettina Kenter
EPISODE 9: THE DAM AND THE DAMNED 26/5/1976
d Peter Weir; *sc* Elizabeth Kata
lp Alfred Bell; Helen Morse;
Shirley Cameron
EPISODE 10: THE HYPOCRITES 2/6/1976
d Hugh David; *sc* John Dorsman
lp Justine Saunders; Stan Roach; Claude Murray
EPISODE 11: DEVIL'S MAN 9/6/1976
d Hugh David; *sc* Tony Morphett
lp Katy Wild; John Mellion; Jack Thompson
EPISODE 12: AN ENEMY TOO MANY 16/6/1976
d Gareth Davies; *sc* Elizabeth Kata
lp Katy Wild; Kevin Miles; James Moss
EPISODE 13: THE PRISONER 23/6/1976
d Ken Hannam; *sc* Tony Morphett
lp Helen Morse; Phillip Ross;
Shirley Cameron

LULU'S BACK IN TOWN
(BBC 21/5–9/7/1968)
Music show with Lulu.
LULU'S BACK IN TOWN 11/6/1968
p John Ammonds; *with* The Everly Brothers,
Les Dawson

M

MACBETH (Thames 4/1/1979)
The Royal Shakespeare Company in Trevor Nunn's production adapted for television.
d Philip Casson; *p* Trevor Nunn
lp Ian McKellen; Judi Dench; Bob Peck;
John Bowen; Susan Drury; Judith Harte

McCORMACK – SPECIAL AGENT
(Yorkshire TV 13/11/1979)
Profile of Mark McCormack – agent for sports superstars.
d Peter Jones; *exec.p* John Fairley;
rep Ian Wooldridge

McHALE'S NAVY
(US Sto-Rev Company 1962–66)
Sitcom about the crew of a PT boat during World War II.

MOVIES ARE YOUR BEST DIVERSION 8/11/1962
d/p Edward J. Montague;
sc Larry Markes, Michael Morris
lp Ernest Borgnine; Joe Flynn;
Tom Conway; Carl Ballantine; Gary Vinson;
Billy Sands; Edson Stroll; Mako

MACKENZIE'S RAIDERS
(US Ziv Television Programs 1958–59)
Syndicated Western series featuring the exploits
of a US Cavalry unit along the Mexican border.
MACKENZIE'S RAIDERS 1958
d Abner Biberman; *p* Elliott Lewis;
sc Bill Driskill; *auth* Russell Reeder
lp Richard Carlson; James Anderson;
Sam Edwards; Manuel Lopez; George Gilbreth;
Robert R. Stephenson; Richard Jury;
John Cason; Jan Stine

MADAM INDIA (BBC 7/3/1966)
Michael Charlton interviews Indira Gandhi
about her life and political opinions.
p Jolyon Wimhurst

MADAME BOVARY (BBC 22/9–13/10/1975)
Four-part serial adapted from the novel by
Gustave Flaubert.
PART 2: FIRST LOVE 29/9/1975
d Rodney Bennett; *p* Richard Benyon;
sc Giles Cooper
lp Francesca Annis; Tom Conti; Ray Smith;
John Cater; Denis Lill; Ivor Roberts

MADE IN BRITAIN (BBC 1966–67)
Documentary series on British-manufactured
goods and exports.
The VALAURISE STORY 18/5/1967

The MAGIC FLUTE (Southern TV 30/12/1978)
The Glyndebourne Festival production of
Mozart's opera, with Leo Goeke, Felicity Lott
and Benjamin Luxon, and The London
Philharmonic Orchestra conducted by Bernard
Haitink.
p David Heather

The MAGIC ROUNDABOUT (BBC 1965–75)
Puppet animation series. Produced in France by
Serge Danot and adapted for BBC transmission.
creator Serge Danot; *sc/nar* Eric Thompson
The MAGIC ROUNDABOUT 5/10/1970
The MAGIC ROUNDABOUT 6/10/1970
The MAGIC ROUNDABOUT 7/10/1970
The MAGIC ROUNDABOUT 8/10/1970
The MAGIC ROUNDABOUT 9/10/1970
The MAGIC ROUNDABOUT 12/10/1970
The MAGIC ROUNDABOUT 13/10/1970
The MAGIC ROUNDABOUT 14/10/1970
The MAGIC ROUNDABOUT 15/10/1970
The MAGIC ROUNDABOUT 16/10/1970

MAGICAL MYSTERY TOUR
(NEMS Enterprises 26/12/1967)
d/sc/lp The Beatles

MAGPIE SPECIAL (Thames)
Irregular series of special editions from the
magazine programme for children, 'Magpie'
(1968–80).
MY BROTHER DAVID 6/7/1971
The life of a mentally retarded boy as seen
through the eyes of his elder sister.
d David Hodgson; *p* Sue Turner
intro Tony Bastable
LIKE ORDINARY CHILDREN 9/10/1973
How normal children and children suffering from
spina bifida regard each other.
d/p David Hodgson;
pres Douglas Rae, Mick Robertson

MAIGRET
(BBC-Winwell Productions 1960–63)
Detective series based on the novels and stories
by Georges Simenon.
regulars Rupert Davies; Ewen Solon;
Helen Shingler
The OLD LADY 28/11/1960
d Eric Tayler; *exec. p* Andrew Osborn;
sc Margot Bennett
lp Marie Ney; Veronica Wells;
Jane Barrett; Kevin Brennan

The GOLDEN FLEECE 4/12/1961
p Rudolph Cartier; *sc* Giles Cooper
lp Al Mulock; Michael Golden;
Dallas Cavell; Michael Brennan
POOR CECILE! 1/10/1963
d Michael Hayes; *p* Andrew Osborn;
sc Donald Bull
lp Neville Jason; Victor Lucas;
Joan Sanderson; Anthony Jacobs; Mary Chester
The FONTENAY MURDERS 8/10/1963
d Alan Bridges; *p* Andrew Osborn;
sc Elaine Morgan
lp Edward Chapman; Alan Wheatley
The CELLARS OF THE MAJESTIC 22/10/1963
d Eric Tayler; *p* Andrew Osborn;
sc Anthony Steven
lp Victor Lucas; Ivor Salter;
Redmond Phillips; Sheila Brennan;
George Coulouris
A MAN CONDEMNED 29/10/1963
d Terence Williams; *p* Andrew Osborn;
sc Roger East
lp Victor Lucas; Patricia Laffan;
Terence De Marney; Ballard Berkeley;
Trader Faulkner
The FLEMISH SHOP 5/11/1963
d Eric Tayler; *p* Andrew Osborn;
sc Rex Tucker
lp Margaret Tyzack; Joyce Carey;
Diana Hoddinott; Olive Kirby; Michael Brennan
A TASTE OF POWER 12/11/1963
d Terence Williams; *p* Andrew Osborn;
sc Donald Bull
lp Neville Jason; Victor Lucas;
John Carson; Terence Alexander;
William Kendall
The LOG OF THE CAP FAGNET 19/11/1963
d Michael Hayes; *p* Andrew Osborn;
sc Elaine Morgan
lp Jerold Wells; Thomas Baptiste;
John Hollis; Victor Platt; Arthur Pentelow
The JUDGE'S HOUSE 26/11/1963
d Terence Dudley; *p* Andrew Osborn;
sc Elaine Morgan
lp Leslie French; Lyn Ashley; Paul Bacon;
Dyson Lovell; Raymond Mason; Patricia Hayes
ANOTHER WORLD 3/12/1963
d Michael Hayes; *p* Andrew Osborn;
sc Donald Bull
lp Neville Jason; Victor Lucas;
Clare Kelly
The CRIME AT LOCK 14 10/12/1963
d/p Andrew Osborn; *sc* Anthony Coburn
lp Neville Jason; Victor Lucas;
Hugh Burden; Isa Miranda; Andrew Faulds
PETER THE LETT 17/12/1963
d Rudolph Cartier; *p* Andrew Osborn;
sc Giles Cooper
lp Victor Lucas; Marius Goring;
Neville Jason; Peter Illing; Roger Delgado;
Magda Miller
MAIGRET'S LITTLE JOKE 24/12/1963
d Terence Williams; *p* Andrew Osborn;
sc Donald Bull
lp Neville Jason; Michael Goodliffe;
Neil McCallum; Stephanie Bidmead;
Constance Wake

The MAIN CHANCE
(Yorkshire TV 1969–75)
Crime series set around a solicitor's office.
A TIME TO LOVE, A TIME TO DIE 14/9/1970
d Christopher Hodson; *exec.p* Peter Willes;
sc Edmund Ward
lp John Stride; Anna Palk; John Arnatt;
Philip Bond; Margaret Ashcroft;
John Wentworth
IT COULD HAPPEN TO YOU 21/9/1970
d Marc Miller; *exec.p* Peter Willes;
sc Edmund Ward
lp John Stride; Anna Palk;
John Wentworth; John Arnatt; Philip Bond;
Bernard Kay

MAKE IT COUNT
(Yorkshire TV 8/1–2/4/1978)
Thirteen-part adult education numeracy
programme.
ADDING, SUBTRACTING, MULTIPLYING AND
DIVIDING 5/2/1978
d/p David Wilson; *pres* Fred Harris

MAKE ME LAUGH
(Jack Hylton TV Productions 1958)
Comedy game show series in which contestants
challenge the comedians to 'Make me laugh'.
pres Chesney Allen;
with The Crazy Gang (Bud Flanagan,
Jimmy Nervo, Teddy Knox, Charlie Naughton,
Jimmy Gold, Eddie Gray)
MAKE ME LAUGH 15/9/1958
d Bill Hitchcock
MAKE ME LAUGH 22/9/1958
d Bill Hitchcock
MAKE ME LAUGH 29/9/1958
d Bill Hitchcock
MAKE ME LAUGH 6/10/1958
d Douglas Hurn; *with* Arthur English,
Davy Kaye
MAKE ME LAUGH 13/10/1958
d Douglas Hurn; *with* Derek Roy,
Davy Kaye, Freddie Sales,
Al Burnett
MAKE ME LAUGH 20/10/1958
d Douglas Hurn; *with* Derek Roy,
Davy Kaye, Freddie Sales, Al Burnett

**The MAKING OF 'BUTCH CASSIDY
AND THE SUNDANCE KID'**
(US Robert Crawford Productions;
BBC *tx* 9/4/1971)
The making of the film 'Butch Cassidy and the
Sundance Kid', with Paul Newman, Robert
Redford, Katherine Ross and director George
Roy Hill.
d/sc Robert Crawford; *p* Ronald Preissman

MAKING OUT (BBC 21/4–23/6/1970)
Ten-part series which examines the work of the
artist in Britain.
DAVID DREW 9/6/1970
Magnus Magnusson interviews choreographer
David Drew about his work.
d Trevor Peters; *p* Nancy Thomas

The MALLENS (Granada 10/6–22/7/1979)
Seven-part drama based on Catherine Cookson's
best-selling novel about the nineteenth-century
Mallen family of Northumberland.
EPISODE 1: 10/6/1979
d Richard Martin; *p* Roy Roberts;
sc Jack Russell
lp John Hallam; David Rintoul;
Sue Burton; Pippa Guard; Julia Chambers;
Caroline Blakiston; Mary Healey;
John Southworth; Gillian Lewis; John Duttine

MAN ABOUT THE HOUSE (Thames 1973–76)
Sitcom set in a flat shared between a man and
two women. Developed into the series
GEORGE AND MILDRED (1976–78) and,
later, ROBIN'S NEST (1977–81).
AND THEN THERE WERE TWO 5/9/1973
d/p Peter Frazer-Jones;
sc Johnnie Mortimer, Brian Cooke
lp Richard O'Sullivan; Paula Wilcox;
Sally Thomsett; Yootha Joyce; Brian Murphy;
Doug Fisher; Jenny Hanley

MAN ALIVE (BBC 1965–82)
Documentary series. See also MAN ALIVE
REPORT (1976–78).
rep Angela Huth, Jeremy James,
John Percival, Trevor Philpott,
Desmond Wilcox, Jim Douglas Henry,
Harold Williamson, Jeanne La Chard,
Gillian Strickland, Denis Tuohy, John Pitman,
Jack Pizzey
MARRIAGE UNDER STRESS: THE BREAKING
POINT 11/1/1967
p Tom Conway
EVERYBODY ELSE IS OUT OF STEP 22/2/1967
Conflicts in which people stand on principle,
stand alone, and stand against the will of society.
p Bill Morton
PUNISHED WOMEN 12/4/1967
The problems facing women prisoners on their
release; interviews with typical cases released
from Holloway prison.
p Bill Morton

MAN ALIVE *cont.*

CONSENTING ADULTS – 1: THE MEN 7/6/1967
Homosexuals talk about the problems they face,
prior to the enactment of the 1967 Sexual
Offences Bill.
p Tom Conway
CONSENTING ADULTS – 2: THE WOMEN
14/6/1967
Lesbians talk about their feelings and problems
prior to the enactment of the 1967 Sexual
Offences Bill.
d Adam Clapham
FOR RICHER FOR POORER... 6/9/1967
Coverage of two weddings – one in the East End
of London, the other in Buckinghamshire.
WORLDS APART 7/5/1968
A review of parent/teenager relationships.
CEREMONIAL MAN 14/5/1968
A portrait of Colonel Eric Hefford, the arranger
of independence ceremonies. The film follows
the organisation of the independence ceremony
for Mauritius.
p Adam Clapham
FROM CASTRO TO COKE 8/1/1969
The problems of Cuban refugees living in
Florida.
PROTEST IN THE RANKS: PART 1: SANCTUARY
12/11/1969
Interviews with American soldiers who took
sanctuary in a church in Honolulu rather than
fight in Vietnam.
d Shirley Fisher
PROTEST IN THE RANKS: PART 2: RESISTANCE
19/11/1969
Opposition to the war in Vietnam amongst
servicemen. Interview with Captain Howard
Levy, the doctor who refused to train Green
Beret soldiers and has served 3 years hard
labour.
d Shirley Fisher
WHAT'S THE TRUTH ABOUT HELL'S ANGELS
AND SKINHEADS 10/12/1969
Interviews with Hell's Angels, Skinheads and
their parents.
p David Filkin
The NAKED EGO 7/1/1970
Encounter groups at the Esalen Institute in
California.
p Tom Conway
The CATHOLIC DILEMMA: PART 1 22/4/1970
Interviews with members of the Catholic clergy
on the question of celibacy.
d Desmond Wilcox
The CATHOLIC DILEMMA: PART 2 29/4/1970
The role of the Catholic church in the twentieth
century.
d Tom Conway
GALE IS DEAD 6/5/1970
The death of a girl from an overdose of drugs.
d Jenny Barraclough
The MOOD OF AMERICA: KENT, OHIO 7/10/1970
Student demonstrations in Kent, Ohio.
p David Filkin
The MOOD OF AMERICA: CLARKESVILLE,
PENNSYLVANIA 14/10/1970
Trade unionism in a troubled coal-mining area.
p David Filkin
The MOOD OF AMERICA: SAUSALITO,
CALIFORNIA 21/10/1970
Schools integration in California.
p David Filkin
The MOOD OF AMERICA: THE WAY AHEAD
28/10/1970
Studio discussion about the future of America.
p David Filkin
DINGLETON 16/6/1971
Dingleton Hospital on the Scottish Borders and
its 'open door' policy.
d Shirley Fisher
FOREIGN LEGION, BEAU GESTE – AND SINCE...
22/9/1971
The present day Foreign Legion.
COULD DO BETTER 12/1/1972
Examines the problems of dyslexic children and
what is being done for them. The importance of
diagnosis is stressed. A discussion programme
about the issues raised was transmitted on
19/1/1972.
d Shirley Fisher

LANDLORD AND TENANT: NO. 1: UP THE RENT
15/3/1972
Housing problems.
p Terence O'Reilly
PLIMPTON: THE MAN ON THE FLYING TRAPEZE
16/8/1972
Reporter George Plimpton joins a trapeze act in
a circus.
p William Kronick
PITY THE CHILDREN 6/12/1972
Cruelty to children. The film follows a man
accused of cruelty through the court case. An
experiment by the NSPCC to help mothers of
child victims is also shown.
d Terence O'Reilly
DEEP SOUTH, DEEP NORTH 15/5/1973
A report on what has happened in both the
South and the North of the USA in the twenty
years since the Supreme Court's historic
desegregation decision on 17/5/1954 (Brown v.
Board of Education) – as seen through the eyes
of a British reporter.
d Tim Slessor
TOUGHER THAN PUNISHMENT 3/10/1973
Pepper Harrow house is a new residence for
disturbed adolescents. The film looks at a new
system of treatment.
p Shirley Fisher
BIG SMILE, PLEASE 21/11/1973
Life at a holiday camp at Selsey, Sussex.
p Jenny Barraclough
SOME LIKE IT HOT 2/1/1974
The work of film stuntmen.
p Brian Trenchard-Smith
PRISON: THE ALTERNATIVE 27/2/1974
Alternatives to prison.
p Sue Boyd
TOP DOG 20/3/1974
A report on the 78th Crufts dog show.
p James Kenelm Clarke
The RISE AND FALL OF WILLIAM STERN
26/9/1974
The collapse of the Nation Life Assurance Co.,
includes an interview with company head
William Stern.
p Philip Geddes
SEX THERAPY – THE NEWEST PROFESSION
31/10/1974
Sex therapy in the United States and its growth
in Britain.
p David Filkin
SOUTH AFRICA: TWO POINTS OF VIEW
12/12/1974
Two views of apartheid in South Africa, 'Last
grave at Dimbaza' and 'Black Man Alive – the
Facts', are followed by a discussion involving the
films' makers and others; chaired by Desmond
Wilcox.
p David Filkin
SOARING LIKE A BIRD 16/1/1975
Gliding in Australia and the preparations by
competitors for the world gliding championships.
p John Walker
PAID OFF, THE STRUGGLE BACK 13/2/1975
The effects of redundancy on middle-aged
executives.
d Henry Murray; *p* Shirley Fisher
STOP THE RAT RACE, I WANT TO GET OFF
10/4/1975
A commune in Suffolk started by people wanting
to get away from town life.
d Brian James
The LAST CHANCE 1/5/1975
Henderson Hospital, Surrey which deals with
'personality disorder' adolescents.
p David Filkin
MURDER WEAPONS 22/5/1975
On the escalation in gun sales in the United
States.
d Lucy Jarvis
MURDER TRIAL 29/5/1975
A filmed record of a one-day murder trial in
Richmond, Kentucky, in which a young man
shot a friend thinking she was an intruder.
d Nell Cox
WE'RE WOMEN – BUT WE'RE WORKERS
26/6/1975
A strike by women workers in a small factory in
the village of Inkersall in Derbyshire.
d Brian Jones

A LIFE FOR A LIFE 5/4/1977
A report on the revival of the death penalty in
the United States and the results of a Gallup poll
in the UK on capital punishment.
p Harry Weisbloom
DEFEAT OR TRIUMPH? 2/10/1979
A report on the Meriden Motorcycle Co-
operative.
p Terence O'Reilly
The CURE 13/11/1979
Nick Ross reports on drug abuse in Britain,
especially barbiturates, and current views on
how to solve the problem.

MAN ALIVE REPORT (BBC 1976–78)
Spin-off documentary series from MAN ALIVE
(1965–82).
POST NATAL DEPRESSION – FROM BABY
BLUES TO BREAKDOWN 25/4/1978
Several women, including Esther Rantzen,
describe post-natal depression. Its causes and
treatment are discussed.
p Ruth Jackson;
rep Jeanne La Chard, Nick Ross

MAN AND WOMAN (Yorkshire TV 1977–78)
Sex education series.
SEX DURING AND AFTER PREGNANCY 4/8/1977
Gaie Houston discusses with a gynaecologist
some of the unnecessary fears that prevent
enjoyment of sexual intercourse during
pregnancy and after the baby is born.
d/p Graham Watts

MAN AT THE TOP (Thames 1970–72)
Drama series about the further exploits of author
John Braine's ruthless anti-hero, Joe Lampton,
the character first featured in the film 'Room at
the Top'.
The FOREMAN'S JOB AT LAST 4/9/1972
d Mike Vardy; *p* Jacqueline Davis;
sc Tom Brennand, Roy Bottomley
lp Kenneth Haigh; Zena Walker;
Stephanie Beacham; John McKelvey;
Paul Hardwick; Richard Easton;
Richard Vernon

MAN AT WORK (BBC 1972–74)
Series about different aspects of work.
ASIANS ON THE SHOP FLOOR 4/10/1972
The result of language training schemes for
Asians together with the supervisors' and shop-
stewards' training sessions on the Asians'
cultural background.
p John Twitchin
DISPUTE: ROUND 1 21/11/1973
Detailed account of an industrial dispute.
Examines the role of the shop stewards.
p Bryn Brooks, John Twitchin
DISPUTE: ROUND 2 28/11/1973
Detailed account of an industrial dispute.
Examines the role of the union.
p Bryn Brooks, John Twitchin

MAN BEFORE ADAM (BBC 19/1/1960)
Kenneth Oakley reports on the discovery of the
earliest known human skull in the Olduvai
Gorge, Tanganyika, by the Leakey Expedition in
July 1959.
d Paul Johnstone; *p* John Irving;
intro David Lutyens

MAN FROM INTERPOL
(Danzigers 1960–61)
Adventures of an Interpol agent seconded to
Scotland Yard.
p Edward J. Danziger, Harry Lee Danziger
regulars Richard Wyler; John Longden
The FEATHERED FRIEND 31/8/1960
d Geoffrey Grayson; *sc* Brian Clemens
lp Peter Elliott; Gerik Schjelderup;
Peggyann Clifford
ODDS ON MURDER 16/9/1960
d Geoffrey Grayson; *sc* Eldon Howard
lp John Le Mesurier; Bill Owen;
Lisa Daniely
SOUL PEDLARS 21/9/1960
d Max Varnel; *sc* George St. George
lp Sandor Eles; Fred Ferris;
Nyree Dawn Porter

The KEY WITNESS 29/9/1960
d Geoffrey Grayson; sc Brian Clemens
lp Robert Arden; Cecil Brock; Jack Taylor
MISSING CHILD 5/10/1960
d Max Varnel; sc Eldon Howard
lp Ferdy Mayne; Lorraine Clewes;
Marion Mathie
The BIG THIRST 20/10/1960
d Geoffrey Grayson
lp Jerold Wells; Margo Mayne;
Robert O'Neil
ESCAPE ROUTE 26/10/1960
d Ernest Morris; sc Stanley Miller
lp James Hayter; Beatrice Varley;
Walter Horsbrugh
The TRAP 3/11/1960
d Geoffrey Grayson; sc Brian Clemens
lp Peter Reynolds; Inia Wiata;
Michael Arlen
NO OTHER WAY 9/11/1960
d Ernest Morris; sc Eldon Howard
lp Leonard Sachs; Peter Howell;
George Roderick
The MURDER RACKET 16/11/1960
d Geoffrey Grayson; sc Brian Clemens
lp Jack Melford; Douglas Jones;
Anthony Jacobs
The MAN WHO SOLD HOPE 7/12/1960
d Robert Lynn; sc Brian Clemens
lp Walter Gotell; Jacques Cey;
John G. Heller
The BIG RACKET 21/12/1960
d Godfrey Grayson
lp Jack Taylor; Gwendoline Watts;
Philip Hollis; Charles Lamb
The MAHARAJAH OF DEN 28/12/1960
d Peter Curran; sc Eldon Howard
lp Francis Matthews; George Pastell;
Nicholas Brady
ALL THE DEAD WERE HARRISONS 4/1/1961
d Godfrey Grayson; sc Mark Grantham
lp Katherine Page; Robert Dorning;
Marguerite Brennan
MURDER BELOW DECK 18/1/1961
d Montgomery Tully
lp Mahmood Mall; Michael Peake;
Bandana Das Gupta
The GOLDEN SHIRRI 8/2/1961
d Montgomery Tully
lp Arthur Gomez; Neil Hallett;
Diane Aubrey; Carl Duering
DEATH IN OILS 23/2/1961
d Godfrey Grayson
lp Ralph Michael; Robert Ayres;
Garard Green; Walter Gotell; Carl Duering
The CASE OF MIKE KRELLO 2/3/1961
d Montgomery Tully
lp Bill O'Connor; Michael Peake;
Diana Chesney; Colin Tapley
MY BROTHER'S KEEPER 16/3/1961
d Geoffrey Grayson
lp John Martin; Neil Hallett;
Charles Lamb
The LAST WORDS 23/3/1961
d Godfrey Grayson; sc Brian Clemens
lp Kevin Stoney; Pete Murray;
Jill Williams; Peter Bennett; Ian Fleming
A WOMAN IN PARIS 30/3/1961
d Montgomery Tully; sc Eldon Howard
lp Francis Matthews; Martine Alexis;
Charles Brodie
LOVE BY EXTORTION 14/4/1961
d Montgomery Tully; sc Brian Clemens
lp Robert Ayres; Noel Dyson; John Serret
INSIDE JOB 20/4/1961
d Geoffrey Grayson; sc Brian Clemens
lp Graham Ashley; Bill O'Connor;
Nyree Dawn Porter
DIPLOMATIC COURIER 28/4/1961
d Montgomery Tully; sc Eldon Howard
lp John McLaren; Nora Gordon;
Catherine Ellison
MISTAKEN IDENTITY 4/5/1961
TIGHT SECRET 18/5/1961
d Geoffrey Grayson; sc Ken Taylor
lp Gerard Heinz; Eira Heath;
Richard Thorpe
INTERNATIONAL DIAMOND INCIDENT 1/6/1961
d Montgomery Tully
lp Paul Carpenter; Jill Melford;
Brian Murray

The CHILD OF EVE 15/6/1961
d Godfrey Grayson; sc Paul Tabori
lp Lisa Daniely; Rowland Bartrop;
Peter Sinclair; Humphrey Lestocq
The ART OF MURDER 6/7/1961
sc Brian Clemens
lp William Marshall; Lionel Ngakane;
John Harrison
The FRONT MAN 13/7/1961
d Peter Curran; sc Stanley Miller
lp Peter Dyneley; Bandana Dar Gupta;
John Serret
MAN ALONE 19/7/1961
Originally scheduled for 29/6/1961.
d Max Varnel; sc Brian Clemens
lp William Ingram; Michael Balfour;
Kenneth Warren; Jack Taylor

A MAN FROM THE SUN (BBC 8/11/1956)
Drama on the problems facing a West Indian
immigrant in London.
p/sc John Elliot

MAN IN A SUITCASE (ITC 1967–68)
Adventure series featuring an ex-CIA agent
turned private investigator.
p Sidney Cole
regular Richard Bradford
SWEET SUE 11/11/1967
d Robert Tronson; sc Philip Broadley
lp Judy Geeson; George A. Cooper;
David Cole; Peter Blythe; Jacqueline Pearce
ESSAY IN EVIL 18/11/1967
d Freddie Francis; sc Kevin Laffan
lp Donald Houston; Peter Vaughan;
John Cairney; Wendy Hall; Maurice Good
DEAD MAN'S SHOES 9/12/1967
d Peter Duffell; sc Edmund Ward
lp Derren Nesbitt; John Carson;
James Villiers; Jayne Sofiano; Noel Howlett;
Gerald Sim
BURDEN OF PROOF 6/1/1968
d Peter Duffell; sc Edmund Ward
lp John Gregson; Nicola Pagett;
Wolfe Morris; Roger Delgado;
Charles Lloyd Pack
BLIND SPOT 10/2/1968
d Jeremy Summers; sc Victor Canning
lp Marius Goring; Felicity Kendal;
Derek Newark; William Dexter; Inigo Jackson;
Michael Bates
NO FRIEND OF MINE 17/2/1968
d Charles Crichton; sc John Stanton
lp Clive Morton; Errol John;
Allan Cuthbertson; Ralph Michael;
Philippa Gail
The REVOLUTIONARIES 16/3/1968
d Peter Duffell; sc Jan Read
lp Hugh Burden; Ferdy Mayne; Sonia Fox;
David Sumner; Barry Shawzin; Bruce Boa
WHO'S MAD NOW? 23/3/1968
d Freddie Francis; sc Roger Parkes
lp Robert Hutton; Audine Leith;
Philip Madoc; John Harvey; Harriett Johns
The JIGSAW MAN 20/4/1968
d Charles Frend;
sc Reed De Rouen, Stanley R. Greenberg
lp Paul Bertoya; Mike Sarne;
Maurice Kauffman; John Bluthal; John Collin;
Bridget Armstrong; Nike Arrighi

MAN IN SOCIETY (BBC 15/1–5/3/1970)
An introduction to the social sciences.
SEEING IS BELIEVING? 15/1/1970
Can we really believe what we see? Two very
different views of the same incident.
d June Steel; p Howard Smith;
intro Derek Hart

MAN IN SPACE (BBC 13/4/1961)
Moscow welcomes Yuri Gagarin after his space
flight.

MAN IN THE NEWS (LWT 1970–71)
Interview series.
BRIAN YOUNG 19/4/1970
Interview with Brian Young, chairman designate
of the Independent Television Authority.
d Bimbi Harris; p Geoffrey Hughes;
interv Alastair Burnet

LORD LONGFORD 30/5/1971
Lord Longford answers questions from a panel
of journalists about his anti-pornography
campaign.
p Geoffrey Hughes; interv Robert Kee
WILLIAM WHITELAW 6/6/1971
William Whitelaw answers questions from a
panel of journalists.
p Geoffrey Hughes; interv Robert Kee
STEPHEN MURPHY
Film censor Stephen Murphy answers questions
from a panel of journalists.
p Geoffrey Hughes; interv Robert Kee
RICHARD NEVILLE 15/8/1971
Richard Neville answers questions from
journalists about the 'Oz' trial and verdict.
p Geoffrey Hughes; interv Alastair Burnet
BRIAN FAULKNER 12/9/1971
Alastair Burnett interviews the Prime Minister of
Northern Ireland, Brian Faulkner.
p Geoffrey Hughes

A MAN OF HIS TIME – GORONWY REES
(HTV 5/9/1978)
The wartime career of Goronwy Rees, and an
account of his friendship with Guy Burgess,
Donald MacLean and Kim Philby.
d/p Jolyon Wimhurst; sc/nar John Morgan

MAN OF NINE MILLION PARTS
(BBC 2/9/1967)
Kenneth Harris interviews George Woodcock,
General Secretary of the Trades Union
Congress, on the eve of the 99th conference in
Brighton.
p Stanley Hyland

MAN OF STRAW (BBC 30/1–5/3/1972)
Six-part adaptation of the Heinrich Mann novel,
set in late nineteenth-century Germany.
UPHOLDERS OF MORALITY 13/2/1972
d Herbert Wise; p Martin Lisemore;
sc Robert Muller
lp Derek Jacobi; Judy Cornwell;
Arnold Peters; Karin MacCarthy;
Elizabeth Bell; Sheila Brennan

MAN OF THE MONTH (ATV 1968–69)
Interview series.
BRIGADIER A.A. AFRIFA 24/6/1969
A portrait of Akwasi Afrifa, chairman of
Ghana's National Liberation Council.
d/p Robin Brown
The LORD MAYOR OF LONDON 25/11/1969
The work involved in being Lord Mayor of
London; with Sir Charles Trinder and Sir Ian
Bowater.
d/p Robin Brown

MAN OF THE SOUTH (Southern TV)
PROFESSOR WAIN 24/4/1972
An interview with the chemist, Professor Ralph
Wain.

MAN OF THE YEAR – NORMAN BORLAUG
(ATV 31/12/1968)
The story of Dr Borlaug, American geneticist,
and his work with grain in Mexico and India.
d/p Robin Brown

The MAN WHO STARTED THE WAR
(BBC 11/11/1965)
Alfred Naujocks, a major of the Nazi Secret
Service, who claims to have faked the broadcast
from a Polish radio station that started the war,
and that he was behind the forged £5 notes
which were intended to ruin the British
economy.
d Bob Symes; p Jeremy James;
sc Gordon Thomas

The MAN WHO TALKS TO CHILDREN
(BBC 12/10/1969)
Harold Williamson is seen in conversation with
children. He explains why he thinks children like
to talk to him.
d Simon Wadleigh; rep Harold Williamson

The MAN WHO WANTED TO LIVE FOREVER (CA Palomar Pictures; US *tx* 15/12/1970)
Made-for-TV thriller about sinister heart transplants at a private research foundation. The above title is the American transmission title; theatrically released under the title 'The Only Way Out is Dead'.
d John Trent; *p* Terence Dene;
sc Henry Denker;
lp Stuart Whitman; Sandy Dennis;
Burl Ives; Tom Harvey; Robert Goodier;
Jack Creley

The MANAGERS (BBC 2–30/10/1966)
Series of five films looking at management.
WHAT DOES A MANAGER DO? 2/10/1966
The jobs of three managers explored in terms of their roles, functions, and problems.
d Michael Blakstad; *p* Gregory Clegg;
intro Christopher Tugendhat;
comm Anthony West, Andrew Life
The USE OF TIME 9/10/1966
An examination of the ways in which managers can make more efficient use of their time.
d Michael Blakstad; *p* Gregory Clegg;
intro Christopher Tugendhat;
comm Jim Horne, David Veall
COMPANY OBJECTIVES 23/10/1966
Asks what managers are in business and discusses the objectives which determine the future of a company.
d Michael Blakstad; *p* Gregory Clegg;
intro Christopher Tugendhat;
comm Sir Joseph Hunt, John Brodrick

MANCHESTER CITY v BOLTON WANDERERS (Granada 17/11/1979)

MANCHESTER CITY v EVERTON (Granada 25/2/1978)

MANCHESTER CITY v NORWICH (Granada 8/9/1973)

MANCHESTER CITY v SOUTHAMPTON (Granada 9/12/1978)

MANCHESTER CITY v SPURS (Granada 7/5/1977)

MANCHESTER CITY v WOLVES (Granada 1/12/1979)

MANHUNT (LWT 2/1–26/6/1970)
Wartime adventure series set in occupied France of 1942.
The DEATH WISH 8/5/1970
d Robert Tronson; *p* Andrew Brown;
sc Arden Winch
lp Peter Barkworth; James Maxwell;
Philip Madoc
LITTLE MAN, WHAT NEXT: PART 1 12/6/1970
d Bill Bain; *p* Andrew Brown;
sc Vincent Tilsley
lp Robert Hardy; Philip Madoc;
Jack Watson; Jane Jordan Rogers

MARC (Granada 1977)
Popular music programme hosted by Marc Bolan.
DAVID BOWIE, THE RODS, GENERATION X, LIP SERVICE 28/9/1977
Marc Bolan and T Rex with guests David Bowie, The Rods, Generation X and Lip Service, and dance group Heart-Throb.
d Nicholas Ferguson; *p* Muriel Young

MARCH OF THE MOVIES (BBC 4/8/1960)
Comedy programme featuring Charlie Drake.
d Sydney Lotterby; *p* G.B. Lupino;
sc Charlie Drake, David Cumming,
Derek Collyer
lp John Fitzgerald; Audrey Nicholson;
Michael Henry; Frank Hawkins;
Robert Mackenzie; Michael Balfour

MARCH OF TIME TELEVISION
(US Time Inc 1951–53)
Early current affairs programme; a successor to the newsfilm 'March Of Time'.

AMERICA'S ARMY – MARCH OF TIME THROUGH THE YEARS 1952
'America's Army 1942'. A March of Time report from 1942 with John Daly. General Omah Bradley discusses the film with reference to the army in 1951 and the Korean War.
rep John Daley
The STATE OF THE NATION 1/10/1952
Autumn and what it means to Americans. Consideration of the race for the presidency between Dwight Eisenhower and Adlai Stevenson.
GERMANY 8/10/1952
Life in West Germany; the post-war reconstruction, relations with the East, and East German refugees.
A NATION DECIDES 15/10/1952
The United States presidential election of 1952. Dr George Gallup, the American pollster, talks to camera. The battle between Adlai Stevenson and Dwight Eisenhower is discussed, as is how various groups in the States are likely to vote. Also includes a look at foreign policy.
CANADIAN BOOM 29/10/1952
Canada and its post-war development in politics and economics.
VIENNA TODAY 19/11/1952
Life in Vienna under the Four-Power Commission; examines the political, military, social and cultural aspects.
The MIDDLE EAST: POWDERKEG ON THE RIM OF THE COMMUNIST WORLD 10/12/1952
Events and trends in Egypt, Iran, Kuwait and Israel.
NEW INDIA'S PEOPLE 31/12/1952
A portrait of contemporary Indian society.
TEXAS! – MARCH OF TIME THROUGH THE YEARS 1953
A review of Texas using past 'March of Time' newsfilm reports. A review of 1941 is seen prior to discussing Texas now. Discussion of Fort Worth newspaper publisher Amon Carter. Also a 1936 report on the rivalry between Fort Worth and Dallas.
rep John Daley
FORMOSA: BLUEPRINT FOR A FREE CHINA 28/1/1953
Formosa (Taiwan); the activities of Chiang Kai-Shek's government and army.
PROGRESS REPORT ON PAKISTAN 4/2/1953
An interview with the Pakistani Ambassador to Washington, Mohammed Ali, who gives reasons for Pakistan's separation from India, and discusses the Muslim faith which holds the nation together.
pres Westbrook Van Voorhis
A CITY IS BORN – LEVITTOWN PA 11/2/1953
The construction of a new town in Pennsylvania. Interviews with the two brothers responsible for its development.
intro Westbrook Van Voorhis
The NEW CONGRESS 18/2/1953
A look at the 83rd Congress of the United States. Joseph Martin, Speaker of The House of Representatives, speaks about the work of the 83rd Congress in which the Republicans under Eisenhower have a majority of 8 and only a majority of 1 in The Senate.
The GREEN PARADISE OF GOA – PORTUGAL'S OUTPOST IN INDIA 18/3/1953
A trip from London to Bombay by Comet, with a brief look at Goa.
A BASEBALL ROOKIE'S BIG CHANCE 25/3/1953
Jim Lemon, a baseball rookie, in spring training with the Cleveland Indians.
OMAHA – RAIL METROPOLIS ON THE PLAINS 1/4/1953
The influence of the railway on Omaha City.
LAS VEGAS – FRONTIER TOWN OF TWO CENTURIES 15/4/1953
A tour of Las Vegas, including the gambling halls and the atomic test sites.
MALAYA: THE FIGHT AGAINST AN UNSEEN ENEMY 6/5/1953
Life in Malaya during the Emergency.
MAKE WAY FOR THE QUEEN 20/5/1953
Preparations for the coronation of Queen Elizabeth II, concentrating on the role of the Earl Marshal the Duke of Norfolk and David Eccles, Minister of Works.

AMERICA'S NEW No. 1 SPORT 18/6/1953
Horse racing in the United States and Canada. Behind the scenes at the Greentree racing stables, with owner Mr Whitney and trainer Mr Gaber.

MARIE CURIE (BBC 1977)
Five-part serial on the life and work of the Nobel Prize-winning discoverer of radium.
d John Glenister; *p* Peter Goodchild;
sc Elaine Morgan
regulars Jane Lapotaire; Nigel Hawthorne
PART 1 16/8/1977
lp Marion Mathie; Natasha Lewer;
Adrienne Byrne; Jack Lynn; James Cornmell;
Robin Halstead
PART 2 23/8/1977
lp James Berwick; Maurice Denham;
Martin Howells; Penelope Lee; Daphne Heard;
Geoffrey Edwards
PART 3 30/8/1977
lp James Berwick; Maurice Denham;
Richard Bebb; Michael Poole; Hugh Dickson;
Sally Home
PART 4 6/9/1977
lp James Berwick; Maurice Denham;
Richard Bebb; Peter Birrel; Hugh Dickson;
Nigel Lambert
PART 5 13/9/1977
lp Hugh Dickson; Clive Graham;
Peter Birrel; Sally Home

MARK SABER (Danzigers 1957–59)
Detective drama series. Followed by SABER OF LONDON (1959–61).
p Edward J. Danziger, Harry Lee Danziger
regulars Donald Gray; Diana Decker;
Patrick Holt; Colin Tapley; Michael Balfour
FILE IT UNDER MURDER 20/6/1957
d Ernest Morris; *sc* Ken Field
lp Hal Osmond; Ronald Leigh-Hunt;
Catherine Finn
IF THIS BE MURDER 27/6/1957
d Ernest Morris; *sc* Ken Field
lp Michael Brill; Basil Dignam;
Eric Pohlmann
SING SOFTLY, SISTER 4/7/1957
d Ernest Morris; *sc* Ken Field
lp Sandra Dorne; Ferdy Mayne;
Nicholas Stuart
RECEIPT FOR MURDER 11/7/1957
d Kieron Moore; *sc* Gilbert Winfield
lp Bill Fraser; Jennifer Jayne;
Denis Shaw; Derek Prentice
AGAINST THE ROPES 18/7/1957
sc Gilbert Winfield
SAFE FOR MURDER 25/7/1957
d Charles Eldridge; *sc* Brian Clemens
lp John Martin Harvey; Catherine Finn;
Michael Ripper; Geoffrey Denton
HOLIDAY FOR HEATHERTON 1/8/1957
d Ernest Morris; *sc* Ken Field
lp John Stuart; June Clyde;
Philip Saville; Frank Sieman
KILL ME, MY LOVE 18/9/1957
d Kieron Moore; *sc* Ken Field
lp Philip Saville; Mary Parker;
Janet Radcliffe Richards
CORPSE IN THE CELLAR 25/9/1957
d Charles Eldridge; *sc* Brian Clemens
lp June Powell; Noel Dyson; Jack Melford
CAGE OF FEAR 2/10/1957
d Ernest Morris; *sc* Brian Clemens
lp Bernard Bresslaw
HATFUL OF TROUBLE 16/10/1957
sc Carol Warner Gluck
RETURN TO DANGER 23/10/1957
d Ernest Morris; *sc* Brian Clemens
lp Denis Quilley; Frank Hawkins;
John Longden; Noel Dyson
The CORPSE WITH A SWORD 20/11/1957
d Charles Eldridge; *sc* Brian Clemens
lp Peter Bathurst; Frank Henderson;
John Barron; Anne Valery
ROOT OF EVIL 18/12/1957
d Ernest Morris; *sc* Brian Clemens
lp John Longden; Jean Aubrey;
Hal Osmond; Tony Quinn
SIGNATURE FOR MURDER 3/1/1958
d Charles Eldridge; *sc* Gilbert Winfield
lp Martine Alexis; John Stone;
Alastair Hunter

DIAMOND JUBILEE 7/2/1958
d Kieron Moore
lp Robert Ayres; John Loder;
Olive Sloane
BLOOD IN THE SKY 6/5/1958
d Ernest Morris; *sc* Brian Clemens
lp Patrick McGoohan; Teresa Thorne;
John Stuart; Kay Callard
COLLECTOR'S ITEM 3/6/1958
d Ernest Morris; *sc* Ken Taylor
lp Teresa Thorne; Frank Hawkins;
Gladys Boot; Jan Holden
DEADLINE FOR MURDER 10/6/1958
d Ernest Morris
lp Sandra Dorne; Teresa Thorne;
Pat Halpin; John Stuart
DEATH NEEDS NO CANE 22/8/1958
d Splinters Deason; *sc* Gilbert Winfield
lp Teresa Thorne; Sandra Dorne
DIAMOND CUT DIAMOND 29/8/1958
d Ernest Morris; *sc* Brian Clemens
lp Teresa Thorne; Trevor Reid;
Eric Pohlmann; Sandra Dorne
FIND A BODY 5/9/1958
d Ernest Morris; *sc* John Roeburt
lp Teresa Thorne; Basil Dignam;
Catherine Finn
FRAME UP WITHOUT GLOVES 12/9/1958
d Ernest Morris
lp Teresa Thorne; Lee Patterson;
Brenda Hogan
HEAR NO EVIL 9/1/1959
d Ernest Morris; *sc* Gwen Davis
lp Nanette Newman; Teresa Thorne;
John Stone; Catherine Finn
KILLER ON THE PROWL 16/1/1959
d Splinters Deason; *sc* Brian Clemens
lp Teresa Thorne; Sandra Dorne; Hal Ayer
A LADY IS MISSING 23/1/1959
d Ernest Morris; *sc* Brian Clemens
lp Teresa Thorne; Robert Ayres;
Trevor Reid
The LONG WAIT 6/2/1959
d Ernest Morris; *sc* Brian Clemens
lp Teresa Thorne; Gary Thorne;
Katherine Page
NO REPLY FROM ROOM 17 20/2/1959
d Ernest Morris;
sc James Eastwood, Kate Barley
lp Teresa Thorne; Frank Hawkins;
Hugh Latimer; Leo Bieber
The SALLY ANKENS STORY 27/2/1959
d Ernest Morris; *sc* Gwen Davis
lp Teresa Thorne; Jill Clifford;
John Stuart; Marne Maitland; Ferdy Mayne;
Peter Arne
The TALL DARK MAN 19/10/1959
d Ernest Morris;
sc James Eastwood, Kate Barley
lp Teresa Thorne; Kay Callard;
Jennifer Jayne; Ann Lancaster; Robert Ayres
WALK SOFTLY FOR MURDER 2/11/1959
d Ernest Morris; *sc* Gwen Davis
lp Frank Hawkins; Teresa Thorne;
Lucie Mannheim; Alan Gifford; Nicholas Stuart

MARK TWAIN'S AMERICA
(US NBC 8/8/1960)
A reconstruction of nineteenth-century America.
p Donald B. Hyatt; *sc* Richard Hanser;
comm Howard Lindsay

MARKHEIM (Scottish TV 24/12/1974)
Adaptation of the Robert Louis Stevenson story.
d Tina Wakerell; *exec.p* Liam Hood;
sc Tom Wright
lp Derek Jacobi; Julian Glover;
Paul Curran; Sally Kinghorn

MARRIAGE GUIDANCE (Thames 17/5/1977)
Three couples seek help from the Marriage
Guidance Council.
d Nicholas Broomfield, Joan Churchill;
p Udi Eichler

The MARRIAGE OF FIGARO
(Southern TV 21/5/1974)
A recording of Peter Hall's 1973 production of
the opera from the Glyndebourne Festival.
d David Heather;
p Peter Hall, Humphrey Burton
with Kiri Te Kanawa, Frederica von Stade,
Ileana Cotrubas, Benjamin Luxon, Knut Skram,
Marius Rintzler, Nucci Condo

MARRIAGE TODAY (BBC 9/9–14/10/1964)
Six-part series on the problems of marriage.
An EXCELLENT MYSTERY 14/10/1964
Views on marriage, from Sir Lewis Casson, Sybil
Thorndike, Rev. Glen Cavaliero, Richard Fox,
A. Ronald Bielby, Margaret Paxon, O.R.
McGregor, Dr Eustace Chesser and Margaret
Mead.
p Lorna Pegram; *intro* Alan Little

MARTY ABROAD (BBC 1/1/1971)
Comedy show featuring the talents of Marty
Feldman.
p Gordon Flemyng;
sc Johnnie Mortimer, Brian Cooke;
with John Junkin, Mary Miller,
Jenny Till, Michael Elwyn, Jon Laurimore,
Caroline Moody, Jim Tyson, Dorian Healy

The MASKED DANCE (ATV 11/5/1976)
Kukrit Pramoj, former Prime Minister of
Thailand, surveys his time in office and his
political struggle with his brother Seni Pramoj.
d Adrian Cowell

The MASQUE OF KINGS (BBC 19/6/1955)
Play set in the Austro-Hungarian Empire of
Emperor Franz Joseph.
p Royston Morley; *auth* Maxwell Anderson
lp Basil Sydney; Jane Barrett;
Frank Windsor; Joan Heath

The MASTER BUILDERS (Grampian 1979)
EDDYSTONE 21/6/1979

MASTER SHEPHERD (Tyne Tees 6/11/1978)
The work of champion shepherd Ray Dent on
his Pennine hill farm.
d James Goldby; *p* David Thomasson

MASTERWORKS (BBC 12/1–14/12/1966)
Music performance series.
FIVE QUINTETS: MOZART'S QUINTET IN G
MINOR 1/6/1966
Mozart's Quintet in G minor played by The
Amadeus String Quartet and Cecil Aronowitz.
d Barrie Gavin
FIVE QUINTETS: SCHUBERT'S 'TROUT'
QUINTET 15/6/1966
Daniel Barenboim and The Melos Ensemble
with Emanuel Hurwitz on violin, Cecil
Aronowitz on viola, Terence Weil on cello and
Adrian Beers on double-bass, playing Schubert's
Quintet in A major.
d Barrie Gavin

MATCH OF THE DAY (BBC 1964–)
Series covering major English football matches.
FA CUP SEMI-FINAL: WEST BROMWICH ALBION
v. LEICESTER CITY 22/3/1969
Highlights of the match played at Hillsborough.
pres David Coleman;
comm Kenneth Wolstenholme
LEEDS v. WOLVES 7/4/1973
pres/comm David Coleman

MATHEMATICS '64 (BBC 1964)
Educational series of twenty programmes – new
trends in maths and the teaching of maths.
TRELLISWORK 7/7/1964
Vectors.
p David Roseveare; *pres* Geoffrey Matthews
LOOKING AHEAD 28/7/1964
Calculating machines.
p David Roseveare; *p* Alan Tammadge

MATHS TODAY: 1ST YEAR (BBC 1967)
Schools programme. Mathematics for secondary
school pupils.

LOOKING FOR PATTERNS 29/3/1967
p John Cain; *intro* David Sturgess
WHICH CLASS? 19/10/1967
p John Cain, Peter Weiss;
intro David Sturgess

A MATTER OF EXPRESSION
(Scottish TV 1/4/1968)
Mime, dance and jazz.
p Bryan Izzard

A MATTER OF LIFE
(Yorkshire TV 30/3–13/4/1976)
Three-part medical documentary series.
BOY IN THE BUBBLE 6/4/1976
Report on a small boy who has no resistance to
disease. Discusses the medical treatment he
receives and reviews the treatment of similar
problems in other countries.
d David Green;
p Kevin Sim, Simon Welfare

MAUPASSANT: WOMEN AND MONEY
(Granada 18/7/1963)
Drama anthology based on three stories by Guy
de Maupassant; A Sale, adapted by Doris
Lessing; A Family Business, adapted by Hugh
Leonard; and The Devil, adapted by Stanley
Miller.
d Gordon Flemyng; *p* Philip Mackie
lp Milo O'Shea; Bryan Pringle;
Barbara Hicks; Keith Marsh; Clare Kelly;
Margaret Boyd; Jack Smethurst;
Beaufoy Milton; Kathleen Bouthall;
Henry Oscar; Alan McClelland

MAVIS...WANTING TO KNOW
(Thames 1978–79)
Interview and discussion series.
BOB GELDOF 12/6/1979
Mavis Nicholson interviews Bob Geldof, lead
singer of the 'new wave' pop group The
Boomtown Rats.
d John Woods

**MAY DAY PARADES AND
DEMONSTRATIONS** (BBC 1/5/1961)
May Day in Moscow; the first direct transmission
via Eurovision.

ME MAMMY (BBC 1969–71)
Comedy series about an Irish family living in
London.
The SACRED CHEMISE OF MISS ARGYLL
21/5/1971
p Sydney Lotterby; *sc* Hugh Leonard
lp Milo O'Shea; Anna Manahan;
Yootha Joyce; Ray McAnally; David Kelly;
J.G. Devlin

MEANWHILE BACK IN SUNDERLAND
(Tyne Tees 5/5/1973)
Records the day on which Sunderland beat
Leeds United in the F.A. Cup Final.
d Ken Stephinson; *exec.p* Leslie Barrett

MEDICINE TODAY (BBC 1965–71)
Monthly series about medical trends.
ILEOSTOMY 17/5/1966
Ileostomy Association spokesmen, Charles
Fletcher, Tom Sturgeon and Bryan Brooke
demonstrate ileostomy appliances and describe
ileostomy surgery and its effects.
d Mary Hoskins; *p* James McCloy
HYPERTENSION AND CORONARY
THROMBOSIS 27/12/1966
d Mary Hoskins; *p* James McCloy
OSTEOPOROSIS 25/4/1967
Defines and discusses osteoporosis with the aid
of x-rays and patient demonstrations. A final
discussion deals with methods of treatment and
possible causes of the condition.
d Peter Riding; *p* James McCloy
RESUSCITATION OF THE NEWBORN 23/4/1968
Drs David Hull, Herbert Barrie and Glyn
Griffiths discuss the problems and procedures of
resuscitation of newborn babies.
d Mary Hoskins; *p* James McCloy

MEET ANDRE PREVIN (LWT 21/3/1969)
An interview with André Previn. He is seen conducting the London Symphony Orchestra and accompanying saxophonist Tubby Hayes on the piano.
d Helen Standage; *p/nar* Humphrey Burton

MEET GEORGE AND ALFRED BLACK
(Tyne Tees 15/1/1959)
Producers George and Alfred Black give a preview of future shows on Tyne Tees Television.

MEET McGRAW
(US M.M. Incorporated 1957–58)
Private detective series.
BARNABY 1957
d Tom Gries;
p Don W. Sharpe, Warren Lewis;
sc E. Jack Neuman, William Koenig
lp Frank Lovejoy; Barton MacLane;
Denver Pyle; Susan Oliver; Douglas Dick;
Dabbs Greer; Dick Rich

MEET THE PEOPLE (Granada 3/5/1956)
Programme from Granada's opening night transmission.

MEET THE PROFESSOR (ATV)
RADIO ISOTOPES 1956
The use of radio-active iodine in the location and treatment of cancer is seen with a patient suffering from a rare form of thyroid cancer.
d Quentin Lawrence

MEET THE QUARE FELLOW
(IE Emmet Dalton Productions 29/11/1960)
Brendan Behan talks about himself, his plays, the Irish, and Dylan Thomas.

MEETING POINT (BBC 1956–68)
Religious series.
The ARCHBISHOP AND THE POPE 27/3/1966
Interview with Dr Michael Ramsey, Archbishop of Canterbury is followed by a recording of the service held at St. Peter's Basilica, Rome, (24/3/66) after the first formal visit of an Archbishop of Canterbury to the Pope in Rome.
comm Tom Fleming
TWO OF A KIND 3/9/1967
Report about two young people who spent a year as community service volunteers; Sophie Cowan worked in an approved school, and Malcolm Stone taught English to immigrant boys.
p Peter Ferres
HOLES IN THE NET? 4/2/1968
Paddy Feeney investigates an unusual voluntary caring scheme.
p Philip Turner

MEETINGS IN BRITAIN
(SU Central Television Studio, Moscow 30/1/1958)
A report on Britain from the correspondents of Moscow television.

MEN AGAINST CANCER
(Rediffusion 26/9/1967)
Ludovic Kennedy reports on the present state of cancer research in Britain.
d Jeremy Murray-Brown; *p* David Windlesham

MEN AGAINST THE MATTERHORN
(BBC 14/7/1965)
A climb to mark the centenary of the first ascent of the Matterhorn by Edward Whymper. British and Swiss mountaineers climb the original route and in addition attempt the North Face.
p Alan Chivers, Walther Pluess;
pres David Dimbleby

The MEN IN BLACK (Rediffusion 27/4/1966)
An examination of Irish priests in the Catholic Church.
d Geoffrey Hughes; *p* Richard De La Mare;
sc Peter Duval Smith

MEN IN THE MIDDLE
(Southern TV 1/11/1977)
A report on the para-military duties of the police force.
d/p Mike Finlason; *nar* Michael Gray

MEN OF IDEAS (BBC 19/1–27/4/1978)
Series of fifteen programmes in which Bryan Magee talks to philosophers.
exec.p Janet Hoenig
An INTRODUCTION TO PHILOSOPHY 19/1/1978
An interview with Sir Isaiah Berlin.
d Tony Tyley
MARCUSE AND THE FRANKFURT SCHOOL 2/2/1978
An interview with Herbert Marcuse.
d Martin L. Bell
The TWO PHILOSOPHIES OF WITTGENSTEIN 16/2/1978
The influence of the philosophies of Ludwig Wittgenstein.
d Tony Tyley

MEN OF OUR TIME (Granada 1963–64)
Documentary series which analyses historical figures of the twentieth century.
RAMSAY MACDONALD 12/6/1963
A compilation on the career of Ramsay MacDonald.
p Patricia Lagone; *pres/sc* Malcolm Muggeridge
MUSSOLINI 19/6/1963
A.J.P. Taylor presents an analysis of Benito Mussolini.
d Patricia Lagone
GANDHI 26/6/1963
Compilation of newsreel film of Gandhi's life; included are filmed interviews with Mahatma Gandhi and some of his contemporaries.
p Patricia Lagone; *sc/nar* James Cameron
STANLEY BALDWIN 27/5/1964
Malcolm Muggeridge gives his personal view of Stanley Baldwin.
p Patricia Lagone

The MEN WHO MADE THE MOVIES
(US WNET Productions 1973; GB *tx* 1975–77)
Documentary series on Hollywood film-makers.
d/p/sc Richard Schickel; *nar* Cliff Robertson
ALFRED HITCHCOCK 1973
Extensive interview footage with Alfred Hitchcock, including extracts from some of his films
RAOUL WALSH 1973
Programme on the work of director Raoul Walsh, with excerpts from some of his films.
VINCENTE MINNELLI 1973
Extensive interview footage with Vincente Minnelli.
HOWARD HAWKS 20/9/1975
Howard Hawks reminisces about some of his most famous films.
WILLIAM WELLMAN 25/10/1975
An interview with William Wellman, who discusses his work.
FRANK CAPRA 29/11/75
Frank Capra reminisces about his career, from early beginnings as a gag-writer for Mack Sennett to his Oscar-winning days with Columbia.
GEORGE CUKOR 17/4/1976
Extensive footage of an interview with George Cukor, with excerpts from some of his films.
KING VIDOR 6/1/1977
Extended interview footage with King Vidor, who talks about his films. Extracts from 'The Big Parade', 'The Crowd', and 'Show People' are included.

MERRY-GO-ROUND (BBC 1963–83)
Educational compendium series/slot for school children aged 7–9.
WHERE WE LIVE: LEICESTER 3/5/1971
With children from the Catherine Junior School, Belper St.
p John Chapple

The MERRY WIVES OF WINDSOR (ACT II)
(BBC 2/10/1955)
Live broadcast from the Stratford Memorial Theatre.
p Glen Byam Shaw
lp Michael Denison; Patrick Wymark;
John Southworth; Edward Atienza;
Geoffrey Bayldon; Ralph Michael;
Angela Baddeley; Keith Michell;
Anthony Quayle

The MERSEY PIRATE (Granada 1979)
Saturday morning programme for children.
The MERSEY PIRATE 14/7/1979
d Stuart Orme;
p Stephen Leahy, Sandy Ross;
with Duggie Brown, Billy Butler,
Frank Carson, Ray Teret, Bernard Wrigley

The MERSEY SOUND (BBC 9/10/1963)
The boom in popular music with The Beatles and Group One and The Undertakers.
d/p Don Haworth; *nar* Michael Barton;
with Bill Harry, Jim Casey, Brian Epstein

The MESSENGERS (Granada 1979)
Programmes for schools.
MODERN ESKIMOS 30/4/1979
Interview with Michael Grigsby, director of ESKIMOS OF POND INLET, DISAPPEARING WORLD series
(*tx* 12/1/1976).
WORLD AT WAR: DAVID ELSTEIN 21/5/1979
Interview with David Elstein, producer-writer on The WORLD AT WAR series (1973–74).
PENNINE PEOPLE 18/6/1979
Interview with Barry Cockcroft, director of Yorkshire Television documentaries CHILDREN OF ESKDALE (1973) and TOO LONG A WINTER (1973).
KATARAGAMA IS A GOD 25/6/1979
Interview with Charlie Nairn, director of KATARAGAMA, DISAPPEARING WORLD series, (*tx* 20/11/1973).

METRO-LAND (BBC 26/2/1973)
Sir John Betjeman looks at the history of the Metropolitan railway from London to Amersham.
p Edward Mirzoeff

MICKEY DUFF: MATCHMAKER
(Thames 28/2/1979)
A month in the life of boxing promoter Mickey Duff.
d/p Tim King

MIDDLE SCHOOL MATHEMATICS
(BBC 1963–65)
Series intended for children aged 13–14.
p Donald Grattan; *pres* David Tahta
BINARY NUMBERS 16/9/1963
TWO STATE SYSTEMS 23/9/1963
A PATTERN OF NUMBERS 30/9/1963
NUMBERS FROM SHAPE 14/10/1963
PATTERN AND GROWTH 12/10/1964
p John Cain

**MIDDLE SCHOOL MATHEMATICS:
FUNCTION** (BBC 1964–65)
Series intended for children aged 13–14.
p John Cain; *intro* Maurice Meredith
DEPENDENCE 27/4/1964
The ways in which two variable quantities can be related.
INEQUALITY 4/5/1964
RESTRICTED AREAS 11/5/1964
The navigation of a vessel on a river is shown graphically in terms of inequalities.

**MIDDLE SCHOOL MATHEMATICS:
PERIODICITY AND LOCI** (BBC 1964)
Educational series intended for children aged 13–14.
p John Cain; *intro* Alan Tammadge
PERIODICITY 1 1/6/1964
PERIODICITY 2 8/6/1964
LOCI 1 15/6/1964
LOCI 2 22/6/1964

MIDDLE SCHOOL MATHEMATICS: STATISTICS (BBC 1964)
Educational series for children aged 13–14. Illustrations of aspects of statistics and an introduction to the understanding of probability and statistical inference.
p John Cain; *intro* Stewart Gartside
FREQUENCY AND THE HISTOGRAM 13/1/1964
AVERAGE AND SPREAD 20/1/1964
SAMPLING 27/1/1964
CORRELATION 10/2/1964

MIDNIGHT IS A PLACE
(Southern TV 12/10/1977–4/1/1978)
Drama series for children set in the mid-nineteenth century.
d/p Chris McMaster; *adapt* Roy Russell;
auth Joan Aiken
EPISODE 1 12/10/1977
lp David Collings; Simon Gipps-Kent; Peggy Aitchison; Erik Chitty; William Squire; Ian Ireland

A MIDSUMMER NIGHT'S DREAM
(Rediffusion 24/6/1964)
d Joan Kemp-Welch
lp Jill Bennett; Maureen Beck; Benny Hill; Patrick Allen; Cyril Luckham; John Fraser; Anna Massey; Peter Wyngarde; Tony Tanner; Alfie Bass; Bernard Bresslaw; Miles Malleson

MIDWEEK (BBC 1972–74)
Current affairs series.
RT. HON. JAMES CALLAGHAN M.P. 4/6/1974
Michael Cockerell interviews James Callaghan about Britain's re-negotiation of her terms of entry into the EEC.
KISSINGER PRESS CONFERENCE 11/6/1974
Henry Kissinger at a press conference in Salzburg, at which he threatens to resign if rumours of his involvement in the Watergate affair persist.
CHRISTOPHER MAYHEW 10/7/1974
Christopher Mayhew discusses his switch from the Labour to the Liberal party. With Robin Day, Brian Walden, and Lord Davies of Leek.
SIR KEITH JOSEPH 22/10/1974
Sir Keith Joseph is interviewed about his speech on declining moral standards.

MIGHTY AND MYSTICAL
(Granada 23/1–13/2/1961)
Four-part documentary series on India.
d Clive Donner; *p* Tim Hewat;
sc Dom Moraes
The CITY 23/1/1961
The daily life of a jute mill worker in Calcutta.
A LITTLE LEARNING 30/1/1961
Dom Moraes, an Indian poet, investigates the problems of education in India.

The MIGHTY CONTINENT
(BBC 12/11/1974–18/2/1975)
Thirteen-part series in which historian John Terraine presents his view of the evolution of Europe during the twentieth century.
FORM, RIFLEMEN, FORM! 14/1/1975
Totalitarianism in Europe.
sc John Terraine; *intro* Peter Ustinov

The MIGHTY MICRO (ATV 29/10–3/12/1979)
Six-part series on microchips and computers.
POLITICAL REVOLUTION 12/11/1979
Social changes caused by the microchip and computers.
d Lawrence Moore

MIKE HAMMER
(US Revue Productions 1957–59)
Syndicated detective series based on the character created by crime writer Mickey Spillane.
The PAPER SHROUD 1958
d Boris Sagal; *sc* Fenton Earnshaw
lp Darren McGavin; Bart Burns; Anthony Caruso; Lisa Montell; George Brenlin; Penny Santon; Jay Lawrence; Eddie Saenz; Jimmy Casino

MILESTONES OR MILLSTONES?
(Ulster TV 1979)
Documentary series on Irish history. Locally transmitted in 1979, ITV transmission in 1980.
p Rory Fitzpatrick
The COMING OF ST. PATRICK 12/6/1979
A discussion about Ireland's national Saint.
NORMANS – INVADERS OR GUESTS? 19/6/1979
The arrival of the Normans in Ireland in 1196.
The FLIGHT OF THE EARLS 26/6/1979
English conquest of Ireland in the seventeenth century. The settlement of Scottish and English in Ireland.
A GRIEVOUS BATTLE 10/7/1979
Battle of the Boyne.
UNITED OR DIVIDED? 17/7/1979
The Act of Union in Ireland in 1800.
CATHOLIC EMANCIPATION 24/7/1979
Daniel O'Connell, the dominant Irish politician in the early nineteenth century, and the passing of the Catholic Emancipation Act freeing Roman Catholics from legal disabilities.
The GREAT FAMINE 31/7/1979
The potato famine of the 1840s.
The FALL OF PARNELL 7/8/1979
Discussion of Irish history with Professor J.C.Beckett and Paul Clark.

MILLENIUM (Border 3/7/1979)
Wynford Vaughan-Thomas looks at how the Isle of Man has developed over the last one thousand years.
d William Cartner; *p* Ken De Vonald

MILLICENT AND ROY
(Rediffusion 5/10/1966)
Variety show starring Millicent Martin and Roy Castle.
d Bill Turner; *p* Buddy Bregman;
sc Ronnie Cass, Alecie Grahame, Barry Cryer, Dick Vosburgh

The MILLION POUND GRAVE (17/8/1965)
The story of the 1939 excavation of the Sutton Hoo ship.
d/p Paul Johnstone; *nar* Nicholas Thomas

MILTON KEYNES – THE MAKING OF A CITY (Anglia 4/12/1975)
The new town of Milton Keynes.

MIND YOUR LANGUAGE (LWT 1977–79)
Sitcom about an English language college course, its teacher and its students.
KILL OR CURE 24/2/1978
p Stuart Allen; *sc* Vince Powell
lp Barry Evans; Zara Nutley; George Camiller; Kevork Malikyan; Françoise Pascal; Robert Lee; Jacki Harding; Albert Moses; Pik-Sen Lim; Dino Shafeek; Ricardo Montez; Jamila Massey

MINDER (Thames 1979–)
Comedy-drama series featuring a shady South London car-dealer and his 'minder'-for-hire.
GUNFIGHT AT THE OK LAUNDERETTE 29/10/1979
d Peter Sasdy;
p Lloyd Shirley, George Taylor;
sc Leon Griffiths
lp Dennis Waterman; George Cole; Dave King; Hilary Mason

The MINERS' STRIKE AND THE AFTERMATH (BBC 28/2/1972)
Alan Watson introduces an all party discussion on the miners' strike.

MINORITIES IN BRITAIN
(BBC 30/5–4/7/1966)
Six-part series surveying minority groups. Shown as part of the 'Outlook' series.
The JEWISH COMMUNITY 30/5/1966
p Michael Bunce; *intro* Stuart Hall;
with Percy Cohen

The MISFIT (ATV 1970–71)
Series in which an old colonial returns to live in 'swinging Britain'.

ON BEING BRITISH 3/3/1970
d James Gatward; *p* Dennis Vance;
sc Roy Clarke
lp Ronald Fraser; Denis Shaw; Jennifer Browne; Simon Ward; Susan Carpenter; Roland Curram; Samantha Birch; Angela Eaton; Windsor Davies

MISLEADING CASES
(BBC 1967–68; 1971)
Comedy series based on the stories of legal absurdities written by A.P. Herbert for 'Punch' magazine.
RIGHT OF WAY 9/10/1968
p John Howard Davies; *sc* Alan Melville
lp Alastair Sim; Roy Dotrice; Avice Landon; Thorley Walters; Paul Whitsun-Jones

MISS WORLD 1971 (BBC 10/11/1971)
Miss World Contest from the Royal Albert Hall, won by 'Miss Brazil'.
p Philip Lewis;
pres Michael Aspel, David Vine

MISSION TO NO-MAN'S LAND
(BBC 13/1/1960)
Yul Brynner reports on a recent visit to European refugee camps.
p Stanley Wright, Anatole Litvak;
sc Stanley Wright

MR. AND MRS. (Border 1969–88)
Game show in which married couples are quizzed on their knowledge of their partner.
p/host Derek Batey
MR. AND MRS. 26/12/1976
MR. AND MRS. 22/9/1977

MISTER LOWRY (Tyne Tees 30/3/1971)
A portrait of the artist L.S. Lowry – his views on death, the savagery of the human race, the comfort of music, and on marriage and children.
d Robert Tyrrell

MR NOAH BEHAVIN' MIGHTY WELL
(BBC 1968)
Bible stories for and by children with mime, puppets and pictures.
MR NOAH HIMSELF 16/6/1968
d Barrie Edgar; *p/sc* Philip Turner
with Tom Coyne, Jean Holden, The Swinging Stewarts

MRS. BROWN AND THE GREAT COMPOSERS (BBC 17/6/1969)
Peter Dorling reports on the case of Rosemary Brown, a South London widow who claims that famous dead composers dictate music to her. Taking part in the programme are Richard Rodney Bennett, Denis Matthews, Hephzibah Menuhin and Dr Malcolm Troup.

MRS GOLDA MEIR (Thames 26/2/1970)
Llew Gardner interviews Golda Meir about the political and military situation in Israel and the prospects for peace in the Middle East.

MRS MARTIN LUTHER KING AT ST. PAUL'S (BBC 16/3/1969)
Mrs Coretta King preaches from the pulpit of St Paul's Cathedral during Evensong.
p Philip Gilbert

MIXED BLESSINGS (LWT 1978–80)
Comedy series focusing on a married couple from different racial backgrounds.
YOU HAVEN'T GOT MUCH HAVE YOU? 17/3/1978
d/p Derrick Goodwin; *sc* Sid Green
lp Muriel Odunton; Christopher Blake; Joan Sanderson; Pauline Delany; Tony Osoba; Sylvia Kay; Carmen Munro; Michael Robbins

The MODEL MILLIONAIRESS
(BBC 7/5/1963)
A profile of Fiona Campbell-Walter and her marriage to Swiss millionaire Heini Thyssen.
p Jack Gold; *rep* Alan Whicker

The MONACO OF PRINCE RAINIER
(BBC *tx* 27/5/1974)
Prince Rainier and Princess Grace talk about
Monaco.
d François Reichenbach

MONGOLIA (Granada 10 & 17/12/1975)
Two-part documentary film about Mongolia.
ON THE EDGE OF THE GOBI 10/12/1975
Life on one of the Gobi's herding collectives.
d/p Brian Moser

MONITOR (BBC 1958–65)
Magazine arts series.
intro Huw Wheldon
LEONIDE MASSINE 14/9/1958
p Peter Newington
A LINE ON SATIRE 21/12/1958
A record of cartoonists Ronald Searle, Osbert
Lancaster and André François.
p Peter Newington
PAUL ROBESON/ FRANK LLOYD WRIGHT
12/4/1959
The Paul Robeson section is an interview about
his interpretation of Othello at Stratford.
p Peter Newington
JEROME ROBBINS 27/9/1959
Peter Brinson interviews Jerome Robbins about
his dance company, and the new approach to
dance he is developing – a synthesis of jazz and
ballet. Erin Martin and John Jones rehearse an
extract from N.Y. Export: Opus Jazz at the
Empire Theatre, Edinburgh, where the
Company performed as part of The Edinburgh
Festival.
d Nancy Thomas; *p* Peter Newington;
nar Robert Prince
MARIE RAMBERT 17/1/1960
Marie Rambert is interviewed by Huw Wheldon.
d Ken Russell; *p* Huw Wheldon
PROFILE OF A QUARTET 27/3/1960
The life and work of The Allegri Quartet.
d Humphrey Burton; *p* Peter Newington
The MINERS' PICNIC 3/7/1960
A brass band carnival and the colliery band
contest at Bedlington, Northumberland.
d Ken Russell
The LIGHT FANTASTIC 18/12/1960
The variety of dance forms which thrive in the
UK including, jive, ballroom, folk dancing and
flamenco.
d Ken Russell; *p* Humphrey Burton;
sc Ron Hitchins
KATINA PAXINOU 15/1/1961
An interview with the Greek actress Katina
Paxinou, including extracts from 'The Trojan
Women'.
p Humphrey Burton
A HOUSE IN BATTERSEA 4/6/1961
Mrs A. Sterling shows her Pre-Raphaelite
paintings at her home in Battersea.
p Nancy Thomas, Humphrey Burton
PROKOFIEV 18/6/1961
A portrait of Sergei Prokofiev.
d Ken Russell
DAME NINETTE DE VALOIS 22/10/1961
Interview with the Director of the Royal Ballet.
Rehearsals of the BBC production of her ballet,
'The Rake's Progress'.
p Nancy Thomas, Humphrey Burton
ANTONIO GAUDI 3/12/1961
A study of Antonio Gaudi discussing his
architecture, including the Church of the Holy
Family in Barcelona, his sources of inspiration,
and his influence on Picasso.
p Nancy Thomas, Humphrey Burton
PAUL TORTELIER 17/12/1961
The French cellist and conductor Paul Tortelier
is interviewed by John Amis.
p Nancy Thomas
RUDOLF NUREYEV 25/2/1962
POP GOES THE EASEL 25/3/1962
A day with four pop artists: Peter Blake, Derek
Boshier, Pauline Boty, and Peter Phillips.
d Ken Russell
FATHER AND SON 28/10/1962
Jean Renoir talks about Auguste Renoir and
their life at Les Collettes.
p Nancy Thomas

ELGAR 11/11/1962
Drama-documentary about the composer Sir
Edward Elgar.
d Ken Russell;
p Nancy Thomas, David Jones
lp George McGrath; Peter Brett
CHANDRA 25/11/1962
The life and work of Avanish Chandra, Indian
painter based in Golders Green.
WATCH THE BIRDIE 9/6/1963
Professional photographer David Hurn.
d Ken Russell
WALKING TALKING LAUGHING DANCE 29/9/1963
Gillian Lynne, whose dance company was
formed to play at The Edinburgh Festival,
receives offers to appear in the West End.
d Melvyn Bragg; *p* David Jones
MAKING THE BEDMAKERS 2/2/1964
The development of a television play from the
earliest script to the actual transmission; with
Huw Wheldon, David Turner (author), Alan
Bridges (director) and the cast of 'The
Bedmakers' (*tx* 1/2/1964).
d/p David Jones
BELA BARTOK 24/5/1964
d Ken Russell; *p* David Jones
The DOTTY WORLD OF JAMES LLOYD 5/7/1964
The work of painter James Lloyd.
d Ken Russell; *p* Nancy Thomas
JB: A PORTRAIT OF SIR JOHN BARBIROLLI
11/3/1965
A portrait of Barbirolli which assesses his
achievements and shows him at work rehearsing
Manchester's Hallé Orchestra.
d Melvyn Bragg; *interv* Charles Reid
ALWAYS ON SUNDAY 29/6/1965
The dramatised life of Henri Rousseau.
d/p Ken Russell
lp James Lloyd; Bryan Pringle

A MONTH IN THE COUNTRY
(Rediffusion 27/9/1955)
d Robert Hamer;
adapt Alwyne Whatsley, Robert Hamer
auth Ivan Turgenev
lp Michael Gough; Frederick Schiffer;
Susan Richmond; Margaret Leighton;
John Bailey; Laurence Harvey;
Audrey Nicholson; Miles Malleson;
Zena Walker; Geoffrey Keen;
Charles Lloyd Pack

MONTY PYTHON'S FLYING CIRCUS
(BBC 1969–74)
Cult comedy/sketch series.
p John Howard Davies, Ian MacNaughton;
sc Graham Chapman, John Cleese,
Terry Gilliam, Eric Idle, Terry Jones,
Michael Palin, *anim* Terry Gilliam
lp Graham Chapman, John Cleese,
Eric Idle, Terry Jones, Michael Palin,
Terry Gilliam, Carol Cleveland
WHITHER CANADA 5/10/1969
SEX AND VIOLENCE 12/10/1969
HOW TO RECOGNISE DIFFERENT TYPES OF
TREES FROM QUITE A LONG WAY AWAY
19/10/1969
OWL STRETCHING TIME 26/10/1969
MAN'S CRISIS OF IDENTITY IN THE LATTER
HALF OF THE 20TH CENTURY 16/11/1969
ZINC STOAT OF BUDAPEST 23/11/1969
YOU'RE NO FUN ANYMORE 30/11/1969
FULL FRONTAL NUDITY 7/12/1969
The ANT, AN INTRODUCTION 14/12/1969
MONTY PYTHON'S FLYING CIRCUS 21/12/1969
MONTY PYTHON'S FLYING CIRCUS 28/12/1969
MONTY PYTHON'S FLYING CIRCUS 4/1/1970
MONTY PYTHON'S FLYING CIRCUS 11/1/1970
MONTY PYTHON'S FLYING CIRCUS 15/9/1970
MONTY PYTHON'S FLYING CIRCUS 22/9/1970
MONTY PYTHON'S FLYING CIRCUS 29/9/1970
MONTY PYTHON'S FLYING CIRCUS 20/10/1970
MONTY PYTHON'S FLYING CIRCUS 27/10/1970
MONTY PYTHON'S FLYING CIRCUS 3/11/1970
MONTY PYTHON'S FLYING CIRCUS 10/11/1970
MONTY PYTHON'S FLYING CIRCUS 17/11/1970
MONTY PYTHON'S FLYING CIRCUS 24/11/1970
MONTY PYTHON'S FLYING CIRCUS 1/12/1970
MONTY PYTHON'S FLYING CIRCUS 8/12/1970

MONTY PYTHON'S FLYING CIRCUS 16/4/1971
Items from the second series of the comedy
programme, compiled as the BBC's entry for the
Montreux Festival.
MONTY PYTHON'S FLYING CIRCUS 18/1/1973

MOONSTRIKE (BBC 21/2–22/8/1963)
Drama series featuring stories about Special
Operations agents during World War II.
A SUNDAY MORNING 2/5/1963
d David Goddard; *p* Gerard Glaister;
sc Robert Barr
lp David Hemmings; Imogen Hassall

MORE THAN MEETS THE EYE
(BBC 4/12/1968)
Michael Ayrton, Professor E.H. Gombrich and
Dr A.R. Jonckheere describe the techniques
used by artists to recreate perspective,
foreshortening, light and shade and also the
physical and psychological analyses of sight.
d Peter Montagnon

**The MORECAMBE AND WISE CHRISTMAS
SHOW** (BBC 25/12/1971)
Seasonal comedy special featuring Eric
Morecambe and Ernie Wise.
p John Ammonds; *sc* Eddie Braben;
with Shirley Bassey, Glenda Jackson,
Francis Matthews, André Previn, Frank Bough,
Robert Dougall, Dick Emery, Cliff Michelmore,
Patrick Moore, Michael Parkinson,
Eddie Waring

**The MORECAMBE AND WISE CHRISTMAS
SHOW** (BBC 25/12/1973)
Seasonal comedy special featuring Eric
Morecambe and Ernie Wise.
p John Ammonds; *sc* Eddie Braben;
with Vanessa Redgrave, Hannah Gordon,
The New Seekers, John Hanson,
Yehudi Menuhin, Rudolf Nureyev,
Laurence Olivier, André Previn

**The MORECAMBE AND WISE CHRISTMAS
SHOW** (BBC 25/12/1976)
Seasonal comedy special featuring Eric
Morecambe and Ernie Wise.
p Ernest Maxin;
sc Barry Cryer, Lawrie Kinsley
with Elton John, John Thaw,
Dennis Waterman, Kate O'Mara,
Marian Montgomery, The Nolans

The MORECAMBE AND WISE SHOW
(BBC 3/6/1971)
Comedy show with Eric Morecambe and Ernie
Wise. Shown as part of the SHOW OF THE
WEEK series (1965–75).
p John Ammonds; *sc* Eddie Braben;
with Glenda Jackson, Mary Hopkin,
Ronnie Hilton, Ann Hamilton, Janet Webb

The MORECAMBE AND WISE SHOW
(BBC 16/2/1973)
Comedy show featuring Eric Morecambe and
Ernie Wise.
p John Ammonds; *sc* Eddie Braben;
with Anita Harris, Anthony Sharp,
Ann Hamilton, Reg Lye

MORNING IN THE STREETS
(BBC 25/3/1959)
Everyday life of the poor in cities in northern
England. Scenes for the film were shot in
Liverpool, Stockport, Salford and Manchester.
d Denis Mitchell, Roy Harris

The MORT SAHL SHOW (BBC 19/7/1961)
Features American comedian Mort Sahl and
singer Georgia Brown.
d Helen Winston; *p* Billy Cotton Jr;
with The Leo Kharibian Dancers,
John Dankworth

A MOSQUE IN THE PARK
(Thames 5/6/1973)
The lives of four Moslem families of different
income groups living in Britain.
d/comm Yavar Abbas; *p* Ian Martin

The Fosters (LWT). Lawrie Mark, Lenny Henry, Norman Beaton, Sharon Rosita, Isabel Lucas.

Above: *Family at War* (Granada). From left to right (standing), Colin Campbell, Trevor Bowen, Barbara Flynn, John McKelvey, Keith Drinkel, Ian Thompson, (seated) Coral Atkins, Colin Douglas, Shelagh Fraser and Lesley Nunnerley.

Right: *Hancock's Half Hour* 4/3/1960 *The Cold* (BBC).

Left: *Emergency – Ward 10* (ATV). From left to right, Charles Tingwell, Rosemary Miller, Frederick Bartman, Jill Browne and John Paul.

Below: *Rising Damp* (Yorkshire TV). Richard Beckinsale, Leonard Rossiter, Frances De La Tour and Don Warrington.

Coronation Street (Granada). Barbara Knox, Julie Goodyear, Anne Kirkbride, Jean Alexander, Eileen Derbyshire, Doris Speed, Betty Driver and Thelma Barlow.

Dixon of Dock Green (BBC). Jack Warner.

MOTHER TERESA OF CALCUTTA
(Thames 5/12/1969)
Macolm Muggeridge looks at the work of
Mother Teresa and her Sisters of Charity in
Calcutta.
d/p Peter Chafer

MOTOR SHOW '66 (Rediffusion 18/10/1966)
The 1966 Motor Show at Earls Court.
d Jim Pople

MOUNTBATTEN (Rediffusion 1969)
Twelve-part documentary history of the life and
times of Lord Mountbatten. Made with the co-
operation of the Imperial War Museum.
d/p Peter Morley; *sc* John Terraine;
nar Alec Mango
EPISODE 1: THE KING'S SHIPS WERE AT SEA
1900–1917 1/1/1969
EPISODE 2: THE KINGS DEPART 1917–1922
8/1/1969
EPISODE 3: THE AZURE MAIN 1922–1936
15/1/1969
EPISODE 4: THE STORMY WINDS 1936–1941
22/1/1969
EPISODE 5: UNITED WE CONQUER 1941–1943
29/1/1969
EPISODE 6: THE IMPERIAL ENEMY 5/2/1969
EPISODE 7: THE MARCH TO VICTORY MARCH–
SEPTEMBER 1945 12/2/1969
EPISODE 8: THE MEANING OF VICTORY 1945–
1947 19/2/1969
EPISODE 9: THE LAST VICEROY FEBRUARY–
AUGUST 1947 26/2/1969
EPISODE 10: FRESH FIELDS 1947–1955 5/3/1969
EPISODE 11: FULL CIRCLE 1955–1965 12/3/1969
EPISODE 12: A MAN OF THIS CENTURY 1900–
1968 19/3/1969

The MOUNTING MILLIONS
(US National Educational Television 6/9/1967)
India's race between progress and population
growth, between food production and famine.
d David Keith Hardy

MOVIE MAGAZINE (TWW)
INTERVIEW WITH HAROLD LLOYD AT CANNES
1960
p Bruce Lewis
INTERVIEW WITH TONY HANCOCK 1960
p Bruce Lewis

The MOVIES (BBC 2/1–10/7/1967)
Documentary series on the film industry.
The WORLD OF JOSEPH VON STERNBERG
16/1/1967
A portrait of Joseph von Sternberg in which he
talks about his work and demonstrates (at
Isleworth Studios) how he achieved his visual
effects.
d/p Barrie Gavin; *nar* Kevin Brownlow
The DESIGNER 30/1/1967
Roger Hudson visits film set designers Ken
Adam and Richard MacDonald.
d Virginia Kent; *p* Barrie Gavin

MUD AND WATER MAN (BBC 5/2/1974)
Self-portrait by English potter Michael Cardew,
who spent over twenty years working with the
traditional potters of West Africa. He revisits
Ghana and Nigeria and talks about his life and
ideas.
d Alister Hallum

MULTI-COLOURED SWAP SHOP
(BBC 1976–81)
Saturday morning show for children.
MULTI-COLOURED SWAP SHOP 7/10/1978
p Crispin Evans;
pres Keith Chegwin, Noel Edmonds,
John Craven

MULTI-RACIAL BRITAIN (BBC 1978–79)
Documentary series.
RACE AND THE INNER CITY 17/7/1978
Professor John Rex discusses race and the inner
city.
p John Twitchin

ASIANS IN BRITAIN: PROBLEM OR
OPPORTUNITY? 19/7/1978
Dr Bhikhu Parekh, in extracts from a talk given
at Hull University, reviews immigration into
Britain and discusses the contributions the
immigrants can make to British life.
p John Twitchin
SCHOOLS AND RACE 20/7/1978
Alan Little discusses schools as the key to a non-
racist society.
p John Twitchin

The MUPPET SHOW (ATV 1976–81)
Comedy-variety show featuring the Henson
'Muppets', with special guests.
JOEL GREY 24/10/1976
d Peter Harris; *p* Jack Burns;
sc Jack Burns, Marc London, Jim Henson,
Jerry Juhl
RITA MORENO 31/10/1976
d Peter Harris; *p* Jack Burns;
sc Jack Burns, Marc London, Jim Henson,
Jerry Juhl
TWIGGY 19/12/1976
d Peter Harris; *p* Jack Burns;
sc Jack Burns, Marc London, Jim Henson,
Jerry Juhl
BRUCE FORSYTH 29/1/1977
d Peter Harris; *p* Jack Burns;
sc Jack Burns, Marc London, Jim Henson,
Jerry Juhl
ELTON JOHN 8/1/1978
d Peter Harris; *p* Jim Henson;
sc Jerry Juhl, Joseph A. Bailey,
Jim Henson, Don Hinkley

MURDER (Yorkshire TV 1976)
Three plays on the theme of murder.
HELLO LOLA 6/6/1976
d Christopher Hodson; *sc* Gerald Vaughan-
Hughes
lp Michael Coles; James Duggan;
Glenn Beck; Jill Bennett; Sebastian Shaw
NOBODY'S CONSCIENCE 13/6/1976
d Christopher Hodson; *sc* Edmund Ward
lp Anthony Bate; Mark Eden;
Patricia Haines; Leslie Sands
A VARIETY OF PASSION 20/6/1976
d John Frankau; *sc* David Ambrose
lp Felicity Kendal; Ralph Michael;
Caroline Blakiston; James Aubrey;
Allan Cuthbertson

The MURUT PEOPLE OF BORNEO
(BBC 3/11/1955)
Murut agriculture in Borneo, filmed by Dr Ivan
Polunin.

The MUSEUM ATTENDANT (BBC 2/8/1973)
Play about an unconventional museum
attendant.
d Derek Bennett; *p* Ann Scott;
sc Michael Abbensetts
lp Joseph Greig; David Battley;
Robin Parkinson; Tony Selby

MUSIC AT HAREWOOD (Yorkshire TV)
Coverage of the Harewood music festival.
SHURA CHERKASSKY 23/5/1977
Shura Cherkassky, pianist, plays Scarlatti's
'Pastorale and Capriccio', Chopin's Scherzo in B
minor Op. 20 and 'Rigoletto Paraphrase' by
Liszt.
d Vernon Lawrence; *p* Ellie Kyle

The MUSIC BOX (Rediffusion 1957)
Variety show.
MUSIC BOX 18/1/1957
d Douglas Hurn; *p* Jack Hylton
with Bud Flanagan
MUSIC BOX 1/2/1957
d Douglas Hurn; *p* Jack Hylton
with The Crazy Gang, Rosalina Neri,
Joyeux Rossignols
MUSIC BOX 8/2/1957
d Eric Fawcett
with Bud Flanagan
MUSIC BOX 15/2/1957
d Eric Fawcett
with Bud Flanagan; Terry-Thomas;
Rosalina Neri

The MUSIC BOX 1/3/1957
d Eric Fawcett
with George Formby, Lauri, Lupino Lane;
George Truzzi; Maggie Fitzgibbon;
Terry Scanlon; The John Tiller Girls

MUSIC FOR YOU (BBC 1958–60)
Music series.
TITO GOBBI 30/3/1960
p Patricia Foy; *intro* Eric Robinson;
with Tito Gobbi, Svetlana Beriosova,
Jacqueline Delman, Rowland Jones

MUSIC IN CAMERA (BBC 15/4/1962)
André Prokovsky and Claire Motte dance scenes
from 'Sylvia'; Marjeta Korosec plays part of
Tchaikovsky's violin concerto; George Malcolm
plays 'Bach Goes To Town' on the harpsichord;
Renato Cioni and John Ford sing excerpts from
'Rigoletto', with the Philharmonia Orchestra.
p Patricia Foy

MUSIC INTERNATIONAL (BBC 1965–68)
Series in which composers/conductors discuss
their views of music.
WILLIAM WALTON CELLO CONCERTO 1967
GIOVANNI MARTINELLI (PRODUCTION
MATERIAL) 5/11/1967
Offcuts from the programme transmitted on
5/11/67 in which Lord Harewood interviews
Giovanni Martinelli about his career. Martinelli
singing in 'La Juive'.
d Kenneth Corden; *pres* Bernard Keeffe;
AARON COPLAND 3/12/1967
Aaron Copland discusses his ideas on modern
American music with Alan Jefferson.
p Kenneth Corden; *intro* Bernard Keeffe
ARCHIE CAMDEN 24/3/1968
A tribute to bassoonist Archie Camden, who is
filmed at his 80th birthday concert playing part
of the Mozart bassoon concerto. Those
appearing include Yehudi Menuhin, Harry
Blech, and The Camden Wind Quartet.
p Kenneth Corden
ALFRED DELLER 19/5/1968
Alfred Deller sings excerpts from songs by
Dowland, Purcell and Wilbye with Desmond
Dupré on the lute, The Deller Consort and with
Walter Bergmann on harpsichord. Includes a
contribution from Sir Michael Tippett.
p Kenneth Corden; *intro* Bernard Keeffe

**The MUSIC OF LENNON AND
McCARTNEY** (Granada 16/12/1965)
Features some of the artists who have recorded
songs by The Beatles. Re-broadcast in 1985 to
herald Granada Television's 30th Anniversary in
1986.
d Philip Casson; *p* John Hamp;
with Peter Sellers, Cilla Black,
Marianne Faithfull, George Martin,
Henry Mancini

MUSIC ON TWO (BBC 1965–73)
Music series.
BALLET RAMBERT STRUGGLES TO SURVIVE
14/3/1966
A film about Ballet Rambert which focuses on
the dancer Maggie Lorraine.
pres Ivor Mills
WORKSHOP – ESPANSIVA 18/1/1970
A portrait of Carl Nielsen.
d Barrie Gavin
The LIFE OF LUDWIG VAN BEETHOVEN
1770–1827: PART 1: MOZART'S SPIRIT FROM
HAYDN'S HANDS 31/5/1970
Beethoven 1770–1804.
The LIFE OF LUDWIG VAN BEETHOVEN
1770–1827: PART 2: FATE BY THE THROAT
7/6/1970
Beethoven 1804–1814.
The LIFE OF LUDWIG VAN BEETHOVEN
1770–1827: PART 3: IT MUST BE 14/6/1970
Beethoven 1814–1827.
d Barrie Gavin;
sc Barrie Gavin, H.C. Robbins Landon;
nar Alan Howard
MUSIC FROM KING'S 25/10/1970
Anthems written by Handel for the coronation
of George II from the chapel of King's College,
Cambridge.
p Brian Large; *intro* Richard Baker

MUSIC ON TWO   cont.

The THREE FACES OF JAZZ 13/12/1970
The evolution of three aspects of jazz music is
traced with the aid of archival film. Those
appearing include Louis Armstrong, Duke
Ellington, Tommy Dorsey, Lester Young,
Charlie Parker, Miles Davis, the Modern Jazz
Quartet, and Dave Brubeck.
p Geoffrey Haydon;
sc Charles Fox, Geoffrey Haydon
BERNSTEIN IN LONDON 21/3/1971
The Vienna Philharmonic Orchestra, conducted
by Leonard Bernstein at the Royal Albert Hall,
plays Schumann's Symphony no.4 and Ravel's
Piano Concerto in G major.
d Brian Large
WORKSHOP: COLIN DAVIS – LIFE AND MUSIC
18/4/1971
Interview with Colin Davis about the musical
experiences which have shaped his career.
d Denis Moriarty; *p* Walter Todds
NIKOLAIS ORIGINAL 27/6/1971
Alwin Nikolais rehearses his company, The
Alwin Nikolais Dance Theatre, for a
performance of a new multi-media work 'The
Relay', specially created for television.
p William Fitzwater
RUGGIERO RICCI PLAYS THE MUSIC OF
PAGANINI 10/10/1971
p Kenneth Corden; *nar* Robert Anderson
with John Williams, Malcolm Henderson,
Denis Nesbitt, and the New Philharmonia
Orchestra conducted by James Lockhart.

MUSIC 625 (BBC 1964–1967)
Music series.
BEETHOVEN'S CHORAL SYMPHONY 8/11/1964
Beethoven's Ninth Symphony, conducted by
Otto Klemperer at the Royal Albert Hall, with
Agnes Giebel (soprano), Marga Hoffgen
(contralto), Ernst Haefliger (tenor), Gustav
Neidlinger (bass), and the New Philharmonia
Chorus and Orchestra.
d Anthony Craxton; *pres* Robert Hudson

MUSICAMERA: PICTURES AT AN
EXHIBITION (BBC 20/7/1969)
The London Symphony Orchestra play
Mussorgsky's 'Pictures at an Exhibition' – the
music is illustrated with views of the modern
world.
d Barrie Gavin;
sc Hilary Carson, Barrie Gavin

MY BROTHER'S KEEPER (HTV 20/1/1972)
A film made by trade unionists on the aims and
values of the trade union movement.
d Jeffrey Milland

MY NAME IS HARRY WORTH
(Thames 22/4–17/6/1974)
Comedy series featuring comedian Harry Worth.
THERE'S NO PLACE LIKE IT 22/4/1974
d/p William G. Stewart; *sc* Ronnie Taylor
lp Lally Bowers; Richard Davies;
James Appleby; Johnny Caesar; Frank Coda
The REFERENCE 29/4/1974
d/p William G. Stewart; *sc* Ronnie Taylor
lp Lally Bowers; Reginald Marsh;
Richard Fraser

MY WIFE NEXT DOOR
(BBC 19/9–12/12/1972)
Thirteen-part comedy series about a newly
divorced couple who find they are neighbours.
MY WIFE NEXT DOOR 1972
p Graeme Muir; *sc* Richard Waring
lp John Alderton; Hannah Gordon

N

NANCY (BBC 28/11/1979)
A film biography of Nancy Astor. Interviews
with her family and associates, including Joyce
Grenfell, Claud Cockburn, Oswald Mosley and
Lord Shinwell.
p Jeremy Bennett; *pres* John Grigg

The NATION DECIDES (ITN 18/6/1970)
The results of the 1970 General Election.
pres Alastair Burnet, David Frost

The NATIONAL DREAM:
BUILDING THE IMPOSSIBLE RAILWAY
(CA CBC; BBC *tx* 19/7–23/8/1975)
A dramatised documentary, in six parts, about
the building of Canada's first intercontinental
railroad.
d James Murray, Eric Till;
p James Murray; *narr* Pierre Berton
EPISODE 1: GREAT LONE LAND AND THE
PACIFIC SCANDAL 19/7/1975
EPISODE 2: HORRID BC BUSINESS AND THE
GREAT DEBATE 26/7/1975
EPISODE 3: RAILWAY GENERAL 2/8/1975
EPISODE 4: SEA OF MOUNTAINS 9/8/1975
EPISODE 5: DESPERATE DAYS 16/8/1975
EPISODE 6: LAST SPIKE 23/8/1975

The NATIONAL DRINK TEST
(Granada 20/6/1979)
Programme devoted to drinking habits based on
a survey of 5,000 people carried out over the
past year. Includes a test of drinking habits that
viewers can do at home.
d Nicholas Ferguson; *p* Jeremy Fox;
sc/pres Laurie Taylor

NATIONAL SAVINGS 50TH ANNIVERSARY
1916–1966 (BBC 19/5/1966)
The Guildhall ceremony 19th May 1966.

The NATION'S FUTURE (US NBC 21/1/1961)
On the day after John F. Kennedy's inauguration
as President, John McCaffery chairs a discussion
on the West's policy towards the USSR and
China. Taking part are Hugh Gaitskell and
Walter Judd. Questions from John Fischer and
Edwin Newman.

NATIONWIDE (BBC 1971–84)
Early-evening news magazine programme.
NATIONWIDE 4/10/1978
pres Frank Bough, Sue Lawley,
John Stapleton, Bob Wellings

The NATIVITY (Rediffusion 23/12/1955)
The Nativity story told through the words of St
Matthew and St Luke, fifteenth-century Flemish
paintings, carols, mime, dance and music
recorded in the Brompton Oratory.
d Graham Young; *p* Cecil Lewis

The NATURE OF PREJUDICE (ATV 1968)
Seven-part documentary examining forms of
prejudice and how they are perpetuated.
d Colin Clark; *p* Stuart Hood;
pres Ludovic Kennedy
The VARIETY OF PREJUDICE 7/1/1968
Ludovic Kennedy attempts to determine a
definition of prejudice.
The DEVELOPMENT OF PREJUDICE AMONG
CHILDREN 14/1/1968
Investigates the foundations of prejudice in
childhood and looks at an experiment in which
children display their prejudices whilst playing.
PREJUDICE AND MEMBERSHIP OF A GROUP
21/1/1968
Groups and group allegiance and the prejudices
they can give rise to, with Professor Hilde
Himmelweit.
STEREOTYPES 28/1/1968
Ludovic Kennedy introduces a discussion with
Professor Henri Tajfel and Dr J. Field about
stereotyping in feature films.
METHODS OF DEALING WITH PREJUDICE
4/2/1968
Ludovic Kennedy, Professor Marie Jahoda and
Anthony Lester discuss whether legislation or
education is the better method of dealing with
prejudice.
THREE PREJUDICED INDIVIDUALS 11/2/1968
Ludovic Kennedy introduces James Mottram,
who gives his views on race and colour; Lady
Dartmouth discusses her views on the effect of
pornography on young people; and Peregrine
Worsthorne gives his views on social elitism.
DISCUSSION ON PREJUDICE 18/2/1968
A studio discussion on the nature of prejudice
and its social implications, with Ludovic
Kennedy, Mark Bonham-Carter and Professors
Henri Tajfel and Alfred J. Ayer.

NAVY LOG (US Gallu Productions 1955–58)
A series of filmed dramas, all re-enactments of
incidents that actually happened to US Navy
personnel, focusing on individuals in both battle
settings and their private lives.
PT 109 13/3/1958
A documentary drama about John Fitzgerald
Kennedy during World War II, specifically the
incident of the sinking of his PT-109 in the South
Pacific.
d/p Samuel Gallu; *sc* Allen E. Sloane;
nar Robert Carson
lp John Baer; Patrick Waltz;
Peter Miller; John Close; Joel Smith;
Skip Killmond

NBC WHITE PAPER (US NBC 1960–)
Documentary news series.
The U.2. AFFAIR 29/11/1960
The aircraft piloted by Francis Powers which was
shot down over the Soviet Union in May 1960.
d/p Al Wasserman
sc Arthur Barron, Al Wasserman;
rep Chet Huntley
SIT-IN 20/12/1960
Black students in Nashville, Tennessee.
d Robert Young; *p* Al Wasserman;
sc Al Wasserman, Robert Young;
rep Chet Huntley

The NEARLY MAN (Granada 4/8/1974)
A public-school educated MP faces difficulties in
his grass roots northern Labour constituency.
d John Irvin; *p* Peter Eckersley;
sc Arthur Hopcraft
lp Tony Britton; Ann Firbank;
Wilfred Pickles; Michael Elphick;
Barrie Gosney; Richard Butler

NEHRU – MAN OF TWO WORLDS
(BBC 27/2/1962)
The life and work of Jawaharlal Nehru.
Interviews with Vijaya Lakshmi Pandit, Indira
Gandhi, Lord Mountbatten, Fenner Brockway
and Sir Grimwood Mears.
d Charles Wheeler, Malcolm Brown,
Philip Donnellan

NEIL YOUNG IN CONCERT
(BBC 26/4/1971)
p Stanley Dorfman

NETWORK (BBC 1970–78)
Documentary series. [Not to be confused with
the BBC-1, 1980s series of programmes about
television]
VIVIAN WHITELEY – ON HER OWN 15/4/1976
The widow from REMEMBER ALL THE
GOOD THINGS (1975) learning to live without
her husband.
p Ray Colley, Alan Murgatroyd

NEVER AND ALWAYS (Granada 15/6/1977)
The director's personal view of life in rural
Norfolk. Shows the effect of time and change on
people's lives in villages and on farms with the
passing of the seasons, and the influence of
world pressures on the traditional way of life.
d Denis Mitchell

NEW ADVENTURES OF CHARLIE CHAN
(ITC 1957–58)
Detective series based on the character created
by author Earl Derr Biggers.
NO FUTURE FOR FREDERICK 7/6/1958
d Don Chaffey; *p* Rudolph Flothow;
sc Terence Maples
lp J. Carrol Naish; Hugh Williams
Derrick de Marney; Maggie McGrath;
Fenine Graham

The NEW AVENGERS (Avengers [Film and
TV] Enterprises-IDTV TV Productions, Paris
1976–77)
Revised version of the 1960s series, The
AVENGERS (1961–69).
p Albert Fennell, Brian Clemens
regulars Patrick Macnee; Gareth Hunt;
Joanna Lumley

EAGLE'S NEST 19/10/1976
d Desmond Davis; *sc* Brian Clemens
lp Derek Farr; Frank Gatliff;
Peter Cushing
The LAST OF THE CYBERNAUTS...? 2/11/1976
d Sidney Hayers; *sc* Brian Clemens
lp Robert Lang; Oscar Quitak;
Gwen Taylor; Basil Hoskins; Robert Gillespie
TARGET 23/11/1976
d Ray Austin; *sc* Dennis Spooner
lp Keith Barron; Robert Beatty; Roy Boyd;
Frederick Jaeger; Malcolm Stoddard; Deep Roy
TO CATCH A RAT 30/11/1976
d James Hill; *sc* Terence Feeley
lp Ian Hendry; Edward Judd;
Robert Fleming; Barry Jackson; Anthony Sharp
The TALE OF THE BIG WHY 7/12/1976
d Robert Fuest; *sc* Brian Clemens
lp Derek Waring; Jenny Runacre;
Roy Marsden; Gary Waldhorn; Rowland Davis
FACES 14/12/1976
d James Hill;
sc Brian Clemens, Dennis Spooner
lp David De Keyser; Edward Petherbridge;
Neil Hallett; Annabel Leventon; David Webb
GNAWS 21/12/1976
d Ray Austin; *sc* Dennis Spooner
lp Julian Holloway; Morgan Shepherd;
Peter Cellier; Anulka Dubinska;
Ronnie Laughlin
SLEEPER 12/1/1977
d Graeme Clifford; *sc* Brian Clemens
lp Keith Buckley; Sara Kestelman;
Mark Jones; Prentis Hancock; Leo Dolan
The THREE-HANDED GAME 19/1/1977
d Ray Austin;
sc Dennis Spooner, Brian Clemens
lp David Wood; Stephen Greif; Tony Vogel;
Michael Petrovitch; Terry Wood;
Gary Raymond
The LION AND THE UNICORN 29/9/1977
d Ray Austin; *sc* John Goldsmith
lp Jean Claudio; Maurice Marsac;
Raymond Bussiéres; Jacques Maury;
Raoul Delfosse
K IS FOR KILL: PART 1: TIGER AWAKES
27/10/1977
d Yvon Marie Coulais; *sc* Brian Clemens
lp Pierre Vernier; Maurice Marsac;
Charles Millot; Paul-Emile Deiber
K IS FOR KILL: PART 2: TIGER BY THE TAIL
3/11/1977
d Yvon Marie Coulais; *sc* Brian Clemens
lp Pierre Vernier; Maurice Marsac;
Charles Millot; Paul-Emile Deiber
COMPLEX 10/11/1977
d Richard Gilbert; *sc* Dennis Spooner
lp Cec Linder; Harvey Atkin;
Vlasta Vrana; Rudy Lipp; Jan Rubes;
Suzette Couture
HOSTAGE 17/11/1977
d Sidney Hayers; *sc* Brian Clemens
lp William Franklyn; Simon Oates;
Michael Culver
FORWARD BASE 24/11/1977
d Don Thompson; *sc* Dennis Spooner
lp Jack Creley; August Schellenberg;
Marilyn Lightstone; Nich Nichols
EMILY 1/12/1977
d Don Thompson; *sc* Dennis Spooner
lp Les Carison; Richard Davidson;
Jane Mallet; Peter Torokvei; Peter Aykroyd
The GLADIATORS 6/9/1978
[Not transmitted as a part of the original series]
d Claude Fournier; *sc* Brian Clemens
lp Louis Zorich; Neil Vipond; Bill Starr;
Peter Boretski; Yanci Bukovec; Jan Muzynski

NEW FACES (ATV 1973–78)
Talent show.
The ALL WINNERS' GALA FINAL 27/7/1975
Talent show final won by Marti Caine, also
featuring Lenny Henry and introduced by Derek
Hobson.
d John Pullen; *p* Les Cocks

NEW LANDMARKS (BBC 1961)
Eucational series for school children.
The KARIBA DAM 5/6/1961
The problems involved in building the dam and
the benefits which it will bring. Discusses the
resettlement of people and animals in the area
affected.
p Peggy Broadhead

**NEW MUSICAL EXPRESS POLL
WINNERS' CONCERT** (ABC 8/11/1964)
Pop concert, featuring performances by the
following: Manfred Mann; Jet Harris; Kathy
Kirby; Billy J. Kramer and The Dakotas;
Merseybeats; Big Dee Irwin; Joe Brown; Gerry
and The Pacemakers; The Beatles.
d Mark Stuart;
pres David Jacobs, Jimmy Savile, Roger Moore

**NEW MUSICAL EXPRESS POLL
WINNERS' CONCERT** (ABC 18/4/1965)
Pop concert featuring performances by the
following: The Moody Blues; Freddie and The
Dreamers; Sounds Incorporated; Twinkle; The
Animals; The Seekers; Herman's Hermits;
Dusty Springfield; The Beatles.
d Mark Stuart; *p* Maurice Kinn;
pres Jimmy Savile, Keith Fordyce,
Cathy McGowan, Tony Bennett

**NEW MUSICAL EXPRESS POLL
WINNERS' CONCERT** (ABC 1966)
Pop concert featuring performances by the
following: Sounds Incorporated; The Fortunes;
Herman's Hermits; Dave Dee, Dozy, Beaky,
Mick & Tich; Crispian St Peter; Alan Price Set;
Dusty Springfield. Award presentations to The
Seekers, The Shadows, The Rolling Stones, and
The Beatles
d Mark Stuart, Royston Mayoh;
pres Jimmy Savile, Keith Fordyce, Pete Murray

The NEW PRESIDENT (BBC 9/11/1960)
Richard Dimbleby introduces the latest news on
the American presidential elections with
Christopher Serpell, Robin Day, Ludovic
Kennedy, John Tidmarsh and David Jacobs in
London, and Douglas Stuart in New York.

NEW RELEASE (BBC 1965–67)
Arts series.
FEDERICO FELLINI 6/1/1966
Ian Dallas interviews Federico Fellini.
d Leo Aylen, Tristram Powell,
John Mapplebeck; *p* Melvyn Bragg;
intro Julian Jebb
A MAN LIKE MY FATHER 11/10/1966
Jean Renoir talks about his life and work.
d Gavin Millar, Tristram Powell;
p Melvyn Bragg; *intro* Alex Glasgow
DAVID MERCER – PLAYWRIGHT 22/11/1966
David Mercer discusses his career as a television,
film and theatre playwright. With R.D. Laing,
David Jones, David Storey and David Warner.
d Gavin Millar, Tristram Powell;
p Melvyn Bragg; *intro* Alex Glasgow

The NEWCOMERS (BBC 30/4–4/6/1964)
Six-part documentary series on the lives of a
young couple in Bristol.
PART 3: OUT THERE IN THE NIGHT 14/5/1964
On Saturday 30th May 1964, Alison Smith gave
birth to twins in the Bristol Maternity Hospital.
This film is an account of happenings in the city
of Bristol during the hours she was in labour.
p John Boorman; *d* Michael Croucher

The NEWCOMERS (BBC 1965–69)
Domestic drama serial focusing on a London
family adapting to life in a country town.
The NEWCOMERS 5/5/1967
d Paddy Russell; *p* Bill Sellars;
sc Patrick Scanlan; *auth* John Cresswell
lp George Woodbridge; Megs Jenkins;
Alan Browning; Naomi Chance; Robert Brown;
June Bland; Sandra Payne; Jeremy Bulloch;
Gladys Henson; Raymond Hunt;
Maggie Fitzgibbon

The NEWCOMERS 26/5/1967
d Ronald Wilson; *p* Bill Sellars;
sc Barry Letts; *auth* John Cresswell
lp Alan Browning; Naomi Chance;
June Bland; Sandra Payne; Jeremy Bulloch;
John Dawson; Michael Collins; Raymond Hunt;
Maggie Fitzgibbon; Gladys Henson;
Wendy Richard; Mona Bruce
The NEWCOMERS 7/12/1967
d Eric Hills; *p* Bill Sellars;
sc Kenneth Hill; *auth* John Cresswell
lp Naomi Chance; June Bland;
Sandra Payne; Jeremy Bulloch; Alan Browning;
Vanda Godsell; Michael Collins;
Raymond Hunt; Maggie Fitzgibbon;
Gladys Henson; Wendy Richard; Robert Brown;
Malcolm McDowell

NEWSDAY (BBC 1974–78)
News summary and current affairs programme.
INTERVIEW WITH ADMIRAL SIR TERENCE
LEWIN 6/10/1975
Features Admiral Sir Terence Lewin, about to
leave his post at NATO as Commander in Chief
Channel Fleet.
p Christopher Capron;
pres Robin Day, Ludovic Kennedy;
rep Angela Rippon

NICHOLAS NICKLEBY (BBC 11/2–5/5/1968)
Thirteen-part serial dramatisation of the Charles
Dickens story.
d Joan Craft; *p* Campbell Logan;
sc Hugh Leonard
regular Martin Jarvis
EPISODE 8: CAPTURED 31/3/1968
lp Gordon Gostelow; Maxwell Shaw;
Derek Francis; Thelma Ruby; Thea Holme;
Susan Brodrick
EPISODE 9: ESCAPE 7/4/1968
lp Gordon Gostelow; Derek Francis;
Thea Holme; Susan Brodrick; Hugh Walters;
Roy Kinnear

NIGERIA – INDEPENDENCE
(Rediffusion 30/9/1960)
Nigeria at the time of Independence, and
celebrations in London, introduced by Antony
Sampson.
d Rollo Gamble; *sc* David Hennessy

A NIGHT AT THE SPEEDWAY
(Tyne Tees 6/7/1979)

NIGHT OF 100 STARS (ITV 5/6/1977)
Gala performance to celebrate Queen Elizabeth
II's Silver Jubilee, performed in the presence of
Princess Alexandra at the National Theatre.
d/p Jon Scoffield;
with Patrick Allen, Moira Anderson,
John Clements, John Dankworth,
Charlie Drake, Geraint Evans, Frank Finlay,
John Gielgud, Stephane Grappelli,
Wendy Hiller, Glenda Jackson, Cleo Laine,
Danny La Rue, Jessie Matthews, John Mills,
Kenneth More, Merle Park, Nyree Dawn Porter,
Beryl Reid

NIGHT OUT AT THE LONDON CASINO
(Thames 20/7–31/8/1977)
Variety series which re-introduces the London
Palladium format incorporating a quiz show.
TWIGGY, PAUL MELBA, JIM DAVIDSON
27/7/1977
d/p Dennis Kirkland; *host* Tom O'Connor

NIGHTINGALE'S BOYS
(Granada 14/1–25/2/1975)
Seven-part drama series about a disillusioned
former schoolteacher and a reunion with his
'star' class of 1949.
TWEETY 14/1/1975
d Richard Everitt; *p* Brian Armstrong;
sc Arthur Hopcraft
lp Derek Farr; Pauline Yates;
Angela Morant; Terry Gilligan;
Bernard Gallagher; Michael Hawkins;
John Barcroft

NIGHTINGALE'S BOYS   cont.

DECISION 25/2/1975
d June Howson; *p* Brian Armstrong;
sc Arthur Hopcraft
lp Derek Farr; Pauline Yates;
Barbara Lott; Angela Morant; Alec Sabin;
John Challis

NINETEEN EIGHTY-FOUR (BBC 12/12/1954)
Dramatisation of the novel by George Orwell.
d/p Rudolph Cartier; *sc* Nigel Kneale
lp Peter Cushing; Yvonne Mitchell;
André Morell; Arnold Diamond;
Donald Pleasence

The NIXON INTERVIEWS (David Paradine
Productions; BBC *tx* 5–26/5/1977)
interv David Frost
NIXON'S VERSION OF WATERGATE 5/5/1977
Richard Nixon is questioned about the
Watergate affair.
NIXON'S FOREIGN POLICY 13/5/1977
United States foreign policy during Nixon's
Presidency.
The VIETNAM WAR 20/5/1977
Why the Vietnam War was fought, its cost and
why it was lost.
FINAL DAYS IN THE WHITE HOUSE 26/5/1977
Richard Nixon talks about the achievements and
humiliations of his time as President.

NO HARD FEELINGS
(Alan Parker Productions 13/6/1976)
Story of a working-class family in East London
during 1939 and 1940.
d/sc Alan Parker
lp Anthony Allen; Mary Larkin;
Joe Gladwin; Kate Williams

NO HIDING PLACE
(Rediffusion 1959–67)
Scotland Yard detective series.
regulars Raymond Francis; Eric Lander;
Johnny Briggs; Michael McStay; Sean Caffrey
ACCESSORIES AFTER THE FACT 15/5/1962
d Douglas Hurn; *p* Ray Dicks;
sc Bill Hitchcock
lp Eric Phillips; Robert Hunter;
Ronald Radd; Barbara Young; Peter Thompson;
Fay Compton
The BEST YEARS OF YOUR LIFE 17/5/1965
d Christopher Hodson; *p* Peter Willes;
sc Jeremy Paul
lp Lynne Barton; Elizabeth Knight;
Martin Matthews; Richard O'Sullivan;
Patrick Tull
A FISTFUL OF TROUBLE 24/5/1965
d Geoffrey Hughes; *p* Peter Willes;
sc Doreen Montgomery
lp Peter Bowles; Jess Conrad;
Janet Kelly; Garfield Morgan; Russell Waters;
Annie Ross
RAT IN A TRAP 7/6/1965
d John Frankau; *p* Peter Willes;
sc Alun Falconer, Colin Holder
lp Gary Bond; David Saire; Jean Kent;
Roger Kemp
CHAIN OF GUILT 17/6/1965
d Christopher Hodson; *p* Peter Willes;
sc Leslie Gann
lp Jerry Desmonde; Deryck Guyler;
Joyce Heron; Peter Murray; Carmen Munro
ONE GOOD MAN AND TRUE 8/7/1965
d John Frankau; *p* Peter Willes;
sc Donald James
lp James Maxwell; Malcolm Patton;
Nicholas Chagrin; George Tovey
The REUNION 15/7/1965
d Richard Doubleday; *p* Peter Willes;
sc Nicholas Jones
lp Henry Gilbert; Ronald Howard;
Joan Benham; Judy Campbell; Imogen Hassall
IT'S ALL HAPPENING 15/3/1967
d Marc Miller; *p* Michael Currer-Briggs;
sc Alun Falconer, Colin Holder
lp David Ashford; Ursula Howells;
Alec Ross; Colette O'Neil; David Garth

NO-HONESTLY (LWT 1974–75)
Comedy series featuring husband-and-wife team
of John Alderton and Pauline Collins.
MORE ROYLE THAN NOBLE REALLY 18/10/1974
d David Askey; *p* Humphrey Barclay;
sc Terence Brady, Charlotte Bingham
lp James Berwick; C. Kenneth Benda;
Roderick Smith

NO LULLABY FOR BROADLAND
(Anglia 20/11/1979)
The threat to the ecology of the Norfolk Broads
caused by massive tourist exploitation.
d/sc Geoffrey Wheeler

NO MAN'S LAND (ATV 3/2–10/3/1973)
Documentary series produced by an all-female
production team which puts forward the
woman's point of view.
WOMEN AND WORK 17/2/1973
Two films, one about the plight of female
graduates, the other about the problems of a low
paid female night office cleaner.
d Dorothy Denham;
p Brigid Segrave, Lis Kustow;
pres Juliet Mitchell

NO MAN'S LAND (HTV 1978–79)
Documentary series on work.
The SHOP FLOOR 1/3/1979
The problems of women at work in factories with
special regard to low pay and the effects of the
Equal Pay Act.
d/p John Mead; *pres* Susan Calland

NO MAN'S LAND (Granada 3/10/1978)
Peter Hall's National Theatre production of
Harold Pinter's play.
d Julian Amyes; *sc* Harold Pinter
lp John Gielgud; Ralph Richardson;
Michael Kitchen; Terence Rigby

NOBEL AND THE PEACE PEOPLE
(Ulster TV 11/12/1977)

NOBODY'S HOUSE
(Tyne Tees 27/9–8/11/1976)
Seven-part fantasy-drama for children.
p Margaret Bottomley;
sc Derrick Sherwin, Martin Hall
regulars Kevin Moreton; Stuart Wilde;
Mandy Woodward; William Gaunt;
Wendy Gifford; Walter Gaunt
THERE'S NOBODY THERE 27/9/1976
d Michael Ferguson
lp John Cater
NOBODY'S FOOL 11/10/1976
d David Green
lp Artro Morris
NOBODY LOVES ME 25/10/1976
d David Green
lp Annabelle Lanyon
NOBODY'S GHOST 8/11/1976
d Michael Ferguson
lp Brian Wilde; John Sanderson;
Mollie Maureen

NOËL COWARD ON ACTING
(BBC 12/3/1966)
Noël Coward talks to Michael MacOwan about
acting techniques and the highlights of his
career.
p Hal Burton

The NORMAN CONQUESTS
(Thames 5/10–19/10/1977)
A trilogy of comedies observing the same
weekend from different vantage points.
TABLE MANNERS 5/10/1977
d Herbert Wise;
p Verity Lambert, David Susskind;
sc Alan Ayckbourn
lp Richard Briers; Tom Conti;
Penelope Keith; Penelope Wilton;
David Troughton; Fiona Walker

NORMAN NICHOLSON – MAN OF MILLOM
(Granada 11/11/1968)
A film about poet and critic Norman Nicholson.

NORTH TONIGHT (Grampian)
Regional news programme.
NORTH TONIGHT 1/6/1979

NORTHERN REPORT (Tyne Tees)
Regional news programme.
TEACHERS AND METRIC MUDDLES 24/6/1979
NUCLEAR POWER 5/11/1979

NORTHERN SCENE
(Tyne Tees 1977–1981)
Regional news programme.
ALAN GOWLING MP 17/10/1977
LIDDLE TOWERS – A CASE TO BE ANSWERED
31/10/1977
OVER THE BORDER 28/11/1977
ONE OF THOSE THINGS WE DO AWFULLY
WELL 30/11/1978
COUNTDOWN AT CONSETT 15/12/1978

NOT A HUNDRED MILES FROM
WEMBLEY (Yorkshire TV 20/6/1979)
The Spalding Tulip Festival, which is held on the
same day as the F.A. Cup Final.
d David St. David Smith;
p John Wilford; *rep* Geoff Druett

NOT ONLY...BUT ALSO PETER COOK
AND DUDLEY MOORE IN AUSTRALIA
(AU ABC; BBC *tx* 18/6/1971)
The first of two comedy programmes with Peter
Cook and Dudley Moore, Barry Humphries and
the Dudley Moore Trio.
sc Peter Cook, Dudley Moore

NOT SO MUCH A PROGRAMME MORE A
WAY OF LIFE (BBC 1964–65)
Revue/sketch satirical programme.
NOT SO MUCH A PROGRAMME MORE A WAY
OF LIFE 13/11/1964
d/p Ned Sherrin; *with* David Frost,
P.J. Kavanagh, William Rushton, Barbara
Evans, Eleanor Bron, Doug Fisher, Roy Hudd
NOT SO MUCH A PROGRAMME MORE A WAY
OF LIFE 11/4/1965
d/p Ned Sherrin; *with* David Frost,
Michael Crawford, Cleo Laine, Roy Hudd
Brian Murphy, Doug Fisher, John Bird

NOT THE NINE O'CLOCK NEWS
(BBC 1979–82)
Comedy sketch series.
NOT THE NINE O'CLOCK NEWS 16/10/1979
d Bill Wilson;
p John Lloyd, Sean Hardie;
with Rowan Atkinson, Chris Langham;
Pamela Stephenson; Mel Smith
NOT THE NINE O'CLOCK NEWS 20/11/1979
d Bill Wilson;
p John Lloyd, Sean Hardie;
with Rowan Atkinson, Chris Langham,
Pamela Stephenson, Mel Smith

NOTHIN' BUT THE BLUES
(Granada 27/12/1966)
Blues music with 'Big' Joe Turner.
d Philip Casson

NOW LOOK HERE... (BBC 1971–73)
Comedy series starring Ronnie Corbett as a
mother-dominated batchelor.
NOW LOOK HERE... 10/12/1971
p Bill Hitchcock;
sc Barry Cryer, Graham Chapman
lp Rosemary Leach; Richard O'Sullivan;
Linda Hayden; Donald Hewlett;
Patricia Hamilton

The NURSES
(US Plautus Productions 1962–64)
Medical drama series featuring two nurses
working in a large metropolitan hospital.
NIGHT SHIFT 27/9/1962
d David Greene; *p* Arthur Lewis;
sc John Vlahos
lp Shirl Conway; Zina Bethune;
Viveca Lindfors; Ruth McDevitt;
Joey Heatherton; Arthur Hill

The NUTCRACKER (BBC 21/12/1958)
Ballet performance with Margot Fonteyn and
Michael Somes. The music is performed by the
Royal Philharmonic Orchestra conducted by
Hugo Rognold. Choreographed by L. Ivanov
p Margaret Dale

NYE! (TWW 7/7/1965)
A documentary of the life of Aneurin Bevan.
d/sc Jack Howells

O

O.S.S.
(US/GB Buckeye-LSQ Productions-Flamingo
Films-ITC 1957–58)
Espionage series set during World War II.
p Jules Buck
regulars Ron Randell; Lionel Murton;
Robert Gallico
OPERATION FRACTURE 14/9/1957
d Peter Maxwell; *sc* Paul Dudley
lp Rene Goddard; Oscar Quitak;
Ryck Rydon; Brian Haines; Murray Kash
OPERATION FOULBALL 21/9/1957
d Robert Siodmak; *sc* Paul Dudley
lp Lyndon Brook; Patrick Holt;
Naomi Chance; Frank Hawkins
OPERATION POWDER PUFF 28/9/1957
d Robert Siodmak; *sc* Paul Dudley
lp Francis Matthews; Sheila Brennan;
Patrick Jordan; Howard Lang; John Heller
OPERATION TULIP 5/10/1957
d Peter Maxwell; *sc* Paul Dudley
lp Denis Shaw; Frederick Piper;
Sandra Dorne; Howard Lang; Harold Lang;
Walter Gotell
OPERATION ORANGE BLOSSOM 12/10/1957
d Lawrence Huntingon; *sc* Paul Dudley
lp Lois Maxwell; Lloyd Lamble;
Irene Prador; Yvonne Warren; John Gabriel
OPERATION DEATH TRAP 19/10/1957
d Lawrence Huntington;
sc Paul Dudley, Robert Spafford
lp Gerard Heinz; Guy Deghy;
Michael David; Stanley Van Beers;
Ronald Fraser; Jeannette Sterke
OPERATION BLUE EYES 2/11/1957
d C.M. Pennington-Richards; *sc* Paul Dudley
lp John Valentine; Bernard Hunter;
Peter Reynolds; Bill Fraser; Lisa Gastoni
OPERATION SWEET TALK 9/11/1957
d C.M. Pennington-Richards; *sc* Paul Dudley
lp Laya Raki; Edwin Richfield;
Robert Perceval; Charles Irwin; Jerold Wells
OPERATION FLINT AXE 23/11/1957
d Robert Siodmak; *sc* Paul Dudley
lp Robert Rietty; Zena Marshall;
Barry Keegan; Donald Stewart
OPERATION LOVEBIRD 30/11/1957
d C.M. Pennington-Richards; *sc* Paul Dudley
lp Edwin Richfield; Jan Holden;
Cyril Chamberlain
OPERATION YO YO 14/12/1957
d C.M. Pennington-Richards; *sc* Paul Dudley
lp John Crawford; Bill Edwards;
David Graham; Don Mason; Franklyn Fox;
Ryck Rydon
OPERATION EEL 11/1/1958
d Robert Siodmak; *sc* Paul Dudley
lp Robert Ayres; James Hayter;
Anton Diffring; Neal Arden; Rupert Davies
OPERATION BARBECUE 18/1/1958
d Allan Davis; *sc* Paul Dudley
lp Basil Dignam; Christopher Rhodes;
Robert Arden; Thomas Gallagher; Diane Todd;
Lionel Ngakane
OPERATION BLACKBIRD 25/1/1958
d Lawrence Huntington; *sc* Paul Dudley
lp Bill Nagy; Sheldon Lawrence;
Gaylord Cavallaro; Franklyn Fox
OPERATION POST OFFICE 1/2/1958
d Lawrence Huntington; *sc* Paul Dudley
lp Richard Bebb; Sandra Dorne;
Reed De Rouen; Gerard Heinz; Conrad Phillips
OPERATION DAGGER 22/2/1958
d C.M. Pennington-Richards; *sc* Paul Dudley
lp Michael Ripper; Esmond Knight;
Nora Swinburne; Geoffrey Bayldon;
Ferdy Mayne

OPERATION MEATBALL 1/3/1958
d Peter Maxwell, Peter Wrestler;
sc Paul Dudley
lp Ryck Rydon; Franklyn Fox;
Gaylord Cavallaro; Lesley Dudley;
Richard Shaw
OPERATION BIG HOUSE 3/3/1958
d Lawrence Huntington;
sc Manning O'Brine, Paul Dudley
lp Roger Delgado; Patrick Waddington;
John Van Eyssen
OPERATION CHOPPING BLOCK 15/3/1958
d Robert Day; *sc* Paul Dudley
lp Morris Sweden; Wolf Frees;
Tony Doonan; John Gabriel; George Tovey;
Max Faulkner

OCCUPATIONS (Granada 1/9/1974)
Drama set in a hotel room in Turin during the
1920 metalworkers' strike.
d Michael Lindsay-Hogg; *p* Jonathan Powell;
sc Trevor Griffiths
lp Donald Pleasence; Jack Shepherd;
Natasha Parry; Georgina Hale; Nigel Hawthorne

The ODD MAN (Granada 1960–63)
Crime-mystery series.
EPISODE 7 30/11/1960
d Gordon Flemyng; *p* Jack Williams;
sc Edward Boyd
lp Geoffrey Toone; Alan Tilvern;
Jan Holden; Moultrie Kelsall; Judith Furse;
Geoffrey Palmer; Roger Delgado;
Richard Vernon
The SAGA OF JOHNNY MAC 26/7/1963
d Richard Everitt; *p* Stuart Latham;
sc Edward Boyd, Harry Driver,
Jack Rosenthal
lp Edwin Richfield; William Mervyn;
Sarah Lawson; Keith Barron; Toke Townley;
Anna Cropper

OH BOY! (ABC 1958–59)
Rock 'n' roll music series.
OH BOY! 30/5/1959
d Rita Gillespie; *p* Jack Good;
sc Trevor Peacock;
pres Tony Hall, Jimmy Henney;
with Cliff Richard, Marty Wilde,
The Dallas Boys Cherry Wainer,
Lord Rockingham's XI, Don Lang, Red Price,
The Vernons Girls, 'Cuddly' Dudley,
Billy Fury, Dickie Pride

OH BOY! (ATV 1979–80)
ATV revival of the 1950s rock 'n' roll music
series.
GBH, DON LANG, FUMBLE 16/7/1979
d Ken O'Neill;
p Ken O'Neill, Richard Leyland;
with Joe Brown, Les Gray, GBH, Don Lang,
Freddie 'Fingers' Lee, Alvin Stardust,
Shakin' Stevens, Johnny Storm, Fumble,
Rockin' Shades

OH BROTHER! (BBC 1968–70)
Comedy series set in a monastery.
BEHOLD THIS DREAMER 2/5/1969
p Harold Snoad;
sc Austin Steele, David Climie
lp Derek Nimmo; Felix Aylmer;
Derek Francis; John Grieve;
Derrick McAlinney; Eddie Malin;
Freddie Wiles; Bernard Archard

The OLD BOY NETWORK (BBC 1978–81)
Series in which veteran stars in show-business
tell their stories and perform.
JOHN LAURIE 21/9/1979
John Laurie recalls his characteristic routines.
p Don Sayer; *sc* Jimmy Perry

The OLD BOYS (ATV 18/2/1969)
The Old Boys' Association of Solihull School
and the background of the members.
d/p Ken Ashton

The OLD GREY WHISTLE TEST
(BBC 1971–85)
Musical documentary and live music programme.
Developed from the series DISCO 2 (1970–71).
p Michael Appleton
pres Richard Williams, Bob Harris
The OLD GREY WHISTLE TEST 7/12/1971
d Colin Strong; *with* Fanny,
Elton John, The Mommas and the Pappas,
The Rolling Stones
DAVID BOWIE 8/2/1972
d Colin Strong
DAVID BOWIE CLIPS 8/2/1972
Production material for above.
BOB HARRIS INTRODUCES MUSIC FROM
DAVID BOWIE 8/2/1972
d Tom Corcoran; *with* David Bowie
The OLD GREY WHISTLE TEST (PRODUCTION
MATERIAL) 8/2/1972 *ntx*
No titles; no introduction by Bob Harris; Bowie
on guitar and piano, Mick Ronson on piano.
d Colin Strong
The OLD GREY WHISTLE TEST 9/1/1973
Joan Armatrading makes her television debut.
Interview with David Geffen of the newly
formed band Asylum.
d Colin Strong;
with J. Geils Band, John Prine,
Barclay James Harvest, Captain Beefheart,
Exuma
The OLD GREY WHISTLE TEST 13/2/1973
d Colin Strong;
with Rory Gallagher, Duncan Browne,
Bette Midler
The OLD GREY WHISTLE TEST 27/11/1973
Includes cartoon of The Band singing 'Promised
Land'
d Colin Strong;
with The New York Dolls
Country Joe MacDonald, Michael Chapman,
B.B. King
JOHN LENNON 18/4/1975
John Lennon is interviewed in New York by
Bob Harris.
d Tom Corcoran
YES AT QPR 26/7/1975
Highlights from the Yes concert at QPR's
ground on 10th May 1975.
d Tom Corcoran
The OLD GREY WHISTLE TEST 24/12/1975
Queen playing live at the Hammersmith Odeon.
d Tom Corcoran
HARD RAIN 28/9/1976
Bob Harris introduces 'Hard Rain', Bob Dylan's
Rolling Thunder Review taped in Fort Collins,
Colorado.
d Tom Corcoran

OLGA (Granada 12/4/1973)
Soviet gymnast Olga Korbut in training and at
home. Appearing in the film are her coaches
Larissa Latynina and Renald Knyfch.
d John Sheppard

The OMEGA FACTOR
(BBC 13/6–15/8/1979)
Thriller serial revolving around the work of a
psychic research centre.
p George Gallaccio
regulars James Hazeldine; Louise Jameson;
John Carlisle
The UNDISCOVERED COUNTRY 13/6/1979
d Paddy Russell; *sc* Jack Gerson
lp Cyril Luckham; Colin Douglas;
Brown Derby; Joanna Tope; Nicholas Coppin
VISITATIONS 20/6/1979
d Norman Stewart; *sc* Eric MacDonald
lp Joanna Tope; Nicholas Coppin;
Natasha Gerson; Paul Young; Alec Heggie;
Martin Cochrane
NIGHT GAMES 27/6/1979
d Ken Grieve; *sc* Nick McCarty
lp Natasha Gerson; Brown Derby;
Nicholas Coppin; Tony Haygarth; Tim Barlow

OMNIBUS (BBC 1967–)
Arts series.
The WORLD OF COPPARD 15/12/1967
Adaptation of three of A.E. Coppard's short
stories: 'The Field of Mustard', 'Adam and Eve
and Pinch Me' and 'Dusky Ruth'.
d/p Jack Gold; *sc* Kit Coppard;
intro Henry Livings
lp Nancy Nevinson; Patricia Lawrence;
David Collings; Frances White; Mike Pratt
DANTE'S INFERNO 22/12/1967
Drama-documentary recreating life among the
Pre-Raphaelites in their country retreat.
d/p Ken Russell
lp Oliver Reed; Judith Paris;
Andrew Faulds; Gala Mitchell; Iza Teller;
Christopher Logue; Pat Ashton; Clive Gordon
DIAGHILEV: THE YEARS ABROAD 2/1/1968
p/sc John Drummond; *intro* Peter Ustinov;
with Tamara Karsavina, Lydia Sokolova,
Marie Rambert, Ninette De Valois,
Sacheverell Sitwell, Léonide Massine,
Nicolas Nabokov, Igor Markevitch,
Cecil Beaton, Cyril Beaumont, Anton Dolin,
Laura Wilson
DIAGHILEV: THE EXILE YEARS 9/1/1968
p/sc John Drummond; *intro* Peter Ustinov;
with participants as above; plus Alicia Markova,
Serge Lifar, Ursula Moreton, Leighton Lucas,
Errol Addison
TOP BRASS 23/1/1968
Three brass bands and their quest for the 1967
National Championship at the Royal Albert
Hall, London. Features the Black Dyke Mills,
G.U.S. (Footwear), and the Woodfalls Silver
Bands.
d/p Ian Engelmann
SONG OF SUMMER 15/9/1968
Drama about the composer Delius.
d/p Ken Russell;
sc Ken Russell, Eric Fenby
lp Max Adrian; Christopher Gable;
Maureen Pryor; David Collings;
Geraldine Sherman; Elizabeth Ercy
The MORE WE ARE TOGETHER 4/5/1969
Suburban housing and one of the designers of
such dwellings, Eric Lyons.
d Barrie Gavin; *sc* Leo Wooding;
nar Robert Cushman
The ACTOR'S CHANGING FACE 25/5/1969
Edith Evans, John Gielgud, Vanessa Redgrave,
and Donald Sinden discuss acting styles of the
twentieth century. Included is archival film of
prominent actors and actresses at work.
p Hal Burton; *intro* Sheridan Morley
The CONFESSIONS OF MARIAN EVANS
23/11/1969
Dramatisation of the life of novelist George
Eliot.
d/sc Don Taylor
lp Sheila Allen; John Garrie;
George A. Cooper; Inigo Jackson;
Christine Hargreaves; Sylvia Kay;
Kathleen Byron
NOËL COWARD – PLAYWRIGHT 7/12/1969
Patrick Garland interviews Noël Coward about
his theatrical career.
p Hal Burton; *intro* Ronald Bryden
A NIGHT'S DARKNESS, A DAY'S SAIL 18/1/1970
The life and work of Virginia Woolf.
Contributors include Elizabeth Bowen, Lord
David Cecil, Duncan Grant, George Rylands
and Raymond Mortimer.
d Julian Webb; *nar* Gavin Millar
with Quentin Bell, Angelica Garnett,
Leonard Woolf
JOHN CLARE: 'I AM ...' 8/2/1970
Film biography of the peasant poet of the
Romantic school.
d/sc David Jones
lp Freddie Jones; Gerald Lawson;
Elizabeth Croft; Martin Howells;
Sharon Gurney; Patrick Stewart
DANCE OF THE SEVEN VEILS 15/2/1970
Ken Russell's subjective impression of Richard
Strauss.
d Ken Russell;
sc Henry Reed, Ken Russell
lp Christopher Gable; Judith Paris;
Kenneth Colley; Vladek Sheybal; James Mellor

HEART OF BRITAIN 20/9/1970
A portrait of Humphrey Jennings, British
documentary film maker. Contributors include
members of his family. Made in collaboration
with the COI and the NFA.
d/sc Robert Vas; *comm* Paul Daneman
with Lindsay Anderson, Marius Goring,
Stuart Legg, Roland Penrose, Kathleen Raine
I REGRET NOTHING 27/12/1970
Film biography of singer Edith Piaf.
p/sc Michael Houldey
with Charles Aznavour, Bruno Coquatrix,
Yves Montand, Eddie Constantine,
Michel Emer, Marcel Blisténe
THREE LOOMS WAITING 13/6/1971
Drama teacher Dorothy Heathcote – a film
portrait about her life and work.
p Ronald Smedley; *comm* Ronald Eyre
FIFTY YEARS ON 7/11/1971
Patrick Garland talks to Sir John Gielgud, on the
50th anniversary of his first appearance on the
English stage.
p Hal Burton
PARADISE RESTORED 2/1/1972
1665: John Milton flees to Chalfont St Giles with
his third wife and three daughters in search of
peace.
d/sc Don Taylor
lp John Neville; Polly James;
Anne Stallybrass; Rosemary McHale;
Jane Hayden; Alan Rowe; Bernard Hepton
ACTOR, I SAID 9/4/1972
Play dramatising the problems of actors.
d/sc Don Taylor
lp Barry Foster; Martin Jarvis;
Ellen Dryden; Tracey Lloyd; Sylvia Coleridge
MORECAMBE AND WISE: FOOLS RUSH IN
18/2/1973
Follows the two weeks of rehearsal that led up to
the recording of the 16/2/1973 edition of The
MORECAMBE AND WISE SHOW.
p Ronald Smedley; *with* John Ammonds,
Eddie Braben, Eric Morecambe, Ernie Wise
The RUNAWAY 18/11/1973
Play about a successful novelist visiting friends in
the country.
d/sc Don Taylor
lp Sylvia Kay; Paul Daneman;
Peter Bowles; Angela Scoular; Malcolm Tierney;
Richard Thorp; Roy Marsden; Tony Aitken
FRANÇOIS TRUFFAUT – FILM MAKER 2/12/1973
A survey of the career of François Truffaut,
which includes interviews with Jeanne Moreau,
Catherine Deneuve, Claude Jade, and Truffaut
himself.
p Michael Darlow;
sc Ann Blaber, Michael Darlow;
nar Brenda Kempner
MUSIC FROM THE FLAMES 10/11/1974
Filmed in 1974 in Moscow and Leningrad,
includes an interview with Shostakovich and
performances of his music by David and Igor
Oistrakh, Sviatoslav Richter and Tatyana
Nikolaeva.
p Ian Engelmann; *sc* Norman Kay
FIND ME 8/12/1974
A drama about an artist in a hostile land.
d Don Taylor; *sc* David Mercer
lp Anthony Hopkins; Sheila Allen;
David Collings; Charlotte Cornwell;
Graham James; Stephen Moore; Rosalyn Elvin
AFRICAN SANCTUS 30/3/1975
The journey made by composer/explorer David
Fanshawe through Africa which inspired his
composition of a Latin Mass.
p Herbert Chappell
ORFEO 17/3/1977
The ballet, created by Robert North, of Thea
Musgrave's work 'Orpheo'; interview with Thea
Musgrave.
d Keith Cheetham; *p* Tony Staveacre
HALF A SMILE FROM STOKE 21/4/1977
Arthur Berry, painter, lives at Wolstanton,
Stoke-on-Trent. He reflects on some walls, some
faces around him, some pictures in front of him,
some memories behind him.
p Philip Donnellan
PURE RADIO 3/11/1977
Film celebrating the group of men and women
who worked in BBC Radio Features 1936–1964.
p/sc Philip Donnellan

The PILGRIMAGE OF TI-JEAN 30/8/1978
French-Canadian Jean Carignan visits Ireland to
search for the music of fiddler Michael Coleman,
who died in 1945.
p Philip Donnellan
DREAD, BEAT AN' BLOOD 7/6/1979
Made for the Arts Council. Features Jamaican
poet, writer and musician Linton Kwesi Johnson
and the black London community to which he
addresses himself.
d/p Franco Rosso
PIG EARTH 21/6/1979
Art critic and photographer John Berger talks
about his new book 'Pig Earth'.
p Michael Dibb; *with* Teodor Shanin
SCHALCKEN THE PAINTER 23/12/1979
Tale of the supernatural set in seventeenth
century Holland, from a story by Sheridan Le
Fanu. Based on the real paintings of Godfried
Schalcken (1643–1706).
d/sc Leslie Megahey; *pres* Charles Gray
lp Maurice Denham; Jeremy Clyde;
John Justin; Cheryl Kennedy; Anthony Sharp;
Ann Tirard; Val Penny; Roy Evans; Eric Francis

OMRI'S BURNING (HTV 16/10/1969)
A Saturday in the life and emotional death of
three people.
d/p Marc Miller; *sc* Ewart Alexander
lp Ian Holm; Diana Coupland; Tessa Wyatt

ON CALL TO A NATION (BBC 22/10/1958)
The work of doctors under the National Health
Service, and the views of GPs on the NHS.
p Richard Cawston

ON CAMERA (BBC)
Regional documentary series from East Anglia.
The UNDEFEATED 22/1/1973
Documentary film concerning a family with a
thalidomide son.
p Douglas Salmon

ON THE BUSES (LWT 1969–73)
Comedy series set around the exploits of a bus
driver, his family and his colleagues at the bus
garage where he works.
p Derrick Goodwin;
sc Ronald Wolfe, Ronald Chesney
regulars Reg Varney; Doris Hare;
Michael Robbins; Anna Karen; Bob Grant;
Stephen Lewis
The OTHER WOMAN 18/12/1970
lp Kate Williams
The BEST MAN 3/10/1971
lp Hugh Walters; Sandra Miller
The INSPECTOR'S PETS 10/10/1971
lp Don McKillop
The EPIDEMIC 17/10/1971
lp Sharon Young; Ruth Kettlewell;
Cheryl Hall; Philip Dunbar
CANTEEN TROUBLE 31/10/1971
lp Andria Lawrence; Fanny Carby;
Glen Whitter; Luan Peters
The NEW NURSE 7/11/1971
lp Hal Dyer; Sandra Miller;
Keith Norrish
STAN'S UNIFORM 21/11/1971
lp Robin Parkinson; Sandra Miller;
Hugh Walters
BOXING DAY SOCIAL 26/12/1971
lp Gillian Lind; Helen Fraser

ON THE INSIDE LOOKING OUT
(BBC 5–19/4/1968)
Looks at three British families who have settled
in Europe.
p/sc Tom Savage
ITALY 5/4/1968
The Harrison family in Italy, following the move
of Peter Harrison from Birmingham to Milan to
work as a salesman for an electrical company.
FRANCE 12/4/1968
The Rye family in France, after Tom Rye had
moved from Bristol to Toulouse to work as a
liaison engineer on the Concorde project.
GERMANY 19/4/1968
Graham Symonds and his family in Germany,
following his move to Cologne to work as a car
designer.

ON THE NATIONAL HEALTH
(BBC 7/10–9/12/1974)
Documentary series on the establishment and
development of the National Health Service of
Britain, and contemporary problems.
p Peter Riding;
pres Michael Reinhold, Anne Lapping
1948 AND ALL THAT 7/10/1974
Lord Hill, Secretary of the British Medical
Association (BMA) at the time of the
negotiations, talks about the compromise
Aneurin Bevan made with the doctors.
WHATEVER IS HAPPENING TO THE FAMILY
DOCTOR? 4/11/1974
The GP and the NHS.
COMMUNITY HOSPITALS – AN OPEN OR SHUT
CASE? 11/11/1974
Should general practitioners be encouraged to
run their own local community hospitals?
d Chris Jelley

ON THE SPOT (BBC 1962)
Quiz programme in which contestants explain
their original business ideas to judges William
Hardcastle, Sir Miles Thomas and Valerie
Hobson.
ON THE SPOT 24/5/1962
p Innes Lloyd; *intro* Peter West

ONCE A KINGDOM (Anglia)
The SHIFTING COAST 17/10/1962
The process of erosion and accretion on the
coastlines of East Anglia, explained by Professor
A.J. Steers.
d Ron Downing

ONCE IN A LIFETIME
(Yorkshire TV 1979–82)
Documentary series.
The VILLAGE THAT WOULD NOT TALK 27/2/1979
Barry Shaw investigates the case of a man who
lived to tell police of his own murder.
d Barry Cockcroft

ONCE UPON A TIME
(Granada 12/8–9/9/1973)
Series of traditional stories for children adding a
different aspect to the traditional story.
BUTTONS 19/8/1973
d Gordon Flemyng; *p* Jonathan Powell;
sc Alun Owen
lp Tommy Steele; Peggy Mount;
Adrienne Posta; Arthur English; John Justin;
Dinsdale Landen; Jenny Runacre; Rula Lenska;
Ken Parry; John Rhys-Davies

ONCE UPON A TIME (Granada 1979–82)
Story-telling series for children.
GOLDILOCKS AND THE THREE BEARS 29/5/1979
d/p Pat Baker; *sc* Barry Hill;
pres Peter Davison

**ONCE UPON A TIME IS NOW...THE STORY
OF PRINCESS GRACE** (US Allyn-Lunney;
GB *tx* 11/12/1977)
A profile of Princess Grace of Monaco. Lee
Grant interviews James Stewart, William
Holden, Raymond Massey, Alfred Hitchcock
and Stanley Kramer.
d Kevin Billington

ONCE UPON A UNION (BBC 12/3/1977)
Reconstructs the events of 1707 when Scotland
and England agreed to the Act of Union.
d Matthew Robinson; *p* Tam Fry;
sc John McGrath;
rep Donald MacCormick, Tom Mangold,
Mike Neville, James Cox, Robert McKenzie
lp Ian McDiarmid; Donald Douglas;
Alex McCrindle; John Bett; Brown Derby;
Iain Cuthbertson; John Grieve;
Leonard Maguire; Peter Howell;
David King; Sean Caffrey

ONE IN EVERY HUNDRED
(Rediffusion 8/6/1966)
The plight of mentally handicapped people in
Canada and Great Britain.
d Maurice Hatton; *p* Richard De La Mare;
sc Paul Barker; *comm* John Stride

ONE MAN AND HIS DOG (BBC 1976–)
Sheepdog trials.
ONE MAN AND HIS DOG 12/1/1977
p Philip Gilbert;
pres Phil Drabble, Eric Halsall

ONE MAN'S HUNGER
(Rediffusion 13/3/1963)
The malnutrition suffered by a farmer and his
family in Soharauna, India.
d Bill Morton; *p* David Windlesham;
sc John Sandilands, James Cameron

ONE PAIR OF EYES (BBC 1967–74; 1984)
Documentary series.
YOU'VE GOT TO WIN 18/11/1967
The British attitude towards sport.
d Peter Robinson; *nar* Peter Wilson
MARTY FELDMAN 7/6/1969
Marty Feldman looks at humour through the
people who create it.
d Francis Megahy; *with* Peter Sellers,
Sandy Powell, Eric Morecambe, Peter Brough,
Dudley Moore, Annie Ross, Johnny Speight,
Denis Norden, Barry Took
RETURN AS A STRANGER 17/10/1970
Poet and author Dom Moraes returns to India,
the land of his birth.
p Anthony De Lotbinière

ONE STEP BEYOND
(US Collier Young Production 1959–61;
GB Lancer Films, syndicated 1961)
Supernatural anthology series; thirteen of which
were produced in Britain.
d John Newland; *p* Peter Marriott
The STRANGER 28/2/1961
sc Larry Marcus
lp Bill Nagy; Peter Dyneley;
Patrick McAlliney; Graham Stark;
Harold Kasket
JUSTICE 7/3/1961
sc Guy Morgan
lp Clifford Evans; Meredith Edwards;
Barbara Mullen; Pauline Jameson;
Edward Evans
The FACE 14/3/1961
sc Derry Quinn
lp Sean Kelly; John Brown;
Penelope Horner; Victor Platt; Robert Cawdron
THAT ROOM UPSTAIRS 21/3/1961
sc Merwin Gerard, Larry Marcus
lp Lois Maxwell; David Knight;
Anthony Oliver; Gilda Emmanueli;
David Markham
SIGNAL RECEIVED 4/4/1961
sc Derry Quinn
lp Mark Eden; Terry Palmer;
Richard Gale; Viola Keats
The CONFESSION 11/4/1961
sc Larry Marcus
lp Donald Pleasence; Adrienne Corri;
Robert Raglan; Raymond Rollett
The AVENGERS 25/4/1961
sc Martin Benson
lp André Morell; Lisa Gastoni;
Stanley Van Beers; Carl Jaffe
The PRISONER 2/5/1961
sc Larry Marcus
lp Anton Diffring; Faith Brook;
Catherine Feller; Sandor Eles
The SORCERER 23/5/1961
sc Derry Quinn
lp Christopher Lee; Martin Benson;
Gabrielli Licudi; Alfred Burke
The VILLA 6/6/1961
sc Derry Quinn
lp Elizabeth Sellars; Geoffrey Toone;
Marla Landi; David Horne; Michael Crawford
The TIGER 20/6/1961
sc Ian Stuart Black
lp Pauline Challenor; Pamela Brown;
Elspeth March; Patsy Smart
NIGHTMARE 27/6/1961
sc Martin Benson
lp Peter Wyngarde; Mary Peach;
Ambrosine Phillpotts; Ferdy Mayne
EYE WITNESS 4/7/1961
sc Derry Quinn
lp John Meillon; Rose Alba;
Anton Rodgers

The ONEDIN LINE (BBC 1971–80)
Drama series telling the story of a young man's
rise to power in the booming Liverpool shipping
business of the mid-nineteenth century.
regulars Peter Gilmore; Anne Stallybrass;
Brian Rawlinson; Jessica Benton; Howard Lang;
Edward Chapman
WHEN MY SHIP COMES HOME 10/12/1971
d Ken Hannam; *p* Peter Graham Scott;
sc David Weir
lp Mary Webster; James Warwick
MUTINY 24/12/1971
d David Cunliffe; *p* Peter Graham Scott;
sc Ian Kennedy Martin
lp Iain Cuthbertson; John Thaw;
Philip Bond; Michael Billington;
Lawrence Douglas
The HARD CASE 17/9/1972
d/p Peter Graham Scott; *sc* Cyril Abraham
lp Philip Bond; Michael Billington
'FRISCO BOUND 12/11/1972
d David Cunliffe; *p* Peter Graham Scott;
sc Allan Prior
lp Philip Bond; Michael Billington;
Richard Hurndall; John Hollis; Paul Lavers;
Alexandra Knowles
ICE AND FIRE 16/12/1973
d David Sullivan Proudfoot;
p Peter Graham Scott; *sc* Allan Prior
lp Michael Billington; Caroline Harris;
Kate Nelligan
LIVERPOOL BOUND 22/7/1979
p Geraint Morris; *sc* Mervyn Haisman
lp Aubrey Richards; Gillian Bailey;
Jill Gascoine; Thomas Heathcote;
Jimmy Gardner
The HOMECOMING 29/7/1979
d David Reynolds; *p* Geraint Morris;
sc Mervyn Haisman
lp Michael Walker; John Wentworth;
Jill Gascoine; Christopher Douglas; Tom Adams
The PADDY WESTERS 5/8/1979
d Pennant Roberts; *p* Geraint Morris;
sc Douglas Watkinson
lp Jill Gascoine; Mary Webster;
Christopher Douglas; Laura Hartong
DIRTY CARGO 12/8/1979
p Geraint Morris; *sc* Nick McCarty
lp John Rapley; Jürgen Andersen;
Maurice Colbourne; Jill Gascoine;
Laura Hartong
TO HONOUR AND OBEY 19/8/1979
d David Reynolds; *p* Geraint Morris;
sc Roger Parkes
lp Keith Jayne; John Justin
RUNNING FREE 26/8/1979
d Pennant Roberts; *p* Geraint Morris;
sc Roger Parkes
lp Michael Walker; Jill Gascoine;
Patricia Prior; Derrick Gilbert; Trevor Martin
STORM CLOUDS 9/9/1979
d David Reynolds; *p* Geraint Morris;
sc Simon Masters
lp Christopher Douglas; Lawrence Douglas;
Michael St. John; Michael Walker;
Laura Hartong
OUTWARD BOUND 16/9/1979
d Pennant Roberts; *p* Geraint Morris;
sc Cyril Abraham
lp Michael Walker; Laura Hartong;
Christopher Douglas; Jeananne Crowley
HOMEWARD BOUND 23/9/1979
d Gerald Blake; *p* Geraint Morris;
sc Cyril Abraham
lp Keith Jayne; Jill Gascoine;
Maurice Colbourne; Patricia Prior;
Valerie Phillips

ONLY WHEN I LAUGH
(Yorkshire TV 1979–82)
Sitcom set in a hospital ward.
d/p Vernon Lawrence; *sc* Eric Chappell
regulars James Bolam; Peter Bowles;
Christopher Strauli; Richard Wilson;
Derrick Branche
A BED WITH A VIEW 29/10/1979
OPERATION NORMAN 5/11/1979
The RUMOUR 12/11/1979
The MAN WITH THE FACE 19/11/1979
lp Stephen Greif; Elin Jenkins
LET THEM EAT CAKE 26/11/1979
lp Robert Gillespie; Pamela Cundell

ONLY WHEN I LAUGH cont.

TANGLED WEB 3/12/1979
lp Sally Osborn
IS THERE A DOCTOR IN THE HOUSE?
10/12/1979
lp John Junkin

OPEN DOOR (BBC 1973–)
Open access series.
GRAPEVINE 6/10/1974
Community sex education programme in north
London.
ONE EVERY 20 SECONDS 10/2/1975
Bristol Victims Support Scheme, a voluntary
group which helps victims of crime. The title
refers to the frequencies of burglaries.
ASSOCIATION FOR NEIGHBOURHOOD
COUNCILS 17/3/1975
The work of the Association for Neighbourhood
Councils.
A PLAYGROUP OF OUR OWN 25/10/1975
A film by the Pre-School Playgroups
Association, a nationwide movement of self-help
groups for families with young children.
SO YOU THINK IT'S A FREE COUNTRY 1/11/1975
The work of the National Council for Civil
Liberties.
comm Peter Despard, Martin Kettle,
Nettie Pollard
TRIBUNAL 6/12/1975
Play about bureaucracy written by a Bradford
lathe operator and enacted by Bradford workers.
auth James Moran
TO A BRIGHTER FUTURE 31/1/1976
The Vegan Society demonstrates the variety and
health aspects of its no-animal products diet.
BRITISH CAMPAIGN TO STOP IMMIGRATION
28/2/1976
Argues against immigration to Great Britain,
made by a right-wing group.
OPEN DOOR: (FOLLOW-UP SURVEY) 29/5/1976
People who took part in the series talk to Chris
Dunkley about what they have achieved with
their programmes.
ALL AGAINST THE BOMB 1/10/1976
Takes the form of a mock news story which tries
to highlight the inadequate treatment which such
issues usually get from the media.
TO LIVE IN PEACE 7/3/1977
Presented by the Anglo-Israeli Friendship
League and explains the future of Israel's right
to exist.
pres Patrick Cosgrave, Paul Johnson
SOUTH AFRICA: THE RIFLE, THE SARACEN
AND THE GALLOWS 20/2/1978
The Anti-Apartheid Movement in South Africa.
Highlights Britain's role in bolstering apartheid.
pres Neil Kinnock
IT AIN'T HALF RACIST, MUM 1/3/1979
The Campaign against Racism in the Media.
pres Maggie Steed
SOUTHALL ON TRIAL 22/9/1979
The work of the Southall Campaign Committee
in the wake of the racial unrest in London which
led to the death of Blair Peach during a
demonstration.
WRECKERS IN THE TOWN HALL 8/12/1979
The Campaign for Demolition Control, on the
ways in which local authorities destroy local
communities by indiscriminate demolition and
ways that this can be combatted.

OPEN NIGHT (Granada 1971–79)
Open discussion programme in which an
audience puts their criticisms of television
programmes to a panel of celebrities.
WHAT VIEWERS WOULD LIKE TO SEE ON
TELEVISION 15/7/1972
Michael Scott chairs a discussion between a
studio audience and representatives from
television.
d Eric Harrison

OPIUM (ATV 9–23/5/1978)
Three-part documentary series on the drug
trade.
d Adrian Cowell
The WHITE POWDER OPERA 9/5/1978
The Triad gangs and the heroin trade in Hong
Kong.

The POLITICIANS 23/5/1978
Investigation into the world's illicit opium trade.
US Congressional Committee holds secret
negotiations with Kun Sar, the most powerful of
the narcotics traffickers, who offers to destroy a
third of the world's opium. US President Jimmy
Carter and aides reject the deal.

OPPORTUNITY KNOCKS!
(ABC 1964–68)
Talent show hosted by Hughie Green.
OPPORTUNITY KNOCKS! 20/7/1968
An all-winners special, bringing back the acts
from previous shows voted into top place,
together with some of the most popular stars
from past series.
p Royston Mayoh

OPPORTUNITY KNOCKS! (Thames 1971–78)
Talent show.
OPPORTUNITY KNOCKS! 30/10/1972
Talent contest featuring previous winners Steven
Smith and father, Kathleen Mooson, Socrates
and Bobby Crush.
d/p Royston Mayoh; *pres* Hughie Green
OPPORTUNITY KNOCKS: THE FINAL SHOW
20/3/1978
d Stuart Hall; *p* Peter Dulay;
pres Hughie Green; *with* Les Dawson,
Peters and Lee, Tom O'Connor, Lena Zavaroni,
Frank Carson, Little and Large, Mary Hopkin,
Pam Ayres, Freddie Davies, Berni Flint

OPTIONS (ATV 17/10/1972)
A comparison of the outlooks and way of life of
a couple who run a traditional grocer's shop near
London, and two men who have dropped out of
society to live in a wood in Surrey.
p Tony Wheeler, Lawrence Moore

The ORANGE AND THE GREEN
(Ulster TV 19/4/1966)
A documentary marking the 50th anniversary of
the Easter Rising in Ireland in 1916. Brian
Connell presents the story of Ireland from the
Rebellion to present times. With Dr G.G.
Lyttle, Denis Ireland, Professor Liam O'Briain,
Cathal O'Seanain, Riobard Langford, The Go-
Luckie Three and The Dubliners.
d/p Jeremy Murray-Brown; *sc* Brian Connell

ORDE WINGATE (BBC 16–30/7/1976)
Drama series of three programmes tracing the
life and career of the controversial leader of the
1943–44 Burma Expeditions.
PART 1: IF I FORGET THEE O JERUSALEM
16/7/1976
d Bill Hays; *p* Innes Lloyd;
sc Don Shaw
lp Barry Foster; Nigel Stock;
Clive Graham; Garrick Hagon; James Cosmo;
John White; Anthony Gardner; Barry Linchan;
Sheila Ruskin

The ORGANIZATION
(Yorkshire TV 16/4–28/5/1972)
Seven-part drama set in the jungle of middle
management.
exec.p Peter Willes; *sc* Philip Mackie
lp Peter Egan; Norman Bird;
Donald Sinden; Philip Stone; Patricia Maynard
MR. PERSHORE AND KEN GRIST 16/4/1972
d James Ormerod
KEN GRIST AND EVE 23/4/1972
d Christopher Hodson
EVE AND RODNEY SPURLING 30/4/1972
d James Ormerod
RODNEY SPURLING AND PETER FRAME
7/5/1972
d Christopher Hodson
PETER FRAME AND VERONICA 14/5/1972
d James Ormerod
VERONICA AND MR. PULMAN 21/5/1972
d Christopher Hodson
MR. PULMAN AND MR. PERSHORE 28/5/1972
d James Ormerod

ORLANDO (Rediffusion 1965–68)
Series for children featuring the character played
by Sam Kydd from the series CRANE (1963–
65).

DANGEROUS WATERS: EPISODE 1: CLUE TO A
CLUE 27/9/1966
d Bryan Shiner; *p* Ronald Marriott;
sc Ivor Jay
lp David Munro; Judy Robinson;
Agnes Lauchlan; John Steiner;
Donald Layne-Smith
DANGEROUS WATERS: EPISODE 3: RHYME –
BUT NO REASON 11/10/1966
d Bryan Shiner; *p* Ronald Marriott;
sc Ivor Jay
lp David Munro; Judy Robinson;
Agnes Lauchlan; John Steiner; Jack Woolgar;
Ben Kingsley

ORSON WELLES SKETCHBOOK NO. 1
(BBC 24/4/1955)
Orson Welles tells stories about his life,
illustrated by his sketches of the places he has
visited.

OSCAR (Tyne Tees 1977–79)
Animated series about Oscar the rabbit.
d Bernard Preston; *p* Bob Murray;
sc Norman Dahl; *voice* Lance Percival
FLYING CARPET 31/3/1977
CARROTS 14/4/1977
ZAGGY DISAPPEARS 22/4/1977
PARTY GAMES 20/7/1977
MAGIC JUNK FLUTE 24/7/1977
GNASHER'S BIRTHDAY 3/8/1977
NO ESCAPE 17/8/1977
OSCAR 4/3/1978
OSCAR 6/4/1978
GNASHERS THE WIZARD 13/4/1978
OSCAR 4/6/1978
TOOTH CLEANING MACHINE 9/1/1979
The SPOOK 11/1/1979

OTHELLO (BBC 15/12/1955)
Production of the Shakespeare play.
p Tony Richardson
lp Gordon Heath; Rosemary Harris;
Paul Rogers; James Maxwell; Edmund Willard;
Robert Hardy; Peter Welch; George Skillan

OTHELLO (BBC 1/10/1959)
A performance of Verdi's opera with the Royal
Philharmonic Orchestra conducted by Bryan
Balkwill, and the Glyndebourne Festival Chorus.
d/p Rudolph Cartier
with John Ford, Charles Holland,
Heidi Krall, Ronald Lewis, Forbes Robinson

The OTHER LINDISFARNE
(Tyne Tees 1/3/1972)
The rock band Lindisfarne discuss their musical
ambitions and the importance of their roots in
Tyneside.
d Ken Stephinson; *exec.p* Leslie Barrett

OTHER PEOPLE'S CHILDREN
(BBC 9/1–15/5/1977)
A series of nineteen programmes for
childminders.
SPARE THE ROD 17/4/1977
Discipline for difficult children.
d Suzanne Davies; *p* David Allen;
with Mavis Nicholson

OTHER PEOPLE'S JOBS (BBC 1950–56)
Documentary series.
SNAPSHOT 2/8/1950
Richard Dimbleby visits Kodak, Harrow and is
shown a variety of different kinds of camera for
different jobs.
The BELL FOUNDER 18/1/1956
The 200–year-old bell foundry at Loughborough,
Leicestershire. Interview with Paul Taylor, bell-
founder about the ancient, dying craft.
p David Martin

The OTHER ROUTE (BBC 31/5–5/7/1966)
Six programmes for teachers and parents on
further education and the opportunities to be
found in it. Part of the 'Outlook' series.

ENGINEERING 7/6/1966
Further education in engineering with
A.S.Williamson, Principal, Ipswich Civic
College; P.R.Bosworth, Group Training Officer,
Truscon Ltd.; M.Smith, Deputy Head, Hartcliffe
School and D.Woosley, Head, Downer
Grammar School.
p Roger Owen

The OTHER SIDE (BBC 27/4–25/5/1979)
Anthology drama series.
ONLY CONNECT 18/5/1979
d Richard Stroud; *p* W. Stephen Gilbert;
sc Noel Greig, Drew Griffiths
lp Joseph O'Conor; Sam Dale;
Christopher Banks; Karl Johnson

The OTHER SIDE OF PARADISE
(AU ABC 15/7/1968)
A report on Fiji.
d Ken Hannam

OUR BELIEVING WORLD (US NBC)
Discussion and religious news programme.
OUR BELIEVING WORLD 9/7/1952
Dr Fisher, The Archbishop of Canterbury, at
Christ Church, Boston, Mass., attending the
57th General Convention of the Episcopal
Church. Dr Fisher's sermon is shown.
d W. Lawrence Baker; *comm* Richard McCann

OUR MAN AT ST. MARK'S
(Rediffusion 1963–65)
Comedy series featuring the activities of an easy-
going country vicar. Title was later changed to
OUR MAN FROM ST. MARK'S (1966).
KNOW THINE ENEMY 19/7/1965
d Richard Doubleday; *p* Eric Maschwitz;
sc James Kelly, Peter Miller
lp Donald Sinden; Joan Hickson;
Harry Fowler; Brian Vaughan; Walter Hall;
Jane Evers; Frank Henderson

OUR MAN FROM ST. MARK'S
(Rediffusion 1966)
Comedy series extending the situation originated
in OUR MAN AT ST. MARK'S (1963–65).
The PEPPERMINT MAN 18/7/1966
d Bill Turner; *p* Eric Maschwitz;
sc James Kelly, Peter Miller
lp Donald Sinden; Joan Hickson;
Clive Morton; Peter Vaughan; Martin Wyldeck;
Margaret Ward; Dorothea Phillips
The SILENT VILLAGE 25/7/1966
d Richard Doubleday; *p* Eric Maschwitz;
sc James Kelly, Peter Miller
lp Donald Sinden; Joan Hickson;
Clive Morton; Peter Vaughan; Martin Wyldeck;
Margaret Ward; Dorothea Phillips

OUR MAN IN LUSAKA (BBC 3/7/1979)
A profile of Leonard Allison, the British High
Commissioner in Zambia.
p Jonathan Stedall

OUR PEOPLE (Thames 11/1–22/2/1979)
Documentary series on immigration.
Production team Tunde Anthony,
Alan Horrox, Annie Kossoff, Gillian McCredie,
John Rowe, Charlie Stafford;
exec. p Diana Potter
IMMIGRANT 11/1/1979
Who are the immigrants and how do the
immigration laws work?
EMPIRE 1/2/1979
How the British Empire has brought about
multi-racial Britain.
A LONG WAY TO WORK 8/2/1979
Life and work of immigrants in France,
Germany, Sweden and Britain.
CARNIVAL 22/2/1979
The Anti-Nazi League Carnival of 1978 – a
demonstration of support for a multi-racial
Britain.

OUR SHOW (LWT 1977–78)
Saturday morning show for children.
OUR SHOW 4/2/1978
d Ted Ayling; *p* Victoria Poushkine-Relf;
pres Elvis Payne, Susan Tully,
Graham Fletcher

OUR TOWN APPLEBY (Border 30/10/1967)
The Westmoreland town of Appleby.
d John Pattison Tomkins; *ed* Alan Pateman;
comm Derek Batey, Alick Cleaver

OUR TOWN KENDAL (Border 11/12/1967)
The Cumbrian town of Kendal.
d John Pattison Tomkins; *ph* Brian Wilson;
comm Allan Cartner

OUT (Euston Films 24/7–28/8/1978)
Six-part crime thriller serial.
EPISODE 1: IT MUST BE THE SUIT 24/7/1978
d Jim Goddard; *p* Barry Hanson;
sc Trevor Preston
lp Tom Bell; Brian Croucher;
Lynn Farleigh; Frank Mills; Peter Blake;
Oscar James; John Junkin; Maurice O'Connell;
Norman Rodway

OUT OF BURNING (ATV 23/5/1962)
Sir Kenneth Clark looks at the new Coventry
Cathedral, and appraises the work of Sir Basil
Spence, Graham Sutherland, John Piper,
Geoffrey Clarke, and John Hutton.
d Stephen Wade

OUT OF STEP
(Rediffusion 18/9–18/12/1957)
Documentary series in which Daniel Farson
looks for unconventional opinions.
d Geoffrey Hughes
OTHER WORLDS ARE WATCHING US 25/9/1957
Interviews with people who believe in the
existence of flying saucers.
sc Elkan Allan
NUDISM 2/10/1957
A report on naturism.
sc Elkan Allan
TUNE IN TO NATURE'S RADIO 13/11/1957
A report on people who attempt to improve
vegetable growth using radio waves.
WITCHCRAFT 4/12/1957
A report on witchcraft in Britain.
sc Daniel Farson, Stanley Craig
The SEVENTH DAY 11/12/1957
A report on the Lord's Day Observance Society.
sc David Kentish
ONE MAN AGAINST THE WORLD 18/12/1957
An interview with Harold Steele, a protestor
against nuclear weapons.

OUT OF THE DARKNESS
(ITV various 1973)
Programmes produced for Advent.
HALF THE BATTLE'S WON (Tyne Tees 2/12/1973)
Michael Partington presents a report on a mental
care centre at Botton, Yorkshire, and its
relationship with the local community.
d Bernard Preston

OUT OF THE UNKNOWN (BBC 1965–71)
Anthology series of science-fiction plays.
The MACHINE STOPS 6/10/1966
d Philip Saville; *p* Irene Shubik;
sc Kenneth Cavander, Clive Donner;
auth E.M. Forster
lp Yvonne Mitchell; Michael Gothard;
Nike Arrighi; Jonathan Hansen

OUT OF THIS WORLD (BBC 25/8/1959)
Hywel Davies reports on the daily lives of the
nuns of a Carmelite convent at Presteigne in
Radnorshire, and interviews the Prioress.
p David J. Thomas

OUT OF THIS WORLD (US European
Broadcasting Union 2/5/1965)
The inaugural programme of the first commercial
communications satellite 'Early Bird' introduced
by Anthony Wedgwood Benn.
d Peter Frazer-Jones, Anton Bowler,
Anthony Flanagan; *pres* Brian Johnson;
interv Richard Dimbleby

OUT OF TOWN
(Southern TV 1963–69; 1972–78)
Documentary series on the countryside.
pres Jack Hargreaves
DUCKSHOOTING 10/8/1973
d George Egan

The MULE'S OPERATION 6/2/1975
Jack Hargreaves and the story of a mule he
bought.
d George Egan
BEE SKIPS 17/3/1978
The technique of making bee skips from straw.

OUTA-SPACE! (BBC 10/2–24/3/1973)
Animation series.
OUTA-SPACE! 17/2/1973
p Paul Ciani;
sc Philip Griffin, Paul Ciani

The OUTER LIMITS
(US Daystar Productions-Villa di Stefano
Productions-United Artists TV 1963–65)
Science-fiction anthology series.
The HUNDRED DAYS OF THE DRAGON
23/9/1963
d Byron Haskin; *p* Joseph Stefano;
sc Allan Balter, Robert Mintz
lp Sidney Blackmer; Richard Loo;
Phillip Pine; Mark Roberts; Nancy Rennick;
Joan Camden; Clarence Lung

OUTLAWS (US NBC 1960–62)
Western set in the Oklahoma Territory in the
1890s.
MY FRIEND THE HORSE THIEF 19/10/1961
d Paul Stanley; *p* Frank Telford;
sc Clair Huffaker
lp Don Collier; Bruce Yarnell;
Barton MacLane; Brian Keith

OUTLOOK (BBC 1958)
Documentary series.
WHAT IS IT LIKE TO BE A DOG? 20/5/1958
The efficiency of a dog's senses and the
possibility of a canine sixth sense. Contributors
are Solly Zuckerman, Konrad Lorenz, Col. J.Y.
Baldwin, E.H. Ashton, D.G. Moulton and A.M.
Warnock.
d Charles Clifford

OUTLOOK (HTV 1979–80)
Current affairs and documentary series on Welsh
issues.
TOO LOW FOR COMFORT 12/1/1979
Report on low-flying RAF aircraft over Wales.
p Geraint Talfan Davies; *p* Cenwyn Edwards
PUBLIC PURSE 15/11/1979
The state of the Welsh economy, discussed on
the day of the Government White Paper
announcing a fixed minimum lending rate, and
plans for public sector cuts.
d David Lloyd;
p Geraint Talfan Davies, Cenwyn Edwards;
pres Max Perkins; *rep* David Williams

The OWL SERVICE
(Granada 21/12/1969–8/2/1970)
Drama serial for children.
EPISODE ONE 21/12/1969
d/p Peter Plummer; *sc* Alan Garner
lp Dorothy Edwards; Gillian Hills;
Michael Holden; Raymond Llewellyn;
Edwin Richfield; Francis Wallis

P

PAGES FROM MEMORY (HTV 30/8/1973)
Emyr Daniel interviews James Griffiths, former
Deputy Leader of the Labour Party and
Secretary of State for Wales, about his career,
and current political issues.
d Owen Griffiths, Terry Delacey

PAGLIACCI (BBC 1/12/1960)
Performance of the opera by Ruiggiero
Leoncavallo, with the London Symphony
Orchestra conducted by Charles Mackerras.
d Michael Leeston-Smith; *p* Vladek Sheybal
with Elaine Malbin, Robert Thomas,
Bernard Turgeon, Kevin Miller, Peter Glossop

The PAINTER AND HIS WORLD
(BBC 6/10–8/12/1963)
A ten-part series introducing European art
1300–1900.

THE PAINTER AND HIS WORLD *cont.*

JAN VAN EYCK 13/10/1963
The work of the Flemish painter Jan van Eyck, especially 'The Betrothal of the Arnolfini'.
p Victor Poole; *pres* Basil Taylor

PANORAMA (BBC 1953–)
Current affairs series.
SALVADOR DALI 5/5/1955
An interview with the Surrealist painter Salvador Dali by Malcolm Muggeridge.
CIVIL DEFENCE MAKES SENSE 1957
Woodrow Wyatt interviews the Home Office Chief Scientist on the likely results of ten H-bombs falling on Britain. He looks at a shelter constructed in an ordinary home, and interviews the housewife, and talks to the Chief of the Civil Defence staff.
PLANNED GIVING 11/7/1960
The director of an American firm which raises funds for charities explains how his company works.
p Michael Peacock
CHILDREN'S NEW ALPHABET 5/12/1960
Film inserts only of the report.
p Michael Peacock
The DALAI LAMA 4/6/1962
The Dalai Lama on Tibet and the United Nations, Sir Robert Menzies on the EEC. Reports on public opinion polls and US foreign policy.
p Jeremy Murray-Brown, Christopher Ralling
BIDAULT INTERVIEW 4/3/1963
An interview with French politician, Georges Bidault, in exile because of his opposition to De Gaulle's Algerian policy.
LYNDON JOHNSON IN TEXAS 25/11/1963
Presented by Robin Day, an examination of America after the assassination of President John F. Kennedy. Includes an interview with Hubert Humphrey about the new President, Lyndon B. Johnson, and an interview with Johnson recorded during his last days as Vice-President. Looks at the potential Republican candidates who will be competing for the Presidency in 1964, including Richard Nixon.
VISIT TO BELSEN 12/4/1965
Richard Dimbleby introduces a report on Belsen, site of the former concentration camp.
p Richard Francis
ADLAI E. STEVENSON 12/7/1965
Robin Day interviews Adlai Stevenson on American foreign policy.
p Richard Francis
RHODESIA – HAROLD WILSON'S VISIT 1/11/1965
A report on Harold Wilson's visit to Rhodesia for talks with Ian Smith.
p Richard Francis
RHODESIA – VIEWPOINTS 15/11/1965
People in the street give their views on the Rhodesian question.
p Richard Francis
RHODESIA – MICHAEL CHARLTON REPORTS 29/11/1965
Michael Charlton reports from Salisbury on the situation in Rhodesia following UDI (Unilateral Declaration of Independence).
p Richard Francis
The SOUTH AFRICAN PRESS 20/12/1965
Michael Charlton looks at the range of newspapers in South Africa and the conditions under which they operate. Includes interviews with journalists in Cape Town and Johannesburg.
p Richard Francis
RHODESIAN OIL EMBARGO 20/12/1965
Harold Wilson talks with Robin Day about the recently imposed sanctions on oil exports to Rhodesia.
p Richard Francis
WELFARE STATE IN ACTION 14/3/1966
Professor Peter Townsend and Anthony Crosland are interviewed on Britain's social services.
p Richard Francis
MENTAL ILLNESS 6/6/1966
An account of mental illness and treatment in Britain today.
d Margaret Douglas; *comm* James Mossman
VIETNAM – JOURNAL OF A WAR 13/6/1966
A survey of the latest developments in the Vietnam War.
p Jo Menell

CALIFORNIA YEAR 2000 4/7/1966 *ntx*
A report on the effects technology has brought to people's lives in California. Postponed and finally transmitted 18/8/1966.
p Peter Rowland; *pres* John Morgan
PROFILE OF ENOCH POWELL 2/12/1968
A profile of the career of politician, Enoch Powell.
VIETNAM 31/3/1969
Julian Pettifer reports on the Vietnam War, as seen by seven American infantrymen.
SPY WARS 24/9/1974
The infiltration of the United Nations by Soviet agents.
ADULT ILLITERACY 13/10/1975
Studio discussion with adults who describe their literacy problems.
WHO'S BEHIND THE PEACE PEOPLE 11/10/1976
The leaders of the rapidly growing peace movement in Northern Ireland.
HOW MUCH 13/12/1976
An interview with the Shah of Iran about oil policy and Iranian politics.
CRISIS INSIDE PRISONS 28/2/1977
The overcrowded state of Britain's prisons.
The BEST DAYS 21/3/1977
Daily life in a comprehensive school in Ealing; the camera follows two classes through a typical school day.
d Angela Pope
ARMS FOR KUWAIT 18/7/1977
Examines British arms dealing in Kuwait and considers the ethics of the trade in general and the government's active promotion of it.
MINDS BEHIND BARS 12/12/1977
Item on the work of Amnesty International, which discusses the treatment of political prisoners in a number of countries including: Chile, USSR, South Africa and Uganda.
p Colin Martin
PANORAMA 30/10/1978
Two items: POLICING THE PEACE, the United Nations peace-keeping force in the Sinai desert; HAS JIM FIXED IT?, the prospects for Labour and the new Parliament.
H-BLOCKS – THE PROPAGANDA PRISON (IRISH LOBBY) 12/2/1979
Report on conditions in the H-Blocks, Long Kesh Prison, and the propaganda campaign surrounding them in the USA. Interview with Roy Mason MP, defending British policies.
p Andrew Clayton
KAREN SILKWOOD: DECEASED 5/3/1979
The case of Karen Silkwood, a plutonium worker who was killed in a car crash on her way to giving journalists evidence of her employer Kerr McGee's breaches of safety regulations.
p Christopher Olgiati; *pres* Philip Tibenham
WHO KILLED GEORGI MARKOV? 9/4/1979
The murder of Bulgarian dissident broadcaster, Georgi Markov.
p Philip Harding; *pres* Michael Cockerell
GUSTAV WAGNER – ANGEL OF DEATH 18/6/1979
The career of Gustav Wagner, the ex-commandant of Sobibor concentration camp in Poland where 250,000 Jews were exterminated between March 1942 and August 1943. Includes an interview with Wagner and Simon Wiesenthal.
p/rep Tom Bower
RHODESIA / NORTHERN IRELAND 17/12/1979

PAPA DOC – THE BLACK SHEEP
(Yorkshire TV 17/6/1969)
Alan Whicker reports on life in Haiti and interviews its President, François Duvalier.
d/p Michael Blakstad; *sc/rep* Alan Whicker

The PAPER LADS (Tyne Tees 1977–79)
The adventures of a group of Geordie children who do a newspaper round.
regulars Andrew Edwards; Gavin Kitchen; Peter Younger; Glynn Edwards; Anne Jameson; Tony Neilson; Judith Pyle
CASH AND CARRY 31/8/1977
d Derek Martinus; *p* John Kaye Cooper;
sc Sid Chaplin
lp Buzz Ford; David McBeth; Paul Luty

ENTER PICASSO 21/9/1977
d John Frankau; *p* John Kaye Cooper;
sc William Corlett
lp Tony Neilson; Dorothy White
PADDY FOR CHAMP 27/11/1978
d Gerry Mill; *p* Keith Richardson;
sc Ian Cullen
lp Barry Braund; Des Young; Dick Irwin;
Hugh Turner
INTRUDERS 4/12/1978
d Gerry Mill; *p* Keith Richardson;
sc Ian Cullen
lp Barry Braund; Nalini Moonasar;
Ian Cullen
A DAY TO REMEMBER 11/12/1978
d Roger Cheveley; *p* Keith Richardson;
sc William Humble
lp Michael Wardle
IT TAKES TWO TO TANGO 15/1/1979
p Keith Richardson
lp Michael Wardle
The SAILOR'S RETURN 22/1/1979
d Gerry Mill; *p* Keith Richardson;
sc William Corlett
lp Michael Wardle

PAPER ROSES (Granada 13/6/1971)
A journalist nearing the end of his career suddenly realises that the end of his career could be the end of him too.
d Barry Davis; *p* Kenith Trodd;
sc Dennis Potter
lp Bill Maynard; John Carson; Donald Gee;
William Simons; Desmond Perry;
Aimée Delamain; Joe Gladwin

PARADE (Granada 1972–74)
Music, dance, theatre performance series.
DUET 3/6/1973
A performance of 'Duet' by the Paul Taylor Dance Company, with Carolyn Adams, Betty DeJong, Senta Driver, Eileen Cropley, Ruby Shang, Monica Morris, Daniel Williams, Nicholas Gunn, and Paul Plummador.
d Basil Coleman
THEODORAKIS CONDUCTS THEODORAKIS 10/6/1973
Mikis Theodorakis conducts a concert in Manchester.
d June Howson; *p* Peter Potter

PARADISE LOST? (Rediffusion 1968)
American Samoa.

PARADISE STREET (Rediffusion 8/9/1965)
The lives of two families: the Widdowson family living in Paradise Street in Newcastle-upon-Tyne, and the Rogers family living in Paradise Road, Stockwell, London.
d Charlie Squires; *p* Cyril Bennett

PARENTS AND CHILDREN (BBC 1973–76)
Documentary series.
YOUR KIDS JOIN, YOU JOIN 27/4/1975
Development of a playgroup on a new housing estate.
d Vivienne King; *p* Dick Foster
WHAT DID YOU LEARN IN SCHOOL TODAY? 18/5/1975
Compares and contrasts the educational methods used in China, Britain and the USSR.
p Dick Foster, Eurfron Gwynne Jones
PART TIME PARENT, FULL TIME JOB 25/5/1975
Society expects parents to be workers and upbringers. Two societies have made an attempt to resolve this conflict between work and family – Sweden and the Israeli kibbutz.
p Dick Foster, Eurfron Gwynne Jones
BREAST FEEDING 8/2/1976
Encourages women to breast feed, now favoured by medical opinion.
p Dick Foster, Suzanne Davies
IF ONLY WE COULD TEACH THEM TOO 29/2/1976
How the National Society for Mentally Handicapped Children organises classes for parents of handicapped children.
p Suzanne Davies, Dick Foster;
comm Paul Bawes

PARKINSON (BBC 1971–82)
Chat show presented by Michael Parkinson.
PARKINSON 17/10/1971
d John Burrowes; *p* Richard Drewett;
with Muhammad Ali
PARKINSON 17/2/1973
d Roger Ordish; *p* Richard Drewett;
with George Best, Sir John Betjeman,
Maggie Smith, Kenneth Williams
PARKINSON AT CHRISTMAS 25/12/1979
Special edition of the show. Features Tommy
Cooper, Barry Humphries and Peter Cook.
d Bruce Millard; *p* John Fisher

PAROSI (BBC 2/10/1977–9/4/1978)
Twenty-six part series in Hindi and English
about the story of two Asian families living in
Britain.
EPISODE 3 16/10/1977
d Paul Kriwaczek; *p* Robert Clamp;
sc Dilip Hiro, Naseem Khan
lp Indira Joshi; Nabeel Gul; Roshan Seth;
Naushaba Khan; Lally Percy; Soni Razdan;
Paul Satvendar; Zohra Segal; Dino Shafeek;
Cleo Sylvestre

PARTY POLITICAL AND ELECTION BROADCASTS: THE AUSTRALIAN LABOR PARTY
TIME FOR ACTION – THE OPEN GATEWAY 1963
The threat of communist expansion from the
North and the opposition's neglect of both the
development of the north of Australia and the
Armed Forces.
TIME FOR ACTION – THE ROAD TO NOWHERE
(Artransa Park Film Studios 19/11/1963)
Gough Whitlam and Arthur Calwell on the
educational shortcomings of Australia.
TIME FOR ACTION – THE HOMELESS ONES
25/11/1963
Gough Whitlam and Arthur Calwell are critical
of the housing record of the Holt-Menzies
Government.
MR. E.G. WHITLAM M.P. 1/11/1967
Gough Whitlam and his relations with world
leaders. He outlines the Party's policies.

PARTY POLITICAL AND ELECTION BROADCASTS: THE CONSERVATIVE PARTY
CONSERVATIVE AND UNIONIST PARTY
6/10/1959
Prime Minister Harold Macmillan comments on
the election campaign, reads extracts from letters
he has received, and speaks on domestic and
foreign affairs.
CONSERVATIVE PARTY 5/6/1970
Election broadcast, an attack on the Labour
Government's claim to be the guardian of a
compassionate society.
CONSERVATIVE PARTY 11/6/1970
Election broadcast aimed at the British
housewife; Iain McLeod attacks the Labour
Party and the price of socialism.

PARTY POLITICAL AND ELECTION BROADCASTS: THE LABOUR PARTY
SIR HARTLEY CROSS, CHRISTOPHER MAYHEW
17/10/1951
The first Labour Party broadcast on television.
CHALLENGE TO BRITAIN 15/10/1953
Hugh Gaitskell introduces the Party's policy
document 'Challenge to Britain'.
MEET THE LABOUR PARTY: A STUDENT'S
JOURNEY 19/3/1954
A student wishing to find out why people join
the Labour Party travels to meet members from
different walks of life.
VALUE FOR MONEY 10/2/1955
Election broadcast. Elaine Burton MP discusses
the value and quality of British goods.
ATTLEE TALKS TO PERCY CUDLIPP 11/5/1955
Clement Attlee and Mrs Attlee discuss a variety
of topics with Daily Herald editor Percy
Cudlipp.
YOUR MONEY'S WORTH 16/5/1955
Election broadcast. Harold Wilson and Dr
Summerskill discuss the price of food under
Labour and the Tories.

ELECTION ROUND UP 1955
20/5/1955
Election broadcast. The panel, James Callaghan,
Herbert Morrison, Lady Megan Lloyd-George
and Hugh Gaitskell, answer questions put to
them by William Pickles.
The WORLD WE LIVE IN 24/2/1956
John Hynd, MP chairs a discussion of foreign
policy issues with Alfred Robens, Richard
Crossman, Kenneth Younger and Denis Healey.
IT'S YOUR COUNTRY 23/3/1956
Herbert Bowden, Labour Chief Whip, chairs a
discussion on home affairs with George Brown,
Hugh Dalton, Tony Greenwood and James
Callaghan.
HOMES OF THE FUTURE 10/1/1957
The Labour Party's housing policy is summed up
by Margaret Herbison.
COMMONWEALTH QUESTIONS 21/2/1957
Dorothy Pitt chairs a discussion between James
Callaghan, Jim Griffiths and Aneurin Bevan and
young people from the Commonwealth.
PRESS CONFERENCE 19/11/1957
Part of a regular press conference given for
London correspondents of foreign newspapers.
QUESTION TIME 11/2/1958
Part of an informal question and answer session
in which Aneurin Bevan replies to foreign policy
issues posed by young members of the Labour
Party.
COUNTRYSIDE QUESTIONS 4/3/1958
Francis Williams chairs a discussion about
agricultural and rural questions posed by an
audience in Steeple Claydon.
EDUCATION 8/4/1958
Percy Cudlip introduces and interviews a number
of people within education. Alice Bacon MP and
Michael Stewart MP answer questions on
Labour's education policy.
PRICES, WAGES AND EMPLOYMENT 29/4/1958
Hugh Gaitskell, Alan Birch and Frank Cousins
answer questions on economic topics put by
Harold Hutchinson and Hugh Cudliffe.
Introduced by William Pickles.
WATFORD FRANKLY SPEAKING 21/4/1959
Woodrow Wyatt asks people in Watford why
they don't like the Labour Party. Hugh Gaitskell
in the studio responds to the public view.
BRISTOL FASHION 6/5/1959
Tony Benn interviews Barbara Castle who
refutes allegations made in an earlier
Conservative Party broadcast. Filmed report of
the achievements of Labour-controlled Bristol.
BRITAIN BELONGS TO YOU NO. 2 26/9/1959
Election broadcast. Tony Benn introduces policy
issues. Contributions from Anthony Greenwood,
Hugh Gaitskell, Christopher Mayhew and
others.
BRITAIN BELONGS TO YOU NO. 3 28/9/1959
Election broadcast. Tony Benn introduces policy
issues, including Richard Crossman on pensions,
Will Carron on union/government relations,
Christopher Mayhew on poor Conservative/
union relations, Hugh Gaitskell on
unemployment and Aneurin Bevan on foreign
affairs.
BRITAIN BELONGS TO YOU NO. 4 1/10/1959
Election broadcast, with Tony Benn,
Christopher Mayhew, Harold Wilson, Albert
Hilton, James Callaghan and Hugh Gaitskell.
BRITAIN BELONGS TO YOU NO. 5 5/10/1959
Election broadcast. Final of series, vox pop of
why people will vote Labour and final
contributions from Aneurin Bevan, Jim
Griffiths, Anthony Crossman, James Callaghan,
Harold Wilson and Hugh Gaitskell.
ANTHONY WEDGWOOD BENN 30/8/1960
Tony Benn outlines the role of the new Minister
of Technology.
RENTS, HOUSING AND PENSIONS 30/11/1960
Sydney Jackson chairs a discussion between
Party members and Margaret Herbison, Robert
Mellish and Harold Collison on rents, housing
and pensions.
PLAIN SPEAKING 22/3/1961
Hugh Gaitskell, Harold Wilson and George
Brown discuss the role of the opposition in
Parliament and use specific examples to illustrate
what can be achieved.
JOURNEY TO WORK 12/4/1961
James Callaghan on the need for a properly
integrated transport system.

PARTY OF THE WHOLE PEOPLE 28/3/1962
James Callaghan introduces a programme about
Labour's support for 'white' as well as 'blue'
collar workers. With Anne Godwin, Alan
Thompson and Richard Marsh.
ENJOYING LIFE 6/6/1962
Tom Driberg introduces John Brown, Denis
Howell, Arnold Wesker, Merlyn Rees, and John
Betjeman on the cultural quality of British life.
SIGNPOSTS FOR THE SIXTIES 12/7/1962
Hugh Gaitskell, Harold Wilson, George Brown
and Richard Crossman in the studio discuss
'Signposts for the Sixties' – the Labour Party's
broad policy document.
The COMMON MARKET 21/9/1962
Hugh Gaitskell on the issues surrounding
Britain's entry into the EEC.
JAMES CALLAGHAN M.P. 7/11/1962
James Callaghan looks at Britain's poor
economic performance since the war and
outlines some of Labour's policies to improve it.
HAROLD WILSON 28/2/1963
Wilson outlines the Labour Party's policy for the
industrial revival of Britain.
RT. HON. HAROLD WILSON M.P. 26/6/1963 *ntx*
Journalists Frank Giles and George Ffitch
interview Harold Wilson on the Profumo affair
and foreign policy issues especially Britain's
relationship with the USSR and USA.
RT. HON. HAROLD WILSON MP 22/10/1963
Harold Wilson is interviewed by Robert
McKenzie and Robin Day about the
appointment of Sir Alec Douglas-Home as Prime
Minister. Contrasts between Wilson and Home
are pointed out.
CHALLENGE TO THE NEW BRITAIN
26/2/1964
Harold Wilson gives a policy broadcast on
homes, rates and education.
The NEW BRITAIN NO. 1 11/9/1964
Election broadcast.
The NEW BRITAIN NO. 2 2/10/1964
Election broadcast.
The NEW BRITAIN NO. 3 5/10/1964
Election broadcast.
The NEW BRITAIN NO. 4 8/10/1964
Election broadcast.
The NEW BRITAIN 12/10/1964
Election broadcast. Clement Attlee's views on
an independent deterrent. Harold Wilson on the
choice before the people in this election.
The PRIME MINISTER (HAROLD WILSON)
12/5/1965
Harold Wilson in his first broadcast as Prime
Minister looks at the Labour Party's
achievements in the first 200 days in office.
PRIME MINISTER (HAROLD WILSON) 22/9/1965
Harold Wilson outlines the Government's social
priorities and stresses the need for improved
economic production.
HERBERT BOWDEN AND JAMES CALLAGHAN
10/11/1965
Ian Coulter interviews James Callaghan and
Herbert Bowden on the choice of legislation
outlined in the Queen's speech.
MARGARET HERBISON AND RICHARD
CROSSMAN 26/1/1966
Herbison on improvements in social security,
Crossman on the Labour Party's housing
achievements in the first 15 months of office.
YOU KNOW LABOUR GOVERNMENT WORKS:
RAY GUNTER 16/3/1966
Journalists Trevor Evans, John Bourne and Alan
Watkins interview Ray Gunter on how the
Labour Party intends to increase industrial
output.
YOU KNOW LABOUR GOVERNMENT WORKS
22/3/1966
Election broadcast. Ministers introduce their
sections from the manifesto, including
presentations from Richard Crossman, Kenneth
Robinson, Richard Marsh and Margaret
Herbison.
YOU KNOW LABOUR GOVERNMENT WORKS
25/3/1966
Election broadcast. George Brown on the
Labour Party's economic achievements and aims
for the future.
The RT. HON. JAMES CALLAGHAN M.P.
23/11/1966
Callaghan looks at the home economic situation
and reviews some current affairs issues.

PARTY POLITICAL AND ELECTION BROADCASTS: THE LABOUR PARTY *cont.*

MICHAEL STEWART 14/12/1966
Keith McDowell interviews Michael Stewart on the problems of low productivity.
The PARLIAMENTARY COMMISSIONER 6/4/1967
Richard Crossman introduces the role of the new Parliamentary Commissioner (Ombudsman).
EDUCATION FOR THE FUTURE 8/11/1967
Mr Rowe, headmaster of David Lister High School, Hull, oulines the benefits of the comprehensive education system.
SECOND CHANCE 15/11/1967
Roy Hattersley on the importance of retraining in areas where traditional industry is giving way to new industry and its importance as part of regional policy.
QUESTION TIME 6/5/1968
Audiences in studios in Manchester, Cardiff and Glasgow put questions to a panel of Labour Party politicians.
pres Norman Hunt
CASTLES IN THE AIR 26/6/1968
Barbara Castle talks to Geoffrey Goodman, 'The Sun's industrial editor, about the prices and incomes policy.
The OTHER WAGE PACKET 25/9/1968
Bill Simpson, General Secretary A.E.F. outlines the increase in the 'social wage' under the Labour Party.
The SHOPPER'S CHARTER 13/11/1968
Gwyneth Dunwoody introduces the Trade Descriptions Act and the benefits which will accrue.
YOUTH ANSWERS BACK 4/12/1968
A pollster's findings about youngsters' views of politics are discussed by Alan Williams MP and three young socialists.
BREAKING UP BRITAIN 9/4/1969
MPs Dickson Mabon, John Morris and John MacKintosh reply to vox pop on why a vote for Scottish/Welsh Nationalist would lead to the election of a Conservative government.
HARRY H. CORBETT, SHIRLEY WILLIAMS AND BOB MELLISH 15/10/1969
Journalist Charles Hodgson puts questions to Williams and Mellish in the light of an accusation by Harry H. Corbett, in his 'Steptoe' character, that all parties are the same.
The RT. HON. GEORGE BROWN M.P. 29/10/1969
George Brown outlines the Labour Party's achievements, questions Conservative promises, and looks to the future.
POLITICAL CHALLENGE 18/3/1970
Based on the television programme UNIVERSITY CHALLENGE, Bernard Donoghue, an academic, introduces teams of new and past voters who are asked questions designed to show the Labour Party's achievements.
WHAT'S AT STAKE? 8/4/1970
George Brown, Bob Mellish and Tony Crosland on the importance of voting in the local elections.
CANTEEN DISCUSSION 4/5/1970
James Callaghan answers questions on a variety of topics in a works canteen in Gateshead.
The PRIME MINISTER 1/6/1970
Election broadcast. Harold Wilson opens the election campaign. Summary of achievements, attack on Tories, and broad pledges.
The RT. HON. EDWARD SHORT 9/6/1970
Election broadcast. A group of young mothers discuss their hopes for their children. Short outlines Labour's policy for youngsters, education and housing in the future.
The CHANCELLOR OF THE EXCHEQUER 12/6/1970
Election broadcast. Roy Jenkins outlines the economic situation which he believes is good and looks at what must be done to move forward to achieve Labour's goals.
The PRIME MINISTER 16/6/1970
Election broadcast. Harold Wilson gives the final broadcast of the series. He outlines Britain's strength and gives his vision of the kind of caring community socialism that the Labour Party is working towards.
JAMES CALLAGHAN AND GEOFFREY GOODMAN 9/12/1970
James Callaghan is interviewed by Goodman about the Conservative Party's handling of the power workers' dispute.

ONE YEAR AFTER 16/6/1971
Harold Wilson looks back on Edward Heath's election pledge to reduce prices.
JOE ASHTON 22/12/1971
Ashton talks to people in Yorkshire.
HAROLD WILSON 3/2/1972
Wilson attacks unemployment and puts forward a 12 point Labour Party plan.
MAYDAY MAYDAY 1/5/1972
Broadcast concerning unemployment, inflation, rents, and school meals.
HAROLD WILSON 12/5/1973
Peter Davis interviews Wilson at home about what needs to be done after the next election and the mistakes the Labour Party made in the 1960s.
RESPONSIBLE GOVERNMENT 7/11/1973
James Callaghan predicts an early election and with the help of Denis Healey and Edward Short attacks the Conservative Party's tax cuts, inflation and pledges a number of policy changes.
LET'S GET TO WORK WITH LABOUR 12/2/1974
James Callaghan looks at the reasons why the country is in the condition it is, offers to improve industrial relations and curb price increases.
HAROLD WILSON AND THE LABOUR TEAM 25/2/1974
Election broadcast. Wilson introduces his team – Roy Jenkins, Michael Foot, Edward Short, Tony Crosland, Tony Benn, Shirley Williams and Denis Healey.
PROGRESS REPORT 1/5/1974
Ten weeks into the new Labour Government, Ministers report on their achievements; includes Denis Healey, Shirley Williams, Michael Foot and Anthony Crosland.
BRITAIN WILL WIN WITH LABOUR 23/9/1974
Election broadcast. Edward Short summarises achievements of seven months of the minority Labour Government. James Callaghan offers a number of proposals.
The SOCIAL CONTRACT 26/9/1974
Election broadcast. The importance of the 'Social Contract' is stressed by Len Murray, Denis Healey, Shirley Williams, Tony Benn and Michael Foot.
SCOTLAND WILL WIN WITH LABOUR 4/10/1974
Election broadcast made by the Scottish Labour Party.
BRITAIN WILL WIN WITH LABOUR (LABOUR'S ACHIEVEMENTS) 8/10/1974
Election broadcast. Bryan Magee assesses the Labour Party's achievements. Harold Wilson rejects confrontation and stresses the need for one nation.
The BETTER PENSIONS BILL 27/3/1975
Barbara Castle with Brian O'Malley introduces the new pensions legislation.
SHIRLEY WILLIAMS 5/5/1975
Prior to local elections Shirley Williams reports that inflation is coming down as a result of government/TUC co-operation.
BRINGING INFLATION UNDER CONTROL 24/6/1975
Denis Healey outlines the improvements in the economy but stresses the need for continued restraint.
MEMBERSHIP OF THE PARTY 16/10/1975
Ron Hayward, Party Secretary, introduces people who explain why they are members of the Labour Party.
COMMUNITY LAND ACT 17/11/1975
John Silkin outlines the measures contained in the Community Land Act.
FIGHTING INFLATION 5/12/1975
Jack Jones and David Basnett outline their support for the wage policy and the Social Contract. Denis Healey stresses the need for the continuation of the policy.
LOCAL GOVERNMENT SPENDING 12/2/1976
Broadcast on local government spending; discussion is led by Anthony Crosland.
The SOCIAL CONTRACT 25/2/1976
Denis Healey talks to Jack Jones about the economic situation.
UNIONS AND GOVERNMENT 19/10/1976
Bry Jones discusses why union leaders Lawrence Daly, John Jones, and Bryan Stanley continue to support the Labour Government.

SHIRLEY WILLIAMS AND PARENTS 23/2/1977
A college principal, Eric Robinson, outlines how the Labour Party has improved education. Shirley Williams talks informally with a group of parents about the Party's policies.
REGENERATION OF INDUSTRY 16/3/1977
MPs Geoffrey Robinson and Gerald Kaufman examine the success of Labour's industrial policy.
The FAMILY 13/9/1978
Austin Mitchell outlines the benefits that the Labour Party's employment policies have brought.
SHIRLEY WILLIAMS AND GEOFFREY ROBINSON 28/3/1979
Against a background of a vote of confidence in the Commons, Shirley Williams and Geoffrey Robinson report on the healthy nature of British industry.
SHIRLEY WILLIAMS 20/4/1979
Election broadcast. Shirley Williams explains the reasons for the 'Winter of Discontent' and outlines the new agreement between the Labour Party and the Unions.
JAMES CALLAGHAN 1/5/1979
Election broadcast: Callaghan stresses the danger of Conservative monetarist policies and outlines Labour's policies.
The TORY RECORD 19/9/1979
Neil Kinnock and Wendy Mantle expose the effects of the first months of Conservative rule.

PARTY POLITICAL AND ELECTION BROADCASTS: THE LIBERAL PARTY

PARTY POLITICAL BROADCAST: LORD SAMUEL 15/10/1951
The first political broadcast on television.
PARTY POLITICAL BROADCAST ON BEHALF OF THE LIBERAL PARTY 1954
LIBERAL PARTY: ARLOTT, BYERS AND SAMUEL 1955
John Arlott, Frank Byers, and Lord Samuel.
LIBERAL PARTY: REA, SYKES AND THORPE 1955
Lord Rea, Manuela Sykes, and Jeremy Thorpe.
PARTY POLITICAL BROADCAST ON BEHALF OF THE LIBERAL PARTY 1/2/1957
Jo Grimond and Frank Byers.
COMING OUR WAY 26/5/1959
Francis Boyd interviews Jo Grimond, Robin Day and Fred Williams.
The LIBERAL CASE 22/9/1959
Election broadcast, with Robin Day, Mark Bonham-Carter, Tegai Hughes and Mrs Renee Soskin, and chairman John Arlott.
LIBERAL PARTY 3/10/1959
Jo Grimond speaks as leader of the Liberal Party.
The RADICAL ALTERNATIVE 4/5/1960
Jo Grimond, Jeremy Thorpe and Mark Bonham-Carter.
The NEXT STEP 29/3/1961
Jo Grimond, Michael Hammond, and David Rees-Williams, 1st Baron Ogmore.
PARTY POLITICAL BROADCAST ON BEHALF OF THE LIBERAL PARTY 1962
Jo Grimond.
PARTY POLITICAL BROADCAST ON BEHALF OF THE LIBERAL PARTY 21/3/1962
PARTY POLITICAL BROADCAST ON BEHALF OF THE LIBERAL PARTY 5/2/1964
Jo Grimond.
NATION OUT OF BALANCE 22/4/1964
Jeremy Thorpe.
QUESTIONS FOR TODAY – THE LIBERAL ANSWERS 29/9/1964
Jeremy Thorpe, Frank Byers, and Mark Bonham-Carter take part in an election broadcast.
NOW VOTE LIBERAL 10/10/1964
Jo Grimond makes an election broadcast.
THINKING ABOUT PEOPLE 5/5/1965
David Steel and David Evans.
A REAL CHANGE 8/12/1965
Jo Grimond.
LIBERAL PARTY 19/3/1966
Ludovic Kennedy.
MIND YOUR OWN BUSINESS 6/5/1966
Dr Michael Winstanley MP.
CAN YOU TELL THE DIFFERENCE? 9/11/1966
Richard Wainwright MP and Terry Lacey.

The RT. HON. JEREMY THORPE M.P. 3/5/1967
The CHOICE IS YOURS 1/5/1968
David Steel, John Pardoe, and Wallace Lawler.
PARTY POLITICAL BROADCAST ON BEHALF OF
THE LIBERAL PARTY 22/10/1969
Jeremy Thorpe.
LIBERALS PROVE THEY CARE 30/4/1970
Jeremy Thorpe, Wallace Lawler and Michael
Meadowcroft.
The LIBERAL VIEW – TOMORROW'S PEOPLE
3/6/1970
Election broadcast with Jeremy Thorpe.
The LIBERAL VIEW – TOMORROW'S PEOPLE
10/6/1970
Election broadcast with Jo Grimond.
WHAT'S THE POINT? 25/11/1970
Jeremy Thorpe and David Steel.
LIBERALS TALK SENSE 5/5/1971
Jeremy Thorpe.
PARTY POLITICAL BROADCAST ON BEHALF OF
THE LIBERAL PARTY 24/11/1971
Jeremy Thorpe and Lord Byers.
PARTY POLITICAL BROADCAST ON BEHALF OF
THE LIBERAL PARTY 1/3/1972
Jeremy Thorpe.
LIBERAL PARTY 13/2/1974
Election broadcast with Jo Grimond, Huw
Thomas and David Steel.
LIBERAL PARTY 20/2/1974
Election broadcast with Huw Thomas, Dr
Michael Winstanley, and Cyril Smith.
LIBERAL PARTY 23/2/1974
Election broadcast with Huw Thomas and
Jeremy Thorpe.
LIBERAL PARTY 25/9/1974
Election broadcast with Jeremy Thorpe, Huw
Thomas, David Steel and Jo Grimond.
LIBERAL PARTY 28/9/1974
Election broadcast with Huw Thomas, John
Briggs, John Pardoe and Alan Watson.
LIBERAL PARTY 2/10/1974
Election broadcast with Huw Thomas, Cyril
Smith, and Dr Michael Winstanley.
LIBERAL PARTY 5/10/1974
An election broadcast with Jeremy Thorpe and
Huw Thomas.

PASSENGERS (Granada 20/5/1973)
Drama concerning a divorced father and his
young daughter on their day out together.
d Howard Baker; *p* James Brabazon;
sc Susan Pleat
lp John Thaw; Robert Bernal;
Tenniel Evans; Elizabeth Holden;
David Warwick; James Bate; John Comer;
Jumoke Debayo; Ian MacKenzie

PAUL TEMPLE (BBC 1969–71)
Thriller series created by crime-suspense writer
Francis Durbridge.
CORRIDA 7/2/1971
d Ken Hannam; *p* Derrick Sherwin;
sc Lindsay Galloway
lp Francis Matthews; Ros Drinkwater;
Edward De Souza; Jeremy Higgins;
George Lambert; Michael Forrest;
Hugh Sullivan; Colette Martin; Frederick Jaeger

PAULINE'S QUIRKES
(Thames 15/11–20/12/1976)
Pop series, with comedy sketches.
PAULINE'S QUIRKES 29/11/1976
d/p Roger Price; *pres* Pauline Quirke;
with Flintlock, Philip Elsmore,
Linda Robson, Nula Conwell

PEBBLE MILL AT ONE (BBC 1972–86)
Daytime magazine programme from the studios
of BBC Birmingham. Series was known simply
as 'Pebble Mill' during 1974–79.
PEBBLE MILL AT ONE 28/11/1979
PEBBLE MILL AT ONE 29/11/1979
PEBBLE MILL AT ONE 3/12/1979

PEKING OPERA (BBC 27/12/1979)
The Shanghai Peking Opera Troupe in
performance during a tour of Britain. The
traditional 'scenes' included in their programme
are 'The Phoenix of Fire', 'The Autumn River'
and 'The Yandang Mountains'. BBC
presentation by Peter Massey.

PENNIES FROM HEAVEN (BBC 1978)
A six-part serial with music which follows the
adventures of a commercial traveller who sells
sheet music.
d Piers Haggard; *p* Kenith Trodd;
sc Dennis Potter
regulars Bob Hoskins; Gemma Craven;
Cheryl Campbell; Kenneth Colley
DOWN SUNNYSIDE LANE 7/3/1978
lp Nigel Havers; Arnold Peters
The SWEETEST THING 14/3/1978
lp Freddie Jones; Peter Cellier;
Spencer Banks; Philip Jackson; Michael Bilton
EASY COME, EASY GO 21/3/1978
lp Freddie Jones; Sam Avent; Bill Dean;
John Malcolm; Philip Jackson
BETTER THINK TWICE 28/3/1978
lp Hywel Bennett; Tony Caunter;
Tudor Davies; Bella Emberg; Jenny Logan
PAINTING THE CLOUDS 4/4/1978
lp Ronald Fraser; Dave King;
Paddy Joyce; Nigel Rathbone
SAYS MY HEART 11/4/1978
lp Peter Bowles; Dave King; Philip Locke;
John Ringham; Steve Ubels

PEOPLE ARE TALKING
(Rediffusion 1957–58)
Irregularly transmitted current affairs,
documentary series.
OUR AMERICAN COUSINS 15/1/1957
Members of the public give their views on the
stationing of American troops in Britain. Atomic
scientist Philip Moon, Julian Huxley, exporter
James Scott, Barbara Castle, American
industrialist James Curry, and Selwyn Lloyd talk
about Anglo-American relations.
d Michael Ingrams
FAN FEVER 1958
Dicky Valentine, Alma Cogan, Denis Lotis, and
Liberace's manager discuss their fans.
d Peter Morley

PEOPLE IN TROUBLE (Rediffusion 1958)
Daniel Farson investigates various problems and
ailments of ordinary people.
d Rollo Gamble
MENTAL HEALTH 1958
METHS ADDICTS 1958
SEX EDUCATION 1958
WITHOUT SIGHT 1958
The problems faced by blind people.
UNMARRIED MOTHERS 30/4/1958
KLEPTOMANIACS 14/5/1958
MIXED MARRIAGES 21/5/1958
EX-PRISONERS 28/5/1958
EPILEPTICS 4/6/1958
SUICIDES 11/6/1958
ILLITERATES 18/6/1958
POVERTY 25/6/1958
SPINSTERS 25/7/1958
CLASS ACCENTS 8/8/1958
POLIO 23/9/1958
STAMMERING 30/9/1958
DEPRESSION 14/10/1958
NO FUTURE 28/10/1958

PEOPLE OF MANY LANDS
(BBC 1959–74)
Educational programmes intended for children
aged 10–11.
GRENADA 23/9/1968
p Peggy Broadhead; *intro* Jeremy Verity
TRINIDAD 30/9/1968
p Peggy Broadhead; *intro* Jeremy Verity
JAMAICA 7/10/1968
p Peggy Broadhead; *intro* Jeremy Verity
IRISH REPUBLIC: DONEGAL WEAVER
14/10/1968
p Harry Cowdy; *intro* Paddy McGill
NEW ZEALAND: THE WIND'S RESTING PLACE
4/11/1968
p F. R. Elwell; *intro* Eugene Fraser
NEW ZEALAND: THE CHANGING LAND
11/11/1968
p F. R. Elwell; *intro* Eugene Fraser
FINLAND: LAND OF WOOD AND WATER
18/11/1968
p Peggy Broadhead; *comm* Christopher Trace
SUMMER IN ICELAND 25/11/1968
p Peggy Broadhead; *comm* Ragnar
Gudmundsson

WINTER IN SWEDEN 2/12/1968
p Peggy Broadhead; *comm* Christopher Trace
UGANDA: FISHING VILLAGE 21/9/1970
p Andrew Neal
TANZANIA: LIFE ON KILIMANJARO 5/10/1970
p Andrew Neal
CEYLON: AMBALANGODA, COASTAL TOWN
30/12/1971
p Peggy Broadhead; *comm* Christopher Trace
CEYLON: LIFE IN THE HILLS 28/2/1972
p Peggy Broadhead; *comm* Christopher Trace

PEOPLE TO WATCH (BBC 23/1–1/5/1966)
Series interviewing major thinkers and
practitioners on their views of future scientific
and social developments.
U THANT 1/5/1966
U Thant, Secretary General of the United
Nations, talks to Robert McKenzie and Erskine
Childers.
p Anthony Smith

PERRY MASON
(US Paisano Productions 1957–66)
Series based on the cases of lawyer Perry Mason
created by author Erle Stanley Gardner.
The CASE OF THE FINAL FADE OUT 22/5/1966
d Jesse Hibbs;
p Arthur Marks, Art Seid;
sc Ernest Frankel
lp Raymond Burr; Barbara Hale;
William Hopper; James Stacy; Marlyn Mason;
Estelle Winwood; Dick Clark;
Erle Stanley Gardner; Denver Pyle

PERSONAL CHOICE (BBC 1967–1974)
Interview series.
MRS MARY WILSON 31/12/1967
Cliff Michelmore interviews Mary Wilson, wife
of Prime Minister Harold Wilson.
p Michael Hill
PATRICK MOYNIHAN 28/1/1968
Robert McKenzie talks to Patrick Moynihan.
p Michael Hill
ALBERT SPEER 4/10/1970
Michael Charlton talks to Nazi Armaments
Minister Albert Speer.
p John Reynolds

PERSONAL IMPRESSIONS
(BBC 4/11–23/12/1949)
A five-part fortnightly transmitted series in which
personalities give their personal impressions.
ROBERT FLAHERTY 18/11/1949
Robert Flaherty talks about his family's
emigration from Ireland to the USA and his
impressions of London.
p Andrew Miller Jones

PERSONAL REPORT (ATV 1977–78)
A series of personal documentary reports. See
also PERSONAL REPORT – PILGER.
JACK TREVOR STORY: I'D TURN BACK IF I
WERE YOU DOROTHY.... 8/8/1977
Author Jack Trevor Story gives a personal view
of Milton Keynes.
d/p Patricia Ingram

PERSONAL REPORT – PILGER
(ATV 5/9–19/9/1977)
Three personal documentaries made by John
Pilger and shown in the PERSONAL REPORT
series.
A FARAWAY COUNTRY...A PEOPLE OF WHOM
WE KNOW NOTHING 5/9/1977
John Pilger and his team secretly film a series of
interviews with members of the Czech
Underground known as the Charter 77
Movement.
p Richard Creasey

The PERSUADERS!
(Tribune Productions 1971–72)
Action-adventure series.
p Robert S. Baker
regulars Roger Moore; Tony Curtis;
Laurence Naismith
OVERTURE 17/9/1971
d Basil Dearden; *sc* Brian Clemens
lp Imogen Hassall; Alex Scott;
Michael Godfrey; Bruno Barnabe; Neal Arden;
John Acheson

THE PERSUADERS! *cont.*

GREENSLEEVES 8/10/1971
d David Greene; *sc* Terence Feely
lp Rosemary Nicols; Cy Grant;
Andrew Keir; Tom Adams; Carmen Munroe
POWERSWITCH 15/10/1971
d Basil Dearden; *sc* John Kruse
lp Annette Andre; Terence Alexander;
Melissa Stribling; Lionel Blair
ANGIE...ANGIE 19/11/1971
d Val Guest; *sc* Milton Gelman
lp Larry Storch; Lionel Murton;
Kirsten Lindholm; John Alderson; Rose Alba
THAT'S ME OVER THERE 3/12/1971
d Leslie Norman; *sc* Brian Clemens
lp Geoffrey Keen; Suzan Farmer;
Allan Cuthbertson; Juliet Harmer;
Terence Edmond
ELEMENT OF RISK 24/12/1971
d Gerald Mayer; *sc* Tony Barwick
lp June Ritchie; Peter Bowles;
William Marlowe; Shane Rimmer; Victor Platt
A HOME OF ONE'S OWN 31/12/1971
d James Hill; *sc* Terry Nation
lp Hannah Gordon; John Ronane;
Leon Greene
FIVE MILES TO MIDNIGHT 7/1/1972
d Val Guest; *sc* Terry Nation
lp Joan Collins; Robert Hutton;
Robert Rietty; Ferdy Mayne; Jean Marsh;
Arnold Diamond; Ian Thompson;
Robert Gallico
READ AND DESTROY 28/1/1972
d Val Guest; *sc* Peter Yeldham
lp Joss Ackland; Nigel Green;
Kate O'Mara; Magda Konopka; George Merritt;
William Mervyn
TO THE DEATH, BABY 18/2/1972
d Basil Dearden; *sc* Donald James
lp Jennie Linden; Terence Morgan;
Thorley Walters; Harold Innocent;
Robert Russell; Roger Delgado; Juan Moreno
SOMEONE WAITING 25/2/1972
d Peter Medak; *sc* Terry Nation
lp Penelope Horner; John Cairney;
Donald Pickering; Lois Maxwell; Maxwell Shaw;
Tim Barrett; Sam Kydd

The PERSUADERS (BBC 26/7–30/8/1979)
Documentary series on advertising.
LAUGHING ALL THE WAY... 26/7/1979
d Mike Healey; *p* David Martin;
rep David Tindall

PESHMERGA – THOSE WHO FACE DEATH (ATV 29/10/1974)
A report on the rebellion of the Kurds against
the Iraqi government, which includes film of the
guerilla warfare and interviews with members of
the provisional independent government.

PETER GUNN
(US Spartan Productions 1958–61)
Private detective series.
The BLIND PIANIST 13/10/1958
d/p Blake Edwards;
sc Blake Edwards, George W. George,
Judy George
lp Craig Stevens; Lola Albright;
Herschel Bernardi; Richard Ney;
Barbara Stuart; Herb Ellis; Barney Phillips;
Ned Glass; E.J. Andre; Elizabeth Talbot-Martin
The YOUNG ASSASSINS 26/10/1959
d Boris Sagal; *p* Blake Edwards
lp Craig Stevens; Dan Easton;
Herschel Bernardi
The PASSENGER 3/10/1960
d Alan Crosland Jr; *p* Blake Edwards;
sc Lewis Reed, Tony Barrett
lp Herschel Bernardi; Craig Stevens;
Lola Albright; Ted De Corsia; Rhys Williams;
Forrest Lewis

PETER USTINOV AT THE NFT
(BBC 25/2/1968)
Peter Ustinov is interviewed by Leslie
Hardcastle at the John Player Lecture held at the
National Film Theatre.

The PHILPOTT FILE (BBC 1969–80)
Documentary series.
rep Trevor Philpott

SOLDIERS OF PITY 22/11/1969
The changing role of the Salvation Army.
p Peter Robinson
The DEVIL TAKES THE YOUNGEST 29/11/1969
The work of the Salvation Army and in
particular of its youngest members.
d Peter Robinson
SOUTH AFRICA FACES TELEVISION: THE END
OF AN ERA 8/7/1976
The last days of the pre-television era in South
Africa; the scale of the South African
entertainment business and the way South
Africans have reacted to the arrival of television.
p Trevor Philpott
SOUTH AFRICA FACES TELEVISION: THE
WHITE WINDOW 15/7/1976
The problems of setting up a television service in
South Africa and the kind of service to be
expected.
p Trevor Philpott
SOUTH AFRICA FACES TELEVISION: THE
BLACK FUTURE 22/7/1976
Soweto township – the way black people
entertain themselves and the sort of programmes
they would, like to see when they get their own
television channel in 1980.
p Trevor Philpott
SOUTH AFRICA FACES TELEVISION: THE FIRST
CASUALTIES 29/7/1976
The impact of television on the prosperous
entertainment industry in South Africa.
p Trevor Philpott

The PHILPOTT FILE – THE SPORTING LIFE (BBC 1973)
Series of film reports.
p/rep Trevor Philpott
The HUNTER 14/5/1973
Hunters and hunting in Britain, Europe and
America.
The FISHERMAN 21/5/1973
The sport of fishing.
The GOLFER 28/5/1973
The game of golf.

The PHOENIX AND THE CARPET
(BBC 29/12/1976–16/2/1977)
Eight-part adaptation of the E. Nesbit story for
children.
d Clive Doig; *p* Dorothea Brooking;
sc John Tully
lp Richard Warner; Gary Russell;
Tamzin Neville; Max Harris; Jane Forster
WHAT TO DO WITH A BURGLAR 2/2/1977
lp Bernard Holley
The HOLE IN THE CARPET 9/2/1977
lp Nigel Lambert
A NIGHT AT THE THEATRE 16/2/1977
lp Bernard Holley

A PHOENIX TOO FREQUENT
(BBC 19/7/1955)
p Owen Reed; *auth* Christopher Fry
lp Noelle Middleton; George Cole;
Jessie Evans

PICARDY AFFAIR (BBC 25/10/1963)
The story of the Battle of Agincourt, 1415.
p Peter Newington; *sc/nar* Robert Hardy
lp Esmond Knight; Michael Culver

PICTURE PARADE (BBC 1956–62)
Documentary series on the cinema.
BEN HUR 7/12/1959
Robert Robinson interviews Charlton Heston,
Haya Hararect and William Wyler about their
recent film 'Ben Hur'.
d Richard Evans
CAMERON MITCHELL 16/2/1960
Keith Fordyce interviews Cameron Mitchell
about his film and stage appearances including
'Love Me or Leave Me', 'The King and I' and
plans for a life of Buddha.
d Richard Evans
MOIRA SHEARER 12/4/1960
Robert Robinson interviews Moira Shearer
about why she gave up dancing, and the new
Roland Petit ballet film.
p Richard Evans

The MOUNTAIN ROAD 10/5/1960
Robert Robinson introduces scenes from the
shooting of 'The Mountain Road', with James
Stewart and Lisa Lu.
d Christopher Doll
JIM BACKUS 7/7/1960
Robert Robinson interviews Jim Backus.
JOHN CARRADINE 18/1/1961
Robert Robinson interviews John Carradine.
p Christopher Doll
ALBERT FINNEY 7/2/1961
Robert Robinson interviews Albert Finney.
p Christopher Doll

PILGER (ATV 1974–76)
Documentary series.
rep John Pilger
THALIDOMIDE, THE 98 WE FORGOT 2/6/1974
The plight of some of the victims of the
thalidomide tragedy.
d Chris Fox
The MOST POWERFUL POLITICIAN IN AMERICA
9/6/1974
John Pilger interviews George Wallace.
p Charles Denton
TO KNOW US IS TO LOVE US 21/8/1975
The reactions of the inhabitants of Fort Smith,
Arkansas to the Vietnamese refugees settling in
the town.
d Richard Marquand
NOD AND A WINK 28/8/1975
The growing use of the conspiracy laws as a
means of political suppression in Britain.
d/p John Ingram

The PILOTS (BBC 5/3/1963)
The crew of a Boeing (BOAC) talk about their
life, work and pay, the types of aircraft they fly
and questions of safety and air traffic control.
p/sc Richard Cawston

PINEAPPLE POLL – THE ROYAL BALLET
(BBC 1/11/1959)
A performance of John Cranko's 'Pineapple
Poll' by the Royal Ballet Company, with David
Blair, Merle Park, Stanley Holden, Brenda
Taylor and Gerd Larsen. Charles Mackerras
conducts the London Symphony Orchestra.
d Margaret Dale

PINKY AND PERKY (BBC 1962–66)
Puppet series.
GUNFIGHT AT MATTRESS SPRINGS 18/10/1964
p Stan Parkinson; *sc* Robert Gray

PIONEERS OF PHOTOGRAPHY
(BBC 15/1–26/3/1975)
Eight-part documentary on the history and
development of photography.
p Ann Turner; *nar* Brian Coe
The PENCIL OF NATURE 15/1/1975
Henry Fox Talbot.
MIRROR WITH A MEMORY 22/1/1975
Daguerreotypes.

The PLANE MAKERS (ATV 1963–65)
Drama series set in the aeroplane manufacture
industry. Followed by the series The POWER
GAME (1965–69).
p Rex Firkin
regulars Patrick Wymark; Barbara Murray;
Robert Urquhart; Jack Watling
DON'T WORRY ABOUT ME 4/2/1963
d Quentin Lawrence; *sc* Edmund Ward
lp Colin Blakely; Ronald Lacey;
Victor Platt; Christopher Beeny; Eric Woodburn
TOO MUCH TO LOSE 16/9/1963
d Quentin Lawrence; *sc* Edmund Ward
lp Reginald Marsh; John Arnatt;
Bernard Brown; Dennis Ramsden;
Martin Wyldeck
NO MAN'S LAND 23/9/1963
d James Ferman; *sc* Leslie Sands
lp Lloyd Pearson; Norma Ronald;
Dennis Ramsden; Tom Macaulay;
Reginald Marsh
QUESTION OF SOURCES 30/9/1963
d John Cooper; *sc* Wilfred Greatorex
lp Geoffrey Chater; Aubrey Richards;
Douglas Muir; Ewan Roberts

ALL PART OF THE JOB 7/10/1963
d James Ferman; *sc* Richard Harris
lp Stanley Meadows; Allan Casley;
Billy Russell; Patricia Haines; Reginald Marsh
DON'T STICK YOUR HEAD OUT 14/10/1963
d Quentin Lawrence; *sc* Peter Draper
lp Reginald Marsh; Fred Ferris;
Rex Robinson; Geoffrey Hinsliffe
OLD BOY NETWORK 21/10/1963
d John Cooper; *sc* Edwin Ranch
lp Patrick Magee; Jeremy Burnham;
Bert Palmer; Justine Lord; Anthony Sagar
ANY MORE FOR THE SKYLARK? 28/10/1963
d James Ferman; *sc* Peter Draper
lp Victor Maddern; Rodney Bewes;
Barbara Windsor; John Woodvine; Fred Ferris
A MATTER OF SELF RESPECT 5/11/1963
d John Cooper; *sc* Leslie Sands
lp Reginald Marsh; Leslie Sands;
Garfield Morgan; Sheila Raynor; John Horsley;
Joan Peart
COSTIGAN'S ROCKET 12/11/1963
d John Nelson Burton; *sc* Edmund Ward
lp Gerald James; Sean Lynch;
Tenniel Evans; Brian Murphy; Jo Rowbottom
The THING ABOUT AUNTIE 19/11/1963
d Geoffrey Nethercott; *sc* Raymond Bowers
lp Norma Ronald; William Devlin;
Tom Criddle
The CAT'S AWAY 26/11/1963
d Hugh Rennie; *sc* John Finch
lp Elizabeth Begley; Sheila Raynor;
Reginald Marsh; John Junkin; Paul Dawkins
STRINGS IN WHITEHALL 3/12/1963
d Quentin Lawrence; *sc* Wilfred Greatorex
lp Richard Vernon; Donald Morley;
Norma Ronald; Michael Ingrams
The BEST OF FRIENDS 10/12/1963
d James Ferman; *sc* Lewis Davidson
lp Reginald Marsh; Bernard Brown;
Zena Walker; Fred Ferris; Aimée Delamain
ONE OUT – ALL OUT! 24/12/1963
d Peter Sasdy; *sc* Leslie Sands
lp Reginald Marsh; John Junkin;
Elizabeth Begley; Norman Tyrrell;
Tom Macaulay
A BUNCH OF FIVES 7/1/1964
d James Ferman; *sc* Peter Nichols
lp Wendy Craig; Barrie Ingham;
Glyn Houston; Frederick Bartman;
Anthea Wyndham
The SMILER 14/1/1964
d Bill Stewart; *sc* John O'Toole
lp Reginald Marsh; James Villiers;
Patrick Magee; Elizabeth Begley; Sheila Raynor
IN THE BOOK 21/1/1964
d Dennis Vance; *sc* Arthur Swinson
lp Reginald Marsh; Michael Gwynn;
Anthony Marlowe; Elizabeth Begley
MISS GÉRALDINE 28/1/1964
d John Cooper; *sc* Arthur Swinson
lp Marie Löhr; Jeremy Burnham;
Norma Ronald; Ruth Kettlewell;
John Boyd Brent
A CONDITION OF SALE 4/2/1964
d James Ferman; *sc* Tony Williamson
lp Reginald Marsh; George A. Cooper;
Elizabeth Begley; Lloyd Lamble; Norma Ronald
A JOB FOR THE MAJOR 25/2/1964
d John Cooper; *sc* John O'Toole
lp Reginald Marsh; Peter Copley;
Fulton Mackay; Elizabeth Begley; Sheila Raynor
A MATTER OF PRIORITIES 3/3/1964
d Eric Price; *sc* Raymond Bowers
lp Margaret Rawlings; Georgina Ward;
Ingrid Hafner; Norma Ronald; James Kerry
BANCROFT'S LAW 10/3/1964
d Bill Stewart; *sc* Geoffrey Stephenson
lp Reginald Marsh; Derrick Sherwin;
Elizabeth Begley; Norma Ronald;
Jerry Desmonde
The HOMECOMING 17/3/1964
d John Cooper; *sc* David Weir
lp Reginald Marsh; Fulton Mackay;
Elizabeth Begley; Sheila Raynor;
Wensley Pithey
SAUCE FOR THE GOOSE 24/3/1964
d Eric Price; *sc* David Weir
lp Murray Hayne; Georgina Cookson;
Robin Hunter; Daniel Moynihan

HOW CAN YOU WIN IF YOU HAVEN'T BOUGHT
A TICKET? 31/3/1964
p Rex Firkin; *sc* Edmund Ward
lp Reginald Marsh; Alan Tilvern;
Elizabeth Begley; Sheila Raynor; Peter Madden
OTHER PEOPLE OWN OUR JUNGLES NOW
27/10/1964
d John Nelson Burton; *sc* Raymond Bowers
lp Peter Jeffrey; Ann Firbank;
William Devlin; Wendy Gifford
A LESSON FOR CORBETT 3/11/1964
d Quentin Lawrence; *sc* David Weir
lp Alan Dobie; Alan Browning;
Philip Latham; Peter Jeffrey; William Devlin
The GOLDEN SILENCE 10/11/1964
d James Ferman; *sc* Raymond Bowers
lp Wendy Gifford; Robert MacLeod;
Peter Jeffrey; William Devlin; Norman Tyrrell
IT'S A FREE COUNTRY – ISN'T IT? 24/11/1964
d John Cooper; *sc* Edmund Ward
lp Sheila Raynor; Cyril Raymond;
Meredith Edwards; Reginald Marsh;
Norman Tyrrell
ONLY A FEW MILLIONS 15/12/1964
p Rex Firkin; *sc* David Weir
lp Alan Dobie; Wendy Gifford;
Norman Tyrrell; William Devlin;
Elizabeth Wallace
The SALESMEN 22/12/1964
d James Ferman; *sc* John Gray
lp Wendy Gifford; Anthony Nicholls;
Peter Jeffrey; Ann Firbank; Norman Tyrrell
The FIRING LINE 12/1/1965
d James Ferman; *sc* Edmund Ward
lp Alan Dobie; Wendy Gifford;
Peter Jeffrey; Ann Firbank; Norman Tyrrell

PLACES WHERE THEY SING
(Yorkshire TV 13/7/1969)
The establishment of a cathedral choir school at
Ripon. The life of the choirboys.
d Patrick Boyle; *p* Tony Scull;
rep Michael Deakin

PLANNING FOR DISCOVERY
(BBC 30/8/1952)
The work of the Cavendish Laboratory,
Cambridge. With Sir Lawrence Bragg and Sir
Edward Appleton.
d John Read

PLAY AWAY (BBC 1971–84)
Series for children.
PLAY AWAY CHRISTMAS SHOW 25/12/1976
d Peter Charlton; *p* Ann Reay;
with Brian Cant, Toni Arthur,
Chlöe Ashcroft, Derek Griffiths

PLAY FOR LOVE
(Yorkshire TV 19/3–23/4/1978)
Collection of plays written for television.
The MARRIAGE COUNSELLOR 9/4/1978
d Marc Miller; *exec.p* Peter Willes;
sc Sheila Sibley
lp Felicity Kendal; James Grout;
Charlie Henley; Vicky Ireland; Richard Heffer;
Gabrielle Drake
The PARTY OF THE FIRST PART 16/4/1978
d Bill Hays; *exec.p* Peter Willes;
sc Alan Plater
lp Anne Stallybrass; Michael Gambon;
Jan Francis; David Parfitt; Martin C. Thurley;
Terence Scully; Sheila Ballantine
The RAGAZZA 23/4/1978
d David Cunliffe; *exec.p* Peter Willes;
sc David Mercer
lp Francesca Annis; Peter Barkworth;
Robert Ashby

PLAY FOR TODAY (BBC 1970–84)
Series of television plays.
The RIGHT PROSPECTUS 22/10/1970
d Alan Cooke; *p* Irene Shubik;
sc John Osborne
lp George Cole; Elvi Hale; Tom Criddle;
Christopher Witty; Allan Warren; John Horsley;
Aubrey Richards; Robert Gillespie

The LIE 29/10/1970
d Alan Bridges; *p* Graeme McDonald;
sc Ingmar Bergman; *adapt* Paul Britten Austin
lp Frank Finlay; Gemma Jones;
John Carson; Mark Dignam; Annette Crosbie;
Caroline Blakiston; Joss Ackland
The PIANO 28/1/1971
d James Cellan Jones; *p* Graeme McDonald;
sc Julia Jones
lp Glyn Owen; Janet Munro; Leo Franklyn;
Hilda Barry; James Cossins; Brian Wilde
WHEN THE BOUGH BREAKS 6/5/1971
d James Ferman; *p* Irene Shubik;
sc Tony Parker
lp Hannah Gordon; Neil McCarthy;
Cheryl Kennedy; Griffith Davies
TRAITOR 14/10/1971
d Alan Bridges; *p* Graeme McDonald;
sc Dennis Potter
lp John Le Mesurier; Jack Hedley;
Neil McCallum; Diana Fairfax; Vincent Ball
EDNA, THE INEBRIATE WOMAN 21/10/1971
d Ted Kotcheff; *p* Irene Shubik;
sc Jeremy Sandford
lp Patricia Hayes; Barbara Jefford;
Pat Nye; June Watson; Denis Carey;
Jerry Verno; Rex Rashley; Walter Sparrow;
Amelia Bayntun
O FAT WHITE WOMAN 4/11/1971
d Philip Saville; *p* Irene Shubik;
sc William Trevor
lp Maureen Pryor; Peter Jeffrey;
William Relton; Roger Hammond;
Martin Boddey; Susan Penhaligon;
Simon Gipps-Kent
MICHAEL REGAN 18/11/1971
d John Gorrie; *p* Irene Shubik;
sc Robert Holles
lp David Burke; Charles Gray;
Julian Glover; Anna Calder Marshall;
Peter Howell; Joan Benham; Noel Johnson;
Geoffrey Palmer
HOME (National Educational TV-CBC 6/1/1972)
d Lindsay Anderson; *sc* David Storey
lp John Gielgud; Ralph Richardson;
Dandy Nichols; Mona Washbourne;
Warren Clarke
STOCKER'S COPPER 20/1/1972
d Jack Gold; *p* Graeme McDonald;
sc Tom Clarke
lp Bryan Marshall; Jane Lapotaire;
Gareth Thomas; Tony Caunter;
Malcolm Tierney
ACKERMAN, DOUGALL AND HARKER 10/2/1972
d Ted Kotcheff; *p* Irene Shubik;
sc Don Shaw
lp Peter Glaze; Keith Marsh; Joe Gladwin;
David Steuart; Jean Taylor Smith
The REPORTERS 9/10/1972
d Michael Apted; *p* Graeme McDonald;
sc Arthur Hopcraft
lp Robert Urquhart; Michael Kitchen;
Barbara Young; Stephanie Turner;
Jacqueline Stanbury; Gavin Richards
TRIPLE EXPOSURE 6/11/1972
d Alan Cooke; *p* Irene Shubik;
sc David Halliwell
lp Alec McCowen; Sheila Allen;
Tom Chadbon; Marguerite Hardiman
The GENERAL'S DAY 20/11/1972
d John Gorrie; *p* Irene Shubik;
sc William Trevor
lp Alastair Sim; Annette Crosbie;
Dandy Nichols; Nan Munro; Norman Shelley;
Julia Goodman
The BANKRUPT 27/11/1972
d Christopher Morahan; *p* Graeme McDonald;
sc David Mercer
lp Joss Ackland; Sheila Allen;
David Waller; Alethea Charlton; Peter Cellier;
Bob Hoskins
KISSES AT FIFTY 22/1/1973
d Michael Apted; *p* Graeme McDonald;
sc Colin Welland
lp Bill Maynard; Rosemarie Dunham;
Lori Wells; Maureen Callaghan;
Andrew Beaumont; Marjorie Yates

ONLY MAKE BELIEVE 12/2/1973
d Robert Knights; *p* Graeme McDonald;
sc Dennis Potter
lp Keith Barron; Georgina Hale;
Alun Armstrong; Susan Richards;
George Howe; Rowena Cooper;
Geoffrey Palmer
HARD LABOUR 12/3/1973
d/sc Mike Leigh; *p* Tony Garnett
lp Liz Smith; Clifford Kershaw;
Polly Hemingway; Bernard Hill;
Alison Steadman; Paula Tilbrook;
Vanessa Harris; Ben Kingsley
BLOOMING YOUTH 18/6/1973
d Les Blair; *p* Tony Garnett
lp Philip Jackson; Colin Higgins;
Peter Kinley; Lydia Lisle; Peter Jonfield;
Carrie Lee-Baker; Rynagh O'Grady; Pat Bee;
William Hoyland; Bruce Taylor
HER MAJESTY'S PLEASURE 25/10/1973
d Barry Davis; *p* Kenith Trodd;
sc Jimmy O'Connor
lp John Bindon; Bob Hoskins;
Yolande Turner; Peter Firth; Derek Griffiths
JACK POINT 1/11/1973
d Michael Apted; *p* Kenith Trodd;
sc Colin Welland
lp Stephen Murray; Isabel Dean;
Gerard Ryder; Basil Lord; Bernard Gallagher;
Vicky Williams
ALL GOOD MEN 31/1/1974
d Michael Lindsay-Hogg; *p* Graeme McDonald;
sc Trevor Griffiths
lp Bill Fraser; Ronald Pickup;
Jack Shepherd; Frances De La Tour
JOE'S ARK 14/2/1974
d Alan Bridges; *p* Graeme McDonald;
sc Dennis Potter
lp Freddie Jones; Angharad Rees;
Dennis Waterman; Christopher Guard;
Patricia Franklin; Edward Evans; Azad Ali;
Colin Rix
The CHEVIOT, THE STAG AND THE BLACK,
BLACK OIL 6/6/1974
d John MacKenzie; *p* Graeme McDonald;
sc John McGrath
lp John Bett; David MacLennan;
Dolina MacLennan; Timothy Martin;
Alex Norton; Bill Paterson; Allan Ross
SCHMOEDIPUS 20/6/1974
d Barry Davis; *p* Kenith Trodd;
sc Dennis Potter
lp Anna Cropper; John Carson; Tim Curry;
John Horsley; Bob Hoskins; Carol MacReady
GANGSTERS 9/1/1975
Play which became the basis for the series
GANGSTERS (1976; 1978).
d Philip Saville; *p* Barry Hanson;
sc Philip Martin
lp Maurice Colbourne; Philip Martin;
Saeed Jaffrey; Ahmed Khalil; Tania Rogers
SUNSET ACROSS THE BAY 20/2/1975
d Stephen Frears; *p* Innes Lloyd;
sc Alan Bennett
lp Harry Markham; Gabrielle Daye;
Bob Peck; Betty Alberge; Albert Mooley;
Madge Hindle; Patricia Mason; Elizabeth Dawn
The SATURDAY PARTY 1/5/1975
d Barry Davis; *p* Mark Shivas;
sc Brian Clark
lp Peter Barkworth; Sheila Gish;
Jan Waters; Judi Bowker; John Welsh
WEDNESDAY LOVE 8/5/1975
d Michael Apted; *p* Graeme McDonald;
sc Arthur Hopcraft
lp Lois Daine; Simon Rouse; Jane Lowe;
Nikolas Simmonds
PLAINTIFFS AND DEFENDANTS 14/10/1975
The first of two Simon Gray plays.
d Michael Lindsay-Hogg; *p* Kenith Trodd;
sc Simon Gray
lp Alan Bates; Dinsdale Landen;
Georgina Hale; Rosemary McHale;
Rosemary Martin; Simon Cadell
TWO SUNDAYS 21/10/1975
Second of two Simon Gray plays.
d Michael Lindsay-Hogg; *p* Kenith Trodd;
sc Simon Gray
lp Alan Bates; Dinsdale Landen;
Georgina Hale; Rosemary Martin; Simon Cadell

THROUGH THE NIGHT 2/12/1975
d Michael Lindsay-Hogg; *p* Ann Scott;
sc Trevor Griffiths
lp Alison Steadman; Jack Shepherd;
Tony Steedman; Thelma Whiteley; Anne Dyson;
Julia Schofield; Dave Hill; Andonia Katsaros
NUTS IN MAY 13/1/1976
d/sc Mike Leigh; *p* David Rose
lp Roger Sloman; Alison Steadman;
Anthony O'Donnell; Sheila Kelley
DOUBLE DARE 6/4/1976
d John MacKenzie; *p* Kenith Trodd;
sc Dennis Potter
lp Alan Dobie; Kika Markham;
Malcolm Terris; Joe Melia; John Hamill
BAR MITZVAH BOY 14/9/1976
d Michael Tuchner; *p* Graeme McDonald;
sc Jack Rosenthal
lp Jeremy Steyn; Kim Clifford;
Mark Herman; Adrienne Posta; Maria Charles;
Bernard Spear; Cyril Shaps; Jack Lynn;
Harry Landis; Pamela Manson; Jonathan Lynn
BUFFET 2/11/1976
d Mike Newell; *p* Graeme McDonald;
sc Rhys Adrian
lp Tony Britton; Amanda Barrie;
Nigel Hawthorne; Robin Bailey; Phyllida Law;
Clive Swift; Maureen Pryor
SCUM 1977 *ntx*
Brutal portrait of a borstal institution. Remade
as a theatrical film by Alan Clarke in 1979.
Original play was later transmitted on
BBC-2 *tx* 27/7/1991.
d Alan Clarke; *p* Margaret Matheson;
sc Roy Minton
lp Raymond Winstone; David Threlfall;
Martin Phillips; Davidson Knight;
Richard Butler; John Judd; John Blundell;
Phil Daniels; Peter Gordon; Ray Burdis
The KISS OF DEATH 11/1/1977
d/sc Mike Leigh; *p* David Rose
lp David Threlfall; Clifford Kershaw;
Angela Curran; John Wheatley; Kay Adshead
SPEND, SPEND, SPEND 15/3/1977
d John Goldschmidt; *p* Graeme McDonald;
sc Jack Rosenthal;
auth Vivian Nicholson, Stephen Smith
lp Susan Littler; John Duttine;
Helen Beck; Joe Belcher; Stephen Bill;
Liz Smith
ABIGAIL'S PARTY 1/11/1977
d/sc Mike Leigh; *p* Margaret Matheson
lp Alison Steadman; Tim Stern;
Janine Duvitski; John Salthouse;
Harriet Reynolds
LICKING HITLER 10/1/1978
d/sc David Hare; *p* David Rose
lp Kate Nelligan; Bill Paterson;
Hugh Fraser; Clive Revill
The SPONGERS 24/1/1978
d Roland Joffé; *p* Tony Garnett;
sc Jim Allen
lp Christine Hargreaves; Bernard Hill;
Peter Kerrigan; Paula McDonagh
DESTINY 31/1/1978
d Mike Newell; *p* Margaret Matheson;
sc David Edgar
lp Colin Jeavons; Iain Cuthbertson;
Frederick Treves; Nigel Hawthorne;
Joseph Blatchley; David Beames; Alan Lake
The LEGION HALL BOMBING 22/8/1978
d Roland Joffé; *p* Margaret Matheson;
sc Caryl Churchill
lp David Kelly; Robert Kavanagh;
Ewen White; May Ollis; Niall Toibin;
Shay Gorman
DINNER AT THE SPORTING CLUB 7/11/1978
d Brian Gibson; *p* Kenith Trodd;
sc Leon Griffiths
lp John Thaw; Billy McColl;
Patrick Durkin; Jonathan Lynn;
Maureen Lipman; Liam Neeson;
Ken Campbell; Terry Downes
BLUE REMEMBERED HILLS 30/1/1979
d Brian Gibson; *p* Kenith Trodd;
sc Dennis Potter
lp Colin Welland; Michael Elphick;
John Bird; Robin Ellis; Helen Mirren;
Janine Duvitski; Colin Jeavons

WHO'S WHO 5/2/1979
d Mike Leigh; *p* Margaret Matheson
lp Simon Chandler; Adam Norton;
Richard Kane; Jeffrey Wickham; Souad Faress;
Philip Davis
LONG DISTANCE INFORMATION 11/10/1979
d Stephen Frears; *p* Richard Eyre;
sc Neville Smith
lp Neville Smith; Pauline Collins;
Freddie 'Fingers' Lee; Malcolm Terris
COMEDIANS 25/10/1979
d/p Richard Eyre; *sc* Trevor Griffiths
lp Bill Fraser; Jonathan Pryce;
David Burke; James Warrior;
Derrick O'Connor; Linal Haft; Edward Peel;
Ralph Nossek; John Barrett
JUST A BOY'S GAME 8/11/1979
d John MacKenzie; *p* Richard Eyre;
sc Peter McDougall
lp Frankie Miller; Ken Hutchinson;
Gregor Fisher; Jean Taylor Smith;
Hector Nichol; Katherine Stark; Jan Wilson
BILLY 13/11/1979
d Charles Stewart; *p* Kenith Trodd;
sc G.F. Newman
lp Jason Plenderleith; Leigh Medcraft;
Terry Andrews; Cindy O'Callaghan;
Chrissy Cottrill; Lee Ashton; Karen Archer;
Tim Brown; Don Warrington
A HOLE IN BABYLON 29/11/1979
d Horace Ové; *p* Graham Benson;
sc Horace Ové, Jim Hawkins
lp Archie Pool; Trevor Thomas;
T-bone Wilson; Carmen Munro; Helen Webb;
Shope Shodeinde; Floella Benjamin
The NETWORK 20/12/1979
d Derek Lister; *p* Anne Head;
sc Stephen Fagan
lp Anthony Bate; Penelope Horner;
Geoffrey Chater; Sara Clee; Natalie Caron;
Michael Barrington; Jean Marlow

PLAY OF THE MONTH (BBC 1965–83)
Series of classic plays.
A PASSAGE TO INDIA 16/11/1965
Adaptation of the play by Santha Rama Rau
from the novel by E.M.Forster.
d Waris Hussein; *p* Peter Luke.
sc John Maynard
lp Sybil Thorndike; Virginia McKenna;
Cyril Cusack; Zia Mohyeddin; Ishaq Bux;
Michael Bates; Ronald Hines;
Allan Cuthbertson; Saeed Jaffrey
LEE OSWALD – ASSASSIN 15/3/1966
d Rudolph Cartier; *p* Peter Luke.
sc Rudolph Cartier, Reed De Rouen;
auth Felix Lützkendorf; *nar* Kenneth Allsop
lp Robert Ayres; Paul Maxwell;
Shane Rimmer; Tony Bill; Callen Angelo;
Harry Tierney; Colin Maitland; John Alderson;
Francis Napier; Patricia Denys;
Harold Goldblatt; Pearl Catlin; Sarah Brackett;
Warren Mitchell; Donald Sutherland
The DEVIL'S EGGSHELL 28/6/1966
d Gareth Davies; *p* Cedric Messina;
sc David Weir; *auth* Alex Comfort
lp Leonard Rossiter; Keith Barron;
David Langton; John Phillips; Nicholas Pennell;
Bernard Hepton
The PARACHUTE 21/1/1968
d Anthony Page; *p* Tony Garnett;
sc David Mercer
lp Alan Badel; Jill Bennett;
John Osborne; Isabel Dean; Esmond Knight;
Drewe Henley; Barry Jackson; Frank Barry
MACBETH 20/9/1970
d John Gorrie; *p* Cedric Messina;
auth William Shakespeare
lp Eric Porter; Janet Suzman; John Thaw;
John Woodvine; John Alderton;
Michael Goodliffe
PLATONOV 23/5/1971
d Christopher Morahan; *p* Cedric Messina;
sc John Elliot; *auth* Anton Chekhov
lp Rex Harrison; Siân Phillips;
Clive Revill; Geoffrey Bayldon;
Joanna Dunham; Patsy Byrne; Donald Eccles;
Willoughby Goddard

The ADVENTURES OF DON QUIXOTE
(BBC-Universal TV 7/1/1973)
d Alvin Rakoff; *p* Gerald Savory;
sc Hugh Whitemore; *auth* Cervantes
lp Rex Harrison; Frank Finlay;
Rosemary Leach; Bernard Hepton;
Ronald Lacey; Roger Delgado
CANDIDE 16/2/1973
d/sc James MacTaggart; *p* Cedric Messina
lp Frank Finlay; Ian Ogilvy; Emrys James;
Angela Richards; Kathleen Helme;
Clifton Jones; Leonard Maguire; Nicholas Jones
ROBINSON CRUSOE 29/12/1974
d/sc James MacTaggart; *p* Cedric Messina
lp Stanley Baker; Ram John Holder;
Jerome Willis
The SCHOOL FOR SCANDAL 16/2/1975
d Stuart Burge; *p* Cedric Messina;
auth Richard Brinsley Sheridan
lp Jeremy Brett; Pauline Collins;
Edward Fox; Bernard Lee; Arthur Lowe;
Bridget Armstrong; Joe Melia; Russell Hunter
KING LEAR 23/3/1975
d Jonathan Miller; *p* Cedric Messina;
auth William Shakespeare
lp Michael Hordern; Sarah Badel;
Angela Down; Michael Jayston;
Frank Middlemass; Anthony Nicholls;
Ronald Pickup; Penelope Wilton
The CHESTER MYSTERY PLAYS 18/4/1976
d Piers Haggard; *p* Cedric Messina;
sc Maurice Hussey
lp Tom Courtenay; Michael Hordern;
Alun Armstrong; Hilda Braid; Keith Chegwin;
Kenneth Colley; Paul Copley; Joe Gladwin;
Brian Glover
FLINT 15/1/1978
d Peter Wood; *p* David Jones;
sc David Mercer
lp John Le Mesurier; Julie Covington;
Peter Bowles; Dandy Nichols; Beryl Reid;
Philip Stone
The WINGS OF THE DOVE 8/4/1979
d John Gorrie; *p* Alan Shallcross;
sc Denis Constanduros; *auth* Henry James
lp Elizabeth Spriggs; Betsy Blair;
John Castle; Suzanne Bertish; Lisa Eichhorn;
Rupert Frazer; Alan Rowe; Gino Melvazzi

PLAY OF THE WEEK (ITV 1956–67)
Series of plays produced by various ITV
companies. [Not to be confused with the BBC
series, 1977–79]
FOR SERVICES RENDERED (Granada 7/7/1959)
auth W. Somerset Maugham
A WOMAN OF NO IMPORTANCE
(Rediffusion 9/2/1960)
d Joan Kemp-Welch; *sc* Paul Dehn;
auth Oscar Wilde
lp Helen Cherry; Griffith Jones;
Charles Lloyd Pack; Nicholas Hannen;
Marian Spencer
SERJEANT MUSGRAVE'S DANCE
(Granada 24/10/1961)
d Stuart Burge; *sc* John Arden
lp Patrick McGoohan; Freda Jackson;
Donal Donnelly; Jeanne Hepple; Denis Carey;
John Thaw
A DOLL'S HOUSE (Rediffusion 31/10/1961)
d Robert Tronson;
sc James Walter McFarlane; *auth* Henrik Ibsen
lp Paul Rogers; Zena Walker;
Kenneth Griffith; Jennifer Wilson;
James Maxwell
A LILY IN LITTLE INDIA (ATV 9/10/1962)
d Peter Wood; *sc* Don Howarth
lp Susan Maryott; Donal Donnelly;
Brenda Bruce; Finlay Currie; Norman Bird
WHEN THE KISSING HAD TO STOP
(Rediffusion 16/10/1962)
d Bill Hitchcock; *sc* Giles Cooper;
auth Constantine Fitzgibbon
lp Frederick Leister; Douglas Wilmer;
Renee Asherson; Eddie Byrne; Denholm Elliott;
Louida Vaughan; Anthony Nicholls;
Patricia Marmont
The BRIMSTONE BUTTERFLY
(Rediffusion 16/4/1963)
d Mark Lawton; *sc* Peter van Greenaway
lp Helen Cherry; John Le Mesurier;
Maurice Kaufmann; Viola Keats; Kevin Stoney

END OF CONFLICT (Anglia 23/7/1963)
d George More O'Ferrall; *sc* Barry England
lp Barry Justice; Derek Newark;
John Woodvine; Robin Parkinson;
Michael Atkinson; Basil Henson; Eric Flynn
WALK ON THE WATER (Rediffusion 25/11/1963)
sc Tom Stoppard
The GUILTY PARTY (ATV 24/2/1964)
d John Llewellyn Moxey;
sc George Ross, Campbell Singer
lp Nigel Davenport; Zena Walker;
Jennifer Daniel; Richard Vernon;
Douglas Wilmer; Laurence Hardy;
Rachel Gurney; Basil Henson; Ewan Roberts
GINA (Rediffusion 27/7/1964)
d Toby Robertson; *sc* Michael Ashe
lp Richard Pearson; Maureen Pryor;
Freddie Jones; Frank Williams; John Barrett;
Susan Richards; John Bailey; Athene Seyler
The BACHELORS (Rediffusion 23/11/1964)
d Tania Lieven; *exec.p* Antony Kearey;
sc Julian Bond
lp David Markham; Max Adrian;
John Le Mesurier; Edward Fox; Marian Spencer
DEEP AND CRISP AND STOLEN
(Rediffusion 21/12/1964)
d Ronald Marriott; *sc* David Freeman
lp Raymond Francis; Dennis Price;
Maggie Fitzgibbon; Robert Dorning;
George Moon; Muriel Young; Joan Hickson;
Arthur Mullard; Dennis Lotis; Grant Taylor
The IMAGE (Rediffusion 25/1/1965)
d John Frankau; *sc* Kenneth Hill
lp Dinsdale Landen; Julia Foster;
John Bown; Elsie Arnold; Derek Smee;
Katy Wild
WHEN THE WIND BLOWS (ATV 2/8/1965)
d Graham Evans; *p* Cecil Clarke;
sc Peter Nichols
lp Alec McCowen; Alison Leggatt;
Ralph Michael; Eileen Atkins

PLAY OF THE WEEK (BBC 1977–79)
Series of plays. [Not to be confused with the
earlier, similarly-titled ITV series, 1956–1967]
PROFESSIONAL FOUL 21/9/1977
d Michael Lindsay-Hogg; *p* Mark Shivas;
sc Tom Stoppard
lp Peter Barkworth; John Shrapnel;
Stephen Rea; Richard O'Callaghan;
Bernard Hill
SHOOTING THE CHANDELIER 26/10/1977
d Jane Howell; *p* Margaret Matheson;
sc David Mercer
lp Edward Fox; Denholm Elliott;
Felicity Dean; Doris Hare
A VISIT FROM MISS PROTHERO 11/1/1978
d Stephen Frears; *p* Innes Lloyd;
sc Alan Bennett
lp Hugh Lloyd; Patricia Routledge
SHE FELL AMONG THIEVES 1/3/1978
d Clive Donner; *p* Mark Shivas;
sc Tom Sharpe; *auth* Dornford Yates
lp Malcolm McDowell; Eileen Atkins;
Michael Jayston; Sarah Badel; Karen Dotrice;
Freda Jackson; Philip Locke; Richard Pearson
FOR TEA ON SUNDAY 29/3/1978
d Don Taylor; *p* Rosemary Hill;
sc David Mercer
lp Debbi Blythe; Alison Fiske;
Rosemary McHale; Ronald Pickup
The LOST BOYS: PART 1: WE SET OUT TO BE
WRECKED 11/10/1978
d Rodney Bennett; *p* Louis Marks;
sc Andrew Birkin
lp Ian Holm; Ann Bell; Maureen O'Brien;
Tim Pigott-Smith
The LOST BOYS: PART 2: DARK AND SINISTER
MAN 18/10/1978
d Rodney Bennett; *p* Louis Marks;
sc Andrew Birkin
lp Ian Holm; Tim Pigott-Smith;
Maureen O'Brien; Ann Bell
The LOST BOYS: PART 3: AN AWFULLY BIG
ADVENTURE 25/10/1978
d Rodney Bennett; *p* Louis Marks;
sc Andrew Birkin
lp Ian Holm; Tim Pigott-Smith;
Maureen O'Brien; Ann Bell

ON GIANT'S SHOULDERS 28/3/1979
d Anthony Simmons; *p* Mark Shivas;
sc William Humble, Anthony Simmons;
auth Marjorie Wallace, Michael Robson
lp Judi Dench; Bryan Pringle;
Terry Wiles; Barbara Keogh; Tim Wylton;
Anna Wing

PLAY SCHOOL (BBC 1964–88)
Series for pre-school children.
USEFUL BOX DAY 14/2/1966
pres Julie Stevens, Brian Cant
with Philip Bate
DRESSING UP DAY 15/2/1966
pres Julie Stevens, Brian Cant
DRESSING UP DAY 4/7/1967
pres Valerie Pitts, Brian Cant
with Ian Wallace
PET'S DAY 5/7/1967
pres Valerie Pitts, Brian Cant
with Ian Wallace
IDEA'S DAY 6/7/1967
pres Valerie Pitts, Brian Cant
with Ian Wallace
PLAY SCHOOL 24/4/1968
pres Johnny Ball, Carole Ward
with Philip Bate
PLAY SCHOOL 23/10/1978
pres Johnny Ball, Carole Ward
with Philip Bate

**PLAY SOCCER – JACK CHARLTON'S
WAY** (Tyne Tees 4/9–16/10/1976)
Seven-part series in which Jack Charlton trains a
group of 30 young people from the North East in
football skills.
d/p Lisle Willis
PLAY SOCCER – JACK CHARLTON'S WAY
4/9/1976
Making better use of sports facilities.
PLAY SOCCER – JACK CHARLTON'S WAY
11/9/1976
Basic passing.
PLAY SOCCER – JACK CHARLTON'S WAY
25/9/1976
Heading and goalkeeping.
PLAY SOCCER – JACK CHARLTON'S WAY
2/10/1976
The correct way to kick a football.
PLAY SOCCER – JACK CHARLTON'S WAY
9/10/1976
The problem of controlling the ball with the
parts of the body above the waist.
PLAY SOCCER – JACK CHARLTON'S WAY
16/10/1976
Dribbling and aggressive running.

PLAYBOARD (BBC 3/10–26/12/1976)
Puppet series.
d/sc Judy Whitfield; *p* Michael Cole;
pres Christopher Lillicrap
The GREAT BIG ENORMOUS TURNIP 10/10/1976
HENNY PENNY 17/10/1976
The THREE LITTLE PIGS 24/10/1976

PLAYDATE (Rediffusion 1961–62)
Drama series.
SOME TALK OF ALEXANDER 5/3/1962
d Ronald Weyman; *sc* Clive Exton;
lp Isa Miranda; Norman Welsh;
Robin Gammell; Maude Whitmore

PLAYHOUSE (ITV various 1967–74)
ITV drama slot. Later called ITV
PLAYHOUSE (1977–82). [Not to be confused
with the BBC series 1976–84].
LADY WINDERMERE'S FAN
(Rediffusion 25/9/1967)
d Joan Kemp-Welch; *exec.p* Peter Willes;
sc Stanley Miller; *auth* Oscar Wilde
lp Barbara Jefford; Joan Benham;
Jennie Linden; Ian Ogilvy; Richard Vernon;
James Villiers; Mia Martin
The BONEGRINDER (Rediffusion 13/5/1968)
d/p Joan Kemp-Welch; *sc* Dennis Potter
lp George Baker; Margaret Tyzack;
Weston Gavin; Eric Dodson; Jeremy Child;
Linda Marlowe

PLAYHOUSE (ITV) *cont.*

The PATRIOT GAME (Thames 13/10/1969)
d Piers Haggard; *p* John Kershaw;
sc Dominic Behan
lp Patrick O'Connell; Roddy McMillan;
Elizabeth Begley; Wesley Murphy; Donal Cox
RUMOUR (Thames 2/3/1970)
d/p/sc Mike Hodges
lp Michael Coles; Ronald Clarke;
Peter Stratford; Vivienne Chandler;
Rita Merkelis; David Cargill
The MOSEDALE HORSESHOE
(Granada 23/3/1971)
d Michael Apted; *p* Peter Eckersley;
sc Arthur Hopcraft
lp Rosemary Leach; Bernard Hepton;
Mary Miller; David Swift; Michael Gover;
Faith Kent
A SPLINTER OF ICE (Granada 29/5/1972)
d Derek Bennett; *sc* Fay Weldon
lp Ian Hendry; Zena Walker;
Annette Crosbie; Judy Loe; Amber Kammer;
Norman Eshley
VINEGAR TRIP (Granada 24/4/1973)
d Brian Mills; *p* Peter Eckersley;
sc Kenneth Cope
lp John Barrie; Stella Moray;
Norman Rossington; Barbara Young;
John Comer
LUCKY (Granada 5/2/1974)
d Gordon Flemyng; *p* Peter Eckersley;
sc Alun Owen
lp Paul Barber; Frederick Treves;
Michael Sheard; Frank Moorey; Doreen Sloane
MR. AXELFORD'S ANGEL
(Yorkshire TV 5/6/1974)
d John Frankau; *sc* Peter Whitbread
lp Julia Foster; Michael Bryant;
Lally Bowers; Jacqueline Stanbury; Katy Wild;
Robert Raglan
LOVE AFFAIR (Anglia 3/7/1974)
d John Jacobs; *sc* William Trevor
lp Celia Johnson; Bill Maynard;
Daphne Slater; Clifford Kershaw; Guy Nicholls;
Shirley Cheriton; Kenneth Cope

PLAYHOUSE (BBC 1976–84)
Drama series. [Not to be confused with the ITV
series 1967–74].
SCHOOL PLAY 7/11/1979
d James Cellan Jones; *p* Richard Broke;
sc Frederic Raphael
lp Denholm Elliott; Jeremy Kemp;
Michael Kitchen; Tim Pigott-Smith;
Jenny Agutter; John Normington;
Richard Warwick; Jeremy Clyde
The BRYLCREEM BOYS 21/11/1979
d Roger Bamford; *p* Innes Lloyd;
sc Peter Durrant
lp David Threlfall; Bunny May;
Stephanie Turner; Spencer Banks;
Stephen Riddle; Stephen Grives; Timothy Spall
SPEED KING 19/12/1979
d Ferdinand Fairfax; *p* Innes Lloyd;
sc Roger Milner
lp Robert Hardy; Jennifer Hilary;
Jack Galloway; Sheila Ruskin; Rosalind Knight;
Derek Martin; Desmond Llewelyn

PLAYS FOR BRITAIN (Thames 1976)
Drama series.
The PARADISE RUN 6/4/1976
d Michael Apted; *p* Barry Hanson;
sc Howard Brenton
lp Kevin McNally; Ian Charleson;
Sarah Porter; Maurice O'Connell
HITTING TOWN 27/4/1976
d Peter Gill; *p* Barry Hanson;
sc Stephen Poliakoff
lp Deborah Norton; Mick Ford;
Lynne Miller; David Bailie
SHUTTLECOCK 11/5/1976
d Philip Saville; *p* Barry Hanson;
sc Henry Livings
lp David Max Vaughan; Carole Nimmons;
Ann Pennington; Dinsdale Landen

PLAYS FOR PLEASURE
(Yorkshire TV 1979–81)
Series of dramas made by Yorkshire TV and
transmitted in the ITV PLAYHOUSE slot.

VILLAGE WOOING 17/4/1979
d/p David Cunliffe; *auth* George Bernard Shaw
lp Judi Dench; Richard Briers
CASTING THE RUNES 24/4/1979
Updated version of the M.R. James story.
d Lawrence Gordon Clark;
exec.p David Cunliffe; *sc* Clive Exton
lp Edward Petherbridge; Christopher Good;
Jan Francis; Joanna Dunham; Iain Cuthbertson
The DAUGHTERS OF ALBION 1/5/1979
Willy Russell's first play for television.
d Pedr James; *sc* Willy Russell
lp Janet Rawson; Kate Fitzgerald;
Annette Ekblom; Ian Burns; Peter Kinley;
Kate Saunders; Alan Igbon

PLAYS OF TODAY
(BBC 11/9–16/10/1969)
Series of six plays.
A VOYAGE AROUND MY FATHER 16/10/1969
d Claude Watham; *p* Ronald Travers;
sc Nesta Pain, John Mortimer
lp Mark Dignam; Ian Richardson;
Arthur Lowe; Trevor Bannister;
Daphne Oxenford

PLAYTIME – THE WHEELBARROWS
(Rediffusion 5/12/1967)
Series for children, with games, songs and
dances.
d Bimbi Harris;
pres Jennifer Naden, Freddie Earlle

The PLAYWRIGHT
(Thames 6/9–11/10/1976)
Documentary series featuring profiles of modern
playwrights.
TREVOR GRIFFITHS 13/9/1976
d Gabrielle Beaumont

PLEASE, SIR! (LWT 1968–72)
Comedy series set in an inner-city school.
d/p Mark Stuart;
sc John Esmonde, Bob Larbey;
regulars John Alderton; Deryck Guyler;
Joan Sanderson; Noel Howlett; Richard Davies;
Erik Chitty; Malcolm McFee; Penny Spencer;
Liz Gebhardt; Peter Cleall
The WELCOME MAT 8/11/1968
MAUREEN BULLOCK LOVES SIR 22/11/1968

PLUM'S PLOTS AND PLANS
(BBC 9–23/12/1977)
Series for children.
IN SEARCH OF SANTA 23/12/1977
d Jeremy Swan; *exec.p* Anna Home;
sc Peter Robinson
lp Arthur Howard; Aubrey Woods;
William Hootkins; Suzanne Tan; Pik-Sen Lim

POINTS OF VIEW (BBC 1961–)
Viewers' written comments are aired on
television.
POINTS OF VIEW 20/11/1968
pres Robert Robinson
POINTS OF VIEW 9/11/1979
pres Barry Took

POLDARK (BBC 1975–77)
Drama serial based on the novels of Winston
Graham and set in eighteenth-century Cornwall.
EPISODE 2 12/10/1975
d Christopher Barry; *p* Morris Barry;
sc Jack Pulman
lp Diana Berriman; Robin Ellis;
Clive Francis; Jill Townsend; Angharad Rees;
Don Henderson

POLICE SURGEON (ABC 1960)
Series following the assignments of a police
surgeon.
EASY MONEY 10/9/1960
d John Knight; *p/sc* Julian Bond
lp Ian Hendry; Diana Kennedy;
Alister Williamson; David Stuart;
Robin Wentworth; Robert Russell;
Michael Crawford; Joseph Tomelty

POLICE SURGEON
(CA Dorian Brentwood Films-CBC 1971–1975;
GB *tx* 1972–73; some regional transmissions
continued into the late 1970s)
Police-medical drama series set in Canada.

LIES 15/4/1977
p Chester Krumholz, Larry Hertzog
lp Sam Groom; Larry D. Mann

POLITICS WEST (Westward 11/7/1979)

PONY EXPRESS (US California National
Productions 1960)
Syndicated Western series set in 1860s
Sacramento and following the investigations of a
Pony Express agent.
The SEARCH 23/3/1960
d Frank McDonald; *p* Tom McKnight;
sc John Meredyth Lucas
lp Grant Sullivan; Ron Hagerty

The POPE IN THE HOLY LAND
(ITN 5/1/1964)
A report, via Eurovision, on the visit of Pope
Paul VI to Jordan and Israel.

POPE PAUL VI (Tyne Tees 6/8/1978)

PORRIDGE (BBC 1974–77)
Comedy series set in a prison and centering on a
veteran inmate and his young, first-time,
cellmate. A sequel, 'Going Straight', was shown
in 1978.
p Sydney Lotterby
sc Dick Clement, Ian La Frenais
regulars Ronnie Barker;
Richard Beckinsale; Brian Wilde;
Fulton Mackay
The HUSTLER 12/9/1974
lp Brian Glover; Ken Jones;
Christopher Biggins
An EVENING IN 19/9/1974
lp Paul McDowell
A DAY OUT 26/9/1974
lp Ken Jones; Paul Angelis;
Philip Jackson
WAYS AND MEANS 3/10/1974
lp Ken Jones; Michael Barrington;
Tony Osoba
MEN WITHOUT WOMEN 10/10/1974
lp Sam Kelly; Brian Glover;
Christopher Biggins; Patricia Brake
JUST DESSERTS 24/10/1975
lp Ken Jones; Sam Kelly; Tony Osoba;
Christopher Biggins; Eric Dodson;
Graham Ashley; John Rudling; Felix Bowness
HEARTBREAK HOTEL 31/10/1975
lp Patricia Brake; Maggie Flint
DISTURBING THE PEACE 7/11/1975
lp Peter Jeffrey; Philip Madoc;
Sam Kelly; Tony Osoba
NO PEACE FOR THE WICKED 14/11/1975
lp David Jason
The HARDER THEY FALL 28/11/1975
lp Peter Vaughan; Cyril Shaps
A STORM IN A TEACUP 18/2/1977
lp Peter Vaughan; Ronald Lacey;
Sam Kelly; Tony Osoba; Christopher Biggins;
John Moore; John Dair
POETIC JUSTICE 25/2/1977
lp Maurice Denham; Ronald Lacey;
Sam Kelly; Tony Osoba; Michael Barrington;
Paul McDowell
ROUGH JUSTICE 4/3/1977
lp Maurice Denham; Ronald Lacey;
Sam Kelly; Tony Osoba
PARDON ME 11/3/1977
lp David Jason; Sam Kelly;
Christopher Biggins; Michael Barrington
A TEST OF CHARACTER 18/3/1977
lp Alun Armstrong; Sam Kelly;
Tony Osoba
FINAL STRETCH 25/3/1977
lp Patricia Brake

The PORTRAIT OF A LADY
(BBC 6/1–10/2/1968)
Six-part dramatisation of the novel by Henry
James.
d James Cellan Jones; *p* David Conroy;
sc Jack Pulman
regulars Richard Chamberlain; Suzanne Neve
EPISODE 1: PROPOSALS 6/1/1968
lp Beatrix Lehmann; Alan Gifford;
Ed Bishop; Edward Fox

EPISODE 6: REVELATIONS 10/2/1968
lp Sarah Brackett; Ed Bishop;
Kathleen Byron; James Maxwell;
Sharon Gurney; Rachel Gurney;
Beatrix Lehmann

PORTRAIT OF A SCHOOL
(Rediffusion 8/5/1957)
A study of a schoolmaster, the problems he faces
in his work, and his relationship with the pupils
in his care.
d Vivian Milroy; *exec.p* Caryl Doncaster;
sc Norman MacKenzie

PORTRAIT OF A VILLAGE
(Anglia 1978–1989)
Regional series exploring villages.
HEYBRIDGE BASIN 8/10/1978
SHINGLE STREET 5/11/1978
WESTMILL 10/12/1978
SWAVESEY 7/1/1979

PORTRAITS OF POWER (BBC 1957–58)
Series illustrating the nature of power.
p Huw Wheldon; *intro* Robert McKenzie
ADOLF HITLER 9/4/1957
with Alan Bullock, Hugh Trevor-Roper,
Ernst Hanfstaengl
KHRUSHCHEV 16/5/1958
with Marshall MacDuffie, Cyril Osborne

PORTUGAL – DREAM OF EMPIRE
(Yorkshire TV 1971)
A two-part documentary on Portugal.
d/p Antony Thomas; *sc* Nicholas Tomalin
PART 1: OUT OF THE LIMBO 19/1/1971
The effects on Portuguese society of its struggles
against insurgents in the African colonies.
PART 2: BREAD AND CIRCUSES 26/1/1971
Portugal's war against insurgents in Angola and
Guinea-Bissau.

POSITIVE SOCCER WITH JACK
CHARLTON (Tyne Tees 1979)
Series in which footballer Jack Charlton advises
on football training and techniques.
d Lewis Williams; *p* David Jones
PRESSURE TRAINING 18/2/1979
COACHING CHILDREN 4/3/1979
AMATEUR – PART TIME COACHING 11/3/1979

POSTSCRIPT TO EMPIRE (Westinghouse
Broadcasting Company 10/1/1962)
Rod MacLeish introduces a study of two
contrasting communities – the Isle of Dogs and
Stevenage, to illustrate how Britain looks to
Americans today.
d Michael Alexander; *p* Michael Sklar

POT BLACK (BBC 1969–86)
The competition for the BBC 2 snooker
championship.
DOUG MOUNTJOY v. CLIFF THORBURN 1/4/1977
First semi-final for the 1977 Pot Black Trophy.
d Jim Dumighan; *p* Reg Perrin;
comm Ted Lowe
The FINALISTS: PERRIE MANS v. DOUG
MOUNTJOY 22/4/1977
The final for the Pot Black Trophy.
d Jim Dumighan; *p* Reg Perrin;
comm Ted Lowe

A POTTER'S WORLD (BBC 23/1/1961)
The work of the potter Bernard Leach.
d John Read

The POWER GAME (ATV 1965–69)
Drama based on political and industrial intrigue.
Sequel to The PLANEMAKERS (1963–65).
The NEW BOY 13/12/1965
d Victor Menzies; *p* Rex Firkin;
sc Edmund Ward
lp Patrick Wymark; Barbara Murray;
William Devlin; Norman Tyrrell;
Peter Barkworth; Clifford Evans; Pauline Loring

POWER IN BRITAIN (ABC 10/1–18/7/1965)
Twenty-six part series examining the government
in theory and practice.

The POWER OF THE PRIME MINISTER 10/1/1965
Norman Hunt and John McKintosh interview
Harold Wilson.
p Geoff Ramsey;
sc Norman Hunt, Isobel Allen;
intro Barry Westwood

POWER OF THE DOLLAR
(GB/US ABC 1968)
Anglo-American co-production on the effect of
American business practices in Europe.
d John Russell; *p* Brian Wenham;
nar Murray Kash
SALES TALK 21/1/1968
The impact of American sales techniques in
Europe and an analysis of the differing
techniques in different European countries.
TECHNOLOGY TRAIL 28/1/1968
Assesses the reasons behind a growing
technology gap between American and
European industries and suggests how Europe
might meet the challenge.
TAKE-OVER TRENDS 4/2/1968
Examines a number of European companies
which have been taken over by American
companies or which have a substantial American
shareholding.
RULES OF THE GAME 11/2/1968
An analysis of the implications of American
investment in Europe and of the problems
entailed in keeping pace with the
internationalisation of business.

PRAISE THE DOG FOR SITTING
(Scottish TV 22/8/1978)
Training of blind students in the use of guide
dogs and the work of the Guide Dogs for the
Blind Training Centre in Tayside.
d/p Patrick Boyle

PREPARING A PLAY
(Rediffusion 21/9–19/10/1966)
Education series of five programmes on
preparing the play, 'Twelfth Night'.
MOVEMENT 5/10/1966)
Scenes from 'Twelfth Night' illustrate how each
actor works to develop movements which
establish characterisation and the mood of a
scene.
d Richard Gilbert; *p* Charles Warren;
pres Mike Hall
with Trevor Martin, Jonathan Elson

PRESENT GRANDEUR (Scottish TV 1965)
Regional current affairs series
DR. LISTER 1965
The story of Joseph Lister.
d Geoff Rimmer
The ROAD AND THE MILES 1965
Dundee since the opening of the Tay Road
Bridge.
sc John Hossack; *nar* Michael Elder
PRESENT GRANDEUR 29/11/1965

PRESIDENT OF EUROPE (HTV 13/1/1977)
Profile of Roy Jenkins in which his friends and
critics appraise his achievements and character.
d Terry Delaney; *p* Gwilym Owen

The PRESIDENT'S LAST TAPE
(BBC 29/6/1974)
d Robert Knights; *p* Mark Shivas;
sc Philip Magdalany
lp Alec McCowen; Elaine Stritch;
Toby Robins; Donald Douglas; James Berwick;
Roy Stephens; Ann Murray; Elliott Sullivan;
Gordon Sterne; Gareth Hunt

PRESS CONFERENCE (BBC)
Interview series.
NEHRU 12/6/1953 *ntx*
p Grace Wyndham Goldie;
interv Kingsley Martin, H.V. Ley Hodson,
Donald McLachlan
GARY COOPER 30/10/1959
Gary Cooper talks to Thomas Wiseman, Eileen
Ashcroft and Francis Williams about his career
in films, his visit to the Soviet Union, and about
bullfighting.
p John Grist

HAROLD MACMILLAN 14/4/1961
Harold Macmillan meets William Hardcastle,
Francis Boyd and John Freeman.
p John Grist

PRETENDERS (HTV 27/2–21/5/1972)
Historical drama series set in the England of
1685.
p Patrick Dromgoole, Leonard White
regulars Frederick Jaeger; Curtis Arden;
Elizabeth Robillard
EPISODE 1: REBELLION 27/2/1972
d Patrick Dromgoole
lp Jonathan Newth; Hedley Goodall;
Constance Chapman; June Barrie
EPISODE 2: NOT A LIVE THING LEFT 5/3/1972
d Patrick Dromgoole; *sc* Christopher Robinson
lp Jack Watson; Maureen Pryor;
Neil McCarthy; Juan Moreno
EPISODE 4: IN SAFE KEEPING 19/3/1972
d Patrick Dromgoole; *sc* Christopher Robinson
lp Jonathan Newth; Hedley Goodall;
Constance Chapman; Frances Cuka
EPISODE 6: SHIPWRECK 2/4/1972
d Patrick Dromgoole; *sc* Martin C. Rodgers
lp William Simons; Rachel Thomas;
James Cossins; Ieuan Rhys Williams
EPISODE 7: The PAYMASTER 9/4/1972
d Bill Bain; *sc* Ivan Benbrook
lp John Thaw; Michael Beint;
James Cossins
EPISODE 8: PRINCE OF AVALON 16/4/1972
d Fred Burnley; *sc* Carole Boyer
lp Jonathan Newth; Hedley Goodall;
James Cossins; Constance Chapman;
Geoffrey Matthews
EPISODE 9: INTO BATTLE 23/4/1972
d Patrick Dromgoole; *sc* A.C.H. Smith
lp Jonathan Newth; Hamilton Dyce;
Carl Bernard; David Spenser; Alaric Cotter
EPISODE 10: The LAST BATTLE 30/4/1972
d Patrick Dromgoole, Terry Harding;
sc A.C.H. Smith, Bob Baker, Dave Martin
lp Jonathan Newth; Hamilton Dyce;
Carl Bernard; David Spenser; David Jackson
EPISODE 11: The EYE OF THE DRUM 7/5/1972
d Terry De Lacey; *sc* Eric Pringle
lp Juan Moreno; Hamilton Dyce;
Robert Bridges; Prunella Ransome
EPISODE 12: PRIZEMEN 14/5/1972
d Bill Bain;
sc Bob Baker, Dave Martin
lp Peter Williams; Hamilton Dyce;
Robert Bridges; Margery Withers;
Jonathan Newth
EPISODE 13: FARE THEE WELL 21/5/1972
d Leonard White; *sc* Denis Constanduros
lp Meadows White; Paul Hansard;
Robert Bridges; Hedley Goodall;
Jonathan Newth; Constance Chapman

The PRETTIEST VILLAGE IN ENGLAND
(BBC 1970)
John Morgan visits Castle Combe to see how it
will cope with increased tourism after it was
voted the prettiest village in England.

The PRICE OF COAL (BBC 29/3 & 5/4/1977)
Two films about life in the Yorkshire pits.
MEET THE PEOPLE 29/3/1977
d Ken Loach; *p* Tony Garnett;
sc Barry Hines
lp Bobby Knutt; Rita May; Paul Chappell;
Jayne Waddington; Haydn Conway;
Jackie Shinn; Duggie Brown

PRIMARY SCHOOL MATHEMATICS
(BBC 1965)
Educational series for schools.
p David Roseveare; *pres* Jim Boucher
ABOUT THIS LONG 4/10/1965
MIRROR IMAGE 8/11/1965

The PRIME MINISTER AND MRS WILSON
(LWT 25/7/1969)
Mary Wilson talks to David Frost about life at 10
Downing Street. Harold Wilson discusses aspects
of his personal life and philosophy.
d Fred Burnley

The PRIME MINISTER – LORD HOME
(BBC 21/10/1963)
Robin Day and Robert McKenzie interview
Lord Home.

A PRIME MINISTER ON PRIME MINISTERS
(Yorkshire TV 5/11/1977–22/2/1978)
Thirteen-part series in which Sir Harold Wilson
looks back at some of his predecessors and some
of his contemporaries.
d/p Peter Morley
RT. HON. HAROLD MACMILLAN O.M. 5/11/1977
David Frost interviews Harold Wilson on Harold
Macmillan.
CLEMENT ATTLEE: PART ONE 15/2/1978
Harold Wilson, in conversation with David
Frost, discusses the achievements of Clement
Attlee.
CLEMENT ATTLEE: PART TWO 22/2/1978
Harold Wilson, in conversation with David
Frost, discusses Clement Attlee's handling of the
granting of Independence to India.

PRIME MINISTER'S BROADCAST ON
RHODESIA (1/12/1965)
Harold Wilson explains the government's
decision to send troops to Zambia and to tighten
trade sanctions against Rhodesia.

The PRIME OF MISS JEAN BRODIE
(Scottish TV 22/1–5/3/1978)
Drama series based on Muriel Spark's novel.
EDINBURGH 29/1/1978
d Mark Cullingham; p Richard Bates;
sc William Pointer
lp Geraldine McEwan; John Castle;
Michael Elder; Georgine Anderson;
George Cormack; Madeleine Christie;
Amanda Kirby

PRINCE CHARLES INTERVIEW
(BBC 26/6/1969)
Brian Connell and Cliff Michelmore interview
Prince Charles about his forthcoming investiture
as Prince of Wales.

The PRISONER
(Everyman Films-ITC 1967–68)
Enigmatic drama series about a government
agent who is kidnapped and interrogated by an
unknown organisation.
p David Tomblin
regulars Patrick McGoohan; Angelo Muscat
The ARRIVAL 1/10/1967
d Don Chaffey;
sc George Markstein, David Tomblin
lp Virginia Maskell; Guy Doleman;
Paul Eddington; George Baker;
Barbara Yu Ling
The CHIMES OF BIG BEN 8/10/1967
d Don Chaffey; sc Vincent Tilsley
lp Leo McKern; Nadia Gray; Finlay Currie;
Richard Wattis; Kevin Stoney
A B AND C 15/10/1967
d Pat Jackson; sc Anthony Skene
lp Katherine Kath; Sheila Allen;
Colin Gordon; Peter Bowles; Georgina Cookson
FREE FOR ALL 22/10/1967
d/sc Patrick McGoohan
lp Eric Portman; Rachel Herbert;
George Benson; Harold Berens; John Cazabon
The SCHIZOID MAN 29/10/1967
d Pat Jackson; sc Terence Feely
lp Anton Rodgers; Jane Merrows;
Earl Cameron; Gay Cameron; David Nettheim
The GENERAL 5/11/1967
d Peter Graham Scott; sc Lewis Greifer
lp Colin Gordon; Conrad Phillips;
John Castle; Peter Howell; Al Mancini;
Betty McDowall
MANY HAPPY RETURNS 12/11/1967
d Patrick McGoohan; sc Anthony Skene
lp Donald Sinden; Patrick Cargill;
Georgina Cookson; Brian Worth;
Richard Caldicot
DANCE OF THE DEAD 26/11/1967
d Don Chaffey; sc Anthony Skene
lp Mary Morris; Duncan Macrae;
Norma West; Aubrey Morris; Bee Duffell;
Camilla Hasse

CHECKMATE 3/12/1967
d Don Chaffey; sc Gerald Kelsey
lp Ronald Radd; Patricia Jessel;
Peter Wyngarde; Rosalie Crutchley;
George Coulouris
HAMMER INTO ANVIL 10/12/1967
d Pat Jackson; sc Roger Woddis
lp Patrick Cargill; Victor Maddern;
Basil Hoskins; Norman Scace; Derek Aylward
IT'S YOUR FUNERAL 17/12/1967
d Robert Asher; sc Michael Cramoy
lp Derren Nesbitt; Annette Andre;
Mark Eden; Andre Van Gyseghem;
Martin Miller; Wanda Ventham
A CHANGE OF MIND 31/12/1967
d Patrick McGoohan; sc Roger Parkes
lp Angela Browne; John Sharp;
George Pravda; Kathleen Breck;
Peter Swanwick
DO NOT FORSAKE ME OH MY DARLING 7/1/1968
d Pat Jackson; sc Vincent Tilsley
lp Zena Walker; Clifford Evans;
Nigel Stock; Hugo Schuster; John Wentworth;
James Bree
LIVING IN HARMONY 14/1/1968
d/p/sc David Tomblin
lp Alexis Kanner; David Bauer;
Valerie French; Gordon Tanner; Gordon Sterne
The GIRL WHO WAS DEATH 21/1/1968
d David Tomblin; sc Terence Feely
lp Kenneth Griffith; Justine Lord;
Christopher Benjamin; Michael Brennan
ONCE UPON A TIME 28/1/1968
d/sc Patrick McGoohan
lp Leo McKern; Peter Swanwick;
John Cazabon; John Maxim
FALL OUT 4/2/1968
d/sc Patrick McGoohan
lp Leo McKern; Kenneth Griffith;
Alexis Kanner; Peter Swanwick; Michael Miller

PRISONERS (BBC 7/4/1971)
Play about creative freedom in the mass media.
d/sc Don Taylor
lp Warren Mitchell, Edward Woodward

The PRIVATE LIFE OF THE KINGFISHER
(BBC 6/12/1967)
A year in the life of a pair of kingfishers on the
River Test.
d Ronald Eastman, Rosemary Eastman;
comm/intro Peter Scott

The PRIVATE LIFE OF THE LARGE WHITE
BUTTERFLY (BBC 5/4/1970)
Life cycle of the Large White butterfly.
d Gerald Thompson, Eric Skinner;
nar Michael Aspel

The PRIVATE LIFE OF THE ROBIN
(BBC 24/12/1969)
Documentary on the robin.
d Ronald Eastman, Rosemary Eastman;
p Suzanne Gibbs, Jeffery Boswall;
comm Hugh Falkus

The PRIVATE LIFE OF THE STARLING
(BBC 22/3/1970)
The life cycle of the starling.
d Ronald Eastman, Rosemary Eastman;
p Jeffery Boswall

The PRIVATE LIFE OF THE WANDERING
ALBATROSS (BBC 29/3/1970)
The life cycle of the wandering albatross.
d Lancelot Tickell; p Jeffery Boswall;
comm Hugh Falkus

PROBATION OFFICER (ATV 12/9/1960)
Drama revolving around the activities of the
probation and welfare service.
d/p Antony Kearey; sc Peter Yeldham
lp Jerold Wells; Patricia Mort;
John Paul; Jessica Spencer; Jack Stewart;
Henry Oscar; Brian Murphy; Patricia Hayes

PROBLEMS (Thames 1976–77)
Discussion series on sexual problems.
PREMATURE EJACULATION 26/1/1976
pres Tony Bastable, Anna Raeburn,
Paul Brolon

The PRODIGAL DAUGHTER
(Anglia 5/1/1975)
Play dealing with the situation that results from
the affections of a young woman for a priest.
d Alastair Reid; p John Jacobs;
sc David Turner
lp Alastair Sim; Jeremy Brett;
Carolyn Seymour; Charles Kay

The PROFESSIONALS
(Avengers Mark 1–LWT 1977–83)
Action-adventure series featuring detectives
from the Criminal Intelligence 5 (CI5) branch.
p Raymond Menmuir
regulars Gordon Jackson; Martin Shaw;
Lewis Collins
BACKTRACK 3/11/1979
d Christopher King; sc Don Houghton
lp Liz Fraser; Michael Elphick;
John Bennett; Anthony Scott
STOPOVER 10/11/1979
d William Brayne; sc John Goldsmith
lp James Laurenson; Michael Gothard;
Morris Perry; Peter Cartwright
DEAD RECKONING 17/11/1979
d Denis Lewiston; sc Philip Loraine
lp Derek Godfrey; Carol Royle;
Alan Tilvern; Milos Kirek
The MADNESS OF MICKEY HAMILTON
24/11/1979
d William Brayne; sc Christopher Wicking
lp Ian McDiarmid; Marjorie Yates;
Barry Stanton; Shaun Curry
A HIDING TO NOTHING 1/12/1979
d Gerry O'Hara; sc Ted Charles
lp Sylvia Kay; Lise Hilboldt;
Nadim Sawalha; Christopher Reich

PROFILE (Rediffusion 1959)
Four-part interview series with prominent
politicians.
d Rollo Gamble; interv Ludovic Kennedy
The RT. HON. VISCOUNT HAILSHAM, Q.C.
18/5/1959
The RT. HON. ANEURIN BEVAN, M.P. 25/5/1959
The RT. HON. R.A. BUTLER, CH, M.P. 1/6/1959
The RT. HON. HUGH GAITSKELL, M.P. 8/6/1959

PROFILE IN MUSIC (BBC 1961–63)
Series featuring musical personalities.
ELISABETH SCHWARZKOPF 21/12/1961
Elisabeth Schwarzkopf talks to John Freeman
about her career and sings operatic arias and
songs with which she is particularly associated.
p Patricia Foy
with Hertha Toepper
VICTORIA DE LOS ANGELES
31/5/1962
Victoria de los Angeles talks to John Freeman
about her life and work and sings excerpts from
'La vida breve', 'The Barber of Seville' and
'Madame Butterfly'.
p Patricia Foy

PROFILE OF ORSON WELLES
(Rediffusion 20/4/1956)
Cecil Lewis looks at the life and work of Orson
Welles.

PROFILES IN POWER (Rediffusion 1963)
Two programmes looking at two of the most
powerful men in the world.
d Bill Morton; pres John Freeman
JOHN FITZGERALD KENNEDY
13/11/1963
The career and presidential record of John
Fitzgerald Kennedy, with John F. Kennedy,
Arthur Schlesinger, James MacGregor Burns,
Henry Reuss, and James Baldwin.
NIKITA SERGEYEVICH KHRUSHCHEV
20/11/1963
The career and personality of Nikita Sergeyevich
Khrushchev, with Harold Wilson, Hubert
Humphrey, K.S. Karol, Roy Thomson, Angus
Wilson, Isaac Deutscher, and Sir Robert
Jackson.

PROSPECTS OF MANKIND
(GB/US BBC-WGBH Boston 29/9/1960)
The defence policy of Great Britain discussed by
Eleanor Roosevelt, Bertrand Russell, Hugh
Gaitskell, Robert McKenzie and Lord Boothby.

The PROTECTORS
(Group Three Productions-ITC 1972–74)
International detective series.
p Gerry Anderson, Reg Hill
regulars Robert Vaughan;
Nyree Dawn Porter; Tony Anholt;
Yasuko Nagazami; Anthony Chinn
2,000FT. TO DIE 15/9/1972
d John Hough; *sc* Terence Feely
lp Harvey Hall; Nicholas Jones;
Jacqueline Stanbury; Paul Stassino;
John Scott
DISAPPEARING TRICK 22/9/1972
d Jeremy Summers; *sc* Brian Clemens
lp David Bauer; Derren Nesbitt;
Chris Malcolm; Don Henderson
CEREMONY FOR THE DEAD 29/9/1972
d Jeremy Summers; *sc* Donald James
lp Stanley Lebor; Toby Robins;
Jennie Lee-Wright
IT WAS ALL OVER IN LEIPZIG 6/10/1972
d Don Chaffey; *sc* Donald James
lp Ron Randell; Phil Brown; Diane Mercer
KING CON 20/10/1972
d Jeremy Summers; *sc* Tony Barwick
lp Anton Rodgers; Peter Cellier;
Ronald Lacey
THINKBACK 27/10/1972
d Cyril Frankel; *sc* Brian Clemens
lp Ian Hendry; Keith Bell;
James Culliford
A KIND OF WILD JUSTICE 3/11/1972
d Jeremy Summers; *sc* Donald James
lp Kubi Chaza; Anna Palk;
Patrick O'Connell; Barry Stanton; Paul Freeman
BROTHER HOOD 10/11/1972
d Don Chaffey; *sc* John Goldsmith
lp Vladek Sheybal; Patrick Troughton;
Jill Balcon; John Cazabon
TRIPLE CROSS 1/12/1972
d John Hough; *sc* Lewis Davidson
lp John Neville; Angharad Rees;
Peter Bowles
BALANCE OF TERROR 8/12/1972
d Don Chaffey; *sc* John Goldsmith
lp Nigel Green; Laurence Naismith;
Angus Lennie
FOR THE REST OF YOUR NATURAL... 15/12/1972
d John Hough; *sc* Tony Barwick
lp Norman Rodway; Damien Thomas
The BODYGUARDS 22/12/1972
d Don Chaffey; *sc* Dennis Spooner
lp Freddie Jones; Manning Redwood;
Ken Watson
A MATTER OF LIFE AND DEATH 5/1/1973
d Don Chaffey; *sc* Donald James
lp Barrie Houghton; Patrick Allen;
Maxwell Shaw; Cyril Shaps
VOCAL 26/1/1973
d Cyril Frankel; *sc* Brian Clemens
lp David Buck; Ian Hogg; Shane Rimmer
YOUR WITNESS 16/2/1973
d Jeremy Summers; *sc* Donald James
lp George Baker; Stephanie Beacham;
Judith Arthy; George Lambert;
Hugo de Vernier
IT COULD BE PRACTICALLY ANYWHERE ON
THE ISLAND 23/2/1973
d Robert Vaughn; *sc* Tony Barwick
lp Sherwood Price; Linda Staab;
Madeline Hinde; Dervis Ward
The FIRST CIRCLE 2/3/1973
d Don Chaffey; *sc* Tony Barwick
lp Ed Bishop; John Collin; Sally Bazely
A CASE FOR THE RIGHT 9/3/1973
d Michael Lindsay-Hogg;
sc Jesse L. Lasky Jr, Pat Silver
lp Milo O'Shea; Jacques Sernas
QUIN 7/4/1973
d Don Leaver; *sc* Trevor Preston
lp Peter Vaughn; Brian Glover
BAGMAN 12/5/1973
d John Hough; *sc* Terry Nation
lp Stephan Chase; Patricia Haines;
Lalla Ward; Oliver Ford Davies
PETARD 9/6/1973
d Cyril Frankel; *sc* Tony Barwick
lp Iain Cuthbertson; Cyril Luckham;
Ralph Bates

BAUBLES, BANGLES AND BEADS 30/6/1973
d Jeremy Summers; *sc* Terry Nation
lp Frederick Jaeger; Yvonne Antrobus;
John Barron
DECOY 14/7/1973
d Michael Lindsay-Hogg; *sc* Brian Clemens
lp Ronald Radd; Mark Damon; Terry Canner
BORDER LINE 21/7/1973
d Charles Crichton; *sc* Anthony Terpiloff
lp Georgia Brown; Oscar Homolka
IMPLICADO 11/8/1973
d Jeremy Summers; *sc* Tony Barwick
lp Patrick Mower; Peter Firth;
Aldo Sambrell; Ruth Trouncer
SUGAR AND SPICE 21/9/1973
d Charles Crichton; *sc* David Butler
lp Derek Anders; Phil Woods;
Norman Ettlinger; John Normington
LENA 5/10/1973
d Don Leaver; *sc* Trevor Preston
lp Roger Lloyd Pack; Judi Bloom;
John Thaw
BURNING BUSH 12/10/1973
d Don Leaver; *sc* Trevor Preston
lp Sinead Cusack; Ken Hutchison;
Madge Ryan; Anthony Steel
The TIGER AND THE GOAT 26/10/1973
d Jeremy Summers; *sc* Trevor Preston
lp Douglas Wilmer; Derek Godfrey;
Derek Newark; Drewe Henley
ROUTE 27 2/11/1973
d Don Leaver; *sc* Terry Nation
lp Michael Coles; Jeremy Wilkin;
Virginia Wetherell
TRIAL 9/11/1973
d Charles Crichton; *sc* Robert Banks Stewart
lp Joss Ackland; Gwen Cherrell;
Richard Hurndall; John Ringham
SHADBOLT 16/11/1973
d John Hough; *sc* Tony Barwick
lp Tom Bell; Georgina Hale

PUBLIC EYE
(ABC 1965–68; Thames 1969–75)
Detective series centred around a seedy private
investigator.
regular Alfred Burke
The MORNING WASN'T SO HOT 10/4/1965
d Kim Mills; *p* John Bryce;
sc Roger Marshall
lp Roland Curram; Carole Ann Ford;
Barry Linehan; Richard Butler; Philip Madoc;
Vic Wise
WORKS WITH CHESS – NOT WITH LIFE
12/8/1966
d Basil Coleman; *p* Richard Bates;
sc Roger Marshall
lp Laurence Hardy; Valerie Bell;
Derek Waring; Jon Croft; Sydney Dobson;
Susan Dowdall
The BROMSGROVE VENUS 16/3/1968
d Jim Goddard; *p* Michael Chapman;
sc Anthony Skene
lp Timothy Carlton; Leon Sinden;
Alan Partington; Sylvia Kay; Elizabeth Benson
WELCOME TO BRIGHTON? 30/7/1969
d/p Kim Mills; *sc* Roger Marshall
lp Michael Graham Cox; Pauline Delany;
George Sewell; John Bindon; John Grieve

PUBLIC PROSECUTOR
(US Jerry Fairbanks Productions 1947–52)
Short mystery films followed by crime writers
and others guessing the solutions.
The DEAD MAN'S VOICE 1948
d Lew Landers; *p* Jerry Fairbanks
lp Walter Sande; Anne Gwynne;
Jane Frazee; David Bruce; Pat Gleason;
John Howard

The PUBLIC'S RIGHT TO KNOW
(Thames 5/3/1974)
Kenneth Griffith describes his experiences with
two television film projects, one about Baden-
Powell, the other about Michael Collins,
(HANG UP YOUR BRIGHTEST COLOURS:
THE LIFE AND DEATH OF MICHAEL
COLLINS 1973) both of which were prevented
from reaching the screen.
d Silvio Narizzano; *with* Jeremy Isaacs,
Ian Martin, William Deedes, Benny Green,
Alan Sapper, Athol Fugard

PULCINELLA (US; BBC *tx* 8/12/1975)
Music by Igor Stravinsky, choreography by
George Balanchine and Jerome Robbins,
performed by the New York City Ballet, with
Edward Villella as Pulcinella. [1975 date is of
repeat GB transmission]
d Hugo Niebeling

PURSUIT OF HAPPINESS
(Rediffusion 1960)
Documentary series in which Daniel Farson
investigates what makes people happy.
RAGS TO GLAMOUR 2/6/1960
Shirley Ann Field talks about the problems of
stardom and personal happiness.
d John Frankau
PEOPLE APART 16/6/1960
An interview with a group of people who have
gone to live on a remote island in order to find
happiness.
d John Frankau
WITHOUT SIGHT 15/9/1960
Lord Fraser of Lonsdale talks about his life since
he was blinded in the First World War.
d Sheila Gregg
WALK ON 29/9/1960
An interview with Christmas Humphreys, an
authority on Zen Buddhism.
d Sheila Gregg
BECAUSE THEY'RE THERE 13/10/1960
An interview with Joe Brown, the rock climber,
who is seen climbing with friends on a Peak
District outcrop.
d Sheila Gregg
MINDS AND HANDS 20/10/1960
Daniel Farson interviews his father, Negley
Farson on his ideas about achieving happiness
through one's work.
d John Frankau
The ARCHBISHOP OF YORK 27/10/1960
An interview with Dr Arthur Michael Ramsey
about happiness and its relation to the purpose
of life.
d David Kentish

Q

Q6 (BBC 6/11–11/12/1975)
Comedy series featuring Spike Milligan.
Q6 6/11/1975
d Ian MacNaughton;
sc Spike Milligan, Neil Shand;
with John Bluthal, Robert Dorning,
Jack Watling
Q6 20/11/1975
p Ian MacNaughton;
sc Spike Milligan, Neil Shand;
with John Bluthal, Robert Dorning,
Peter Jones, David Lodge

QUATERMASS (Thames 24/10–14/11/1979)
Fourth entry in Nigel Kneale's Quatermass
television serials. A four-part story set in the
near future.
EPISODE 1 24/10/1979
d Piers Haggard; *p* Ted Childs;
sc Nigel Kneale
lp John Mills; Barbara Kellermann;
Simon MacCorkindale; Ralph Arliss;
Paul Rosebury; Jane Bertish

QUATERMASS AND THE PIT
(BBC 1958–59)
Third of the Quatermass serials, presenting a six-
part story blending supernatural elements with
science-fiction.
p Rudolph Cartier; *sc* Nigel Kneale
regulars André Morell; Cec Linder;
Anthony Bushell; John Stratton; Christine Finn
EPISODE 1: HALFMEN 22/12/1958
lp Robert Perceval; Michael Ripper;
Ian Ainsley; Harold Goodwin; Victor Platt
EPISODE 2: GHOSTS 29/12/1958
lp Michael Ripper; Harold Goodwin;
Victor Platt; John Walker; Hilda Barry;
Howell Davies; Madge Brindley
EPISODE 3: IMPS AND DEMONS 5/1/1959
lp John Walker; Michael Ripper;
Harold Goodwin; Tony Quinn; Keith Banks;
Brian Worth; Richard Shaw

EPISODE 4: ENCHANTED 12/1/1959
lp Michael Ripper; Harold Goodwin;
Brian Worth; Kenneth Seeger; Tony Quinn;
Richard Shaw; Robert Perceval; Ian Ainsley;
Noel Howlett
EPISODE 5: WILD HUNT 19/1/1959
lp Michael Ripper; Harold Goodwin;
Richard Shaw; Noel Howlett; Brian Worth;
Robert Perceval; Harold Siddons
EPISODE 6: HOB 26/1/1959
lp Harold Siddons; Brian Worth;
Ian Ainsley; Edward Burnham;
Anthony Pendrell; Richard Shaw; Budd Knapp;
Stuart Nichol; Tony Quinn

The QUATERMASS EXPERIMENT
(BBC 18/7–22/8/1953)
The first Quatermass television serial, revolving
around a failed rocket experiment and its chilling
consequences.
EPISODE 1: CONTACT HAS BEEN
ESTABLISHED 18/7/1953
p Rudolph Cartier; *sc* Nigel Kneale
lp Reginald Tate; Isabel Dean;
Duncan Lamont; Hugh Kelly; Moray Watson;
W. Thorp Devereux; Van Boolen; Iris Ballard;
Neil Wilson; Katie Johnson; Oliver Johnston
EPISODE 2: PERSONS REPORTED MISSING
25/7/1953
p Rudolph Cartier; *sc* Nigel Kneale
lp Reginald Tate; Isabel Dean; Duncan Lamont;
Hugh Kelly; Moray Watson; John Glen;
Ian Colin; Frank Hawkins; Christopher Rhodes;
Peter Bathurst; Enid Lindsay; Oliver Johnston

QUATERMASS II (BBC 1955)
Continuing the Quatermass serials in a six-part
story about the invasion of earth by alien
creatures.
p Rudolph Cartier; *sc* Nigel Kneale
regulars John Robinson; Monica Grey;
Hugh Griffith; John Stone
EPISODE 1: BOLTS 22/10/1955
lp Brian Hayes; Tony Lyons; Eric Lugg;
Hilda Barry; Herbert Lomas; Richard Cuthbert
EPISODE 2: MARK 29/10/1955
lp Rupert Davies; Austin Trevor;
John Miller; Wilfrid Brambell;
Michael Brennan; Sheila Martin;
Michael Collins; Diana Chesney
EPISODE 3: FOOD 5/11/1955
lp Rupert Davies; Austin Trevor;
John Miller; Derek Aylward; John Cazabon;
Margaret Flint; Ilona Ference; Sydney Bromley;
Melvyn Hayes; Trevor Reid
EPISODE 4: COMING 12/11/1955
lp Austin Trevor; Roger Delgado;
Michael Golden; John Rae; Elsie Arnold;
Ian Wilson; Desmond Jordan
EPISODE 5: FRENZY 19/11/1955
lp Michael Golden; John Rae;
Desmond Jordan; Ian Wilson
EPISODE 6: DESTROYERS 26/11/1955
lp Dennis McCarthy; Cyril Shaps

The QUEEN (25/12/1957)
Queen Elizabeth's first televised Christmas Day
broadcast. She recalls the countries she has
visited during the year and reads a passage from
'Pilgrim's Progress'. The choir of Westminster
Abbey sing the National Anthem.

The QUEEN (25/12/1963)
The Queen's Christmas Day broadcast.

The QUEEN (25/12/1970)
The Queen's Christmas Day broadcast.

The QUEEN (25/12/1971)
The Queen's Christmas Day broadcast.
p Richard Cawston

The QUEEN (25/12/1972)
The Queen's Christmas Day broadcast, in which
she refers to the Ulster situation and Britain's
entry to the EEC.

The QUEEN (25/12/1973)
The Queen's Christmas Day broadcast.
p Richard Cawston

The QUEEN (25/12/1974)
The Queen's Christmas Day broadcast.
p Richard Cawston

The QUEEN (25/12/1975)
The Queen's Christmas Day broadcast, filmed in
Buckingham Palace gardens.
p Richard Cawston

The QUEEN (25/12/1975 *ntx*)
The Queen's Christmas Day broadcast, filmed in
the Regency Room, Buckingham Palace, as an
alternative to the transmitted version.
p Richard Cawston

The QUEEN (25/12/1976)
The Queen's Christmas Day broadcast.
p Richard Cawston

The QUEEN (25/12/1977)
The Queen's Christmas Day broadcast.
p Richard Cawston

The QUEEN (25/12/1978)
The Queen's Christmas Day broadcast.
p Richard Cawston

The QUEEN (25/12/1979)
The Queen's Christmas Day broadcast.
p Richard Cawston

**The QUEEN OF THE NETHERLANDS'
ARRIVAL** (BBC 21/11/1950)
The Queen of The Netherlands' arrival at
Victoria station where King George VI and
Queen Elizabeth wait to greet her.

QUEEN'S CHAMPION (BBC 20/7–7/9/1958)
Drama series for children set on the eve of the
Spanish Armada.
EPISODE 1: THE BETRAYAL 20/7/1958
p/sc Shaun Sutton
lp Patrick Cargill; Michael Anderson;
Roger Delgado; John Woodnutt;
Paul Whitsun-Jones; Nigel Arkwright;
Colin Douglas; Frazer Hines

The QUEEN'S SILVER JUBILEE VISIT
(Yorkshire TV 13/7/1977)
Queen Elizabeth II's tour of Yorkshire and
Humberside.
d Charles Flynn; *p* John Meade

QUEST FOR GANDHI (BBC 13/7/1969)
On the 100th anniversary of Gandhi's birth
Malcolm Muggeridge explores his life and work.
d/p Peter Chafer

QUEST OF EAGLES
(Tyne Tees 11/11–23/12/1979)
Seven-part adventure serial for children about a
boy on the trail of a priceless treasure.
d Bob Hird; *p* Margaret Bottomley;
sc Richard Cooper
lp Robert Urquhart; Ferdy Mayne;
Michael Yeaman; Michael Williams;
Vladek Sheybal
EPISODE 1 11/11/1979
EPISODE 6 16/12/1979
EPISODE 7 23/12/1979

A QUESTION OF EUROPE (BBC 3/6/1975)
Oxford Union debate on the EEC.
p Philip Gilbert, Tam Fry

A QUESTION OF SEX
(LWT 15/6–27/7/1979)
Documentary series examining the difference
between the sexes and offering sex education.
SEX 15/6/1979
Clive James and Anna Raeburn discuss sex and
the emotional differences between men and
women.
d David Crossman; *p* Jane Hewland

The QUIET WAR (Rediffusion 3/5/1961)
The background to the early years of the
Vietnam War.
d Bill Morton; *sc* Elkan Allan

The QUIET WAYS OF WALES
(HTV 1978)
Travels along the canals of Wales.
sc/nar/pres Wynford Vaughan-Thomas
The LLANGOLLEN CANAL 3/7/1978
Wynford Vaughan-Thomas journeys along the
Llangollen canal in a narrow boat.
d/p John Mead
MONTGOMERY CANAL 10/7/1978
The Montgomery Canal, preserved by
volunteers, and some of the places on the canal's
route.
d Peter Farrell; *p* John Mead
BRECON AND MONMOUTHSHIRE CANAL
23/10/1978
A record of the Brecon and Monmouthshire
Canal, currently separate from the rest of the
British canal system, which is to be changed by
canal preservation and re-activation groups.
d John Mead, Peter Farrell, Jack Howells;
p John Mead

QUO VADIS (Scottish TV 6/2/1966)
James Gordon and David Campbell talk to Sir
Compton Mackenzie after his 83rd birthday.
d Geoff Rimmer

R

R.C.M.P.
(CA Crawley Films-CBC-BBC 1960)
Drama series following the exploits of the Royal
Canadian Mounted Police.
NUMBER 34 1960
d George Gorman; *p* Bernard Girard;
sc Vincent Tilsley
lp Gilles Pelletier; John Perkins;
Joseph Boley; Aileen Seaton; Robert Rivard;
Helen Winston; Don Francks; Jim Terrell
DAY OF RECKONING GB *tx* 16/12/1960
d Fergus McDonell; *sc* Vincent Tilsley
lp Gilles Pelletier; John Perkins;
Don Francks; Gene Persson; Ann Helm;
Ed McNamara; Ivor Barry; Shane Rimmer;
Ruth Springford

The RACE APART
(Southern TV 2/4/1974)
The 1973 Round the World Yacht Race and an
insight into the motivation of some of the
participants.
d Michael Finlason; *nar* Barry Westwood

The RACING GAME
(Yorkshire TV 21/11/79–9/1/80)
Six-part series about an ex-jockey turned
detective; based on the stories by Dick Francis.
p Jacky Stoller
regular Mike Gwilym
ODDS AGAINST 21/11/1979
d Lawrence Gordon Clark; *sc* Terence Feely
lp James Maxwell; Gerald Flood;
Rachel Davies; Mick Ford; Susan Wooldridge
TRACKDOWN 28/11/1979
d Lawrence Gordon Clark; *sc* Terence Feely
lp Leslie Sands; Jeremy Clyde;
Mick Ford; Carol Royle; David Calder
GAMBLING LADY 5/12/1979
d Peter Duffell; *sc* Evan Jones
lp Caroline Blakiston; James Maxwell;
Mick Ford; Anthony Steel; Susan Wooldridge
HORSES FOR COURSES 12/12/1979
d John Mackenzie; *sc* Leon Griffiths
lp Jan Francis; Maurice O'Connell;
Mick Ford; Geoffrey Tomlinson; John Bindon
HORSENAP 19/12/1979
d Colin Bucksey; *sc* Trevor Preston
lp Iain Cuthbertson; Mick Ford;
Susan Penhaligon; Larry Lamb; Peter Blake

RAFFLES (Yorkshire TV 25/2–20/5/77)
The adventures of the gentleman thief A.J.
Raffles; from the stories by E.W. Hornung.
p Jacky Stoller; *sc* Philip Mackie
regulars Anthony Valentine; Christopher Strauli
The FIRST STEP 25/2/1977
d Christopher Hodson
lp Thorley Walters; Jeremy Clyde;
David Firth; Susan Skipper

RAFFLES *cont.*

A COSTUME PIECE 4/3/1977
d Christopher Hodson
lp Brian Glover; Alfred Marks;
Jill Gascoine
The SPOILS OF SACRILEGE 11/3/1977
d Christopher Hodson
lp William Mervyn; Barbara Hicks;
Sally Osborn; William Humbert
The GOLD CUP 18/3/1977
d David Cunliffe
lp Peter Sallis; Tony Britton;
Diana Weston
A CHEST OF SILVER 25/3/1977
d Alan Gibson
lp Geoffrey Hutchings; Victor Carin;
Peter Dean; Robert Dorning
The LAST LAUGH 1/4/1977
d Jim Goddard
lp Victor Carin; Cyril Shaps;
Robert Lang; Marina Sirtis; Bruce Robinson
A TRAP TO CATCH A CRACKSMAN 8/4/1977
d John Davies
lp John Stratton; Christopher Malcolm;
Lloyd Lamble; Carol Drinkwater
TO CATCH A THIEF 15/4/1977
d Christopher Hodson
lp Robert Hardy; Victor Carin;
David Parfitt; John Flint
A BAD NIGHT 22/4/1977
d Christopher Hodson
lp Norman Bird; Jan Francis;
Brenda Cowling
HOME AFFAIRS 6/5/1977
d Jim Goddard
lp Victor Carin; Graham Crowden;
Claire Davenport; Erik Chitty
The GIFT OF THE EMPEROR 13/5/1977
d Jim Goddard
lp Victor Carin; John Hallam;
John Carson
An OLD FLAME 20/5/1977
d Jim Goddard
lp Gerald Flood; Caroline Blakiston;
Victor Carin

The RAG TRADE (LWT 1977–78)
Sitcom featuring the colourful characters in a
clothing factory. Originally a BBC series in the
early 1960s, the programme was revived by
LWT.
The GUVNOR'S WIFE 13/11/1977
d/p Bryan Izzard;
sc Ronald Wolfe, Ronald Chesney
lp Miriam Karlin; Peter Jones;
Christopher Beeny; Anna Karen;
Diane Langton; Rowena Cooper;
Deddie Davies; Lucita Lijertwood;
Gillian Taylforth

The RAGGED REVOLUTION
(Yorkshire TV 16/6/1970)
The Mexican Revolution of 1910/11. Includes
film shot in and around Mexico City at the time,
and at the Battle of Chihuahua.
d/p Tony Essex; *nar* Alec Mango

RAGING CALM (Granada 7/1–18/2/1974)
Drama series based on Stan Barstow's novel of
the same name.
A VOTE FOR PROGRESS 18/2/1974
d June Howson; *p* Brian Armstrong;
sc Stan Barstow
lp Alan Badel; Diana Coupland;
Michael Williams; Frances White; Basil Dignam;
Donald Morley

RAGTIME (BBC 1973)
Series for children.
RAGTIME 10/10/1973
p Michael Cole; *sc* Michael Cole;
pres Maggie Henderson; Fred Harris

RAILWAY ROUNDABOUT (BBC 1957–1963)
Magazine programme for railway enthusiasts.
d Patrick Whitehouse, John Adams
LOCO SPOTTERS AT KING'S CROSS AND
EUSTON 1957
The BRISTOLIAN IN THE AGE OF STEAM
17/6/1958
A journey on The Bristolian Express on British
Rail's Western Region, hauled by Castle class
loco 'Drysllwyn Castle'.

FISHGUARD HARBOUR 7/10/1958
A passenger boat arrives at Fishguard Harbour.
The passengers disembark and board the
London train pulled by a Hall class locomotive.
THREE BRANCH LINES 4/11/1958
A Terrier locomotive at work on the Hayling
Island branch lines.
TRAINS ON THE LICKEY INCLINE 2/12/1958
Depicts a typical summer Saturday in 1958 on
the Lickey Incline, with scenes at Bromsgrove
and en route to Blackwell.
The SKYE LINE 1959
A journey from Fort William to Mallaig behind a
K2 class 2-6-0.
ROTHER VALLEY SPECIAL 31/1/1959
The special run over the old Kent and Sussex
Railway from Robertsbridge to Tenterden.
CLOSING OF THE WYE VALLEY LINE 7/4/1959
Made on the last operational day of the railway
line from Ross-on-Wye to Chepstow via
Monmouth.
WORCESTERSHIRE BRANCH LINE 5/5/1959
The story of one of the last official workings of a
Midland Compound between Barnt Green and
Ashchurch.
A VISIT TO KING'S CROSS SHED 30/6/1959
E4 AT CAMBRIDGE 30/6/1959
Shows the last of the E4 class 2-4-0's at work in
Cambridge.
G.N. TANK NO. 1247 28/7/1959
Great Northern 0-6-0 locomotive no. 1247
filmed at Hatfield and on a run to St Albans
MIDLAND COMPOUND 1000 30/9/1959
The rebuilding of the Midland Compound, its
trials and first official run.
TWO GLENS TO FORT WILLIAM 8/12/1959
Historic film of Glen Loy and Glen Falloch
working mail between Glasgow and Fort
William.
BUTLER HENDERSON 1960
SPECIAL OPERATION ON THE LICKEY 1960
TWO DUKEDOGS TO BARMOUTH 20/4/1960
Working the 1959 Talyllyn Special from
Shrewsbury to Towyn and taking empty stock to
Barmouth.
CALEY BOGIES FROM PERTH TO AVIEMORE
15/11/1960
Two Pickergill 4-4-0s being prepared at Perth
and then working an express from Perth to
Aviemore.
BY SLIP COACH TO BICESTER 15/11/1960
The operation of the slip coach system on British
Rail's Western Region.
FROM BATH TO EVERCREECH JUNCTION
13/12/1960
A train is hauled by ex-Somerset and Dorset
class 2-8-0s and shows banking performed by
ex-LMS 0-6-0T engines.
BANK HOLIDAY AT BEWDLEY 1961
The comings and goings of trains and people on
an August Bank Holiday at Bewdley.
TRAINS AT NEWCASTLE-UPON-TYNE 11/4/1961
GORDON HIGHLANDER ON THE SPEY VALLEY
11/4/1961
4-4-0 locomotive no. 49, ex Great North of
Scotland Railway, on the run from Craigellachie
to Boat of Garten.
The LOCOMOTIVES OF LONDON TRANSPORT
6/6/1961
Steam locomotion at Neasden Shed;
Rickmansworth, the change-over from steam to
electric traction.
BEWDLEY–TENBURY BRANCH 10/10/1961
The train working on the Bewdley–Tenbury
branch railway between Bewdley, Tenbury Wells
and Woofferton Junction in the last season of
full service.
The SEMMERING LINE 10/10/1961
The electrification of this line in Austria with
both steam and electric locomotives.
The JONES GOODS FROM KYLE TO DINGWALL
25/4/1962
The famous Highland Railway engine no. 103
making a journey from Kyle of Lochalsh to
Dingwall.
A JOURNEY FROM RYDE TO VENTNOR
25/4/1962
KIRTLEY, JOHNSON AND CO. 25/4/1962
The preserved engines from the Derby works
make a journey to Wirksworth.
d Patrick Whitehouse, John Adams

A DAY AT SEATON JUNCTION 18/7/1962
A typical collection of steam-hauled locomotives
on the old Southern Railway.
NEWTON HEATH SHED 18/7/1962
A selection of LM locomotives including some
rare L and Y classes.
YUGOSLAV NARROW GAUGE 15/8/1962
The narrow gauge line from Sarajevo to
Dubrovnik.
The SNOW TRAIN 1/5/1963
The re-opening operations and snow clearance
with steam locomotives of the Swiss Narrow
Gauge Furka Oberalp Bahn from Brig to
Disentis.

RAINBOW CITY (BBC 5/7–9/8/1967)
Six-part serial about a Jamaican lawyer and
other immigrants living in and around
Birmingham.
d/p John Elliot;
sc John Elliot, Horace James
regulars Horace James; Errol John;
Gemma Jones
EPISODE 1: WHAT SORT OF A BOY? 5/7/1967
lp Colin Skipp; Calvin Butler;
Graham Weston; Ianthe Agelasto;
Frank Veasey; Leslie Dunn; Myrtle Robinson;
Frances Dunne; Nina Baden-Semper;
Dolores Mantez
EPISODE 2: WHY YOU MARRY? 12/7/1967
lp George Woolley; Raymond Hill;
Annie Perkins; Mitzi Townshend; Cecil Gray;
Leonie Forbes; Buddy Pouatt; Yvonne Jones;
Beverley Anderson; George Madden
EPISODE 3: BETTER FORTUNE 19/7/1967
lp Carmen Munroe; David Stevens
EPISODE 4: BEARDS AND TURBANS 26/7/1967
d Mike Bowen; *p* Alan Rees
lp Robin Wentworth; Renu Setna;
Fiona Duncan; Shay Gorman; Charles Hyatt;
Ysanne Churchman; Roger Milner

RAINBOW MOVES HOUSE
(Thames 9/4/1979)
Programme for children. The Holton family
move house, Steven aged five and Julia aged
three face special problems.

The RAKE'S PROGRESS (BBC 30/10/1961)
A studio performance of Gavin Gordon's ballet,
inspired by William Hogarth's paintings. The
ballet charts the path to the madhouse trodden
by an eighteenth-century profligate.
d/p Margaret Dale; *choreo* Ninette de Valois
with Donald Britton, Elizabeth Anderton,
Gordon Aitken, Alan Alder, Alan Beale,
Alexander Bennett, Christopher Gable,
Brian Shaw, Lorna Mossford

RANDALL & HOPKIRK (DECEASED)
(ITC 1969–71)
Fantasy-detective series revolving around the
partnership of a private detective and the ghost
of his dead partner.
p Monty Berman
regulars Mike Pratt; Kenneth Cope;
Annette Andre
MY LATE, LAMENTED, FRIEND AND PARTNER
21/9/1969
d Cyril Frankel; *sc* Ralph Smart
lp Frank Windsor; Ronald Lacey;
Dolores Mantez; Harry Locke
NEVER TRUST A GHOST 12/10/1969
d Leslie Norman; *sc* Tony Williamson
lp Peter Vaughan; Caroline Blakiston;
Philip Madoc; Edina Ronay
THAT'S HOW MURDER SNOWBALLS 19/10/1969
d Paul Dickson; *sc* Ray Austin
lp Grazina Frame; Arthur Brough;
Patrick Holt; Harold Berens; Valerie Leon;
Michael Griffiths; David Jason; John Cazabon
The GHOST WHO SAVED THE BANK AT MONTE
CARLO 30/11/1969
d Jeremy Summers; *sc* Tony Williamson
lp Mary Merrall; Brian Blessed;
Veronica Carlson; John Sharp
FOR THE GIRL WHO HAS EVERYTHING
7/12/1969
d Cyril Frankel; *sc* Donald James
lp Lois Maxwell; Marjorie Rhodes;
Freddie Jones; Michael Coles

BUT WHAT A SWEET LITTLE ROOM 14/12/1969
d Roy Ward Baker; sc Ralph Smart
lp Michael Goodliffe; Doris Hare;
Norman Bird; Frances Bennett
The MAN FROM NOWHERE 28/12/1969
d Robert Tronson; sc Donald James
lp Ray Brooks; Michael Gwynn;
Patrick Newell; Neil McCarthy
WHEN THE SPIRIT MOVES YOU 2/1/1970
d Ray Austin; sc Tony Williamson
lp Ivor Dean; Kieron Moore;
Anton Rodgers; Michael Gothard
SOMEBODY JUST WALKED OVER MY GRAVE
9/1/1970
d Cyril Frankel; sc Donald James
lp George Murcell; Bernard Kay;
Patricia Haines; Nigel Terry
COULD YOU RECOGNISE THAT MAN AGAIN?
16/1/1970
d Jeremy Summers; sc Donald James
lp Ivor Dean; Madge Ryan;
Stanley Meadows; Dudley Sutton
A SENTIMENTAL JOURNEY 23/1/1970
d Leslie Norman; sc Donald James
lp William Squire; Tracey Crisp;
Victor Maddern; Drewe Henley
The GHOST TALKS 6/2/1970
d Cyril Frankel; sc Gerald Kelsey
lp Alan MacNaughtan; John Collin;
Jack MacGowran; Marne Maitland
IT'S SUPPOSED TO BE THICKER THAN WATER
13/2/1970
d Leslie Norman; sc Donald James
lp Liz Fraser; Felix Aylmer; John Hallam;
Neil McCallum
The TROUBLE WITH WOMEN 20/2/1970
d Cyril Frankel; sc Tony Williamson
lp Paul Maxwell; Denise Buckley;
Edward Brayshaw; Robert Russell; Nik Zaran;
Gwen Nelson
VENDETTA FOR A DEAD MAN 27/2/1970
d Cyril Frankel; sc Donald James
lp George Sewell; Barrie Ingham;
Ann Castle; Timothy West; Richard Owens
SMILE BEHIND THE VEIL 13/3/1970
d Jeremy Summers; sc Gerald Kelsey
lp Alex Scott; Hilary Tindall;
Gary Watson; Freda Jackson; Peter Jesson

The RANK AND FILE (BBC 20/5/1971)
Dramatised documentary of the Pilkington's
glass factory strike.
d Ken Loach; p Graeme McDonald;
sc Jim Allen
lp Peter Kerrigan; Billy Dean;
Joan Flood; Johnny Gee; Mike Hayden;
Tommy Summers

The RAT CATCHERS
(Rediffusion 1966–67)
Espionage series following the adventures of
three British spies.
TICKET TO MADRID 31/1/1966
d James Ormerod; p Cyril Coke;
sc Raymond Bowers
lp Gerald Flood; Glyn Owen; Norman Scace;
Ian Gardiner; Jeffrey Gardiner; Philip Stone

RAWHIDE (US CBS 1959–66)
Western series set against a cattle drive during
the 1870s.
INCIDENT OF THE TOWN IN TERROR 6/3/1959
d Ted Post; p Charles Marquis Warren;
sc Oliver Crawford
lp Eric Fleming; Clint Eastwood;
Margaret O'Brien

RAY GUNTER ON ECONOMIC POLICY
(Border 17/11/1967)

REACH FOR TOMORROW
(JP Nippon Television Network Corporation;
GB tx 1/9/1976)
The Japanese entry for the 1976 Italia Prize,
telling the story of a thalidomide baby. English
version by Michael Bakewell, with commentary
by Harold Williamson.
d Toshio Ikematsu

READY, STEADY, GO!
(Rediffusion 1963–66)
Pop music programme.
READY, STEADY, GO! 4/10/1963
d Robert Fleming; pres Keith Fordyce;
with Dusty Springfield, The Beatles,
Tony Meehan, Helen Shapiro, Eden Kane
READY, STEADY, GO! 20/11/1964
d Daphne Shadwell;
pres Keith Fordyce, Cathy McGowan;
with Marvin Gaye, Kenny Lynch,
Jerry Lee Lewis, Samantha Jones,
The Rolling Stones, Them, The Zephyrs
READY, STEADY, GO! 30/11/1966
The final section of the programme, in which
Cathy McGowan introduces The Rolling Stones,
who perform 'I Am Waiting,' 'Under My
Thumb' and 'Paint It Black'.
d Michael Lindsay-Hogg; p Francis Hitching

REARDON ON SNOOKER
(HTV 8/10–22/10/1977)
Ray Reardon demonstrates how to play better
snooker.
d/p Euryn Ogwen Williams
REARDON ON SNOOKER 8/10/1977
REARDON ON SNOOKER 15/10/1977

REBECCA (BBC 17/1–7/2/1979)
Four-part dramatisation of the novel by Daphne
Du Maurier.
PART 1 17/1/1979
d Simon Langton; p Richard Beynon;
sc Hugh Whitemore
lp Jeremy Brett; Joanna David;
Elspeth March; Peter Carlisle; Claude Le Sache;
Hugh Morton; Anna Massey

The REBEL (US Rebel Company 1959–61)
Adventures of an American Civil War veteran in
the post-war West.
The CHAMP 2/10/1960
d Bernard L. Kowalski; p Andrew J. Fenady;
sc Sam Ross
lp Nick Adams; Edward Kemmer;
William Harlow; Chuck Hicks; Red Morgan;
John Indrisano; Paul Rhone; Eric Alden;
Michael Ansara

REBELLION (ATV 8/7/1969)
The events leading up to Irish independence and
partition are recalled with the aid of archival
film.
d George Morrison

REBELLION AT EASTER
(Rediffusion 6/4/1966)
The 50th anniversary of the Easter Rising in
Dublin, using songs of the time as commentary.
Singers include Dominic Behan, Billy Boyle,
James Caffrey, Eileen Colgan, and Gerry Fox.
d John Sheppard

The RECORD BREAKERS (BBC 1973–)
Programme for children based on the 'Guinness
Book of Records'.
The RECORD BREAKERS 24/10/1978
p Alan Russell;
pres Norris McWhirter, Roy Castle

The RED BARON (US; GB tx 31/7/1975)
Documentary about aircraft in World War I and
the aerial dog fights. Contains original archive
footage. Film opens at Rhinebeck Airfield New
York where air battles are recreated.

RED LETTER DAY
(Granada 11/1–22/2/1976)
Series of seven plays devised by Jack Rosenthal.
AMAZING STORIES 1/2/1976
d Peter Plummer; p Michael Dunlop;
sc Howard Schuman
lp Joe Melia; John Normington;
Harold Kasket; Ian McDiarmid;
Maryann Turner; Herbert Ramskill;
Richard Willis; Rula Lenska

REDGAUNTLET (Scottish TV 1970)
Serialisation of Sir Walter Scott's adventure.
d/p Clarke Tait; sc Ian Stuart Black
regulars Jack Watson; Roddy McMillan;
Isobel Black; James Grant; Andrew Robertson
EPISODE 1: MAN WITH THE SWORD 7/1/1970
lp James Copeland; Isabel Begg;
Marjorie Thompson; Leonard Maguire;
Brian Pettifer
EPISODE 2: WARNING FROM A LADY 14/1/1970
lp Leonard Maguire; James Gibson;
Jean Taylor Smith
EPISODE 3: RACE AGAINST THE TIDE 21/1/1970
lp John Laurie; Leonard Maguire;
James Gibson
EPISODE 4: HELD PRISONER 28/1/1970
lp Douglas Murchie; Margaret Leslie;
Wallace Campbell
EPISODE 5: TRIAL 4/2/1970
lp John Laurie; Callum Mill;
Phill McCall
EPISODE 7: REBELS 18/2/1970
lp John Laurie; Callum Mill;
Michael O'Halloran
EPISODE 8: DEATH OF A TRAITOR 25/2/1970
lp John Laurie; Callum Mill;
Ewan Roberts; Michael O'Halloran

REDIFFUSION GOLF TOURNAMENT
(Rediffusion 3/10/1965)
Highlights of the golf tournament from
La Moye, Jersey.
d Grahame Turner

REDISCOVERING THE IMAGE
(ATV 1/2–15/2/1965)
Sir Kenneth Clark talks about three artists;
Gauguin, Rousseau and Munch.
PAUL GAUGUIN 1/2/1965
p H.K. Lewenhak

**A REFERENDUM CAMPAIGN
BROADCAST ON BEHALF OF BRITAIN IN
EUROPE** (22/5/1975)

REFLECTIONS (BBC 1977)
Religious series.
CHRISTIANS IN ACTION 16/9/1977
Dr Anthony Barker talks about his life at a Zulu
mission hospital and how he views the hospital
and its work.

REGAN (Euston Films 4/6/1974)
London-based police drama. Pilot for the series
The SWEENEY (1975–78).
d Tom Clegg; p Ted Childs;
sc Ian Kennedy Martin
lp John Thaw; Dennis Waterman;
Lee Montague; Garfield Morgan;
David Daker; Janet Key

RELEASE (BBC 1967–69)
Magazine arts series.
RELEASE 25/11/1967
Two items: a modern ballet 'Ziggurat'; and the
tercentenary of the birth of Jonathan Swift. With
Glen Tetley and Michael Foot.
p Colin Nears; ed Lorna Pegram
RELEASE 16/12/1967
Interview with film director Richard Fleischer.
p Colin Nears

REMBRANDT
(NL European Colour Productions 1976)
Four-part series examining the artist and his life.
d Colin Clark; pres Kenneth Clark
SELF PORTRAITS 29/6/1976
SUCCESS 13/7/1976
Rembrandt's success as a portrait painter in
Amsterdam, which culminated in the
commission for the portrait group known as 'The
Night Watch'.
WITHDRAWAL 20/7/1976
Rembrandt by the age of fifty was threatened
with bankruptcy. The prosperous years gave way
to a time of spiritual withdrawal and this was the
period of his greatest work.
The BIBLE 27/7/1976
Rembrandt as illustrator of The Bible.

REMEMBER ALL THE GOOD THINGS
(BBC 30/3/1975)
Film about the emotional problems of a family
facing up to the approaching death of the father
from lung cancer.
d Alan Murgatroyd;
p Alan Murgatroyd, Ray Colley

RENTAGHOST (BBC 1976–84)
Series for children featuring the misadventures
of a group of ghosts.
RENTAGHOST 13/1/1976
d David Crichton; *p* Paul Ciani;
sc Bob Block
lp Anthony Jackson; Michael Darbyshire;
Michael Staniforth; Betty Alberge;
John Dawson; Ian Collier; Elizabeth Day

REPORT (Thames 1969–71)
Current affairs programme.
ST ANN'S 4/3/1969
A decayed inner area of Nottingham. The lives
of two families and the primary school are
examined.
d Stephen Frears; *p* Ian Martin
A LIFE WORTH LIVING? 8/4/1969
The life of victims of brain and head injuries
following road accidents. Filmed at the
Birmingham Accident Hospital.
d Ted Childs; *p* Ian Martin;
comm Victor Henry
IT'S A BATTLEGROUND 6/5/1969
Examination of the fundamental thinking of
education; what the role of the teacher should be
and the experiment of one school.
IT'S LIKE THIS, DOCTOR 21/10/1969
The work of a general practitioner in the Notting
Hill district of London.
d Ted Childs; *p* Ian Martin
NOW THAT THE BUFFALO'S GONE 8/11/1969
The American Indian.
d/p Ross Devenish; *comm* Marlon Brando
AND ON THE EIGHTH DAY 27/1/1970
Contemporary environmental conditions and the
concern with problems of pollution.
d Richard Broad; *p* Ian Martin
The GREEN IS WEARING 17/3/1970
The changes brought about in Eire by the
economic development of recent years, and how
traditional Republican attitudes to the North
have altered.
d Ted Childs; *p* Ian Martin
HARD TIMES 3/11/1970
A report on the problem of poverty in Britain, as
found in the slum areas of London, Liverpool
and Birmingham.
d Richard Broad; *p* Ian Martin
PHOENIX HOUSE 1971
A drug addiction centre in South London run by
ex-addicts.
d Richard Broad; *p* Tom Steel

REPORTING '67 (ITN)
Documentary series.
APOLLO MOON SHOT 1967
The Apollo spacecraft and preparations for the
Apollo Mission at Moon Port in Florida,
including the training of the astronauts.
The HIPPIES OF SAN FRANCISCO 20/4/1967
The way of life and creed of the hippies of San
Francisco; introduced by Andrew Gardner.

REPORTS ACTION (Granada 1976–81)
Community action programme, in which
community problems are highlighted and viewers
are urged to help.
CRIME VICTIMS, BLACK SPOTS, HOMELESS
CHILDREN 21/11/1976
Joan Bakewell and Bob Greaves ask for viewers'
assistance in helping crime victims, cleaning up
black spots and looking after homeless children.
d Charles Sturridge; *p* Jim Walker

REPORTS POLITICS (Granada 1976–80)
Regional current affairs series.
REPORTS POLITICS 1/11/1976
d Peter Carr

REPRESENTING THE UNION
(BBC 2/10–7/12/1969)
Ten-part documentary series. A trade unionist's
guide to productivity bargaining and
management techniques.
COSTS AND THE PAYPACKET 26/10/1969
What a trade union negotiator needs to know
about a firm's costs.
p Tony Matthews; *comm* Bob Houlton
A FAIR DAY'S PAY 30/11/1969
The problems of changing to a new pay scheme.
d Ian Woolf; *p* Tony Matthews;
comm Bob Houlton

RESEARCH REPORT (BBC 1964)
Science documentary series.
The DAM BUILDERS 3/11/1964
The research, science and technology that goes
into the construction of a dam.
p Brenda Horsfield
SEEING IN THE DARK 15/12/1964
A look at infra-red radiation – an advance
recently made by the Signals Research and
Development Establishment, Christchurch.
d Peter R. Smith; *p* Brenda Horsfield

The RESISTIBLE RISE OF ARTURO UI
(BBC 7/11/1972)
d Jack Gold; *p* Tony Garnett;
sc George Tabori; *auth* Bertolt Brecht
lp Nicol Williamson; Sam Wanamaker;
Peter Frye; Phil Brown; Al Mancini;
Jill Townsend; Bruce Boa

The RESTLESS SPHERE (BBC 30/6/1957)
The story of the International Geophysical Year
told by the Duke of Edinburgh at the invitation
of the Royal Society.
d Tom Millett; *p* Aubrey Singer;
comm Richard Dimbleby

RETURN OF THE GUNFIGHTER
(US King Bros. Productions 29/1/1967)
Western about a retired gunfighter's return to
avenge the murder of an old friend.
d James Neilson;
p Frank King, Maurice King;
sc Robert Buckner;
auth Burt Kennedy, Robert Buckner
lp Robert Taylor; Ana Martin;
Chad Everett; Mort Mills; Lyle Bettger;
John Davis Chandler; Michael Pate;
Barry Atwater

RETURN OF THE SAINT
(ITC 1978–79)
Revival of the Leslie Charteris character
originally featured in The SAINT series
(1962–69).
p Anthony Spinner
regular Ian Ogilvy
The JUDAS GAME 10/9/1978
d Jeremy Summers; *sc* Leslie Charteris
lp Judy Geeson; Olga Karlatos;
Maurice Roëves; Mona Bruce; Richard Wyler;
Moray Watson
ASSAULT FORCE 15/10/1978
d Peter Sasdy; *sc* Moris Farhi
lp Kate O'Mara; Bryan Marshall;
Carolle Rousseau; Neil Stacy; Burt Kwouk
YESTERDAY'S HERO 22/10/1978
d Roy Ward Baker; *sc* John Kruse;
auth Roger Parkes
lp Ian Hendry; Annette Andre;
Gerald Flood; Norman Eshley; Matthew Ryan;
Tony Vogel
The POPPY CHAIN 29/10/1978
d Charles Crichton; *sc* John Kruse
lp Laurence Naismith; Grégoire Aslan;
Jenny Hanley; Christopher Timothy
SIGNAL STOP 26/11/1978
d Ray Austin; *sc* John Kruse
lp Ciaran Madden; Frederick Jaeger;
Brian Glover; Ian Cullen; Heather Wright

**The RETURN OF ULYSSES TO HIS
HOMELAND** (Southern TV 24/8/1975)
A performance of Monteverdi's 'Il Ritorno
d'Ulisse in Patria', with Janet Baker, Benjamin
Luxon, Anne Howells, Richard Lewis, the
Glyndebourne Festival Chorus and the London
Philharmonic Orchestra conducted by Raymond
Leppard.
d David Heather; *p/intro* Humphrey Burton

RETURN TO THE EDGE OF THE WORLD
(BBC 7/5/1979)
In 1978 director Michael Powell returned to the
island of Foula in the Shetland Islands to see
what changes had occurred. While there he
made an introduction and epilogue to his original
film 'Edge of the World'.
d Michael Powell; *with* John Laurie

RETURN TO THE RHONDDA
(TWW 22/9/1965)
Stanley Baker, Jimmy Wilde, Tommy Farr and
Gwyn Thomas return to their native Rhondda
valley.

REVIEW (BBC 1969–72)
Arts series.
The ELIZABETHAN IMAGE 6/12/1969
An exhibition of Elizabethan paintings at the
Tate Gallery.
d Anne James;
p Darrol Blake, Christopher Martin,
Peter Adam
WHAT USE PHILOSOPHY? 30/4/1971
James Mossman interviews Stuart Hampshire,
the Warden of Wadham College, Oxford, on the
uses and value of philosophy.
d Michael MacIntyre;
p Peter Adam, Tony Staveacre;
intro David Jones
A NEW KING LEAR 1/10/1971
Edward Bond talks about his new play 'Lear',
which is opening with Harry Andrews in the lead
role. Play extracts directed by Alan Yentob.
p Tony Staveacre, Peter Adam, Barrie Gavin
LENI RIEFENSTAHL 23/6/1972
An interview with Leni Riefenstahl about her
film making in Nazi Germany and her current
photographic work in Africa.
p Peter Adam, Tony Cash, Michael MacIntyre

REVOLUTION IN HUNGARY
(BBC 20/10/1966)
A compilation of newsreel material on the
Hungarian Revolution of 1956. Including
interviews with Tamas Aczel, Anna Kethly,
Peter Fryer, Bela Szasz, John Sadovy and Sir
William Hayter.
p Christopher Ralling

REVOLUTION 1917
(Rediffusion 18–22/9/1967)
Five-part lecture series on the Russian
Revolution by A.J.P. Taylor.
FEBRUARY: REVOLUTION OLD STYLE 19/9/1967
p Sheila Gregg

REVOLVER (ATV 1978)
Pop music series.
d Chris Tookey; *p* Mickie Most;
pres Peter Cook
REVOLVER (PILOT) 20/5/1978
Pilot programme of the pop and rock music
show.
with X.T.C., Steel Pulse, John Dowie,
Rich Kidds, Kate Bush, Ricky Cool and The
Icebergs, Tom Robinson Band
REVOLVER 29/7/1978
pres Chris Hill, Les Ross;
with Roy Hill Band, Vibrators,
Siouxsie and The Banshees, Ian Dury and The
Blockheads, Bonnie Tyler, Buzzcocks

**RICHARD DIAMOND PRIVATE
DETECTIVE** (US Four Star Films 1957–60)
Private eye drama series.

The SPACE SOCIETY 2/1/1958
d Stuart Rosenberg; p David Heilweil;
sc David Chandler
lp David Janssen; Ruta Lee; Walter Sande;
Joi Lansing; Paul Bryar

RICHARD DIMBLEBY TRIBUTE
(BBC 22/12/1965)
Cliff Michelmore and Huw Wheldon pay tribute
to broadcaster Richard Dimbleby following the
announcement of his death.

RICHARD OF BORDEAUX
(BBC 29/12/1955)
Presentation of the 1933 play by crime author
Josephine Tey [Elizabeth MacKintosh] writing as
'Gordon Daviot'.
p Victor Menzies; sc Gordon Daviot
lp Peter Cushing; Jeannette Sterke;
Joseph O'Conor; Maurice Colbourne;
Charles Lloyd Pack; George Woodbridge;
Robin Bailey

RICHARD THE LIONHEART
(Danziger Productions 1961–62)
Historical action-drama series. [London-area
transmission included some episode premieres
during 1965 and 1968]
d Ernest Morris;
p Edward J. Danziger, Harry Lee Danziger
regulars Dermot Walsh; Sheila Whittington;
Iain Gregory; Robin Hunter; Trader Faulkner;
Francis de Wolff; Glyn Owen; Anne Lawson
LONG LIVE THE KING 20/11/1961
sc Paul Tabori, Stanley Miller
lp Alan Haywood; Peter Reynolds;
Tony Doonan; Howard Greene; Lisa Daniely
The ROBBERS OF ASHDOWN FOREST 4/12/1961
sc Paul Tabori, Stanley Miller
lp Alan Haywood; John Gabriel;
Raymond Rollett
The WOLF OF BANBURY 11/12/1961
sc Stanley Miller, Paul Tabori
lp Alan Haywood; Larry Taylor;
Frank Sieman; Katharine Page;
Juliet Alexander; Humphrey Lestocq
The ALCHEMIST OF ROUEN 18/12/1961
sc Stanley Miller, Paul Tabori
lp Alan Haywood; Soraya Rafat;
Juliet Alexander
SCHOOL FOR A KING 1/1/1962
sc Stanley Miller, Paul Tabori
lp Alan Haywood; Peter Illing;
Dawn Beret; Jill Hyem; Derrick Sherwin;
Edgar K. Bruce; Reginald Hearne
CROWN IN DANGER 8/1/1962
sc Stanley Miller, Paul Tabori
lp Alan Haywood; Peter Reynolds;
Tony Doonan; Howard Greene; Kevin Brennan;
Patricia Rogers
The PIRATE KING 15/1/1962
sc Stanley Miller, Paul Tabori
lp Alan Haywood; Martin Benson;
Michael Peake; John Longden; Juliet Alexander
The KING'S CHAMPION 22/1/1962
sc Stanley Miller, Paul Tabori
lp Alan Haywood; John Scott; Ian Fleming;
John Lewis; John Bay; John Longden
KING ARTHUR'S SWORD 29/1/1962
sc Stanley Miller, Paul Tabori
lp Alan Haywood; Ferdy Mayne;
David Davenport; Prudence Hyman;
Daphne Anderson; Ian Fleming
The CHALLENGE 5/2/1962
sc Paul Tabori, Stanley Miller
lp Alan Haywood; Jeremy Bisley;
Ian Curry; Paul Craig; Zena Marshall;
John Longden; Eric Dodson
The BRIDE 12/2/1962
sc Stanley Miller, Paul Tabori
lp Alan Haywood; Susan Shaw;
David Davenport; Michael Ashlin;
John Brooking; Ian Fleming;
John Longden; John Serret
The GREAT ENTERPRISE 19/2/1962
sc Stanley Miller, Paul Tabori
lp Susan Shaw; Richard Shaw;
Olaf Pooley; Michael McStay; Ian Fleming
The NORMAN KING 26/2/1962
sc David Nicholl
lp Elwyn Brook-Jones; Roger Delgado;
John Cater

WHEN CHAMPIONS MEET 5/3/1962
sc David Nicholl
lp Robert Rietty; Marne Maitland;
Michael Peake; Conrad Phillips; Martin Benson
The WARRIOR FROM SCOTLAND 12/3/1962
sc Stanley Miller
lp Alan Haywood; Anton Rodgers;
Jennifer Daniel; Michael Peake; Max Faulkner;
Brian McDermott; Peter Vaughan; Roy Kinnear
The CONJUROR 19/3/1962
sc Mark Grantham
lp Max Faulkner; Riggs O'Hara;
George Pastell; Eric Dodson;
Christopher Carlos; Steve Plytas; Tom Gill
LORD OF KERAK 26/3/1962
sc David Nicholl
lp Willoughby Goddard; Hugh David;
Jack May; Francis Matthews; Michael Peake;
Nadja Regin
The SARACEN PHYSICIAN 2/4/1962
sc Stanley Miller
lp Marne Maitland; Michael Peake;
Jennifer Daniel; Anton Rodgers; Peter Elliott
A MARRIAGE OF CONVENIENCE 9/4/1962
sc Stanley Miller
lp Marne Maitland; Conrad Phillips;
Michael Peake; Anton Rodgers; Jennifer Daniel
QUEEN IN DANGER 16/4/1962
sc David Nicholl
lp Michael Peake; John Bennett;
Laurence Hardy
The STRANGE MONKS OF LATROUN 23/4/1962
sc Stanley Miller
lp Edgar Wreford; Alister Williamson;
Olaf Pooley; Max Faulkner; Maurice Reyna
PRINCE OTTO 30/4/1962
sc Stanley Miller
lp Alan Haywood; Jill Ireland;
Walter Gotell; Max Faulkner; Michael Peake;
Brian McDermott
The VISION FADES 27/5/1965
sc Stanley Miller;
lp Alan Haywood; Max Faulkner;
Anton Rodgers; Brian McDermott;
Conrad Phillips; Anna Gerber
The FUGITIVE 3/6/1965
sc Stanley Miller
lp Elwyn Brook-Jones
KNIGHT ERRANT AT LARGE 10/6/1965
sc David Nicholl
lp David Davies; April Olrich;
Derek Tansley
GUARDIAN OF THE TEMPLE 17/6/1965
sc David Nicholl
lp Ernest Clark; Richard Shaw;
Ken Wayne; Alan Rolfe
A KING'S RANSOM 1/7/1965
sc David Nicholl
lp Alan Haywood; Joan Haythorne;
Elwyn Brook-Jones; Ian Fleming
The DEVIL IS UNLOOSED 15/7/1965
sc David Nicholl
lp Alan Haywood; Ronald Howard;
Robert Perceval; Ralph Michael; Colin Tapley
LITTLE PEOPLE OF LINTOR 29/7/1965
sc Paul Tabori, Stanley Miller
lp Alan Haywood; John Scott;
Jocelyn Britton; Bartlett Mullins;
Jack Smethurst; Roy Kinnear;
Humphrey Lestocq; Ian Fleming
An EYE FOR AN EYE 5/8/1965
sc Paul Tabori; Stanley Miller
lp Alan Haywood, David Davies;
Jennifer Jayne; Sean Kelly
The CAVEMAN 19/8/1965
sc Mark Grantham
lp June Thorburn; Nigel Green;
Mark Burns; Guy Deghy; David King
The RAIDERS 2/9/1965
sc Mark Grantham
lp Philip Latham; Robert Raglan;
Neil Hallett; Bill Nagy; Jill Williams
A YEAR AND A DAY 9/9/1965
sc Paul Tabori, Stanley Miller
lp Richard Caldicot; Ellen Pollock;
Derrick Sherwin; Eira Heath; Roy Patrick;
Michael O'Brien; Bernard Martin
The CROWN JEWELS 23/9/1965
sc Mark Grantham
lp Lisa Daniely; Maurice Kaufmann;
Sean Lynch; Alan Haywood; John Gill;
Peter Sinclair; Richard Huggett

The MAN WHO SOLD PARDONS 30/9/1965
sc David Nicholl
lp Nigel Green; Noel Coleman;
Barry Shawzin; Garard Green; Leon Cortez
The HEIR OF ENGLAND 7/10/1965
sc David Nicholl
lp Margaretta Scott; Christopher Witty;
William Fox; Patrick MacAlliney;
Victor Spinetti; Petra Davies; Larry Taylor
The PEOPLE'S KING 14/10/1965
sc David Nicholl
lp Alan Haywood; Jane Hylton;
Anthony Jacobs; Malcolm Knight;
Howard Douglas; David Davenport;
Max Faulkner

RING A DING (BBC 1973)
Story series for children.
RING A DING 23/2/1973
d/sc Peter Charlton; pres Derek Griffiths

RIPPING YARNS
(BBC 27/9–25/10/1977; 10–24/10/1979)
Comedy series featuring Michael Palin which
parodies popular fictional themes.
sc Michael Palin, Terry Jones
TOMKINSON'S SCHOOLDAYS 7/1/1976
Pilot programme for the series.
p Terry Hughes
lp Terry Jones; Gwen Watford; Ian Ogilvy;
John Wentworth; Sarah Grazebrook; Chai Lee
The TESTING OF ERIC OLTHWAITE 27/9/1977
d Jim Franklin
lp Kenneth Colley; Liz Smith;
Barbara New; John Barrett; Reg Lye;
Petra Markham; Anita Carey
ESCAPE FROM STALAG LUFT 112B 4/10/1977
d Jim Franklin; nar Ronald Fletcher
lp Roy Kinnear; John Phillips;
Timothy Carlton; David Griffin; Julian Hough
GOLDEN GORDON 17/10/1979
d Alan J.W. Bell
lp Bill Fraser; Gwen Taylor; Ken Kitson;
David Leland
ROGER OF THE RAJ 24/10/1979
d Alan J.W. Bell
lp Richard Vernon; Joan Sanderson;
Roger Brierley; Jan Francis; John Le Mesurier

RIPTIDE (AU Trans Pacific Enterprises-
Artransa Park Studios 1969; GB tx 1971–73)
Adventure series.
p Ralph Smart
regular Ty Hardin
BOUND FROM CALIFORNIA 9/7/1971
lp Patricia Sullivan; John Gray;
Willie Fennel; Ron Graham; Gordon Boyd
NORTH OF THE HEADLAND 23/7/1971
The MCQUADE MYTH 20/8/1971
lp Gordon Boyd
JUMP HIGH LAND EASY 24/12/1971
BRETHREN ISLAND 31/3/1972
lp Helen Morse; Ross Thompson;
Ron Haddrick; Neva Carr-Glyn
HAGAN'S KINGDOM 21/12/1972
lp Tony Ward
DEAD BUT NOT FORGOTTEN 19/7/1973
DOWN AT THE BAY 9/8/1973
lp Tony Ingersent; Jessica Noad;
Enid Lorimer
GAME FOR THREE HANDS 22/8/1973
lp Peter Reynolds; Beryl Cheers;
Suzy Kendall; Maggie Stuart; Anthony Bazell
BLACK FRIDAY 30/8/1973
lp Norman Yemm; Brian Anderson;
Linal Haft; Doreen Warburton; Don Pascoe;
Shirley Smith
FLIGHT OF THE CURLEW 5/9/1973
lp Suzy Kendall; Owen Weingott;
John Meillon; Robert Bruning; Jack Thompson;
Don McNiven

The RISE AND RISE OF LAURA ASHLEY
(ATV 17/12/1976)
A tribute to the life and career of Laura Ashley;
re-broadcast in September 1985 as a memorial
following her death.
d/p Peter Batty

RISING DAMP (Yorkshire TV 1974–78)
Sitcom set around offbeat characters resident in a run-down boarding house.
d/p Ronnie Baxter (1974–77);
Vernon Lawrence (1978); *sc* Eric Chappell
regulars Leonard Rossiter;
Richard Beckinsale; Don Warrington;
Frances De La Tour
RISING DAMP 2/9/1974
p Ian MacNaughton
BLACK MAGIC 13/12/1974
A NIGHT OUT 20/12/1974
lp Frank Gatliff; Derek Newark
CHARISMA 27/12/1974
lp Liz Edmiston
ALL OUR YESTERDAYS 3/1/1975
d Len Lurcuck
lp Derek Newark
The PROWLER 10/1/1975
lp George Sewell; Michael Stainton
The PERMISSIVE SOCIETY 7/11/1975
lp George A. Cooper
GOOD GLORIOUS GOOD 14/11/1975
A BODY LIKE MINE 21/11/1975
MOONLIGHT & ROSES 28/11/1975
lp Robin Parkinson; Gay Rose
The PERFECT GENTLEMAN 5/12/1975
lp Henry McGee
The LAST OF THE BIG SPENDERS 12/12/1975
lp Gay Rose; Campbell Singer
THINGS THAT GO BUMP IN THE NIGHT
19/12/1975
p Len Lurcuck
lp Gay Rose; Norman Bird; David Rowlands
FOR THE MAN WHO HAS EVERYTHING
26/12/1975
THAT'S MY BOY 12/4/1977
lp Ann Beach; David Baker
STAGE STRUCK 19/4/1977
lp Peter Bowles
CLUNK CLICK 26/4/1977
lp Derek Francis; Judy Buxton
The GOOD SAMARITANS 3/5/1977
lp David Swift; John Clive
FAWCETT'S PYTHON 10/5/1977
lp Jonathan Elsom; Andonia Katsaros
The COCKTAIL HOUR 17/5/1977
lp Judy Buxton; Diana King
SUDDENLY AT HOME 24/5/1977
lp Roger Brierley
HELLO YOUNG LOVERS 4/4/1978
lp Deborah Watling; Alun Lewis;
Robert Dorning
FIRE AND BRIMSTONE 11/4/1978
GREAT EXPECTATIONS 18/4/1978
lp Avis Bunnage; Andrew Sachs
PINK CARNATIONS 25/4/1978
lp Joan Sanderson
UNDER THE INFLUENCE 2/5/1978
lp Peter Jeffrey
COME ON IN THE WATER'S LOVELY 9/5/1978
lp Brian Peck; Fanny Rowe

The RISK BUSINESS (BBC 1976–81)
Documentary series for industry outlining the combination of technological advancement with economic reality.
DEMOCRACY AT WORK 26/8/1976
Worker participation and industrial democracy.
d John Gorman; *p* Tony Edwards;
pres Raymond Baxter; *rep* William Woollard

The RIVER NILE (US NBC 25/3/1964)
The Aswan high dam and the threatened temples of the Nile.
nar James Mason

RIVERBOAT
(US Meladare Co.-Revue Productions 1959–61)
Western series set on board a paddle steamer on the Mississippi and Missouri rivers during the 1840s.
HANG THE MAN HIGH 21/3/1960
d Hollingsworth Morse; *p* John Larkin;
sc Jerry Adelman
lp Darren McGavin; Stephen McNally;
Jack Lambert; Karen Steele; Dick Wessel

ROAD TO BLAYDON (Tyne Tees 11/11/1968)
The rehousing of the residents of Scotswood Road, Newcastle, after the area was demolished and renovated.

The ROAD TO CAREY STREET
(BBC 10/11/1960)
Dramatised documentary on bankruptcy.
p Donald Taylor; *sc* Arthur Swinson

The ROAD TO WIGAN PIER
(Thames 16/10/1973)
Using Orwell's own words, contemporary archive film, still photographs taken by Bill Brandt and traditional working-class songs sung by Bob Davenport and the Morriston Orpheus Choir, documents life in the North of England as portrayed in Orwell's novel.
d/p Frank Cvitanovich; *nar* Michael Jayston

The ROADS TO FREEDOM
(BBC 4/10–27/12/1970)
Thirteen-part serial based on Jean-Paul Sartre's trilogy.
d James Cellan Jones; *p* David Conroy;
sc David Turner
regulars Michael Bryant; Donald Burton;
Daniel Massey
EPISODE 1 4/10/1970
lp Rosemary Leach; Robert Tayman;
Alfred Hoffman; Heather Canning; Alison Fiske
EPISODE 2 11/10/1970
lp Georgia Brown; Alison Fiske;
Anthony Corlan; Bella Emberg; Clifford Rose;
Rosemary Leach; Roger Lloyd Pack

ROAR OF THE CROWD
(BBC 23/3–24/10/1969)
Ten-part documentary series on aspects of sport.
GAME, SET AND CASH 20/6/1969
Tennis celebrities discuss the 'politics' of the game.
d Bob Abrahams; *p* Phil Pilley

The ROARING 20s
(US Warner Bros TV 1960–62)
Period crime series set in New York and featuring two newspaper reporters and their fight against organised crime.
ANOTHER TIME, ANOTHER WAR 4/11/1961
d Robert Sparr; *p* Boris Ingster;
sc Shirl Hendry
lp Eddie Bracken; Donald May;
Dorothy Provine; Mike Road;
Grace Lee Whitney; Jack Collins;
Sheldon Allman

The ROBERT DHERY SHOW
(Rediffusion 1957–58)
Variety show originally billed under the 'Jack Hylton Presents' banner.
The ROBERT DHERY SHOW 22/2/1957
d/p Robert Dhéry, Eric Fawcett;
with Robert Dhéry, Pierre Olaf,
Jacques Legras, Roger Caccia, Philippe Dumat
The ROBERT DHERY SHOW 8/3/1957
d Robert Dhéry; Eric Fawcett;
with Robert Dhéry, Pierre Olaf,
Jacques Legras, Roger Caccia, Philippe Dumat
The ROBERT DHERY SHOW 22/3/1957
d Robert Dhéry, Eric Fawcett;
with Robert Dhéry, Pierre Olaf,
Jacques Legras, Roger Caccia, Philippe Dumat
The ROBERT DHERY SHOW 29/3/1957
d Robert Dhéry, Eric Fawcett;
with Robert Dhéry, Pierre Olaf,
Jacques Legras, Roger Caccia, Philippe Dumat
The ROBERT DHERY SHOW 19/5/1958
d Bill Hitchcock; *sc* Robert Dhéry;
with Robert Dhéry, Pierre Olaf,
Jacques Legras, Roger Caccia, Ross Parker

ROBERT VAS: FILM-MAKER, 1931–1978
(BBC 3/5/1978)
An obituary on documentary film-maker Robert Vas by his fellow Hungarian and friend Karel Reisz.
p Barrie Gavin, Peter West

ROBIN'S NEST (Thames 1977–81)
Sitcom developed from MAN ABOUT THE HOUSE (1973–76).

The BISTRO KIDS 18/1/1977
d/p Peter Frazer-Jones;
sc Johnnie Mortimer, Brian Cooke
lp Richard O'Sullivan; Tessa Wyatt;
Tony Britton; Duncan Lamont;
Michael Hawkins

ROCK FOLLIES
(Thames 24/2–30/3/1976)
The fortunes of three girls when they trade show business for rock music.
p Andrew Brown; *sc* Howard Schuman
regulars Charlotte Cornwell;
Julie Covington; Rula Lenska
EPISODE 1: SHOW BUSINESS 24/2/1976
d Jon Scoffield
lp Jeffrey Gardiner; John Blythe;
Larry Burns; Emlyn Price; Peter Hill;
Michael J. Shannon; Stephen Moore
EPISODE 3: ROAD 9/3/1976
d Jon Scoffield
lp Iain Blair; Emlyn Price;
James Warwick; Christopher Neil;
Stephen Moore; Dustin Gee

ROCK FOLLIES OF '77
(Thames 4/5–18/5/1977; 22/11–6/12/1977)
Sequel to the earlier series.
p Andrew Brown; *sc* Howard Schuman
regulars Julie Covington; Rula Lenska;
Charlotte Cornwell
The BAND WHO WOULDN'T DIE 4/5/1977
d Brian Farnham
lp Derek Thompson; Maurice O'Connell;
Tim Curry; Little Nell; Beth Porter
The EMPIRE 11/5/1977
d Bill Hays
lp Beth Porter; Gregory Floy;
Derek Thompson; Ian Charleson; Little Nell;
Denis Lawson
The REAL LIFE 6/12/1977
d Bill Hays
lp Adrian Shergold; Sue Jones-Davies;
Beth Porter; Little Nell; Denis Lawson;
Derek Thompson; Bob Hoskins

ROCKY JONES, SPACE RANGER
(US Roland Reed Productions 1954)
Syndicated science-fiction adventure series for children featuring Rocky Jones, head of the Space Rangers in the twenty-first century.
d Hollingsworth Morse; *p* Roland Reed
lp Richard Crane; Scotty Beckett;
Sally Mansfield
ESCAPE IN SPACE 1954
lp Maurice Cass
FORBIDDEN MOON 1954
KIPS PRIVATE WAR 1954

ROGUE MALE (BBC 22/9/1976)
An English aristocrat attempts to assassinate Adolf Hitler just prior to the outbreak of World War II.
d Clive Donner; *p* Mark Shivas;
sc Frederic Raphael; *auth* Geoffrey Household
lp Peter O'Toole; Alastair Sim; Cyd Hayman;
Harold Pinter; John Standing; Michael Sheard;
Hugh Manning; Robert Lang; Michael Byrne;
Mark McManus

The ROGUES
(US Four Star-Giyo Productions 1964–65)
The adventures of an international group of conmen.
The STEFANINI STORY 27/9/1964
d Hy Averback; *p* Collier Young;
sc Marion Hargrove
lp Gig Young; Charles Boyer;
Gladys Cooper; Robert Coote;
Susan Strasberg; Fritz Weaver

The ROLF HARRIS SHOW (BBC 1967–70)
Variety series.
The ROLF HARRIS SHOW 4/2/1967
p Stewart Morris; *with* Sandie Shaw
Del Shannon, The Morgan-James Duo,
Georges Schlick
The ROLF HARRIS SHOW 15/2/1969
p Stewart Morris; *with* Roy Castle,
Massiel, Jon Pertwee, The Young Generation

The ROLF HARRIS SHOW 29/3/1969
p Stewart Morris; *sc* Peter Robinson;
with Noel Harrison, Russ Conway,
Nana Mouskouri, The Young Generation

ROLL ON FOUR O'CLOCK
(Granada 20/12/1970)
Drama on life in a secondary modern school.
d Roy Battersby; *p* Kenith Trodd;
sc Colin Welland
lp George A. Cooper; Bill Dean;
Colin Edwynn; John Malcolm; Tony Melody;
Tom O'Connor; Jack Shepherd; Clive Swift;
Kenneth Watson; Colin Welland

The ROMANTIC YOUNG LADY
(BBC 5/7/1955)
A romantic comedy by Gregorio Martinez
Sierra.
p Harold Clayton;
adapt Helen Granville-Barker, Harley Granville-
Barker
lp Sylvia Syms; John Breslin; Eric Lander;
Marjorie Fielding; Tony Britton; Margaret Boyd

RONNIE BARKER PLAYHOUSE
(Rediffusion 3/4–8/5/1968)
Six comedy plays starring Ronnie Barker.
ALEXANDER 8/5/1968
d Michael Lindsay-Hogg; *p* Stella Richman;
sc Alun Owen
lp Molly Urquhart; Pauline Yates;
Pamela Ann Davy; Anthony Trent

A ROOF OVER OUR HEADS
(Granada 3/10/1962)
An examination of the housing situation at a
time when one person in five lives in a home
officially listed as unfit for human habitation.
d Michael Scott; *p* Elaine Grand;
intro Bill Grundy

ROOM SERVICE (Thames 2/1–13/2/1979)
Seven-part comedy series set in an hotel.
ROOM SERVICE 23/1/1979
d/p Michael Mills; *sc* Jimmy Perry
lp Bryan Pringle; Freddie Earlle;
Jeillo Edwards; Chris Gannon; Matthew Kelly;
Gertan Klauber; Basil Lord; Judi Maynard;
Penelope Nice; Michael Petrovitch

ROOTS, ROCK, REGGAE
(Harcourt Films 29/8/1977)
Documentary on reggae music and its origins.
d Jeremy Marre; *with* Bob Marley and The
Wailers, Scratch

ROOTS: THE NEXT GENERATIONS
(US A David L. Wolper Production
18–23 & 25/2/1979)
Fictionalised account of the continuing history of
Alex Haley's family, covering the period 1882 to
date, particularly the author's own direct life
story.
d John Erman, Charles Dubin,
Lloyd Richards, Georg Stanford Brown;
p Stan Margulies;
sc Ernest Kinoy, Sidney A. Glass;
Thad Mumford, Dan Wilcox, John McGreevey
lp Georg Stanford Brown; Henry Fonda;
Richard Thomas; Debbi Morgan; Lynne Moody;
Olivia De Havilland; Marc Singer; Avon Long;
Brian Mitchell; Greg Morris; Paul Koslo;
Beah Richards; Stan Shaw; Roger E. Mosley;
Harry Morgan; Ossie Davis; Ruby Dee;
James Earl Jones; Debbie Allen; Norman Fell;
Andy Griffith; Diahann Carroll; Brock Peters;
Dina Merrill; Pam Grier; Percy Rodrigues;
Al Freeman Jr; Marlon Brando

The ROSALINA NERI SHOW
(Jack Hylton TV Productions 1959)
Variety series starring Rosalina Neri; originally
billed under the 'Jack Hylton Presents' banner.
The ROSALINA NERI SHOW 1959
with Pilar Lopez
The ROSALINA NERI SHOW 25/2/1959
d Milo Lewis; *with* Ivor Emmanuel,
Jacques Chazot, René Bon, Peter Pit
The ROSALINA NERI SHOW 26/3/1959
d Milo Lewis; *with* Ivor Emmanuel

The ROSALINA NERI SHOW 2/4/1959
d Mark Lawton; *with* Ivor Emmanuel,
Antoinette Sibley, Graham Usher
The ROSALINA NERI SHOW 25/9/1959
d Mark Lawton; *with* Ivor Emmanuel,
Dennis Egan, Gerald Mordon, Gilbert Vernon,
Virginia Mason, Pamela Barrie, Joyce Quealley
The ROSALINA NERI SHOW 2/10/1959
d Mark Lawton; *with* Dennis Egan,
Gerald Mordon, Gilbert Vernon,
Virginia Mason, Ivor Emmanuel
The ROSALINA NERI SHOW 16/10/1959
d Mark Lawton; *with* Ivor Emmanuel,
Pamela Barrie, Dennis Egan, Virginia Mason,
Gerald Mordon, Joyce Quealley,
Gilbert Vernon, Barney Gilbraith Singers
The ROSALINA NERI SHOW 23/10/1959
d Mark Lawton; *with* Ivor Emmanuel
Juanita Lorina, Gerald Mordon,
Virginia Mason, Dennis Egan, Joyce Quealley,
Barney Gilbraith Singers

ROSLA AND AFTER – SPRING TERM
(BBC 1972)
In-service education project for teachers.
The CURRICULUM: PART I 18/1/1972
What should we be teaching young adults? The
role of separate subjects and integrated areas.
Curriculum renewal and development. Looks at
two contrasting case studies which raise
questions about the 'right' curriculum for early
school leavers.
p Michael Lumley, David Allen;
intro Angus Stewart

ROSTROPOVITCH AND RICHTER
(BBC 13/12/1964)
Mstislav Rostropovich and Sviatoslav Richter
perform Sonata No 3 in A major by Beethoven
at the Usher Hall, Edinburgh. Filmed at the
1964 Edinburgh Festival.
p Alan Rees

Die ROTE KAPELLE
(DE Bavaria Atelier Gesellschaft 16/7/1975)
d Franz Peter Wirth

The ROUGH AND READY LOT
(BBC 22/9/1959)
Adaptation of Owen's stage play, set in a
Spanish-American republic shortly after the
American Civil War.
d/p Casper Wrede; *sc* Charles Lawrence;
auth Alun Owen
lp Jack MacGowran; Patrick Allen;
Rupert Davies; Alan Dobie; Ronald Harwood;
June Brown

ROUND THE WORLD IN FORTY
MINUTES (BBC 17/5/1957)
Prince Philip talks about his world tour of 1956–
57. Scenes in Ceylon, Australia, Antarctica and
the Gambia.
p Antony Craxton

ROVING REPORT (ITN 1957–64)
Current affairs series.
DOMINICAN REPUBLIC 12/4/1962
Life in the Dominican Republic after the
assassination of Rafael Trujillo, and the impact
of propaganda from Cuba.
p Edwin Morrisby
WILD FIRE 3/5/1962
Brian Widlake reports on the extinguishing of an
oil well which has been burning for several
months in the Sahara.
p Robert Tyrrell
BRITISH GUIANA 17/5/1962
Dr Cheddi Jagan, Prime Minister of British
Guiana, talks about the social and racial
problems of the colony and its hopes for full
independence.
p Edwin Morrisby
OUTLOOK UNSETTLED 26/7/1962
Racial conflict in Kenya.
p Edwin Morrisby
KENYA ELECTIONS 22/5/1963
The first election in Kenya; interviews with R.G.
Ngala, Jomo Kenyatta and Thomas Joseph
Mboya.

ROWAN AND MARTIN'S LAUGH-IN
(US NBC 1967–73)
Offbeat, high-speed comedy series.
ROWAN AND MARTIN'S LAUGH-IN 16/11/1969
with Dan Rowan, Dick Martin,
Diana Ross, Goldie Hawn

The ROYAL FAMILY
(BBC-ITV 21/6/1969)
A year in the life of the British royal family.
d Richard Cawston; *comm* Michael Flanders

ROYAL HERITAGE (BBC 21/4–16/6/1977)
Documentary series on the British monarchy and
its treasures and legacy.
d David Heycock; *p* Michael Gill;
sc/comm Huw Wheldon
The TUDORS 28/4/1977
VICTORIA AND ALBERT 2/6/1977
VICTORIA, QUEEN AND EMPRESS 9/6/1977

The ROYAL PALACES OF BRITAIN
(BBC 25/12/1966)
Sir Kenneth Clark conducts a tour of Windsor
Castle, Buckingham Palace and Holyrood
House, with music composed by Sir Arthur
Bliss.
d Anthony De Lotbinière

The ROYAL PHILHARMONIC SOCIETY
(BBC 13/2/1957)
The first performance in this country of William
Walton's Cello Concerto played by Gregor
Piatigorsky at the Royal Festival Hall, with the
BBC Symphony Orchestra, conducted by
Malcolm Sargent.
p Antony Craxton; *intro* Alvar Lidell

The ROYAL SOCIETY TERCENTENARY
(BBC 19/7/1960)
Queen Elizabeth II at the Royal Albert Hall for
the formal opening of the Royal Society
tercentenary celebrations, with Sir Cyril
Hinshelwood and Gustav VI, King of Sweden.
p Humphrey Fisher

The ROYAL TOURNAMENT – 1965
(BBC 24/7/1965)
A visit to the Royal Tournament at Earl's Court,
featuring the massed bands of the RAF, a
gymnastic display by the Army Physical Training
Corps, the police dogs of the RAF and the Fiji
Military Band with dancers.
p John Vernon; *comm* Geoffrey Wheeler

The ROYAL VARIETY PERFORMANCE
(ATV 22/5/1960)
First television transmission of the Royal Variety
Performance, from the Victoria Palace Theatre
in the presence of Queen Elizabeth II and Prince
Philip.
d Bill Ward; *p* Jack Hylton

ROYAL VISIT TO ULSTER
(Ulster TV 10/8/1977)
The Queen's and Duke of Edinburgh's visit to
Northern Ireland, 10–11th August 1977. Arrival
of the Queen and the Duke of Edinburgh, the
day's events.

ROYAL WEDDING (Thames 14/11/1973)
The wedding of Princess Anne and Captain
Mark Phillips.
p Bob Service

RUBOVIA (BBC 1963)
Puppet series.
A CRANKY BANQUET 22/1/1963
d/p Gordon Murray
FIRE, FIRE, FIRE 13/8/1963
d/p Gordon Murray

RUDY SCHOKKER CRIES NO MORE
(NL VPRO Television 31/3/1977)
Based on the story by Gerben Hellinga. Strange
happenings occur in a street in Amsterdam one
night when a young couple and their baby are
evicted from their home.
d Pieter Verhoeff
lp Jan Rudd Ruiter; Fritz Van Moorselaar;
Vera Weels

RUGBY SPECIAL (BBC)
p Alan Mouncer; *pres* Cliff Morgan
HIGHLIGHTS OF THE SEASON 1966–67 1967
RUGBY SPECIAL 23/11/1968
1968–69 County Championships, South-Western Division.
PRIDE OF THE LIONS, A REVIEW OF THE BRITISH LIONS' TOUR OF NEW ZEALAND 4/9/1971
WARWICK v. GLOUCESTER 11/3/1972
FRANCE v. WALES 15/3/1972
MIDDLESEX SEVENS 6/5/1972
WALES v. NEW ZEALAND ALL BLACKS 2/12/1972
N.E. COUNTIES v. ALL BLACKS 9/12/1972
WALES v. ENGLAND 20/1/1973
IRELAND v. ENGLAND 10/2/1973
MIDLANDS v. LANCASHIRE 3/3/1973
WALES v. IRELAND 10/3/1973
SCOTTISH RUGBY UNION CENTENARY INTERNATIONAL SEVEN A SIDE 7/4/1973
WALES v. AUSTRALIA 10/11/1973
WALES v. SCOTLAND AND FRANCE v. IRELAND 19/1/1974
ENGLISH SCHOOLBOYS v. AUSTRALIAN SCHOOLBOYS 26/1/1974
SCOTLAND v. ENGLAND AND WALES v. IRELAND 2/2/1974
WALES v. FRANCE AND ENGLAND v. IRELAND 16/2/1974
FRANCE v. ENGLAND AND IRELAND v. SCOTLAND 2/3/1974
SCOTLAND v. FRANCE AND ENGLAND v. WALES 16/3/1974
MIDDLESEX SEVENS 4/5/1974
SCOTLAND v. TONGA 28/9/1974
WALES v. TONGA 19/10/1974
IRELAND v. ALL BLACKS 23/11/1974
BARBARIANS v. NEW ZEALAND 30/11/1974
FRANCE v. WALES AND IRELAND v. ENGLAND 18/1/1975
SCOTLAND v. IRELAND AND ENGLAND v. FRANCE 1/2/1975
SCOTLAND v. WALES AND IRELAND v. FRANCE 1/3/1975
SCOTLAND v. AUSTRALIA 6/12/1975
FRANCE v. IRELAND 7/2/1976
MIDDLESEX SEVENS 8/5/1976
WALES v. IRELAND 16/1/1977
IRELAND v. ENGLAND 2/2/1977
FRANCE v. SCOTLAND 6/3/1977
WALES v. ENGLAND 6/3/1977
LONDON WELSH v. GOSFORTH 3/4/1977
GOSFORTH v. WATERLOO 17/4/1977
FRANCE v. NEW ZEALAND 20/11/1977
WALES v. SCOTLAND 19/2/1978
IRELAND v. FRANCE 19/2/1978
SCOTLAND v. ENGLAND 5/3/1978
WALES v. FRANCE 19/3/1978
GLOUCESTER v. LEICESTER 16/4/1978
MIDDLESEX SEVENS 29/4/1978
SCOTLAND v. WALES 21/1/1979
FRANCE v. WALES 18/2/1979
WALES v. ROUMANIA 7/10/1979
SCOTLAND v. NEW ZEALAND 11/11/1979

RUMPOLE OF THE BAILEY
(Thames 1978–)
Legal comedy/drama series based on the character created by John Mortimer. Developed from a PLAY FOR TODAY *tx* 1975.
RUMPOLE AND THE FASCIST BEAST 19/6/1979
d Robert Knights; *p* Jacqueline Davis;
sc John Mortimer
lp Leo McKern; Robert Lang; Roger Sloman; Michael O'Hagan; Douglas Reith; Peggy Thorpe-Bates; Patricia Hodge; Julian Curry; Richard Murdoch; Peter Bowles

RUSSELL HARTY (LWT 1974–79)
Chat show with Russell Harty. Developed from RUSSELL HARTY PLUS (1972–74).
INGRID BERGMAN, RITA HUNTER 29/11/1974
d Mike Mansfield
GRACIE FIELDS 17/1/1975
d Mike Mansfield
JEAN SIMMONS, HELEN BRADLEY 21/3/1975
d Mike Mansfield
DENNIS POTTER 1/10/1976
d Mike Mansfield; *p* Nicholas Barrett
OLIVER REED, MRS. VICTOR BRUCE, HEATH BARNES 4/3/1977
d Mike Mansfield; *p* Nicholas Barrett

JOHN MORTIMER 2/6/1979
d Mike Mansfield; *p* Nicholas Barrett

RUSSELL HARTY PLUS (LWT 1972–74)
Chat show with Russell Harty. Later developed into RUSSELL HARTY (1974–79).
RUDOLPH NUREYEV 10/2/1973
d Bruce Gowers

RUTLAND (Anglia 22/4/1968)
A portrait of the county of Rutland and a discussion of the proposed merger with surrounding larger counties.
d Harry Aldous

RUTLAND WEEKEND TELEVISION
(BBC 1975–76)
Comedy sketch series.
RUTLAND WEEKEND TELEVISION 2/6/1975
p Ian Keill; *sc* Eric Idle;
with Eric Idle, Bridget Armstrong, Neil Innes, David Battley, Henry Woolf, Andy Roberts

The RUTLES
(Rutle Corps Production 27/3/1978)
Parody of the Beatles' rise to fame. Developed from a sketch first featured in RUTLAND WEEKEND TELEVISION (1975–76).
d Gary Weis; Eric Idle;
sc Eric Idle
lp Eric Idle; Michael Palin; Neil Innes; Mick Jagger; Ron Wood

S

SABER OF LONDON
(Danziger Productions 1959–62)
British crime series. Followed on from the MARK SABER (1957–59) series.
[Syndicated *tx* in US 1957–60]
p Edward J. Danziger, Harry Lee Danziger
regulars Donald Gray; Neil McCallum; Robert Arden
GIRL FROM ROME 1959
lp Neil McCallum
The MISSING HOURS 14/12/1959
d Ernest Morris; *sc* Brian Clemens
lp Norma Parnell; Gary Thorne; Noel Dyson; Ernest Clark; Bernard Cribbins
GIRLS AND DIAMONDS 4/1/1960
d Ernest Morris; *sc* Eldon Howard
lp Jean Aubrey; Diane Aubrey; Colin Tapley; Arnold Bell
MURDER SHALL SPEAK 11/1/1960
d Godfrey Grayson; *sc* George St. George
lp Silvia Herklots
HOUR OF DECISION 25/1/1960
d Max Varnel; *sc* John Roeburt
CHEATING CHEATERS 28/3/1960
d Max Varnel; *sc* John Roeburt
lp Colin Tapley; Robert Raikes; Bernard Bresslaw; Ian Fleming
SIX MONTHS TO TALK 4/4/1960
d Max Varnel; *sc* Eldon Howard
lp Colin Tapley; Edwin Richfield
CODE TO MURDER 2/5/1960
d Max Varnel; *sc* Eldon Howard
lp Leslie Kyle; John Harvey; Peter Elliott
CALLING CHARLIE – EMERGENCY 9/5/1960
d Max Varnel; *sc* Eldon Howard
lp Colin Tapley; Bill Nagy; Peter Bathurst
The VISITOR 16/5/1960
d Max Varnel; *sc* James Eastwood
lp Colin Tapley; John Loder; Mila Parely; Wendy Hutchinson
DIAMOND FOLLIES 22/8/1960
lp Jan Holden; Gordon Tanner
A DIPLOMATIC AFFAIR 29/8/1960
d Max Varnel; *sc* Brian Clemens
lp Ellen Blueth; John Le Mesurier
BLACK PAWN, WHITE PAWN 5/9/1960
lp Gordon Tanner; Basil Dignam; Denis Shaw
DEAD MAN'S HANDS 7/11/1960
lp Gordon Tanner; Mary Jones

BEYOND FEAR 21/11/1960
d Max Varnel
lp Harold Lang; Jennifer Jayne; Edwin Richfield; John Stuart; Frank Henderson; Arnold Bell
DON'T LOSE YOUR SHIRT 28/11/1960
d Max Varnel
lp Gordon Tanner; Patrick Holt
PAID OFF 12/12/1960
d Geoffrey Grayson
lp Jacques Cey; Michael Ripper; Robert Raikes; Patricia Driscoll
DEATH AT HIS FINGERTIPS 26/6/1961
d Max Varnel; *sc* Brian Clemens
lp Francis Matthews; Vera Fusek
The CURSE OF DEATH 10/7/1961
d Geoffrey Grayson
lp Howard Pays; Robert Raikes
LADY DOESN'T SCARE 31/7/1961
d Geoffrey Grayson
lp Honor Blackman; Colin Tapley; Denis Shaw
The BLACK WIDOW 7/8/1961
d Geoffrey Grayson
lp Colin Tapley; John McLaren
The KILLER AND THE KID 14/8/1961
lp Harry Fowler; Richard Williams; Patrick Holt
UNDER SUSPICION 4/9/1961
d Max Varnel
lp Kenneth Edwards; Howard Lang; Jan Holden
HOUR OF RECKONING 25/9/1961
d Max Varnel
lp Jean Aubrey; Brian Nissen
TROUBLE FOR HARRY 9/10/1961
d Geoffrey Grayson; *sc* Eldon Howard
lp John McLaren; Roberta Huby; Hal Osmond
COME OUT FIGHTING 13/11/1961
d Geoffrey Grayson; *sc* Brian Clemens
lp Neil Hallett; Peter Sinclair; Hal Osmond
SILENT ACCUSATION 1/1/1962
d Godfrey Grayson; *sc* Stanley Miller
lp John Stuart; Neil Hallett; Honor Shepherd
JOCKEY MISSING 15/1/1962
d Godfrey Grayson; *sc* Mark Grantham
lp Ann Sears; William Hodge
SWITCH TO MURDER 12/2/1962
d Godfrey Grayson;
sc Stanley Miller, Gilbert Winfield
lp Francis Matthews
BROKEN JOURNEY 5/3/1962
d Godfrey Grayson; *sc* Brian Clemens
lp Garry Thorne; Colin Tapley; Paddy Webster
ORDEAL OF FEAR 26/3/1962
d Godfrey Grayson;
sc Paul Tabori, James Eastwood
lp Garry Thorne; John Gabriel; Honor Shepherd
The SCREAM IN THE NIGHT 23/4/1962
d Geoffrey Grayson; *sc* George St. George
lp John Stuart; Robert Raikes

The SACRED FLAME (BBC 10/7/1955)
p Hal Burton; *auth* W. Somerset Maugham
lp Emrys Jones; Mark Dignam; Marie Ney; Irene Worth; Amy Dalby; Julian d'Albie; Anne Crawford; Dermot Walsh

SADIE, IT'S COLD OUTSIDE
(Thames 21/4–25/6/1975)
Six-part comedy series based on the life of a middle-aged, married couple.
SADIE, IT'S COLD OUTSIDE 21/4/1975
d/p Les Chatfield; *sc* Jack Rosenthal
lp Rosemary Leach; Bernard Hepton; Lesley Joseph; Bernard Stone

SAILOR (BBC 5/8–7/10/1976)
Ten-part documentary series on life aboard the aircraft carrier HMS Ark Royal.
LAST RUN ASHORE 5/8/1976
The last night ashore for the sailors of Ark Royal and the beginning of the voyage.
p John Purdie
HAPPY BIRTHDAY 19/8/1976
A celebration of the Ark Royal's twenty-first birthday.
p John Purdie

SAILOR OF FORTUNE

(ATV-Michael Sadlier Productions 1955–56)
Adventure series featuring the exploits of the captain of a freighter.
CRESCENT AND STAR 7/12/1956
d Michael McCarthy;
p Michael Sadlier, Ted Holliday
lp Lorne Greene; Rupert Davies;
Jack MacGowran; Betty McDowall;
Robert Cawdron; Russell Waters;
André Maranne; Ewen Solon; Sean Connery
TANGIER 15/6/1957
d John Guillermin;
p Michael Sadlier, Ted Holliday
lp Lorne Greene; Paul Carpenter;
Michael Goodliffe; Alec Mango;
Jack MacGowran

The SAINT

(ATV-New World-ITC-Bamore Production 1962–69)
The adventures of Simon Templar – 'The Saint'.
From the character created in the novels of Leslie Charteris.
p Robert S. Baker, Monty Norman
regulars Roger Moore; Ivor Dean
The TALENTED HUSBAND 30/9/1962
d Michael Truman; sc Jack Sanders
lp Derek Farr; Shirley Eaton;
Patricia Roc
The CAREFUL TERRORIST 14/10/1962
d John Ainsworth;
sc Gerald Kelsey, Dick Sharples
lp David Kossoff; Peter Dyneley;
Allan Gifford
COVETOUS HEADMAN 21/10/1962
d Michael Truman; sc John Roddick
lp Barbara Shelley; Eugene Deckers;
George Pastell; Esmond Knight;
Robert Cawdron
The LOADED TOURIST 28/10/1962
d Jeremy Summers; sc Richard Harris
lp Barbara Bates; Edward Evans; Guy Deghy
The PEARLS OF PEACE 11/11/1962
d David Greene; sc Richard Harris
lp Bob Kanter; Erica Rogers; Djna Paisner
ELEMENT OF DOUBT 18/11/1962
d John Ainsworth; sc Norman Borisoff
lp David Bauer; Alan Gifford;
Margaret Vines; Bill Nagy; Ken Wayne;
Anita West
ARROW OF GOD 25/11/1962
d John Paddy Carstairs; sc Julian Bond
lp Elspeth March; Ronald Leigh-Hunt;
Honor Blackman; Tony Wright;
Anthony Dawson
The MAN WHO WAS LUCKY 16/12/1962
d/sc John Gilling
lp Eddie Byrne; Delphi Lawrence;
Campbell Singer; Vera Day; Harry Towb;
Charles Houston
The SAINT SEES IT THROUGH 10/3/1963
d Robert S. Baker; sc Ian Kennedy Martin
lp Margit Saad; Joseph Furst;
Elspeth March; Guy Deghy; Larry Cross;
Gordon Sterne
The FELLOW TRAVELLER 29/9/1963
d Peter Yates; sc Harry H. Junkin
lp Dawn Addams; Neil McCallum; Ray Austin
STARRING THE SAINT 6/10/1963
d James Hill; sc Harry H. Junkin
lp Ronald Radd; Alfred Burke;
Wensley Pithey; Monica Stevenson;
Alexander Davion
TERESA 20/10/1963
d Roy Ward Baker; sc John Kruse
lp Lana Morris; Eric Pohlmann;
Marne Maitland; Lawrence Dane; Marie Burke
MARCIA 3/11/1963
d John Krish; sc Harry H. Junkin
lp Samantha Eggar; Johnny Briggs;
Philip Stone
WORK OF ART 17/11/1963
d Peter Yates; sc Harry H. Junkin
lp Yolande Turner; Alex Scott;
Martin Benson; John Bailey; Robert Cawdron
IRIS 24/11/1963
d John Gilling; sc Bill Strutton
lp Barbara Murray; David Bauer;
Ivor Dean; Cyril Luckham; Ferdy Mayne;
John Ronane

KING OF THE BEGGARS 1/12/1963
d/sc John Gilling
lp Maxine Audley; Oliver Reed;
Yvonne Romain; Warren Mitchell;
Ronnie Corbett
ROUGH DIAMONDS 8/12/1963
d Peter Yates; sc Bill Strutton
lp Douglas Wilmer; Ivor Dean;
George A. Cooper; Vanda Godsell;
Paul Stassino; Jemma Hyde
The SAINT PLAYS WITH FIRE 15/12/1963
d Robert S. Baker; sc John Kruse
lp Joseph Furst; Justine Lord
BENEVOLENT BURGLARY 22/12/1963
d Jeremy Summers; sc Larry Forrester
lp John Barrie; Gary Cockrell;
Rachel Gurney; Suzanne Neve;
Raymond Adamson; Arnold Diamond
The WONDERFUL WAR 26/1/1964
d Robert S. Baker; sc John Graeme
lp Renee Houston; Noel Purcell;
Alfred Burke; Alec Mango
NOBLE SPORTSMAN 2/2/1964
d Peter Yates; sc John Graeme
lp Sylvia Syms; Anthony Quayle;
Francis Matthews; Paul Curran; Jane Asher
LAWLESS LADY 16/2/1964
d Jeremy Summers; sc Harry H. Junkin
lp Dawn Addams; Julian Glover
SOPHIA 6/3/1964
d Roger Moore; sc Robert Stewart
lp Oliver Reed; Imogen Hassall;
Peter Kriss; Tommy Duggan; John Wentworth
GOOD MEDICINE 23/4/1964
d Roy Ward Baker; sc Norman Borisoff
lp Barbara Murray; Anthony Newlands;
Jean Marsh; Bill Nagy; John Bennet;
Veronica Turleigh
The MIRACLE TEA PARTY 27/9/1964
d Roger Moore; sc Paddy Manning O'Brine
lp Nanette Newman; Fabia Drake;
Conrad Phillips
LIDA 4/10/1964
d Leslie Norman; sc Michael Cramoy
lp Erica Rogers; Jeanne Moody;
Barry Keegan; Peter Bowles; Marne Maitland;
Aubrey Morris
The SCORPION 18/10/1964
d Roy Ward Baker; sc Paul Erickson
lp Catherine Woodville;
Nyree Dawn Porter; Dudley Sutton;
Philip Latham
REVOLUTION RACKET 25/10/1964
d Pat Jackson; sc Harry H. Junkin
lp Eric Pohlmann; Peter Arne;
Suzanne Lloyd
The MAN WHO LIKED TOYS 22/11/1964
d John Gilling; sc Basil Dawson
lp John Paul; Maurice Kaufmann
HI-JACKERS 13/12/1964
d David Eady; sc Paul Erickson
lp Ingrid Schoeller; Neil McCallum;
Walter Gotell
The DAMSEL IN DISTRESS 3/1/1965
d Peter Yates; sc Paul Erickson
lp Richard Wyler; Catherine Woodville
The CONTRACT 10/1/1965
d Roger Moore; sc Terry Nation
lp Dick Haymes; Robert Hutton
The RHINE MAIDEN 30/1/1965
d James Hill; sc Brian Degas
lp Stephanie Randall; Nigel Davenport;
Anthony Booth
The INESCAPABLE WORD 6/2/1965
d Roy Ward Baker; sc Terry Nation
lp Ann Bell; James Maxwell;
Maurice Hedley
SIGN OF THE CLAW 20/2/1965
d Leslie Norman; sc Terry Nation
lp Suzan Farmer; Peter Copley;
Godfrey Quigley; Geoffrey Frederick;
Leo Leyden
SIBAO 6/3/1965
d Peter Yates; sc Terry Nation
lp John Carson; Jeanne Roland;
Christopher Carlos
HAPPY SUICIDE 20/3/1965
d Robert Tronson; sc Brian Degas
lp Jane Merrow; John Bluthal;
William Sylvester; Donald Sutherland;
Annie Ross

The ABDUCTORS 3/7/1965
d Jeremy Summers; sc Brian Degas
lp Annette Andre; Robert Urquhart;
Dudley Foster
The MAN WHO COULD NOT DIE 31/7/1965
d Roger Moore; sc Terry Nation
lp Patrick Allen; Robin Phillips
The SAINT BIDS DIAMONDS 7/8/1965
d Leslie Norman; sc Norman Hudis
lp Eunice Gayson
OLD TREASURE STORY 21/8/1965
d Roger Moore; sc Monty Berman
lp Jack Hedley; Robert Hutton;
Erica Rogers; Reg Lye; Frank Wolff; Jill Curzon
The RELUCTANT REVOLUTION 16/10/1966
d Leslie Norman; sc John Stanton
lp Jennie Linden; Barry Morse;
Peter Illing
CONVENIENT MONSTER 30/10/1966
d Leslie Norman; sc Michael Cramoy
lp Suzan Farmer; Laurence Payne;
Caroline Blakiston; Fulton Mackay
ANGEL'S EYE 6/11/1966
d Leslie Norman; sc Paul Erickson
lp Liam Richmond; Jane Merrow;
T.P. McKenna
The DEATH GAME 29/1/1967
d Leslie Norman; sc John Kruse
lp Angela Douglas; George Murcell
COUNTERFEIT COUNTESS 5/3/1967
d Leslie Norman; sc Philip Broadley
lp Kate O'Mara; Alexandra Bastedo;
Philip Madoc; Derek Newark
ISLAND OF CHANCE 9/4/1967
d Leslie Norman; sc John Stanton
lp Sue Lloyd; David Bauer; Alex Scott
The ROMANTIC MATRON 16/4/1967
d John Paddy Carstairs; sc Larry Forrester
lp Ann Gillis; John Carson;
Patrick Troughton
GADGET LOVERS 23/4/1967
d Jim O'Connolly; sc John Kruse
lp Mary Peach; Campbell Singer;
Glynn Edwards; Nicholas Donnelly;
John Bennett
The INVISIBLE MILLIONAIRE 30/4/1967
d Jeremy Summers; sc Kenneth Hayles
lp Katharine Blake; Michael Goodliffe;
Nigel Stock
POWER ARTIST 21/5/1967
d Leslie Norman; sc John Kruse
lp Pauline Munro; George Murcell;
Tristram Jellinek; Peter Bourne; John Bown
The GADIC COLLECTION 25/6/1967
d Freddie Francis; sc Philip Broadley
lp Georgia Brown; Peter Wyngarde;
Michael Ripper
LEGACY FOR THE SAINT 18/11/1968
d Roy Ward Baker; sc Michael Winder
lp Reginald Marsh; Alan MacNaughton
DESPERATE DIPLOMAT 25/11/1968
d Ray Austin; sc Terry Nation
lp John Robinson; Suzan Farmer
The DOUBLE TAKE 9/12/1968
d Leslie Norman; sc John Kruse
lp Gregoire Aslan; Kate O'Mara;
Denise Buckley
The TIME TO DIE 16/12/1968
d Robert Tronson; sc Terry Nation
lp Suzanne Lloyd; Maurice Good;
John Barcroft; Terence Rigby; Freddie Jones
The MASTER PLAN 8/1/1969
d Leslie Norman; sc Harry H. Junkin
lp Lyn Ashley; John Turner; Burt Kwouk;
Christopher Benjamin; Robert Morris
The PEOPLE IMPORTERS 15/1/1969
d Ray Austin; sc Donald James
lp Susan Travers; Neil Hallett;
Gary Miller; Ray Lonnen; Salmaan Peer;
Imogen Hassall
The SCALES OF JUSTICE 22/1/1969
d Robert Asher; sc Robert Holmes
lp Andrew Keir; Jean Marsh; Mark Burns;
Gillian Lind; John Barron; Geoffrey Chater
The EX-KING OF DIAMONDS 5/2/1969
d Alvin Rakoff; sc John Kruse
lp Ronald Radd; Isla Blair; Stuart Damon
The MAN WHO GAMBLED WITH LIFE 26/2/1969
d Freddie Francis; sc Harry H. Junkin
lp Clifford Evans; Jayne Sofiano;
Veronica Carlson; Steven Berkoff

The SAINT cont.

The WORLD BEATER 5/3/1969
d Leslie Norman; sc Donald James
lp Patricia Haines; John Ronane;
James Kerry; George A. Cooper; Eddie Byrne
INVITATION TO DANGER 12/3/1969
d Roger Moore; sc Terry Nation
lp Shirley Eaton; Robert Hutton;
Julian Glover

ST. CLOUD – PRIX JEAN DE CHAUDENAY
(FR BBC 22/5/1972)
Horse race.

ST. IVES (BBC 30/10–4/12/1955)
Six-part serial from the novel by Robert Louis
Stevenson.
EPISODE 1: LION RAMPANT 30/10/1955
p/sc Rex Tucker
lp Roger Delgado; William Russell;
Anthony Sharp; Joan Sanderson;
Noelle Middleton

ST. PAUL'S MEMORIAL SERVICE TO
KING GEORGE VI (BBC 17/2/1952)

SAINTS ALIVE (ATV 1975–77)
Religious series.
SAINTS ALIVE 24/7/1977
Rev. Houston talks about the plain language
used in the Good News Bible; Revs. Green and
Watson discuss evangelism; Mary Whitehouse
talks about her book 'Whatever Happened To
Sex'.
p Sam Fairhall

SAKI (Granada 6/7/1962–16/1/1963)
Dramatisation of the stories by H.H. Munro.
SAKI 6/7/1962
d Gordon Flemyng; p Philip Mackie;
sc Hugh Leonard, Edward Boyd
lp William Mervyn; Richard Vernon;
Jane Eccles; Martita Hunt; Mark Burns;
Fenella Fielding; Nora Nicholson;
Rosamund Greenwood

SALUTE
(ATV; US tx 13/6/1975; GB tx 20/6/1975)
A show business tribute to Sir Lew Grade.
d Dwight Hemion; p Dick Schneider

SALUTE TO A.P. (BBC 19/3/1954)
The development of the television broadcasting
service at Alexandra Palace from 1936 to 1954.
Extracts from BBC transmissions of the period,
including the first programme transmitted, the
coronation of George VI, the final transmission
before World War II, a Mickey Mouse cartoon,
variety shows after the War and two plays,
'Promise of Tomorrow' and 'Drums of
Deliverance'.
p Ray Dicks; pres Keith Rogers;
comm Berkeley Smith

SAM (Granada 1973–75)
Drama series about a boy growing up in a mining
town.
HOME FROM HOME 21/8/1973
d Richard Doubleday, Alan Grint;
p Michael Cox; sc John Finch
lp Michael Goodliffe; Maggie Jones;
Ray Smith; Alethea Charlton; James Hazeldine
BREADWINNERS 4/9/1973
d Colin Cant; p Michael Cox;
sc John Finch
lp Michael Goodliffe; Maggie Jones;
Ray Smith; Alethea Charlton; James Hazeldine
MOVING ON 8/8/1974
d Roland Joffé; p Michael Cox;
sc John Finch
lp Mark McManus; Jennifer Hilary;
Michael Goodliffe; Alethea Charlton; Ray Smith

SANCTUARY (Rediffusion 1967–68)
Drama series about an order of nuns involved in
social work.
The MISSION 28/6/1967
d Joan Kemp-Welch; p John Harrison;
sc Philip Levine, Noel Robinson
lp Fay Compton; Alison Leggatt;
Peggy Thorpe-Bates; Joanna Dunham;
Mona Bruce; Rudolph Walker; Hilda Fenemore

SANDBAGGERS (Yorkshire TV 1978–80)
Espionage series about a special operations team
of the S.I.S. (Secret Intelligence Service).
sc Ian MacKintosh
regulars Roy Marsden; Richard Vernon;
Ray Lonnen; Alan MacNaughtan;
Elizabeth Bennett; Jerome Willis
FIRST PRINCIPLES 18/9/1978
d/p Michael Ferguson
lp Bob Sherman; David Glyder;
Olaf Pooley; Brian Haines
A PROPER FUNCTION OF GOVERNMENT
25/9/1978
d/p Michael Ferguson
lp Laurence Payne; Brian Osborne;
Michael O'Hagan; Steven Grives;
Barkley Johnson
IS YOUR JOURNEY REALLY NECESSARY?
2/10/1978
d/p Derek Bennett
lp Steven Grives; David Glyder;
Michael O'Hagan; Brian Osborne;
Brenda Cavendish; Andrew Bradford
The MOST SUITABLE PERSON 9/10/1978
d David Reynolds; p Michael Ferguson
lp Bob Sherman; Diane Keen; Jonathan Coy;
Christopher Benjamin; Stephen Greif;
John F. Landry
ALWAYS GLAD TO HELP 16/10/1978
d David Reynolds; p Michael Ferguson
lp Bob Sherman; Diane Keen; Gerald James;
Terence Longdon; Peter Miles; Brian Osborne;
Alan Thompson
SPECIAL RELATIONSHIP 30/10/1978
d/p Michael Ferguson
lp Bob Sherman; Diane Keen

The SANDIE SHAW SUPPLEMENT
(BBC 10/9–5/11/1968)
Six-part pop music series, with each programme
presenting a different theme.
QUICKSAND 17/9/1968
The second programme concentrates on travel.
p Mel Cornish; with John Walker

SAPPHIRE AND STEEL (ATV 1979–81)
Fantasy science-fiction series about the
adventures of two 'time detectives'.
HELPING TWO CHILDREN 10/7/1979
d/p Shaun O'Riordan; sc P.J. Hammond
lp David McCallum; Joanna Lumley;
Steven O'Shea; Tamasin Bridge;
Felicity Harrison; John Golightly

SARAH (Yorkshire TV 21/1/1973)
d John Frankau; sc Guy Cullingford
lp Pheona McLellan; Richard Vernon;
Ursula Howells; Pat Heywood; Mark Kingston;
Kathleen Michael

SATURDAY NIGHT AT THE MILL
(BBC 1976–81)
Entertainment series.
SATURDAY NIGHT AT THE MILL 25/2/1979
d Roy Norton; p Roy Ronnie;
pres Bob Langley; with Bernard Miles,
Kate Bush, Kenny Ball and his Jazzmen

SATURDAY NIGHT THEATRE
(ITV various 1969–70)
Anthology drama series.
BANGELSTEIN'S BOYS (ATV 18/1/1969)
d John Mackenzie; p Kenith Trodd;
sc Colin Welland
lp Donald Webster; Del Henney;
Christine Hargreaves; Colin Welland;
Ray Smith; Bruce Myles; Terence Rigby;
June Ellis; Jill Kerman
MACNEIL (ATV 1/2/1969)
d Charles Jarrott; sc Alun Owen;
intro Laurence Olivier
lp Sean Connery; Anna Calder-Marshall;
Katharine Blake; Roddy McMillan;
Jo Rowbottom; Maggie McGrath;
Katharine Page
CORNELIUS (ATV 8/2/1969)
d Charles Jarrott; sc Alun Owen;
intro Laurence Olivier
lp Michael Caine; Anna Calder-Marshall;
Michael Bates; Janet Key

EMLYN (ATV 15/2/1969)
d Anthony Page; sc Alun Owen;
intro Laurence Olivier
lp Paul Scofield; Anna Calder-Marshall;
Geoffrey Chater; George Howe;
Kynaston Reeves; Kate Coleridge
MOONLIGHT ON THE HIGHWAY
(LWT 12/4/1969)
d James MacTaggart; p Kenith Trodd;
sc Dennis Potter
lp Ian Holm; Anthony Bate; Deborah Grant;
Robin Wentworth; Frederick Peisley;
Wally Patch
The TALKING HEAD (LWT 30/8/1969)
d James Gatward; p Kenith Trodd;
sc Jim Allen
lp Michael Craig; Ann Lynn; Ralph Ball;
Godfrey James; John Thaw; Robert Cawdrin;
Alex Donald; Edwin Richfield
FAITH AND HENRY (LWT 6/12/1969)
d Jack Gold; p Kenith Trodd;
sc Julia Jones
lp Hilary Baker; John Baron; Joe Gladwin;
Allan Surtees; Julia Jones; Myrtle Robinson;
Charles Hyatt
LAY DOWN YOUR ARMS (LWT 23/5/1970)
d Christopher Morahan; p Kenith Trodd;
sc Dennis Potter
lp Nikolas Simmonds; John Bloomfield;
Tucker McGuire; Will Stampe; Leonard Trolley;
Ken Wayne; John Warner; Graham Armitage;
George Layton

SATURDAY PLAYHOUSE (BBC 1958–61)
Anthology drama series.
GOING LIKE A FOX 13/2/1960
p David J. Thomas; sc Alun Richards
lp Rupert Davies; Maureen Pryor;
Ralph Michael; Peter Gill; Beckett Bould

SATURDAY SHAKE-UP (Tyne Tees 1979)
Saturday morning series for children.
with Alastair Pirrie, Graham Thornton,
Christine Anderson
SATURDAY SHAKE-UP 9/2/1979
SATURDAY SHAKE-UP 24/3/1979
SATURDAY SHAKE-UP 14/7/1979
SATURDAY SHAKE-UP 17/11/1979

The SATURDAY SPECIAL
(ITV various 1968–69)
Series of music programmes, both popular and
classical, and revues.
A NIGHT OUT WITH DANNY LA RUE
(LWT 7/12/1968)
d David Bell;
sc Barry Cryer, Dick Vosburgh;
with Toni Palmer, Valerie Walsh,
Jenny Logan, Ronnie Corbett, Richard Wattis.
KING OF VIOLINISTS (LWT 14/12/1968)
David Oistrakh plays Beethoven's violin
concerto, with the London Symphony Orchestra
conducted by Sir Adrian Boult.
d/nar Humphrey Burton
MRS WILSON'S DIARY (LWT 4/1/1969)
Satirical revue of life at No. 10 Downing St.,
based on Joan Littlewood's stage production.
d/p Stuart Allen;
sc Richard Ingrams, John Wells
lp Myvanwy Jenn; Bill Wallis;
Nigel Hawthorne; Stephen Lewis; Bob Grant;
Peter Reeves; Toni Palmer

The SATURDAY SPECIAL
(ITV various 1977)
Series of special entertainment programmes.
The EDINBURGH FESTIVAL
(Scottish TV 24/9/1977)
Highlights from the 1977 Edinburgh Festival.
d Tony Palmer; p Chris Fox;
with Max Wall, Claudio Abbado,
Rex Harrison, Placido Domingo,
Natalia Makarova, Paul Tortelier,
Dorothy Tutin, Billy Connolly

SAVAGES
(US Spelling-Goldberg Productions 11/9/1974)
Made-for-TV film. A deranged hunter stalks his
young guide.
d Lee H. Katzin;
p Aaron Spelling, Leonard Goldberg;
sc William Wood; *auth* Robb White
lp Andy Griffith; Sam Bottoms;
Noah Beery Jr; Jim Antonio; Jim Chandler;
James Best

SCENE (BBC 1967–)
Schools programme consisting of plays or reports
on topical issues of interest to teenagers.
UNDERGROUND 8/3/1967
Paul McCartney introduces and concludes the
film. Poetry reading at the Royal Albert Hall
5/5/1965 (amateur film) with Allen Ginsberg and
Lawrence Ferlinghetti. Pink Floyd playing at the
UFO club.
TERRY 30/1/1969
d Michael Simpson; *p* Ronald Smedley;
sc Alan Plater
lp Dennis Waterman; Bill Owen
TWO WAY TRAFFIC 13/11/1969
p Ronald Smedley; *sc* Allan Prior
lp Wilfred Pickles; Clare Sutcliffe
QUIET AFTERNOON 5/10/1972
A play about a missing baby.
p Ronald Smedley
lp Paula Wilcox; David Lincoln;
James Culliford; Jan Carey
JAMES IS OUR BROTHER 20/2/1975
The family life of a 16 year-old mongol boy
living at home with his parents and two younger
brothers.
p Roger Tonge
AND THEY ALL LIVED HAPPILY TOGETHER
13/1/1977
Adoption and its effects on four families.
p Roy Thompson; *comm* Nick Ross

SCENER UR ETT ÅKTENSKAP
(SE Sveriges Radio 1973; GB *tx* 1975)
Made for Swedish television in six parts and later
re-edited into a feature film. Shown on British
television under the title 'Six Scenes from a
Marriage'.
d/p/sc Ingmar Bergman
lp Liv Ullmann; Erland Josephson;
Bibi Andersson; Jan Malmsjo
OSKULD OCH PANIK 11/4/1973
KUNSTEN ATT SOPA UNDER MATTEN 18/4/1973
PAULA 25/4/1973
TÅREDALEN 2/5/1973
ANALFABETERNA 9/5/1973
MITT I NATTEN I ETT MÖRKT HUS
NÅGONSTANS I VÄRLDEN 16/5/1973

The SCHOOLS (BBC 18/9/1962)
Britain's school system and the problems
teachers face in schools.
p/sc Richard Cawston

SCIENCE INTERNATIONAL
(BBC 1–8/12/1959)
The first of two programmes examining cells and
their structure.
WHAT IS LIFE? 1/12/1959
Michael Swann and Raymond Baxter report on
world-wide research into the living cell and the
origins of life.
d Humphrey Fisher, Aubrey Singer

The SCIENTISTS (Yorkshire TV 1970–73)
Documentary series on scientific developments.
The FLESH HARVESTERS 15/4/1972
The scientific research behind the breeding of
animals for food.
d Harris Watts; *p* Sid Waddell, David Taylor;
rep Peter Moth
The HEIRS OF KING CANUTE 22/4/1972
A report from London and Venice on the
scientific research being carried out into the
prevention of flooding and erosion by the sea.
d Barry Cockcroft; *exec.p* John Fairley;
rep Austin Mitchell
MAGNUS AND THE BEANSTEAK 6/5/1972
The work of food technologist Magnus Pyke.
d Harris Watts; *p* David Taylor, Sid Waddell;
rep Peter Moth

An EXPERIMENT IN TIME 29/4/1973
A programme about biorhythms. Dr Janet
Harker of Cambridge University claims to have
found the first living clock ever isolated in an
animal.
d Lis Kustow; *p* David Taylor;
rep Simon Welfare

SCOTLAND TODAY (Scottish TV)
Regional news programme.
SCOTLAND TODAY 18/6/1975
Regional news bulletin, including reports on the
annual conference of the Scottish miners and on
the National Health Service in Scotland.

SCOTLAND YARD (BBC 12/4–5/7/1960)
Series of dramatised documentaries about the
London Metropolitan Police.
PROTECTION 5/7/1960
An account of a 'protection racket' which
operates when crooks step out of line.
p David E. Rose; *sc* Robert Barr

SCOUTS AND GUIDES OF ALL NATIONS
(BBC 1950)
Scouts on a boat trip from Southend to the
Tower of London.

**SCREAM QUIETLY OR THE NEIGHBOURS
WILL HEAR** (Thames 26/2/1974)
Examines the plight of battered wives. In
particular, looks at the experiences of a group of
women who with their children were receiving
temporary refuge in a house run – without
official help – by a woman from Chiswick
Women's Aid.
d Michael Whyte; *p* Roger Hacker

SCREENPLAY (Granada 1979)
Anthology drama series.
GOSSIP FROM THE FOREST 29/7/1979
d/sc Brian Gibson; *p* Michael Dunlop;
auth Thomas Keneally
lp Hugh Burden; Ronald Hines;
Michael Jayston; John Shrapnel;
Vernon Dobtcheff
TALENT 5/8/1979
Victoria Wood's first play for television. Music
and lyrics are also by Victoria Wood.
d Baz Taylor; *p* Peter Eckersley;
sc Victoria Wood
lp Victoria Wood; Julie Walters;
Nat Jackley; Bill Waddington; Kevin Lloyd;
Peter Ellis

SEA WAR (Rank Organisation 1960)
Documentary series about British naval
operations in World War II.
p George Grafton Green; *sc* Jack Broome;
pres Caspar John; *nar* Roy Foster-Brown;
OPENING BID 10/9/1960
Hitler's invasion of Norway in 1940.
LIFE LINE 17/9/1960
Battle of the Atlantic.
SECOND GENERATION 24/9/1960
The pursuit and destruction of two German
warships, the 'Scharnhorst' and the 'Gneisenau'.
BROUGHT TO THE BOIL 1/10/1960
The threat to Britain's Mediterranean bases from
Mussolini's forces, who became Hitler's allies in
1940.
WINGS OVER THE WATER 15/10/1960
The role of the Fleet Air Arm and the story of
'HMS Ark Royal'.
DIVIDED BY THREE 22/10/1960
The story of the German armed merchant raider
'Atlantis' and the scuttling of the pocket
battleship 'Graf Spee'.
TO RUSSIA WITH LUCK 29/10/1960
In June 1941 Germany invaded Russia and Stalin
appealed for weapons. Series writer Captain
Jack Broome commanded the ship escorting the
ill-fated British Convoy PQ17 sent in response.
ONE ENEMY BATTLESHIP 5/11/1960
The 'Bismarck' and the 'Tirpitz' were, for
Britain, the biggest dangers.
The SUBMARINERS 12/11/1960
British submariners in World War II.
EIGHTEEN BY EIGHT 19/11/1960
British naval operations at Malta in
World War II.

TIMELY ARRIVAL 26/11/1960
The back-room boys come to the aid of the Navy
with radar, Asdic and longer range aircraft.
The WATER'S EDGE 3/12/1960
The Navy's contribution to land warfare – from
the evacuation of troops from Dunkirk to the
Normandy invasion.
SINGAPORE AND BACK 10/12/1960
The fall of Hong Kong and Singapore, the
sinking of the 'Prince of Wales' and the
'Repulse' and the Japanese surrender.

The SEARCH FOR THE NILE
(BBC 22/9–27/10/1971)
Dramatised documentary series about the search
for the source of the Nile in the nineteenth
century.
p Christopher Ralling; *nar* James Mason
The DREAM OF THE WANDERER 22/9/1971
d Fred Burnley, Christopher Ralling;
sc Derek Marlowe
lp Kenneth Haigh; John Quentin;
Barbara Leigh-Hunt; Andre Van Gyseghem;
Michael Gough; Elizabeth Proud;
Doran Godwin
The SECRET FOUNTAINS 6/10/1971
d Richard Marquand; *sc* Derek Marlowe
lp Kenneth Haigh; John Quentin;
Ian McCulloch; Oliver Litondo;
Barbara Leigh-Hunt; Norman Rossington
CONQUEST AND DEATH 27/10/1971
d Richard Marquand; *sc* Michael Hastings
lp Kenneth Haigh; Oliver Litondo;
Barbara Leigh-Hunt; Keith Buckley;
Martin Echitemi; David Field

SECOND CITY FIRSTS
(BBC 1973–78)
Series of single plays from Birmingham by new
writers.
The MEDIUM 15/10/1973
d Michael Simpson; *p* Barry Hanson;
sc Denise Robertson
lp Nora Fulton; Valerie Georgeson
GIRL 25/2/1974
d Peter Gill; *p* Barry Hanson;
sc James Robson
lp Myra Frances; Alison Steadman;
Eileen McCallum; Stella Moray
EARLY TO BED 20/3/1975
d Les Blair; *sc* Alan Bleasdale
lp David Warwick; Alison Steadman;
Patricia Leach; Johnny Meadows;
Clifford Kershaw
JACK FLEA'S BIRTHDAY CELEBRATION
10/4/1976
d Mike Newell; *p* Tara Prem;
sc Ian McEwan
lp Sara Kestelman; David Wilkinson;
Eileen McCallum; Ivor Roberts
KNOCK FOR KNOCK 21/11/1976
d/sc Mike Leigh; *p* Tara Prem
lp Sam Kelly; Anthony O'Donnell;
Meryl Hampton

SECOND CITY REPORTS
(Granada 3/3–7/4/1964)
Six-part series of satirical sketches, each part
based on a particular theme.
d David Cunliffe; *p* Bernard Sahlins;
sc Michael Frayn, John Bird, Ian Davidson
regulars David Battley; Kathleen Breck;
Eleanor Bron; David Buck; Pamela Ann Davy;
Jeremy Geidt; Gordon Gostelow; Barry Letts
SECOND CITY REPORTS: EXTRACTS 1964
SEEMS LIKE ONLY YESTERDAY 1964
CRAZES 17/3/1964
EXCLUSION 31/3/1964
LOVE 7/4/1964

2ND HOUSE (BBC 1973–75)
Arts programme. Initially several items and
presented by Melvyn Bragg. Latterly mostly one
subject. The first issue was titled 'Second
House'. Derives from the series 'Full House'.
The WHO 5/10/1974
Interview with Pete Townshend and footage of
the rock band, The Who, in concert.
p Tony Staveacre
ISAAC BASHEVIS SINGER 19/10/1974
Isaac Bashevis Singer talks about his life and
work.

Right: *Citizen '63* 28/8/1963 Barry Langford (BBC)

Below: *This Week* 18/10/1973 *The Unknown Famine* (Thames).

Face to Face 18/9/1960 Gilbert Harding (BBC).

Panorama (BBC). Richard Dimbleby.

Party Political Broadcast: The Labour Party 17/10/1951 Sir Hartley Shawcross, Christopher Mayhew (BBC).

That Was The Week That Was (BBC). David Frost, Roy Kinnear, Kenneth Cope, Lance Percival and William Rushton.

Survival (Anglia). Producer Aubrey Buxton with Turkana fisherman at Lake Rudolf.

ATHOL FUGARD 30/11/1974
The work of playwright Athol Fugard, includes extracts from 'Hello and Goodbye', 'The Blood Knot', 'Boesman and Lena', 'Sizwe Bansi is Dead', 'The Island', and 'Statements After an Arrest Under the Immorality Act'.
p Tristram Powell;
with Ben Kingsley, Janet Suzman, Niall Buggy, Alton Kumalo, Yvonne Bryceland, Athol Fugard, John Kani, Winston Ntshoni, Wilson Dunster
WITH GUN AND CAMERA 15/3/1975
'The Real Thing', an exhibition about the history and rediscovery of British photography; and an appraisal of the work of the Victorian photographer Dr P.H.Emerson.
FANSHEN 18/10/1975
Production of the play by David Hare, adapted from the novel by William Hinton about a village in North China, 1945–48.
d Ben Rea
lp Marty Cruickshank; Paul Freeman; Cecily Hobbs; Paul Kember
MIRROR ON CLASS 29/5/1976
Richard Hoggart talks to Melvyn Bragg about what television reveals about social class in Britain.
p Tony Cash

The SECOND MRS. TANQUERAY
(BBC 9/3/1962)
p Dorothea Brooking; *auth* Arthur W. Pinero
lp Elizabeth Sellars; Peter Williams; Margaretta Scott; Bernard Archard; Jennifer Wilson; Fiona Duncan; Desmond Llewelyn

The SECRET HOSPITAL
(Yorkshire TV 1979)
Two-part film about Rampton Hospital.
d/p John Willis
RAMPTON – THE BIG HOUSE 22/5/1979
Investigates allegations of cruelty at Rampton Hospital.
EASTDALE – THE WAY OUT 23/5/1979
The progress of Len Harding, an ex-patient of Rampton Hospital, during his stay at the Eastdale Experimental Unit.

The SECRET LIFE OF EDWARD JAMES
(ATV 26/7/1978)
Portrait of millionaire eccentric Edward James, patron of the Surrealists, who now lives with his adopted family in Mexico. James owns the world's largest collection of Surrealist paintings.
d/p Patrick Boyle

SEE IT NOW (US CBS 1951–58)
Current affairs series.
p Edward R. Murrow, Fred W. Friendly
pres Edward R. Murrow
SEE IT NOW 16/12/1951
Theodore Caudle hearing in Washington, D.C. Korean orphans. Brain research at the Massachusetts Institute of Technology. Howard K. Smith comments on the Schuman Plan for European economic cooperation. Senator Joseph McCarthy opens his campaign with a testimonial dinner.
rep Howard K. Smith
SEE IT NOW 3/2/1952
An instruments-only landing at New York's Idlewild Airport. Governor Adlai Stevenson on his presidential candidacy. Irving Berlin sings 'I like Ike'. Daily life in Berlin.
SEE IT NOW 10/2/1952
Carl Sandburg at the Lincoln Memorial. Queen Elizabeth II's proclamation following the King's death. Republican rally at Georgetown. US Sabre jet pilots in Korea.
SEE IT NOW 17/2/1952
Funeral of George VI. Korea: the ruins of Seoul. Detroit's 'baby depression': unemployment.
SEE IT NOW 25/5/1952
Averill Harriman's campaign tour of New York. Interview with Thomas Dewey. The Suez Canal controversy with scenes of British soldiers guarding the canal.

SEE IT NOW 8/6/1952
Eisenhower's activities in Washington, D.C., New York City and Abilene, Kansas. Textile industry slump in Lancashire: Nye Bevan comments on Sen. Taft; Taft comments.
SEE IT NOW 22/6/1952
Eisenhower's speech in Dallas. Sen. Taft's press conference at Washington's National Press Club. Sidney Hertzberg interviews Indian Prime Minister Jawaharlal Nehru in Delhi. Yugoslavia's break with Moscow.
SEE IT NOW 7/9/1952
Charlie Company, a Marine division at Beetle Gulch in Korea. Coach Alonzo Stagg discusses football at Susquehanna University. The presidential campaign between Eisenhower and Stevenson.
SEE IT NOW 14/9/1952
Presidential campaign. Sen. Robert Taft in Cincinatti on the Republican candidates. Canadian uranium rush.
SEE IT NOW 2/11/1952
Voting machines at Seward Park. Last-minute campaigning in the Missouri Valley, in New York City's garment district and with both Eisenhower and Stevenson at Madison Square Garden. Election opinions of milkmen in Buffalo, New York. Eisenhower and Stevenson offering opposing views on Korea and Communism.
SEE IT NOW 9/11/1952
Election night in Eisenhower's home town of Abilene, Kansas. Adlai Stevenson comments on his defeat. Michael Quill reports on the New York transit workers' strike. Bell Telephone Laboratory: two minute silence.
rep Michael Quill
SEE IT NOW 21/12/1952
Robert Trout reports from Kitty Hawk, North Carolina on the anniversary of the US Air Force. Ed Murrow and Joe Wershba report from Anchorage on US jet interjections. Bill Downs reports from Shemya (Aleutian Islands). Larry LeSueur aboard a plane flying over the international date line. Charles Collingwood reports on French Morocco; US air bases; living conditions in North Africa; the Sultan of Morocco and El Glouie.
SEE IT NOW 11/1/1953
Pre-inauguration events and preparations in Washington. Korean troops in action. Murrow interviews NATO Chief General Matthew Ridgway.
SEE IT NOW 18/1/1953
David Schoenbrun interviews French Premier René Mayer. White House correspondents 'briefing' President Eisenhower. Mock bombing of New York City demonstrating destruction after attack: last item a repeat of 29/6/52.
rep David Schoenbrun
SEE IT NOW 1/2/1953
Report from Formosa on the military strength of Nationalist China; Formosa Strait; Eisenhower speech. Report on the processing and handling of East German refugees in West Berlin.
SEE IT NOW 8/2/1953
Flood devastation in England. Former President Truman at a church supper in Independence, Missouri. Thomas Edison's New Jersey studio.
SEE IT NOW 1/3/1953
Report on Marine medal winners in Korea; film of Navy testing cold weather equipment at Mt. Washington; Italy and New York: briar pipes, tariffs, and reciprocal trade.
SEE IT NOW 15/3/1953
Judsonia, Arkansas: one year since a tornado devastated the town. Miss Parker's Social School for Washingtonians. Discussion between Ed Murrow, Averell Harriman and Ernst Reuter.
SEE IT NOW 29/3/1953
Panmunjon Cemetery in Korea. Italian land reform efforts; compares the conditions of farmers who have and have not been given their own land.
SEE IT NOW 5/4/1953
How news of peace in Korea affected the stock market in the U.S. Richard C. Hottelot interviews Konrad Adenauer on the eve of his visit to Washington. A refugee Passover service in West Berlin.

SEE IT NOW 19/4/1953
A POW's family in Rutland, Vermont; church service. Robert Pierpont reports (audio only) from Panmunjon on release of US POW's. Comment from Representatives Martin and Rayburn.
SEE IT NOW 26/4/1953
Freed US POW's at Freedom Village in Panmunjon and leaving for Tokyo. Drs Karl Menninger, Irving S. Wright and Cornelius Rhodes discuss heart disease and cancer.
SEE IT NOW 17/5/1953
Sen. William Knowland on Winston Churchill's speech. Restoration of Williamsburg, Virginia highlighted by Eisenhower's visit.
SEE IT NOW 24/5/1953
Pan-Am flight to London. Interview with General George Marshall in Leesburg.
SEE IT NOW 31/5/1953
Howard K. Smith, Ned Calmer and Richard C. Hottelet report from London on the preparations for the Coronation of Queen Elizabeth II.
rep Howard K. Smith, Ned Calmer, Richard C. Hottelet
SEE IT NOW 7/6/1953
The building of the H-Bomb plant on the Savannah river; Dr Harold Urey in Chicago discusses heavy hydrogen. Segregation in adult education classes at Shreveport, Louisiana.
BERLIN: CITY WITHOUT A COUNTRY 22/9/1953
The Cold War, focusing on Berlin.
SEE IT NOW 6/10/1953
Murrow interviews California Governor Earl Warren. 'India, 1953': report on the political, social and economic climate including an interview with Nehru.
SEE IT NOW 13/10/1953
Effects of drought in Amarillo, Texas; Agriculture Secretary Ezra Taft Benson comments. Winston Churchill at Margate.
SEE IT NOW 3/11/1953
Reports from the campaign headquarters of various New York candidates for office. Murrow interviews Gen. George C. Marshall on his Nobel Peace Prize. Joe Wershba interviews former President Truman on Gen. Marshall. Truman attacks Sen. Joe McCarthy for the Senator's attacks on Marshall. Interview with Lt. Quinn on brainwashing.
rep Joe Wershba
TRIESTE 10/11/1953
Trieste, Italy. Interviews with GIs stationed there, Italian Prime Minister Giuseppe Pella, a farmer, a restaurant owner and newspaper editors.
SEE IT NOW 24/11/1953
Air Force Secretary Harold E. Talbott admits that Lt. Milo Radulovich is not a security risk. The local American Legion's opposition to the formation of a chapter of the American Civil Liberties Union.
SEE IT NOW 1/12/1953
A debate on wiretapping between Republican Majority Leader Rep. Charles Halleck and former Federal Communications Commission Chairman James Lawrence Fly. How aluminium is made; Murrow reports from Alcoa's plant at Wenachee, Washington and Ed Scott reports from Surinam where bauxite is mined (to commemorate the 3rd year of Alcoa's sponsorship of the programme).
SEE IT NOW 5/1/1954
Horace Underwood and Percy Chen on Communist China. The influx of refugees to Hong Kong and the problems caused.
CORRESPONDENTS ON THE BIG FOUR CONFERENCE OF FOREIGN MINISTERS 16/2/1954
Discussion between Ed Murrow and reporters covering the Foreign Ministers' Berlin conference. With Don Hollenbeck, Richard C. Hottelet, Howard K. Smith of CBS, Marian Podkowinski of the Polish paper 'Express Wiczorav' and Richard Scott of the 'Manchester Guardian'.
A STUDY OF TWO CITIES 25/2/1954
Segregation in two Southern towns: Gastonia, North Carolina and Natchitoches, Louisiana.
MENTAL HEALTH 27/4/1954
Report on a mental health clinic in Louisville, Kentucky.

The FIFTH AMENDMENT AND SELF-INCRIMINATION 1/6/1954
Professors Ralph Sharp Brown of Yale and Edwin P. McManus of Georgetown debate the proper use of the Fifth Amendment. Debate includes discussion of repeal possibility and the conduct of congressional committees. (Reissued under the educational series 'Problems of Democracy').
SEE IT NOW 7/9/1954
Conversation with French Premier Pierre Mendès-France; and with the West German Chancellor Konrad Adenauer.
SEE IT NOW 28/9/1954
A 'Pro America' meeting in East Orange, New Jersey. Segregation in schools in Milford, Delaware.
A VISIT TO FLAT ROCK: CARL SANDBURG 5/10/1954
Poet Carl Sandburg on his North Carolina farm. He and Ed Murrow discuss Lincoln, language and history. He sings 'Eating Goober Peas', a Confederate song.
SEE IT NOW 7/12/1954
Interview with Professor Thomas Bailey of Stanford University. The arrival of television in Waterbury, Vermont.
STOCKMOBILE 11/1/1955
The mobile offices of Merrill, Lynch, Pierce, Fenner and Beane, which operates in towns throughout Massachusetts. Also, Columbia University professors Courtney Brown and Benjamin Graham and Senator Fulbright discuss the Stock Exchange.
REPORT ON POLIO 22/2/1955
Interview with Dr Jonas Salk about his search for a vaccine against poliomyelitis.
SEE IT NOW 8/3/1955
The McCarran-Walter Immigration Act; interview with the co-sponsor, Rep. Walter.
The SALK VACCINE 12/4/1955
Ed Murrow interviews Dr Jonas Salk and his colleagues on the day of their vaccine breakthrough against poliomyelitis.
IMMIGRATION AND RELIEF PROGRAM 17/5/1955
Interviews with people on Bedloe Island; people at a refugee centre in Berlin; E. D. Jones of Racine, Wisconsin; and a report by Scott McLeod, administrator of the programme.
REPORT ON CIGARETTES AND LUNG CANCER, PART 1 31/5/1955
First of two reports presenting cigarette-cancer arguments. Opinions from Drs Paul Kotkin, John R. Heller, Clarence Cook Little, Charles Cameron and Dr E. Cuyler Hammond of the American Cancer Society whose recent report refuelled the controversy. Also Timothy V. Hartnett of the Tobacco Industry Research Committee.
REPORT ON CIGARETTES AND LUNG CANCER, PART 2 7/6/1955
Second of two reports on smoking and cancer featuring medical and industry spokesmen including Dr Elmer Hess of the American Medical Association.
SEE IT NOW 14/6/1955
The status of subscription television in America; interviews with Dean James M. Landis, Brooklyn Dodgers owner Walter O'Malley, Robert Sherwood, CBS President Dr Frank Stanton, P.A.Sugg and a man in an Oklahoma City street.
SEE IT NOW 5/7/1955
SEE IT NOW's final broadcast as a regularly scheduled programme. Features excerpts from the past season's shows.
The SECRET LIFE OF DANNY KAYE 2/12/1956
Danny Kaye's 50,000 mile trip abroad as ambassador for UNICEF. He interviews Sir Anthony Eden, David Ben-Gurion, Marshal Tito and French President René Coty.

CLINTON AND THE LAW: A STUDY IN DESEGREGATION 6/1/1957
The problems confronting communities attempting to comply with the 1954 Supreme Court order on desegregation in public schools. Interviews with townspeople of Clinton, Tennessee on the events leading to the assault on a Baptist minister who escorted six Negro youngsters to Clinton High school, which led to the state militia coming in with tanks and tear gas.
rep Arthur Morse
BURMA, BUDDHISM AND NEUTRALISM 3/2/1957
Looks at Burma. Includes interview with Premier U Nu, leader of the anti-fascist People's Freedom League, the country's governing political party. Nu explains the nature of Buddhism and leads a tour of Burma's religious centres. Also shows films of the Burmese parliament and cabinet in session; a look at the life of a rice farmer; a visit with Dr Gordon Seagrave, famed 'Burma Surgeon' of World War II, at his hospital in Namkham.
pres Paul Niven
POLAND, 1957 31/3/1957
Report on the Polish political climate since the 1956 revolution. Religion; rock 'n' roll; the rise of anti-Semitism. Interviews with Premier Joseph Cyrankiewicz, Polish journalists, Jewish families about to emigrate to Israel, and workers who participated in the Poznan riots. A sermon by Cardinal Wyszynski; the opening of the Polish Parliament; Warsaw University,; nightclubs; TV studios; the Frederic Chopin Society.
rep Daniel Schorr
PUERTO RICANS: AMERICANS ON THE MOVE 5/5/1957
The migration of Puerto Ricans to the USA and the problems caused. In Puerto Rica: San Juan slums; interview with Governor Luis Munoz-Mari and a report on his 'Operation Bootstrap' self-help program for housing, industry and education. In New York City: housing, racial and assimilation problems; discussion with government officials, social workers and Puerto Ricans; adult education classes; a Bronx factory where almost all the employees are Puerto Rican immigrants.
ATOMIC TIMETABLE: FISSION, FUSION AND ABUNDANCE 24/11/1957
First of two 'ATOMIC TIMETABLE' programmes exploring recent developments in the adaptation of atomic energy to peaceful uses, such as food preservation, uranium reclamation and nuclear power. Interviews with AEC Chairman Adm. Lewis L. Strauss, Rear Adm. Hyman G. Rickover, physicist Dr Edward Teller, and British scientists Sir John Cockcroft and Sir Christopher Hinton.
rep Charles Collingwood, Arthur Morse
ATOMIC TIMETABLE: RADIATION AND FALLOUT 30/3/1958
The second of two 'ATOMIC TIMETABLE' programmes. Looks at whether atomic testing should be halted because of the dangers of radioactive fallout. Shows a plane flying through a mushroom cloud; the underground detonation of a nuclear device; the 'Lucky Dragon', the Japanese fishing craft whose crew became accidental fallout victims; microscopic films of human cells affected by radiation; experiments on animals and humans; how fallout is measured and the benefits of radioactive isotopes. Interviews with geneticist Hermann Muller, chemist J. Laurence Kulp and AEC officials Willard Libby and Merrill Eisenbud.
WATCH ON THE RUHR 7/7/1958
Post-war Germany and its industrial rejuvenation: interviews with Defence Minister Franz Josef Strauss; Economy Minister Ludwig Erhard; labour, business and press spokespeople. An assessment of Germany's moral feeling: interviews with soldiers on their feelings about Hitler; students at Cologne University; the reaction of a Dusseldorf audience to the play 'The Diary of Anne Frank'.

SEGOVIA AT LOS OLIVOS (BBC 5/5/1968)
Andres Segovia, at his home in Andalusia, reflects on his career, and plays several guitar pieces.
d/comm Christopher Nupen

SEND FOSTER
(Rediffusion 6/7–22/9/1967)
Series for children.
HOLE IN THE ROAD 6/7/1967
d/p Geoffrey Hughes; *sc* George Markstein
lp Hayward Morse; Polly James; Patrick Newell; Garfield Morgan; Frank Tregear; Peter Macann

SET OF SIX (Granada 1972)
Regional series of six programmes of pop music.
SET OF SIX 24/5/1972
d Terry Heneberry; *p* M. Young

SEVEN ARTISTS (BBC 11/7–22/8/1979)
Seven-part documentary series on contemporary artists.
exec.p Julia Cave, Barrie Gavin
ROY LICHTENSTEIN 11/7/1979
d Geoffrey Haydon
ANTONI TAPIES 18/7/1979
d David Gladwell
VICTOR PASMORE 25/7/1979
p/sc John Mansfield
DUANE HANSON 8/8/1979
d Ian Sharp
JULIO LE PARC 15/8/1979
d John Hooper
EDWARD RUSCHA 22/8/1979
d Geoffrey Haydon

SEVEN DEADLY SINS
(Rediffusion 1966)
Anthology drama series.
MY FRIEND CORBY 9/5/1966
d Christopher Hodson; *sc* Paul Jones
lp Nigel Stock; Vivien Merchant; Patrick Allen
The ERPINGHAM CAMP 27/6/1966
d James Ormerod; *sc* Joe Orton
lp Reginald Marsh; Peter Reeves; Faith Kent; Angela Pleasence

SEVEN DEADLY VIRTUES
(Rediffusion 1967)
Anthology drama series.
exec.p Peter Willes
IT'S YOUR MOVE 30/3/1967
d Christopher Hodson; *sc* Bill Naughton
lp Colin Blakely; Avis Bunnage; Christopher Mitchell; Jack Watson; James Kerry; Michael Robbins; Russell Waters
The GOOD AND FAITHFUL SERVANT 6/4/1967
d James Ormerod; *sc* Joe Orton
lp Donald Pleasence; Hermione Baddeley; Patricia Routledge; Sheila White; Richard O'Callaghan; Jack Bligh
The WHOLE TRUTH 27/4/1967
d James Ormerod; *sc* John Bowen
lp Kenneth Farrington; John Nettleton; Vivian Pickles; Angela Pleasence; Tim Preece; Robert Urquhart; Windsor Davies

SEVEN FACES OF WOMAN
(LWT 2/6–14/7/1974)
Series of seven plays.
POLLY PUT THE KETTLE ON 23/6/1974
d Michael Lindsay-Hogg; *p* Richard Doubleday; *sc* Jack Rosenthal
lp Sylvia Kay; Susan Penhaligon; John Rae; David Ryall; David Lincoln; Eric Carte; Linda Regan

SEVEN MEN
(Granada 27/2–8/5/1971)
Interview series.
QUENTIN CRISP 13/3/1971
Made for Granada Television in 1970 as one of a series of 'personal portraits'. It is an interview with Quentin Crisp before he became famous as 'The Naked Civil Servant'. It represents a departure from Mitchell's familiar style of filmmaking in that it is a continuous interview with a single subject and shot on location in Crisp's small flat in Soho. It was also the director's first programme to be made in colour.
d/p Denis Mitchell

SEVEN PLUS SEVEN
(Granada 15/12/1970)
A sequel to SEVEN UP where children with different backgrounds were interviewed. (Shown in the WORLD IN ACTION series *tx* 5/5/1964). See also TWENTY ONE UP (1977). This film shows the same children at the age of fourteen. The interviews are intercut with parts of the original film of the children aged seven showing how they and their attitudes have changed.
d Michael Apted

SEVEN TO ONE (BBC 17/2–7/4/1979)
Interview/discussion series in which seven members of the public talk to a celebrity of their choice.
ANNA RAEBURN 7/4/1979
d Peter Hamilton; *p* Derek Towers

SEVENTH WINTER OLYMPICS – SLALOM AND FIGURE SKATING (BBC 31/1/1956)
The slalom and figure skating events from the Winter Olympics at Cortina D'Ampezzo. Competitors include Michael Booker, Hays Jenkins and Ronnie Robertson.

77 SUNSET STRIP
(US Warner Bros. 1958–64)
Inspired by the novel 'The Double Take' by Roy Huggins about a private detective agency run by Stuart Bailey.
regulars Efrem Zimbalist Jr; Roger Smith; Edward Byrnes
LOVELY LADY, PITY ME 17/10/1958
d Stuart Heisler; *p* Howie Horwitz
lp Kathleen Crowley; Peter Breck; Jeanne Cooper
A NICE SOCIAL EVENING 24/10/1958
d Stuart Heisler; *p* Howie Horwitz
lp Ray Danton
The BOUNCING CHIP 7/11/1958
d Leslie H. Martinson; *p* Roy Huggins
lp Brad Dexter; Ruta Lee; Ray Teal; Russ Conway
The KOOKIE CAPER 9/10/1959
p Roy Huggins
lp Will Hutchins; Sherry Jackson
TIGER BY THE TAIL 3/3/1961
d Sutton Roley; *p* Howie Horwitz;
sc Fenton Earnshaw
lp Louis Quinn; John Van Dreelen; Sharon Hugueny; Merry Anders; Theodore Marcuse

SEX EDUCATION IN PRIMARY SCHOOLS
(BBC 13/1–10/2/1970)
Five-part series, for parents and teachers, previewing an instructional series designed for 8–9 year olds.
d Anita Sterner; *p* Geoffrey Hall;
pres Magnus Magnusson
GROWING UP 20/1/1970
BEGINNING 27/1/1970
BIRTH 3/2/1970
FULL CIRCLE 10/2/1970

The SEXTET (BBC 13/6–1/8/1972)
Series of eight individual plays performed by the same group of six actors.
FOLLOW THE YELLOW BRICK ROAD 4/7/1972
d Alan Bridges; *p* Rod Graham;
sc Dennis Potter
lp Denholm Elliott; Michele Dotrice; Ruth Dunning; Nicolette Pendrell; Billie Whitelaw; Maureen Nelson; Richard Vernon; Dennis Waterman

SEXTON BLAKE (Rediffusion 1967–69)
Detective series for children.
The FIND THE LADY AFFAIR: EPISODE 1: THE LADY VANISHES 25/9/1967
d Adrian Cooper; *p* Ronald Marriott;
sc Max Oberman
lp Laurence Payne; Roger Foss; Dorothea Phillips; Wallas Eaton; Hugh Futcher; Ernest Clark

SEZ LES (Yorkshire TV 1969–76)
Comedy show starring Les Dawson, with Roy Barraclough.

SEZ LES 25/1/1974
d David Mallett; *p* Bill Hitchcock;
with Eli Woods, John Cleese, Lulu
SEZ LES 1/2/1974
d David Mallett; *p* Bill Hitchcock;
with Eli Woods, John Cleese, Marian Montgomery
SEZ LES 8/2/1974
d David Mallett; *p* Bill Hitchcock;
with Eli Woods, John Cleese, Francis Van Dyke
SEZ LES 15/2/1974
d David Mallett; *p* Bill Hitchcock;
with Eli Woods, John Cleese, Kenny Ball and his Jazzmen
SEZ LES 1/3/1974
d David Mallett; *p* Bill Hitchcock;
with Eli Woods, John Cleese, Salena Jones
SEZ LES 8/3/1974
d David Mallett; *with* Eli Woods, John Cleese
SEZ LES 22/11/1974
d David Mallett; *with* Eli Woods, Lynsey De Paul, John Cleese
SEZ LES 19/10/1976
d/p Vernon Lawrence

SHADES OF GREENE (Thames 1975–76)
Series of adaptations of Graham Greene stories.
The BLUE FILM 14/10/1975
d Philip Saville; *p* Alan Cooke;
sc John Mortimer
lp Betsy Blair; Brian Cox; Koo Stark; Al Lampert
The OVERNIGHT BAG 3/2/1976
d Peter Hammond; *p* Alan Cooke;
sc Clive Exton
lp Tim Brooke-Taylor; Joyce Carey; Eleanor Summerfield; Dudley Sutton
UNDER THE GARDEN 10/2/1976
d/p Alan Cooke; *sc* Robin Chapman
lp Denholm Elliott; Vivian Pickles; Bruce Purchase; Arthur Lowe; George Roubicek; Tony Steedman

SHADOW IN THE CLOUDS
(BBC 18/7/1966)
A history of airships.
p Harry Hastings; *sc* Douglas Botting;
nar Anthony Smith

SHADOW OF AN IRON MAN
(Scottish TV 22/7/1973)
Zambia, its geography, economy, education and the effects of missionary work begun by Livingstone. Introduced by Colin Morris.
d Richmond Harding; *voice* Simon Lach

SHADOWS (Thames 1975–76; 1978)
Series of plays for children dealing with the supernatural.
The MAN WHO HATED CHILDREN 18/10/1978
d Neville Green; *p* Pamela Lonsdale;
sc Brian Patten
lp George A. Cooper; Brian Wilde; Charles Morgan; James Ottaway; Paul Watson

SHAKESPEARE IN PERSPECTIVE
(BBC 1978–85)
Series designed to back up the BBC TELEVISION SHAKESPEARE series. Writers, critics, politicians and entertainers offer their personal views on specific Shakespeare plays, usually to be transmitted later the same evening.
RICHARD II 10/12/1978
d Barbara Derkow; *p* Victor Poole;
pres Paul Johnson

SHANG A LANG (Granada 1/4–26/8/1975)
Pop music show featuring The Bay City Rollers.
SHANG A LANG 1/4/1975
d David Warwick; *p* Muriel Young;
with Lieutenant Pigeon, Big Jim Sullivan

SHARON (Granada 9/12/1964)
A divine healing campaign at the Sharon Full Gospel Church, Manchester, with pastors William Barratt and Arthur Williams.
p Denis Mitchell

A SHARP INTAKE OF BREATH (ATV 1979)
Comedy series centered around a newly-married couple.
YOUR VERY GOOD HEALTH 26/2/1979
d/p Les Chatfield; *sc* Ronnie Taylor
lp David Jason; Jacqueline Clarke; Richard Wilson; Alun Armstrong; Maggie Jones; Nigel Humphreys; Tamar Cooper

SHE (LWT 17/4–22/5/1977)
Six-part series of plays based on a central female character.
ANXIOUS ANNE 15/5/1977
d Gerry Mill; *sc* Howard Schuman
lp Beth Porter; Phyllida Law; Donald Sumpter; Charlotte Mitchell; Harold Kasket; Denis Lawson; Lynda Marchal; Julie Covington

SHELLEY (Thames 1979–)
Comedy series about a cynical, unemployed Londoner.
The NELSON TOUCH 19/7/1979
d/p Anthony Parker; *sc* Peter Tilbury
lp Hywel Bennett; Belinda Sinclair; Josephine Tewson; Rowena Roberts; Kenneth Cope; Nicholas Le Prevost

SHEPHERD (Anglia 20/1/1968)
The work done by the modern-day shepherd.
d Harry Aldous

SHIRLEY BASSEY (BBC 1976; 1979)
Variety show.
SHIRLEY BASSEY 13/11/1976
p Stewart Morris; *with* Johnny Nash
SHIRLEY BASSEY 27/11/1976
p Stewart Morris; *with* Mel Tormé, Clive Westlake

SHIRLEY'S WORLD (ATV 1972)
The adventures of Shirley Logan, a globetrotting photographer.
p Barry Delmaine
regulars Shirley Maclaine; John Gregson
THOU SHALT NOT BE FOUND OUT 28/1/1972
d Ray Austin; *sc* Peter Miller
lp Nigel Davenport; Lelia Goldoni; Jeremy Lloyd
The DEFECTIVE DEFECTOR 4/2/1972
d Ray Austin;
sc John Muir, Brian Degas
lp Stuart Damon; Bill Nagy
The LOVERS 11/2/1972
d Ray Austin; *sc* Peter Miller
lp Akiko Wakabayashi; Tetsu Nakamura; Riko Miura; Shinzo Hotta; Koji Kawamura
The ISLANDERS 18/2/1972
d Charles Crichton; *sc* Lewis Schwarz
lp Peter Dyneley; Sally Thomsett; Roddy McMillan; Gerald Sim; Ronald Adam; Derek Anders
FOLLOW THAT RICKSHAW 26/3/1972
d Ralph Levy;
sc Tom Brennand, Roy Bottomley
lp Joe Baker; Murray Head; Barbara Yu Ling
A GIRL LIKE YOU 9/4/1972
d Ray Austin; *sc* Anthony Skene
lp Rodney Bewes; Una Stubbs; Yoko Tani
EVIDENCE IN CAMERA 16/4/1972
d Ralph Levy; *sc* T.E.B. Clarke
lp Kathy Eu; Norman Bird; Kim Smith
The RALLY 23/4/1972
d Peter Hunt; *sc* Peter Miller
lp Neil Hallett; Aimi MacDonald; Ann Beach; John Glyn-Jones; Kim Smith
FIGURATIVELY SPEAKING 30/4/1972
d Ralph Levy; *sc* Patrick Alexander
lp Jacqui Chan; Patrick Newell; Robert Rothman
KNIGHTMARE 7/5/1972
d Peter Sasdy; *sc* Jeremy Burnham
lp John Neville; Brian Blessed; James Villiers; Graham Crowden; Fabia Drake

The SHOALS OF HERRING
(BBC 15/9/1972)
A documentary based on 'Singing the Fishing' by Ewan MacColl, Peggy Seeger and Charles Parker which won the Italian Press Association for radio documentary, Italia 1960. The programme uses music and voices of the radio ballad and sets them against archive film to tell the story of the rise and decline of the herring industry on the east coast of Scotland and England.
p/sc Philip Donnellan;
with Ewan MacColl, A.L. Lloyd, Ian Campbell, Peggy Seeger

SHOESTRING (BBC 1979–80)
Private eye series.
regulars Trevor Eve; Michael Medwin, Doran Godwin; Liz Crowther
PRIVATE EAR 30/9/1979
d Douglas Camfield; *p/sc* Robert Banks Stewart
lp William Russell
KNOCK FOR KNOCK 7/10/1979
d Roger Tucker; *sc* Bob Baker
lp Shirley Anne Field; Cassie McFarlane;
Dominic Guard; Christopher Guard;
Mervyn Johns; Aimée Delamain;
Malcolm Terris
HIGHER GROUND 14/10/1979
d Marek Kanievska; *sc* Dave Humphries
lp Glyn Houston; Anna Cropper;
Derek Anders
NINE TENTHS OF THE LAW 4/11/1979
d Marek Kanievska; *sc* Peter Miller
lp Harry H. Corbett; Geraldine James;
Neil Campbell; Karl Johnson; Fiona Scott
The LINK-UP 11/11/1979
d Douglas Camfield; *sc* Peter King
lp Janet Key; John Gregg; John Woodnutt;
Keith Buckley; Mela White
FIND THE LADY 2/12/1979
d Marek Kanievska; *sc* Philip Martin
lp Christopher Biggins; Gary Holton;
Toyah Willcox; Peter Dean; Lynda Bellingham;
Diana Weston

The SHOOT (Thames 1/2/1978)
Documentary on the gamekeeper's year.
d/p Richard Broad

SHOP FLOOR (BBC 6/10–18/11/1965)
A series of eight programmes examining problems in labour relations. Shown in the 'Outlook' series.
The WORKS COMMUNITY 6/10/1965
Factors influencing the sharply contrasting labour relations at the Leeds & Kirkby works of Yorkshire Imperial Metals.
d Nancy Thomas; *p* Tony Mathews

The SHOP OF GHOSTS
(Tyne Tees 2/1/1977)
Richard Todd reads G.K.Chesterton's story for Christmas.
d Lisle Willis

SHORT STORY
(Scottish TV 16/4–29/7/1972)
Anthology play series.
SANCTUARY 1972
sc David Edgar
lp Thorley Walters; Michael Balfour
BLOCH'S PLAY 11/6/1972
d/p Brian Mahoney; *sc* Cecil P. Taylor
lp Roddy McMillan; Maggie Jordan

SHOTGUN (BBC 11/7/1966)
d/p John McGrath;
sc John McGrath, Christopher Williams
lp Nigel Davenport; Shirley Anne Field;
Zena Walker; Petra Markham; Edward Fox;
Clive Graham; Wendy Varnals;
Patricia Garwood

SHOUDU BAIWAN JUN-MIN LONGZHONG JIHUI QINGZHU DA SHENGLI (CN Beijing Television 1976)
A rally in Tiananmen Square to celebrate the overthrow and arrest of the 'Gang of Four'. Title translates as: A Million Troops and Civilians Celebrate A Great Victory in the Capital.

SHOULDER TO SHOULDER
(BBC 3/4–8/5/1974)
Six-part series dramatising the Suffragette Movement.
p Verity Lambert
The PANKHURSTS 3/4/1974
d Waris Hussein; *sc* Ken Taylor
lp Siân Phillips; Angela Down;
Kenneth McClennan; Sylvia Kay; Jane Knowles;
Patricia Quinn
ANNIE KENNEY 10/4/1974
d Waris Hussein; *sc* Alan Plater
lp Georgia Brown; Siân Phillips;
Angela Down; Patricia Quinn; Sheila Allen;
Ronald Hines; Fulton Mackay; Anne Dyson
LADY CONSTANCE LYTTON 17/4/1974
d Waris Hussein; *sc* Douglas Livingstone
lp Judy Parfitt; Georgia Brown;
Siân Phillips; Patricia Quinn;
Patience Collier; Sheila Allen; Jonathan Newth;
Pam St. Clement
CHRISTABEL PANKHURST 24/4/1974
d Moira Armstrong; *sc* Ken Taylor
lp Patricia Quinn; Georgia Brown;
Siân Phillips; Angela Down; Sheila Allen;
Ronald Hines; Robert Hardy; Fulton Mackay;
Maureen Pryor
OUTRAGE 1/5/1974
d Moira Armstrong; *sc* Hugh Whitemore
lp Siân Phillips; Georgia Brown;
Angela Down; Patricia Quinn; Maureen Pryor;
Sheila Ballantine; Bob Hoskins
SYLVIA PANKHURST 8/5/1974
d Waris Hussein; *sc* Ken Taylor
lp Angela Down; Georgia Brown;
Siân Phillips; Patricia Quinn; Fulton Mackay;
Andonia Katsaros; Michael Gough

A SHOW CALLED FRED
(Rediffusion 1956)
Comedy series. Follow-up series was SON OF FRED.
d Richard Lester; *sc* Spike Milligan;
with Peter Sellers, Spike Milligan,
Valentine Dyall, Kenneth Connor,
Graham Stark, Patti Lewis, Max Geldray
A SHOW CALLED FRED 2/5/1956
A SHOW CALLED FRED 9/5/1956
A SHOW CALLED FRED 30/5/1956

SHOW OF THE WEEK (BBC 1965–75)
Series of variety shows.
IN ALL DIRECTIONS 26/4/1966
Sketch comedy show.
p Michael Mills; *with* Peter Ustinov,
Peter Jones
TONY BENNETT AND COUNT BASIE 15/6/1969
Music 'spectacular' featuring Tony Bennett and Count Basie.
p Terry Henebery
DAVE ALLEN AT LARGE 12/3/1973
Comedy show with Dave Allen, Jacqueline Clarke, Ronnie Brody, Michael Sharvell-Martin, Peter Hawkins and Robert East.
p Peter Whitmore

SHOWTIME (BBC 4/10–13/12/1959)
Variety show hosted by David Nixon.
SHOWTIME 4/10/1959
d Graeme Muir; *with* Chico Marx,
Eve Boswell, Mata and Hari.

SHUT THAT DOOR! (ATV 1972–73)
Comedy show hosted by Larry Grayson.
SHUT THAT DOOR! 22/9/1972
p Colin Clews; *with* Diana Dors

SIBERIA – THE GREAT EXPERIMENT
(BBC 28/4/1966)
A record of life and work in the Akademgorodok, the academic community established near Novosibirsk.
d Philip Daly

SIGHT AND SOUND IN CONCERT
(BBC 1972–78)
Series of popular music broadcasts.
The following editions are all *d* Tom Corcoran;
p Michael Appleton, except where noted.
JOHN MILES 5/2/1977
GALLAGHER AND LYLE 5/3/1977
CAMEL 1/10/1977
ELKIE BROOKS 8/10/1977
RACING CARS AND JOHN MARTYN 15/10/1977
SPLIT ENZ AND LEO KOTTKE 22/10/1977
LONE STAR AND THE PAT TRAVERS BAND 5/11/1977
SUPERTRAMP 19/11/1977
The STEVE GIBBONS BAND 26/11/1977
NAZARETH 3/12/1977
d John Burrows
DR FEELGOOD AND IAN DURY AND THE BLOCKHEADS 10/12/1977
ALBERTO Y LOST TRIOS PARANOIAS 17/12/1977
COLOSSEUM II AND RICHARD DIGANCE 14/1/1978
GENTLE GIANT 21/1/1978
GORDON GILTRAP AND MICHAEL CHAPMAN 28/1/1978
BE-BOP DELUXE AND JENNY DARREN 4/2/1978
GILBERT O'SULLIVAN AND CHRIS DE BURGH 11/2/1978
The STRAWBS 18/2/1978
LOUDON WAINWRIGHT III 25/2/1978
STEEL PULSE AND XTC 25/3/1978
d John Burrows
FRANKIE MILLER AND SAMMY MITCHELL 1/4/1978

The SIGNALMAN (BBC 22/12/1976)
Dramatisation of the story by Charles Dickens.
d Lawrence Gordon Clark; *p* Rosemary Hill;
sc Andrew Davies
lp Denholm Elliott; Bernard Lloyd;
Carina Wyeth; Reginald Jessup

The SILVER COLLECTION
(Granada 23/5/1971)
Play about a young couple who are attracted to each other yet, intellectually, are miles apart.
d Alan Gibson; *p* James Brabazon;
sc Susan Pleat
lp Helen Mirren; Billy Murray;
Cyril Luckham; Bill Gavin; Elizabeth Bennett;
Dorothea Rundle

The SILVER JUBILEE REVIEW AT SPITHEAD (Southern TV 28/6/1977)
Queen Elizabeth II reviews the fleet at Spithead.
pres Cliff Michelmore, Barry Westwood

The SILVER SWORD (BBC 1957–58)
Seven-part serial telling the story of some Polish children who were made homeless by World War II.
p Shaun Sutton; *sc* C.E. Webber;
auth Ian Serraillier
regulars Pat Pleasance; Melvyn Hayes;
Ingrid Sylvester
EPISODE 1: ESCAPE FROM THE NAZIS 24/11/1957
lp Barry Letts; Gwen Watford;
Barbara Cavan; Garth Adams; Patrick Cargill;
Alan Browning; Richard Carpenter
EPISODE 2: ESCAPE FROM PRISON 1/12/1957
lp Barry Letts; John Woodnutt;
John Heller; Gladys Spencer; Philip Morant;
Helen Misener; Frazer Hines
EPISODE 3: BURNING OF THE CITY 8/12/1957
lp Michael Kent; Gertan Klauber;
Frazer Hines; Graham Harper; Judy Horn;
Colin Douglas; Tim Hudson
EPISODE 4: RETURN OF EDEK 15/12/1957
lp Frazer Hines; Nigel Arkwright;
Carl Bernard; Sally Travers; Bruce Stewart;
Alaric Cotter; Enid Lindsey

EPISODE 5: JAN IN TROUBLE 22/12/1957
lp Frazer Hines; Reed De Rouen;
Bill Edwards; Gordon Tanner; Alan Tilvern;
Richard Carpenter
EPISODE 6: ESCAPE FROM BAVARIA 29/12/1957
lp George Woodbridge; Frazer Hines;
Brenda Dunrich; Peter Bull; Roger Delgado
EPISODE 7: THE LAST LAP 5/1/1958
lp Frazer Hines; Michael Balfour;
Peggy Thorpe-Bates; Philip Latham; Ivor Salter;
Barry Letts; Gwen Watford

SINBAD JR.
(US American International Productions 1965)
Animation series.
SINBAD JR. AND THE POACHED POACHERS
1965
d Sid Marcus; *exec.p* Sam Singer
SINBAD JR. IN SHAKE THE BOTTLE 1965
d Reuben Timmins; *exec.p* Sam Singer
SINBAD JR. OUT WEST 1965
d Reuben Timmins; *exec.p* Sam Singer
SINBAD JR. WITH S.K. MOE 1965
d Reuben Timmins; *exec.p* Sam Singer

SINFONIA (Tyne Tees 1979)
Series featuring the Northern Sinfonia.
BEHIND BOW TIES 14/5/1979

SINGING FOR YOUR SUPPER
(Scottish TV 6/8–8/10/1968)
Nine-part introduction to opera.
FULL CIRCLE 8/10/1968
A performance of Robin Orr's one-act opera
'Full Circle', with the Scottish Opera Chamber
Orchestra conducted by Alexander Gibson.
d Bryan Izzard

The SINNERS (Granada 1970–71)
Series of comedy plays set in Ireland.
IN THE BOSOM OF THE COUNTRY 9/9/1970
d Barry Davis; *p/sc* Brian Armstrong;
auth Sean O'Faolain
lp Barbara Jefford; John Carson;
Cyril Cusack; Elizabeth Tyrell; Will Leighton

SIR MICHAEL BALCON – FILM MAKER
(Thames 12/6/1969)
Sir Michael Balcon is interviewed by Shaw
Taylor at the National Film Theatre. Extracts
are shown from some of his productions.
p Steve Minchin

SIX (BBC 12/12/1964–16/1/1965)
A series of six plays.
DIARY OF A NOBODY 12/12/1964
Comedy based on the novel by George and
Weedon Grossmith.
d Ken Russell; *p* John McGrath;
sc Ken Russell, John McGrath
lp Bryan Pringle; Avril Elgar;
Murray Melvin; Brian Murphy; Jonathan Cecil;
Anne Jameson; Vivian Pickles

SIX DATES WITH BARKER
(LWT 8/1–12/2/1971)
Comedy series featuring Ronnie Barker.
The ODD JOB 22/1/1971
d Maurice Murphy; *p* Humphrey Barclay;
sc Bernard McKenna
lp Ronnie Barker; Joan Sims; David Jason

SIX DAYS IN SEPTEMBER
(BBC 29/9/1979)
Made while a major retrospective of the work of
abstract artist John Hoyland was in preparation
at the Serpentine Gallery in 1979, the film
follows the painting of 'Offspring' for six days in
his studio, from a blank canvas to its hanging in
the exhibition.
d Judy Marle; *p* Alan Yentob

SIX DAYS OF JUSTICE
(Thames 1972–75)
Series of courtroom dramas.
WE'LL SUPPORT YOU EVERMORE 15/5/1973
d Piers Haggard; *p* Peter Duguid;
sc Shane Connaughton
lp Mona Washbourne; Norman Atkyns;
Joyce Parry; Tony Caunter; Christopher Good;
Brian Pettifer; Peter Hugo Daly;
Gretchen Franklin

SIX FACES OF ROYALTY
(BBC 5/1–9/2/1973)
Six-part series in which Roy Strong discusses the
portraits of six British monarchs.
CHARLES II – THE NEW IMAGE OF MONARCHY
26/1/1973
p Derek Trimby

SIX-FIVE SPECIAL (BBC 1957–58)
Pop music series. Follow-up series was 'Dig
This!'.
SIX-FIVE SPECIAL 22/11/1958
The last edition of the pop music show.
p Russell Turner; *intro* Jim Dale;
with The Six-Five Dates, Joan Regan,
Lita Roza, Malcolm Vaughan, The Mudlarks,
Ronnie Carroll, Don Rennie, Des O'Connor,
Jerry Angelo, Sheila Clarke, The Avon Sisters,
Tony Osborne and his Brasshats,
The Tito Burns 6.5ers

The SIX WIVES OF HENRY VIII
(BBC 1/1–5/2/1970)
Historical drama.
p Ronald Travers, Mark Shivas
regular Keith Michell
CATHERINE OF ARAGON 1/1/1970
d John Glenister; *sc* Rosemary Anne Sisson
lp Annette Crosbie; Dorothy Tutin;
Patrick Troughton; John Woodnutt;
Ken Wynne; Sally Travers; Donald Bisset;
Margaret Ford
ANNE BOLEYN 8/1/1970
d Naomi Capon, John Glenister;
sc Nick McCarty
lp Dorothy Tutin; Anne Stallybrass;
Patrick Troughton; Sheila Burrell;
Michael Osborne; Hilary Mason;
Jonathan Newth
JANE SEYMOUR 15/1/1970
d John Glenister; *sc* Ian Thorne
lp Anne Stallybrass; Patrick Troughton;
Sheila Burrell; Daniel Moynihan; Gillian Bailey;
Dorothy Black; John Ronane; Bernard Hepton
ANNE OF CLEVES 22/1/1970
d John Glenister; *sc* Jean Morris
lp Elvi Hale; Angela Pleasence;
Patrick Troughton; Sheila Burrell;
Bernard Hepton; Wolfe Morris; Basil Dignam;
Patrick Godfrey
CATHERINE HOWARD 29/1/1970
d Naomi Capon; *sc* Beverley Cross
lp Angela Pleasence; Patrick Troughton;
Sheila Burrell; Julia Cornelius; Catherine Lacey;
Ralph Bates; Howard Goorney; Sue Bishop
CATHERINE PARR 5/2/1970
d Naomi Capon; *sc* John Prebble
lp Rosalie Crutchley; John Ronane;
Howard Goorney; Daniel Moynihan;
Basil Dignam; Bernard Hepton;
Patrick Godfrey; Alison Frazer

**The SIXTH PAUL: THE POPE IN THE
MIDDLE** (Rediffusion 9/7/1968)
A report on Pope Paul VI and the Catholic
Church.
d Randal Beattie; *p* Jeremy Isaacs;
nar George Scott

SKIPPY THE BUSH KANGAROO
(AU Norfolk International Films 1966–68)
Series about a family with a pet kangaroo.
d Eric Fullilove;
p Lee Robinson, Joy Cavill
regulars Ed Devereaux; Tony Bonner;
Ken James; Liza Goddard
BON VOYAGE 1968
COBBER 1968
HI-FI 1968
TIGER 1968
TREASURE HUNT 1968

The SKY AT NIGHT (BBC 1957–)
Astronomy series.
ASTRONOMY IN RUSSIA 7/11/1960
Patrick Moore talks about his recent visit to the
principal observatories in the USSR.
d Peter Bennet Stronc; *p* Paul Johnstone
LIFE ON MARS 20/3/1961
Patrick Moore and Dr F.L. Jackson discuss the
planet Mars.
d Michael Johnston

The SLAUGHTER OF ST. TERESA'S DAY
(BBC 6/4/1962)
Play about a tough, female bookie who holds a
party where the guests are people she has
quarrelled with in the past year.
p John Jacobs; *sc* Peter Kenna
lp Susannah York; Madge Ryan;
Molly Urquhart; Margaret Wedlake;
Ethel Gabriel; Maggie Fitzgibbon;
Johnny Briggs; Vincent Ball; John Tate;
Reg Lye; J.G. Devlin

The SLEEPING BEAUTY
(BBC 20/12/1959)
A performance of Tchaikovsky's 'The Sleeping
Beauty', with Margot Fonteyn, Michael Somes,
Lucette Aldous, Yvonne Cartier, Antoinette
Sibley, Audrey Farris, June Lesley and Prudence
Rodney. The Royal Opera House Orchestra is
conducted by John Lanchbery.
d/p Margaret Dale

The SLIMMING DISEASE (ATV 31/1/1974)
A report on anorexia nervosa in Britain.
d Robin Brown

SMALL BUILDER (BBC 1971)
Series for principals and managers of small
construction firms.
d Mike Weatherley; *p* Michael Garrod
BUILDING A BUSINESS 10/1/1971
BUILDING IN TIMBER 31/1/1971

SMALL TIME (Rediffusion 1963)
Puppet series for children.
The MUSICAL BOX 1963
with Muriel Young, Wally Whyton

SMALL WORLD (US CBS 1958–60)
Discussion programme. Edward R. Murrow in
New York linked via telephone and radio with
internationally known figures in different parts of
the world.
d Edward R. Murrow, Fred W. Friendly
SMALL WORLD 7/12/1958
With pianist Artur Rubinstein in Paris; poet
Archibald MacLeish in Washington, D.C.; and
President of the Union of Polish Writers, Antoni
Slonimski, in Warsaw.
SMALL WORLD 3/4/1960
With British historian Arnold Toynbee in
London; British author Robert Graves in
Washington, D.C.; and American writer Phillip
Wylie in Miami. Eric Sevareid moderates a
discussion on ethics and morality in the atomic
age.
SMALL WORLD 9/4/1960
Discussion on the H-bomb, nuclear tests and
freedom of speech.
SMALL WORLD 30/4/1960
Second programme which discusses the H-bomb,
nuclear tests and freedom of speech.

SMASHING DAY (BBC 17/8/1962)
Play about a young man's drift from diffidence
into marriage and responsibility.
p Vivian A. Daniels; *sc* Alan Plater
lp Alfred Lynch; June Barry; Angela Douglas;
John Thaw; Charles Denville; Mary Quinn;
Douglas Ives

SMUGA CIENIA
(PL/GB Film Polski-Thames; GB *tx* 1/7/1976)
Dramatised documentary about Joseph Conrad's
adventures as a young British sea captain in the
1880s. Shown on ITV as 'The Shadow Line'.
d Michael Darlow, Andrzej Wajda;
p Barbara Pec-Slesicka, Jolyon Wimhurst;
sc Boleslaw Sulik
lp Marek Kondrat; Graham Lines;
Tom Wilkinson; Bernard Archard;
John Bennett; Martin Wyldeck;
Richard Bartlett; Peter Cartwright

SNADER TELESCRIPTIONS
(US Snader Telescriptions Corporation 1950–53)
Series of musical shorts featuring an artist
performing a particular song.
AIN'T SEEN NOTHING LIKE YOU
The Four Freshman.
ALL GOD'S CHILLUN GOT RHYTHM
June Christy.

ALWAYS YOU
Nat King Cole, supported by a string band.
AMERICAN PATROL
Red Nichols and his Five Pennies.
ANDY'S BOOGIE
Charlie Barnet and his Orchestra, and Helen
Carr, with Charlie Barnet soloing on soprano
sax.
APRIL SHOWERS
Mel Tormé.
BABY WON'T YOU PLEASE COME HOME
Herb Jeffries.
BACK ROOM BLUES
Red Nichols and his Five Pennies.
BASIE BOOGIE
Count Basie and his Sextet.
BASIE'S CONVERSATION
Count Basie and his Sextet.
BASIN STREET BLUES
Herb Jeffries singing with an unidentified band.
BATTLE HYMN OF THE REPUBLIC
Red Nichols and his Five Pennies.
BECAUSE OF RAIN
Nat King Cole, supported by a string band.
BEULAH'S BOOGIE
Lionel Hampton and his Orchestra.
BIG NOISE FROM WINNETKA
The Bobcats.
BILLBOARD MARCH
Les Brown and his Band of Renown, with Butch
Stone, Stumpy Brown, and Lucy Ann Polk.
BONGO INTERLUDE
Lionel Hampton and his Orchestra.
BRASS BELL
The Firehouse Five Plus Two.
CALLOWAY BOOGIE
Cab Calloway and his Cabaliers.
CARAVAN
Duke Ellington and his Orchestra with a solo on
valve trombone by Juan Tizol.
CHEROKEE
Charlie Barnet and his Orchestra, and Helen
Carr.
COBB'S IDEA
Lionel Hampton and his Orchestra and Betty
Carter singing.
COMPLAININ'
The Bobcats.
CONCEPTION
The George Shearing Quintet.
DAILY TROUBLE
Pete Daily and his Chicagoans.
DANCE OF RENOWN
Les Brown and his Band of Renown, with Butch
Stone, Stumpy Brown, and Lucy Ann Polk.
DARK EYES
Jack Teagarden and his Sextet.
DING DONG BABY
Lionel Hampton and his Orchestra.
DON'T WORRY 'BOUT STRANGERS
Tony Pastor and his Orchestra.
DREAM
The Pied Pipers and the Ernie Felice Quartet.
ENTRANCE OF THE GLADIATORS
Red Nichols and his Five Pennies.
ESPECIALLY FOR YOU
Bonnie Baker and an unidentified band.
ETIQUETTE BLUES
Les Brown and his Band of Renown, with vocal
by Butch Stone.
EVERYBODY LOVES MY BABY
The Firehouse Five Plus Two.
FIREHOUSE STOMP
The Firehouse Five Plus Two.
FLAMINGO
GEORGIA ON MY MIND
Jack Teagarden and his Sextet.
GHOST OF A CHANCE
Ginny Simms.
GIANNINA MIA
Ralph Flanagan and his Orchestra, with Harry
Prime.
GOAT BLUES
Pete Daily and his Chicagoans.
The GYPSY
The Ink Spots.
The HAWK TALKS
Duke Ellington and his Orchestra and a drum
solo by Louie Bellson.
HOME
Nat King Cole and his Trio.

HOOK AND LADDER BLUES
The Firehouse Five Plus Two.
I CAN'T GIVE YOU ANYTHING BUT LOVE
Cab Calloway and his Cabaliers, including Jonah
Jones on trumpet, Milt Hilton on bass and
'Panama' Francis on drums.
I CRIED FOR YOU
Helen Humes singing with the Count Basie
Sextet.
I DON'T KNOW ENOUGH ABOUT YOU
Peggy Lee and the Dave Barbour Quartet.
I ONLY HAVE EYES FOR YOU
Peggy Lee and the Dave Barbour Quartet.
I'LL BE AROUND
The George Shearing Quintet.
I'LL NEVER SMILE AGAIN
The George Shearing Quintet.
I'M NOBODY'S SWEETHEART NOW
Connee (Connie) Boswell.
I'VE GOT THE WORLD ON A STRING
Les Brown and his Band of Renown, with vocal
by Lucy Ann Polk.
IMAGINATION 1950
June Christy.
INDIANA
Ada Leonard and her Orchestra.
IT DON'T MEAN A THING IF IT AIN'T GOT THAT
SWING
Connie Haines.
IT'S A GOOD DAY
Peggy Lee and the Dave Barbour Quartet.
JACK ARMSTRONG BLUES
Jack Teagarden and his Sextet.
JOSHUA
Ralph Flanagan and his Orchestra, with Harry
Prime.
JUST ONE MORE CHANCE
Ralph Flanagan and his Orchestra with Harry
Prime.
LITTLE GIRL
Nat King Cole, supported by a string group.
LOVE'S GOT ME IN A LAZY MOOD
The Bobcats.
LOVE YOU LIKE MAD, LOVE YOU LIKE CRAZY
Lionel Hampton and his Orchestra.
LOVER
Jack Teagarden and his Sextet.
MAÑANA
Peggy Lee and the Dave Barbour Quartet.
MARCH OF THE BOBCATS
The Bobcats.
MARGIE
Tony Pastor and his Orchestra.
MIDNIGHT SUN
Lionel Hampton and his Orchestra.
MINNIE THE MOOCHER
Cab Calloway and his Cabaliers, including Jonah
Jones on trumpet, Milt Hinton on bass, and
'Panama' Francis on drums.
MONA LISA
Nat King Cole and his Trio.
The MOOCH
Duke Ellington and his Orchestra.
MOOD INDIGO
Duke Ellington and his Orchestra, with solo
performances from Russell Procope on clarinet,
Willie Cook on trumpet and Duke Ellington on
piano.
MOVE
The George Shearing Quintet.
MUSIC, MUSIC, MUSIC
Teresa Brewer.
MUSKRAT RAMBLE
The Bobcats.
MY OLD FLAME
Charlie Barnet and his Orchestra, and Helen
Carr.
NATURE BOY
Nat King Cole, supported by a string band.
The NEARNESS OF YOU
Sarah Vaughan.
O TANNENBAUM
Pete Daily and his Chicagoans.
ONE FOR MY BABY
Cab Calloway and his Cabaliers performing the
song in a nightclub setting.
ONE O'CLOCK JUMP
Count Basie and his Sextet.
OVER THE WAVES
Pete Daily and his Chicagoans.
PANAMA
The Bobcats.

PLEASE DON'T TALK ABOUT ME WHEN I'M
GONE
Pete Daily and his Chicagoans.
POINCIANA
The Four Freshman.
RED HOT RIVER VALLEY
The Firehouse Five Plus Two.
ROCKIN' CHAIR
Jack Teagarden and his Sextet.
ROUTE 66
Nat King Cole.
S'POSIN'
June Christy.
ST JAMES INFIRMARY
Cab Calloway and his Cabaliers, including Jonah
Jones on trumpet, Milt Hinton on bass and
'Panama' Francis on drums.
SAVOY BLUES
The Bobcats.
SHE'S FUNNY THAT WAY
June Christy.
SKYLINER 1
Charlie Barnet and his Orchestra, and Helen
Carr.
SLIDE, HAMP, SLIDE
Lionel Hampton and his Orchestra.
SOLITUDE
Duke Ellington and his Orchestra and Jimmie
Grissom on vocals.
SOLITUDE
Herb Jeffries.
SOPHISTICATED LADY
Duke Ellington and his Orchestra with solo
performances from Harry Carney on bass
clarinet, Willie Smith on alto sax, and Duke
Ellington on piano.
SOUTH
The Firehouse Five Plus Two.
STARS FELL ON ALABAMA
Jack Teagarden and his Sextet.
SWEDISH PASTRY
The George Shearing Quintet.
SWEET LORRAINE
Nat King Cole.
T.V. SPECIAL
Lionel Hampton and his Orchestra.
TAKING A CHANCE ON LOVE
June Christy.
THAT'S A PLENTY
Jack Teagarden and his Sextet.
THAT'S MY DESIRE
The Four Freshman.
THESE THINGS I OFFER YOU
Sarah Vaughan.
THREE BEARS
The Paul Cavanaugh Trio.
THREE BLIND MICE
Red Nichols and his Five Pennies.
TIME TAKES CARE OF EVERYTHING
Les Brown and his Band of Renown, with Butch
Stone, Stumpy Brown, and Lucy Ann Polk.
TROUBLE IS A GIRL 1
Mel Tormé.
The TROUBLE WITH ME IS YOU
Nat King Cole and his Trio.
V.I.P's BOOGIE 1952
Duke Ellington and his Orchestra.
VIENI SU
Carl Ravazza.
WHAT MORE CAN A WOMAN DO
Peggy Lee and the Dave Barbour Quartet.
WHEN I WRITE MY SONG
Herb Jeffries.
WHILE WE'RE YOUNG
Peggy Lee and the Dave Barbour Quartet.
WHO'S SORRY NOW
The Bobcats.
WHY DON'T YOU DO RIGHT
Peggy Lee and the Dave Barbour Quartet.
WOLVERINE BLUES
Jack Teagarden and his Sextet.
YOU DON'T KNOW WHAT LOVE IS
Fran Warren.
YOU OUGHTA BE IN PICTURES
Mel Tormé.
YOU WAS RIGHT, BABY
Peggy Lee and the Dave Barbour Quartet.
YOU'RE A CHARACTER, DEAR
The Dinning Sisters.
YOU'RE DRIVING ME CRAZY
Mel Tormé.

YOU'RE MINE, YOU
Sarah Vaughan.
YOU'RE NOT THE KIND
Sarah Vaughan.

The SNOW QUEEN (BBC 25/12/1976)
d Andrew Gosling; *p* Ian Keill;
auth Hans Christian Andersen
lp Linda Slater; Joshua Le Touzel;
Hilda Barry; Mercedes Burleigh

SO IT GOES (Granada 1976–77)
Pop music series.
d Peter Carr, Eric Harrison;
p Geoff Moore
SO IT GOES CLIPS 1977
Compilation of clips of 'punk rock' performers
from the Granada Television series SO IT
GOES, featuring Elvis Costello, The Stranglers,
The Sex Pistols, and The Clash.
IGGY POP 29/10/1977
Iggy Pop in concert at the Apollo Theatre,
Manchester.
The STRANGLERS 5/11/1977
TOM ROBINSON BAND 5/11/1977
The CLASH 10/12/1977

SOFTLY, SOFTLY (BBC 1966–70)
Police series developed from Z CARS
(1962–78). The series, itself became the basis for
SOFTLY, SOFTLY: TASK FORCE (1970–76).
IT DOESN'T GROW ON TREES 26/1/1966
d Leonard Lewis; *p* David E. Rose;
sc Robert Barr
lp Garfield Morgan; Frank Windsor;
Alexis Kanner; Robert Keegan; John Welsh;
Aubrey Richards
IN AT THE DEATH 25/9/1969
d Vere Lorrimer; *p* Leonard Lewis;
sc Robert Barr
lp Philip Brack; Norman Bowler;
Howell Evans; John Barron; James Cosmo;
Pippa Rowe; Laurence Hardy
ARRIVAL 20/11/1969
d Peter Cregeen; *p* Leonard Lewis;
sc Elwyn Jones
lp Stratford Johns; David Allister;
Norman Bowler; David Lloyd Meredith;
Terence Rigby; Susan Tebbs
TASK FORCE: DIVERSION 4/12/1969
d Vere Lorrimer; *p* Leonard Lewis;
sc Robert Barr
lp Stratford Johns; Frank Windsor;
Norman Bowler; David Allister;
David Lloyd Meredith; Susan Tebbs

SOFTLY, SOFTLY: TASK FORCE
(BBC 1970–76)
Police series developed from SOFTLY,
SOFTLY (1966–70).
PRIVATE MISCHIEF 22/1/1970
d Ben Rae; *p* Leonard Lewis;
sc Elwyn Jones
lp Frank Windsor; David Allister;
David Lloyd Meredith; Jeremy Young;
Ann Penfold; Stratford Johns
The POWER OF THE PRESS 19/2/1970
d Brian Parker; *p* Leonard Lewis;
sc Elwyn Jones
lp Stratford Johns; Norman Bowler;
David Lloyd Meredith; David Allister;
Walter Gotell; Gary Waldhorn; Kenneth Waller
ESCORT 12/3/1970
d Frank Cox; *p* Leonard Lewis;
sc Elwyn Jones
lp Stratford Johns; Frank Windsor;
Norman Bowler; David Allister;
David Lloyd Meredith; Susan Tebbs;
Terence Rigby; Walter Gotell; Jack Shepherd
JUST A WHISPER? 24/11/1976
d Martyn Friend; *p* Geraint Morris;
sc Elwyn Jones
lp Frank Windsor; Norman Bowler;
Peter Childs; John Flanagan; Philippa Howell;
Jane Baxter; Nicholas McArdle;
Michael Mundell

A SOHO STORY
(Denis Mitchell Films 22/4/1959)
Mac the busker talks of his life as a painter and
as an entertainer of theatre queues in Soho.
d Denis Mitchell

**SOLEMN OPENING OF LIVERPOOL
CATHEDRAL** (ABC 14/5/1967)
The dedication and consecration of Liverpool's
Roman Catholic Cathedral.
d David Southwood

SOLITAIRE (BBC 19/6/1961)
A study of loneliness and greed.
d/p Naomi Capon; *sc* Lucienne Hill;
auth Henri Troyat
lp Sonia Dresdel; Colin Jeavons;
Françoise Rosay; Tamara Hinchco;
Cameron Hall

SOME MOTHERS DO 'AVE 'EM
(BBC 1973–78)
Comedy series.
p Michael Mills; *sc* Raymond Allen
regulars Michael Crawford; Michele Dotrice
SOME MOTHERS DO 'AVE 'EM 6/12/1973
lp James Cossins; Ralph Watson;
Kevin Moran; Zulema Dene;
Christopher Biggins; Jill Damas
SOME MOTHERS DO 'AVE 'EM 13/12/1973
lp Sydney Tafler; Charles Lamb;
Christopher Holmes; Anthony Woodruff;
Christopher Timothy; Julia Breck
SOME MOTHERS DO 'AVE 'EM 27/12/1973
lp Richard Caldicot; Cyril Luckham;
Eric Francis; Alison Coleridge; Diane Holland;
John D. Collins; Anthony Woodruff
JESSICA'S FIRST CHRISTMAS 25/12/1974
lp Bryan Pringle; Cyril Luckham;
Emma Ware; Brian Hayes; Bartlett Mullins;
Alan Bowerman; Ian Milton; Tony Bateman
SOME MOTHERS DO 'AVE 'EM 11/11/1978
lp Glynn Edwards; Glyn Houston;
Milton Johns; Jean Boht; Royston Tickner;
Michael Redfern; Babar Bhatti; Andrew Lane
SOME MOTHERS DO 'AVE 'EM 18/11/1978
lp Richard Wilson; Hazel Bainbridge;
Eric Dodson; Carl Andrews; John Malcolm;
Norman Chappell; Sheila Keith
SOME MOTHERS DO 'AVE 'EM 25/11/1978
lp Roland Curram; Norman Jones;
Harriet Reynolds; Andrew Downie; Eric Mason;
Jean Boht
SOME MOTHERS DO 'AVE 'EM 2/12/1978
lp Derek Farr; Glynn Edwards;
Dick Bentley; Roger Kemp; Bunny May;
Linda James; Johnny Allan; Norman Hartley
SOME MOTHERS DO 'AVE 'EM 9/12/1978
lp Derek Farr; Bernard Gallagher;
Derek Newark; Geoffrey Chater; John Harvey;
Ellis Dale; Patrick McAlinney; David Ryall;
Gretchen Franklin
SOME MOTHERS DO 'AVE 'EM 16/12/1978
lp Edward Hardwicke; Glynn Edwards;
Diana King; Dick Bentley; David Rose

SOME WOMEN (BBC 27/8/1969)
A film about four women who have been in
prison. [A revised version of a film previously
called 'Five Women'].
d Roy Battersby; *p* Tony Garnett;
sc Tony Parker
lp Fionnuala Flanagan; Natalie Kemp;
Edith MacArthur; Cleo Sylvestre; Bella Emberg

SOMETHING IN THE CITY
(Jack Hylton TV Productions 1959)
Sitcom series.
d Kenneth Carter
regulars Eric Barker; Joan Benham;
Pearl Hackney; Deryck Guyler;
Peter Hammond; Diane Hart
SOMETHING IN THE CITY 6/7/1959
SOMETHING IN THE CITY 13/7/1959
SOMETHING IN THE CITY 20/7/1959
lp Michael Bird
SOMETHING IN THE CITY 27/7/1959
SOMETHING IN THE CITY 3/8/1959

SOMETHING TO SAY
(Rediffusion 1964)
Interview series with Daniel Farson.
DRUGS 1964
GERALD GARDINER Q.C. 6/1/1964
d Rollo Gamble
ADELINE BOURNE 13/1/1964
d Rollo Gamble
GWYN THOMAS 20/1/1964
d Rollo Gamble
WILLIAM BURROUGHS AND ALEXANDER
TROCCHI 27/1/1964
d Randal Beattie
The REV. DAVID SHEPPARD 3/2/1964
d Randal Beattie
TREVOR HOWARD 10/2/1964
d Randal Beattie
LORD ROBENS 30/3/1964
d Randal Beattie
DR. BARNES WALLIS 13/4/1964
d Randal Beattie
HENRY WILLIAMSON 4/5/1964
d Randal Beattie
ROBERT CARRIER 5/10/1964
d Peter Robinson
GODFREY WINN 26/10/1964
d Peter Robinson
SHIRLEY BASSEY 2/11/1964
d Peter Robinson

SOMETHING TO SAY (Thames 1972–73)
Discussion programme chaired by Bryan Magee.
EVOLUTIONARY ACCIDENT OR SPIRITUAL
MAN? 1/6/1972
Jaques Monod and Sir John Eccles on the nature
of man.
d Ken Craig
LIMITS OF GROWTH DISCUSSION 6/6/1972
Experts answer questions phoned-in by viewers
of the television programme The LIMITS OF
GROWTH.
d Ken Craig
DEMOCRATIC COMMUNISM OR WISHFUL
THINKING? 22/6/1972
Herbert Marcuse and Raymond Aron discuss
Communism.
d Ken Craig
The FUTURE OF ULSTER 23/11/1972
Conor Cruise O'Brien and John Hume discuss
the Ulster situation.
d George Sawford
IS MARXISM ENOUGH? 7/12/1972
Professor Eric Hobsbawm discusses Marxism.
WILL THE REAL RONNIE LAING STAND UP?
21/12/1972
Professor G.M. Carstairs questions R.D. Laing
about his ideas on psychiatry, mental health and
family life.
d George Sawford; *p* Udi Eichler

SON OF FRED (Rediffusion 1956)
Comedy series which followed on from A
SHOW CALLED FRED.
SON OF FRED 1956

The SONG PARADE (Granada 1959)
Variety series.
SONG PARADE 26/6/1959
Song and dance show with singers The
Granadiers, The Dance Paraders and Peter
Knight and his Orchestra.
d Mark Stuart

SONGS OF PRAISE (BBC 1961–)
Religious programme.
ST. MARTIN-IN-THE-FIELDS 14/2/1968
SONGS OF PRAISE 20/3/1971
Church service from St. John's Roman Catholic
Church, Bath, Avon.
p John Dobson; *pres* Geoffrey Wheeler

The SONGWRITERS
(BBC 16/6–10/8/1978)
Series celebrating eighty years of British popular
music.
LENNON AND McCARTNEY 27/7/1978
d Keith Cheetham; *p/sc* Tony Staveacre

SOOTY (BBC 1952–68)
Glove puppet series for young children. See also
The SOOTY SHOW.
SOOTY 24/7/1955

The SOOTY SHOW (Thames 1968–)
Puppet series.
The SOOTY SHOW 6/10/1976
d/p Daphne Shadwell
with Harry Corbett, Matthew Corbett,
Freddie Davies

The SOUTH AFRICAN EXPERIENCE
(ATV 30/11–21/12/1977)
Four-part documentary series on aspects of
South Africa.
The SEARCH FOR SANDRA LAING 30/11/1977
The classification of a girl of white parentage as
black.
d/nar Antony Thomas
WHERE TO FROM HERE? 21/12/1977
Studio debate about South Africa.
d Nigel Warrack; *p* Peter Farrel

SOUTH AMERICA (Thames 24/5–7/6/1979)
Three films on aspects of South America.
PERU – THE REVOLUTION THAT NEVER WAS
31/5/1979
How the peasants of Cuzco in the Andes have
fared since an army coup in 1969.
d Peter Tiffin; *p* David Elstein
BRAZIL – CHILDREN OF THE MIRACLE 7/6/1979
Social and economic conditions in São Paolo,
Brazil.
d Peter Tiffin; *p* David Elstein

The SOUTH BANK SHOW (LWT 1978–)
Arts programme. Developed from AQUARIUS
(1970–77).
pres/ed Melvyn Bragg
DENNIS POTTER: MAN OF TELEVISION
11/2/1978
Dennis Potter talks to Melvyn Bragg about his
plays and the ideas and experiences which led to
them.
d Peter L. Walker;
p Alan Benson, Tony Cash, Andrew Snell
HAROLD PINTER 22/4/1978
Harold Pinter is interviewed by Melvyn Bragg.
d Andrew Snell;
p Andrew Snell, Alan Benson
MACMILLAN'S MAYERLING 17/6/1978
The evolution of Kenneth MacMillan's ballet;
with excerpts.
d/p Derek Bailey
INTERVIEW WITH WOODY ALLEN 10/12/1978
Woody Allen discusses his film 'Interiors' as well
as the nature of screen comedy.
BERYL COOK 25/3/1979
A record of the work of painter Beryl Cook.
The RISE AND FALL OF THE SINGLE PLAY
8/4/1979
A survey of the changes in television drama,
including writing, acting and technology, over
the previous twenty years. Includes interviews
with producers Kenith Trodd, Sidney Newman
and Barry Hanson.
d/p Gerry Harrison
FRANCIS COPPOLA 2/12/1979
Features an interview with Coppola on his work,
and on his most recent film, 'Apocalypse Now'.
p Alan Benson

SOUTH RIDING
(Yorkshire TV 16/9–9/12/1974)
Thirteen-part serial based on the best-selling
novel by Winifred Holtby.
p James Ormerod; *sc* Stan Barstow
regulars Dorothy Tutin; Nigel Davenport;
Judi Bowker; John Cater; Clive Swift;
Norman Jones; Lesley Dunlop; Ray Mort
The POWERS THAT BE 16/9/1974
d Alastair Reid
lp Hermione Baddeley; Roy Kinnear;
Richard Borthwick
A LAND OF HOPE AND GLORY 23/9/1974
d James Ormerod
lp Peter Madden; Ingrid Hafner; Maggie Flint
THOSE FOR AND THOSE AGAINST 30/9/1974
d James Ormerod
A TIME TO LIVE AND A TIME TO DIE 7/10/1974
d Alastair Reid
The FACTS OF LIFE 14/10/1974
d Alastair Reid
lp Bernard Kay; June Brown; Michael Bilton
IN SICKNESS AND IN HEALTH 21/10/1974

DREAMS AND DESTINATIONS 28/10/1974
d Alastair Reid
BEGGARS AND CHOOSERS 4/11/1974
d James Ormerod
lp Michael Barrington; June Brown;
Milton Johns
TAKE WHAT YOU WANT – AND PAY FOR IT
11/11/1974
d Alastair Reid
lp Brenda Cowling; Liz Smith; Gillian Lind
The LORD GIVETH AND THE LORD TAKETH
AWAY 18/11/1974
d James Ormerod
lp Paul Haley; Sheila Raynor;
Michelle Cerowski
The NUMBER OF OUR DAYS 25/11/1974
d Alastair Reid
lp Bernard Kay; June Brown; Peter Madden
FORGIVE US OUR TRESPASSES 2/12/1974
d James Ormerod
GIVE US THIS DAY 9/12/1974
d Alastair Reid
lp Amanda Broadley; Margaret Whitelam;
Bernard Kay

**SOUTH VIETNAM: A QUESTION OF
TORTURE** (Granada 7/5/1973)
An investigation into allegations of torture made
by political prisoners in South Vietnam, accusing
officials of President Thieu's regime, and the
Americans who help to run the country's
prisons.
d/p Michael Beckham

The SOVIET PRIME MINISTER
(BBC 10/2/1967)
Kenneth Harris interviews Alexei Kosygin.
p Paul Fox

The SPACE BETWEEN WORDS
(GB/US BBC-KCET TV 8/2–7/3/1972)
Five-part series concerned with situations which
depend on good communications.
p Roger Graef
WORK 8/2/1972
An account of a possible strike at an electronics
factory in Wales.
FAMILY 15/2/1972
Film, using verité techniques, about
communication within a family.
SCHOOL 22/2/1972
The problems of teaching a 4th year class at a
comprehensive school. Educational psychologist
Richard Suchman talks to the children and their
teachers.
DIPLOMACY 7/3/1972
The progress of meetings of the United Nations
Economic and Social Council to discuss a British/
American plan to establish a UN disaster relief
co-ordinator.

SPAGHETTI TWO-STEP
(Yorkshire TV 18/1/1977)
Drama about restaurants and restaurant folk.
d David Cunliffe; *exec p* Peter Willes;
sc Jack Rosenthal
lp Paul John Geoffrey; Nicholas Amer;
Stephen Greif; Louis Mansi; John Bluthal;
Connie Booth

SPANISH RIDING SCHOOL OF VIENNA
(BBC 23/10/1969)
The first complete performance in Britain of the
Spanish Riding School of Vienna demonstrating
the classical art of riding as practised at the
Imperial Court, Vienna.
d Derek Burrell-Davis; *nar* Dorian Williams

**The SPEAKER OF THE HOUSE OF
COMMONS** (BBC 11/4/1966)
Robin Day talks to Dr Horace King about his
position as Speaker of the House of Commons.
p Anthony Smith

SPEAKING FRANKLY (Border 1965)
Interview series.
SIR HUGH GREENE 19/3/1965
An interview with Sir Hugh Greene, Director-
General of the BBC.
interv Maurice Lindsay

SPEARHEAD (Southern TV 1978–79)
Drama series about the life of an army regiment.
regulars Roy Holder; Gordon Case;
George Sweeney; Charles Cork; Robin Davies
JACKAL 8/8/1978
d Derek Martinus; *p* James Ormerod;
sc Nick McCarty
lp Michael Billington; Stafford Gordon;
Lawrence Davidson; Kevin Lloyd
REPERCUSSIONS 16/7/1979
d/p James Ormerod; *sc* Nick McCarty
lp Martyn Jacobs; Martin Read;
Eamon Boland; James Kerry
WAITING GAMES 23/7/1979
d/p James Ormerod; *sc* Nick McCarty
lp Peter Turner; Stafford Gordon;
Eamon Boland

The SPECIAL BRAIN OF KARL KROYER
(Yorkshire TV 1/11/1972)
A portrait of Danish inventor Karl Kroyer,
holder of over two hundred patents.
d Barry Cockcroft

The SPECIAL CHILD
(Yorkshire TV 1977; 1979)
Documentary series about the mentally
handicapped.
p Richard Handford; *pres* Kenneth Day
PARENTS TALKING 23/1/1977
Three families discuss their personal experiences
in coping with mentally handicapped children.
The SPECIAL CHILD 30/1/1977
The causes and nature of mental handicap.
FIRST STEPS 6/2/1977
Cliff Cunningham, psychologist at the Hester
Adrian Research Centre, Manchester
University, shows how to develop the
capabilities of mentally handicapped children.
PLAY AND LANGUAGE 13/2/1977
The role of play in the development of mentally
handicapped children with psychologist Cliff
Cunningham.
PHYSICAL HANDICAPS 20/2/1977
The problems of cerebral palsy.
WITH A LITTLE HELP 27/2/1977
Outside agencies which may be able to help
parents with mentally handicapped children.
LOOKING AHEAD 6/3/1977
Looks forward to schooling and adult facilities
available to the mentally handicapped.

**The SPECIAL LONDON BRIDGE
SPECIAL** (US Winters-Rosen Production;
GB *tx* 15/3/1973)
Light entertainment musical programme about
the moving of London Bridge to Arizona, USA.
d David Winters;
sc Marty Farrell, Marc B. Rayrell,
Ronnie Cassell, Donald Rossell
with Tom Jones, Jennifer O'Neill,
Kirk Douglas, Hermione Gingold, Elliot Gould,
The Carpenters, Rudolf Nureyev, Merle Park

The SPINNERS AT THE PHIL
(BBC 20/12/1971)
Part of a public concert recorded in the
Liverpool Philharmonic Hall.
p Nick Hunter

SPIRIT OF THE AGE
(BBC 31/10–19/12/1975)
Eight-part documentary series on eight centuries
of British architecture.
p Christopher Martin
The MEDIEVAL AGE 31/10/1975
The achievements of the medieval builders.
sc/nar Alec Clifton-Taylor
The CULT OF GRANDEUR 14/11/1975
Restoration architecture – the work of Sir
Christopher Wren, Sir John Vanbrugh and
Nicholas Hawksmoor; St Paul's Cathedral, City
of London, Blenheim Palace and Castle
Howard.
sc/nar Robert Furneaux Jordan
A SENSE OF PROPORTION 21/11/1975
The value of moderation, self-confidence and
proportion expressed in the mid-eighteenth
century both in Italy under Palladio in the
sixteenth century and in England two centuries
later.
p David Heycock; *sc/nar* John Julius Norwich

ALL THAT MONEY COULD BUY 5/12/1975
The social and architectural consequences of the wealth of the Victorians, most particularly at St. Pancras Station designed by Sir Gilbert Scott.
sc/nar Mark Girouard
A FULL LIFE AND AN HONEST PLACE 12/12/1975
The Arts and Crafts Movement. Discusses the influence of William Morris on the Movement and looks at Bedford Park, Glasgow School of Art, Lindisfarne Castle, Cragside House and Letchworth Garden City.
sc/nar Patrick Nuttgens
DREAMS AND AWAKENINGS 19/12/1975
Architecture in Britain in the twentieth century.
sc/nar Hugh Casson

The SPIRIT OF THE TWENTIES
(BBC 7/9/1968)
A historical film compilation to introduce BBC-2's new series of plays based on the 1920s – 'The Jazz Age'.
p Thérèse Denny; *comm* Malcolm Muggeridge

SPIRO AGNEW ANSWERS BERNARD LEVIN (ATV 30/6/1970)
Bernard Levin interviews Spiro Agnew.
p Robin Brown

SPOONER'S PATCH (ATV 1979–82)
Sitcom about Inspector Spooner of the Metropolitan Police.
The MORNING AFTER 16/7/1979
d/p William G. Stewart;
sc Ray Galton, Johnny Speight
lp Ronald Fraser; Peter Cleall;
Norman Rossington; John Lyons; Dermot Kelly;
Wendy Richard; Mavis Pugh; Donald Morley

SPORTS ARENA (LWT)
Sports documentary series.
SIR ALF RAMSEY 27/4/1969
Sir Alf Ramsey is interviewed about his career in football.

SPORTS REVIEW OF 1959
(BBC 16/12/1959)
Peter Dimmock introduces a review of the year's sporting highlights, and the presentation of the BBC 'Sportsview Personality of the Year Award'.
d Bryan Cowgill

SPORTSNIGHT (BBC 1970–)
Sports series.
N.W. COUNTIES v. ALL BLACKS 22/11/1972
Rugby Union.
p Jonathan Martin;
pres Alan Mouncer, David Coleman;
comm Cliff Morgan

SPORTSPOT (Rediffusion)
Sports series.
BOWLING 11/6/1956
An instructional film on cricket and practical advice on how to improve your bowling.
intro Trevor Bailey

SPOTLIGHT ON ANTHONY ASQUITH
(Rediffusion 30/4/1958)
The work of director Anthony Asquith, with extracts from some of his films, including 'Orders to Kill'.
d Jim Pople

SPRING IN ETHIOPIA
(Rediffusion 28/3/1967)
How Ethiopia is developing in the twentieth century.
d/nar Denis Mitchell; *p* Richard De La Mare

SPRING, SUMMER AND AUTUMN...50 YEARS IN SHOWBUSINESS
(Thames 26/10/1977)
Profile of Jimmy Jewel.
d Roy Lomas; *p* Jim Pople;
intro Roy Hudd

The SPRINGS OF LEARNING
(BBC 1966)
Series looking at the development of children in their first five years.
d George Inger; *p* Eileen Molony

The EARLY YEARS 4/10/1966
BABYHOOD 11/10/1966
RISING TWO 18/10/1966
IDEAS OF THEIR OWN 25/10/1966
PLAYING TOGETHER 1/11/1966
The PRE-SCHOOL CHILD 8/11/1966

SPROUT (Thames 1/7/1974)
Comedy about a couple of out-of-work flatmates.
d/p Anthony Parker;
sc Anthony Matheson, Peter Tilbury
lp John Alderton; Julian Holloway;
Geoffrey Chater; Jenny Cox; Clare Sutcliffe

SPYCATCHER (BBC 1959–60)
Series of true stories of the search for spies in wartime Britain, based on the experiences of Lt.-Col. Oreste Pinto.
p Terence Cook; *sc* Robert Barr
lp Bernard Archard
LOUISE 8/10/1959
ABSENT FRIEND 24/3/1960
INFERNAL TRIANGLE 31/3/1960

STAGECOACH – NOT SO MUCH A THEATRE MORE A WAY OF LIFE
(Tyne Tees 19/4/1973)
The touring theatre company, Stagecoach, which operates in the north of England.
d Ken Stephinson

The STANLEY BAXTER BIG PICTURE SHOW (LWT 21/12/1973)
Comedy show featuring Stanley Baxter in a variety of satires on films and television programmes.
p David Bell; *sc* Ken Hoare

The STANLEY BAXTER MOVING PICTURE SHOW (LWT 7/9/1974)
Comedy programme featuring Stanley Baxter in a variety of satirical impersonations of show business stars.
d/p David Bell; *sc* Ken Hoare

STANLEY BAXTER ON TELEVISION
(LWT 1/4/1979)
Stanley Baxter parodying other television programmes.
d/p John Kaye Cooper

The STANLEY BAXTER PICTURE SHOW
(LWT 8/10/1972)
Comedy programme featuring mimic Stanley Baxter.
d/p David Bell;
sc Ken Hoare, Bill Solly, Eric Merriman

The STANLEY BAXTER PICTURE SHOW PART III (LWT 19/9/1975)
Comedy programme featuring Stanley Baxter in a variety of satirical impersonations, with Denise Coffey.
d Jon Scoffield; *sc* Ken Hoare

STANLEY SPENCER: COOKHAM VILLAGE (BBC 30/5/1956)
Stanley Spencer talks about his life and work.
d/p/sc John Read; *nar* Robert Reid

STANLEY SPENCER: WAR AND PEACE
(BBC 20/6/1956)
Stanley Spencer talks about his paintings in the Burghclere Memorial Chapel and discusses his work in Port Glasgow.
d/p/sc John Read; *nar* Robert Reid

STAR PERFORMANCE
(Rediffusion 1966–68)
The HUMAN VOICE 30/11/1966
Television version of Cocteau's play.
d Ted Kotcheff;
p David Susskind, Lars Schmidt;
sc Clive Exton
lp Ingrid Bergman

NOON WINE 9/4/1968
d/sc Sam Peckinpah; *p* Daniel Melnick;
auth Katherine Anne Porter
lp Jason Robards; Olivia De Havilland;
Theodore Bikel; Per Oscarsson;
Robert Emhardt; Steve Sanders; Ben Johnson;
Peter Robbins; L.Q. Jones
SATURDAY NIGHT AROUND THE WORLD 16/4/1968
Young couples' Saturday night entertainment in New York, London, Lisbon, Tel Aviv, Nairobi, Tokyo, and Paris. Appearing are Tom Jones, The Supremes, Amalia Rodrigues, and The Peddlars.
d George Freedland; *p* Irvine Gitlin
AT THE DROP OF ANOTHER HAT 30/4/1968
d Ted Kotcheff;
exec.p David Susskind; Alexander H. Cohen;
with Michael Flanders, Donald Swann
DIAL 'M' FOR MURDER 7/5/1968
d John Llewellyn Moxey; *p* David Susskind;
sc/auth Frederick Knott
lp Laurence Harvey; Diane Cilento;
Hugh O'Brian; Cyril Cusack; Nigel Davenport;
Glynn Edwards; Gary Marsh
FROM CHEKHOV WITH LOVE 14/6/1968
d Bill Turner; *p* David Susskind;
sc Jonathan Miller
lp Peggy Ashcroft; Nigel Davenport;
Maurice Denham; John Gielgud; Wendy Hiller;
Dorothy Tutin
DARE I WEEP, DARE I MOURN 2/7/1968
d Ted Kotcheff; *p* Anthony Perry;
sc Stanley Mann; *auth* John Le Carré
lp James Mason; Jill Bennett;
Hugh Griffith; Kay Walsh; Maureen Pryor;
Hamilton Dyce; Derek Francis

STAR SOCCER (ATV)
Football series.
WEST BROMWICH ALBION v EVERTON 19/5/1968
Highlights of the 1968 F.A. Cup Final at Wembley Stadium.
WEST BROMWICH ALBION v. ARSENAL 1970
Highlights of the football match.
WEST BROMWICH ALBION v. MANCHESTER CITY 8/3/1970
Highlights of the League Cup final played at Wembley Stadium, 7/3/1970.
DERBY v. MANCHESTER UNITED 1971
Highlights of the football match.
ARSENAL v. STOKE 28/3/1971
Highlights of the F.A. Cup semi-final.
ARSENAL v. LIVERPOOL 9/5/1971
Highlights of the F.A. Cup Final played at Wembley, 8/5/1971. After-match analysis by Brian Moore and a panel including Derek Dougan and Malcolm Allison.
ENGLAND v. SCOTLAND 23/5/1971
Highlights of the soccer international played at Wembley, 22/5/1971.
LIVERPOOL v. DERBY 1972
Highlights of the football match.
CHELSEA v. STOKE 5/3/1972
The League Cup final at Wembley Stadium, 4/3/1972.

STAR TURN CHALLENGE (BBC 1979)
Game show featuring celebrities.
STAR TURN CHALLENGE 30/9/1979
p Peter Charlton; *pres* Graeme Garden;
with Michael Rodd, Judith Hann,
Kieran Prendiville, Kenneth Williams,
June Whitfield, Alfred Marks

STARS ACROSS THE WATER
(Ulster TV 17/3/1979)
A musical spectacular for St Patrick's Day.
d John Scholz-Conway

STARS AND GARTERS
(Rediffusion 1963–65)
Pub entertainment including singers and comedians.
STARS AND GARTERS 1/2/1964
d Rollo Gamble
STARS AND GARTERS 12/4/1964
d Rollo Gamble

STARS IN THEIR EYES
(Tyne Tees 31/1/1979)
Documentary film about the Italia Conti Stage
School.
d Tony Kysh; *p* Andrea Wonfor;
with Ruth Davies, Lena Zavaroni,
Bonnie Langford

STARS OF THE BALLET
(BBC 12/5/1959)
Ballet performances, introduced by Peggy Van
Praagh, with Carla Fracci and John Gilpin.
p Naomi Capon

STARS OF THE BOLSHOI BALLET
(BBC 24/7/1960)
A studio presentation of highlights from the
repertoire of the Bolshoi Ballet. Dancers include
Nina Timofeyeva, Georgiy Farmanyants, Irina
Tikhomirovna, Rimma Karelskaya, Susanna
Zvyagina, Margarita Smirnova, Bori Khokhlov
and Vladimir Levashev.
d Margaret Dale

STARS ON SUNDAY
(Yorkshire TV 1969–79)
Religious series.
STARS ON SUNDAY 9/1/1972
Religious songs and stories. Featuring James
Mason, Nina, Max Jaffa, Barry Crocker, Bobby
Bennett and Gracie Fields.
d David Millard, Len Lurcuck;
pres Jess Yates
STARS ON SUNDAY 16/1/1972
Religious songs and stories. Featuring Petula
Clark, Lovelace Watkins, Brendan O'Dowda,
Bobby Bennet, Violet Carson and the
Archbishop of Canterbury.
d David Millard, Len Lurcuck;
pres Jess Yates
STARS ON SUNDAY 15/12/1974
Religious songs and stories. Featuring Dr
Donald Coggan, Douglas Fairbanks, Rolf
Harris, John Lawrenson, and Ireen Sheer.
d Ian Bolt; *pres* Robert Dougall

The STARS RISE IN THE WEST
(TWW 1964)
Variety show with Tessie O'Shea, Donald
Houston, Stanley Baker, Ralph Reader, Donald
Sinden, Sir Ralph Richardson, Petula Clark,
Harry Secombe and Tommy Cooper.
d Ernest Borneman

**The STATE FUNERAL OF SIR WINSTON
CHURCHILL** (BBC 30/1/1965)

The STATE OF THE NATION
(Granada 1966–79)
Current affairs series. See also The STATE OF
THE NATION: THE PARTY IN POWER and
The STATE OF THE NATION: THE
BOUNDS OF FREEDOM.
A LAW IN THE MAKING: FOUR MONTHS INSIDE
A MINISTRY 23/7/1973
A record of the progress of the Fair Trading Bill
at the Standing Committee stage at the
Department of Trade and Industry. MPs seen at
work include Sir Geoffrey Howe, Peter Emery,
Alan Williams, George Darling, Sally
Oppenheim, and Edward Taylor.
d Roger Graef
LAW-MAKING AND PUBLIC MONEY: HAS
PARLIAMENT LOST CONTROL? 24/7/1973
The ways MPs scrutinise the Government's
activities.
d Peter Mullings, Royston Morley
A DEBATE: ARE M.P.s TOO IGNORANT TO DO
THEIR JOB? 25/7/1973
A discussion of the quality of information
available to MPs under the British Parliamentary
system. Taking part are Richard Crossman,
Enoch Powell, Michael Foot, Edward Du Cann,
Brian Walden, Reginald Maudling, Anthony
Crosland, Nicholas Scott, Angus Maude, John
Selwyn Gummer, Charles Pannell, John
Mackintosh and John Jennings.
d Eric Harrison, Peter Mullings

**The STATE OF THE NATION: THE PARTY
IN POWER** (Granada 13–27/6/1976)
Three-part documentary report on the problems
of passing into law proposed government
legislation.
LABOUR'S LAND POLICY 1964 13/6/1976
Fred Willey, Evelyn Sharp, Sir Fredrick Bishop
and John MacKintosh discuss the
implementation of the Labour Government's
land policy in 1964.
d Eric Harrison

**The STATE OF THE NATION: THE
BOUNDS OF FREEDOM**
(Granada 17/6–22/7/1979)
Six-part documentary/current affairs series on
aspects of 'freedom' with regard to the press,
information and television.
d Eric Harrison; *p* Brian Lapping
The TREATMENT OF RAPE IN A TV DRAMA
1/7/1979
A panel of journalists, television people and
lawyers discuss a hypothetical television play
about rape.
FREEDOM OF INFORMATION 15/7/1979
Free speech in the British media. Ministers, civil
servants, journalists and television producers in
discussion.
TERRORISM 22/7/1979
Senior politicians, judges, police and army
officers join newspaper and television journalists
to explore their responses to an imaginary case.

The STATE OF THE UNION (ATV 4/7/1962)
Made for American Independence Day, tracing
America's history and illustrating how far
Americans have succeeded in achieving their
hopes and ideals through independence.
p James Bredin; *sc* Ian Trethowan;
comm Frank Duncan

The STATE OPENING OF PARLIAMENT
(Rediffusion 21/4/1966)
The opening of Parliament by Queen
Elizabeth II.
comm Alastair Burnet

STATE VISIT OF KING FEISAL II OF IRAQ
(BBC 16/7/1956)
King Feisal's arrival at Victoria Station and the
drive to Buckingham Palace.
nar Alexander Moyes

The STATE VISIT TO DENMARK
(BBC 22/5/1957)
Queen Elizabeth II and the Duke of Edinburgh
attend a gala performance of the Danish Royal
Ballet at the Royal Theatre, Copenhagen. An
excerpt from Act III of 'Napoli', choreographed
by Auguste Bournonville.
comm Richard Dimbleby

STEPTOE AND SON (BBC 1962–74)
Comedy series featuring a couple of rag-and-
bone men.
p Duncan Wood (1962–70);
sc Ray Galton, Alan Simpson
regulars Wilfrid Brambell; Harry H. Corbett
The ECONOMIST 28/6/1962
lp Frank Thornton
The BATH 10/1/1963
lp Yootha Joyce; Marjie Lawrence
A MUSICAL EVENING 31/1/1963
HOMES FIT FOR HEROES 7/1/1964
lp Peggy Thorpe-Bates; Marie Makino
STEPTOE A LA CARTE 28/1/1964
lp Gwendolyn Watts; Frank Thornton;
Lala Lloyd
SUNDAY FOR SEVEN DAYS 4/2/1964
lp Michael Brennan; Michael Stainton;
Mark Singleton; Damaris Hayman; George
Betton;
Billy Maxam; Alec Bregonzi; Kathleen Heath
AND AFTERWARDS AT 4/10/1965
lp George A. Cooper; Joan Newell;
Mollie Sugden; Rose Hill; Rita Webb;
Gretchen Franklin
MY OLD MAN'S A TORY 8/11/1965
lp Dudley Foster; Damaris Hayman;
Howard Douglas; Evelyn Lund; Peter
Thompson
A WINTER'S TALE 13/3/1970

STEPTOE AND SON AND SON 27/3/1970
lp Ann Beach; Glynn Edwards
The COLOUR PROBLEM 3/4/1970
lp Anthony Sharp; Geoffrey Adams;
Carmel Cryan
COME DANCING 9/11/1970
lp Tony Melody
TWO'S COMPANY 16/11/1970
lp Jean Kent
TEA FOR TWO 23/11/1970
lp Geoffrey Chater; Robert Raglan
WITHOUT PREJUDICE 30/11/1970
lp Gerald Flood; Norman Bird
POT BLACK 7/12/1970
lp George Tovey; Alf Mangan
The THREE FEATHERS 14/12/1970
lp John Arnatt; John Bailey
MEN OF LETTERS 12/2/1972
p John Howard Davies
lp Anthony Sharp
BACK IN FASHION 4/9/1974
p Douglas Argent
lp Madeleine Smith; Roy Holder;
Peter Birrel
STEPTOE AND SON 26/12/1974
p Douglas Argent
lp Leon Eagles

STICKS AND BONES
(US New York Shakespeare Festival 17/8/1973)
A black comedy about the homecoming of a
blind Vietnam veteran. Broadcast by CBS
network television in 1973, the play was so
controversial that many of the CBS affiliates
refused to put it on air.
d Robert Downey; *p/intro* Joseph Papp;
sc David Rabe
lp Tom Aldredge; Anne Jackson;
Alan Cauldwell; Joe Fields; Cliff De Young;
Asa Gim; Brad Sullivan; Ron Nealy;
Stan Levine

STINGRAY
(AP Films Production-ATV 1964–65)
Science-fiction puppet series.
p Gerry Anderson
voices Don Mason; Robert Easton;
Ray Barrett; Lois Maxwell
STINGRAY – PILOT 10/4/1964
d Alan Pattillo;
sc Gerry Anderson, Sylvia Anderson
COUNT DOWN 9/5/1965
d Alan Pattillo; *sc* Dennis Spooner

The STONE FLOWER ACT 1 (BBC 6/8/1961)
The first part of the ballet danced by the
Leningrad State Kirov Ballet at the Royal Opera
House, Covent Garden. Choreography by Yuri
Grigorovich. The Covent Garden Orchestra is
conducted by Niazi.
d Margaret Dale

The STONE TAPE (BBC 25/12/1972)
d Peter Sasdy; *p* Innes Lloyd;
sc Nigel Kneale
lp Michael Bryant; Jane Asher;
Iain Cuthertson; Michael Bates; Tom Chadbon;
John Forgeham; James Cosmo;
Philip Trewinnard; Neil Wilson;
Hilda Fenemore; Peggy Marshall;
Reginald Marsh

STONES IN THE PARK
(Granada 2/9/1969)
A record of the free concert given by The
Rolling Stones in Hyde Park.
d Jo Durden-Smith, Leslie Woodhead;
p Jo Durden-Smith

The STORIES OF D.H. LAWRENCE
(Granada 3/1–21/2/1966)
Series of adaptations of the stories of D.H.
Lawrence.
The WHITE STOCKING 3/1/1966
d Claude Whatham; *p* Margaret Morris;
sc James Saunders
lp David Langton; Brian Smith;
Celestine Randall; Shirley Stelfox;
Warren Clarke

118

STORM BELL (BBC 1/11/1955)
Play for children.
p Peter Newington; *sc* Robert Moss
lp Fred Johnson; Colin Douglas;
Julia Puccini; Robin Willett;
Richard Wordsworth; Michael Segal;
Michael Corcoran; Jeremy Geidt;
Gordon Whiting

The STORY BEHIND THE STORY
(BBC 19/9–24/10/1973)
Documentary series for children about legends.
p Molly Cox; *pres* John Craven
KING ARTHUR AND THE HOLY GRAIL 19/9/1973
MONSTER IN THE LABYRINTH 26/9/1973
The MEN OF GOLD 3/10/1973
WILD MEN FROM THE NORTH 10/10/1973
The ISLAND THAT VANISHED 17/10/1973
The WALLS THAT FELL 24/10/1973

The STORY BENEATH THE SANDS
(BBC 1978)
Six-part series in which John Coston explores the origins of six legends concerning ancient civilizations, the remains of which have been uncovered in the Middle East. The legends are retold and linked with the monuments which survive today.
d Charles Davies; *p* Molly Cox;
nar Ray Smith
The KING OF THE OTHER WORLD 12/9/1978
The LOST PALACES OF NINEVEH 19/9/1978
The EMPEROR FROM AFRICA 26/9/1978
The LOST GLORY OF IRAN 3/10/1978
The SACRED FIRES 10/10/1978
The DESERT QUEEN 17/10/1978

The STORY OF THE QUEEN MARY
(BBC 26/9/1967)
The liner 'Queen Mary' and what life was like on the North Atlantic run.
d Richard Cawston; *sc* Anthony Lawrence;
nar Kenneth More

The STORY-TELLER (ABC)
Anthology drama series.
The HEROISM OF THOMAS CHADWICK
23/9/1967
A specially commissioned production based on stories by Arnold Bennett from the Victoria Theatre, Stoke-on-Trent.
d Mike Vardy; *p* Peter Cheeseman;
sc Peter Terson
lp Ken Campbell; Anne Raitt;
Gillian Brown; Edward Clayton; Ellis Dale;
Susan Glanville; Terence Davies

STRANGE REPORT
(Arena Productions 1968–69)
Criminologist/mystery series.
p Robert 'Buzz' Berger
regulars Anthony Quayle; Kaz Garas;
Anneke Wills; Charles Lloyd Pack
REPORT 0846: LONELY HEARTS – WHO KILLED DAN CUPID? 26/9/1969
d Peter Duffell; *sc* Roger Parkes
lp Donald Douglas; John Bennett
REPORT 0649: SKELETON – LET SLEEPING HEROES LIE 3/10/1969
d Peter Medak;
sc Brian Degas, Tudor Gates
lp Eric Portman; Hugh Burden; Tom Adams;
Edward Cast; Sylvia Kaye
REPORT 2641: HOSTAGE – IF YOU WON'T LEARN, DIE! 17/10/1969
d Charles Crichton; *sc* John Kruse
lp Kenneth Haigh; Eric Young;
Peggy Thorpe-Bates; Peter Craze; Gerald Sim;
Robert Lee; Lockwood West
REPORT 1021: SHRAPNEL – THE WISH IN THE DREAM 24/10/1969
d Brian Smedley-Aston; *sc* Jan Read
lp Sylvia Syms; Gerald Flood;
Leo Genn; Bryan Marshall; Barry Fantoni
REPORT 8944: HAND – A MATTER OF WITCHCRAFT? 31/10/1969
d Peter Duffell; *sc* Edward De Blasio
lp Renee Asherson; Keith Barron;
Cecilia Darby; Helen Lindsay;
Rosalind Atkinson; Alfred Bell;
Carleton Hobbs; Richard Coe

REPORT 1553: RACIST – A MOST DANGEROUS PROPOSAL 7/11/1969
d Peter Duffell; *sc* Arthur Dales
lp Jane Merrow; Guy Doleman;
Griffith Jones; Karl Held; Clive Francis;
Cleo Sylvestre; Ram John Holder;
Sarah Marshall; Phillip Ross
REPORT 7931: SNIPER – WHEN IS YOUR COUSIN NOT? 14/11/1969
d Peter Medak; *sc* Nicholas Palmer
lp Lelia Goldoni; Vladek Sheybal;
Kika Markham; Martin Shaw;
Alan MacNaughton; Sandor Eles
REPORT 4821: X-RAY – WHO WEEPS FOR THE DOCTOR? 21/11/1969
d Charles Crichton; *sc* Roger Parkes
lp Ann Firbank; John Laurie;
Trisha Mortimer; Ewan Hooper; Nicholas Selby;
Richard Carpenter
REPORT 4407: HEART – NO CHOICE FOR THE DONOR 5/12/1969
d Robert Asher; *sc* Edward De Blasio
lp Kenneth Griffith; Barbara Murray;
Robert Hardy; Peter Cellier
REPORT 3906: COVER GIRLS – LAST YEAR'S MODEL 12/12/1969
d Peter Duffell; *sc* Terence Maples
lp Elaine Taylor; Lisa Daniely;
Richard Vanstone; David Healy; Ron Pember;
Doreen Mantle

STRANGERS (Granada 1978–82)
CID officers are drafted into a Northern police force to form a new team, Unit 23, to infiltrate areas of crime where local detectives might be recognized.
p Richard Everitt
regulars Don Henderson; Dennis Blanch;
John Ronane; Mark McManus;
Frances Tomelty; Fiona Mollison;
Thorley Walters
The PARADISE SET 5/6/1978
d Carol Wilks; *sc* Murray Smith
BRISCOE 3/7/1978
d Brian Mills; *sc* Leslie Duxbury
lp Michael Byrne; Michael Turner;
David Neilson
PAYING GUESTS 17/7/1978
d Quentin Lawrence; *sc* Leslie Duxbury
lp John Tordoff; Amanda Barrie;
Michael Byrne
WHEELER DEALERS 9/1/1979
d Carol Wilks; *sc* Murray Smith
lp Anne Kristen; Jo Beadle; Neil Johnson
CLEVER DICK 23/1/1979
d Quentin Lawrence; *sc* Brian Finch
lp John Duttine; Neil Stacy;
Gunnar Mollar; Geoffrey Chater
FRIENDS IN HIGH PLACES 30/1/1979
d Bill Gilmour; *sc* Murray Smith
lp Anthony Steel; Freddie Jones;
Derek Fowlds

The STRAUSS FAMILY
(ATV 7/11–19/12/1972)
Seven-part series about the Strauss family of Vienna.
ANNA 7/11/1972
d David Giles; *p* David Reid;
sc Anthony Skene
lp Eric Woofe; Stuart Wilson;
Anne Stallybrass; Barbara Ferris; Derek Jacobi;
Christopher Benjamin; Jeffrey Segal;
Max Latimer; Arthur Pentelow;
David De Keyser; Carleton Hobbs; Sam Kelly

The STRUGGLE FOR CHINA
(Yorkshire TV 11/11/1969)
Compilation film on the history of China, 1900–1949.
p Tony Essex, Michael Deakin;
comm James Mason, Cyril Luckham,
Alec Mango, David Bauer

STUDENTS IN REVOLT
(BBC 13/6/1968)
Robert McKenzie introduces a discussion between leading left wing students from all over the world, including Daniel Cohn-Bendit, Tariq Ali, Yasuo Ishii, Lewis Cole, Karl Dietrich Wolff, Dragana Stavijel, Luca Martin de Hijas, Ekkehart Krippendorf, Alain Geismar and Leo Nauweds.
p Anthony Smith; *interv* Robert McKenzie

STUDIO FIVE (Rediffusion 9/6/1960)
The story and official opening of Studio 5, the world's largest television studio; with John Spencer Wills, Chairman of Associated-Rediffusion
d Bill Morton; *p* Ray Dicks

The STUDIO 4 (BBC 1962)
Drama series.
The VICTORIAN CHAISE LONGUE 19/3/1962
d/p/sc James MacTaggart; *auth* Marghanita Laski
lp Frances White; Nora Laidlaw;
John Boxer; Denise Coffey; Richard Vernon;
Michael Culver; Jerome Willis

STUDIO '64 (ATV 1964)
Drama series.
BETTER LUCK NEXT TIME 2/2/1964
d Silvio Narizzano; *exec.p* Stuart Burge;
sc Stanley Mann
lp Zohra Lampert; Michael Bryant;
Helen Horton; Guy Deghy; Chuck Julian;
Bruce Boa

STUFF AND NONSENSE (BBC 9/8/1960)
p Brandon Acton-Bond; *sc* David Perry
lp Richard Pearson; Patsy Rowlands;
Dandy Nichols; Gretchen Franklin; Charles Lamb

A SUBJECT OF STRUGGLE
(Granada 26/9/1972)
A dramatised reconstruction of the downfall and interrogation of Wang Kuang-Mei, wife of Liu Shao-Chi, during the Cultural Revolution in China.
d Leslie Woodhead

SUCCESS STORY (Rediffusion 1959)
Daniel Farson examines the quality of success by interviewing successful people.
d Rollo Gamble
HANK JANSSEN 1959
The western/crime writer.
HYPERION 1959
The race horse Hyperion.
LADY LEWISHAM 5/1/1959
Raine Legge, her mother Barbara Cartland, and grandmother Polly Cartland.
FATHER JOSEPH CHRISTIE 12/1/1959
The Jesuit priest, Father Joseph Christie, discusses the success of the Roman Catholic Church in Britain.
HARRY EDWARDS 19/1/1959
Spiritual healer.
ALICK DICK 2/2/1959
Alick Dick, who became Managing Director of Standard Motors at the age of 37, discusses his position.
SHELAGH DELANEY 9/2/1959
The playwright Shelagh Delaney.
HERBERT MORRISON 9/3/1959
Herbert Morrison discusses his political career.
The CRADOCKS 16/3/1959
Cookery experts, John and Fanny Cradock.
CHARLES FORTE 23/3/1959
Sir Charles Forte talks about his success in the restaurant and catering industry.
MAURICE WOODRUFF 30/3/1959
Clairvoyant Maurice Woodruff; Diane Cilento and Peter Sellers discuss why they consult him.

SUEZ 1956 (BBC 25/11/1979)
Play based on the Suez Crisis of 1956.
d Michael Darlow; *p* Cedric Messina;
sc Ian Curteis
lp Michael Gough; Robert Stephens;
Richard Vernon; Wensley Pithey;
Seymour Green; Peter Cellier;
Edward Burnham; Patrick Troughton;
Mark Dignam

SUGARFOOT
(US Warner Bros. 1957–61)
Western action series.
The TRIAL OF THE CANARY KID 15/9/1959
lp Will Hutchins; Wayde Preston;
Peter Brown; Ty Hardin

The SUMMER IN GOSSENSASS
(BBC 15/9/1964)
Reconstruction of the relationship between
Henrik Ibsen and Emilie Bardach at Colle Isarco
in the Tirol.
d Casper Wrede;
sc Michael Meyer, Casper Wrede

SUMMER OF 79 (Westward 3/8/1979)

SUMMONED BY BELLS (BBC 29/8/1976)
Based on Sir John Betjeman's verse
autobiography and produced to celebrate his
70th birthday.
d Jonathan Stedall

The SUN TV AWARDS (Thames 14/5/1970)
d Bob Service; *intro* Keith Fordyce

SUNDAY AND MONDAY IN SILENCE
(Thames 29/5/1973)
The problems faced by two families affected by
deafness.
d David Hodgson; *exec.p* Ian Martin

The SUNDAY DRAMA (Yorkshire TV)
Anthology drama series.
SISTER DORA 26/6–10/7/1977
Three-part play by Christopher Fry, from the
book by Jo Manton. Based on the true story of
Sister Dora – Dorothy Pattison – one of the
world's greatest nurses and set in Walsall in the
mid-nineteenth century.
d/p Marc Miller; *sc* Christopher Fry;
auth Jo Manton
lp Dorothy Tutin; Bernard Archard;
Peter Cellier; Patricia Garwood;
Stephen Yardley
WHY HERE? 7/8/1977
d Robert Knights; *p* Nicholas Palmer;
sc David Cook
lp Andrew Ray; Carol Gillies;
Dickie Arnold; Geoffrey Greenhill
A SUPERSTITION 14/8/1977
d David Cunliffe; *p* Peter Willes;
sc David Mercer
lp Hugh Burden; Anthony Andrews;
John Stratton; John Nolan
TREATS 11/12/1977
d/p John Frankau; *sc* Christopher Hampton
lp John Hurt; Tom Conti; Kate Nelligan
CITY SUGAR 6/8/1978
d Mike Vardy; *exec.p* Robert Love;
sc Stephen Poliakoff
lp Tim Curry; Jon Morrison;
Veronica Quilligan; Frances Low;
Debbie Wheeler; Joseph Greig; Roy Boutcher;
Robert Trotter; Jimmy Chisholm; Ian Dewar

SUNDAY IN SEPTEMBER
(Granada 18/9/1961)
The nuclear disarmament demonstration in
Trafalgar Square, Sunday 17th September 1961.
p Tim Hewat

SUNDAY NIGHT (BBC)
Anthology drama series.
The QUARRY 27/2/1966
d/sc John Boorman
lp John Franklyn-Robbins; Sheila Allen;
Peter Bowles; Alexandra Malcolm;
Ingrid Hafner; David De Keyser;
Alexander Cranfield Abbott; George Tute;
Catherine Rodgers; Richard Howard;
John Boorman

The SUNDAY NIGHT PLAY (BBC 1960–63)
Anthology drama series.
The CHOPPING BLOCK 23/10/1960
d Vivian Matalon; *p/sc* Vincent Tilsley
lp Ursula Howells; Glyn Houston;
Barbara Young; Robert Perceval;
Jacqueline Hill; Pauline Taylor; Marion Mathie;
Angela Crow; Arnold Bell

LOOKING FOR GARROW 30/10/1960
p Terence Dudley; *sc* Elaine Morgan
lp Margaret Johnston; McDonald Hobley;
Donald Stewart; Olive Milbourne;
Jack Smethurst; Armine Sandford
A SUBJECT OF SCANDAL AND CONCERN
6/11/1960
p Tony Richardson; *sc* John Osborne;
nar John Freeman
lp Richard Burton; Rachel Roberts;
George Devine; William Devlin; George Howe;
Colin Douglas; Donald Eccles;
Willoughby Goddard; John Ruddock;
Nigel Davenport; Andrew Keir
The WIND AND THE SUN 13/11/1960
p Gilchrist Calder; *sc* Colin Morris
lp Katharine Blake; Scott Forbes;
Francesca Annis; Wilfrid Brambell;
Michael Bird
The WRONG SIDE OF THE PARK 19/3/1961
d Stuart Burge; *sc* John Mortimer
lp Brenda Bruce; Nigel Stock;
James Villiers; Ann Lynn; Charles Heslop;
Marie Ney

SUNDAY NIGHT THEATRE (BBC 1955–59)
Anthology drama series.
The WHITE FALCON 5/2/1956
p Rudolph Cartier;
sc Neilson Gattey, Jordan Lawrence
lp Marius Goring; Paul Rogers;
Jeannette Sterke; Margaretta Scott;
Patrick Troughton; Rupert Davies; Julia James;
Eric Lander; Enid Lindsay; Cyril Shaps;
Roger Delgado; Jennifer Browne
MRS. PATTERSON 17/6/1956
p Anthony Pélissier;
sc Charles Sebree, Greer Johnson
lp Eartha Kitt; Estelle Winwood;
Elisabeth Welch; Evelyn Dove; Neville Crabbe;
Rita Stevens; John Harrison
The COLD LIGHT 29/7/1956
d/p Rudolph Cartier; *sc* Judith Kerr;
auth Carl Zuckmayer; *trsl* Elizabeth Montagu
lp Marius Goring; John Longden;
Anton Diffring; Ewen Solon; John Van Eyssen;
Roger Delgado; Vera Fusek
The TEMPEST 14/10/1956
p Ian Atkins, Robert Atkins;
auth William Shakespeare
lp Robert Atkins; Robert Eddison;
Douglas Wilmer; Charles Lloyd Pack;
Olaf Pooley; Patti Brooks
The LARK 11/11/1956
p Julian Amyes; *sc* Christopher Fry;
auth Jean Anouilh
lp Hazel Penwarden; Robert Harris;
Michael Goodliffe; John Arnatt; Michael Caine
The GREEN PASTURES 14/9/1958
p Eric Fawcett; *sc* Marc Connelly
lp William Marshall; Berril Briggs;
Nadia Cattouse; Ansel Bernard; Curtis Auguste;
Locksley Booth; Barbara Bernard
A MIDSUMMER NIGHT'S DREAM 9/11/1958
p Rudolph Cartier; *sc* Eric Crozier;
auth William Shakespeare
lp Paul Rogers; Natasha Parry;
John Justin; Miles Malleson; Ronald Fraser;
Peter Sallis; Gillian Lynne; Michael Bates
WATERS OF THE MOON 27/12/1959
p Harold Clayton; *sc* N.C. Hunter
lp Edith Evans; Sybil Thorndike;
Kathleen Harrison; Lewis Casson;
Margaret Tyzack; Jean Anderson;
Cyril Raymond; George Pravda

SUNDAY STORY (BBC 1962)
Bible story-telling series.
EARTHA KITT TELLS STORIES FROM DANIEL:
1–THE FIERY FURNACE 27/5/1962
d John Elphinstone-Fyffe
EARTHA KITT TELLS STORIES FROM DANIEL:
2–THE KING'S DREAMS 3/6/1962
d John Elphinstone-Fyffe
EARTHA KITT TELLS STORIES FROM DANIEL:
3–THE DEN OF LIONS 10/6/1962
d John Elphinstone-Fyffe

SUNDAY, SWEET SUNDAY: ITALY
(Westward 28/10/1979)
How an Italian family in Milan spend their
Sunday.

SUNDERLAND v MANCHESTER CITY
(Granada 18/9/1976)

SUNLEY'S DAUGHTER
(Yorkshire TV 14/5/1974)
The traditional way of life still maintained by
farming families in the east Cleveland area of
Yorkshire.
d Barry Cockcroft; *exec.p* John Fairley

SUPERSONIC (LWT 1975–77)
Pop music series.
SUPERSONIC 27/12/1975
d/p Mike Mansfield
with Alvin Stardust, Gary Glitter,
Marc Bolan, Roxy Music, Slade, Mud,
Leo Sayer, Linda Lewis, Sweet, David Essex,
The Bay City Rollers, Justin Hayward,
John Lodge.

SUPERVISORS (BBC 6/11–4/12/1966)
Five-part series on management.
IN CHARGE OF MEN 13/11/1966
The problems faced when supervising people and
production.
d Paul Ellis

SURVIVAL (Anglia 1961–)
Wildlife programme. See also SURVIVAL
SPECIAL.
WILDLIFE IN LONDON 1/2/1961
d Bill Morton; *intro* Aubrey Buxton
SOS RHINO 21/6/1961
The measures being taken to save the white
rhino from extinction.
d Stanley Joseph; *p* Aubrey Buxton;
sc Colin Willock;
comm Aubrey Buxton, Dick Graham
LAST STRONGHOLD 25/2/1963
Birds, especially vultures and eagles, are under
threat in an area of Southern Spain due to be
developed.
d Stanley Joseph; *p* Aubrey Buxton
The EIGHTH WONDER OF THE WORLD
7/10/1963
The extinct volcano of Ngoronoro in Tanganyika
provides huge grazing grounds for one of the
greatest collections of game animals in Africa.
d Stanley Joseph; *p* Aubrey Buxton;
sc Colin Willock
The LIVING MOUNTAIN 26/5/1965
Wildlife in the Austrian Alps throughout the
year: ospreys catching fish; and red deer fighting
during the mating season.
p Heinz Nitsche, J.A. Holman
KARAMOJA 2/3/1966
Life among the Jie tribe of Karamoja, Uganda.
d Stanley Joseph; *sc* Colin Willock;
nar Duncan Carse
ROO! 8/4/1966
Rolf Harris narrates and sings the commentary
to a programme about kangaroos.
d Stanley Joseph; *sc* Colin Willock
KILL BY KINDNESS 26/9/1967
The problem of the overpopulation of elephants
in the Murchison Falls National Park.
sc Colin Willock; *intro* Duncan Carse
MONUMENTS IN MANGROVES 17/10/1967
A detailed study of a tiny mangrove island off
the coast of Florida, showing how it became the
first wildlife refuge in the USA, and
concentrating in particular on the birdlife.
d Stanley Joseph; *sc* Colin Willock;
intro Patrick Allen
The LONELIEST PLACE IN THE WORLD 2/1/1968
The way of life of the islanders of Tristan da
Cunha. The bird life on the islands.
d/p Stanley Joseph; *sc* Colin Willock;
comm Duncan Carse
FIRST CATCH YOUR UNICORN 12/1/1969
The straight-horned oryx of the Namib desert.
p Stanley Joseph; *sc* Colin Willock;
intro Duncan Carse
The YEAR OF THE DRAGONS 23/2/1969
The hazards faced by colonies of nesting herons
and egrets on an island in a stream east of
Pretoria in South Africa. Close by is a modern
factory, but the main danger to the birds are
monitor lizards.
d Stanley Joseph; *sc* Colin Willock;
intro Patrick Allen

LAND ABOVE THE CLOUDS 22/6/1969
p Stanley Joseph; *sc* Colin Willock;
pres Patrick Allen
DEATH OF A ZEBRA 12/4/1970
The danger to the wildlife of the Etosha Pan
National Park in South Africa posed by an
outbreak of anthrax and the work of the wardens
in trying to pinpoint the source of the diseases.
d Stanley Joseph; *sc* Colin Willock
STRIPED HORSE IN A RED COLLAR 19/4/1970
The wildlife in Etosha Pan National Park,
particularly the zebra herd, and an experiment
involving marking a zebra with a red collar to
help rangers to track the anticlockwise migration
pattern of zebras.
d Stanley Joseph; *intro* Duncan Carse
The LONG DRY SUMMER 26/4/1970
The threat posed to the wildlife in Etosha, a Pan
National Park in South Africa, by the late arrival
of the rainy season. It highlights the perils for
the flamingo colony and the rare black-faced
impala antelope.
d Stanley Joseph; *sc* Colin Willock;
intro Duncan Carse
The V.I.P.s 3/5/1970
A sequel to The LONG DRY SUMMER. Looks
at the transportation of the rare black-faced
impala antelope into the Etosha Pan National
Park, from an outside area where they were
threatened by drought and poachers.
d Stanley Joseph; *sc* Colin Willock
The SEA OF CORTEZ 7/6/1970
Wildlife in and around the Gulf of California
including finback whales, sealions and terns.
p Stanley Joseph; *sc* Colin Willock
PARADISE LOST? 6/9/1970
The work of the Ocean Science Foundation in
protecting whales and dolphins that inhabit the
waters around the Hawaiian Islands.
p Stanley Joseph; *sc* Hugh De Las Casas;
intro Patrick Allen
WAR OF THE ROSES 13/9/1970
The fight against the greenfly by rose growers.
p Stanley Joseph; *sc* Hugh De Las Casas;
pres Dick Graham
The ISLAND THAT CAME BACK TO LIFE
20/9/1970
Shows how a delicate balance has been achieved
between the human and seabird communities on
the island of St. Kilda. The island is the location
for an Army radar establishment.
p Stanley Joseph; *sc* Hugh De Las Casas
WATER, WATER EVERYWHERE 27/9/1970
Shows the areas set aside for wildfowl
affected by the draining of the Zuider Zee and
suggests that the Dutch example in conservation
is one that Britain should follow when
undertaking similar land reclamation schemes.
d Stanley Joseph; *sc* Colin Willock;
pres Duncan Carse
JEZEBEL 4/10/1970
The story of a young Swaziland farmer who
turned his farm into a wildlife reserve and
stocked it with animals which had become
extinct in the district in recent times.
d Stanley Joseph; *sc* Colin Willock;
pres Dick Graham
OKAVANGO 18/10/1970
The wildlife of the Okavango Swamp in
Botswana which is threatened by the diversion of
the river which feeds the swamp.
p Stanley Joseph;
sc Colin Willock, Caroline Weaver;
pres Dick Graham
ALL FOR THEIR OWN GOOD 13/3/1971
Looks at how some American biologists are
saving endangered species.
d Stanley Joseph; *sc* Colin Willock;
nar Rolf Harris
MAN-MADE FOR NATURE 30/7/1972
Chew Valley Lake is a large reservoir in
Somerset which serves the city of Bristol. The
lake has been stocked with fish and nature
reserves have been created around its edges.
p Stanley Joseph; *sc* Colin Willock;
comm Flora Robson

FLIGHT OF THE SNOW GEESE 25/12/1972
Yearly migrations of America's blue and snow
geese from Hudson Bay to the 'Deep South' of
America.
d Jen Bartlett, Des Bartlett;
sc Colin Willock; *comm* Peter Scott
A WEALTH OF WILDFOWL 1973
The wildfowl to be found on the Ouse washes in
the East Anglian Fenlands, home to 25,000
ducks and 1000 swans, in particular at the birds
that visit the new sanctuary of the Wildfowl
Trust at Welney.
d/p Ron Downing; *sc* Colin Willock;
intro Peter Scott
SAGA OF THE SEA OTTER 7/2/1973
The life and behaviour of the sea otter, filmed
off the coast of Southern California, and the
threat to its existence posed by local fishermen.
p Aubrey Buxton;
sc Colin Willock, Caroline Weaver;
intro Peter Scott
ALDABRA REPRIEVED 5/8/1973
The range of of wildlife, including giant
tortoises, on Aldabra Island in the Indian Ocean
which was at one time threatened by a proposed
Anglo-US air base.
p Stanley Joseph; *sc* Colin Willock
INDUSTRIAL ACTION 16/10/1974
A study of the honey bee.
sc Malcolm Penny; *intro* Peter Scott
The ODYSSEY OF ARGULUS 1/10/1975
A study of the argulus, a fish lice. It shows what
happens when a stickleback swallows an argulus
and a pike swallows the stickleback.
d/p Colin Willock
The LITTLE GENTLEMEN IN BLACK VELVET
26/6/1977
Documentary on moles.
d Malcolm Penny, David Thompson;
p Colin Willock; *nar* Richard Briers
CHILDREN OF THE STORM 3/7/1977
The survival of young grey seals off Ramsey
Island.
d/p Colin Willock; *sc* Malcolm Penny;
nar Alan Dobie
DEAD OR ALIVE? 16/4/1978
The Aye-Aye in the Malagasy Republic.
d Elizabeth Bomford, Anthony Bomford,
Colin Willock; *p* Colin Willock;
sc Malcolm Penny; *nar* Anthony Valentine

SURVIVAL SPECIAL (Anglia)
Wildlife programme. See also SURVIVAL.
The FORBIDDEN DESERT OF THE DANAKIL
8/5/1973
Retraces the journey made in 1934 by explorer
Wilfred Thesiger tracing the course of the
previously uncharted Awash River in the
Danakil desert of Ethiopia and looks at the life
of the Danakil people. Wilfred Thesiger
recollects his own experiences.
d/sc Colin Willock; *p* Aubrey Buxton;
nar David Niven
The FAMILY THAT LIVES WITH ELEPHANTS
29/2/1976
Scientist Iain Douglas-Hamilton and his wife
who brought up their children among 500
elephants in the African bush.
d Colin Willock; *intro* David Niven
HUMPBACK – THE GENTLE GIANTS 24/3/1978
A study of humpback whales.
p/sc Colin Willock; *nar* Patrick Allen
CASTLES OF CLAY 31/3/1978
A study of termite colonies and the ecological
role they play.
d/p/sc Alan Root; *nar* Derek Jacobi
The LAST KINGDOM OF THE ELEPHANTS
27/10/1978
Documentary about the animals in Zambia's
Luangwa Valley, especially the elephants; filmed
by Cindy Buxton.
d/p/sc Colin Willock; *nar* Orson Welles
The LEOPARD THAT CHANGED ITS SPOTS
22/12/1978
Story of how Billy Arjan Singh, an Indian
conservationist who specialises in knowing and
understanding big cats, successfully reared a
female leopard who returned to the wild and had
cubs, then took them back to his house to rear.
Includes footage of wild leopards.
p Colin Willock; *nar* Andrew Sachs

SURVIVORS (BBC 1975–77)
Science-fantasy drama series about the world
depopulated by a virulent disease.
NEW WORLD 23/6/1976
d Terence Williams; *p* Terence Dudley;
sc Martin Worth
lp Gordon Salkilld; Lucy Fleming;
Ian McCulloch; Stephen Tate; Heather Wright;
John Abineri; Tanya Ronder

SWALLOWS AND AMAZONS
(Windsor Films Production-BBC 1963)
Six-part serial based on the story by Arthur
Ransome.
d Peter Saunders; *p* John Robins;
sc Anthony Steven
regulars David Lott; Siobhan Taylor;
John Paul; Susan George; Shane Younger;
Christine Reeve; Amanda Coxell; Paula Boyd
EPISODE 1: SAILING ORDERS 3/9/1963
lp Mary Kenton
EPISODE 2: THE ALLIANCE 10/9/1963
lp George Roderick; Anthony Sagar;
Ruth Kettlewell; Natalie Kent
EPISODE 3: THE SERPENT 17/9/1963
lp Michael Ripper; Sam Kydd;
Natalie Kent
EPISODE 4: NIGHT RAIDERS 24/9/1963
lp Mary Kenton; George Roderick;
Anthony Sagar
EPISODE 5: TABLES TURNED 1/10/1963
lp Mary Kenton; George Roderick;
Anthony Sagar; Ruth Kettlewell; Bernard Kay
EPISODE 6: STORM 8/10/1963
lp Mary Kenton; George Roderick;
Anthony Sagar

SWAN LAKE (BBC 9/6/1954)
Robert Irving introduces Margot Fonteyn and
Michael Somes in the pas de deux from Act II
and III of 'Swan Lake'. Irving discusses the
ballet and sets the pas de deux in context. He
also comments on the score and conducts
excerpts from it.
p Christian Simpson; *with* Arnott Mader

SWEDISH LOOK (Tyne Tees 2/11/1966)

The SWEENEY (Thames 1975–78)
Police drama series about Scotland Yard's tough
Flying Squad (nicknamed 'The Sweeney').
Developed from the film REGAN.
p Ted Childs
regulars John Thaw; Dennis Waterman;
Garfield Morgan
JACKPOT 9/1/1975
d Tom Clegg; *sc* Tony Marsh
lp Ed Devereaux; Morris Perry;
John Flanagan; Richard Davies;
Morgan Sheppard; Carolyn Jones
The PLACER 13/2/1975
d Ted Childs; *sc* Trevor Preston
lp Stanley Meadows; Tony Steedman;
Carl Rigg
COUNTRY BOY 17/11/1975
d Jim Goddard; *sc* Andrew Wilson
lp Robert Swan; Myra Frances;
Christine Shaw; Andonia Katsaros;
Leslie Schofield
SELECTED TARGET 6/9/1976
d Tom Clegg; *sc* Troy Kennedy Martin
lp Lee Montague; Ronald Fraser;
James Aubrey; Peter Schofield;
Maureen Lipman; Jonathan Elsom;
Basil Dignam
DOWN TO YOU, BROTHER 22/11/1976
d Chris Menaul; *sc* Richard Harris
lp Derek Francis; Terence Budd;
Tina Heath; Kenny Lynch; Malcolm Tierney;
Simon Callow
MESSENGER OF THE GODS 7/9/1978
d Terry Green; *sc* Trevor Preston
lp Diana Dors; Malcolm McFee;
Dawn Perlman; James Ottaway;
Richard Adams; Rosemary Martin
HARD MEN 14/9/1978
d Graham Baker; *sc* Troy Kennedy Martin
lp James Cosmo; James Warrior;
Stewart Preston; Alex Norton; Brian Hoskin

The SWEENEY *cont.*

DRAG ACT 21/9/1978
d Tom Clegg; *sc* Ted Childs
lp Katherine Fahy; Albert Welling; Benjamin Whitrow; Patrick Malahide; Peter Kerrigan
NIGHTMARE 5/10/1978
d David Wickes; *sc* Ranald Graham
lp Paul Antrim; Tony Rohr; Barry Philips; David Gillies
MONEY, MONEY, MONEY 12/10/1978
d Sid Roberson; *sc* Trevor Preston
lp Edward Judd; Vilma Hollingbery; Tina Martin; Glynn Owen; Michael Culver; John Cater
The BIGGER THEY ARE 26/10/1978
d Mike Vardy; *sc* Tony Hoare
lp Colin Jeavons; Jenny Runacre; Tony Steedman; Donald Burton; Richard Wilson
FEET OF CLAY 2/11/1978
d Chris Burt; *sc* Roger Marshall
lp Joss Ackland; Thelma Whiteley; Brian Capron; David Wilkinson; Cheryl Campbell; Geoffrey Palmer; John Junkin; Diana Weston; Carol Drinkwater
ONE OF YOUR OWN 9/11/1978
d Chris Menaul; *sc* Tony Hoare
lp Michael Elphick; John Alkin; Nick Stringer; Sion Probert; Rachel Davies; John Turner
LATIN LADY 30/11/1978
d Peter Smith; *sc* Ted Childs
lp Meg Davies; Stuart Wilson; Donald Morley; Benjamin Whitrow; James Warrior

SYBIL THORNDIKE REMEMBERS
(BBC 30/12/1970)
Frank Hauser interviews Sybil Thorndike about her life in the theatre.
p Hal Burton

The SYLPHIDE (BBC 2/4/1961)
Ballet of Auguste Bournonville with principal dancers Lucette Aldous and Flemming Flindt. Music by Løvenskjold performed by the London Symphony Orchestra conducted by David Ellenberg.
d Margaret Dale

Les SYLPHIDES (BBC 3/4/1953)
Performance by the Royal Ballet. The Covent Garden Orchestra conducted by Eric Robinson.
p Christian Simpson; *pres* Tamara Karsavina; *with* Alicia Markova, Violetta Elvin, Svetlana Beriosova, John Field

T

T.E. LAWRENCE 1888–1935
(BBC 27/11/1962)
The life of Thomas Edward Lawrence. With Professor Arnold Lawrence, Sir Alec Kirkbride, Lowell Thomas, Air Commodore Sydney Smith, Henry Williamson, David Garnett and Siegfried Sassoon.
p Malcolm Brown, Philip Donnellan

TAKE HART (BBC 1977–84)
Series for children with artist Tony Hart who shows different ways of creating art.
TAKE HART 7/3/1979
d Christopher Pilkington; *p* Patrick Dowling

TAKE SIX (Thames 1978; 1981)
Series in which young film-makers are given the opportunity to make a film for television.
HACKNEY MARSHES 8/8/1978
Living in a tower block in Hackney.
d John Smith

TAKE THREE GIRLS
(BBC 17/11/1969–2/2/1970; 24/3–11/6/1971)
Drama series following the problems of three women friends.
RELEASE 11/6/1971
d Michael Hayes; *sc* Robert Muller
lp Liza Goddard; Barra Grant; Carolyn Seymour; Elisabeth Bergner; Peter Halliday; Ernst Walder; Gerard Heinz; Hilde-Maria Demlova; Peter Arne; Roger Mutton

TAKE YOUR PICK (Rediffusion 1955–68)
Quiz show hosted by Michael Miles.
voice Bob Danvers-Walker
TAKE YOUR PICK 1955
TAKE YOUR PICK 7/10/1966
d Audrey Starrett; *with* Jane Murray
TAKE YOUR PICK 26/1/1968
d Audrey Starrett; *p* Michael Miles
TAKE YOUR PICK 26/7/1968
d John P. Hamilton; *p* Michael Miles

A TALE OF CANTERBURY
(Rediffusion 25/12/1967)
Canterbury Cathedral and its history.
d John Rhodes; *p* Peter Hunt; *with* John Betjeman

A TALE OF TWO HAWKERS
(Tyne Tees 10/5/1972)
The rag-and-bone trade in the north-east of England.
d Jeremy Lack

A TALE OF TWO STREETS
(ATV 16/11/1966)
The contemporary fashion business of Carnaby Street compared with the traditions of Savile Row.
d Ken Ashton

TALES FROM SOHO (BBC 21/1–25/2/1956)
A series of six plays.
The FIDDLE 21/1/1956
d John Nelson Burton; *p* Tony Richardson; *sc* Berkely Mather
lp Meier Tzelniker; Alfie Bass; Lucie Mannheim; Gerard Heinz

TALES OF INDIA
(BBC 8/5–12/6/1978)
A six-part documentary series in which people are interviewed about the British in India during the 1920s and '30s.
p Stephen Peet
MEMSAHIBS 8/5/1978
Three memsahibs who joined their husbands in India between the wars, recall what it was like to be a woman in what was traditionally considered a man's country.
d/nar Christopher Cook
FRONTIER OUTRAGE 15/5/1978
The North-West Frontier in 1923.
p/nar Stephen Peet
SOLDIERS THREE 22/5/1978
Life in the British Army in the 1930s is described by a fusilier, a drummer and a private.
p/nar Stephen Peet
FIGHTING TERRORISTS 29/5/1978
An account of dedicated revolutionaries in Bengal who, in opposition to the pacifist policies of Gandhi, believed that political assassination and indiscriminate bombings were the only way to drive the British from India.
d/nar Christopher Cook
SAHIBS 5/6/1978
Three British sahibs recall their time in 'a man's country'. An Indian civil servant, a Gurkha officer and a Bengal pilot remember work and leisure during the last days of the British Raj.
d/nar Christopher Cook
ONE OF THE COMMUNITY 12/6/1978
Irene Green, now Mrs Irene Edwards, recalls her childhood in the Anglo-Indian community and her adventurous time as a nursing sister in the North-West Frontier of the 1930s.
d/nar Christopher Cook

TALES OF THE UNEXPECTED
(Anglia 1979–84)
Drama series.
p John Rosenberg
MAN FROM THE SOUTH 24/3/1979
d Michael Tuchner; *sc* Kevin Goldstein-Jackson; *auth* Roald Dahl
lp José Ferrer; Michael Ontkean; Katy Jurado; Cyril Luckham; Pamela Stephenson
MRS. BIXBY AND THE COLONEL'S COAT 31/3/1979
d Simon Langton; *sc* Roald Dahl
lp Julie Harris; Michael Hordern; Richard Greene

WILLIAM AND MARY 7/4/1979
d Donald McWhinnie; *sc* Ronald Harwood; *auth* Roald Dahl
lp Elaine Stritch; Marius Goring; Richard Hampton
LAMB TO THE SLAUGHTER 14/4/1979
d John Davies; *sc* Robin Chapman; *auth* Roald Dahl
lp Susan George; Brian Blessed; Michael Byrne; Mark Jones; George Little; Hugh Cross; Andrew Fell; David English
The LANDLADY 21/4/1979
d Herbert Wise; *sc* Robin Chapman; *auth* Roald Dahl
lp Siobhan McKenna; Leonard Preston; Anthony Dawes; John Bryant; Jess Davies
NECK 28/4/1979
d Christopher Miles; *sc* Robin Chapman; *auth* Roald Dahl
lp John Gielgud; Joan Collins; Michael Aldridge; Peter Bowles; Paul Herzberg

TALES OF WELLS FARGO
(US Overland Productions 1957–62)
Western series featuring a Wells Fargo company troubleshooter.
regular Dale Robertson
RIDE WITH A KILLER 2/12/1957
The THIN ROPE 2/6/1958
d Leslie H. Martinson; *p* Nat Holt; *sc* N.B. Stone Jr; *nar* Dale Robertson;
lp Chuck Connors; Russell Thorson; Jacqueline Holt; Arthur Space; Robert Burton; Kit Carson
RED RANSOM 8/2/1960

TALKBACK (BBC 1967–72)
Series about television in which David Coleman (1967–68) then Cliff Michelmore chaired a discussion between television programme makers and a selected audience of viewers.
TALKBACK 22/4/1969
p Michael Townson
TALKBACK 15/7/1969
p Michael Townson

The TAMER TAMED (BBC 7/2/1956)
Drama continuing the story of Katharina, Petruchio, Baptista, Hortensio and Bianca based on Shakespeare's 'The Taming of the Shrew'.
p Anthony Pélissier; *sc* Elaine Morgan
lp Judy Campbell; Robert Urquhart; Bruno Barnabe; Aubrey Dexter; John Gatrell; Annabel Maule; Hugh Latimer

TARGET (BBC 1977–78)
Detective series featuring a tough Regional Crime Squad.
p Philip Hinchcliffe
regulars Patrick Mower; Philip Madoc; Brendan Price; Vivien Heilbron
SHIPMENT 9/9/1977
d David Wickes;
sc David Wickes, Philip Hinchcliffe
lp Carl Rigg; Ania Marson; Jon Laurimore; Peter Godfrey; Keith James
BLOW OUT 16/9/1977
d Douglas Camfield; *sc* David Agnew
lp Sandy Ratcliff; Maurice Roëves; Kenneth Colley; Christopher Benjamin; Ron Pember; Hilary Crane; Dorothy White
BIG ELEPHANT 23/9/1977
d Douglas Camfield;
sc Bob Baker, Dave Martin
lp Ken Hutchinson; Katy Manning; Walter Randall; Hugh Fraser
HUNTING PARTIES 30/9/1977
d Chris Menaul; *sc* David Agnew
lp Carl Rigg; Lee Montague; Janet Amsden; Roy Marsden; Ian MacKenzie; Tina Heath; Andrew McCulloch; Davyd Harries
VANDRAGGERS 14/10/1977
d Francis Megahy;
sc Francis Megahy, Bernie Cooper
lp David Daker; Bernard Spear; Ania Marson

ROGUES' GALLERY 15/9/1978
d Mike Vardy;
sc Bob Baker; Dave Martin
lp Jan Francis, Lewis Fiander;
Michael J. Shannon; Stephen Bent; Tony Osoba;
Glyn Houston; Ian Thompson; Diana Weston;
Anna Nygh
A GOOD AND FAITHFUL WOMAN 22/9/1978
d Ben Bolt; *sc* Richard Harris
lp Dave King; Prunella Scales;
Ronald Lacey; Tom Chadbon
QUEEN'S PARDON 29/9/1978
d/sc David Wickes
lp Max Wall; Ray Smith; Lance Percival;
Ted Moult
FRINGE BANKING 13/10/1978
d Terry Green; *sc* Ken Follett
lp John Judd; Leslie Sarony;
Neville Barber; Yvonne Antrobus;
John Malcolm; Gwen Cherrell;
John Rhys-Davies
PROMISES 20/10/1978
d Gordon Flemyng; *sc* Tony Hoare
lp Donald Sumpter; Mark McManus;
Katherine Fahy; Maurice O'Connell; Peter Dean
TROUBLE WITH CHARLIE 27/10/1978
d Peter Smith; *sc* Dave Humphries
lp Cheryl Kennedy; John Nolan;
David Dixon; Mark Jones; Ben Howard;
Elin Jenkins; David Sibley
FIGURES OF IMPORTANCE 3/11/1978
d/sc Chris Menaul
lp Alfred Marks; Patricia Hodge;
David Beckett; Virginia Stride; Renee Goddard
The RUN 10/11/1978
d Terry Green; *sc* P.J. Hammond
lp Christopher Neame; Jonathan Elsom;
David Lodge; Tony Caunter

TARGET: THE CORRUPTORS
(US Four Star-Velie-Burrows-Ackerman
1961–62)
Drama series set in a newspaper office and
following the adventures of an investigative
reporter.
MILLION DOLLAR DUMP 29/9/1961
d Don Medford;
sc Palmer Thompson, Don Brinkley,
Christopher Knopf
lp Stephen McNally; Robert Harland;
Peter Falk; Walter Matthau

TASTE FOR ADVENTURE (BBC 1975–77)
Documentary series.
FISTS OF FIRE 16/1/1975
The Hong Kong movie empire and the people
who make it work; including Run Run Shaw and
David Chiang.
p Colin Luke

TELEGOONS (Grosvenor Films 1963–64)
Puppet series based on the radio show 'The
Goon Show'.
d/p Tony Young; *sc* Spike Milligan;
adapt Maurice Wiltshire
voice Peter Sellers, Harry Secombe,
Spike Milligan
The LOST COLONY 12/10/1963
The HASTINGS FLYER 7/12/1963
The MYSTERY OF THE MARIE CELESTE –
SOLVED 14/12/1963
sc Spike Milligan, Eric Sykes
The INTERNATIONAL CHRISTMAS PUDDING
21/12/1963
The CHOKING HORROR 28/12/1963
SCRADGE 28/3/1964
d Bill Freshman
The BOOTED GORILLA 4/4/1964
sc Spike Milligan, Eric Sykes
TALES OF OLD DARTMOOR 25/4/1964
sc Spike Milligan, Eric Sykes
LURGI STRIKES BRITAIN 2/5/1964
The FIRST ALBERT MEMORIAL TO THE MOON
16/5/1964
d Bill Freshman;
sc Spike Milligan, Larry Stephens
The WHISTLING SPY ENIGMA 23/5/1964
TALES OF MONTMARTRE 30/5/1964
The AFRICA SHIP CANAL 6/6/1964
d Mike Wilson;
sc Spike Milligan, Larry Stephens

The AFFAIR OF THE LONE BANANA 13/6/1964
d Bill Freshman
The TERRIBLE REVENGE OF FRED FU MANCHU
20/6/1964
The SIEGE OF FORT KNIGHT or THE
UNDERWATER GAS STOVE 18/7/1964
The CHINA STORY 15/8/1964
The CANAL 22/8/1964
d Bill Freshman

TELEVISION AND THE WORLD
(BBC 31/10/1961)
The impact of television in different countries:
Italy, Egypt, Thailand, Japan, USA, Russia,
Poland, Brazil and Nigeria.
d/p/sc Richard Cawston; *comm* Michael Flanders

TELEVISION COMES TO LONDON
(BBC 1936)
The preparation and transmission of the first
television programmes from Alexandra Palace,
2/11/1936.
p Gerald Cock, Dallas Bower; *sc* Cecil Lewis;
comm Leslie Mitchell;
with Adele Dixon, The Television Orchestra

TELEVISION DEMONSTRATION FILM
(BBC 1937)
A film survey of television programmes during
the first six months of operation, November
1936–May 1937. Intended for manufacturers and
retailers to show sample types of programmes
transmitted.
d/p Dallas Bower;
comm Leslie Mitchell, Jasmine Bligh,
Elizabeth Cowell

TELEVISION FOR CHILDREN
(Rediffusion 1959)
Examples of the range of programmes for
children produced by Rediffusion. Includes
'Lucky Dip', 'The Little Ship', 'Francis Storm
Investigates', 'Musical Box', 'Our Street', 'Brock
and Bruin', 'Nature Page', and 'Music Parade'.
d Bill Morton; *p* Ray Dicks;
sc Stanley Joseph

TELEVISION PLAYHOUSE
(ITV various 1956–63)
Anthology drama series.
NO FIXED ABODE (Granada 30/1/1959)
d James Ormerod; *sc* Clive Exton
lp Robin Wentworth; Wilfrid Brambell;
Michael Gwynn; Jack Hedley; Jack Rodney
PROMENADE (Granada 22/5/1959)
d Julian Amyes; *sc* Peter Nichols
lp Susannah York; William Young;
Tom Bell; Trader Faulkner; Pauline Yates;
Peter McEnery
MR. BROWN COMES HOME
(Rediffusion 10/7/1959)
d David Boisseau; *sc* Paul Jones
lp Donald Pleasence; Gwen Watford
MY SIDE OF THE STORY (Rediffusion 7/8/1959)
d Michael Westmore; *sc* Robert Gould
lp Valerie White; Andre van Gyseghem
OGGIE (Rediffusion 13/11/1959)
d Ronald Marriott; *sc* Roy Jennings
lp John Merivale; Peter Vaughan;
Gordon Jackson; Wendy Craig; Alfred Burke;
Robert Desmond; Max Butterfield;
Martin Wyldeck; Edward Cast
The ADVOCATE (Rediffusion 11/12/1959)
d Christopher Hodson; *sc* Peter Van Greenaway
lp Harold Kasket; Mary Morris;
Keith Buckley; Carol Booth; Sam Kydd;
Erik Chitty; Edward Hardwicke
AT HOME (Rediffusion 18/3/1960)
d Robert Tronson; *sc* Paul Jones
lp Renee Asherson; Emrys Jones
BEN SPRAY (Granada 23/2/1961)
d Cliff Owen; *sc* Peter Nichols
lp Ian Hendry; Lockwood West;
John Arnatt; Jane Jordan Rogers; Philip Bond;
Derrick Sherwin; Betty Huntley-Wright;
Felicity Young
The RECEPTION (Granada 18/5/1961)
d Julian Amyes; *sc* Peter Nichols
lp Olga Lindo; Wensley Pithey;
Jennifer Wright; Michael Blakemore;
Julie Webb; Philip Bond; Jan Holden

The DIFFERENT DRUM (Rediffusion 6/7/1961)
d Peter Graham Scott; *sc* Frederick Aicken
lp Eric Portman; Douglas Wilmer;
Joyce Heron; Cavan Kendall;
Christopher Beeny; Jean Alexander
The DUMB WAITER (Granada 10/8/1961)
d Paul Almond; *sc* Harold Pinter
lp Roddy McMillan; Kenneth J. Warren
The PALETO CONFESSION
(Rediffusion 25/1/1963)
d Michael Currer-Briggs; *sc* Patrick Ryan
lp Patrick Wymark; Bernard Archard;
Martin Benson; Roy Holder; Anna Burden
BEN AGAIN (Granada 22/3/1963)
d Gordon Flemyng; *sc* Peter Nichols
lp Dinsdale Landen; Ann Bell;
John Bonney; Joyce Heron; William Kendall;
Philip Locke; Diana Coupland
TOO OLD FOR DONKEYS (ATV 4/4/1963)
d Peter Potter; *sc* Rhys Adrian
lp Ann Lynn; Leslie Sands; Patrick Magee;
Peter Furnell; Patrick Godfrey
The TWO-SEATER BACHELOR DAYS
(Rediffusion 11/4/1963)
d Michael Currer-Briggs; *sc* Paul Jones
lp Dinsdale Landen; Zena Walker;
Ann Bell; Henry McGee; Peter Cellier;
Derek Partridge
RETURN TO THE REGIMENT (ATV 2/5/1963)
d John Llewellyn Moxey; *sc* Arden Winch
lp Michael Redgrave; Nigel Davenport;
Barry Foster; Thomas Heathcote;
Anthony Sagar; Antony Carrick

TELEVISION WORLD THEATRE
(BBC 1957–58)
Anthology drama series.
The CLANDESTINE MARRIAGE 16/3/1958
p Hal Burton;
auth George Colman; David Garrick
lp Doreen Aris; Rosalind Knight;
Eric Lander; Esmond Knight; Helen Lindsay;
Hermione Baddeley; Elizabeth Thorndike;
Charles Lloyd Pack

TELFORD'S CHANGE
(Astramead-BBC 7/1–11/3/1979)
Ten-part drama serial about an international
banker who decides to change his career and
manage a provincial branch of the bank.
EPISODE 1 7/1/1979
d Barry Davies; *p* Mark Shivas;
sc Brian Clark
lp Peter Barkworth; Hannah Gordon;
Martin Benson; Julian Holloway;
Michael Maloney; Holly Palance;
Paul Williamson; Patrick Barr; Gerry Cowper;
Nula Conwell

TELL ME WHY (Tyne Tees 1978)
Series in which a group of 20 young people
debate social and ethical questions.
MARY WHITEHOUSE 11/7/1978

TELLING IT LIKE IT IS: CUDLIPP'S
CRUSADE (ATV 23/10/1974)
Sir Hugh Cudlipp looks back at his career in
journalism. (This programme was postponed
from its original transmission date 17/9/1974
because of its closeness to a General Election.)
d/p John Goldschmidt

TEMPO (ABC 1961–67)
Arts series.
CAROLS MEAN CHRISTMAS 22/12/1963
Collegium Musicum Oxoniense rehearse carols
at Merton College, Oxford.
p Reginald Collin; *sc* Louis Marks;
intro Leonard Maguire
POSTSCRIPT TO THE BALLET 5/4/1964
Dance programme specially written by Peter
Brinson as a tribute to Dame Ninette de Valois
and the Royal Ballet.
d Pamela Lonsdale; *p* Reginald Collin;
intro David Mahlowe
The MIME OF JACQUES LECOQ 24/5/1964
Lecoq and his company perform 'The
Separation' and 'The Swimming Pool'.
p Reginald Collin; *sc* Peter Brinson;
intro David Mahlowe

TEMPO *cont.*

The PRINCE MAKER 13/9/1964
Zeffirelli rehearses a scene from his National
Theatre production of 'Hamlet'. The same scene
on film from the Italian production.
p Reginald Collin; *sc* Derek Prouse;
intro David Mahlowe
The BLUES CAME WALKIN': PART 1 6/12/1964
The Third American Folk Blues Festival in
Manchester, featuring Sonny Boy Williamson,
Lightning Hopkins, Willie Dixon and Sunnyland
Slim.
d Helen Standage; *p* Reginald Collin;
intro David Mahlowe
The BLUES CAME WALKIN': PART 2 13/12/1964
Further music (see Part 1) from the Third
American Folk Blues Festival held at
Manchester, featuring Sleepy John Estes,
Howlin' Wolf and Sugar Pie Desanto.
d Helen Standage; *p* Reginald Collin;
intro David Mahlowe
BOSS GUITAR 6/6/1965
Jazz guitarist Wes Montgomery, with Ronnie
Scott, Stan Tracey, Rick Laird and Jackie
Dougan.
p Reginald Collin; *intro* David Mahlowe
HAROLD PINTER 3/10/1965
A portrait of playwright Harold Pinter.
d Jim Goddard; *p* Mike Hodges;
nar John Kershaw
A TALE OF TWO TALENTS 6/2/1966
Contrasts the careers of Tom Jones, the Welsh
pop singer and Lynn Seymour, a Canadian
dancer with the Royal Ballet Company.
d Jim Goddard; *p* Mike Hodges;
nar Alan Dell

TEMPO – PERFORMER AND COMPOSER
(ABC)
Music series.
DANIEL BARENBOIM ON BEETHOVEN 6/8/1967
d Helen Standage; *p* John Irwin;
intro Antony Hopkins
GEORGE MALCOLM ON SCARLATTI 13/8/1967
d Helen Standage; *p* John Irwin;
intro Antony Hopkins
GERVASE DE PEYER ON BRAHMS 20/8/1967
d Helen Standage; *p* John Irwin;
intro Antony Hopkins
VLADO PERLEMUTER ON RAVEL 24/9/1967
d Helen Standage; *p* John Irwin;
intro Antony Hopkins
JANET BAKER ON SCHUMANN 8/10/1967
d Helen Standage; *p* John Irwin;
intro Antony Hopkins

TEMPO – THE ACTOR AND THE ROLE
(ABC)
Actors and actresses discuss and illustrate great
roles.
IRENE WORTH 3/3/1968
Irene Worth as Celia Copplestone from T.S.
Eliot's 'The Cocktail Party' with Robert Flemyng
as Edward Chamberlayne and Sir Henry
Harcourt-Reilly.
d Pamela Lonsdale; *p* John Irwin;
intro Derek Hart
EDITH EVANS 17/3/1968
Dame Edith Evans as Lady Pitts from 'Daphne
Laureola' by James Bridie, with David Buck as
Ernest.
d Helen Standage; *p* John Irwin;
intro Derek Hart
SYBIL THORNDIKE 7/4/1968
Dame Sybil Thorndike in the role of Medea by
Euripedes.
d Helen Standage; *p* John Irwin;
intro Derek Hart
MICHAEL HORDERN 14/4/1968
Michael Hordern discusses the role of Prospero
from Shakespeare's 'The Tempest' and acts in
sequences from the play, with Jane Asher as
Miranda and Freda Dowie as Ariel.
d Helen Standage; *p* John Irwin;
intro Derek Hart

TEN DAYS THAT SHOOK THE WORLD
(Granada 6/11/1967)
Compilation of archive film from seven
countries, and specially shot all over Europe;
relates the history of Russia from the Coronation
of Tsar Nicholas II in 1896 to the October
Revolution of 1917.
p Norman Swallow, Grigori V. Alexandrov;
sc Grigori V. Alexandrov, Derek Granger,
Mike Murphy; *nar* Orson Welles

TEN MILLION STRONG
(AU ABC 26/11/1963)
A report on Malaysia.
d John Gray

**10 THOUSAND DAYS, 93 THOUSAND
HOURS, 33 YEARS OF EFFORT**
(BBC 6/6/1965)
Sculptor Ferdinand Cheval has built a palace in
his back garden.
d/p Michael Gill; *sc/nar* John Berger

TEN YEARS A QUEEN
(Rediffusion 6/2/1962)
The tenth anniversary of the reign of Queen
Elizabeth II.
d Rollo Gamble

TEN YEARS OF LONDON WEEKEND
(LWT 1/9/1978)
Denis Norden takes a personal look at the first
ten years of London Weekend Television.
d David MacMahon

The TERRACOTTA HORSE
(BBC 1973)
Six-part children's adventure serial.
p Bill Sellars; *sc* Christopher Bond
regulars Godfrey James; Kristine Howarth;
Lindy Howard; Patrick Murray; Norman Scace;
Constantin De Goguel; James Warwick;
David Scheuer; Nadim Sawalha; Jeffrey Sirr
PART 1: SEAL OF SOLOMON 12/11/1973
PART 2: THIRD PENTANGLE 19/11/1973
PART 3: LEGEND OF THE GRAIL 26/11/1973
PART 4: HOUSE OF COLUMNS 3/12/1973
PART 5: STONES OF AIN KHALIFA 10/12/1973
PART 6: PLACE OF SOLOMON'S SEAL
17/12/1973

TESTAMENT OF YOUTH (BBC 1979)
Five-part serial based on the Vera Brittain's
autobiography during the years 1913–1925.
d Moira Armstrong; *p* Jonathan Powell;
sc Elaine Morgan
regulars Cheryl Campbell; Emrys James;
Jane Wenham; Rupert Frazer; Michael
Troughton
PART 1: BUXTON 1913 4/11/1979
lp Peter Woodward; Rosalie Crutchley;
William Russell
PART 2: BUXTON 1914 11/11/1979
lp Peter Woodward; Rosalie Crutchley;
June Tobin; Hazel Douglas; Janet Davies;
Geoffrey Burridge; Tricia George;
Joanna Foster; Elizabeth Rider;
Kristine Howarth; Roger Monk
PART 3: 1915 18/11/1979
lp Peter Woodward; Tricia George;
Kenneth Gilbert; June Tobin; Victor Lucas;
Geoffrey Burridge; Rosalie Crutchley;
Audrey Muir; Annabel Petrie; Guy Hassan
PART 4: 1917 25/11/1979
lp Peter Woodward; Kenneth Gilbert;
Victor Lucas; Thelma Whiteley; Jane Booker;
Susan Bovell
PART 5: 1918 2/12/1979
lp Joanna McCallum; Rosalie Crutchley;
Frances Tomelty; Denis Carey;
Peter Woodward; Elizabeth Spender; Jill Cowles

The TEXAN
(US Desilu Productions-Rorvic Productions
1958–60)
Western drama series starring Rory Calhoun
who was also the executive producer.
RETURN TO FRIENDLY 1958
d Erle C. Kenton; *p* Jerry Stagg;
sc Harry Kronman
lp James Philbrook; Mary Webster;
Anthony Warde; John Harmon; John Anderson

THANK YOU COMRADES (BBC 19/12/1978)
Based on real events in Russia and America
between 1918 and 1921, recounts how Roberto
Cibrario cheated the Soviet Government out of
one million dollars.
d Jack Gold; *p* Graham Benson;
sc Jim Hawkins
lp Ben Kingsley; Connie Booth;
Lee Montague; Stephen Rea; Richard Ireson;
Derek Godfrey; Charles Keating

THANK YOU, RON (ATV 30/10/1973)
Joan Bakewell investigates the scientology
movement and visits its headquarters at Saint
Hill Manor, East Grinstead.
d David Foster

THANK YOUR LUCKY STARS
(ABC 1961–66)
Pop music series.
THANK YOUR LUCKY STARS 14/5/1966
Jim Dale introduces The Rolling Stones, Tom
Jones, The Koobas, Deano, The Morgan-James
Duo, The Kentuckians, Lorne Lesley, Ronnie
Carroll, and The Londonaires.
d Peter Frazer-Jones
FAREWELL LUCKY STARS 25/6/1966
Last programme of series. Features Keith
Fordyce, Brian Matthews, Janice Nicholls, Pete
Murray, Jim Dale, The Beatles, Roy C, Ray
Ellington, Herman's Hermits, The Ivy League,
Cleo Laine, Peter and Gordon, Gene Pitney,
and Helen Shapiro.

THAT OLD BLACK MAGIC
(Rediffusion 2/2/1967)
Paul Jones's last television play, about a black
medical student rooming in the household of a
family desperate to prove how liberal-minded
they are.
d Peter Moffatt; *sc* Paul Jones
lp George Cole; Joan Sims; Julia Foster;
Johnny Sekka

THAT WAS THE WEEK THAT WAS
(BBC 1962–63)
Series treating the week's news in a satirical and
humorous manner.
p Ned Sherrin
with David Frost, Millicent Martin,
Kenneth Cope, David Kernan, Roy Kinnear,
Bernard Levin, Lance Percival,
William Rushton, Timothy Birdsall, Al Mancini
THAT WAS THE WEEK THAT WAS 8/12/1962
Includes an item on Harold Macmillan which
makes use of actuality footage.
THAT WAS THE WEEK THAT WAS 15/12/1962
THAT WAS THE WEEK THAT WAS 20/4/1963
THAT WAS THE WEEK THAT WAS – TRIBUTE
TO PRESIDENT KENNEDY 23/11/1963
Tribute to John Fitzgerald Kennedy following his
assassination.

**THAT WELL KNOWN STORE IN
KNIGHTSBRIDGE** (BBC 1/6/1971)
A behind-the-scenes look at Harrods, showing
the elaborate work that goes into running the
store.
p Harry Hastings

THAT'S LIFE (BBC 1973–)
Consumer affairs magazine programme.
p Esther Rantzen;
pres Esther Rantzen, Bob Wellings (1973),
George Layton (1973), Kieran Prendiville
(1974–78), Glyn Worsnip (1974–78),
Cyril Fletcher (1974–1978)
THAT'S LIFE 26/5/1973
d Simon Wadleigh
THAT'S LIFE 9/6/1973
d Simon Wadleigh
THAT'S LIFE 14/7/1973
d Simon Wadleigh
THAT'S LIFE 23/3/1974
d Mark Patterson
THAT'S LIFE 20/4/1974
d Mark Patterson
THAT'S LIFE 3/8/1974
d Mike Catherwood
THAT'S LIFE 17/8/1974
d Mike Catherwood
THAT'S LIFE 19/4/1975

THAT'S LIFE 28/6/1975
THAT'S LIFE 18/1/1976
THAT'S LIFE 22/2/1976
THAT'S LIFE 23/5/1976
d Peter Morpurgo
THAT'S LIFE 2/1/1977
d Peter Morpurgo
THAT'S LIFE 20/2/1977
d Peter Morpurgo
THAT'S LIFE 14/5/1977
d Peter Morpurgo

THEATRE ROYAL
(Towers of London 1955–56)
Anthology drama series.
The COLONEL 15/1/1956
d Don Chaffey; *p* Roger Proudlock
lp Andrew Cruickshank; Majorie Stewart;
Harold Young; Graham Stuart; Van Boolen;
David Rush; Nigel Davenport; Victor Platt;
Roderick Lovell; Robert Raikes
The ASSASSIN 29/1/1956
d Don Chaffey; *p* Roger Proudlock;
sc Winston Clewes
lp André Morell; Willoughby Goddard;
Brian Wilde; William Russell; Julie Somers;
Eddie Malin; Richard Marner; Michael Ingrams
The OLD MAN OF THE AIR 19/2/1956
d Don Chaffey; *p* Edward Lloyd;
sc Berkeley Mather
lp Lionel Murton; Anne Castle;
Michael Brooke; Eddie Byrne; Robert Cawdron;
Michael Collins; John Phillips; Vivian Matalon
The ENDS OF JUSTICE 27/4/1956
d/sc Warren Jenkins; *auth* G. Fielden Hughes
lp Felix Aylmer; Kenneth Griffith;
Dorothy Gordon; Robert Raglan;
Patrick Troughton; Barbara Lott; Frank Sieman;
John Paul; Russell Waters; Ivor Dean;
Philip Lennard; Glyn Houston; Ian Fleming

THEATRE 625 (BBC 1964–68)
Anthology drama series.
A MAN LIKE THAT 27/2/1966
d Peter Duguid; *p* Cedric Messina;
sc H.S. Eveling
lp Irene Handl; Norman Bird;
Annette Crosbie; Jeanne Moody; Colin Ellis;
Margaret Nolan
TWELFTH HOUR 3/4/1966
d Alan Cooke; *p* Cedric Messina;
auth Aleksei Arbuzov; *trsl* Ariadne Nicolaeff
lp Clifford Evans; Michael Goodliffe;
Sheila Allen; Dudley Foster; Walter Brown;
Hannah Gordon
GIRL OF MY DREAMS 31/7/1966
d Bill Hays; *p* Cedric Messina;
sc Hugh Whitemore
lp Nicholas Pennell; Chela Matthison;
Edward Fox; James Grout; Kathleen Michael;
Anne Brooks; Jennifer Jayne;
George A. Cooper
TALKING TO A STRANGER: PART 1: ANYTIME
YOU'RE READY I'LL SPARKLE 2/10/1966
d Christopher Morahan; *p* Michael Bakewell;
sc John Hopkins
lp Judi Dench; Michael Bryant;
Maurice Denham; Margery Mason;
Pinkie Johnstone; Emrys James;
Timothy Carlton; Calvin Lockhart
TALKING TO A STRANGER: PART 2: NO SKILL
OR SPECIAL KNOWLEDGE REQUIRED 9/10/1966
lp Judi Dench; Michael Bryant;
Maurice Denham; Margery Mason;
Frederick Pyne; Barry Stanton; Gaynor Jones;
Emrys James; Ann Mitchell; Keith Kent
TALKING TO A STRANGER: PART 3: GLADLY,
MY CROSS-EYED BEAR 16/10/1966
lp Judi Dench; Michael Bryant;
Maurice Denham; Terry Leigh; Windsor Davies;
Maryann Turner
TALKING TO A STRANGER: PART 4: THE
INNOCENT MUST SUFFER 23/10/1966
lp Judi Dench; Michael Bryant;
Margery Mason; Maurice Denham;
Maryann Turner
KAIN 17/4/1967
d/p Lionel Harris; *sc* Alan Poolman
lp Keith Michell; J.G. Devlin;
Audine Leith; Alan White; Candy Devine;
Roger Cox; Teddy Plummer

STAN'S DAY OUT 13/8/1967
d James MacTaggart; *p* Michael Bakewell;
sc Rhys Adrian
lp Leslie Dwyer; Alfie Bass;
Roddy McMillan; Bryan Pringle;
Michael Robbins
The LOST YEARS OF BRIAN HOOPER 8/10/1967
d Alan Gibson; *p* Michael Bakewell;
sc Bernard Kops
lp Hugh Burden; Margery Mason;
Sheila Reid; Ray Brooks; Alan MacNaughtan;
Susan George
The INCANTATION OF CASANOVA 22/10/1967
d Herbert Wise; *p* Michael Bakewell;
sc Ken Taylor
lp Jeremy Brett; Anthony Webb;
Geoffrey Bayldon; Anne Cunningham;
Patrick O'Connell; Jacqueline Pearce
The FANATICS 29/4/1968
d Rudolph Cartier; *p* Michael Bakewell;
sc Max Marquis;
auth Stellio Lorenzi, André Castelot,
Alain Decaux
lp Leonard Rossiter; Alan Badel;
Rosalie Crutchley; John Paul; Alex Scott;
Cyril Shaps
ALL'S WELL THAT ENDS WELL 3/6/1968
d Claude Whatham; *p* Ronald Travers;
auth William Shakespeare
lp Catherine Lacey; Ian Richardson;
Brewster Mason; Lynn Fairleigh;
Sebastian Shaw; Ian Hogg; Daniel Moynihan;
David Ashford; David Bailie; Elizabeth Spriggs;
Natalie Kent; Caroline Hunt

THEATRE '60 (ATV 1960–61)
Anthology drama series.
The GOLD INSIDE 24/9/1960
p Quentin Lawrence; *sc* Jacques Gillies
lp André Morell; Richard Warner;
Rosemary Giles; Max Faulkner; Michael Logan;
Richard Vernon; Edward Jewesbury

THEN AND NOW (BBC 1973)
Six plays, three set in the 1930s and three in the
1970s.
TIGERS ARE BETTER LOOKING 1/10/1973
d John Glenister; *p* Anne Head;
sc Alan Seymour; *auth* Jean Rhys
lp Peter Miles; Ken Halliwell;
John Stratton; Rhoda Lewis; Alex Marshall

THERE GO I (HTV 11/6–16/7/1972)
Quasi-religious documentary series looking at
people's reactions to other people.
I WAS A STRANGER 11/6/1972
Religious programme presented by Neil Stacy
and Angela Pleasence.
d Jeffrey Milland

THERE WAS THIS FELLA...
(Granada 7/12/1971)
A profile of club comedians in the north of
England, with Bernard Manning and Charlie
Williams.
p Gus MacDonald

**THEY CAME TO AN ISLAND IN LOVE
WITH CREATION** (Tyne Tees 27/6/1976)
A visit to the Inner Farne Islands, a pilgrimage
centre and bird sanctuary.
d Jeremy Lack; *p* Maxwell Deas

THEY MADE HISTORY (BBC 1960–61)
Dramatised reconstructions of historical events
and the lives of personalities.
The VAN MEEGEREN STORY 11/8/1960
A dramatised reconstruction of the life and work
of the Dutch art forger Han van Meegeren.
p Bill Duncalf; *nar* Richard Attenborough

THEY MET IN A CITY (BBC 28/3–25/4/1961)
Anthology drama series based on the theme of a
man and a woman meeting.
The ENCYCLOPAEDIST 4/4/1961
p Hal Burton; *sc* John Mortimer
lp Cy Grant; Elizabeth Shepherd

THEY SANK THE LUSITANIA
(US CBS 20/10/1964)
The causes and effects of Germany's policy of
unrestricted submarine warfare in World War I,
focusing on the Lusitania, the submarine that
sank it in the USA and reaction in England.
Includes a look at life aboard a German U-boat.
p Isaac Kleinerman, John Sharnik;
sc Burton Benjamin; *nar* Robert Ryan

THEY'LL NEVER GET IT TO FLY
(Westward 29/8/1978)
Historical footage of helicopter development and
interviews with aircraft designer Igor Sikorski.
d/sc John Phillips; *pres* Kenneth More

THICK AS THIEVES (HTV 29/2/1972)
Drama about a hard-bitten professional criminal
and his partner who aspire to greatness in the
profession.
d/p Patrick Dromgoole;
sc Bob Baker, Dave Martin
lp Leonard Rossiter; Corin Redgrave;
Rosemary McHale; George Woodbridge;
Daphne Heard; Horace James; June Barrie;
Nina Baden-Semper

THICK AS THIEVES (LWT 1974)
Comedy series about two small-time criminals.
regulars John Thaw; Bob Hoskins
The HOME COMING 1/6/1974
p Derrick Goodwin;
sc Dick Clement, Ian La Frenais
lp Johnny Briggs
GOOD CONDUCT 15/6/1974
d/p Derrick Goodwin;
sc Ian La Frenais, Dick Clement
lp Pat Ashton; Michael Robbins;
Johnny Briggs; Philip Anthony; Kenneth Scott

The THIRD MAN (GB/US BBC 1959–65)
Drama series featuring a globe-trotting freelance
adventurer; loosely derived from the Graham
Greene story and 1949 film.
p Felix Jackson
regulars Michael Rennie; Jonathan Harris
ONE KIND WORD 2/10/1959
d Cliff Owen; *sc* Iain MacCormick
lp Mai Zetterling; George Pastell;
Eric Pohlmann; Bud Knapp; Anne Blake;
Rupert Davies
The BEST POLICY 23/10/1959
d Julian Amyes; *sc* John Player
lp Venetia Stevenson; Andre Van Gyseghem;
David Lander; Miki Iveria; Lee Hamilton;
Kevin Stoney; Fiona Clyne
THREE DANCING TURTLES 13/11/1959
d Julian Amyes; *sc* John Kruse
lp Louise Collins; Bill Nagy;
Michael Mulcaster; Robert Robinson;
Yvonne Warren; Andrea Malandrinos;
George Eugeniou; Arthur Gomez
QUESTION OF PRICE 27/11/1959
d David Orrick McDearmon; *sc* Harry Brown
lp Viveca Lindfors; Simon Oakland;
Rudolph Anders; Frank De Kova;
Tom Greenway; Len Lesser; Cece Whitney;
Martin Garralaga; Robert Sherman
The IMPORTANCE OF BEING HARRY LIME
4/12/1959
d Julian Amyes; *sc* Iain MacCormick
lp Jeannette Sterke; Bernard Rebel;
George Roderick; Maxine Audley; Alan Tilvern;
Ivan Craig; Naomi Chance; Rupert Davies
AS THE TWIG IS BENT 3/6/1960
d Arthur Hiller; *sc* David Chandler
lp Eduardo Ciannelli; Ziva Rodann;
Frank Puglia; Vito Scotti; Ruggero Romor;
Oreste Seragnoli
CALCULATED RISK 30/3/1963
d Paul Henreid; *p* Irving Asher;
sc Frank Schiller, Mary C. McCall Jr
lp Alan Caillou; Linda Wong;
Jim Howe; George Pelling
WHO KILLED HARRY LIME? 24/8/1963
d Robert M. Leeds; *p* Irving Asher;
sc Philip Saltzman
lp Virginia Gregg; Bernie Gozier;
Ann Atmar; Weaver Lee

THIRTY MINUTE THEATRE
(ITV various 1962–65)
Anthology drama series.
INTERVIEW FOR WIVES (TWW 1962)
d David Boisseau; *sc* Leo Lehman
lp Robert Shaw; Jill Dixon
A MATTER OF PRINCIPLE (Southern TV 1965)
d Stuart Burge; *sc* Lukas Heller;
lp Peter Woodthorpe; Reed De Rouen;
Michael Gough; Thomas Heathcote;
Harry Towb; Ralph Munday

THIRTY MINUTE THEATRE (BBC 1965–73)
Anthology drama series.
The WARMONGER 13/11/1970
d Mischa Scorer; *p* Innes Lloyd;
sc Keith Waterhouse
lp Nicholas Osborn; Paul Jacobs;
Alan Baverstock; Nicholas Rymills; Martin Cox
SAID THE PREACHER 6/3/1972
d Michael Apted; *p* David Rose;
sc Arthur Hopcraft
lp Victor Henry; Madge Hindle;
Frank Crompton; Mark Dignam;
Bernard Wrigley
UNDER THE AGE 20/3/1972
d Alan Clarke; *p* David Rose;
sc E.A. Whitehead
lp Paul Angelis; Michael Angelis;
Stephen Bent; David Lincoln; Rosalind Elliot;
Sylvia Brayshay
THRILLS GALORE 4/9/1972
d Donald McWhinnie; *p* Tim Aspinall;
sc Rhys Adrian
lp Bryan Pringle; Patrick Magee;
Rosalind Ayers; Charles Lamb; Harry Landis
KRAPP'S LAST TAPE 29/11/1972
d Donald McWhinnie; *p* Tim Aspinall;
sc Samuel Beckett
lp Patrick Magee
YOU AND ME AND HIM 22/2/1973
d Barry Hanson; *p* David Rose;
sc David Mercer
lp Peter Vaughan

THIRTY MINUTES WORTH
(Thames 1972–73)
Comedy series with Harry Worth.
THIRTY MINUTES WORTH 8/8/1973
d/p William G. Stewart;
sc Mike Craig, Lawrie Kinsley,
Ron McDonnell, Roy Tuvey, Maurice Sellar,
George Martin;
with Hugh Paddick, Ronnie Brody,
Guy Deghy, Brenda Duncan, Louis Mansi,
Harry Littlewood

THIS DAY IN FEAR (BBC 1/7/1958)
Drama focusing on a reformed IRA member
whose past comes back to haunt him.
p George R. Foa;
sc Malcolm Hulke, Eric Paice
lp Patrick McGoohan; Billie Whitelaw;
Allan McClelland; Kevin Stoney;
Donal Donnelly; Larry Burns; David Morrell;
Marcella Burgoyne; Hugh Moxey;
Harold Berens; Bartlett Mullins;
Gladys Spencer; Paddy Joyce

THIS ENGLAND
(Granada 1965–67; 1977–80)
Documentary series.
ELEGY 24/3/1967
The decline of the influence of the chapel in the
Yorkshire mining village of Hebden.
d David Wheeler; *exec.p* Denis Mitchell
NUCLEAR CATHEDRAL 21/4/1967
A working day on the nuclear power station site
at Wylfa, Anglesey.
d Gerard Dynevor; *exec.p* Denis Mitchell;
p David Naden
The MIGHTY WURLITZER 2/10/1978
The history of the cinema organ.
d Tony Palmer

THIS IS CHARLES LAUGHTON
(US Sherman Harris Production 1953)
Charles Laughton, in front of a microphone,
reads extracts from various books including The
Bible, tells stories, recites poems and jokes.
d/p Paul Gregory

THIS IS SCOTLAND
(Scottish TV 31/8/1957)
The opening night of Scottish Television, live
form the Theatre Royal Glasow. Introduced by
Jimmy Nairn and hosted by James Robertson
Justice, with Deborah Kerr, David Niven, Jack
Buchanan, Alastair Sim, Moira Shearer, Jimmy
Logan, Stanley Baxter, Kenneth McKellar,
Andrew Keir, Ludovic Kennedy, The Starlets,
The Mitchell Singers and Geraldo and his
Orchestra.
d/p Rai Purdey

THIS IS THE BBC (BBC 27/11/1959)
The work of the British Broadcasting
Corporation over a twenty-four hour period,
showing the preparations for and the variety of
radio and television programmes broadcast.
d/p/sc Richard Cawston
with Flora Robson, Beryl Grey,
Isaiah Berlin, Richard Murdoch,
Eamonn Andrews

THIS IS WAUGH (ATV 9–23/8/1976)
Auberon Waugh's highly personalised, three-
part social and political look at Britain.
d/p Derek Hart
VIEWS ON THE WORKING CLASS 9/8/1976
Housing problems, trade union attitudes and
unemployment among the working class.
The CHANGING NATURE OF SOCIETY 16/8/1976
Socialism and the working class, and its effects
on the middle and upper classes.

THIS IS YOUR LIFE (BBC 1955–64)
Series which looks at the lives of surprise
celebrity guests. Taken over by Thames in 1969.
p T. Leslie Jackson; *pres* Eamonn Andrews
EAMONN ANDREWS 29/7/1955
The first British edition of the series made
famous in America by Ralph Edwards, who
introduces this programme. As the planned
'victim' learned of his fate in advance, it turned
out to be a THIS IS YOUR LIFE for presenter
Eamonn Andrews.
MAJOR FLOOD 29/4/1957
T.E.B. CLARKE 31/10/1960
MAX BYGRAVES 2/10/1961
BARBARA MULLEN 3/3/1964

THIS IS YOUR LIFE (Thames 1969–)
Series which looks at the lives of surprise
celebrity guests. Previously produced by the
BBC.
pres Eamonn Andrews
DES O'CONNOR 19/11/1969
HUGHIE GREEN 16/2/1972
d Margery Baker
MAJOR PAT REID 21/2/1973
d Margery Baker
RAY MILLAND 19/11/1975
d Royston Mayoh
ARNOLD RIDLEY 10/3/1976
d Philip Casson, Michael Dormer
FRANKIE HOWERD 27/10/1976
d Royston Mayoh, Terry Yarwood;
p Jack Crawshaw
LORD LOUIS MOUNTBATTEN 27/4/1977
d Terry Yarwood; *p* Jack Crawshaw
RICHARD BECKINSALE 23/11/1977
p Jack Crawshaw
BOB PAISLEY 28/12/1977
p Jack Crawshaw

THIS QUESTION OF PRESSURES
(BBC 7/10–4/11/1969)
Five-part discussion series on topical issues.
The VOICE OF THE TORTOISE 14/10/1969
Conservationists' concern over the atoll Aldabra
in the Indian Ocean where a RAF staging post is
planned.
p John Eidinow

THIS WAS THE FUTURE (BBC 31/12/1957)
Compilation of BBC transmissions from 1936 to
1957.
p Geoffrey Baines; *nar* Robert Donat

THIS WEEK (Rediffusion 1956–68)
Current affairs programme. The programme
format consisted of a number of film reports and
live studio interviews and links. The Archive
largely holds the film reports. The series was
taken over by Thames in 1968. See also THIS
WEEK SPECIAL, THIS WEEK NATIONAL
and THIS WEEK – THE ARTS.
POLYGAMY 6/1/1956
The first programme of the current affairs series.
p Caryl Doncaster; *intro* René Cutforth
FENCHURCH 2/3/1956
The Southend to Fenchurch Street Railway line.
p Caryl Doncaster; *rep* Ian Fordyce
TEDDY BOYS 2/3/1956
Micky Wood explains how he won the co-
operation of the Teddy Boys and follows their
extraordinary lives.
p Caryl Doncaster
GRETNA GREEN 23/3/1956
Ian Fordyce reports from Gretna Green on the
runaway couples attempting to marry.
p Caryl Doncaster
GIBRALTAR 4/5/1956
p Caryl Doncaster
S.O.S. 4/5/1956
A scheme to help old people.
p Caryl Doncaster
SPAIN TOURISM 18/5/1956
Report on passports to Spain.
p Caryl Doncaster
SS UNITED STATES 18/5/1956
p Caryl Doncaster
USTINOV 18/5/1956
A report on Peter Ustinov appearing at the
Piccadilly Theatre in 'Romanoff and Juliet'.
p Caryl Doncaster; *rep* Elkan Allan
BUSSANA VECCHIA 25/5/1956
Municipal elections in Italy. Voting intentions in
the rural community of Bussana Vecchia.
p Caryl Doncaster
GAITSKELL 25/5/1956
p Caryl Doncaster
EISENHOWER INTERVIEWS 8/6/1956
p Caryl Doncaster
TITANIC 8/6/1956
p Caryl Doncaster
ROYAL WEST KENTS 15/6/1956
Report on the return to Britain of the Royal
West Kent Regiment after two years in
Germany: looks at one unit in Luneberg.
p Caryl Doncaster
SQUATTERS 15/6/1956
p Caryl Doncaster; *rep* Ian Forsythe
BLUEBELL TRAIN 10/8/1956
ISRAEL STORY 10/8/1956
The growth in Israel's economy, despite Arab
determination to restore Palestine.
COLONEL NASSER 24/8/1956
Report on the Suez conference, includes an
interview with Krishna Menon.
p Caryl Doncaster
HYRAM CANTOR 24/8/1956
Daniel Farson meets American millionaire
Hyram B. Cantor in London.
p Caryl Doncaster
SPITFIRE STORY 14/9/1956
The Battle of Britain and the Spitfire.
p Caryl Doncaster
ZANZIBAR 14/9/1956 *ntx*
Princess Margaret's visit to East Africa.
p Caryl Doncaster
ITV FIRST YEAR 21/9/1956
A report on ITV's first year by William
Hardcastle.
p Peter Hunt
MR HAROLD MACMILLAN 21/9/1956
A report on the Chancellor of the Exchequer.
p Peter Hunt
SELWYN LLOYD 28/9/1956
Maurice Edelman interviews Selwyn Lloyd,
Foreign Secretary.
p Peter Hunt
CRISIS INTERVIEWS 2/11/1956
Suez crisis interviews, with four journalists from
the USA, France, Israel and Egypt.
NOEL BARBER 9/11/1956
Norman McKenzie interviews Noel Barber on
the Russian invasion of Hungary.
p Caryl Doncaster
PRESCRIPTIONS 30/11/1956
p Peter Hunt

SIR WINSTON CHURCHILL 30/11/1956
p Peter Hunt
THIS WEEK 4/1/1957
Includes shots of the new German Army.
p Peter Hunt
ROD STEIGER 18/1/1957
p Peter Hunt
EMPIRE FOODS 24/5/1957
p Peter Hunt
MUSIC HALL 7/6/1957
p Peter Hunt
BEVAN INTERVIEW 11/10/1957
Aneurin Bevan is interviewed by Kenneth Harris
on the Labour Party, China and the USSR.
d John Rhodes; p Michael Westmore
INDONESIA 13/12/1957
p Peter Hunt
LORD RUSSELL 9/1/1958
Lord Russell is interviewed by Kenneth Harris.
d John Rhodes
TEENAGE GIRL (ATTACKS) 23/1/1958
d John Rhodes
THORNEYCROFT 23/1/1958
The resignation of Peter Thorneycroft,
Chancellor of the Exchequer.
d John Rhodes
FASHIONS 6/2/1958
The fashions for 1958.
d John Rhodes
MAKARIOS 6/2/1958
Archbishop Makarios of Cyprus.
d John Rhodes
VENEZUELA 6/2/1958
d John Rhodes
MRS ARMSTRONG 27/3/1958
Michael Westmore interviews Janet Armstrong,
wife of Dr John Armstrong, following her
confession to a newspaper that she, and not her
husband, was responsible for killing their son.
d John Rhodes
SOHO STRIPTEASE CLUBS 24/4/1958
Daniel Farson reports on the lunchtime shows at
Soho striptease clubs, and interviews a club
owner and three of the girls.
d John Rhodes
The RENAISSANCE OF TATTOOING 8/5/1958
d Ian Fordyce
TRANSPORT OF DELIGHT 8/5/1958
d Ian Fordyce
FALL OF FRANCE 22/5/1958
The political turmoil in France over possible
independence of Algeria.
d Ian Fordyce
BIDAULT INTERVIEW 29/5/1958
Interview with Georges Bidault.
d Ian Fordyce
POLICE CARS 5/6/1958
d Ian Fordyce
ANGLO-AMERICAN RELATIONSHIPS 12/6/1958
d Ian Fordyce
MAU MAU STORY 12/6/1958
d Ian Fordyce
AUSTRIAN REFUGEES 3/7/1958
d Ian Fordyce; intro Ludovic Kennedy
LEAMINGTON SPA TEDDY BOYS 3/7/1958
d Ian Fordyce
COLOUR BAR 28/8/1958
Extension of apartheid in South Africa.
d Ian Fordyce
NAUTILUS STORY 28/8/1958
The trip under the Arctic ice cap by the nuclear-
powered submarine.
d Ian Fordyce
LITTLE ROCK 4/9/1958
Desegregation of education in Arkansas.
d Sheila Gregg; p Peter Hunt
FORMOSA 11/9/1958
The attack by China on Chinese Nationalist
islands.
p Peter Hunt
NORMAN MANLEY 11/9/1958
Chief Minister and Minister of Development of
Jamaica.
p Peter Hunt
DOUGLAS SCHOOL 25/9/1958
A finishing school in London.
d Alan Morris; p Peter Hunt
GAITSKELL 25/9/1958
Hugh Gaitskell is interviewed by Robin Day. He
is questioned on the Liverpool local elections,
Cyprus and Formosa policy.
d Alan Morris

RENAULT STORY 25/9/1958
d Alan Morris; p Peter Hunt
HIS HOLINESS POPE PIUS XII 9/10/1958
The Pope's reign reviewed.
d Alan Morris
POOLS 9/10/1958
Interview with a football 'pools' winner.
d Alan Morris
BERLIN 13/11/1958
East and West Berlin.
d Ian Fordyce
KALEIDOSCOPE 13/11/1958
Review of King Hussein and the situation in
Jordan, including the Army and refugee camps.
Interviews with journalists and ambassadors.
d Ian Fordyce
BERLIN 20/11/1958
d Sheila Gregg
LIONEL EDWARDS 20/11/1958
d Sheila Gregg
BERLIN 11/12/1958
d Ian Fordyce
NEHRU INTERVIEW 18/12/1958
Nehru discusses the need to disarm, he states
that he is not frightened of China and that he
will not retire.
d Sheila Gregg
PROTESTS 15/1/1959
d Sheila Gregg
COMET FLIGHT SIMULATOR 15/1/1959
d Sheila Gregg
SOVIET 21ST CONGRESS 29/1/1959
d Sheila Gregg
H-BOMB: INTERVIEWS AGAINST 12/2/1959
d Sheila Gregg
BURGESS IN MOSCOW 26/2/1959
d Alan Morris; p Peter Hunt
MOSCOW (MACMILLAN) 5/3/1959
Harold Macmillan's visit to the USSR.
d Sheila Gregg; p Peter Hunt;
pres Ludovic Kennedy
R.A.F. NOW 18/3/1959
d Sheila Gregg
CHILDREN IN PARIS 13/5/1959
The political future in France, one year after
General De Gaulle returned to power.
d Sheila Gregg
TU 104 20/5/1959
The Russian jet airliner.
d Sheila Gregg
MENZIES 10/6/1959
Interview with Australian Prime Minister Robert
Menzies.
d Sheila Gregg
PRINTING STORY 24/6/1959
d Sheila Gregg
TRADE UNION CONFERENCE 15/7/1959
d Sheila Gregg
AINTREE 22/7/1959
Motor racing at Aintree.
BOER WAR 22/7/1959
ADENAUER 26/8/1959
d Sheila Gregg
HOP PICKING 9/9/1959
d Peter Robinson
YEMEN 22/10/1959
d Sheila Gregg
ADEN 29/10/1959
d Sheila Gregg
FRANCE 29/10/1959
Round-up of opinion about De Gaulle one year
after taking up office.
d Sheila Gregg
GARY COOPER 29/10/1959
Gary Cooper is interviewed about his
forthcoming trip to Moscow.
d Sheila Gregg
ADEN 5/11/1959
d Geoffrey Hughes
FIREWORKS 5/11/1959
d Geoffrey Hughes
NEHRU STORY 5/11/1959
d Geoffrey Hughes
OXFORD 12/11/1959
d Geoffrey Hughes
POLICE 19/11/1959
d Geoffrey Hughes
ANIMAL ASTRONAUTS 26/11/1959
d Geoffrey Hughes

APARTHEID 4/2/1960
South African Home Spokesman and black and
white groups define Apartheid.
d Geoffrey Hughes; p Elkan Allan
GENEVA DISARMAMENT TALKS 31/3/1960
d Geoffrey Hughes
MAC AND IKE 31/3/1960
Harold Macmillan and President Eisenhower
meet at Camp David for talks on the nuclear test
ban treaty.
d Geoffrey Hughes
DR. HASTINGS BANDA 7/4/1960
Interview with Dr Hastings Banda.
d Geoffrey Hughes
SOUTH AFRICAN PROPAGANDA 5/5/1960
d Geoffrey Hughes
TONY ARMSTRONG JONES 5/5/1960
d Geoffrey Hughes
AL CAPP ON IKE 12/5/1960
Al Capp comments on President Eisenhower.
d Geoffrey Hughes
DIARY OF THE SUMMIT 19/5/1960
The Paris Summit.
d Geoffrey Hughes
PROJECT MERCURY 26/8/1960
The first American manned space programme.
d Geoffrey Hughes
NASSER 2/9/1960
d Geoffrey Hughes
RHODESIA 3/3/1961
d Peter Robinson
KENNEDY V. KHRUSCHEV 2/6/1961
The meeting between John F. Kennedy and
Nikita Khruschev in Vienna.
d Peter Robinson
GERMAN TROOPS 11/8/1961
p Peter Morley
STALIN 3/11/1961
p Peter Morley
BERLIN WALL 29/12/1961
p Peter Morley
INDIA – BIRTH CONTROL 5/4/1962
Paul Johnson discusses India and birth control
with Dr Khanna.
p Peter Morley
PRINCE PHILIP'S TOUR OF SOUTH AMERICA
19/4/1962
The Duke of Edinburgh, following his two
month tour to 11 South American countries,
reports on opportunities for Britain. Includes
film of his tour.
p Peter Morley
BRITISH ARMY ON THE RHINE 14/6/1962
Bryan Magee and Desmond Wilcox talk to Lt.
Gen. Darling and Herr Max Quarg, editor of
'Minden Tagblatt'.
p Peter Morley
NEW YORK TOURIST CENTRE 30/8/1962
p Peter Morley
SICILY STORY 6/9/1962
p Peter Morley
ALGERIA 20/9/1962
p Peter Morley
HUNGARY 27/9/1962
p Peter Morley
CUBAN CRISIS 25/10/1962
p Peter Morley
NEHRU INTERVIEW 13/12/1962
p Peter Morley
UNITED NATIONS 27/12/1962
Includes shots of J.F.Kennedy, the visit of the
Laotian Prime Minister to China, Mao-Tse-
Tung, De Gaulle, Khruschev, and the U.N.
Secretary General in debate.
p Peter Morley
ISRAEL 2/5/1963
Israel on the 15th anniversary of Independence;
interview with the Minister of Education, Abba
Eban.
p Peter Morley, Cyril Bennett
BLACK MUSLIMS 9/5/1963
A report on the Black Muslim movement, and
interviews with two of its leaders, Malcolm X
and Elijah Muhammed. Includes newsreel film
from 1962.
AL CAPP ON DICK GREGORY 16/5/1963
Al Capp reports on the political activities of
Dick Gregory during the racial demonstrations
in Alabama.
p Peter Morley; Cyril Bennett

THIS WEEK (Rediffusion) *cont.*

SEX AND THE SINGLE GIRL 6/6/1963
Models and working girls are interviewed on
their attitudes towards sex.
p Peter Morley, Cyril Bennett
rep Desmond Wilcox
STEPHEN WARD 6/6/1963
The Profumo/Christine Keeler story; Desmond
Wilcox interviews Stephen Ward.
p Peter Morley
KENTUCKY – THE LOUISVILLE STORY 27/6/1963
Desmond Wilcox reports on aspects of racial
integration in Louisville, Kentucky.
p Peter Morley, Cyril Bennett
AL CAPP ON PROFUMO 11/7/1963
Al Capp talks about the Profumo Affair and
whether something of a similar nature could
occur in the USA.
p Peter Morley, Cyril Bennett
BEIRUT 11/7/1963
p Peter Morley, Cyril Bennett
LAW ENQUIRY 7/8/1963
The setting up of the Denning report into the
Profumo affair.
d James Butler;
p Peter Morley, Cyril Bennett
JUSTICE ON TRIAL 8/8/1963
Ronna Ricardo, Joe Wade and John Capstick
are interviewed in connection with the Profumo
Affair.
d James Butler;
p Peter Morley, Cyril Bennett
CAR INSURANCE 15/8/1963
Report on Fire Auto and Marine Insurance's
tactics to avoid paying out on claims, and an
interview with ex-owner of London Cheshire
Insurance Company, now going into liquidation.
d James Butler
SLEEPING PILLS 15/8/1963 *ntx*
Inquiry into the increase in suicides and
accidents through sleeping pills.
d James Butler
SAIGON/VIETNAM 12/9/1963
With Hoang Xuan Yen, Madame Ngu and
President Diem.
p Jeremy Isaacs
MALAYSIA/INDONESIA 19/9/1963
Russell Spurr interviews Tunku Abdul Rahman,
Prime Minister of Malaysia. Bryan Magee
interviews Peter Thorneycroft and Burhanudin
Mohamed Diah.
p Jeremy Isaacs
AFTER DENNING WHAT? 26/9/1963
A report on Lord Denning's enquiry into the
Profumo Affair. George Ffitch is in the studio
with two Conservative MPs, Sir Lionel Hugh and
Mr Aubrey Jones. Desmond Wilcox with George
Wigg (Labour MP). David Butler explains
Parliamentary procedure.
d James Butler, John Phillips;
p Jeremy Isaacs
BIRTH CONTROL 3/10/1963
p Jeremy Isaacs
GERMANY 10/10/1963
p Jeremy Isaacs
MACMILLAN 10/10/1963
Harold Macmillan's illness and announcement
that he would not lead the Conservative Party in
the next election.
p Jeremy Isaacs
NEW PRIME MINISTER 17/10/1963
James Cameron reviews the contenders before
Macmillan and after the choice of Alec Douglas-
Home.
d James Butler; *p* Jeremy Isaacs;
rep James Cameron
TELEPHONES 17/10/1963
The modernisation of telephones, including
subscriber trunk dialling.
d James Butler; *p* Jeremy Isaacs
LEEDS UNIVERSITY 24/10/1963
d James Butler; *p* Jeremy Isaacs
KINROSS BY-ELECTION 31/10/1963
COLD WEATHER 31/10/1963
p Jeremy Isaacs
BEATLEMANIA 7/11/1963
p Jeremy Isaacs
NORTH EAST DEVELOPMENT 14/11/1963
TRADING STAMP WARS 14/11/1963
CAMBERLEY 21/11/1963
p Jeremy Isaacs
POLICE ENQUIRY 21/11/1963
p Jeremy Isaacs

POLICE REPORT 21/11/1963
p Jeremy Isaacs
DALLAS 28/11/1963
The assassination of John F. Kennedy.
p Jeremy Isaacs
AVIATION 5/12/1963
A report on BEA and BOAC.
d James Butler
BRITAIN'S POPULATION GROWTH 12/12/1963
p Jeremy Isaacs
KENYA INDEPENDENCE 12/12/1963
p Jeremy Isaacs
AFRO-CHINA RELATIONS 19/12/1963
BERLIN WALL (XMAS OPENING) 19/12/1963
The SATIRE BOOM 26/12/1963
d Randal Beattie; *p* Jeremy Isaacs;
pres Bryan Magee; *with* Peter Cook,
Jonathan Miller, Michael Frayn,
William Rushton, John Bird
COMMUNITY CARE OF THE MENTALLY SICK
1964
Shows hospital conditions and workings of the
mental welfare services.
d Stephen Peet; *p* Jeremy Isaacs;
comm Desmond Wilcox
ROAD DEATHS 2/1/1964
p Jeremy Isaacs
BRITISH ARMY 9/1/1964
p Jeremy Isaacs
UNEMPLOYMENT IN CORNWALL 9/1/1964
p Jeremy Isaacs
MR HAROLD WILSON 16/1/1964
d John Phillips; *p* Jeremy Isaacs;
interv George Ffitch, Bryan Magee,
William Rees-Mogg
LEUKAEMIA 23/1/1964
p Jeremy Isaacs
SARAWAK 23/1/1964
p Jeremy Isaacs
EAST AFRICAN DISCUSSION 30/1/1964
p Jeremy Isaacs
CUNARD 6/2/1964
p Jeremy Isaacs
DR. STRANGELOVE 6/2/1964
p Jeremy Isaacs
DUTCH ROYAL FAMILY 6/2/1964
p Jeremy Isaacs
KENTUCKY 13/2/1964
Poverty in the USA.
p Jeremy Isaacs
The PRIME MINISTER SIR ALEC DOUGLAS-
HOME 20/2/1964
p Jeremy Isaacs; *interv* George Ffitch,
Bryan Magee, William Rees-Mogg
'FANNY HILL' (OBSCENE PUBLICATIONS ACT)
27/2/1964
p Jeremy Isaacs
TV AND POLITICS 5/3/1964
p Jeremy Isaacs
METHS ADDICTS 12/3/1964
p Jeremy Isaacs; *rep* Desmond Wilcox
DE GAULLE 19/3/1964
p Jeremy Isaacs
RACE HORSE DOPING 19/3/1964
p Jeremy Isaacs
BATTLE FOR LONDON 26/3/1964
p Jeremy Isaacs
PSYCHOPATHS 26/3/1964
p Jeremy Isaacs
PURPLE HEARTS 2/4/1964
p Jeremy Isaacs
BABY MINDERS 16/4/1964
p Jeremy Isaacs
PRISON SENTENCES 16/4/1964
p Jeremy Isaacs
RADIO CAROLINE 23/4/1964
p Jeremy Isaacs
TEACHING MACHINES 30/4/1964
Paul Johnson reports on teaching with the aid of
machines.
d James Butler; *p* Jeremy Isaacs
MODERN ART 14/5/1964
d James Butler; *p* Jeremy Isaacs
YEMEN 14/5/1964
d James Butler; *p* Jeremy Isaacs
FATHERLESS FAMILIES 21/5/1964
d James Butler; *p* Jeremy Isaacs
FACTORY FARMING 28/5/1964
d James Butler; *p* Jeremy Isaacs
INDIA AFTER NEHRU 28/5/1964
d James Butler; *p* Jeremy Isaacs

NEHRU (FUNERAL PYRE AND SHASTRI)
4/6/1964
d James Butler; *p* Jeremy Isaacs
CANCER – FACTS AND FILMS 11/6/1964
d James Butler; *p* Jeremy Isaacs
EXCLUSIVE BRETHREN 11/6/1964
d James Butler; *p* Jeremy Isaacs
The NEXT STEP FORWARD IN FAMILY
PLANNING 11/6/1964
d James Butler; *p* Jeremy Isaacs
GENEVA CONFERENCE 18/6/1964
George Ffitch reports on the Geneva
Conference.
d James Butler
WELFARE STATE 18/6/1964
Enoch Powell and Peter Townsend discuss
poverty.
d James Butler; *pres* Robert Kee
CANADA'S NEW FLAG 25/6/1964
d James Butler; *p* Jeremy Isaacs
RUMANIA 25/6/1964
d James Butler; *p* Jeremy Isaacs
DIVORCE LAWS 9/7/1964
d James Butler; *p* Jeremy Isaacs
KANSAS 16/7/1964
d James Butler; *p* Jeremy Isaacs
The MEANING OF BARRY GOLDWATER
16/7/1964
A record of the campaign for the American
Presidency by Barry Goldwater.
d James Butler; *p* Jeremy Isaacs; *rep* George
Ffitch; Bryan Magee
The NATION'S TEETH 23/7/1964
p Jeremy Isaacs
PARLIAMENT IN RETROSPECT 30/7/1964
d Anthony Isaacs; *p* Jeremy Isaacs
PARTY CONFERENCE 30/7/1964
d Anthony Isaacs; *p* Jeremy Isaacs
HITCHHIKERS 6/8/1964
d Anthony Isaacs; *p* Jeremy Isaacs
VIETNAM 6/8/1964
d Anthony Isaacs; *p* Jeremy Isaacs
BRAZIL 13/8/1964
James Cameron examines Brazil's move to the
Right.
p Jeremy Isaacs
BOLIVIA 20/8/1964
James Cameron considers what happened to the
Bolivian Revolution.
p Jeremy Isaacs
CHILE 27/8/1964
James Cameron examines how far to the Left
Chile is going.
p Jeremy Isaacs
SOUTHERN RHODESIA TUC – MR GODBER
3/9/1964
d Anthony Isaacs; *p* Jeremy Isaacs
MENTAL ILLNESS IN GREAT BRITAIN 10/9/1964
d Anthony Isaacs; *p* Jeremy Isaacs
HOUSING 17/9/1964
Russell Spurr interviews residents of a suburban
housing estate.
d James Butler; *p* Jeremy Isaacs
COLOURED VOTING – HIDDEN ISSUE 24/9/1964
d James Butler; *p* Jeremy Isaacs
STEEL 1/10/1964
p Jeremy Isaacs
COST OF LIVING 8/10/1964
d James Butler; *p* Jeremy Isaacs
HALIFAX 8/10/1964
d James Butler; *p* Jeremy Isaacs
HOMOSEXUALS 22/10/1964
The problems encountered by homosexuals in
the UK and a comparison with Holland where
homosexuality is not illegal.
d James Butler; *p* Jeremy Isaacs;
rep Bryan Magee
CAR SAFETY 29/10/1964
d James Butler; *p* Jeremy Isaacs;
rep Bryan Magee
AMERICAN ELECTIONS 5/11/1964
d Peter Robinson; *p* Jeremy Isaacs
COMPREHENSIVE SCHOOLS 12/11/1964
d Peter Robinson; *p* Jeremy Isaacs
G.P.O. 19/11/1964
d Peter Robinson; *p* Jeremy Isaacs
LONDON DOCKERS 26/11/1964
d Peter Robinson; *p* Jeremy Isaacs
PRIME MINISTER (H. WILSON) 3/12/1964
d Robert Fleming
NORTHERN IRELAND 10/12/1964
d Peter Robinson; *p* Jeremy Isaacs

BERLIN CRISIS 17/12/1964
d Peter Robinson
ROAD SAFETY 17/12/1964
A report on likely deaths this Christmas.
d Peter Robinson; p Jeremy Isaacs;
rep Desmond Wilcox
PRISONERS OF CONSCIENCE 24/12/1964
Political prisoners, mainly in South Africa and
East Germany, featuring Nelson Mandela and an
East German prisoner released after a long
sentence – Heinz Brandt.
d Peter Robinson; p Jeremy Isaacs;
rep James Cameron
1964 COMPILATION 31/12/1964
d Peter Robinson; p Jeremy Isaacs
LESBIANS 7/1/1965
d John Phillips; p Jeremy Isaacs;
rep Bryan Magee
B.A.C. CRISIS 14/1/1965
d Peter Robinson; p Jeremy Isaacs
RELIGION IN SCHOOLS 21/1/1965
d Peter Robinson; p Jeremy Isaacs
ETHIOPIA 28/1/1965
d Peter Robinson; p Jeremy Isaacs
ABORTION – A LAW FOR THE RICH? 4/2/1965
The laws relating to abortion are discussed by
doctors. Girls who have had abortions talk about
their feelings and describe the ordeal.
d Stephen Peet; p Jeremy Isaacs;
comm Desmond Wilcox
SUDAN 11/2/1965
The Sudanese helping to get arms through to the
rebels in the Congo.
d Peter Robinson
UNITED NATIONS 18/2/1965
James Cameron discusses how the United
Nations has survived another monetary crisis.
d Peter Robinson
A PLAIN MAN'S GUIDE TO THE ECONOMY AND
WHAT TO DO ABOUT IT 25/2/1965
d Peter Robinson
CONSERVATIVE CENTRAL OFFICE 4/3/1965
d Peter Robinson; p Jeremy Isaacs
ROMAN CATHOLIC BIRTH CONTROL 11/3/1965
d Peter Robinson; p Jeremy Isaacs
MEDICARE 18/3/1965
SOUTH VIETNAM 1/4/1965
INCOMES POLICY 8/4/1965
TRAINING IN INDUSTRY 15/4/1965
GERMAN 'IMMIGRANT WORKERS' 22/4/1965
GAMBLING FEVER 29/4/1965
An examination of motives behind gambling.
DOMINICAN REPUBLIC 13/5/1965
Reports from the Dominican Republic where the
Americans have invaded the island in order to
head off a revolution.
d Peter Robinson; p Jeremy Isaacs
CREDIT (HP) 20/5/1965
d Peter Robinson; p Jeremy Isaacs
RE-UNIFICATION OF GERMANY 27/5/1965
Queen Elizabeth II's ten day visit to West
Germany in which she supported reunification in
a speech.
d Peter Robinson; p Jeremy Isaacs
CITY (BUSINESS TAX) 3/6/1965
The City's reaction to corporation tax in the
Labour Government Finance Bill, including an
interview with the Chancellor, James Callaghan.
d Peter Robinson
BURGLARY 10/6/1965
d Peter Robinson
MAURITIUS 17/6/1965
d Peter Robinson
100 YEARS OF THE SALVATION ARMY 24/6/1965
d John Phillips
The PRIME MINISTER (H. WILSON) 1/7/1965
d John Phillips
VIETNAM 8/7/1965
d John Phillips; p Cyril Bennett
ISRAELI ARMY 15/7/1965
d Peter Robinson
SIR ALEC DOUGLAS-HOME 22/7/1965
d John Phillips
CRUELTY 29/7/1965
A report on cruelty to children.
d Peter Robinson
EDWARD HEATH 5/8/1965
Interview with Edward Heath about his politics,
his policy towards Europe and the support of the
American presence in Vietnam.
d Peter Robinson

LBJ – THE PRESIDENT IN ACTION 12/8/1965
d Peter Robinson; p Cyril Bennett
The NEGRO NEXT DOOR 19/8/1965
Race relations in Leeds.
d Peter Robinson; p Cyril Bennett;
rep Desmond Wilcox
JAMAICA 26/8/1965
A report from Jamaica by James Cameron; with
Donald Sangster, John Maxwell and Michael
Manley.
JOHN LINDSAY 2/9/1965
A study of John Lindsay, a candidate for the
Mayor of New York City.
d Peter Robinson
WOODCOCK ON 'THE WORKERS' 9/9/1965
Robert Kee and Bernard Levin interview
George Woodcock about the problems of trade
unions in Britain.
d Peter Robinson
NATIONAL DEVELOPMENT PLAN 16/9/1965
d Peter Robinson
FERTILITY PROBLEM 23/9/1965
INDIA – PAKISTAN 30/9/1965
d Peter Robinson; p Cyril Bennett
MR. SMITH (RHODESIA) 7/10/1965
An interview with Ian Smith about the future of
Rhodesia.
d Peter Robinson
BRITAIN'S JEWS 14/10/1965
Godfrey Hodgson and James Cameron report on
some of the problems facing Jews in Britain,
including religous schisms and an increase in
mixed marriages.
d Peter Robinson
RHODESIA – OUR KITH AND KIN 21/10/1965
d Peter Robinson; p Cyril Bennett;
rep Robert Kee
RHODESIA 28/10/1965
d Peter Robinson; p Cyril Bennett
COLOURED SCHOOL LEAVERS 4/11/1965
School leavers in Birmingham and London and
teaching staff discuss the possibility of black
students suffering discrimination when searching
for jobs.
d Peter Robinson
RHODESIA – U.D.I. DECLARED 11/11/1965
A report on the Unilateral Declaration of
Independence (U.D.I) by Rhodesia with George
Ffitch, Alastair Burnet, Edward Heath, Jo
Grimond, Ian Smith and the Rev. Ndabaningi
Sithole.
d Peter Robinson; p Cyril Bennett
RHODESIA – U.D.I. + 1 18/11/1965
d Peter Robinson; p Cyril Bennett
ZAMBIA 25/11/1965
d Peter Robinson; p Cyril Bennett
The NATIONAL HOUSING PLAN 25/11/1965
d Peter Robinson; p Alasdair Milne
FRENCH ELECTIONS 2/12/1965
The build-up to the French presidential elections
of 5th December, with François Mitterand, Jean
Louis Tixier-Vignancour and Jean Lecanuet.
d Theo Richmond
NOBODY'S CHILD 9/12/1965
d Theo Richmond
The PROTESTERS (AMERICA) 16/12/1965
Civil rights and Vietnam protests at Berkeley
University, California.
d James Butler; p Alasdair Milne
POOR FAMILIES 23/12/1965
d James Butler; p Alasdair Milne
JAMES CAMERON'S YEAR 30/12/1965
d Peter Robinson; p Alasdair Milne;
pres James Cameron
HALF A LIFETIME 1966
The life of a heroin addict. The addict was
filmed again in the programme The ADDICT
ALONE in the same series tx 18/5/1967.
ECONOMY 6/1/1966
d Peter Robinson; p Alasdair Milne
The VANDALS 13/1/1966
An investigation into the motivation of people
who commit acts of vandalism.
d Peter Robinson
MINES 20/1/1966
d Peter Robinson
HULL BY-ELECTIONS 27/1/1966
d Peter Robinson
LAW IN ACTION (POLICE) 3/2/1966
d Peter Robinson
LAW IN ACTION (JUSTICE) 10/2/1966
d Peter Robinson

ROY JENKINS 17/2/1966
d Peter Robinson
GHANA – COUP 3/3/1966
d Peter Robinson; rep Alastair Burnet
The UNION AND THE PARTIES 10/3/1966
Interviews with David Steel, Ron Smith and
Harry Nichols.
d Peter Robinson; rep Alastair Burnet
CONFRONTATION 17/3/1966
d Peter Robinson; rep Alastair Burnet
EDUCATION 24/3/1966
d Peter Robinson; rep Alastair Burnet
GIFTED CHILDREN 7/4/1966
Advocates special units for gifted children which
are not available in primary or secondary
schools. Interviews some gifted children and
their parents and describes those who 'fail' at
secondary modern schools.
d John P. Hamilton; p Cliff Morgan
UNITED NATIONS 14/4/1966
d John P. Hamilton; p Cliff Morgan
KENYA 21/4/1966
d John P. Hamilton; p Cliff Morgan
The HIGHLANDS 28/4/1966
d Peter Robinson; rep Alastair Burnet
DOCTORS' PAY 5/5/1966
A studio discussion in which Alastair Burnet
talks to four doctors and a dentist about the new
pay awards.
d Peter Robinson; p Cliff Morgan
OXFORD – THE FRANKS REPORT 12/5/1966
On the future of Oxford University.
d Peter Robinson; p Cliff Morgan
INDIA – YEAR OF CRISIS 19/5/1966
Famine threatens India because of the failure of
the monsoon. Includes an interview with Mrs
Gandhi.
d James Butler
WORKING MUMS 26/5/1966
d Robert Fleming; p Cliff Morgan
INDIA – GOVERNMENT 2/6/1966
d Robert Fleming; p Cliff Morgan
SEAMEN'S STRIKE DAY 25 9/6/1966
Alastair Burnet reports on the 25th day of the
seamen's strike, including interviews with the
people concerned.
d James Butler; p Cliff Morgan
The SEAMEN'S STRIKE – WHO WANTS IT?
16/6/1966
A discussion with seamen on the 32nd day of
their strike. Taking part are John White, John
Cullinane, Charles Anderman, Leonard Smale,
Desmond Dalton and Edward Simons.
d James Butler; p Cliff Morgan; rep Alastair
Burnet, George Ffitch
BRAZIL – FOOTBALL 23/6/1966
d Robert Fleming; p Cliff Morgan
VIETNAM 30/6/1966
d Peter Robinson; p Cliff Morgan
ULSTER 7/7/1966
p Cliff Morgan
TEENAGE MARRIAGE 14/7/1966
The problems facing young teenage married
couples.
d Ian McFarlane; p Cliff Morgan
COLOURED FOSTER CHILDREN 21/7/1966
d Peter Robinson; p Cliff Morgan
EDWARD HEATH 28/7/1966
d Peter Robinson; p Cliff Morgan
SIKHS 4/8/1966
d Peter Robinson; p Cliff Morgan
BERLIN 11/8/1966
d Peter Robinson; p Cliff Morgan
The FREEZE 18/8/1966
d Peter Robinson; p Cliff Morgan
DIVORCE 1/9/1966
d Peter Robinson
RHODESIA 8/9/1966
d Peter Robinson; p Cliff Morgan
PRIME MINISTER (H. WILSON) 15/9/1966
d Peter Robinson; p Cliff Morgan
The PILL 22/9/1966
d Peter Robinson
ACCIDENTS 29/9/1966
Accidents in the home and on the roads caused
by fire and drunken drivers.
d Ian McFarlane; p Cliff Morgan;
with Ralph Stoney
The NATIONAL HEALTH SERVICE IN FINE
FOCUS 6/10/1966
The National Health Service in Halifax.
d Peter Robinson

THIS WEEK (Rediffusion) *cont.*

DR MARTIN LUTHER KING 13/10/1966
Robert Kee and James Cameron interview Dr
Martin Luther King in Chicago concerning the
violence three years after his 'I have a dream'
speech.
d Jim Pople, James Butler;
p Cliff Morgan
DEATH OF A VALLEY 20/10/1966
d Peter Robinson; *p* Cliff Morgan
AMERICAN ELECTIONS 10/11/1966
d Peter Robinson; *p* Cliff Morgan
NEO-NAZI PARTY GERMANY – N.D.F. 17/11/1966
d Peter Robinson; *p* Cliff Morgan
YUGOSLAVIA 24/11/1966
d Vic Hughes
ISLE OF MAN 1/12/1966
d Vic Hughes
RHODESIA 8/12/1966
d Vic Hughes
SOUTH AFRICA 15/12/1966
d Vic Hughes
PRISON SECURITY 22/12/1966
d Vic Hughes; *p* Barry Westwood
LOOKING BACK AT '66 29/12/1966
d Vic Hughes; *p* Barry Westwood
SLUM HOUSING 1967
The Gorbals in Glasgow.
d Ian McFarlane; *p* Barry Westwood
DONALD CAMPBELL: THE LAST 48 HOURS
5/1/1967
The death of Donald Campbell.
TANZANIA 12/1/1967
d Vic Hughes; *p* Barry Westwood
DISABLED 19/1/1967
d Vic Hughes; *p* Barry Westwood
CHINA 26/1/1967
d Vic Hughes; *p* Barry Westwood
ABERFAN RESETTLEMENT AND
COMPENSATION 2/2/1967
d Vic Hughes; *p* Barry Westwood
MALTA 9/2/1967
Llew Gardner reports on the effects on Malta of
the withdrawal of British troops.
d John Phillips
SPARKBROOK 16/2/1967
d Vic Hughes; *p* Barry Westwood
GAMBLING 9/3/1967
A report on gambling in England with Alfred
Salkin, George Winberg, Alfred Barnet and
Maurice Kendall.
d David Hodgson
PRIME MINISTER 16/3/1967
Harold Wilson is interviewed by Paul Johnson
and Alastair Burnet. Issues discussed include
prices and income control, the Common Market
and Vietnam.
d Terry Yarwood; *p* Barry Westwood
VIET FLYER 23/3/1967
d Terry Yarwood; *p* Barry Westwood
GLASGOW HOUSING 6/4/1967
d Terry Yarwood
NIGERIA 13/4/1967
d Terry Yarwood
RACIAL DISCRIMINATION 20/4/1967
d Terry Yarwood; *p* Barry Westwood
COMMON MARKET – EUROPE – NO! 27/4/1967
A discussion about Britain joining the EEC with
Labour MP Samuel Silkin, Conservative MP
Peter Hordern and Liberal MP James Davidson.
d Terry Yarwood; *p* James Butler
COMMON MARKET – EUROPE – YES! 4/5/1967
Interviews with people on the streets on why
Britain should join the EEC. In the studio are
Ernest Marples, Sir Frank Kirton, and David
Marghend.
d Terry Yarwood
GREECE 11/5/1967
A report about the Junta that was taken over by
the Military ten days before the elections were to
be held. Interview with Colonel Nikloaos
Makarezos, one of the Junta.
d Terry Yarwood; *p* James Butler
The ADDICT ALONE 18/5/1967
A heroin addict talks about himself. His brother,
who shared the same background and is not an
addict, also speaks. Continuation of the
programme HALF A LIFETIME in the same
series, *tx* 1966.
d David Hodgson
TURMOIL IN THE MIDDLE EAST 25/5/1967
d Terry Yarwood; *p* Phillip Whitehead

AMERICA 1/6/1967
d Terry Yarwood
ULSTER 22/6/1967
d Terry Yarwood; *p* Phillip Whitehead
The FUTURE OF OCCUPIED JORDAN 6/7/1967
d Terry Yarwood; *p* Phillip Whitehead
The FIRE THIS TIME 13/7/1967
The problems of negroes in New York and
Cleveland, Ohio; the solutions that are being
proposed particularly by Stokely Carmichael and
the violence in Atlanta, Georgia.
d Ian McFarlane; *p* Phillip Whitehead;
rep Godfrey Hodgson
ADEN – THE LAST POST 20/7/1967
The situation in Aden. Includes an interview
with Colonel Colin Campbell 'Mad Mitch'
Mitchell.
d Ian McFarlane; *p* Phillip Whitehead;
rep Llew Gardner
CANNABIS 10/8/1967
d Terry Yarwood; *p* Phillip Whitehead
DESERTERS – THE WAY OUT 17/8/1967
A report on US soldiers in the Rhine Army who
desert because they are about to be drafted/sent
to Vietnam.
d Terry Yarwood; *p* Phillip Whitehead
SHOPLIFTING 24/8/1967
d Ian McFarlane
BRITAIN AND CHINA 31/8/1967
d Terry Yarwood; *p* Phillip Whitehead
BLACK JACK (LAST EXIT: CONGO) 14/9/1967
Mercenaries in the Belgian Congo before
independence.
d Terry Yarwood; *p* Phillip Whitehead
IS LABOUR'S LOVE LOST? 5/10/1967
The Labour Party Conference in Scarborough
including speeches from Michael Foot and James
Callaghan. Includes coverage of the social side of
the Conference.
d Terry Yarwood; *p* Phillip Whitehead
HONG KONG 12/10/1967
Measures being taken against Communism in
Hong Kong. With Sir David Trench, P.S. Woo,
David Lai, Elsie Elliott, and Police
Commissioner T.C. Eates
d Randal Beattie
DIVORCE 26/10/1967
d Terry Yarwood
RUSSIA – DAUGHTERS OF THE REVOLUTION
2/11/1967
d Terry Yarwood
SCOTTISH NATIONALISTS 9/11/1967
A report on nationalism in Scotland.
d Terry Yarwood
The SPECIAL WORLD OF NIGEL HUNT
30/11/1967
The achievements and progress that can be made
by a Down's syndrome child with the help of
parents and teachers.
d Ian McFarlane; Terry Yarwood
MISSING FROM HOME 28/12/1967
d Terry Yarwood
EDWARD HEATH 4/1/1968
d Terry Yarwood
A HILL IN VIETNAM 11/1/1968
d Terry Yarwood; *p* Phillip Whitehead
RUSSIAN UNDERGROUND 18/1/1968
BLACK POWER 25/1/1968
d Terry Yarwood; *p* Phillip Whitehead
UNMARRIED MOTHERS 1/2/1968
d Terry Yarwood
IF LONDON FLOODS 8/2/1968
A report on the danger of flooding in London;
interviews with the public and the Greater
London Council's Flood Prevention Officer.
d Ken Ashton; *p* Phillip Whitehead
GERMANY: THE NEW EXTREMISTS 15/2/1968
VIETNAM: THE YEAR OF THE MONKEY
22/2/1968
VIETNAM: LAND WITHOUT JOY 22/2/1968
FRANCE (AMERICAN CHALLENGE) 4/3/1968
AMERICAN ELECTIONS '68 (WHO VOTES FOR
PEACE) 7/3/1968
Eugene McCarthy's campaign against L.B.
Johnson, centering on New Hampshire.
d Terry Yarwood
EGYPT 21/3/1968
Egypt six months after the war with Israel,
including interviews with Egyptian politicians.
d Terry Yarwood
CZECHOSLOVAKIA 28/3/1968
d Terry Yarwood

L.B. JOHNSON 4/4/1968
d Terry Yarwood
MISTAKEN IDENTITY 11/4/1968
d Terry Yarwood
PORTRAIT OF A MILITANT – HUGH SCANLON
25/4/1968
d Terry Yarwood
KENNEDY: WHEN I'M THROUGH, HOW ABOUT
YOU? 2/5/1968
d Terry Yarwood; *p* Phillip Whitehead
MARLON BRANDO 16/5/1968
d Terry Yarwood; *p* Phillip Whitehead
FRANCE 23/5/1968
Robert Kee interviews 'les Erenerents'
approximately four weeks after the first sit-ins.
Scenes of De Gaulle's return.
d Terry Yarwood; *p* Phillip Whitehead
The DAYS THAT SHOOK DE GAULLE 30/5/1968
d Terry Yarwood
NEWARK : 'WHITE POWER' 6/6/1968
d Terry Yarwood
ARGYLLS 13/6/1968
d Terry Yarwood
WALLACE 20/6/1968
A report by Godfrey Hodgson on George
Wallace's campaign; Wallace is the 'racist'
candidate and 'third horse' in the American
presidential campaign.
d Terry Yarwood

THIS WEEK (Thames 1968–92)
Current affairs programme; continuing the
Rediffusion series. See also THIS WEEK
SPECIAL.
CRIME AND VIOLENCE: PART 1 8/8/1968
An interview with a confessed criminal who
states that he would agree to kill someone for
the sum of five thousand pounds.
p Phillip Whitehead
An INTERVIEW WITH THE PRIME MINISTER
3/10/1968
Harold Wilson is interviewed at the time of the
Labour Party Conference.
p Phillip Whitehead
MILOVAN DJILAS – PORTRAIT OF A
COMMUNIST 30/12/1968
A portrait of the Yugoslav writer and politician
Milovan Djilas.
The GROUP 24/7/1969
The work of the German scientists at the NASA
space flights centre at Huntsville, Alabama, and
an interview with its director, Wernher Von
Braun.
p Phillip Whitehead
EDWARD KENNEDY – THE WRONG TURNING
31/7/1969
The circumstances surrounding the accident to
Edward Kennedy and his passenger on July 18th
1969, on Chappaquiddick Island, Massachusetts.
d Phillip Whitehead
WHAT WAS LOST, WHAT WAS WON? 21/8/1969
An examination of the 'B' Specials and the
problem of law and order in Ulster.
The ARMY IN ULSTER – THE MEN IN THE
MIDDLE 18/9/1969
An examination of the role of the British Army
during the civil disturbances in Ulster.
FORTRESS ISRAEL 25/9/1969
A report on how senior Israeli politicians and
soldiers see Israel's position.
p Phillip Whitehead
A ROOM IN PEKING 30/10/1969
Reuters correspondent Anthony Grey describes
his experiences during his two years in prison in
Peking.
p Phillip Whitehead
The POLITICS OF SPORT 6/11/1969
John Morgan reports on the implications of the
proposed tour of Britain by the South African
rugby team.
p Phillip Whitehead
CAMBODIA – THE PRINCE 20/11/1969
A survey of the political situation in Cambodia
in relation to the war in Vietnam, which includes
an interview with Prince Sihanouk.
d Chris Goddard
LAOS – THE NEXT DOMINO 4/12/1969
The political situation in Laos; the state of the
Pathet Lao; the Ho Chi Minh trail.
p Phillip Whitehead
DRUGS 18/12/1969
d Phillip Whitehead

THIS WEEK (Thames) *cont.*

EDWARD HEATH 10/6/1970
An interview with Edward Heath during the run-up to the General Election.
EDWARD HEATH 24/9/1970
An interview with Edward Heath, the new Prime Minister.
p Jo Menell
ALL OUR MISS STEADMANS 15/10/1970
The problems of old people waiting for admission to hospital.
d David Gill
DO SOMETHING! 22/10/1970
How the action of a group of local people in Islington, without particular influence, started an adventure playground.
d Ross Devenish;
p Jo Menell, Ross Devenish
ACCIDENT DEPARTMENT 17/12/1970
A day in the accident ward of a large London hospital.
d David Gill; *p* Jo Menell
V.D. OUT OF CONTROL 11/3/1971
The spread of venereal disease.
SOMETHING ABOUT A SOLDIER 1/7/1971
John Edwards interviews Lt. Col. Anthony Herbert, a professional American soldier who accuses the American army of war crimes in Vietnam.
d Ted Childs
MEN OF THE CLYDE 8/7/1971
A report from Clydebank on the problems of the Upper Clyde shipyard, with Sir John Toothill.
d Chris Goddard; *p* Ian Martin
PARENTS AND THE PILL 22/7/1971
A discussion chaired by Alastair Burnet between a panel of experts and an audience of parents and children on the issue of providing the contraceptive pill. Panel members include Michael Schofield and Helen Brook.
d Udi Eichler, David Elstein
RALPH NADER – PUBLIC CITIZEN 29/7/1971
A profile of Ralph Nader and his consumer protection campaigning in the USA.
d David Elstein
BOTH PRACTICABLE AND REASONABLE 2/9/1971
A report by Alan Hargreaves on the failure by various authorities to implement the provisions of the Chronically Sick and Disabled Act, with Alf Morris.
d Richard Broad
DEATH IN THE PRISON YARD 23/9/1971
A report on the death of George Jackson in San Quentin prison. Interviews with the Warden, a guard, Angela Davis and Jackson's mother. Includes a recording of an earlier American interview with Jackson.
d Chris Goddard
A MOTHER'S REPORT 23/12/1971
Actuality study of a poor family in a large northern city, showing the problems faced by the mother as she strives to keep her family together.
WE ARE THE YOUNG ONES 1972
The Raising Of the School Leaving Age (ROSLA) has created problems for teachers of children who would have preferred to leave.
The MINERS' LAST STAND 20/1/1972
A report on the background to the miners' strike. A young miner living in a pit village in Yorkshire gives his views on the issues involved.
d Tom Steel
The TIMOTHY DAVEY AFFAIR 2/3/1972
An interview with Timothy Davey, a 14-year-old English boy sentenced to six years' imprisonment by a Turkish court on a drugs charge.
d Vanya Kewley
JIMMY REID UNLIMITED 11/5/1972
A profile of Scottish trade unionist Jimmy Reid, leader of the work-in at the John Brown shipyard on Clydebank, and newly elected Rector of Glasgow University.
d Tom Steel
WHO WANTS TO BE A MILLIONAIRE? 29/6/1972
The asset stripping activities of business tycoon John Bentley. The views of a shop steward at the Merton toy factory taken over by Bentley.
d Peter Tiffin

TWO BROTHERS 24/8/1972
How their experiences in Vietnam have altered the lives of two war veterans living in Boston, Massachusetts.
d Tom Steel
The NATIVES ARE GETTING RESTLESS 12/10/1972
A report on grass roots opinion in the Conservative Party, as expressed by party workers in the constituencies of Ashton-under-Lyne and Billericay.
d Peter Tiffin
WASTED LIVES 19/10/1972
Women who have needlessly spent their lives in mental hospitals.
d David Gill
EVEREST – THE FIGHT FOR THE FACE 23/11/1972
The unsuccessful British attempt on the south-west face of Everest, led by Chris Bonington. Expedition members include Dougal Haston, Hamish MacInnes and Doug Scott.
CHILDREN IN CARE: PART 1: OTHER PEOPLE'S CHILDREN 1/2/1973
The effects of institutionalised life on children taken into care.
d David Gill; *rep* Peter Williams
CHILDREN IN CARE: PART 2: TAKE THREE GIRLS 8/2/1973
A study of three sisters who have spent most of their lives in children's homes.
d David Gill
DAVID CASSIDY – WEEKEND AT WEMBLEY 22/3/1973
A report on the visit to Britain of pop singer David Cassidy.
d David Gill; *p* John Edwards;
rep Peter Taylor
PRISONER OF WAR 5/4/1973
James Lindbergh Hughes, a colonel in the American army, relates how he was imprisoned and tortured by the North Vietnamese.
p John Edwards
S.P.G. 12/4/1973
A report on the work of Special Patrol Group (SPG), a police unit working in London, and its use of firearms.
d Peter Tiffin
WINDOW ON THE WORLD 12/7/1973
An operation to restore a patient's sight by means of the 'plastic window' technique, performed at Southend General Hospital by Peter Choyce.
d Peter Tiffin
MAN FROM THE MOON 20/9/1973
An interview with astronaut Edwin 'Buzz' Aldrin, who suffered a nervous breakdown following his moon flight.
d John Edwards
The GREATEST HI-JACK EVER 4/10/1973
A report on the kidnapping by Arabs of Jewish passengers from a train in transit to Vienna; Dr. Kreisky, Moshe Dayan and Golda Meir at a press conference.
The UNKNOWN FAMINE 18/10/1973
A report on the famine in Ethiopia by Jonathan Dimbleby.
d Ian Stuttard
GLASGOW FIREMEN'S STRIKE 1/11/1973
A report on the firemen's strike in Glasgow.
p John Edwards
ONCE A MINER... 8/11/1973
A report on coal mining in Britain and why miners are leaving the industry.
d David Elstein
The PRESS AND THE PRESIDENT 29/11/1973
A report on the relationship between President Nixon and the press in the USA.
ELECTION SPECIAL 7/2/1974
Interviews with Edward Heath, Harold Wilson, and Jeremy Thorpe on the day the February 1974 General Election was announced.
interv Robert Kee
JEREMY THORPE 14/2/1974
Llew Gardner interviews Jeremy Thorpe during the run up to the February 1974 General Election.
HAROLD WILSON 20/2/1974
Llew Gardner interviews Harold Wilson during the run up to the General Election of February 1974.

EDWARD HEATH 21/2/1974
Llew Gardner interviews Edward Heath during the build-up to the General Election of February 1974.
TUG OF LOVE 28/2/1974
A report on the struggle for possession of Demetreous Palmer, a foster child reclaimed by his parents. The head of Health and Social services in Coventry, Tom White, gives his views on the case.
d Ian Stuttard
RETURN TO ETHIOPIA 14/3/1974
Jonathan Dimbleby reports on the famine in Ethiopia.
The NATIONAL FRONT 5/9/1974
d Michael Ruggins; *rep* Peter Williams
DEALING WITH TERRORISTS – ROY JENKINS 12/12/1974
Peter Taylor reports on the new measures introduced by the Home Secretary to deal with the I.R.A., Roy Jenkins discusses the measures.
d Michael Dormer
JOBS FOR THE BOYS 30/1/1975
John Fielding reports on a workers' co-operative set up at Kirkby, Lancashire with the aid of a government grant. Tony Benn states why he supported the enterprise.
d Ian Stuttard; *p* David Elstein
LEARNING ABOUT SEX: PART 1: SEX AND THE 14-YEAR OLD 20/2/1975
The work of Dr Christopher in Haringey who gives sex education classes and advice in the Borough's schools.
PORTUGAL: LURCH TO THE LEFT 20/3/1975
John Fielding reports on the political struggle in Portugal.
d Ken Craig
DYING FOR A FAG 3/4/1975
Peter Taylor reports on the links between smoking and lung cancer.
d Martin Smith; *p* David Elstein
LICENSED TO KILL 10/4/1975
The debate over cigarette advertising. Includes comments from Minister of Health, David Owen.
d Martin Smith; *p* David Elstein;
rep Peter Taylor
PORTUGAL AND THE REVOLT AGAINST THE COMMUNISTS 24/7/1975
A report on the anti-communist demonstrations in Portugal, including the burning of the communist headquarters at Alcobaca.
d Martin Smith; *rep* John Fielding
ETHIOPIA – A REVOLUTION IS DECLARED 31/7/1975
Jonathan Dimbleby reports from Ethiopia on the socialist measures being taken by the military government.
d Ian Stuttard
ETHIOPIA: FAMINE AND WAR 7/8/1975
Jonathan Dimbleby reports from Ethiopia on the problems faced by the military government.
d Ian Stuttard
ASHES TO ASHES 11/9/1975
An investigation into the damage to health caused by smoking.
ARGENTINA – STATE OF SIEGE 6/11/1975
John Fielding reports on the problems faced by Isabel Peron in Argentina, and on the violence being used by the police and right-wing groups.
d Martin Smith
LEADER OF THE OPPOSITION 5/2/1976
Llew Gardner interviews Margaret Thatcher.
d Terry Yarwood; *p* David Elstein
HERE COME THE CUTS 19/2/1976
An interview with Denis Healey on the day of publication of the Government White Paper announcing widespread cuts in the Social Services.
d Peter Tiffin; *p* David Elstein
STONES ON THE ROAD 27/5/1976
The Rolling Stones on tour.
d Bruce Gowers; *p* David Elstein
ULSTER: IN FRIENDSHIP AND FORGIVENESS? 26/8/1977
Political events in Ulster in reaction to the Queen's visit.
d Ian Stuttard; *p* David Elstein
LIFE BEHIND THE WIRE 22/9/1977
A report on the activities of Special Category prisoners in the Maze Prison, Northern Ireland.
d Ian Stuttard; *p* David Elstein

THIS WEEK (Thames) *cont.*

NAMIBIA – THE FRONT LINE 16/2/1978
South Africa's military involvement in Namibia.
p David Elstein
BREAKING THE LINK? 7/3/1978
Interviews with Irish politicians concerning Jack
Lynch's call for Irish unification.
d Michael Dormer

THIS WEEK 1844 – THE UNION AND THE BOND (Thames 21/1/1975)
On April 5, 1844, 30,000 coal miners in
Northumberland and Co. Durham, went on
strike. This film creates an historical
reconstruction of events during the strike as
though a current affairs programme were in
existence to give it coverage at the time.
d Richard Broad; *pres* Allan Hargreaves
lp Freddie Jones; Sean Garrad;
Roger Avon; James Garbutt; Gordon Faith;
John Malcolm; William Maxwell; Neil McCaul;
Lizzie McKenzie

THIS WEEK NATIONAL
(Rediffusion 1966–67)
Rediffusion current affairs programme.
Transmitted Tuesdays, initially weekly, then
fortnightly, while THIS WEEK was transmitted
on Thursdays.
PRODUCTIVITY 27/9/1966
d Sheila Gregg
LABOUR PARTY CONFERENCE 4/10/1966
d Sheila Gregg; *p* Lewis Rudd
REDEPLOYMENT 18/10/1966
d Sheila Gregg; *p* Lewis Rudd
RACE RELATIONS BOARD 1/11/1966
d Sheila Gregg; *p* Lewis Rudd
INTRUSION BY TELEVISION 8/11/1966
d Sheila Gregg; *p* Lewis Rudd
COMMON MARKET 15/11/1966
d Sheila Gregg; *p* Lewis Rudd
SANCTIONS ON RHODESIA 29/11/1966
d Sheila Gregg; *p* Lewis Rudd
UNEMPLOYED EXECUTIVES 6/12/1966
d Sheila Gregg; *p* Jeremy Taylor
The G.L.C. 31/1/1967
d Sheila Gregg
DEFENCE WHITE PAPER 16/2/1967
Presenter Alastair Burnet in a studio discussion
with Enoch Powell and Dennis Healey
concerning the implications of the defence cuts
announced in the White Paper. Also, George
Ffitch interviews Christopher Mayhew about his
reaction.
d Vic Hughes; *p* Barry Westwood
YOUNG POLITICIANS 28/2/1967
d Sheila Gregg; *p* Jeremy Taylor;
rep Llew Gardner; George Scott;
with George Ffitch
POLLOCK 7/3/1967
d Sheila Gregg; *p* Jeremy Taylor
FOOTBALL 14/3/1967
d Sheila Gregg; *p* Jeremy Taylor
ADEN 21/3/1967
The violence against the British presence in
Aden and the future of the South Arabian
Federation. Llew Gardner speaks to the
Secretary-General of the South Arabian League
in Aden and Robert Kee speaks to Duncan
Sandys and Christopher Mayhew in the studio.
d Sheila Gregg; *p* Jeremy Taylor
STANSTED 'LONDON AIRPORT' 9/5/1967
d Terry Yarwood; *p* Jeremy Taylor
PARIS 16/5/1967
Interviews in the street with French people
giving their views about Britain joining the EEC.
d Terry Yarwood; *p* Jeremy Taylor
COMPUTER DATING 30/5/1967
The 'night hours' use of UNIVAC Computer in
the City by the computer dating firm 'Operation
Match'.
d Terry Yarwood; *p* Jeremy Taylor

THIS WEEK SPECIAL (Rediffusion 1964–68)
Series of special reports from the THIS WEEK
team.
PICK THE WINNER 2/6/1964
Preview of the Derby horserace.
d Grahame Turner; *p* Jeremy Isaacs
GENERAL ELECTION 15/9/1964
p Jeremy Isaacs

WE WISH YOU A MERRY CHRISTMAS 23/12/1966
The contrasting Christmases spent by a rich
family, Mr and Mrs Robert Maxwell, and a poor
one.
d Peter Robinson, Vic Hughes;
p Barry Westwood

THIS WEEK SPECIAL (Thames 1968–92)
Special reports from the THIS WEEK team.
MARTIN LUTHER KING 5/4/1968
MANHUNT 23/4/1968
The police investigation into the 1967 murder of
7–year-old Christine Darby on Cannock Chase
in Staffordshire, the biggest manhunt in British
criminal history.
d Ken Ashton; *p* Phillip Whitehead;
rep Peter Williams
REMEMBER CZECHOSLOVAKIA 30/12/1968
Robert Kee reviews the past fifty years of Czech
history and considers the implications of the
Warsaw Pact intervention.
p Phillip Whitehead
The WAR IS OVER 22/1/1970
Robert Kee reports on the prospects for a united
Nigeria, and the relations between its main
tribes.
ULSTER – THE LAST FIVE YEARS 8/8/1974
A survey of the troubles in Ulster since 1969.
d David Elstein
The WORLD'S WORST AIR CRASH – THE
AVOIDABLE ACCIDENT? 19/2/1975
A report on the causes of the crash of a Turkish
Airline's DC10 outside Paris in March 1974, and
interviews with Charles Miller, John Shaffer, and
Senator Vance Hartke about the decision to
modify the DC10's cargo door.
d Peter Tiffin; *p* David Elstein;
rep Peter Williams
ABORTION 15/10/1975
How a National Health Service hospital conducts
abortions; a discussion of the issues involved
with Jonathan Dimbleby, David Steel, Leo
Abse, and a studio audience.
d Richard Broad; *p* David Elstein;
rep Jenny Wilkes

THIS WEEK – THE ARTS
(Rediffusion 1966– 67)
Fortnightly spin-off from the THIS WEEK
series.
THIS WEEK – THE ARTS 26/9/1966
d John Phillips
GUITARS 10/10/1966
d John Phillips
PAPERBACKS 24/10/1966
d John Phillips; *pres* Bryan Magee
THIS WEEK – THE ARTS 7/11/1966
d John Phillips
BALLET RAMBERT 21/11/1966
d John Phillips; *pres* Bryan Magee
IRISH CENSORSHIP 5/12/1966
d John Phillips; *pres* Bryan Magee
ART SCHOOLS 9/1/1967
d John Phillips; *pres* Bryan Magee
BURNS CULT 23/1/1967
d John Phillips; *pres* Bryan Magee
WILLIAM SHAKESPEARE/MARTHA GRAHAM
7/4/1967
d John Phillips; *pres* Bryan Magee
TURNER: TATE GALLERY 14/4/1967
pres Bryan Magee
ROYAL ACADEMY: CHANDOS INTERVIEW
28/4/1967
d Terry Yarwood; *pres* Bryan Magee
STRUCTURES: SONORES 5/5/1967
d Terry Yarwood; *pres* Bryan Magee
MICHAEL AYRTON STORY 12/5/1967
d Terry Yarwood; *pres* Bryan Magee
CANNON HILL 26/5/1967
d Terry Yarwood; *pres* Bryan Magee
PICASSO SCULPTURE 9/6/1967
Tracking shots around sculptures in an
exhibition, with Sir Roland Penrose, Picasso's
friend and biographer.
d Terry Yarwood
HENRY MOORE 14/7/1967
Henry Moore exhibits at Marlborough Art
Gallery.
d Terry Yarwood

THIS WONDERFUL WORLD
(Scottish TV 1958–65)
The wonderful things the camera has seen on all
frontiers of human observation, introduced by
John Grierson.
THIS WONDERFUL WORLD 1960

THIS YEAR NEXT YEAR
(Granada 25/1–19/4/1977)
Thirteen-part drama series that centres on the
life of Harry Shaw, who moved from the
Yorkshire Dales to compete in the affluent
society of London.
PARTING OF THE WAYS 25/1/1977
d Alan Grint; *p* Howard Baker;
sc John Finch
lp Ronald Hines; Michael Elphick;
Jill Summers; Teddy Turner; Anne Stallybrass

THOMAS AND SARAH
(LWT 14/1–8/4/1979)
Period drama series; a spin-off from the series
UPSTAIRS DOWNSTAIRS (1970–75).
The POOR YOUNG WIDOW OF PECKHAM
4/3/1979
d Marek Kanievska; *p* Christopher Hodson;
sc Jeremy Paul
lp John Alderton; Pauline Collins;
John Moore; Eve Pearce; Hilary Gasson;
Norman Jones

THOSE WONDERFUL TV TIMES
(Tyne Tees 1976–78)
Quiz show in which celebrities answer questions
on ITV programmes.
with Barry Cryer
THOSE WONDERFUL TV TIMES 2/4/1976
d Lisle Willis; *with* Sylvia Syms,
Hughie Green, Shaun Usher
THOSE WONDERFUL TV TIMES 29/4/1977
d Lisle Willis; *p* Tony Sandford;
with Nerys Hughes, Patrick Mower,
Marjorie Proops
THOSE WONDERFUL TV TIMES 20/5/1977
d Lisle Willis; *p* Tony Sandford;
with Fenella Fielding, Robin Nedwell,
Tessa Wyatt
THOSE WONDERFUL TV TIMES 15/7/1977
d Lisle Willis; *with* Jack Haig,
Joan Turner, Kenneth Cope
THOSE WONDERFUL TV TIMES 13/8/1978
d Anthony J. Bacon; *exec.p* Tony Sandford;
pres Norman Vaughan;
with Joan Bakewell, Fanny Cradock,
Alan Freeman, Shirley Anne Field,
David Jacobs, Carmel McSharry

The THREAD OF LIFE
(BBC 4/1–7/3/1964)
Ten-part introduction to molecular biology.
pres John Kendrew
The REVOLUTION IN BIOLOGY 4/1/1964
The importance of DNA with Dr Andrew Kerr.
p Alan Sleath

THREE COMEDIES OF MARRIAGE
(Thames 3/7–17/7/1975)
Trilogy of plays.
FEELING HIS WAY 10/7/1975
d/p Peter Duguid; *sc* Donald Churchill
lp Michael Bryant; Wendy Gifford;
Geoffrey Palmer; Sandra Dickinson;
Kathleen Heath; Joanna Craig

THREE DAYS IN SZCZECIN
(Granada 21/9/1976)
A reconstruction of the shipyard workers' strike
in Poland in 1971.
d/p Leslie Woodhead; *sc* Boleslaw Sulik
lp Leslie Sands; Kenneth Colley;
Patrick Durkin; George Irving; Neil Johnston;
Barry Hart; James Tomlinson; Dinah Stabb;
Roger Walker

The THREE HOSTAGES (BBC 27/12/1977)
Made-for-TV film, based on the novel by John
Buchan and featuring his espionage hero
Richard Hannay.
d Clive Donner; *p* Mark Shivas;
sc John Prebble
lp Barry Foster; Diana Quick;
John Castle; Peter Blythe; Hilary Mason;
Constance Chapman; Donald Pickering;
John Shrapnel

The THREE KISSES (BBC 28/12/1978)
Drama adapted from Jerome K. Jerome's
'Malvina of Brittany'.
d John Prowse; *exec.p* Anna Home;
sc Ben Steed
lp Damian Earle; Julia Schopflin;
Ian Hogg; Lynn Farleigh; Ian Gelder;
Natalie Ogle; Margaret D'Arcy; Amanda Bell;
Frank Jarvis; John Rapley; Beth Harris;
Jill Gascoine

THREE MEN IN A BOAT
(BBC 31/12/1975)
Dramatisation of the novel by Jerome K.
Jerome.
d Stephen Frears; *p* Rosemary Hill;
sc Tom Stoppard
lp Tim Curry; Stephen Moore;
Michael Palin; Michael Elphick; Bill Stewart;
John Blain; George Innes; Russell Dixon;
Mary McLeod; Clifford Kershaw

3–2–1 (Yorkshire 1978–82)
Game show based on a Spanish programme.
3–2–1 29/7/1978
d David Millard; *p* Derek Burrell-Davis;
pres Ted Rogers

THRILLER
(US Hubbell Robinson Pictures 1960–62)
Horror-fantasy anthology series hosted by Boris
Karloff.
p William Frye
The PURPLE ROOM 25/10/1960
d Douglas Heyes
lp Rip Torn; Patricia Barry;
Richard Anderson
The PREDICTION 22/11/1960
d John Brahm; *sc* Donald S. Sanford
lp Audrey Dalton; Alex Davion
The CHEATERS 27/12/1960
d John Brahm; *sc* Donald S. Sanford;
auth Robert Bloch
lp Jack Weston; Miriam Olcott;
Harry Townes; Henry Daniell; Paul Newlan;
Mildred Dunnock

THUNDERBIRDS
(AP Films Productions-ATV 1965–66)
Science-fiction puppet animation series.
p Gerry Anderson, Reg Hill
voice Ray Barrett; Peter Dyneley;
David Graham; Sylvia Anderson;
Christine Finn; David Holliday;
Shane Rimmer; Matter Zimmerman
TRAPPED IN THE SKY 2/10/1965
d Alan Pattillo;
sc Gerry Anderson, Sylvia Anderson
DAY OF DISASTER 6/11/1965
d David Elliott; *sc* Dennis Spooner

TILL DEATH US DO PART
(BBC 1966–75)
Sitcom series about a London East End family.
Revived by ATV in 1981 as 'Till Death…' and
the BBC produced a sequel 'In Sickness and in
Health' in 1985.
p Dennis Main Wilson; *sc* Johnny Speight
regulars Warren Mitchell; Dandy Nichols;
Anthony Booth; Una Stubbs
A HOUSE WITH LOVE IN IT 20/6/1966
d Douglas Argent
lp John Junkin; Jacques Cey;
Will Stampe; Charlie Bird
INTOLERANCE 27/6/1966
d Douglas Argent
lp Thomas Baptiste; Ian St. John;
Willie Stevenson
The BLOOD DONOR 12/1/1968
PIGEON RACING 20/9/1972
lp Joan Sims; Bill Maynard

TIME FOR BAXTER (BBC 1/1/1972)
Comedy-variety show.
p David Bell; *sc* Ken Hoare;
with Stanley Baxter; Clodagh Rodgers

A TIME TO REMEMBER (Thames 1969–71)
Documentary series covering the period 1896–
1945 compiled from the Pathé News Library.
The TIME OF THE SUFFRAGETTES 14/5/1969
d Peter Baylis; *nar* Edith Evans

TIME TO SPARE (Tyne Tees 1979)
Regional series for children which looks at how
spare time may be usefully filled.
TIME TO SPARE 10/7/1979

TIMES REMEMBERED (BBC 1971)
Documentary series in which people are
interviewed about their lives.
HARRY BUTTON 17/11/1971
Harry Button looks back over his working life in
the steel industry.
d Terence O'Reilly

TINKER, TAILOR, SOLDIER, SPY
(BBC-Paramount Television 10/9–22/10/1979)
Seven-part espionage serial adapted from the
story by John Le Carré.
d John Irvin; *p* Jonathan Powell;
sc Arthur Hopcraft
regulars Alec Guinness; Bernard Hepton
EPISODE 1 10/9/1979
lp Terence Rigby; Michael Aldridge;
Ian Richardson; Alexander Knox;
George Sewell; Ian Bannen; Michael Jayston;
Nigel Stock; Anthony Bate; Hywel Bennett;
Milos Kirek; Eugene Lipinski; Alec Sabin;
Brian Hawksley
EPISODE 2 17/9/1979
lp Thorley Walters; Susan Kodicek;
Hilary Minster; Pauline Letts; Stephen Earle
EPISODE 3 24/9/1979
lp Beryl Reid; Frank Compton;
Frank Moorey; Jean Rimmer
EPISODE 4 1/10/1979
lp Patrick Stewart; Warren Clarke;
Alec Sabin; Marjorie Hogan; Joe Praml
EPISODE 5 8/10/1979
lp John Standing; Mandy Cuthbert;
Duncan Jones; Daniel Beecher
EPISODE 6 15/10/1979
lp Joss Ackland; John Wells; Betty Hardy;
Guy Standeven; Duncan Jones; Daniel Beecher;
Jo Apted; Alec Sabin
EPISODE 7 22/10/1979
lp Siân Phillips; George Pravda;
Alec Sabin; Duncan Jones; Daniel Beecher

TO BE SEVEN IN BELFAST
(ATV 6/4/1975)
A camera team visited three Catholic and three
Protestant children all aged seven.
d John Sheppard; *p* Richard Creasey

TO ENCOURAGE THE OTHERS
(BBC 28/3/1972)
Dramatised reconstruction of the Craig and
Bentley murder case of 1952.
d Alan Clarke; *p* Mark Shivas;
sc David Yallop
lp Billy Hamon; Charles Bolton;
Roland Culver; Philip Stone; Wensley Pithey;
Arthur Lovegrove; Carmel McSharry;
John Ringham; Ken Halliwell; Michael Sheard;
Christopher Coll; Derrick Slater;
Barbara Hickmott

TO THE MANOR BORN (BBC 1979–81)
Sitcom about an impoverished lady of the
manor.
TO THE MANOR BORN 14/10/1979
p Gareth Gwenlan; *sc* Peter Spence
lp Penelope Keith; Peter Bowles;
Angela Thorne; Daphne Heard; Gerald Sim;
John Rudling; Michael Bilton
The HUNT BALL 28/10/1979
p Gareth Gwenlan; *sc* Peter Spence
lp Penelope Keith; Peter Bowles;
Angela Thorne; Anthony Sharp;
Daphne Oxenford; John Rudling; Paul Barber

**TO THE SOUTH POLE WITH PETER
SCOTT** (BBC 26/5/1966)
Peter Scott, son of Captain Robert Scott, takes
part in an expedition from New Zealand to the
South Pole.
p Christopher Ralling

TOBIAS AND THE ANGEL (BBC 19/5/1960)
An opera specially commissioned for television;
with libretto by Christopher Hassall; after the
Apocryphal Book of Tobit; with music by
Arthur Bliss.
p Rudolph Cartier
with Elaine Malbin; John Ford;
Richard Golding; Roy Patrick;
William Lyon Brown

TOESTANDEN (NL NOS 5/7/1978)
An innovatory improvised drama based on the
work of an actor's collective situations project by
the Dutch Worktheatre.
d Thijs Chanowski

TOGETHER AGAIN
(Rediffusion 5/4–14/6/1957)
Six-part variety-comedy series (shown under the
'Jack Hylton Presents' banner) featuring Bud
Flanagan and Chesney Allen.
d John Phillips
TOGETHER AGAIN 5/4/1957
TOGETHER AGAIN 19/4/1957
TOGETHER AGAIN 3/5/1957
TOGETHER AGAIN 17/5/1957
TOGETHER AGAIN 31/5/1957
TOGETHER AGAIN 14/6/1957

TOLSTOY – FROM RICHES TO RAGS
(BBC 18/3/1972)
Biography of Tolstoy, which was filmed in the
Soviet Union with a Russian film crew. Uses
photographs and manuscripts from the Tolstoy
Literary Museum in Moscow and archive
footage. Includes interviews with Malcolm
Muggeridge and Theodore Roszak and footage
of Tolstoy's funeral at Yas Maya Polyana.
p Jonathan Stedall;
sc Jonathan Stedall, Theodore Roszak;
comm Richard Hurndall

TOM BROWN'S SCHOOLDAYS
(BBC 14/11–12/12/1971)
Five-part adaptation of the novel by Thomas
Hughes.
PART 3 28/11/1971
d Gareth Davies; *p* John McRae;
sc Anthony Steven
lp Anthony Murphy; Iain Cuthbertson;
Richard Morant; Gerald Flood; Simon Turner;
Christopher Guard; Geoffrey Edwards;
Valerie Holliman

TOMMY COOPER'S CHRISTMAS
(Thames 25/12/1973)
Comedy-variety show.
d/p Peter Frazer-Jones;
sc Johnnie Mortimer, Brian Cooke;
with Tommy Cooper, Sacha Distel,
Clodagh Rodgers, Allan Cuthbertson

TOMMY STEELE AND A SHOW
(Thames 28/9/1977)
Show to celebrate Tommy Steele's 21st
anniversary in show business with Ronnie Brody,
David Samuels, Susan Gene, The Mike Sammes
Singers, The Irving Davies Dancers, and Peter
Knight and his Orchestra.
d/p Keith Beckett; *sc* Eric Merriman

TOMORROW'S WORLD (BBC 1965–)
Series presenting inventions which would
eventually aid the public.
TOMORROW'S WORLD FROM AUSTRALIA
4/4/1972
A report on new inventions in Australia.
p Brian Johnson; *rep* Raymond Baxter

TOMORROW'S WORLD SPECIAL
(BBC)
Special editions of TOMORROW'S WORLD
that looked at one technological/scientific issue
rather than the series' usual magazine
programme format.

TOMORROW'S WORLD SPECIAL *cont.*

CHALLENGE 1964
Scientific and ecological problems of the 1960s.
p Roy Battersby; *pres* Raymond Baxter

TONIGHT (BBC 1957–65)
Topical magazine series.
pres Cliff Michelmore; *rep* Derek Hart,
Geoffrey Johnson Smith, MacDonald Hastings,
Alan Whicker, Fyfe Robertson, Trevor Philpott,
Julian Pettifer, Kenneth Allsop, Brian Redhead,
Christopher Brasher, Cathal O'Shannon,
Magnus Magnusson
ANDRE MAUROIS 16/7/1959
An interview with Maurois following the recent
publication of his biography of Sir Alexander
Fleming. Maurois speaks of his other
biographical writings and on the nature of
Fleming and his achievements.
p Donald Baverstock;
interv Geoffrey Johnson Smith
PEACE CORPS 25/10/1962
SHRIMP FISHING 3/12/1962
AUTOMATIC SWING DOOR 4/12/1962
HIROSHIMA 17/12/1962
WEST INDIANS 1963
Early race relations in Britain. Tells the story of
a West Indian man as he makes his way from the
false equality of an England v. West Indies
cricket match to the reality of trying to find
accommodation in a hostile and prejudiced
London.
d Jack Gold
IRAQ AND GENERAL KASSIM/SNOW/U.N.
8/2/1963
WITHYWOOD YOUTH CLUB, BRISTOL 13/9/1963
OUTCAST VILLAGE 4/12/1963
FREE SCHOOL OUTSIDE LEICESTER 16/12/1963
EGYPTIAN YOUTH 16/1/1964
LINEN INDUSTRY IN IRELAND 10/3/1964
DEATH IN THE MORNING 17/3/1964
A report on fox-hunting in Leicestershire.
p Jack Gold; *rep* Alan Whicker
BARBADOS 24/3/1964
PREFABRICATED FLATS 25/3/1964
BANANAS IN JAMAICA/JETS 14/5/1964
STRIKE AT BASILDON 30/10/1964
HYPOTHERMIA 26/11/1964
PEACE CORPS IN MALAYSIA 20/1/1965
THESE HUMBLE SHORES 21/1/1965
Alan Whicker in Monte Carlo.
d/p Kevin Billington
TOBRUK 9/3/1965
GHADAMES, LIBYA 31/3/1965
NOMADS IN TURKEY 11/6/1965
TINKERS IN SCOTLAND 16/6/1965

TONIGHT (BBC 1975–79)
Current affairs series.
pres Sue Lawley, Denis Tuohy,
Donald MacCormick
The FUTURE OF THE MOTOR BIKE INDUSTRY
2/9/1975
Government plans for motor cycle industry.
p Keith Clements
ALCOHOLISM 9/9/1975
A discussion from Liverpool about drinking and
the risks of becoming an alcoholic.
MONASTEREVAN 5/11/1975
Report on a police siege at Monasterevan (in
connection with kidnapping of Tiede Herrema).
p David Hannington
VON DANIKEN 13/4/1976
Erich Von Daniken talks about his book
'Chariots of the Gods' with Sue Lawley.
ALLEGED INTERROGATION METHODS IN N.
IRELAND BY THE R.U.C. 2/3/1977
Keith Kyle reports on interrogation methods
used by the Royal Ulster Constabulary in Ulster;
with Bernard O'Connor and Michael Lavelle.
p Christopher Capron; *pres* John Timpson
ULSTER 'SPOTLIGHT' DISCUSSION 22/3/1977
A discussion produced by the BBC Belfast
programme 'Spotlight' about alleged torture by
the Royal Ulster Constabulary. Chaired by
George Scott and with Keith Kyle, William
Deedes, Harold Evans and Roy Lilley.
pres John Timpson

TONIGHT IN AMERICA
(Rediffusion 3/5/1965)
George Ffitch reports from Washington D.C. on
the day's political events; Russell Spurr reports
on the changing face of Philadelphia.
d Peter Robinson; *p* Cyril Bennett

The TONY HANCOCK SHOW
(Rediffusion 27/4–1/6/1956)
Comedy and variety series.
d Kenneth Carter; *exec.p* Roland Gillett;
sc Eric Sykes
with Tony Hancock, June Whitfield
The TONY HANCOCK SHOW 27/4/1956
The TONY HANCOCK SHOW 4/5/1956
The TONY HANCOCK SHOW 11/5/1956
The TONY HANCOCK SHOW 18/5/1956
The TONY HANCOCK SHOW 25/5/1956
The TONY HANCOCK SHOW 1/6/1956

TOO GOOD TO BE TRUE?
(Granada 20/2/1979)
A profile of new wave rock performer Tom
Robinson which attempts to uncover his political
involvement in Gay Liberation and Anti-Nazi
League organisations.
d Mick Gold; *p* Chris Pye

TOO LONG A WINTER
(Yorkshire TV 30/1/1973)
Documentary on the hard lives led by those still
living off small farms in the High Pennines,
Yorkshire. The programme focuses on Hannah
Hauxwell, who lives alone in a dilapidated
farmhouse without electricity or running water
on less than £250 per year.
d/p Barry Cockcroft; *rep* Peter Moth

TOO MANY MANSIONS
(Anglia 3/12/1978)
Asks whether we should save our churches.
d/sc Geoffrey Weaver; *nar* Eric Thompson

TOO NEAR THE SUN (BBC 9/6/1966)
The development of the hydrogen bomb by
American scientists and the role played by J.
Robert Oppenheimer.
p/sc Robert Reid;
nar Robert Beatty, Ronald Baddiley

**TOO OLD TO ROCK 'N' ROLL, TOO
YOUNG TO DIE** (LWT 16/7/1976)
Concert by rock band Jethro Tull.
d/p Mike Mansfield

TOP CROWN (BBC 1976–)
BBC bowls competition.
DENNIS MERCER v. DEREK RIPLEY 18/11/1976
The opening match at the start of the 1976 BBC
2 Masters' Trophy Tournament.
p Nick Hunter; *comm* Harry Rigby
intro Colin Welland
NORMAN DAWKES v. TONY POOLE 30/12/1976
The final of the 1976 BBC 2 Masters' Trophy
Tournament.
p Nick Hunter; *comm* Harry Rigby
intro Colin Welland
TOP CROWN 19/10/1977
Noel Burrows of Manchester plays Reg Pointon
of the North Midlands.
p Nick Hunter; *intro* Colin Welland

TOP OF THE BILL (ABC 5/10/1957)
Variety show with George Formby, Edna
Savage, The Chas McDevitt Skiffle Group,
Shirley Douglas, Gordon Franks, and Dennis
Ringrowe and his Orchestra.
d/p Arthur Lane

TOP OF THE FORM (BBC 1962–75)
School quiz show.
TOP OF THE FORM 29/10/1964
The girls of Portsmouth High School and the
boys of Liverpool Institute High School.
p Innes Lloyd
TOP OF THE FORM 9/6/1966
Final of the Spring series.
p Bill Wright

TOP OF THE FORM 19/10/1966
The girls of Leamington Spa College and the
boys of St. Phillip's Grammar School,
Birmingham.
p Bill Wright
TOP OF THE FORM 7/12/1966
Colston's Girls' School Bristol and the girls of
Arnold High School, Blackpool.
p Bill Wright

TOP OF THE POPS (BBC 1964–)
Weekly programme of popular music, stars and
news from the week's Top 30.
TOP OF THE POPS '67: PART 2 26/12/1967
p Johnnie Stewart; *with* The Bee Gees,
The Monkees, The Rolling Stones,
Long John Baldry, Dave Dee, Dozy, Beaky,
Mick & Tich, Lulu, Scott McKenzie,
Diana Ross, The Supremes, Cliff Richard,
Procol Harum, The Beatles,
Engelbert Humperdinck, Gojos
TOP OF THE POPS '71: PART 2 27/12/1971
p Johnnie Stewart; *pres* Tony Blackburn;
with T. Rex, Elton John, The Tams,
Benny Hill, Slade, The Rolling Stones,
Ashton, Gardner and Dyke, Diana Ross,
New Seekers, Rod Stewart, Pan's People
TOP OF THE POPS '72: PART 2 28/12/1972
p Johnnie Stewart;
pres Tony Blackburn, Noel Edmonds;
with Chuck Berry, Gary Glitter,
Donny Osmond, Alice Cooper,
Lieutenant Pigeon, Roberta Flack, Slade,
Benny Hill, Chicory Tip, The Osmonds,
Michael Jackson, T. Rex, Pan's People
TOP OF THE POPS 25/1/1973
p Johnnie Stewart; *pres* Jimmy Savile;
with Dandy Livingstone, Colin Bluntstone,
The Strawbs, The Sweet, Gary Glitter,
Elton John, Pan's People
TOP OF THE POPS '73 25/12/1973
Christmas edition reviewing the number one hits
of the year.
p Robin Nash;
pres Noel Edmonds, Tony Blackburn;
with The Sweet, Donny Osmond,
Suzi Quatro, Simon Park Orchestra, Slade,
Dawn, Gilbert O'Sullivan, Gary Glitter,
David Cassidy, 10 CC, Peters and Lee,
Wizzard, Pan's People
TOP OF THE POPS '73 (PRODUCTION
MATERIAL) 25/12/1973
A review of 1973's number one hits. Includes
technical breakdowns.
p Robin Nash;
pres Tony Blackburn, Noel Edmonds;
with Gary Glitter, Slade, Donny Osmond,
Suzi Quatro, Jimmy Osmond, Dawn,
David Cassidy, 10 CC, Peters and Lee, Wizzard,
Pan's People
TEN YEARS OF TOP OF THE POPS 1964–1974
27/12/1973
Jimmy Savile introduces a mixtures of clips from
the decade and 1973 performances in the studio.
d Bruce Milliard; *p* Robin Nash;
pres Jimmy Savile;
with The Dave Clark Five, Billy J. Kramer,
The Supremes, The Beatles, The Bachelors,
The Who, The Rolling Stones,
The Righteous Brothers, Sonny and Cher,
Jonathan King, Sandie Shaw, Scott McKenzie,
Procol Harum, The Tremeloes, Dave Dee,
Dozy, Beaky, Mick & Tich, Joe Cocker,
Status Quo, Alan Price, Arthur Brown,
Julie Driscoll, The Move, Marmalade, Free,
The Faces, David Bowie, Wizzard, Pan's People
TOP OF THE POPS 25/12/1974
Christmas edition featuring the number one
records of 1974.
p Robin Nash;
pres Tony Blackburn, Jimmy Savile;
with Slade, Mud, The Osmonds,
Sweet Sensation, David Essex, Paper Lace,
The Three Degrees, Ken Boothe, Abba,
Charles Aznavour, Pan's People

TOP OF THE POPS 27/12/1974
Special edition of the pop music charts
programme featuring the number one hits of
1974.
d Bruce Milliard; *p* Robin Nash;
pres Noel Edmonds, Dave Lee Travis;
with John Denver, Carl Douglas,
Gary Glitter, George McCrae, Mud,
Pan's People, Suzi Quatro, The Rubettes,
Alvin Stardust, Ray Stevens,
Stephanie De Sykes, Sparks, Sylvia, Queen,
Terry Jacks

TOPPER
(US John W. Loveton, Bernard L. Schubert
1953–55)
Comedy series based on the characters originally
created by Thorne Smith.
HAPPY NEW YEAR 1954
d Lew Landers
lp Leo G. Carroll; Anne Jeffreys;
Robert Sterling
JURY DUTY 26/11/1954
d Philip Rapp
lp Leo G. Carroll; Anne Jeffreys
TOPPER IN MEXICO 1955
d Lew Landers; *p* John W. Loveton;
sc Robert Riley Crutcher
lp Leo G. Carroll; Anne Jeffreys

TOPPER'S TALES
(Yorkshire TV 28/9–21/12/1978)
Thirteen-part children's animation series.
TOPPER'S PET 2/11/1978
p Joy Whitby; *sc* Julian Orchard

TOTAL ECLIPSE (BBC 15/2/1961)
An attempt to use the Eurovision link-up to
follow the eclipse of the sun across Europe.
d Paul Johnstone; *intro* Tom Margerison

A TOUR OF THE WHITE HOUSE
(US CBS 27/3/1962)
Jacqueline Kennedy tours the White House.

TOUS CEUX QUI TOMBENT
(FR ORTF 25/1/1963)
d Michel Mitrani; *auth* Samuel Beckett
lp Guy Trejean; Alice Sapritch

TOWARDS TOMORROW (BBC 1967–69)
Documentary series on scientific and
technological ideas.
A PLAGUE ON YOUR CHILDREN 6/6/1968
A report on the Chemical Warfare
Establishment at Porton Down, which set in
motion investigations by Dennis Healey,
Minister of Defence.
p Alan Malone; *nar* Alan Dobie

TOWN MEETING OF THE WORLD
(US CBS 1963–67)
CBS series of transatlantic discussions making
use of the Telstar II communications satellite.
TRANSATLANTIC TEACH-IN 26/10/1965
Former President Eisenhower, UN Ambassador
Arthur J. Goldberg and Solicitor-General
Thurgood Marshall discuss Vietnam, civil rights,
NATO, Latin America, the UN and other topics
with students in London, Mexico City, Paris and
Belgrade.
p Don Hewitt, William K. McClure;
pres Charles Collingwood;
rep Dan Rather, Burt Quint, Bernard Kalb,
Daniel Schorr
HOW TO STOP THE SPREAD OF NUCLEAR
WEAPONS 1/1/1966
Senator Robert Kennedy, General Pierre
Gallois, Lord Chalfont and Franz-Josef Strauss
in discussion.
pres Eric Sevareid

The TRAIL BLAZERS (BBC 1/11/1963)
The story of the aviators from the earliest
explorers to the present day astronauts.
Including Alcock and Brown, Kingsford Smith,
Charles Lindbergh, Amy Johnson, Jim
Mollinson and Amelia Earhart.
p Peter Bale; *comm* Richard Hurndall

TRAITOR IN A STEEL HELMET
(BBC 18/9/1961)
Play about soldiers during an Army training
exercise.
p Patrick Dromgoole; *sc* Charles Wood
lp Brian Bedford; Patrick McAlinney;
Frank Windsor

TRAVELLER'S TALES (BBC 1956–68)
Travel and exploration series.
PERISCOPE INTO THE PAST 27/7/1964
The Roman Road expedition, led by Victor Von
Hagen, showing Etruscan tombs in Tarquini
before they were vandalised, and the devices
developed by Carlo Lerici for seeing inside the
tombs.
d Victor von Hagen, Richmond Lawrence

TREASURE HOUSE OF BOOKS
(BBC 10/3/1969)
George Painter, a member of the library staff,
guides a tour of the British Museum Library.
p John Furness

TREASURE HUNT (Westward 16/1/1979)

TREASURE OVER THE WATER
(BBC 14–28/2/1972)
Three-part adaptation of the children's book
'Minnow on the Say' by Philippa Pearce.
EPISODE 2: THE TREASURE WAS TAKEN
21/2/1972
d Marilyn Fox
lp Andrew Balcombe; Justin Swan;
Carol Hollands; Dorothy Gordon; Philip Ray;
John Line; Jean Challis; Godfrey Jackman;
Michael Raghan
EPISODE 3: THE SINGLE ROSE 28/2/1972
d Marilyn Fox
lp Andrew Balcombe; Justin Swan;
Carol Hollands; Dorothy Gordon; Philip Ray;
John Line; Jean Challis; Godfrey Jackman;
Michael Raghan

TREASURES IN STORE
(ITV various 1976–79)
Series about museums made by different ITV
companies.
NATIONAL RAILWAY MUSEUM
(Tyne Tees 9/3/1976)
The National Railway Museum in York
including the locomotive Mallard.
d Malcolm Dickinson; *exec.p* Leslie Barrett;
pres Alec Taylor
BOWES MUSEUM (Tyne Tees 21/7/1977)
The Bowes Museum and its collection.
d Tony Kysh; *p* Alan Powell
GULBENKIAN MUSEUM (Tyne Tees 31/10/1978)
The Gulbenkian Museum in Durham has one of
the finest collections of oriental art in Britain.
Philip Rawson, the curator, looks at the
paintings, sculpture and pottery.
d Tony Kysh; *d* Andrea Wonfor

TREASURES OF BRITAIN
(LWT 7/9–28/9/1975)
Four-part documentary on castles, houses,
gardens and the cathedrals of Britain.
CASTLES 7/9/1975
The history of the fortified house in Britain. Jack
Hargreaves interviews the Duke of Norfolk at
Arundel, and Joan Bakewell interviews the
Duke and Duchess of Northumberland at
Alnwick.
d Charlie Squires

TREASURES OF THE BRITISH MUSEUM
(Thames 24/11/1971–16/2/1972)
Thirteen-part documentary series looking at the
collections of the British Museum.
The HOUSE 24/11/1971
Sir John Betjeman looks at the history and
architecture of the British Museum. Sir John
Wolfenden talks about some of its treasures.
d John Pett

TRIANGLE (Border)
Regional documentary series.
TRIANGLE 6/4/1979
TRIANGLE 1/6/1979

The TRIBE THAT HIDES FROM MAN
(ATV 17/2/1970)
Documentary recalling the story of an expedition
into hitherto unexplored areas of the Amazon
jungle to make contact with the Kreen-Akrore
Indians, one of the few remaining tribes that has
had no contact with the outside world.
d/p/sc/nar Adrian Cowell;
with Orlando Villas Boas, Claudio Villas Boas

TRIBES
(US Marvin Schwartz Productions 10/11/1970)
Made-for-TV film concerning a hippie drafted
into the Marines, and the relationship between
him and the tough drill instructor. Shown
theatrically outside the USA as 'The Soldier
Who Declared Peace'.
d Joseph Sargent; *p* Marvin Schwartz;
sc Tracy Keenan Wynn, Marvin Schwartz
lp Darren McGavin; Earl Holliman;
Jan-Michael Vincent; John Gruber;
Danny Goldman; Richard Yniguez;
Antone Curtis; Peter Hooten;
David Buchanan; Rick Weaver

TRIBUTE TO A WRITER
(ATV 15/5/1974)
Ted Willis and his career as a writer for
television.
p Nicholas Palmer

TRIBUTE TO GARY COOPER
(BBC 14/5/1961)
A tribute to actor Gary Cooper, shown on his
death, includes an item from the PRESS
CONFERENCE series *tx* 30/10/1959.

TRIBUTE TO PRESIDENT KENNEDY
(ITN 22/11/1963)
p Cyril Bennett, Peter Morley

TRIBUTE TO RICHARD MASSINGHAM
(BBC 1954)
The life and work of Richard Massingham,
including excerpts from some of his films.
intro Nicholas Bentley

TRIBUTE TO THE BBC
(Granada 3/5/1956)
A programme from Granada's opening night
transmission.

TRINITY TALES (BBC 21/11–26/12/1975)
Six-part modern update of the 'Canterbury
Tales'.
The DRIVER'S TALE 21/11/1975
d Tristan De Vere Cole; *p* David Rose;
sc Alan Plater
lp Bill Maynard; Francis Matthews;
Colin Farrell; Gaye Brown; John Stratton;
Susan Littler; Paul Copley

The TROUBLES (Granada 9/10/1963)
The Irish Rebellion against the English, 1916–
1923, the civil strife and development of present
attitudes to the English.
p Jeremy Isaacs; *sc/nar* Brian Inglis;
voice Ray McAnally, Robert Holness

TROUBLESHOOTERS (BBC 1966–72)
Drama series set around the multiple activities of
an international oil empire.
THIS PLACE IS A PARADISE, MISTER 30/6/1969
d Malcolm Taylor; *p* Anthony Read;
sc David Weir
lp Ray Barrett; Geoffrey Keen;
Philip Latham; Jayne Sofiano; Iain Cuthbertson;
Sheila Steafel

TRUMPETS OF MAJESTY (LWT 14/6/1969)
A performance of the Berlioz 'Te Deum' by the
London Symphony Orchestra and the BBC
Choral Society at St. Paul's Cathedral. Colin
Davis conducts.
d Humphrey Burton

TUESDAY'S DOCUMENTARY
(BBC 1968–79)
Documentary series.
The HEART OF APARTHEID 10/9/1968
Apartheid in South Africa as seen by non-whites.
p Hugh Burnett
WAR UNDER THE SEA 20/1/1970
The submarine and its tactical evolution.
Newsreel shows the development of submarine warfare.
p Harry Hastings
AFRIKANER 14/4/1970
A portrait of Afrikaner society in South Africa.
d Hugh Burnett
SHETLAND : BRITAIN'S FARTHEST NORTH 19/5/1970
The month of January on the island of Shetland culminating in the great Viking fire-festival of Up-Helly-Aa.
p/sc Malcolm Brown; *nar* Duncan Carse
LLOYD'S OF LONDON 24/11/1970
Lloyd's Insurance Company.
p Anthony De Lotbinière; *nar* Michael Adams
The UNBORN CHILD: A NEW DILEMMA 15/6/1971
Developments in pre-natal genetic diagnosis enable doctors to trace signs of Mongolism and other defects, which under the new Abortion Act enables them to terminate pregnancies.
p Philip Daly
The BLOCK 19/9/1972
Living conditions of those who live below the poverty line – at Chaucer House in Southwark.
p Paul Watson
The PRICE OF VIOLENCE 14/11/1972
Harold Williamson talks to Protestants and Catholics whose friends or family have been the victims of terrorist attacks in Ulster.
p Tony Broughton
The LONGEST DRINK 6/2/1973
How water is processed before it reaches the consumer in Manchester.
d/p Don Haworth; *comm* David Mahlowe
The SABOTEURS OF TELEMARK 27/2/1973
The destroying of heavy water stocks for atomic experiments in Norway 1943, includes actual footage as well as reconstruction sequences.
p Jeremy Bennett
SOMEONE FROM THE WELFARE 24/4/1973
The work and attitudes of social workers in Camden.
p Jenny Barraclough; *rep* Esther Rantzen
The ENERGY CRUNCH: PART 1: THE BOTTOM OF THE OIL BARREL 12/6/1973
Attempts to analyse the likely effects of the speed with which man is using his resources, in this case oil.
p/sc Simon Campbell-Jones
CHILDREN IN CROSSFIRE 12/3/1974
The effect of the troubles in Ulster on the children growing up there.
p Michael Blakstad
The BROKEN BRIDGE 2/7/1974
The story of Irene Kassorla's work with mentally handicapped children.
p/sc Robert Reid;
nar Christopher Chataway, Frank Gillard
SADAT – PRESIDENT OF EGYPT 16/7/1974
Interview with Anwar el-Sadat, President of Egypt.
The RISE AND FALL OF D.D.T. 13/8/1974
The dangers of the pesticide DDT.
p Alec Nisbett, Robin Bootle
The BOMB DISPOSAL MEN 29/10/1974
The training of the Army's bomb disposal squads and their work in Ulster.
p Jenny Barraclough; *rep* Jack Pizzey
The FACE OF FAMINE 18/3/1975
Examines the cause of famine and the problems of food distribution.
p Simon Campbell-Jones; *comm* Ray Moore
TOMORROW'S SAUDI ARABIA 22/4/1975
Documentary transmitted shortly after the assassination of King Faisal.
p Patrick Uden
The SHAH OF IRAN 17/6/1975
An interview with the Shah of Iran and Empress Farah.
p Malcolm Brown

EVERYTHING NEW UNDER THE SUN 23/9/1975
Documentary on the accelerated development of the newly-rich oil state of Abu Dhabi.
p Patricia Meehan

The TUNNEL (US NBC 31/10/1962 *ntx*)
Students dig a tunnel under the Berlin Wall enabling 59 people to escape to the West. Original transmission was postponed owing to the Cuban Crisis. Finally transmitted 10/12/1962.
d Reuven Frank;
sc/nar Piers Anderton, Reuven Frank

The TURN OF THE SCREW
(Rediffusion 25/12/1959)
Benjamin Britten's opera performed by the English Opera Group Orchestra conducted by Charles Mackerras and Paul Hamburger.
p Peter Morley
with Raymond Nilsson, Jennifer Vyvyan, Tom Bevan, Janette Miller, Judith Pierce, Arda Mandikian

TURNING POINT (ATV 11–25/7/1972)
Three documentaries looking at the turning points of modern history.
The SIEGE OF DIEN BIEN PHU 25/7/1972
The defeat of the French by the Vietnamese at the battle of Dien Bien Phu. Includes actuality footage taken by the Vietnamese.
p Ross Devenish

TURNING YEAR TALES
(BBC 24/6–5/8/1979)
Series of seven plays.
BIG JIM AND THE FIGARO CLUB 24/6/1979
Basis for 1981 series of the same name.
d Colin Rose; *p* Alastair Reid;
sc Ted Walker; *nar* Bob Hoskins
lp Patrick Murray; Norman Rossington; David Beckett; Sylvester McCoy; Helen Keating; Roland Curram; Gordon Rollings
FOLLOW THE RIVER DOWN 1/7/1979
d Colin Godman; *p* Alastair Reid;
sc David Pownall
lp George A. Cooper; Robert McIntosh; Michael St. John; Ted Morris
CLUBS 15/7/1979
d Colin Godman; *p* Alastair Reid;
sc Philip Martin
lp Robert Dorning; John Arnatt; Paul Darrow; Andrew Crawford; Brian Capron
The ESSAY 22/7/1979
p Alastair Reid; *sc* David Fitzsimmons
lp Sean Puckle; Fraser Hall; Carol Kirkland; Barry Jackson; Diana Dean; David Trevena; Timothy Knightley
MAY BLOSSOMS 29/7/1979
d Colin Rose; *p* Alastair Reid;
sc Tom Hadaway
lp Tom Hadaway; Jean Heywood; Peggy Gosschalk; Gwen Doran; Harry Herring
JACK FLETCHER 5/8/1979
p Alastair Reid; *sc* Dominic Cooper
lp David Collings; Vernon Dobtcheff; Elizabeth Cassidy; Brian Pettifer

TUTANKHAMUN'S EGYPT
(BBC 2/4–25/6/1972)
Thirteen-part series decribing the civilisation of Ancient Egypt at the time of Tutankhamun. Introduced from the Tutankhamun Exhibition at the British Museum.
d Paul Jordan; *p* Paul Johnstone;
comm Eric Porter
PHARAOH 2/4/1972
The role of the Pharaoh in Ancient Egypt.
LAND 9/4/1972
Argues that the most significant achievement of the Ancient Egyptians were based upon the farming of their narrow zone of fertile soil.
WARRIOR PHARAOHS 7/5/1972
The introduction of the horse-drawn chariot in the eighteenth century BC enabled the Pharoah to lead his armies in battle.
LIFE AND TIMES OF TUTANKHAMUN 25/6/1972

TV EYE (Thames 1978–86)
Documentary/current affairs programme. Previously called THIS WEEK, reverted to that name in 1986.

FRONT LINE RHODESIA 28/9/1978
The Rhodesian Army in operation against Nationalist guerillas.
The SHAH v. THE MULLAHS 14/12/1978
The Iranian crisis with interviews with members of the Shah's government immediately before his leaving the country.
p Norman Fenton
HOSPITAL IN CRISIS 15/2/1979
Two weeks of an industrial dispute at St. Andrew's Hospital, Bow.
WHAT'S ON THE SATELLITE TONIGHT? 15/3/1979
Future developments in broadcasting television.
SOLDIERS UNDER STRESS 12/4/1979
British troops in Ulster.
PIRATE WHALER S.S. SIERRA 21/6/1979
WHY HAVEN'T THE POLICE CAUGHT THE YORKSHIRE RIPPER? 22/11/1979
Report on the police investigation of the 'Yorkshire Ripper' case.
The SHAH OR THE HOSTAGES? 6/12/1979
Report on the American hostages in the American Embassy in Tehran and interviews with the Iranian students holding the Embassy.

TWELFTH NIGHT
(Rediffusion 21/1–18/3/1959)
Nine-part programme for schools which examines Shakespeare's play.
HIS VERY GENIUS 21/1/1959
A scene from Act II, Scene iii in which Malvolio interrupts the revellers.
d Peter Robinson; *sc* Martin Worth;
intro John Westbrook
lp George A. Cooper; Geoffrey Bayldon; Gillian Raine; Prunella Scales; Terence Soall; Peter Vaughan

12 O'CLOCK HIGH
(US Quinn Martin 1964–5)
Drama series about USAF squadrons in Britain during World War II. Format based on 1949 feature film.
The HOTSHOT 18/10/1965
d Richard Donner; *p* William D. Gordon;
sc Robert Lewin
lp Paul Burke; Frank Overton; Chris Robinson; Warren Oates; Jill Haworth; Andrew Duggan; Jill Ireland; Walter Brooke

The TWENTIETH CENTURY
(US CBS 1957–66)
Series presenting filmed reports of the major events, movements, and personalities that shaped the history of the twentieth century. Replaced by 'The 21st Century' in 1967.
The RED SELL: THE PROPAGANDA MILL 26/10/1958
The first of two evaluations of the Soviet Union's propaganda techniques. Excerpts from propaganda films. How students are trained for propaganda work.
p Burton Benjamin, Isaac Kleinerman;
sc Marvin Kalb, Marshall Flaum;
pres Walter Cronkite; *comm* Daniel Schorr
The RED SELL: REPORT FROM THE TARGETS 2/11/1958
The second of two reports. Analyses the effectiveness of Soviet propaganda in India, South East Asia, Finland, South America and the Middle East.
p Burton Benjamin, Isaac Kleinerman;
sc Marvin Kalb, Marshall Flaum;
pres Walter Cronkite;
rep Arthur Bonner, Peter Kalischer, Austin Goodrich, Richard C. Hottelet, Frank Kearns
The RUSSO-FINNISH WAR 16/11/1958
The first battles fought by the Russian Army since 1917: the attack on Finland in 1939.
p Burton Benjamin, Isaac Kleinerman;
sc Burton Benjamin; *pres* Walter Cronkite
PERON AND EVITA 23/11/1958
The rise and fall of the Perons.
p Burton Benjamin, Isaac Kleinerman;
sc Ray Josephs; *pres* Walter Cronkite

The REMAGEN BRIDGE 4/1/1959
An account of the March 1945 attempt by the
Germans to keep the bridge from falling into
Allied hands. Interviews with Sgt. Alexander
Dravnik, the first American soldier to cross after
the battle; American infantry leader Major
Charles Gerhardt and Captain Willi Bratge, the
German officer assigned to blow up the bridge.
p Burton Benjamin, Isaac Kleinerman;
sc Hal Boyle; *pres* Walter Cronkite
PARIS IN THE TWENTIES 17/4/1960
Paris as the centre for American intellectuals and
tourists.
p Burton Benjamin
TURN OF THE CENTURY 1/8/1960
Historic figures who lived 1900 to 1914.
p Burton Benjamin
IRELAND: THE TEAR AND THE SMILE: PART 1
29/1/1961
Part one of a two-part documentary. Discussion
of the traditions and problems of modern Ireland
with Irish Republic President Eamon de Valera,
Prime Minister Sean Lemass, author Sean
O'Faolain, playwright Brendan Behan, editor
Alec Newman and former Lord Mayor of
Dublin, Robert Briscoe.
d Willard Van Dyke;
p Burton Benjamin, Isaac Kleinerman;
sc Elizabeth Bowen; *pres* Walter Cronkite;
rep Alexander Kendrick
CITY UNDER THE ICE 15/8/1961
The United States Army 'Camp Century' in
Greenland.
d Norton Bloom
HUNGARY TODAY 29/10/1961
Hungary five years after the 1956 Revolution.
Daily life; interviews with Communist Youth
League members and a journalist for the
newspaper 'Nepszabadsag'.
d Av Westin; *p* Isaac Kleinerman;
sc Daniel Schorr; *pres* Walter Cronkite
The SATELLITE THAT TALKS 6/5/1962
A preview of Telstar, the communications
satellite that will enable live telecasts to the USA
from Europe and Asia and its effect on television
and telephone communications.
d Peter Poor; Av Westin; *p* Isaac Kleinerman;
sc Richard Witkin; *pres* Walter Cronkite
RHODES SCHOLAR 17/3/1963
Oxford University's Rhodes Scholarship
programme. The curriculum and how scholars
are selected. Student Winston J. Churchill, Jr of
Pennsylvania goes about his daily routine.
d Robert K. Sharpe; *p* Isaac Kleinerman;
sc James Benjamin; *pres* Walter Cronkite;
rep Alexander Kendrick
ETHIOPIA: THE LION AND THE CROSS: PART 1
31/3/1963
The first of two reports on Ethiopia's efforts to
modernise. Interview with Emperor Haile
Selassie; views of city and rural life; discussions
with American Peace Corps volunteers.
d/sc Harry Rasky; *p* Isaac Kleinerman;
pres Walter Cronkite; *rep* Blaine Littell
ETHIOPIA: THE LION AND THE CROSS: PART 2
7/4/1963
Interview with Haile Selassie on Ethiopia's needs
and its role in Africa's future. The city of Axum;
a new highway construction programme.
d Harry Rasky; *p* Isaac Kleinerman;
sc Blaine Littell; *pres* Walter Cronkite
ANTHONY EDEN 27/12/1964
An interview on topics ranging from today's
leaders to his own career.
d Burton Benjamin; *p* Isaac Kleinerman;
pres Walter Cronkite; *rep* Alexander Kendrick
MAN WITH A VIOLIN: ISAAC STERN 28/3/1965
An interview with the violinist. Included are
films of Stern with his family and in performance
with the Hartford Symphony Orchestra. Looks
at Stern's efforts to save Carnegie Hall, as leader
of the American-Israeli Cultural Foundation and
as a supporter of UN-sponsored cultural
exchanges.
d Roger Englander; *p* Isaac Kleinerman;
rep Daniel Schorr

TWENTIETH CENTURY FOCUS
(BBC 1966–74)
Series for school children.
DROP OUTS 16/11/1970
p Bernard Adams; *comm* Guy Slater

MENTAL HEALTH – WHO CARES? 23/10/1972
The mental health provisions in Croydon, Surrey
and particularly the attempt to bring the patients
more into the community.
p Suzanne Davies; *comm* Michael Rodd
HEALTH HAZARDS – VD 12/3/1973
A short history of venereal disease and an
account of how clinics operate.
d Gordon Croton

The TWENTIETH CENTURY-FOX HOUR
(US Twentieth Century-Fox Television
Productions 1955–57)
Drama anthology series.
The OX-BOW INCIDENT 2/11/1955
d Gerd Oswald; *p* Jules Bricken;
sc Lamar Trotti; *auth* Walter van Tilburg Clark
lp Robert Wagner; Cameron Mitchell;
E.G. Marshall; Raymond Burr; Wallace Ford;
Hope Emerson
DECEPTION 7/3/1956
d Jules Bricken; *p* Samuel Marx;
sc Alec Waugh
lp Linda Darnell; Trevor Howard;
John Williams; Alan Napier; Gavin Muir
BROKEN ARROW 2/5/1956
d Robert Stevenson; *p* Peter Packer;
sc Michael Blankfort; *auth* Elliott Arnold
lp Ricardo Montalban; Rita Moreno;
John Lupton; Robert F. Simon;
Robert Warwick; Roy Roberts;
Donald Randolph
OVERNIGHT HAUL 16/5/1956
d Jules Bricken; *p* Peter Packer;
sc Leonard Freeman;
auth Peter Packer, Gabrielle Upton
lp Richard Conte; Lizabeth Scott;
Richard Eyer; James Griffith; Clarence Muse;
Forrest Lewis

TWENTIETH CENTURY MESSIAH
(BBC 27/1/1979)
A contemporary view of the world, set to a new
performance of Handel's Messiah, performed at
St John's Smith Square, London, conducted by
Colin Davis.
d Humphrey Hinshelwood

TWENTY-FOUR HOURS (BBC 1965–72)
Nightly programme with coverage of topical
news items. See also TWENTY-FOUR HOURS
SPECIAL.
LABOUR PARTY CONFERENCE BRIGHTON
1966–1ST DAY 3/10/1966
Report on the opening day of the conference.
Extracts from Walter Padley's opening speech.
Robin Day sums up the transport debate.
Barbara Castle on transport matters.
LABOUR PARTY CONFERENCE BRIGHTON
1966–2ND DAY 4/10/1966
Robin Day interviews Harold Wilson, Kenneth
Harris interviews Michael Stewart and Harry
Nicholson. Extracts from the Wilson speech and
from the social services debate.
LABOUR PARTY CONFERENCE BRIGHTON
1966–3RD DAY 5/10/1966
Extracts from the economic debate. Kenneth
Harris interviews Ray Gunter on the
implications of some of the motions passed.
LABOUR PARTY CONFERENCE BRIGHTON
1966–4TH DAY 6/10/1966
Kenneth Harris interviews Harold Wilson.
Extracts from the foreign affairs debate. George
Brown makes a speech as Foreign Secretary and
is interviewed by Robin Day.
TWENTY-FOUR HOURS 19/4/1967
TWENTY-FOUR HOURS 6/6/1968
On the day of Robert Kennedy's death friends
and colleagues in England and the USA pay
tribute to him.
SUMMERHILL SCHOOL 19/6/1968
A report on Summerhill school in Suffolk, run
by Alexander Neill.
DEMOCRATIC CONVENTION IN CHICAGO, 1968
29/8/1968
Report on the violent demonstrations at the
Democratic Party Convention in Chicago; a
profile of candidate Hubert Humphrey.
CHOU EN-LAI INTERVIEW 24/4/1972
Felix Greene interviews Chou En-Lai.

TWENTY-FOUR HOURS SPECIAL
(BBC)
Documentaries from the TWENTY-FOUR
HOURS series.
ASSASSINATION OF ROBERT KENNEDY
5/6/1968
Special programme on Robert Kennedy
immediately after his assassination, reporting on
this and the problem of curbing the availability
of firearms in the USA.
CZECH INVASION 21/8/1968
Eurovision monitored film of the intervention of
Warsaw Pact forces in Czechoslovakia.
Comments on the situation from Michael
Stewart MP, Milan Glozar, Victor Zorza, Jiri
Pelikan, Thomas Vybiral, Josef Jostan and
others.

TWENTY ONE UP (Granada 9/5/1977)
Documentary on a group of 21–year-olds who
were previously interviewed by a WORLD IN
ACTION team at the age of 7. Sequel to
SEVEN PLUS SEVEN (1970) and SEVEN UP
(WORLD IN ACTION series tx 5/5/1964).
d/p Michael Apted, Margaret Bottomley

TWENTY ONE YEARS
(Southern TV 28/12/1979)
Several of the key figures in Southern
Television's history recall the previous 21 years
of the Company's broadcasting.
p Paul Smith

TWILIGHT OF EMPIRE (BBC 10/11/1964)
A TONIGHT presentation. Forty years after his
first visit to India Malcolm Muggeridge returns
to meet old frinds and relive the experiences of
the last days of the British Raj.
d Kevin Billington

TWO BROTHERS (BBC 16/8/1959)
Ballet Rambert performance of Norman
Morrice's dance drama, with Gillian Martlew,
John Chesworth and Norman Morrice.
Dohnanyi's music performed by the Aeolian
String Quartet.
p Christian Simpson

The 250TH ANNIVERSARY OF
WESTMINSTER HOSPITAL
(Rediffusion 14/1/1956)
Commemoration service at Westminster Abbey,
conducted by the Dean, Eric S. Abbott.
d Jim Pople

TWO PEOPLE (LWT 10/11–15/12/1979)
Drama series about two 15 year-old lovers and
the problems they encounter.
BLUEPRINTS 10/11/1979
lp Ray Brooks; Steven O'Shea;
Charlotte Coleman; Stephen Garlick;
Bridget Turner; David Daker; Gerry Cowper;
Sheila Raynor; Veronica Strong;
Nicholas Lyndhurst
BACK TO EARTH 15/12/1979
d Tony Wharmby; *p* Paul Knight;
sc Alick Rowe
lp Stephen Garlick; Gerry Cowper;
Bridget Turner; David Daker; Hilda Fenemore;
Stephanie Cole; Ray Brooks; Charlotte Coleman

The TWO RONNIES (BBC 1971–86)
Comedy/variety series starring Ronnie Corbett
and Ronnie Barker.
The TWO RONNIES 10/4/1971
p Terry Hughes;
sc Tim Brooke-Taylor, Eric Idle,
Terry Jones, Spike Mullins, David Nobbs,
Michael Palin, Bill Solly, Peter Vincent,
Dick Vosburgh, Gerald Wiley;
with Tina Charles, Madeleine Smith
The TWO RONNIES 24/4/1971
p Terry Hughes;
sc Tim Brooke-Taylor, Barry Cryer,
Eric Idle, Spike Mullins, David Nobbs,
Michael Palin, Terry Jones, Bill Solly,
Peter Vincent, Dick Vosburgh, Gerald Wiley;
with Tina Charles, Madeleine Smith,
New World

The TWO RONNIES *cont.*

The TWO RONNIES 29/5/1971
p Terry Hughes;
sc Eric Idle, Spike Mullins,
David Nobbs, Bill Solly, Peter Vincent,
Dick Vosburgh, Gerald Wiley;
with Tina Charles, Madeleine Smith

TWO WEEKS CLEAR
(Yorkshire TV 5/8/1974)
Simon Welfare follows three miners from Denby
Grange on their annual week's holiday: one acts
as a clown at the James Brothers circus at
Mablethorpe; another competes at the
Wakefield Horticultural Show; the third takes his
family to Bridlington.
d Barry Cockcroft

TWO WOMEN (Thames 28/11/1972)
The experience of two women living on opposite
sides of the Iron Curtain.
d Mira Hamermesh; *p* Ian Martin

TWO'S COMPANY (LWT 1975–79)
Sitcom featuring a London-based American
writer and her English 'gentleman's gentleman'.
The HOUSEKEEPING 13/9/1975
p Stuart Allen; *sc* Bill McIlwraith
lp Elaine Stritch; Donald Sinden;
Peter Carlisle; Helen Horton

U

U.F.O.
(Century 21 Pictures-ATV 1971–72)
Science-fiction series revolving around a defence
organisation and their fight against alien
invaders.
p Reg Hill
regulars Ed Bishop; George Sewell;
Michael Billington; Gabrielle Drake;
Dolores Mantez; Antonia Ellis; Wanda Ventham
IDENTIFIED 18/9/1971
d Gerry Anderson;
sc Gerry Anderson, Sylvia Anderson,
Tony Barwick
lp Peter Gordeno; Grant Taylor;
Basil Dignam; Shane Rimmer; Michael Mundell;
Gary Files; Matthew Robertson; Maxwell Shaw
EXPOSED 25/9/1971
d David Lane; *sc* Tony Barwick
lp Norma Ronald; Robin Bailey;
Jean Marsh; Matt Zimmerman; Basil Moss;
Sue Gerrard; Arthur Cox
CONFLICT 2/10/1971
d Ken Turner; *sc* Ruric Powell
lp Alan Tucker; Drewe Henley;
Michael Kilgarriff
SURVIVAL 9/10/1971
d Alan Perry; *sc* Tony Barwick
lp Robert Swann; Harry Baird;
Suzan Farmer; Ray Armstrong; David Weston
The PSYCHOBOMBS 16/10/1971
d Jeremy Summers; *sc* Tony Barwick
lp Ayshea Brough; Deborah Grant;
David Collings; Mike Pratt; Tom Adams;
Alex Davion; Christopher Timothy
DESTRUCTION 23/10/1971
d Ken Turner; *sc* Dennis Spooner
lp Stephanie Beacham; Philip Madoc;
Edwin Richfield; David Warbeck;
Steven Berkoff
The SQUARE TRIANGLE 30/10/1971
d David Lane; *sc* Alan Pattillo
lp Adrienne Corri; Gary Myers;
Keith Alexander; Patrick Mower;
Godfrey James; Anthony Chinn;
Allan Cuthbertson; Norma Ronald
CLOSE UP 6/11/1971
d Alan Perry; *sc* Tony Barwick
lp Jeremy Wilkin; Keith Alexander;
Alan Tucker; James Beckett; Jon Kelley;
Neil Hallett; Grant Taylor; Mark Hawkins
E.S.P. 20/11/1971
d Ken Turner; *sc* Alan Fennell
lp John Stratton; Deborah Stanford;
Douglas Wilmer; Maxwell Shaw; Donald Tandy
KILL STRAKER! 4/12/1971
d Alan Perry; *sc* Donald James
lp Keith Alexander; David Sumner;
Harry Baird; Grant Taylor; Vladek Sheybal;
Steve Cory; Louise Pajo

The COMPUTER AFFAIR 18/12/1971
d David Lane; *sc* Tony Barwick
lp Michael Mundell; Maxwell Shaw;
Peter Burton; Nigel Lambert
The CONFETTI CHECK A-OK 1/1/1972
d David Lane; *sc* Tony Barwick
lp Keith Alexander; Julian Grant;
Suzanne Neve; Geoffrey Hinsliff;
Michael Forrest; Grant Taylor; Jack May
The DALOTEK AFFAIR 15/1/1972
d Alan Perry; *sc* Ruric Powell
lp Tracy Reed; Clinton Greyn;
David Weston; Philip Latham; John Breslin;
Basil Moss
REFLECTIONS IN THE WATER 29/1/1972
d/sc David Tomblin
lp Gordon Sterne; Conrad Phillips;
Richard Caldicot; James Cosmo; Mark Griffith;
Steven Berkoff
The CAT WITH TEN LIVES 26/11/1972
d/sc David Tomblin
lp Alexis Kanner; Al Mancini;
Windsor Davies; Geraldine Moffat;
Colin Gordon; Lois Maxwell
MINDBENDER 3/12/1972
d Ken Turner; *sc* Tony Barwick
lp Charles Tingwell; Stuart Damon;
Anouska Hempel
TIMELASH 17/12/1972
d Cyril Frankel; *sc* Terence Feely
lp Ron Bember; Jean Vladon;
Kirsten Lindholm; Patrick Allen

U.S.S.R. NOW
(Rediffusion 28/1/1958)
Michael Ingrams reports on life in the Soviet
Union, and talks to Soviet citizens in various
walks of life.
d Michael Ingrams

UKRAINIAN STATE DANCE COMPANY
(BBC 5/11/1961)
A programme of dances including 'Polzunets', a
Cossack comic dance; 'Needlewomen'; 'The
Whalers'; 'Podolianochia'; 'The Joys of
Tchumak life!'; and 'Gopak'.
d Margaret Dale

ULSTER REPORTS (Ulster TV)
Local news programme.
ULSTER REPORTS 12/7/1978

ULSTER: THE RIGHT TO STRIKE
(Ulster TV 19/5/1977)
An examination of the response of a large cross-
section of people and opinion in Ulster to the
strike called by the Loyalist parties under the
leadership of Ian Paisley in May 1977.

UNIVERSITY CHALLENGE
(Granada 1962–87)
Quiz show in which undergraduate teams from
Britain compete.
pres Bamber Gascoigne
UNIVERSITY COLLEGE, OXFORD v. KEBLE
COLLEGE, OXFORD 9/7/1972
d Peter Mullings
UNIVERSITY CHALLENGE v. COLLEGE BOWL
28/12/1978
A play-off between the winners of University
Challenge and College Bowl, the original
American show on which it is based.

The UNLUCKY AUSTRALIANS
(ATV 25/9/1973)
The seven-year long attempt by Aborigines of
the Gurindji tribe of Northern Territories to
regain their tribal lands.
d John Goldschmidt

The UNRECORDED JASPER CARROTT
(LWT 18/2/1979)
Comedian Jasper Carrott's live show at the
Theatre Royal, Drury Lane, London.
d/p Paul Smith

UNTIL ARMAGEDDON (BBC 10/8/1969)
The six-day 'Peace on Earth' assembly of
Jehovah's Witnesses at Wembley in July 1969.
Includes a report on the group's beliefs and
philosophies.
p Peter Chafer; *rep* Esther Rantzen

UP POMPEII (BBC 1970)
Comedy series featuring Frankie Howerd as a
slave in ancient Pompeii.
p David Croft; *sc* Talbot Rothwell
regulars Frankie Howerd; Jeanne Mockford;
Max Adrian; Elizabeth Larner;
William Rushton; Kerry Gardner
EXODUS 1970
JAMES BONDUS 1970
The LEGACY 1970
The LOVE POTION 1970
ROMAN HOLIDAY 1970
UP POMPEII! 1970
VESTAL VIRGINS 1970

UP SUNDAY (BBC 1972–73)
Topical revue series.
IN SEARCH OF MERRY ENGLAND 25/11/1973
Satirical revue with John Wells, William
Rushton, John Fortune, Clive James, James
Cameron, and Adge Cutler and The Wurzels.
d Tom Corcoran

The UPCHAT LINE
(Thames 26/9–7/11/1977)
Comedy series.
HOME IS THE HUNTER 7/11/1977
d/p Robert Reed; *sc* Keith Waterhouse
lp John Alderton; Gabrielle Drake;
Daphne Heard; Annette Kerr; Pippa Sparkes;
Ray Marioni

UPSTAIRS, DOWNSTAIRS (LWT 1971–75)
Drama series which looks at life in a fashionable
London household at the turn of the century
from the point of view of both the masters and
servants.
p John Hawkesworth
regulars Pauline Collins; Gordon Jackson;
Jean Marsh; Angela Baddeley; George Innes;
David Langton; Christopher Beeny;
Simon Williams; Gareth Hunt;
Lesley-Anne Down; Jenny Tomasin;
Hannah Gordon; Karen Dotrice;
Jacqueline Tong
ON TRIAL 10/10/1971
d Raymond Menmuir; *sc* Fay Weldon
lp Evin Crowley; Rachel Gurney;
Patsy Smart; Brian Osborne; Patsy Crowther
GUEST OF HONOUR 17/11/1972
d Bill Bain; *sc* Alfred Shaughnessy
lp Rachel Gurney; Patsy Smart;
Joan Benham; Ailsa Grahame; Elvi Hale;
Lockwood West; Mary Kenton;
Anthony Woodruff
A CHANGE OF SCENE 10/11/1973
d Bill Bain; *sc* Rosemary Anne Sisson
lp Meg Wynn Owen; Anthony Ainley;
Clive Morton; Richard Vernon; Helen Lindsay;
John Quayle; Celia Bannerman;
Annette Wollett
The SUDDEN STORM 19/1/1974
d Bill Bain; *sc* John Hawkesworth
lp Meg Wynn Owen; Frank Middlemass;
Paul Alexander; Raymond Barry; Peter Honri;
Paul Haley; Avril Fane
WOMEN SHALL NOT WEEP 5/10/1974
d Christopher Hodson; *sc* Alfred Shaughnessy
ON WITH THE DANCE 7/9/1975
d Bill Bain; *sc* Alfred Shaughnessy
lp Anne Yarker; Jonathan Seely
A PLACE IN THE WORLD 14/9/1975
d Christopher Hodson; *sc* Jeremy Paul
lp Raymond Huntley; Michael Logan;
Ann Mitchell; Jay Neill; Jack Le White;
Derek Martin; Una Brandon Jones; Brian Nolan
LAUGH A LITTLE LOUDER, PLEASE 21/9/1975
d Derek Bennet; *sc* Rosemary Anne Sisson
lp Celia Bannerman; Madeleine Cannon;
Osmund Bullock; Jonathan Seely; Anne Yarker;
Shirley Cain; John Quayle; Victor Langley
The JOY RIDE 28/9/1975
d Bill Bain; *sc* Alfred Shaughnessy
lp Joan Benham
WANTED, A GOOD HOME 5/10/1975
d Christopher Hodson; *sc* John Hawkesworth
lp Shirley Cain; Anne Yarker;
Jonathan Seely; Peter Forest; Tracey Childs

An OLD FLAME 12/10/1975
d Derek Bennett; *sc* John Hawkesworth
lp Celia Bannerman; John Quayle;
Mike McKenzie; Tom Chatto; John Caesar;
Georgina Hale
DISILLUSION 19/10/1975
d Bill Bain; *sc* Alfred Shaughnessy
SUCH A LOVELY MAN 26/10/1975
d Christopher Hodson; *sc* Rosemary Anne
Sisson
lp Robert Hardy; Polly Adams;
Joan Benham; John Normington;
Leonard Kavanagh
The NINE DAY WONDER 2/11/1975
d Simon Langton; *sc* Jeremy Paul
lp Joan Benham; Martin Wimbush;
Tommy Wright; John Breslin; Roy Pattison
The UNDERSTUDY 9/11/1975
d James Ormerod; *sc* Jeremy Paul
lp Anthony Woodruff; André Charise;
Barbara Bolton; Natalie Caron
ALBERTO 16/11/1975
d Christopher Hodson; *sc* Alfred Shaughnessy
lp Joan Benham; Madeleine Cannon;
Seymour Green; Rowland Davies
WILL YE NO' COME BACK AGAIN 23/11/1975
d Bill Bain; *sc* Rosemary Anne Sisson
lp Georgine Anderson; Jack Watson
JOKE OVER 30/11/1975
d Bill Bain; *sc* Rosemary Anne Sisson
lp Nigel Havers; Madeleine Cannon;
Patsy Blower; Terence Bayler;
Anthony Andrews; Raymond Huntley;
Barry Stanton; Bernard Barnsley;
Robert Hartley; Daphne Lawson;
Kenneth Thornett
NOBLESSE OBLIGE 7/12/1975
d Cyril Coke; *sc* John Hawkesworth
lp Elaine Donnelly; Anthony Andrews;
Ursula Howells; Joan Sanderson;
Deddie Davies; Frank Duncan
ALL THE KING'S HORSES 14/12/1975
d Simon Langton; *sc* Jeremy Paul
lp Pippa Page; Lindsay Campbell
WHITHER SHALL I WANDER 21/12/1975
d Bill Bain; *sc* John Hawkesworth
lp Pippa Page; Raymond Huntley;
Joan Benham; Ursula Howells; Anne Yarker;
Anthony Andrews

V

The VAL DOONICAN SHOW
(BBC 26/12/1976)
Music-variety show.
p Yvonne Littlewood; *sc* Bryan Blackburn;
with Val Doonican, Tony Blackburn,
Nana Mouskouri, James Galway, Pete Murray,
Terry Wogan, Arthur Askey, Janet Brown,
Henry Cooper, Cliff Michelmore

The VALE OF SHADOWS (BBC 26/7/1955)
A television version of Anouilh's 'Eurydice'.
d Rudolph Cartier; *sc* Lothian Small
lp Laurence Payne; Philip Stainton;
Jeannette Sterke; Ellen Pollock; Anthony Sharp;
Roger Delgado; Eric Pohlmann; Arthur Lowe;
Andre Van Gyseghem

The VALIANT MAN (Rediffusion 26/1/1966)
An edited outside broadcast of the funeral of Sir
Winston Churchill.
d Peter Morley

VANDAL RULE – O.K.? (HTV 12/7/1977)
Vandalism in Cardiff.
d/p Terry Delacey

VARIETY CLUB LUNCH (Granada 7/5/1963)
p Stephen Peet

The VARIETY YEARS (Thames 30/4/1975)
Denis Norden looks back at variety
entertainment in the late 1930's with the aid of
archival footage of many famous acts, and with
recollections from Ted Ray, Arthur Askey,
Jimmy Jewel, and Sandy Powell.
d John Robins

VERDI'S MACBETH (Southern TV 27/12/1972)
A performance of Verdi's 'Macbeth', recorded at
Glyndebourne. John Pritchard conducts the
London Philharmonic Orchestra.
d David Heather; *p* Humphrey Burton
with Kostas Paskalis, James Morris,
Josephine Barstow, Keith Erwen, Ian Caley,
Geoffrey Gilbertson

A VERY HUMBLE PRINCE (Thames 2/1/1970)
John Morgan interviews Prince Norodom
Sihanouk of Cambodia. The Prince discusses his
career and the threat to his country posed by the
Vietnam War.
d Chris Goddard

VICTOR FEATHER (T.U.C.)
(Yorkshire TV 23/2/1971)
A profile of Vic Feather, General Secretary of
the Trades Union Congress (TUC). In an
interview with Peter Jay he explains his
opposition to current legislation on industrial
relations.
p Michael Deakin

VIEWPOINT (BBC 1959–73)
Religious series.
ELLY JANSEN 25/7/1963
The achievements of Elly Jansen, founder of the
Richmond Fellowship, in the after-care of
mentally ill patients.
p Peter Ferres

VIEWPOINT (Thames 23/9–2/12/1975)
Series of ten films for school children looking at
the functions of mass communications and how
they reinforce the sets of values and beliefs that
are specific to a free enterprise society.
p Douglas Lowndes, Gillian Skirrow,
Alan Horrox
BELIEVE ME 23/9/1975
MONEY TALKS 7/10/1975
Argues that advertising mass produces a
symbolic language which sells a system of values.

The VIOLENT EARTH (ATV 13/1/1970)
The nature of volcanoes. Includes sequences
filmed by Cine-Documents Tazieff, a company
run by Haroun Tazieff.
sc Leslie Mallory, James Hamilton-Paterson;
nar Graham Lines

The VISE (Danziger Productions)
British half-hour films released theatrically in
Britain 1954–5 (not a series). Transmitted in the
USA 1954–55 as The VISE series; transmitted in
Britain 1962–63 under the series title 'Tension';
anthology hosted by Ron Randell. Format later
changed to accommodate MARK SABER series
(1955–56; with Donald Gray).
p Edward J. Danziger, Harry Lee Danziger
ONE JUST MAN 1/10/1954
d David MacDonald
lp Alexander Knox; Maureen Swanson;
Eunice Gayson; Peter Reynolds
SET A MURDERER 8/10/1954
d David MacDonald;
sc James Eastwood, Paul Tabori
lp Clifford Evans; Honor Blackman;
Martin Boddey; Bill Nagy
DR DAMON'S EXPERIMENT 22/10/1954
d David MacDonald; *sc* Paul Tabori
lp Laurence Naismith; Sandra Dorne;
Brian Worth
DEATH PAYS NO DIVIDENDS 29/10/1954
lp Peter Reynolds; Eunice Gayson
GABRIEL'S CHOICE 5/11/1954
d David MacDonald;
sc Kate Barley; Paul Tabori
lp Clifford Evans; Lee Patterson
The SECRET PLACE 19/11/1954
d David MacDonald
lp Margaret Rawlings; John Stuart;
Georgina Cookson
The EAVESDROPPER 3/12/1954
lp Mila Parely; Frederick Leister;
Terrence Brook
The YELLOW ROBE 17/12/1954
d David MacDonald; *sc* George St. George
lp Robert Raglan; Anthony Pendrell;
Iris Russell; Peter Neil; Arthur Ridley;
Nicholas Hill

LUCKY MAN 24/12/1954
d David MacDonald; *sc* Paul Tabori
lp Leslie Phillips; Ann Stephens;
Raymond Rollet; Colin Gordon
HOSTAGE 1955
MAN HUNT 1955
MURDER BY DESIGN 1955
The SUCKER GAME 1955
BLIND MAN'S BLUFF 28/1/1955
lp Patrick Holt; Eunice Gayson; John Bentley
The EIGHTH WINDOW 4/2/1955
d David MacDonald
lp Robert Arden; Beverly Brooks;
Guy Dehgy
BROKEN HONEYMOON 11/2/1955
lp Adrienne Corri; Robert Ayres
DEATH ON THE BOARDS 18/2/1955
d David MacDonald;
sc James Eastwood, Paul Tabori
lp Brian Worth
BEHIND THE MASK 25/2/1955
d Paul Gerrard
lp Betta St. John; Philip Friend;
Ronald Hunt
The CRUEL TEST 11/3/1955
d David MacDonald; *sc* Paul Tabori
lp Mark Dignam; Joyce Heron;
Ian Whittaker
The DECEPTION 18/3/1955
lp Marjorie Stewart; Ann Stephens;
Mary Parker; Ronan O'Casey
The WEEKEND GUEST 25/3/1955
d David MacDonald; *sc* James Eastwood
lp Mary Hinton; Kenneth Haigh;
Brenda Hogan
The FAME AND THE FURY 1/4/1955
d David MacDonald;
sc Kate Barley, James Eastwood
lp Patrick Holt; Sandra Dorne;
David Horne
The IMPERFECT GENTLEMAN 15/4/1955
d David MacDonald
lp Jack Watling; June Rodney; Tony Quinn
DOUBLE PAY-OFF 29/4/1955
d David MacDonald; *sc* Paul Tabori
lp Robert Raikes; Mary Scott; Denis Shaw;
Howard Pays
ACCOUNT CLOSED 6/5/1955
d David MacDonald
lp Dennis Price; Helen Backlin
The SERPENT BENEATH 13/5/1955
d David MacDonald; *sc* Kate Barley
lp Dennis Price; Zena Marshall;
Ronan O'Casey; John Stuart; Jacqueline Ellis
DEATH WALKS BY NIGHT 22/5/1955
d David MacDonald
lp Julian Sherrier; Patrick Jordan;
Robert Perceval; Joy Adamson;
Nanette Newman
The MAN IN DEMAND 27/5/1955
d David MacDonald
lp Dorothy Gordon; Enid Lorimer;
Brian Worth
The HOMING CHINAMAN 3/6/1955
d David MacDonald
lp Colin Tapley; Cameron Hall; Chin Yu;
Michael Kelly; Ronald Adam; Sam Kydd
MURDER OF A HAM 17/6/1955
d David MacDonald
lp Leslie Dwyer; Walter Gotell;
April Olrich
The BETTER CHANCE 24/6/1955
d David MacDonald; *sc* Paul Tabori
lp Kay Callard; Leslie Phillips;
John Witty; Josephine Douglas; Norah Gordon
DIPLOMATIC ERROR 1/7/1955
d David MacDonald
lp Sandra Dorne; Patrick Holt; Carl Jaffe
STRANGLEHOLD 8/7/1955
d Ernest Morris; *sc* Ken Taylor
lp John Bentley; Maureen Swanson;
Christopher Lee; Mary Laura Wood;
Colin Tapley
The CORPSE IN ROOM 13 15/7/1955
d David MacDonald; *sc* John Roeburt
lp Phil Brown; Margaret Anderson
DEATH IN WHITE 19/8/1955
lp Ronald Leigh-Hunt; Jill Clifford
SIDE ENTRANCE 23/9/1955
lp John Loder; Thea Gregory;
Philip Friend; Jennifer Jayne

The VISE *cont.*

SEARCH FOR MARTHA HARRIS 30/9/1955
lp Jenny Laird; Lloyd Lamble
TWO OF A KIND 14/10/1955
lp Donald Wolfit; Aleta Morrison
CROSS CHANNEL 21/10/1955
lp Patrick Holt; Paula Byrne
DEAD MAN'S EVIDENCE 4/11/1955
lp John Stone; Honor Blackman; Brenda Hogan
GOOD NAME MURDER 4/11/1955 *ntx*
lp Sylvia Pemberton; Ronald Briggs
STRANGER IN TOWN 11/11/1955
lp Shirley Lawrence; Neil Hallett;
Barry Keegan
BY PERSONS UNKNOWN 18/11/1955
lp Laurence Naismith; Brenda Hogan
WRONG TIME MURDER 2/12/1955
lp John Loder; Peter Reynolds; Jean Aubrey
A GIFT FROM HEAVEN 9/12/1955
lp Colin Croft; Patrick McGoohan;
Mary Laura Wood
SNAPSHOT 16/12/1955
lp Dorothy Gordon; Rosamund Waring;
Philip Friend
RING OF GREED 29/6/1962
d David MacDonald; *sc* Frank Atkinson;
auth Mabel Constanduros
lp Megs Jenkins; Clifford Evans;
Betty Ann Davies

VISION ON (BBC 1971–76)
Series designed for deaf children.
VISION ON 1/2/1972
p Patrick Dowling; *with* Tony Hart
WAVES 5/2/1974
d Clive Doig; *p* Patrick Dowling;
with Tony Hart, Pat Keysell
WEIGHTS 10/2/1976
d Clive Doig; *p* Patrick Dowling;
with Tony Hart, Pat Keysell, Sylvester McCoy

VISIT TO THE ADMIRALTY
(Rediffusion 27/6/1962)
Ian Trethowan looks at the work of the
Admiralty.
d Graham Watts

The VOLUNTEERS (Rediffusion 9/1/1968)
Young people in Malawi working for the
Voluntary Service Overseas organization.
d Fred Burnley; *nar* Andrew Faulds

VOLUNTEERS (BBC 10/10–12/12/1977)
Ten-part documentary on aspects of voluntary
work.
d Susanna Capon; *p* Ian Woolf;
pres Mavis Nicholson
'HANDS' – COMMUNITY CARE GROUP
10/10/1977
The variety of welfare work undertaken by
volunteers in the 'Hands' community care group
started by the Rev. Peter Absolon in 1968 in
Strood, Kent.
VOLUNTARY ASSOCIATES 17/10/1977
Young married couples who are involved in
voluntary work in association with probation
officers in the rehabilitation of offenders.
ROSLA PROJECT – BRISTOL 24/10/1977
A scheme in Bristol where a small group of
children spend one day a week at the Avon
Youth Centre with volunteers and students.
W.R.V.S. 31/10/1977
Mrs Pat Andrews, the local volunteer organiser
in the Holme Valley, West Yorkshire.
RATHBONE PROJECT – LEEDS 7/11/1977
An experimental scheme in which volunteers
work alongside teachers in a school for
educationally subnormal children.
MARRIAGE GUIDANCE COUNSELLOR
14/11/1977
The satisfaction and the risks involved in
becoming a marriage guidance counsellor.
OUTDOORS 21/11/1977
Volunteer activity in conservation.
ST. CRISPIN – PSYCHIATRIC HOSPITAL
28/11/1977
COMMUNITY RELATIONS – PETERBOROUGH
5/12/1977
The variety of work undertaken by the
Community Relations Council in Peterborough.

ONE PARENT FAMILIES – EDINBURGH
12/12/1977
An experimental scheme started by the Guild
Service in Edinburgh, in which volunteers work
with one parent families.

Le VOYAGE DU JERICHO
(Rediffusion 10/1–7/3/1967)
Nine-part French-language schools serial
following the adventures of a young French
family on holiday along the canals of Brittany.
EPISODE 6: LE BON POT-AU-FEU 14/2/1967
d Bob Gray; *p* Robert Stead;
sc Max Bellancourt
lp Paulette Preney; Xavier Renoult;
Pascal Dufar; Katy Fraysse

VOYAGE TO THE BOTTOM OF THE SEA
(US Twentieth Century-Fox TV-Irwin Allen
Productions 1964–68)
Science-fiction series about the crew of a nuclear
submarine.
regulars Richard Basehart; David Hedison;
Robert Dowdell; Terry Becker; Del Monroe
ESCAPE FROM VENICE 17/10/1965
d Alex March; *sc* Charles Bennett
lp Renzo Cesana; Vincent Gardenia;
Danica D'Handt; Delphi Lawrence
TERROR ON DINOSAUR ISLAND 26/12/1965
d Leonard Horn; *sc* William Welch
lp Paul Carr

W

The WACKERS
(Thames 19/3–23/4/1975)
Six-part comedy series set in Liverpool.
OUT OF THE FRYING PAN 19/3/1975
d/p Anthony Parker; *sc* Vince Powell
lp Ken Jones; Sheila Fay; Bill Dean;
Joe Gladwin; Pearl Hackney; Alison Steadman;
Keith Chegwin

WAGON TRAIN
(US Revue Productions 1957–65)
Western drama series following the adventures
of the members of a wagon train going west in
the pioneer days.
The JOHN CAMERON STORY 2/10/1957
d George waGGner (sic); *sc* E. Jack Neuman
lp Ward Bond; Robert Horton;
Michael Rennie; Carolyn Jones

The WAKEFIELD SHEPHERDS' PLAY
(BBC 28/11/1961)
p/trsl Ronald Eyre
lp Timothy Bateson; Barbara Hicks;
Dudley Foster; Neil McCarthy;
Michael Williams

The WAKEY WAKEY TAVERN
(BBC 21/2/1959)
The 50th BILLY COTTON BAND SHOW
(1956–65) featuring Billy Cotton, with guests
Alan Breeze, The Leslie Roberts Silhouettes,
The Rita Williams Singers, Kathie Kay, Max
Bygraves, The Mudlarks, and Russ Conway.
p Billy Cotton Jr

WALK DOWN ANY STREET
(Rediffusion 24/11/1965)
The Snow family and their experiences of three
major events: the death of a grandparent, the
coming of age of a son, and the birth of a baby.
d Charlie Squires

WALTER SICKERT (BBC 7/6/1954)
A study of the life and work of the artist Walter
Sickert.
d/sc John Read; *comm* Robert Reid

WAR AND PEACE (Granada 26/3/1963)
d Silvio Narizzano; *sc* Robert David MacDonald;
adapt Alfred Neumann, Erwin Piscator,
Guntram Prufer; *auth* Leo Tolstoy;
nar John Franklyn Robbins
lp Nicol Williamson; Kenneth Griffith;
Tim Pearce; Steve Plytas; Daniel Massey;
Clifford Evans; Ann Bell; Valerie Sarruf;
Mary Hinton; Gary Bond; Tom Adams

WAR AND PEACE (BBC 1972–73)
Serial in twenty parts based on Leo Tolstoy's
novel.
d John Howard Davies; *p* David Conroy;
sc Jack Pulman
regulars Morag Hood; Anthony Hopkins;
Alan Dobie; David Swift; Fiona Gaunt;
Rupert Davies; Colin Baker
PART 1: NAME DAY 28/9/1972
lp Hugh Cross; Maurice Quick;
Faith Brook; Patricia Shakesby; Anne Blake;
Sally Lahee; Candida Fawsitt; Sylvester Morand;
Barnaby Shaw; Joanna David; Basil Henson;
Neil Stacy; Josie Kidd; Michael Billington;
Robert Sansom; Gideon Kolb; Archie Wilson;
Keith Campbell
PART 3: SKIRMISH AT SCHÖNGRABEN
12/10/1972
lp Richard Poore; Jerome Willis;
Frank Middlemass; David Beale; Michael
Mulcaster;
John Cobner; Brian Justice; Brian Watson;
Sylvester Morand; Colin Fisher; Derek Chafer;
Joseph Wise; Tenniel Evans; Giles Phibbs;
John Sterland; James Appleby; Gerard Hely;
Haydn Jones; Julian Herington
PART 4: LETTER AND TWO PROPOSALS
19/10/1972
lp Anne Blake; Joanna David; Barnaby Shaw;
Faith Brook; Patricia Shakesby; Barbara Young;
Basil Henson; Edith Sharpe; Josie Kidd;
Margaret Ward; John Lawrence;
Anthony Jacobs; Will Leighton; Angela Down;
Alison Frazer; Athene Fielding
PART 5: AUSTERLITZ 26/10/1972
lp Geoffrey Morris; John Ringham;
Sylvester Morand; Gary Watson; Neil Stacy;
Michael Billington; Malcolm Bullivant;
Terry Wright; Donald Douglas; Philip Morant;
Michael Beint; Frank Middlemass; Gerard Hely;
John Lincoln Wright; Tony Steedman;
Tenniel Evans; Richard Poore; Joseph Wise;
James Appleby; Hubert Cross
PART 6: REUNIONS 2/11/1972
lp Angela Down; Will Leighton;
Anthony Jacobs; Athene Fielding;
Alison Frazer; Edmund Bailey;
Sylvester Morand; Gary Watson; Joanna David;
Faith Brook; Anne Blake; Patricia Shakesby;
Barnaby Shaw; Donald Burton; Douglas Storm;
Michael Billington; Jean Heywood
PART 7: NEW BEGINNINGS 9/11/1972
lp Frank Middlemass; Sylvester Morand;
Gary Watson; Donald Burton; Andrew Carr;
Kevin Lindsay; Philip Lowrie; Edmund Bailey;
Joanna David; Barnaby Shaw; Faith Brook;
Arnold Peters; Carleton Hobbs; Geoffrey Lewis;
Christopher Owen; Terence Lodge;
Pat Gorman; Richard Poore; Neil Stacy;
Martin Carroll; Joseph Wise
PART 8: BEAUTIFUL TALE 16/11/1972
lp Anthony Woodruff; Derek Ware;
Joanna David; Edmund Bailey; Faith Brook;
Anne Blake; Patricia Shakesby;
Michael Billington; Basil Dignam;
Geoffrey Denton; Mary Chester; Judith Pollard;
Donald Douglas; Neil Stacy
PART 9: LEAVE OF ABSENCE 23/11/1972
lp Anthony Jacobs; Joanna David;
Faith Brook; Neil Stacy; Sylvester Morand;
Rufus Frampton; Hugh Cross; Patrick Holt
PART 10: MADNESS 30/11/1972
lp Joanna David; Beatrix Lehmann;
Anthony Jacobs; Athene Fielding;
Angela Down; Frank Middlemass;
Donald Burton; Elma Soiron; Terry Nelson;
Joy Hope
PART 11: MEN OF DESTINY 7/12/1972
lp Geoffrey Morris; Morris Perry;
Angela Down; Toby Bridge; Anthony Jacobs;
Athene Fielding; Joanna David;
Donald Douglas; Peter Bathurst; John Cazabon;
Michael Gover; Rufus Frampton
PART 12: FORTUNES OF WAR 14/12/1972
lp Richard Hurndall; Rufus Frampton;
Guy Graham; Geoffrey Denton;
Anthony Jacobs; Angela Down;
Athene Fielding; Will Leighton;
Peter Cartwright; Michael Moore;
Charles Morgan; Victor Brooks; Gerard Hely;
Tony Steedman; John Baker; Sylvester Morand;
Denis Cleary; David Fennell

Rawhide (CBS). From left to right, Ruta Lee, Clint Eastwood and Eric Fleming.

Betjeman's London (Rediffusion).

Alan Bennett (Channel 4).

Aquarius 11/11/1973 *Hello Dali!* (LWT) Salvador Dali

Tempo (ABC). Script conference with left to right, Kenneth Tynan, Lord Harewood, Clive Goodwin, Reginald Collin.

Monitor (BBC). Huw Wheldon with Ken Russell.

Dennis Potter
(BBC).

The WEDNESDAY PLAY   *cont.*

IN CAMERA 4/11/1964
d Philip Saville; *p* Peter Luke;
sc Philip Saville; *auth* Jean-Paul Sartre
lp Harold Pinter; Jane Arden;
Catherine Woodville; Jonathan Hansen;
Andre Boulay; David De Keyser;
Alison Seebohm; Rodney Goodall
TAP ON THE SHOULDER 6/1/1965
d Ken Loach; *p* James MacTaggart;
sc James O'Connor
lp Lee Montague; Richard Shaw;
Tony Selby; Judith Smith; Griffith Davies;
George Tovey
THREE CLEAR SUNDAYS 7/4/1965
d Ken Loach; *p* James MacTaggart;
sc James O'Connor
lp Tony Selby; Rita Webb; Glynn Edwards;
George Sewell; Kim Peacock;
Finuala O'Shannon
AND DID THOSE FEET? 2/6/1965
d Don Taylor; *p* James MacTaggart;
sc David Mercer
lp Kenneth Haigh; Patrick Troughton;
Anna Wing; Diana Coupland; Victor Lucas;
David Markham; Willoughby Goddard;
Anna Bentinck
ALICE 13/10/1965
d Gareth Davies; *p* James MacTaggart;
sc Dennis Potter
lp George Baker; Rosalie Crutchley;
David Langton; Deborah Watling
UP THE JUNCTION 3/11/1965
d Ken Loach; *p* James MacTaggart;
sc Nell Dunn
lp Carol White; Geraldine Sherman;
Vickery Turner; Tony Selby; Michael Standing;
Ray Barron; Rita Webb; George Sewell
STAND UP, NIGEL BARTON 8/12/1965
d Gareth Davies; *p* James MacTaggart;
sc Dennis Potter
lp Keith Barron; Jack Woolgar;
Barbara Keogh; Janet Henfrey; Terence Soall
VOTE, VOTE, VOTE, FOR NIGEL BARTON
15/12/1965
d Gareth Davies; *p* James MacTaggart;
sc Dennis Potter
lp Keith Barron; Valerie Gearon;
John Bailey; Cyril Luckham
The COMING OUT PARTY 22/12/1965
d Ken Loach; *p* James MacTaggart;
sc James O'Connor
lp Toni Palmer; George Sewell;
Dennis Golding; Wally Patch; Carol White
A MAN ON HER BACK 12/1/1966
d Waris Hussein; *p/sc* Peter Luke;
auth William Sansom
lp Norman Rodway; Valerie Gearon;
Barrie Ingham; Jo Rowbottom
The PORTSMOUTH DEFENCE 30/3/1966
d James MacTaggart; *p* Peter Luke;
sc Nemone Lethbridge
lp Emrys James; Fanny Carby; Michael Coles;
Frederick Farley; David Hutcheson;
Anthony Newlands
The CONNOISSEUR 4/5/1966
d Waris Hussein; *p* Peter Luke;
sc Hugo Charteris
lp Derek Francis; Rosalie Crutchley;
Michael Goodliffe; Richard O'Sullivan;
Ian Ogilvy; Rosalie Westwater
WHERE THE BUFFALO ROAM 2/11/1966
d Gareth Davies; *p* Lionel Harris;
sc Dennis Potter
lp Megs Jenkins; Hywel Bennett;
Glyn Houston; Aubrey Richards;
Richard Davies
CATHY COME HOME 16/11/1966
d Ken Loach; *p* Tony Garnett;
sc Jeremy Sandford
lp Carol White; Ray Brooks;
Emmett Hennessy; Adrienne Frame;
Wally Patch; Winifred Dennis; Alec Coleman;
Gabrielle Hamilton
The LUMP 1/2/1967
d Jack Gold; *p* Tony Garnett;
sc Jim Allen
lp Leslie Sands; Colin Farrell;
Joby Blanshard; James Caffrey; Chris Canavan

IN TWO MINDS 1/3/1967
d Ken Loach; *p* Tony Garnett;
sc David Mercer
lp Anna Cropper; Brian Phelan;
George A. Cooper; Helen Booth;
Christine Hargreaves
DEATH OF A PRIVATE 13/12/1967
d James Ferman; *p* Irene Shubik;
sc Robert Muller
lp Dudley Sutton; Liam Redmond;
John Nettleton; Geraldine Sherman;
Harry Fowler; Kenneth Cranham
An OFFICER OF THE COURT 20/12/1967
d James MacTaggart; *p* Tony Garnett;
sc Nemone Lethbridge
lp Tommy Godfrey; Yootha Joyce;
Bryan Pringle; Ronald Radd; Glynn Edwards
HOUSE OF CHARACTER 10/1/1968
d Alan Cooke; *p* Irene Shubik;
sc David Rudkin
lp Alfred Lynch; Shelagh Fraser;
John Collin; Rex Garner
LET'S MURDER VIVALDI 10/4/1968
d Alan Bridges; *p* Graeme McDonald;
sc David Mercer
lp Gwen Watford; Denholm Elliott;
Glenda Jackson
MRS. LAWRENCE WILL LOOK AFTER IT
21/8/1968
d John MacKenzie; *p* Irene Shubik;
sc Tony Parker
lp Constance Chapman; Barry Jackson;
Mary Miller; Ray Smith; Christine Hargreaves
The GORGE 4/9/1968
d Christopher Morahan; *p* Tony Garnett;
sc Peter Nichols
lp Billy Hamon; Constance Chapman;
Reg Lye; Neil Wilson; Betty Alberge
A BEAST WITH TWO BACKS 20/11/1968
d Lionel Harris; *p* Graeme McDonald;
sc Dennis Potter
lp Patrick Barr; Denis Carey;
Basil Henson; Madeleine Newbury;
Geraldine Newman
ON THE EVE OF PUBLICATION 27/11/1968
d Alan Bridges; *p* Graeme McDonald;
sc David Mercer
lp Leo McKern; Thorley Walters;
Michele Dotrice; Rosalind Knight;
Kay Newman; Pauline Devaney;
Mischa De La Motte; Geraldine Gwyther;
Alfred Hoffman; Winifred Hill
The BIG FLAME 19/2/1969
d Ken Loach; *p* Tony Garnett;
sc Jim Allen
lp Godfrey Quigley; Norman Rossington;
Peter Kerrigan; Ken Jones; David Stephens;
Tommy Summers; Meredith Edwards;
Michael Forrest; Neville Smith
SLING YOUR HOOK 2/4/1969
d Michael Tuchner; *p* Irene Shubik;
sc Roy Minton
lp Michael Bates; Joe Gladwin;
Patrick O'Connell; Jo Rowbottom;
Kenneth Cranham; Geraldine Moffatt
SON OF MAN 16/4/1969
d Gareth Davies; *p* Graeme McDonald;
sc Dennis Potter
lp Colin Blakely; Robert Hardy;
Bernard Hepton; Brian Blessed;
Edward Hardwicke; Godfrey Quigley;
Patricia Lawrence; Gawn Grainger
The LAST TRAIN THROUGH THE HARECASTLE
TUNNEL 1/10/1969
d Alan Clarke; *p* Irene Shubik;
sc Peter Terson
lp Richard O'Callaghan; John Le Mesurier;
Joe Gladwin; Angela Pleasence; Shelagh Fraser
MAD JACK 4/2/1970
d Jack Gold; *p* Graeme McDonald;
sc Tom Clarke
lp Michael Jayston; Michael Pennington;
Clive Swift; Peter Gale; Anna Barry
The CELLAR AND THE ALMOND TREE 4/3/1970
d Alan Bridges; *p* Graeme McDonald;
sc David Mercer
lp Celia Johnson; Peter Vaughan;
Sydney Tafler; Patsy Byrne; Bernard Kay;
Richard Beaumont; Peter Jesson; John Rollason

EMMA'S TIME 13/5/1970
d Alan Bridges; *p* Graeme McDonald;
sc David Mercer
lp Michele Dotrice; Andrew Keir;
Peter Vaughan; Ian Holm; Pauline Yates

WEDNESDAY SPECIAL (Thames)
Series featuring drama, music and factual
programmes.
The NAKED CIVIL SERVANT 17/12/1975
Drama-documentary on the life of Quentin
Crisp.
d Jack Gold; *p* Barry Hanson;
sc Philip Mackie; *auth/intro* Quentin Crisp
lp John Hurt; Liz Gebhardt;
Patricia Hodge; Stanley Lebor;
Katharine Schofield; Colin Higgins;
John Rhys-Davies; Lloyd Lamble; Joan Ryan
ODDS AGAINST 15/9/1976
English racing – the background to the current
crisis facing the bloodstock and horse-racing
industries.
d Graham Hurley; *nar* Ivor Herbert
ST. NICOLAS-CANTATA OPUS 42 BY BENJAMIN
BRITTEN 22/12/1976
Special performance for the centenary of
Lancing College, recorded at St. Albans
Cathedral with Wandsworth School Choir, led
by Russell Burgess and soloist Ian Partridge.
d/p Margery Baker; *sc* Eric Crozier
IF THE SHOOTING STARTS 18/5/1977
A report on the weaknesses in Britain's military
contribution to NATO.
d/p Graham Hurley

WEEKEND WORLD (LWT 1972–88)
Current affairs series.
p John Birt, Nick Elliott, David Elstein,
Karl Francis, Francis Fuchs, Nelson Mews
ASPECTS OF THE MEDIA 26/11/1972
An examination of some aspects of the press and
television in Britain illustrating contemporary
viewpoints. Taking part are Donal O'Morain,
Tony Benn, Richard Briginshaw, Richard
Neville and Alan Sapper.
ANGRY BRIGADE 10/12/1972
The activities of the anarchist group known as
the 'Angry Brigade'. The views of the four
defendants acquitted in the Angry Brigade trial,
Stuart Christie, Angela Weir, Christopher Bott
and Kate McClean.
INTERVIEW WITH PROFESSOR SIR MICHAEL
SWANN 17/12/1972
An interview with Michael Swann, the new
Chairman of the BBC.
LONRHO 4/3/1973
A report on the affairs of the Lonrho company.
With Tiny Rowland, Gerald Percy, and Sir Basil
Smallpeice.
INTERVIEW WITH GRACE WYNDHAM GOLDIE
4/3/1973
interv Peter Jay
The MINERS 27/1/1974
A report on the miners' strike. With Derek
Robinson of the Pay Board, Professor Ben
Roberts, David Basnett of the GMWU and
Eddie Robertson of the CBI.
WEEKEND WORLD 7/4/1974
Interviews with Ronald Milhench and Philip
Moore-Clague about the 'land deal scandal'.
Garret Fitzgerald and William Craig are
interviewed about the situation in Ulster. Film of
a meeting between Sammy Smith of the UDA
and Rory O'Bradaigh of Provisional Sinn Fein.
EDWARD HEATH 5/5/1974
interv Peter Jay
POLITICAL COVER OF JAMES CALLAGHAN
28/3/1976
An INTERVIEW BETWEEN PETER JAY AND THE
RT. HON MICHAEL FOOT M.P 4/4/1976
An interview held at the time of the Labour
Party leadership contest.
The EDUCATION SYSTEM 19/12/1976
The British educational system and why so few
sixth formers are entering into the engineering
and manufacturing industries.

DAVID OWEN 3/4/1977
Foreign policy in the twentieth century and how
Britain's role has changed in the world; interview
with David Owen about Britain's role in Europe;
discussion on his forthcoming trip to South
Africa.
d John Longley, Howard Ross, Ian Wyatt
INTERVIEW WITH MARGARET THATCHER
18/9/1977
interv Brian Walden
PRENTICE DEFECTS/AFTER POLARIS 9/10/1977
Brian Walden interviews Reg Prentice about his
switch from the Labour Party to the
Conservative Party; a debate on Britain's nuclear
deterrents.
NORTHERN IRELAND 15/1/1978
A discussion of the stand taken by Prime
Minister Lynch on Northern Ireland. Those
taking part include Mary Holland and Conor
Cruise O'Brien.
pres Brian Walden
WEEKEND WORLD 11/3/1979
Justice in Northern Ireland.
WEEKEND WORLD 8/4/1979
Election special – the role of the unions.
WEEKEND WORLD 22/4/1979
Election special – the problem of cutting tax.
WEEKEND WORLD 16/12/1979
Hostage crisis in Iran.
pres Brian Walden

The **WEEPING MADONNA** (BBC 8/1/1956)
Comedy play set in an Italian fishing village.
p Alan Bromly; *sc* Iain MacCormick
lp Sandra Alfred; Eddie Leslie;
Michael Balfour; Ina De La Haye; Ruth Shiell;
Peter Swanwick; Kevin Stoney; Philip Stainton;
Douglas Wilmer; Cyril Shaps; Richard Pearson;
Alan Rolfe; Bill Nagy; Wolfe Morris

WELL ANYWAY (BBC 24/9–5/11/1976)
Comedy series about two men sharing a flat.
STILL 24/9/1976
p Denis Main Wilson;
sc John Bird, John Fortune
lp John Bird; John Fortune;
Dennis Waterman; Annabel Leventon;
Bernard Bresslaw; Hugh Walters

WESSEX TALES (BBC 1973)
Series of plays adapted from the stories of
Thomas Hardy.
The WITHERED ARM 7/11/1973
d Desmond Davis; *p* Irene Shubik;
sc Rhys Adrian
lp Billie Whitelaw; Yvonne Antrobus;
Edward Hardwicke; William Relton;
John Welsh; Esmond Knight
The FELLOW TOWNSMEN 14/11/1973
d Barry Davis; *p* Irene Shubik;
sc Douglas Livingstone
lp Kenneth Haigh; Jane Asher;
Terence Frisby; Susan Fleetwood;
John McKelvey; Ann Curthoys; Robert Hartley;
William Simons; Colin Edwyn;
Anthony Edwards
A TRAGEDY OF TWO AMBITIONS 21/11/1973
d Michael Tuchner; *p* Irene Shubik;
sc Dennis Potter
lp Paul Rogers; John Hurt;
David Troughton; Lynne Frederick;
Heather Canning; Edward Petherbridge;
Betty Cooper; Dan Meaden
An IMAGINATIVE WOMAN 28/11/1973
d Gavin Millar; *p* Irene Shubik;
sc William Trevor
lp Claire Bloom; Norman Rodway;
Maureen Pryor; Paul Dawkins;
Barbara Kellermann; Anne-Louise Wakefield
The MELANCHOLY HUSSAR 5/12/1973
d Mike Newell; *p* Irene Shubik;
sc Ken Taylor
lp Mary Larkin; Ben Cross; Emrys James;
Richard Kay
BARBARA OF THE HOUSE OF GREBE
12/12/1973
d David Jones; *p* Irene Shubik;
sc David Mercer
lp Joanna McCallum; Nick Brimble;
Ben Kingsley; Leslie Sands; Sheila Allen;
Richard Cornish; Jean Gilpin; John Boswall

WESTMINSTER FILE (Tyne Tees 1975–77)
Regional current affairs series.
WILLIAM WHITELAW 27/2/1975
WESTMINSTER FILE 16/3/1975
NORTH EAST METRO 1976
RT HON GEORGE THOMAS MP 17/5/1976
SIR KEITH JOSEPH 3/6/1976
WESTMINSTER FILE 1/7/1976
The QUIET MAN OF THE WILSON YEARS
11/10/1976
Profile of Ted Short.
LORD SHINWELL 18/4/1977
SIR TIMOTHY KITSON 25/4/1977
COMMON MARKET 2/5/1977
DEVOLUTION 23/5/1977

WHACK-O! (BBC 1956–62)
Comedy set in a public school.
The POOLS 22/11/1962
p Eric Fawcett;
sc Frank Muir, Denis Norden
lp Jimmy Edwards; Edwin Apps;
Arthur Howard; Keith Smith; Gordon Phillott

WHAT ABOUT THE WORKERS?
(Granada 6–20/11/1972)
Three-part documentary series.
The MEN AND MACHINES OF THE RAILWAYS
20/11/1972
Railwaymen past and present recall the days of
steam and talk about the future of the railway
industry.
p Brian Trueman

WHAT FETTLE (Tyne Tees)
Regional magazine programme.
WEARSIDE 13/1/1977
NORTHUMBERLAND 27/1/1977
WHAT FETTLE 29/1/1977
Poems, songs, an exhibition at Jarrow, local
comedians, sword dances, Harry Thompson talks
about the television image of 'Geordies'.
d Tony Kysh; *p* Heather Ging
SUPERSTITION 3/3/1977
COAL 31/3/1977
HARTLEPOOL 2/2/1978
WOMEN 2/3/1978
Women are interviewed about the 'Andy Capp-
mentality' in the north east of England.
d Tony Kysh; *p* Heather Ging

WHAT IS PROGRAMMED LEARNING?
(BBC 27/4–25/5/1965)
A series of five programmes for teachers.
SUBJECT ANALYSIS AND PROGRAMME
VALIDATION 18/5/1965
The case history of an OHM's law programme
prepared for technical school students.
p Peter Montagnon

WHAT MAKES JOHNNIE RUN?
(Rediffusion 8/7/1968)
British athletes discuss their motivation while
preparing for the Mexico Olympics at a high
altitude training camp in the French Pyrenees.
d Grahame Turner

WHAT PRICE OIL? (Grampian 4/5/1973)
A discussion between representatives of the oil
companies and Scottish local government
officials on the effects on the north of Scotland
of the massive oil-related developments planned
for the area.

WHAT'S IN A GAME (LWT 12/4–24/5/1970)
Seven-part documentary series looking at the
morality in children's games.
COPS AND ROBBERS 19/4/1970
Marjorie Sigley talks to children playing 'Cops
and Robbers'.
d Helen Standage

WHAT SHALL WE TELL THE CHILDREN?
(Thames 6/8/1968)
The problems facing parents and schools in
teaching children about sex.
d Francis Megahy

WHAT THE PAPERS SAY (Granada 1956–)
Looks at the ways in which national newspapers
have treated recent topics.

WHAT THE PAPERS SAY 8/4/1966
d David Warwick; *pres* Bill Grundy
WHAT THE PAPERS SAY 3/8/1978
d Peter Mullings; *p* Mike Murphy

**WHATEVER HAPPENED TO THE LIKELY
LADS?** (BBC 1973–74)
Sequel to The LIKELY LADS (1964–66).
sc Dick Clement, Ian La Frenais
regulars Rodney Bewes; James Bolam;
Brigit Forsyth
STRANGERS ON A TRAIN 9/1/1973
p James Gilbert
lp Deidre Costello; James Mellor;
Angelique Ashly
COUNT DOWN 20/3/1973
p James Gilbert
lp Bill Owen; Joan Hickson; Anita Carey
ABSENT FRIENDS 1/1/1974
p Bernard Thompson
lp Bill Owen; Anita Carey; Terry Scully;
Constantin De Goguel

WHAT'S A GIRL LIKE YOU ...?
(LWT 19/12/1969)
Female impersonators performing in clubs and
pubs.
d Charlie Squires

WHAT'S MY LINE? (BBC 1951–74)
Game show developed from the American
format in which guests guess the occupation of
the candidates.
WHAT'S MY LINE? 15/1/1961
Panel game chaired by Eamonn Andrews, with
Cyril Fletcher, Isobel Barnett, Barbara Kelly
and Roy Foster Brown, with guest Van Johnson.
d Bill Parry Jones

WHEELBASE (BBC 1964–71)
Motoring magazine programme.
ELEVEN PENCE A MILE 13/5/1966
Compares the prices of ferry crossings between
the Humber and Gothenburg and from Dover to
Calais.
d Brian Robins
SNOW IN SEPTEMBER 8/9/1967
The 28th annual Coupes Des Alpes rally through
2,500 miles of mountains from Marseilles to
Menton.
d Jonathan M. Mills, Tony Salmon
The BEST CAR IN THE WORLD 17/11/1967
Gordon Wilkins reports on whether the Rolls
Royce is still the best car in the world.
d Jonathan M. Mills
SEE YOU IN MONTE 1/2/1968
The Monte Carlo Rally.
d Tony Salmon
WHICH WAY WILL THE CAT JUMP? 27/9/1968
The new cars for 1969 produced by Jaguar with
Sir William Lyons, Chairman of Jaguar Daimler.
d Chris Berry, Tony Salmon; *p* Brian Robins;
rep Gordon Williams, Michael Frostick
ONE WEEKEND IN JUNE 16/6/1969
The Le Mans 24 Hour Race.
p Brian Robins
FIFTY YEARS OF THE BENTLEY 10/10/1969
The celebrations to mark the 50th anniversary of
the founding of the Bentley firm: vintage
Bentleys racing at Le Mans; interviews with the
President of the Bentley Drivers Club, Stanley
Sedgwick; 1927 Le Mans winner Sammy Davis;
and W.O. Bentley.
d Chris Berry, Tony Salmon;
p Brian Robins;
rep Gordon Wilkins, Michael Frostick

**WHEELTAPPERS' AND SHUNTERS'
SOCIAL CLUB** (Granada 1974–76)
Variety show based on the concept of the north
of England working men's clubs.
WHEELTAPPERS' AND SHUNTERS' SOCIAL
CLUB 20/4/1974
With Colin Crompton, Ronnie Hilton, and Bill
Haley and The Comets.
d David Warwick, John Scholz-Conway;
p John Hamp; *pres* Bernard Manning
WHEELTAPPERS' AND SHUNTERS' SOCIAL
CLUB 22/2/1975
d David Warwick; *p* John Hamp;
pres Colin Crompton, Bernard Manning

WHEELTAPPERS' AND SHUNTERS' SOCIAL CLUB *cont.*

WHEELTAPPERS' AND SHUNTERS' SOCIAL
CLUB 15/5/1976
d David Warwick; *p* John Hamp;
pres Colin Crompton, Bernard Manning

WHEN THE BOAT COMES IN
(BBC 1976–81)
Period drama series set in a fictional north east
of England town.
FISH IN WOOLLY JUMPERS 22/1/1976
d Paul Ciappessoni; *p* Leonard Lewis;
sc James Mitchell
lp James Bolam; Susan Jameson;
James Garbutt; Jean Heywood;
John Nightingale; Michelle Newell
LOOK UP AND SEE THE SKY 3/11/1977
d Michael Hayes; *p* Andrew Osborn;
sc James Mitchell
lp James Bolam; James Garbutt;
Jean Heywood; John Nightingale;
Edward Wilson; Vernon Drake; David King

WHERE ADAM STOOD (BBC 21/4/1976)
Play based on 'Father and Son' by Edmund
Gosse.
d Brian Gibson; *p* Kenith Trodd;
sc Dennis Potter
lp Alan Badel; Max Harris; Ronald Hines;
Heather Canning; Gareth Forwood; Jean Boht;
Hubert Rees

WHERE THE DIFFERENCE BEGINS
(BBC 15/12/1961)
Play concerning a moment of crisis in the lives of
a Wakefield family. First in a trilogy of plays,
followed by A CLIMATE OF FEAR (1962),
and 'The Birth of a Private Man' (1963).
p Don Taylor; *sc* David Mercer
lp Nigel Stock; Leslie Sands;
Barry Foster; Hylda Baker; Olive McFarland;
Pauline Letts

WHERE THE HOUSES USED TO BE
(Thames 29/6/1971)
Looks at the people living in a vast housing
estate in Wandsworth, London.
d Carlo Passini; *p* Jeremy Isaacs

WHICKER IN THE ARGENTINE
(Yorkshire TV 1969)
AFTER US – WHAT? PENGUINS 9/3/1969
Alan Whicker reports on the changes taking
place in Argentina.
d Michael Blakstad

WHICKER WAY OUT WEST
(Yorkshire TV 1973)
The LORD IS MY SHEPHERD AND HE KNOWS
I'M GAY 2/10/1973
Alan Whicker reports on homosexuality in
California.
d Michael Deakin

WHICKER WITHIN A WOMAN'S WORLD
(Yorkshire TV 1972)
A GIRL GETS TEMPTATIONS – BUT I WANTED
TO GIVE MYSELF TO GOD 2/8/1972
Alan Whicker looks at the life of the Poor Clare
nuns at their convent at Baddesley Clinton.
d Ian McFarlane; *exec.p* John Fairley
GOD FORGIVE ME FOR WHAT I'VE DONE – BUT
IT WAS ALL VERY ENJOYABLE... 9/8/1972
Alan Whicker talks to a woman criminal.
d Ian McFarlane; *p* John Lloyd

WHICKER'S ORIENT (Yorkshire TV 1972)
WHAT MAKES SHAW RUN RUN? 25/1/1972
Alan Whicker looks at the work of Hong Kong
film-maker Run Run Shaw.
d Ian McFarlane; *exec.p* Tony Essex

WHICKER'S WORLD DOWN UNDER
(Yorkshire TV 1976)
MANY PEOPLE CURTSY – BUT WE DON'T
EXPECT IT 19/5/1976
Alan Whicker meets Leonard and Shirley Casley
who, following an argument with the
government, declared their farm in the outback
to be an independent nation with its own stamps,
currency and airforce. Whicker visits the Hutt
River Province in Australia.
d John Willis, Nigel Turner; *exec.p* John Fairley

WE HOPE WE CAN LET OFF A NICE SAFE
HYDROGEN BOMB... 26/5/1976
Alan Whicker meets multi-millionaire mineral
prospector, Lang Hancock, and discusses his
plans for opening up the outback of the north-
west, his battle against government and
bureaucracy and his plan for his 21 year old
daughter Gina to eventually take control of the
business.
exec.p John Fairley
The TOMATO SAUCE LIST WAS BIGGER THAN
THE WINE LIST... 2/6/1976
Alan Whicker meets migrants who have found
success in Australia.
d John Willis, Mike Weigall;
exec.p John Fairley
YOU STOPPED BEING A PIGEON – WHEN YOU
GOT YOUR THROAT CUT 9/6/1976
Alan Whicker visits the opal town of Coober
Pedy in Australia's Central Desert.
d Michael Weigall; *exec.p* John Fairley
WHEN YOU BECOME A BUSH BISHOP THEY
SAY – TOUGH LUCK! 16/6/1976
Alan Whicker meets some migrants who retain
their old world individuality but also manage to
conform to Australia's materialistic society.
d John Willis; *exec.p* John Fairley
The OCKERS HAVE ARRIVED – NOW WE DON'T
ALL HAVE TO BE BRAIN SURGEONS! 23/6/1976
Alan Whicker discovers the Ocker – a term
describing the new-style aggressive Australian
who cocks a snook at his British origins and the
rest of the world.
d Michael Weigall; *exec.p* John Fairley

WHIPLASH (AU/GB ITC 1960)
Western-type series set in Australia during the
1850s.
p Ben Fox
regulars Peter Graves; Anthony Wickert
ACT OF COURAGE 1960
d Ben Fox; *sc* Gerry Day
lp Guy Doleman; Margo Lee; Brett Hart;
Terry McDermott; Ric Hutton; Janette Craig;
Brian Hungerford; Tony Madigan
BARBED WIRE 1960
d Peter Maxwell
lp Gerry Duggan; Phillip Ross;
Grant Taylor; Eric Reiman
LOVE STORY IN GOLD 1960
d John Meredyth Lucas; *sc* James Clavell
lp Neva Carr-Glyn; Owen Weingott;
Margaret Mewkill; Keith Silver
The WRECKERS 1960
d John Meredyth Lucas; *sc* Daphne Field
lp Guy Doleman; Robert Tudawali;
Hugh Stewart; Nat Levison
EPISODE IN BATHURST 10/9/1960
d Peter Maxwell
CONVICT TOWN 17/9/1960
d Peter Maxwell
SARONG 8/10/1960
d John Meredyth Lucas; *sc* Gene Roddenberry
lp Joe McCormack; Julian Flett;
John Fegan
DUTCHMAN'S REEF 15/10/1960
d Peter Maxwell; *sc* Gene Roddenberry
lp Leonard Teale; Queenie Ashton;
Derani Scarr; Jerome White
The OTHER SIDE OF THE SWAN 22/10/1960
d Peter Maxwell; *sc* Michael Plant
lp Nigel Lovell; Margo Lee; Ken Fraser
The ACTRESS 29/10/1960
d Peter Maxwell; *p* Maury Geraghty;
sc Gene Roddenberry
lp Lew Luton; Jennifer Jayne; Cherry Butlin
The BONE THAT WHISPERED 5/11/1960
d John Meredyth Lucas; *sc* Michael Plant
lp Nigel Lovell; Gwenda Pippen; Reg Lye;
Robert Tudawali; Jack Kelly
SECRET OF THE SCREAMING HILLS 12/11/1960
d Peter Maxwell; *sc* Don Ingalls
lp Marion Johns; Frank Waters;
James Elliott; George Roubicek; Pat Wedge
Veronica Rouse
The TWISTED ROAD 7/1/1961
d Peter Maxwell; *sc* Michael Plant
lp Tom Farley; Ben Gabriel; Rachel Lloyd
The SOLID GOLD BRIGADE 4/2/1961
d Maury Geraghty; *p* Ted Holliday;
sc Michael Plant
lp John Gray; Don Pascoe; Tony Arpino

STAGE FOR TWO 11/2/1961
d Peter Maxwell; *sc* Terry Maples
lp Leonard Teale; Peter Guest; Vaughan Tracy
CANOOMBA INCIDENT 18/2/1961
d Peter Maxwell; *sc* Richard Grey
lp Janette Craig; Stewart Ginn; Lew Luton
The RUSHING HANDS 25/2/1961
d Peter Maxwell; *sc* Michael Plant
lp Gordon Glenwright; Barry Linehan;
Nevil Thurgood
The HUNTERS 11/3/1961
d John Meredyth Lucas; *sc* Morris L. West
lp Bettina Welch; Philip Ross;
Robert Tudawali
The LEGACY 18/3/1961
d John Meredyth Lucas; *sc* Bill Templeton
lp Betty Lucas; Moray Powell;
Reginald Livermore
STAGE FREIGHT 8/4/1961
d Peter Maxwell; *sc* Ralph Peterson
lp Barry Linehan; Margo Lee;
Eric Reiman
PORTRAIT IN GUNPOWDER 22/4/1961
d John Meredyth Lucas; *sc* Michael Plant
lp Stuart Wagstaff; Therese Talbert;
Alan Light
RIBBONS AND WHEELS 29/4/1961
d Peter Maxwell; *sc* Ralph Peterson
lp Tom Farley; Ursula Finlay; Grant Taylor
FLOOD TIDE 6/5/1961
d Ben Fox; *sc* Michael Plant
lp Shirley Broadway; Barry Linehan
DILEMMA IN WOOL 20/5/1961
d Peter Maxwell; *sc* Ralph Peterson
lp Janette Craig; Neil Fitzpatrick;
Nigel Lovell
MAGIC WIRE 27/5/1961
d Peter Maxwell; *sc* Ralph Petersen
lp Peter Aanensen; Terry McDermott;
Robert Tudawali

WHISPERING SMITH
(US Whispering Co. 1961)
Western detective series.
STAKE OUT 29/5/1961
d Christian I. Nyby; *p* Joseph Hoffman;
sc Harold Swanton, Borden Chase
lp Audie Murphy; Guy Mitchell;
John Cliff; Sam Buffington; Joyce Taylor;
Richard Devon; Billy McLean; Lyn Thomas

WHITE HUNTER
(Beaconsfield Productions 1958–60)
Safari series filmed partly in Kenya and based on
the life of John A. Hunter.
p Norman Williams
regular Rhodes Reason
DEAD MAN'S TALE 6/7/1958
d Ernest Morris
lp Harry Baird; Lloyd Lamble;
Arnold Diamond; Martin Benson
The VALLEY OF THE DEAD 13/7/1958
d Ernest Morris
lp Alec Mango; Lawrence Taylor;
Edwina Carroll; Billy Milton; Harry Baird;
Donovan Wynter; Frank Hawkins;
Max Faulkner
BIG BWANA BRADY 20/7/1958
lp Harry Baird; Faith Brook;
Robert Ayres; John Crawford
GUN DUEL 27/7/1958
d Ernest Morris
lp Francis De Wolff; Harry Baird
ONE FATAL WEAKNESS 3/8/1958
d Max Varnel; *sc* Lee Erwin
lp Adrienne Corri; Mervyn Johns;
Julian Strange
LET MY PEOPLE GO 10/8/1958
d D'Arcy Conyers;
sc Gordon Wellesley, Charlotte Hastings
lp Frank Singuineau; Danny Daniels;
Jack Lambert; Lloyd Lamble; Harry Baird;
Orlando Martins; Edna McKenzie
DAY OF RECKONING 17/8/1958
d D'Arcy Conyers
lp Jill Adams; Barry Keegan;
Ivor Salter; Orlando Martins
The TREASURE OF TIPPU TIB 24/8/1958
d Ernest Morris; *sc* Lee Loeb
lp John Loder; Leslie Perrins;
Peter Sinclair

ROGUE MAN 31/8/1958
d Peter Maxwell; *sc* Herb Purdom
lp Edwin Richfield; Gwen Watford;
John Longden
WEB OF DEATH 7/9/1958
d D'Arcy Conyers; *sc* Ken Taylor
lp Jeannette Sterke; Peter Illing;
Peter Reynolds; Harry Baird
The SICKNESS OF KILIMANJARO 1959
The JACKALS 14/6/1959
d D'Arcy Conyers
INSIDE STORY 28/6/1959
d Joseph Sterling; *sc* Ellis Marcus
lp Barbara Shelley; Phil Brown; Cy Crane
PEGASUS 5/7/1959
OPERATION TRANSFER 2/8/1959
d D'Arcy Conyers; *sc* Frank L. Moss
The STEPFATHERS 9/8/1959
The LONG KNIFE 16/8/1959
d Ernest Morris; *sc* Ian Stuart Black
lp Patrick Holt; Barbara Shelley;
Jack Lambert; Harry Baird
The PLAGUE 23/8/1959
d Ernest Morris; *sc* Donn Mullally
lp William Lucas; Jennifer Jayne;
Harry Baird; Robert Perceval
DEADFALL 30/8/1959
d Peter Maxwell
lp Ronan O'Casey; Harry Baird;
Patricia Dainton; Conrad Phillips
The PRISONER 19/6/1960
d Ernest Morris; *sc* Lee Loeb
lp Catherine Boyle; David Oxley;
Peter Sinclair
FOREST OF THE NIGHT 3/7/1960
d Bernard Lewis; *sc* Robert Yale Libott
lp Marianne Brauns; Wolf Frees; John Rae
MARKED MAN 10/7/1960
d D'Arcy Conyers; *sc* Lee Loeb
lp Jack Hedley; Kay Callard; Gordon Sterne
The FUGITIVE 17/7/1960
d Peter Maxwell; *sc* Lee Erwin
lp Charles Houston; Tim Turner;
Earl Cameron
RUN TO EARTH 24/7/1960
d Maurice Elvey; *sc* Robert Yale Libbott
lp Peter Bathurst; Sandra Dorne;
Harry Fowler; Arnold Ridley;
Madeline Thomas; Frances Guthrie;
Hugh Moxey; Jack Lambert; Michael Mellinger;
André Morell
SQUIRE OF THE SERENGETI 31/7/1960
d Ernest Morris; *sc* Donn Mullally
lp Rona Anderson; John Witty;
Denis Shaw; Phillip Rose; Samuel Mansaray
VOODOO WEDDING 7/8/1960
d Ernest Morris; *sc* Lee Loeb
lp Edward Judd; Robert Shaw;
Gene Anderson
The LONELY PLACE 14/8/1960
d Ernest Morris;
sc Donn Mullally, Alan Caillou
lp André Morell; Harry Baird; Barbara Brown;
Richard Peel
SISTER MY SPOUSE 21/8/1960
d Ernest Morris; *sc* Donn Mullally
lp Barbara Mullen; Thomas Baptiste;
Harry Baird; Arthur Lawrence
OUT OF THE WIND 28/8/1960
d Joseph Sterling; *sc* Ken Taylor
lp Harry Baird; Patricia Dainton;
Ronan O'Casey; Trevor Reid
GIRL HUNT 4/9/1960
d D'Arcy Conyers
lp Harry Baird; Beth Rogan;
Robert Cawdron; John Longden

WHITE MISSIONARY (BBC 3/2/1966)
The church in Tanzania, its missionary work,
and its work in helping to alleviate poverty and
leprosy.
d/p Michael Gill; *nar* Erskine Childer

The WHITE TRIBE OF AFRICA
(BBC 8/1–29/1/79)
Series of four films about the Afrikaners.
The TREKKERS 8/1/1979
The Afrikaans community of South Africa and
its history
pres David Dimbleby

The GRAND DESIGN 22/1/1979
Introduction of the policy of Apartheid by the
Afrikaner Nationalists. 30 years later, how it has
worked.
d Francis Gerard; *p* David Harrison

WHO DO YOU DO? (LWT 1972–74)
Comedy show based on impersonations.
WHO DO YOU DO? 4/5/1973
With Freddie Starr, Paul Melba, Dailey and
Wayne, Roger Kitter, Dustin Gee, Arthur
Mullard, Lance Percival and Johnny More.
p Jon Scoffield;
sc Barry Cryer, Dick Vosburgh, Wally Malston

WHO PAYS THE PIPER? (BBC 13/10/1960)
A dramatised documentary about the lives and
work of the performers and administrators of a
local orchestra.
d/p David E. Rose

A WHOLE SCENE GOING (BBC 1966)
Popular music magazine programme for young
people.
A WHOLE SCENE GOING 8/6/1966
A visit to Paris with Dave Dee, Dozy, Beaky,
Mick and Tich; looks at bed-sits and flats in
London; talks to Ravi Shankar about Indian
'pop' music; music from The Yardbirds and The
Kinks; plus an interview with Charlton Heston.
d Tom Savage; *p* Elizabeth Cowley;
pres Wendy Varnals, Barry Fantoni

The WHOLE UNIVERSE SHOW
(BBC 7/7–25/8/1977)
Eight-part series on the beginnings of the
universe.
EXPLODING STARS 14/7/1977
An examination, for children, of the 'big bang'
theory.
p Stuart Harris; *sc* Nigel Calder

WHOOSH (BBC 15/9/1966)
A partially dramatised review of the first twenty
years in the life of H.G. Wells. Contributors
include Vincent Brome, Michael Foot, Odette
Keun, Patrick Moore, Frank Swinnerton, A.J.P.
Taylor, Professor G.P. Wells and Frank Wells.
d/sc Christopher Burstall
lp Sarah Miles; Murray Melvin

WHOSE LIFE IS IT ANYWAY?
(Granada 12/3/1972)
Play debating the point: does a hospital have the
right to battle for the life of a man who refuses
to carry on living?
d Richard Everitt; *p* Peter Eckersley;
sc Brian Clark
lp Ian McShane; Suzanne Neve; John Welsh;
Philip Latham; Hal Dyer; Julian Curry

WHY CAN'T I GO HOME?
(ATV 18/6–26/11/1979)
Children's drama series about life in a hospital
ward.
The STORY OF A CHILDREN'S WARD 30/7/1979
d Chris Tookey; *p* Royston Morley;
auth Max Marquis
lp Fiannula O'Shannon; Vivienne Avramoff;
Pat Wainwright; Ian Thompson; David Baron;
Craig McFarlane; Catherine Kirkwood;
Hazel Clyne; Charles Cork; Dawn Perllman;
Oona Kirsch; Paul Humpoletz

WICKET KEEPING AND FIELDING
(Rediffusion 28/5/1956)
Shown as part of the 'Sportspot' series. Trevor
Bailey presents the fourth programme on cricket
coaching.

WILD AND FREE – TWICE DAILY
(ATV 28/10/1969)
The running of the Roberts Brothers circus and
the lives of its artistes.
d Chris Menges

The WILD WEST SHOW
(BBC 26/9–31/10/1975)
Series of six plays about a small town rugby
team.

MELVYN'S MARAUDERS 10/10/1975
d Jim Goddard; *p* Kenith Trodd;
sc Colin Welland
lp Brian Glover; Juliet Cooke;
Joe Lynch; Henry Livings; Patrick Durkin;
Peter Martin

WILDE ALLIANCE
(Yorkshire TV 17/1–11/4/1978)
Thirteen-part comedy thriller.
p Ian Mackintosh
regulars John Stride; Julia Foster; John Lee;
Patrick Newell
QUESTION OF RESEARCH 17/1/1978
d Derek Bennett; *sc* Ian Mackintosh
lp Jerome Willis; Donald Burton; Judy Buxton
FLOWER POWER 24/1/1978
d Bob Hird; *sc* Anthony Skene
lp Ambrosine Phillpotts; James Villiers;
Gwyneth Owen; June Ellis
THINGS THAT GO BUMP 7/2/1978
d Marc Miller; *sc* Philip Broadley
lp Marius Goring; Janina Faye;
Sean Arnold; Donald Layne-Smith
The PRIVATE ARMY OF COLONEL STONE
14/2/1978
d Matthew Robinson; *sc* Jacques Gillies
lp John Fraser; Hilary Mason;
Anthony Dutton; Philip McGough
DANNY BOY 21/2/1978
d Bob Hird; *sc* Ian Mackintosh
lp Ed Bishop; Jacqui Sullivan;
David King; Leon Lissek
WELL ENOUGH ALONE 28/2/1978
d David Reynolds; *sc* Anthony Skene
lp Caroline Blakiston; Edward De Souza;
Roger Brierley; Desmond Llewelyn
EXPRESS FROM ROME 7/3/1978
d Marc Miller; *sc* Philip Broadley
lp David Swift; Madeline Hinde;
Timothy Morand; Alex Davion; Tony Anholt
A GAME FOR TWO PLAYERS 14/3/1978
d David Reynolds; *sc* John Bowen
lp Cherith Mellor; Jeff Rawle; David Corti
TIME AND AGAIN 21/3/1978
d Marc Miller; *sc* Anthony Skene
lp Anthony Bate; Diana Coupland;
Richard Shaw; Freddie Earlle
AFFRAY IN AMSTERDAM 28/3/1978
d David Reynolds; *sc* Philip Broadley
lp Diane Keen; Damien Thomas;
Christopher Benjamin; Paul Lavers
A SUSPICION OF SUDDEN DEATH 4/4/1978
d Leonard Lewis; *sc* Jacques Gillies
lp Philip Stone; Moira Redmond;
Cyril Shaps; Ruth Trouncer
SOME TRUST IN CHARIOTS 11/4/1978
d Derek Bennett; *sc* Ian Mackintosh
lp Mela White; Pat Astley; Mark Eden

WILDERNESS (BBC 8/11–23/12/1974)
Eight-part series showing eight journeys in
various wildernesses undertaken by zoologist
Anthony Smith.
p Ned Kelly, Peter Bale
The HIMALAYAS 8/11/1974
The MATO GROSSO OF BRAZIL 15/11/1974
ANTARCTICA 22/11/1974
The GIBSON DESERT OF AUSTRALIA 29/11/1974
LAKE RUDOLF 6/12/1974
CANADA'S ARCTIC TUNDRA 13/12/1974
The SUDD 20/12/1974

WILDLIFE ON ONE (BBC 1977–)
Series of natural history programmes.
The AMERICAN EAGLE 3/2/1977
A study of the bald eagle filmed over a period of
three years
d/p Steve Smith; *nar* David Attenborough
A SAFE POLAR BEAR IS A DISTANT POLAR
BEAR 17/2/1977
The annual influx of polar bears to the town of
Churchill, Northern Manitoba, waiting to move
onto the pack ice in the surrounding sea.
d/p Douglas Thomas; *intro* David Attenborough
SOME OF MY BEST FRIENDS ARE VULTURES
9/8/1977
The Griffon vulture in the sierras of Seville.
d John Elliot

WILDLIFE ON ONE cont.

BIG BILL – THE STORY OF A HERON 20/4/1978
The life of Big Bill, a European grey heron, raised in a heronry.
d Anthony Bomford, Hugh Miles;
p Hugh Miles; *nar* Eric Thompson
SQUIRREL ON MY SHOULDER 31/5/1979
The light-hearted story of an abandoned baby grey squirrel who is fostered by a domestic cat and causes chaos in the home.
p John Paling; *nar* David Attenborough
The REAL MR. RATTY 7/6/1979
The life of a water vole, filmed among the wildlife of a Devon river bank. Extracts from Kenneth Grahame's 'Wind in the Willows' are read by Felicity Kendal.
p Maurice Tibbles; *nar* David Attenborough
SCORPION 21/6/1979
Studies the scorpion and examines its reputation as a symbol of secrecy and death.
p/sc Tony Edwards; *nar* David Attenborough

WILLY (ATV 3/6/1973)
Drama. After an accident in which he suffered brain damage, a man lies in a hospital intensive care unit as his mother and girl friend try to talk him back to consciousness.
d Vivian Matalon; *p* Nicholas Palmer;
sc David Cook
lp Christopher Gable; Anna Massey;
Maureen Pryor; Gwyneth Powell; George Innes;
Paul Copley; Sheila Ferris

WILTON'S: THE HANDSOMEST HALL IN TOWN (BBC 26/12/1970)
Re-opening of Wilton's, the famous music hall, 90 years after its closure, in Whitechapel.
d Michael Mills

The WIND OF CHANGE (BBC 10–12/4/1960)
Three documentary films about Africa.
d/p Denis Mitchell
MAIN STREET AFRICA 10/4/1960
Potgietersrus, a small community in the Transvaal.
A VIEW FROM THE FARM 11/4/1960
The life of Devonshire-born Hugh Tracey, authority on African music, who farms near Johannesburg.
BETWEEN TWO WORLDS 12/4/1960
How a college education in Dar es-Salaam is changing the lifestyle of Victor Kimeseru, a Masai tribesman from Tanganyika.

WINDSOR WORLD CAMP (BBC 1957)
Scenes at the international camp at Windsor in 1957.

WITHIN THESE FOUR WALLS
(BBC 15/1–19/3/1971)
Ten-part series looking at museums in Britain.
PATRICK MOORE 12/2/1971
Television astronomer Patrick Moore visits the old Royal Observatory at the National Maritime Museum, Greenwich.
d Peter R. Smith; *p* Brenda Horsfield

WODEHOUSE PLAYHOUSE
(BBC 1975–76; 1978)
Adaptations of the P.G. Wodehouse stories.
regulars John Alderton; Pauline Collins
PORTRAIT OF A DISCIPLINARIAN 7/5/1975
p David Askey; *sc* David Climie
lp William Gaunt; Vicki Woolf; Daphne Heard
ANSELM GETS HIS CHANCE 26/3/1976
p Michael Mills; *sc* David Climie
lp Desmond Llewellyn; Thorley Walters;
Paul Curran
The NODDER 30/4/1976
p Michael Mills; *sc* David Climie
lp Don Fellows; Jonathan Cecil;
Sydney Tafler; David Healy
The CODE OF THE MULLINERS 7/5/1976
p Michael Mills; *sc* David Climie
lp David Quilter; Gabrielle Drake;
Walter Gotell; Daphne Oxenford
The LUCK OF THE STIFFHAMS 21/11/1978
p Gareth Gwenlan; *sc* David Climie
lp Liza Goddard; Leslie Sands;
David Healy; Paul McDowell

MULLINER'S BUCK-U-UPPO 12/12/1978
p Gareth Gwenlan; *sc* David Climie
lp Belinda Carroll; John Barron;
Cyril Luckham; Avis Bunnage; Beatrix Mackey

WOMEN IN LOVE (Rediffusion 24/9/1958)
Six short plays introduced by George Sanders with continental leading ladies and settings. Produced as part of the celebrations for the third anniversary of Rediffusion. The earliest surviving example of a programme made on videotape. The titles are as follows:- After So Long; Willi; The Return; Song Without Words; A Candle for The Madonna; The Stowaway. The Archive holds the following:
AFTER SO LONG
sc Bridget Boland
lp Terence Morgan; Scilla Gabel
SONG WITHOUT WORDS
sc Michael Meyer
lp John Fraser; Ann-Marie Gyllenspetz
The STOWAWAY
sc Charles Terrot
lp Daniel Massey; Yvonne Monlaur

WOMEN IN PRISON (Rediffusion 12/8/1964)
An investigation into women in prisons, visiting Holloway, Askham Grange and Styal.
d Stephen Peet; *sc* Martin Worth;
nar Andrew Faulds

WON'T GET FOOLED AGAIN
(Yorkshire TV 25/11/1979)
The rock band The Who.

WOODY ALLEN (Granada 10/2/1965)
Comedy show.
d Philip Casson; *p* John Hamp;
with Woody Allen

WORDPOWER (BBC 1977)
Ten-part series about communicating by the spoken word.
UNACCUSTOMED AS I AM... 7/3/1977
The art of public speaking, with Jean Howell and Rex Swindall.
p Bernard Adams

The WORKER (ATV 1965; 1969–70)
Comedy series set in a Labour Exchange. Several sketches were repeated in the 'Bruce Forsyth's Big Night' series.
regulars Charlie Drake; Henry McGee
A PUNTING WE WILL GO 23/10/1965
d Shaun O'Riordan; *p* Alan Tarrant;
sc Lewis Schwarz, Charlie Drake
lp Glyn Houston; Eddie Byrne;
Peter Hager; Jean Marlow; Barry Lowe
BREED IN FOR SPEED, BREED OUT FOR STAMINA 13/8/1970
d John Sholtz-Conway; *p* Shaun O'Riordan;
sc Lewis Schwarz, Charlie Drake
lp Willoughby Goddard; Kathleen Byron;
Nicholas Phipps; Blake Butler;
William Lyon Brown; Celestine Burden
The SAUCERER'S APPRENTICE 27/8/1970
d/p Shaun O'Riordan;
sc Lewis Schwarz, Charlie Drake
lp Cyril Cross; Fred Hugh;
Celestine Burden; Edwin Brown;
Jean Challis; Marcia Warren;
Matthew Robertson

WORKSHOP (BBC 1964–81)
Music series
The GOLDEN RING 16/5/1965
A recording session in Vienna of Wagner's 'Götterdämmerung'. Georg Solti conducts the Vienna Philharmonic Orchestra, and the performers include Birgit Nilsson, Wolfgang Windgassen, Gottlob Frick, Dietrich Fischer-Dieskau and Claire Watson.
p Humphrey Burton
DOUBLE CONCERTO 4/4/1966
Vladimir Ashkenazy and Daniel Barenboim, with the English Chamber Orchestra in rehearsal and performance of Mozart's Concerto in E Flat for two pianos at the Fairfield Hall, Croydon.
p Brian Large, Christopher Nupen

PIERRE BOULEZ 22/8/1966
Pierre Boulez talks about his life and music to Basil Moss, and conducts a performance of his 'Improvisation No.2 On Mallarmé', with Halina Lukomska and The New Music Ensemble.
d Barrie Gavin
BERNSTEIN IN REHEARSAL 6/1/1967
Leonard Bernstein rehearsing the London Symphony Orchestra for a performance of the Symphony No. 5 by Shostakovich. Bernstein also talks about his conducting.
p Herbert Chappell
The DARING YOUNG MAN ON THE BLACK AND WHITE KEYS 11/2/1968
A study of piano virtuosity past and present, featuring Charles Rosen. Introduced by Robin Ray. With film of Cziffra, Michelangeli and Paderewski playing the piano.
d Herbert Chappell
SCHUBERT 22/9/1968
Schubert's life and music. Taking part are Janet Baker, Paul Hamburger, Paul Badura-Skoda, Jörg Demus, Alfred Brendel, John Shirley-Quirk, Peter Pears, Benjamin Britten, H.C. Robbins Landon, The Muller Quartet, The Linz Tramway Band.
d Jamila Patten; *p* Barrie Gavin
SCHUBERT – SOUND AND SENSE 29/9/1968
An anthology of comment on the character and nature of his music. Taking part are Hans Keller with The Darlington String Quartet, Janet Baker, Alfred Brendel, Les Black and Paul Hamburger (on the Great C major Symphony) and Benjamin Britten and Peter Pears on Winterreise.
d Jamila Patten; *p* Barrie Gavin
SCHUBERT – AN EVENING OF HIS MUSIC 6/10/1968
Taking part are Janet Baker, Paul Hamburger, John Shirley-Quirk, Martin Isepp, Paul Badura-Skoda, The Weller Quartet, The Willi Boskowsky Ensemble, and The Linz Tramways Band.
d Jamila Patten; *p* Barrie Gavin
sc Leo Black; *nar* Gary Watson
TELEMARTEAU 20/10/1968
Pierre Boulez conducts and explains his composition 'Le Marteau sans Maitre'.
d Barrie Gavin
O.A.M.D.G. 23/2/1969
Omnia ad Majorem Dei Gloria (All to the Greater Glory of God) – the life and music of Anton Bruckner.
d Barrie Gavin
BERLIOZ: A SINGULAR OBSESSION 9/3/1969
Michael Ayrton's personal obsession with the life and works of Berlioz.
p Kenneth Corden
with Jean-Louis Barrault, Josephine Veasey, Ryland Davies, Michael Rippon
The NEW RHYTHM OF MUSIC 12/9/1969
Pierre Boulez on Bartok and Stravinsky and their place in twentieth-century music with extracts from 'Music for Strings, Percussion, and Celesta' by Bartok and 'The Rite of Spring' by Stravinsky, performed by the BBC Symphony Orchestra.
d Barrie Gavin; *nar* Gary Watson
The MOST MAGNIFICENT AND EXPENSIVE DIVERSION 26/8/1973
Raymond Leppard describes the early days of opera and shows how the Venetian extravaganzas of Monteverdi and Cavalli can be staged today. Ends with first known performance since 1643 of 'L'Egisto' by Cavalli (final scene).
d Barrie Gavin;
with Kenneth Bowen, Anne Howells, Richard Angas, Patricia Grieg, Rosannne Creffield, Ann Murray, Norma Burrowes, Academia Cavalli

WORKTALK (BBC 11/10–8/11/1976)
Five-part training series.
d Paul Kriwaczek; *p* John Twitchin
FRED BARKER GOES TO CHINA 18/10/1976
A dramatisation of Fred Barker's emigration to China to take up a job in a hospital as an ancillary worker, demonstrating the range of misunderstandings that can arise from a language barrier and cultural differences.
intro Elizabeth Laird

SINGH 171 25/10/1976
A dramatisation about a Sikh worker, Gurdial Singh, who hopes for promotion to chargehand in a plastics factory. Illustrates the misunderstandings arising from the different cultural backgrounds of the participants.
T'AINT WHAT YOU SAY, IT'S THE WAY THAT YOU SAY IT... 1/11/1976
Explores the role of language in communications at work.

The WORLD ABOUT US (BBC 1967–87)
Documentary series about animals and exploration.
The LAST GREAT JOURNEY ON EARTH 20/10/1968
A journey by hovercraft from the Amazon to the Orinoco through the rain forests of Brazil and Venezuela.
d/p/sc/comm Brian Branston
INCREDIBLE HUMMINGBIRDS 4/1/1970
d/p Richard Brock; *nar* Peter Scott
SAGA: ICELAND AS THE VIKINGS SAW IT 8/8/1971
Iceland as it would have appeared to the Vikings.
p Brian Branston; *nar* William Franklyn
The FOALS OF EPONA 24/9/1972
A look at the mountain and moorland ponies of Britain.
p Suzanne Gibbs
FLAMENCO TRIANGLE 23/1/1973
The wildlife in the south-west of Spain.
p Richard Brock
SACRED COWES 3/2/1974
The 1973 Regatta at Cowes.
p Bob Saunders
The TENDER TRAP 22/9/1974
Four carnivorous plants; venus fly trap; sundews; bladderwort; and pitcher plant.
nar Hugh Falkus
3,900 MILLION AND ONE 8/12/1974
The women's role in an extended family in South India.
p Anthony Mayer
The ROMANCE OF INDIAN RAILWAYS 4/5/1975
A celebration of the 150th anniversary of railways. Michael Satow, retired Managing Director of ICI, travels to India in search of steam locomotives for the first railway museum in Asia.
p Colin Luke; *sc/nar* James Cameron
The HYENA STORY 11/5/1975
Portrait of the spotted hyena in Africa.
d Bill Travers, Hugo Van Lawick; *nar* David Attenborough
The GREAT TURTLE MYSTERY 6/6/1976
Mass meeting of turtles on Costa Rican beach.
d Ned Kelly
The ELEPHANT RUN 9/6/1977
The decline of the African elephant population, largely due to ivory poachers.
p/nar Julian Mounter
SALMO – THE LEAPER 11/9/1977
The sea trout and the Atlantic salmon. Filmed in Eskdale and in Scottish locations, including the Tey and the Spey rivers.
p/sc/intro Hugh Falkus
The DAY OF THE ZEBRA 19/9/1976
How zebras survive.
p John Sparks; *nar* Robert Powell
The CURIOUS CAT 29/4/1979
A colony of cats living in a Devon farmyard is studied by a full-time researcher for a year.
p/sc Peter Crawford; *nar* Eleanor Bron
KATHMANDU: A THREATENED BEAUTY 6/5/1979
The problems for Nepal of preserving the Kathmandu Valley.
p Richard Taylor
BUTTERFLIES 10/6/1979
p/sc Robin Crane; *nar* Tom Fleming
The LAST CHANCE WAGON TRAIN 5/12/1979
A scheme for young offenders in Arizona. They are given a choice between staying in prison or taking part in a trek across the desert to Denver, Colorado.
p Bob Saunders; *sc* Desmond Wilcox

The WORLD AT WAR (Thames 1973–74)
A history of World War II in twenty-six episodes. Uses archive film from national and private sources and includes interviews with statesmen and military leaders of the time.
p Jeremy Isaacs; *nar* Laurence Olivier
A NEW GERMANY: 1933–1939 31/10/1973
Hitler's rise to power.
d Hugh Raggett; *sc* Neal Ascherson
The DISTANT WAR: 1939–1940 7/11/1973
Hitler attacks Poland and Britain finds itself at war. The Nazi terror begins in Eastern Europe.
p David Elstein; *sc* Laurence Thompson
FRANCE FALLS: MAY–JUNE 1940 14/11/1973
France has prepared for another war like World War I, counting on the defences of the Maginot Line. But the Germans fight a new war – Blitzkrieg.
p/sc Peter Batty
ALONE: 1940–1941 21/11/1973
After Dunkirk, Britain faces the German onslaught. Germany prepares to invade but must first win mastery of the air. The RAF holds on and wins the Battle of Britain.
p David Elstein; *sc* Laurence Thompson
BARBAROSSA: JUNE–DECEMBER 1941 28/11/1973
Hitler attempts to conquer Russia.
p/sc Peter Batty
BANZAI!: JAPAN 1931–1942 5/12/1973
The Japanese covet the wealth of South East Asia, the oil and rubber to fuel their unending war with China. They hope for easy victories over Imperial powers Britain and Holland, weakened by their wars in Europe. The Japanese attack the USA at Pearl Harbor; Malaya, Philippines and Singapore fall to their armies.
p/sc Peter Batty
ON OUR WAY: USA: DECEMBER 1941–AUGUST 1942 12/12/1973
America joins the war.
p/sc Peter Batty
DESERT 1940–1943 19/12/1973
The battle at El Alamein – a British victory in Egypt.
p/sc Peter Batty
STALINGRAD: JUNE 1942 – FEBRUARY 1943 2/1/1974
The battle for Stalingrad; includes film taken by a German soldier.
d Hugh Raggett; *sc* Jerome Kuehl
WOLF PACK: U-BOATS IN THE NORTH ATLANTIC 1939–1943 9/1/1974
German attacks by U-boats on British and Allied ships.
p Ted Childs; *sc* J.P.W. Mallalieu
RED STAR: SOVIET UNION, 1941–1943 16/1/1974
The two-year battle between Russia and Germany on Russian soil.
p Martin Smith; *sc* Neal Ascherson
WHIRLWIND: BOMBING GERMANY, SEPTEMBER 1939–APRIL 1944 23/1/1974
Bomber Command raids on Germany described by Sir Arthur 'Bomber' Harris who directed them.
p Ted Childs; *sc* Charles Douglas-Home
TOUGH OLD GUT: ITALY, NOVEMBER 1942 – JUNE 1944 30/1/1974
The two-year fight for Italy.
p Ben Shephard; *sc* David Wheeler
IT'S A LOVELY DAY TOMORROW: BURMA 1942–1944 6/2/1974
The British Army learns to master the jungle and fights the Japanese on the borders of India.
p John Pett; *sc* John Williams
HOME FIRES: BRITAIN 1940–1944 13/2/1974
British people during World War II become used to the ARP, gas masks, 'Dig for Victory', 'ITMA', and The Land Army.
p Phillip Whitehead; *sc* Angus Calder
INSIDE THE REICH: GERMANY 1940–1944 20/2/1974
The fear of defeat by the German people after the failure of the Blitzkrieg against Russia, and the devastation of German cities by bombs.
p Phillip Whitehead; *sc* Neal Ascherson
MORNING: JUNE–AUGUST 1944 27/2/1974
D-Day. The assembling of the invasion fleet.
p John Pett; *sc* John Williams

OCCUPATION: HOLLAND 1940–1944 13/3/1974
Occupied Holland and its effect on the invaded people.
p Michael Darlow; *sc* Charles Bloomberg
PINCERS: AUGUST 1944–MARCH 1945 20/3/1974
Events leading up to the defeat of the Germans.
p/sc Peter Batty
GENOCIDE: 1941–1945 27/3/1974
Survivors of Auschwitz and S.S. men talk about their experience of the genocide perpetrated by the Nazis upon Jews.
p Michael Darlow; *sc* Charles Bloomberg
NEMESIS: GERMANY FEBRUARY–MAY 1945 3/4/1974
Hitler's suicide.
p Martin Smith; *sc* Stuart Hood
JAPAN: 1941–1945 10/4/1974
p Hugh Raggett; *sc* Courtney Browne
PACIFIC: FEBRUARY 1942 – JULY 1945 17/4/1974
The American-Japanese war.
p John Pett; *sc* David Wheeler
The BOMB: FEBRUARY – SEPTEMBER 1945 24/4/1974
The B29 bomber 'Enola Gay' dropped the atomic bomb on Hiroshima on August 6, 1945. The pilot, Col. Paul Tibbetts, talks about the mission.
p/sc David Elstein
RECKONING: 1945...AND AFTER 1/5/1974
The end of the War, and the beginning of the Cold War.
p/sc Jerome Kuehl
REMEMBER 8/5/1974
Final programme remembers the millions of men and women who died during World War II.
p/sc Jeremy Isaacs

The WORLD CUP FINAL 1966
(BBC 30/7/1966)
England v. West Germany at Wembley.
exec.p Bryan Cowgill, Alan Chivers; *intro* David Coleman; *comm* Kenneth Wolstenholme

WORLD IN ACTION (Granada 1963–)
Current affairs programme. See also WORLD IN ACTION SPECIAL.
EAST GERMANY 21/1/1963
A report on the lives of families in the German Democratic Republic.
p Bill Grundy;
nar Derek Cooper, Wilfrid Thomas
TIBET 11/3/1963
A report from Tibet on the aftermath of the Chinese take-over.
nar Derek Cooper, Wilfrid Thomas
The GUNS 11/9/1963
The sale of arms to African states by Britain.
p Tim Hewat
LIVING IN THE SLUMS 22/10/1963
The living conditions of a family in a British slum area.
d Gordon Flemyng; *p* Tim Hewat
The PRIME MINISTER, SIR ALEC DOUGLAS-HOME 12/11/1963
The Prime Minister's family and their reactions to his new status.
p Tim Hewat
The SHADOWS 19/11/1963
Report on the politicians likely to make up Labour's front bench.
p Tim Hewat;
nar Derek Cooper, Wilfrid Thomas
DALLAS 3/12/1963
A report on Dallas and its inhabitants six days after the assassination of President John F. Kennedy.
exec.p Tim Hewat;
comm Derek Cooper, Wilfrid Thomas
PRESIDENT JOHNSON 10/12/1963
A profile of Lyndon B. Johnson on becoming President of the United States on the death of John F. Kennedy.
exec.p Tim Hewat;
nar Derek Cooper, Wilfrid Thomas
US IN UK 1964
Shows the growing influence of the United States on Britain from the Playboy Clubs to industrial matters.
exec.p Derek Granger

TRUTH ABOUT SPAIN 7/1/1964
Spain under Franco since the Spanish Civil War.
Franco's home near Madrid; Manuel Fraga,
Minister of Information and Tourism,
interviewed about political prisoners; interview
with Alberto Ullastres, Minister of Commerce,
on the booming tourist trade.
nar Derek Cooper, Wilfrid Thomas
LAKONIA – THE FACTS 14/1/1964
An investigation into the sinking of the Greek
liner 'Lakonia'.
nar Derek Cooper, Wilfrid Thomas
The POWER OF THE NANNY 11/2/1964
The work and influence of nannies.
CYPRUS 18/2/1964
SEVEN UP! 5/5/1964
A group of seven-year-olds from different social
backgrounds exchange views and attitudes about
the country today. See also SEVEN PLUS
SEVEN (1970) and TWENTY ONE UP (1977).
p Paul Almond; *comm* Douglas Keay
The STORY OF THE SUN 15/9/1964
The launching of 'The Sun' newspaper; with
Hugh Cudlipp.
p Alex Valentine;
nar Derek Cooper, Wilfrid Thomas
VIETNAM 3/11/1964
The history and people of Vietnam and the
effects of American involvement, with Senator
Barry Goldwater, Robert McNamara, Senator
Wayne Morse, and Lord Avon.
p Mike Hodges
SMETHWICK 17/11/1964
Racial problems in Britain.
STATE OF THE UNIONS 1/12/1964
Compares the trade union system of Britain with
that of the United States. Examines the
membership, structure and background of the
giant United Auto Workers of America, and its
British counterpart, the 22 separate trade unions
which represent the British car industry.
p Mike Hodges, Brian Winston
LABOUR PARTY CONFERENCE 1964 15/12/1964
Report from the second day of the Labour
Party's conference in Brighton 12–13th
December 1964.
p Alex Valentine;
comm Derek Cooper, Wilfrid Thomas
The ENGLISH DISEASE 1965
The causes, symptoms, results and treatment of
bronchitis in Britain.
d Alex Valentine
The NIGHT DRIVERS 2/3/1965
The work of long distance lorry drivers.
The OTHER WORLD 29/6/1965
A report on spiritualism and extra-sensory
perception (ESP).
DUKES 6/7/1965
The different ways of life of the Dukes of Atholl,
Bedford, Grafton and Leinster.
p David Plowright
The £.S.D. OF MPH 13/7/1965
Portrait of the champion racing driver Jim Clark
and an investigation of the relevance of motor
sport development to the ordinary motorist.
d/p Leslie Woodhead
TIME OFF 1966
Increased leisure because of more automation
and how it is changing peoples lives.
SOME GRAINS OF TRUTH 10/7/1967
The black market importation of marijuana and
heroin from ships in port in Liverpool.
p Leslie Woodhead, David Plowright
A DUEL IN THE SUN 17/7/1967
A report on Anguilla, with Robert Bradshaw
and Sir Frederick Phillips.
p Brian Armstrong, Russell Spurr
MICK JAGGER 31/7/1967
Mick Jagger is interviewed by William Rees-
Mogg, the Bishop of Woolwich, Dr. John
Robinson, Father Thomas Corbishley, and Lord
Stow Hill.
p John Sheppard, Leslie Woodhead, John Birt
The THIRD WORLD 7/8/1967
A report on Stokeley Carmichael's visit to
England, with Mark Bonham-Carter.
p Jo Durden-Smith
SCIENTOLOGY 14/8/1967
Report on scientology from Saint Hill Manor,
Sussex, the world headquarters of the
movement.
p Jo Durden-Smith, Charlie Nairn

COLONELS' DEMOCRACY 21/8/1967
Interviews with Brigadier Stylanios Patakos and
Colonel George Papadopolous following the
military coup in Greece which brought them into
power.
p Jo Durden-Smith, Russell Spurr
BORN LOSERS 18/9/1967
The story of a Manchester family with nine
children and how they exist on £13 a week dole
money.
p Michael Murphy
SMITH'S BACK DOOR 2/10/1967
An examination of sanctions-busting in
Rhodesia.
p Leslie Woodhead, Jeremy Wallington
ISLAND UNDER ARMS 16/10/1967
A report on the situation in Cyprus; with
Archbishop Makarios and the leader of the
Turkish community, Dr Fazil Kutchuk.
p Jo Durden-Smith
KING OF KINGS 23/10/1967
A report from Iran three days before Queen
Farah was crowned Empress; includes interviews
with the Queen and the Shah.
p Brian Armstrong, Ingrid Floering
WE KNOW WHAT WE SAW 30/10/1967
Examines the question of whether Unidentified
Flying Objects (UFOs) exist and investigates the
attitudes of American scientists to the
phenomenon.
p John Mcdonald
EAST OF ADEN 27/11/1967
The British military presence in Bahrain,
Sharjah and Abu Dhabi, and the reasons behind
it.
p Ingrid Floering, Brian Armstrong
MOTHERS IN ACTION 4/12/1967
Unmarried mothers discuss their problems with
Quintin Hogg, MP.
d Leslie Woodhead;
p Ingrid Floering, Brian Armstrong
END OF A REVOLUTION 11/12/1967
A report on the death of Che Guevara, killed
whilst fighting a guerilla war in Bolivia, and the
trial of French journalist Regis Debray.
p Brian Moser
An OUTLAW'S LIFE 1/1/1968
An investigation into the problems of Britain's
gypsies.
p Charlie Nairn
ALAS POOR HIPPIES, LOVE IS DEAD 15/1/1968
A record of the development of hippy drug
addicts in the USA after the introduction of new
drugs.
p John MacDonald
The TWELVE YEAR ENGAGEMENT 5/2/1968
The lives of teenagers who enlist with the armed
forces for 12–year engagements.
p Charlie Nairn
DEATH BY INSTALMENTS 12/2/1968
A report on drug addiction in Britain. Minister
of Health, Kenneth Robinson, is interviewed
about proposed legislation.
p Mike Murphy
CAUGHT FOR A BABY 19/2/1968
Family planning for the unmarried, following the
National Health Family Planning Act of 1967.
d John Ponsford; *p* Russell Spurr
COLD WAR, WARM WATER 26/2/1968
A report on the current threatening presence of
Russian shipping in the Mediterranean, from the
US Sixth Fleet attack carrier Shangri-La.
p Leslie Woodhead, Brian Amstrong
RICHARD NIXON'S LAST HURRAH 11/3/1968
A report on the presidential election campaign
of Richard Nixon.
p John MacDonald
GROSVENOR SQUARE DEMONSTRATION
18/3/1968
A report on the violence at the anti-Vietnam war
demonstration outside the American Embassy in
London's Grosvenor Square.
exec.p David Plowright
WAKE UP AND WORK TOGETHER 15/4/1968
Belize facing a take-over bid by neighbouring
Guatemala.
p Brian Moser
The FLAME IN SPAIN 29/4/1968
A record of social conditions in contemporary
Spain and interviews with opponents of Franco's
regime.
p Charlie Nairn, Michael Wall

STAGE FOR A REVOLUTION 13/5/1968
Student demonstration in Berlin on May 1, 1968,
and events leading up to it. Interviews with
students and leaders of student movements
p Jo Durden-Smith
WARD F.13 20/5/1968
The appalling conditions in a geriatric wing of a
hospital and how present care for the aged
results from general lack of concern.
p David Plowright, Charlie Nairn
The GUINEA PIGS 17/6/1968
An experiment carried out by Wiltshire
education committee in which secondary and
grammar school boys were admitted to
Marlborough College public school.
p Michael Beckham
The BOTTOM OF THE LIST 8/7/1968
A report on the housing and educational
problems facing coloured immigrants in
Wolverhampton and an investigation of colour
prejudice in the allocation of council housing.
p Ingrid Floering
SPIES FOR HIRE 16/9/1968
An exposé of the industrial espionage business.
Hidden cameras record the moves of spies as
they bug a telephone and photograph secret
blueprints in a north London electronic factory.
d Michael Beckham
NEW DRUGS, SAME NEEDLE 7/10/1968
Methedrine has now been banned: looks at the
problem of 'Methheads,' the disastrous effects of
the drug and the addicts' search for an
alternative.
p Dennis Woolf
NASSER'S FORTIFIED DITCH 11/11/1968
Egyptian defences on the Suez canal.
p Ingrid Floering
A CITY STUMBLES 25/11/1968
An analysis of the troubles and the difficulties of
administration in New York.
p Russell Spurr
ALL CHANGE AT NEWRY 20/1/1969
An examination of the causes of the violence
which occurred in Newry, Northern Ireland,
during a civil rights march in January 1969.
p Russell Spurr, Michael Ryan, Charlie Nairn
A NEW SCHOOL OF THOUGHT 27/1/1969
The movement by a group of older pupils at
Bedales school for more self-government, and
the abolition of uniform and corporal
punishment.
p Michael Beckham
DEATH OF A STUDENT 3/2/1969
Events in Prague following the suicide and
funeral of Jan Palach.
p Brian Armstrong
UNTRIED, INSIDE 8/9/1969
Investigates the remand system in Britain, under
which unconvicted prisoners can be held in jail,
often without compensation.
p Michael Ryan
PUT TO THE TEST 13/10/1969
The work of the mobile health unit, providing
examination and screening facilities in a London
street.
p Vanya Kewley
STATE OF THE LION 20/10/1969
An examination of the current state of Ethiopia.
p John Sheppard
UNKNOWN SOLDIER 27/10/1969
A report on a special American military group
and interviews with members of the force.
p Michael Ryan
WEDNESDAY'S CHILDREN 15/12/1969
Seventeen teenagers in a British hospital are
suffering from muscular dystrophy. Reports on
the research being carried out to help these boys
and the other 20,000 sufferers from this disease.
p Brian Armstrong
The NANCECUKE DOSSIER 22/12/1969
Investigates the secrecy which surrounds the
British Chemical Research Establishment.
p Michael Ryan
COLD COMFORT 19/1/1970
Every year in Britain, 9,000 old people freeze to
death in their own homes. Investigates the
causes and results of hypothermia, the low body-
temperature condition that can kill.
p Richard Martin

ST. MUNGO'S PEOPLE 23/2/1970
An investigation into the problem of derelicts and outcasts of both sexes who sleep rough every night.
p Denis Mitchell
The STATE OF DENMARK 23/3/1970
A study of how Denmark feels about the abolition of laws that cover pornography.
p Charles Denton
IAN PAISLEY 21/4/1970
A profile of Protestant leader Ian Paisley, who is seen addressing his congregation at the Martyrs Memorial Free Presbyterian Church in Belfast and campaigning during elections in the Bannside constituency.
p David Boulton, Denis Mitchell
QUENTIN CRISP 6/7/1970
An interview with author Quentin Crisp.
p Denis Mitchell
ACT OF GOD 20/7/1970
The effects of the earthquake in Peru and the country's recovery programme.
p Leslie Woodhead, Brian Moser
EVERYBODY'S CHILDREN 21/9/1970
A drama project by fourth formers at Farnworth Comprehensive school, Lancashire, based on the idea of 'Freedom'. Extracts from the performance are shown as well as interviews with the teacher involved.
d David Boulton
The QUIET MUTINY 28/9/1970
John Pilger reports from Vietnam on the disaffection of some of the frontline American soldiers.
p Charles Denton, John Pilger
THEY'RE ONLY HUMAN BEINGS LIKE EVERYBODY ELSE 19/10/1970
Investigates the treatment of the physically disabled in Britain and in particular the claim that they are segregated from the rest of society.
d/p Su Dalgleish
GOODBYE MR SMITH? 9/11/1970
Peter Le Marchant reports from Rhodesia on the workings of the Land Tenure Act. Includes interviews with Ian Smith, Bishop La Monte, Lance Smith and Sir Robert Tredgold.
p Michael Ryan, Peter Le Marchant
The DUMPING GROUNDS 21/12/1970
Living conditions in the African homelands of South Africa.
d/sc John Shepherd; p Leslie Woodhead;
rep Stephen Clarke
SOUTH OF THE BORDER 1971
Attitudes in Eire to the IRA and the situation in Ulster
p David Boulton
The VILLAGE THAT QUIT 25/1/1971
An attempt by the villagers of Longnor, Staffordshire, to give up cigarette smoking over a period of one week. See also the programme tx 6/9/1971.
d Michael Ryan
The MONDAY CLUB 1/2/1971
The activities of the 'Monday Club' (a right wing ginger group). Contains samples of speeches by several prominent members, which deal with South Africa, race relations and dangers of communism.
d John Shepherd
The BREAKING POINT 8/2/1971
A follow-up to two reports transmitted earlier both examining apartheid discrimination in Southern Africa.
p Leslie Woodhead, Stephen Clarke
SQUARE ONE 15/2/1971
The history of the Republican struggle to unite Ireland and the present conflict in Ulster.
p David Boulton
The TRUANTS 8/3/1971
Truancy in Britain. See also updated programme tx 1/11/1976.
p Dennis Woolf
SAILORS' JAIL 26/4/1971
The Royal Navy's detention quarters at Portsmouth.
p Vanya Kewley
The TANZAM RAILWAY 10/5/1971
A report on the construction of the railway between Kpiri Mposhi in Zambia and Dar es-Salaam in Tanzania, and the involvement of China in the project.
p John Sheppard

CONVERSATION WITH A WORKING MAN 7/6/1971
John Pilger talks to a dye worker about his life as a trade unionist in a poorly paid industry and about his aspirations.
p Michael Beckham
The VILLAGE THAT QUIT, WELL NOT EXACTLY 6/9/1971
A visit to the village of Longnor, Staffordshire, six months after a week-long no smoking experiment. Update to the programme tx 25/1/1971.
p Michael Ryan
SOUNDS OF THE CLYDE 13/9/1971
A report on the situation at the Upper Clyde shipyard and the problems of the British shipbuilding industry.
p Gus MacDonald
DOES AN M.P. HAVE THE RIGHT? 25/10/1971
The difference of opinion between Labour MP Dick Taverne and his constituency party over the question of British membership of the EEC.
d Dennis Woolf;
p John Birt, Brian Lapping
The MOST WIDELY USED DRUG IN THE WORLD 15/11/1971
The problems caused by the ready availability of drugs in the home.
p Dennis Woolf; with Alastair G. MacGregor
The BACKSEAT GENERALS 29/11/1971
The backing given to Meo tribesmen by the Central Intelligence Agency to fight against the communist forces in Laos.
p Leslie Woodhead, Stephen Clarke
WORKING THE LAND 10/1/1972
A farm worker's day on a farm in Suffolk and the financial problems faced by agricultural labourers.
p Michael Grigsby
WAITING FOR THE PACKAGE 20/3/1972
Attitudes in Ulster to the British Government's proposals for direct rule, with Glen Barr, William Craig and Billy Hull.
p Richard Creasey, Stephen Clarke
The LUMP 27/3/1972
A dispute between management, union and workers at a Birmingham building site over the operation of the 'lump' system, the hiring of non-union, self-employed workers by sub-contractors.
p David Hart
HET DORP 10/4/1972
A report on Het Dorp, a village in Holland built for and run by handicapped persons.
p Leslie Woodhead
The CONTAINER ROW 1/5/1972
Investigation into the dispute where Liverpool dockers refused to handle containerised cargo.
p David Hart
The RUNCORN EXPERIMENT 22/5/1972
A government-sponsored experiment to provide free contraception and vasectomies in Runcorn, Cheshire. Appearing in the programme are Baroness Birk and Sir John Peel.
p John Slater
The PROTESTANT SUCCESSION 12/6/1972
Protestant opinion in Ulster with mass rallies addressed by Ian Paisley, Enoch Powell and William Craig. Includes interviews with Brian Faulkner and Billy Hull.
p David Boulton, Richard Martin
The DOCKS DISPUTE 19/6/1972
The dispute at London docks over containerised cargo.
p David Hart
IN SEARCH OF GUSTY SPENCE 10/7/1972
An interview with Gusty Spence, Irish protestant terrorist, convicted of murder and kidnapped while on parole.
p Richard Martin, David Boulton
HOW TO STEAL A PARTY 18/7/1972
A report on the Democratic Party convention in Miami, at which George McGovern won the nomination as presidential candidate.
p Leslie Woodhead, David Hart
CAUGHT IN THE ACT 7/8/1972
The refusal of Camden Council to implement the Housing Finance (Fair Rents) Act of 1972. Includes film of the council meeting at which the implementation of the Act was rejected.
p David Boulton

SEE FOR YOURSELF! 11/9/1972
A shop steward from Smithfield opposed to further immigration is taken to Uganda to witness the plight of the Asian community. He talks to Africans and to the Asians who want to go to Britain.
p David Boulton
A QUESTION OF TORTURE 25/9/1972
A report on the methods used to interrogate internees in Ulster.
p Stephen Clarke
The CASE OF LEOPOLD TREPPER – MASTER SPY 20/11/1972
The Soviet espionage network organised by Leopold Trepper in German-occupied Europe during World War II.
p Stephen Clarke
A DAY IN THE LIFE OF KEVIN DONNELLON 4/12/1972
The problems faced by a thalidomide child.
p Allan Segal
The ANGRY BRIGADE 7/12/1972
The activities of the anarchist group known as the 'Angry Brigade' as revealed in interviews with two members of the group, Anna Mendelson and Hilary Creek, found guilty in the Angry Brigade trial.
p Michael Ryan
CONVERSATIONS WITH A GAY LIBERAL 5/3/1973
A Durham Councillor, Sam Green, talks about his homosexuality.
d Brian Blake
The PROTESTANT SUCCESSION NO. 2 26/3/1973
The struggle between Brian Faulkner, Ian Paisley and William Craig for the leadership of Ulster's protestants, following the publication of the Government's White Paper of March 20th.
p David Boulton
The COST OF A CUP OF TEA 24/9/1973
Report on conditions under which workers live on British-owned tea plantations in Ceylon (Sri Lanka). See also the updated programme tx 17/3/1975.
p David Hart
HER MAJESTY'S OPPOSITION 5/11/1973
A portrait of anti-monarchist MP Willie Hamilton.
p Brian Blake
A POLITICAL JOURNEY: PART I 11/2/1974
Sir John Foster and Richard Crossman discuss their days in the House of Commons and plan how they will report the election for the programme.
p David Boulton, Leslie Woodhead
A POLITICAL JOURNEY: PART II 18/2/1974
Richard Crossman and Sir John Foster follow the general election campaigns of the party leaders Edward Heath, Harold Wilson, and Jeremy Thorpe, and talk to miners and their families.
p Leslie Woodhead, David Boulton
A POLITICAL JOURNEY: PART III 25/2/1974
Sir John Foster and Richard Crossman continue their report on the election by visiting the north of England and Scotland and returning to a lunch in Oxfordshire.
p Leslie Woodhead, David Boulton
HAROLD WILSON 8/4/1974
An interview with Prime Minster, Harold Wilson.
The BEN HUNTER WAY 13/5/1974
The difficulties of finding foster parents for many of the children in care in Britain. Californian Ben Hunter demonstrates his own method of offering children for adoption on television.
p Sue Woodford
The DAY THE TORTURE STOPPED 20/5/1974
A report on the use of torture by the recently overthrown dictatorship in Portugal.
p Stephen Clarke, David Hart
The GRANADA 500 7/10/1974
Harold Wilson, Edward Heath and Jeremy Thorpe answer questions from an invited audience during the run-up to the General Election of October 1974. Michael Scott acts as chairman.
BIRTH OF A NATION 21/10/1974
A report on the situation in Mozambique following the victory of the Frelimo forces.
p Michael Beckham

WORLD IN ACTION *cont.*

ON THE TRAIL OF THE TORTURERS 4/11/1974
A report on the torture of political opponents by the Greek junta.
p Michael Ryan
The TRIALS IN ZANZIBAR 18/11/1974
The political situation in Zanzibar; includes a videotape recording of a treason trial in which the prosecution admit that admissions were obtained under torture. Interviews are conducted with Attorney-General Wolf Dourado and Aboud Jumbe.
p Allan Segal, Stephen Clarke
WHO RUNS ULSTER? 25/11/1974
A week in the life of Northern Ireland Secretary of State, Merlyn Rees.
p Linda MacDougall
WHY I WANT TO BE LEADER: BY MARGARET THATCHER 3/2/1975
On the eve of the first ballot for the Tory Party leadership, discusses the character and career of Margaret Thatcher, one of the principal contenders in the leadership struggle. Includes an interview with Mrs Thatcher
p Linda MacDougall
WANTED: A HOME OF THEIR OWN 10/2/1975
Reports on what happened to four children offered for adoption in an earlier programme The BEN HUNTER WAY (*tx* 13/5/1974), and shows three more children available for adoption or fostering.
p Sue Woodford
The SIEGE OF PHNOM PENH 24/2/1975
A report from Phnom Penh, capital city of Cambodia, shot in February 1975 when the city was under siege by the Khmer Rouge, Cambodia's communist guerrilla army.
p Michael Beckham
TEA: THE DEADLY COST 17/3/1975
A follow-up to the programme The COST OF A CUP OF TEA (*tx* 24/9/1973) which revisits the plantation of Ceylon to see whether conditions have improved for the workers. They were found to be no better off than before, some facing starvation and death.
p David Hart
HERE IS THE NEWS 5/5/1975
The first day of production of the Scottish Daily News, a co-operatively produced national paper, and a visit by Tony Benn.
p Steve Morrison
A BUS ROUND THE MARKET 27/5/1975
Michael Scott takes a busload of Britons on a tour of Bruges, Brussels, Frankfurt, Mannheim, Strasbourg and Milan in the company of Lord George-Brown and Clive Jenkins, to look at aspects of the EEC.
p Leslie Woodhead; *rep* Michael Scott
A BUS ROUND THE MARKET 3/6/1975
Michael Scott takes a busload of Britons from Italy to France, in the company of Lord George-Brown and Clive Jenkins, to look at aspects of the EEC.
p Leslie Woodhead; *rep* Michael Scott
JOBLESS IN BATLEY 6/10/1975
Unemployment in Batley.
p Allan Segal
CHRYSLER AND THE CABINET: HOW THE DEAL WAS DONE 9/2/1976
Six leading political journalists present views involved in the Chrysler debate.
d Baz Taylor; *p* Brian Lapping
A SCHOOL OF THOUGHT 11/10/1976
The operation of a progressive comprehensive school, Countesthorpe College, and the reactions of parents, pupils and teachers to the school.
d Steve Morrison
YESTERDAY'S TRUANTS 1/11/1976
Follow-up report on The TRUANTS (8/3/1971).
d Brian Blake
The NATIONAL PARTY 22/11/1976
The growth and practises of the National Party in Blackburn.
d Sue Woodford
The LAWBREAKERS 6/12/1976
The treatment by South African police of schoolchildren in black township schools.
d Michael Ryan; David Hart

STARTING ON THE DOLE 27/6/1977
Report from Liverpool on teenage unemployment. Interviews with school-leavers who are unemployed and those on Job Creation projects.
d Simon Albury
A REPORT FROM SIEGE CITY 1978
Presents the views of Bernard Nossiter, financial reporter on the Washington Post on Britain's present economic situation, as he visits the port of Hull during the strike by lorry drivers.
d Simon Albury
THATCHER INTERVIEW 30/1/1978
An interview with Margaret Thatcher as she outlines her Party's policies.
d Eric Harrison; *interv* Gordon Burns
BLACK TO FRONT 24/4/1978
Report on race relations in Brixton immediately following the by-election there.
d/p Linda MacDougall
LIABLE TO PROSECUTION 31/7/1978
An investigation of the evidence that Shell and BP had broken sanctions by supplying oil to Rhodesia.
rep Michael Gillard
NO USEFUL PURPOSE WOULD BE SERVED 7/8/1978
Investigation into the British Government's knowledge of oil sanctions being broken by British firms; includes an interview with Lord Thomson.
d Stephen Clarke, Chris Curling;
rep Michael Gillard
KIDS UNITED 27/11/1978
Problems of children in care and the growing protest movement to demand more consultation in running their lives.
d Sue Woodford
A TALE OF TWO CITIES 26/3/1979
Steel workers facing redundancy.
d Michael Ryan
BANGED UP 2/4/1979
A report on the overcrowded conditions in Strangeways Prison.
d John Blake
The LUCK OF THE IRISH 11/6/1979
The Common Agricultural Policy and the prosperity it has brought to Irish farmers.
d Michael Beckham
The OTHER PROFESSIONALS 12/7/1979
The British Army's assessment of the Provisional IRA.
d Stephen Clarke

WORLD IN ACTION SPECIAL
(Granada 1973–)
Current affairs programme. See also WORLD IN ACTION.
The RISE AND FALL OF JOHN L. POULSON 30/4/1973
The bankruptcy proceedings involving architect John Poulson; an investigation into his dealings with local councillors and civil servants.
p Brian Blake
INSIDE AMIN'S TERROR MACHINE 13/6/1979
A report on Idi Amin's State Research Centre, and interviews with survivors of Amin's regime.
d/p Michael Ryan

The WORLD IS OURS (BBC 1954–56)
Intermittent documentary series.
The WAITING PEOPLE 8/10/1954
The problem of displaced persons and refugees in Europe and the Middle East. The relief work undertaken by the United Nations.
d Norman Swallow
The FORGOTTEN INDIANS 28/11/1956
The efforts of the International Labour Organization (ILO) to help the Indians of Peru and Bolivia to improve their standard of living through education and new methods of collective farming.
d Anthony De Lotbinière

The WORLD OF BOB HOPE (BBC 8/10/1970)
Bob Hope's annual 100,000 mile tour of America.
p Denis Pitts;
with Cary Grant, Gregory Peck, David Janssen, Jack Benny, Les Brown and his Band of Renown

A WORLD OF MY OWN (Tyne Tees 1969)
Interview series.
CATHERINE COOKSON 14/5/1969
JOHN BRAINE 28/5/1969
BASIL BUNTING 11/6/1969
EMANUEL SHINWELL MP 3/11/1969
DAME IRENE WARD 15/12/1969

The WORLD OF PAM AYRES
(LWT 2/9–25/11/1977)
Thirteen-part entertainment show, presented by poet Pam Ayres.
ARTHUR MULLARD 7/10/1977
d/p Keith Beckett

The WORLD OF TELEVISION
(Yorkshire TV 4/6–9/7/1975)
Six-part documentary series looking at the medium of television through interviews with executives, producers, performers and viewers.
The BEAUTIFUL BUSINESS 4/6/1975
The television industry in Hollywood.
p/sc Peter Batty; *nar* Nigel Pegram

The WORLD TOMORROW
(Granada 1966–67)
Documentary and current affairs series.
DROUGHT 11/1/1966
Spraying clouds with chemicals; desalination plants in California and Kuwait; plans to build a dam in Wales (Clywedog) and channel water across the Chilterns into the Thames.
d Eric Harrison;
p Dietrich Koch, Russell Spurr
TRAINS – HIGH SPEED TRAVEL 29/3/1966
d Eric Harrison
The MOST AMAZING HUNT EVER KNOWN 19/4/1966
Operation of the American Government to fish an H-bomb off the Mediterranean seabed in the Bay of Palomares.
d Eric Harrison
ASTRONAUTS' HEALTH 17/5/1966
Investigations into the effects of space travel on the health of the astronauts.
d Peter Heinze, Russell Spurr, John MacDonald
The BLACK OASIS 30/9/1966
A report from Basutoland shortly before it became the independent state of Lesotho on October 4th, 1966.
p David Plowright;
rep Bill Grundy, Chris Kelly
RUNNING FOR GOVERNOR 4/11/1966
Ronald Reagan during his campaign for election as Governor of California; includes film of Democratic Governor Edmund G. 'Pat' Brown, and Bob Kline, Paul Adams, Julian Foster, and Gene Barry.
p David Plowright
IT'S A HAPPENING, A HAPPENING, A HAPPENING 18/11/1966
Holland's provos and their methods of drawing attention to social problems.
p David Plowright
INDONESIA 1967
The recent history and future prospects of the collection of over 3,000 islands and islets that comprises this South-East Asian republic.
p Russell Spurr
The SILENT WAR 6/1/1967
The concern felt by the scientific community at developments in biological and chemical warfare. Eric Heddon, Director of the Chemical Defence Establishment, is interviewed.
p David Plowright;
comm Chris Kelly, Bill Grundy
A BIRD CALLED HARMONY 13/1/1967
A report on the progress of the Concorde aircraft and the risks of supersonic flight.
p David Plowright
SOUND OR MUSIC? 10/2/1967
A report on new recording techniques. Among those appearing are: The Hollies, George Martin, Tristram Carey, Sir Michael Tippett, Yehudi Menuhin, Daphne Oram and Roger Smalley.
p David Plowright

A NEW KIND OF MATCH 10/3/1967
A survey of housing conditions and public health services for Pakistanis in Bradford. The schooling provided for Pakistani children.
p David Plowright

The WORLD TONIGHT (Granada 1965)
Current affairs series.
SINGAPORE – UNCERTAIN OUTPOST 1965
A report on the political situation in Singapore with Lee Siew Choh, Tunku Abdul Rahman, Sir John Frandy and Lee Kuan Yew.
p Russell Spurr
The LUNATIC OLYMPICS 19/10/1965
A look at the 'test Olympics' at Mexico City to see if altitude will be a problem in the forthcoming Olympic Games.
d Eric Harrison;
p Dietrich Koch, Russell Spurr, Peter Heinze, John MacDonald, John Maher, Hugh Pitt, Joan Harrison
The WORD WAR 9/11/1965
The uses and influence of international broadcasting.
d Eric Harrison
FARMING 16/11/1965
New methods of farming and breeding being used in Britain, Japan, the USA and Kenya.
d Eric Harrison
MAFIA 30/11/1965
Reports from Italy, the USA and Australia assessing the strength of the Mafia.
d Eric Harrison

WORLDWIDE (BBC 1974–77)
Documentary series on television around the world.
CUBA: THE PEOPLE'S TELEVISION 3/11/1975
Television programming in Cuba.
p Maryse Addison; *intro* Frank Gillard
TELEVISION IN BLACK AFRICA: PART 1 14/12/1976
Television in Nigeria, Ivory Coast, Zaire, Zanzibar and Kenya; how governments use television and priorities for news and information; includes film of total eclipse of the sun seen in Zanzibar
p Maryse Addison; *rep* Richard Kershaw
TELEVISION IN BLACK AFRICA: PART 2 4/1/1977
How television is being used to educate and entertain in Nigeria, Zaire, Zanzibar and Kenya.
p Maryse Addison; *rep* Richard Kershaw
TOP VALUE TELEVISION 19/4/1977
Portrait of TVTV, Top Value Television, an American fringe video organisation who use small portable equipment to make documentaries.
p Jack Saltman; *pres* Frank Gillard

WORZEL GUMMIDGE (Southern TV 1978–81)
Series for children about the adventures of the eponymous scarecrow and his friends.
The SCARECROW HOP 8/4/1979
d James Hill;
sc Keith Waterhouse, Willis Hall
lp Jon Pertwee; Una Stubbs; Joan Sims; Charlotte Coleman; Jeremy Austin; Mike Berry; Michael Ripper; Norman Mitchell; Norman Bird; Megs Jenkins; Denis Gilmore; Bill Pertwee; Geoffrey Bayldon

WRITE ON! (BBC 17/10–19/12/1976)
Ten-part series in which members of the public air their views.
WRITE ON! 28/11/1976

WUTHERING HEIGHTS (BBC 11/5/1962)
p Rudolph Cartier; *auth* Emily Brontë
lp Claire Bloom; Keith Michell; Ronald Howard; Frank Crawshaw; June Thorburn; Jean Anderson; Horace Sequeira; Patrick Troughton; David McCallum; Kenneth Edwards; Peter Augustine; Desmond Cullum-Jones

WUTHERING HEIGHTS
(BBC 24/9–22/10/1978)
d Peter Hammond; *p* Jonathan Powell;
auth Emily Brontë
regulars Ken Hutchison; Cathryn Harrison; David Wilkinson; Brian Wilde; Pat Heywood; John Duttine; Kay Adshead

EPISODE 1 24/9/1978
sc Hugh Leonard
lp Richard Kay; John Collin; Patricia Healey; Paul Dawkins; Maggie Wilkinson; Dennis Burgess; Wendy Williams; Barry Hart
EPISODE 2 1/10/1978
sc David Snodin
lp Maggie Wilkinson; Dennis Burgess; Wendy Williams; Judith Byfield; John Golightly; David Robb; Paul Dawkins; Caroline Langrishe
EPISODE 3 8/10/1978
sc David Snodin
lp David Robb; Caroline Langrishe; Kate David; John Golightly; Simon Massey
EPISODE 4 15/10/1978
sc David Snodin
lp David Robb; Caroline Langrishe; John Golightly; Norman Rutherford; Barbara Keogh; Andrew Burleigh

Y

YANCY DERRINGER
(US Derringer Productions 1958–59)
The story of an ex-Confederate soldier in New Orleans after the American Civil War.
The LOUISIANA DUDE 1959
d William F. Claxton;
exec.p Don W. Sharpe, Warren Lewis;
sc Coles Trapnell
lp Jock Mahoney; Kevin Hagen; X Brands; Hillary Brooke; John Cliff; Harry Swoger; Addison Richards; Steve Pendleton; James Anderson; Woodrow Chambliss; Booth Colman

YANKS GO HOME (Granada 1976–77)
Drama series about the arrival of the U.S. Air Force to Britain during World War II.
SOMEWHERE IN ENGLAND 22/11/1976
d/p Eric Prytherch; *sc* Michael Carter
lp Alan MacNaughtan; Bruce Boa; Stuart Damon; Meg Johnson; Catherine Neilson; Richard Oldfield; Norman Bird
OFF LIMITS 29/11/1976
d/p Eric Prytherch; *sc* John Stevenson
lp Alan MacNaughtan; Bruce Boa; Stuart Damon; Meg Johnson; Catherine Neilson; Richard Oldfield; Norman Bird

The YEAR OF KILLING (Granada 21/12/1971)
A report from East Pakistan on the effects of the floods and the civil war.
p Michael Beckham

YEAR OF OBSERVATION
(Rediffusion 16/5–11/7/1957)
Eight-part scientific survey series for schools.
A ROCKET REPORTS 27/6/1957
Redvers Kyle introduces a programme for schools about the principles and uses of the rocket. With Professor H.S.W. Massey and W.H. Stevens.
d John Frankau

YEAR ZERO: THE SILENT DEATH OF CAMBODIA (ATV 30/10/1979)
The first account by a Western television team of the Cambodian situation since the Vietnamese routed the Khmer Rouge regime.
d/p David Munro; *rep* John Pilger

YEAR OF CRISIS (US CBS 12/12/1964)
The 16th annual broadcast. CBS News reporters round the world appraise major international developments. Items discussed are: the possible waning of American influence in the world; and the growing concern by Americans about the Vietnamese crisis.
d Vern Diamond; *p* Av Westin;
rep Eric Serareid, Charles Collingwood, Marvin Kalb, Alexander Kendrick, Bernard Kalb, Daniel Schorr, Stuart Nevins

YEHUDI AND HEPHZIBAH MENUHIN
(BBC 17/1/1960)
Yehudi and Hephzibah Menuhin play Franck's Sonata in A for violin and piano.
pres Walter Todds

YEHUDI MENUHIN AND DAVID OISTRAKH
(BBC 23/9/1962)
Yehudi Menuhin and David Oistrakh in a performance with the Royal Philharmonic Orchestra of Bach's double violin concerto.
p Anthony Craxton; *intro* Kenneth Kendall

YES, IT'S THE CATHODE-RAY TUBE SHOW! (Rediffusion 11/2/1957)
Two comedy sketches featuring Peter Sellers.
d/p Kenneth Carter;
sc Michael Bentine; David Nettheim
with Michael Bentine

YESTERDAY'S GIRL (Granada 18/7/1973)
Drama. Shown as part of 'Late Night Theatre'.
d Peter L. Walker; *p* Dennis Woolf;
sc Adrian Henri
lp Geoffrey Evans; Mike Savage; Jacob Witkin; Adrian Henri; Tina Heath; Noreen Kershaw; Valerie Holliman; Christine Buckley

YESTERDAY'S WITNESS (BBC 1969–79)
Documentary series in which participants recollect various incidents from the past.
I HAVE FLOWN AND IT'S MARVELLOUS 24/3/1969
Pioneer aviators recall their first experiences of powered flight; includes Richard Atcherley, Alan Cobham, Thomas Sopwith, C.H. Watkins, Charles Dollfus, E.C. Gordon England and Cecil Pashley.
d Ian Keill; *p* Stephen Peet
TOLSTOY REMEMBERED BY HIS DAUGHTER 11/5/1970
Alexandra Tolstoy recalls the years she was Leo Tolstoy's secretary and confidant.
d Michael Rabiger; *p* Stephen Peet
The SHELL HOUSE RAID 20/8/1973
The RAF raid on the Gestapo headquarters in Copenhagen, March 21st 1945, recollected by Air Chief Marshall Sir Basil Embry and others who took part in the raid, and by members of the Danish resistance.
p Stephen Peet
A CAUSE WORTH FIGHTING FOR 27/8/1973
Members of the International Brigade recall their experiences in the Spanish Civil War. With Claud Cockburn, Bob Cooney, Tony Gilbert, Margaret Lesser, Will Paynter, Jim Prendergast, Bessie Wild, and Sam Wild.
d Michael Rabiger; *p* Stephen Peet;
nar James Cameron
FIVE YEARS' NIGHTMARE 3/9/1973
Gergana Taneva recalls her escape from the Gestapo in wartime Europe.
p Stephen Peet
The IOLAIRE DISASTER 10/9/1973
Survivors of the 'Iolaire' disaster of January 1st, 1919, in which two hundred men were drowned, describe how the admiralty yacht came to sink off Stornoway harbour.
p Stephen Peet
ENGLISH NURSE WITH THE TSAR'S ARMY 25/9/1974
Florence Farmborough recalls her experiences during World War I as a Red Cross nurse with the Russian armies.
d Christopher Cook
STAND UP AND BE COUNTED 23/7/1977
Some dramatic moments of dissent in Britain, including miners' protests during the General Stike of 1926, conscientious objectors in World War I, a protest against Church tithes by East Anglian farmers in the 1930s and East End protests against fascism.
p Stephen Peet; *nar* James Cameron

YOU AND ME (BBC 1974–92)
Story series for children.
p Barbara Parker;
pres Jacqui McDonald, Christopher Neil, Kim Goody, Malcolm McFee, Tony Hughes, Michael Maynard
TOUCH WOOD 17/5/1974
I SPY SOMETHING IN THE SKY 5/2/1976
SHOW ME...GOATS GALORE! 20/5/1976
WHAT SHAPE IS A SUN? 12/10/1976
SEE! 28/4/1977
1 26/1/1978
4 31/1/1978

YOU AND ME *cont.*

U 9/2/1978
HERBERT THE HANDYMAN FIXES THE SINK
6/2/1979
UP/DOWN 4/10/1979

YOU ARE THERE (US CBS 1953–57)
Historical events recreated in a dramatic way as news events.
DEATH OF SOCRATES 3/5/1953
Historical reconstruction of the death of Socrates (399 B.C.)
rep Walter Cronkite
lp Paul Newman; Robert Culp;
Shepperd Strudwick; John Cassavetes;
Philip Bourneuf; Richard Kiley; E.G. Marshall

YOU BET YOUR LIFE (US NBC 1/1/1956)
Quiz show compered by Groucho Marx.
d Robert Dwan, Bernie Smith

YOU CAN MAKE IT (Tyne Tees 1977–79)
Series designed to give children the opportunity to make films about subjects that interest them.
FERRETS 15/11/1977
The DAY THE PIT WHEEL STOPPED: SHOULD MINERS RETIRE AT FIFTY FIVE? 22/11/1977
SAVE THE WHALES 24/7/1978
YOU CAN MAKE IT 2/1/1979
YOU CAN MAKE IT 23/1/1979
YOU CAN MAKE IT 29/11/1979

The YOUNG MUSIC MAKERS
(Tyne Tees 1976)
A series featuring music performed by schoolchildren from the Tyne Tees region.
The YOUNG MUSIC MAKERS 26/8/1976
d Malcolm Dickinson; *p* Lisle Willis

The YOUNG TIGERS
(Rediffusion 8/6–3/8/1964)
Series of interviews with young people who have achieved wealth and fame before the age of thirty.
JOHN BLOOM 8/6/1964
Jack Hargreaves interviews John Bloom, washing-machine tycoon, about his life.
d Bill Morton
PETER HALL 27/7/1964
Jack Hargreaves interviews Peter Hall, director of the Royal Shakespeare Company, about his life and work.
d Bill Morton

YOUR CHILDREN'S PLAY (BBC 1956)
The TODDLER 9/10/1956
Phyllis Hostler talks about young children's play.
p Beryl Radley

YOUR LIFE IN THEIR HANDS
(BBC 1958–64)
A series of visits to various hospitals to observe medical practices and procedures.
HAMMERSMITH HOSPITAL 22/3/1961
Open heart surgery.
p Bill Duncalf

YOUR NATIONAL THEATRE
(LWT 21/8/1976)
The story of the National Theatre's development.
d/p Derek Bailey; *nar* Albert Finney;
with Laurence Olivier, Sybil Thorndike,
Peggy Ashcroft, Ralph Richardson,
John Gielgud, Peter Hall, Denys Lasdun

YOUR WITNESS (BBC 1967–73)
Discussion series.
EXISTENCE OF GOD 17/6/1967
John Mortimer and Quintin Hogg debate the existence of God, Mortimer being against the motion 'God does not exist' and Hogg being for.
CENSORSHIP 24/6/1967
A debate between Sir John Hobson and Ned Sherrin on censorship, under the motion 'That the Arts are too important to be left to the artists', both being allowed to call witnesses to substantiate their arguments. Sir John Hobson is for censorship, Ned Sherrin against.
d Michael Townson; *p* Anthony Smith;
pres Ludovic Kennedy

YOU'RE A LONG TIME DEAD
(BBC 17/7/1960)
Restaging of Elaine Morgan's play; originally presented under the billing of 'Summer Theatre'.
p Patrick Dromgoole; *sc* Elaine Morgan
lp Kenneth Griffith; Rachel Roberts;
Harry Locke; Gillian Vaughan; Michael Ellison;
Constance Chapman

YOU'RE ONLY YOUNG TWICE
(Yorkshire TV 1977–81)
Comedy series set in a superior residence for retired gentle-folk – 'Paradise Lodge'.
d/p Graeme Muir;
sc Pam Valentine, Michael Ashton
regulars Peggy Mount; Pat Coombs;
Diana King; Lally Bowers; Charmian May;
Georgina Moon
STRANGER IN PARADISE 6/9/1977
RAISING THE ROOF 13/9/1977
ONE OF LIFE'S WINNERS 20/9/1977
The BALL GAME 27/9/1977
The BIRTHDAY GIRL 4/10/1977
TOO MANY COOKS 18/10/1977
The BOX NUMBER 29/5/1978
The WINDFALL 5/6/1978
The COMMERCIAL 12/6/1978
The WHITE ELEPHANT 19/6/1978
The FOUNDLING 26/6/1978
The DEPUTY 3/7/1978
The SPRING FAYRE 10/7/1978
AND CISSIE MAKES THREE 31/5/1979
The DESPERATE HOURS 7/6/1979
WHO'S CALLING? 14/6/1979
USE OF BATH 21/6/1979
JOBS FOR THE GIRLS 28/6/1979
The OUTING 5/7/1979
CISSIE'S LAST CHANCE 12/7/1979

YURI GAGARIN (BBC 11/7/1961)
A press conference at the Russian Exhibition at Earls Court.

YURI GAGARIN (BBC 14/7/1961)
Richard Dimbleby interviews Yuri Gagarin at the Russian Exhibition at Earls Court.

Z

Z CARS (BBC 1962–78)
Police drama series set in the fictional north of England town, Newtown. Series developed from JACK AND KNAVES (1961), with later spin-off series SOFTLY, SOFTLY (1966–70), SOFTLY SOFTLY: TASK FORCE (1970–76) and BARLOW AT LARGE (1971–73).
regulars James Ellis; Brian Blessed;
Jeremy Kemp; Joseph Brady; Terence Edmond;
Colin Welland; Stratford Johns; Frank Windsor;
John Slater; Douglas Fielding; Derek Waring;
Ian Cullen
FOUR OF A KIND 2/1/1962
d John McGrath; *p* David E. Rose;
sc Troy Kennedy Martin
The BIG CATCH 30/1/1962
d Morris Barry; *p* David E. Rose;
sc Allan Prior
FRIDAY NIGHT 6/2/1962
d John McGrath; *p* David E. Rose;
sc Troy Kennedy Martin
PEOPLE'S PROPERTY 15/5/1962
d/sc John McGrath; *p* David E. Rose
INCIDENT REPORTED 29/5/1962
d/p David E. Rose; *sc* John Hopkins
A PLACE OF SAFETY 24/6/1964
d Michael Simpson; *p* David E. Rose;
sc John Hopkins
lp Johnny Sekka; Alaknanda Samarth
ACCORDING TO PLAN: PART 1 4/8/1969
d Timothy Combe; *p* Richard Beynon;
sc Robert Barr
lp John Flanagan; Paul Darrow;
Donald Webster; Brendan Barry; Reg Pritchard;
Robert Hartley; Jennie Goossens
NIGHT OUT: PART 1 11/5/1970
d Ron Craddock; *sc* P.J. Hammond
lp Bernard Holley; Richard Steele;
John Swindells; Graham Roberts; Natalie Kent;
Julie Booth; John Colclough; Lane Meddick
NIGHT OUT: PART 2 12/5/1970
d Ron Craddock; *sc* P.J. Hammond

lp Bernard Holley; Richard Steele;
John Swindells; Graham Roberts; Natalie Kent
A BIG SHADOW: PART 1 5/10/1970
d Michael Hart; *p* Ron Craddock;
sc Bill Barron
lp Bernard Holley; Neil McCarthy;
Edward Cast; Jennie Goossens; George Baker;
Dorothy Gordon
A BIG SHADOW: PART 2 6/10/1970
d Michael Hart; *p* Ron Craddock;
sc Bill Barron
lp Bernard Holley; Neil McCarthy;
Edward Cast; Jennie Goossens; George Baker;
Dorothy Gordon
HUNCH 22/3/1976
d Fiona Cumming; *p* Rod Graham;
sc Allan Prior
lp John Collin; Ray Lonnen;
Brian Grellis; David Jackson; Pat Gorman;
Vicky Ireland; Ronald Mayer; John Bryans;
John Labanowski; John Rapley;
Cynthia Etherington
JUVENILE 5/7/1977
d Derrick Goodwin; *p* Rod Graham;
sc Ted Lewis
lp Brian Grellis; Allan O'Keefe;
Alan Guy; Pat Ashton; Philip Dunbar;
Paul Rosebury; Don McKillop; Gwyneth Strong;
Josie Kidd; Bunny May
PRESSURE 20/9/1978
d John McGrath; *p* Ron Craddock;
sc Troy Kennedy Martin
lp John Phillips; Allan O'Keefe;
Paul Stewart; Tony Haygarth; Gavin Richards;
Alun Armstrong; Michael Gordon;
Chris Darwin; Philip Jackson;
Christine Hargreaves; Neville Smith

ZAMBEZI (BBC 9/8–23/8/1965)
Three-part documentary covering a journey along the Zambezi river.
d/nar David Attenborough
LORD OF THE LAND 9/8/1965
The ANCIENT HIGHWAY 16/8/1965

ZOO TIME (Granada 1956–68)
Documentary series about animals filmed at London Zoo.
pres Desmond Morris
ZOO TIME 7/8/1963
p David Warwick
ZOO TIME 12/9/1963
Desmond Morris visits the new cattle pen at London Zoo.
p David Warwick

Alternative Title Index

ABIGAIL'S PARTY
PLAY FOR TODAY 1/11/1977

ABU SIMBEL
CHRONICLE 5/8/1967

ACCOUNT CLOSED
The VISE 6/5/1955

ACKERMAN, DOUGALL AND HARKER
PLAY FOR TODAY 10/2/1972

The ACTOR'S CHANGING FACE
OMNIBUS 25/5/1969

ACTOR, I SAID
OMNIBUS 9/4/1972

The ADVENTURES OF DON QUIXOTE
PLAY OF THE MONTH 7/1/1973

The ADVOCATE
TELEVISION PLAYHOUSE 11/12/1959

AFRICAN SANCTUS
OMNIBUS 30/3/1975

AFTER SO LONG
WOMEN IN LOVE

AFTER THE FUNERAL
ARMCHAIR THEATRE 3/4/1960

AFTER THE SHOW
ARMCHAIR THEATRE 20/9/1959

AFTERNOON OF A NYMPH
ARMCHAIR THEATRE 30/9/1962

AFTERNOON OFF
BY ALAN BENNETT – SIX PLAYS 3/2/1979

ALCOA PRESENTS
ONE STEP BEYOND

ALEXANDER
RONNIE BARKER PLAYHOUSE 8/5/1968

ALICE
The WEDNESDAY PLAY 13/10/1965

ALICE TRYING
HEARTLAND 10/8/1979

ALICK DICK
SUCCESS STORY 2/2/1959

ALL GOOD MEN
PLAY FOR TODAY 31/1/1974

ALL'S WELL THAT ENDS WELL
THEATRE 625 3/6/1968

ALLERGY
CONFESSION 28/8/1970

ALWAYS ON SUNDAY
MONITOR 29/6/1965

ALWAYS SOMETHING HOT
ARMCHAIR THEATRE 28/10/1962

The AMATEUR SCIENTIST
HORIZON 19/10/1964

AMAZING STORIES
RED LETTER DAY 1/2/1976

AND DID THOSE FEET?
The WEDNESDAY PLAY 2/6/1965

...AND WHERE WILL THE CHILDREN
PLAY?
HORIZON 1/3/1973

ANDY PANDY
WATCH WITH MOTHER 8/1/1957

ANSELM GETS HIS CHANCE
WODEHOUSE PLAYHOUSE 26/3/1976

ANTONIO GAUDI
MONITOR 3/12/1961

ANXIOUS ANNE
SHE 15/5/1977

The APOLLO OF BELLAC
APPOINTMENT WITH DRAMA 12/8/1955

ARTHUR
ALFRED HITCHCOCK PRESENTS 27/9/1959

ARTICLE 5
CENTRE PLAY 1975

AS YOU LIKE IT
BBC TELEVISION SHAKESPEARE
17/12/1978

An ASPIDISTRA IN BABYLON
COUNTRY MATTERS 25/2/1973

The ASSASSIN
Der ATTENTÄTER

The ASSASSIN
THEATRE ROYAL 29/1/1956

AT HOME
TELEVISION PLAYHOUSE 18/3/1960

AT THE DROP OF ANOTHER HAT
STAR PERFORMANCE 30/4/1968

The AVENGERS
ONE STEP BEYOND 25/4/1961

The ARCHITECTS OF FEAR
The OUTER LIMITS 7/10/1963

The BACHELORS
PLAY OF THE WEEK 23/11/1964

BACKSTAGE AT THE REP
MONITOR 28/9/1958

BALLOON FROM ZANZIBAR
ADVENTURE 23/8/1962

BANGELSTEIN'S BOYS
SATURDAY NIGHT THEATRE 18/1/1969

The BANKRUPT
PLAY FOR TODAY 27/11/1972

BANQUO'S CHAIR
ALFRED HITCHCOCK PRESENTS 3/5/1959

BAR MITZVAH BOY
PLAY FOR TODAY 14/9/1976

BARBARA OF THE HOUSE OF GREBE
WESSEX TALES 12/12/1973

BARTOK
MONITOR 24/5/1964 BELA BARTOK

A BEAST WITH TWO BACKS
The WEDNESDAY PLAY 20/11/1968

The BEATLES LIVE
AROUND THE BEATLES

The BEERSHEVA EXPERIMENT
HORIZON 3/11/1978

BEHIND THE MASK
The VISE 25/2/1955

BELA BARTOK
MONITOR 24/5/1964

BELOVED STRANGER
DOUGLAS FAIRBANKS JR., PRESENTS
3/9/1956

BEN AGAIN
TELEVISION PLAYHOUSE 22/3/1963

BEN KOKHBA
CHRONICLE 12/2/1976
The SCROLLS FROM THE SON OF A STAR

BEN SPRAY
TELEVISION PLAYHOUSE 23/2/1961

BERLIOZ: A SINGULAR OBSESSION
WORKSHOP 9/3/1969

BERNSTEIN IN REHEARSAL
WORKSHOP 6/1/1967

The BEST PLAY OF...
LAURENCE OLIVIER PRESENTS

The BETTER CHANCE
The VISE 24/6/1955

BETTER LUCK NEXT TIME
STUDIO '64 2/2/1964

BETTER MOUSETRAPS
DOUGLAS FAIRBANKS JR., PRESENTS
6/2/1956

BIG BEAT '64
**NEW MUSICAL EXPRESS POLL
WINNERS' CONCERT**

The BIG DRAGNET
DRAGNET

The BIG FLAME
The WEDNESDAY PLAY 19/2/1969

BIG JIM AND THE FIGARO CLUB
TURNING YEAR TALES 24/6/1979

BILLION DOLLAR BUBBLE
HORIZON 8/11/1976

BILLY
PLAY FOR TODAY 13/11/1979

BIRD BRAIN – THE MYSTERY OF BIRD
NAVIGATATION
HORIZON 14/1/1974

A BIT OF A LIFT
ARMCHAIR THEATRE 25/9/1973

The BLACK DOG
COUNTRY MATTERS 4/2/1973

The BLACK HOLES OF GRAVITY
HORIZON 15/10/1973

The BLACKTOFT DIARIES – TRUE OR
FALSE?
ITV PLAYHOUSE 10/4/1979

BLASPHEMY AT THE OLD BAILEY
EVERYMAN 18/9/1977

BLIND MAN'S BLUFF
The VISE 28/1/1955

BLOCH'S PLAY
SHORT STORY 11/6/1972

The BLOOD KNOT
ARMCHAIR THEATRE 1968

BLOOMING YOUTH
PLAY FOR TODAY 18/6/1973

The BLUE FILM
SHADES OF GREENE 14/10/1975

BLUE REMEMBERED HILLS
PLAY FOR TODAY 30/1/1979

The BLUES CAME WALKIN': PART 1
TEMPO 6/12/1964

The BLUES CAME WALKIN': PART 2
TEMPO 13/12/1964

The BONEGRINDER
PLAYHOUSE 13/5/1968

BOSS GUITAR
TEMPO 6/6/1965

BRAZIL: THE MEHINACU
DISAPPEARING WORLD 20/11/1974
The MEHINACU

BREACH OF MARRIAGE
ARMCHAIR THEATRE 4/5/1958

BREEZE ANSTEY
COUNTRY MATTERS 24/9/1972

The BRIDGE
The GAMBLERS 21/12/1967

The BRIMSTONE BUTTERFLY
PLAY OF THE WEEK 16/4/1963

BRITISH STUDENTS ORCHESTRA
MONITOR 20/7/1958

BROKEN ARROW
The TWENTIETH CENTURY FOX HOUR
2/5/1956

The BROKEN BRIDGE
HORIZON 24/10/1968

BROKEN HONEYMOON
The VISE 11/2/1955

BRONZE AGE BLAST-OFF
HORIZON 26/3/1979

BUFFET
PLAY FOR TODAY 2/11/1976

BUG
HALF HOUR STORY 13/9/1967

The BUILDINGS OF ENGLAND
CONTRASTS 3/12/1968

BUT THE CLOUDS...
The LIVELY ARTS 17/4/1977

BY PERSONS UNKNOWN
The VISE 18/11/1955

CALL ME DADDY
ARMCHAIR THEATRE 8/4/1967

CALLAN: A MAGNUM FOR SCHNEIDER
ARMCHAIR THEATRE 4/2/1967
A MAGNUM FOR SCHNEIDER

CANCER – THE SMOKER'S GAMBLE
HORIZON 20/6/1967

CANCER NOW
HORIZON 10/11/1969

CANDIDE
PLAY OF THE MONTH 16/2/1973

CANNES FILM FESTIVAL
MONITOR 25/5/1958

CAPTAIN VIDEO'S STORY
ARMCHAIR THIRTY 27/11/1973

CAR ALONG THE PASS
GALTON AND SIMPSON PLAYHOUSE
17/2/1977

CARBON COPY
AGAINST THE CROWD 3/8/1975

CAROLS MEAN CHRISTMAS
TEMPO 22/12/1963

CASCADE
KASKAD

The CASE OF THE ANCIENT
ASTRONAUTS
HORIZON SPECIAL 25/11/1977

CASTING THE RUNES
PLAYS FOR PLEASURE 24/4/1979

The CATACOMBS OF SAKKARA
CHRONICLE 11/4/1970

The CATHODE-RAY TUBE SHOW
**YES, IT'S THE CATHODE-RAY TUBE
SHOW!**

CATHY COME HOME
The WEDNESDAY PLAY 16/11/1966

CBS TOWN MEETING OF THE WORLD
TOWN MEETING OF THE WORLD

The CELLAR AND THE ALMOND TREE
The WEDNESDAY PLAY 4/3/1970 ·

The CHANGE OF LIFE
HORIZON 17/2/1975

CHARIOT OF THE GODS
HORIZON SPECIAL 25/11/1977
The CASE OF THE ANCIENT ASTRONAUTS

CHARLIE DRAKE – MARCH OF THE
MOVIES
MARCH OF THE MOVIES

The CHEATERS
THRILLER 27/12/1960

The CHERRY ON THE TOP
ARMCHAIR THEATRE 27/9/1964
The CHERRY ON TOP

The CHERRY ON TOP
ARMCHAIR THEATRE 27/9/1964

The CHESTER MYSTERY PLAYS
PLAY OF THE MONTH 18/4/1976

The CHEVIOT, THE STAG AND THE
BLACK, BLACK OIL
PLAY FOR TODAY 6/6/1974

CHICAGO
CHICAGO: PORTRAIT OF A CITY

The CHOPPING BLOCK
The SUNDAY NIGHT PLAY 23/10/1960

A CHRISTMAS STORY WITH MUSIC
AMAHL AND THE NIGHT VISITORS

CIRCUS
MONITOR 2/2/1958

CITY SUGAR
The SUNDAY DRAMA 6/8/1978

The CLANDESTINE MARRIAGE
TELEVISION WORLD THEATRE 16/3/1958

A CLEARING IN THE JUNGLE
DISAPPEARING WORLD 19/5/1970

CLUBS
TURNING YEAR TALES 15/7/1979

The CODE OF THE MULLINERS
WODEHOUSE PLAYHOUSE 7/5/1976

COLD HARBOUR
ITV PLAYHOUSE 25/4/1978

The COLD LIGHT
SUNDAY NIGHT THEATRE 29/7/1956

A COLD PEACE
ARMCHAIR THEATRE 18/12/1965

The COLLECTION
LAURENCE OLIVIER PRESENTS 5/12/1976

The COLONEL
THEATRE ROYAL 15/1/1956

COMEDIANS
PLAY FOR TODAY 25/10/1979

The COMING OUT PARTY
The WEDNESDAY PLAY 22/12/1965

The CONFESSION
ONE STEP BEYOND 11/4/1961

The CONFESSIONS OF MARIAN EVANS
OMNIBUS 23/11/1969

The CONNOISSEUR
The WEDNESDAY PLAY 4/5/1966

CONSECRATION OF LIVERPOOL
METROPOLITAN R.C. CATHEDRAL
**SOLEMN OPENING OF LIVERPOOL
CATHEDRAL**

CORNELIUS
SATURDAY NIGHT THEATRE 8/2/1969

The CORPSE IN ROOM 13
The VISE 15/7/1955

COUNTESS MARITZA
GAY OPERETTA 6/11/1959

COVENTRY CATHEDRAL
ACT OF FAITH

A CRACK IN THE ICE
The WEDNESDAY PLAY 28/10/1964

CRACKING THE STONE AGE CODE
CHRONICLE 31/10/1970

The CRADLE SONG
HALLMARK HALL OF FAME 6/5/1956

CRAVEN ARMS
COUNTRY MATTERS 20/8/1972

CRAWFORD MYSTERY THEATRE
PUBLIC PROSECUTOR

CRIPPLED BLOOM
COUNTRY MATTERS 10/9/1972

CROSS CHANNEL
The VISE 21/10/1955

CROWD OF THE DAY: AUSTRALIA V.
WEST INDIES
CROWD OF THE DAY

The CRUEL TEST
The VISE 11/3/1955

The CRYSTAL TRENCH
ALFRED HITCHCOCK PRESENTS 1/1/1959

CUT YOURSELF A SLICE OF THROAT
BLACKMAIL 15/10/1965

DALAI LAMA
ADVENTURE 29/6/1962

DANTE'S INFERNO
OMNIBUS 22/12/1967

DARE I WEEP, DARE I MOURN
STAR PERFORMANCE 2/7/1968

The DAUGHTERS OF ALBION
PLAYS FOR PLEASURE 1/5/1979

DAVE ALLEN AT LARGE
SHOW OF THE WEEK 12/3/1973

DEAD MAN'S EVIDENCE
The VISE 4/11/1955

DEADLY ROULETTE
HOW I SPENT MY SUMMER VACATION

DEAL IN DIVING
AS I WAS SAYING 1/10/1955

DEATH IN WHITE
The VISE 19/8/1955

DEATH OF A HAM
The VISE 17/6/1955
MURDER OF A HAM

DEATH OF A PRIVATE
The WEDNESDAY PLAY 13/12/1967

DEATH ON THE BOARDS
The VISE 18/2/1955

DEATH PAYS NO DIVIDENDS
The VISE 29/10/1954

DEATH WALKS BY NIGHT
The VISE 22/5/1955

The DECEPTION
The VISE 18/3/1955

DECEPTION
The TWENTIETH CENTURY FOX HOUR
7/3/1956

DEEP AND CRISP AND STOLEN
PLAY OF THE WEEK 21/12/1964

DENIS MITCHELL: TELEVISION'S
MASTER FILM MAKER
AQUARIUS 17/10/1970

DENNIS POTTER: MAN OF TELEVISION
The SOUTH BANK SHOW 11/2/1978

The DESPERATE PEOPLE
FRANCIS DURBRIDGE PRESENTS

DESTINY
PLAY FOR TODAY 31/1/1978

The DETECTIVES, STARRING ROBERT
TAYLOR
The DETECTIVES

The DEVIL
MAUPASSANT: WOMEN AND MONEY

The DEVIL'S EGGSHELL
PLAY OF THE MONTH 28/6/1966

DIAGHILEV: THE EXILE YEARS
OMNIBUS 9/1/1968

DIAGHILEV: THE YEARS ABROAD
OMNIBUS 2/1/1968

DIAL M FOR MURDER
STAR PERFORMANCE 7/5/1968

DIARY OF A NOBODY
SIX 12/12/1964

The DIFFERENT DRUM
TELEVISION PLAYHOUSE 6/7/1961

DINNER AT THE SPORTING CLUB
PLAY FOR TODAY 7/11/1978

A DIP IN THE POOL
ALFRED HITCHCOCK PRESENTS 1/6/1958

DIPLOMATIC ERROR
The VISE 1/7/1955

DIVERS DO IT DEEPER
HORIZON 10/11/1978

DO NOT ADJUST YOUR STOCKING
DO NOT ADJUST YOUR SET 25/12/1968

DR DAMON'S EXPERIMENT
The VISE 22/10/1954

DR. SIMON LOCKE
POLICE SURGEON

DOING IT THEIR WAY
ARENA 12/3/1979 MY WAY

A DOLL'S HOUSE
PLAY OF THE WEEK 31/10/1961

DON'T CACKLE, LAY EGGS
HORIZON 1/12/1969

The DOTTY WORLD OF JAMES LLOYD
MONITOR 5/7/1964

DOUBLE DARE
PLAY FOR TODAY 6/4/1976

DOUBLE PAY-OFF
The VISE 29/4/1955

DOUGLAS FAIRBANKS PRESENTS
DOUGLAS FAIRBANKS JR., PRESENTS

DREAD, BEAT AN' BLOOD
OMNIBUS 7/6/1979

The DRIVER'S TALE
TRINITY TALES 21/11/1975

DUE TO LACK OF INTEREST
TOMORROW HAS BEEN CANCELLED
HORIZON 8/3/1971

The DUMB WAITER
TELEVISION PLAYHOUSE 10/8/1961

DURING BARTY'S PARTY
BEASTS 23/10/1976

EARLY TO BED
SECOND CITY FIRSTS 20/3/1975

EASIER IN THE DARK
ARMCHAIR THEATRE 25/2/1967

EAST AFRICA – MASAI WOMEN
DISAPPEARING WORLD 27/11/1974
MASAI WOMEN

The EAVESDROPPER
The VISE 3/12/1954

The EAVESDROPPERS
The VISE 3/12/1954
The EAVESDROPPER

ED AND ZED!
EDANDZED!

The EDINBURGH FESTIVAL
The SATURDAY SPECIAL 24/9/1977

EDNA, THE INEBRIATE WOMAN
PLAY FOR TODAY 21/10/1971

The EDUCATION OF CORPORAL
HALLIDAY
ARMCHAIR THEATRE 5/8/1967

The EIGHTH WINDOW
The VISE 4/2/1955

ELGAR
MONITOR 11/11/1962

ELVIS
The FABULOUS ELVIS

EMBERA – THE END OF THE ROAD
DISAPPEARING WORLD 15/6/1971

EMLYN
SATURDAY NIGHT THEATRE 15/2/1969

EMMA'S TIME
The WEDNESDAY PLAY 13/5/1970

EMMERDALE
EMMERDALE FARM

The EMPEROR JONES
ARMCHAIR THEATRE 30/3/1958

The ENCYCLOPAEDIST
THEY MET IN A CITY 4/4/1961

END OF CONFLICT
PLAY OF THE WEEK 23/7/1963

The ENDS OF JUSTICE
THEATRE ROYAL 27/4/1956

END OF THE LINE
JOHNNY GO HOME

ENGLAND MY ENGLAND
ARMCHAIR THRILLER 29/4/1967

The ERPINGHAM CAMP
SEVEN DEADLY SINS 27/6/1966

ESKIMOS OF POND INLET – THE
PEOPLE'S LAND
DISAPPEARING WORLD 12/1/1976

The ESSAY
TURNING YEAR TALES 22/7/1979

EXECUTION NIGHT
CONFLICT 28/5/1957

EXPLOSION
WARNER BROTHERS PRESENTS 27/3/1956

EYE FOR DETAIL
AS I WAS SAYING 10/9/1955

EYE WITNESS
ARMCHAIR MYSTERY THEATRE 5/6/1960

EYE WITNESS
ONE STEP BEYOND 4/7/1961

FABIAN OF SCOTLAND YARD
FABIAN OF THE YARD

The FACE
ONE STEP BEYOND 14/3/1961

A FAIR SHARE OF WHAT LITTLE WE
HAVE
HORIZON 19/1/1976

FAITH AND HENRY
SATURDAY NIGHT THEATRE 6/12/1969

FAME AND THE FURY
The VISE 1/4/1955

A FAMILY BUSINESS
MAUPASSANT: WOMEN AND MONEY

FAMOUS FIVE
ENID BLYTON'S FAMOUS FIVE

The FANATICS
THEATRE 625 29/4/1968

FANSHEN
2ND HOUSE 18/10/1975

FAREWELL LUCKY STARS
THANK YOUR LUCKY STARS 25/6/1966

The FAT IN THE FIRE
HORIZON 10/12/1979

FATHER AND SON
MONITOR 28/10/1962

A FEAR OF STRANGERS
DRAMA '64 10/5/1964

FEELING HIS WAY
THREE COMEDIES OF MARRIAGE
10/7/1975

The FELLOW TOWNSMEN
WESSEX TALES 14/11/1973

The FERRYMAN
HAUNTED 23/12/1974

A FEW NOTES ON OUR FOOD PROBLEMS
A FEW NOTES ON OUR FOOD PROBLEM

The FIDDLE
TALES FROM SOHO 21/1/1956

The FIFTY-SEVENTH SATURDAY
HALF HOUR STORY 3/7/1968

FIFTY YEARS ON
OMNIBUS 7/11/1971

The FIGHT TO BE MALE
HORIZON 21/5/1979

FIND ME
OMNIBUS 8/12/1974

FIRE
HORIZON 30/11/1972

FIRST DAY
DOUGLAS FAIRBANKS JR., PRESENTS
19/3/1956

The FIRST LADY AT HOME
A TOUR OF THE WHITE HOUSE

FIVE WOMEN
SOME WOMEN

FLIGHT FROM TREASON
ARMCHAIR MYSTERY THEATRE 10/7/1960

FLINT
PLAY OF THE MONTH 15/1/1978

The FLOATING POPULATION
ARMCHAIR THEATRE 28/1/1967

The FLOWERPOT MEN
WATCH WITH MOTHER 1952

FOLLOW THE RIVER DOWN
TURNING YEAR TALES 1/7/1979

FOLLOW THE YELLOW BRICK ROAD
The SEXTET 4/7/1972

FOR SERVICES RENDERED
PLAY OF THE WEEK 7/7/1959

FOR TEA ON SUNDAY
PLAY OF THE WEEK 29/3/1978

The 45TH UNMARRIED MOTHER
HALF HOUR STORY 9/8/1967

FORTY YEARS OF MURDER
HORIZON 16/9/1977

The FOUR BEAUTIES
COUNTRY MATTERS 11/3/1973

FRANÇOIS TRUFFAUT – FILM MAKER
OMNIBUS 2/12/1973

FRIENDS
HALF HOUR STORY 6/9/1967

FROM CHEKHOV WITH LOVE
STAR PERFORMANCE 14/6/1968

GABRIEL'S CHOICE
The VISE 5/11/1954

GALE IS DEAD
MAN ALIVE 6/5/1970

The GANGSTER SHOW
The RESISTIBLE RISE OF ARTURO UI

GANGSTERS
PLAY FOR TODAY 9/1/1975

The GENERAL'S DAY
PLAY FOR TODAY 20/11/1972

GEORGE'S ROOM
HALF HOUR STORY 5/2/1971

GHOST TRIO
The LIVELY ARTS 17/4/1977

A GIFT FROM HEAVEN
The VISE 9/12/1955

GINA
PLAY OF THE WEEK 27/7/1964

The GIPSY BARON
GAY OPERETTA 27/11/1959

GIRL
SECOND CITY FIRSTS 25/2/1974

GIRL OF MY DREAMS
THEATRE 625 31/7/1966

GIRL OF MY DREAMS
JOURNEY TO THE UNKOWN 26/9/1968

GIRL ON THE SUBWAY
CONFLICT 8/1/1957

GLADLY MY CROSS-EYED BEAR
THEATRE 625 16/10/1966
TALKING TO A STRANGER

GLYNDEBOURNE FESTIVAL OPERA
PERFORM 'LE NOZZE DI FIGARO'
The MARRIAGE OF FIGARO

GO-SLOW ON THE BRIGHTON LINE
**LONDON TO BRIGHTON IN FOUR
MINUTES**

GOING LIKE A FOX
SATURDAY PLAYHOUSE 13/2/1960

The GOLD INSIDE
THEATRE '60 24/9/1960

GOLDEN HOUR
CALLAS SINGS TOSCA

The GOLDEN RING
WORKSHOP 16/5/1965

The GOLDEN ROSE 1962
KASKAD

The GOOD AND FAITHFUL SERVANT
SEVEN DEADLY VIRTUES 6/4/1967

GOOD NAME MURDER
The VISE 4/11/1955

GOODNIGHT ALBERT
HALF HOUR STORY 6/2/1968

The GORGE
The WEDNESDAY PLAY 4/9/1968

GOSSIP FROM THE FOREST
SCREENPLAY 29/7/1979

GRADUATION BALL
**LONDON'S FESTIVAL BALLET IN
GRADUATION BALL**

The GREATEST MAN IN THE WORLD
ARMCHAIR THEATRE 9/11/1958

The GREEN PASTURES
SUNDAY NIGHT THEATRE 14/9/1958

GUILTY PARTY
PLAY OF THE WEEK 24/2/1964

The GUV'NOR
LONDON PLAYHOUSE 19/1/1956

The GYPSY BARON
GAY OPERETTA 27/11/1959
The GIPSY BARON

HACKNEY MARSHES
TAKE SIX 8/8/1978

HALF A SMILE FROM STOKE
OMNIBUS 21/4/1977

HAMLET
HALLMARK HALL OF FAME 17/11/1970

HANG OUT YOUR BRIGHTEST
COLOURS...THE LIFE AND DEATH OF
MICHAEL COLLINS
**HANG UP YOUR BRIGHTEST
COLOURS...THE LIFE AND DEATH OF
MICHAEL COLLINS**

HAPPY ANNIVERSARY
HALF HOUR STORY 10/7/1968

The HARD KNOCK
ARMCHAIR THEATRE 8/7/1962

HARD LABOUR
PLAY FOR TODAY 12/3/1973

HAROLD PINTER
TEMPO 3/10/1965

HAWKS AND DOVES
HALF HOUR STORY 19/7/1967

HEAD OF STATE
The GUARDIANS 24/7/1971

HEAR THE TIGER SEE THE BAY
ARMCHAIR THEATRE 23/12/1962

HEART OF BRITAIN
OMNIBUS 20/9/1970

HELLO LOLA
MURDER 6/6/1976

HENRY IV PART TWO
BBC TELEVISION SHAKESPEARE
16/12/1979

HENRY V
BBC TELEVISION SHAKESPEARE
23/12/1979

HER MAJESTY'S PLEASURE
PLAY FOR TODAY 25/10/1973

The HEROISM OF THOMAS CHADWICK
The STORY-TELLER 23/9/1967

The HIGGLER
COUNTRY MATTERS 11/12/1973

HINDLE WAKES
LAURENCE OLIVIER PRESENTS 19/12/1976

HITTING TOWN
PLAYS FOR BRITAIN 27/4/1976

HOLD AUTUMN IN YOUR HAND
The SOUTHERNER

A HOLE IN BABYLON
PLAY FOR TODAY 29/11/1979

HOME
PLAY FOR TODAY 6/1/1972

A HOME LIKE OURS...A STORY OF FOUR
CHILDREN
HORIZON 7/6/1976

HOMECOMING
DOUGLAS FAIRBANKS JR., PRESENTS
12/11/1956

The HOMING CHINAMAN
The VISE 3/6/1955

HONEYMOON POSTPONED
ARMCHAIR THEATRE 29/1/1961

HOSPITAL: 1922
HORIZON 12/10/1972

HOSTAGE
The VISE 1955

HOT SUMMER NIGHT
ARMCHAIR THEATRE 1/2/1959

The HOUSE IN ATHENS
LONDON PLAYHOUSE 1956

A HOUSE IN BATTERSEA
MONITOR 4/6/1961

HOUSE OF CHARACTER
The WEDNESDAY PLAY 10/1/1968

HOUSTON...WE'VE GOT A PROBLEM
A LIFE AT STAKE 31/3/1978

HOW DO YOU READ ?
HORIZON 14/7/1975

HOW IS IT IN CRACOW?
EVERYMAN 22/10/1978

The HUMAN VOICE
STAR PERFORMANCE 30/11/1966

The HUNDRED DAYS OF THE DRAGON
The OUTER LIMITS 23/9/1963

The HUNTING OF AUBREY HOPKISS
BLACKMAIL 7/11/1966

HURRICANE!
The DUPONT SHOW OF THE WEEK
27/5/1962

I AM OSANGO
ARMCHAIR THEATRE 15/4/1967

I DON'T WANT TO BE A BURDEN
HORIZON 27/1/1978

I KNOW WHAT I MEANT
LATE NIGHT DRAMA 10/7/1974

I REGRET NOTHING
OMNIBUS 27/12/1970

I TOOK MY LITTLE WORLD AWAY
ARMCHAIR THEATRE 14/3/1965

I'LL HAVE YOU TO REMEMBER
ARMCHAIR THEATRE 23/10/1960

I'M A DREAMER MONTREAL
ITV PLAYHOUSE 6/3/1979

IF THE SHOOTING STARTS
WEDNESDAY SPECIAL 18/5/1977

The IMAGE
PLAY OF THE WEEK 25/1/1965

An IMAGINATIVE WOMAN
WESSEX TALES 28/11/1973

The IMMORTALISTS
EVERYMAN 11/11/1979

The IMPERFECT GENTLEMAN
The VISE 15/4/1955

The IMPORTANCE OF BEING EARNEST
ARMCHAIR THEATRE 15/11/1964

IN ALL DIRECTIONS
SHOW OF THE WEEK 26/4/1966

IN CAMERA
The WEDNESDAY PLAY 4/11/1964

IN LOVING MEMORY OF...
HALF HOUR STORY 2/1/1968

IN THE BOSOM OF THE COUNTRY
The SAINNERS 9/9/1970

IN TWO MINDS
The WEDNESDAY PLAY 1/3/1967

The INCANTATION OF CASANOVA
THEATRE 625 22/10/1967

The INNOCENT MUST SUFFER
THEATRE 625 23/10/1966
TALKING TO A STRANGER

The INSECT WAR
HORIZON 9/11/1970

INTERVIEW FOR WIVES
THIRTY MINUTE THEATRE 1962

INTO THE DARK
ARMCHAIR THEATRE 3/2/1963

The INTRUDER
DOUGLAS FAIRBANKS JR., PRESENTS
2/4/1956

ISRAEL'S VICTORY
The LIGHTNING WAR

ITALIAN OPERA COMPANY
MONITOR 30/3/1958

ITEM
LATE NIGHT DRAMA 7/8/1974

IT'S YOUR MOVE
SEVEN DEADLY VIRTUES 30/3/1967

JACK FLEA'S BIRTHDAY CELEBRATION
SECOND CITY FIRSTS 10/4/1976

JACK FLETCHER
TURNING YEAR TALES 5/8/1979

JACK POINT
PLAY FOR TODAY 1/11/1973

JASON'S HOUSE
DOUGLAS FAIRBANKS JR., PRESENTS
20/2/1956

JB: A PORTRAIT OF SIR JOHN
BARBIROLLI
MONITOR 11/3/1965

JOE'S ARK
PLAY FOR TODAY 14/2/1974

JOEY
HORIZON 9/12/1974

JOHN CLARE: 'I AM...'
OMNIBUS 8/2/1970

JUST A BOY'S GAME
PLAY FOR TODAY 8/11/1979

JUSTICE
ONE STEP BEYOND 7/3/1961

KAIN
THEATRE 625 17/4/1967

KATARAGAMA
DISAPPEARING WORLD 20/11/1973

The KEYS OF PARADISE
HORIZON 12/3/1979

KILL ME
BLACKMAIL 17/9/1965

KING LEAR
PLAY OF THE MONTH 23/3/1975

KING OF VIOLINISTS
The SATURDAY SPECIAL 14/12/i968

KING RICHARD II
HALLMARK HALL OF FAME 24/1/1954

The KISS OF DEATH
PLAY FOR TODAY 11/1/1977

KISSES AT FIFTY
PLAY FOR TODAY 22/1/1973

The KITCHEN
KOK

KNOCK KNOCK
SECOND CITY FIRSTS 21/11/1976

KRAPP'S LAST TAPE
THIRTY MINUTE THEATRE 29/11/1972

L.S. LOWRY – LANCASHIRE ARTIST
L.S. LOWRY

The LADY OF THE CAMELLIAS
ARMCHAIR THEATRE 16/2/1958

LADY WINDERMERE'S FAN
PLAYHOUSE 25/9/1967

LAMB TO THE SLAUGHTER
ALFRED HITCHCOCK PRESENTS 13/4/1958

LAMB TO THE SLAUGHTER
TALES OF THE UNEXPECTED 14/4/1979

The LANDLADY
TALES OF THE UNEXPECTED 21/4/1979

The LARK
SUNDAY NIGHT THEATRE 11/11/1956

The LAST OF THE BRAVE
ARMCHAIR THEATRE 15/11/1959

The LAST OF THE CUIVA
DISAPPEARING WORLD 8/6/1971

The LAST OF THE SUMMER WINE
COMEDY PLAYHOUSE 4/1/1973

LAST SUMMER
ITV PLAYHOUSE 21/6/1977

LAST TOUR
DOUGLAS FAIRBANKS JR., PRESENTS
15/10/1956
THIS LAST TOUR

The LAST TRAIN THROUGH THE
HARECASTLE TUNNEL
The WEDNESDAY PLAY 1/10/1969

LAUGH-IN
ROWAN AND MARTIN'S LAUGH-IN

The LAUGHING MAN
**Der LACHENDE MANN: BEKENNTNISSE
EINES MÖRDERS**

LAY DOWN YOUR ARMS
SATURDAY NIGHT THEATRE 23/5/1970

LEE OSWALD – ASSASSIN
PLAY OF THE MONTH 10/3/1966

The LEGION HALL BOMBING
PLAY FOR TODAY 22/8/1978

LENA, O MY LENA
ARMCHAIR THEATRE 25/9/1960

LET'S MURDER VIVALDI
The WEDNESDAY PLAY 10/4/1968

LICKING HITLER
PLAY FOR TODAY 10/1/1978

The LIE
PLAY FOR TODAY 29/10/1970

A LILY IN LITTLE INDIA
PLAY OF THE WEEK 9/10/1962

A LINE ON SATIRE
MONITOR 21/12/1958

LITTLE BIG SHOT
DOUGLAS FAIRBANKS JR., PRESENTS
18/5/1955

LITTLE DORIS
ARMCHAIR THEATRE 13/10/1963

The LITTLE FARM
COUNTRY MATTERS 28/1/1973

LITTLE MAN LASSE
GLOBE THEATRE 3/12/1974

LONESOME ROAD
DRAMA '62 21/1/1962

LONG BOW
CHRONICLE 12/2/1973

LONG DISTANCE INFORMATION
PLAY FOR TODAY 11/10/1979

The LONG VALLEY
HORIZON 6/12/1976

LOOKING FOR GARROW
The SUNDAY NIGHT PLAY 30/10/1960

LORD ARTHUR SAVILE'S CRIME
ARMCHAIR THEATRE 3/1/1960

The LORDS OF THE LABYRINTH
HORIZON 22/2/1976

LORDS OF THE SEA
HORIZON 10/10/1967

The LOST BOYS
PLAY OF THE WEEK 11/10/1978

The LOST WATERS OF THE NILE
HORIZON 22/10/1979

The LOST WORLD OF THE MAYA
CHRONICLE 6/10/1972

The LOST YEARS OF BRIAN HOOPER
THEATRE 625 8/10/1967

LOVE AFFAIR
PLAYHOUSE 3/7/1974

LOVE LIFE
ARMCHAIR THEATRE 29/7/1967

The LOVING LESSON
ARMCHAIR THEATRE 31/8/1971

The LUCK OF THE STIFFHAMS
WODEHOUSE PLAYHOUSE 21/11/1978

LUCKY
PLAYHOUSE 5/2/1974

LUCKY MAN
The VISE 24/12/1954

The LUMP
The WEDNESDAY PLAY 1/2/1967

MACBETH
HALLMARK HALL OF FAME 28/11/1954

MACBETH
PLAY OF THE MONTH 20/9/1970

The MACHINE STOPS
OUT OF THE UNKNOWN 6/10/1966

MACNEIL
SATURDAY NIGHT THEATRE 1/2/1969

MAD JACK
The WEDNESDAY PLAY 4/2/1970

A MAGNUM FOR SCHNEIDER
ARMCHAIR THEATRE 4/2/1967

MAKE IT A HABIT
LOVE STORY 8/7/1963

The MAKING OF A NATURAL HISTORY
FILM
HORIZON 23/11/1972

MAKING THE BEDMAKERS
MONITOR 2/2/1964

MAN AND SUPERMAN
HALLMARK HALL OF FAME 25/11/1956

MAN BEANEATH
The GAMBLERS 7/12/1967

MAN FROM THE SOUTH
TALES OF THE UNEXPECTED 24/3/1979

MAN HUNT
The VISE 1955

The MAN IN DEMAND
The VISE 27/5/1955

A MAN LIKE THAT
THEATRE 625 27/2/1966

MAN-MADE LAKES OF AFRICA
HORIZON 20/3/1972

A MAN ON HER BACK
The WEDNESDAY PLAY 12/1/1966

The MAN WHO HATED CHILDREN
SHADOWS 18/10/1978

The MAN WHO WANTED TO LIVE
FOREVER
The ONLY WAY OUT IS DEAD

The MAN WHO WAS GIVEN A GASWORKS
CHRONICLE 20/4/1968

MAN WITHOUT A MORTGAGE
ARMCHAIR THEATRE 19/3/1966

The MARRIAGE COUNSELLOR
PLAY FOR LOVE 9/4/1978

MASAI MANHOOD
DISAPPEARING WORLD 8/4/1975

MASAI WOMAN
DISAPPEARING WORLD 27/11/1974

MASTERCLASS
JACQUELINE DU PRE MASTERCLASS

The MATE MARKET
COMEDY PLAYHOUSE 3/1/1964

A MATTER OF PRINCIPLE
THIRTY MINUTE THEATRE 1965

MAY BLOSSOMS
TURNING YEAR TALES 29/7/1979

ME AND MY BIKE
DYLAN THOMAS'S ME AND MY BIKE

MEASURE FOR MEASURE
BBC TELEVISION SHAKESPEARE
18/2/1979

A MEDITERRANEAN PROSPECT
HORIZON 9/4/1979

The MEDIUM
SECOND CITY FIRSTS 15/10/1973

The MEHINACU
DISAPPEARING WORLD 20/11/1974

The MELANCHOLY HUSSAR
WESSEX TALES 5/12/1973

MELISSA
FRANCIS DURBRIDGE PRESENTS
26/4/1964

MEO
DISAPPEARING WORLD 4/7/1972

The MERRY WIDOW
GAY OPERETTA 13/11/1959

MESSIAH
TWENTIETH CENTURY MESSIAH

MEXICAN OIL DANCE
HORIZON 24/9/1979

MICHAEL REGAN
PLAY FOR TODAY 18/11/1971

MICKEY SPILLANE'S MIKE HAMMER
MIKE HAMMER

A MIDSUMMER NIGHT'S DREAM
SUNDAY NIGHT THEATRE 9/11/1958

The MILL
COUNTRY MATTERS 27/8/1972

The MIME OF JACQUES LECOQ
TEMPO 24/5/1964

MISS PAISLEY'S CAT
ALFRED HITCHCOCK PRESENTS
22/12/1957

The MISSION
SANCTUARY 28/6/1967

MR. AXELFORD'S ANGEL
PLAYHOUSE 5/6/1974

MR. BLANCHARD'S SECRET
ALFRED HITCHCOCK PRESENTS
23/12/1956

MR. BROWN COMES HOME
TELEVISION PLAYHOUSE 10/7/1959

MR LUDWIG'S TROPICAL DREAMLAND
HORIZON 30/4/1979

MRS. BIXBY AND THE COLONEL'S COAT
ALFRED HITCHCOCK PRESENTS 27/9/1960

MRS. BIXBY AND THE COLONEL'S COAT
TALES OF THE UNEXPECTED 31/3/1979

MRS. LAWRENCE WILL LOOK AFTER IT
The WEDNESDAY PLAY 21/8/1968

MRS. PATTERSON
SUNDAY NIGHT THEATRE 17/6/1956

MRS WILSON'S DIARY
The SATURDAY SPECIAL 4/1/1969

MOONLIGHT ON THE HIGHWAY
SATURDAY NIGHT THEATRE 12/4/1969

The MORE WE ARE TOGETHER
OMNIBUS 4/5/1969

MORECAMBE AND WISE: FOOLS RUSH
IN
OMNIBUS 18/2/1973

The MOSEDALE HORSESHOE
PLAYHOUSE 23/3/1971

MS OR JILL AND JACK
LATE NIGHT DRAMA 11/9/1974

MULLINER'S BUCK-U-UPPO
WODEHOUSE PLAYHOUSE 12/12/1978

MURDER BY DESIGN
The VISE 1955

MURDER OF A HAM
The VISE 17/6/1955

The MURDER OF BILLY TWO-TONE
JOHNNY GO HOME 22/7/1975

MUSIC FROM THE FLAMES
OMNIBUS 10/11/1974

La MUSICA
LOVE STORY 6/12/1965

MY FRIEND CORBY
SEVEN DEADLY SINS 9/5/1966

MY SIDE OF THE STORY
TELEVISION PLAYHOUSE 7/8/1959

MY WAY
ARENA 12/3/1979

MYSELF, I'VE GOT NOTHING AGAINST
SOUTH KEN
HALF HOUR STORY 9/6/1967

The NAKED CIVIL SERVANT
WEDNESDAY SPECIAL 17/12/1975

The NATIVITY OF JESUS CHRIST
The NATIVITY

NATURAL JUSTICE
HALF HOUR STORY 13/3/1968

NECK
TALES OF THE UNEXPECTED 28/4/1979

The NEGLECTED HARVEST
HORIZON 16/12/1974

The NETWORK
PLAY FOR TODAY 20/12/1979

NEVER COME NIGHT
The INCREDIBLE ROBERT BALDICK

NEVER TURN YOUR BACK ON A FRIEND
ESPIONAGE 4/1/1964

NEWSROUND
JOHN CRAVEN'S NEWSROUND

The NIGHT BEFORE THE MORNING
AFTER
ARMCHAIR THEATRE 2/4/1966

NIGHT CONSPIRATORS
ARMCHAIR THEATRE 6/5/1962

A NIGHT OUT
ARMCHAIR THEATRE 24/4/1960

A NIGHT OUT WITH DANNY LA RUE
The SATURDAY SPECIAL 7/12/1968

NIGHT SCHOOL
DO YOU REMEMBER? 14/5/1978

A NIGHT'S DARKNESS, A DAY'S SAIL
OMNIBUS 18/1/1970

NIGHTMARE
ONE STEP BEYOND 27/6/1961

NO FIXED ABODE
TELEVISION PLAYHOUSE 30/1/1959

NO MAMA NO
ITV PLAYHOUSE 27/3/1979

NO MAN'S ROAD
CONFLICT 30/4/1957

NO SAMPLES
DOUGLAS FAIRBANKS JR., PRESENTS
27/2/1956

NOBODY'S CONSCIENCE
MURDER 13/6/1976

The NODDER
WODEHOUSE PLAYHOUSE 30/4/1976

NOEL COWARD – PLAYWRIGHT
OMNIBUS 7/12/1969

NOON WINE
STAR PERFORMANCE 9/4/1968

NOT I
The LIVELY ARTS 17/4/1977

NOW LET HIM GO
ARMCHAIR THEATRE 15/9/1957

NUTS IN MAY
PLAY FOR TODAY 13/1/1976

O FAT WHITE WOMAN
PLAY FOR TODAY 4/11/1971

The ODD JOB
SIX DATES WITH BARKER 22/1/1971

ODDS AGAINST
WEDNESDAY SPECIAL 15/9/1976

The OFFER
COMEDY PLAYHOUSE 5/1/1962

An OFFICER OF THE COURT
The WEDNESDAY PLAY 20/12/1967

OGGIE
TELEVISION PLAYHOUSE 13/11/1959

The OLD CROWD
BY ALAN BENNETT – SIX PLAYS 27/1/1979

The OLD MAN OF THE AIR
THEATRE ROYAL 19/2/1956

ON GIANT'S SHOULDERS
PLAY OF THE WEEK 28/3/1979

ON THE EVE OF PUBLICATION
The WEDNESDAY PLAY 27/11/1968

ON THE ROAD WITH BOB HOPE
The WORLD OF BOB HOPE

ONE CAN'T HELP FEELING SORRY
DOUGLAS FAIRBANKS JR., PRESENTS
29/10/1956

The ONE EYED MONSTER
ARMCHAIR THEATRE 6/8/1966

ONE JUST MAN
The VISE 1/10/1954

ONE MAN AGAINST THE WORLD
OUT OF STEP 18/12/1957

ONE OF NATURE'S HOTELS
HORIZON 11/3/1977

ONE THING LEADS TO ANOTHER
SQUARE TWO 14/1/1970

ONLY CONNECT
The OTHER SIDE 18/5/1979

ONLY MAKE BELIEVE
PLAY FOR TODAY 12/2/1973

OPENING NIGHT OF SCOTTISH TV
THIS IS SCOTLAND

ORFEO
OMNIBUS 17/3/1977

The OTHER WAY
HORIZON 11/11/1974

OTHER WORLDS ARE WATCHING US
OUT OF STEP 25/9/1957

The OVERNIGHT BAG
SHADES OF GREENE 3/2/1976

OVERNIGHT HAUL
The TWENTIETH CENTURY FOX HOUR
16/5/1956

The OX-BOW INCIDENT
The TWENTIETH CENTURY FOX HOUR
2/11/1955

The PALETO CONFESSION
TELEVISION PLAYHOUSE 25/1/1963

The PARACHUTE
PLAY OF THE MONTH 21/1/1968

PARADISE RESTORED
OMNIBUS 2/1/1972

The PARADISE RUN
PLAYS FOR BRITAIN 6/4/1976

The PARADISE SUITE
ARMCHAIR THEATRE 17/2/1963

The PARAFFIN SEASON
ARMCHAIR THEATRE 4/12/1965

The PARTY OF THE FIRST PART
PLAY FOR LOVE 16/4/1978

A PASSAGE TO INDIA
PLAY OF THE MONTH 16/11/1965

The PATRIOT GAME
PLAYHOUSE 13/10/1969

PATTERN FOR VIOLENCE
CONFLICT 14/5/1957

The PERFECT CRIME
ALFRED HITCHCOCK PRESENTS
20/10/1957

PHILBY, BURGESS & MACLEAN
ITV PLAYHOUSE 31/5/1977

The PIANO
PLAY FOR TODAY 28/1/1971

PICTURE BOOK
WATCH WITH MOTHER 4/2/1957

PIG EARTH
OMNIBUS 21/6/1979

The PILGRIMAGE OF TI-JEAN
OMNIBUS 30/8/1978

The PITY OF IT ALL
ARMCHAIR THEATRE 22/1/1966

PLAINTIFFS AND DEFENDANTS
PLAY FOR TODAY 14/10/1975

PLATONOV
PLAY OF THE MONTH 23/5/1971

PLEASURE WHERE SHE FINDS IT
ARMCHAIR THEATRE 3/5/1964

POLLY PUT THE KETTLE ON
SEVEN FACES OF WOMAN 23/6/1974

POOR BABY
AGAINST THE CROWD 20/7/1975

POOR CHERRY
ARMCHAIR THEATRE 9/9/1967

POP GOES THE EASEL
MONITOR 25/3/1962

PORTRAIT OF A DISCIPLINARIAN
WODEHOUSE PLAYHOUSE 7/5/1975

PORTRAIT OF A SOVIET COMPOSER
MONITOR 18/6/1961
PROKOFIEV

The PORTSMOUTH DEFENCE
The WEDNESDAY PLAY 30/3/1966

POSTSCRIPT TO THE BALLET
TEMPO 5/4/1964

The PREDICTION
THRILLER 22/11/1960

The PRESENT
DOUGLAS FAIRBANKS JR., PRESENTS
13/2/1956

PRETTY POLLY
ARMCHAIR THEATRE 23/7/1966

The PRINCE MAKER
TEMPO 13/9/1964

The PRISONER
ONE STEP BEYOND 2/5/1961

PRISONER AND ESCORT
ARMCHAIR THEATRE 5/4/1964

PROFESSIONAL FOUL
PLAY OF THE WEEK 21/9/1977

PROKOFIEV
MONITOR 18/6/1961

PROMENADE
TELEVISION PLAYHOUSE 22/5/1959

PT 109
NAVY LOG 13/3/1958

The PUB FIGHTER
HALF HOUR STORY 27/2/1968

PURE RADIO
OMNIBUS 3/11/1977

The PURPLE ROOM
THRILLER 25/10/1960

The QUARRY
SUNDAY NIGHT 27/2/1966

The QUARRYMEN
Y CHWARELWR

QUESTION OF LOYALTY
CONFLICT 2/4/1957

A QUESTION OF TORTURE – SOUTH
VIETNAM
**SOUTH VIETNAM: A QUESTION OF
TORTURE**

QUIET AFTERNOON
SCENE 5/10/1972

The RACE FOR THE DOUBLE HELIX
HORIZON 8/7/1974

RAG, TAG AND BOBTAIL
WATCH WITH MOTHER

The RAGAZZA
PLAY FOR LOVE 23/4/1978

RAIL CRASH
HORIZON 8/5/1972

The RANDOLPH FAMILY
DEAR OCTOPUS

RASTAMAN
EVERYMAN 26/6/1977

The RECEPTION
TELEVISION PLAYHOUSE 18/5/1961

The RED DEER OF RHUM
HORIZON 29/12/1978

RED SEA CORAL AND THE CROWN-OF-
THORNS
HORIZON 12/4/1973

RENDEZVOUS AT DAWN
DOUGLAS FAIRBANKS JR., PRESENTS
19/11/1956

The REPORTERS
PLAY FOR TODAY 9/10/1972

RETURN AS A STRANGER
ONE PAIR OF EYES 17/10/1970

RETURN TO THE REGIMENT
TELEVISION PLAYHOUSE 2/5/1963

The REVENGE OF DR. DEATH
MADHOUSE

REX HARRISON IN THE ADVENTURES
OF DON QUIXOTE
PLAY OF THE MONTH 7/1/1973
The ADVENTURES OF DON QUIXOTE

RICHARD II
BBC TELEVISION SHAKESPEARE
10/12/1978

RICHARD II
SHAKESPEARE IN PERSPECTIVE
10/12/1978

The RIGHT PROSPECTUS
PLAY FOR TODAY 22/10/1970

The RIME OF THE ANCIENT MARINER
CLOUDS OF GLORY 16/7/1978

RING OF GREED
The VISE 29/6/1962

The RING OF TRUTH
COUNTRY MATTERS 4/3/1973

The RIVER THAT CAME CLEAN
HORIZON 2/9/1977

ROALD DAHL'S TALES OF THE
UNEXPECTED
TALES OF THE UNEXPECTED

ROBERT TAYLOR'S DETECTIVES
The DETECTIVES

ROBINSON CRUSOE
PLAY OF THE MONTH 29/12/1974

The ROBOTS ARE COMING
HORIZON 28/5/1979

ROMEO AND JULIET
BBC TELEVISION SHAKESPEARE
3/12/1978

The ROSE AFFAIR
ARMCHAIR THEATRE 8/10/1961

The ROYAL BALLET: THE RAKE'S
PROGRESS
The RAKE'S PROGRESS

ROYAL CANADIAN MOUNTED POLICE
R.C.M.P.

ROYAL TOUR
ACROSS THE HEART

ROYAL WELSH 1904–1979
**BEASTLY TIME: ROYAL WELSH
1904–1979** 22/7/1977

RUMOUR
PLAYHOUSE 2/3/1970

The RUNAWAY
OMNIBUS 18/11/1973

SAID THE PREACHER
THIRTY MINUTE THEATRE 6/3/1972

ST. NICOLAS-CANTATA OPUS 42 BY
BENJAMIN BRITTEN
WEDNESDAY SPECIAL 22/12/1976

SAKI: THE STORIES OF H.H. MUNRO
SAKI

A SALE
MAUPASSANT: WOMEN AND MONEY

SALUTE TO SIR LEW – THE MASTER
SHOWMAN
SALUTE

SAN FRANCISCO BEAT
The LINEUP

SANCTUARY
SHORT STORY 1972

SATURDAY NIGHT AROUND THE
WORLD
STAR PERFORMANCE 16/4/1968

The SATURDAY PARTY
PLAY FOR TODAY 1/5/1975

SAY GOODNIGHT TO YOUR GRANDMA
ARMCHAIR THEATRE 27/10/1970

SCENES FROM A MARRIAGE
SCENER UR ETT KTENSKAP

The SCENT OF FEAR
ARMCHAIR THEATRE 13/9/1959

SCHALCKEN THE PAINTER
OMNIBUS 23/12/1979

SCHMOEDIPUS
PLAY FOR TODAY 20/6/1974

The SCHOOL FOR SCANDAL
PLAY OF THE MONTH 16/2/1975

SCHOOL PLAY
PLAYHOUSE 7/11/1979

SCIENCE ON SAFARI
HORIZON 15/9/1969

The SCROLLS FROM THE SON OF A STAR
CHRONICLE 12/2/1976

SCUM
PLAY FOR TODAY 1977

SEARCH FOR MARTHA HARRIS
The VISE 30/9/1955

The SECRET PLACE
The VISE 19/11/1954

SECRETS
BLACK AND BLUE 14/8/1973

SERJEANT MUSGRAVE'S DANCE
PLAY OF THE WEEK 24/10/1961

The SERPENT BENEATH
The VISE 13/5/1955

SERVANT OF TWO MASTERS
ARLECCHINO

SET A MURDERER
The VISE 8/10/1954

SHADES: THREE PLAYS BY SAMUEL
BECKETT
The LIVELY ARTS 17/4/1977

The SHADOW LINE
SMUGA CIENIA

The SHAKESPEARE PLAYS
BBC TELEVISION SHAKESPEARE

SHARP AT FOUR
ARMCHAIR THEATRE 12/1/1964

SHE FELL AMONG THIEVES
PLAY OF THE WEEK 1/3/1978

SHELTER
HALF HOUR STORY 19/5/1967

SHIPWRECK
CHRONICLE 11/5/1979

The SHIRLEY MACLAINE SHOW
SHIRLEY'S WORLD

SHOOTING THE CHANDELIER
PLAY OF THE WEEK 26/10/1977

SHUTTLECOCK
PLAYS FOR BRITAIN 11/5/1976

SIDE ENTRANCE
The VISE 23/9/1955

SIEGE
WARNER BROTHERS PRESENTS 14/2/1956

SIGNAL RECEIVED
ONE STEP BEYOND 4/4/1961

The SILENT MAN
DOUGLAS FAIRBANKS JR., PRESENTS
27/1/1954

SILENT SPEECH
HORIZON 29/7/1977

The SILVER MASK
BETWEEN THE WARS 15/6/1973

The SIMPLE LIFE
COUNTRY MATTERS 18/2/1973

SIR MORTIMER: DIGGING UP PEOPLE
CHRONICLE 26/3/1973

SIR MORTIMER: THE VICEROY SENT
FOR ME
CHRONICLE 2/4/1973

SISTER DORA
The SUNDAY DRAMA 10/7/1977

The SISTERS
Las HERMANAS

SIX PEOPLE, NO MUSIC
ALFRED HITCHCOCK PRESENTS 4/1/1959

SIX SCENES FROM A MARRIAGE
SCENER UR ETT KTENSKAP

SLING YOUR HOOK
The WEDNESDAY PLAY 2/4/1969

SMALL FISH ARE SWEET
ARMCHAIR THEATRE 8/11/1959

A SMILE FOR THE CROCODILE
HORIZON 7/1/1977

SMOG
GLOBE THEATRE 5/11/1974

SNAKES AND LADDERS
BLACKMAIL 5/11/1965

SNAPSHOT
The VISE 16/12/1955

SOME TALK OF ALEXANDER
PLAYDATE 5/3/1962

SOME WOMENOF MARRAKESH
DISAPPEARING WORLD 26/1/1977

SOMEONE OUTSIDE
DOUGLAS FAIRBANKS JR., PRESENTS
22/10/1956

SON OF MAN
The WEDNESDAY PLAY 16/4/1969

SONG OF SUMMER
OMNIBUS 15/9/1968

SONG WITHOUT WORDS
WOMEN IN LOVE

The SONGS THEY SANG WERE OF
IRELAND FREE
REBELLION AT EASTER

The SORCERER
ONE STEP BEYOND 23/5/1961

SPEED KING
PLAYHOUSE 19/12/1979

SPEND, SPEND, SPEND
PLAY FOR TODAY 15/3/1977

A SPLINTER OF ICE
PLAYHOUSE 29/5/1972

The SPONGERS
PLAY FOR TODAY 24/1/1978

SPY CATCHER
SPYCATCHER

STACCATO
JOHNNY STACCATO

STAN'S DAY OUT
THEATRE 625 13/8/1967

STAND UP, NIGEL BARTON
The WEDNESDAY PLAY 8/12/1965

STARMAKER
LATE NIGHT DRAMA 4/9/1974

STELLA
HALF HOUR STORY 19/6/1968

STOCKER'S COPPER
PLAY FOR TODAY 20/1/1972

The STORY OF THE RED ORCHESTRA
Die ROTE KAPELLE

The STOWAWAY
WOMEN IN LOVE

STRANGENESS MINUS THREE
HORIZON 25/7/1964

The STRANGER
ONE STEP BEYOND 28/2/1961

STRANGER IN TOWN
The VISE 11/11/1955

STRANGLEHOLD
The VISE 8/7/1955

A SUBJECT OF SCANDAL AND CONCERN
The SUNDAY NIGHT PLAY 6/11/1960

The SUCKER GAME
The VISE 1955

The SULLENS SISTERS
COUNTRY MATTERS 3/9/1972

SUNSET ACROSS THE BAY
PLAY FOR TODAY 20/2/1975

A SUPERSTITION
The SUNDAY DRAMA 14/8/1977

SUTTON HOO
The MILLION POUND GRAVE

SWEET SOLUTIONS
HORIZON 19/3/1979

Ein TAG
EIN TAG

A TALE OF TWO TALENTS
TEMPO 6/2/1966

TALENT
SCREENPLAY 5/8/1979

TALES OF THE PLAINSMAN
The LAW OF THE PLAINSMAN

The TALKING HEAD
SATURDAY NIGHT THEATRE 30/8/1969

TALKING TO A STRANGER
THEATRE 625 2/10/1966–23/10/1966

The TAMING OF THE SHREW
HALLMARK HALL OF FAME 18/3/1956

The TAMING OF TROOPER TANNER
BLACKMAIL 25/11/1965

TAP ON THE SHOULDER
The WEDNESDAY PLAY 6/1/1965

TEA LADIES
GALTON & SPEIGHT'S TEA LADIES

The TEA PARTY
The LARGEST THEATRE IN THE WORLD
25/3/1965

The TEMPEST
SUNDAY NIGHT THEATRE 14/10/1956

TENDERFOOT
SUGARFOOT

TENSION
The VISE

The TERRORIST
ARMCHAIR THEATRE 26/10/1958

TERRY
SCENE 30/1/1969

THAT ROOM UPSTAIRS
ONE STEP BEYOND 21/3/1961

THAT'S WHERE THE TOWN'S GOING
ARMCHAIR THEATRE 7/6/1964

'THERE IS NO CONQUEROR...' THE
STORY OF THE MOORS IN SPAIN
CHRONICLE 11/10/1969

The THIRSTLAND
The LOST WORLD OF THE KALAHARI

THIRTY STRETCH
The GAMBLERS 28/2/1968

THIS LAST TOUR
DOUGLAS FAIRBANKS JR., PRESENTS
15/10/1956

THIS WEEK ARTS
THIS WEEK – THE ARTS

THIS YANKEE DODGE BEATS
MESMERISM HOLLOW – THE STORY OF
ANAESTHETICS
HORIZON 29/4/1974

THIS YEAR'S GIRL
FOUR OF HEARTS 11/10/1965

THREE CLEAR SUNDAYS
The WEDNESDAY PLAY 7/4/1965

THREE LOOMS WAITING
OMNIBUS 13/6/1971

THRILLS GALORE
THIRTY MINUTE THEATRE 4/9/1972

THROUGH THE NIGHT
PLAY FOR TODAY 2/12/1975

The TIGER
ONE STEP BEYOND 20/6/1961

TIGERS ARE BETTER LOOKING
THEN AND NOW 1/10/1973

The TIME OF YOUR LIFE
GLOBE THEATRE 26/7/1978

TIME OUT OF MIND
ARMCHAIR MYSTERY THEATRE 19/7/1964

TIMMY THE SHANKS
DOUGLAS FAIRBANKS JR., PRESENTS
17/9/1956

TO WHAT GREAT HEIGHTS
DOUGLAS FAIRBANKS JR., PRESENTS
3/12/1956

TOMB OF THE LOST KING
CHRONICLE 20/4/1979

TONY BENNETT AND COUNT BASIE
SHOW OF THE WEEK 15/6/1969

TOO OLD FOR DONKEYS
TELEVISION PLAYHOUSE 4/4/1963

TOP BRASS
OMNIBUS 23/1/1968

A TOUCH OF SENSITIVITY
HORIZON 5/11/1979

A TOUCH OF THE JUMBOS
BIG BROTHER 4/10/1970

A TRAGEDY OF TWO AMBITIONS
WESSEX TALES 21/11/1973

TRAITOR
PLAY FOR TODAY 14/10/1971

The TRANSPLANT EXPERIENCE
HORIZON 5/1/1976

The TREASURE OF PRIAM
CHRONICLE 3/12/1966

A TREASURY OF TREES
HORIZON 12/11/1979

TREATS
The SUNDAY DRAMA 11/12/1977

The TRIAL OF DR. FANCY
ARMCHAIR THEATRE 13/9/1964

TRIPLE EXPOSURE
PLAY FOR TODAY 6/11/1972

The TROUBLE WITH OUR IVY
ARMCHAIR THEATRE 19/11/1961

TUNE IN TO NATURE'S RADIO
OUT OF STEP 13/11/1957

TUNNEL OF FEAR
FOUR STAR PLAYHOUSE 19/1/1956

TUNNEL UNDER THE WALL
The TUNNEL

The TUAREGS
DISAPPEARING WORLD 18/4/1972

TWELFTH HOUR
THEATRE 625 3/4/1966

TWELFTH NIGHT
HALLMARK HALL OF FAME 15/12/1957

The TWELVE POUND LOOK
BARRIE WITH LOVE 27/6/1973

TWENTY ONE
TWENTY ONE UP

TWO OF A KIND
The VISE 14/10/1955

The TWO-SEATER BACHELOR DAYS
TELEVISION PLAYHOUSE 11/4/1963

TWO SUNDAYS
PLAY FOR TODAY 21/10/1975

TWO WAY TRAFFIC
SCENE 13/11/1969

TYCOON OF THE YEAR
The GAMBLERS 23/11/1967

TYGER TYGER
OMNIBUS 10/11/1967

UNDER THE AGE
THIRTY MINUTE THEATRE 20/3/1972

UNDER THE GARDEN
SHADES OF GREENE 10/2/1976

UNDERGROUND
SCENE 8/3/1967

UP THE JUNCTION
The WEDNESDAY PLAY 3/11/1965

The VALIANT YEARS
WINSTON CHURCHILL

A VARIETY OF PASSION
MURDER 20/6/1976

VENUS RISING
HALF HOUR STORY 13/2/1968

The VICTORIAN CHAISE LONGUE
The STUDIO 4 19/3/1962

VIETNAM : A QUESTION OF TORTURE
SOUTH VIETNAM: A QUESTION OF TORTURE

The VILLA
ONE STEP BEYOND 6/6/1961

VILLAGE OF FEAR
DICK POWELL'S ZANE GREY THEATRE
1/3/1957

VILLAGE WOOING
PLAYS FOR PLEASURE 17/4/1979

VINEGAR TRIP
PLAYHOUSE 24/4/1973

The VIRGINS
ARMCHAIR THEATRE 25/6/1974

VIRUS
HORIZON 14/9/1970

A VISIT FROM MISS PROTHERO
PLAY OF THE WEEK 11/1/1978

VOTE, VOTE, VOTE, FOR NIGEL BARTON
The WEDNESDAY PLAY 15/12/1965

VERITE
ARMCHAIR THEATRE 23/10/1973

The VOYAGE AROUND MY FATHER
PLAYS OF TODAY 16/10/1969

A WALK IN THE WILDERNESS
DOUGLAS FAIRBANKS JR., PRESENTS
5/3/1956

WALK ON THE WATER
PLAY OF THE WEEK 25/11/1963

WALK WITH DESTINY
The GATHERING STORM

WAR OF THE GODS
DISAPPEARING WORLD 22/6/1971

The WARMONGER
THIRTY MINUTE THEATRE 13/11/1970

WATCH THE BIRDIE
MONITOR 9/6/1963

The WATERCRESS GIRL
COUNTRY MATTERS 17/9/1972

WATERS OF THE MOON
SUNDAY NIGHT THEATRE 27/12/1959

A WAY OF LIVING
ARMCHAIR THEATRE 22/12/1963

The WAYS OF LOVE
ARMCHAIR THEATRE 9/4/1961

WE ARE ALL GUILTY
AGAINST THE CROWD 17/8/1975

WEDNESDAY LOVE
PLAY FOR TODAY 8/5/1975

The WEEKEND GUEST
The VISE 25/3/1955

WHALES, DOLPHINS AND MEN
HORIZON 6/3/1972

WHAT A WASTE!
HORIZON 24/5/1973

WHAT DO YOU THINK OF IT SO FAR?
FESTIVAL 40 29/8/1976

WHAT'S WRONG WITH HUMPTY
DUMPTY?
ARMCHAIR THEATRE 11/2/1967

WHAT'S WRONG WITH THE SUN?
HORIZON 14/6/1976

WHEN THE BOUGH BREAKS
PLAY FOR TODAY 6/5/1971

WHEN THE BREEDING HAS TO STOP
HORIZON 8/2/1973

WHEN THE KISSING HAD TO STOP
PLAY OF THE WEEK 16/10/1962

WHEN THE WIND BLOWS
PLAY OF THE WEEK 2/8/1965

WHERE I LIVE
ARMCHAIR THEATRE 10/1/1960

WHERE THE BUFFALO ROAM
The WEDNESDAY PLAY 2/11/1966

The WHITE FALCON
SUNDAY NIGHT THEATRE 5/2/1956

The WHITE STOCKING
The STORIES OF D.H. LAWRENCE 3/1/1966

The WHO SPECIAL
WON'T GET FOOLED AGAIN

WHO'S WHO
PLAY FOR TODAY 5/2/1979

WHOLE LOTTA SHAKIN' GOIN' ON
DON'T KNOCK THE ROCK

The WHOLE TRUTH
SEVEN DEADLY VIRTUES 27/4/1967

WHY DID STUART DIE?
HORIZON 3/5/1976

WHY HERE?
The SUNDAY DRAMA 7/8/1977

WILLIAM AND DOROTHY
CLOUDS OF GLORY 9/7/1978

WILLIAM AND MARY
TALES OF THE UNEXPECTED 7/4/1979

The WIND AND THE SUN
The SUNDAY NIGHT PLAY 13/11/1960

The WIND IN A TALL PAPER CHIMNEY
ARMCHAIR THEATRE 7/2/1968

The WINGS OF THE DOVE
PLAY OF THE MONTH 8/4/1979

The WITHERED ARM
WESSEX TALES 7/11/1973

WOLF PACK
ARMCHAIR THEATRE 13/4/1958

A WOMAN OF NO IMPORTANCE
PLAY OF THE WEEK 9/2/1960

A WOMAN SOBBING
DEAD OF NIGHT 17/12/1972

WOMEN AND MONEY
MAUPASSANT: WOMEN AND MONEY

The WORLD OF COPPARD
OMNIBUS 15/12/1967

WORLDS IN COLLISION
HORIZON 11/1/1973

The WRITING ON THE WALL
HORIZON 11/2/1974

The WRONG SIDE OF THE PARK
The SUNDAY NIGHT PLAY 19/3/1961

WRONG TIME MURDER
The VISE 2/12/1955

The YELLOW ROBE
The VISE 17/12/1954

YELLOWBELLY
FOUR STAR PLAYHOUSE 12/7/1956

YOU AND ME AND HIM
THIRTY MINUTE THEATRE 22/2/1973

Genre Index

ADVENTURE

ADVERTISING

AGRICULTURE

ANIMATION

ANTHOLOGY DRAMA

ANTHROPOLOGY

ARCHAEOLOGY

ARCHITECTURE

ARTS

AVIATION AND SPACE TRAVEL

AWARD CEREMONIES

BALLET see DANCE

BLACK AND ASIAN CULTURE

BOARDROOM DRAMAS

BREAKFAST TELEVISON

BUSINESS AND ECONOMICS

CARTOONS see ANIMATION or PUPPETS

CHAT SHOWS

CHILDREN'S DRAMA

CHILDREN'S PROGRAMMES

CINEMA, TELEVISION AND RADIO

COMEDY

CONSUMER PROGRAMMES

CRAFTS

CRIME (Fiction)

CURRENT AFFAIRS

DANCE

DAYTIME TELEVISION

DETECTIVE

DISCUSSION

DRAMA

DRAMA DOCUMENTARIES

ECONOMICS see BUSINESS AND ECONOMICS

EDUCATION (Documentaries)

EDUCATION (Fiction)

ELECTIONS

ESPIONAGE

EXPLORATION

FANTASY

FASHION

GAME SHOWS

HEALTH AND MEDICINE

HISTORICAL DRAMAS

HISTORY

HOUSING

INDUSTRY

INSTRUCTIONAL

INTERVIEW

LAW (Documentaries)

LAW (Fiction)

LITERATURE

MAGAZINE PROGRAMMES

MANAGEMENT see BUSINESS AND ECONOMICS

MEDICAL (Fiction)

MEDICINE see HEALTH AND MEDICINE

MINI-SERIES

MILITARY (Documentaries)

MILITARY (Fiction)

MUSIC

MUSIC – CLASSICAL

MUSIC – JAZZ AND BLUES

MUSIC – OPERAS AND OPERETTAS

MUSIC – POPULAR

NATURAL HISTORY

NEWS

OPEN ACCESS PROGRAMMES

PAINTING AND SCULPTURE

PARTY POLITICAL CONFERENCES

PHOTOGRAPHY

POLICE

POLITICAL AND MINISTERIAL BROADCASTS

POLITICAL DOCUMENTARIES

PRESS

PUPPETS

QUIZ SHOWS see GAME SHOWS

RAILWAYS

REGIONAL NEWS

REGIONAL PROGRAMMES

RELIGION AND ETHICS

ROYALTY

SATIRE

SCHOOL PROGRAMMES

SCIENCE AND TECHNOLOGY

SCIENCE-FICTION

SCULPTURE see PAINTING AND SCULPTURE

SHIPS AND SHIPPING

SITCOMS

SOAP OPERAS

SOCIAL DOCUMENTARIES

SPORT

STATE OCCASIONS

TALENT SHOWS

TELEVISION COMPANY HISTORY

TELEVISION FILMS

THEATRE

TRADE UNIONISM

TRANSPORT

TRAVEL

VARIETY

WAR (Documentaries)

WAR (Fiction)

WESTERNS

WILDLIFE see NATURAL HISTORY

ADVENTURE
The ADVENTURER
ADVENTURES OF AGGIE
The ADVENTURES OF ROBIN HOOD
The ADVENTURES OF THE SCARLET
  PIMPERNEL
ASSIGNMENT FOREIGN LEGION
The AVENGERS
The BARON
BEARCATS
BOLD VENTURE
The BORDERERS
BOY DOMINIC
CALLAN
CANNONBALL
CASABLANCA
The CHAMPIONS
The COUNT OF MONTE CRISTO
CRANE
DANGER MAN
DOMINIC
HAND IN GLOVE
The HILL OF THE RED FOX
JASON KING
LUKE'S KINGDOM
The NEW AVENGERS
The PERSUADERS!
QUEEN'S CHAMPION
QUEST OF EAGLES
RAFFLES
REDGAUNTLET
RETURN OF THE SAINT
RICHARD THE LIONHEART
RIPTIDE
SAILOR OF FORTUNE
The SAINT
ST. IVES
The TERRACOTTA HORSE
The THIRD MAN
The VISE
WHIPLASH
WHITE HUNTER
WILDE ALLIANCE

ADVERTISING
The GROUP 9/11/1965
  The EGGHEADS
LEVIN INTERVIEW 5/4/1966
  DR. JOHN TREASURE
LOOKING AT TELEVISION 22/6/1977
  GIVE US A BREAK
The PERSUADERS
THIS WEEK 10/4/1975
  LICENSED TO KILL
VIEWPOINT 7/10/1975
  MONEY TALKS
WAYS OF SEEING: PART 4

AGRICULTURE
ABOUT BRITAIN 7/1/1976
  BUCCLEUCHS OF THE BORDER
ABOUT BRITAIN 12/2/1979
  An HONEST DAY'S TOIL
BEASTLY TIME: ROYAL WELSH 1904–1979
BEAUTY, BONNY, DAISY, VIOLET, GRACE AND
  GEOFFREY MORTON
BITTER HARVEST
CBS REPORTS 21/3/1961
  HARVEST OF SHAME
CHILDREN OF ESKDALE
COUNTRY FOCUS
The DALE THAT DIED
EMMERDALE FARM
ENOUGH TO EAT
FARM AND COUNTRY NEWS
FARMING OUTLOOK
A FEW NOTES ON OUR FOOD PROBLEM
MAN OF THE YEAR – NORMAN BORLAUG
MASTER SHEPHERD
The MURUT PEOPLE OF BORNEO
NEVER AND ALWAYS
OUT OF TOWN 17/3/1978
  BEE SKIPS
SHEPHERD
The SHOOT
SUNLEY'S DAUGHTER
THIS WEEK 28/5/1964
  FACTORY FARMING
TOO LONG A WINTER
WORLD IS OURS 28/11/1956
  The FORGOTTEN INDIANS

WORLD IN ACTION 10/1/1972
  WORKING THE LAND
WORLD IN ACTION 11/6/1979
  The LUCK OF THE IRISH
WORLD TONIGHT 16/11/1965
  FARMING

ANIMATION
see also PUPPETS
CAPTAIN PUGWASH
CINEMA 20/12/1973
  RAY HARRYHAUSEN
The DO-IT-YOURSELF FILM ANIMATION SHOW
The FANTASTIC FOUR
FESTIVAL OF FAMILY CLASSICS
The HUNTING OF THE SNARK
IT'S A SQUARE WORLD
JAMIE AND THE MAGIC TORCH
LITTLE BLUE
OSCAR
OUTA-SPACE!
SINBAD JR.
TOPPER'S TALES

ANTHOLOGY DRAMA
AGAINST THE CROWD
ALFRED HITCHCOCK PRESENTS
APPOINTMENT WITH DRAMA
ARMCHAIR MYSTERY THEATRE
ARMCHAIR THEATRE
ARMCHAIR 30
ARMCHAIR THRILLER
AS I WAS SAYING
BEASTS
BETWEEN THE WARS
BIG BROTHER
BLACK AND BLUE
BY ALAN BENNETT – SIX PLAYS
CENTRE PLAY
CHILDHOOD
COMEDY PLAYHOUSE
CONFESSION
CONFLICT
COUNTRY MATTERS
DICK POWELL'S ZANE GREY THEATRE
DO YOU REMEMBER?
DOUGLAS FAIRBANKS JR., PRESENTS
DRAMA '64
DRAMA '62
ESPIONAGE
FOUR OF HEARTS
FOUR STAR PLAYHOUSE
THE FRIGHTENERS
The GAMBLERS
GLOBE THEATRE
HALF HOUR STORY
HALLMARK HALL OF FAME
HEARTLAND
ITV PLAYHOUSE
LATE NIGHT DRAMA
LAURENCE OLIVIER PRESENTS
LONDON PLAYHOUSE
LOVE STORY
MAUPASSANT: WOMEN AND MONEY
MURDER
ONE STEP BEYOND
The OTHER SIDE
OUT OF THE UNKNOWN
The OUTER LIMITS
PLAY FOR LOVE
PLAY FOR TODAY
PLAY OF THE WEEK (ITV)
PLAY OF THE WEEK (BBC)
PLAY OF THE MONTH
PLAYDATE
PLAYHOUSE (ITV)
PLAYHOUSE (BBC)
PLAYS FOR BRITAIN
PLAYS FOR PLEASURE
PLAYS OF TODAY
RED LETTER DAY
SATURDAY NIGHT THEATRE
SATURDAY PLAYHOUSE
SCREENPLAY
SECOND CITY FIRSTS
SEVEN DEADLY SINS
SEVEN DEADLY VIRTUES
SEVEN FACES OF WOMAN
The SEXTET
SHADES OF GREENE
SHADOWS
SHE

SHORT STORY
The SINNERS
SIX
The STORY-TELLER
The STUDIO 4
STUDIO '64
The SUNDAY DRAMA
SUNDAY NIGHT
SUNDAY NIGHT THEATRE
The SUNDAY NIGHT PLAY
TALES FROM SOHO
TALES OF THE UNEXPECTED
TELEVISION PLAYHOUSE
TELEVISION WORLD THEATRE
THEATRE ROYAL
THEATRE 625
THEATRE '60
THEN AND NOW
THEY MET IN A CITY
THIRTY MINUTE THEATRE (ITV)
THIRTY MINUTE THEATRE (BBC)
THRILLER
TURNING YEAR TALES
The TWENTIETH CENTURY FOX HOUR
WARNER BROTHERS PRESENTS
The WEDNESDAY PLAY

ANTHROPOLOGY
ADVENTURE
ALCHERINGA
The CITY ON THE STEPPE
The CONGO I KNEW
DESTRUCTION OF THE INDIAN
DISAPPEARING WORLD
The EMPTY QUARTER
THE FAMILY OF MAN
KINGDOM IN THE JUNGLE
The LOST WORLD OF THE KALAHARI
MAN BEFORE ADAM
MONGOLIA
The MURUT PEOPLE OF BORNEO
PARADISE LOST?
REPORT 8/11/1969
  NOW THAT THE BUFFALO'S GONE
SURVIVAL 2/3/1966
  KARAMOJA
SURVIVAL SPECIAL 8/5/1973
  The FORBIDDEN DESERT OF THE DANAKIL
The TRIBE THAT HIDES FROM MAN
TUESDAY'S DOCUMENTARY 19/5/1970
  SHETLAND: BRITAIN'S FARTHEST NORTH
The UNLUCKY AUSTRALIANS

ARCHAEOLOGY
see also HISTORY
ANCIENT MONUMENTS OF EGYPT
CHRONICLE
CRADLE OF ENGLAND
HORIZON 22/2/1976
  The LORDS OF THE LABYRINTH
HORIZON 26/3/1979
  BRONZE AGE BLAST-OFF
HORIZON SPECIAL 25/11/1977
  The CASE OF THE ANCIENT ASTRONAUTS
INDUSTRIAL GRAND TOUR
The LIVING WALL
MAN BEFORE ADAM
The MILLION POUND GRAVE
The RIVER NILE
The STORY BENEATH THE SANDS
TRAVELLER'S TALES 27/7/1964
  PERISCOPE INTO THE PAST
TUTANKHAMUN'S EGYPT

ARCHITECTURE
ACT OF FAITH
ALL OUR YESTERDAYS 18/3/1972
  TOWN PLANNING IN POST-WAR BRITAIN
AQUARIUS 2/3/1975
  The GREAT GONDOLA RACE: PART 1
BETJEMAN'S LONDON
CIVILISATION 9/3/1969
  ROMANCE AND REALITY
CIVILISATION 6/4/1969
  GRANDEUR AND OBEDIENCE
CONTRASTS
The FIGHT FOR YORK MINSTER
The GIFT
The GROWING TOWN
HORIZON 11/2/1974
  The WRITING ON THE WALL
HOUSE FOR THE FUTURE

SCIENCE-FICTION *cont.*

SURVIVORS
THUNDERBIRDS
U.F.O.
VOYAGE TO THE BOTTOM OF THE SEA

SHIPS AND SHIPPING

ALL IN A DAY 25/8/1971
   The LAUNCH
CONTRACT 736
SAILOR
SEA WAR
The SILVER JUBILEE REVIEW AT SPITHEAD
The STORY OF THE QUEEN MARY
THEY SANK THE LUSITANIA
THIS WEEK 18/5/1956
   SS UNITED STATES
THIS WEEK 8/6/1956
   TITANIC
THIS WEEK 28/8/1958
   NAUTILUS STORY
THIS WEEK 8/7/1971
   MEN OF THE CLYDE
WARSHIP EAGLE
WORLD IN ACTION 14/1/1964
   LAKONIA – THE FACTS
WORLD IN ACTION 13/9/1971
   SOUNDS OF THE CLYDE
YESTERDAY'S WITNESS 10/9/1973
   The IOLAIRE DISASTER

SITCOMS

see also COMEDY
The ADDAMS FAMILY
AGONY
...AND MOTHER MAKES THREE
ARE YOU BEING SERVED?
BACKS TO THE LAND
The BEVERLY HILLBILLIES
BILLY LIAR
BIRDS ON THE WING
BLESS ME, FATHER
BLESS THIS HOUSE
BOOTSIE AND SNUDGE
CAR 54, WHERE ARE YOU?
CHALK AND CHEESE
CITIZEN SMITH
COME BACK MRS NOAH
CURRY AND CHIPS
DAD'S ARMY
DENNIS THE MENACE
DICK AND THE DUCHESS
THE DICKIE HENDERSON SHOW
DOCTOR AT LARGE
DOCTOR IN CHARGE
DOCTOR IN THE HOUSE
DOCTOR ON THE GO
The DOUBLE LIFE OF HENRY PHYFE
The FALL AND RISE OF REGINALD PERRIN
FATHER, DEAR FATHER
FAWLTY TOWERS
FOR THE LOVE OF ADA
THE FOSTERS SERIES
FROM A BIRD'S EYE VIEW
GEORGE AND MILDRED
GERT AND DAISY
GET SOME IN
GILLIGAN'S ISLAND
The GLUMS
The GOOD LIFE
HOW'S YOUR FATHER?
IN LOVING MEMORY
IT AIN'T HALF HOT MUM
LAST OF THE BASKETS
LAST OF THE SUMMER WINE
LIFE BEGINS AT FORTY
LIFE WITH THE LYONS
The LIKELY LADS
The LIVER BIRDS
LOVE THY NEIGHBOUR
LOVELY COUPLE
The LOVERS
McHALE'S NAVY
MAN ABOUT THE HOUSE
ME MAMMY
MIND YOUR LANGUAGE
The MISFIT
MIXED BLESSINGS
MY WIFE NEXT DOOR
NOW LOOK HERE...
OH BROTHER!
ON THE BUSES
ONLY WHEN I LAUGH

OUR MAN AT ST. MARK'S
OUR MAN FROM ST. MARK'S
PLEASE, SIR!
PORRIDGE
The RAG TRADE
RISING DAMP
ROBIN'S NEST
ROOM SERVICE
A SHARP INTAKE OF BREATH
SOMETHING IN THE CITY
SPOONER'S PATCH
STEPTOE AND SON
TILL DEATH US DO PART
TO THE MANOR BORN
TWO'S COMPANY
WELL ANYWAY
WHACK-O!
WHATEVER HAPPENED TO THE LIKELY LADS?
The WORKER
YOU'RE ONLY YOUNG TWICE

SOAP OPERAS

ANGELS
The CEDAR TREE
COMPACT
CORONATION STREET
CROSSROADS
EMERGENCY – WARD 10
EMMERDALE FARM
EMPIRE ROAD
GARNOCK WAY
GENERAL HOSPITAL
The NEWCOMERS (1965)

SOCIAL DOCUMENTARIES

see also BLACK AND ASIAN CULTURE
       EDUCATION (Documentaries)
       HEALTH AND MEDICINE
       HOUSING
       LAW (Documentaries)
       POLITICAL DOCUMENTARIES
       TRADE UNIONISM
ABOUT BRITAIN
ADVENTURE PLAYGROUND
AFTER MIDNIGHT
AIRPORT 64
THE ALCOHOLIC
ALL IN A DAY
ALL OUR YESTERDAYS
AMERICA NOW
AMERICA – ON THE EDGE OF ABUNDANCE
AMERICA – THE DOLLAR POOR
The ARAB EXPERIENCE
ASIAN HIGHWAY
B-P SERVICE IN WESTMINSTER ABBEY
BEAUTY, BONNY, DAISY, VIOLET, GRACE AND
   GEOFFREY MORTON
BEFORE THE MONSOON
BEHIND THE LINES: ERITREA
BETWEEN TWO RIVERS
BIG JACK'S OTHER WORLD
BILLY – VIOLENCE IN A FAMILY
BIRD'S EYE VIEW
BLACK MAN'S BURDEN
BORN CHINESE
BORN TO BE SMALL
BROAD ACRES
BROKEN HILL – WALLED CITY
BYGONES
CALL FOR ACTION
The CANADIANS
A CASE FOR EXPANSION
The CASE OF YOLANDE MCSHANE
CBS REPORTS
CBS SPECIAL REPORTS
CHECK IT OUT 31/7/1979
CHELSEA FLOWER SHOW
CHICAGO: PORTRAIT OF A CITY
CHILD OF THE SIXTIES
The CHILD WANTS A HOME
A CHILD'S PLACE
CHILDREN GROWING UP
CHILDREN GROWING UP – FIVE PLUS
CHILDREN OF REVOLUTION
CHILDREN OF ESKDALE
CHILDREN OF ABERFAN
CHINA NOW
CHRISTIANS AT WAR – TWO FAMILIES IN
   BELFAST
CITIZEN 63
CITY
The CITY ON THE STEPPE

CITY ON THE BORDER
A CLAN FOR ALL SEASONS
CLASS OF '74
COME OUT ALAN BROWNING – WE KNOW
   YOU'RE IN THERE
A COMPLETELY DIFFERENT WAY OF LIFE?
CONSETT – THE END OF THE ROAD
CONTRACT 736
COULD YOUR STREET BE NEXT?
A COURIS THING
The DALE THAT DIED
The DAY BEFORE YESTERDAY
The DEAD END LADS
DEATH BY MISADVENTURE?
DERBY DAY
DESTINATION AMERICA
DIVIDED WE STAND
The DO GOODERS
DO YOU REMEMBER VIETNAM?
DOUBLE SENTENCE
DUMMY
The DUPONT SHOW OF THE WEEK
EDEN AND AFTER
ENGLAND THEIR ENGLAND
The ENTERTAINERS (1964)
EYE TO EYE
FACES OF COMMUNISM
FAMILY BY CHOICE
The FAMILY OF MAN
The FAMILY
FAMINE
FANATICS
A FAR BETTER PLACE
FAREWELL ARABIA
FARSON'S GUIDE TO THE BRITISH
A FEW NOTES ON OUR FOOD PROBLEM
FORMAT V
FORTY MILLION SHOES
14TH JULY – PARIS
FRANCE
The FRANCE I LOVE
FREEDOM ROAD: SONGS OF NEGRO PROTEST
FROST PROGRAMME 30/1/1972
   The MINERS' STRIKE
FROST PROGRAMME 4/11/1973
   LIFE BEGINS AT SEVENTY
The GAMBLING CITY
GAYS: SPEAKING UP
GENERAL STRIKE REPORT
GENERATIONS APART
GENETTE
GERMAINE GREER v. USA
GO GO GO SAID THE BIRD
The GOLD RUN
GOOD AFTERNOON 17/3/1977
   APRIL ASHLEY
GOODBYE LONGFELLOW ROAD
The GRAFTERS
GRASS ROOTS
The GREAT DEBATE – ENOCH POWELL AND
   TREVOR HUDDLESTON
The GROUP
HEAD ON
The HEARTBEAT OF FRANCE
The HECKLERS
HERE AND NOW 5/7/1962
   LADY MAYORESS
HOSPITAL (1969)
HOSPITAL (1977)
A HOUSE IN BAYSWATER
HOW WE USED TO LIVE
I'M GOING TO ASK YOU TO GET UP OUT OF
   YOUR SEAT
The IMPORTANT THING IS LOVE
INSIDE STORY
IT NEVER SEEMED TO RAIN
ITALIAN WAY
IT'S DARK DOWN THERE
The JAPANESE EXPERIENCE
JIM BULLOCK – MINER EXTRAORDINARY
JIM'LL FIX IT 1977
   OLAVE, LADY BADEN-POWELL AND JIM'LL FIX IT
   INTERVIEW
JOHNNY GO HOME
The JUMPERS
JUST ONE KID
KAREN – A TODAY REPORT
KEEPING IN STEP
KIDS
KILVERT'S DIARY
KIND OF EXILE
KING

KINGDOM IN THE NORTH
KIRKBY: A SELF PORTRAIT
KIRKBY, PORTRAIT OF A TOWN
LADIES NIGHT 22/2/1978
    GAY WOMEN
The LAST HUNTERS
The LAST LIGHTHOUSE
LEVIN INTERVIEW 13/7/1966
    ANTON WALLICH-CLIFFORD
A LIFE APART
LIFESTYLE
LIFESTYLE 5/1/1978
    WORKING MEN'S CLUB
The LIMITS OF GROWTH
The LINEHAMS OF FOSDYKE
The LIVING CAMERA
LIVING FOR KICKS
LIVING WITH DANGER
LIVING WITH THE GERMANS
LONDON HEATHROW
LONDONERS
The LONG STRUGGLE: THE RISE OF THE
    WELFARE STATE
The LONGEST DECADE
LOOK IN
LOOK IN ON LONDON
LOOK OUT OF LONDON – NORTHERN
    JOURNEY
LOOK STRANGER
LOOKOUT
MAN ALIVE
MAN ALIVE REPORT
MAN IN SOCIETY
MAN IN THE NEWS 30/5/1971
    LORD LONGFORD
MAN OF NINE MILLION PARTS
The MAN WHO TALKS TO CHILDREN
MARCH OF TIME TELEVISION
MARRIAGE GUIDANCE
MARRIAGE TODAY
MEETING POINT 3/9/1967
    TWO OF A KIND
MEETING POINT 4/2/1968
    HOLES IN THE NET?
MEETINGS IN BRITAIN
MIDWEEK
MIGHTY AND MYSTICAL
The MINERS' STRIKE AND THE AFTERMATH
MINORITIES IN BRITAIN
MISSION TO NO-MAN'S LAND
MRS. BROWN AND THE GREAT COMPOSERS
MRS MARTIN LUTHER KING AT ST. PAUL'S
The MODEL MILLIONAIRESS
MORNING IN THE STREETS
A MOSQUE IN THE PARK
MOTHER TERESA OF CALCUTTA
The MOUNTING MILLIONS
MY BROTHER'S KEEPER
The NATIONAL DRINK TEST
NATIONAL SAVINGS 50TH ANNIVERSARY
    1916–1966
The NATURE OF PREJUDICE
NETWORK
NEVER AND ALWAYS
NEW LANDMARKS
The NEWCOMERS (1964)
NO LULLABY FOR BROADLAND
NO MAN'S LAND (1973)
NO MAN'S LAND (1978–79)
NOBEL AND THE PEACE PEOPLE
NOT A HUNDRED MILES FROM WEMBLEY
NYE!
The OLD BOYS
ON CAMERA
ON THE INSIDE LOOKING OUT
ONCE IN A LIFETIME
ONE MAN'S HUNGER
ONE PAIR OF EYES
OPEN DOOR 6/10/1974
    GRAPEVINE
OPEN DOOR 17/3/1975
    ASSOCIATION FOR NEIGHBOURHOOD COUNCILS
OPEN DOOR 25/10/1975
    A PLAYGROUP OF OUR OWN
OPEN DOOR 1/10/1976
    ALL AGAINST THE BOMB
OPEN DOOR 8/12/1979
    WRECKERS IN THE TOWN HALL
OPTIONS
OTHER PEOPLE'S JOBS
The OTHER SIDE OF PARADISE
OUR PEOPLE

OUR TOWN APPLEBY
OUR TOWN KENDAL
OUT OF STEP
OUT OF THE DARKNESS
OUTLOOK
OUTLOOK: MINORITIES IN BRITAIN
PANORAMA
PARADISE STREET
PARENTS AND CHILDREN
PEOPLE ARE TALKING
PEOPLE IN TROUBLE
PEOPLE TO WATCH
PERSONAL IMPRESSIONS
PERSONAL REPORT
PERSONAL REPORT – PILGER
The PHILPOTT FILE
PILGER
POSTSCRIPT TO EMPIRE
PRAISE THE DOG FOR SITTING
The PRETTIEST VILLAGE IN ENGLAND
The PRICE OF COAL
PURSUIT OF HAPPINESS
QUEST FOR GANDHI
QUO VADIS
RAINBOW MOVES HOUSE
REMEMBER ALL THE GOOD THINGS
REPORT 4/3/1969
    ST ANN'S
REPORTING '67 20/4/1967
    The HIPPIES OF SAN FRANCISCO
REPORTS ACTION
RETURN TO THE EDGE OF THE WORLD
RETURN TO THE RHONDDA
The RIVER NILE
The ROAD TO WIGAN PIER
A ROOF OVER OUR HEADS
ROVING REPORT 12/4/1962
    DOMINICAN REPUBLIC
RUTLAND
SCENE 20/2/1975
    JAMES IS OUR BROTHER
SCENE 13/1/1977
    AND THEY ALL LIVED HAPPILY TOGETHER
SCOUTS AND GUIDES OF ALL NATIONS
SCREAM QUIETLY OR THE NEIGHBOURS WILL
    HEAR
2ND HOUSE 29/5/1976
    MIRROR ON CLASS
The SECRET LIFE OF EDWARD JAMES
SEVEN PLUS SEVEN
SHADOW OF AN IRON MAN
The SHOALS OF HERRING
SIBERIA – THE GREAT EXPERIMENT
A SOHO STORY
The SOUTH AFRICAN EXPERIENCE
SOUTH AMERICA
The SPACE BETWEEN WORDS
The SPIRIT OF THE TWENTIES
SPRING IN ETHIOPIA
SUNDAY IN SEPTEMBER
SUNDAY, SWEET SUNDAY: ITALY
SUNLEY'S DAUGHTER
A TALE OF TWO HAWKERS
TALES OF INDIA
TASTE FOR ADVENTURE
TELL ME WHY
TEN MILLION STRONG
THAT WELL KNOWN STORE IN
    KNIGHTSBRIDGE
THERE WAS THIS FELLA.....
THIS ENGLAND
THIS IS WAUGH
THIS QUESTION OF PRESSURES 14/10/1969
    The VOICE OF THE TORTOISE
THIS WEEK (Rediffusion)
THIS WEEK (Thames)
THIS WEEK NATIONAL
THIS WEEK SPECIAL (Rediffusion)
THIS WEEK SPECIAL (Thames)
TIMES REMEMBERED
TO BE SEVEN IN BELFAST
TOO LONG A WINTER
A TOUR OF THE WHITE HOUSE
TUESDAY'S DOCUMENTARY
TV EYE
TWENTY ONE UP
TWILIGHT OF EMPIRE
TWO WEEKS CLEAR
TWO WOMEN
U.S.S.R. NOW
VANDAL RULE – O.K.?
The VOLUNTEERS

VOLUNTEERS
WALK DOWN ANY STREET
WE WAS ALL ONE
A WEDDING ON SATURDAY
WHAT ABOUT THE WORKERS?
WHAT'S A GIRL LIKE YOU ...
WHAT'S IN A GAME
WHICKER IN THE ARGENTINE
WHICKER WAY OUT WEST 2/10/1973
    The LORD IS MY SHEPHERD AND HE KNOWS I'M GAY
WHICKER WITHIN A WOMAN'S WORLD
WHICKER'S ORIENT
WHICKER'S WORLD DOWN UNDER
WHITE MISSIONARY
THE WHITE TRIBE OF AFRICA
The WIND OF CHANGE
WORLD ABOUT US 8/12/1974
    3,900 MILLION AND ONE THREE THOUSAND NINE
    HUNDRED
WORLD IN ACTION
WORLD IN ACTION SPECIAL
The WORLD IS OURS
The YEAR OF KILLING

SPORT
ABOUT BRITAIN 20/5/1977
    TELL THEM YOU COME FROM GOSFORTH
ABOUT BRITAIN 20/8/1975
    EVERYONE'S A WINNER IN GATESHEAD
ALL OUR YESTERDAYS 5/1/1972
    J.L. MANNING
ANOTHER SUNDAY AND SWEET F.A.
AQUARIUS 2/3/1975
    The GREAT GONDOLA RACE: PART 1
AQUARIUS 9/3/1975
    The GREAT GONDOLA RACE: PART 2
BARRY SHEENE – DAYTONA 1975
BOLTON WANDERERS v MANCHESTER CITY
CHALLENGE OF THE SEXES
The CHARLTON BOYS
CHARLTON'S CHAMPIONS
COME OUT FIGHTING
CRICKET WITH TREVOR BAILEY
CROWD OF THE DAY
CUT AND THRUST
ENGLAND v. HUNGARY
ENGLAND v. POLAND
ENGLAND v. ROMANIA
ENGLAND v. SPAIN
ENGLAND v. WEST GERMANY
ENGLAND v. YUGOSLAVIA
The EUROPEAN CHAMPIONS' CUP FINAL (1969)
The EUROPEAN CHAMPIONS' CUP FINAL (1977)
EUROPEAN CUP FINAL: BENFICA v.
    MANCHESTER UNITED
EUROPEAN CUP WINNERS' CUP FINAL:
    LIVERPOOL v. BORUSSIA (DORTMUND)
The FAVOURITES
The FIGHT GAME: IS IT SPORT – OR WAR?
FOOTBALL LEAGUE CUP FINAL: MANCHESTER
    CITY v NEWCASTLE UNITED
FOR THE RECORD 31/1/1969
    GEORGE BEST
GOOD SAILING
GRANDSTAND
The HARDEST WAY UP
HERE AND NOW 23/3/1962
    BILLY WALKER
HUNT v. LAUDA
HURRICANE HIGGINS
The INDOOR LEAGUE
INTERNATIONAL FOOTBALL: ENGLAND v.
    RUMANIA
INTERNATIONAL FOOTBALL: ENGLISH LEAGUE
    v. SCOTTISH LEAGUE
INTERNATIONAL FOOTBALL: HOLLAND vs.
    ENGLAND
INTERVIEW WITH PRINCESS ANNE
JACKIE 'TV' PALLO v. BOBBY GRAHAM
The JOHN CURRY ICE SPECTACULAR
The JUMPERS
The LAST WORD
LIVING CAMERA 1960
    EDDIE
LIVING CAMERA 1961
    MOONEY vs. FOWLE
LONGCHAMP RACES
McCORMACK – SPECIAL AGENT
MAN ALIVE 16/1/1975
    SOARING LIKE A BIRD
MANCHESTER CITY v BOLTON WANDERERS
MANCHESTER CITY v EVERTON

SPORT cont.

MANCHESTER CITY v NORWICH
MANCHESTER CITY v SOUTHAMPTON
MANCHESTER CITY v SPURS
MANCHESTER CITY v WOLVES
MARCH OF TIME TELEVISION 25/3/1953
   A BASEBALL ROOKIE'S BIG CHANCE
MARCH OF TIME TELEVISION 18/6/1953
   AMERICA'S NEW NO. 1 SPORT
MATCH OF THE DAY
MEANWHILE BACK IN SUNDERLAND
MICKEY DUFF: MATCHMAKER
A NIGHT AT THE SPEEDWAY
OLGA
ONE PAIR OF EYES 18/11/1967
   YOU'VE GOT TO WIN
The PHILPOTT FILE – THE SPORTING LIFE
PLAY SOCCER – JACK CHARLTON'S WAY
POSITIVE SOCCER WITH JACK CHARLTON
POT BLACK
THE RACE APART
The RACING GAME
REARDON ON SNOOKER
REDIFFUSION GOLF TOURNAMENT
ROAR OF THE CROWD
RUGBY SPECIAL
ST. CLOUD – PRIX JEAN DE CHAUDENAY
SEVENTH WINTER OLYMPICS – SLALOM AND
   FIGURE SKATING
SPANISH RIDING SCHOOL OF VIENNA
SPORTS ARENA
SPORTS REVIEW OF 1959
SPORTSNIGHT
SPORTSPOT
STAR SOCCER
SUNDERLAND v MANCHESTER CITY
THIS WEEK 22/7/1959
   AINTREE
THIS WEEK 23/6/1966
   BRAZIL – FOOTBALL
THIS WEEK 6/11/1969
   The POLITICS OF SPORT
THIS WEEK SPECIAL 2/6/1964
   PICK THE WINNER
TOP CROWN
WEDNESDAY SPECIAL 15/9/1976
   ODDS AGAINST
WHAT MAKES JOHNNIE RUN?
WHEELBASE 8/9/1967
   SNOW IN SEPTEMBER
WHEELBASE 1/2/1968
   SEE YOU IN MONTE
WHEELBASE 16/6/1969
   ONE WEEKEND IN JUNE
WICKET KEEPING AND FIELDING
The WILD WEST SHOW
WORLD CUP FINAL 1966
WORLD IN ACTION 13/7/1965
   The £.S.D. OF MPH
WORLD TONIGHT 19/10/1965
   The LUNATIC OLYMPICS

STATE OCCASIONS

ACROSS THE HEART
ADVENTURE 29/6/1962
   DALAI LAMA
AT NO. 10 DOWNING STREET
CHURCHILL FUNERAL
The CONSECRATION OF COVENTRY
   CATHEDRAL
The CORONATION
ENTHRONEMENT OF THE ARCHBISHOP OF
   CANTERBURY
A HERO'S RETURN
INVESTITURE AT CAERNARVON
MAN ALIVE 14/5/1968
   CEREMONIAL MAN
MAN IN SPACE
MAY DAY PARADES AND DEMONSTRATIONS
The QUEEN OF THE NETHERLANDS' ARRIVAL
ROUND THE WORLD IN FORTY MINUTES
ROYAL VISIT TO ULSTER
ROYAL WEDDING
ST. PAUL'S MEMORIAL SERVICE TO KING
   GEORGE VI
The SILVER JUBILEE REVIEW AT SPITHEAD
STATE FUNERAL OF SIR WINSTON CHURCHILL
The STATE OPENING OF PARLIAMENT
STATE VISIT OF KING FEISAL II OF IRAQ
The STATE VISIT TO DENMARK
THIS WEEK 27/5/1965
   RE-UNIFICATION OF GERMANY
The VALIANT MAN

TALENT SHOWS

NEW FACES
OPPORTUNITY KNOCKS! (ABC 1964–68)
OPPORTUNITY KNOCKS! (Thames 1971–78)

TELEVISION COMPANY HISTORY

see also CINEMA, TELEVISION AND RADIO
ABC OF ABC: SOUVENIR WITH MUSIC
ALL GOOD THINGS
ANGLIA TELEVISION OPENING NIGHT
   TRANSMISSION
The BIRTH OF ITV
....COME TO AN END
COUGH AND YOU'LL DEAFEN THOUSANDS
DEMONSTRATION FILM OPENING OF MIDLAND
   TELEVISION STUDIOS
EAMONN ANDREWS SHOW 8/5/1966
FESTIVAL 40
5TH ANNIVERSARY
The ITN STORY
ITV OPENING NIGHT AT THE GUILDHALL
ITV OPENING NIGHT – TRAILER
ITV OPENING NIGHT – PREVIEW OF
   REDIFFUSION AND ABC PROGRAMMES
LORD DERBY
MEET GEORGE AND ALFRED BLACK
MEET THE PEOPLE
SALUTE TO A.P.
STUDIO FIVE
TELEVISION COMES TO LONDON
TELEVISION DEMONSTRATION FILM
TELEVISION FOR CHILDREN
TEN YEARS OF LONDON WEEKEND
THIS IS SCOTLAND
THIS IS THE BBC
THIS WAS THE FUTURE
THIS WEEK 21/9/1956
   ITV FIRST YEAR
TRIBUTE TO THE BBC
TWENTY ONE YEARS

TELEVISION FILMS

The ANDERSONVILLE TRIAL
La BELLE VIE
BIG BOB JOHNSON AND HIS FANTASTIC SPEED
   CIRCUS
The DANGEROUS DAYS OF KIOWA JONES
The DOOMSDAY FLIGHT
The FIRECHASERS
HARDCASE
The HERO OF MY LIFE
HONKY TONK
HOW I SPENT MY SUMMER VACATION
ISTANBUL EXPRESS
The MAN WHO WANTED TO LIVE FOREVER
RETURN OF THE GUNFIGHTER
SAVAGES
The THREE HOSTAGES
TRIBES

THEATRE

ACCOLADE
ALL OUR YESTERDAYS 29/8/1971
   CYRIL CONNOLLY
ANTHONY QUINN
AQUARIUS 3/10/1970
   A PINTER PREMIERE
COME IN, IF YOU CAN GET IN 30/3/1979
The DICK CAVETT SHOW 17/2/1974
   SIR LAURENCE OLIVIER
EDITH EVANS
FAREWELL TO THE VIC
GOLDEN DRAMA
GREAT ACTING
HAMLET AT ELSINORE
LIVELY ARTS 17/4/1977
   SHADES: THREE PLAYS BY SAMUEL BECKETT
   SAMUEL BECKETT PREMIERE
LOOK OUT OF LONDON – NORTHERN
   JOURNEY 4/12/1956
   REPERTORY
MONITOR 12/4/1959
   PAUL ROBESON/ FRANK LLOYD WRIGHT
MONITOR 15/1/1961
   KATINA PAXINOU
NEW RELEASE 22/11/1966
   DAVID MERCER – PLAYWRIGHT
NOËL COWARD ON ACTING
OMNIBUS 25/5/1969
   The ACTOR'S CHANGING FACE
OMNIBUS 7/12/1969
   NOEL COWARD – PLAYWRIGHT

OMNIBUS 13/6/1971
   THREE LOOMS WAITING
OMNIBUS 7/11/1971
   FIFTY YEARS ON
OMNIBUS 9/4/1972
   ACTOR, I SAID
PARADE
The PLAYWRIGHT
PREPARING A PLAY
REVIEW 1/10/1971
   A NEW KING LEAR
SATURDAY SPECIAL 4/1/1969
   MRS WILSON'S DIARY
2ND HOUSE 30/11/1974
   ATHOL FUGARD
SHAKESPEARE IN PERSPECTIVE
The SOUTH BANK SHOW 22/4/1978
   HAROLD PINTER
STAGECOACH – NOT SO MUCH A THEATRE
   MORE A WAY OF LIFE
STARS IN THEIR EYES
SUCCESS STORY 9/2/1959
   SHELAGH DELANEY
SYBIL THORNDIKE REMEMBERS
TEMPO – THE ACTOR AND THE ROLE
TEMPO 13/9/1964
   The PRINCE MAKER
THIS WEEK 18/5/1956
   USTINOV
TOESTANDEN
TWELFTH NIGHT
WILTON'S: THE HANDSOMEST HALL IN TOWN
YOUNG TIGERS 27/7/1964
   PETER HALL
YOUR NATIONAL THEATRE

TRADE UNIONISM

BITTER HARVEST
DEMOCRACY AT WORK
DISPUTE
FOR THE RECORD 24/1/1969
   JACK DASH TALKS TO ALAN WATSON
GENERAL STRIKE REPORT
HOSPITAL 30/11/1977
   INDUSTRIAL ACTION
JIM BULLOCK – MINER EXTRAORDINARY
MAN ALIVE 14/10/1970
   The MOOD OF AMERICA: CLARKESVILLE,
     PENNSYLVANIA
MAN AT WORK 21/11/1973
   DISPUTE: ROUND 1
MAN AT WORK 28/11/1973
   DISPUTE: ROUND 2
MAN OF NINE MILLION PARTS
MY BROTHER'S KEEPER
REPRESENTING THE UNION
SHOP FLOOR
THIS WEEK 15/7/1959
   TRADE UNION CONFERENCE
THIS WEEK 9/9/1965
   WOODCOCK ON "THE WORKERS'
THIS WEEK 9/6/1966
   SEAMEN'S STRIKE DAY 25
THIS WEEK 16/6/1966
   The SEAMEN'S STRIKE – WHO WANTS IT?
THIS WEEK 25/4/1968
   PORTRAIT OF A MILITANT – HUGH SCANLON
THIS WEEK 20/1/1972
   The MINERS' LAST STAND
THIS WEEK 11/5/1972
   JIMMY REID UNLIMITED
THIS WEEK 1844–THE UNION AND THE BOND
THREE DAYS IN SZCZECIN
TV EYE 15/2/1979
   HOSPITAL IN CRISIS
VICTOR FEATHER (T.U.C.)
WEDNESDAY PLAY 1/2/1967
   The LUMP
WEDNESDAY PLAY 19/2/1969
   The BIG FLAME
WEEKEND WORLD 8/4/1979
WORLD IN ACTION 1/12/1964
   STATE OF THE UNIONS
WORLD IN ACTION 7/6/1971
   CONVERSATION WITH A WORKING MAN
WORLD IN ACTION 27/3/1972
   The LUMP
WORLD IN ACTION 1/5/1972
   The CONTAINER ROW CONTAINERS
WORLD IN ACTION 19/6/1972
   The DOCKS DISPUTE DOCKERS

WESTERNS *cont.*

The LAW OF THE PLAINSMAN
MACKENZIE'S RAIDERS
OUTLAWS
PONY EXPRESS
RAWHIDE
The REBEL
RETURN OF THE GUNFIGHTER
RIVERBOAT
SUGARFOOT
TALES OF WELLS FARGO
The TEXAN
WAGON TRAIN
WHIPLASH
WHISPERING SMITH
YANCY DERRINGER

University College of
Ripon & York St. John
YORK CAMPUS
REFERENCE ONLY
NOT TO BE TAKEN OUT
OF THE LIBRARY